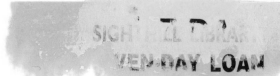

Global Marketing Strategies

INTERNATIONAL
STUDENT EDITION

GLOBAL MARKETING STRATEGIES

Second Edition

Jean-Pierre Jeannet

Walter H. Carpenter Professor of Marketing and
  International Business
Babson College, Wellesley, Massachusetts

Professor of Marketing and Global Business Strategies
International Management Development Institute,
  Lausanne, Switzerland

Hubert D. Hennessey

Associate Professor of Marketing
Babson College, Wellesley, Massachusetts

Associate
Ashridge Management College, Berkhamsted,
  United Kingdom

HOUGHTON MIFFLIN COMPANY
Boston   London   Melbourne

To Our Students

This book is to be sold only in the territory to which it has been consigned. It is not for sale in the United States and its territories or in Canada.

CREDITS

Figure 7.3: Adapted from *Internationalization of Business* by Richard D. Robinson, copyright ©1984 by The Dryden Press, reprinted by permission of the publisher.

Figure 13.3: From *International Business Management* Second Edition by Richard D. Robinson, copyright ©1978 by the Dryden Press, reprinted by permission of the publisher.

Printed in the U.S.A.

Library of Congress Catalog Card Number: 91-72094
ISBN: 0-395-62839-3

BCDEFGHIJ-D-95432

Contents

P A R T   O N E

Understanding the Global Marketing Environment

2

3

4

P A R T   T W O

Analyzing Global Opportunities

5

6

7

P A R T   T H R E E

Developing Global Marketing Strategies

8

9

P A R T   F O U R

Global Marketing Programs

10

11

12

13

P A R T   F I V E

Managing the Global Marketing Effort

16

17

18

Cases

Preface

In the 1980s, international marketing was revolutionized by the concept of globalization. Economically and politically, the world has changed with the initiative of the European Community to reach economic integration (1992 initiative) and the liberalization of Eastern Europe, culminating with the dramatic events in the Soviet Union in August 1991. As authors, we have benefited enormously from being close to these changes, both through our contacts as well as our extended trips and teaching assignments in Europe. In addition, we have worked extensively with companies who are about to embark on new types of global strategies. Given these substantial changes, it became very clear that substantial changes in the text material were necessary. In *Global Marketing Strategies,* Second Edition, we have combined the successful organization of our first edition with new material that reflects the radically changed business environment faced by globally active marketing professionals.

Major Features of the Text

A number of features in the book serve the new breed of global marketing manager. Most importantly, our approach is managerial: we look at the global marketing task through the eyes of the marketing manager. The book emphasizes aspects of global and international marketing that apply to managers from any industry sector, or from anywhere in the world. Furthermore, we maintain a strategic focus throughout the text. We believe that success in global markets today is not only a function of broad cultural understanding but also modern strategic planning. Finally, the book emphasizes the practical aspects of global marketing by including numerous recent examples from well-known companies, as well as full-length cases that probe international marketing issues in great depth.

Major Changes in the Second Edition

While we retained important aspects from our first edition, this second edition has nevertheless seen some very important changes. First of all, we have changed the title of the text to better reflect the global orientation of the material. We do not view Global Marketing simply as a new term for the more traditional International Marketing. Instead, we believe that global marketing issues are of a different nature, and need to be viewed in addition to the more traditional international marketing concepts. We have taken care to add the specific global concerns throughout the text. In fact, the highlighting of specific global strategy issues as distinct from the international marketing issues represents a major strength of this text.

Aside from the global issues, this new edition gives ample attention to the European integration (Europe 1992) and its impact on international marketing. Furthermore, we have included a considerable amount of material on Eastern Europe and the liberalization process and added examples of international firms' activities in those countries.

Overall, the book's organization has remained intact. The Part Opening chart has been improved. We have eliminated the chapter on Financing International Marketing Operations (Chapter 18 in the first edition) and integrated the material on barter and nonfinancial pricing into Chapter 13 of this edition (Pricing for International and Global Markets.) Chapter 1 (Global Marketing: An Overview), Chapter 8 (Global Marketing Strategies), and Chapter 13 have been substantially changed. All other chapters have seen a considerable amount of updating, with a majority of the examples concentrating on the 1988–1991 period. Reference readings and citations have also been updated. We have retained the strengths of the first edition and combined them with new material, maintaining an increasingly global point of view and taking into consideration such new developments as Europe 1992 and the liberalization of Eastern Europe.

The case section of the text has undergone several changes. We have introduced four new cases and eliminated three of the older ones. With 15 cases, the section represents a full range of issues. The new cases, Gillette Trac II, Wiltech India, World Paint Industry, and ICI Paints, should be of interest to a diverse student body and should strengthen the already present consumer goods cases. Furthermore, we have substantially improved the Swatch and Tissot cases.

The Instructor's Resource Manual has been strengthened to include test questions for each chapter. In addition, we include suggestions and ideas on how to structure student projects, both for an entire semester or for individual topics. The IRM contains case notes with transparency masters for all text cases, as well as four additional cases.

This second edition has been written for students of global and international marketing both in the United States and abroad. It is intended for use at the undergraduate, graduate, and executive program level. However, the text is written in such a way that even experienced practitioners will be able to profit from its approach.

Much of the material has been extensively class tested, both in the United States and abroad.

Acknowledgments

To write a new edition of a textbook on global marketing is a major undertaking that could not have been completed without the active support and help of a great many people. This process was made especially difficult by the fact that both authors spent most of the time working on this revision during extended overseas projects. However, we hope that this has added to the global content of the material.

We are indebted to our home institution, Babson College, for generously supporting us in the manuscript stage and allowing us the flexibility to spend time overseas to develop the material for this book. To International Management Development Institute (IMD), we are indebted for their support of our case research and for allowing us to publish IMD cases in the text. To Ashridge Management College we are thankful for providing access to its extensive data base, which proved helpful in updating this new edition. And finally, we would like to express our gratitude to our colleagues at Babson, IMD, and Ashridge for their support and willingness to discuss global marketing issues that have helped us in clarifying many of our concepts.

The content of the cases would not have been possible without the generous participation of a number of companies and executives: Rune Glimenius and David Webster at Alfa-Laval; Ernst Thomke and Franz Sprecher from SMH (Swatch and Tissot cases); Ian Souter at Nestlé; Mr. Nakamoto of American Hospital Supply—Japan; Hansruedi Bieri at Bieri Pumps; John Sweeney at Puritan-Bennett; Harold Todd, Masahiro Horita, and Brian Taylor at Nippon Vicks K.K.; and Herman Scopes and John Thompson at ICI Paints. These executives and others who prefer to remain anonymous gave generously of their time so that other practicing as well as future managers could learn from their own experiences. We would also like to thank Silvia Farmanfarma, case librarian at IMD, who has provided us crucial support in guiding our cases through the approval, release, and copyright process.

To turn the collected material and data into readable form we could always count on a number of students, graduate assistants, and research associates. Babson College students Peter Mark, David Rittenhouse, Maricel Blum, John Bleh, and Sameer Kaji wrote parts of the cases used in this text. Rebecca Houpt researched material for a number of chapters. Susan Nye served both as graduate assistant at Babson and as research associate at IMD. Barbara Priovolos and Robert Howard wrote several of the cases at IMD. Faith Towle provided helpful editorial assistance on our new cases. John Marthinsen, Professor of Economics and International Business at Babson College, contributed the original version of Chapter 2. We also thank Allen S. Marber of the University of Bridgeport for writing the test questions for the Instructor's Resource Manual.

Throughout the development of this edition, as well as the previous edition, a number of reviewers have made important contributions. These reviews were extremely important in the revision and improvement of the text. We especially thank the following people.

B. G. Bizzell
Stephen F. Austin University

Jean Boddewyn
CUNY-Bernard M. Baruch College

Sharon Browning
Northwest Missouri State University

Roger J. Calantone
Michigan State University

Alex Christofides
Ohio State University

William Cunningham
Southwest Missouri State

Charles de Mortanges
University of New Hampshire

Susan P. Douglas
New York University

Adel I. El-Ansary
The George Washington University

Jeffrey A. Fadiman
San Jose State University

Kate Gillespie
University of Texas at Austin

John L. Hazard
Michigan State University

Joby John
Bentley College

H. Ralph Jones
Miami University

A. H. Kizilbash
Northern Illinois University

Saul Klein
Northeastern University

G. P. Lauter
The George Washington University

Joseph L. Massie
University of Kentucky

James McCullough
The University of Arizona

Taylor W. Meloan
University of Southern California

Aubrey Mendelow
Duquesne University

Joseph Miller
Indiana University at Bloomington

Zahir A. Quraeshi
Western Michigan University

Samuel Rabino
Northeastern University

Pradeep Rau
University of Delaware

Michael Steiner
University of Wisconsin—Eau Claire

Gordon P. Stiegler
University of Southern California

Ruth Lesher Taylor
Southwest Texas State University

L. Trankiem
California State University at Los Angeles

Phillip D. White
University of Colorado at Boulder

Van R. Wood
Texas Tech University

Attila Yaprak
Wayne State University

We are grateful to our publisher, Houghton Mifflin Company. Over time we had the pleasure of working with a number of their editors who have seen this project through to its completion. We thank them for their patience, their encouragement, and their professionalism in supporting our writing efforts. Houghton Mifflin has also provided us with a first-class staff in turning the manuscript into its final form. The marketing, production, art, editorial, permissions, and manufacturing staffs have substantially added to the quality of this finished book.

A number of people have been instrumental in the preparation of the manuscript of this book. In particular we would like to thank our department secretary, Marion Power, who patiently typed this manuscript. Her efforts and willingness to deal with our numerous revisions are most appreciated.

We especially would like to thank our wives, Patricia and Ellen, who encouraged us during the normal ups and downs that are inherent in such an extensive writing project. Finally, we extend our greatest gratitude to our students at Babson College, at International Management Development Institute, and at Ashridge Management College for their constant help and inspiration. Their interest in global marketing issues inspired us to undertake and complete this project. Therefore, we are happy to dedicate this book to our students.

J.-P.J.
H.D.H.

Global
Marketing
Strategies

Introduction

1

Global Marketing: An Overview

IN THIS FIRST chapter of the text, we provide an introduction to the field of global marketing. An overview of the most important global marketing decisions is given, and the major problems likely to be encountered by international firms are highlighted. This introduction to the text also explains the conceptual framework we used to develop the book. Understanding this underlying plan will help you to quickly integrate these concepts into an overall framework for global marketing. It should also make it easier for you to appreciate the complexities of global marketing.

1

Global Marketing: An Overview

● **THIS FIRST CHAPTER** *is intended to introduce you to the field of global marketing. Initially we concentrate on the scope of global marketing, using several examples to illustrate that it is a broad-based process encompassing many types of participating firms and a wide range of activities. We next present definitions that will relate global marketing to other fields of study. We examine the differences between domestic and global marketing and explain why domestic companies often have difficulty marketing abroad. The chapter continues with a description of the major participants in global marketing. We also provide an explanation of why mastering global marketing skills can be valuable to your future career. A conceptual outline of the book concludes the chapter.*

FROM INTERNATIONAL MARKETING TO GLOBAL MARKETING

The term *global marketing* has only been used for some ten years and began to assume widespread use in 1983 with the seminal article by Ted Levitt.[1] Prior to that, international marketing or multinational marketing was the term used most often to describe international marketing activities. However, global marketing is not just a new term for an old phenomenon; there are real differences between international marketing and global marketing. In many ways global marketing is a subcategory of

1. Theodore Levitt, "The Globalization of Markets," *Harvard Business Review,* May–June 1983, pp. 92–102.

international marketing with special importance in our present world. It has captured the attention of marketing academics and business practitioners alike and, as indicated by the title of our book, we attach considerable importance to this new type of international marketing. However, before we explain global marketing in greater detail, let us first look at the historical development of international marketing as a field and gain a better understanding of the phases through which it has passed.

Domestic Marketing

Marketing that is aimed at a single market, the firm's domestic market, is referred to as *domestic marketing.* In domestic marketing, the firm faces only one set of competitive, economic, and market issues and, essentially, must deal with only one set of customers, although the company may serve several segments in this one market. The marketing concepts that apply to domestic or single-country marketing are those we expect our readers are well versed in and will not be covered further in this book.[2]

Export Marketing

The field of export marketing covers all those marketing activities involved when a firm markets its products outside its main (domestic) base of operation and when products are physically shipped from one market or country to another. Although the domestic marketing operation remains of primary importance, the major challenges of export marketing are the selection of appropriate markets or countries through marketing research, the determination of appropriate product modifications to meet the demand requirements of export markets, and the development of export channels through which the company can market its products abroad. In this phase, the firm may concentrate mostly on the product modifications and run the export operations as a welcome and profitable by-product of its domestic strategy. Because the movement of goods across national borders is a major part of an exporting strategy, the required skills include knowledge of shipping and export documentation.[3] Although export marketing probably represents the most traditional and least involved form of international marketing, it remains an important aspect for many firms. As a result, we have devoted Chapter 18 exclusively to this topic.

International Marketing

When practicing international marketing, a company goes beyond exporting and becomes much more directly involved in the local marketing environment within a

2. Philip Kotler, *Marketing Management: Analysis, Planning, Implementation and Control,* 7th ed. (Englewood Cliffs, N.J.: Prentice-Hall, 1991).

3. Gerald Albaum, Jesper Strandskov, Edwin Duerr, and Laurence Dowd, *International Marketing and Export Management* (Reading, Mass.: Addison-Wesley, 1989).

given country or market. The international marketer is likely to have its own sales subsidiaries and will participate in and develop entire marketing strategies for foreign markets. At this point, the necessary adaptation to the firm's domestic marketing strategies become a main concern. Companies going international now will have to find out how they must adjust an entire marketing strategy, including how they sell, advertise, and distribute, in order to fit new market demands.

An important challenge for the international marketing phase of a firm becomes the need to understand the different environments the company needs to operate in. Understanding different cultural, economic, and political environments becomes necessary for success. This is generally described as part of a company's internationalization process, whereby a firm becomes more experienced to operate in various foreign markets. It is typical to find a considerable emphasis on the environmental component at this stage. Typically, much of the field of international marketing has been devoted to making the environment understandable and to assist managers in navigating through the differences. The development of the cultural/environmental approach to international marketing is an expression of this particular phase.[4]

Multinational Marketing

The focus on multinational marketing came as a result of the development of the multinational corporation. These companies are characterized by extensive development of assets abroad and operate in a number of foreign countries or markets as if they were local companies. Such development led to the creation of many domestic strategies, thus the name multidomestic strategy whereby a multinational firm competes with many strategies, each one tailored to a particular local market. The major challenge of the multinational marketer is to find the best possible adaptation of a complete marketing strategy to an individual country. This approach to international marketing leads to a maximum amount of localization and to a large variety of marketing strategies. The attempt of multinational corporations to appear "local" wherever they compete, often results in the duplication of some key resources. The major benefits are the ability to completely tailor a marketing strategy to the local requirements.[5]

Multiregional Marketing

Given the diseconomies of scale of individualized marketing strategies, each tailored to a specific local environment, companies have begun to emphasize strategies for larger regions. These regional strategies encompass a number of markets, such as Euro-strategies for Western Europe, and have come about as a result of regional economic and political integration. Such integration is apparent in North America, where the United States and Canada have signed a far-reaching trade pact and the

4. Philip R. Cateora, *International Marketing,* 7th ed. (Homewood, Ill.: Irwin, 1990).
5. Warren J. Keegan, *Multinational Marketing Management,* 3rd ed. (Englewood Cliffs, N.J.: Prentice-Hall, 1984).

inclusion of Mexico is discussed, or in the Pacific Rim, where a number of countries have made great progress in their economic development. Nowhere has the development been faster than in Europe through the impetus of Europe 1992, a series of political and economic measures aimed at total integration of the European Community. Companies considering regional strategies look to tie together operations in one region, rather than around the globe, the aim being increased efficiency. Many firms are presently working on such solutions, moving from many multidomestic strategies in Europe toward Pan-European strategies.

Global Marketing

Over the years, academics and international companies alike have become aware that opportunities for economies of scale and enhanced competitiveness are greater if they can manage to integrate and create marketing strategies on a global scale. A global marketing strategy involves the creation of a single strategy for a product, service, or company, for the entire global market, that encompasses many markets or countries simultaneously and is aimed at leveraging the commonalties across many markets. Rather than tailor a strategy perfectly to any individual market, the company aims at settling on one general strategy that will guide itself through the world market. The management challenge is to design marketing strategies that work well across many markets. It is driven not only by the fact that markets appear increasingly similar in environmental and customer requirements, but, even more so, by the fact that large investments in technology, logistics, or other key functions force the companies to expand their market coverage.

Thus global marketing is the last stage in the development of the field of international marketing. While global marketers face their own unique challenges that stem from finding marketing strategies that fit many countries, the skills and concepts of the earlier stages are very important and continue to be needed. In fact, companies that take a global marketing approach will be good exporters because they will include some exporting in their strategies. Such firms will also have to be good at international marketing because designing one global strategy requires a sound understanding of the cultural, economic, and political environment of many countries. Furthermore, few global marketing strategies can exist without some local tailoring, which is the hallmark of multinational marketing. As a result, global marketing is but the last of a series of skills, all included under the broad concept of international marketing.

THE SCOPE OF INTERNATIONAL AND GLOBAL MARKETING

It is generally understood that a company like Boeing, the world's largest commercial airline manufacturer and one of the leading exporters from the United States, engages in international marketing when it sells its airplanes to airlines across the globe.[6] Likewise, Ford Motor Company, which operates large manufacturing plants in several countries, engages in international marketing even though a major part of its output is sold in the country where it is manufactured.

Today, however, the scope of international marketing is broader and includes many other business activities. Those of large U.S. department store chains, such as K mart and Bloomingdale's, include a substantial amount of importing. When these stores search for new products abroad to sell in the United States, they practice another form of international marketing. A whole range of service industries are involved in international marketing; many large advertising firms, banks, investment bankers, public accounting firms, consulting companies, hotel chains, and airlines now market their services worldwide.

The success of the U.S.-made pop culture is a good example of how broad the range of products and services sold internationally is.[7] Madonna sells two and a half times more albums abroad than in the United States. The U.S. music business, consisting largely of rock & roll style music, is a $20 billion a year industry with about 70 percent of its revenue coming from overseas. European revenues for U.S.-made television series amount to about $600 million annually. Over the past five years, overseas revenues of U.S. film studios doubled, resulting in several acquisitions from Japanese and European investors who see this business as one with strategic worldwide potential. The companies that run these businesses, both domestically and internationally, are engaging in international marketing in the same way that exporters of airplanes, computers, or medical equipment do.

Also, Disney, the large U.S.-based entertainment company, is engaging in international and global marketing.[8] The company is building a new theme park in Europe which is expected to be ready for 1992 and has licensed another one in Japan. Disney's film revenue from overseas sales already accounts for some $500 million annually and is growing rapidly. The company has plans to enter the home video market in some forty-five countries. Its European comic book sales reach some 17 million customers each week. Disney also is combining efforts with major international companies, such as Carrefour, France's leading retailer of large supermarkets, and Nestlé, the large international food company. Although Disney does engage in the traditional sales of products overseas, most of its activities, such as theme parks and publishing, involve the exploitation of concepts that can be adapted around the world. In doing so, the company becomes a major player in international and global marketing.

Definitions of International and Global Marketing Management

Although much conceptual work has been accomplished in global marketing, the use of the word *global* remains unclear among many marketing academics and execu-

6. "Overseas Sales Take Off At Last," *Fortune,* July 16, 1990, p. 76.
7. "America's Hottest Export: Pop Culture," *Fortune,* December 31, 1990, p. 50.
8. "Disney's Global Goals," *Marketing,* May 17, 1990, p. 22.

tives. For many, global is just a new term or replacement term for international. Since it does mean something new and different to us, we plan to make use of the term in a judicious way. For us, global marketing is a subset, albeit different and distinct, of international marketing. In general, we still use the term international more often to describe factors that relate to the entire field, and to use global mainly when it refers to the specific new phenomena in international marketing. The term global was selected because it indicates clearly that a significant portion of this text will deal specifically with new concepts and strategies without neglecting the standard concepts dealing with export, international, or multinational marketing.

Having examined the scope of international and global marketing, we are now able to define it more accurately. Any definition has to be built, however, on basic definitions of marketing and marketing management, with an added explanation of the international dimension. We understand *marketing* as the performance of business activities directing the flow of products and services from producer to consumer. A successful performance of the marketing function by a firm is contingent upon the adoption of the marketing concept, consisting of (a) a market focus, (b) a customer orientation, (c) an integrated marketing organization, and (d) customer satisfaction.[9] *Marketing management* is the execution of a company's marketing operation. Management responsibilities consist of planning, organizing, and controlling the marketing program of the firm. To accomplish this job, marketing management is assigned decision-making authority over product strategy, communication strategy, distribution strategy, and pricing strategy. The combination of these four aspects of marketing is referred to as the *marketing mix.*

For international and global marketing management, the basic goals of marketing and the responsibilities described above remain unchanged. What is different is the execution of these activities in more than one country. Consequently, we define *international marketing management* as *the performance of marketing activities across two or more countries.* We are moving from single-country decisions to multicountry decisions. As we see in Figure 1.1, in some situations, only one or two countries are involved; in other situations, dozens of countries are involved simultaneously, particularly when we speak of global marketing.

A U.S. firm exporting products to Mexico is engaged in a marketing effort across two countries: the United States and Mexico. Another U.S. firm operating a subsidiary in Mexico that manufactures and markets locally under the direction of the head office in the United States is also engaged in international marketing to the extent that the head office staff directs and supervises this effort. Consequently, international marketing does not always require the physical movement of products across national borders. International marketing occurs whenever marketing decisions are made that encompass two or more countries.

9. Philip Kotler, *Marketing Management,* 7th ed. (Englewood Cliffs, N.J.: Prentice-Hall, 1991, p. 16–20.

FIGURE 1.1 ● International and Global Marketing

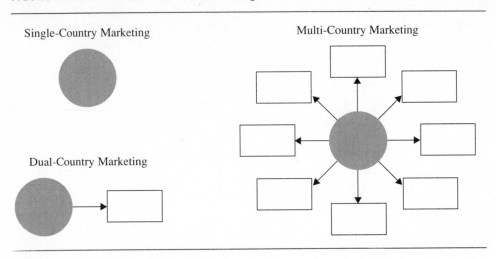

Single-Country Marketing

Multi-Country Marketing

Dual-Country Marketing

Relationships With Other Fields of Study

The field of international marketing is related to other fields of study. In its broadest terms, international marketing is a subset of *international business,* which is defined as the performance of all business functions across national boundaries. International business includes all functional areas such as international production, international financial management, and international marketing (see Figure 1.2).

International trade theory, which explains why nations trade with each other, is a related concept. This theory is aimed at understanding product flows between countries, either in the form of exports or imports. A U.S. corporation exporting machinery to Japan would find its transactions recorded as an export in the United States whereas the same transaction is treated as an import in Japan. In this situation, international marketing and international trade are concerned with the same phenomenon.

Should the same U.S. company produce its machinery in Japan and sell locally, however, there would be no exchange of goods between the two countries. Consequently, there would be no recognized international trading activity. However, as we have seen earlier, the U.S. company's decision to build machinery in Japan and sell it there is still considered an international marketing decision. Therefore we can conclude that international marketing goes beyond strict definitions of international trading and includes a wider range of activities.

International marketing should not be confused with *foreign marketing* which consists of marketing activities carried out by foreign firms within their own countries. Marketing by Brazilian firms in Brazil is, therefore, defined as foreign marketing and is not the principle focus of this book. However, Brazilian firms engaged in marketing their products in the United States are engaged in international marketing and are subject to the same concepts and principles that U.S. firms marketing in Brazil are subject to.

DIFFERENCES BETWEEN INTERNATIONAL AND DOMESTIC MARKETING

Companies that market products or services abroad have always had to deal with a wider range of issues than those encountered by domestic firms. The following section gives some insight into the special difficulties encountered in the international market.

Using a Domestic Strategy Abroad: Risk or Opportunity?

When a company uses an initial marketing strategy abroad, its success or failure depends greatly on the market where it is used. In 1977, Apple Computer Company began distribution of its personal computer in Japan. At that time there were no other personal computer products on the market. However, by 1985 Apple still had only a very small market share, and the company had failed to achieve any significant market penetration. Japanese competitors and IBM had begun to market Japanese-language machines. The Apple could only be used by Japanese who understood English very well, thus its market was limited to a small group. It was years later when

FIGURE 1.2 ● International Marketing and Related Fields of Study

Apple brought in a team of technicians from its head office to adapt its products to the Japanese language and built a subsidiary staff with local managers.[10]

Although Apple did poorly in Japan, it operated very successfully in France. There, Apple became the leader in personal computers. In France, Apple used many of the high-visibility promotions begun in the United States by adapting them to the French environment. Apple did extremely well by focusing on in-home businesses and independent professionals, such as doctors and lawyers, achieving a market share of 35 percent in 1984 compared to 27 percent for IBM.[11]

Apple's market position internationally had improved over the years and had actually grown more abroad to about 10 percent while it dropped in the U.S. from about 15 percent to about 13 percent in 1989.[12] In Europe, Apple had done particularly well, almost tripling sales in 2 years to about $1.2 billion in 1989, which amounts to almost one quarter of its worldwide sales. The success in Europe has also influenced executive positions at Apple's head office in the United States. The architects of Apple's success in France and in Europe, Jean-Louis Gassee and Michael Spindler from France and Germany respectively, were promoted to senior positions partly to enhance Apple's competitiveness in the U.S. market.[13]

In the two examples described above, Apple tried to duplicate a marketing strategy that had been successful in its home market. It failed in Japan, whereas in France it succeeded, with Apple achieving a higher market share than in its home market. The success in its European markets also caused the company to bring back to the United States the lessons learned abroad by transferring executives from abroad. Apple's example does show that success in international markets does not always require the complete adaptation of a company's strategy nor does it show that you will never have to change anything. The Apple situation does however, support a pattern where managers will have to evaluate situations and sometimes change, sometimes adapt, and other times extend the same strategy abroad. The reasons for these patterns are explained in the next section.

FACTORS LIMITING STANDARDIZATION OF INTERNATIONAL AND GLOBAL MARKETING STRATEGIES

From an international marketing manager's point of view, the most cost-effective method to market products or services worldwide is to use the same program in every

10. "Apple Loser in Japan Computer Market, Tries to Recoup by Redesigning Its Models," *Wall Street Journal,* June 21, 1985, p. 30.

11. "Can Apple Transplant Its Sexy French Marketing?" *Business Week,* June 10, 1985, p. 10.

12. "Apple's Woes Can't Just Be Reshuffled Away," *Business Week,* February 12, 1990, p. 32.

13. "The Toughest Job in the Computer Business," *Business Week,* March 19, 1990, p. 118.

country, provided environmental conditions favor such an approach. However, invariably, as we have seen in the previous section, local market characteristics exist that may require some form of adaptation to local conditions. One of the challenges of international marketing is to be able to determine the extent to which a standardized approach may be used for any given local market. To do this, the international marketing manager must become aware of any factors that limit standardization. Such factors can be categorized into four major groups: market characteristics, industry conditions, marketing institutions, and legal restrictions.[14]

The debate over the amount or extent of standardization is one of the longest in the field of international marketing. Some see markets as becoming more similar, and increasingly more global, such as those espoused by Levitt.[15] Others point out the difficulties in using a standardized approach as has been the experience of many companies and the research of many academics.[16]

Market Characteristics

Market characteristics can have a profound effect on international marketing strategy. The *physical environment* of any country—determined by its climate, product use conditions, and population size—often forces marketers to make adjustments to products to fit local conditions. Many cars in Canada come equipped with a built-in heating system that is connected to an electrical outlet to keep the engine from freezing while turned off. In warmer climates, cars are not equipped with such a heating unit but are more likely to require air conditioning. The product use conditions for washing machines in Europe differ from country to country. In Germany, manufacturers have been forced to add built-in heaters because homemakers prefer to boil the water during the regular washing cycle and use a cold-water fill. British homemakers prefer to fill washing machines with hot water directly from a house boiler, making a built-in heating unit unnecessary.[17] In Japan, washing is done frequently with cold tap water or left-over bath water. Procter & Gamble, marketing its Cheer all-temperature brand in Japan, soon learned that cold washing was required and that the product had to be reformulated to allow for the addition of fabric softener with cold water. The old Cheer formula produced insufficient suds.[18]

14. This section draws heavily on Robert D. Buzzell's classic article, "Can You Standardize Multinational Marketing?" See *Harvard Business Review,* November–December 1968, pp. 102–113.

15. Theodore Levitt, "The Globalization of Markets," *Harvard Business Review,* May–June 1983, pp. 92–102.

16. See Kamran Kashani, "Beware of the Pitfalls of Global Marketing," *Harvard Business Review,* September–October 1989, pp. 91–98; also, "Marketers Turn Sour on Global Sales Pitch Harvard Guru Makes," *Wall Street Journal,* May 12, 1988, p. 1.

17. See "Hoover (A)," Harvard Business School, *Harvard Case Clearing House,* 9-582-102.

18. "After Early Stumbles, P&G Is Making Inroads Overseas," *Wall Street Journal,* February 6, 1989, p. B1.

A country's *population* will affect the market size in terms of volume, allowing for lower prices in larger markets. Market size or expected sales volume greatly affect channel strategy. Company-owned manufacturing and sales subsidiaries are often possible in larger markets, whereas independent distributors are often used in smaller countries.

Macroeconomic factors also greatly affect international marketing strategy. The income level, or gross national product (GNP) per capita, varies widely among nations—from below $100 per year for some of the world's poorest nations to above $20,000 per year for rich countries such as Kuwait, Sweden, and the United States. Countries have been categorized according to stages of economic development, ranging from a preindustrial stage to full economic maturity.[19] As can be expected, marketing environments will differ considerably according to income level. If the population's level of technical skill is low, a marketer may be forced to simplify product design to suit the local market. Pricing may be affected to the extent to which countries with lower income levels show higher price elasticities for many products compared to more developed countries. Furthermore, convenient access to credit is often restricted to buyers in developing countries. This has negative impact on the sale of capital goods and consumer durables.

Exchange rate fluctuations distort prices among countries for many products that otherwise would sell at similar prices. This leads to the problem of cross shipping products to take advantage of price gaps. With specialization among channel members differing widely among various countries, depending on macroeconomic factors, companies often find themselves forced to adjust channel policies to compensate for the absence of the middleman they normally rely on in their home country. Wage levels and the availability of manpower may influence a company to choose a different approach for its sales force. Since the motivation to purchase some products depends on a country's income level, advertising and promotion strategies may have to be adjusted for such changes.

Cultural and social factors are less predictable influences on the marketing environment, and they often have frustrated many international marketers. Customs and traditions have the greatest effect on product categories when a country's population has had prior experience with a given product category. Although Coca-Cola has been very successful transferring its Coke brand into many countries, it has also run into difficulties with other products. Its canned coffee drink, Georgia Coffee, which had met with success in Japan, did not find any acceptance elsewhere. And a soy drink that did very well in Hong Kong did not take off in the United States.[20] Erno Laszlo, a U.S. skin care product, was marketed successfully in the United States by convincing American women to use it as part of a daily "regimen." Such efforts

19. W. W. Rostow, *The Stages of Economic Growth* (London: Cambridge University Press, 1960).

20. "Marketers Turn Sour on Global Sales Pitch Harvard Guru Makes," *Wall Street Journal,* May 12, 1988, p. 1.

failed completely in both European and Asian markets where skin care customs varied widely from country to country.[21]

Language can be another hurdle for international marketing to get over and international marketers are focusing their attention on this problem. There are many examples of poor translations of promotional material. When McDonald's expanded into Puerto Rico in the early 1980s, the company employed American TV commercials dubbed in Spanish. When prospective customers objected, the company eventually relented and developed a Spanish language campaign just for Puerto Rico. Sales showed a considerable increase.[22] This experience shows that when it comes to language, not even simple translation is sometimes enough. Slight differences in idioms can exist that are not known to the uninitiated which, if neglected, may result in poor marketing results.

Industry Conditions

Industry conditions often vary by country since products frequently are in varying stages of the product life cycle. New product introduction in a country without prior experience may affect the degree of product differentiation since only one or two versions of the product may be introduced initially. Also, a company may find itself in a situation where limited awareness or prior experience of a country require a considerable missionary sales effort and primary demand stimulation, whereas in more mature markets the promotional strategy is likely to concentrate on brand differentiation. The level of local competition can be expected to vary substantially by country. The higher the technological level of the competition, the more an international company must improve the quality level of its products. The varying prices of local substitutes or low local production costs can be expected to influence pricing policy. In countries where competitors control channels and maintain a strong sales force, the strategy of a multinational company may differ significantly from that in a country where the company holds a competitive advantage.

How difficult it can sometimes be to break into local competition was illustrated by Allied Signal, a U.S.-based technology company trying to sell a new technology through a joint-venture operation with a large Japanese trading company. Allied had developed a new process for amorphous metals that allows key electronic components to be made much smaller than before and electric transformers in utility poles could become more efficient. Allied had hoped to convince Japanese utility companies that they were estimated to be able to use about $65 million worth of such products, as many have already done in the United States. After four years of trying, Allied quit because it could not get any local utility to use the new product in volume. The powerful Japanese steel companies, threatened by this venture, were believed to have rushed their own development to head off the U.S. incursion. Even though the

21. Ibid., p. 4.
22. Ibid., p. 4.

venture was managed by a Japanese-American manager who spoke fluent Japanese, sales remained at a low level and costs could not be met.[23]

Marketing Institutions

For historic and economic reasons, marketing institutions have assumed different forms in different countries. Practices in distribution systems often entail different margins for the same product, requiring a change in company pricing strategy. Availability of outlets is also likely to vary by country. Mass merchandisers such as supermarkets, discount stores, and department stores are widely available in the United States and other industrialized countries but are largely absent in less developed nations in southern Europe, Latin America, and other parts of the world. Such variations may lead to considerably different distribution strategies. Likewise, advertising agencies and the media are not equally accessible in all countries; and the absence of mass media channels in some countries makes a "pull" strategy less effective.

Presently, Eastern Europe is an area where many companies find they have to adapt to a much less developed marketing infrastructure. Xerox, in expanding its business in Czechoslovakia, found it difficult to expand its sales to independent copy shops. All copying was previously done by government-owned shops where customers had to show identification. Sales were only through three government-owned sales outlets. Although a sufficient number of government-employed service technicians existed in the country, the company found it very difficult to find independent people willing to start copy shops or even independent dealers for local sales.[24] The opening of Eastern Europe during 1991 completely changed this situation, resulting in the opportunity for numerous independent dealers.

Legal Restrictions

Legal restrictions also require consideration for the development of an international marketing strategy. Product standards issued by local governments must be observed. To the extent that they differ from one country to another, unified product design often becomes an impossibility. Tariffs and taxes may require adjustments in pricing to the extent that a product can no longer be sold on a high-volume basis. Specific restrictions may also be problematic. In Europe, restrictions on advertising make it impossible to mention a competitor's name, despite the fact that such an approach may be an integral part of the advertising strategy in the United States.

To carry out the international marketing task successfully, international managers have to be cognizant of all the factors that influence the local marketing envi-

23. "Frustrated and Defeated, a U.S. Businessman Says Farewell to Japan," *International Herald Tribune,* June 24, 1989, p. 1.
24. "Dilemma of a Salesman in Prague," *New York Times,* December 27, 1990, p. D1.

ronment. Frequently, they need to target special marketing programs for each country.

MAJOR PARTICIPANTS IN INTERNATIONAL MARKETING

Several types of companies are major participants in international and global marketing. Among the leaders are multinational corporations (MNCs), exporters, importers, and service companies. These firms may be engaged in manufacturing consumer or industrial goods, in trading, or in the performance of a full range of services. What all participants have in common is a need to deal with the complexities of the international marketplace.

Multinational Corporations

Multinational corporations (MNCs) are companies that manufacture and market products or services in several countries. Typically an MNC operates a number of plants abroad and markets products through a large network of fully owned subsidiaries. Although no clearly acceptable definition exists, MNCs are also referred to as global companies, transnational firms, or stateless corporations. For the purpose of this text, we have chosen the terms international, multinational, or global corporation. We use the term international to indicate a company with some international activities. The term MNC is reserved for a company with extensive overseas operations including overseas manufacturing in several companies. We would call a company global if its operations span the globe and are active in most major markets for its industry. Since multinational (MNC) or global tend to be more specific terms, we have chosen to use the term international firm when the issues apply to all types of firms.

Fortune's list of the world's largest one hundred companies shows how much international business has developed outside the United States by large, growing firms across the world. Of the largest corporations, only thirty-nine are based in the United States, Japan has fifteen and Germany twelve, with a total of fifteen countries represented on the list.[25]

Fortune's list of the largest 500 foreign corporations lists the largest non-U.S.-based firms and includes 159 firms from Japan, 74 from the U.K., 53 from Germany, 39 from France, 28 from Canada, 20 from Sweden, and 13 each from Australia and Switzerland. Several of the largest firms are based in countries that only recently have spawned large international businesses. They include South Korea (11 firms), Taiwan (4 firms), India (7 firms) and Brazil (5 firms).[26]

One of the newcomers to the field of international business, Daewoo from

25. "The New Shape of Global Business," *Fortune,* July 31, 1989, p. 280.
26. "The 500 International," *Fortune,* July 31, 1989, p. 312.

Korea, is an excellent example of a company that has risen to a strong international position in just a few years. The company, a large conglomerate with 1989 sales of $19.98 billion and ranking 47th among the world's largest corporations, is active in a number of fields. Daewoo Heavy Industries (DHI) produces products such as diesel engines, fork lift trucks, excavators, machine tools, and precision machines. Exports rose from less than 10 percent of sales in 1983 to almost one-third of sales in 1986. The company has a number of licensing agreements with foreign firms such as Caterpillar of the United States for whom DHI is becoming a major producer.[27] Another rapidly growing division is Daewoo Telecom, which designed and engineered a personal computer sold in the United States as the Leading Edge Model D. It became one of the best-selling, IBM-compatible personal computers on the market.[28]

The interest of foreign MNCs in the U.S. market continues to grow. Perrier, the French bottled-water company, acquired Poland Spring, Calistoga, Oasis Water, Zephyr Hill, and most recently Arrowhead, all local brands. By 1989, Perrier sales had reached $100 million at wholesale level and the brand accounted for about 50 percent of all imported bottled water. Following the complete recall of Perrier in 1990 due to traces of benzene, Perrier sales ended up at $60 million for 1990, down 40 percent, and its market share has been cut in half. Perrier has found it difficult to reestablish its position.[29]

Foreign investment in the United States increased rapidly during the 1980s. Great Britain with some $100 billion in direct investments accounted for the largest portion of foreign direct investments in the United States. For several large British firms, U.S. sales account for a large portion of their global sales. For ICI (chemicals) it amounts to 29 percent and for Grand Met (acquired Pillsbury and Burger King) the amount was 40 percent. For the two large German chemical firms, BASF and Hoechst, U.S. sales account for some 22 percent of corporate volume. For Swedish Electrolux, the U.S. volume rose to 30 percent through the acquisition of White Westinghouse. Pechiney of France has 42 percent of its corporate sales in the United States. Even some Japanese firms, such as Honda (48 percent), Mitsubishi Electric (49 percent) and Nissan (23 percent), have become dependent to a large degree on U.S. sales.[30]

Global Companies

Global companies differ from MNCs in that they pursue integrated strategies on a worldwide scale rather than separate strategies on a country-by-country basis. They

---

27. "Daewoo Gets Ready to Play World Role," *Financial Times,* May 9, 1986, p. 23.

28. "Foreign Clones Spark a Mid-Life Crisis," *Financial Times,* June 9, 1986, p. 28.

29. "Perrier Finds Mystique Hard to Restore," *Wall Street Journal,* December 12, 1990, p. B1.

30. "Nice View From Up Here," *The Economist,* November 24, 1990, p. 68.

tend to look at the whole world as one market and move products, manufacturing, capital, or even personnel wherever it can gain an advantage. Global firms also tend to have a strong base in all of the major economic regions of North America, Europe, and Asia's Pacific Rim countries. Their products are developed for the entire world market and their organization has undergone changes in order to be able to move from regional to product line-based profit centers. Many of their senior executives come from foreign countries.

General Electric, one of the largest U.S. corporations, is pursuing its own strategy to become a global company. Each of the company's businesses is expected to reach the number one or number two position worldwide in its respective area. A number of GE's businesses have already reached this goal, such as its aircraft engine business, its plastics business, and its turbine business. The medical division, concentrating on computer tomography, was formed only recently to reach its goal of becoming dominant in its segment worldwide. The division was formed out of GE's own medical division, the acquisition of Thompson's medical business in France, and a majority ownership of Yokogawa Medical Systems in Japan. Product development was streamlined with the French company concentrating on X rays, the United States on CT and magnetic resonance equipment, and the Japanese firm concentrating on the cheaper lines. This integrated business was now ahead of Siemens of Germany, Philips of the Netherlands, and Toshiba of Japan, in diagnostic imaging devices. The acquisition of the French medical business was only made possible through the trade of GE's consumer electronics business which fit better into the French company's portfolio and thus allowed the French company to become a major player in that segment.[31]

Texas Instruments is pursuing globalization to compete in the very tough market for memory chips. The company has designated a single design center and factory worldwide for each type of memory chip. TI has built two of its four new memory chip plants in Taiwan and Japan to take advantage of lower capital costs. An alliance with Hitachi of Japan helps share research costs. The global responsibility for TI's memory business is assigned to its country manager for Japan, a Japanese executive.[32]

ICI, Britain's largest manufacturing company and one of the world's largest chemical companies, is an excellent example of a foreign-based global company. With one of the broadest product lines in the chemical industry, ICI began to shift its traditional country-by-country organization in 1983 toward a product line organization with worldwide business units. Several of these business units were headquartered outside of the United Kingdom, two of them in the United States in Wilmington, Delaware. In ICI Pharmaceuticals, worldwide responsibility for new projects allowed the company to reduce the time lag for new product introductions

31. "How To Go Global—and Why," *Fortune,* August 28, 1989, p. 72.
32. Ibid., p. 76.

of drugs to different countries from as much as a dozen years to one or two. The eventual goal is to have simultaneous introductions worldwide.[33] More recently the company announced that, in the future, it will put its resources behind those world-wide businesses that globally have a good chance to obtain a competitive position. The businesses will retain strategy-making responsibility and the various country organizations will be asked to support these businesses in their individual countries in order to execute those strategies rather than have to create new strategies country-by-country as was the case in previous decades.

Service Companies

The early MNCs and global companies were largely manufacturers of industrial equipment and consumer products. Many of the newer MNCs are service compa-nies. Commercial banks, investment bankers, and brokers have turned themselves into global service networks. Airlines and hotel companies have gained global status. Less noticeable are the global networks of public accounting firms, consulting com-panies, advertising agencies, and a host of other service-related industries. This glob-alization of the service sector has not been restricted to the United States alone but has been mirrored in many other countries as well.

Examples of U.S. service companies with international involvement abound. McDonald's has increased its international sales from 20 percent in 1985 to 31 per-cent in 1989 amounting to a volume of more than $5 billion. Its international busi-ness is growing much faster than U.S. sales where the company may have reached saturation. It is believed that the company may pass the 40 percent mark for inter-national volume by 1992.[34] Other major services exports include American Inter-national Group (50 percent of revenue abroad), Citicorp (40 percent), Time Warner (communications and entertainment, 23 percent), Disney (20 percent), American Express (19 percent), Federal Express (19 percent), and Merrill Lynch (15 percent).[35] Today's service company is apt to be as global or international as any manufactur-ing company.

Exporters

Exports are an important aspect of international and global marketing. In 1989, the U.S. exported goods worth some $360 billion, of which $44 billion went to Japan, doubling that volume over four years ago.[36] This surge in exporting was largely due

---

33. Ibid., p. 72.
34. "McD's Faces U.S. Slowdown," *Advertising Age,* May 14, 1990, p. 1.
35. "The Stateless Corporation," *Business Week,* May 14, 1990, p. 58.
36. "Overseas Sales Take Off at Last," *Fortune,* July 16, 1990, p. 76.

to U.S. performance in manufactured products that increased from $168 billion in 1985 to $287 billion in 1989, reducing the trade deficit from $150 billion to $100 billion.[37]

Exporters are firms that market products abroad but produce largely in their home country. Most large exporters have evolved into multinational companies. However, multinational companies, by shipping products between subsidiaries, have maintained some of the largest export operations. Consistently, the United States' largest exporter, Boeing, had export sales of $11 billion in 1989 representing almost 55 percent of total sales.[38] Other leading exporters included General Motors, Ford Motors, General Electric, and IBM, who all exported more than $5 billion in 1989 but whose export sales were less than 15 percent of corporate sales. Much of their international business was transacted through foreign subsidiaries produced abroad and would, thus, not be registered as U.S. exports. A newcomer to the list of top U.S. exporters was Sun Microsystems which exported about 42 percent of its volume amounting to $751 million in exports in 1989.[39] Many U.S. companies that follow a strict export-only policy are smaller firms. Some may have foreign subsidiaries devoted only to marketing and sales. Even some of the foreign subsidiaries operating in the U.S. market can become exporters. Honda Motor Co. has been exporting the Gold Wing 1,200cc motorcycle from its U.S. plant since 1980. After selling it in fourteen overseas markets, Honda started to ship these motorcycles to Japan in 1987.[40]

Importers

As described earlier, importing is as much an international marketing decision as exporting. Companies that neither export nor have multinational status may still participate in international marketing through their importing operations. Many of the largest U.S. retail chains maintain import departments that are in contact with suppliers in many overseas countries. Other major importers are MNCs that obtain products from their own plants abroad or from other clients. Among the largest U.S. importers are oil companies and subsidiaries of foreign MNCs, particularly those of European and Japanese origin.

For the purpose of this text, we will use *international company* or *international firm* as umbrella terms that may include MNCs, global firms, exporters, importers, and service companies.

37. "Anchors Away, My Boys," *The Economist,* January 12, 1991, p. 59.
38. "Overseas Sales Take Off at Last," *Fortune,* July 16, 1990, p. 76.
39. Ibid., p. 76.
40. "Honda Will Ship to Japan Motorcycles Made in the U.S.," *Wall Street Journal,* July 3, 1987, p. 25.

THE IMPORTANCE OF INTERNATIONAL AND
GLOBAL MARKETING

International and global marketing is a very broad activity and it is expanding rapidly. The dollar value of world trade grew by an average of 13 percent annually between 1970 and 1987.[41] As we discussed earlier, international trade is one of the important components of international and global marketing. For 1990, total world trade in merchandise was estimated to have reached $3,500 billion, a 13 percent rise over the previous year.[42] Some 55 percent of this volume was in manufactured products compared to about 43 percent in primary products.[43] Table 1.1 compares world exports of manufactured products in the years 1973, 1980, 1981, and 1985. The table shows a clear upward trend in the world trade of manufactured goods. Most of this world trade was concentrated in heavy machinery, transport equipment, motor vehicles, specialized machinery, and office and telecommunications equipment, and this did not include the local business of foreign-owned subsidiaries.

World trade in services—in shipping, insurance, banking, and other service-related industries—increased to $690 billion in 1989[44] and now accounts for about 20 percent of total world trade. Service trade is referred to as "invisible trade" because the traded goods are abstract and difficult to quantify. Major components of service trade are transport, travel, banking, and insurance. The U.S. Department of Commerce has estimated the foreign business of U.S. service industries at about $144 billion in exports and $122 billion in imports.[45] This invisible sector of total world trade is expanding quickly and is expected to grow at a faster rate than world trade in manufactured goods and commodities. For 1989, revised U.S. export figures for services were estimated at over $100 billion, accounting for about 22 percent of U.S. exports.[46] Even education is an important service export for the U.S. economy. The tuition income of U.S. educational institutions derived from foreign students has passed $5 billion annually and accounts for an important portion of the budget of many universities. China, Taiwan, Japan, India, and Korea each supply between 20,000 and 30,000 students. About half of the foreign students take graduate studies. Engineering and business administration are the favorite subjects.[47]

A substantial portion of international marketing operations does not get recorded in international trade statistics. In particular, MNC overseas sales of locally manufactured and locally sold products are not included in world trade figures. Consequently, total volume in international marketing far exceeds the volume of $2,400

---

41. "Economic and Financial Indicators: Trade," *The Economist,* February 4, 1989, p. 102.

42. "Economic and Financial Judication," *The Economist,* April 27, 1991, p. 110.

43. "Statistical Trends: World Trade," *Financial Times,* April 25, 1983, p. 5.

44. Economic and Financial Indicators: Trade in Services," *The Economist,* December 8, 1990, p. 118.

45. "Services—The Star of U.S. Trade," *New York Times,* September 14, 1986, p. 74.

46. "Nothing To Lose But Its Chains," *The Economist,* September 22, 1990, p. 36.

47. "Foreign Students: Who Are They?," *New York Times,* November 29, 1989.

TABLE 1.1 ● World Exports of Manufactured Products (in Billions of Dollars)

	1973	1980	1981	1985
Iron and steel	28.5	76.2	74.0	69.3
Chemicals	41.9	153.0	148.5	163.4
Other semi-manufacturers	29.0	92.7	88.5	86.4
Engineering products	188.0	593.0	615.0	682.0
Specialized industry machinery	52.5	159.0	160.5	150.6
Office and telecommunications equipment	17.2	59.6	62.0	97.9
Road motor vehicles	41.0	127.4	129.5	158.3
Other machinery/transportation equipment	62.0	198.7	211.0	216.3
Household appliances	15.3	48.3	52.0	58.9
Textiles	23.4	55.4	53.5	55.4
Clothing	12.6	40.2	41.0	49.2
Other consumer goods	24.3	83.7	82.5	91.6
Total manufactures	347.5	1,094.1	1,103.0	1,197.3
Percent of world exports	60%	55%	56%	62%

Source: Data from *GATT International Trade 1981/1982,* as published in *Financial Times,* April 25, 1983, p. 5. 1985 data from *GATT International Trade 1985/1986,* p. 157.

billion for total world trade in 1989. The U.S. Department of Commerce estimated that the 1981 income of foreign affiliates of U.S. service firms amounted to about $100 billion, compared with export earnings of $40 billion for the same year.[48] Although no detailed statistics are available, this pattern suggests that the overall volume of international marketing amounts to a multiple of world trade volume.

Why Companies Become Involved in Global Marketing

Companies become involved in international markets for a variety of reasons. Some firms simply respond to orders from abroad without any organized efforts of their own, but most companies take a more active role because they have determined that it is to their advantage to pursue export business on an incremental basis. The profitability of a company can increase when fixed manufacturing costs are already committed and additional economies of scale are achieved. OshKosh B'Gosh Inc., the U.S.-based maker of children's clothing, had European sales of only 2 percent of its corporate volume of $250 million for 1988. Despite its low sales, the

48. "GATT State Set for Reagan to Break Down Services Trade Bars," *Financial Times,* November 22, 1982, p. 3.

company's trademark and clothing were well known in Europe. Through a joint venture with a European clothing manufacturer, the company will get local production for its styles and sell them under its own name throughout Europe. The foreign expansion is expected to reach about 12 percent of total sales within four years. This extra volume will essentially be made under an already existing strong brand umbrella.[49]

Some companies pursue growth in other countries after their domestic market has reached maturity. Coca-Cola, a market leader worldwide in the soft drink business, finds that foreign consumers drink only 14 percent as much as Americans do. This suggests an enormous market potential outside the United States. The company already earns as much as 80 percent of its operating earnings outside the U.S. and expects strong growth to come from Europe.[50] In eastern Germany, where Coke could only be sold after the liberalization of 1989, sales may reach $1 billion within just a few years.[51]

Companies move into foreign markets to get additional volume. H. J. Heinz, the U.S.-based food producer, achieved about one third of its sales abroad, mostly in Europe, Australia, and New Zealand.[52] However, the company's entire sales of more than $3 billion were achieved with only 15 percent of the world's population. As a result, Heinz has aggressively looked for opportunities in Third-World countries, with the goal of sales in those areas reaching $1 billion by 1990.

When a company's customers move overseas, many firms follow suit. Major U.S. banks have shifted to serve their U.S. clients in key financial centers around the world by opening branches. Advertising agencies in the United States have created networks to serve the interests of their multinational clients. As some Japanese manufacturers opened plants in the United States, many of their component suppliers followed and built operations nearby. Not following these clients would have meant a loss of business.

Companies also enter the international arena for purely defensive purposes. Those that are concerned about foreign competition, in particular certain U.S. companies such as Texas Instruments or Kodak, have launched businesses in Japan to check the advance of Japanese competitors. Others such as Olivetti of Italy entered the United States to learn from the most advanced market in the office equipment industry. Whether companies participate for the pursuit of new opportunities or for any other reason, most have been able to enhance their overall competitiveness as a result of pursuing foreign ventures.

49. "OshKosh B'Gosh Sets European Venture," *Wall Street Journal,* November 8, 1989, p. B6.

50. "As a Global Marketer, Coke Excels by Being Tough and Consistent," *Wall Street Journal,* December 19, 1989, p. 1.

51. "Coke Gets Off Its Can in Europe," *Fortune,* August 13, 1990, p. 68.

52. "Heinz Sets Out to Expand in Africa and Asia, Seeking New Markets, Sources of Materials," *Wall Street Journal,* September 27, 1983.

WHY STUDY GLOBAL MARKETING?

You have probably asked yourself why you should study global marketing. You also may have wondered about the value of this knowledge to your future career. While it is not very likely that many university graduates find an entry-level position in international or global marketing, it is nevertheless a fact that each year U.S.-based international companies hire large numbers of marketing professionals. Since many of these firms are becoming increasingly globalized, competence in global marketing will become even more important in the future—and many marketing executives will be pursuing global marketing as a career. Other career opportunities exist with a large number of exporters, and candidates will require international marketing skills. Furthermore, each year many university graduates are hired for the marketing efforts of foreign-based companies in the United States. These companies are also looking for international and global competence within their managerial ranks.

With the U.S. service sector becoming increasingly globalized, many graduates joining service industries have found themselves confronted with international opportunities at early stages of their careers. Today, consulting engineers, bankers, brokers, and public accountants are all in need of international and global marketing skills to compete in a rapidly changing environment. Consequently, a solid understanding and appreciation of global marketing will benefit the careers of most business students, regardless of the field or industry they choose to enter.

A Need for More Globetrotters

Compared to other industrialized nations, the United States severely lacks a sufficient number of international marketing professionals. The professionals and the firms actively participating in international and global marketing through exporting, importing, or production abroad have been called globetrotters.[53] Globetrotters, as active participants in international and global marketing, play a key role in the success of international firms. In this competitive business, the United States has seen its share of world exports steadily decline. In 1953, the United States accounted for 19 percent of total world exports, more than twice the share of the second-ranked United Kingdom with about 8 percent. At that time, Japan accounted for only 2 percent of world exports. The U.S. share of world export was back to 12 percent in 1988 which saw the United States tied with Germany and ahead of Japan with a 10 percent share. France, the U.K. and Italy followed with shares of about 5 percent each.[54]

There are other indications that the United States is lagging behind other countries in globetrotting. From 1870 to 1970, the United States almost always reported

53. Hans Thorelli and Helmut Becker, *International Marketing Strategy,* rev. ed. (New York: Pergamon Press, 1980), p. 14.
54. "America's Place in World Competition," *Fortune,* November 6, 1989, p. 83.

a positive trade balance, exporting more goods than importing. This began to change in the 1970s, and despite the large increase in earnings of the service industry, the overall balance of trade has turned substantially negative (see Figure 1.3).[55] It has been estimated that a trade deficit of this size has cost the United States several million jobs. Although many reasons for this lagging performance lie beyond the control of individual companies, there is much that company management can do to redress the imbalance. Foreign companies fight much harder than U.S. firms to retain foreign markets. Because the foreign firms' domestic markets are usually smaller than the U.S. market, foreign firms are more motivated than U.S. firms to succeed abroad.

Despite this problem, foreign trade or international marketing is still not given enough attention by large sectors of United States society. Whereas university graduates in other countries learn one or more foreign languages as a matter of course, U.S. graduates usually have no foreign language competence. About 50,000 Japanese business professionals work in New York, all with a good understanding of English. Only about 500 U.S. business professionals working in Tokyo have a good command of the Japanese language. Although it is too simplistic to associate foreign language capabilities with effective globetrotting, this comparison nevertheless serves as an indicator of interest in international business.

A Need for More Globe Watchers

Few of us can avoid the impact of international competition today. Many of our domestic industries have fallen on hard times. Foreign competition has made enormous inroads in the manufacture of apparel, textiles, shoes, electronic equipment, and steel. As a result, these industries have become globalized (see Figure 1.4). Although foreign competition for many consumer goods has been evident for years, inroads by foreign firms in investment goods industries have been equally spectacular. By 1985, imports accounted for 20 percent of the U.S. market for industrial goods.[56] The U.S. machine tool industry found it had to appeal to the U.S. government for help because imported machine tools increased their share of domestic consumption from 25 percent in 1982 to 55 percent in 1986.[57] Management of companies competing with foreign firms requires globe watching skill: an ability to judge the next move of foreign competitors by observing them abroad, in order to be better prepared to compete at home.

Import competition has been rising even in industries that used to be reserved largely for domestic companies. Nissin, a Japanese maker of instant noodles, started to make its dry soup called Oodles of Noodles in 1976 and, by expanding its manufacturing to a plant on each coast, now accounts for 4 percent share of the U.S. soup market estimated at $2.3 billion. The company competes with Lipton, a traditional

55. "US Economy Grows Ever More Vulnerable to Foreign Influences," *Wall Street Journal,* October 27, 1986, pp. 1, 16.

56. "America's War on Imports," *Fortune,* August 19, 1985, pp. 26–29.

57. "Cost-Cutting Will Still Be the Watchword," *Business Week,* January 12, 1987.

FIGURE 1.3 ● U.S. Trade Deficit 1973–1990

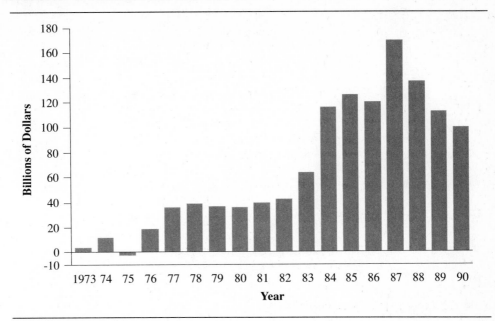

Source: Reprinted from the August 29, 1983 issue of *Business Week* by special permission, © 1983 by McGraw-Hill, Inc. 1973–1983 data from Commerce Department, Data Resources Inc.; 1984–1986 data from the United Nations, *World Economic Survey 1986;* p. 46; 1987–1988 data from *Business Week,* February 27, 1989, p. 86; 1989 *Survey of Current Business,* March 1990, p. 50; and 1990 *The Economist,* March 9, 1991, p. 108.

supplier of dry soups, by shipping smaller quantities to retailers. This results in faster product turnover at the retail level and a fresher product. Although the initial results were not successful, Nissin stayed in for the long haul and is now a successful competitor in the United States.[58] In 1983, processed food imports by the United States exceeded processed food exports for the first time.[59]

Even the service industry is not immune from foreign competition. For decades, Nielsen, the leading U.S. marketing research company, enjoyed a near-monopoly in the rating of television programs. Now it is facing serious competition from a newcomer from the United Kingdom, AGB. This U.K. company gained a competitive edge with its "people reader," which allows the company to record viewership automatically in each connected television set. Nielsen still relies on selected viewers to record in diaries what they watch.[60]

58. "Japan's Next Push in U.S. Markets," *Fortune,* September 26, 1988, p. 135.
59. "U.S. Food Firms Face More Imports and Rise in Foreign Plants Here," *Wall Street Journal,* November 18, 1986, p. 1.
60. "ABG Breaks into U.S. Networks," *Financial Times,* October 16, 1986, p. 16.

FIGURE 1.4 ● Globalization of Selected Industries

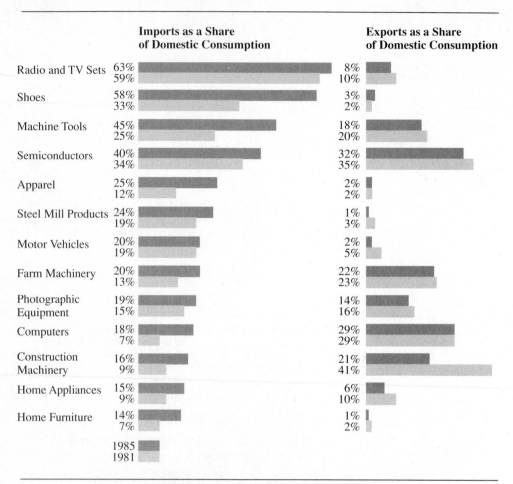

	Imports as a Share of Domestic Consumption	Exports as a Share of Domestic Consumption
Radio and TV Sets	63% / 59%	8% / 10%
Shoes	58% / 33%	3% / 2%
Machine Tools	45% / 25%	18% / 20%
Semiconductors	40% / 34%	32% / 35%
Apparel	25% / 12%	2% / 2%
Steel Mill Products	24% / 19%	1% / 3%
Motor Vehicles	20% / 19%	2% / 5%
Farm Machinery	20% / 13%	22% / 23%
Photographic Equipment	19% / 15%	14% / 16%
Computers	18% / 7%	29% / 29%
Construction Machinery	16% / 9%	21% / 41%
Home Appliances	15% / 9%	6% / 10%
Home Furniture	14% / 7%	1% / 2%
	1985 / 1981	

Source: Data from U.S. Commerce Department, National Association of Manufacturers, as published in *The Wall Street Journal,* October 27, 1986. Reprinted by permission of *The Wall Street Journal,* © 1986 Dow Jones & Company, Inc. All Rights Reserved Worldwide.

Foreign competition has also reached U.S. retailers. IKEA, a Swedish furniture retailing chain with some ninety stores worldwide in twenty-two countries and total sales of $3.2 billion, has expanded its operation into the United States. The stores have the size of six normal supermarkets and specialize in disassembled furniture. IKEA has decided on a major expansion on both coasts and its stores have done well despite the stagnant sales in the U.S. furniture industry. In its most recent opening in New Jersey, consumers snapped up the furniture priced 20 to 40 percent below competitive prices as the managers conceded that they had underestimated demand by 40 percent.[61]

The need to become more competitive in a global economy will force many changes on the typical company. Companies will have to become international and compete in global markets to define their own domestic markets and to keep up with global competitors based in other countries. These firms will need an increasing cadre of managers who can think with a global perspective.[62] This requires not only a knowledge about other countries, economies, or cultures, but a clear understanding of how the global economy works. Managers with a global perspective will also have to integrate developments from one part of the world with actions somewhere else. This means that a U.S. executive will be required to use input, facts, or ideas from all other countries for decisions in the United States so that the most efficient and best products may be marketed.

Managers with a global perspective will also be challenged to deal with new strategies that were not part of the domestic or older international business scene. These concepts, created and developed over the past ten years, have been included in our text and will become apparent to the reader on a chapter by chapter basis. As a result, the reader will come to appreciate that the term "global" is more than just a replacement for "international." It is a combination of a new perspective on the world and a series of new strategic concepts that add to the competitiveness of global marketing strategies. Mastering both this new outlook and the concepts will become a requirement for firms who aspire to a position of global player in their chosen industries or market segments.

THE ORGANIZATION OF THIS BOOK

This text is structured around the basic requirements for making sound international marketing decisions. It takes into account the need to develop several types of competencies to analyze international marketing issues. The global marketer must be able to deal with decision areas on various levels of complexity. We will first discuss each of these dimensions of the global marketing task before we discuss the outline for this text.

Competencies

To compete successfully in today's international marketplace, companies and their management must master certain areas. *Environmental competence* is needed to

61. "IKEA's Got 'Em Lining Up," *Fortune,* March 11, 1991, p. 72.
62. Jean-Pierre Jeannet, "International Management: The Age of the Global Mind," *Die Unternehmung,* March 1991.

perform in the international economy. It includes a knowledge of the dynamics of world economy, of major national markets, and of social and cultural environments. *Analytic competence* is needed to pull together a vast array of information and data and to assemble relevant facts. *Strategic competence* helps executives focus on the strategic or long-term requirements of their firms as opposed to short-term, opportunistic decisions. A global marketer must also possess *functional competence,* or a thorough background in all areas of marketing. Finally, *managerial competence* is the ability to implement programs and organize effectively on a global scale.

Managers with domestic responsibility will also need analytic, strategic, functional, and managerial competence. They do not need international competence. Consequently, we can isolate one component that sets the international executive apart from his or her domestic counterpart.

Decision Areas

Successful international marketing requires the ability to make decisions not typically faced by single-country firms. These decision groupings include environmental analysis, opportunity analysis, international marketing strategies, international marketing programs, and international marketing management. Managers continuously must assess foreign environments and perform *environmental analyses* relevant to their businesses. In a second step, managers need to do an *opportunity analysis* that will tell them which products to pursue in which markets. Once opportunities have been identified, *global marketing strategies* are designed to define long-term efforts of the firm. The company then may design *global marketing programs* to determine the marketing mix. Finally, international marketing must *manage the global marketing effort,* which requires attention to planning, personnel, and organization.

Our five competence levels are closely related to the five major global marketing decision areas described above. Environmental competence is needed to perform an analysis of the international environment. Analytic competence is the basis for opportunity analysis. Sound global marketing strategies are based on strategic competence. To design global marketing programs one needs functional competence. Finally, managerial competence is needed for managing the international marketing effort.

Chapter Organization

This text is organized around the flow of decisions as depicted in Figure 1.5. The five decision areas are treated in several chapters that delineate the respective competence levels most appropriate for each decision area.

Chapter 1 provides an introduction and overview of global marketing and its challenges today.

Part 1, Chapters 2 through 4, is concerned with the global environment. In order to build environmental competence, special emphasis is given to the economic,

FIGURE 1.5 ● International Marketing Management

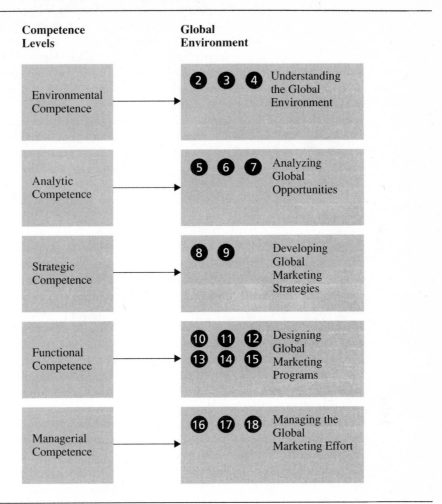

cultural, social, political, and legal forces companies must contend with in order to be successful.

Part 2, Chapters 5 through 7, concentrates on the global opportunity analysis. Chapters in this section highlight international markets or countries, international buyers, and the research or analysis necessary to pinpoint opportunities globally.

Chapters 8 and 9, which make up Part 3, deal with strategic issues. Chapter 8 introduces the elements of global marketing strategy. Chapter 9 describes how companies can enter markets they have decided to target.

Part 4, consisting of Chapters 10 through 15, aims at developing the competence to design global marketing programs consistent with a global strategy. The chapters in this section cover product strategies, product development, pricing, channel management, communications, and advertising.

The chapter material concludes with Part 5, Chapters 16 through 18. Here the emphasis is on building managerial competence in a global environment. Chapters 16, 17, and 18 deal with organizational and controlling issues and also with the technical aspects of the export and import trade process.

Finally the cases at the back of the book address international and global marketing issues and will allow you to practice the concepts developed in the text. These cases feature a range of complexity levels and address different decision areas of the global marketing process. They are all based on real situations, although the names of some of the companies are disguised.

CONCLUSIONS

As a separate activity of business, global marketing is of great importance to nations, to individual companies, and to prospective managers. With markets and industries becoming increasingly globalized, most companies have to become active participants in global marketing. The competitive positions of most companies, both abroad and in their domestic markets, rests on their ability to succeed in global markets. At the same time, the economies of entire countries rest on the global marketing skills of its managers. The standard of living of many people will depend on how well local industry does in the international market place. These forces will place a premium on executive talent that is able to direct marketing operations from a global perspective. It is clear that many business professionals will need to understand the global dimension as it pertains to their functions if they are to progress in their careers.

When it comes to a trained cadre of professional global marketing executives, the United States has typically lagged behind other countries. The U.S. market is so large that domestic problems tend to overshadow global marketing opportunities. As a result, most U.S. executives develop their careers largely in a domestic setting and have little direct exposure to foreign markets. Executives in foreign countries are more apt to have traveled abroad and tend to speak one or two foreign languages. Thus, their ability to understand global complexities is more developed than it is in their U.S. counterparts. All of this gives many foreign firms a considerable edge in competing for global dominance.

Although the need to develop a global competence may be clear, the circumstances that determine successful marketing practices for foreign markets are far less clear. The foreign marketing environment is characterized by a wide range of variables not typically encountered by domestic firms. This makes the job of global marketing extremely difficult. However, despite the complexities involved, there are concepts and analytic tools that can help international marketers. By learning to use these concepts and tools, you can enhance your own international and global competence—you will be able to contribute to the marketing operations of a wide range of firms, both domestic and foreign.

Questions for Discussion

1. Explain the scope of global marketing.
2. How and why does global marketing differ from domestic marketing?
3. Which do you think would be the most relevant factors limiting international marketing standardization of yogurts, automobiles, and desk-top personal computers?
4. How does global marketing as a field relate to your future career in business? How would you expect to come in contact with global marketing activities?
5. Why are so many U.S. industries facing import competition?
6. Investigate one or two U.S. firms that do well abroad and analyze why they are successful.
7. Explain the major roles of multinationals (MNCs) and global corporations as well as other types of firms in international marketing and how they participate in this activity.
8. What do you think are the essential skills of successful "globetrotting"?
9. Which are the important skills for successful "globe watching"?
10. List ten items most important to you that you hope to be able to understand or accomplish after studying this book.

For Further Reading

Alden, Vernon R. "Who Says You Can't Crack Japanese Markets." *Harvard Business Review,* January–February 1987, pp. 52–56.

Bolt, James F. "Global Competitors: Some Criteria for Success." *Business Horizons,* January–February 1988, pp. 34–41.

Buzzell, Robert D. "Can You Standardize Multinational Marketing?" *Harvard Business Review,* November–December 1968, pp. 102–113.

Davidson, William H. *Global Strategic Management.* New York: John Wiley and Sons, 1982.

Henzler, Herbert, and Wilhelm Rall. "Facing Up to the Globalization Challenge." *The McKinsey Quarterly,* Winter 1986, pp. 52–68.

Kashani, Kamran. "Beware of Pitfalls in Global Marketing" *Harvard Business Review,* September–October 1989, pp. 91–98.

Kotler, Philip. "Global Standardization—Courting Danger." *The Journal of Consumer Marketing* (Spring 1986), pp. 13–15.

Levitt, Theodore. "The Globalization of Markets." *Harvard Business Review* (May–June 1983), pp. 92–102.

Ohmae, Kenichi. *The Borderless World.* New York: Harper & Row, 1990.

Ohmae, Kenichi. "Managing in a Borderless World." *Harvard Business Review,* May–June 1989, pp. 152–161.

Porter, Michael E. "The Strategic Role of International Marketing." *The Journal of Consumer Marketing* (Spring 1986), pp. 17–21.

Rau, Pradeep A., and John F. Reble. "Standardization of Marketing Strategy by Multinationals." *International Marketing Review,* Autumn 1987, p. 18–28.

Simon-Miller, Francoise. "World Marketing: Going Global or Acting Local? Five Expert Viewpoints." *The Journal of Consumer Marketing* (Spring 1986), pp. 5–7.

van Mesdag, Martin. "Winging It In Foreign Market." *Harvard Business Review,* January–February 1987, pp. 71–74.

Wind, Yoram, and Howard Perlmutter. "On the Identification of Frontier Issues in Multinational Marketing." *Columbia Journal of World Business* (Winter 1977), pp. 131–139.

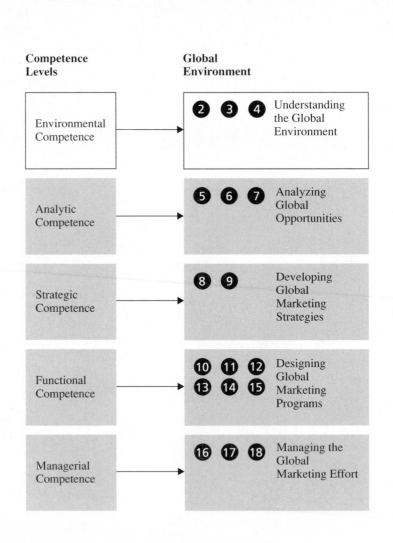

PART
ONE

Understanding the Global Environment

THIS PART OF the book introduces you to the environmental factors that influence international marketing decisions. Throughout Part 2 we maintain an analytical emphasis so that general concepts can be applied from country to country. Rather than describe a large number of environmental differences, we focus on several approaches that companies have adopted to cope with these differences. Our aim is to maintain a managerial point of view throughout.

In Chapter 2 we explain the nature of the various economic forces that shape developments within individual countries as well as within the international economy. In Chapter 3 we describe the social and cultural influences that shape the local marketing environment, and in Chapter 4 we discuss the political and legal forces that affect international firms, focusing on how companies cope with these forces.

2

The International Economy

BILLIONS OF DOLLARS *in goods and services are traded between nations each day. Businesses establish operations and borrow funds in locations throughout the world. Financial investors expeditiously purchase stocks and bonds on U.S., European, and Asian markets. Banks lend and arbitrage currencies worldwide. It is only when these transactions are interrupted or threatened that the scope and significance of the international economy are appreciated.*

The nations of the world are linked by a multidimensional network of economic, social, and political ties. As these connections become more important and complex, countries will find themselves richer but more vulnerable to foreign disturbances, and this vulnerability increasingly will move the issues surrounding international trade and finance into the political arena.

This chapter introduces you to the important aspects of world trade and finance. We begin by explaining comparative advantage, which is the basis for international trade. Then, we explain the international system to monitor world trade, particularly the balance of payments measurement system. From this base, we describe the workings of the foreign exchange market and the cause of exchange rate movements. Finally, we discuss the international agencies that promote economic and monetary stability, as well as the strategies that countries use to protect their own economies.

INTERNATIONAL TRADE: AN OVERVIEW

Few individuals in the world are totally self-sufficient. Why should they be? Restricting consumption to self-made goods lowers living standards by narrowing the range and reducing the quality of goods we consume. For this reason, few nations have economies independent from the rest of the world, and it would be difficult to find a national leader willing or able to impose such an economic hardship on a country.

Foreign goods are central to the living standards of all nations. But as Table 2.1 shows, there is considerable variation among countries concerning their reliance on foreign trade. Imports are less than 15 percent of the gross national product (GNP) of Japan, Mexico, or the United States, whereas the Netherlands and Belgium have import-to-GNP ratios of 47 percent or more.

Even in countries that seemingly do not have a great reliance on imports (such as the United States), foreign goods and services do play an important role. In the United States, exports account for 75 percent of manufacturing growth.[1] For example:

> Peter Johnson, a student, is awakened in the morning by his Sony clock radio. After showering, he puts on an Italian-made jacket while listening to the latest release by Tears for Fears, a British singing group. At breakfast, he has a cup of Brazilian coffee, a bowl of cereal made from American-grown wheat, and a Colombian banana. A quick glance at his Swiss watch shows him that he will have to hurry if he wants to be on time for his first class. He drives to campus in a Toyota, stopping on the way to fill the tank with gas from Saudi Arabian oil. Once in class, he rushes to take a seat with the other students, 30 percent of whom hold non-U.S. passports.

The figures given in Table 2.1 are useful for identifying the international dependence of nations, but they should be viewed as rough indicators only. If there were a disruption of international trade, there is little doubt that the United States would be harmed much less than the Netherlands. But how about Japan? Japan is a nation with relatively few natural resources. It survives by importing raw materials, processing them, and then exporting the finished products. Japan's import-to-GNP ratio is small (which indicates a lack of reliance on foreign trade) only because its exports are so large—therefore making its GNP large. Thus Japan would be a major victim of trade curtailment.

So far the focus has been on world trade for goods. Services also are an important and growing part of the world's economy. Services make up approximately 20 percent of the world's exports. Industries such as banking, telecommunications, insurance, construction, transportation, tourism, and consulting make up over half the national income of many rich economies. Services account for 70 percent of GDP in the United States and 75 percent of the employed. The leading exporters of com-

1. Susan Lee, "Are We Building New Berlin Walls," *Forbes,* January 7, 1991, p. 87.

TABLE 2.1 ● Imports and Exports as a Percentage of GDP, 1990 Estimates (in Billions of Dollars)

	GDP	Imports	Imports/GDP	Exports	Exports/GDP
Industrial					
Australia*	283	40	14%	37	13%
Belgium	196	121	61	120	61
Canada	594	118	20	127	21
Germany	1617	337	21	402	25
Japan	2932	225	8	270	9
Netherlands	272	127	47	130	48
Norway	105	28	27	33	31
United States	5550	510	9	392	7
Switzerland	228	73	32	66	29
Developing					
Greece	67	18	27%	6	9%
Mexico	230	27	12	26	11
Pakistan	40	7	18	5	13
Romania*	43	1	2	4	9
Saudi Arabia	104	22	21	48	46
South Korea	235	71	30	65	28
Venezuela	47	8	17	17	36

*Figures reflect 1989 data due to the unavailability of 1990 information.

Note: Estimates of GDP in local currency were converted to dollars using the yearly average exchange rate. Figures are rounded to the nearest billion in dollars. Please note that GDP is similar to GNP, which is explained in detail in Chapter 7, page 229. Percentages were calculated by the authors.

Source: Adapted from *World Outlook 1991.* London: The Economist Intelligence Unit, January 1991.

mercial services are shown in Figure 2.1. The United States, France, and Great Britain are the largest exporters of services. Countries like Spain, Austria, and Norway depend heavily on services, which represent over 30 percent of their exports. As the world market for services grows, developing countries fear that the powerful global service companies will steal business away from their less efficient domestic suppliers. At recent trade talks the United States has pressed for the inclusion of services in the General Agreement on Tariffs and Trade (GATT). While not decided on yet, it is anticipated that services will come under the principles of GATT in the near future.[2] Other transactions play an equally important role in world trade.

2. "The Survey of World Trade," *The Economist,* September 22, 1990, p. 36.

FIGURE 2.1 ● Leading Exporters of Commercial Services, 1988

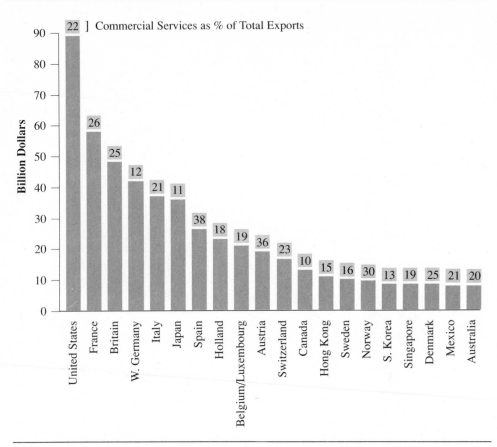

Source: "The Survey of World Trade", *The Economist,* September 22, 1990, p. 36. © 1990 The Economist Newspaper Limited. Reprinted with permission.

International investments, foreign borrowing and lending, and grants-in-aid are essential to the health and well-being of all nations.

The Growth in World Trade

World trade has grown rapidly from about $50 billion in 1950 to over $4 trillion today. This growth has been fuelled by the opening of world markets. The Bretton Woods conference of world leaders in 1944 led to the establishment of GATT, which will be discussed in detail later. The original group of twenty-three countries has expanded to almost one hundred. GATT has helped to reduce tariffs from 40 percent in 1947 to less than 5 percent in 1990. The reduction of tariffs and the relatively free flow of goods has increased trade by 500 percent, of which global output has gone up

200 percent.[3] The principle of free trade has led to the building of market interdependencies. As shown in Figure 2.2, major interdependencies have grown among the major trading blocks—North America, Europe, Asia, and the rest of the world. If one member behaves unfairly (for example by giving government support to a domestic industry and, thereby, lowering its costs, or by protecting a domestic industry by not allowing or making it difficult for foreign suppliers to enter the market, or by letting a manufacturer dump its product overseas at cut rate prices), then other members can retaliate by excluding or limiting the culprit. Unfortunately this practice of retaliation is growing, particularly in the United States. The Omnibus Trade and Competitiveness Act of 1988 includes a section called super-301 which gives the U.S. trade representative the power to negotiate a settlement or issue a duty to offset any alleged damage. The U.S. government has used its large potential market and the power of super-301 retaliation to obtain a number of voluntary export restraints covering textiles, steel, clothing, cars, shoes, machinery, and electronics.[4] Many economists argue that by protecting domestic industry, consumers usually pay higher prices. Understanding the economics of trade is critical to understanding the need for free trade flows from country to country.

3. "The Survey of World Trade," *The Economist,* September 22, 1990, p. 7.
4. Ibid., pp. 8–11.

FIGURE 2.2 ● World Trade Flows, 1989 (in Billions of Dollars)

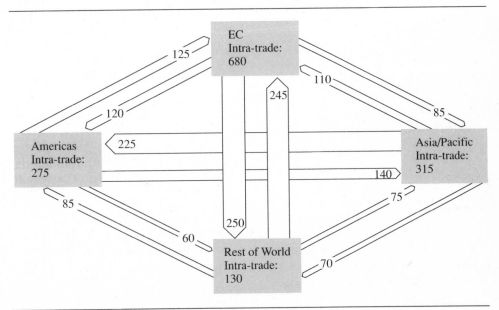

THE BASIS FOR TRADE: ABSOLUTE VERSUS COMPARATIVE ADVANTAGE

Internationally traded goods and services are important to most countries as shown in Table 2.1. Because jobs and standard of living seem to be so closely tied to these inflows and outflows, there is much debate about why particular countries find their competitive advantages in certain goods and not others, whereas other countries have different advantages and disadvantages.

Over the past twenty years, not only has there been a dramatic rise in the volume of trade, but numerous changes have been made in its patterns as well. Countries that once exported vast amounts of steel, such as the United States, are now net importers of the metal. Other nations such as Japan, once known for inexpensive, handmade products, now compete globally in high-tech products. What caused these trade pattern changes? Why do countries that are able to produce virtually any product choose to specialize in only certain goods? Where do international cost advantages originate? In the twenty-first century, will we still think of South Korea and China as having the greatest advantage in handmade goods or, in the future, will they be like Japan and Taiwan are today?

The early work of Adam Smith provides the foundation for understanding trade today. Smith saw trade as a way to promote efficiency because it fostered competition, led to specialization, and resulted in economies of scale. Specialization supports the concept of absolute advantage, that is, sell to other countries the goods that utilize your special skills and resources and buy the rest from those who have some advantage. This theory of selling what you are best at is known as *absolute advantage.* But what if you have no advantages? Will all your manufacturers be driven out of business? David Ricardo in his 1817 publication, *Principles of Political Economy,* offered his theory of comparative advantage.[5] This theory maintains that it is still possible to produce what one is best at even if someone else is better. The following sections further develop the concepts of absolute and comparative advantage, the economic basis of free trade.

Absolute Advantage

While there are many variables that may be listed as the primary determinants of international trade, productivity differences rank high on the list. Take, for example, two countries—Spain and Germany. Suppose the average Spanish worker can produce either 400 machines or 1,600 pounds of tomatoes in one year. Over the same time period, the average German worker can produce either 500 machines or 500 pounds of tomatoes. (This information is summarized in Table 2.2.) In this case, German workers can produce more machinery, *absolutely,* than Spanish workers; whereas Spanish workers can produce more tomatoes, *absolutely,* than their German counterparts.

5. "The Economies of Free Trade," *The Economist,* September 22, 1990, p. 12.

TABLE 2.2 ● Worker Productivity: Example 1

	Machinery	*Tomatoes*
Spain	400	1,600
Germany	500	500

TABLE 2.3 ● Worker Productivity: Example 2

	Machinery	*Tomatoes*
Spain	200	800
Germany	500	1,000

Given these figures, Spain is the obvious low-cost producer of tomatoes and should export them to Germany. Similarly, Germany is the low-cost producer of machines and should export them to Spain.[6]

We should not conclude from the previous example that absolute differences in production capabilities are necessary for trade to occur. Consider the same two countries—Spain and Germany. Now assume that the average Spanish worker can produce either 200 machines or 800 pounds of tomatoes each year whereas the average German worker can produce either 500 machines or 1,000 pounds of tomatoes (see Table 2.3). Germany has an absolute advantage in both goods, and it appears as though Spain will benefit from trade because it can buy from Germany cheaper goods than Spain can make for itself. However, the basis for mutually advantageous trade is present, even here. The reason lies in the concept of *comparative advantage.*

Comparative Advantage

Comparative advantage measures a product's cost of production, not in monetary terms but in terms of the foregone opportunity to produce something else. It focuses on tradeoffs. To illustrate, the production of machines means that resources cannot be devoted to the production of tomatoes. In Germany, the worker who produces 500 machines will not be able to grow 1,000 pounds of tomatoes. Alternatively, if we standardize, the cost can be stated as follows: each pound of tomatoes costs 0.5 machines; or 1 machine costs 2 pounds of tomatoes. In Spain, producing 200 machines forces the sacrifice of 800 pounds of tomatoes. Alternatively, this means

6. The concept of absolute advantage can be found in Adam Smith, *The Wealth of Nations* (New York: Modern Library, 1937). Originally published in 1776.

TABLE 2.4 ● Opportunity Costs of Production

Spain	Germany
1 machine costs 4 pounds of tomatoes	1 machine costs 2 pounds of tomatoes
1 pound of tomatoes costs 0.25 machines	1 pound of tomatoes costs 0.50 machines

TABLE 2.5 ● Mutually Advantageous Trading Ratios

Tomatoes	Machines
1 pound tomatoes = 0.50 machines	1 machine = 4 pounds tomatoes
↕	↕
1 pound tomatoes = 0.25 machines	1 machine = 2 pounds tomatoes

that 1 pound of tomatoes costs 0.25 machines; or 1 machine costs 4 pounds of tomatoes (see Table 2.4).[7]

From the example above we see that even though Spain has an absolute disadvantage in both commodities, it still has a comparative advantage in tomatoes. For Spain, the cost of producing a pound of tomatoes is 0.25 machines while for Germany, the cost is 0.5 machines. Similarly, even though Germany has an absolute advantage in both products, it has a comparative cost advantage only in machines. It costs Germany only 2 pounds of tomatoes to produce a single machine while in Spain the cost is 4 pounds of tomatoes.

The last step in the discussion of the comparative advantage concept is to choose a mutually advantageous trading ratio and to show how it can benefit both countries. Any trading ratio between 1 machine = 2 pounds of tomatoes (Spain's domestic trading ratio) and 1 machine = 4 pounds of tomatoes (Germany's domestic trading ratio) will benefit both nations (see Table 2.5). Suppose we choose 1 machine = 3 pounds tomatoes. Since Germany will be exporting machinery, it gains by getting 3 pounds of tomatoes rather than the 2 pounds it would have produced domestically. Likewise, because Spain will be exporting tomatoes, it gains because 1 machine can be imported for the sacrifice of only 3 pounds, rather than 4 pounds, of tomatoes if it made the machine in Spain.

Another way to think of it is in terms of the value of labor. If workers are paid relative to their output, at the end of a year a German worker could have 500

7. David Ricardo, "Principles of Political Economy and Taxation" in *The Works and Correspondence of David Ricardo,* ed. Pierro Sraffa and Maurice H. Dobb (Cambridge, England: The University Press, 1951–1955), Chapter 7.

machines or 1,000 pounds of tomatoes, and a Spanish worker 200 machines or 800 pounds of tomatoes. Given the relative output of each, a German worker could trade 1 machine for 2 pounds in Germany or 4 pounds in Spain. The Spanish worker could trade a pound of tomatoes for .25 machines in Spain or .50 machines in Germany. In the end, the Spanish worker will end up with less goods, because productivity is less, which means he or she will be paid less, so the goods will be cheaper than in Germany where the output per worker is higher and, therefore, more expensive.

The discussion of comparative advantage illustrates that relative rather than absolute differences in productivity can form a determining basis for international trade. Although the concept of comparative advantage provides a powerful tool for explaining the rationale for mutually advantageous trade, it gives little insight into the source of the relative productivity differences. Specifically, why does a country find its comparative advantage in one particular good or service rather than another product? Is it by chance that the United States is a net exporter of aircraft, machinery, and chemicals but a net importer of steel, textiles, and consumer electronic products? Or can we find some systematic explanations for this pattern?

The answers to these questions are of more than just academic concern because they have an impact on the standard of living and livelihood of millions of people. The importance of understanding productivity differences is especially apparent in countries where trade barriers (for example, tariffs and quotas) are about to be either erected or dismantled. For instance, during the formative years of the European Common Market, discussions centered on the economic disruptions that would occur when Germany, Italy, and France dropped their tariff barriers and permitted free trade among them. These issues have resurfaced each time a new country (such as Greece, Spain, or Portugal) has applied for membership to the European Community. They were hotly debated in 1982 when the U.S. government proposed trade liberalization measures for Latin American countries in the Caribbean Basin Initiative. Similarly, they were at the center during the Uruguay round of GATT trade talks which ran into difficulty over the elimination of farm subsidies by member countries.

The notion of comparative advantage requires that nations make intensive use of those factors they possess in abundance. They export *these* goods and import *those* goods for which they have a comparative disadvantage. So South Korea with its low cost labor will export labor intensive goods like textiles and electronic assemblies, and Sweden with its high quality iron ore deposits will export high grade steel. Michael Porter argues that while the theory of comparative advantage has appeal, it is limited just to the factors of production on land, labor, natural resources, and capital. His study of ten trading nations which account for 50 percent of world exports and one hundred industries resulted in a new theory. This theory postulates that the country will have a significant impact on the competitive advantage of an industry depending on the following factors:

1. The factors of production
2. The nature of domestic demand

3. The presence of appropriate suppliers or related industry

4. The conditions in the country that govern how companies are created, organized, and managed as well as the nature of domestic rivalry[8]

This view of competitive advantage does not refute the theory of comparative advantage, rather it helps explain why industries have a comparative advantage.

Many theories have been advanced to explain the composition of international trade, but only three of them have gained a widespread following: the *labor productivity* theory, the *factor proportions* theory, and the *product life cycle* theory. Each of these explanations provides some insight into this issue.

The Labor Productivity Theory   The oldest, and perhaps simplest, explanation of the source of comparative advantage focuses on international differences in labor productivity. The reasoning is as follows: if it takes the average Japanese worker less time to produce a good than it takes his or her counterpart in France, then Japan should have a competitive advantage in producing this commodity. The savings in labor should be reflected in the relative costs that determine international trade. Therefore, under this theory, the key to understanding comparative advantage is in determining why labor productivities among nations differ.[9]

The strength of this theory lies in its appeal to common sense and in its ability to be tested empirically. Over the years, numerous studies have shown a strong correlation between trade flows and labor productivity.[10] The theory's major problem is that it gives no insight into *why* the labor in one country should be more productive than it is elsewhere. Moreover, it seems to imply that labor is the only important input used in producing goods—surely, it is not. The production process also requires capital, natural resources, and an entrepreneur. The factor proportions theory gives some clarification of all of these requirements.

The Factor Proportions Theory[11]   The factor proportions theory provides another common sense explanation for the patterns of international trade. It rests on two

8. Michael E. Porter, *The Competitive Advantage of Nations* (New York: MacMillan, 1990). pp. 69–175.

9. The labor productivity theory can be found in the works of both Adam Smith and David Ricardo. See Smith, *The Wealth of Nations,* and *The Works and Correspondence of David Ricardo,* ed. Sraffa and Dobb.

10. See Eli Heckscher, "The Effect of Foreign Trade on the Distribution of Income," *Economisk Tidskrift,* vol. 21, 1919; Bertil Ohlin, *Interregional and International Trade* (Cambridge, Mass.: Harvard University Press, 1933).

11. The factor proportions theory can be found in G. D. A. MacDougal, "British and American Exports: A Study Suggested by the Theory of Comparative Costs," *Economic Journal,* December 1951 and September 1952; Bela Balassa, "An Empirical Demonstration of Classical Comparative Cost Theory," *Review of Economics and Statistics,* August 1963; Robert M. Stern, "British and American Productivity and Comparative Costs in International Trade," *Oxford Economic Papers,* October 1962.

very realistic assumptions and a deductive conclusion. First, it assumes that different products have different relative input requirements. For example, both machinery and textiles require capital and labor in their production processes, but relatively more capital is needed for each unit of labor in the production of machinery than in the production of textiles.

The second assumption is that, just as commodities differ in their relative input requirements, countries differ in their relative resource endowments. Many of the Asian, African, and Latin American countries are distinguished by their large and growing populations. In comparison to the more developed countries (the United States, Germany, and Switzerland), these nations employ far less capital per worker. Consequently, the factor proportions theory predicts that countries with high labor-to-capital ratios will have relatively cheap labor and, therefore, will be able to produce and export labor-intensive goods. Similarly, nations relatively rich in capital will be able to export capital-intensive goods.

The logic in this theory is compelling. By couching international trade in terms of both relative resource endowments and relative commodity requirements, it provides an explanation for a vast array of international transactions. Using it, one is able to explain some of the obvious trade flows in primary products. For example, South Africa trades gold and Canada trades nickel because these resources exist in highest relative abundance. The theory also helps to explain why the United States produces machinery, aircraft, and chemicals (all capital- and education-intensive products), but imports steel, textiles, and shoes (both more labor-intensive and low-skill oriented).

If the factor proportions theory is correct, then a country wishing to change its comparative advantage would have to focus (over a period of time) on modifying its relative, rather than absolute, resource endowments. Such a task may be more difficult than simply changing the absolute amount of a single resource, but certainly not impossible. For example Japan, once the producer of low-quality, labor-intensive goods, has been able to change its relative resource endowment by educating its population and devoting considerable resources to obtaining capital. Today it is an industrial giant and has gained the reputation for being one of the economic miracles of the twentieth century.

Although the factor proportions theory has been useful in explaining international trade patterns (both at any time and over time), a third explanation, the product life cycle theory, more effectively deals with certain types of products. This theory is dynamic in nature and stresses both technological changes and variations in production input requirements. It is mainly concerned with high technology products that have been invented and produced by industrial countries.

The Product Life Cycle Theory   The patterns of international trade shift like grains of sand. Perhaps it is inevitable. For example, the United States once enjoyed a substantial international comparative advantage in steel, radios, televisions, semiconductors, electronic products, and motion pictures, but this advantage has slipped away. Why did this shift occur? Some may argue that it was due to management errors or inefficiencies, and they may be partly correct. However, another explanation, the product life cycle theory, demonstrates that changes in comparative advantage will be inevitable with many high technology products.[12]

This theory focuses on the role of technology, economies of scale, transportation costs, and changing input requirements. To best explain it, imagine a hypothetical, high-tech product being introduced by a Boston-based firm. In the early stages of production, success is uncertain. Mass production is difficult because the market has not been developed and experimentation with the product's design and production process are needed. Moreover, highly skilled engineers and other technical support must be used to assist in design changes. As a result, production facilities are located near the market they serve and only the richest domestic markets are targeted for product introduction.

Once the market is identified and developed, exports to high-income foreign countries (for example, the United Kingdom, Germany, and Switzerland) begin. With these increased sales come the cost-saving gains associated with large-scale production. While competition may begin at this stage, the cost advantages bestowed by patents, trade secrecy, and the product's novelty are sufficient to keep most of this competition at bay.

As time passes, the product and its process become more standardized. There is no longer a need for highly skilled labor to make product modifications. Furthermore, since the market has been already developed, a significant barrier to entry is reduced. As a result, in the foreign markets where the product has been introduced, import-competing firms are created. They survive initially because they do not have to pay the relatively large transportation costs borne by the U.S.-based company. They are often given tariff protection by their respective governments as well. These two cost advantages are sufficient to offset the economies of scale enjoyed by the initiating (U.S.) firm.

At first, foreign competitors sell exclusively within their own markets. Since these imitators must bear similar transportation costs and face the same tariff barriers as the U.S. firm, sales to third countries are difficult. Once production volume increases, these foreign competitors begin to enjoy cost-saving economies of scale. Using their domestic markets as a base, they expand into new foreign markets. Gradually, they take on a larger share of the world market, and competition becomes most intense in Third-World countries. Although foreign producers may now have certain advantages over the United States, they still have not made significant inroads into the U.S. market, but this final phase of the cycle is not long in coming.

With further standardization of the production process and with the market better defined, production gravitates toward nations with the cheapest relative labor costs or with the greatest relative abundance of needed resources (just as the factor

---

12. The product life cycle theory can be found in Raymond Vernon, "International Investment and International Trade in the Product Cycle," *Quarterly Journal of Economics,* May 1966; W. Gruber, D. Mehta, and R. Vernon, "The R&D Factor in International Trade and Investment of United States Industries," *Journal of Political Economy,* February 1967.

proportions theory would predict). At this point, the inventor country (the United States) becomes a net importer, unless a new innovation or invention can set off another wave of the production/consumption cycle.

This dynamic theory of trade implies that comparative advantage in high technology goods may, in the early stages of production, be transitory. For industrial nations, such as the United States or Germany, this is important because it means that a strong export position in these products can only be achieved by a high rate of new product invention and innovation or a slow rate of product imitation. In either case, the end results are the same. Comparative advantage weakens over time.

BALANCE OF PAYMENTS

Newspapers, magazines, and nightly T.V. news programs are filled with stories relating to aspects of international business. Often media coverage centers on the implications of a nation's trade deficit/surplus or on the economic consequences of an undervalued/overvalued currency. What are trade deficits? What factors will cause a currency's international value to change? The first step in answering these questions is to gain a clear understanding of the contents and meaning of a nation's balance of payments.

The balance of payments is an accounting record of the transactions between the residents of one country and the residents of the rest of the world over a given period of time.[13] It resembles a company's sources and uses of funds statement. Transactions in which domestic residents either purchase assets (goods and services) from abroad or reduce foreign liabilities are considered uses (outflows) of funds because payments abroad must be made. Similarly, transactions in which domestic residents either sell assets to foreign residents or increase their liabilities to foreigners are sources (inflows) of funds because payments from abroad are received.

Listed in Table 2.6 are the principal parts of the balance of payments statement: the current account, the capital account, and the official transactions account. There are three items under the current account. The goods category states the monetary values of a nation's international transactions in physical goods. The services category shows the values of a wide variety of transactions such as transportation services, consulting, travel, passenger fares, fees, royalties, rent, and investment income. Finally, unilateral transfers include all transactions for which there is no quid pro quo (that is, gifts). Private remittances, personal gifts, philanthropic donations, relief, and aid are included within this account.

The capital account category is divided into two parts on the basis of time. Short-term transactions refer to maturities less than or equal to one year and

13. An excellent source of historical and internationally comparable data can be found in the *Balance of Payments Yearbook* published yearly by the International Monetary Fund.

TABLE 2.6 ● Balance of Payments

	Uses of funds	*Sources of funds*
Current Account		
1. Goods	Imports	Exports
2. Services	Imports	Exports
3. Unilateral transfers	Paid abroad	From abroad
Capital Account		
1. Short-term investment	Made abroad	From abroad
2. Long-term investments	Made abroad	From abroad
a. Portfolio investment		
b. Direct investment		
Official Transactions Account		
1. Official reserve changes	Gained	Lost

long-term transactions refer to maturities longer than one year. Purchases of treasury bills, certificates of deposit, foreign exchange, and commercial paper are typical short-term investments. Long-term investments are separated further into portfolio investments and direct investments.

In general, portfolio investments imply that no ownership rights are held by the purchaser over the foreign investment. Debt securities such as notes and bonds would be included under this heading. Direct investments are long-term ownership interests, such as business capital outlays in foreign subsidiaries and branches. Stock purchases are included as well, but only if such ownership entails substantial control over the foreign company. Countries differ in the percentage of total outstanding stock an individual must hold in order for an investment to be considered a direct investment in the balance of payments statements. The International Monetary Fund reports that these values range from 10 percent for widely dispersed holdings to 25 percent.[14]

Because it is recorded in double-entry bookkeeping form, the balance of payments as a whole must always have its inflows (sources of funds) equal all its outflows (uses of funds). Therefore, the concept of a deficit or surplus refers only to selected parts of the entire statement. A deficit occurs when the particular outflows (uses of funds) exceed the particular inflows (sources of funds). A surplus occurs when the inflows considered exceed the corresponding outflows. In this sense, a nation's surplus or deficit is similar to that of individuals, governments, or businesses. If we

14. International Monetary Fund, *Balance of Payments Manual,* 4th ed. (Washington D.C.: International Monetary Fund, 1977), pp. 137–138.

spend more than we earn, we are in a deficit position. If we earn more than we spend, we are running a surplus.

Balance of Payments Measures

Three balance of payments measures are considered to be important by many businesspeople, government officials, and economists. These are the balance on merchandise trade, the balance on goods and services, and the balance on current account.[15] The balance on merchandise trade is the narrowest measure because it considers only internationally traded goods. For this reason, critics feel that it is of the least practical value. They argue that the balance on merchandise trade is a vestigial remnant of the seventeenth century mercantilist conviction that if one country gained from trade, the other lost.[16] In those war-torn times, domestic economic policies were geared toward ensuring that exports exceeded imports. In so doing, domestic jobs were provided and the excess funds (usually precious metals) earned through the surpluses could be used to support armies and navies for imperialist expansions—or to defend against them. However, if jobs are the goal, there seems to be little point in separating goods from services. Both activities give jobs to willing workers.

Defenders of the measure feel that jobs connected to physical goods are more important than service-oriented jobs and, therefore, the balance on merchandise trade is a useful economic indicator. They contend that if an international disruption occurred, it would be better to live in a country with textile factories, steel mills, farms, and electronics firms rather than live in a country with a labor force of insurance clerks, computer consultants, and tourist guides.

The balance on goods and services has a direct link to most national income accounting systems. It is reported in the national income and national product statements as "net exports." If this figure is positive, a net transfer of resources is taking place from the surplus nation to the debtor nations. Many analysts feel that if the balance is negative, it is an indication that a nation is not living within its means. To have such a deficit position, the country would have to be a net borrower of foreign funds or a net recipient of foreign aid.

The most widely used measure of a nation's international payments position is the balance on current account statement. As with the balance on goods and services statement, it shows whether a nation is living within or beyond its means. Because it includes unilateral transfers, deficits (in the absence of government intervention)

15. The classic discussion of balance of payments is found in James Meade, *The Balance of Payments* (London: Oxford University Press, 1951).

16. Examples of mercantilist thought can be found in Thomas Mun, "England's Treasure by Foreign Trade," in *Early English Tracts in Commerce,* ed. John McCullock (Norwich: Jarrold and Sons, 1952). See also Joseph Schumpeter, *History of Economic Analysis* (New York: Oxford University Press, 1954).

must be financed by international borrowing or by selling foreign investments. Therefore, the measure is considered to be a reflection of the change in a nation's financial claims on other countries.

Exchange Rates

The purchase of a foreign good or service can be thought of as involving two sequential transactions—the purchase of the foreign currency followed by the purchase of the foreign item itself. If the cost of buying either the foreign currency or the foreign item rises, the price to the importer increases. A ratio that measures the value of one currency in terms of another currency is called an *exchange rate*. With it, one is able to compare domestic and foreign prices.

When a currency rises in value, it is said to *appreciate*. If it falls in value, it is said to *depreciate*. Therefore, a change in the value of the U.S. dollar exchange rate from 0.50 British pounds to 0.65 British pounds is an appreciation of the dollar and a depreciation of the pound. After all, the dollar now commands more pounds while a greater number of pounds must be spent to purchase one dollar.

The strength of a domestic currency against the currency of your trading partners can have a negative effect. For example, the Swiss franc was strong versus the dollar, pound, and yen in 1990 so when Nestle converted its sales into dollars in the United States, yen in Japan, and pounds in the United Kingdom, it all equaled less in Swiss francs. Nestle reported a 3.5 percent decline in sales in 1990 due to the strong Swiss franc.[17] Rossignol, the French ski manufacturer, is predicting difficulty in 1991 as the French franc strengthens against the dollar and yen, its two biggest markets.[18]

The Foreign Exchange Market   Unlike major stock markets where trading is done on central exchanges (for example, the New York Stock Exchange and the London Stock Exchange), foreign exchange transactions are handled on an over-the-counter market, largely by phone, teletype, and telex. Private and commercial customers, as well as banks, brokers, and central banks, conduct millions of transactions on this worldwide market daily.

As Figure 2.3 shows, the foreign exchange market has a hierarchical structure. Private customers deal mainly with banks in the retail market, and banks stand ready to either buy or sell foreign exchange as long as a free and active market for the currency exists.

Not all banks participate directly in the foreign exchange market. In the United States, a bank must have a substantial volume of international business to justify

17. "Nestlé Turnover Falls by 3.5%," *Financial Times,* January 19, 1991, p. 22.
18. Ian Frasen, "Out of the Slush and Into the Bunker," *Eurobusiness,* December 1990, p. 29.

FIGURE 2.3 ● Structure of the Foreign Exchange Market

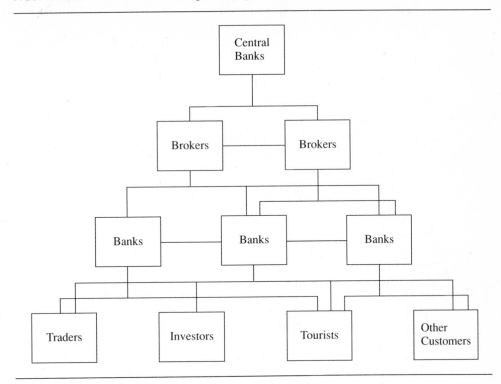

setting up a foreign exchange department. Thus, most small financial intermediaries handle customers' business through correspondent banks.

Banks that have foreign exchange departments trade with private commercial customers on the retail market, but they also deal with other banks (domestic or foreign) and brokers on the wholesale market. Generally, these wholesale transactions are for amounts of one million dollars or more. Many of these trades are made on the basis of verbal agreements and it is only some days later that written documentation is formally exchanged.

The foreign exchange market is probably as close as one can get to the economist's proverbial ideal of pure competition. There are many buyers and sellers, no one buyer or seller can influence the price, the product is homogeneous, there is relatively free entry into and exit from the market, and there is virtually perfect worldwide information. If prices among banks differed by even a fraction of a cent, arbitragers would immediately step in for the profits they could earn risk free. Through telex machines, telephone calls, and voice boxes that lead directly into the trading rooms of other banks and brokers, participants keep abreast of the market. Positions are opened and closed minute-by-minute, and the pace of activity in a foreign exchange dealing room can be quite frantic.

Central banks play a key role in the foreign exchange markets because they are the ultimate controllers of domestic money supplies. When they enter the market to directly influence the exchange rate value, they deal mainly with brokers and large money market banks. Their trading is not done to make a profit but to attain some macroeconomic goal such as altering the exchange rate value, reducing inflation, or changing domestic interest rates. In general, even if central banks do not intervene in the foreign exchange markets, their actions influence exchange rate values because large increases in a nation's money supply will increase its inflation rate and lower the international value of its currency.

Causes of Exchange Rate Movements   Exchange rates are among the most closely watched and politically sensitive economic variables. Regardless of which way the rates move, some groups are hurt while other groups are helped. If a currency's value rises, domestic businesses will find it more difficult to compete internationally and the domestic unemployment rate may rise. If the value of the currency falls, foreign goods become more expensive, the cost of living increases, and goods become cheaper to foreign buyers. What are the causes of these exchange rate movements and to what extent can governments influence them?

Market exchange rates are determined by the forces of supply and demand. The greater the supply of a currency to the foreign exchange market or the lesser its demand, the lower will be its international value. Similarly, the greater the demand for a currency in the foreign exchange market or the lower its supply, the higher will be its international value. Therefore, to predict movements in a currency's international value, one must identify the participants whose transactions affect these supply and demand forces and determine which factors will cause them to change their behavior.

Identifying the international participants is a relatively easy matter since they have been implicitly mentioned already in the discussion of the balance of payments. Recall that the balance of payments is nothing more than a summary of a nation's international transactions. In the current account and the capital account, traders, speculators, and investors are the major players. To this list, we will add government participants. The following sections will show how these groups act and react to overlapping market signals.

Traders   International trade in goods and services is influenced mainly by changes in relative international prices and relative income levels. If, for example, the U.S. inflation rate exceeds that of Germany, then U.S. goods will become progressively more expensive than German goods. Consequently, U.S. consumers will begin to demand more of these foreign goods, thereby increasing the supply of dollars to the foreign exchange market (that is, increasing the demand for German marks). For the same reason, German consumers will reduce their demand for dollars (that is, reduce their supply of marks) as they purchase fewer U.S. goods. Therefore, relatively high inflation in the United States will cause the international value of the dollar to fall and the value of other currencies to rise.

Consumption is constrained by income, the ability to borrow, and the availability of credit. This is true both for individuals and nations. However, when speaking of a country's income, gross national product (GNP) is the most widely used measure. An increase in GNP will give the citizens of a nation the wherewithal to purchase more goods and services. Since many of the newly purchased goods are likely to be foreign, increases in GNP will raise the demand for foreign products and therefore raise the demand for foreign currencies. If, for example, the U.S. growth rate exceeds that of Germany, there will be a net increase in the demand for German marks and a lowering of the dollar's international value.[19]

Speculators   Speculators buy and sell currencies in anticipation of changing future values. If there were a widespread expectation that the Japanese yen would rise in relative value to the dollar, speculators would try to purchase yen now (that is, sell dollars) in anticipation of that change. As the demand for yen increased in the spot market and the supply of yen for dollars fell, the yen's exchange rate value would rise. (A spot market is for the immediate delivery of currency within two days of the transaction.) Similarly, as the supply of dollars increased and the demand for them decreased, the international value of the dollar relative to yen would fall. Consequently, spot market rates are very much influenced by future expectations.

Investors   One of the main factors influencing investors' decisions is the differential between international interest rates. If, for example, Italian interest rates were greater than U.S. interest rates (adjusted for such things as risk, taxability, and maturity), then investors would have an incentive to place their funds where they earned the highest return—in Italy. The supply of dollars in the foreign exchange market would rise (as U.S. investors purchased Italian securities) and the demand for dollars would fall (as Italians purchase domestic rather than U.S. securities). The effect of these investments would be to lower the value of the dollar relative to the lira.

As important as relative interest rates are to the international investment decision, expected changes in exchange rates are equally important. There can be a substantial difference between the interest rate at which funds are placed in foreign investments and the net return after repatriation. The gains made on higher foreign

19. For an alternative point of view, see Jacob A. Frenkel and Harry Johnson, "The Monetary Approach to the Balance of Payments: Essential Concepts and Historical Origins" in *The Monetary Approach to the Balance of Payments,* ed. J. A. Frenkel and H. G. Johnson (Toronto: University of Toronto Press, 1976).

interest rates can be partially or fully offset by changes in a currency's value. This risk may be eliminated by contracting on the forward exchange market; but in general the forward rates are arbitraged to the point where these rates completely offset the interest rate advantage. This is why relative inflation rates reappear as an important determinant of international transactions. A relatively high domestic inflation rate is one of the major causes of a depreciation in the exchange value of a currency.[20] Therefore, a high inflation rate implies that the currency carries high nominal interest rates, an expensive spot exchange value, and a relatively cheap forward exchange rate value.

Governments   Governments enter foreign exchange markets in a variety of ways, ranging from the international purchase of goods and services to the granting of foreign aid. Perhaps the most pronounced impact governments have is as discretionary interveners in foreign exchange markets. Suppose the United States and Japan agreed to lower the dollar's value relative to the yen. To do so, dollars would have to be supplied—and yen demanded—in the foreign exchange markets.

For the United States, this would mean putting upward pressure on the domestic money supply as newly created dollars were exchanged for circulating Japanese yen. For Japan, this type of intervention would mean putting downward pressure on its money supply as dollar reserves were used to take yen off the market. Because governments have such strong and direct controls over domestic money supplies, subsequent changes in other economic variables (for example, inflation or interest rates) will result from this activity.

INTERNATIONAL AGENCIES FOR PROMOTING ECONOMIC AND MONETARY STABILITY

Stability in the international economy is a prerequisite for worldwide peace and prosperity. It was for this reason that at the end of World War II, a group of countries met at Bretton Woods, a small ski resort in New Hampshire, and formed both the International Monetary Fund and the World Bank (the International Bank for Reconstruction and Development). With headquarters in Washington, D.C., these two agencies continue to play major roles in the international scene. Although they have accomplished many notable achievements, perhaps their most important con-

---

20. The purchasing power parity theory explains that exchange rates can be predicted by estimating relative international inflation rates. See Gustav Cassel, *The World's Monetary Problems* (London: Constable, 1921); Jacob A. Frenkel, "Purchasing Power Parity: Doctrinal Perspective and Evidence from the 1920s," *Journal of International Economics,* vol. 8, May 1978; and Jacob A. Frenkel, "The Collapse of Purchasing Power Parity During the 1970s," *European Economic Review,* vol. 16, May 1981.

tribution has been to initiate forums for summit discussions of controversial financial topics.

International Monetary Fund

The major goals of the International Monetary Fund (IMF) are to promote orderly and stable foreign exchange markets, maintain free convertibility among the currencies of member nations, reduce international impediments to trade, and provide liquidity to counteract temporary balance of payments disequilibria. While the IMF has no legal powers to enforce its decisions, strong and subtle pressures can be brought to bear on noncomplying nations.

In the early years following its creation, the IMF focused its attention on restoring currency convertibility among members and ensuring that adequate liquidity existed for countries experiencing balance of payments difficulties. Free convertibility was regained by 1958, but the liquidity issue was a much more difficult problem to solve. International trade expanded rapidly over the post-war period, but international reserves in both dollars and gold grew less rapidly. To increase the amount of international liquidity and to take some of the pressure off these reserve assets, the IMF in 1970 began issuing Special Drawing Rights (SDRs) to member nations. These SDRs (mutual book credits) gave nations the right to purchase foreign currencies, and with these currencies they could finance temporary balance of payments deficits.

In 1973, major trading nations abandoned the fixed exchange rate system set up at Bretton Woods in 1944. As a result, the need for increases in world liquidity to finance balance of payments deficits was reduced substantially. Today, the IMF has taken on some different tasks and has a somewhat new image. Prior to the 1970s, the agency funded operations with contributions from member nations, but this changed as the IMF began selling some of its gold reserves and banking part of the capital gain. In the 1980s, the IMF took another step away from the past by borrowing in the private capital markets.

Over the past decade, the IMF has begun to extend longer term credits to the developing nations rather than only short-term balance of payments aid. To qualify for such loans the Fund may require that countries take drastic economic steps, such as reducing tariff barriers, making businesses independent, curbing domestic inflation, and cutting government expenditures. While many nations have resented such intervention, banks worldwide have used the IMF as a screening device for their private loans to many developing countries. If countries qualify for IMF loans, they are considered for private credit.

World Bank (International Bank for Reconstruction and Development)

The World Bank along with its sister organizations, the International Finance Corporation and the International Development Association, give long-term loans mainly to developing nations. In this sense, these three institutions are like merchant bankers (that is, suppliers of capital) for the developing nations.

The World Bank acts as an intermediary between the private capital markets and the developing nations. It makes long-term loans (usually fifteen or twenty-five years) carrying rates that reflect prevailing market conditions. By virtue of its AAA credit rating, the bank is able to borrow private funds at relatively low market rates and pass the savings off to the developing nations. However, because it must borrow to obtain capital and is not funded by members' contributions, the World Bank must raise lending rates when its costs (that is, market interest rates) rise.

The International Finance Corporation (IFC) provides risk capital to fledgling companies in developing nations. For its investments, the IFC acquires stocks or bonds in the newly established businesses. After the company becomes solvent, the IFC tries to sell these securities on the domestic capital markets and to reinvest the receipts into other projects worldwide.

The International Development Association lends what may be termed *soft money* to developing nations. Funds used for these loans do not come directly from the private capital markets but are donated by member nations—meaning that they are usually taxpayer financed. Loan maturities are for fifty years and a grace period may be granted on all payments for up to ten years. Moreover, the interest that IDA charges to debtor nations is only 0.75 percent above the agency's cost of funds.

Together these agencies have tried to encourage entrepreneurial endeavors in underdeveloped parts of the world. Their loans have focused on areas that promote domestic industry and employment. The idea is age old: "If you give a starving man a fish, you will feed him for a day. If you teach him how to fish, you will feed him for a lifetime."

Group of Seven

The world's leading industrial nations have established a Group of Seven, which meets regularly to discuss the world economy. Finance ministers and central bank governors from the countries of the United States, Japan, Germany, France, Britain, Italy, and Canada make up this group referred to as G7. The group works together informally to help stabilize the world economy and reduce extreme disruptions. For example G7 met in late January 1991 after the start of the Gulf War and issued the following statement.[21]

> Ministers and governors reviewed their economic policies and prospects and reaffirmed their support for economic policy coordination at this critical time. They noted that although growth in all their economies had slowed, expansion of the world economy continues, and the pace of activity could be expected to pick up late this year. They noted that growth remains particularly strong in Germany and Japan. Implementation

21. "G7 Pledges to Strengthen Cooperation," *Financial Times,* January 22, 1991, p. 7.

of sound fiscal policies, combined with stability-oriented monetary policies, should create conditions favorable to lower global interest rates and a stronger world economy. They also stressed the importance of a timely and successful completion of the Uruguay Round (of multilateral trade talks). The ministers and governors also discussed the situation of global financial markets in the light of uncertainties arising from the Gulf War and developments in the Soviet Union. They agreed to strengthen cooperation and to monitor developments in exchange markets. Ministers and governors are prepared to respond as appropriate to maintain stability in international financial markets.

European Monetary System

In the early 1970s, a group of European countries established the European Joint Float agreement. The values of the currencies were fixed against one another in a narrow range of plus or minus 2.25 percent. The movement of these currencies back and forth within this range became known as the snake. The early system was later replaced by the European Monetary System (EMS) which includes the twelve members of the European Community (EC). Britain was the last to join in late 1990. The EMS includes a set of features to force member countries to regulate their economies so that their currency stays within 2.25% of the central rates. If a currency slips out of this band, it may be required to increase or lower interest rates to stay in line with the other currencies. The German mark is EMS's strong currency so the exchange rate between each individual currency and the German mark is closely monitored. The EC countries have all contributed to the European Monetary Cooperation Fund which has a pool of over $30 billion to buy or sell currency in order to keep all currencies within their acceptable band. The EMS has also developed a new currency called the European Currency Unit (ECU), which is made up of a weighted average of twelve currencies from the EC countries. The next stage after EMS is the formation of a European Monetary Union. This would include much closer regulation of economies and the eventual replacement of the twelve currencies with the ECU.

There are plans for the ECU to be issued as a currency in 1996 and traded as the single European currency in 1997.[22] Many doubt that either Britain or Germany will give up its own currency in favor of ECU.

Mr. Mulford, undersecretary of the U.S. Treasury, welcomes the idea of the European Monetary Union. As the Group of Seven attempts to coordinate the monetary policies of the industrialized world, it will be much easier to focus on the dollar, the yen, and the ECU.[23] With the cooperation of world leaders, a managed global economy may be possible by the year 2000. This would reduce the likelihood of recession and minimize exchange rate fluctuations.

22. "Plotting Monetary Union," *The Economist,* May 19, 1990, pp. 119–120.
23. "Power to the Centre," *The Economist,* July 7, 1990, p. 25.

INTERNATIONAL TRADE: DOES IT DESERVE SPECIAL TREATMENT?

The principles of comparative advantage can be applied to any type of trade—international, intranational, or interpersonal. But if this is true, why is there so much concern about the international sector? Few residents of Massachusetts complain about the jobs that Pennsylvania, California, or Michigan factories take away from the New England area. Is the problem that people perceive international trade as an "us against them" situation while they perceive domestic trade as "us against us"? Or are there legitimate differences when one goes beyond the national borders?[24]

There seem to be some obvious factors one can point to in differentiating international from intranational trade. Varying currencies, languages, traditions, and cultures are just a few examples. But how significant are they? Switzerland, a developed, but relatively small Western European country, has four official languages—German, French, Italian, and Romansch—and an assortment of widely differing dialects. The country is divided into twenty-six cantons and in most respects, each canton wields more authority than does the national government. The result is a nation where rules and regulations vary canton by canton. In regards to its currency, Switzerland is bordered by Germany, France, Austria, Italy, and Lichtenstein. While the Swiss franc is the national currency, many merchants throughout the country accept payment in any of these neighboring currencies. What factors distinguish foreign from domestic trade in Switzerland? It seems that there are few, if any, distinguishing characteristics. Certainly, the ones listed above are more apparent than real. If, in general, this is true, then international trade becomes nothing more than a simple subset of broader trade issues.

PROTECTIONISM AND TRADE RESTRICTIONS

Economists have spent considerable time identifying and quantifying the net gains from free international trade. In large part, the benefits are obvious. After all, trade by its very nature involves a voluntary exchange of assets between two parties. In the absence of coercion, the motives behind this exchange must be for mutual benefit. The controversy surfaces when domestic producers are considered. Foreign imports seem to take business away from domestic firms and to increase the domestic unemployment rate.[25]

Free trade, like all competitive or technological changes, creates and destroys; it gives and it takes away. By increasing competition, free trade lowers the price of the

24. See Lester Thurow, *The Zero Sum Society: Distribution and the Possibilities for Economic Change* (New York: Basic Books, 1980).

25. For details on the arguments against protectionism, see Robert Z. Lawrence and Robert E. Litan, "Why Protectionism Doesn't Pay," *Harvard Business Review,* May–June 1987, pp. 60–67.

imported goods and raises the demand for efficiently produced domestic goods. In these newly stimulated export industries, sales will increase, profits will rise, and stock prices will climb. Clearly, consumers of the imported good and producers of the exported good benefit by these new conditions. However, it is equally clear that there are groups that are harmed as well. Domestic producers of the import-competing good are one of the most visible groups. They experience noticeable declines in market share, falling profits, and deteriorating stock prices.

It is a fact of life that there are both beneficiaries and victims from free trade, just as there are when virtually any change is made. For instance, if someone were to discover a way for people to grow three or four sets of teeth in a lifetime, most people would benefit from this discovery. Nevertheless, there exists a group of people—dentists, oral surgeons, and periodontists—who would be hurt. Should this invention be withheld from the market because this group is hurt? The true test of a discovery is not whether or not victims exist, but whether the benefits outweigh the inevitable losses.[26]

Herein lies the major reason for protectionist legislation. The victims of free trade are highly visible and their losses quantifiable. Governments use protectionism as a means of lessening the harm done to this easily identified group. The individuals who are helped by free trade tend to be dispersed throughout the nation rather than concentrated in one particular region. Moreover, their monetary gain is only a fraction of the total purchase price of the commodity.

A recent study by Australia's Center for International Economies (CIE) prepared a detailed model of the international trading system in order to measure the impact of reduced protectionism on world trade. If the countries in GATT reduced their tariff and nontariff barriers by 50 percent, CIE estimates that trade would increase $750 billion—$208 billion in the United States, $245 billion in Europe, and $287 billion in Asia/Pacific.[27]

Protectionist legislation tends to be in the form of either tariffs, quotas, or qualitative trade restrictions. The following sections describe these barriers and their economic effects.

Tariffs

Tariffs are taxes on goods moving across an economic or political boundary. They can be imposed on imports, exports, or on goods in transit through a country on their way to some other destination. In the United States, export tariffs are constitutionally prohibited, but in other parts of the world they are quite common. Of course, the most common type of tariff is the import tariff, and it is on this tariff that we focus our attention.

26. Leland Yeager and David G. Tuerck, *Foreign Trade and U.S. Policy* (New York: Praeger Publishers, 1976), pp. 1–11, 40–88.
27. "Once and Future GATT," *The Economist,* September 22, 1990, p. 39.

Import tariffs have a dual economic effect. First, they tend to raise the price of imported goods and, thereby, protect domestic industries from foreign competition. Second, they generate tax revenues for the governments imposing them. It is important to recognize this duality because, oftentimes, the situations resulting from the tariffs are quite different from what was originally intended. Moreover, regardless of what the goals are (for example, increasing tax revenue or raising employment), tariffs may not be the most direct or effective means of attaining them.

Today, most nations impose import duties for the purpose of protecting domestic manufacturers. In some cases (as when they are imposed on expensive-to-store agricultural products), foreign sellers will lower their prices to offset any tariff increase. The net effect is for the consumer-paid price to differ only slightly, if at all, from the pretariff level. Consequently, the nation has greater tariff revenues but little additional protection for the domestic producers.

When tariffs do raise the price of the imported good, consumers of the imported good develop a disadvantage, whereas the import-competing industries are helped. Quite often, another unintended group is hampered as well. This group is made up of domestic producers (for example, automobile manufacturers) that use the imported good (steel) in their production processes. For example, when Torrington Company, a domestic manufacturer of ball bearings, asked the U.S. government to put a tariff on imports, Caterpillar and Hewlett Packard objected. They said the tariffs would raise the cost of their inputs, making their products less competitive on the world market.[28] Tariffs permit foreign businesses to acquire these material inputs at the cheaper international price. Therefore, restrictive duties may put domestic companies at a competitive disadvantage.[29] Occasionally, this unintended side effect leads to subsequent layers of tariff protection to compensate for the higher prices.

Quotas

Quotas are physical limits on the *amount* of goods that can be imported into a country. Unlike tariffs that restrict trade by directly increasing prices, quotas increase prices by directly restricting trade. Naturally, to have such an effect, imports must be restricted to levels below the free trade level.

For domestic producers, quotas are a much surer means of protection. Once the limit has been reached, imports cease to enter the domestic market regardless of whether foreign exporters lower their prices. Consumers have the most to lose with the imposition of quotas. Not only are their product choices limited and the prices increased, the goods that are imported carry the highest profit margins. Restrictions on imported automobiles, for instance, will bring in more luxury models with high-cost accessories.

28. "When One Man's Dumping Is Another's Good Price," *Financial Times,* May 9, 1990, p. 8.
29. W. Max Corden, "The Structure of a Tariff System and the Effective Protective Rate," *Journal of Political Economy,* vol. 74, June 1966, pp. 221–237.

Like tariffs, quotas have both revenue and protection effects. The protection effects are the most apparent since trade is unequivocally being curtailed. The revenue effects are less obvious. When a government imposes arbitrary restrictions on imported goods, companies vie for the right to conduct this limited trade. One source estimated that the net effects of the U.S. quota system on product categories such as apparel or steel cost U.S. consumers about $10 billion in 1985. Quotas protect foreign companies from competition among themselves and also tend to limit the impact on prices set by U.S. firms that can be assured a certain volume.[30] One option is for the government to auction these rights to the highest bidder. In this way, the government gains revenues similar to those earned under a tariff.[31] However, if these rights are given away (as has been done in the United States on occasion), the revenue that was earned by the government is reported as windfall profits by the domestic importers and foreign exporters.

Orderly Marketing Arrangements and Voluntary Export Restrictions

Over the years, certain words in our vocabulary have become associated with a strongly objectionable mental image. One such word is *depression.* In the years immediately prior to the 1930s, economic downturns were called depressions but now they are called *recessions.* Why is this? The answer, in large part, is due to the strong psychological associations the word *depression* has to the Great Depression. Because no president or Congress would want to be considered responsible for such a grave situation, the new term, *recession,* was coined. Though downturns are the same, the name to describe them has changed.[32]

In the same sense, the word *quota* has come to be associated with the most selfish of protectionist legislation. There can be strong political and economic repercussions associated with such unilateral, beggar-thy-neighbor policies. To avoid these problems, the new terms, *orderly marketing arrangement* and *voluntary export restriction,* have been invented.[33] In general, an orderly marketing arrangement is an agreement between countries to share markets by limiting foreign export sales. Usually, these arrangements have a set duration and provide for some annual increase in foreign sales to the domestic market. Korea and Taiwan are two countries that have negotiated orderly marketing agreements with the United States. In 1987, Korea pledged a number of steps to keep the U.S. trade deficit with that country to $7 billion. Taiwan granted more liberalized trade concessions, including a currency appreciation, to keep its trade surplus with the United States in 1987 from passing $18

30. "Tariffs Aren't Great, But Quotas Are Worse," *Business Week,* March 16, 1987, p. 64.

31. Monica Langley, "The Idea of Auctioning Import Rights Appeals to Lawmakers Faced with Trade, Budget Gaps," *Wall Street Journal,* February 6, 1987, p. 44.

32. See John K. Galbraith, *Money: Whence It Came, Where It Went* (Boston: Houghton Mifflin, 1975).

33. See Kent Jones, *Politics versus Economics in World Steel Trade* (London: George Allen & Unwin, 1986).

billion.[34] Voluntary restraints can take a funny twist. Mazak, a Japanese tool maker with a factory in Kentucky, has used the voluntary restraint agreement to limit Japanese imports into the United States. In fact, Mazak prepared a video of Japanese screwdriver (assembly only) factories to show how his Tokyo competitors were circumventing the agreement.[35]

The euphemistic terms are intended to give the impression of fairness. After all, who can be against anything that is orderly or voluntary? But when one scratches beneath the surface of these so-called negotiated settlements, a different image appears. First, the negotiations are initiated by the importing country with the implicit threat that, unless concessions are made, stronger unilateral sanctions will be imposed. They are really neither orderly nor voluntary. They are quotas in the guise of negotiated agreements.

The Omnibus Trade and Competitiveness Act of 1988 gave presidents of the United States the right to negotiate orderly marketing arrangements and set countervailing duties to deal with the problems of trade deficits, protected markets, and dumping. The use of these voluntary export restraints (VERs) has spread to textiles, clothing, steel, cars, shoes, machinery, and consumer electronics. There are approximately 300 VERs worldwide, most protecting the United States and Europe. Over fifty agreements affect exports from Japan and another thirty-five affect South Korea.[36] Some researchers argue that the cost of these VERs to consumers far exceeds the cost of the jobs they protect. See, for example, the jobs-saved cost in the following industries:

Industry	Cost/Job saved
Carbon steel	$750,000
Shipping	$270,000
Dairy	$220,000
Meat	$160,000
Autos	$105,000
Textiles	$ 42,000[37]

Often the real impact of VERs is hidden in higher costs to the consumer. The voluntary restraint of Japanese cars into the United States forced Japan to send higher priced cars since they wanted to generate the maximum revenue per unit while staying within the quota. U.S. car manufacturers continued to raise their prices

34. "Where Sanctions Against Japan Are Really Working," *Business Week,* May 11, 1987. p. 61.

35. "Look Who's Taking Japan to Task," *Business Week,* June 4, 1990, p. 26.

36. "A Survey of World Trade," *The Economist,* September 22, 1990, p. 8.

37. Michael McFadden, "Protectionism Can't Protect Jobs," *Fortune,* May 11, 1987, p. 125.

and the consumer paid an additional $15.7 billion from 1981 to 1984.[38] Where was the savings? Now, years later, the U.S. car manufacturers are still struggling and Japan has over 30 percent of the market.

Commodity Agreements

In theory, the purpose of a commodity agreement is to stabilize market prices over an extended period of time. Agricultural goods and mining resources are the products chosen most often for these agreements because their supplies are inflexible in the short run and their demands can be both volatile and price insensitive. The agreement can be made either exclusively by only producers of the good or between the major buyers and sellers.

Producer agreements ordinarily restrict or control output by means of production quotas. Ideally, production limits should be increased in years when market demand is high and reduced when market demand is low. In this manner, the roller coaster, up-and-down movement of prices may be avoided.

Commodity agreements between buyers and sellers generally operate through a stabilization agency. The agency buys up surplus production in years when prices are likely to decline and then supplies the market from its stockpile when prices are likely to rise. In general, these agreements do not last very long. Members too often try to set prices at levels that are unrealistically high. The result is that the stabilization agency's stockpile grows from year to year and the costs associated with buying and storing these products soar.[39]

Under the producer agreements, unity tends to be strongest when demand is strong; but as market strength weakens, so does the will to abide by the output restrictions. Voluntary export limits require that members restrict their production for the well-being of the organization, but each participant in the agreement is aware that, as a single seller, more output can be sold if there is a way to circumvent or evade the export quotas. Consequently, it is common to see illegal actions and price concessions when markets decline.

Formal and Administrative Nontariff Trade Barriers

The final category of trade restrictions is perhaps the most problematic and certainly the least quantifiable. As Table 2.7 (sections D, E, and F) shows, there is a virtual potpourri of rules and taxes that impede international trade. Not all of these barriers are discriminatory and protectionist. Restrictions dealing with public health and

38. U.S. International Trade Commission, *The Internationalization of the Automobile Industry and Its Effects on the U.S. Automobile Industry,* U.S. ITC Publication 1712 (Washington D.C., 1985), p. xiv.

39. A recent example is the International Tin Agreement that collapsed in late 1985. See "Death Rattle of an Old Tin Market?" *The Economist,* December 2, 1985, pp. 81–82.

TABLE 2.7 ● Nontariff Trade Barriers

Formal trade restrictions	*Administrative trade restrictions*
A. NONTARIFF IMPORT RESTRICTIONS (PRICE-RELATED MEASURES) Surcharges at border Port and statistical taxes Nondiscriminatory excise taxes and registration charges Discriminatory excise taxes, government insurance requirements Nondiscriminatory turnover taxes Discriminatory turnover taxes Import deposit Variable levies Consular fees Stamp taxes Various special taxes and surcharges	D. STATE PARTICIPATION IN TRADE Subsidies and other government support Government trade, government monopolies, and granting of concessions or licenses Laws and ordinances discouraging imports Problems relating to general government policy Government procurement Tax relief, granting of credit and guarantees Boycott
B. QUANTITATIVE RESTRICTIONS AND SIMILAR SPECIFIC TRADE LIMITATIONS (QUANTITY-RELATED MEASURES) Licensing regulations Ceilings and quotas Embargoes Export restrictions and prohibitions Foreign exchange and other monetary or financial controls Government price setting and surveillance Purchase and performance requirements Restrictive business conditions Discriminatory bilateral arrangements Discriminatory regulations regarding countries of origin International cartels Orderly marketing agreements Various related regulations	E. TECHNICAL NORMS, STANDARDS AND CONSUMER PROTECTION REGULATIONS Health and safety regulations Pharmaceutical control regulations Product design regulations Industrial standards Size and weight regulations Packing and labeling regulations Package marking regulations Regulations pertaining to use Regulations for the protection of intellectual property Trademark regulations
C. DISCRIMINATORY FREIGHT RATES (FLAG PROTECTIONISM)	F. CUSTOMS PROCESSING AND OTHER ADMINISTRATIVE REGULATIONS Antidumping policy Customs calculation bases Formalities required by consular officials Certification regulations Administrative obstacles Merchandise classification Regulations regarding sample shipment, return shipments, and re-exports Countervailing duties and taxes Appeal law Emergency law

Source: Beatrice Bondy, *Protectionism: Challenge of the Eighties* (Zurich, Union Bank of Switzerland, 1983), p. 19. Reprinted by permission.

safety are certainly legitimate, but the line between social well-being and protection is a fine one.

At what point do consular fees, import restrictions, packaging regulations, performance requirements, licensing rules, and government procurement procedures discriminate against foreign producers? Is a French tax on automobile horsepower targeted against powerful U.S. cars or is it simply a tax on inefficiency and pollution? Are U.S. automobile safety standards unfair to German, Japanese, and other foreign car manufacturers? Does a French ban on advertising bourbon and Scotch (but not cognac) serve the public's best interest?

Sometimes, nontariff barriers can have considerable impact on foreign competition. For decades, West German authorities forbade the sale of beer in Germany unless it was brewed from barley malt, hops, yeast, and water. If any other additives were used—a common practice elsewhere—German authorities denied foreign brewers the right to label their products as beer. Only recently has the law been struck down by the European Court of Justice.[40]

The General Agreement on Tariffs and Trade—GATT

Because of the deleterious effects of protectionism, which were most painfully felt during the Great Depression of the 1930s, twenty-three nations banded together in 1947 to form the General Agreement on Tariffs and Trade (GATT). Over its life, GATT has been a major forum for the liberalization and promotion of nondiscriminatory international trade between participating nations. Liberalization is promoted through periodic trade rounds or negotiations.

The principles of a world economy embodied in the articles of GATT are reciprocity, nondiscrimination, and transparency. The idea of reciprocity is simple. If one country lowers its tariffs against another's exports, then it can expect the other country to do the same. This practice of reciprocity has been important in the bargaining process to reduce tariffs. Nondiscrimination means that one country should not give one member or group of members preferential treatment over other members of the group. Referred to as the most favored nation status, it does not mean you are *most* favored, but rather favored the same as the others. Transparency refers to the GATT policy that nations replace nontariff barriers (like quotas) with tariffs and then to bind the tariff, which means to agree not to raise it. Nontariff barriers do much more harm to trade than tariffs especially when bound. Tariffs reduce uncertainty and are out in the open so they are easier to negotiate down in the future.[41] Through these principles, trade restrictions have been effectively reduced and price distortions have been minimized.

Although GATT's most notable gains have been in reducing tariff and quota barriers on certain goods, GATT has also helped to simplify and homogenize trade

40. "EC Claims Victory as Court Overturns Germany's Age-Old Ban on Beer Imports," *The Wall Street Journal,* March 13, 1987, p. 29.
41. "The ITO That Never Was," *The Economist,* September 22, 1990, pp. 7–8.

documentation procedures, reduce qualitative trade barriers, curtail dumping (that is, selling abroad at a cost less than the cost of production),[42] and discourage government subsidies. While GATT has reduced tariffs from 40 percent in 1947 to under 5 percent in 1990, there are still opportunities to improve world trade. Ambassador Carla A. Hills, the U.S. Trade Representative, has recommended the following improvements in GATT for 1991 and beyond.[43]

1. Expand market access further by reducing tariff and nontariff business by one-third, which would increase global output by $4 trillion over the next ten years.
2. Develop rules of fair play for services, investments, and intellectual property.
3. Eliminate the billions of government subsidies to industries, which distort the market.
4. Expand the rules to developing countries not yet part of GATT.
5. Create a swift and effective way to resolve trade disputes.
6. Reform agricultural policy in an effort to eliminate subsidies.

These are key issues for the continuation of the Uruguay round of talks. The major stumbling block has been the agricultural policy, as both Japan and Europe have a strong system of protection for their farmers.

ECONOMIC INTEGRATION AS A MEANS OF PROMOTING TRADE

There is little argument that free trade bestows net gains on trading nations—especially in the long run. The problem is that with so many entrenched, vested interest groups, it is difficult to update existing trading rules. A reduction of protectionist legislation causes considerable short-term dislocations, putting much economic and political pressure on a nation's power structure.

As a partial step in the trade liberalization process, countries have begun to move toward limited forms of economic integration. While the degree of economic integration can vary considerably from one organization to another, four major types of integration can be identified: free trade areas, customs unions, common markets, and monetary unions. Some of these concepts will be covered in greater detail in Chapter 5.

---

42. Economists prefer to define *dumping* as selling below the variable cost per unit because only in such cases is the decision uneconomical.
43. Carla A. Hills, "Time to Free Up," in *The World in 1991* (London: The Economist Publications Ltd., 1991), p. 42.

Free Trade Areas

The simplest form of integration is a *free trade area*. Within a free trade area, nations agree to drop trade barriers among themselves, but each nation is permitted to maintain independent trade relations with nongroup countries. There is little attempt, at this level, to coordinate such things as domestic tax rates, environmental regulations, and commercial codes; and, generally, such areas do not permit resources (that is, labor and capital) to flow freely across national borders. Moreover, because each country has autonomy over its money supply, exchange rates can fluctuate relative to both member and nonmember countries.

Examples of free trade areas are the Latin American Free Trade Area and the European Free Trade Area. The United States–Canada Free Trade agreement, one of the newest free trade areas, became effective on January 1, 1989.[44] The countries are each other's biggest customers, with the United States consuming 74 percent of Canada's exports and Canada claiming 22 percent of U.S. exports.[45] The Free Trade Agreement is expected to boost trade for both countries and strengthen North America's position when negotiating with the European Community.

Customs Unions

Customs unions, a more advanced form of economic integration, possess the characteristics of a free trade area but with the added feature of a common external tariff/trade barrier for the member nations. Individual countries relinquish the right to set their nongroup trade agreements independently. Rather, a supranational policy-making committee makes these decisions. An historic example of a customs union was the 1834 German Zollverein that was composed of several German states and paved the way for the eventual uniting of Germany in 1870.

Common Markets

The third level of economic integration is a common market. Here, countries have all the characteristics of a customs union but, in addition, the organization encourages resources (labor and capital) to flow freely among the member nations. For example, if jobs are plentiful in Germany but scarce in Italy, workers can move from Italy to Germany without having to worry about severe immigration restrictions. In a common market, there is usually an attempt to coordinate tax codes, social welfare systems, and other legislation that influences resource allocation. Finally, while each nation still has the right to print and coin its own money, exchange rates among nations are oftentimes fixed or permitted to fluctuate only within a narrow band. The

44. Louis Kraar, "North America's New Trade Punch," *Fortune,* May 22, 1989, pp. 123–127.
45. *Vital World Statistics* (London: The Economist Books, 1990), p. 158.

most notable example of a common market is the European Economic Community (EEC). Established in 1957, the EEC has been an active organization for trade liberalization and continues to increase its membership size.

Monetary Unions

The highest form of economic integration is a *monetary union.* A monetary union is a common market in which member countries no longer regulate their own currencies. Rather, member country currencies are replaced by a common currency regulated by a supranational central bank. To date, no good examples of a monetary union exist, even though some of the initiators of the European Common Market had envisioned this as an ultimate step for its members.

The Global Economy

The global economy is in a state of transition from a set of strong national economics to a set of interlinked trading groups. This transition has accelerated over the past few years with the fall of the Berlin Wall, the collapse of communism, and the strengthening of the European Community into a single market. The investment by Europeans, Japanese, and Americans in each other's economies is unprecedented. U.S. companies create and sell over $80 billion per year in goods and services in Japan. Britain bought 640 companies in the United States from 1978–1989 and had a direct foreign investment of $250 billion in the United States, making it the biggest foreign owner of business followed by the Dutch and Japanese.[46] There are eleven Japanese automobile assembly plants in North America, some of which will be shipping finished cars to Europe in 1991.[47] As companies globalize, manufacturing becomes more flexible, and engineers have instant access to the latest technology, we will see microchips designed in California, sent to Scotland to be fabricated, shipped to the Far East to be tested and assembled, and returned to the United States to be sold.[48]

There is no doubt the world is moving toward a single global economy. Of course there are major difficulties on the horizon, such as the development of a market-based economy in Eastern Europe, a reduction of hostilities and the establishment of political stability in the Middle East, and a renewal of GATT talks continuing the trend toward free trade. The global marketer needs to understand the interdependencies that make up the world economy in order to understand how a drop in the U.S. discount rate will affect business in Stockholm, or how Britain join-

46. John Naisbitt and Patricia Aburdene, *Mega Trends 2000* (London: Sidgwick & Jackson, 1990), pp. 9–28.
47. Kevin Done, "Big Three Batten Down the Hatches," *Financial Times,* February 5, 1991, p. 18.
48. William Van Dusen Wishard, "The 21st Century Economy," *The Futurist,* May–June 1987, p. 23.

ing the European Monetary System will affect sales in London. As the speed of change accelerates, successful companies will be able to anticipate the trends and take advantage of them or respond to them quickly. Other companies will watch the changes going on around them and wake up one day to a different marketplace with new rules.

CONCLUSIONS

We learn from the study of economics that changes in rules or in financial circumstances help some groups and hurt others. Therefore, it is important to understand that papers and speeches have particular points of view. Exchange rate movements, tariffs, quotas, and customs unions can be viewed as alternative ways to achieve economic goals. The issue is not will a change take place but rather *which* change will provide the most benefit with the least cost.

This chapter describes the fundamentals of international trade and finance. An understanding of the fundamentals will enable you to comprehend the technical issues raised by the media and formulate your own views. With such an understanding you will be able to *analyze* international economic events and to *evaluate* critically the proliferation of articles that are being written about them.

Questions for Discussion

1. If a nation has a balance on merchandise trade deficit, can it be said that the nation has a weak currency in the international markets as well?

2. Regarding question 1, examine both the balance of payments statistics and the foreign exchange rate statistics presented in the International Monetary Fund's *International Financial Statistics*. What link, if any, do you see between Switzerland's balance on merchandise trade and the value of the Swiss franc over the past five years?

3. Calculate your individual balance of payments over the past month. What were your balance on merchandise trade, balance on goods and services, and your current account balance?

4. Exchange rate changes have been called a "double-edged sword" because they hurt some sectors of the nation while helping other sectors. Explain why this is true.

5. If interest rates in the United Kingdom rise while those in Germany remain unchanged, explain what pressure this will put on the British pound per the German mark exchange rate.

6. Suppose the U.S. Federal Reserve reduces the rate of growth of the money supply causing the U.S. inflation rate to fall, interest rates to rise, and

economic growth to decline. What impact will these economic changes have on the actions of the participants in the foreign exchange market?

7. The concept of *comparative advantage* is one of the most powerful in all of economic theory (both at the domestic level and the international level). Explain why this is true. What does the concept show? What are its implications for international and intranational trade?

8. Suppose that Brazil can produce with an equal amount of resources either 100 units of steel or 10 computers. At the same time, Germany can produce either 150 units of steel or 10 computers. Explain which nation has a comparative advantage in the production of computers. Choose a mutually advantageous trading ratio and explain why this ratio increases the welfare of both nations.

9. In April 1987, President Reagan imposed a tariff on goods imported into the United States made with Japanese semiconductors. Explain which groups in the United States were helped by this action and which groups were hurt by this action. Explain why a tax on semiconductors alone would have actually lowered the level of protection given to computer manufacturers in the United States. Do you believe this action is evidence of good economic thinking?

10. In terms of their economic effects on a nation's economy, explain the similarities and differences between tariffs and quotas.

11. Based on each of the following distinct and separate cases, explain which trade theory best describes the trading pattern cited. Briefly explain why you chose the theory you did.

   a. The opening of trade between the United States and China has resulted in the importation of textiles and other hand-made craftwork by the United States from China and the exportation of machinery and steel from the United States to China.

   b. Currently, the United States is a major importer of televisions from Japan. It once was a major exporter of televisions to Japan.

For Further Reading

Aggarwal, Raj, "The Strategic Challenge of the Evolving Global Economy." *Business Horizons* (July–August 1987), pp. 38–44.

Foreign Exchange Information: A Worldwide Summary. New York: Price Waterhouse, 1990.

"Getting a Grip on the GATT." *Financial Times,* February 5, 1991, p. 18.

Hollerman, Leon. *Japan Disincorporated: The Economic Liberalization Process.* Stanford, Calif: Hoover Institution Press, 1988.

Kindleberger, Charles P. and Peter H. Lindert. *International Economics.* 7th ed. Homewood, Ill.: Irwin, 1984.

Nevin, John J. "Doorstop for Free Trade." *Harvard Business Review,* (March–April 1983), p. 91.

Porter, Michael E. *The Competitive Advantage of Nations.* New York: Macmillan, 1990.

Rabino, Samuel. "An Attitudinal Evaluation of an Export Incentive Program: The Case of Disc." *Columbia Journal of World Trade,* (Spring 1980), p. 61.

Root, Franklin R. *International Trade and Investment.* 5th ed. Cincinnati: Southwestern, 1984.

Rostow, W. W. *The Stages of Economic Growth.* 2nd ed. Cambridge, England: The University Press, 1971.

Schneeweis, Thomas. "A Note on International Trade and Market Structure." *Journal of International Business Studies,* 16 (Summer 1985), pp. 139–152.

The Omnibus Trade and Competitiveness Act of 1988. Washington, D.C.: The International Division, U.S. Department of Commerce, 1988.

Tolchin, Martin. *Buying into America: How Foreign Money Is Changing the Face of Our Nation.* New York: Time Books, 1988.

Vernon, Raymond, "Can the U.S. Negotiate Trade Equality," *Harvard Business Review,* (May–June 1989), pp. 96–101.

Vernon, Raymond and Debora L. Spar, *Beyond Globalism: Remaking American Foreign Policy.* New York: Free Press, 1989.

Wells, Louis T., Jr. "A Product Life Cycle for International Trade?" *Journal of Marketing,* (July 1968), pp. 1–6.

"World Industrial Survey," *Financial Times,* January 15, 1991, Section III pp. 1–4.

3

Cultural and Social Forces

● **IN CHAPTER 1** *we explained that the complexities of international marketing are partially caused by societal and cultural forces. In Chapter 3 we describe some of these cultural and societal influences in more detail. However, since it is not possible to list all of them—or even to fully describe the major cultures of the world—only the more salient forces are highlighted. Figure 3.1 shows the components of culture that are described in this chapter. We also provide an analytical framework that suggests to the international marketing practitioner what to look for. Thus, rather than suggest all the possible cultural or societal factors that may affect international marketers, we concentrate on the analytical processes marketers can use to identify and monitor any of the large number of cultural influences encountered around the globe.*

A DEFINITION OF CULTURE

Anthropology, the study of humans, is a discipline that focuses on the understanding of human behavior. Cultural anthropology examines all human behaviors that have been learned, including social, linguistic, and family behaviors.[1] *Culture* includes the entire heritage of a society transmitted by word, literature, or any other form. It includes all traditions, habits, religion, art, and language. Children born anywhere in

1. Charles Winick, "Anthropology's Contributions to Marketing," *Journal of Marketing,* July 1961, p. 54.

FIGURE 3.1 ● Cultural Analysis

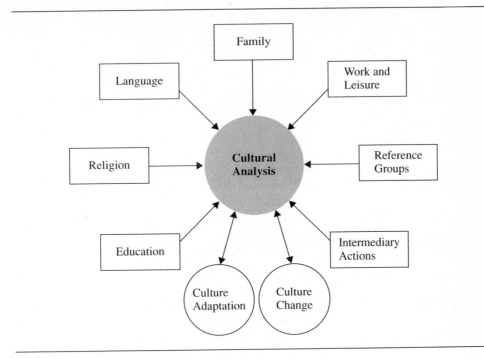

the world have the same essential needs for food, shelter, and clothing. But as they grow, children will develop desires for nonessential things. The development and priority of these *wants* are based on messages from families and peers and, thus, are said to be a result of the culture. Culture reflects the human aspect of a person's environment; it consists of beliefs, morals, customs, and habits learned from others.

Cultural Influences on Marketing

The function of marketing is to earn profits from the satisfaction of human wants and needs. In order to understand and influence the consumer's wants and needs, marketers must understand the culture, especially in an international environment. Figure 3.2 is a diagram of how culture affects human behavior. As the figure shows, culture is embedded in elements of the society such as religion, language, history, and education. These elements send direct and indirect messages to consumers regarding the selection of goods and services. The culture we live in answers such questions as: Is tea or coffee the preferred drink? Is black or white worn at a funeral? What type of food is eaten for breakfast?

For example, the effect of culture was illustrated in a 1975 survey of six European countries (with similar per capita income) to determine preferences in con-

FIGURE 3.2 ● Cultural Influences on Buyer Behavior

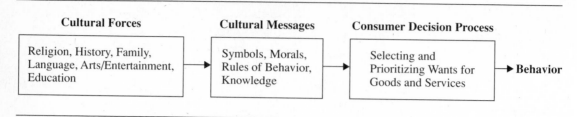

sumer durables. Households having an automatic clothes washer ranged from 67 percent in Italy to 25 percent in the United Kingdom. The use of freezers ranged from 31 percent in Germany to 13 percent in France. Household ownership of vacuum cleaners ranged from 99 percent in the Netherlands to 29 percent in Italy.[2] Behavior in these countries was different due to cultural preferences with regard to methods of cleaning, the use of fresh foods, and so on. An understanding of the culture will help marketers better understand consumer behavior and the need for products and services.

Isolating Cultural Influences

One of the most difficult tasks for international marketers is the assessment of the cultural influences that affect their operations. In the actual marketplace there are always several factors working simultaneously, and it is extremely difficult to isolate any one factor. Frequently, *cultural differences* generally have been held accountable for any noticeable differences between countries. However, when environmental factors differ, what is thought to be *cultural* may in fact be attributable to other factors. Quite often, when countries with both economic and cultural differences are compared, the differences are credited solely to the varying cultural systems. The analyst should be aware that though many of the differences are culturally based, other environmental factors, such as the level of economic development, political system, or legal system, may be responsible for these differences. (These other aspects of the environment will be discussed in Chapters 4 and 5.)

LANGUAGE

Language is a key component of culture because most of a society's culture finds its way into its spoken language. Thus, in many ways language embodies the culture of

2. *Consumer Europe* (London: Euromonitor Publications, 1976), p. 36.

the society. Knowing the language of a society can become the key to understanding its culture. But language is not merely a collection of words or terms. Language expresses the thinking pattern of a culture—and to some extent even forms the thinking. Linguists have found that cultures with more primitive languages or a limited range of expression are more likely to be limited in their thought patterns. Many languages cannot accommodate modern technological or business concepts, forcing the cultural elite to work in a different language.

Forms of Address

The English language has one form of address: all persons are addressed with the pronoun *you.* Not so in many other languages. In the Germanic and Romance languages there are always two forms, the personal and the formal address. In Japanese there are three forms. Depending on status, a Japanese person will speak differently to a superior, a colleague, or a subordinate, and there are different forms for male and female in many expressions. These differences in language represent different ways of interacting. English, particularly as it is spoken in the United States, is much less formal than Japanese. At a recent management development course at a university in the United States with participants from many countries, the Japanese participants had first considered some Americanized nicknames. As it turned out, most of the Japanese participants preferred the Japanese way of address, which is a combination of the last name with "san" attached, for example, Endo-san for Mr. Endo.[3] Consequently, knowing the Japanese language gives a foreigner a better understanding of the cultural mores regarding social status and authority. Of course, one can develop a cultural understanding or empathy by learning about a culture directly. However, just learning a foreign language substantially can help develop cultural empathy.

Overcoming the Language Barrier

International marketing communications are heavily affected by the existence of different languages. Advertising has to be adjusted to each language, and personal contacts are made difficult by a widely existing language barrier. To overcome this language barrier, businesspeople all over the world have relied on three approaches: the direct translation of written material, interpreters, or the acquisition of foreign language skills.

Translations are made for a wide range of documents, including sales literature, catalogues, advertising, and contracts. Though this increases the initial costs of entering a market, few companies can conduct their business over the long run without translating material into the language of their customers. If a company does not have a local subsidiary, competent translation agencies are available in most countries.

3. "How 21 Men Got Global in 35 Days," *Fortune,* November 6, 1989, p. 71.

Some companies even route their foreign correspondence through a translation firm, thus communicating with foreign clients on all matters in their own language. This often increases the likelihood of concluding a deal.

The use of translators is usually restricted to higher level executives because of the higher cost. Traveling with executives and attending meetings, translators perform a very useful function when a complete language barrier exists. They are best used for a limited time only, however, and cannot realistically overcome long-term communication problems.

Both translation services and translators depend on translating one foreign language into another. Experience shows that this also involves risks.[4] In many situations it is almost impossible to translate fully a given meaning into a second language. When the original idea, or thought, is not part of the second culture, the translation may be meaningless. Brand names have been particularly affected by this, since they are not normally translated. Consequently, a company may get into difficulty with the use of a product name in a foreign country even though its advertising message is fully translated. General Motors' experience with its Nova model is typical here. Though it could easily be pronounced in Spanish, the literal meaning is *no va,* or "does not go." That was certainly not the right attribute for a car.[5] Today, companies tend to carefully choose product names in advance to ensure that the meaning in all major languages is neutral and positive. They also want to make sure that the name can be easily pronounced. Language differences may have caused many blunders during the period of rapid business expansion after World War II, but careful translations have now reduced the number of international marketing mistakes. However, the language barrier still remains, and companies that do more to overcome this barrier frequently achieve better results.

Another approach to the problem is to learn a foreign language. Citizens of the United States in general have been remiss in learning foreign languages, whereas citizens of other nations have invested much time and effort in language study. Although international business is increasingly being transacted in English, it should not be assumed that all foreign executives speak it. Furthermore, not all foreign executives speak English well enough to have serious business discussions, and still fewer can communicate fluently in written English. As a result, native English-speaking executives should not use the excuse that their counterparts speak English anyway. True, it is difficult to select a suitable language to learn. Some languages, such as Japanese or German, are spoken in only one geographic area, whereas others, such as Spanish or French, are spoken in many countries. But if marketers really believe in the saying that "you have to speak the language of your customer," then there is every advantage in finding a way to communicate in the client's native language. If one considers the value of developing cultural empathy through learning a foreign

4. David A. Ricks, *Big Business Blunders: Mistakes in Multinational Marketing* (Homewood, Ill.: Dow Jones-Irwin, 1983) pp. 75–95.
5. Ibid., p. 83.

language, an argument can be made that learning any language will develop such cultural skills. Looking at foreign languages from that point of view allows the student to approach learning as a developmental skill that can be applied in many ways. In a sense, by learning one foreign language, the student can learn to appreciate all different cultures. Whenever two executives get together and speak their respective languages to some extent, the chosen language is frequently that one that is better spoken. If an American executive meets an Italian executive, and the Italian speaks better English than the American speaks Italian, it would be normal for the two to speak in English. Thus, as more and more executives abroad learn English, they, at the same time, raise the required level at which the American executive must make use of the foreign language. This is often frustrating to those who have learned a few sentences with difficulty.

Even when executives understand each other's language, there can still be plenty of room for misunderstanding. When an American executive means "yes" in a negotiation, this usually means "yes, I accept the terms." However, in Asian countries "yes" may mean four different things. First, it may mean that the other side recognizes that one is talking to them, but not necessarily that they understand what is said. Secondly, it could mean that what was said was understood and was clear, but not that it was agreed to. Thirdly, it may mean that the other party has understood the proposal and will consult with others about it. And finally, "yes" may mean total agreement. It takes skill to understand just what "yes" means in any type of negotiation.[6]

However, achieving some fluency in a foreign language is not the only cultural barrier to cross. At least as important is the use of nonverbal communications or *body language.* Sometimes referred to as the "silent language," this includes such elements as touching, the distance between speakers, facial expressions, and speech inflection, as well as arm and hand gestures. Particularly the latter vary greatly according to culture.[7] The head of worldwide marketing of Parker Pen once went for a stroll with his Saudi distributor in Jeddah. Suddenly, the Saudi distributor took the American's hand and they continued to walk through the streets swinging hands. The U.S. executive found out later that this was a sign of great respect and admiration and that pulling away would have meant a great insult.[8]

We can now draw two major conclusions about the impact of language on international marketing. First, a firm must adjust its communication program and design communications to include the languages used by its customers. Second, the firm must be aware that a foreign language may contain different thinking patterns or indicate varying motivations on the part of prospective clients. This is much more

6. Carl R. Ruthstrom and Ken Matejka, "The Meaning of 'Yes' in the Far East," *Industrial Marketing Management,* vol. 19, no. 3, August 1990, p. 191.

7. Robert Moran, "Cross-Cultural Contact: Watch Your Body Language," *International Management,* May 1990, p. 84.

8. "When in Rome, or Jeddah, or Tokyo," *USA Today/International,* March 31, 1990, p. 4A.

difficult. To the extent that such differences occur, the simple mechanical translation of messages will not suffice. Instead, the company may have to change the entire marketing message to reflect the different cultural patterns.

RELIGION

Many businesspeople ignore the influence religion may have on the marketing environment. But even in the United States, religion has had a profound impact, though we are not aware of it on a daily basis. Historically, the religious tradition in the United States, based on Christianity and Judaism, emphasizes hard work, thriftiness, and a simple lifestyle. These religious values have certainly altered over time; many of our modern marketing activities would not exist if these older values persisted. Thrift, for instance, presumes that a person will save hard-earned wages and use these savings for purchases later on. Today ample credit facilities exist to supplement or even supplant savings. Hard work is no longer the *raison d'etre* for many U.S. consumers; more time and energy are given to leisure activities. The simple lifestyle has given way to conspicuous consumption. This latter development also affects purchasing and consumption patterns.

Christian Traditions

There still are, however, religious customs that remain a major factor in marketing today, both here and abroad. Christmas is one Christian tradition that, at least in respect to consumption, remains an important event for many consumer goods industries. Retailers traditionally have their largest sales around that time. Christmas can be used as an illustration of the substantial differences among even largely Christian societies. A large U.S.-based retailer of consumer electronics found out about these differences the hard way when it opened its first retail outlet in the Netherlands. The company planned the opening to coincide with the start of the Christmas selling season, as this would allow the firm to show a profit in the first year, and advertising space was bought accordingly in late November and December. The results were less than satisfactory, however, because major gift giving in Holland takes place not around December 25, Christmas Day, but on St. Nicholas Day, December 6, the Dutch traditional day of gift giving. Thus, the opening of the company's retail operation was late and missed the major buying season.

Many other variations surrounding Christmas gift giving can be found. In France, it is traditional to exchange gifts on January 6, often called "Little Christmas." Also different are the personages who bring the gifts. In the United States, as in the United Kingdom, Santa Claus brings the Christmas gifts; but in German-speaking countries, gifts are brought by an angel representing the Christ Child. In German areas, Santa Claus or St. Nicholas comes on December 6 to bring small gifts and food to those children who behaved. All of these examples show that local variations of religious traditions can have a substantial impact on international marketing activities.

Islam

Religion's impact on international marketing becomes more apparent when the observer compares one religion to another. It is beyond the scope of this text to give a complete description of all world religions with specific implications for marketing. However, by using one non-Christian religion, Islam, some of the potential impact can be documented. We chose Islam to discuss in view of its growing influence in many countries.

With about 767 million followers, Islam is the religion of 20 percent of the world's population.[9] Islam was established by the prophet Mohammed in Mecca in A.D. 610. Thirteen years later, when Mohammed had to flee to nearby Medina, he established the first Islamic city-state.[10] By his death in 632, the holy book of Islam, the *Koran*, had been completely revealed. It is believed to contain God's own words. The *Koran* was supplemented by the *Hadith* and *Sunna* which contain the reported words and actions of the prophet Mohammed. These works contain the primary sources of guidance for all Muslims on all aspects of life.

With the expansion of the Islamic state, additional guidance was needed; and as a result the *Sharia*, or legal system, emerged. Based on the *Koran*, the *Sharia* gives details of required duties and outlines all types of human interactions. It essentially constitutes what elsewhere would be considered criminal, personal, and commercial law. These Islamic guidelines cover all aspects of human life and categorize human behavior as obligatory, merely desirable, forbidden, merely undesirable, or neutral. The principal goal is to guide human beings in their quest for salvation because the basic purpose of human existence is to serve God. Divine guidance is to be accepted as given; and it is believed to meet both the spiritual and psychological needs of individuals, making them better social beings. The nonritual divine guidance covers, among other areas, the economic activities of society. This latter guidance offers people a wide range of choices while protecting them from evil. A set of basic values restricts economic action and should not be violated or transgressed.

The Islamic value system, as it relates to economic activities, requires a commitment to God and a constant awareness of God's presence even while engaged in material work. Wealth is considered a favor of God to be appreciated; it cannot be regarded as a final goal. Wealth is to be used to satisfy basic needs in moderation. With the real ownership of wealth belonging to God, man is considered only a tem-

9. Mushtaq Luqmani, Zahir Quraeshi, and Linda Delene, "Marketing in Islamic Countries: A Viewpoint," *MSU Business Topics,* Summer 1980, p. 17.

10. Muhammad Abdul-Rauf, "The Ten Commandments of Islamic Economics," *Across the Board,* August 1979, p. 7.

porary trustee. Thus, material advancement does not entail higher status or merit. In Islam, all people are created equal and have the right of life, the right of liberty, the right of ownership, the right of dignity, and the right of education. For the true Muslim, the achievement of goals is both a result of individual efforts and a blessing from God. A Muslim should therefore not neglect the duty of working hard to earn a living.

In their work, Muslims are required to uphold the Islamic virtues of truth, honesty, respect for the rights of others, pursuit of moderation, sacrifice, and hard work. Moderation applies to virtually all situations. The resulting Islamic welfare economy is based on the bond of universal brotherhood in which the individuals, while pursuing their own good, avoid wrongdoing to others. In their economc pursuits, true Muslims not only have their own material needs in mind but accept their social obligations and, thereby, improve their own position with God. The Islamic culture has many specific implications for international marketers. A summary of these implications is shown in Table 3.1.

The prohibition of usury has led to quite different practices with respect to lending in Arab societies.[11] Since this law prohibits interest payments, special Islamic banks were formed. These banks maintain three types of accounts: nonprofit accounts with a very small minimum deposit and the right of immediate withdrawal without notice, profit-sharing deposit accounts, and social services funds. These banks do not charge a fixed rate of interest on loans. Instead, the "interest payment" is levied according to the profits derived from the funds employed. Thus, the depositors get earnings on their deposits depending on the amount of profits earned by the bank. Such Islamic banks now exist in many countries, particularly Egypt, Saudi Arabia, Kuwait, Sudan, Dubai, and Jordan. In Pakistan, where the population is 97 percent Moslem, the Murree Brewery Company operates at only 27 percent of capacity. Only non-Moslems and visitors can purchase alcohol; and they are limited to six bottles of beer and one bottle of liquor each month. Moslems caught with alcohol are subject to flogging.[12]

The influence of Islamic habits on business even outside the Islamic world was demonstrated in the construction of a new luxury hotel in Paris. The hotel, a renovated building near the center of Paris, was selected partially for the reason that some of the rooms face Mecca. Decorated in the latest interior style, some rooms are equipped with buttons that bring down shades with engraved minarets on them. According to the hotel management, one-third of the hotel guests are expected to come from the Middle East.[13]

Certainly, international marketers require a keen awareness of how religion can influence business. They need to search actively for any such possible influences even

11. Ibid., pp. 15–16.
12. "Teetotaling but Tolerant, Pakistan Lets Its Only Brewery Totter Along," *Wall Street Journal,* April 14, 1987, p. 28.
13. "Nouveaux-riches Elysees," *The Economist,* February 27, 1982, p. 66.

TABLE 3.1 ● Marketing in an Islamic Framework

Elements	*Implications for marketing*

I. *Fundamental Islamic Concepts*

A. Unity.
(Concept of centrality, oneness of God, harmony in life.)

Product standardization, mass media techniques, central balance, unity in advertising copy and layout, strong brand loyalties, a smaller evoked size set, loyalty to company, opportunities for brand-extension strategies.

B. Legitimacy.
(Fair dealings, reasonable level of profits.)

Less formal product warranties, need for institutional advertising and/or advocacy advertising, especially by foreign firms, and a switch from profit maximizing to a profit satisficing strategy.

C. Zakaat.
(2.5 percent per annum compulsory tax binding on all classified as "not poor.")

Use of "excessive" profits, if any, for charitable acts; corporate donations for charity, institutional advertising.

D. Usury.
(Cannot charge interest on loans. A general interpretation of this law defines "excessive interest" charged on loans as not permissible.)

Avoid direct use of credit as a marketing tool; establish a consumer policy of paying cash for low value products; for high value products, offer discounts for cash payments and raise prices of products on an installment basis; sometimes possible to conduct interest transactions between local/foreign firm in other non-Islamic countries; banks in some Islamic countries take equity in financing ventures, sharing resultant profits (and losses).

E. Supremacy of human life.
(Compared to other forms of life, objects, human life is of supreme importance.)

Pet food and/or products less important; avoid use of statues, busts—interpreted as forms of idolatry; symbols in advertising and/or promotion should reflect high human values; use floral designs and artwork in advertising as representation of aesthetic values.

F. Community.
(All Muslims should strive to achieve universal brotherhood—with allegiance to the "one God." One way of expressing community is the required pilgrimage to Mecca for all Muslims at least once in their lifetime, if able to do so.)

Formation of an Islamic Economic Community—development of an "Islamic consumer" served with Islamic-oriented products and services, for example, "kosher" meat packages, gifts exchanged at Muslim festivals, and so forth; development of community services—need for marketing or nonprofit organizations and skills.

G. Equality of peoples.

Participative communication systems; roles and authority structures may be rigidly defined but accessibility at any level relatively easy.

TABLE 3.1 ● Marketing in an Islamic Framework (*cont.*)

Elements	*Implications for marketing*
H. Abstinence. (During the month of Ramadan, Muslims are required to fast without food or drink from the first streak of dawn to sunset—a reminder to those who are more fortunate to be kind to the less fortunate and as an exercise in self-control.)	Products that are nutritious, cool, and digested easily can be formulated for Sehr and Iftar (beginning and end of the fast).
Consumption of alcohol and pork is forbidden; so is gambling.	Opportunities for developing nonalcoholic items and beverages (for example, soft drinks, ice cream, milk shakes, fruit juices) and nonchance social games, such as Scrabble; food products should use vegetable or beef shortening.
I. Environmentalism. (The universe created by God was pure. Consequently, the land, air, and water should be held as sacred elements.)	Anticipate environmental, antipollution acts; opportunities for companies involved in maintaining a clean environment; easier acceptance of pollution-control devices in the community (for example, recent efforts in Turkey have been well received by the local communities).
J. Worship. (Five times a day; timing of prayers varies.)	Need to take into account the variability and shift in prayer timings in planning sales calls, work schedules, business hours, customer traffic, and so forth.
II. *Islamic Culture*	
A. Obligation to family and tribal traditions.	Importance of respected members in the family or tribe as opinion leaders; word-of-mouth communication, customer referrals may be critical; social or clan allegiances, affiliations, and associations may be possible surrogates for reference groups; advertising home-oriented products stressing family roles may be highly effective, for example, electronic games.
B. Obligations toward parents are sacred.	The image of functional products should be enhanced with advertisements that stress parental advice or approval; even with children's products, there should be less emphasis on children as decision makers.
C. Obligation to extend hospitality to both insiders and outsiders.	Product designs that are symbols of hospitality, outwardly open in expression; rate of new product acceptance may be accelerated and eased by appeals based on community.
D. Obligation to conform to codes of sexual conduct and social interaction.	

TABLE 3.1 ● Marketing in an Islamic Framework (*cont.*)

Elements	*Implications for marketing*
These may include the following: 1. Modest dress for women in public.	More colorful clothing and accessories are worn by women at home; so promotion of products for use in private homes could be more intimate—such audiences could be reached effectively through women's magazines; avoid use of immodest exposure and sexual implications in public settings.
2. Separation of male and female audiences (in some cases).	Access to female consumers can often be gained only through women as selling agents, salespersons, catalogs, home demonstrations, and women's specialty shops.
E. Obligations to religious occasions. (For example, there are two major religious observances that are celebrated—Eid-ul-Fitr, Eid-ul-Adha.)	Tied to purchase of new shoes, clothing, sweets, and preparation of food items for family reunions, Muslim gatherings. There has been a practice of giving money in place of gifts. Increasingly, however, a shift is taking place to more gift giving; due to lunar calendar, dates are not fixed.

Source: Mushtaq Luqmani, Zahir A. Quraeshi, and Linda Delene, "Marketing in Islamic Countries: A Viewpoint," *MSU Business Topics,* Summer 1980, pp. 20–21. Reprinted by permission.

when the influences are not very apparent. Developing an intitial awareness of the impact religion has on one's own culture is often very helpful in developing cultural sensitivity.

EDUCATION

Though the educational system of a country largely reflects its own culture and heritage, education can have a major impact on how receptive consumers are to foreign marketing techniques. Education shapes people's outlooks, desires, and motivation. To the extent that educational systems differ by country, we can expect differences among consumers. However, education not only affects potential consumers, it also shapes potential employees for foreign companies and for the business community overall. This will influence business practices and competitive behavior.

Executives who have been educated in one country are frequently poorly informed about educational systems elsewhere. In this section, we will indicate some of the major differences in educational systems throughout the world and explain their impact on international marketing.

Levels of Participation

In the United States, although compulsory education ends at age 16, virtually all students who obtain a high school diploma stay in school until age 18 (see Table 3.2). While at high school, some 25 percent take vocational training courses. After high school, students either go on to college or find a job. About half of the high school graduates go on to some type of college.

TABLE 3.2 ● Educational Statistics of Selected Countries (in Percentages)

Countries	Participation in secondary education	Literacy rates
United States	98	99
Canada	104	99
United Kingdom	83	99
Germany	84	99
France	92	99
Italy	75	93
Netherlands	104	99
Spain	102	97
Yugoslavia	80	90.5
Sweden	91	99
Japan	96	99
Korea	89	90
Australia	98	98.5
India	39	36
Mexico	53	88
Brazil	38	76
Venezuela	54	85.6
Afghanistan	7	12
Israel	83	88*/70†
Egypt	69	45
Nigeria	NA	42.4
Kenya	23	59.2
South Africa	?	100**/50††
Tunisia	40	62

*Jews   **whites   †Arabs   ††blacks

Sources: Statistical Yearbook 1988, pp. 3-17–3-67; Copyright, United Nations 1988. Reproduced by permission. *The World Fact Book* 1990 (Washington, D.C.: CIA, June 1990) pp. 1–351. Reprinted by permission.

This pattern is not shared by all countries. The large majority of students in Europe go to school only until age 16; then they join an apprenticeship program. This is particularly the case in Germany, where formal apprenticeship programs exist for about 450 job categories. These programs are under tight government supervision and typically last three years. They include on-the-job training, with one day a week of full-time school. About two-thirds of young Germans enter such a program after compulsory full-time education.[14] During the first year they can expect to earn about 25 percent of the wages earned by a fully trained craftsman in their field. Only about 30 percent of young Germans finish university schooling.

In Great Britain the majority of young people take a job directly in industry and receive informal on-the-job training. In Japan, as in the United States, apprenticeships attract only a small percentage of the youth. In both the United States and Japan, companies provide a substantial amount of in-house training. Some comparative statistics are contained in Figure 3.3.

Participation in secondary education affects literacy levels and economic development. Even with similar levels of participation in secondary education, the attitudes of some countries about the quantity and quality of education differ. For example, Japanese high school students attend class 240 days per year whereas students in the United States attend class 180 days per year. Also, only 35 percent of Japanese high school seniors spend less than five hours per week on homework, but as many as 76 percent of students in the United States spend less than five hours on homework each week.[15]

Literacy and Economic Development

The extent of education affects marketing on two levels. First there is the problem of literacy. In societies where the average level of participation in the educational process is low, one typically finds a low level of literacy (see Table 3.2). This not only affects earning potential, and thus the level of consumption, but it determines the communication options for marketing programs, as we will see in Chapters 14 and 15. A second concern is for how much young people earn. In countries like Germany, where much of its youth have considerable earnings by age 20, the value or potential of the youth market is quite different from that in the United States, where a substantial number of youths do not enter the job market until age 21 or 22.

Recent studies by The Organization for Economic Cooperation and Development have found a definite link between the percentage of sixteen-year-olds staying in school beyond the minimum leaving age and a country's economic well being. Countries like Japan, Holland, West Germany, Austria, and the United States get a high return on their educational expenses since so many young people stay in school, either in traditional or vocational schools. Portugal, Spain, Britain, and New Zea-

14. "School's Out," *The Economist,* December 12, 1981, p. 91.
15. "High Schools in U.S. Lack Drive of Japan's But Show Spontaneity," *Wall Street Journal,* March 10, 1987, p. 20.

FIGURE 3.3 ● Percentage Distribution of Young People After Compulsory Education

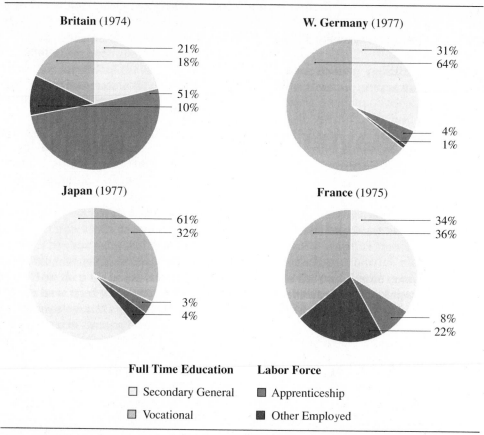

Britain (1974)

21%
18%
51%
10%

W. Germany (1977)

31%
64%
4%
1%

Japan (1977)

61%
32%
3%
4%

France (1975)

34%
36%
8%
22%

Full Time Education
☐ Secondary General
☐ Vocational

Labor Force
◼ Apprenticeship
◼ Other Employed

Source: The Economist, December 12, 1981, p. 91. © 1981 The Economist Newspaper Limited. Reprinted with permission.

land get a poor return on their educational expenses because so few young people continue their education.[16]

The educational system also affects the type of employees and executive talent. The typical career path of a U.S. executive involves a four-year-college program and, in many cases, a post-degree, masters in business administration (MBA) program. This type of executive education is rare outside the United States. Top management talent may have university degrees in other fields. For example, law is among the more popular degrees. In many areas of the world, it may be impossible to hire university graduates. In the United States, the sales organizations of many large com-

16. "The Wealth of Nations," *The Economist,* December 20, 1986, p. 101.

panies are staffed strictly with university graduates. In many other countries, sales as a profession has a lower status, and it can be difficult to attract university graduates.

Different countries have substantially different ideas about education in general, and management education in particular. In general, though differences exist between countries, traditional European education emphasizes the mastery of a subject through knowledge acquisition. In contrast, the U.S. approach emphasizes analytic ability and an understanding of concepts. Students passing through the two educational systems will probably develop different thinking patterns and attitudes. It requires a considerable amount of cultural sensitivity for an international manager to understand these differences and to make the best use of the human resources that are available.

THE FAMILY

The role of the family varies greatly between cultures, as do the roles that the various family members play. Across cultures, we find differences in family sizes, in the employment of women, and in many other factors that are of great interest to marketers. Particularly since the family is a primary reference group and has always been considered an important determinant of purchasing behavior, these differences are of interest.[17] Companies familiar with family interactions in Western society cannot assume that they will find the same patterns elsewhere. For example, the Chinese value family above individuals or even country. People have strong ties with family members. Within a family an individual has no rights or property—expenses are shared.[18] Therefore, product advertising appeals must focus on family benefits, not individual benefits.

One development centers around the nature of the nuclear family. The term *nuclear family* is used with reference to the immediate family group—father, mother, and children living together.[19] In the United States, and to some degree in Western Europe as well, we have found strong trends toward the dissolution of the traditional nuclear family.[20] As a result of an increasing divorce rate, the "typical" family of father, mother, and children living in one dwelling is rapidly becoming a thing of the past or "atypical." Furthermore, families are smaller than they used to be due to the drop in fertility rates. Also, an increasing number of women are working outside the home (see Table 3.3). These circumstances have substantially changed purchasing patterns, especially among U.S. families.

17. J. Barry Mason and Hazel F. Ezell, *Marketing Principles and Strategy* (Plano, Tex.: Business Publications, 1987), p. 266.

18. Ester Lee Yao, "Cultivating Guan-xi (Personal Relationships) with Chinese Partners," *Business Marketing,* January 1987, p. 64.

19. John C. Mowen, *Consumer Behavior* (New York: Macmillan, 1987), p. 399.

20. Fabian Linder, "The Nuclear Family Is Splitting," *Across the Board,* July 1980, p. 52.

TABLE 3.3 ● Family Statistics of Selected Countries

Country	Fertility rates[1]	Average size of household[2]	Active women† as a percent of total female population[5]
United States	61.0	2.7	41.8
Canada	55.5	3.1	54.3*
United Kingdom	52.8	2.7	37.4
Germany	40.1	2.4[3]	35.3
France	62.5	2.9	34.8
Italy	46.5	3.0	28.2
Netherlands	46.2	2.5[4]	35.9*
Spain	73.1	3.5[3]	16.5
Yugoslavia	64.2	N/A	32.9
Sweden	47.1	2.4	68.0
Japan	49.2	3.2	38.6
Korea	82.0	4.5	29.3
Australia	62.2	3.1	45.7
India	136.7	N/A	19.8
Mexico	99.8	5.5[3]	18.2
Brazil	94.0	4.9	26.6*
Venezuela	138.8	5.8[4]	18.7
Afghanistan	232.5	6.2	4.9
Israel	104.5	3.8	26.2
Egypt	160.7	5.2	12.5
Nigeria	N/A	N/A	20.6
Kenya	N/A	N/A	N/A
South Africa	N/A	N/A	22.8
Tunisia	151.9	5.5[4]	11.5

*Data is for women 15 years and older only.

†"Active" refers to employed

N/A = Not Available.

Source: [1] Adapted from *1984 Demographic Yearbook,* 36th Edition. Copyright United Nations 1984; [2] *1982 Demographic Yearbook,* 34th Issue. Copyright, United Nations 1982; [3] *Statistical Yearbook 1982/1983;* [4] *Compendium of Human Settlement Statistics;* [5] Data is for different years 1980–1985 and from different sources, such as census, household surveys, official estimates, and so on. See *1986 Year Book of Labor Statistics* (Geneva: International Labor Office). Copyright © 1987, International Labor Organization, Geneva.

Marketers who have dealt only with U.S. consumers should not expect to find the same type of family structure elsewhere. In many societies, the role of the male as head of household is more pronounced; and in some cultures (as in Asia or Latin America), the differences tend to be substantial. This male dominance coincides with a lower rate of participation by women in the labor force outside the home. On the average, this results in a lower family income, since double wage earners increase the average family incomes. The number of children per family also shows substantial variations by country or culture. In many Eastern European countries and in Germany, one child per family is fast approaching the rule, whereas families in many developing countries are still large by Western standards.

So far we have discussed only the nuclear family. However for many cultures, the extended family—including grandparents, in-laws, aunts, uncles, and so on—is of considerable importance. In the United States, older parents usually live alone, either in individually owned housing, in special housing for the elderly, or in nursing homes (for those who can no longer care for themselves). In countries with lower income levels and in rural areas, the extended family still plays a major role, further increasing the size of the average household.

Because the family plays such an important role as a consumption unit, marketers need to understand family roles and composition as they differ from country to country. At this point we are not so much concerned with the demographic aspects, though they will concern us as we discuss the various market opportunities in Chapters 5 and 6. Here, the primary emphasis is on the roles the individual family members play, their respective influences on each other, and the society's expectation as to what role each family member ought to play. Such an understanding is crucial for the marketing of consumer products and tends to affect both communication policy and product policy.

WORK AND LEISURE

The attitudes a society holds toward work have been documented to have a substantial impact on a society's or culture's economic performance. David McClelland has maintained that it is not a country's external resources that determine its economic rise, but its level of entrepreneurial spirit to exploit existing resources.[21] What was found to be crucial was the orientation or attitudes toward achievement and work. Cultures with a high level of achievement motivation were found to show a faster rise in economic development than those with low achievement motivation.

A well-known German sociologist, Max Weber, investigated the relationship between attitudes toward work and religion. In his famous work published in 1904, *The Protestant Ethic and the Spirit of Capitalism,* Weber was one of the first to spec-

21. David C. McClelland and David G. Winter, *Motivating Economic Achievement* (New York: Free Press, 1969).

ulate on the influence of religion on the work ethic by demonstrating differences between Protestant and Catholic attitudes toward work. McClelland later expanded Weber's theory to cover all religions and found that economies with a more Protestant orientation exceeded economies with a Catholic orientation in per capita income. McClelland ascribed this to the Protestant (particularly Calvinist) belief that man did not necessarily receive salvation from God through work, but that success in work could be viewed as an indication of God's grace. Consequently, accumulating wealth was not viewed as a shameful activity that needed to be hidden. Traditional Catholic doctrine viewed money making in more negative terms. It was Weber's theory that this difference in attitude toward wealth caused Protestant societies to outperform Catholic societies in economic terms.

Thus religion appears to be a primary influence on attitudes toward work. Observers have theorized that the Shinto religion encourages the Japanese people to have a strong patriotic attitude, which is in part responsible for Japan's excellent economic performance.[22] The low rate of economic performance in some developing countries can be attributed in part to their different attitudes toward work as dictated by their religions.

A discussion on work will usually lead to a discussion of its opposite—leisure. Different societies have different views about the amount of leisure time that is acceptable. In most economically developed countries, particularly where work has become a routine activity, leisure has become a major aspect of life. In such countries the development of the leisure industries is an indication that leisure can be as intensely consumed as any other product. In Western European countries it is typical for employees and management alike to receive three to five weeks of vacation time and to embark on trips away from home. In Japan, official vacations may reach the same number of weeks, but employees only take a portion of it. In the United States vacations are shorter, so people tend to use up their allotted time off. These differences in the usage of leisure time to some degree reflect differences in attitudes toward work.

REFERENCE GROUPS

The impact of reference groups on buying behavior has been documented by many writers in marketing.[23] Past experience clearly indicates that the concept of reference group influence applies to many cultures. Differences can be found in the types of relevant reference groups and in the nature of their influence on individual consumers.

22. Vern Terpstra, *International Marketing* (New York: Dryden Press, 1987), p. 101.

23. Leon G. Schiffman and Leslie Lazar Kanuk, *Consumer Behavior,* 3rd ed. (Englewood Cliffs, N.J.: Prentice-Hall, 1987), p. 374.

Peer Groups

The account of a U.S. journalist traveling in the U.S.S.R. gives an excellent illustration of the different types of peer reference groups found abroad. The journalist became curious about the fact that many young people in Russia were wearing the same type of blue jeans and T-shirts that young people were wearing in the United States. In fact, some of the items had been acquired at very high prices on the black market. After several personal conversations, the reporter concluded that those who wore this clothing were viewed as having a sense of fashion-mindedness, and they derived a high level of status within their social groups. In contrast, U.S. consumers who wore blue jeans and T-shirts normally conveyed a sense of informality and casualness about their appearance. Indeed, the U.S. consumers wanted the opposite of their Russian counterparts. Consequently, we can observe the influence of different reference groups on the same product category, as they induce consumption but satisfy different purposes. International marketers are well advised to ensure that communication programs based on specific reference groups are consistent with the cultural and social environment of that reference group in the foreign market.

Role Models

Famous sportspersons traditionally have been used in order to exploit the reference group concept. The idea is to use the prestige of accomplished athletes to promote certain products. However, not all sports are equally popular in all parts of the world. The enormous interest in baseball in the United States is shared only by certain Latin American and Asian nations, and not at all in Europe. On the other hand, soccer dominates only in Europe and Latin America, and not in the United States. Some sports, such as tennis or golf, have an international following but do not attract large segments of the population. Consequently, it is difficult to find a sports personality who is recognized equally around the world.

There are some reference groups of U.S. origin that appear to have substantial universal appeal. The "American way of life" is one phenomenon that may explain the success of many U.S. consumer products elsewhere. Though not always clearly defined, it does represent an attraction to large groups of people in most countries. What is considered American may in fact only be a cover for a modern or high-income lifestyle. Consequently, foreign consumers aspire to a high level of economic status as exemplified by the U.S. lifestyle, or the commonly held image of such a life. In any case, some companies have successfully capitalized on this lifestyle, and Americans have become a reference group for numerous products in markets abroad.

Another U.S. symbol with international appeal is the American cowboy of the "Wild West." The image of a cowboy on horseback triggers substantially similar reactions in most countries, even where the cultural background is otherwise diverse. The cowboy may very well be one of the few commonly shared symbols around the world and this may account for the success of the well-known Philip-Morris Marlboro campaign featuring western scenes.

Country Image

The success of the U.S. company Levi Strauss in foreign markets can partially be credited to the penchant of foreign consumers for western-style clothing. Texas Boot Co., a division of U.S. Shoe Corp., found a growing market for boots in Europe by emphasizing leisure and sportswear shoes.[24] Other U.S. firms have had more difficulty, partially because of the image foreign consumers have of shoes manufactured in the United States. Market research revealed that French manufacturers were viewed as leading in high-fashion women's shoes, whereas Italian companies dominated the market for light-weight men's shoes. Europeans viewed shoes manufactured in the United States as stiff, heavy, boxy, and lacking a variety in styles. Manufacturers in the United States took the lead only with western boots. Once a strong image exists, it is extremely difficult to change a prevailing view.

On an international level, countries can assume the position of a reference group. Over time, various countries, or the residents of various countries, have become known for achievements in some aspects of life, culture, or industry. Other countries, thus, may attach a special quality to the behavior of these consumers or to products that originate in these countries. When the German beer, Beck, was touted in the United States as "the German beer that is number one in Germany," the idea was to capitalize on the image of German beer drinkers as being the most discriminating. BSN-Gervais, Danone, the French company that brewed Kronenbourg, was attempting to take on Heineken, the leading exporter to the United States, by claiming "Europeans like Heineken, but they love Kronenbourg." This campaign tried to take advantage of the fact that Kronenbourg was the largest selling bottled beer in Europe. BSN decided not to emphasize French Alsace as the origin of the beer. Since the brand name Kronenbourg sounded German to most U.S. consumers, the company was banking on the positive image of German beers in general.[25]

The U.S. brewer Anheuser-Busch faced a different problem when entering the European market. Anheuser-Busch marketed its beer as the beer brewed with "high-country barley" from Wyoming, using the German voice used in John Wayne films as the narrator. The same western theme was used in France, where Busch beer was advertised as "the beer of the men of the West." Because the United States was not recognized by Europeans as a major beer-brewing country, the company took advantage of already existing images familiar to European consumers.[26]

The perfume industry, for decades dominated by French firms, has been greatly affected by the "Made in Paris" phenomenon. Consumers all over the world have come to admire and expect more of perfumes made by French companies. American firms have tried to overcome this handicap with aggressive marketing policies and

24. "An Export Foothold for U.S. Made Shoes," *Business Week,* September 4, 1978, p. 74.
25. "Big Battle Is Brewing As French Beer Aims to Topple Heineken," *Wall Street Journal,* February 22, 1980, p. 24.
26. "Anheuser Tries Light Beer Again," *Business Week,* June 29, 1981, p. 140.

the creation of new products based on market research and new insights into perfume-making chemistry. Still, it has proved to be very difficult to enter this high-prestige market, and some U.S. cosmetic leaders have not been able to duplicate their domestic success abroad. To overcome the "Made in Paris" mystique, foreign companies have acquired French cosmetic firms. Foreign firms are now said to control about 25 percent of the French perfume market.[27]

Shiseido, the leading Japanese cosmetics firm, avoided a direct attack on the top French firms by primarily emphasizing skin care products. Traditionally, Japanese cosmetics have emphasized skin care, whereas Western cosmetics have concentrated on fragrances and makeup. When Shiseido entered the German market, the company's message was that Japanese women had concentrated on skin care for generations, thus establishing that the Japanese were experts in skin care products.[28] After various cosmetic firms campaigned heavily against the French industry, some two dozen French firms formed a trade group designed to enhance their image worldwide. Under the name "Prestige de la Parfumerie Francaise," the group planned over several years to spend several million French francs to hold onto the German market, the most important export market for French cosmetics and perfumes.[29]

Research has shown that buyers attach certain values to "made in" labels. A study found that 70 percent of the Japanese business leaders surveyed were concerned about building factories in the United States because of their doubts about the "quality of labor."[30] Actually, these Japanese businesspersons expressed a concern about the quality of U.S. products in general; the quality of labor was only a subelement. A survey conducted by the American Society for Quality Control of 7,000 heads of households in the United States found that about 75 percent believed foreign products were equal to or better than U.S.-made products.[31]

Belarus, a Russian tractor company selling in the United States, was fighting the strongly established shoddy image of Russian goods in the U.S. market. It sold its tractors at prices that were about 10 percent below the leading U.S. models but had been able to sell only 4,000 between 1975 and 1980. Though the buyers of Belarus tractors appeared satisfied with the product, the "Made in Russia" label presented an enormous handicap for the company.[32] This experience, and that of other companies, indicates that a company has to consider the possible impact of its label on the image of its products. While a company or product image may be within the control of an international firm, country images may have to be accepted as given.

27. "Die Parfumeurs unter Konkurrenzdruck," (The Perfume Companies Under Pressure), *Neue Zurcher Zeitung,* March 21–22, 1981, p. 17.

28. Ibid.

29. Ibid.

30. "To Japan 'Made in the U.S.' Means Products Aren't the Very Best," *Wall Street Journal,* February 19, 1981, p. 34.

31. "American-Made Products Get Poor Ratings in Poll," *Wall Street Journal,* December 10, 1980, p. 20.

32. "This Tractor Is Russian. It's Stalled," *The New York Times,* March 9, 1980, p. 1F.

Where the country has a positive image, the origin of the product or company can be exploited. In other cases, the international firm may be advised to select a strategy that plays down the origin of the product. As international cosmetic firms have demonstrated in France, a positive country label can be obtained by opening operations in a particular country known for its achievements in a certain industry.

THE CHALLENGE OF CULTURAL CHANGE

Sometimes, what may appear to be a cultural difference may in fact be due to other influences, particularly economic influences. These other influences are subject to considerable change over short periods of time. Some examples follow.

Although Kellogg has sold Kellogg's Corn Flakes in France since 1935, it has only recently penetrated the breakfast market. The slow growth of demand for corn flakes was related to two aspects of French culinary habits. First, the French did not eat corn; 80 percent of the corn harvested in France was fed to pigs and chickens.[33] Second, of those who ate cereal for breakfast, 40 percent poured on warm milk, which didn't do much for the crunchiness or taste of corn flakes. To overcome these cultural biases, Kellogg put instructions on its cereal boxes and radically boosted television advertising with "Tony le Tigre." The average French person ate 10 ounces of cereal in 1985; and Kellogg expected consumption to increase by 25 percent each year until 1990. However, the consumption of corn flakes in France had a long way to go to reach the average consumption of 9 pounds in the United States, 12 pounds in England, and 13 pounds in Australia.[34]

The United States-based multinational corporation, Pillsbury, for some time dominated the refrigerated dough business in the United States. Expansion into Germany was very successful despite a long tradition of homemakers making their own dough for baked products or buying these products at local bakeries. Germans, who had always eaten rolls for breakfast, found that small bakers were initially stopping deliveries and later closing up shop in large numbers due to economic pressures. The innovation of refrigerated dough, developed for German tastes, thus reached the market at a crucial time when economic problems were overcoming the traditional suppliers of dough and baked products.[35]

Perrier, the French producer of bottled mineral spring water, successfully launched its product in the United States despite this market's practice of consuming soft drinks, beer, or tap water instead. United States per capita consumption of bottled water was less than one liter compared to 55 liters each in France and Italy. Despite these cultural hurdles, the French company started a major push in 1976 and

33. "While Americans Take to Croissants, Kellogg Pushes Corn Flakes on France," *Wall Street Journal,* November 11, 1986, p. 40.

34. Ibid.

35. Barrows Mussey, "Pillsbury Hits Big Jackpot with German Refrigerator Dough," *Advertising Age,* May 19, 1975, p. 34.

increased its annual volume from 3 million to 200 million bottles in 1979, achieving a one percent share of the U.S. soft drink market. Though these figures may not indicate a large volume, they nevertheless indicated a considerable change in U.S. consumption habits.[36]

American fast-food chains have been particularly successful in Japan. In fact, most of the new restaurant concepts in Japan came from the United States. Some concepts, such as home delivery for pizza, were difficult to adopt in a city such as Tokyo where street names or consecutive numbers on houses are nonexistent. However, Japanese consumers have readily accepted new American restaurant forms because they tend to have a great interest in the U.S. lifestyle.[37]

A more dramatic change was triggered by technological innovation. The Japanese have now shifted from using hand-operated abacuses to operating hand-held electronic calculators. Though abacus production declined only from 3.1 million in 1965 to 2 million in 1978, Japanese calculator sales rose from 4,000 to 42.3 million over the same period. Within a few years, the way mathematical operations were carried out by an entire nation had been fundamentally changed.[38]

There are many challenges for marketers seeking to change cultural habits. The New Zealand Meat Board, the world's largest exporter of lamb, traced its inability to penetrate important markets to consumer resistance to the strong flavor and odor of lamb meat. Following several years of research, government scientists found the natural cause of this taste and developed a special grain diet for lambs before slaughter. This solution was considered for some markets only; traditional lamb-purchasing areas such as the United Kingdom, the Mediterranean, and Middle East countries continued to prefer the stronger taste.[39]

In 1980, Brazilian multinational beverage companies made huge investments in vineyards in the hope of changing wine-drinking patterns. Annual per capita wine consumption in Brazil amounted to only one half-gallon. By contrast, neighboring Argentina had a consumption of 23 gallons. Even a modest increase in per capita consumption within a population of 120 million will represent a substantial volume increase.[40]

When Lotus Development Corporation, one of the largest software companies in the world, entered the Japanese market it did not expect the landslide acceptance it achieved in the United States. According to the president of Lotus Development—Japan, "You can't push Japanese management people to use the keyboard. . . . The

36. "Perrier Sales Lose Momentum as Hard Times Hit U.S. Market," *Business Standard,* July 4, 1980, p. 3.

37. "Family in Japan Plays Big Role in Importing Fast Food from U.S.," *Wall Street Journal,* March 3, 1987, p. 11.

38. "Japan's Abacus Makers Begin to Breathe Easier a Decade After the Advent of Electronic Calculators," *Wall Street Journal,* September 14, 1979, p. 44.

39. "New Zealand Hopes to Aid Lamb Exports in Bid to Cut Meat's Odor, Strong Flavor," *Wall Street Journal,* September 13, 1976, p. 38.

40. "Multinationals Push to Turn Brazilians into Wine Drinkers," *Wall Street Journal,* April 8, 1980, p. 19.

Japanese way of working is totally different."[41] In Japanese offices it was unusual to see anyone but a secretary working on a personal computer. Lotus advertisements showed a group of samurai warriors around another warrior holding a floppy disk. As Lotus hoped to start the office productivity revolution in Japan, their new president in Tokyo expected it would be successful with the young managers.

The companies in these examples have viewed the absence or low level of consumption as an indication of potential for growth, rather than as a given cultural trait not subject to change. Many companies have not pursued this goal. International marketers must determine whether observed differences are actually permanent or subject to influence, either by the company itself or by other societal trends.

ADAPTING TO CULTURAL DIFFERENCES

Some companies have made special efforts to adapt their products or services to various cultural environments. Nowhere are these strategies more apparent than in Japan, where foreign companies have to compete in an economically developed market with greatly differing cultural patterns. One critical cultural trait of the Japanese is to resist outside influence. Such resistance is not met by foreign companies alone. New Japanese companies face the same barrier. To overcome such resistance, U.S.-based Procter & Gamble obtained access to the Japanese distribution channel by first buying into and later acquiring a Japanese soap manufacturer, Nippon Sunhome. The acquired company's existing salesforce provided the needed link to the wholesale distribution channel. P&G could exploit the personal contacts that Nippon Sunhome's salesforce had built up over time.[42]

Some companies found that their products needed special adaptations to the cultural requirement of the Japanese market. General Mills, in its attempt to penetrate the Japanese cake mix market, was looking for a mix that could be baked without the traditional electric oven present in most American or European homes. The company developed a cake mix that could be prepared in an electric rice cooker. However, the product turned out to be unsuccessful because Japanese homemakers believed the cake mix might contaminate the purity of their rice flavor.[43] Levi Strauss was another company that had to find a unique strategy for Japan. To compete against Japanese companies, Levi Strauss attempted to establish its product as the most authentic by using film clips of old John Wayne movies in its commercials. The jeans, however, were made in Japan to satisfy the tighter fit desired by Japanese consumers. To gain the cooperation of local retailers, the company delivered weekly and offered free training courses to help store managers run their business more efficiently.[44]

41. "Can Lotus Make Japanese Executives Love PC's?" *New York Times,* November 30, 1986, p. 6F.
42. "Inside Japan's 'Open' Market," *Fortune,* October 5, 1981, p. 124.
43. Ibid., p. 122.
44. Ibid., p. 126.

American Express had to devise a unique strategy in Japan to overcome the Japanese preference for paying in cash. Though there were about 70 million credit cards in circulation in Japan in 1980, they were rarely used. Annual charges averaged $400 compared to $1,500 in the United States. The Japanese appeared embarrassed if they could not pay in cash when out for dinner. For company entertainment, top executives frequently had their bills sent to the company; and junior executives obtained a cash advance before taking out clients. Research showed that Japanese businesspeople wanted primarily cash and security when traveling abroad. As a result, American Express offered a card that, in addition to normal charges, allowed customers to draw $2,200 in cash each month. This adaptation to Japanese requirements expanded the American Express credit card business in Japan.[45]

After years of trying, Japanese appear finally to be warming up to credit cards, too. Particularly younger consumers are now becoming frequent users of credit cards, and besides American Express, Visa and MasterCard are well represented.[46]

INTERMEDIARY RELATIONS

The most common roles found in almost any marketing system are wholesalers, retailers, and salespeople. We find that these roles are played differently in each country. Frequently the differences are due to culture, though there may be other influences that cause different role behavior.

Again, Japan offers some excellent examples of unique role expectations. In the late 1950s, Sony experienced market resistance in a few prefectures in northeastern Japan. Sales appeared to have reached a plateau. The national product manager happened to come across a salesperson's field report indicating that one retailer had determined through an experiment that National Panasonic radios outperformed Sony radios. On further checking, the product manager found that the experiment had been conducted in a washing machine! Informed that the experiment outcome depended on how the radio was placed in the washing machine, the product manager flew out to the store together with the local salesperson and the Research and Development engineer. The store owner was honored to receive such distinguished guests, and he gladly repeated the experiment for the company engineer. The retailer, already impressed by the Sony executive visit, appeared very impressed with the Sony radio performance. The product manager knew that in a few days a large retailer meeting was to take place in the region. He also knew that the Sony experiment would become common knowledge among retailers. The experiment brought Sony closer to many retailers, and sales increased by about 20 percent.[47] This example demonstrates how executives, salespeople, and retailers relate to one another in

45. Ibid., p. 127.

46. "Japanese Consumers, Long Known Savers, Catch on to Credit," *Wall Street Journal,* April 10, 1989, p. 1.

47. Masaaki Imai, "Emotional Aspect Figures Larger in Resolving Problems in Japan," *Japan Economic Journal,* March 27, 1979, p. 12.

Japan. The personal visit showed care and sincerity on the part of the large company. On purely analytical grounds, the solution adopted by the Japanese product manager was emotionally oriented and may not make much sense. However, the mutual expectations that participants in a marketing system have of one another are not the same for all countries.

CULTURAL ANALYSIS FOR INTERNATIONAL MARKETING

We do not feel it is sufficient to describe cultural differences by citing only past experiences of companies. Clearly, we could never cover all of the possible mistakes or cultural differences that international firms may experience abroad. Consequently, we have restricted ourselves to a few examples indicating the kind of problems international firms face. However, because it is impossible to predict all the possible problems that can be encountered abroad, it becomes necessary to provide some analytical framework to deal with cultural differences.

In a classic article, James E. Lee exposed the natural tendency among executives to fall prey to a *self-reference criterion.* Lee defines the self-reference criterion as an "unconscious reference to one's own cultural values."[48] How does this work? Within each culture, we have come to expect certain truths or basic facts. These facts have become part of our experience and are, therefore, rarely challenged. As we continue our experience in one culture only, there are few occasions when such inherent beliefs can be exposed. The self-reference criterion also helps us under new circumstances. Whenever we face an unknown situation, we have an inherent tendency to fall back on prior experience to solve the new problem. There is one substantial handicap to this automatic reflex: if the new situation takes place in a different cultural environment, then the self-reference criterion may invoke past experience that is not applicable.

To avoid the trap of the self-reference criterion habit, Lee suggests that executives approach problems using a four-step analysis. In the first step, the problem is to be defined in terms of the executive's home cultural traits, habits, or norms. Here the analyst can invoke the self-reference criterion. In a second step, the problem is to be defined in terms of the foreign cultural traits, habits, or norms. Value judgements should be avoided at this step. In the third step, the executive is to isolate the personal biases relating to the problem and determine if or how they complicate the problem. Finally, in the fourth step, the problem is to be redefined without the self-reference criterion influence in a search for the optimum solution. Consequently, the four-step approach is designed to avoid culture-bound thinking on the part of executives or companies. (We will further develop this approach in Chapter 7, where a model to analyze the entire international environment is presented.)

48. James E. Lee, "Cultural Analysis in Overseas Operations," *Harvard Business Review,* March–April 1966, pp. 106–114.

Businesspeople moving to another culture will experience stress and tension, often called culture shock. When an individual enters a different culture, he or she must learn to cope with a vast array of new cultural cues and expectations as well as identify which old ones no longer work.

The authors of *Managing Cultural Differences* offer the following ten tips to deflate the stress and tension of cultural shock:

Be culturally prepared.

Learn local communication complexities.

Mix with the host and nationals.

Be creative and experimental.

Be culturally sensitive.

Recognize complexities in host cultures.

Perceive one's self as a culture bearer.

Be patient, understanding, and accepting of one's self and hosts.

Be most realistic in expectations.

Accept the challenge of intercultural experiences.[49]

CONCLUSIONS

In this chapter we introduced you to the wide variety of possible cultural and social influences present in international marketing operations. What we have presented here represents only the tip of the iceberg, a very small sample of all the potential factors.

It is essential for international marketers to avoid a cultural bias, or the self-reference criterion, when dealing with business operations in more than one culture. As the president of a large industrial company in Osaka, Japan, once explained, our cultures are 80 percent identical and 20 percent different. The successful business-person is the one who can identify the differences and deal with them. Of course, this is a very difficult task, and few executives ever reach the stage where they can claim to be completely sensitive to cultural differences. The analytical concepts presented at the end of the chapter will help you to deal with cultural differences. These concepts will be refined further in Chapter 7.

Questions for Discussion

1. Explain the difference between innate wants and needs and wants and needs that are culturally derived.

49. Philip R. Harris and Robert T. Moran, *Managing Cultural Differences,* 2nd ed. (Houston: Gulf Publishing, 1987), pp. 212–215.

2. What process can a marketer use to ensure that an advertisement or brochure gives the desired message in an unfamiliar language?

3. How would marketing automobiles to a predominantly Islamic population differ from marketing to a predominantly Christian population?

4. How do the educational systems of the United States, Japan, England, and Germany affect the marketing of banking services to young adults aged 16–22?

5. What aspects of the culture influence the marketing of women's designer blue jeans in different countries? How do these cultural influences affect magazine advertising?

6. The country of origin of a product is said to influence consumer demand. Why do we prefer specific products from certain countries, for example perfume from France, electronics from Japan, and beer from Germany?

7. When entering a new market, how can one "learn" the culture?

For Further Reading

Cavusgil, S. Tamer, and Pervez N. Ghauri, *Doing Business in Developing Countries.* Lincolnwood, IL: Routledge, 1990.

De Mente, Boye, *How to Do Business with the Japanese.* NTC Business Books, 1989.

De Mente, Boye, *Chinese Etiquette and Ethics in Business.* NTC Business Books, 1989.

Douglas, Susan, and Bernard Dubois, "Looking at the Cultural Environment for International Marketing Opportunities." *Columbia Journal of World Business* (Winter 1977), p. 102.

Douglas, Susan P. "Cross-National Comparisons and Consumer Stereotypes: A Case Study of Working and Nonworking Wives in the U.S. and France." *Journal of Consumer Research* (June 1976), pp. 12–20.

Geert, Hofstede. "National Cultures Revisited." *Asia-Pacific Journal of Management* (September 1984), pp. 22–29.

Graham, John L. "The Influence of Culture on Business Negotiations." *Journal of International Business Studies* (Spring 1985), pp. 81–96.

Hall, Edward T. *Beyond Culture.* Garden City, N.Y.: Anchor Press, 1976.

Harris, D. George. "How National Cultures Shape Management Styles." *Management Review* (July 1982), pp. 58–61.

Harris, Philip R., and Robert T. Moran. *Managing Cultural Differences.* 2nd ed. Houston: Gulf Publishing, 1987.

Martenson, Rita. "Is Standardization of Marketing Feasible in Culture-Bound Industries? A European Case Study." *International Marketing Review* (Autumn 1987), p. 7–17.

Reynolds, John I. "Developing Policy Responses to Cultural Differences." *Business Horizons* (August 1978), pp. 30, 31.

Terpstra, Vern, and Kenneth David. *The Cultural Environment of International Business.* 2nd ed. Cincinnati: South-Western, 1985.

4

Political and Legal Forces

● **BY THE VERY** *nature of their jobs, international marketing executives interact with a multitude of political and legal systems that substantially complicate their jobs. The purpose of this chapter is to identify these political and legal forces. A conceptual framework is provided to assist you in identifying the relevant political and legal factors as they pertain to each situation. Figure 4.1 maps out the elements covered in the chapter and shows the relationships between them.*

Dealing simultaneously with several political and legal systems makes the job of the international marketing executive a complex one. Because of these factors, many problems exist that increase the level of risk that exists in the international marketplace. Global companies have learned to cope with such complexities by developing risk reduction strategies. These strategies are explained toward the end of the chapter.

The first part of this chapter primarily is concerned with political factors, and the second part is devoted to the legal aspects of international marketing. The emphasis is on the regulations or laws that affect international marketing business transactions. It is difficult to separate political from legal forces since many laws are actually politically inspired or motivated. Nevertheless, some separation of the two areas is made to allow for a better organization of the subject matter.

FIGURE 4.1 ● Analyzing Political Forces

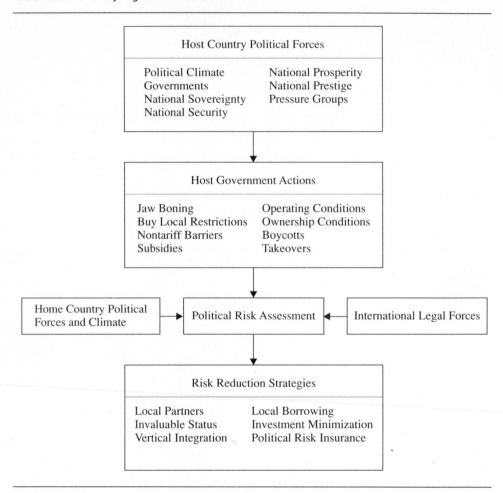

HOST COUNTRY POLITICIAL FORCES

The rapidly changing nature of the international political scene is evident to anyone who regularly reads, listens to, or watches the various news media. Political upheavals, revolutions, or changes in government policy occur daily and can have an enormous effect on international business. As governments change, opportunities for new business may be lost or, just as often, newly gained. For the executive, this means constant adjustments to maximize new opportunities and minimize losses.

Besides the international company, the principal players in the political arena are the host country governments, the home country governments, and the transnational bodies or agencies. The respective interactions of these groups result in a given political climate that may positively or negatively affect the operations of an international business. The difficulty for the international company stems from the fact that the firm simultaneously is subject to all these forces, often having conflicting influence; whereas a strictly domestic corporation only has to deal with one, namely the home country political climate. The situation is further complicated by the fact that companies maintain operations in scores of countries—meaning that companies must be able to simultaneously manage many sets of political relationships. In the following sections of this chapter, we will discuss the host country political climate, the home country political climate, and transnational legal forces that regulate international trade. We also focus on political risk assessment and analyze the types of risk reduction strategies that may be employed to manage in such a complex world.

Political Climate

Any country that contains an operational unit (manufacturing, finance, sales office, and so on) of an international company can be defined as a host country. By definition, international companies deal with many different host countries, each with its own political climate. In each country, the political climate is largely determined by the way the various participants interact with each other. It is influenced by the actions of the host-country government and local special interest groups, as well as by the prevailing political philosophy. The type of economic system—capitalistic or socialistic—will often dictate the political system.

Capitalistic systems depend on a market allocation system, where consumers determine demand through consumption of desired goods. Socialistic systems normally depend on command allocation systems, where the government decides what type and how many products will be made. The two systems differ greatly in deciding how resources will be allocated, with the consumers deciding in capitalistic systems and the government deciding in socialist systems, which also reflects the role of the consumer in these societies.

Stable political climates are those in which the presently existing relationships among the key players are not expected to change. Conversely, political climates are termed unstable when the nature of the interactions or their outcomes are unpredictable. Though the political climate of a country can be analyzed with respect to various segments of a society, for the purpose of this text we restrict ourselves to those aspects that relate to the business sectors.

Governments

Businesses operate in another country at the discretion of the government. The government can encourage or discourage foreign businesses through a variety of measures. The government plays the principal role in host countries in initiating and implementing policies regarding the operation, conduct, and ownership of businesses. Today there are over 150 nations accepted as full members at the United Nations, a number that should give some indication as to the large number of independent countries that exist at this time. Although each government may give the impression of acting as a single and homogeneous force, governments in most countries represent a collection of various, and at times conflicting, interests. Governments are sharply influenced by the prevailing political philosophy, existing local pressure groups or special interest groups, and the government's own self-interest. All of these factors lead to government actions that international companies must not only recognize but also actively incorporate into their marketing strategies. What is of prime importance, then, is the ability to understand the rationale behind government actions.

To evaluate the political risk in a country and understand how decisions are made, it is useful to examine the political structure. Is it a democracy, dictatorship, monarchy, or communist government? Knowing the political system helps understand the relationship between business and government. One way to classify governments is by the degree of representation of its population in government. Parliamentary government holds regular elections so that government policies reflect the will of the people. All democracies are classified as parliamentary. On the other hand, absolutist goverments such as monarchies and dictatorships do not necessarily reflect the will of the people. Absolutist governments are often found in newly formed nations. There is a trend away from absolutist governments. The overthrow of the Nicolae Ceaușescu regime in Romania and the fall of the Sandinistas in Nicaragua, to be replaced by Violeta Chamorro, are examples of the trend away from the absolutist toward parliamentary government.

Understanding governmental behavior only makes sense if there is a rational basis for leaders' actions and decisions. As many political scientists have pointed out, these actions usually flow from the government's interpretation of its own self-interest. This self-interest, often called national interest, may be expected to differ from nation to nation, but it typically includes the following goals:

1. *Self-preservation.* This is the prime goal of any entity, including states or governments.

2. *Security.* To the extent possible, each entity seeks to maximize the opportunity for continued existence and to minimize threats from the outside.

3. *Prosperity.* Improved living conditions for a country's citizens is an important and constant concern.

4. *Prestige.* Most governments or countries seek this either as an end in itself or to help reach other objectives.

5. *Ideology.* Governments frequently protect or promote an ideology in combination with other goals.[1]

1. Vern Terpstra and Kenneth David, *The Cultural Environment of International Business,* 3rd ed. (Cincinnati: South-Western, 1991), p. 203.

The interaction of governments with foreign business interests can be understood through a basic appreciation of their national interest. The goals cited above are frequently the source of governmental actions either encouraging or limiting the business activities of international companies. Many executives erroneously believe that such limiting actions will mostly occur in developing countries. On the contrary, there are as many examples of restrictive government actions in the most developed countries, which indicates the universal nature of this type of governmental behavior. Such restrictive behavior most often occurs when a government perceives the attainment of its own goals threatened by the activities or existence of a body beyond its total control, namely the foreign subsidiary of a company.

National Sovereignty and the Goal of Self-Preservation

A country's self-preservation is most threatened when its national sovereignty is at stake. Sovereignty gives a nation complete control within a given geographic area, including the ability to pass laws and regulations and the power to use necessary reinforcement. Governments or countries frequently view the existence of sovereignty as a key to reaching the goal of self-preservation. Though sovereignty may, of course, be threatened by a number of factors, it is the relationship between a government's attempt to protect its sovereignty and a company's policies to achieve its own goals that are of primary interest to us.

Due to the fact that subsidiaries, or branch offices, of international companies are substantially controlled or influenced by decisions made in headquarters beyond the physical or legal control of the host government, such foreign companies are frequently viewed as a danger to the host country's national sovereignty. (It is important to recognize in this context that perceptions on the part of host countries are typically more important than actual facts.)

One of the best examples of a conflict between a local government and the local units of an international company took place in Canada. Due to its long border with the United States, Canada had become a popular market for subsidiaries of U.S. companies. Through local operations, these companies could circumvent the tariff barrier erected decades ago. It is a fact that there were more foreign companies operating in Canada than in any other country in the world. For such important industry segments as food, chemicals, refining, automobiles, and textiles, foreign companies controlled more than 50 percent of the assets. In the crucial energy segment, foreign companies controlled about 70 percent.[2]

To redress this imbalance in key industries, Canada's government passed a number of laws and instituted some new regulations that are aimed at reasserting control over Canada's industry. Now, the Foreign Investment Review Agency (FIRA) must accept any change in ownership of foreign subsidiaries or the opening of new investments in Canada.[3]

2. "Trudeau's War on U.S. Business," *Fortune,* April 6, 1981, pp. 74–82.
3. Ibid.

Canada's attempt to limit foreign control of its industry showed significant results in several key economic sectors. As a result, the application of the law has been relaxed. However, this was also partially in response to a ruling of the General Agreements on Tariffs and Trade (GATT), of which Canada is a member, that some of Canada's policies were in violation of GATT rules.[4] Recall that GATT, originally signed after World War II, is an agreement of the member nations to reduce tariffs and solve trade disputes.

Most countries limit foreign ownership of newspapers, television and radio stations, for reasons of national sovereignty. Countries fear that if a foreign company controlled these media, they could influence public opinion and limit national sovereignty. It is believed that Rupert Murdoch, the well-known Australian, became a U.S. citizen to avoid the foreign ownership limits in the U.S.[5] The U.K. Monopolies and Mergers Commission disallowed the sale of ICI's fertilizer business to the state-owned Finnish company Kemira Oy. Mr. Peter Lilley, the U.K. Secretary of State for Trade and Industry, feels that selling a U.K. business to a state-owned business is a "form of Nationalization through the back door."[6]

As many emerging nations attempt to control their own political and economic destiny, attempts to restrict foreign companies will continue. Large industrial complexes like mines, telephone companies, or steel works are much more likely to be affected by this than smaller companies out of the public eye. Often the periods of tight control of international companies are followed by periods of liberalization, reflecting the need for a long-term perspective and investment by companies.

The Need for National Security

It is natural for a government to strive to protect its country's borders from outside forces. Typically, the military establishment becomes a country's principal tool to prevent outside interference. Consequently, many concerns about national security have to do with a country's armed forces or related agencies. Other areas sensitive to the national security are aspects of a country's infrastructure, its essential resources, utilities, and the supply of crucial raw materials, particularly oil. To ensure their security, host governments tend to strive for control of these sensitive areas and resist any influence foreign firms may gain over such companies or agencies.

Examples of such government influence abound. The U.S. government, for one, does not typically purchase military material from foreign controlled firms, even if they have subsidiaries in the United States. Other foreign governments give preference to their own arms industry to achieve a certain measure of independence from outside interference. For example, the Japan Defense Agency planned to have Mitsubishi Heavy Industries build a new jet fighter with home-grown technology rather

4. "Canada Eases Curbs on Foreign Investment," *Financial Times,* February 7, 1984, p. 5.
5. "Rupert Murdoch—The Exile," *The Economist,* September 29, 1990, pp. 93–94.
6. "ICI Ready to Close Leith Plant After Government Veto of Finnish Takeover," *Sunday Times,* Feburary 3, 1991, p. 35.

than buy an existing one from General Dynamics or McDonnell Douglas in the United States. Although Japan was being pressured to buy from the United States, Japanese officials felt that if they continued to rely on foreign technology, Japan's defense capability would be diminished.[7] The protection of national security interests such as defense and telecommunications through regulations requiring local sourcing is declining. This change has been influenced by two issues. First, it is not economical for each country to have its own defense and telecommunications industry. The high cost of research and development means that in many cases the small local defense supplier will have inferior technologies. Second, the European Community has agreed to open up public spending to all EC companies. This opening of the European public spending has caused many American and Japanese firms to form alliances with European partners as well as encourage the U.S. and Japanese governments to open up their public spending markets so their industries are not shut out of European markets. For example, Japan recently agreed to open its $3 billion telecommunications market, after heavy lobbying by the U.S. government.[8]

Fostering National Prosperity

A key goal for government is to ensure the material prosperity of its citizens. Prosperity is usually expressed in national income or GNP, and comparisons between countries are frequently made with respect to per capita income or GNP per capita figures. However prosperity is measured, most governments strive to provide full employment and an increasing standard of living. Part of this goal is to enact an economic policy that will stimulate the economic output of businesses active within its borders. International companies can assume an important role inasmuch as they add to a host country's GNP and thus enhance its income. However, any action that runs contrary to the host government's goals, though it may be in the best interest of the company, will likely cause a conflict between the foreign company and the host country government. Furthermore, a host country may take actions that unilaterally favor local industry over foreign competitors to protect its own standard of living and prosperity.

For many countries, a high level of imports represents a drain on their monetary resources and lost opportunities to expand their own industrial base. Under such circumstances, a host country may move towards a restriction of imports beyond the imposition of tariffs or customs duties. It puts up what are called nontariff barriers. Both the Italian and French governments have protected their local automobile industries from Japanese competition by using nontariff barriers. The Italian government has for many years restricted the import of Japanese automobiles to a total of 2,000 units annually. The French government, through selective use of import

7. "U.S. Urges Japan to Import Jet Fighter Rather Than Develop One Domestically," *Wall Street Journal,* March 16, 1987, p. 19.

8. "Japan Agrees to Open Market for Telecoms," *International Herald Tribune,* August 3, 1990, p. 11.

licenses, has limited Japanese producers to only 3 percent of the market. The Germans also prohibit the import of high-leaded gasoline needed by French and Italian cars, therefore restricting imports. A new agreement between Japan and the European Community will allow more Japanese cars into Europe, although France and Italy are expected to keep Japanese imports to a minimum.[9] As these examples have shown, government actions can frequently close an otherwise attractive market to a company.

Most host governments try to enhance a nation's prosperity by increasing its exports. To do this, some governments have sponsored export-credit arrangements combined with some form of political risk insurance. (Some other methods of increasing exports are described in more detail in Chapter 18). Particularly in Europe, heads of governments often engage in state visits to encourage major export transactions. Political observers often have pointed out that both the French president and the German chancellor spend a substantial amount of their state visits on business and trade affairs, more so than is typically the case for the president of the United States. Attracting international companies with a high export potential to open up operations in their countries is of critical interest to host governments. Frequently, such companies can expect special treatment or subsidies. The Irish government established the Irish Development Agency whose principal aim is to attract international companies with export potential to Ireland. Companies can expect tax-free status for many years and low-interest loans to finance capital expenditures. In some cases, host governments may even request an export quota commitment before they grant permission to companies to build a local operation.

The host government's export policy is of interest to companies considering locating operations in a particular country. By collecting information on a government's policies or orientation, a company can make an optimal choice that may give it access to benefits not available in some other countries.

Enhancing Prestige

The pursuit of prestige can take many forms; it does not always take the form of industrial achievement. While the governments of some countries choose to support team sports or individual athletes to enhance national prestige, other host governments choose to influence the business climate for the same reason. Having a national airline gives rise to national prestige. Other developed countries may prefer to see their industries achieve leadership in certain technologies such as telecommunications, electronics, robotics, or aerospace.

A host government trying to enhance its country's prestige will frequently encourage local or national companies at the expense of a foreign company. One example was the French government's intervention on behalf of the vineyard Chateau Margaux. On the grounds that it would damage national prestige to do otherwise, the Bordeaux winery was sold to a French supermarket chain despite the fact

9. "EC Car Imports—Fiasco Turbo," *The Economist,* September 29, 1990, pp. 90–92.

that a U.S. buyer had offered a higher price.[10] In another case, the U.S. Secretary of Interior raised a number of objections to the Japanese ownership of the concessions in the Yosemite National Park. While the concessions are not a big business, the idea of part of Yosemite being in foreign hands did challenge the nation's sense of prestige.[11]

In the future, companies will need to develop a keen sense for what constitutes national prestige as perceived by host governments. Businesspeople cannot expect that host governments will have an explicit policy on such issues. Instead, they will have to derive from a series of overt or covert government actions some notions on national prestige. Once a company has a clear definition or idea of what prestige constitutes for a host government, it can avoid policies that are in direct conflict with government intentions or aspirations and emphasize those actions that tend to enhance the host country's prestige.

Host Country Pressure Groups

Host country governments are not the only ones able to influence the political climate and, thus, able to affect the operations of foreign companies. There are other groups that have a stake in the treatment of companies or in political and economic decisions that indirectly affect foreign businesses. In most instances, they cannot act unilaterally. Thus, they try to pressure either the host government or the foreign businesses to conform to their views. Such pressure groups exist in most countries and may be made up of ad hoc groups or permanently structured associations. Political parties are a common pressure group, though they frequently cannot exert much influence outside the government. Parties generally associated with a leftist point of view frequently advocate policies restricting foreign companies. Environmental groups have had a major influence on consumers around the world raising concerns about nuclear energy, oil transportation, waste disposal, rainforest destruction, fishing techniques, global warming, and so on. For example, scientists report that 1990 was the earth's warmest year on record since 1850 when people started recording the planet's temperature. The increased temperature is thought to be caused by human activities related to the escape of carbon dioxide, chlorofluorocarbons, and methane. There is a fear that this warming will have a drastic effect on climate, agriculture, and sea levels.[12] DuPont, one of the world's largest producers of chlorofluorocarbons (CFC), announced in 1988 it would stop making CFCs by 2000, hoping to offer alternatives.[13] Environmental groups also forced McDonald's to reduce its use of plastic

10. "France's Erratic Policies on Investments by Foreigners Confuse Many U.S. Firms," *Wall Street Journal,* April 7, 1980, p. 24.

11. "That Tough New Line on Foreign Investment Is Only a Mirage," *Business Week,* January 21, 1991, p. 43.

12. William K. Stevens, "Separate Studies Rank '90 as World's Warmest Year," *New York Times,* January 10, 1991, p. 1.

13. "Setting the Rules," *The Economist,* September 8, 1990, p. 22.

and styrofoam packing. While McDonald's internal market research shows that environmental issues will have neither a positive nor negative impact on sales, they have agreed to work with the Environmental Defense Fund, an environmental pressure group, to reduce unnecessary and harmful waste.[14]

Some of the most potent pressure groups are found among the local business community itself. These include local industry associations and occasionally local unions. When local companies get into trouble due to foreign competition, they frequently petition the government to help by placing restrictions on the foreign competitors. In the United States, industry groups have in the past attempted to block some imports in textiles, shoes, consumer electronics, and steel. For example, the National Knitwear and Sportswear Association, which represents U.S. manufacturers of sweaters, filed a dumping complaint with the U.S. International Trade Commission against manufacturers of sweaters made in Taiwan, Hong Kong, and South Korea. The Commission found in favor of the U.S. trade group and imposed duties of 21 percent for Taiwan, 6 percent for Hong Kong, and 1.3 percent for South Korea.[15]

HOST GOVERNMENT ACTIONS

In the previous section, we focused on various governmental concerns and the underlying motivations for certain political actions. In this section, we analyze some of the typical policies host governments may choose to control foreign-based businesses. The relationships between the underlying motivations and the chosen policies are also discussed. The host governments' policies are presented in order of their severity, from the least to the most severe.

Jaw Boning

When governments intervene in the business process in an informal way, often without a legal basis, it is called *jaw boning.* Governments use this form of intervention to prevent an act that, though legal, is perceived to be contrary to their own interests or goals. The effectiveness of jaw boning lies in the possibility of stronger action at a later time should the "culprit" not fall into line.

The European Community held discussions with politicians and bureaucrats in Tokyo for over a year to arrive at voluntary import quotas for cars that are expected to be imported from Japan in 1992 through 1997. The Japanese will be allowed to increase exports to Europe from 9.4 percent of the European Market to 18.7 percent by 1997 (of which 10 percent will be from factories in Britain and Spain and the other

14. Martha M. Hamilton, "Will the Golden Arches Adopt a Green Tint?" *International Herald Tribune,* August 3, 1990, p. 11.
15. Nancy Dunne, "U.S. Sweater Makers Elated by Anti-Dumping Victory," *Financial Times,* September 7, 1990, p. 7.

8.7 percent will be from Japan). After 1997 the market will become fully open to the Japanese. The jaw boning efforts of the EC give the European manufacturers seven years of protection to prepare for the open market in 1998.[16]

The leverage of host governments comes from the fact that foreign companies depend on permits and approvals issued by host governments. Such favored treatment may be at risk if a company proceeds against the expressed wishes of the host government despite the fact that no laws were violated.

"Buy Local" Restrictions

Since governments are important customers of industry in virtually every country, they can use this purchasing power to favor certain suppliers. Frequently, local companies are favored over foreign imports. An industry that is particularly subject to such local favoritism is the telecommunications industry because telephone companies are state run in most countries. For foreign companies, the case of Japan's Nippon Telegraph & Telephone Public Corp. (NTT) was particularly problematic. For years, NTT granted contracts exclusively to a few local suppliers, virtually shutting out foreign-based companies. Pressures from foreign governments led to international agreements under the umbrella of GATT, and other international organizations have established new rules that tend to prevent direct government intervention except for cases of national security and a few other exemptions. This has also opened up opportunities for foreign firms with Japan's NTT.[17]

Nontariff Barriers

Under this heading we can include any government action that is not an official custom tariff but that nevertheless inhibits the free flow of products between countries. (See Table 2.7 for a detailed listing.) These barriers may not necessarily add to landed costs but are more likely to result in a limitation on product flows. To a large extent nontariff barriers are used by governments to keep imports from freely entering the home market. There are many types of measures that may be taken. A common one is import restrictions or quotas. The Brazilian government introduced strong action to stem the flow of imports in 1976. As part of a plan to limit imports to only 20 percent of the previous year's total, fiscal incentives and tax exemptions on capital goods were abolished. Payments of 360 days in advance for imports with the Central Bank added to their costs. While such measures had an immediate effect, companies that depend on imports for part of their supplies were suddenly forced to develop local sources.[18]

16. "EC Car Imports," *The Economist,* September 19, 1990, pp. 90–92.
17. "Japan Agrees to Open Market for Telecoms," *International Herald Tribune,* August 3, 1990, p. 11.
18. "Brazil: Tough Import Controls Shake-Up Business," *Business Week,* January 12, 1976, p. 38.

Whiskey spirits face a tax of 220 percent in Japan, so an imported bottle of Scotch would include a tax of 2000 yen ($15.70). Meanwhile, Japanese whiskey which only includes 10 percent of whiskey spirit only pays 10 percent of the tax, but importers are not allowed to mix their spirits to gain this advantage. Japan plans to eliminate this discrimination against imports so they will compete on equal footing in the future.[19]

There has been a growth in nontariff barriers. The world bank estimates that nontariff barriers increased from 15 percent of industrial countries' imports in 1981 to 18 percent by 1986. The Institute of International Economies estimates that if nontariff barriers were eliminated, world trade would increase by $330 billion.[20]

Subsidies

Government subsidies represent free gifts that host governments make available with the intention that the overall benefits to the economy by far exceed such grants. They are a popular instrument used both to encourage exports and attract international companies to a certain country. In a study compiled by the U.S. Department of Commerce, 26 percent of U.S. subsidiaries abroad were reported to have received investment incentives while another 20 percent were offered tax breaks. Incentives vary by countries. Seventy percent of U.S. subsidiaries in Ireland are receiving incentives. In South Korea, 53 percent received incentives; and around 40 percent received incentives in Israel, Taiwan, and Brazil. Developed countries such as Britain, Spain, Sweden, and Australia granted incentives to about one-third of U.S. subsidiaries operating there. The figure for Japan was only 9 percent.[21] All of these actions were intended to attract operations to their countries with the expectation of higher employment and exports.

Governments may also use direct or indirect subsidies to encourage industries that will be major exporters. Exporters have multiple benefits, since they provide employment as well as increase revenue into the country through export sales. An example of a direct subsidy is when a government agrees to pay $1.00 for each pair of shoes to help a local producer compete more effectively in foreign markets. GATT agreements outlaw direct export subsidies but do not usually prohibit indirect subsidies. An indirect subsidy is the result of a subsidy on a component of the exported product. For example, a government may provide a subsidy on the canvas used to manufacture tents, which are then exported.

Subsidies are one way for government to support local industries. In most countries subsidies amount to 2–3.5 percent of the value of industrial output. The rate of subsidy in the United States is estimated to be .5 percent while it is 1.0 percent in Japan. In Europe, subsidies range from 2 percent of industrial output in Germany

19. "Foreign Business in Japan—Whiskey versus 'Whiskey,'" *The Economist,* October 29, 1988, p. 66.
20. "A Survey of World Trade," *The Economist,* September 22, 1990, p. 8.
21. *The Economist,* December 12, 1981, p. 73.

and Britain, to as much as 6–8 percent in Sweden and Ireland.[22] The logic of the subsidies are to improve international competitiveness and create or protect jobs. The European Community has tightened its policy on state aid to industry. In cases where the state aid reduces or distorts competition, the EC can intervene and require the business to pay back the aid to the government. Peugeot, Alfa Romeo, Rover, and Renault have all been required to pay back aid they received from their governments.[23]

Operating Conditions

Host governments have a direct influence on the operations of a foreign subsidiary by imposing specific conditions on the company's operations. According to a report issued by the U.S. Department of Commerce, such conditions became more common. Of the 23,641 U.S. subsidiaries operating abroad, 14 percent had to accept at least one type of operating restriction. Such conditions imposed typically included a pledge about the share of jobs going to local nationals. There were fewer conditions imposed on the amount of sales exported. Performance pledges were most common in Latin America, however, where typically one-third to one-half of operating U.S. subsidiaries had made pledges.[24]

Even Canada imposed conditions on U.S. subsidiaries through its Foreign Investment and Review Agency, FIRA, in 1981. When Apple Computer applied to enter the Canadian market it won an approval by pledging to build a factory in Canada, to share data on potential clients with Canadian companies, and by promising to use Canada's Telidon videotex technology worldwide in home information products.[25] Similarly, the U.S. media concern, Gannett Co., won approval to acquire a Canadian outdoor advertising company, Mediacom Inc., only after the U.S. company agreed to source newsprint for a planned national U.S. newspaper from Canada. Gannett was also required to sell its laser printing technology, which had cost Gannett $14 million to develop, to a Canadian company for the sum of one dollar.[26]

The rules of conducting business may also challenge the international company. For example, the requirement of Mitbestimmung (co-determination) in Germany requires the participation of labor on the management committee.[27] The limited store opening hours challenge retailers in many countries. In Germany there is a ban on bakers working from 10:00 P.M. to 4:00 A.M. The ban dates back to World War I

22. "From the Sublime to the Subsidy," *The Economist,* February 24, 1990, p. 85.

23. "European State Aid—Loaded Down with Lolly," *The Economist,* November 18, 1989, p. 127.

24. "Bait for Multinationals," *The Economist,* December 12, 1981, p. 73.

25. "Canada Widens Its Grip on U.S. Investment," *Business Week,* November 23, 1981, p. 43.

26. Ibid.

27. David Goodhart, "Unruffled Chairman of the Club," *Financial Times,* January 7, 1991, p. 26.

when supplies were short and authorities noticed that people ate less day old bread than fresh bread. Borden, the U.S. company which owns Wilhelm Weber, GmbH has circumvented the night use of bakers through the use of automation, including robots.[28]

Ownership Conditions

Host governments sometimes pursue the policy of requiring that local nationals become part owners of the foreign company. These governments believe that this guarantees fair contributions to the local economy. The restrictions can range from an outright prohibition of full foreign ownership, as is the case in primarily communist countries in Eastern Europe, to selective policies aimed at key industries.

One country that has used ownership conditions extensively is India. India's Foreign Exchange Regulation Act of 1973 stipulates that foreign ownership may not exceed 40 percent unless the foreign firm or Indian company belongs to a key industry, manufacturing materials such as chemicals, turbines, machinery, tractors, or fertilizers. Additional exceptions can be granted for companies that export more than 60 percent of their output or that have incorporated high technologies. For companies that qualify for such exemptions, the maximum percentage may, however, not exceed 74 percent.[29] Since 1976 there exists an intermediate solution that allows foreign ownership of maximum 51 percent as long as 60 percent of sales take place in key industries or high technology with an export content of 10 percent.[30]

Colgate Palmolive (India) followed the requirements of the law and reduced its equity participation and continued to prosper in a growing market. Ciba-Geigy used the restructuring of the company to raise capital by 27 percent, therefore increasing production and doubling sales of Hindustan Ciba-Geigy.[31] International Business Machines Corp. decided to leave rather than give up control. However, later changes in the government have brought a softening of India's stance and the country is again courting firms that can contribute new technologies.[32] Coca-Cola also decided to leave rather than share their secret formula with the Indians. In 1988, Coke began negotiations to return to India without revealing the formula, but as of 1991 they had not entered the Indian market of 860 million consumers due to the political sensitivity of their return, and the difficulty of finding an appropriate partner.[33]

28. Miriam Widman, "Automating the Off-Limit Hours," *International Herald Tribune,* June 9, 1989, p. 13.

29. "Auslandskapital in Indien Unerwunscht" (Foreign Investors Declared Undesirable in India), *Neue Zucher Zeitung,* March 8, 1978, p. 21.

30. Ibid.

31. Denis J. Encarnation and Susbil Vachani, "Foreign Ownership: When Host Changes the Rules," *Harvard Business Review,* September–October 1985, pp. 152–160.

32. "India: Reviving the Welcome for U.S. Business," *Business Week,* March 1, 1982, p. 31.

33. "Coca-Cola Seeking to Re-Enter Huge Indian Market After 11 Years," *Asian Wall Street Journal,* November 21, 1988, p. 23 and "The Real Thing Returns to India," *Financial Times,* April 17, 1991, p. 22.

Boycotts

The previously discussed policies are aimed at restricting or limiting the freedom of action of foreign firms. Boycotts, however, tend to completely shut out some companies from a given market. Typically, politically motivated boycotts tend to be directed at companies of certain origin or companies that have engaged in transactions with political enemies.

One of the most publicized boycott campaigns was the boycott waged by some Arab countries in 1975 against firms that had engaged in business beyond simple export transactions with Israel. The boycott was administered by the Arab League. For example, one U.S. company on the Arab boycott list was Ford Motor Company, which supplied an Israeli car assembler with flat-packed cars for local assembly. Xerox was placed on the list after having financed a documentary on Israel, and the Coca-Cola Company was added to the boycott list for having licensed an Israeli bottler. The embargo did not always include all Arab League member nations. The actual enforcement was, therefore, quite selective and differed by industry. Manufacturers of military hardware sold equally to both Israel and Arab countries. Hilton maintained hotels in both Israel and Arab countries, just as IBM was in a position to do business with both camps.[34]

Boycotts can have very visible effects. The 1990 boycott against tuna caught in nets that also trap and kill dolphins caused Heinz, owners of Star-Kist, to switch to dolphin-safe tuna. The other manufacturers quickly followed suit. Avon gave in to the efforts of the People for Ethical Treatment of Animals, agreeing not to use animals in testing its products. Procter and Gamble, manufacturer of Folger's coffee, did not give in to the boycott by a political advocacy group called Neighbor to Neighbor. The group accused P&G of indirectly financing a brutal civil war in El Salvador because it buys its coffee beans there. Neighbor to Neighbor ran an advertisement with a cup of Folger's coffee which turns to blood when it is poured. P&G denied the claims and pulled its advertising from WHDH-TV in Boston for running the commercial.[35]

Takeovers

No action a host government can take is more drastic than a takeover. Broadly defined, takeovers are any actions that a host government initiates that result in a loss of ownership or direct control by the foreign company. There are, of course, several types of takeovers.[36] *Expropriation* is used to describe a formal, or legal, taking over of an operation with or without the payment of compensation. Even when compensation is paid, there are often concerns about the adequacy of the amount,

---

34. "That Curious Barrier on the Arab Frontiers," *Fortune,* July 1975, p. 82.
35. "P&G Can Get Mad, Sure, But Does it Have to Get Even?" *Business Week,* June 4, 1990, p. 27.
36. Richard D. Robinson, *International Business Management* (New York: Dryden, 1973), p. 374.

timeliness of the payment, and form of payment. *Confiscation* is an expropriation without any compensation. The term *domestication* is used to describe the limiting of certain economic activities to local citizens; this means a takeover by either expropriation, confiscation, or forced sales. Governments may domesticate industry by imposing one of the following requirements: transfer of partial ownership to nationals, promotion of nationals to higher levels of management, and purchase of raw materials or components produced locally. If the company cannot meet these requirements, it may be forced to sell its operations in that country.

Several studies have been made to suggest that takeovers are becoming more frequent and are a major threat to companies operating abroad. In a study compiled by Hawkins, Mintz, and Provissiero in 1975, a total of 170 foreign takeovers of U.S. subsidiaries were registered for the period 1946 to 1973. Comparing these findings with the total of 23,282 U.S. subsidiaries operating outside the United States gives us a takeover rate of about 6 percent. Though this is a small percentage, it is important to note that takeover rates varied substantially by region: 6.4 percent for Africa, 2.2 percent for Latin America, 3.0 percent for the Middle East, and 1.3 percent for Asia. In absolute numbers, three Latin American countries accounted for over one-third of these takeovers: Argentina, 13; Chile, 36; and Peru, 14. Only 38 countries had takeovers, with the vast majority having had none at all.[37] These statistics were supported by a broader survey of all countries by the United Nations in which 875 takeovers were identified for the 1960–1974 period.[38] Ten countries had accounted for two-thirds of all takeovers, and 50 countries registered none at all. The above statistics highlight the fact that takeovers are usually limited to a specific country. A recent study of capital flows in Latin American countries found that there is not a ripple effect from expropriations. That is, a major expropriation in one country did not reduce capital flows into neighboring countries.[39]

The takeovers of U.S. subsidiaries were most frequently associated with a change in government, typically a move to the left. More recently, the proportion of

37. See Franklin R. Root, "The Expropriation of American Companies," *Nationalization, Expropriation, and Other Takings of the United States and Certain Foreign Property Since 1960* (Washington: U.S. Department of State, Bureau of Intelligence and Research, Research Study RECS-14, November 30, 1971); *Business Horizons,* April 1968, p. 69; John F. Truit, "Expropriation of Private Foreign Investment: A Framework to Consider the Post World War II Experience of British and American Investors," Ph.D. diss., Graduate School of Business, Indiana University, 1969, revised and published as *Expropriation of Private Investment,* International Business Research Series No. 3, Indiana University, 1974; *Permanent Sovereignty over Natural Resources,* Report of the Economic and Social Council to the Secretary-General (A/9716), New York, United Nations, 1974; and Robert G. Hawkins, Norman Mintz, and Michael Provissiero, "Government Takeovers of U.S. Foreign Affiliates," *Journal of International Business Studies,* Spring 1976, pp. 3–16.

38. Ibid.

39. Geiger T. Linwood, "Expropriation and External Capital Flows." *Economic Development and Cultural Change,* vol. 37, issue 3, April 1989, pp. 535–556.

TABLE 4.1 ● Host Government Goal and Policy Actions

	Self-preservation	*Security*	*Prosperity*	*Prestige*	*Ideology*
Actions					
Jaw boning	X	X	X	X	X
"Buy local"	X	X	X		
Nontariff barriers	X		X		
Subsidies	X		X		
Operating restrictions	X	X	X		
Ownership conditions		X			
Boycotts					X
Takeovers	X	X	X		X

X = Likelihood of using given action to accomplish certain goals.

takeovers of manufacturing operations has increased. Hawkins, Mintz, and Provissiero classified the majority of the takeovers in their survey as expropriations.[40]

Though all of these above cited reports covered periods up to 1974, takeovers have happened since then in consistently large numbers. Takeovers more recently took place in Iran and Nicaragua; and some are even taking place in France where the French subsidiary of ITT was nationalized.[41] How companies can deal with such risks in the future will be dealt with in a later segment of this chapter.

This section on host government actions was intended to illustrate how host governments can impact on the local operations of international companies. The section before this concentrated more on the motivations behind these governmental actions. Table 4.1 is a chart identifying and relating certain policy actions to the underlying goals discussed in this chapter. Though any combination of goal and action is possible, past history tends to suggest that certain actions are more often associated with specific goals.

HOME COUNTRY POLITICAL FORCES

Managers of international companies need not only be concerned about political developments abroad. Many developments take place at home that can have a great impact on what a company can do internationally. The political development in a

40. Hawkins, Mintz, and Provissiero, "Government Takeovers of U.S. Foreign Affiliates," pp. 3–16.
41. "Nationalization Without Tears," *The Economist,* December 19, 1981, p. 77.

company's home country tends to affect either the role of the company in general, or, more often, some particular aspects of their operations. Consequently, restrictions can be placed on companies not only by host countries but by home countries as well. Therefore, an astute international manager must be able to monitor political developments both at home and abroad.

This section of the chapter will emphasize home country policies and actions directed at international companies. Some of these actions are unique and have only recently come into existence to any large extent.

Home Country Actions

Home countries are essentially guided by the same six interests described earlier in this chapter: national sovereignty, national security, prosperity, prestige, ideology, and power. In general, a home country government wishes to have its country's international companies accept its national priorities. As a result, home country governments at times look towards international companies to help them achieve political goals. They may engage in any or all the actions outlined earlier: jaw boning, nontariff barriers, subsidies, operating restrictions, and so on.

How then do home country policies differ? In the past, home country governments have tried to prevent companies from doing business on ideological, political, or national security grounds. In the extreme, this can result in an embargo on trade with a certain country. Following the unilateral declaration of independence of Rhodesia from the British Empire under white minority rule, most nations followed the United Nations' resolutions and trade embargoes with Rhodesia, thus prohibiting companies located within their borders to engage in any business with Rhodesian firms. This embargo was lifted when black majority rule was won under a new government in what is now called Zimbabwe. Many African nations prohibit any trade with South Africa, and Arab countries prohibit any trade between their countries and Israel. Recent changes in the political structure of South Africa are likely to overturn the trade embargo.

Home Country Pressure Groups

The kind of pressures that international companies are subject to in their home countries are frequently different from the types of pressures brought to bear on them abroad. In many ways, international companies had to deal with special interest groups abroad for a long time. But the type of special interest groups found domestically have only come into existence over the last ten to fifteen years. Such groups are usually well organized, tend to get extensive media coverage, and have succeeded in catching many companies unprepared. While part of their actions has always been geared toward mobilizing support to get the home country government to sponsor specific regulations favorable to their point of view, they have also managed to place companies directly under pressure.

International companies can come under pressure for two major reasons: (1) for the choice of their markets and (2) for their methods of business. The controversy surrounding the involvement of international companies in South Africa is a typical example of this first type of pressure. Most citizens of Western countries abhor the political system and race separation in South Africa. They have attacked companies for their tacit approval of the system in working under South African regulations. The controversy spread to several countries but was particularly debated in the United States. Civil Rights groups and church groups began to show up at annual meetings. During IBM's 1975 annual meeting in Pittsburgh, some shareholders had proposed that IBM completely halt its activities in South Africa.[42] Following a fifty-minute debate, the proposal was voted down by a large margin. But the public debate persisted and other companies started to be drawn into the controversy. Then, in 1976, riots broke out in Soweto near Johannesburg. These developments prompted a dozen U.S. companies in 1977 to accept a code established by the Reverend Dr. Leon Sullivan from Philadelphia, who also happened to be a member of the board at General Motors.[43] The Sullivan Principles covered six basic areas:

- Nonsegregation of races in all eating, comfort, and work facilities
- Equal and fair employment practices
- Equal pay for comparable work
- Training programs to prepare blacks and other nonwhites for supervisory, administrative, clerical, and technical jobs in substantial numbers
- More blacks and other nonwhites in management and supervisory positions
- Improving employees' lives outside the work environment in such areas as housing, transportation, scheduling, recreation, and health.[44]

Many of the 350 U.S. companies active in South Africa eventually joined in signing the Sullivan Principles despite the fact that its implementation in many ways was in violation of official South African laws and labor regulations. In mid-1987, Reverend Sullivan changed his position and recommended complete divestment rather than his original principles.

When political troubles in South Africa intensified, some of the U.S. companies decided to reduce their involvement. Among those who decided to disinvest were Ford Motor Company, Coca-Cola, PepsiCo, and Perkin-Elmer.[45] A total of fifty-five U.S. companies have closed or sold their South African operations since 1984.[46] The release of Nelson Mandela and the pledge by South Africa to repeal apartheid legislation is expected to reduce the impact of the South African boycott. In fact, Austra-

---

42. *New York Times,* April 29, 1975.

43. Herman Nickel "The Case for Doing Business in South Africa," *Fortune,* June 19, 1978, p. 70.

44. Herman Nickel, *Fortune,* © 1978 Times Inc. All rights reserved.

45. "U.S. Companies Are Pulling Out—But Apartheid Is Likely to Stay," *Business Week,* June 24, 1985.

46. "Out of Africa? Well, Not Really," *New York Times,* August 17, 1986, p. 4F.

lia and the U.K. are both optimistic that the announcement by South Africa will lead to the early lifting of sanctions.[47]

A second source of controversy involves the business practices of international companies in three areas: product strategies, promotion practices, and pricing practices. Product strategies include the decision to cease marketing a certain product (such as pesticides or pharmaceuticals), usually for safety reasons. Promotional practices include the way the products are advertised or pushed through distribution channels. Pricing practices refer to the policy of charging higher or unfair prices.

The infant formula controversy of the early 1980s involved participants from many countries and serves as a good example of the type of pressure sometimes placed on international companies. Infant formula was being sold all over the world as a substitute or supplement for breast-feeding. Though even the producers of infant formula agreed that breast-feeding was superior to bottle-feeding, changes started to take place in Western society decades ago that brought about the decline of infant breast-feeding. Following World War II, several companies expanded their infant formula productions in Third-World countries where birth rates were much higher than in the West. Companies that had intended their products to be helpful found themselves embroiled in controversy. Critics blasted the product, saying it was unsafe under Third-World conditions. Because the formula had to be mixed with water, the critics charged that the sanitary conditions and contaminated water in developing countries led to many deaths. As a result, the critics requested an immediate stop to all promotional activities, such as nurses visiting mothers and the distribution of free samples.

Nestlé Company, as one of the leading infant-formula manufacturers, became the target of a boycott by consumer action groups in the United States and elsewhere. Under the leadership of INFACT, the Infant Formula Action Coalition, a consumer boycott of all Nestlé products was organized to force the company to change its marketing practices.[48] The constant public pressure resulted in the development of a code sponsored by the World Health Organization (WHO). This code, accepted by the Thirty-fourth WHO General Assembly in 1981 (with the sole dissenting vote from the United States), primarily covered the methods used to market infant formula. Producers and distributors could not give away any free samples, had to avoid contact with consumers, and were not allowed to do any promotion geared toward the general public. The code was subject to voluntary participation by the WHO member governments.[49] The effect of this controversy was that new regulations, or codes, eventually became part of the legal system. Thus, today's executive must be prepared to deal with issues in home markets that may not be echoed abroad.

47. Ivo Dawnay, "Australia Presses for Early Easing of South African Sanctions," *Financial Times,* February 6, 1991, p. 24.

48. "The Corporation Haters," *Fortune,* June 16, 1980, p. 126.

49. For a detailed background on the infant-formula issue, see "Nestle and the Infant Food Controversy" (A) and (B), by Christopher Gale, George Taucher, and Michael Pearce, *IMEDE,* Lausanne, Switzerland, and University of Western Ontario, London, Ontario, Canada.

CHANGES IN THE POLITICAL CLIMATE

The presence of political risk means that a foreign company can lose part or all of its investment in another country due to some political actions on the part of either the host country government or other pressure groups. The previous sections have detailed the various elements of political risk by describing the participants, their motivation, and their available options to participate and determine the political climate of a country. As we emphasized in the section on takeovers, the political climate of a country is hardly ever static. Instead, key decisions are often made during sudden and radical changes in the political climate of a host country. Sudden changes of power, especially when the new leadership is committed to a leftist economic and political philosophy, have frequently lead to hostile political climates and takeovers. Such changes in government can happen as a result of open elections or unexpected coup d'etats or revolutions.

The fall of the Iranian shah in 1980 is a typical example of a sudden change that caught many companies by surprise. The impact on U.S. business included a total of 3,848 claims—and a full 518 were for more than $250,000. The claims are being settled by The Hague Tribunal, which is dispersing funds from one billion dollars of Iranian assets, which were set aside after the release of the American diplomats who had been held hostage for fourteen months. The largest single settlement was $49.8 million paid to R. J. Reynolds.[50] The damage was not only to U.S. companies. Many companies operating from Europe and Japan were forced to close either all or parts of their operations. The following war between Iran and Iraq further limited the attractiveness of the area and caused additional losses to foreign investors.

Even during periods of war and civil unrest, business goes on. In 1979, U.S. investment in El Salvador reached $150 million in U.S. dollars. By 1984, this was reduced to about $50 million. Many U.S. firms quit the country as it became embroiled in a bitter civil war that saw many of their executives kidnapped or held hostage. But despite these trying circumstances, AVX Corp.'s local subsidiary assembling electronic components was rated better than the company's other eight foreign plants. Operations were maintained by changing shifts to allow workers to be home during hours of high risk. Texas Instruments responded by consolidating its two operations into one and by hiring a full-time professional security force.[51]

Of particular concern to companies operating in various parts of the world is the increasing international terrorism. A U.S. business organization published figures that placed the number of worldwide terrorist incidents at 572 in 1975, 728 in 1976, 1,255 in 1977 and 1,500 in 1978.[52] A full 55 percent of the U.S. citizens kidnapped overseas have been businesspeople. Companies have replied by hiring special security personnel, purchasing kidnap insurance, and employing specialized

50. "Slow Progress on Iran Claims," *New York Times,* November 14, 1984, pp. D1, D5.

51. "U.S. Corporations Are Hoping for a More Stable Environment After Today's Elections," *New York Times,* March 25, 1984, p. 6.

52. *Overseas Business Trends,* Rhode Island Hospital Trust National Bank, February 1980.

firms to negotiate with terrorists in case of a kidnapping. Ransom demands have been rising with amounts in excess of one million dollars becoming more frequent.[53]

The taking of hostages in the Middle East began in 1979 with the storming of the U.S. Embassy in Tehran, Iran. The hostages were held for 444 days and activist groups realized the potential impact of hostage-taking on political opinion. Lebanese gangs have kidnapped 90 foreigners since 1984. Of these, 61 have escaped or were released, 11 died or were murdered and 15 are still being held. These include 7 Americans, 3 British, 2 Germans, 2 Swiss and 1 Italian.[54] International terrorist incidents logged by the U.S. State Department dropped from 856 in 1988 to 528 in 1989. The first quarter 1990 incidents fell to 132, versus 165 in 1989. The opening of Eastern Europe has helped reduce terrorism. Czechoslovakia is no longer supplying Semtex, the plastic explosive, to terrorists. Romania and Hungary are no longer safe havens for terrorists, as police officials cooperate with the West. Iran and Syria both seem to have stopped supporting terrorists. All these activities are reducing terrorism.[55] The Provisional IRA is still active, as shown by the February 7, 1991 mortar attack on 10 Downing Street while the British Cabinet was meeting.[56] Other terrorists located in Lebanon and Libya are expected to be active, and could help lead a resurgence of terrorism in the Middle East and Europe.[57]

A major concern for international companies is the financial aspect of investment. Changes in the political climate and financial structure of a country can result in policies that can make a profitable operation unprofitable. Edward Roberts, the manager of International Credit at Union Carbide reports, "The big problem we're facing now is not with expropriation of assets, but rather with the ability to repatriate funds for material we shipped in."[58] American Motors' joint venture in China, Beijing Jeep Corporation, was shut down for seven weeks in 1986 due to Chinese government restrictions on joint venture foreign purchases. Beijing Jeep imports 90 percent of its parts to assemble the Jeep Cherokee, but it could not get enough hard currency due to the new regulations. The problem was eventually resolved when AMC agreed to start using more locally produced parts.[59]

Faced with such a changing political climate, what can companies do? Internationally active companies have reacted on two fronts. First, they have started to perfect their own intelligence system to prevent situations where they get caught

53. "Terrorism: Why Business Is Now a Prime Target," *International Management Europe,* p. 20.

54. "Out from the Cellar," *The Economist,* April 28, 1990, pp. 77–78.

55. "Terrorism: A Glimmer of Hope," *The World in 1991—The Economist,* 1991, p. 81.

56. "The Day Job—Major Misses His Lunch," *Sunday Times,* February 10, 1991, pp. 10–11.

57. "Terrorism: A Glimmer of Hope," *The World in 1991-The Economist,* 1991, p. 81.

58. "Real-Life Risky Business," *Business Marketing,* January 1987, p. 50.

59. Ibid., p. 52

unaware. Secondly, they have developed several risk reducing business strategies that will help to limit the exposure, or losses, should a sudden change occur. The following sections will concentrate on these two solutions.

POLITICAL RISK ASSESSMENT

Because more than 60 percent of U.S.-based companies suffered some type of politically motivated damage between 1975 and 1980, many companies established systems to systematically analyze political risk.[60] One piece of evidence that political risk assessment was coming of age was the formation of the Association of Political Risk Analysts (APRA) in 1981 with about 200 members.[61] For a company to establish an effective political risk assessment (PRA) system, it has to decide first on the objectives of the system. Another aspect concerns the internal organization, or the assignment of responsibility within the company. Finally, some agreement has to be reached on how the analysis is to be done.

The Objectives of Political Risk Assessment

Potential risks have been described in detail in earlier sections of this chapter. Of course, companies everywhere would like to know about impending governmental instabilities so that no new investments will be placed in those countries. But even more important is the monitoring of existing operations and their political environment. Particularly with existing operations, not much is gained by knowing in advance of potential changes in the political climate unless such advanced knowledge can also be used for future action. As a result, political risk assessment is slowly moving from predicting events to developing strategies to help companies cope with changes.[62] But first, political risk assessment has to deal with the potential political changes. Questions must be answered such as: Should we enter a particular country? Should we stay in a particular country? What can we do with our operations in country X given that development Y can occur?

The Organization of Political Risk Assessment

Although Professor Root found little evidence of systematic political risk assessment in a study he conducted in 1968, more than half of the large U.S.-based international

60. "More Firms Are Hiring Own Political Analysts to Limit Risks Abroad," *Wall Street Journal,* March 30, 1981, p. 17.

61. Bob Donath, "Handicapping and Hedging the Foreign Investment," *Industrial Marketing Management,* February 1981, p. 56.

62. "The Post-Shah Surge in Political-Risk Studies," *Business Week,* December 1, 1980, p. 69.

companies surveyed by the Conference Board indicated that company internal groups were reviewing the political climate of both newly proposed and current operations. In companies that did not have any formalized systems for political risk assessment, top executives tended to obtain first-hand information through direct contact by traveling and talking with other businesspeople.[63]

This informal and unstructured approach once spelled trouble for a U.S. company. Eaton, a diversified U.S. manufacturer, built a plant in southern Normandy, France, that was notorious for its troublesome communist union.[64] If the company had known about the labor situation, it would never have built there, of course. As a result of this and other unsatisfactory experiences, Eaton established a group of full-time political analysts at its headquarters that included former government employees with an extensive background in political risk assessment. Other companies with a full-time corporate staff include Gulf Oil, General Motors, American Can, TRW, and General Electric.[65]

The way Gulf Oil was able to make use of its political risk assessment serves as an example of the power of correct information. Gulf's small team of analysts warned of the Iranian shah's probable fall several months before it was generally anticipated. The same group supported an exploration venture in Pakistan despite the Soviet invasion of Afghanistan that had just taken place. More risky was Gulf's decision to proceed with its operations in Angola. Prior to the civil war in Angola, Gulf's analyst foresaw that a Marxist group would emerge as the most powerful force among the three factions vying for control of the country. Gulf managers felt, however, that the Marxist government would provide both a stable and reasonable government, so they decided to invest. Angola has since become one of Gulf's most important overseas production sources.[66]

Rather than rely on a centralized corporate staff, some companies prefer to delegate political risk assessment responsibility to executives or analysts located in the particular region. Exxon and Xerox both use their subsidiary and regional managers as a major source. The use of distinguished foreign policy advisors is practiced by another group. Bechtel, the large California-based engineering company, made use of the services of Richard Helms, a former CIA director and U.S. ambassador in Iran. Henry Kissinger, a former U.S. Secretary of State, has advised Merck, Goldman, Sachs, and the Chase Manhattan Bank. General Motors and Caterpillar have also maintained outside advisory panels.[67]

63. Franklin Root, "U.S. Business Abroad and Political Risks," *MSU Business Topics,* Winter 1968, pp. 73–80; and Stephen J. Kobrin, et al., "The Assessment and Evaluation of Noneconomic Environments by American Firms: A Preliminary Report," *Journal of International Business Studies,* Spring/Summer 1980, pp. 32–47.

64. "The Multinationals Get Smarter About Political Risks," *Fortune,* March 24, 1980, p. 88.

65. "The Post-Shah Surge in Political-Risk Studies," p. 69.

66. "The Multinationals Get Smarter," p. 87.

67. Ibid.

Information Needs

Though expropriations and takeovers have been a major problem for companies in the past, companies now view other political actions as actually more dangerous. Delayed payments or restrictions on profit repatriation was viewed as the major problem in a study done by a U.S. consulting firm, Heidrick & Struggles, Inc.[68] A study of business executives revealed that political stability, foreign investment, climate, profit remittance, and taxation were all more important than the fear of expropriation, as shown in Table 4.2. An executive of General Motors even went so far as to state that his firm was more concerned about "indigenization," or required local content, leading General Motors away from general political risk studies to studies of the country's regulatory processes.[69]

Professor Root, one of the first academics to take an interest in political risk assessement, suggested that international companies look for answers to six broad key questions:

1. How stable is the host country's political system?

68. "More Firms Are Hiring Own Political Analysts to Limit Risks Abroad," p. 1.
69. "The Post-Shah Surge in Political-Risk Studies," p. 69.

TABLE 4.2 ● Most Important Aspects of the Overseas Environment*

	Percent of respondents
Political stability	79.5
Foreign investment climate	79.5
Profit remittances and exchange controls	69.4
Taxation	51.4
Expropriation	28.4
Political party attitudes toward foreign investors	24.2
Labor strikes and unrest	21.1
Administrative procedures	15.8
Public sector industrial activities	13.2
Public image of the firm	5.3

*Respondents were asked to select four. Aspects listed in rank order.

Source: Stephen J. Kobrin, John Basek, Stephen Blank, Joseph La Palombara, "The Assessment and Evaluation of Noneconomic Environments by American Firms: A Preliminary Report," *Journal of International Business Studies,* Spring/Summer 1980, p. 41. Reprinted by permission.

2. How strong is the host government's commitment to specific rules of the game, such as ownership or contractual rights, given its ideology and power position?

3. How long is the government likely to remain in power?

4. If the present government is succeeded, how would the specific rules of the game change?

5. What would be the effects of any expected changes in the specific rules of the game?

6. In light of those effects, what decisions and actions should be taken now?[70]

Another approach used by Lawrence Bloom, an independent consultant on political risk, concentrated on viewing each country in terms of its political issues and the major political actors. The analysis was to determine which one of these actors would have the greatest influence with respect to important decisions.[71]

One of the most common approaches in political risk assessment is the use of "risk indices" available from specialized country risk assessment services. A survey of fifty-nine companies located in nine countries found that 76 percent used outside risk evaluation services, such as BERI, S.A., Business International, The Economist Intelligence Unit, or Frost & Sullivan.[72] Business International (BI) surveyed about 70 countries twice each year.[73] BI correspondents and other specialists rated the countries on 55 topics, each carrying a specific weight for an index. The countries were than ranked according to risk probability and operating conditions. The report also included discount factors to be applied to projects in various countries. Some experts expect that political risk will increase over the next decade. The balance of power and relative stability that has existed worldwide for the past forty-five years appears to be endangered. History has shown that the dissolution of an existing order increases the likelihood of economic, political and social conflict. As a new political and economic order develops in the 1990s the risks inherent to trading and investing abroad may grow.[74]

Another well-known service is available from Frost & Sullivan (F&S).[75] The research company ranks individual "actors" according to the nature and importance of their opinions on specific issues in any given country. The results for a 1980–1981 survey are contained in Figure 4.2. The figure charts 61 countries according to their likelihood of restricting business activities and their relative political stability.

70. Donath, "Handicapping and Hedging the Foreign Investment," *Industrial Marketing Management,* February 1981, p. 57.

71. "The Multinationals Get Smarter," p. 98.

72. F. T. Haner with John S. Ewing, *Country Risk Assessment* (New York: Praeger, 1985), p. 170.

73. "The Post-Shah Surge," p. 69.

74. Daniel Wagner, "Why Political Risk Insurance will grow in the 1990's," *Risk Management,* vol. 37, no. 10, October 1990, pp. 34–39.

75. Donath, "Handicapping and Hedging the Foreign Investment," p. 57.

FIGURE 4.2 ● Sixty-One Countries Classified by Instability and Restrictions on Business

Restrictions On Business

		High	Medium	Low
Political Instability	High	El Salvador Iran Zaire	Philippines	Bolivia
	Medium	Libya Kenya Nicaragua Nigeria Zambia	Argentina Dominican Republic Canada Ecuador Egypt Indonesia Morocco Pakistan Panama Peru Portugal Tunisia Turkey Yugoslavia	Brazil Colombia India Italy South Africa Spain Thailand Uruguay Zimbabwe
	Low	China	Algeria Greece Mexico Saudi Arabia Venezuela	Australia Austria Chile Denmark Finland France Ireland Japan Kuwait Malaysia Netherlands New Zealand Norway Singapore South Korea Sweden Taiwan United Kingdom United States West Germany

Source: Reprinted by permission of the publisher from "Handicapping and Hedging the Foreign Investment" by Bob Donath, *Industrial Marketing Management,* vol. 66, no. 2, p. 58. Copyright 1981 by Elsevier Science Publishing Co., Inc.

Motorola would often use consultants to determine political risk. For example, in 1987, Motorola used consultants to evaluate the investment risk for a facility in a Southeast Asian country. A Far Eastern business information service reported on how other businesses were responding to the political climate. Another consultant analyzed financial risks. An academic analyzed factors relating to operating costs.[76]

What companies do with their assessment depends on the data they collect. Exxon, for one, integrated its political assessment with its financial plans. In cases where Exxon expects a higher political risk, the company may add 1 to 5 percent to its required return on investment.[77] The political risk assessment should also help the company stay out of a certain country when it is necessary. However the collected data should be carefully differentiated so that the best decision can be made. Recall Gulf's decision to go into Angola despite the Marxist government there.

RISK REDUCTION STRATEGIES

Determining or assessing political risk should not be a goal in itself. The value of political risk assessment is its integration of risk-reducing strategies that eventually enable companies to enter a market or remain in business. Many companies have experimented with different forms of ownership arrangements, production, and financing that were geared towards reducing political risks to an acceptable minimum. We will enlarge upon these alternatives with a discussion of the tools managers can use to deal with political risk rather than leave a market or refuse to enter one.[78]

Local Partners

To rely on local partners with excellent contacts to the host country governing elite is a strategy that has been used effectively by many companies. This may range from placing local nationals on the board of foreign subsidiaries to accepting a substantial capital participation from local investors. According to a survey done for a U.S. research organization, The Conference Board, some 40 percent of U.S. companies with sales in excess of $100 million engaged in some type of joint ventures with local partners. About half of these companies claimed that their joint ventures were just as profitable as fully-owned subsidiaries, and 12 percent viewed their joint ventures even more profitable.[79] Though many host countries require some form of local par-

76. "How MNCs Are Aligning Country-Risk Assessment with Bottom-Line Concerns," *Business International Weekly Report to Managers of Worldwide Organizations,* June 1, 1987, pp. 169–170.

77. "The Multinationals Get Smarter," p. 88.

78. The following sections are adapted from *Insurance Decisions,* published by the CIGNA companies, Philadelphia. Reprinted by permission.

79. Donath, "Handicapping and Hedging the Foreign Investment," p. 61.

ticipation as a condition for entering their market, there are many firms that do so voluntarily. Diamond Shamrock, a U.S.-based company, built its chemical plant in South Korea with the help of a local partner to get more favorable operating conditions.[80]

Invaluable Status

Achieving a status of indispensability is an effective strategy for firms that have exclusive access to high technology or specific products. Such companies keep research and development out of the reach of their politically vulnerable subsidiaries and, at the same time, enhance their bargaining power with host governments by emphasizing their contributions to the economy. When Texas Instruments wanted to open an operation in Japan more than twenty years ago, the company was able to resist pressures to take on a local partner due to its advanced technology. This occurred at a time when many other foreign companies were forced to accept local partners.[81] The appearance of being irreplaceable obviously helps reduce political risk.

Vertical Integration

Companies that maintain specialized plants in various countries, each dependent on each other, are expected to incur fewer political risks than firms with fully integrated and independent plants in each country. A firm practicing this form of distributed sourcing can offer economies of scale to a local operation. This can become crucial for success in many industries. If a host government were to take over such a plant, its output level would be spread over too many units, products, or components, thus rendering the local company uncompetitive due to a cost disadvantage. Further risk can be reduced by having at least two units engage in the same operation to prevent the company itself from becoming hostage to overspecialization. Unless multiple sourcing exists, a company could be virtually shut down if only one of its plants were affected negatively.

Local Borrowing

One of the reasons why Cabot Corp. prefers local partners is that they are then able to borrow locally instead of bringing foreign exchange to a host country.[82] Financing local operations from indigenous banks and maintaining a high level of local accounts payable maximizes the negative effect on the local economy if adverse political actions were taken. Typically, host governments do not expropriate themselves, and they are reluctant to cause problems for their local financial institutions.

80. "More Firms Are Hiring Own Political Analysts," p. 17.
81. Yves L. Doz and C. K. Prahalad, "How MNCs Cope with Host Government Intervention," *Harvard Business Review,* March–April 1980, p. 152.
82. "The Multinationals Get Smarter," p. 98.

Local borrowing, however, is not always possible due to restrictions placed on foreign companies who may otherwise crowd local companies out of the credit markets.

Minimizing Fixed Investments

Political risk of course is always related to the amount of capital at risk. Given equal political risk, an alternative with comparably lower exposed capital amounts is preferable. A company can decide to lease facilities instead of buying them, or they can rely more on outside suppliers provided they exist. In any case, companies should keep exposed assets to a minimum to limit damage due to political risk.

Political Risk Insurance

As a final recourse, international companies can purchase insurance to cover their political risk. With the political developments in Iran and Nicaragua in rapid succession and the assassinations of President Park of Korea and President Sadat of Egypt all taking place between 1979 and 1981, many companies began to change their attitudes on risk insurance. Political risk insurance can offset large potential loses. For example, as a result of the United Nations Security Council's worldwide embargo on Iraq until it withdrew from Kuwait, companies will collect $100–200 million from private insurers and billions from government owned insurers.[83]

Companies based in the United States have two sources for such insurance: government insurance or private insurance. The Overseas Private Investment Corporation (OPIC) was formed in 1969 by the U.S. government to facilitate the participation of private U.S. firms in the development of less developed countries. OPIC offers three kinds of political risk insurance in one hundred developing countries. The agency covers losses caused by currency inconvertibility, expropriation, and bellicose actions such as war and revolution. Because "developing countries are all in hock up to their ears, about 98 percent of our clients buy currency inconvertibility coverage," says Robert L. Jordan, OPIC's director of public affairs.[84] To obtain coverage for an investment, a corporation must demonstrate that the project satisfies both U.S. foreign policy objectives and the aspirations of the host country. This includes an examination of the employment effect, balance of payments impact, environments, and human rights among many other factors. Union Carbide's use of OPIC in Sudan illustrates how the program works. Although Sudan is the largest nation in Africa, it is hampered by a lack of infrastructure. Union Carbide entered a joint venture for the production of dry-cell batteries in Sudan. The project has been very successful and expanded three times. The original project and the three expansions have all been OPIC-insured.[85]

83. "Political Risk Insurers Fear Crisis Escalation," *Business Insurance,* vol. 24, no. 33a, August 13, 1990, p.1.
84. Kate Bertrand, "Real-Life Risky Business," *Business Marketing,* January 1987, p. 53.
85. *The Overseas Private Investment Corporation 1985 Annual Report,* Washington, D.C.: OPIC, 1985, p. 20.

Although some companies did have insurance against political risks, others did not. Among those that did was Cabot Corp. who used initially joint-venture partners and local borrowings to reduce its own investment. Cabot's own capital contribution was insured, just as it was elsewhere. Thus, the firm's investment of $3 million in its Iran venture was well covered by insurance. Earlier, Cabot had been able to recoup its losses both in Argentina and Colombia.[86] Starrett Housing Corp., a company with little foreign experience, got involved in Iran in 1975 with the help of some local partners who were closely connected to the shah. The company had to leave Iran, leaving the residential construction unfinished. To cover its investment of $38 million, the company relied on an Iranian bank closely linked with the shah's business interests. Starrett decided against OPIC insurance due to price considerations. It now has turned out rather difficult to collect against Starrett's letter of guarantee since the local bank's management changed during the Iranian revolution.[87] The price of risk insurance depends, of course, on the country. Rates range from as low as 0.5 percent for the best areas to about 3 percent for risky countries, and they can go as high as 9 percent for high risks. The average risk premium paid is about 1 percent of contract value.

INTERNATIONAL LEGAL FORCES

In many ways, the legal framework of nations is the result of a particular political philosophy or ideology. Just as each country has its own political climate, so does the legal system change from country to country. The legal systems of the world are based on one of four sources—common law derived from English law found in the United Kingdom, the United States, Canada, and countries previously part of the English Commonwealth; civil or code law, which is based on the Roman law of written rules found in non-Islamic and non-Marxist countries; Socialist law derived from the Marxist-Socialist system found in China, Russia, and other socialist nations; and Islamic law derived from the Koran found in Iran, Iraq, Pakistan, and other Islamic nations. Thus, internationally active companies find themselves in a situation where they have to conform to more than one legal system. Although this is complex enough, the difficulty of determining whose laws apply in some cases adds further to an already complex environment.

Here we discuss some of the current major legal challenges that require adjustment and consideration at the corporate level. In later chapters, we will present the specific legal requirements covering certain aspects of the international marketing program. Such material has been added to the chapters on pricing, advertising, and export mechanics, among others.

Of particular interest to us in this chapter are the laws pertaining to commercial

86. "The Multinationals Get Smarter," p. 98.
87. Ibid., p. 95.

behavior, such as laws against bribery and laws regulating competition and product liability. We also discuss the emergence of international courts.

Laws Against Bribery and Corrupt Practices

Though bribery in international business has been known to exist for years, the publicity surrounding some bribery scandals in the early 1970s has caused a public furor about the practice in the United States. For example, in 1975 the U.S.-based company, United Brands, was accused of paying a bribe of $1.25 million in 1974 to a high government official in Honduras later identified as that country's president.[88] The bribe had been paid to obtain a reduction of an export tax levied by Honduras on each box of bananas. United Brands was a major banana exporter that marketed its products worldwide under the Chiquita label. Despite the public outcry about the affair that resulted in the replacement of the Honduran president, United Brands' only violation of U.S. laws was the failure to have reported the payments by concealing them in the books of its subsidiaries.[89] As a result of these revelations, scores of U.S. companies voluntarily declare such payments to the SEC. According to some sources, more than 300 U.S. corporations voluntarily declared illicit payments.

The flood of declarations triggered a new federal law, The Foreign Corrupt Practices Act of 1977, intended to stop the payments of bribes. Though the act covered the whole range of record keeping and control activities of a company both in the United States and abroad, its best known section specifically prohibited U.S. companies, their subsidiaries, and representatives from making payments to high ranking, foreign government officials or political parties. Specifically, the FCPA stated: "Prohibited are the use of an instrumentality of interstate commerce (such as the telephone or the mails) in the furtherance of a payment or even an offer to pay 'anything of value,' directly or indirectly, to any foreign official with discretion or to any foreign political party or foreign political candidate, if the purpose of the payment is the 'corrupt' one of getting the recipient to act (or to refrain from acting) in such a way as to assist the company in obtaining or retaining business for or with or directing business to any person." This portion of the FCPA applied to all U.S. concerns and was not exclusively limited to companies subject to SEC jurisdiction.[90] The penalties for violation can be very stiff: an executive who violates the FCPA may be imprisoned for up to five years and fined up to $10,000. The company involved may be fined up to one million dollars. Though the law prohibits outright bribery, small facilitating payments are not outlawed as long as they are made to government clerks without any policy-making responsibility.

One of the principal reasons why payoffs continue is due to the different attitude toward bribery by various governments. Contrary to U.S. law, the German govern-

---

88. "Honduran Bribery," *Time,* April 21, 1975, p. 74.
89. "Honduras: A Genuine Banana Coup," *Time,* May 5, 1975, p. 29.
90. Hurd Baruch, "The Foreign Corrupt Practices Act," *Harvard Business Review,* January–February 1979, p. 44.

ment considers payoffs legal as long as they are made outside Germany. Furthermore, any such payments are tax deductible. As a result, many U.S.-based companies consider themselves at a disadvantage when competing for business in certain parts of the world where kickbacks are common. Some efforts have been made to help U.S. companies distinguish illegal from legal payments. The U.S. Justice Department reviews proposed transactions and lets the companies know about the legal consequences.[91] There is little likelihood that other governments would come around to accepting the U.S. positions. Europeans and Japanese view such payments as a cost of business.

In a study of U.S. and Australian business people, both groups reported that bribery was a major ethical problem facing international business managers.[92] There has been criticism that the FCPA has had a negative impact on U.S. companies versus their competitors who are not held to the same standard. This criticism is refuted by a macroeconomic study which found that the FCPA had not had a negative impact on U.S. export trade.[93]

To avoid any conflict with the law, some U.S. companies have developed their own guidelines. DuPont Co. had adopted its own code of ethics before the FCPA became law in 1977 and, according to company officials, it is said to be even more stringent.[94] Other companies that have spelled out in detail what employees can or cannot do include General Motors and Lockheed Corp.[95] Companies with a clear technological lead such as IBM typically do not have to make payoffs to sell their products.[96] And one official at a U.S. aircraft company stated that since the passing of the FCPA in 1977 the requests for payoff were down by 80 percent.[97] The Omnibus Trade and Competitiveness Act of 1988 amended the FCPA to clarify the level of detail and assurance a company should take to avoid illegal payments. The revision also increased the civil and criminal penalties for violation of FCPA.[98]

Rejection of a request for a payoff often puts the executive in a difficult position. One strategy is to transform the private payoff into a public gift of funds for a hospital, services for the public good, or jobs for the unemployed. These actions may satisfy the request for funds while not violating the provisions of the FCPA.[99]

91. "U.S. Outlines its Review of Foreign Payments," *New York Times,* March 25, 1980, p. D1.

92. Robert W. Armstrong, et al. "International Marketing Ethics," *European Journal of Marketing,* 24 (10), 1990, p. 10.

93. John L. Graham, "The Foreign Corrupt Practices Act: A New Perspective," *Journal of International Business Studies,* Winter 1984, pp. 107–121.

94. *Wall Street Journal,* August 2, 1979.

95. "Misinterpreting the Antibribery Law," *Business Week,* September 3, 1979, p. 150.

96. "The Global Costs of Bribery," *Business Week,* March 15, 1976, p. 22.

97. *Wall Street Journal,* August 2, 1979, p. 19.

98. Ronald Gray, "The Foreign Corrupt Practices Act: Revisited and Amended." *Business Society,* vol. 29, no. 1, Spring 1990, pp. 11–17.

99. Jeffrey A. Fadiman, "A Traveler's Guide to Gifts and Bribes," *Harvard Business Review,* July–August 1986, pp. 122–136.

Laws Regulating Competitive Behavior

Many countries have adopted laws that govern the competitive behavior of their firms. In some cases, as for the European Community (EC), supranational bodies enforce their own laws. Unfortunately for international companies, these antitrust laws are frequently contradictory or differently enforced, adding great complexity to the job of the international executive. The United States, with its long-standing tradition of antitrust enforcement, has had considerable impact on the multinational operations of U.S. companies and increasingly on those of foreign-based companies operating in the United States.

But foreign companies entering the U.S. market may also have to deal with U.S. antitrust legislation. When Nippon Sanso attempted to buy Semi-Gas Systems, the San Jose Californian manufacturer of semiconductor equipment, the U.S. Justice Department blocked the takeover. The government said that the purchase would give Nippon Sanso 48 percent of the U.S. market, therefore reducing competition.[100]

In other countries, antitrust legislation may be enforced differently than in the United States. For example, the Office of Fair Trading in the United Kingdom has investigated anticompetitive practices in the U.K. copier market for the second time in the past decade. Practices such as requiring customers to only buy toner from the manufacturer and not selling spare parts to parties who repair and service machines, may be why the top five suppliers have 66 percent of the market.[101] Though each member country of the EC has some antitrust laws, the Common Market Commission, which functions to some extent as a government, enforces its antitrust legislation on a European level. Starting rather slowly, enforcement and convictions increased in the early 1970s to reach about twenty convictions each year.[102] According to the EC agreement, companies are not allowed to abuse the dominant market position in either the entire EC territory or a significant part of it. Several large companies have been convicted for various violations in the areas of pricing, distribution policies, or mergers.

One of the firms under investigation was International Business Machines Corp., which came under attack for some of its marketing practices.[103] Several U.S. and European computer firms selling plug-compatible equipment for IBM customers complained to the European Commission that IBM suddenly changed its selling practices. IBM had been restricting operating information on how to connect computer units and had been inducing its clients to buy only IBM software by refusing to price memories and software separately from the overall cost of a computer. The case was settled in 1984 and IBM was required to publish within four months of a

100. "That Tough Line on Foreign Investment Is Only a Mirage," *Business Week,* January 21, 1991, p. 43.

101. Michael Skapinker, "U.K. Examines Anti-Competitive Practices in Photocopier Sales," *Financial Times,* September 13, 1990, p. 24.

102. "Trustbusting in Europe," *New York Times,* January 18, 1976, p. 17.

103. "The Brussels Threat to IBM," *The Economist,* February 6, 1982, p. 47.

new product announcement any information required by competitors to develop compatible equipment.[104] In another case, European manufacturers have brought a complaint against Korean car radio manufacturers, claiming they are dumping car radios in Europe at prices below their Korean home market. Korean imports into Europe have increased from 1.1 to 5.8 million radios while European manufacturers' share of market has dropped from 49 percent in 1985 to 23 percent in 1988. The European Commission is evaluating the case.[105]

Product Liability

Though there are regulations or laws that directly affect all aspects of international marketing, regulations on product liability are included here because of their enormous impact on all firms. Specific regulatory acts, or laws, pertaining to other aspects of the marketing mix, namely pricing, distribution, and promotion, have been included in other chapters.

Regulations on product liability are relatively recent and started first in the United States. Other countries have laws on product liability as well; one of the major problems for international marketers involves the differences in laws in different countries or regions. In the United States, product liability is viewed in the broadest sense, or along the lines of strict liability. For a product sold in defective condition that becomes unreasonably dangerous for the user, both producer and distributor can be held accountable.

Product liability laws have changed in Europe as well. In the mid-1970s, the European Commission proposed a set of regulations that was to supersede each member country's laws. Traditionally, the individual country laws had been rather lax by U.S. standards. The new regulations have been described as even tougher than those in the United States.[106] In the United States, the plaintiff must prove that the product was defective at the time it left the producer's hand, whereas under the EC guidelines it is the manufacturer who must prove that the product was not defective when it left his control. Nevertheless, there are differences due to the different legal and social systems. In the EC, trials are decided by judges and not common jurors. And the existing extensive welfare system will automatically absorb many of the medical costs that are subject to litigation in the United States. Furthermore, it is typical for the loser in a court judgment in Europe to bear the legal costs. In the case of product liability cases, if a company is found to owe damages to a plaintiff, then it also will have to pay the plaintiff's legal costs according to typical fee standards. This differs substantially from the U.S. system in which a winning plaintiff's lawyer

104. "The Road is Clear for IBM's Probe into Europe," *Business Week,* August 20, 1984, p. 44.
105. "When One Man's Dumping Is Another's Good Price," *Financial Times,* May 9, 1990, p. 8.
106. "Common Market Nations Likely to Adopt Harsher Product-Liability Codes for Firms," *Wall Street Journal,* March 3, 1977.

typically is compensated through a predetermined percentage of the awarded damages, a practice that in the eyes of many experts has raised award damages and, as a result, liablity insurance costs. `

The rapid spread of product liability litigation, however, forces companies with international operations to carefully review their potential liabilities and to acquire appropriate insurance policies. Although an international marketing manager cannot be expected to know all the respective rules and regulations, executives must nevertheless anticipate potential exposure and, by asking themselves the appropriate questions, make sure that their firms consider all possible aspects.

Bankruptcy Laws

Bankruptcy laws vary from country to country. In the United Kingdom, Canada, and France the laws of bankruptcy favor the creditors. When a firm enters bankruptcy, an administrator is appointed. The adminstrator's job is to recover the creditors' money. In the U.S. bankruptcy tends to protect the business from the creditors. Under Chapter 11, the management prepares a reorganization plan which is voted on by the creditors. In Germany and Japan, bankruptcies are often handled by the banks behind closed doors. The national bankruptcy systems have a wide variety of standards of openness to others. Also, creditor preference varies from country to country. For example, Swiss law gives preference to Swiss creditors. There is a need for a global bankruptcy law, but until establishment of world accountancy standards, there is little chance of a global bankruptcy code.[107]

Patents and Trademarks

Patents and trademarks are used to protect products, processes, and symbols. Patents and trademarks are issued by each individual country, so marketers must register every product in every country they intend to trade in. The International Convention for the Protection of Industrial Property, honored by forty-five countries, gives all nationals the same privileges when applying for patents and trademarks. Also, the agreement gives patent coverage for one year after the trademark or patent is applied for in one country, thus limiting pirating of the product in other countries. The United States has an extensive patent system open to anyone. In fact, 48 percent of the patents issued in 1988 were to foreigners. The firms receiving the most U.S. patents in 1988 were Hitachi, Toshiba, Canon, GE, Fuji Film, Philips, Siemens, IBM, Mitsubishi, and Bayer. The only U.S. firms in the top 10 were GE and IBM.[108] It does not seem that some of our biggest trading partners have as open and accessible patent systems. For example, Allied Signal took eleven years to get its patent on amorphous metal alloys approved in Japan. Allied Signal alleges that the Japanese patent office

107. "Bankruptcy Laws," *The Economist,* February 24, 1990, pp. 93–94.
108. "America's Patent System—Not Invented Here," *The Economist,* October 24, 1989, p. 104.

dragged its feet while the Ministry for Trade and Industry (MITI) launched a catch-up program with thirty-four Japanese companies.[109] The U.S. Trade Representative watches its trading partners to assure they are protecting intellectual property. Countries on the priority watch list—that is, subject to scrutiny—are Brazil, India, China, and Thailand.[110]

Pirating products has become a significant problem in the 1980s affecting computers, watches, designer clothes, and industrial products. The sale of counterfeit goods ranging from Louis Vuitton bags and Rolex watches to car parts and medicines is estimated to be a hefty $150 billion a year. The United States and other industrialized countries are working together to stop this illicit trade. Washington has forced a proposal for trade-related aspects of intellectual property (TRIP) on the agenda of the Uruguay round of GATT talks. The Western countries want the TRIP proposal to be approved to strengthen the regulation and enforcement of intellectual property rights.[111] Patents, trademarks, and pirating will be discussed in more detail in Chapter 10.

International Court Judgments

One of the great difficulties with international law is the task of determining which law applies where. In the United States, state courts will enforce each other's judgments automatically. This is normally not the case with international judgments. One exception, however, involves judgments within the European Community. A French court will uphold a decision of a German court and can enforce it even though the legal basis for the judgment may be different. How far this can go is illustrated by a suit filed in Austria against Jean-Claude Killy, the former French skiing champion.[112] According to both German and Austrian law, anyone who has any amount of personal property, however small, in those countries can leave himself or herself open for a suit. When Jean-Claude Killy left a pair of shorts once in an Austrian ski resort, it was sufficient to be able to bring a suit against him in an Austrian court. Such a judgment has to be enforced by other European courts that can attach property. In the case of a U.S. firm, it can mean that a judgment against it in Italy, for example, can be enforced against property the firm owns in Germany. To avoid being subject to often much stricter European law, the U.S. government concluded a treaty with the British government to recognize each other's court judgments. As a consequence, U.K. courts do not have to enforce EC judgments against U.S. firms made in other EC member states.[113]

The International Court in The Hague, Netherlands, will render judgments on

109. "American-Japanese Trade—Low Tricks in High Tech," *The Economist,* September 29, 1990, p. 90.

110. "Call for Stronger Action to Protect Copyrights," *Financial Times,* May 1, 1990, p. 4.

111. Frances Williams, "Foiling the Fakers," *Eurobusiness,* September 1990, pp. 11–14.

112. "Court Judgments Go International," *Business Week,* February 1977, p. 50.

113. Ibid.

international business disputes, but its judgments are not automatically binding to the parties involved. The European Court, situated in Luxembourg, renders judgments that are only binding in the EC member states. To deal with this lack of a generally accepted and binding court, companies frequently use a predetermined format of arbitration panels. They may consist of specially appointed representatives, or the firms may use panels available from the International Chamber of Commerce. In any event, companies are advised to include in major contracts specific rules of how they expect to solve contract disputes. A simple dependence on national courts is often insufficient.

Global Trends in Politics Affecting Trade

The impetus for the Single European Market was to protect Western Europe from the Soviets. The prospect of 1992 and a fortified Europe encouraged the United States-Canada Trade Agreement, which has been followed by similar talks between the United States and Mexico, Chile and Colombia, Ecuador and Bolivia. This can lead to a strong American bloc. The third trading bloc will encompass the Pacific— Japan, Hong Kong, Singapore, Taiwan, South Korea, and maybe North Korea. The world may be moving toward these three strong trading blocs which will encourage free trade within the blocs, while protectionism faces the countries outside the bloc. The recent future of the Uruguay round of GATT talks indicates a major problem with eliminating these strong regional interests in place of a global move to free trade. While GATT has helped reduce the average tariff from 40 percent in 1947 to less than 5 percent in 1990, there are still strong protectionist tendencies. In the United States where exports account for 70 percent of manufacturing growth and 12 percent of GNP, there still appears to be a need to protect domestic production. The share of total imports into the United States subject to quotas or restraints went from 9 percent in 1980 to 15 percent in 1990.[114]

CONCLUSIONS

In this chapter we have outlined the major political and regulatory forces facing international companies. Our approach was not so much to identify and list all possible influences or actions that may have an impact on international marketing operations. Instead, we have provided only a sample of potential acts. It is up to executives with international responsibility to devise structures and systems that systematically deal with these environmental influences. What is important to our discussion is to recognize that companies can adopt risk reduction strategies to compensate for some of these risks, but certainly not for all of them. For effective international marketing management, executives must be forward looking, anticipate

114. Susan Lee, "Are We Building New Berlin Walls," *Forbes,* January 7, 1991, pp. 86–89.

potentially adversarial *or* positive changes in the environment, and not wait until changes occur. To accomplish this, a systematic monitoring system that encompasses both political and legal developments must be implemented.

Questions for Discussion

1. The telecommunications industry in Japan has traditionally been tightly controlled, with very little non-Japanese equipment allowed. What aspects of Japan's political forces may have influenced this control over the Japanese telecommunications market?

2. In 1987 Japan began to open its telecommunications market, especially to United States and European firms. How did political forces influence this change?

3. How could a country develop its own expertise in a product that is primarily imported, for example, automobiles in Egypt?

4. With executives in a variety of different countries, what strategies can be used to protect against terrorist activities?

5. What are the different methods that a company can use to develop/obtain political risk assessment information?

6. John Deere has decided to enter the tractor market in Central America. What strategies could it use to reduce the possible effects of political risk?

7. While attempting to deliver a large computer system (selling price $1.4 million) to a foreign government, the Minister of Transportation advises that a fee of $20,000 is required to assure proper coordination of the custom clearance delivery process. What would you do?

For Further Reading

Akhter, Humayum and Robert F. Lusch. "Political Risk and the Evolution of the Control of Foreign Business: Equity, Earnings, and the Marketing Mix." *Journal of Global Marketing* (Spring 1988) pp. 109–127.

Bradley, David G. "Managing Against Expropriation." *Harvard Business Review* (July–August 1977), pp. 75–83.

Brewer, Thomas L., ed. *Political Risks in International Business.* New York: Praeger, 1985.

Cao, A. O. "Nontariff Barriers to U.S. Manufactured Exports." *Columbia Journal of World Business* (Summer 1980), p. 95.

Davidow, Joel. "Multinationals, Host Governments and Regulation of Restrictive Business Practices." *Columbia Journal of World Business* (Summer 1980), pp. 14–19.

Doz, Yves L. and C. K. Prahalad. "How Multinational Corporations Cope with Host Government Intervention," *Harvard Business Review* (March–April, 1980), pp. 149–157.

Encarnation, Dennis J. and Sushil Vachani. "Foreign Ownership: When Hosts Change the Rules." *Harvard Business Review* (September–October 1985), pp. 152–160.

Graham, John L. "The Foreign Corrupt Practices Act." *Journal of International Business Studies* (Winter 1984), pp. 107–121.

Harvey, Michael G. and Ilkka A. Ronkainen. "International Counterfeiters: Marketing Success Without the Cost and the Risk." *Columbia Journal of World Business* (Fall 1985), pp. 37–45.

Hauptman, Gunter. "Intellectual Property Rights." *International Marketing Review* (Spring 1987), pp. 61–64.

Kaikati, Jack G. "The Export Trading Company Act." *California Management Review* (Fall 1984), pp. 59–69.

Kaikati, Jack G. and Wayne A. Label. "American Bribery Legislation: An Obstacle to International Marketing." *Journal of Marketing* (Fall 1980), pp. 38–43.

Kim, Chan W. "Competition and the Management of Host Government Intervention." *Sloan Management Review* (Spring 1987), pp. 33–39.

Kobrin, Stephen J. "Assessing Political Risk Overseas." *The Wharton Magazine* (Winter 1981/1982), pp. 25–31.

Lodge, George C. and Erza F. Vogel. *Ideology and National Competitiveness.* Boston: Harvard Business School Press, 1987.

Raddock, David M. *"Assessing Corporate Political Risk."* Totowa, N. J.: Roowman and Littlefield, 1986.

Shapiro, Alan C. "Managing Political Risk: A Policy Approach." *Columbia Journal of World Business* (Fall 1981), pp. 63–70.

Simon, Jeffery D. "Theoretical Prospective on Political Risk." *Journal of International Business Studies* (Winter 1984), pp. 123–143.

Simon, Jeffery D. "Political Risk Assessment: Past Trends and Future Prospects." *Columbia Journal of World Business* (Fall 1982), pp. 62–71.

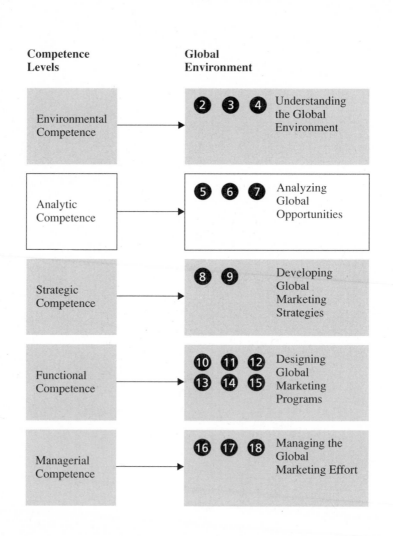

Competence Levels

Environmental Competence

Analytic Competence

Strategic Competence

Functional Competence

Managerial Competence

Global Environment

2 3 4 Understanding the Global Environment

5 6 7 Analyzing Global Opportunities

8 9 Developing Global Marketing Strategies

10 11 12 Designing Global Marketing Programs
13 14 15

16 17 18 Managing the Global Marketing Effort

P A R T

T W O

Analyzing Global Opportunities

THE GLOBAL marketplace is large, with more than 150 countries or territories. Given this large opportunity, international companies are constantly searching for the most appropriate markets and the best opportunities for their firms. Analyzing, classifying, and selecting opportunities for future business is an important aspect of international marketing management. In Part 2, we concentrate on the skills necessary to do this job well.

Chapter 5 provides analytic concepts to analyze opportunities within countries and groups of countries. In Chapter 6, we discuss the major market segments within each country's consumer, industrial, and government sectors and analyze the differences in these segments from market to market. In the final chapter of this section, Chapter 7, we cover the methods by which international companies collect market data, and we discuss ways to analyze this market research data for decision making.

We have given this section a largely analytic focus. Our aim in doing this has been to encourage analytic competence, which is so necessary for success in international and global marketing.

5

International Markets

AN IMPORTANT ASPECT *of international marketing is the assessment of market opportunities. Every time a company decides to expand into foreign markets it must systematically evaluate possible markets to identify the country or group of countries with the greatest opportunities. This process of evaluating worldwide opportunities is complicated for a number of reasons. First, there are some 150 countries in the world; obviously, it is difficult to examine all these opportunities. Second, due to the number of countries and resource limitations, the initial screening process is usually limited to the analysis of published data. Third, many possible markets are small, with little data available about specific consumer, business, or government needs.*

In this chapter, which is outlined in Figure 5.1, we first discuss the process for selecting markets to include both the selection techniques and the selection criteria. Then, to illustrate the screening process, we present a detailed example of how this process can be used to select a market for dialysis equipment. In the final sections of the chapter, we discuss the rationale for grouping countries together and present the market groups in existence around the world today.

SCREENING INTERNATIONAL MARKETING OPPORTUNITIES

The assessment of international marketing opportunities usually begins with a screening process that involves gathering relevant information on each country and filtering out the less desirable countries. A model for selecting foreign markets is shown in Figure 5.2.

FIGURE 5.1 ● International Markets

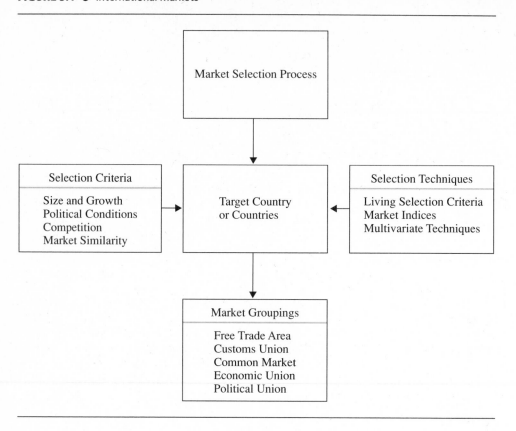

The model includes a series of four filters to screen out countries. It is necessary to break the process down into a series of steps due to the large number of market opportunities. Although a firm does not want to miss a potential opportunity, it is not possible to conduct extensive market research studies in every one of the 150 countries of the world. (The World Bank Atlas includes 185 countries and territories.)[1] The screening process is used to identify good prospects. Two common errors of country screening are (1) ignoring countries that offer good potential for the company's products and (2) spending too much time investigating countries that are poor prospects.[2] Thus the screening process allows an international company to quickly

1. The World Bank Atlas 1990 (Washington, D.C.: The World Bank, 1990).
2. Franklin R. Root, *Entry Strategies for International Market* (Lexington, Mass.: Lexington Books, 1987), p. 33.

FIGURE 5.2 ● A Model for Selecting Foreign Markets

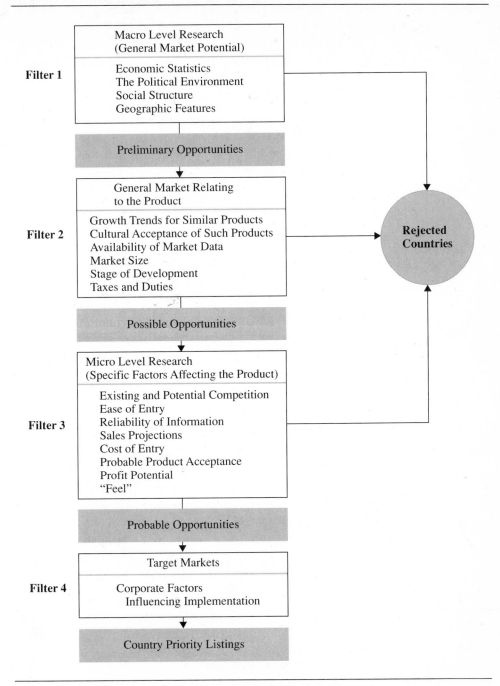

Source: R. Wayne Walvoord, "Export Market Research," *Global Trade Magazine,* May 1980, p. 83. Reprinted by permission.

focus efforts on a few of the most promising market opportunities by using published secondary sources available in most business libraries.[3]

The first stage of the selection process uses macro variables to discriminate between countries that represent basic opportunities and countries with little or no opportunity or with excessive risk. Macro variables describe the total market in terms of economic, social, geographic, and political information. Often macro economic statistics indicate that the country is too small, as described by the gross national (or domestic) product. Possibly the gross national product seems large enough, but the personal disposable income per household may be too low. Political instability can also be used to remove a country from the set of possible opportunities.

In the second stage of the selection process variables that indicate the potential market size and acceptance of the product or similar products are used. Often proxy variables are used in this screening process. A proxy variable is a similar or related product that indicates a demand for your product. For example, if you are attempting to measure the potential market size and receptivity for satellite television reception equipment, possible proxy variables may be the number of televisions per household, total sales of VCRs, or total sales of microwave ovens. The number of televisions and VCRs indicates the potential for home entertainment and the sales of microwave ovens indicates a propensity to use advanced technologies in place of traditional appliance technology. The year-to-year growth rates and the total sales of similar or proxy products are good predictors of market size and growth. Other factors in the second stage of the selection process can also be used to screen out countries, such as the stage of economic development, taxes, and duty requirements. If you do not plan to manufacture locally, a high import duty may eliminate a country from consideration in the second stage of the screening process.

The third stage of the screening process focuses on micro-level considerations such as competitors, ease of entry, cost of entry, and profit potential. Micro-level factors influence the success or failure of a specific product in a market. At this stage of the screening process marketers may only be considering a small number of countries, so it is feasible to get more detailed, up-to-date information from the U.S. Department of Commerce, the U.S. State Department, and from other companies currently operating in that country. The International Trade Administration of the Department of Commerce has an office in most major cities and can provide information and contacts for many markets. Also customs brokers and freight forwarders can help at this stage of the process.

The focus of the screening process switches from total market size to profitability. For example, based on the current and potential competitors, how much would you need to invest to gain a particular market share? Given the prices currently charged in the market, what margin can your company expect? Given the cost of entry and the expected sales, what is the expected profit? This stage of the analysis

3. See Susan P. Douglas and C. Samuel Craig, *International Marketing Research* (Englewood Cliffs, N.J.: Prentice-Hall, 1983), pp. 306–325 for a detailed listing of secondary sources of information.

focuses on the quantitative profit expected; but many subjective judgments are made to arrive at the expected profit. For example, an Israeli manufacturer of pipe insulation found that the market price in the United Kingdom was $10/kilo while its cost was less than $5/kilo. This indicated a good profit potential if the company could gain access to the market.

The fourth stage of the screening process is an evaluation and rank ordering of the potential target countries based on corporate resources, objectives, and strategies. For example, although South Africa may have the same expected potential as Venezuela, Venezuela may be given a higher priority since successful entry into Venezuela can later be followed by entry into Colombia and Bolivia.

Criteria for Selecting Target Countries

The process of selecting target countries through the screening process requires that the companies identify the criteria to be used to differentiate desirable countries from less desirable countries. Research on international investment decisions has shown that the four critical factors affecting market selection are market size and growth, political conditions, competition, and market similarity.[4] In the following section of the chapter we will explain each of these factors and their uses in the market selection process.

Market Size and Growth   It is obvious that the potential market size and growth would be an important factor in selecting markets. The larger the potential demand for a product in a country the more attractive it will be to a company.

Measures of market size and growth can be on both a macro and a micro basis. On a macro basis, it may be determined that the country needs a minimum set of potential resources to be worth further consideration. Table 5.1 shows a summary of potential macro indicators of market size. There are a variety of readily available statistics that are macro indicators of market size. If you are screening countries for a firm that sells microwave ovens, you may decide not to consider any country with a personal disposable income per household of less than $10,000 per year. The logic of this criterion is that if the average household has less than $10,000, the potential for a luxury item like a microwave oven will not be great. However, a single statistic can sometimes be deceptive. For example, a country may have an average household income of $8,000, but there may be one million households with an income of over $10,000. These one million households will be potential buyers of microwaves. One commercially available report on the attractiveness of different countries for business is the World Competitiveness Report. Published annually, this report analyzes 300 criteria to determine the overall competitiveness of the country and its strength by industry. The report is published by the World Economic Forum and IMD in Lausanne, Switzerland.

The macro indicators of market potential and growth are usually used in the first

4. William H. Davidson, "Market Similarity and Market Selection: Implications for International Market Strategy," *Journal of Business Research,* December 1983, pp. 439–456.

TABLE 5.1 ● Macro Indicators of Market Size

GEOGRAPHIC INDICATORS
  Size of the country, in terms of geographic area
  Climatic conditions
  Topographical characteristics
DEMOGRAPHIC CHARACTERISTICS
  Total population
  Population growth rate
  Age distribution of the population
  Degree of population density
ECONOMIC CHARACTERISTICS
  Total gross national product
  Per capita gross national product
  Per capita income (also income growth rate)
  Personal or household disposable income
  Income distribution

stage of the screening process, because the data are readily available and can be used to quickly eliminate countries with little or no potential demand. The macro indicators focus on the total potential demand (population) and ability to afford a product (per capita income). However, because the macro indicators of market size are general and crude, they do not necessarily indicate a perceived need for the product. For example, a country such as Italy may have the population and income to indicate a large potential for deodorants, but the consumers may not feel a perceived need for the product. In the third stage of the screening process it is recommended that micro indicators of market potential be used. Micro indicators usually indicate actual consumption of a company's product or a similar product, therefore indicating a perceived need. Table 5.2 shows an example of micro indicators of market size.

These micro indicators can be used to estimate market size. The number of households with televisions indicates the potential market size for televisions, if every household purchased a new television. Depending on the life of the average television in use, one can estimate the annual demand. Although the actual consumption statistics may not be available for a certain product category, often the consumption of similar or substitute products are used as proxy variables. For example, in determining the market size for surgical sutures, marketers may use the number of hospital beds or doctors as a proxy variable. The number of farms may indicate the potential demand for tractors.

The macro and micro indicators of market size allow the marketer to determine or infer the potential market size. Next the marketer needs to evaluate the risk associated with each market opportunity.

TABLE 5.2 ● Micro Indicators of Market Size

Radios	Hotel Beds
Televisions	Telephones
Cinema seats	Tourist arrivals
Scientists and engineers	Passenger cars
Hospitals	Civil airline passengers
Hospital beds	Steel production
Physicians	Rice production
Alcoholic liquor consumption	Number of farms
Coffee consumption	Land under civilization
Gasoline consumption	Electricity consumption

TABLE 5.3 ● Indicators of Political Risk

Probability of nationalization	Percent of the voters in the Communist party
Bureaucratic delays	Restrictions on capital movement
Number of expropriations	Government intervention
Number of riots or assassinations	Limits on foreign ownership
Political executions	Soldier/civilian ratio
Number of Socialist seats in the legislature	

Political Conditions   The impact of a host country's political condition on market selection is described in studies by Stephan J. Kobrin and Franklin R. Root.[5] The influence of the host country's political environment was described in detail in Chapter 4. Though political risk tends to be more subjective than the quantitative indicators of market size, it is equally important. For example, the invasion of Kuwait in 1990 resulted in the exposure of millions of dollars of U.S. assets.

Any company can be hurt by political risk, from limitations on the number of foreign company officials, limits on the amount of profits paid to the parent company, or outright takeovers. There are a number of indicators that can be used to assess political risk.[6] Table 5.3 shows some indicators of political risk that may be used in country selection.

5. S. J. Kobrin, "The Environmental Determinants of Foreign Direct Manufacturing Investment: An Ex-Post Empirical Analysis," *Journal of Business Studies,* Fall-Winter 1976, pp. 29–42; F. R. Root, "U.S. Business Abroad and Political Risks," *MSU Business Topics,* Winter 1968, pp. 73–80.

6. R. Rummel and David Heenan, "How Multinationals Analyze Political Risk," *Harvard Business Review,* January-February 1978, pp. 67–76.

Historically, extractive industries such as oil and mining have been susceptible to the political risk of expropriation. More recently, the financial, insurance, communication, and transportation industries have been targets of expropriation. As shown in Table 5.3, many aspects of political risk assessment can be analyzed based on historical data. Unfortunately, historical indicators are not always that accurate, since political conditions can change radically with a new government. As we mentioned in Chapter 4, some companies have in-house staff to assess political risk. American Can (now Primerica), United Technologies, and Borg Warner are three such companies.[7] We also noted some of the syndicated services that rate the political risk of most countries in the world. Major sources of information are the World Political Risk Forecast by Frost & Sullivan; Business International Rating of 57 Countries; Business Environment Risk Index and Political Risk Index of BERI, Ltd.; and the Economist Intelligence Unit. In addition to these major sources of information, many international companies often consult banks, accounting firms, and domestic government agencies for political risk information.[8] The risk assessment services provided by Business International, Frost & Sullivan, BERI, and others are all useful long-term measures of risk. These do not preclude the need to keep attuned to the current events of the day, be they the collapse of the Berlin Wall, the invasion of Kuwait, or the developments in Tiananmen Square. Each of these critical events may not have been predicted by the risk assessment services, yet they all had a profound effect on business.

Competition   The number, size, and quality of the competition in a particular country affects a firm's ability to enter and compete profitably.[9] In general, it is more difficult to determine the competitive structure of foreign countries than it is to determine the market size or political risk. Because of the difficulty of obtaining information, competitive analysis is usually done in the last stages of the screening process when a small number of countries are being considered.

Some secondary sources are available that describe the competitive nature of a marketplace. The Findex Directory publishes a listing of the most readily available research reports. These reports tend to concentrate on North America and Europe, but there are some reports available on Japan, the Middle East, and South America. These research reports usually cost between $500 and $5,000, with the average report being about $1,200. In some cases, there may not be a research report covering a specific country or product category, or it may be too expensive. Another good source of information is the U.S. government. The U.S. Department of Commerce and the U.S. State Department may be able to provide information on the compet-

7. Douglas and Craig, *International Marketing Research.*

8. F.T. Haner with John S. Ewing, *Country Risk Assessment* (New York: Praeger, 1985), p. 171.

9. Igal Ayal and Zif Jehiel, "Competitive Market Choice Strategies in International Marketing," *Columbia Journal of World Business,* Fall 1978, pp. 72–81.

itive situation. Also, in almost every country, the U.S. embassy employs a commercial attaché whose main function is to assist U.S. companies entering that foreign marketplace. Embassies of the foreign country being investigated may also be able to help marketers in their analysis. For example, in investigating the competition for farm implements in Spain, you can call or write the Spanish embassy in Washington, D.C. and ask for a list of manufacturers of farm implements in Spain.

Other sources of competitive information vary widely depending on the size of the country and the product. Many of the larger countries have Chambers of Commerce or other in-country organizations that may be able to assist potential investors. For example, if you were investigating the Japanese market for electronic measuring devices, the following groups could assist you in determining the competitive structure of the market in Japan:

- U.S. Chamber of Commerce in Japan
- Japan External Trade Organization (JETRO)
- American Electronics Association in Japan
- Japan Electronic Industry Development Association
- Electronic Industries Association of Japan
- Japan Electronic Measuring Instrument Manufacturers Association

The final and usually most expensive way to assess the market is to go to the country and interview potential customers and competitors to determine the size and strength of the competition. As a trip to a potential market is always required before a final decision is made, it should not be overlooked as an important part of the screening process. If you are well prepared in advance, two to three days in a country talking to distributors, large buyers, and trade officials can be extremely valuable to assess the competitiveness of the market and the potential profitability.

Market Similarity Strong evidence exists that market similarity can be used for country selection. A study of 954 product introductions by fifty-seven U.S. firms found a significant correlation between market selection and market similarity.[10]

The concept of market similarity is simple. A firm tends to select countries based on their similarity to the home market. Therefore, when a company decides to enter foreign markets, it will enter the markets first that are most similar. For example, a U.S. firm will enter Canada, Australia, and the United Kingdom before entering less similar markets like Spain, South Korea, or India. Measures of similarity are (1) aggregate production and transportation, (2) personal consumption, (3) trade, and (4) health and education.[11]

As shown in Table 5.4, the selection of foreign markets tends to follow similarity

10. Davidson, "Market Similarity and Market Selection: Implications for International Market Strategy."
11. Ibid.

TABLE 5.4 ● Similarity to the United States and Position in the Entry Sequence

	Similarity to the United States	*Position in investment sequence*
Canada	1	2
Australia	2	3
United Kindgom	3	1
West Germany	4	6
France	5	4
Belgium	6	10
Italy	7	9
Japan	8	5
Netherlands	9	12
Argentina	10	15
Mexico	11	8
Spain	12	13
India	13	16
Brazil	14	7
South Africa	15	14
Philippines	16	17
South Korea	17	18
Colombia	18	11

Source: Reprinted by permission of the publisher from "Market Similarity and Market Selection: Implications for International Market Strategy" by William H. Davidson, *Journal of Business Research,* vol. 11, no. 4, p. 446. Copyright 1983 by Elsevier Science Publishing Co., Inc.

very closely. Although language similarities were not measured in the study, it is worth noting that the top three markets all use the same language. Using market similarity as a selection variable is relatively simple. Once can use the similarity ranking shown in Table 5.4, update it with the most recent economic data, or develop other criteria for determining similarity.

The premise behind the selection of similar markets is the desire of a company to minimize risk in the face of uncertainty. Entering a market that has the same language, a similar distribution system, and similar customers is less difficult than entering a market in which all these variables are different.

TECHNIQUES OF MAKING MARKET SELECTION DECISIONS

The framework for making market selection decisions usually follows the systematic screening process shown in Figure 5.2. There are different techniques that can be used to accomplish the screening processes. These techniques vary from simple listings of selection criteria to complex combinations of different criteria into an index. These techniques will be discussed individually.

Listing of Selection Criteria

The simplest way to screen countries is to develop a set of criteria that are required as a minimum for a country to move through the stages of the screening process. To illustrate the screening methodology, we have outlined the screening process that can be used by a manufacturer of kidney dialysis equipment (see Table 5.5).

The minimum cut-off number for each criterion will be established by management. As we move through the screening process, the criteria become more specific. The following text will give the rationale for each of the screening criteria and cut-off point.

Macro Level Gross National Product Introduction of dialysis equipment in a new market requires a significant support function including salespeople, service people, replacement parts inventory, and an assured continuous supply of dialyses, dialysate fluid, needles, tubing, and so on. Some countries lack the technical infrastructure to support such high-level technology. Therefore, management may decide only to consider countries having a minimum size of $15 billion GDP or GNP, thus excluding many of the developing economies of the world from consideration. (Note the dialysis screening was done with 1985 data.) Also, dialysis requires substantial government support. A tradeoff then develops between acceptable expenditures for dialysis and acceptable kidney-related death rates. GDP per capita is an indicator of the level at which this tradeoff will occur. The lower the GDP per capita, the lower the

---

TABLE 5.5 ● Screening Process to Target Countries for Kidney Dialysis Equipment

---

FILTER 1: Macro-Level Research
  Gross domestic product over $15 billion
  Gross domestic product per capita over $1,500

FILTER 2: General Market Factors Relating to the Product
  Less than 200 people per hospital bed
  Less than 1,000 people per doctor
  Government expenditures for the health care over $100 million
  Government expenditures for health care per capita over $20

FILTER 3: Micro Level Factors Specific to the Product
  Kidney-related deaths over 1,000
  Patient use of dialysis equipment—
  Over 40 percent growth in treated population

FILTER 4: Final Screening of Targe Markets
  Number of competitors
  Political stability

---

expected government expenditure for dialysis equipment, given other pressing societal needs such as food, shelter, and so on. Therefore, the GDP per capita over $1,500 will be set as a minimum. These economic factors will limit the market to the following twenty-eight countries in the world, excluding North America:

> All of Europe except Hungary,
> Iceland, Ireland, Luxembourg
> U.S.S.R.
> New Zealand
> South Africa
> Brazil
> Venezuela
> Australia
> Iran
> Argentina
> Iraq

General Market Factors Related to the Product—Medical Concentration

Hemodialysis is a sophisticated procedure that requires medical personnel with advanced training. In order for a country to support advanced medical equipment, it will require a high level of medical specialization. Higher levels of medical concentration allow doctors the luxury of specialization in a field such as nephrology (the study of kidneys).

Management may determine that a population of less than 1,000 per doctor and a population of less than 200 per hospital bed indicate that medical personnel will be able to achieve the level of specialization needed to support a hemodialysis program. This second step of the screening process will eliminate Iran, Iraq, Brazil, and Venezuela. As can be expected, the majority of countries with high GNP and GDP per capita have a high level of medical concentration.

Public health expenditures show the government's contribution to the medical care of its citizens—a factor of obvious importance in hemodialysis. Management may believe that countries that do not invest substantially in the health care of their population generally will not be interested in making an even more substantial investment in a hemodialysis program. Thus, countries that do not have a minimum of $20 expenditure per capita or $100 million in total expenditures for health care will be eliminated from consideration. This would screen out Austria, Portugal, Yugoslavia, the U.S.S.R., and South Africa. Thus, nineteen countries will have the ability to purchase and satisfactorily support dialysis equipment. Dialysis programs were already under way in most of these countries.

The third stage of the screening process will identify which countries will provide the best opportunities for the sale of kidney dialysis machines.

Micro-Level Factors Specific to the Product Management may decide that there are two micro-level factors to consider: (1) the number of kidney-related deaths and (2) the growth rate of the treated patient population.

  1. *Kidney-Related Deaths.* The number of deaths due to kidney failure is a good indicator of the number of people in each country who could have used dialysis equipment. The company only will be interested in countries with a minimum of 1,000 deaths per year due to kidney-related causes. A lower death rate indicates that the country has little need for dialysis equipment or that the market is currently being well-served by competitive equipment. The Netherlands, Argentina, Norway, Switzerland, and Sweden will be eliminated from analysis on these grounds.
  2. *Growth Rate of the Treated Patient Population.* Analysis of the growth rate of the kidney treatment population demonstrates a growth in potential demand. Newly opened markets, with the greatest growth potential are the best targets for a new supplier of dialysis equipment. These are the countries in which the treated patient population continues to grow at a minimum of 40 percent per year. This criterion will exclude all but the following: Italy, with 75.1 percent; Greece, with 63.4 percent; and Spain, with 60.1 percent. Competition in all three of these markets is substantially less than in the United States, Japan, and the remainder of Western Europe.

Final Screening of Target Markets The screening process has identified three target countries. To select one of these countries, an analysis of the competition and political stability will be conducted. Discussions with the five major suppliers of dialysis equipment may indicate that Italy already has two local suppliers. Greece is being served by the four major European suppliers. Spain has a strong preference for U.S. equipment and is served only by one supplier. An evaluation of the political environment in each country will indicate that Greece has a stable government. Italy's government is stable but is not increasing medical expenditures. Spain is making a transition to a stable democracy.

After evaluating the data, management will most likely select Spain for the initial market entry. The final decision will be based on the following review of each market.

Greece will be discounted as a potential market for the following reasons:

  1. There is significant competition from other companies.
  2. The corporate income tax is higher than that of Spain.
  3. Products are subject to a "turnover" tax.
  4. There is a high inflation rate.

Similarly, Italy will be discounted for these reasons:

  1. There is extensive foreign as well as local competition.
  2. The projected growth for dialysis equipment is slower than it was in Spain.
  3. Products are subject to a 14 percent value-added tax.

4. There is an extremely high inflation rate.

Spain will be chosen for the following reasons:

1. The political outlook is stable. It appears that the transition to democracy will continue.

2. There is aggressive government support for health care.

3. There is a very high growth rate predicted for kidney equipment (23 percent).

4. Competition at this time is minimal.

5. There is no value-added tax.

6. Government subsidies for home use of dialysis equipment will stimulate demand.

7. The inflation rate is lower than in Italy or Greece.

8. U.S. products and firms have a good reputation in the country.

The screening of markets for dialysis equipment is an example of how to analyze the world market and select a few countries for entry. The screening process must be tailored to the specific product or service.

Market Indices for Country Selection

Another technique for analyzing country selection criteria is to develop indices that combine statistical data and allow the marketer to look at a large number of variables quickly. For example, for the past thirty years *Business International* has published market indicators that allow managers to quickly compare country opportunities. There are three indices which *Business International* publishes: market size, market growth, and market intensity.

Market size is the measure of total potential based on the total population (double-weighted), urban population, private consumption expenditure, steel consumption, cement and electricity production, and ownership of telephones, cars, and televisions. Market growth is an indicator of the rate of increase in the size of the market. The growth is determined based on an average of several indicators over five years: population, steel consumption, cement and electricity production, ownership of passenger cars, trucks, buses, televisions, and telephones. The market intensity index measures the richness of a market or the concentration of the purchasing power. The average world intensity is designated as 1.0 and each country is calculated in proportion to the average world intensity. The intensity is calculated for each market by averaging the per capita consumption of steel, ownership of telephones and televisions, the production of cement and electricity levels, private consumption expenditure (double-weight), ownership of passenger cars (double-weight), and the proportion of urban population (double-weight). Figure 5.3 shows the twenty largest countries and their percentage of the world market. The size of the circle represents the relative market size.

FIGURE 5.3 ● *Business International* Market Indices: Size, Growth, and Intensity of the Twenty Largest Markets

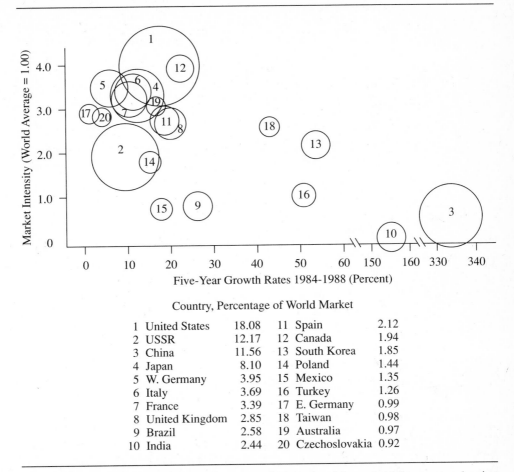

Country, Percentage of World Market

1 United States	18.08	11 Spain	2.12
2 USSR	12.17	12 Canada	1.94
3 China	11.56	13 South Korea	1.85
4 Japan	8.10	14 Poland	1.44
5 W. Germany	3.95	15 Mexico	1.35
6 Italy	3.69	16 Turkey	1.26
7 France	3.39	17 E. Germany	0.99
8 United Kingdom	2.85	18 Taiwan	0.98
9 Brazil	2.58	19 Australia	0.97
10 India	2.44	20 Czechoslovakia	0.92

Note: The position of the center of each circle shows the intensity of the market (when measured against the vertical axis) and its cumulative growth over the 1984–88 period (when measured against the horizontal axis). The size of the circles indicates the relative size of the markets as a percentage of the total world market. See text for definitions and methodology.

Source: Business International. 1990 edition. Reprinted by permission.

Customized Weighted Multivariate Technique

Every company has particular needs and interests when selecting market opportunities. They relate to the product line, the corporate strategy and objectives, and the normal entry strategy. For example, a company that usually builds a new plant in each country will be more sensitive to the political risk variable than a company that exports. Larger companies develop a screening and monitoring system that includes a large number of variables weighted specifically for that firm.

American Can had developed a system called PRISM which reduces two hundred variables collected from various data sources to an index of economic desirability and an index of risk payback. The information collected includes the macro indicators of investment climate, such as per capita income, market size, and inflation, as well as indicators of the quality of the infrastructure, such as capital availability, bureaucratic delays, and enforceability of contracts. Table 5.6 shows the factors that are included in the American Can system.[12]

12. Douglas and Craig, *International Marketing Research.*

TABLE 5.6 ● American Can Company's Relative Factor Weights for Major Indexes

Payback index	Percentage	Desirability index	Percentage
Political stability	26.0	Quality of infrastructure	13.6
Political freedom	7.0	Availability of financing	10.1
Civil liberties	7.0	Labor situation	9.1
Quality of infrastructure	6.7	Market growth	8.6
Nationalization probability	6.3	Currency convertibility	6.6
Desire for foreign investment	5.6	Per capita income	7.1
Bureaucratic delays	5.4	Market size	7.1
Market size and growth	4.4	Inflation	6.8
Inflation	3.6	Physical quality of life	6.0
Labor situation	3.5	Bureaucratic delays—Red tape	5.1
Currency stability	3.3	Enforceability of contracts	4.4
Balance of payments	3.3	Balance of payments	3.4
Likelihood of internal disorder	3.2	Currency history	3.2
Availability of financing	2.4	Corporate tax level	2.2
Restrictions on capital movements	2.3	Local management	2.0
Enforceability of contracts	1.8	Cultural interaction	1.7
Government intervention	1.5	Reserves imports ratio	1.3
Limits on foreign ownership	1.4	Government intervention	0.8
Cultural interaction	1.4		
Limits on expansion	1.1		
Local management and partners	1.0		
Physical quality of life	1.0		
Corporate tax level	0.8		

Source: Susan P. Douglas and C. Samuel Craig, *International Marketing Research* (Englewood Cliffs, N.J.: Prentice-Hall, 1983), pp. 289–292. Reprinted by permission of American National Can Company.

Notice the difference in the importance of each factor in the scales. The variables are weighted based on their importance to management with particular emphasis given to items that will mean a short-term change in the investment climate. A number of factors are used in both the payback (risk) index and the desirability index. Political stability is most important in the payback index, weighted three times more important than the next item. In the desirability index, quality of the infrastructure and availability of financing are the two most important factors. In all of the screening systems we have discussed, the industrialized Western nations will rate the highest due to consumer buying power.

Ongoing Market Screening

The market screening process requires a significant amount of effort. After the target country is selected there is a tendency to focus on the selected markets and ignore the rejected countries. The world market is continually changing and countries that were rejected last year may provide significant opportunities just one year later. For example, Finland has long favored domestic banks making it very difficult for foreign banks to operate. The move toward a single European market has caused Finland to become concerned about the limited access it provides to its banking market. So Finland's financial markets are suddenly much more accessible. The events in Eastern Europe have also made countries such as Poland, Hungary, Czechoslovakia, and Romania more attractive.

Political and economic events can also make an attractive market suddenly undesirable. Iraq and Jordan became less attractive after the invasion of Kuwait as did Argentina after it invaded the Falkland Islands and its anti-Western sentiment increased. For most companies, it is necessary to have an ongoing monitoring and screening of world markets to spot new emerging opportunities as well as to identify potential risks.

GROUPING INTERNATIONAL MARKETS

There are many ways to group international markets. The chapters on the political, economic, and cultural environments demonstrated that the interaction between these variables causes each country to be unique, therefore making it difficult to group countries together. Despite these difficulties, it is often necessary to group countries together to be considered as a single market or as a group of similar markets. In this segment of the chapter, we explore the rationale for grouping markets and the various ways that marketers can group countries together.

Rationale for Grouping Markets

The two principles that often drive the need for larger market groupings are critical mass and economies of scale. *Critical mass,* a term used in physics and military strategy, indicates that a minimum amount of effort is necessary before any impact will be achieved. *Economies of scale* is a term used in production situations; it means that greater levels of production result in lower costs per unit, which obviously increases profitability.

The costs of marketing products within a group of countries are lower for three reasons. First, the potential volume to be sold in a group of countries is sufficient to support a full marketing effort. Second, the geographic proximity makes it easy to travel from one country to another often in two hours or less. Third, the barriers to entry are often the same in countries within an economic grouping, for example, the European Community. Finally, in pursuing countries with similar markets, a company gains leverage with marketing programs.

Marketing Activities Influenced by Country Groupings

The major activities used to enter a new market are market research, product development or product modification, distribution, and promotion. Each of these activities can be influenced by economies of scale and critical mass. The following section of the chapter will show how each of these four activities relate to country groupings.[13]

Market Research   In the screening process, marketers use many secondary sources of market information, which are readily available. As stated previously, these secondary sources are acceptable for selecting target countries, but they are not sufficient to develop a marketing strategy to penetrate a specific market. Before entering a new market, the company will need to invest in the acquisition of knowledge about the specific aspects of marketing the product in each country. Normally the following questions must be answered:

1. Who makes the purchase decisions?
2. What decision criteria do consumers use to select the product?
3. How must the product be modified?
4. What are the channels of distribution?
5. What are the competitive price levels?

These and many other questions must be answered before the first product can be shipped. The cost of this knowledge will often be higher than domestic market research due to the distance to travel, cultural differences, and language differences. Given the sizable investment required to obtain this first-hand market knowledge, there are economies of scale if two or more countries can be included in the same market research study.

13. Vern Terpstra, "Critical Mass and International Marketing Strategy," *Journal of Academy of Marketing Sciences,* Summer 1983.

Product Development/Product Modification The development of new products and the modifications of current products require a large investment. Given the cost, there are obvious economies of scale when these costs are spread over a number of markets. This is particularly true if the markets are similar, so that the same modified product can be sold in a number of markets. For example, Procter & Gamble's Head & Shoulders Dandruff Shampoo is manufactured in a single European plant; however, the company takes advantage of European Community regulations by selling the product throughout Europe with a "Eurobottle" label in eight languages.[14]

Distribution The distribution aspect of marketing is particularly important in serving international markets. In the case of exporting, the marketer is faced with all the mechanics of getting the product from the domestic market to the foreign market, which includes documentations, insurance, and financial arrangements. Also, the shipping rates will vary, depending on the size of the shipment. Less than carload or container size orders will be at a higher price per pound than full carloads or containers. The mechanics and shipping aspects of exporting are influenced by economies of scale and critical mass. If one only plans to ship a small amount each month to a South American country, it may not be worth the effort. Without a critical mass of business, it is not worth the effort of learning the mechanics and processing the paperwork. Also, if you do not have sufficient volumes to ship, transportation costs will escalate.

The distribution systems within foreign markets also are influenced by the number of markets served. Many distributors and dealers in foreign markets handle numerous markets. For example Caps Gemini, a large software development and distribution firm, has operations in every European country. Given the multicountry nature of many distributors, it is usually beneficial to enter a group of similar markets through the same distribution channels.

Promotion A major task of the international company is promotion, which includes advertising and personal selling. Advertising is used as a communications device to give customers a message about a product via television, radio, or print media. In many parts of the world these three forms of communication cross country boundaries; for example, a message on German television will be seen in Switzerland. For this reason there may be economies of scale in grouping two or more markets together when entering a new area.

Selling is a very important part of the promotional process, which usually requires a local sales force. Establishing and managing a sales force is a large fixed cost expense that lends itself to economies of scale. Spreading the cost of a sales office, rent, secretarial staff, sales support, sales managers, and sometimes the salesperson, over two or three countries can be very cost-effective.

14. "Unilever Aims to Bolster Lines in US" *Wall Street Journal,* June 19, 1987, p. 6.

GROWTH OF FORMAL MARKET GROUPS

Countries have used the concept of market groupings for centuries. The British Commonwealth preference system linked the markets of the United Kingdom, Canada, Australia, New Zealand, India, and former colonies in Africa, Asia, and the Middle East. The growth of market groups since World War II was encouraged by the success of the European Economic Community, now called the European Community (EC). As discussed in Chapter 2, a market group is created when two or more countries agree to reduce trade and tariff barriers between themselves, therefore creating a trade unit.

Successful trade units or market groups are based on favorable economic, political, or geographic factors. A country will agree to join a trade unit based on one or more of these factors, *if* the expected benefits of becoming part of the trade unit exceed the disadvantages and loss of sovereignty caused by joining the group.

Economic Factors

The major benefit of every market group is usually economic. Member countries of the group experience reduced or eliminated tariffs and duties that stimulate trade between member countries. They also have common tariff barriers against firms from nonmember countries. Joining together with other countries gives members a greater economic security, reducing the impact of competition from member countries and increasing the group's strength against foreign competitors. For example, when the United States planned to impose tariffs on French cheese, Italian wine, Greek olives, and Danish ham, the twelve-nation European Economic Community was ready to retaliate with tariffs on U.S. wheat, rice, and corn.[15]

Consumers benefit from the reduced trade barriers through lower prices. Economies that are complementary rather than directly competitive tend to make better members of a market group. Most of the problems within the European Community have revolved around agricultural products; member countries are threatened by products from other member countries, such as eggs, milk, and chicken.

Political Factors

In most countries, the political system and its ideology are dominant environmental forces. The political system usually reflects the aspirations of the nation. It's easy to see, then, why market groups are made up of countries with similar political aspirations. A major impetus for the original formation of the European Community was the need for a unified entity to protect against the political threat of the U.S.S.R.

15. "A Duty to Pay for Government Items," *Insight,* January 26, 1987, p. 46.

Geographic Factors

Countries that share common borders tend to function better in a market group for the simple fact that it is easier to move goods back and forth across the truck and railroad systems. Also, countries that share boundaries have experienced each other's cultures and probably have had a history of trade.

Types of Market Groups

There are five different types of market groups: the free trade area, customs union, common market, economic union, and political union. A country may enter an agreement with another country or group of countries using one of these five types of groups. The level of integration and cooperation between countries will depend on the type of group they form. Figure 5.4 shows which aspects of international integration are included in each type of agreement.

FIGURE 5.4 ● Forms of International Integration

| | Removal of Internal Tariffs | Common External Tariffs | Free Flow of Capital and Labor | Harmonization of Economic Policy | Political Integration |

Free Trade Area
Customs Union
Common Market
Economic Union
Political Union

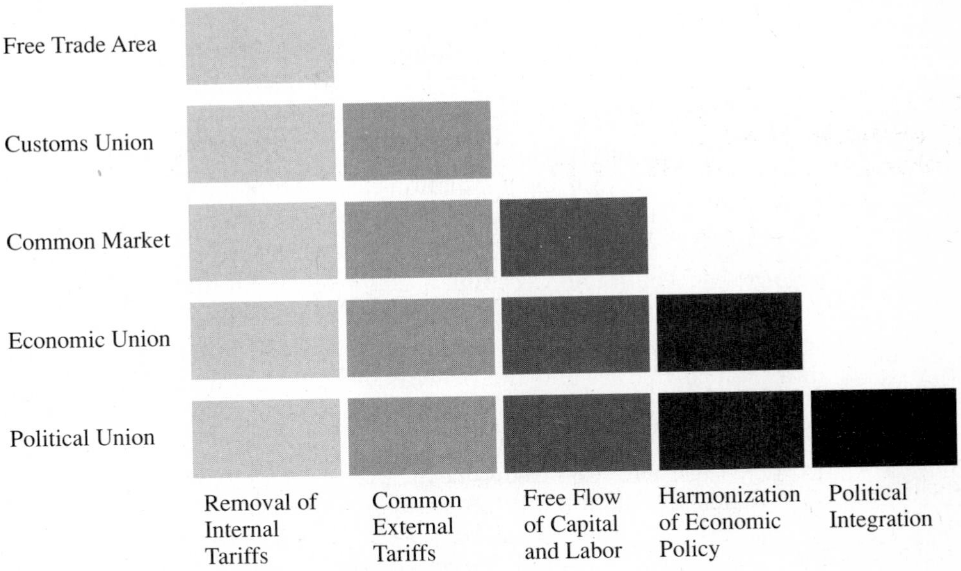

Source: Ruel K. Kahler and Roland L. Kramer, *International Marketing,* 5th ed., p. 343. Reprinted by permission of South-Western Publishing Company.

Major Market Groups

Market agreements that formed the major market groups are shown in Table 5.7. The next sections describe these market groups and the agreements that brought them together. The sections are divided according to geographic area.

Europe   Europe has three major market groups: the European Community (EC), the European Free Trade Association (EFTA), and the Council for Mutual Economic Assistance (COMECON).

The European Community (EC), originally called the European Common Market when it was established in 1958, is a true common market. The EC has grown from the original six countries to twelve countries, and there is the possible addition of other countries in the future. The EC also has preferential trade agreements with the European Free Trade Association, and a number of Caribbean, Pacific, and African countries. The EC has increased its role over time through the establishment of the European Parliament, The Court of Justice, and the creation of the European Currency Unit. Because of this increased economic and monetary power, most would agree that the EC has become an economic union.

The relaunch of the European Community and the creation of The Single European Market, often referred to as "1992," were initiated by Lord Cockfield. He was the British Commissioner to the EC and authored the Internal Market White Paper published on June 14, 1985.[16] The White Paper explained the logic for a single market and summarized the impediments into three areas: physical business at frontiers, technical barriers within different countries, and barriers designed to protect fiscal regimes. It took two years for the White Paper to be approved by the twelve members of the EC and become the Single Market Act. There was a strong logic for the Single Market. Europe, while bigger than the United States and Japan in population, was underperforming its two largest competitors on almost every measure. In 1987, 11.7 percent of the EC working population was unemployed, compared to 6.7 percent in the United States and 3.2 percent in Japan.[17]

The EC commissioned a number of studies to measure the potential impact of a Single Market. Paolo Cecchini, a senior official of the EC, coordinated thirty different studies and published the economics of 1992 in the Spring of 1988.[18] This report became known as the Cecchini report and documented the costs of continuing in a divided market and the benefits of building an integrated one.[19] The report

---

16. Lord Cockfield, "Completing the Internal Market," White Paper to the European Council. Luxembourg: Office of Publications of the European Communities, 1985.

17. Catherine Taylor and Alison Press, *1992: The Facts and Challenges* (London: The Industrial Society, 1988), p. XI.

18. Nicholas Colchester and David Buchan, *Europe Relaunched* (London: The Economist Books, 1990), p. 32–33.

19. Paolo Cecchini, *The European Challenge 1992: The Benefits of a Single Market* (London: Wildwood House, 1988).

TABLE 5.7 ● Summary of Market Agreements

Member countries		Population (in millions)	GNP (in billions of U.S. dollars)	GNP per capita (in U.S. dollars)	Daily calorie supply per capita	Life expectancy	Total fertility[1]
EUROPEAN AGREEMENTS							
European Community (EC) (Customs union)	Belgium	9.9	162.0	16,390	3,942	75	1.6
	Denmark	5.1	105.3	20,510	3,577	75	1.5
	France	56.1	1,000.9	17,830	3,310	77	1.8
	Germany	61.3	1,272.9	20,750	3,514	75	1.5
	Ireland	3.5	30.0	8,500	3,699	74	2.3
	Italy	57.5	871.9	15,150	3,566	77	1.3
	Luxembourg	.4	9.4	24,860	3,942	75	1.6
	United Kingdom	57.3	834.5	14,570	3,252	76	1.8
	Portugal	10.3	44.1	4,260	3,382	75	1.6
	Spain	39.2	358.4	9,150	3,543	77	1.6
	The Netherlands	14.8	237.4	16,010	3,354	77	1.6
	Greece	10.0	53.6	5,340	3,699	77	1.6
	Total	325.4	5,305.5	16,305	—	—	—
European Free Trade Association (EFTA) (Free trade area)	Austria	7.6	131.9	17,360	3,478	76	1.5
	Finland	5.0	109.7	22,060	3,170	75	1.7
	Iceland	.3	5.4	21,240	3,352	78	2.1
	Liechtenstein	.03	.5	16,964	—	—	—
	Norway	4.2	92.1	21,850	3,253	77	1.8
	Sweden	8.5	184.2	21,710	3,007	77	2.0
	Switzerland	6.5	198.0	30,270	3,547	77	1.6
	Total	32.1	721.3	22,470	—	—	—

TABLE 5.7 ● Summary of Market Agreements (cont.)

	Member countries	Population (in millions)	GNP (in billions of U.S. dollars)	GNP per capita (in U.S. dollars)	Daily calorie supply per capita	Life expectancy	Total fertility[1]
EUROPEAN AGREEMENTS							
Council for Mutual Economic Assistance (COMECON) (Political union)	Cuba	10.4	—	—	3,103	76	1.9
	Bulgaria	9.0	20.8	2,320	3,614	72	1.9
	Czechoslovakia	15.6	—	—	3,564	71	2.0
	East Germany	16.7	—	—	3,890	74	1.8
	Hungary	10.6	27.1	2,560	3,601	71	1.8
	Mongolia	2.1	—	—	2,458	62	4.8
	Poland	38.0	66.9	1,760	3,451	72	2.2
	Romania	23.1	—	—	3,357	71	2.1
	U.S.S.R.	287.6	—	—	3,386	70	2.3
	Vietnam	65.7	—	—	2,233	66	4.0
	Total	478.8	—	—	—	—	—
AFRICAN AGREEMENTS							
Afro-Malagasy Economic Union (Economic union)	Benin	4.6	1.7	380	2,145	51	6.3
	Cameroon	11.6	11.7	1,010	2,161	57	6.4
	Central African Republic	3.0	1.1	390	1,980	51	5.7
	Chad	5.5	1.0	190	1,852	46	5.9
	Congo, People's Rep.	2.2	2.0	930	2,512	54	6.5
	Gabon	1.1	3.1	2,770	2,396	53	5.6
	Ivory Coast	11.7	9.3	790	2,365	53	7.3
	Mali	8.2	2.1	260	2,181	48	7.0
	Mauritania	2.0	1.0	490	2,528	46	6.5
	Niger	7.5	2.2	290	2,340	45	7.1
	Total	57.4	35.2	613	—	—	—

Group	Country						
East Africa Customs Union (Customs union)	Ethiopia	48.8	6.0	120	1,658	48	7.5
	Kenya	23.3	8.8	380	1,973	59	6.8
	Sudan	24.4	10.1	420	1,996	50	6.3
	Tanzania	25.6	3.1	120	2,151	54	6.7
	Uganda	16.7	4.3	250	2,013	49	7.3
	Zambia	7.8	3.1	390	2,026	54	6.7
	Total	146.6	35.4	241	—	—	—
West African Economic Community (WAEC) (Common market)	Burkina Faso	8.7	2.7	310	2,061	48	6.5
	Ivory Coast	11.7	9.3	790	2,365	53	7.3
	Mali	8.2	2.1	260	2,181	48	7.0
	Mauritania	2.0	1.0	490	2,528	46	6.5
	Niger	7.5	2.2	290	2,340	45	7.1
	Senegal	7.2	4.7	650	1,989	48	6.5
	Total	45.3	22.0	486	—	—	—
Maghreb Economic Community (Common market)	Algeria	24.5	53.1	2,170	2,726	65	5.3
	Libya	4.4	22.9	5,410	3,384	62	6.7
	Morocco	24.6	22.0	900	2,820	61	4.7
	Tunisia	8.0	10.1	1,260	2,964	66	4.0
	Total	61.5	108.1	1,758	—	—	—
Casablanca Group (Free trade area)	Egypt	51.4	32.5	630	3,213	63	4.5
	Ghana	14.4	5.5	380	2,209	54	6.2
	Guinea	5.5	2.3	430	2,042	43	6.5
	Morocco	24.6	22.0	900	2,820	61	4.7
	Total	95.9	62.3	650	—	—	—
Economic Community of West African States (ECOWAS) (Customs union)	Benin	4.6	1.7	380	2,145	51	6.3
	Burkina Faso	8.8	2.7	310	2,061	48	6.5
	Cape Verde	.4	.3	760	2,436	66	5.0
	The Gambia	.8	.2	230	2,360	44	6.5
	Ghana	14.4	5.5	380	2,209	54	6.2
	Guinea	5.5	2.3	430	2,042	43	6.5

TABLE 5.7 ● Summary of Market Agreements (cont.)

Member countries	Population (in millions)	GNP (in billions of U.S. dollars)	GNP per capita (in U.S. dollars)	Daily calorie supply per capita	Life expectancy	Total fertility[1]
AFRICAN AGREEMENTS						
Guinea-Bissau	1.0	.2	180	2,690	40	6.0
Ivory Coast	11.7	9.3	790	2,365	53	7.3
Liberia	2.5	—	—	2,270	50	6.3
Mali	8.2	2.1	260	2,181	48	7.0
Mauritania	2.0	1.0	490	2,528	46	6.5
Niger	7.5	2.2	290	2,340	45	7.1
Nigeria	113.7	28.3	250	2,039	51	6.5
Senegal	7.2	4.7	650	1,989	48	6.5
Sierra Leone	4.0	.8	200	1,806	42	6.5
Togo	3.5	1.4	390	2,133	54	6.6
Total	195.8	62.7	324	—	—	—
LATIN AMERICAN AGREEMENTS						
Latin American Integration Association (LAIA) (Free trade area)						
Argentina	31.8	68.8	2,160	3,118	71	2.9
Bolivia	7.1	4.3	600	2,086	54	5.9
Brazil	147.3	375.1	2,550	2,709	66	3.3
Chile	13.0	22.9	1,770	2,584	72	2.6
Colombia	32.3	38.6	1,190	2,561	69	3.0
Ecuador	10.3	10.7	1,040	2,338	66	4.1
Mexico	85.4	170.1	1,990	3,135	69	3.4
Paraguay	4.1	4.3	1,030	2,816	67	4.5
Peru	21.1	23.0	1,090	2,269	62	3.9
Uruguay	3.1	8.1	2,620	2,770	72	2.3
Venezuela	19.2	47.2	2,450	2,547	70	3.6
Total	374.7	773.1	2,063	—	—	—

Central American Common Market (Common market)						
Costa Rica	2.7	4.9	1,790	2,782	75	3.1
El Salvador	5.1	5.4	1,040	2,415	63	4.7
Guatemala	8.9	8.2	920	2,352	63	5.6
Honduras	5.0	4.5	900	2,164	65	5.4
Nicaragua	3.7	—	—	2,361	64	5.3
Total	25.4	23.0	1,060	—	—	—
Andean Common Market (ANCOM) (Common market)						
Bolivia	7.1	4.3	600	2,086	54	5.9
Colombia	32.3	38.6	1,190	2,561	69	3.0
Ecuador	10.3	10.7	1,040	2,338	66	4.1
Peru	21.1	23.0	1,090	2,269	62	3.9
Venezuela	19.2	47.2	2,450	2,547	70	3.6
Total	90.0	123.8	1,375	—	—	—
Southern Common Market (Common market)						
Argentina	31.8	68.8	2,160	3,118	71	2.9
Brazil	147.3	375.1	2,550	2,709	66	3.5
Paraguay	4.1	4.3	1,030	2,816	67	4.5
Uruguay	3.1	8.1	2,620	2,770	72	2.3
Total	186.3	456.3	2,449	—	—	—
Caribbean Community and Common Market (CARACOM) (Common market)						
Antigua and Barbuda	0.8	.30	3,880	2,222	73	1.9
Barbados	.26	1.62	6,370	3,228	75	1.8
Belize	.18	.29	1,600	2,649	67	4.8
Dominica	.08	.14	1,670	2,877	75	3.0
Grenada	.09	.18	1,900	2,979	69	3.1
Guyana	.80	.25	310	2,375	64	2.9
Jamaica	2.40	3.01	1,260	2,572	73	2.5
Trinidad & Tobago	1.3	4.00	3,160	2,960	71	2.9
St. Kitts-Nevis	.04	.12	2,860	2,801	69	2.7
St. Lucia	.15	.27	1,810	2,821	71	3.3
St. Vincent	.11	.13	1,200	2,818	70	2.7
Total	5.49	10.31	1,878	—	—	—

TABLE 5.7 ● Summary of Market Agreements (cont.)

Member countries	Population (in millions)	GNP (in billions of U.S. dollars)	GNP per capita (in U.S. dollars)	Daily calorie supply per capita	Life expectancy	Total fertility[1]
ASIAN AGREEMENTS						
Arab Common Market (ACM) (Common market)						
Egypt	51.4	32.5	630	3,213	63	4.5
Iraq	18.3	—	—	2,962	64	6.2
Jordan	4.0	5.3	1,730	2,907	67	6.3
Syria	12.1	12.4	1,020	3,168	66	6.6
Kuwait	2.0	33.1	16,380	3,132	74	3.6
Total	87.8	83.3	1,199	—	—	—
Regional Cooperation for Development (RDC) (Ad hoc arrangement)						
Iran	50.2	—	—	3,100	63	5.5
Pakistan	109.9	40.1	370	2,200	55	6.5
Turkey	54.9	74.7	1,360	3,080	65	3.7
Total	215.0	114.8	534	—	—	—
Association of South East Asian Nations (ASEAN) (Free trade area)						
Brunei	.2	—	—	2,819	75	3.6
Indonesia	178.2	87.9	490	2,670	61	3.3
Malaysia	17.3	37.0	2,130	2,686	70	3.7
Singapore	2.7	28.1	10,450	2,892	74	1.9
Philippines	61.2	42.8	700	2,255	64	3.7
Thailand	55.2	64.4	1,170	2,287	66	2.5
Total	314.8	260.2	827	—	—	—

Australia	16.8	242.1	14,440	3,322	77	1.9
Canada	26.3	500.4	19,020	3,447	77	1.7
China	1,105	393.0	360	2,632	70	2.4
Hong Kong	5.7	59.2	10,320	2,899	77	1.6
India	832.5	287.3	350	2,104	59	4.1
Israel	4.5	44.1	9,750	3,138	76	2.9
Japan	123.0	2,920.3	23,730	2,848	79	1.7
Korea, Rep	42.3	186.4	4,400	2,878	70	1.8
New Zealand	3.3	39.4	11,800	3,459	75	1.9
Saudi Arabia	13.6	90.0	6,230	2,832	64	7.0
South Africa	34.9	86.0	2,460	3,035	61	4.3
United States	248.2	5,237.7	21,100	3,666	76	1.9
Yugoslavia	23.7	59.1	2,490	3,505	72	2.0

Source: Adapted from *The World Bank Atlas 1990.* Reprinted by permission of the World Bank. All data is for 1989.

1. Total Fertility is the number of children a woman will bear during her lifetime.

summarized the economic gains if the EC implemented the Single Market as follows:

- A rejuvenation of the EC economy adding 4.5 percent to GDP
- A reduction in inflation with a fall in consumer prices of 6.1 percent
- A reduction in the cost of public programs through open bidding
- The creation of 1.8 million new jobs in the EC, reducing unemployment[20]

The potential gains were also documented by industry section, therefore triggering curiosity and enthusiasm. The concept of 1992 was the major business topic of 1988 to 1991. It became the leading topic in the business press. Business conferences were held for every major industry on the impact of 1992. Thousands of articles were written on 1992 along with many books. The publicity has caused most companies around the globe to consider the potential impact of 1992 on their business and to develop strategies to take advantage of the single European market.

The original Single Market White Paper outlined 282 pieces of legislation needed to remove physical, technical, and fiscal business between member countries. This legislation will remove internal border controls, unify technical standards for products, and bring national value-added taxes and excise taxes by member countries closer together. As of mid-1991, all 282 pieces of legislation had been written and presented to the Council of Ministers of the European Commission. The Council of Ministers had approved 189 acts and 75 acts had been implemented by all twelve countries. One of the first acts to be implemented was a Single Customs document replacing seventy forms for a transborder shipment!

To illustrate the potential impact of 1992, we will look at the pharmaceutical industry. The drug industry has a separate regulatory body, applying its own criteria for approving medicines and mutual approval of licenses is nonexistent. Each country has a different system for pricing and paying for drugs. Also, rules regarding drug advertising vary from country to country. Within the spirit of the single market, the European Commission is moving on several fronts to harmonize the EC drug industry. There are plans for a central European Medicines Agency to open in 1993. This agency will test drugs for use throughout the EC. Also, the twelve member countries will still be able to test and license drugs, but after a company has approval in one country, the drug manufacturer will be able to request a license from the other member states based on the principle of mutual recognition. The European Commission has also stated that it plans to develop a European drug pricing system, but specific proposals have not been issued.[21] If the new approach to drug licensing is implemented, it will radically reduce the cost and time to launch drugs in Europe.

The EC has fostered a great deal of public and private crossborder cooperation,

20. James W. Dudley, *1992 Strategies for the Single Market* (London: Kogan Page, 1989), p. 34–35.

21. Clive Cookson, "In Search of Harmony to Cure Europe's Ills," *Financial Times,* March 11, 1991, p. 4.

which resulted in Airbus and many other multicountry alliances. Some executives are beginning to refer to the European Marketplace as Europe Inc., reflecting its development into a unified entity.[22]

The European Free Trade Association (EFTA) was created in 1959 by countries that did not join the EC. The EFTA, consisting of Austria, Finland, Iceland, Liechtenstein, Norway, Sweden, and Switzerland, operates as a free trade area. As the EC single market becomes a reality in 1992, the EFTA countries are quickly negotiating to assure they are not blocked access to the large EC market. In 1990, negotiations took place to form the European Economic Space (EES) or European Economic Area (EEA). The concept of EES or EEA is to give EFTA countries as much access to the EC, with free movement of goods, capital, services, and people as possible—short of full membership.[23] The leaders of EFTA and EC held a series of meetings in 1990 and 1991 to establish the EES. The goal of both parties is to have an agreement in place by January 1, 1993. The challenge facing EFTA countries is the need to accept over 1,400 legal acts covering more than 10,000 pages that represent over thirty years of EC legislation. While most of the legal acts are acceptable, EFTA has raised questions on issues related to the acquisition of real estate, land transport, free movement of people, telecommunications, audio-visual services, insurance, administrative assistance, company law, and social policy. EFTA has also raised concern over health, safety, environment, and consumer affairs as EFTA has achieved a higher level of protection in these areas.[24]

The major stumbling block to the talks between EFTA and the EC is how EFTA can participate in EC decision making without becoming a member of the EC. The opinion of Mr. Cohen, the EC Commission negotiator, is that the EFTA/EC agreement will be for a free trade area, but not a full customs union with a common external tariff. EFTA tariffs for industrial goods average 3 percent compared with 4.2 percent for the EC. In order to create a full customs union, the EFTA countries would need to increase tariffs to the rest of the world which will raise problems with GATT.[25]

EFTA's cooperative agreement with Yugoslavia set the pattern for the Declarations of Cooperations with Czechoslovakia, Hungary, and Poland that were signed at the Gothenburg Summit in June 1990. EFTA has agreed to cooperate with these four countries on trade; economic, industrial, and scientific cooperation; tourism; transport and communication; and environmental pollution.

The long-term role of EFTA may be in jeopardy. Austria has already applied for

22. Business International, "Europe Inc.—No Longer a Fantasy," *Executive Focus/Europe,* June 22, 1987, p. 1.

23. Bengt Jonsson, "Those Other Europeans," *The World in 1991* (The Economist Publications), 1991, p. 56.

24. "The EFTA-EC Negotiations Are Now Firmly on Track," EFTA Bulletin, No. 3, July/September, 1990, p. 2.

25. Peter Montagnon, "EFTA Gives Trade Policy Pledge," *Financial Times,* January 17, 1991, p. 6.

membership to the EC, indicating they prefer the benefits of EC membership over EFTA. If the EFTA/EC agreement does not give EFTA members any decision-making authority or real influence in the EC, Sweden and Norway may decide to apply for EC membership, leaving EFTA as a small appendage to the EC with little economic influence.[26]

The Council for Mutual Economic Assistance (COMECON) was formed in 1949 as a political union of eight Eastern European communist countries, later joined by Cuba and Vietnam. Until 1990, these ten countries were tightly controlled by the Soviet Union and COMECON operated as an enforced political group. The COMECON countries depended on the U.S.S.R. as a major customer. In exchange, the U.S.S.R. provided defenses against NATO forces and oil. COMECON countries were dissatisfied with their forced cooperation with the U.S.S.R. At a COMECON summit in 1988 they complained about intra-country pricing, lack of currency convertibility, and slow economic growth. Matters were made worse in 1989, when the Soviets decided that trade with COMECON should be at world market pricing based on hard currency instead of roubles (the COMECON Unit of Account).[27] So in January 1991 the Eastern European countries had to start paying for Soviet oil at world prices in hard currency. Prior to that they were exchanging manufactured goods for Russian oil.[28] In addition to these problems, suddenly the demand for goods from East Germany and the U.S.S.R dropped. As East and West Germany merged, East German factories struggled for survival in the new Germany and cancelled contracts with their former COMECON partners.[29] Many Soviet contracts also evaporated. For example, the Ikarus bus factory in Hungary almost closed as they lost most of the Soviet buyers of 15,000 buses per year.[30]

The free elections of 1990 put the status of COMECON in doubt. As Yugoslavia, Hungary, Poland, and Czechoslovakia strengthen their relationship with EFTA, it is doubtful that COMECON will continue to exist. Also, the breakup of the Soviet Union and declaration of independence of many of the 15 republics will radically change the process of doing business in the former U.S.S.R.

Africa   The continent of Africa has seven major market agreements in force: Afro-Malagasy Economic Union, East Africa Customs Union, Maghreb Economic Community, Casablanca Group, Economic Community of West African States, West African Economic Community, and Customs and Economic Union of Central

---

26. "Europe—The Makings of a New Constellation," *The Economist,* August 4, 1990, p. 31.

27. "COMECON—Busting Open Eastern Europe," *The Economist,* December 16, 1989, p. 84.

28. Daniel Franklin, "Eastern Europe's Gloomy Boom," *The World in 1991* (London: The Economist Publications, 1991), p. 60.

29. Anthony Robinson, "Forward to a New Society," Survey—Eastern Europe in Transition, *Financial Times,* February 4, 1991, p. 11.

30. "Welcome to this Cruel, Competitive World," *The Economist,* August 11, 1990, p. 41.

Africa. The success of the EC has prompted African countries to get together to form these groups. Unfortunately, however, the groups have had little success in promoting trade and economic progress because most African nations are small with limited economic infrastructure to produce goods.

Latin America There are four major market agreements in Latin America: Andean Common Market, Central American Common Market, Caribbean Community and Common Market, Latin American Integration Association and the Southern Common Market. Latin America faces a number of problems that make it difficult to achieve significant economic integration and cooperation between countries. The low level of economic activity, political turmoil, and the extreme differences in economic development from country to country are stumbling blocks to the success of these market agreements. The five presidents of the Andean member countries met in Caracas in May 1991 and signed an accord designed to implement a full free trade zone by the end of 1995. The Andean Common Market also agreed to begin negotiating with the United States to take advantage of the Enterprise for the Americas initiative. The Andean Pact, set up in 1973, has been slow to reach a full common market, but the negotiations between the United States and Mexico as well as the recent establishment of the Southern Common Market (Argentina, Brazil, Paraguay and Uruguay) has encouraged regional integration.[31]

North America The United States and Canada formed the largest free trade area in the world through the U.S.-Canada Free Trade Agreement. The agreement, which became effective in 1989, removes barriers to trade and investment for most agricultural, industrial, and service businesses. The agreement eliminates tariffs for products manufactured in either country then exported to the other. If less than 50 percent of the manufacturing cost takes place in the United States or Canada, then the goods are subject to the normal tariff. As two-thirds of Canada's imports from the United States were already duty-free, the agreement has not had a large economic impact. The main impact of the agreement is a psychological "kick in the backside" according to Mr. Rutley, economist of the Canadian Manufacturing Association.[32]

The North American Free Trade Agreement (NAFTA) is on the horizon for 1992. If the United States, Canada, and Mexico successfully complete negotiations and enact this agreement, North America will become a free trade zone. The Mexican car industry is optimistic about NAFTA, which could double the production of Mexican cars by the mid-1999s, as labor is less expensive than in the United States or Canada.[33]

31. Joe Mann, "Andean Leaders Breathe Fresh Life into Regional Pact," *Financial Times,* May 20, 1991, p. 4.

32. Bernard Simon, "Trade Pact Brings Canada New Hopes and Fears," *Financial Times,* February 12, 1991, p. 3.

33. Damian Fraser, "Free Trade No Brake on Mexican Car Sales," *Financial Times,* March 12, 1991, p. 3.

Middle East There are two market agreements in the Middle East: Arab Common Market and the Regional Cooperation for Economic Development. The Arab Common Market was formed in 1964 by Egypt, Iraq, Kuwait, Jordan, and Syria. Progress has been achieved toward the development of free trade and eliminations of tariffs between member countries. Equalization of external tariff is expected in the future. The Regional Cooperative for Economic Development (RCD) was formed in 1964 between Iran, Pakistan, and Turkey. The RCD was originally established to provide hydroelectric power and future economic development.

Asia The Association of South East Asian Nations (ASEAN) includes Brunei, Indonesia, Malaysia, Singapore, the Philippines, and Thailand. All the ASEAN countries, except Singapore, have an abundance of labor and developing economies. ASEAN is seeking closer economic integration and cooperation between the member countries. While ASEAN has a population of 315 million, its combined GNP of $260 million is less than 10 percent of Japan's GNP, giving the group very little economic clout. ASEAN is economically the fastest growing area of the world.

The Asia Pacific Economic Cooperative (APEC) initiative is a grouping of the members of the ASEAN and the United States, Australia, Canada, New Zealand, Japan, and South Korea. APEC was started by the U.S. and Australia to promote the multilateral interests of the member countries, especially at the Uruguay Round of GATT talks.

Malaysia has proposed the East Asia Economic Grouping (EAEG) which will include the six members of ASEAN plus North Korea, South Korea, Japan, Taiwan, Hong Kong, Vietnam, China, Australia, and New Zealand. ASEAN meets in mid-1991 to discuss the concept of EAEG and decide which countries should be included. Singapore, initially rejected the idea of EAEG, but later agreed if the new group will be consistent with both GATT rules and the objectives of APEC. The inclusion of China, Hong Kong, or Taiwan in the group will raise some sovereignty problems as none of these countries currently belongs to GATT.[34]

The future of country groupings in Asia is unclear. ASEAN is a weak grouping that has not been able to harmonize its own tariff structure. APEC is a weak collection of countries to promote trade, but it is not any type of formal union. EAEG is just a proposal, no agreements have been formatted. Some of the most successful trading countries in the world are in Asia. The four dragons—Japan, Taiwan, Singapore, and Hong Kong—all have developed their expertise without the protection of a market grouping. Some argue that Japan may gain space when negotiating with the United States or Europe by belonging to a trade group such as EAEG.[35]

34. Lim Siong Hoon, "Mahathir Brain Child Proves Problem for Partners," *Financial Times,* February 9, 1991, p. 8.
35. Ibid., p. 8.

CONCLUSIONS

The world marketplace is large and complex. The international company needs to systematically evaluate the entire world market on a regular basis to be sure that company assets are directed toward the countries with the best opportunities. The basis for an evaluation of countries should be a comparative analysis of different countries. Certain countries may be unsuitable because of their unstable political situation, and other countries may have little potential because their population is small or the per capita income is low. The screening process gives the firm information about market size, competition, trade regulations, and distribution systems that will form the basis for the development of a market strategy.

The nature of the world marketplace has changed as a result of the development of major regional market groups. The economic integration of a number of countries offers great opportunities to companies. Many national markets such as those in Europe that are too small individually become significant when combined with other countries. By locating production facilities in one country of a market group, the international company has access to the other markets with little or no trade restrictions. The market groups also increase competition. Local producers who for years completely dominated their national markets due to tariff protection now face competition from many other member countries.

The development of these market groups can also have negative effects on international companies. If a company is unable or unwilling to build a manufacturing plant in a certain market group, it may be unprofitable to export to that market. There are often more regulations between market groups, making it more complicated and expensive to move goods from one group to another. Also, the market group does not necessarily reduce the complexity of the consumer and cultural differences. For example, while Germany and Spain are both in the EC, the marketing programs, products, and strategies for success in each market will probably be different.

The success of market groups formed after World War II, particularly the EC, indicates that market groups will continue to grow in the future. The potential entry of some Eastern European countries into the EFTA/EC, as well as the expansion of the U.S.-Canada EFTA to include Mexico, support the growth of market groups and the growing interdependence of trading partners. International companies need to monitor the development of new groups and any changes in the structure of current groups, since changes within market groups will result in changes in market size and competition.

Questions for Discussion

1. Searching for the best international opportunity often requires an analysis of all the countries of the world. How will the initial screening differ from the final screening of possible countries to enter?

2. If you were evaluating opportunities for caviar, but found that no countries had data on caviar consumption, what other indicators of market size would you use to evaluate the size of each country's market?

3. Using Figure 5.3, compare the potential for caviar consumption in Germany, India, and S. Korea?

4. In the sale of hair shampoo, what are the advantages of grouping countries together rather than marketing to each country individually?

5. What are the differences between a free trade area, a customs union, and a common market? If you were marketing to a grouping of countries but only had a manufacturing plant in one of the countries, which of the three types of agreements would you prefer?

6. What are the reasons for the growth in the establishment of country groupings?

For Further Reading

Auguier, Antoine A. *French Industry's Reaction to the European Common Market.* New York: Garland, 1984.

Behrman, Jack N. "Transnational Corporations in the New Economic Order." *Journal of International Business Studies,* Spring/Summer, 1981, pp. 29–42.

Boisot, Max, "Territorial Strategies in a Competitive World: The Emerging Challenges to Regional Authorities," *European Management Journal,* September 1990, pp. 394–401.

Cracco, Etienne, and Guy Robert. *"The Uncommon Common Market."* In Ronald C. Curhan, *1974 Combined Proceedings.* Chicago: American Marketing Association, 1975.

Fishburn, Dudley, ed. *The World in 1991.* London: The Economist Publications, 1991.

"Here Come the Multinationals of the Third World." *The Economist,* July 23, 1983, p. 55.

Hertzfeld, Jeffrey M. "Joint Ventures: Saving the Soviets from Perestroika," *Harvard Business Review,* January and February 1991, pp. 80–91.

Kirkland, Richard I., Jr., "Who Gains from the New Europe," *Fortune,* December 18, 1989, pp. 48–54.

Lasserre, Philippe. "The New Industralizing Countries of Asia: Perspectives and Opportunities." *Long Range Planning,* June 1981, pp. 36–43.

Levy, Brian, "Korean and Taiwanese Firms as International Competitors: The Challenges Ahead," *Columbia Journal of World Business,* Spring 1988, pp. 43–52.

Lipsey, R. "The Theory of Customs Unions: A General Survey." *Economic Journal,* 70 (1960), pp. 496–513.

Luqman, Mushtag, A. Quraeshi, and Linda Delene. "Marketing in Islamic Countries." *MSU Business Topic,* 3 (1980), pp. 17–26.

Sethi, S. Prakash. "Comparative Cluster Analysis for World Markets." *Journal of Marketing Research,* August 1971, pp. 348–354.

Sethi, S. Prakash, and Richard H. Holton, "Review of Comparative Analysis for International Marketing." *Journal of Marketing Records,* November 1969, pp. 502–503.

Smith-Morris, Miles, ed. *Book of Vital World Statistics.* London: The Economist Books, 1990.

Staude, Gavin. "Marketing to the African Segment of the South African Market." *European Journal of Marketing,* 6 (1978), pp. 400–412.

"Survey of the Third World." *The Economist,* September 23, 1989, pp. 1–58.

6

International Buyers

IF ALL BUYERS *around the globe acted in the same way, then international marketing would not be as challenging or difficult as it is. If all buyers were the same, international marketers could use the same marketing program to meet all their needs. However, buyers are different—and there are major variations from country to country, often even within countries. Also, the international buyer can be a consumer, a business, or a government; and each differs from market to market as a result of distinct economic, cultural, social, and political structures. The international marketing manager's job is further complicated by the interaction of these dimensions in an ever-changing context. Whereas the previous sections analyzed the impact of the cultural, economic, and political structures, this chapter synthesizes these systems and demonstrates how they relate to buyer behavior patterns.*

It is important for the international marketer to identify the similarities and differences of international buyers. These similarities and differences dictate the need for product modifications and adaptations. Also, the marketing strategy will need to be modified to be successful with different sets of consumers. Figure 6.1 summarizes the chapter and shows factors that influence each type of buyer.

THE PURCHASE DECISION PROCESS

All buyers go through a similar process to select a product or service for purchase. While the process will be similar from country to country, the final purchase decision will vary because of the differences in the social, economic, and cultural systems.

FIGURE 6.1 ● International Buyers

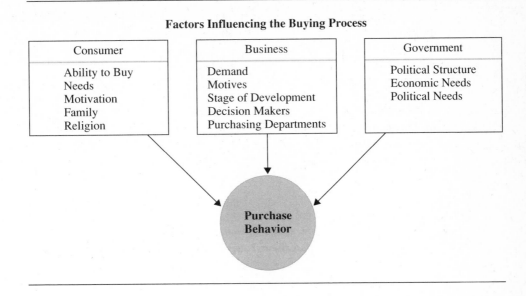

Factors Influencing the Buying Process

Consumer	Business	Government
Ability to Buy Needs Motivation Family Religion	Demand Motives Stage of Development Decision Makers Purchasing Departments	Political Structure Economic Needs Political Needs

Purchase
Behavior

International buyers differ by whom actually makes the decision to buy, what they buy, why they buy, how they buy, when they buy, and where they buy. Assuming that buyers in different countries use the same buying processes and the same selection criteria can be disastrous. When launching baby diapers worldwide, P&G established a global marketing team in Cincinnati, believing babies' diaper needs should be the same worldwide. They later found out that while mothers in most countries are concerned about keeping their babies' bottoms dry, Japanese mothers had different needs. In Japan, babies are changed so frequently that thick absorbent diapers were not necessary and could be replaced by thin diapers that take up less space in the small Japanese home.[1] This chapter provides a framework to evaluate the buying process for consumers, businesses, and governments.

ANALYZING THE INTERNATIONAL BUYER

In every marketing situation it is important to understand potential buyers and the process they use to select one product over another. Most of the elements of a marketing program are designed to influence the buyer to choose your product versus a

1. Brian Dumaine, "P&G Rewrites The Rules of Marketing," *Fortune,* November 6, 1989, p. 48.

competitor's product. Figure 6.2 summarizes a process that can be used to analyze the buyer.

In the case of each type of buyer—consumer, business, or government—the marketer must be able to identify who the buyers are, what is the size of the potential market, and how do they make a purchase decision. For example, in purchasing automobiles in Italy, who usually makes the decision, the husband or wife? When a Japanese company purchases a computer system, what type of people are involved? Is price more important than the reputation of the computer manufacturer? When a young man in Germany decides to open a savings account, what information sources does he use to select a bank?

Having set a framework for understanding international buyers, we will examine each type of buyer—consumers, businesses, and governments.

FIGURE 6.2 ● International Buyer Analysis Process

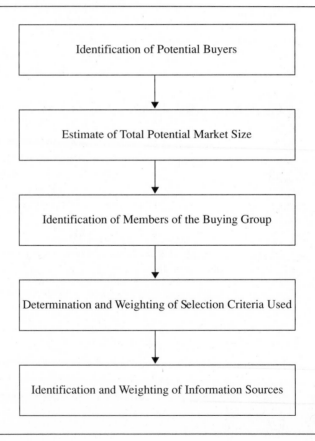

Identification of Potential Buyers

Estimate of Total Potential Market Size

Identification of Members of the Buying Group

Determination and Weighting of Selection Criteria Used

Identification and Weighting of Information Sources

CONSUMERS

Consumers around the world have many similar needs. All people must eat, drink, and be sheltered from the elements. Once these basic needs are met, consumers will seek to improve their standard of living with a more comfortable environment, more leisure time, and an increased social status. While basic needs and the desire for an improved standard of living are universal throughout the world, people's ability to achieve these objectives is not universal. The economic, political, and social structure of countries affects the ability and method consumers use to fulfill their needs. To understand a consumer market, one must examine the following four aspects of consumer behavior:

1. The ability of people to buy

2. Consumer needs

3. Buying motives

4. The buying process

Figure 6.3 illustrates consumer buying behavior in terms of these four aspects.

Ability to Buy

In order for a consumer to purchase a product, he or she must have the ability to buy. The medium of exchange in most societies is currency. The ability to buy a product is affected by the amount of wealth a country possesses and the distribution of the wealth. As shown in Figure 6.3, a country accumulates wealth by the sale of goods to other countries (exports) and the sale of goods within the country. These inflows of money are offset by the outflows of money to pay for necessary imports.

A very important indicator of total consumer potential is gross national product (GNP) because it indicates the value of production in a country, which is an indicator of market size. The GNP per capita shows the value of production per consumer, which is a crude indicator of potential per consumer. The per capita national income is better than the GNP, as a measure of gross consumer purchasing power, because it eliminates capital consumption and business taxes which are not part of personal income. As shown in Table 6.1 (on page 189), GNP and GNP per capita can vary significantly from country to country.

The total wealth in a country is an important indicator of market potential. With a GNP per capita of $23,730 in Japan and $21,710 in Sweden, it is expected the demand for automobiles will be greater than in Zaire or India with GNP per capita below $400.

The accumulated income (GNP) is thus divided among the members of a society. The government has a major influence on the distribution of wealth. A large government will take a large share of the wealth through taxes or ownership of industries. The government also sets policies and laws to regulate the distribution of wealth. For example, a graduated income tax with a 60 to 90 percent tax on high levels of income and no taxes on low levels of income will help to evenly distribute the income. The revenue that remains in the private sector will be distributed to

FIGURE 6.3 ● Consumer Buying Behavior

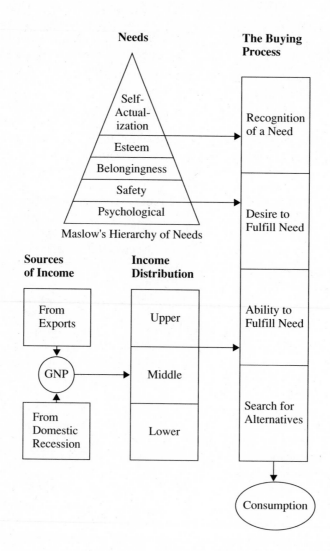

workers, managers, and owners of the industries. Low labor wages and unemployment will tend to increase the size of the lower income class. Concentration of business ownership in a few families will decrease the size of the upper class. The social structure of the country can also affect income distribution. For example, in Japan where an emphasis is placed on group versus individual needs, 95 percent of the population reports that they are in the middle class.

Table 6.2 compares the distribution of family income in the United States, the United Kingdom, and India. The United States has a large middle class whereas the greatest portion of India's population is in the lower income class. The rate of change in economic levels also affects the ability to buy. It is harder for an Indian to move from the lower to the middle class than it is for a U.S. citizen because of the caste structure which makes upward mobility difficult. The amount a consumer has to spend is not solely accounted for by disposable income; it also reflects the availability and use of consumer financing. The United States is becoming a cashless society and many purchases are financed through private credit organizations, such as banks, finance companies, store financing, automobile credit, and so on. Cultural attitudes can affect the use of credit. The German avoids credit, so only 15 to 20 percent of retail purchases are made using credit, while 80 percent of U.S. purchases are paid for with credit cards.[2] Governments also subsidize spending through social programs

2. "Frugal Foreigners," *Wall Street Journal,* December 17, 1986, pp. 1, 14.

TABLE 6.1 ● Selected Data on Potential Consumer Buying Power (In U.S. Dollars for 1989)

	GNP (in billions)	GNP/capita (in billions)
U.S.	5,238	21,100
U.K.	834	14,570
France	1,001	17,830
Japan	2,920	23,730
Sweden	184	21,710
Kuwait	33	16,380
Colombia	39	1,190
Egypt	33	630
Zaire	9	260
India	287	350
Kenya	9	380

Source: The World Bank Atlas 1990; The World Bank, 1990, pp. 6–9. Reprinted by permission.

TABLE 6.2 ● Percent Distribution of Family Income

*Household income**	*U.S.*	*U.K.*	*India*
Under $5,000	7.9	18.2	99.0
$5,000 to $9,999	13.2	35.1	1.0
$10,000 to $14,999	12.2	29.8	—
$15,000 to $19,999	11.4	7.9	—
$20,000 to $24,999	10.4	5.1	—
$25,000 to $34,999	16.9	2.9	—
$35,000 to $49,999	15.3	0.8	—
$50,000 and over	12.8	0.2	—

*All figures show gross income.

Source: Statistical Abstract of the United States, 1986 (106th) Edition (Washington, D.C.: U.S. Bureau of the Census, 1985), p. 445; *Annual Abstract of Statistics, 1987 Edition* (London: Board of Inland Revenue, 1987), p. 258; *Household Income and Its Disposition* (New Delhi: National Council of Applied Economic Research, 1980), p. 243.

such as unemployment income and national health care. Long-term demographics can also affect income distribution. For example, in 1980 11.2 percent of the U.S. population was over 65 years old versus 15.5 percent in Germany and 9.0 percent in Japan. The number of people over 65 will change radically over the next 30 years. In the year 2010, 13.8 percent of the U.S. population will be over 65 compared to 20.7 percent in Germany and 18.2 percent in Japan.[3]

Consumer Needs

Money is spent to fulfill basic human needs. One framework of consumer needs was developed by Abraham Maslow. Maslow's hierarchy of needs model explains that humans will tend to satisfy lower-level needs, such as the physiological need for food, clothing, and shelter, before attempting to satisfy higher-level needs such as safety, belongingness, or esteem (see Figure 6.3). Figure 6.4 illustrates Maslow's theory in terms of the consumption patterns within different countries. The figure shows that the structure of consumption for each country varies depending on the income per capita. A developing country, such as China, spends over 50 percent on food whereas developed countries, such as France or the United States, spend less than 20 percent on food. While it is possible to generalize about the order of consumer purchases based on Maslow's hierarchy of needs, the patterns may vary by country.

Buyer Motivation

The ability to buy is influenced by a variety of economic elements, which are much easier to identify and qualify than the motivation to buy. As mentioned earlier, all consumers have some similarities as members of the human race. Unfortunately, however, buyer behavior is not uniform among all humans. Buyer behavior is learned, primarily from the culture. As a marketer moves from culture to culture (within and between countries), buyer behavior will differ.

Consumer behavior is a complex process in any culture. Figure 6.5 shows the environmental influences that affect a consumer during the buying process. These factors will vary from country to country.

As we discussed in Chapter 3, culture refers to widely shared norms or patterns of behavior within a large group of people.[4] These norms can directly affect product usage. For example, mothers in Brazil feel that only they can properly prepare foods for their babies and, therefore, they are reluctant to buy processed foods. This cultural norm in Brazil caused difficulty for Gerber Products despite the fact that their products were selling well in other Latin American countries.[5] Social class is a group-

---

3. Japan Economic Institute, "Projected Demographic Changes in the Major Industrial Countries," *Japan Economic Report,* March 27, 1987, p. 5.

4. Henry Assael, *Consumer Behavior and Marketing Action,* 3rd ed. (Boston: Kent, 1987), p. 15.

5. Ann Helmings, "Culture Shocks," *Advertising Age,* May 17, 1982, p. M-9.

FIGURE 6.4 ● Consumer Expenditure Patterns of Selected Countries, 1987/1988 Percentage of Total Spending

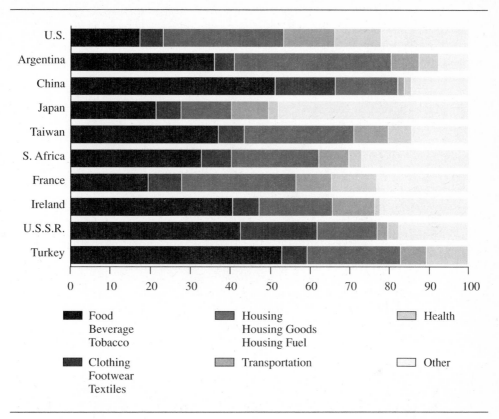

Source: International Marketing Data and Statistics, 1990 London: Euromonitor Publications Ltd., 1990, Table Number 1103. p. 391; *European Marketing Data and Statistics, 1991* London Euromonitor Publications Ltd., 1991, Table Number 1103, pp. 254–255. Reprinted by permission.

ing of consumers based on income, education, and occupation. Consumers in the same social class tend to have similar purchase patterns. The perceived class structure and the distribution of income will affect purchase behavior. Culture not only influences the consumer behavior. It also affects the conduct of businesses. Professors Harris and Moran suggest that cross cultural training is very important for managers to be successful in dealing with business people of different cultures.[6]

Consumers belong to a variety of different groups that also influence purchase behavior. For example, in Moslem countries it is difficult to sell insurance because

6. Philip R. Harris and Robert T. Moran, *Managing Cultural Differences,* 2nd ed. (Houston, Texas: Gulf Publishing, 1987), pp. 3-24.

FIGURE 6.5 ● Environmental Influences on Consumer Behavior

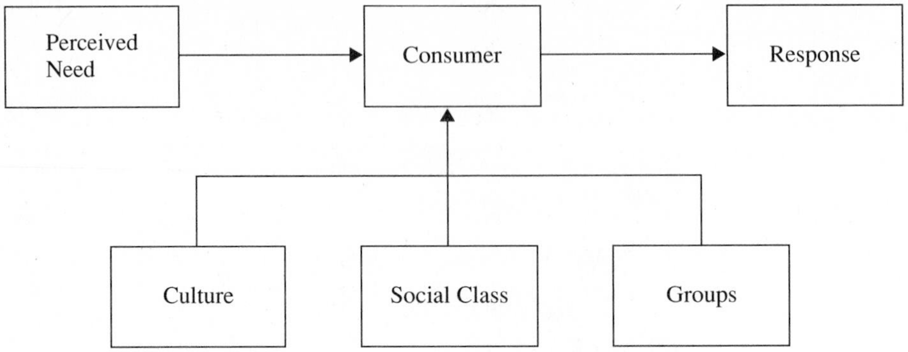

religious leaders claim it is a form of usury and gambling, both of which are explicitly prohibited in the Koran.[7]

Family Structure The structure of the family and the roles assigned to each member play an important part in determining who makes a decision and who does the influencing. Table 6.3 shows the results of a study that examined and compared decision-making roles in families from the United States and Venezuela. Nine products/ services were picked and each family within the survey was asked to identify which member made the decision to purchase the product. The overriding contrast between the two samples involved the role of the husband. More joint decisions regarding major purchases were made in the United States than in Venezuela. In all purchase decisions, except groceries and savings, the Venezuelan husband made more decisions than the U.S. husband. Families in the United States make more joint decisions than Venezuelan families.

International marketers must be aware that variations in family purchasing roles may exist in foreign markets due to the social and cultural differences. Marketing strategy may change based on the respective role of family members. For example, a U.S. manufacturer of appliances or furniture may find it advisable to incorporate the husband into its Venezuelan marketing strategy to a larger extent than in the United States.

Family structure, particularly the number of two-parent families (versus single-parent families), will also affect the level of household income. Also, families with two working parents will have a higher level of pooled income than single-parent or one-working-parent families. The pooling of incomes will positively influence the demand for consumer durables and luxury goods.

7. D. E. Allen, "Anthropological Insights into Consumer Behavior," *European Journal of Marketing,* vol. 5 (Summer 1971), p. 54.

TABLE 6.3 ● Mean Number of Purchase Decisions
by Product Type

Product	United States	Venezuela
Groceries		
Husband	.23	.23
Joint	.60	.69
Wife	3.20	3.08
Furniture		
Husband	.41	1.16
Joint	3.41	2.71
Wife	2.23	2.16
Major Appliances		
Husband	.98	1.97
Joint	3.21	2.10
Wife	.85	.93
Life Insurance		
Husband	2.65	3.38
Joint	1.23	.55
Wife	.15	.05
Automobiles		
Husband	2.59	4.16
Joint	3.06	1.42
Wife	.41	.40
Vacations		
Husband	1.00	1.51
Joint	3.68	3.18
Wife	.40	.41
Savings		
Husband	1.00	1.07
Joint	1.61	1.60
Wife	.44	.34
Housing		
Husband	.34	.87
Joint	2.47	1.82
Wife	.34	.39
Doctor		
Husband	.03	.10
Joint	.35	.42
Wife	.62	.49

Source: Robert T. Green and Isabella Cunningham,
"Family Purchasing Roles in Two Countries, *Journal of
International Business Studies,* Spring/Summer 1980,
p. 95. Reprinted by permission.

Religion   As we noted in Chapter 3, religion affects behavior patterns by establishing moral codes and taboos. What, when, and how consumers buy is a function of their religion. Traditional Catholics do not eat meat on Fridays during Lent and Orthodox Jews are forbidden to eat pork. The Christian sabbath is on Sunday, Jewish sabbath on Saturday, and the Moslem sabbath on Friday. Religion influences the attitudes and beliefs of people with regard to interests, work, leisure, family size, family relationships, and so on. Many of these influences affect the type of products people purchase, why they buy them, and even which newspapers they read. For example, in some countries if too much attention is given to the body in advertisements, the product may be rejected as immoral.

Educational Systems   Formal education involves public or private schools or institutions where learning takes place in a structured environment. The literacy rate is the standard measurement used to assess the extent and success of educational systems, and it normally varies directly with economic development.

In Europe and Japan the literacy rate exceeds 90 percent (see Table 3.2), whereas in some developing countries it is below 50 percent. Low levels of literacy affect marketers in two ways: first, it reduces the market for products that require reading, such as books and magazines; second, it reduces the effectiveness of advertising.

Education includes the process of transmitting skills, ideas, attitudes, and knowledge. The educational process in effect transmits the existing culture and traditions to the next generation. Often, the goals of an educational system will include broader political goals, such as India's programs to improve agriculture and reduce the birth rate.

The international company is impacted by the educational system of the markets it serves. The educational system will determine the nature of the consumer market and the kinds of marketing personnel available. Some of the major implications of dealing with poorer educational systems are as follows:

- If consumers are largely illiterate, advertising programs and package labels will need to be adapted.
- Conducting marketing research can be difficult, both in communicating with consumers and in getting qualified researchers.
- Products that are complex or need written instructions may need to be modified to meet the educational attainments of members in the channel.
- Relations with, and cooperation from, the distribution channel will depend partly on the educational and skill levels of the market.
- The nature and quality of marketing support services, such as advertising agencies, will depend on how well the educational system prepares people for such occupations.[8]

---

8. Vern Terpstra and Sarathy Revi, *International Marketing,* 5th ed. (Hinsdale, IL: Dryden Press, 1991), p. 109.

Innovativeness of Countries The rate at which people accept a new product is defined as the adoption rate. The adoption rate is determined by the innovativeness of the potential adopters. Early adopters are very innovative, laggards are not innovative. Research had determined that high levels of innovativeness are associated with high education levels, low levels of centralized government, a positive attitude toward science, and frequent travel. A study by Professor Lee, based on the adoption rate of black and white televisions, found that there is a difference from country to country on their level of innovativeness and, therefore, the rate of adoption of new products.[9] Table 6.4 shows the categorization of seventy countries by their adoption rate of new products. When developing a global strategy for a new product, the decision on where to launch the product should take into account the innovativeness of the potential markets.

Consumption Patterns

It is difficult to generalize about consumer behavior in each country of the world and for every product category because consumption patterns vary considerably. The differences in consumption patterns are caused by consumers' ability to buy and their motivation to buy. Table 6.5 shows consumption patterns for a number of consumer items in selected countries.

9. Chol Lee, "Determinants of National Innovativeness and International Market Segmentation," *International Marketing Review,* vol. 7, no. 5 (1990), pp. 39–49.

TABLE 6.4 ● International Market Segmentation Based on National Innovativeness

Adopter category	*Countries*
Innovators	Japan, US.
Early Adopters	Canada, Denmark, Sweden, Switzerland, West Germany.
Early Majority	Australia, Austria, Belgium, Finland, France, Greece, Hong Kong, Israel, Italy, Korea, Kuwait, Netherlands, New Zealand, Norway, Portugal, Singapore, Spain, United Kingdom.
Late Majority	Argentina, Brazil, Bulgaria, Burma, Colombia, Costa Rica, Cuba, Czechoslovakia, Dominica, Dominican Republic, Ecuador, Hungary, Guyana, Ireland, Malaysia, Malta, Mauritania, Panama, Paraguay, Peru, Philippines, Poland, Sri Lanka, Thailand, Turkey, Uruguay, Venezuela, Yugoslavia.
Laggards	Algeria, China, Congo, Ghana, Haiti, India, Indonesia, Ivory Coast, Kenya, Madagascar, Pakistan, Rwanda, Senegal, Sudan, Syria, Togo, Zambia.

Source: Chol Lee, "Determinants of National Innovativeness and International Market Segmentation," *International Marketing Review,* vol. 7, no. 5, 1990, pp. 39–49, MCB University Press Ltd. Used with permission.

TABLE 6.5 ● Consumption Patterns in Selected Countries (1989)

	Poultry (kilograms/capita)	Potatoes (kilograms/capita)	Cigarettes (number/capita)	Washing products (kilograms/capita)
Argentina	11.7	64.0	1064.0	1.3
Australia	24.7	56.0	2126.0	15.2
Canada	28.7	63.0	1939.0	16.0
China	1.9	17.0	2300.0	N.A.
Israel	35.8	37.0	1500.0	N.A.
Japan	14.2	14.0	2490.0	9.3
South Africa	15.4	15.0	950.0	N.A.
United States	36.8	29.0	2240.0	N.A.
Belgium	17.2	99.1	1713.0	10.1
France	20.2	74.5	1648.0	9.8
West Germany	11.3	70.6	1883.0	10.6
Italy	19.5	38.2	1645.0	6.9
Spain	21.4	107.0	1966.0	13.3
United Kingdom	18.2	108.3	1677.0	6.1
Finland	6.2	64.1	1511.0	5.0
Switzerland	10.9	50.2	1955.0	9.2
Czechoslovakia	N.A.	73.0	1628.0	N.A.
Poland	N.A.	143.0	2608.0	N.A.

N.A. = Not Applicable

Source: European Marketing Data and Statistics 1991, London: Euromonitor Publications Ltd, 1991, Tables 1401, 1402, 1408, 1409; *Interntional Marketing Data and Statistics 1991,* London: Euromonitor Publications Ltd, 1991, Tables 1401, 1404, 1406. Reprinted by permission.

The differences from country to country are tremendous. In China and Finland the poultry consumption per year is under 7 kilograms whereas it is over 35 kilograms in the United States and Israel. These statistics are critical to an exporter of poultry. Consider the difference in market size caused by consumers who use over 15 kilograms of washing products each year (Australia and Canada) versus the consumers who use less than 10 kilograms (Argentina, Japan, France, Italy, the United Kingdom, Finland, or Switzerland).

The consumption patterns for wine vary tremendously from country to country. For example, in France the average consumption is 73 litres (19 gallons) per person versus 1.6 litres in Japan or 8 litres in the United States as shown in Figure 6.6. Consumption of wine in Britain has doubled during the 1980s to 13 litres per person.

The high consumption of wine in Europe versus the United States is offset by the high consumption of soft drinks. The average American drinks five times as

FIGURE 6.6 ● Wine Consumption for Selected Countries (in Litres per Head 1989–1990)

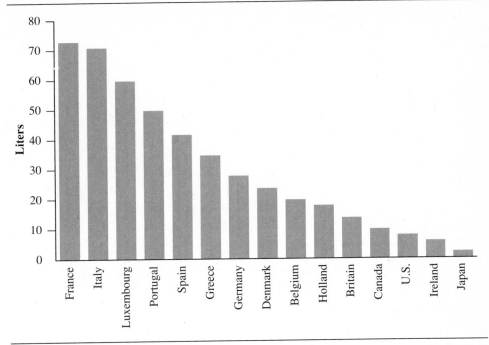

Source: The Economist, December 22, 1990, p. 139. © 1990 The Economist Newspaper Limited. Reprinted by permission.

many soft drinks as a Frenchman, three times as many as an Italian, and two-and-one-half times as many as a German.[10]

Different customs and attitudes in foreign countries will affect product usage rates. See Table 6.6 for the results of a survey in a number of different countries regarding housecleaning, children, and deodorant. These differences in attitudes will influence the marketing strategy. An advertising campaign that depicts a floor cleaner as a timesaving device in the United States may need to be changed or modified for Italian homemakers, showing how the cleaner gives the cleanest floor and receives the highest praise.

Advertising messages that deodorant is a social requirement are accepted in the United States but may be overlooked in Australia. The differences in attitudes also affect consumption. In France and Great Britain the annual consumption of deodorants is about $3.75 per person versus $7.85 in the United States.[11]

10. *Beverage Industry Annual Manual* (Cleveland: Harcourt, Brace, Jovanovich Publications, 1987), p. 16.
11. "Unilever Aims to Bolster Lives in U.S.," *Wall Street Journal,* June 19, 1987, p. 6.

TABLE 6.6 ● Cross-cultural Attitudes Toward Housecleaning, Children, and Deodorants

"A house should be dusted and polished three times a week." Agreement rate	*"My children are the most important thing in my life."* Agreement rate	*"Everyone should use a deodorant."* Agreement rate
86% Italy	86% Germany	89% U.S.A.
59% U.K.	84% Italy/French Canada	81% French Canada
55% France	74% Denmark	77% English Canada
53% Spain	73% France	71% U.K.
45% Germany	71% U.S.A.	69% Italy
33% Australia	67% Spain	59% France
25% U.S.A.	57% U.K.	53% Australia
	56% English Canada	
	53% South Africa	
	48% Australia	

Source: Joseph T. Plummer, "Consumer Focus in Cross-National Research," *Journal of Advertising,* vol. 6, Spring 1977, pp. 10–11. Reprinted by permission.

The patterns of consumption also vary with services. For example, about 15 percent of the world's countries have 95 percent of telephones. The United Nations has established a fund to speed up the adoption of telephones around the world. Studies by the Brookings Institute, the University of Texas, Stanford University, the University of Cairo, and the Massachusetts Institute of Technology indicate that telephones have significant economic benefits to the consumer in excess of the cost and contribute to a rise in per capita income. For example, The World Bank reported that when Sri Lankan farmers received telephones, prices of produce increased from 55 percent of Colombian prices to 85 percent due to better information.[12]

BUSINESS MARKETS

Business buyers around the world are much more predictable than consumers because they are more influenced by the economic considerations of cost and less by social or cultural factors. For example, a purchasing agent in Japan who is purchasing specialty steel for his company will attempt to get the best possible product at the

12. "Third World Telephones," *The Economist,* December 17, 1983, pp. 82–85.

lowest cost, which is similar to how a purchasing agent in the United States or Germany would act. The criteria that business buyers use will be much the same around the world. However, the buying process used by business buyers and the negotiation process will be influenced by local culture and will vary from country to country. The terms *business buyer* and *industrial buyer* are used interchangeably in this chapter, although business buyers normally include all types of businesses, whereas industrial buyers are limited to manufacturing businesses.

Buying Motives

Industrial buying is less affected by such cultural factors as social roles, religion, and language than is consumer buying. The purchasing agent, regardless of his or her background, will be primarily influenced by the use of the product, its cost, and delivery.

Industrial products, such as raw materials or machinery, are sold to businesses to be used in a manufacturing process to produce other goods. Given that the objective of the manufacturer is to maximize profit, the critical buying criterion will focus on the performance of the product purchased versus its cost. This is called the *cost-performance criterion,* and it is used along with other buying criteria such as service, dependability, knowledge of the selling company, and so on.

Because the cost-performance criterion is critical, the economic situation in the purchasing country will affect the decision process. Cost performance is a function of the local cost of labor and the scale of operation. As can be seen in Figure 6.7, which lists manufacturing labor cost averages in selected countries, wage levels vary from country to country. Thus, selling an industrial robot that replaces three workers in the manufacturing of a certain product will be more easily justified in Norway or Germany, where average labor costs are 20 percent more than in the United States, than it will be in Britain where labor cost is less than 80 percent of the U.S. labor rate.

Labor costs play a key role in the level and type of manufacturing. Countries with a surplus of labor normally have lower labor costs, as supply exceeds demand. These lower pay rates result in a certain type of manufacturing which is labor intensive. Therefore, they will be less apt to purchase sophisticated automatic machinery because the same job can get done with the cheaper labor. China's main objective, for example, is to import technology that optimizes its vast population. Companies wishing to export to labor intensive countries must be aware that labor-saving measures may not be appreciated or readily applied. On the other hand, highly developed countries with a high labor rate are prime targets for automated manufacturing equipment. Countries with high labor rates have begun to see an emergence of service industries, which require human labor instead of machines. Labor in these areas is expensive, for a great deal of expertise is needed. Thus, a country normally moves from labor-intensive industry to capital-intensive and then to technical-intensive industry.

FIGURE 6.7 ● Manufacturing Labor Costs per Man-Hour for Selected Countries

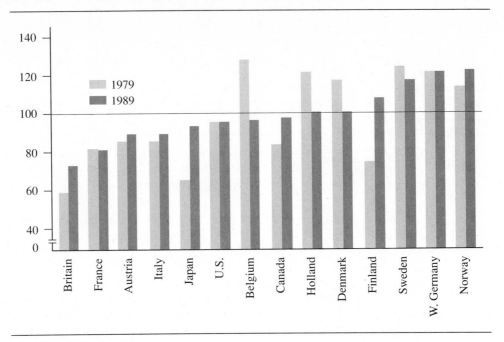

Note: United States = 100
Source: *The Economist,* January 20, 1990, p. 139. © 1990 The Economist Newspaper Limited. Reprinted by permission.

Stage of Economic Development

The nature of the industrial structure varies from country to country. The size and type of industry in a country depends on the level of economic development. While it is dangerous to generalize about countries, the level of economic development is a good indicator of the types of industrial products a country will need and the sophistication of its industrial infrastructure.

Each country basically goes through five stages of economic development and each stage relates to the extent of production capability (see Table 6.7). The stage of economic development is a function of the cost of labor, technical capability of the buyers, scale of operations, interest rates, and level of product sophistication.

It is difficult to use the stages of economic development as a device to segment markets because many countries are in a state of change and can overlap two stages at a time. Also the level of development may not be a good indicator for all product lines. For example, a Third-World country in the first stage may purchase advanced

TABLE 6.7 ● Stages of Economic Development

STAGE 1. THE TRADITIONAL SOCIETY

One with limited production functions, primarily agricultural. The level of productivity in manufacture as in agriculture is limited by the inaccessibility of modern science, its applications, and its frame of mind.

STAGE 2. THE PRECONDITIONS FOR TAKE-OFF

Societies in transition toward modernization. Some investment in infrastructure occurs and there is a widening scope of internal and external commerce. Some modern manufacturing appears but the society is still mainly characterized by the old social structure and values.

STAGE 3. THE TAKE-OFF

Resistance to change lessens and the forces for economic growth come to dominate the society. Industries expand rapidly, requiring new investment. New techniques spread in agriculture as well as industry.

STAGE 4. THE DRIVE TO MATURITY

Continuing growth extends modern technology over the whole range of economic activity. The make-up of the economy changes unceasingly as technique improves, new industries grow and older ones level off. The economy extends its range into more complex technologies.

STAGE 5. THE AGE OF HIGH MASS CONSUMPTION

The leading sectors shift toward durable consumers' goods and services. The structure of the working force changes with more employed in offices or in skilled factory jobs. The extension of modern technology as an objective is joined with a desire to improve social welfare and security.

Source: Walt W. Rostow, *The Stages of Economic Growth,* 2nd ed. Copyright © 1971 by Cambridge University Press. Reprinted by permission.

technology like telecommunication satellites, computer systems, or nuclear power to speed up its industrialization.[13]

The international company must adjust its product offerings to the stage of economic development in potential markets. For example, if a company manufactures buses for sale to countries in all stages of economic development, the product line may vary from high quality luxury buses for countries in advanced stages of development to small, simple buses that offer basic transportation at a minimal price for countries in the early stages of development.

The Buying Process

Industrial buying is a complex process that includes a number of different people. The people involved in the buying process are members of the *buying center.*[14] The

---

13. Norman W. McGuiness and Blair Little, "The Influence of Product Characteristics on the Export Performance of New Industrial Products," *Journal of Marketing,* Spring 1981, pp. 110–122.

14. Frederick E. Webster, Jr. and Yorman Wind, *Organizational Buying Behavior* (Englewood Cliffs, N.J.: Prentice-Hall, 1972), p. 6.

size of the buying center can vary from one person to fifty people depending on the complexity of the buying company, the importance of the decision, and the value of the purchase. It is not unusual to encounter groups of fifteen to twenty individuals involved in the purchase process.[15] One of the major tasks of a marketer is to determine who is involved in the purchase process so that communications through the mail, media, or salesperson can be directed at the appropriate people in the company. The people involved in the buying process can be described by the role they play. The most common roles follow:

Initiators. Persons who first recognize or anticipate a problem that may be solved by buying a good or service.

Gatekeepers. Persons who control information or access, or both, to decision makers.

Influencers. Persons who have some positive or negative input into what is to be bought.

Deciders. Persons who actually say yes or no to a contemplated purchase.

Purchasers. Persons who process the paperwork and place the order.

Users. Persons who ultimately will use the product or service being bought.[16]

The different members of the buying center can be found in companies throughout the world. Although the objective of purchasing the best value at the lowest cost may be universal, the composition of the buying center and the interactions between members of the buying center will vary by country.

Decision Making by Industrial Buyers   In the international marketplace it is often difficult to identify the members of the buying center and their role in the buying process. Often the success of a company will depend on the sales staff's ability to identify the key individuals, determine their role, and communicate the appropriate information to them. Less-developed countries may not have well-developed staff functions, such as engineering or purchasing, so purchase decisions may be made by a line manager, such as a production manager or plant manager. In Japan, where companies are organized with a great deal of attention given to age and seniority, the decision maker may appear to be a senior-level, older person, but the real decision may be made by a younger, lower-level manager. These differences in the decision process from country to country are very important to the international company.

Around the world, purchasing is often a separate function. Efficient purchasing consists of the efficient use of production resources. Developing countries and industrialized countries with a small domestic market must purchase goods and services from other countries. The efficient use of these foreign sources of supply is critical

15. G. Van Der Most, "Purchasing Process: Researching Influences Is Basic to Marketing Planning," *Industrial Marketing,* October 1976, p. 120.

16. Thomas V. Bonoma, "Major Sales: Who Really Does the Buying?" *Harvard Business Review,* May-June 1982, p. 113.

for profitability.[17] The level of purchasing expertise and efficiency varies from country to country, and it will change over time. Two elements that influence the purchasing process are the organizational factors related to purchasing and the decision-making process.

The international company must also be aware that the process of decision making varies in different countries. It is important to know who the decision maker will be, what the relationship is between the decision maker and the other members of management, and what process is used to make decisions. Table 6.8 summarizes the corporate decision-making styles of managers in the United States, Japan, Mexico, and the Middle Eastern countries. As shown in the table, the decision process is somewhat different in each country. For example, in the United States and Japan, subordinates and other managers are likely to be involved in a major purchase decision, whereas in Mexico or the Middle East the decision will be made at a high level with little or no subordinate input. Understanding these differences will help make the marketer a success in different markets.

Factors Influencing International Purchasing In many situations a buyer will have the choice of purchasing a domestic product/service or a foreign product/service. The buyer's perceptions of product quality may be influenced by the product's country of origin, feelings of nationalism, and the firm's competence with international transactions. Although it is assumed that industrial buyers will be completely rational and purchase products based on concrete decision criteria such as price, quality, and performance, research has shown that professional purchases are also influenced by the country of origin even when all other variables are held constant.[18]

The international company must recognize the country of origin stereotypes and use this information when developing a marketing strategy. Highly nationalistic countries tend to encourage economic self-sufficiency even at the expense of economic efficiency, which will have a negative effect on the international company. A study of purchasing behavior by Swedish companies found that buyers preferred to deal with domestic suppliers but would use foreign suppliers when necessary.[19] The study also found that the purchasing firm's competence for international business is positively related to the use of international suppliers. International purchasers will generally have broad market knowledge, an ability to handle foreign cultural patterns, and a knowledge of international trade techniques.[20] Given the results of this

17. Lars Hallen, "International Purchasing in a Small Country: An Exploratory Study of Five Swedish Firms," *Journal of International Business Studies,* Winter 1982, p. 99.

18. Phillip D. White and Edward W. Cundiff, "Assessing the Quality of Industrial Products," *Journal of Marketing,* January 1978, pp. 80–86.

19. Hallen, "International Purchasing in a Small Country: An Exploratory Study of Five Swedish Firms," pp. 99–111.

20. Ibid.

TABLE 6.8 ● Contrasts in Managers' Decision-Making Styles

	U.S. firms	Japanese firms	Mexican firms	Middle Eastern firms
Delegation of authority	Yes. Believed to be essential in increasing subordinates' capabilities.	Yes. Subordinate development is a primary management function; worker suggestions for improvement are sought and accepted.	No. Authoritarian style reflects manager's individualism; subordinate development is not manager's responsibility.	No. Authority rests at the top; delegation depends on personal relationship.
Participation in decision making	Yes. Subordinates contribute to decisions; believed to improve motivation and performance.	Yes. Subordinates participate in and initiate decisions; consensus of all employees is sought.	No. May indicate to subordinates that manager is unsure of own job; maintaining social distance is important.	No. Chain of command is rigidly followed.
Importance of planning	High. Problem solving is valued, planning is a tool for decision making emphasis on short-term planning.	High. Planning is valued, more emphasis on long-term planning.	Low. Plans appear to restrict the manager's personal expression.	Low. Ad hoc planning.
Emphasis in communication style	Direct and frank.	Polite, respectful; patience in difficult topics.	Maintenance of pleasant relations; avoidance of difficult issues.	Tone depends on position, power, or family influence.
Commitment to firm's objectives	Doing well for the firm is an essential component of career success.	Firm's and manager's goals are one and the same; manager identifies with firm.	Career success is based on personal relations with superiors.	Reluctance to take risks inherent in decision making; success dependent on contacts and being of the "right" social position.

Sources: Adapted from Eugene C. McCann, "Anglo-American and Mexican Management Philosophies," *MSU Business Topics,* Summer 1970, pp. 28–37. William Ouchi, *Theory Z: How American Business Can Meet the Japanese Challenge,* Reading, Mass.: Addison-Wesley, © 1981, p. 58; M. L. Dadawy, "Styles of Mideastern Manager," Reprinted/condensed from the *California Management Review,* vol. 22, no. 3. © 1980 by The Regents of the University of California.

analysis, the international company should pay close attention to the level of nationalism in a country, the country of origin stereotypes, and the competence level of the purchasing function to deal with international suppliers.

GOVERNMENT MARKETS

A large number of international business transactions involve governments. For example, 80 percent of all international trade of agricultural products is handled by governments. The U.S. government buys more goods and services than any other government, business, industry, or organization in the world.[21] Selling to governments can be both time consuming and frustrating. However governments are large purchasers and selling to them can provide enormous returns.

The size of government purchases depends on the economic or political orientation of the country. In highly developed, free-market countries, the government has less of a role than in state-controlled markets, like the U.S.S.R., where all buying is under direct control of the state. Less-developed countries lack the economic infrastructure to facilitate private companies, thus governments play a major role in overseeing the purchase of foreign products. The amount of government purchases is also a function of state-owned operations. For example, in the United States, the only government-owned operation is the postal system, whereas in India, the government not only owns the postal system, but also the telecommunications, electric, gas, oil, coal, railway, airline, and shipbuilding industries.

The Buying Process

Governmental buying processes tend to be highly bureaucratic. In order to sell to the U.S. Department of Defense, a firm has to get on a bidding list for each branch of the armed forces. These bidding lists are issued on an annual basis; thus, if a firm is not able to get on the list, it must wait a full year to try again.

Governments make it harder for a foreign firm to sell to them; many place their own domestic firms ahead of foreign operations. Also, negotiating with foreign governments can be a very formal process. Understanding cultural differences is essential in order not to overstep boundaries.

Government procurement processes vary from country to country. The following sections describe purchasing processes in Belgium, the European Community, China, and state controlled economies.

Marketing to the Belgian Government[22]   In Belgium, 90 percent of all public contracts are awarded to the lowest bidder. The remaining 10 percent are granted

---

21. *Selling to the Government Markets: Local, State, Federal* (Cleveland: Government Product News, 1975), p. 2.

22. The information in this section has been drawn from Business International, "How to Sell to Belgium's Public Sector," *Business Europe,* October 2, 1981, pp. 314–315.

through "invitation to tender," where factors other than price are taken into consideration. These other factors may include the company's financial viability, technical competence, and post-sale service. Central government supplies, excluding data processing and telecommunications, must be bought through the Central Supplies Office. Regional, local, and quasi-governmental bodies, such as Sabena Airlines, purchase supplies independently. Here are several recommendations to companies that wish to sell to the Belgian government:

- Manufacture in Belgium. Preference is given to a local supplier if other things are equal.
- Develop a European image. A strong EC image has favored companies such as Siemens and Philips.
- Use the appropriate language. Although both Flemish and French are officially accepted, ask which is preferred in the department that is accepting the bid.
- Emphasize the recruitment of labor following the winning of a contract. Companies are favored if they will employ Belgian people.
- When new technology is involved, get in at the beginning. It is often difficult and expensive for the government to change to a different technology at a later date.
- Whenever possible, use local contractors. The Belgian government likes a bidder to use as many local contractors as possible.

Obviously, bidding for Belgian government work is particularly difficult for suppliers with no local participation of subcontractors or manufacturing in Belgium or the EC. However, every government market has some limitations.

Public Procurement in European Community   One of the major objectives of the 1992 Single European Market is the opening up of the public procurement markets in the European Community. Public procurement made up 15.5 percent of Gross European Product. Governments of Europe are only importing a small portion of their total consumption. Governments made almost no foreign purchases unless the goods were unavailable in local markets. For example, in 1988 the U.K. government only imported .4 percent of its requirements, in Italy it was .3 percent, in France 1.6 percent, and in Belgium 2.6 percent.[23] The European Community has actively encouraged its members to open up their government markets for the following reasons:

1. It will reduce costs of public utilities, transportation, and telecommunications through competitive bidding.

---

23. Bernard Cova and Philippe Cova, "ECC Public Procurement Directives: Dropping Competitive Values," *European Management Journal,* September 1990, p. 334.

2. The cost of public administration will decline, therefore taxes and inflation will be reduced.

3. Companies supplying government will become more cost competitive, and their opportunity to serve customers outside the community will, therefore, be improved.

4. Open procurement will increase GDP by .5 percent and create 400,000 new jobs.[24]

To implement an open procurement policy the EC has issued a number of directives. For example, all EC governments have agreed to remove restrictions on the purchasing of materials and to open bidding of public works projects. There is still some resistance of EC members to open up bidding on sensitive defense-related projects.

Marketing to the Chinese Government   Before 1978, China had a simple system whereby all purchasing was delegated by the Ministry of Foreign Trade to the large state trading companies. Negotiations took place at the biannual Canton Trade Fair between the state trading companies and the importers.[25] There was minimal, if any, contact with the respective province end-user, and after-sale service was nonexistent.[26]

By 1979, this structure was decentralized, giving the authority for importing to the various ministries. Most of these ministries established their own trading companies. Also major factories were given authority to deal directly with foreigners. This means that foreign businesses can now deal with either a trading corporation of one of the ministries or with the end-user. Also, the power to conduct trade has been granted to provinces and municipalities.

Although businesspersons have a wider range of contacts than they did in the 1950s, they must make sure that the project they are interested in is being handled by the correct organization. Provinces are still not given carte blanche in what they can do, and they are generally placed under some sort of financial limit.[27] Thus, although contact is easier, coordination between contacts is harder. Figure 6.8 shows the various Chinese government organizations that are responsible for developing trade. As can be seen in the figure, some ministries may conflict with others. For example, the China National Technical Import Export Corporation may conflict with the China National Instruments Corporation.

The Chinese government has given the international company numerous gov-

24. James W. Dudley, *1992 Strategies for the Single Market* (London: Kogan Page, 1989), p. 38.

25. Judith Lubman, "The Helps and Hindrances of Decentralization," *Financial Times,* October 19, 1983, p. IX, China Section.

26. Adam Williams, "Picking a Way Through the Maze," *Financial Times,* October 19, 1983, p. IX, China Section.

27. Ibid.

FIGURE 6.8 ● The Chinese Trade Ministry and Its Subsidiary Import Export Corporations

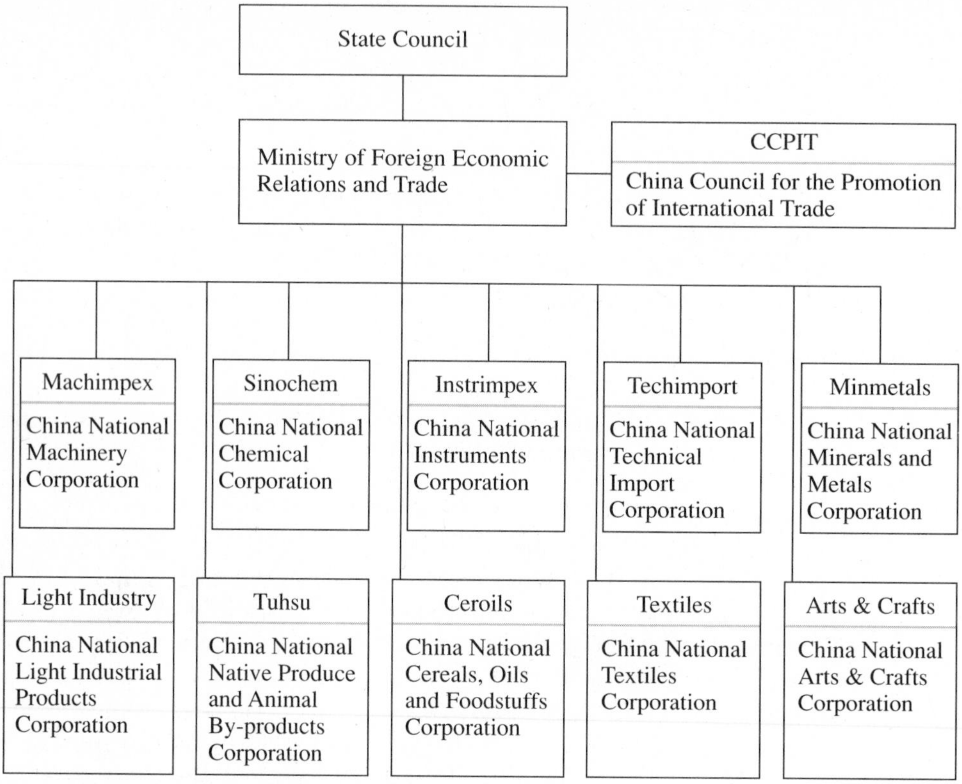

```
                        ┌──────────────────────┐
                        │    State Council     │
                        └──────────┬───────────┘
                                   │
         ┌─────────────────────────┴──────┬──────────────────────────────┐
┌────────────────────────────┐   ┌───────────────────────────────────┐
│ Ministry of Foreign Economic│   │              CCPIT                 │
│ Relations and Trade         │   │ China Council for the Promotion    │
│                             │   │ of International Trade             │
└────────────┬────────────────┘   └───────────────────────────────────┘
```

Machimpex	Sinochem	Instrimpex	Techimport	Minmetals
China National Machinery Corporation	China National Chemical Corporation	China National Instruments Corporation	China National Technical Import Corporation	China National Minerals and Metals Corporation

Light Industry	Tuhsu	Ceroils	Textiles	Arts & Crafts
China National Light Industrial Products Corporation	China National Native Produce and Animal By-products Corporation	China National Cereals, Oils and Foodstuffs Corporation	China National Textiles Corporation	China National Arts & Crafts Corporation

Source: Adam Williams, "Picking a Way Through the Maze," *Financial Times,* October 19, 1983, p. IX—China Section. Reprinted by permission.

ernment organizations to negotiate with on national and provincial levels. The businessperson approaching China today must be aware of these increased options and be alert to the potential confusion between central and provincial organizations, and then pick his or her contacts very carefully.

Although most governments purchase airplanes, office supplies, and military equipment, even the sale of products such as Avon facial cream and Heinz baby food must be negotiated with the Chinese government. After three years of negotiation, Avon reached an agreement to sell one of its 700 products in Chinese department stores.[28] H. J. Heinz recently signed a joint venture agreement with the General Cor-

28. "Avon Adds China to Its List of Foreign Markets," *Marketing News,* October 15, 1982, p. 1.

poration of Agriculture, Industry, and Commerce to build a baby-food factory in Guanghou. The president and CEO of Heinz stated, "This is a tremendous growth opportunity . . . the U.S. produces 3.5 million babies per year. China produces 16 million."[29] After two years of negotiation with the Ministry of Light Industry, Coca-Cola Company reached an agreement for Coke to be sold in China.[30]

Authorities offer the following suggestions for marketing to the Chinese government:

- Before going to China, conduct research with other companies, the Department of Commerce, and other consultants to determine the correct Chinese organization to approach.
- If possible bring your own translator.
- Be patient. The Chinese as negotiators are not in a hurry. Chinese negotiators want to show their superiors they are shrewd negotiators.
- Physical distribution is a critical limitation in China. The road system is poor; the airlines are used to transport people not cargo; and the national rail and water transportation systems are for bulk food, coal, and building materials. Be sure to discuss the transportation and distribution of your product in China with your trading partner.
- Repatriation of profits is extremely difficult since China has a limited supply of hard currency. Products, agreements, and joint ventures that will increase China's exports will help improve the likelihood of getting profits out of the country.
- Recognize the importance of good *guanxi* (connections). The trade representative in the U.S. Embassy can help you establish relationships with people who can help with all the difficulties of doing business in China, such as getting a hotel room, arranging travel, getting to the correct ministry, and so on.[31]

Doing business in China is complex and requires an understanding of the culture and the process of management decision making in China. The events of 1989 illustrate China's strong commitment to socialism and rejection of capitalism. To be successful in China, cross-cultural training is very important in order to understand the cultural factors of guanxi, face, deference to age, group orientation, and primacy of the Party.[32]

29. "Heinz, China Agree on Baby Food Plant," *Wall Street Journal,* September 4, 1984, p.5.
30. Joseph O. Eastlack, Jr. and Roberta Lucker, "Is China Moving from Marx to Mastercard?" *Journal of Consumer Marketing,* Summer 1986, p. 9.
31. Ibid., pp. 14–17.
32. Gregory E. Osland, "Doing Business in China: A Framework for Cross Cultural Understanding," *Marketing Intelligence and Planning,* vol. 8, no. 4 (1990), pp. 4-14.

Marketing to State Controlled Economies[33]   COMECON countries (Cuba, Bulgaria, Czechoslovakia, Hungary, Mongolia, Poland, Romania, the U.S.S.R., and Vietnam) share common political and economic ideals. Although these countries together are a vast market, dealing with these countries is extremely difficult.

As the Berlin Wall came down in late 1990, extraordinary political and economic reforms have opened up the market of the U.S.S.R. and Eastern Europe. This market of 430 million people accounted for over 15 percent of world GNP in 1989.[34] A survey of U.S. executives revealed that 68 percent felt their companies would be conducting more business with the U.S.S.R. over the next two years. Seventy-seven percent reported that Eastern Europe was a major market, which would be comparable to Western Europe within twenty years.[35]

While Eastern Europe offers great opportunities, it is not without major difficulties. The transformation of a socialist system to a market system is a difficult one. Eastern Europe has poor transportation and communications systems. There is limited knowledge of contract laws, accounting, or management. Given these deficiencies, it will be difficult to set up and operate businesses in Eastern Europe in the near future.

It will also be difficult to export to Eastern Europe in the near term. First, the governments have restrictions on payment in hard currency. Second, Coordinating Committee for Multilateral Export Controls (COCOM) puts limits on the export of advanced technology products to Eastern Europe, thus the potential market for defense products is limited. Given the reduced security threat of Eastern Europe, COCOM is expected to reduce its restrictions. For example, Digital Equipment Corporation, which has been unable to ship state of the art computers to Eastern Europe, has been given permission to sell to Hungary.[36]

Direct investment in Eastern Europe is another way to enter the market. As most countries do not want to give foreign companies access without retaining some control, direct investment often requires a joint venture. There were 3,345 joint venture agreements between COMECON countries and Western countries in place in 1989. The increase in joint ventures is fueled by Eastern Europe's interest in acquiring hard currency and the West's interest in getting into this new market before it takes off. Also, the first companies into Eastern Europe may benefit from the development of brand recognition. There are a number of Western products that already have strong brand recognition in Eastern Europe. A survey of 600 Soviets, Czechs, Poles, Yugoslavs, East Germans, and Hungarians revealed strong brand recognition.

---

33. The information in this section is drawn from John A. Quelch, Erich Joachimsthalen, and Jose Luis Nueno, "After the Wall: Marketing Guidelines for Eastern Europe," *Sloan Management Review* (Winter 1991), pp. 82–93.

34. Ibid. p. 82.

35. M. Alput, "Wary Hope on Eastern Europe," *Fortune,* January 29, 1990, pp. 125–126.

36. A. Cane, "DEC Secures First Base in Eastern Europe," *Financial Times,* February 13, 1990, p. 18.

The top twelve products were as follows:

Product	*Country*
1. Pepsi	U.S.
2. Coke	U.S.
3. Nescafé	Switzerland
4. Nivea Cream	Germany
5. Chanel Perfumes	France
6. Levi's Jeans	U.S.
7. Johnnie Walker	U.S.
8. Maggi/Knorr Soups	Switzerland/U.S.
9. Guinness Books of Records	Britain
10. McDonald's	U.S.
11. Philips Electronics	U.S.
12. Gillette Razor Blades	U.S.[37]

Surprisingly the top twelve most recognized brands did not include any Japanese products; Sony, Panasonic, Hitachi, and Toshiba placed fourteenth to seventeenth by Eastern European consumers.

Marketing products in Eastern European markets requires minimal adaptation. While East Europeans will not accept low quality obsolete goods, there is a demand for mass market, good quality products. Western brand names should be retained. Many consumers are familiar with the brands and view them favorably. Of course, usage instructions need to be in the local language. Distribution systems in many East European countries are weak, so it is suggested they be located initially in major cities. Television advertising is not considered trustworthy by most citizens, therefore, advertisements should be straightforward and factual. Trade shows are a popular way to communicate with both consumers and industrial buyers. Colgate-Palmolive found that Moscow consumers would wait for hours to receive free samples and information on Colgate's products. Industrial companies can be reached through the international trade fairs held in Leipzig, Budapest, and other industrial centers.

There are different strategies to organize marketing efforts for Eastern Europe. One approach is to have one European headquarters for all of Europe. For example, Digital has its Eastern European staff in its European headquarters. This assures that the entire European strategy is consistent. Another approach is to locate the Eastern European staff in the international headquarters. There is usually a staff of people experienced in joint ventures, negotiations, and sophisticated financial arrangements in the international headquarters. A third approach is to locate the

37. "East Rates West," *Fortune,* January 28, 1991, p. 10. © 1991 The Time Inc. Magazine Company. All rights reserved. Original market research study done by MIA.

sales staff in Austria or Switzerland. These countries are well located to serve Eastern Europe, but overcome the difficulty of having executives live in poorly developed Eastern European countries.

The long-term opportunities in Eastern Europe are great, but they should not be exaggerated in the short term. While U.S. trade with Eastern Europe has increased from $2.5 billion in 1987 to $6.5 billion in 1989, it still only accounts for 3 percent of trade. Given the lack of an infrastructure, the lack of hard currency, and difficulty of switching from a centrally controlled to a market economy, the opportunities should be considered for the long term.

Economic and Political Needs of Governments

Firms involved in selling to foreign governments must not only have an understanding of the political and economic structures, they must also be able to evaluate a country's industrial trends vis-à-vis the national system. Factors to be considered involve what the government's responsibility is to industry; what the government priorities are; national defense; high-tech, industrial efficiency; and financial self-sufficiency. The level of economic development involves not only the GNP but the state of production. China, for example, is pushing for modernization but does not want production techniques at the expense of its large labor pool. The desire to lessen unemployment is a major interest to most countries. Governments are also confronted with balance of payments problems. Trade deficits—importing more than exporting—will affect the position of a country's currency with respect to foreign currencies. The more the government imports, the more expensive the products become because the government must use more foreign exchange.

Governments tend to protect their domestic industry to reduce high unemployment and GNP deficits. Whether products are for consumer, industrial, or government use, protection in the form of tariffs, subsidiaries, and quotas are levied if domestic industries are threatened. Because the government looks out for its domestic companies, they will stay clear of those products and services for which restrictions are imposed.

Protection of domestic products and services extends beyond that imposed by foreign governments. The threat of reducing national security has governments of domestic firms employing restrictions on various products. The transfer of technology such as nuclear plants, computers, telecommunications, or military weapons is usually restricted so that these critical technologies do not get into the wrong hands.

CONCLUSIONS

If an international firm wants to succeed, it must know who the potential buyer is and how this buyer will make the decision to purchase. Consumers can be radically different from country to country because of their ability to buy and their cultural preferences.

The largest business markets for U.S. goods are in countries that have a sophisticated industrial infrastructure, such as Canada, Japan, Germany, and England. These countries have a large industrial base, a financial basis, and a transportation network. These countries are large importers and exporters of goods and services.

Developing countries offer a different type of market opportunity. They have specific economic needs that must be met with limited financial resources. In these situations the government is likely to get involved in the purchase process, offering concessions to get the correct product or agreement. In many cases the government will be the decision maker.

As international firms evaluate different consumer, business, and government market opportunities, they must be aware of the nature of the differences between countries.

Questions for Discussion

1. What are the critical factors that influence a consumer's ability to purchase a product such as a stereo system?

2. Given the data on family decision making in the United States and Venezuela in Table 6.3, how will the marketing of automobiles be different in the two countries?

3. What causes the large difference in washing products (shown in Table 6.5) in Argentina, Australia, Italy, and Spain?

4. If you were marketing typewriters worldwide, how would the stages of economic development influence the marketing mix?

5. Will the buying process be more similar from country to country for deodorant or delivery vans? Why?

6. If selling a product like nuclear power plants, which are purchased mostly by governments, how would a marketer prepare to sell to Belgium, Egypt, or Mexico? What process should be used to understand the government buying process in each of these countries?

For Further Reading

Bilkey, Warren J., and Erik Nes. "Country-of-Origin: Effects on Product Evaluation." *Journal of International Business Studies,* Spring/Summer 1982, pp. 89–99.

Bonoma, Thomas, and Benson Shapiro. *Segmenting the Industrial Market.* Lexington, Mass.: D.C. Heath, 1983.

Green, Robert T., and Eric Langeard. "A Cross-National Comparison of Consumer Habits and Innovator Characteristics." *Journal of Marketing,* July 1975, pp. 34–41.

Guthery, Dennis Alan. "Income and Social Class as Indicators of Buyer Behavior in an Advanced LDC: A Case Study of Durable Good Purchases in Porto Alegre, Brazil." A paper presented at the Academy of International Business Annual Meeting, Washington, D.C., 1982.

Mitchell, Vincent W., and Michael Grentorex. "Consumer Purchasing in Foreign Countries: A Perceived Risk Perspective." *International Journal of Advertising,* vol. 9, no. 4 (1990), pp. 295–307.

Moriarty, Rowland T. *Industrial Buying Behavior.* Lexington, Mass.: D.C. Heath, 1983.

Papadopoulos, Nicolas, Louise A. Heslop and Jozsef Beracs. "National Stereotypes and Product Evaluation in a Socialist Country." *International Marketing Review,* vol. 7, no. 1 (1990), pp. 32–47.

Poser, Gunter, and Zoher Shipchandler. "Impact of Inflation on Consumer Life Style." *European Journal of Marketing,* vol. 13, no. 3 (1979), pp. 103–112.

Quelch, John, Erich Joachimsthalen and Jose Luis Nueno. "After the Wall: Marketing Guidelines for Eastern Europe." *Sloan Management Review,* vol. 32, no. 2 (Winter 1991), pp. 82–93.

Shipchandler, Zoher. "Change in Demand for Consumer Goods in International Markets." In Subhash Jain and Lewis Tooker, Jr., eds. *International Marketing.* 2nd ed. Boston: Kent, 1986.

Shipchandler, Zoher. "Keeping Down with the Joneses: Stagflation and Buyer Behavior." *Business Horizons,* vol. 25, no. 6 (1982), pp. 32–38.

Tillinghast, Charles C. Jr. "Competing Against State-Owned Enterprises." Paper presented at the Academy of International Business Annual Meeting, Las Vegas, June 1979.

Vernon, Ivan R. "The International Aspects of State Owned Enterprises." *Journal of International Business Studies* (Winter 1979), pp. 7–15.

International and Global Marketing Research

● **PREVIOUSLY, WE INTRODUCED** *you to a variety of consumers, markets, and environments. Our main purpose in Chapter 7 is to provide you with a method for collecting the appropriate data and a framework in which to analyze the environment, the market, and the consumers for your product. Figure 7.1 is an overview of international market research.*

Although this chapter is written around the research issues in an international environment, our emphasis is a managerial one rather than a technical one. Throughout the chapter, we focus on how companies can obtain the useful and accurate information that will help them to make more informed strategic and marketing decisions described in later chapters.

THE SCOPE OF INTERNATIONAL MARKETING RESEARCH

International marketing research is meant to provide adequate data and cogent analysis for effective decision making on a global scale. In contrast to marketing research that has a domestic focus, international research covers a multitude of environments, and there is a scarcity of comparable, relevant data. Because of this, in many cases, flexibility, resourcefulness, and ingenuity on the part of the researcher are required in order to overcome the numerous obstacles encountered in carrying out the research task.

The analytical research techniques practiced by domestic businesses also apply to international marketing projects. The key difference is in the complexity of

FIGURE 7.1 ● International Marketing Research and Analysis

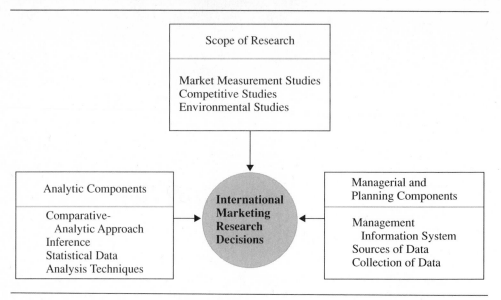

assignments due to the additional variables that must be dealt with. Global marketers have to judge the comparability of their data across a number of markets. They frequently are faced with making decisions based on limited data. As a result, international marketing research can aptly be described as making the best out of limited resources. Traditionally, marketing research has been charged with the following three broad areas of responsibility:

1. *Market Measurement Studies.* One of the most frequent tasks of researchers is to determine the size of a market or its potential as well as a firm's sales potential. Included in this area are sales forecasts for a product. A firm's expected sales for a product in a country or set of countries is an important input into the development of an international marketing program.

2. *Competitive Studies.* To provide insights about competitors, both domestic and foreign, is an important assignment for the international marketing researcher. The researcher must study the general competitive behavior of industries in the various markets within which the firm will compete.

3. *Environmental Studies.* Given the added environmental complexity of global marketing, managers need factual and timely input on the international environment—particularly relating to the economic, political, and legal elements of the potential markets.

International marketing research is used to make both strategic and tactical decisions. Strategic decisions include the selection of what markets to enter, how to

TABLE 7.1 ● International Marketing Decisions Requiring Marketing Research

Marketing mix decision	Type of research
Product policy decisions	Focus groups and qualitative research to generate ideas for new products
	Survey research to evaluate new product ideas
	Concept testing, test marketing
	Product benefit and attitude research
	Product formulation and feature testing
Pricing decisions	Price sensitivity studies
Distribution decisions	Survey of shopping patterns and behavior
	Consumer attitudes to different store types
	Survey of distributor attitudes and policies
Advertising decisions	Advertising pretesting
	Advertising posttesting, recall scores
	Surveys of media habits
Sales promotion decisions	Surveys of response to alternative types of promotion
Sales force decisions	Tests of alternative sales presentations

Source: Susan P. Douglas and C. Samuel Craig, *International Marketing Research,* © 1983, p. 32. Reprinted by permission of Prentice-Hall, Inc., Englewood Cliffs, New Jersey.

enter the markets (exporting licensing, joint venture), and where to locate production facilities. Tactical decisions are decisions about the specific marketing mix to be used in a country. Table 7.1 shows the various types of tactical marketing decisions and the types of research used to collect the necessary data.

New product development or product adaptation will require product benefit research and product testing to meet environmental conditions, customer tastes, and competitive constraints. Advertising, sales promotion, and sales force decisions will all require data from the local market in the form of testing. The type of information required is often the same as that required in domestic marketing research, but the process is more complex due to the variety of cultures and environments.

THE IMPORTANCE OF INTERNATIONAL MARKETING RESEARCH

The complexity of the international marketplace, the extreme differences that exist from country to country, and the frequent lack of familiarity with foreign markets accentuate the importance of international marketing research. Before making market entry, product position, or market mix decisions, accurate information is needed about the market size, market needs, competition, and so on. Marketing research provides the necessary information to avoid the costly mistakes of poor strategies or lost opportunities.

Marketing research can guide product development for a foreign market. Based on a research study conducted in the United States, one U.S. firm introduced a new cake mix in England. Believing that homemakers wanted to feel that they participated in the preparation of the cake, the U.S. marketers devised a mix that required homemakers to add an egg. Given the success in the U.S. market, the marketers confidently introduced the product in England. The product failed, however, because the British did not like the fancy American cakes. They preferred cakes that were tough and spongy and could accompany afternoon tea. The technique of having homemakers add an egg to the mix did not eliminate basic taste and stylistic differences.[1]

CHALLENGES IN PLANNING INTERNATIONAL RESEARCH

International marketing researchers face the following five principal challenges:

1. Complexity of research design
2. Lack of secondary data
3. Costs of collecting primary data
4. Coordination of research and data collection across countries
5. Difficulty of establishing comparability and equivalence[2]

While domestic research is limited to one country, international research includes many countries. The research design is made more complex because in defining the possible target market, the researcher must choose which countries or segments should be researched. This initial step in the research process is further complicated by the fact that there is limited secondary information. Even if the appropriate secondary information exists, it may be difficult to locate and acquire. Thus researchers are forced either to spend considerable resources finding such data or to accept the limited secondary data that is available. In many countries, the cost of collecting primary data is substantially higher than in the domestic market. This is particularly the case for developing countries. Consequently, researchers have to make tradeoffs between the need for more accurate data and the limited resources available to accomplish the tasks.

Even gathering demographics from country to country is no easy task. There are a wide variety of problems with using national census data. For example, the United States census is taken every ten years. Canada and Japan do one every five years. Germany did one in 1987, twenty-seven years after its previous census in

1. David A. Ricks, *Big Business Blunders: Mistakes in Multinational Marketing* (Homewood, Ill.: Dow Jones—Irwin, 1983), pp. 129–130.

2. Susan P. Douglas and C. Samuel Craig, *International Marketing Research* (Englewood Cliffs, N.J.: Prentice Hall, 1983), pp. 16–19.

1960. While the United States, Canada, Australia, New Zealand, Mexico, Sweden, and Finland collect income data, most countries do not. Educational levels can be used to determine socioeconomic status, but educational systems vary widely from country to country making comparisons very crude. Switzerland and Germany publish data on noncitizens. Canada collects data on religion. Both these topics are excluded from the U.S. census. Marital status and head of household information vary from country to country. Ireland only recognizes single, married, or widowed. Latin America often combines cohabiting with marital categories. These major differences from country to country make even the simplest demographic analysis very challenging.[3]

Because companies can ill afford for each subsidiary to obtain its own expensive primary data, coordination of research and data collection across countries becomes necessary. Companies that can successfully manage this task will be in a situation to avoid costly duplication of research. The borrowing of research results from one country to another is hindered by the general difficulty of establishing comparability and equivalence among various research data. Definitions of housewives, socioeconomic status, incomes, and customers vary widely in Europe, even where the research is measuring the same thing.[4] Full comparability can only be achieved when identical procedures are used. A recent study found that, even with the same scales measuring the same attributes of products, different cultures exhibit different degrees of reliability due to different levels of awareness, knowledge, and familiarity.[5] With research capabilities differing from country to country, global marketing research administration becomes a real challenge. Along with all the problems of data collection and comparability, balancing between the needs of the national subsidiaries and the headquarters of the multinationals can pose a challenge. Market research agencies report that treading the diplomatic path between head office staff and national subsidiaries of multinational firms is probably the biggest problem they face on global research projects. This obstacle is increasingly recognized as companies make the conceptual switch to treating Europe as a single market.[6]

A CONCEPTUAL FRAMEWORK FOR INTERNATIONAL MARKET RESEARCH: THE COMPARATIVE ANALYTIC APPROACH

In the first part of this chapter we discussed the scope of marketing research situations and the difficulties encountered in conducting research. Although an understanding of the difficulties of collecting information for foreign markets helps to increase the quality of information obtained, an overall conceptual framework is necessary to

3. Donald B. Pittenger, "Gathering Foreign Demographics Is No Easy Task," *Marketing News,* January 8, 1991, p. 23.
4. Tom Lester, "Common Markets," *Marketing,* November 9, 1989, p. 41.
5. Ravi Parameswaran and Attila Yaprak, "A Cross-National Comparison of Consumer Research Measures," *Journal of International Business Studies,* Spring 1987, p. 45.
6. Robin Cobb, "Client Diplomacy," *Marketing,* May 17, 1990, p. 31.

provide the analyst with the relevant questions to ask. Consequently, this section of the chapter focuses on building a framework that can guide international marketing managers in the formulation of market research studies.

Pioneered by T. A. Hagler in the late 1950s, comparative research actually led to the establishment of international marketing as a discipline.[7] Comparative marketing focuses on the entire marketing system, but this macro approach becomes less important as specific problems at the company level need to be analyzed. However, the comparative approach can be adapted to specific micro-marketing problems.

Marketing as a Function of the Environment

The comparative marketing analysis emphasizes the study of the marketing process in its relationship to the environment. The marketing process is viewed as a direct function of environment. Under changed environmental conditions, the existing marketing processes are also expected to change. In a dual-country analysis employing the comparative approach, the marketing environment in one country is investigated with respect to its effect on the marketing process. The resulting functional relationship is transferred to a second country whose environment may be known but whose marketing process will be assessed based on the earlier analysis of the relationship between the marketing process and the environment in another country.

This situation is illustrated in Figure 7.2.[8] The comparative marketing analysis allows the researcher to understand the relationship between the environment and the marketing process in one country and then to transfer that knowledge to another country, *adjusting* for differences in the environment.

An Example: McDonald's   We can illustrate this concept by using McDonald's as an example. A tremendous success in the United States (the home country), McDonald's obtained its success by way of an aggressive and well-structured marketing mix. The elements may be described as follows:

Product/Service Design. A standardized product of high and consistent quality emphasizing speed of service and long opening hours.

Price. A low price policy.

Distribution. Placing restaurants in areas where customers primarily live— suburban and urban locations.

Promotion. A strong advertising campaign that focuses on the consumer, particularly young people, via heavy use of television promotion.

---

7. Jean Boddeyn, "A Framework for Comparative Marketing Research," *Journal of Marketing Research,* May 1966, pp. 149–153; and *Comparative Management and Marketing.* (Glenview, Ill.: Scott, Foresman, 1969).

8. Jean-Pierre Jeannet, "International Marketing Analysis: A Comparative-Analytic Approach," working paper, 1981.

**FIGURE 7.2 ● ** Managerial Approach to Comparative Analysis

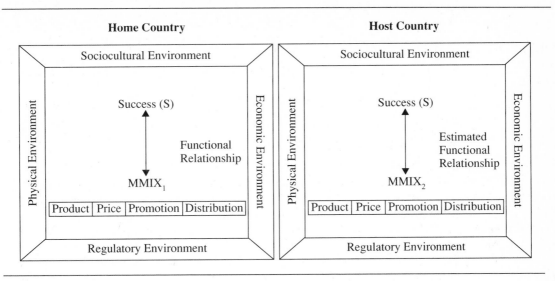

With this marketing mix, McDonald's has been extremely successful in the United States. In the early 1970s, several other countries were targeted for possible expansion and an assessment had to be made as to the best approach for McDonald's to pursue. The traditional approach views success in the United States as a function of McDonald's effective marketing strategy or as a direct result of the company's own efforts. The comparative-analytic approach advanced here, however, views McDonald's success as a function of a given set of marketing mix variables that are effective due to the country's environment. This view puts the main emphasis on the environmental variables that allowed McDonald's marketing mix to be successful.

The difference between the two approaches is important. The comparative-analytic view sees McDonald's primarily as having been able to take advantage of an existing opportunity, whereas the traditional approach views McDonald's success primarily as a direct result of its own efforts.

Viewing the Marketing Mix as a Function of the Environment   Viewing the marketing mix as a function of the existing environment emphasizes an environmental view of the marketing process.[9] The emphasis now is on the existing environment that enables a given marketing mix to be successful. This view is of great importance, since success is no longer defined as unilateral or solely a function of the marketing mix. Thus, the company is viewed as taking advantage of a given opportunity rather

9. Robert Bartels, "Are Domestic and International Marketing Dissimilar?" *Journal of Marketing,* July 1968, pp. 56–61.

than creating one by its own actions. The first step is to look at the environmental factors.

Understanding the Components of the Marketing Environment

The critical environmental variables may be grouped into four major categories: physical, social, economic, and regulatory.

Physical Environmental Variables   Included in this category are the physical constraints with respect to the conditions of the product's use or the physical properties of the particular market. These are population, population density, geographic area, climate, and the physical conditions of the product's use (surroundings, space and size requirements, and so on). Variables such as population have an effect on the absolute size of any target market and, similar to climate, tend to be subject to little change over time. The physical use conditions relate to a product's function in any given environment. As a result, we view the consumption of the product or service as a *physical event* directly influenced by physical environmental variables that have to be recognized to determine a marketing mix.

Turning again to the McDonald's example, several variables from the physical environment have contributed toward McDonald's success in the United States. An important influence on McDonald's distribution or location policies was the concentration of the U.S. population in suburbia. Opening 4,000 units in the United States was possible due to the absolute size of the population, which is about 248 million people. It is important to recognize that the market size is often finite, and that any country with a different population would, of course, not offer the same opportunities, all things being equal. The physical use conditions of McDonald's are less restrictive because they are directly shaped by the firm's policies and the building of outlets. The situation is different in cases where consumers take products home for consumption and are restricted by their own physical environments, such as apartment or kitchen size.

Social Environmental Variables   This category includes all relevant factors from the social and cultural background of any given marketing environment, including: cultural background (race, religion, customs, habits, and languages), the educational system, and social structure (the individual roles, family structure, social classes, and reference groups).

As we have mentioned before, the social environment is a primary influence on the role expectations of buyers and sellers, regardless of the differences in the physical environment. Since the social environment does not change rapidly over time, many domestic marketers can lose sight of the fact that they've subconsciously chosen a marketing mix that incorporates many social values. Defining the social forces that impact on a marketing mix is the first step in shedding the cultural bias that affects so many managers unknowingly.

In the case of McDonald's there were several social and cultural forces that greatly affected its success. For one, the value that U.S. society placed on time favored the consumption of meals with minimum time effort. Saving time, in fact, created the desire for meals purchased outside the home on an unplanned or impulse basis. The result was a burgeoning demand for low-priced food that was available any time and that could be purchased with minimum shopping effort. Another important factor was the prevailing family structure in the United States and the trend towards a youth-oriented culture. In the 1960s and 1970s, the decision-making role had been changed to such an extent that often children made the selection of a place to eat. McDonald's special emphasis on children and teenagers as advertising targets has been successful largely because the strategy capitalized on these existing social trends.

The changing role of the wife in the typical, U.S. household has resulted in an ever-increasing number of women accepting employment outside the home. Whether this resulted in a lower valuation of the home-cooked meal in a social sense is debatable; nevertheless, it greatly increased the acceptability of eating meals outside the home as compared to home-cooked meals.

Not to be underestimated is the habit or heritage of the hamburger itself. Truly, the hamburger represents a long-standing tradition of the U.S. food and restaurant scene, and hamburger made up the daily meal of many Americans before McDonald's arrived on the scene. It is fair to state, then, that the product's success stemmed, to a considerable degree, from the selection of an already existing and widely popular product. Aside from the type of service, the product did not represent an innovation. Of course, there are other reasons for dining out, and U.S. customers often make other choices, but the social and cultural influences to a large extent prepared the ground for the success of an operation such as McDonald's.

What is important then is to isolate the salient social and cultural variables that have an impact on the success of a company's products or services. The combined sociocultural variables create the *sociocultural event* that becomes an essential part of the consumption and use of any product or service. Understanding the nature of the sociocultural event in one country as the starting point for analyzing the respective variables in another country is the basis of the comparative-analytic model.

Economic Environmental Variables   Under this category we include all aspects of the economic environment, both on a macro- and micro-level, such as GNP, GNP per capita, price levels, income distribution, and prices of competitive products and services.

Economic considerations affect most consumption or buying decisions. To the extent that income levels of consumers differ from country to country, the trade-offs consumers make in order to maximize economic satisfaction are different. Different price levels for products also cause changes in buying behavior even under a constant income level. The international marketer must isolate the specific income and price variables to arrive at a given combination, termed the *economic event,* that affects the success of a given product or service. The analytic-comparative model suggests that the elements and nature of the economic event with regard to a another market can largely be found by first investigating the relevant factors in a company's home market.

For McDonald's, a significant variable of the economic environment was the income level of the U.S. population and the resulting disposable income available for frequent visits to fast-food restaurants. It is still more expensive to frequent a fast-food outlet than to prepare an equivalent meal at home; consequently, the success of fast-food outlets does not so much stem from their price advantage over food purchased in stores. Instead, it was the *relative price advantage* of fast-food restaurants compared to the more traditional or simple diner-type restaurants that ensured their tremendous success. Consuming a meal at a place such as McDonald's becomes an economic event to the extent that economic variables are introduced into the consumer's decision-making process affecting the particular product or service choice.

Regulatory Environmental Variables The regulatory environment includes all actions of governments or agencies influencing business transactions such as commercial law or codes, consumer protection laws, product liability laws, regulatory agencies (for example, the FDA, CAB, or ICC), local regulations, and zoning laws.

Regulations do not tend to stimulate needs or demands for services and products. Instead, they act in an *enabling manner* (or disabling manner, depending on point of view) by restricting choices for the international corporation or prescribing the nature of its marketing effort. Companies have to be aware of the particular regulations that make an existing marketing program effective since such an approach may not be duplicated in other countries, even if it were desirable from a business point of view.

The possible effect of the regulatory environment can be illustrated by turning to our example. Certainly, the use of television advertising to reach children was one of the reasons for McDonald's success in the United States. But in many other countries, particularly those in Europe, such advertising is banned outright. On an operational level, it may be difficult to get teenage help in some countries or impossible to keep operating during hours customary in the United States. Since the United States has in many ways a more liberal regulatory environment, companies often face situations where operations cannot be carried out in the accustomed fashion. This is true even when the target customers in other countries would respond positively to U.S. methods or practices and the relevant physical, economic, and social events indicate that their use would be beneficial.

Analyzing Environmental Variables

The importance of these environmental variables has been emphasized by previous writers with respect to international marketing. Robert Bartels has highlighted physical, social, and economic variables in his environmental marketing concept.[10] Robert Buzzell included a similar set of variables in his analysis of elements that may

10. Ibid.

prevent a standardization of marketing programs across several countries.[11] Furthermore, Warren Keegan has concentrated on the same variables as influencing extension versus adaptation decisions for product design or communications strategy.[12] The comparative-analytic approach is different in that it focuses on the situational and it selects the salient environmental variables that may affect the product's or service's success in any country. Since the selected environmental variables are the ones most clearly related to the success of a product or service in the home country, they can be referred to as *success factors.*

Traditionally, marketers have viewed success factors as variables under marketing management's control. With the comparative-analytic approach, success factors are treated as a function of the environment, which means that success is recognized as a function of a given scenario of outside factors not always subject to management's control. Typically, marketing programs succeed because managements take advantage of opportunities or positive constellations of success factors. Therefore, we are "allowed" to be successful provided we spot the opportunity. This view results in a greater appreciation of the role that environmental variables play in marketing and also tends to avoid traditional tendencies to overestimate the impact of management's own actions in the marketplace.

The comparative-analytical approach provides a methodology for marketers to analyze their success in current markets as a function of the marketing mix and the environment. It also provides an approach for isolating the critical environmental variables. These variables become the focus of the international market research process. In the McDonald's example, the variables we analyzed were population, population density, the family structure, role of the mother, income levels, and the availability of advertising media to reach children. As we look at other countries, we must examine these environmental variables and adjust McDonald's marketing mix appropriately.

THE INTERNATIONAL MARKETING RESEARCH PROCESS

Although conducting marketing research internationally usually adds to the complexity of the research task, the basic approach remains the same for domestic and international assignments. International or domestic market research is a four-step process consisting of the following:

1. Problem definition and development of research objectives

2. Determination of the sources of information

11. Robert D. Buzzell, "Can You Standardize Multinational Marketing?" *Harvard Business Review,* November–December 1968, pp. 102–113.

12. Warren J. Keegan, "Multinational Product Planning: Strategic Alternatives," *Journal of Marketing,* January 1969, p. 58.

3. Collection of the data from primary and secondary sources

4. Analysis of the data and presentation of the results

While these four steps may be the same for both international and domestic research, problems in implementation may occur because of cultural and economic differences from country to country.

Problem Definition and Development of Research Objectives

In any market research project, the most important task is to define what information you are after. This process, which can take weeks or months, determines the choice of methodologies, the types of people you wish to interview, and the appropriate time frame in which to conduct your research.[13]

Problems may not be the same in different countries or cultures. This may reflect differences in socioeconomic conditions, levels of economic development, cultural forces, or the competitive market structure.[14] For example, bicycles in a developed country may be competing with other recreational goods, such as skis, baseball gloves, or exercise equipment; whereas in a developing country, they may be a form of basic transportation competing with small cars, mopeds, and scooters.

The comparative-analytic approach can be used to isolate the critical environmental variables in the home market. These variables should be included in the problem definition and research objectives.

Determination of Sources of Data

For each assignment, researchers may choose to base their analyses on primary data (data collected specifically for this assignment) or use secondary data (already collected and available data). Since costs tend to be higher for research based on primary data, researchers usually exhaust secondary data first. Often called desk research or library research, this approach depends on the availability of material and its reliability. Secondary sources may include government publications, trade journals, and data from international agencies or service establishments such as banks or advertisement agencies. Although a substantial body of data exists from the most advanced industrial nations, secondary data are less available for developing countries. Not every country publishes a census, and some published data are not considered reliable. For example, in Nigeria, the total population is of such political importance that published census data are generally believed to be highly suspect. For reasons such as this, companies sometimes have to proceed with the collection of primary data in developing countries at a much earlier stage than in the most industrialized nations.

13. Michael Brizz, "How to Learn What Japanese Buyers Really Want," *Business Marketing,* January 1987, p. 72.
14. Douglas and Craig, *International Marketing Research,* pp. 16–19.

Data Collection

The collection of data from secondary sources includes the task of calling, writing, or visiting the potential secondary sources. Often, one source will lead to another source until you find the information desired or determine that the information does not exist. A good approach to locating secondary sources is to ask yourself who would know about most sources of information on a specific market. For example, if you wanted to locate secondary information on fibers used for tires in Europe, you may consider asking the editor of a trade magazine on the tire industry, or the executive director of the tire manufacturing association or the company librarian for AKZO, a Dutch company that manufactures fibers. Also, most business libraries will have some type of directory of secondary information such as:

International Directory of Published Research, Vol. 14. London: Arlington Management Publications Limited, 1990.

Directory of U.S. and Canadian Marketing Surveys and Services. Kline Publishing, 1990.

Findex: Directory of Market Research Reports, Studies and Surveys, 1990.

On line databases, microfilm, and compact disks are also excellent sources of information available in most business libraries. Searches on these systems can quickly identify articles, books, and financial information on most business topics, marketing, and companies. Some of these online data sources follow:

Datastream International, Dun and Bradstreet Company

Textline, Reuters Limited

DunsPrint, Dun and Bradstreet

Harvest, Marketing Research, Harvest Information Services

ABI/Inform, University Microfilms, Inc.

Collecting Secondary Data   For any marketing research problem, the analysis of secondary data should be a first step. Although not available for all variables, often data is available from public and private sources at a fraction of the cost for obtaining primary data. It would be impractical to include a listing of all the secondary data sources available on international markets, but some secondary data sources would be banks, consulates, embassies, foreign chambers of commerce, libraries with foreign information sections, foreign magazines, public accounting firms, security brokers, and state development offices in foreign countries. A good business library and the local U.S. Department of Commerce are always good places to start a search for secondary data. Table 7.2 lists some of the major sources of published secondary data.

There are problems associated with the use of secondary data, namely: (1) the lack of necessary data, (2) the level of accuracy of the data, (3) the lack of comparability of the data, and (4) the age of the data. In some cases, no data have been

TABLE 7.2 ● Major Sources of Secondary Data

U.S. DEPT. OF COMMERCE

  Foreign Trade Report (U.S. exports by commodity and by country)

  Global Market Surveys (Global market research on targeted industries)

  Country Market Surveys (Detailed reports on promising countries covering 15 industries)

  Business America (Magazine presenting domestic and international business news)

  Overseas Marketing Report (Prepared for all countries, includes trade forecasts, regulations, and market profiles)

INTERNATIONAL MONETARY FUND

  International Financial Statistics (Monthly report on exchange rates, inflation, deflation, country liquidity, etc.)

NATIONAL TECHNICAL INFORMATION SERVICES

  Market Share Reports (Reports the size of 88 markets and identifies export opportunities)

UNITED NATIONS

  Yearbook of Industrial Statistics (Statistics of minerals, manufactured goods, electricity, and gas)

  Statistical Yearbook (Population, production, education, trade, wages)

  Demographic Yearbook (Population, income, marriages, deaths, literacy)

WORLD BANK

  Country Economic Reports (Macroeconomic and industry trends)

  World Development Report (Population, investment, balance of reports, defense expenditures)

BUSINESS INTERNATIONAL

  Business International Data Base (Economic indicators, GNP, wages, foreign trade, production, and consumption)

EUROMONITOR PUBLICATIONS

  European Marketing Data and Statistics (Population, employment, production, trade, standard of living, consumption, housing, communication)

PREDICASTS

  Worldcasts (Economics, production, utilities)

THE ECONOMIST

  E.I.U. World Outlook (Forecasts of trends for 160 countries)

  Marketing in Europe (Product markets in Europe—food, clothing, furniture, household goods, appliances)

---

collected. For example, in many countries, there is little data on the number of retailers, wholesalers, and distributors. In Ethiopia and Chad, no population statistics are available. The accuracy of the data varies from country to country, with the data from highly industrialized nations likely to be more accurate than data from developing countries.[15] This is a result of the mechanism for collecting data. In industrialized nations, relatively reliable procedures are used for national accounting and for collecting population and industry statistics. In developing countries, where a major portion of the population is illiterate, the data may be based on estimates or rudimentary procedures.

Furthermore, data may not be directly comparable from country to country. The population statistics in the United States are collected every ten years, whereas population statistics in Bolivia are collected every twenty-five years. Also, countries may calculate the same statistic but in different ways. For example, there are a number of indicators of national wealth. Gross National Product (GNP) is the gross value of production in a country. Gross Domestic Product (GDP) is the value of all goods and services produced and is often used in place of GNP. Net material product (NMP) is the measure of national wealth used by communist countries. NMP is based on the Marxian perception of value and productivity which consists of physical production and services related to the delivery of goods like transport. NMP excludes nonproductive services like health, education, banking, and defense. Not only does NMP exclude large amounts of economic activity, but centrally planned economies are not known for accurate statistics. In the past, NMP figures were inflated for political reasons. Recently, countries have deflated estimates to gain preferential custom duties or soft loans from international institutions like the World Bank.

In 1990 *The Economist* examined ten reports on the economies of Eastern Europe. The GDP ranged from $4,000 per person to $13,000 per person for East Germany. The use of gross statistics of national production is very challenging. These crude measures of national wealth can often be very misleading.[16] Finally, the age of the data is a constant problem. Population statistics are usually two to five years old. Industrial production statistics can be one to two years old. With different growth rates, it is difficult to use older data to make decisions.

To test the quality of secondary data, marketers should investigate the following:

1. When was the data collected?

2. How was the data collected?

3. What is the expected level of accuracy?

4. Who collected the data, and for what purpose was it collected?

15. Ibid., p. 79.
16. "Grossly Deceptive Product," *The Economist,* March 10, 1990, p. 99.

If secondary data is not available or usable, the marketer will need to collect primary data. Experienced global researchers indicate that while secondary data may be available, it may sometimes be less expensive in the long run to go directly to potential consumers, distributors, and retailers, than to spend considerable time in libraries, embassies, and trade associations.

Collecting Primary Data   Once secondary sources of information have been exhausted, the next step is to collect primary data that will meet the specific information requirements for making the management decision. Sources of primary data are the people in the target country who will purchase or influence the purchase of products. These are consumers, businesses, or governments. Collecting the appropriate data requires the development of a process to do so. The collection of primary data involves the process of developing a research instrument, selecting a sample, collecting the data, and analyzing the results. These steps are the same in domestic and multinational environments. The process of collecting data in different cultures creates a number of challenges for the international marketer. These challenges include comparability of data, willingness of the potential respondent to participate, and the ability of the respondent to understand and communicate.

Comparability of data is important irrespective of whether research is conducted in a single-country or multi-country context. Research conducted in a single country may be used at a later date to compare with the results of research in another country.[17] For example, if a product is tested in France and is successful, the company may decide to test the Italian market. The test used for the Italian market must be comparable with the test in the French market to assess the possible outcome in Italy.

A second challenge in research is the willingness of the potential respondent. For example, in many cultures a man will consider it inappropriate to discuss his shaving habits with anyone, especially with a female interviewer. Respondents in the Netherlands or Germany are notoriously reluctant to divulge information on their personal financial habits. The Dutch are more willing to discuss sex than money. Through careful planning, researchers can design instruments and techniques to overcome or avoid cultural limitations.[18] For example, in some cultures, it may be necessary to enlist the aid of a local person to obtain cooperation.

Another challenge in survey research involves the translation from one language to another. Translation equivalence is important, first to assure that the respondents understand the question and second to assure that the researcher understands the response. Idiomatic expressions and colloquialisms are often translated incorrectly. For example, the French translation of a *full* airplane became a *pregnant* airplane and in German a *"Body by Fisher"* became a *corpse by Fisher.*[19] In a recent case,

17. Douglas and Craig, *International Marketing Research,* p. 132.
18. Robin Cobb, "Marketing Shares," *Marketing,* February 22, 1990, p. 44.
19. Ricks, *Big Business Blunders,* p. 83.

Braniff found its translation of *to be seated in leather* became *to be seated naked* in Spanish.[20] In order to avoid these translation errors, experts suggest the technique of back-translation.[21] First, the questionnaire is translated from the home language into the language of the country where it will be used by a bilingual who is a native speaker of the foreign country. Then, this version is translated back to the home language by a bilingual who is a native speaker of the home language. Another translation technique is parallel translation, in which two or more translators translate the questionnaire. The results are compared, and differences are discussed and resolved.

Data can be collected by mail, telephone, or face-to-face. The technique for collecting the data will vary by country. The European Society for Opinion and Market Research (ESOMAR) recently reported on interviewing techniques used in Europe. As shown in Table 7.3, face-to-face interviews at home or work are very popular in Switzerland and the United Kingdom, while interviews in shopping areas are popular in France and the Netherlands. Telephone interviewing dominates Swedish data collection.[22] In Japan, it is recommended that personal, face-to-face discussion be used instead of telephone or mail questionnaires.[23] Although personal interviews are expensive and time consuming, the Japanese preference for face-to-face contact suggests that personal interviews yield better information than data collected by mail or telephone. In fact, many Japanese managers are skeptical about Western-style

20. "Braniff, Inc.'s Spanish Ad Bears Cause for Laughter," *Wall Street Journal,* February 9, 1987, p. 5.

21. R. Brislin, "Back-Translation for Cross-Cultural Research," *Journal of Cross Cultural Psychology,* vol. 1 (1970), pp. 185–216.

22. Emanual H. Demby, "ESOMAR Urges Changes in Reporting Demographics, Issues Worldwide Report," *Marketing News,* January 8, 1990, p. 24.

23. Brizz, "How to Learn What Japanese Buyers Really Want," p. 72.

TABLE 7.3 ● Comparison of European Data Collection Methods

	France	*The Netherlands*	*Sweden*	*Switzerland*	*U.K.*
Mail	4%	33%	23%	8%	9%
Telephone	15	18	44	21	16
Central location/streets	52	37	—	—	—
Home/work	—	—	8	44	54
Groups	13	—	5	6	11
Depth interviews	12	12	2	8	—
Secondary	4	—	4	8	—

Source: Emanuel H. Demby, "ESOMAR Urges Changes in Reporting Demographics, Issues Worldwide Report." *Marketing News,* January 8, 1990, p. 24. Reprinted by permission of the American Marketing Association.

marketing research. Senior and middle managers will often go into the field and speak directly with consumers and distributors. This technique of collecting information called "soft-data," though less rigorous than large scale consumer studies, gives the manager a real feel for the market and the consumers.[24]

Another technique for collecting marketing research data is focus groups. The researcher assembles a set of six to twelve carefully selected respondents to discuss a product. The focus group is often used at the early stage of a new product concept to gain valuable insights from potential consumers. The research company assembles the participants and leads the discussion, avoiding the potential bias from a company representative. Of course, the discussion leader must speak in the mother tongue of the participants. Representatives of the company can observe the focus group via video or audio taping, through a one-way mirror or sitting in the room. In some countries such as Japan, it may be difficult to get participants to criticize a potential product. Experienced focus group companies are resourceful at using questioning techniques and interpreting body language to get the full value from this research technique.[25]

Sample Selection   After developing the instrument and converting it to the appropriate language, the researcher will determine the appropriate sample design. Due to its advantage of predicting the margin of error, researchers generally prefer to use probability sampling. The great power of a probability sample lies in the possibility of predicting the corresponding errors: (1) sampling errors or the chance of not receiving a true sample of the group investigated; (2) response errors or the deviation of responses from the facts due to either incorrect recall or unwillingness to tell the truth; and (3) nonresponse errors or uncertainty of the views held by members of the sample that were never reached.[26] For these reasons, probability samples are generally preferred by researchers.

However, in many foreign countries the existing market infrastructure and the lack of available data or information substantially interferes with attempts to use probability samples. Sampling of larger populations requires the availability of detailed census data, called *census tracks,* and maps from which probability samples can be drawn. Where such data is available it is often out of date. Thus, stratification is prevented.[27] Further difficulties arise from inadequate transportation that may pre-

24. Johny K. Johansson and Ikujiro Nonaka, "Market Research the Japanese Way," *Harvard Business Review,* May–June 1987, pp. 16–22.

25. Catherine Bond, "Market Research—Spy in a Corner," *Marketing,* August 17, 1989, p. 35.

26. Paul E. Green and Donald S. Tull, *Research for Marketing Decisions,* 4th ed. (Englewood Cliffs, N.J.: Prentice-Hall, 1978), pp. 111–112.

27. W. Boyd Harper, Jr., Ronald E. Frank, William F. Massy, and Mostafa Zoheir, "On the Use of Marketing Research in the Emerging Economies," *Journal of Marketing Research,* vol. 1 (November 1964), pp. 20–23.

vent field workers from actually reaching selected census tracks in some areas of the country. Sampling is particularly difficult in countries having several spoken languages because it is impractical to carry out a nationwide survey.

Due to the special circumstances of international sampling, Charles Mayer has defined three additional errors over and above those previously described.[28] These are (a) definitional errors, (b) instrument errors, and (c) frame errors.

The *definitional error* is caused by the different ways a research problem may be defined in each country. Conceptual equivalence cannot be automatically assumed because different countries view products in different conceptual terms; bicycles and motorcycles, for example, are viewed as means of transportation in one country and as leisure vehicles in another. When a research project is carried out in several countries, care must be taken to assure definitional equivalence with respect to the product or service considered. In Japan, for instance, noncarbonated fruit drinks are consumed with great frequency as alternatives to soft drinks. In doing a soft drink study in Japan, fruit drinks would have to be included in the list of alternatives, while the same would not necessarily be true in the United States. Consequently, researchers must be careful to consider and define the products in relation to competing products, as they may vary from country to country.

Temporal equivalence may be hard to achieve because time lags may exist between research in the various countries causing additional errors. And finally, market structure equivalence, another source of definitional error, may be caused due to differing market sizes, penetration rates, channel structures, or competition. In a survey conducted in Europe, French and German consumers were reported to have consumed more spaghetti than Italian consumers. This result was caused by asking about the consumption of branded spaghetti only, the typical method of marketing spaghetti in France and Germany. In Italy, most spaghetti was consumed in loose and unbranded form, causing a response that would have to be interpreted with great care.[29]

Instrument error may be caused by either the instrument chosen for data collection or the interviewer involved. The absence of linguistic equivalence is one cause, but this can be achieved through careful translation of the instrument. Also, the participants' perceptions of each other may be different from country to country, making it difficult to reach contextual equivalence. This is particularly the case where perceptions of the social status of either the interviewer or the respondent vary substantially among countries. Of particular importance is the achievement of instrumental equivalence. Researchers must be aware that some survey instruments may not work equally well across countries. Telephone interviews are not reliable where a substantial portion of the society does not own a telephone. In some countries, mail

28. Charles S. Mayer, "Multinational Marketing Research: Methodological Problems," in *International Marketing Strategy,* eds. Hans Thorelli and Helmut Becker (New York: Pergamon Press, 1980), pp. 162–171.

29. Ibid., p. 166.

service is so unreliable that other methods of surveying or data collection have to be used. And finally, response-style equivalence may be difficult to reach because the social conventions in some countries tend to produce more nay-sayers or yea-sayers.

Frame errors are caused by the selection of samples from different sources or lists in each country. Since the same census track data may not be available elsewhere, other public data may be used as a basis to randomly select respondents. Though the sample may be properly arrived at for each country, comparability can be endangered due to the frame error.

INTERNATIONAL MARKETING RESEARCH TECHNIQUES

There are a variety of analytic techniques that can be used in international marketing research. These techniques may be used in domestic marketing research, but they are often modified to deal with the complexities of international markets.

Demand Analysis

Demand for products or services can be measured at two levels: aggregate demand for an entire market or country and company demand as represented by actual sales. The former is generally termed the *market potential* whereas the latter is referred to as *sales potential.* A very useful concept developed by Richard Robinson views both market and sales potential as a filtering process (see Figure 7.3). According to Robinson, demand or potential demand can be measured at six successive levels, the last and final level representing actual sales by the firm.[30] The six levels of demand are explained as follows.

Potential Need   The potential need for a product or service is primarily determined by the demographic and physical characteristics of a country. The determinant factors are a country's population, climate, geography, natural resources, land use, life expectancy, and other factors that we have termed part of the physical environment.

The potential need could only be realized if all consumers in a country used a product to the fullest extent regardless of social, cultural, or economic barriers. This represents the ideal case that actually may never be reached. Of course, the country's consumers would not purchase the product if there were no need. Therefore, the researcher has to pose the question: Is there a potential need, either now or in the future?

Felt Need   Though a potential need as defined above may exist to the uninvolved observer, one should not assume that everyone in a market actually feels a need for the product or service under investigation. Due to different lifestyles, some consum-

---

30. Richard D. Robinson, *Internationalization of Business,* 2nd ed. (Chicago: The Dryden Press, 1984), p. 36.

FIGURE 7.3 ● Market Potential and Sales Potential Filter

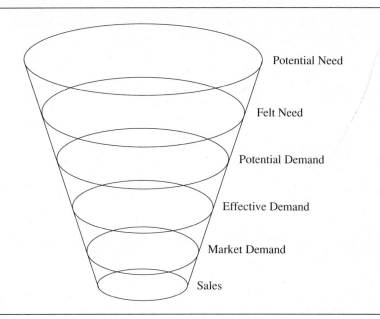

Potential Need

Felt Need

Potential Demand

Effective Demand

Market Demand

Sales

Source: Richard D. Robinson, *Internationalization of Business,* 2nd ed. (Chicago: The Dryden Press, 1984), p. 36. Copyright © 1984 by the Dryden Press. Reprinted by permission of the publisher.

ers may not feel a need for a product. For instance, though a farmer in a developing country who drives his produce to a local market in an animal-drawn cart potentially has a use for a pick-up truck, he actually may not feel the need for one. Thus, the felt need is substantially influenced by the cultural and social environment, including the amount of exposure the consumers or buyers have to modern communications. The key task for the researcher is to evaluate the extent to which the potential need is culturally and socially appropriate among the target customers.

Potential Demand   The felt need represents the aggregate desire of a target population to purchase a product. However, the lack of sufficient income may prevent some of the customers from actually purchasing the product or service. The result is potential demand or the total amount the market would be ready to absorb. The economic variables preventing the realization of sales are generally beyond the control of any individual company. For example, the average income per household may seem to indicate a large demand for washing machines, but the distribution of income is skewed so that 10 percent of the population has 90 percent of the wealth. To identify if potential demand is blocked, a firm must look at income distribution data.

Effective Demand Though potential demand may exist, regulatory factors may prevent prospective customers from being able to satisfy their demand. Included are regulations on imports, tariffs, and foreign exchange; specific regulations on product standards with respect to safety, health, pollution; legal aspects such as patents, copyrights, trademarks; fiscal controls such as taxes, subsidies, or rationing and allocations; economic regulations including price controls and wage controls; political regulations including restrictions on buying foreign goods, the role of the government in the economy, and the power of the government to impose controls.

The presence of any of the above cited factors can cause the potential demand to be reduced to a lower level, in other words, to effective demand. Therefore, marketing research should uncover the extent to which regulatory factors are present and determine the possible actions a firm may take to avoid some of the impact on demand.

Market Demand The extent to which the effective demand can be realized depends substantially on the marketing infrastructure available to competing firms in a country. The degree to which a country's transportation system has been developed is important as well as its efficiency in terms of cost to users. Additional services that marketers use regularly are storage facilities, banking facilities (particularly for consumer credit), available wholesale and retail structure, and advertising infrastructure. The absence of a fully developed marketing infrastructure will cause market demand to be substantially below effective demand. Marketing research will determine the effectiveness of the present marketing system and locate the presence of any inhibiting factors.

Sales Potential The actual sales volume that a company will realize in any country is essentially determined by its competitive offering vis-à-vis other firms who also compete for a share of the same market. The resulting market share is determined by the relative effectiveness of the company's marketing mix. In determining a company's sales potential the researcher will have to assess whether the company can meet the competition in terms of product quality and features, price, distribution, and promotion. The assessment should result in an estimate of the company's market share, given the assumptions about the company's mode of entry (see Chapter 9) and marketing strategy (see Chapter 8).[31]

The difficulty, of course, lies in the determination of the various demand levels and the collection of the facts that can be used to determine actual potential and sales forecasts. Consider a situation in which a company is investigating a market that already has had experience with the product to be introduced. In such a case, the research effort is aimed at uncovering the data on present sales, usage, or production to arrive at the market demand (see Figure 7.3). Consequently, this is primarily an

31. Franklin R. Root, *Entry Strategies for International Markets* (Lexington, Mass.: Lexington Books, 1987), p. 41.

effort in collecting data from secondary information sources or commissioning professional marketing research through independent agencies when necessary.

Analysis by Inference

Available data from secondary sources are frequently of an aggregate nature and do not satisfy the specific needs of a firm focusing on just one product at a time. A company must usually assess market size based on very limited data on foreign markets. In such cases, market *assessment by inference* becomes a necessity. This technique uses available facts about related products or other foreign markets as a basis for inferring the necessary information for the market under analysis. Market assessment by inference is a low cost method that is analysis based and should take place before a company engages in any primary data collection at a substantial cost. Inferences can be made based on related products, related markets' sales, and related environmental factors.

Inferences based on related products. Few products are consumed or used alone without any ties to other prior purchases or products in use. Such relationships exist, for example, between replacement tires and automobiles on the road and electricity consumption and the use of appliances. In some situations, it may be possible to obtain data on related products and their uses as a basis for inferred usage of the particular product to be marketed. From experience in other similar markets, the analyst is able to apply usage ratios that can provide for low cost estimates. For example, the analyst can determine the number of replacement tires needed per X automobiles on the road. A clear understanding of usage patterns can be gained from performing a comparative analysis as described earlier.

Inferences based on related markets' size. Quite frequently, if market size data are available for other countries, this information can be used to derive estimates for the particular country under investigation. For example, consider that market size is known for the United States and estimates are required for Canada, a country with a comparable economic system and consumption patterns. Statistics for the United States can be scaled down by the relative size of either GNP, population, or other factors to about one-tenth of U.S. figures. Similar relationships exist in Europe where the known market size of one country can provide a basis for an inference about a related country. Of course, the results are not exact, but they provide a basis for further analysis. The cost and time lag for collecting primary market data often forces the analyst to use the inference approach.

Inferences based on related environmental factors. A more comprehensive analysis can be provided following a full comparative analysis as outlined previously. After collecting data on the relevant environmental variables for a given product, an inference may be made on the market potential. The estimate's reliability would depend on the type of data available on the success factors. Actual data on success factors are of course preferable to inferences based on the demand structure in a related market. Reed Moyer described a series of additional methods suited for forecasting purposes which often involve the use of historic data.[32] Some of these methods are described in abbreviated form.

Analysis of demand patterns. By analyzing industrial growth patterns for various countries, insights can be gained into the relationship of consumption patterns to industrial growth. Relationships can be plotted between gross domestic product per capita, GNP per capita, and the percent of total manufacturing production accounted for by major industries. During earlier growth stages with corresponding low per capita incomes, manufacturing tends to center on necessities such as food, beverages, textiles, and light manufacturing. With growing incomes, the role of these industries tends to decline and heavy industry assumes a greater importance. By analyzing such manufacturing patterns, forecasts for various product groups can be made for countries at lower income levels since they often repeat the growth patterns of more developed economies.

Similar trends can be observed for a country's import composition. With increasing industrialization, countries develop similar patterns only modified by a country's own natural resources. Energy-poor countries must import increasing quantities of energy as industrialization proceeds, whereas energy-rich countries can embark on an industrialization path without significant energy imports. Industrialized countries import relatively more food products and industrial materials than manufactured goods, which are more important for the less industrialized countries. Understanding these relationships can help the analyst in determining future trends for a country's economy and may help determine future market potential and sales prospects.

Multiple Factor Indexes

This technique has already been successfully used by domestic marketers. It entails the use of proxies to estimate demand if the situation should prevent the direct computation of a product's market potential. A multiple factor measures potential indirectly, using proxy variables that intuition or statistical analysis reveal to be closely correlated to the potential for the product under review.

A good example for such an approach is Ford Motor Company's analysis for its overseas tractor business.[33] To evaluate the attractiveness of its various overseas markets, the company developed a scale and rated each country based on country attractiveness and competitive strength. These two dimensions were measured based on the following:

Country attractiveness	*Competitive strength*
1. Market size	*1.* Market share

32. Reed Moyer, "International Market Analysis," *Journal of Marketing Research,* vol. 5 (November 1968), pp. 353–360.

33. Gilbert D. Harrell, and Richard O. Kiefer, "Multinational Strategic Market Portfolios," *MSU Business Topics,* Winter 1981, pp. 5–15.

Country attractiveness	*Competitive strength*
2. Market growth rate	2. Product fit

3. Government regulations
   Price controls
   Nontariff barrier
   Local content
	3. Contribution margin
	   Profit per unit
	   Profit percentage, net of dealer
	   cost

4. Economic and political stability
   Inflation
   Trade balance
   Political stability
	4. Market support
	   Quality of distribution system
	   Advertising versus competition

These items were evaluated by Ford's executives and rated on a 10-point scale for each item. The items are combined based on the relative weight of each item to determine the coordinates of the X and Y axis. Figure 7.4 illustrates Ford's use of the market evaluation system for Ford's key countries. The weights are indicative of the firm's effort to rank markets via multiple factor indexes.

Competitive Studies

As every marketer knows, the results in the marketplace do not only depend on researching buyer characteristics and meeting buyer needs. To a considerable extent, success in the marketplace is influenced by a firm's competition. Companies competing on an international level have to be particularly careful with monitoring competition since some of the competing firms will most likely be located abroad, thus creating additional difficulties in keeping abreast of the latest developments.

When Honda first entered the U.S. motorcycle industry in 1959, the British and American motorcycle firms that dominated the industry did not pay much attention. Honda's entry with a 50 cc bike posed little threat to the macho bikes by Harley Davidson and Triumph. But thirty years later 80 percent of the bikes are Japanese competing from 50 cc to 1,400 cc. Many companies fail to spot competitors until it is too late. Swiss watchmakers were blindsided by competitors, not even in the same business. While the Swiss were making increasingly more complex mechanized watches, Casio launched basic digital watches which sold at half the price of cheap mechanical watches. Only with the launch of the fashionable electronic Swatch watch in 1985 were the Swiss able to regain some of their lost market.[34]

First, a company will have to determine who its competitors are. The domestic market will certainly provide some input here. However, it is of great importance to include any foreign company that either presently is or may become a competitor in the future. For many firms, the constellation of competitors will most likely change over time. One U.S. company, Caterpillar, could consider other domestic competitors its major competitors both domestically and abroad. More recently, the

34. "Competing with Tomorrow," *The Economist,* May 12, 1990, p. 85.

FIGURE 7.4 ● Key-Country Matrix

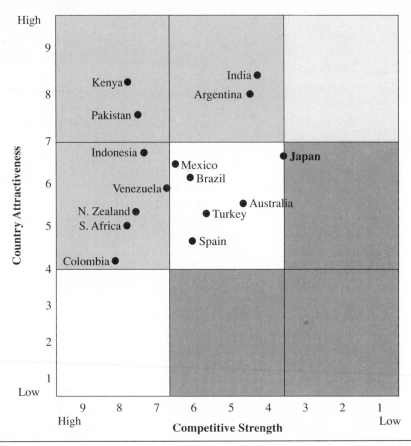

Source: Gilbert D. Harrell and Richard O. Kieter, "Multinational Strategic Market Portfolios," MSU Business Topics, Winter 1981, p. 13. Reprinted by permission.

Japanese firm Komatsu has established itself as the second largest firm for earth-moving equipment, forcing Caterpillar to concentrate more resources on this new competitor.[35] Therefore, included in a company's monitoring system should be *all* major competitors, both domestic and foreign. The monitoring should not be restricted to activity in the competitors' domestic market only but must include competitors' moves anywhere in the world. Many foreign firms first innovate in their home markets, expanding abroad only when the initial debugging of the product has been completed. Therefore, a U.S. firm would lose valuable time if, say, a Japanese

35. "Komatsu on the Track of Cat," *Fortune,* September 20, 1981, pp. 164–174.

competitor's action would only be picked up on entry of the U.S. market. Any monitoring system needs to be structured in such a way as to ensure that competitors' actions will be spotted wherever they tend to occur first. Komatsu, Caterpillar's major competitor worldwide, subscribed to the *Journal Star,* the major daily newspaper in Caterpillar's hometown, Peoria, Illinois. Also important are the actions taken by subsidiaries because they may signal future moves elsewhere in a company's global network of subsidiaries.

Table 7.4 contains a list of the type of information a company may wish to collect on its competitors. Aside from the general business statistics, a competitor's profitability may shed some light on the capacity to pursue new business in the future. Learning about others' marketing operations will allow the investigating company to assess, among other things, the market share to be gained in any given market.

TABLE 7.4 ● Monitoring Competition: Facts to be Collected

OVERALL COMPANY STATISTICS
   Sales and market share profits
   Balance sheet
   Capital expenditures
   Number of employees
   Production capacity
   Research and development capability
MARKETING OPERATIONS
   Types of products (quality, performance, features)
   Service and/or warranty granted
   Prices and pricing strategy
   Advertising strategy and budgets
   Size and type of sales force
   Distribution system (includes entry strategy)
   Delivery schedules (also spare parts)
   Sales territory (geographic)
FUTURE INTENTIONS
   New product developments
   Current test markets
   Scheduled plant capacity expansions
   Planned capital expenditures
   Planned entry into new markets/countries
COMPETITIVE BEHAVIOR
   Pricing behavior
   Reaction to competitive moves, past and expected

Whenever major actions are planned, it is extremely helpful to know what the likely reaction of competitive firms will be and to include them in a company's contingency planning. And, of course, monitoring a competitor's new products or expansion programs may give early hints on future competitive threats.

Analysis that focuses on studying the products of key competitors can often miss the real strength of the competitor. To understand an industry and where it is headed over the next five years, it is important to study the core competencies in an industry. For example, Chaparral Steel, a profitable American steel maker, sends its managers and engineers to visit competitors, customers and suppliers' factories to identify the trends and skills that will lead steel making in the future. Chaparral also attends trade shows and visits university research departments to spot new competencies that may offer an opportunity or pose a threat.[36]

There are numerous ways to monitor competitor's activities. Thorough study of trade or industry journals is an obvious starting point. Also, frequent visits can be made to major trade fairs where competitors exhibit their products. At one such recent fair in Texas, engineers of Caterpillar were seen measuring Komatsu equipment.[37] Other important information can be gathered from the company's foreign subsidiaries located in the home markets of major competitors. The Italian office equipment manufacturer, Olivetti, assigned a major intelligence function to its U.S. subsidiary because of the subsidiary's direct access to competitive products in the U.S. marketplace.

A different approach was adopted by the Japanese pharmaceutical company, Esei, which opened a liaison office in Switzerland, home base to several of the world's leading pharmaceutical companies. There is a widespread impression that American and European firms are much less vigilant than their Asian competitors. For example, Mitsubishi has between 650 and 800 employees in New York to gather intelligence information about their American competitors. The South Koreans are not far behind. The intelligence systems of their three largest trading companies were developed by an ex-colonel of the South Korean military intelligence. The systems require real time reporting to a central processing unit by every branch manager around the world.[38] The examples from Japan and Korea suggest that a business intelligence system requires a coordinated effort that draws on the knowledge of the entire organization. To keep track of a firm's competitors is an important international research function. The effort is most effectively performed on a permanent basis rather than ad hoc. To achieve the status of a permanent monitoring operation, responsibilities need to be assigned to personnel well placed to carry out this important activity.

36. C. K. Prahalad and Gary Hamel, "The Core Competence of the Corporation," *Harvard Business Review,* May–June 1990, pp. 79–91.

37. Ibid.

38. Benjamin Gilad, "The Role of Organized Competitive Intelligence in Corporate Strategy," *Columbia Journal of World Business,* Winter 1989, p. 32.

Environmental Studies

Frequently it becomes necessary to study the international environment beyond the customary monitoring function that most international executives perform. Of particular interest are the economic, physical, sociocultural, and political environments.

When focusing on the economic environment, the primary interest will be on the economic activity in target countries. Major economic indicators are GNP growth, interest levels, industrial output, employment levels, and the monetary policy of the country under investigation. Studies focusing on one country are frequently undertaken when a major decision regarding that country has to be made. This could include a move to enter the country or to significantly increase the firm's presence in that market through large new investments.

Also frequently studied are the international economy and the role of the various supranational organizations, as these affect the business climate for international companies. For example, it is important for companies active in Europe to learn about the possible impact or likelihood of new regulations or decisions of the European Community. Frequently, reviews of such agencies or groups are ordered when a major move is imminent and information is needed on the potential impact of these decisions.

Since the physical environment tends to be the most stable aspect of the foreign marketing environment, such studies are frequently made for major market entry decisions or when the introduction of a new product requires a special analysis of that particular aspect of the environment. Included within the physical environment are population and related statistics on growth, age composition, birthrates, and life expectancy, as well as data on the climate and geography of a country.

Of particular interest is the sociocultural environment already described in some detail in Chapter 3. The salient factors include social classes, family life, lifestyles, role expectations of the sexes, reference groups, religion, education, language, customs, and traditions. Market researchers have classified these statistics as psychographics. The primary interest to the international company is the potential effect of these variables on the sale of its products. Since the sociocultural environment is also unlikely to change over the short run, and since changes that do occur tend to be of a more gradual nature, such studies are most likely ordered when a major marketing decision in the local market is contemplated. As a company gains experience in any given country, its staff and local organization accumulate considerable data on the social and cultural situation that can be tapped whenever needed. Therefore a full study of these environmental variables is most useful when the company does not already have a base in that country and past experience is limited.

Frequently management will investigate the regulatory environment of a given country because those influences can substantially affect marketing operations anywhere. Today, regulatory influences can originate both with national and supranational organizations. National bodies tend to influence the marketing scene within the borders of one country only whereas supranational agencies have a reach beyond any individual country. National regulations may include particular rulings affecting all businesses, such as product liability laws, or may be targeted at individual industries only. In the United States, the latter type would include regulatory agencies such as the U.S. Food and Drug Administration (FDA) or the Civil Aeronautics Board (CAB). Examples of supranational regulations are those issued by the European Community (EC) with respect to business within the member nations or the United Nations' Center for Transnational Corporations that has issued a nonbinding code of conduct for international companies.

Regulatory trends can be of great importance to international companies and may even lead to new opportunities. It is generally accepted by most observers that U.S. safety and emission control regulations for passenger automobiles are the most stringent to be found anywhere in the world. Recognizing this fact, the French company Peugeot has maintained a small beachhead in the U.S. market, even with a small and insignificant sales volume, primarily to gain the experience of engineering cars under these stringent conditions. The company feels that this experience can be usefully applied elsewhere as other countries adopt similar regulations. Consequently, a company will not monitor the regulatory environment to adopt products and marketing operations to meet only with local success. In addition, firms may find it useful to keep informed about the latest regulations regarding their business in countries that have preceded other countries with pertinent legislation even if they may not conduct any business there.

The Macro Survey Technique

The lack of market data has led to the use of a specially designed method for the identification of primary data: the *macro survey*. Developed for anthropological research, this method attempts to identify market potential of rural trading areas by observing the presence or absence of certain types of specialized institutions.[39] Such an approach was adapted in Thailand by the U.S. Department of Commerce desiring to promote U.S. products in rural areas. The market potential was assessed by developing a macro survey scale consisting of five steps. Each step depended on the presence of certain public, religious, or commercial building(s), as shown in Table 7.5. Each next higher step naturally included the characteristics of the previous step. The scales were developed from the Commerce Department personnel's detailed knowledge of the region. Other scales can be developed based on empirical data or research in a small sample area to be later extended to a much larger region. Once a scale exists, research only needs to identify the absence or presence of the indicated key items to establish the potential for a given product category.

The data collection on the presence of key items for a macro survey is as unconventional as the method itself. One important method is area photography to discern visible key items from the air, such as temples, schools, and so on. Aerial photography, even via satellite, is quick and relatively inexpensive. A second method for

39. Richard P. Carr, Jr., "Identifying Trade Areas for Consumer Goods in Foreign Markets," *Journal of Marketing,* October 1978, pp. 76–80.

TABLE 7.5 ● Macro Survey for Rural Thailand

Step number	Item content	Population estimate	Markets
1	Market Square	1,000 to 3,000	Piece-good cloth and light agricultural implements (shovels)
2	Fair ground agricultural support shops, food shops	3,000 to 8,000	Manufactured clothes, canned and dried foods, radios, bicycles, mopeds
3	Raimie fiber mill and pond, Buddhist temple, elementary school, urban support shops (auto repair shops)	5,000 to 10,000	Service for mopeds, hardware (e.g., hammers, saws, roofing material); school supplies; one-man motorized agricultural equipment (e.g., front end tiller)
4	Government administration building; ambulatory health care, secondary school, police services	7,000 to 10,000	Window/door screen material glass; social dresses, primitive plumbing equipment (e.g., lavatories, shower heads, etc., with support piping)
5	Raimie sack mill and water reservoir; high school and/ or technical college; sewer and water purification systems	22,000 to 30,000	Light industrial machinery (welding, pipe threading equipment); air conditioning; cement; construction services; office supplies and equipment

Source: Richard P. Carr, Jr., "Identifying Trade Areas for Consumer Goods in Foreign Markets." Reprinted from *Journal of Marketing,* October 1978, p. 79, published by the American Marketing Association.

ascertaining the step or level of a given trade area is the use of yellow pages telephone directories. Available for purchase from many countries, yellow pages allow the researcher to check on the availability of commercial establishments and make analogies accordingly. Of course, a community visit allows for a more comprehensive check.

DEVELOPING A GLOBAL INFORMATION SYSTEM

Companies that have or plan to become global marketers must look at the world market place to identify global opportunities. To evaluate the full range of opportunities requires a global perspective for market research. While many of the global players started in the triad of North America, Japan, and Europe this only represents 15 percent of the planet's population. Eastern Europe offers interesting opportunities with a combined GNP from the former East Germany, Hungary, and

Czechoslovakia which is larger than the GNP of China. This region has relatively well-trained and low-paid workers. Indonesia, the fifth most populated country in the world, has recently cut government paperwork by 67 percent in an effort to stimulate growth and attract foreign investors. India, the second largest country with 800 million people, has been eliminating regulations to open its markets. For example, in 1988, Indians bought 6 million television sets, up from only 150,000 sets a decade earlier.[40] In approaching the market place from a global perspective, companies need to look at not only countries, but industries and segments.

The forces that affect industry should be analyzed to determine the competitiveness of the industry and the role of the major forces such as buyers, suppliers, new entrants, substitutes and competitors.[41] In addition, companies need to look for global industry shifts and position themselves to take advantage of them. For example, a retailer examining the do-it-yourself market may notice that the car servicing industry is shifting due to changes in automotive technology. With the mechanical reliability of modern cars, the maintenance needs of second-hand car owners beyond the warranty are limited to a few options that do not require skilled labor on complex equipment. These repairs can be done in specialty workshops at a lower cost and more conveniently than at the authorized dealer.[42] Predicting this type of industry shift opens opportunities for the vigilant company.

Globalization also means that companies are looking for new ways to segment markets, especially where demographics fail. There is a trend toward classifying consumers based on lifestyles, attitudes, and preferences rather than nationalities. If you plan to build a global brand, you need segments that are similar regardless of nationality.[43]

Another challenge to the global company is the sharing of information regarding customers, markets, competitors, and marketing approaches. For example, if the marketing manager for the chemical divison is evaluating the global tape industry, he should have easy access to research done by other parts of the company who may have also looked at that business. While it sounds like an easy task, it is not. Imperial Chemical Industries (ICI) with 130,000 employees worldwide has recently launched an "Experience Databank" to capture its marketing knowledge. The database stores information from all over the world, covering every part of the market process. It draws on the experience of different businesses, territories, and functions within ICI as well as from other international companies. Anyone in the country can contact the Market Focus Bureau which manages the service to search the database for their needs. This is one approach to helping share the experience throughout the company.

40. Thomas A. Stewart, "How to Manage in a New Era," *Fortune,* January 15, 1990, p. 29.

41. Michael E. Porter, *Competitive Strategy: Techniques for Analyzing Industries and Competitors* (New York: Free Press, 1980).

42. Xavier Gilbert and Paul Stebel, "Taking Advantage of Industry Shifts," *European Management Journal,* vol. 7, no. 4 (1990), p. 399.

43. Mary Goodyear, "Bold Approaches to Brave New Worlds," *Marketing Week,* March 23, 1990, pp. 52–55.

The demand for quality multicountry research has spurred the market research industry to expand beyond traditional national boundaries. Mintel, primarily a U.K.-based market research company changed its name to Mintel International to reflect its concentration on the world market. Industry experts expect a rapid increase in the demand for multicountry research.[44]

Nielsen introduced its first pan-European research service called Quartz, which provides simulated market tests based upon consumer reactions in five European countries. Twenty-five multinationals, including Nestlé, Procter & Gamble, and BSN, have already signed up for the service. Europanel, a consortium of Europe's leading consumer panel companies has developed a pan-European service called The European Market Measurement Database. It tracks the movement of consumer goods throughout Western Europe based on information from 55,000 households. The global research companies have purchased a number of national market research companies. For example, Nielsen bought companies in Denmark, Holland, and Italy to expand their European operations. With the acquisitions, Nielsen reports to track 25,000 European householders on an ongoing basis.[45]

The global market research companies often publish monthly industry reports that cover specific product categories. They supply the industry with a wide variety of secondary research. Also, they can be called on to conduct primary research where necessary. The largest international research companies are shown in Table 7.6.

44. Donna Dawson, "Booming Reports," *Marketing,* December 14, 1989, p. 37.
45. Elena Bowers, "Powerhouses Tear Down Europe Borders," *Advertising Age,* June 11, 1990, pp. S-14–16.

TABLE 7.6 ● Top Market Research Companies*

	1989—$ Million
A.C. Nielsen	542
IMS International	221
Research International	82
MRB Group	42
Millward Brown	30
Associated Market Research	30
Information Resources	23
Louis Harris and Associates	12
National Research Group	3
McCollum/Spielman Worldwide	2

*1989 International Non-U.S. Revenue.
Source: Elena Bowers, "Researchers look Eastward." Reprinted with permission from *Advertising Age,* June 11, 1990, copyright Crain Communications, Inc. All rights reserved.

To assist decision making about marketing on a global scale, researchers must provide more than data on strictly local factors within each country. All firms that market their products in overseas markets, require information that allows analysis across several countries or markets. However, leaving each local subsidiary or market to develop its own data base does not usually result in an integrated marketing information system (MIS). Instead, authority to develop a centrally managed MIS must be assigned to a central location, with reports given directly to the firm's chief international marketing officer. Jagdish Sheth made a very effective case for a centralized marketing research staff that would monitor buyer needs on a worldwide basis.[46] Sheth favors the establishment of a longitudinal panel in selected geographical areas encompassing all major markets, present and potential. By assessing client needs on a worldwide basis, the company ensures that products and services are designed with all buyers in mind. This avoids the traditional pattern of initially designing products for the company's home market and looking at export or foreign opportunities only once a product has been designed.

A principal requirement for a worldwide MIS is a standardized set of data to be collected from each market or country. Though the actual data collection can be left to a firm's local units, they will do so according to central and uniform specifications.

CONCLUSIONS

In this chapter, we discussed the major challenges and difficulties in securing necessary data for international marketing. We have shown that effective marketing research is based on a conceptual framework combined with a thorough but flexible use of conventional marketing research practices. The major difficulties are the lack of basic data on many markets and the likelihood that research methods will have to be adapted to local environments. The final challenge of international marketing research is to provide managers with a uniform data base covering all the firm's present and potential market. This will allow for cross-country comparisons and analysis as well as the incorporation of worldwide consumer needs into the initial product design process. Given the difficulties in data collection, to achieve this international comparability of data is indeed a challenge for even the most experienced professionals.

Questions for Discussion

1. Why is it so difficult to do marketing research in multi-country settings?

2. Comparative marketing analysis is a powerful technique that provides the

46. Jagdish N. Sheth, "A Conceptual Model of Long-Range Multinational Marketing Planning," *Management International Review,* no. 4–5 (1971), pp. 3–10.

basis for the study of international marketing. What is the comparative approach and how do you apply it to multi-country environments?

3. What are the advantages and disadvantages of secondary and primary data in international marketing?

4. How would you protect against definitional, instrument, and frame error in international marketing research?

5. If you were estimating the demand for bathroom cleaners, what type of inference analysis would you use? Give a specific example.

6. If you headed Kodak, how would you monitor reactions around the world to a major competitor such as Fuji Film?

For Further Reading

Davis, Harry L., Susan P. Douglas, and Alvin J. Silk. "Measure Unreliability: Hidden Threat to Cross-National Marketing Research." *Journal of Marketing,* Spring 1981, pp. 98–109.

Douglas, Susan P., and Samuel Craig. *International Marketing Research.* Englewood Cliffs, New Jersey: Prentice-Hall, 1983.

Green, Robert, and Philip D. White. "Methodological Considerations in Cross National Consumer Research." *Journal of International Business Studies,* Fall-Winter 1976, pp. 81–88.

Jaffee, E. D. "Multinational Marketing Intelligence: An Information Requirements Model." *Management International Review,* 19, no. 2 (1979), pp. 53–60.

Kracmar, John Z. *Marketing Research in the Developing Countries.* New York: Praeger, 1971.

Mayer, Charles S. "The Lessons of Multinational Marketing Research." *Business Horizons* (December 1978), pp. 7–13.

Moyer, Reed. "International Market Analysis." *Journal of Marketing Research* (November 1968), pp. 353–360.

Murray, J. Alex. "Intelligence Systems of the MNCs." *Columbia Journal of World Business* (September–October 1972), pp. 63–71.

Permut, Steven F. "The European View of Marketing Research." *Columbia Journal of World Business* (Fall 1977), p. 94.

Samli, A. Coskun. "An Approach to Estimating Market Potential in East Europe." *Journal of International Business Studies* (Fall-Winter 1977), pp. 49–55.

Wind, Yoram, and Susan Douglas. "International Market Segmentation." *European Journal of Marketing,* 6, no. 1 (1972), p. 18.

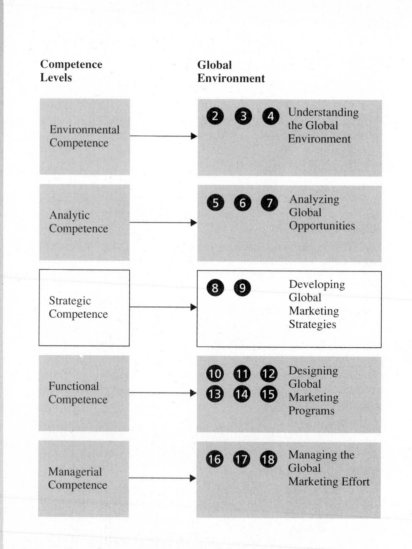

Competence Levels

Global Environment

Environmental Competence → ② ③ ④ Understanding the Global Environment

Analytic Competence → ⑤ ⑥ ⑦ Analyzing Global Opportunities

Strategic Competence → ⑧ ⑨ Developing Global Marketing Strategies

Functional Competence → ⑩ ⑪ ⑫ ⑬ ⑭ ⑮ Designing Global Marketing Programs

Managerial Competence → ⑯ ⑰ ⑱ Managing the Global Marketing Effort

P A R T
T H R E E

Developing Global Marketing Strategies

INCREASINGLY, INTERNATIONAL COMPANIES are being asked to design their business strategies from a global point of view. Globalized business strategies require an ability to look at business and competitive developments all over the world and to digest often conflicting information into a workable plan. Global strategies require skills and conceptual understanding that are different from those required for developing domestic strategies.

In this section, we concentrate on the global strategies international firms must be able to develop in order to be successful. No company can be all things to all people, and international managers have to learn to focus and build on their company's strengths. Future international marketing managers need to have the strategic competence necessary to develop global marketing programs that will ensure the success of their firms.

Chapter 8 concentrates on the major strategic decisions faced by firms active in global marketing. The chapter will introduce the most recent concepts on globalization of marketing strategies. The various alternative entry strategies will be the subject of Chapter 9.

8

Global Marketing Strategies

● **COMPANIES WILL NEED** *to make a number of strategic decisions concerning their international and global marketing operations. At first, there is the decision to become an international company and eventually a global firm. Second, an international company will have to decide on the geographic concentration of its business, that is, whether the business or operations should be located in developing or in industrialized countries. Third, a company will need to decide which particular countries it will enter. Closely related is the type of entry strategy a firm will adopt for each country selected. Another strategic decision concerns the marketing mix the firm intends to employ for its international operations. Finally, companies will have to address key organizational and planning issues. When designing a strategy, companies need to develop generic strategies in terms of geographic expansion, product or markets, and competitive strategies. The purpose of this chapter is to describe the nature of these strategic decisions, with a particular emphasis on the first three topics. The other topics will be introduced as they are treated in greater detail in separate chapters. Figure 8.1 shows the decision elements involved in international marketing.*

FIGURE 8.1 ● International and Global Marketing Strategies

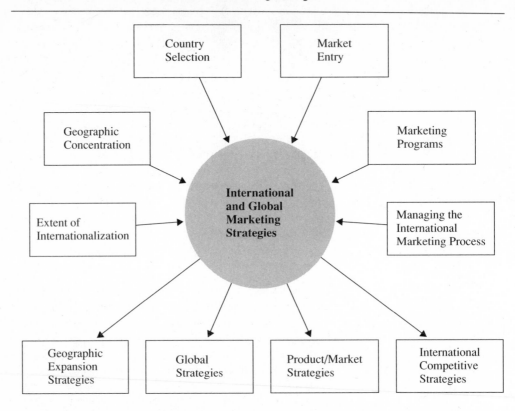

REASONS FOR INTERNATIONALIZATION

Whether a company wants to compete internationally is a strategic decision that will affect the firm fundamentally including its operations and its management. For many companies, the decision to internationalize remains an important and difficult one. Typically, there are many issues behind a company's decision to begin to compete in foreign markets. For some firms, going abroad is the result of a deliberate policy decision, whereas for others it is a reaction to a specific business opportunity or a competitive challenge.

Opportunistic Development

Probably the most common reason for international expansion is the recognition that opportunities exist in foreign markets. Many companies, particularly those in the United States, promote their products in trade journals or through other media to their U.S. customers. These publications are also read by foreign business executives, orders are made that are initially unsolicited. Because these transactions are usually more complicated and more involved than a routine shipment to domestic customers, the firm has to make the decision whether or not to respond at that time. The company can also adopt a more aggressive policy and actively pursue foreign customers, moving beyond filling unsolicited orders. Thus, some firms have built sizable foreign businesses by first responding to orders and by taking a more proactive approach later on. Most of today's large internationally active companies were built initially around an opportunistic strategy, although today these firms have moved to a more orchestrated and deliberate strategy in their approach to international marketing.

The United States counts about 100,000 active exporters among its companies. Of those, 86,500 firms make fewer than nine export shipments per year and, thus, are classified as occasional exporters. Only 15 percent of all U.S. exporters fall into the active category, making on average 116 shipments or more.[1]

Following Customers Abroad

For a company whose business is concentrated on a few large customers, the decision to internationalize is usually made when one of its key customers moves abroad to pursue international opportunities. Many of the major U.S. automobile component suppliers are operating plants abroad to supply their customers in foreign locations. PPG Industries, a major U.S.-based supplier of car body paints to the U.S. automobile industry, did little overseas business other than licensing its technology to other foreign paint makers. In the early 1980s, the company began to follow its major customers abroad and began to directly service them in Europe and elsewhere. The company began to sell to non-U.S. car companies as well and achieved the leading position in supplying paints to car manufacturers worldwide.[2] Similar trends can be observed as Japanese and European automobile manufacturers set up their own operations in the United States. These moves tend to be followed by a series of component suppliers who do not want to lose out on a new business opportunity.

The service sector has seen similar expansions triggered by client moves overseas. The establishment of international branch networks of major U.S. banks, such as Citibank or Chase Manhattan, was motivated by a desire to service key domestic clients overseas. Major U.S. advertising agencies and accounting firms have set up extensive networks of foreign offices for the same reasons. Thus, as a firm's customer base becomes international, so will the firm's own operations if it wants to maintain its business.

1. "The Little Guys are Making it Big Overseas," *Business Week,* February 27, 1989, p. 96.
2. "Remarkable Resurgence of a Highly Respected Company," World Paints and Coatings (Special Survey), *Financial Times,* March 27, 1991, p. 11.

Pursuing Geographic Diversification

A need to diversify beyond a single country can also be behind moves to internationalize a company. Although this is less of a factor for U.S.-based companies, firms in other parts of the world often do not want their operations to be dominated or become overly dependent on the economies of a single country. Saint-Gobain, a large French company with a long-standing tradition in glass and building materials, for years followed a strategy to break out of its France-only position. Acquiring large companies in the same field in Germany and the United Kingdom, the company was able to reduce French sales to 30 percent of corporate but gain 36 percent in the rest of Europe. The acquisition of Norton Company, a U.S.-based maker of abrasives and ceramics, significantly strengthened Saint-Gobain's position in the U.S., which accounted for only 20 percent of its sales before the Norton acquisition and turned a Europe-wide group into a world-wide group.[3]

International Market Extension for Incremental Profit

A deliberate international expansion policy is pursued by firms who are motivated by profit potential through market extension. In industries where investment in research and development is high, companies often want to harvest past investment by introducing established products into other countries. Such a strategy is particularly profitable when additional market entries do not require substantial investments in product changes or additional research and development. This is the case for much of the computer industry where products are substantially standardized around the world.

Ferro, a U.S.-based company in ceramics, specialty chemicals and plastics, achieved international sales of more than 55 percent of total volume. The company followed a strategy of aggressively pursuing additional payoffs for products successfully launched in the United States. This type of "profit leverage" was intended to use the company's foreign business to strengthen its overall competitive position, both domestically and abroad.[4]

Taking Advantage of Different Growth Rates of Economies

Growth rates among countries are subject to wide variations. In situations where a company is based in a low-growth country, the firm may suffer a competitive disadvantage and may want to expand into faster growing countries to take advantage of growth opportunities. For those reasons, many European companies looked for new business opportunities in the United States during the mid-1970s and 1980s. A similar rush of companies to the Middle East was noticeable during the time period following the first substantial oil price increases in 1973 and 1974. The area of the

3. "Saint-Gobain Pushing Worldwide Growth," *New York Times,* April 26, 1990, p. D5.
4. "Ferro's Global Position Sparks Intrigue," *Wall Street Journal,* March 17, 1989, p. A7.

Pacific Rim (which includes Japan, Korea, Taiwan, China, Hong Kong, Thailand, Singapore, Malaysia, and Indonesia) had experienced above average growth rates in the second half of the 1980s, which in turn prompted many international firms to invest heavily in expanding in that region.[5]

The Coca-Cola Company, experiencing growth rates in Europe that were twice its U.S. market rate in the late 1980s, decided to place additional emphasis in Europe where substantial potential exists in connection with the 1992 European integration initiative and the opening of the Eastern European economies. As a result, the company feels the 1990s will be the decade of Europe.[6]

Exploiting Product Life Cycle Differences

When the market for a firm's product becomes saturated, a company can open new opportunities by entering into foreign markets where the product may not be very well known. Thus adding new markets works like an extension of the product's life cycle. Among U.S. firms following this strategy are many consumer goods marketers, such as Philip Morris, Coca-Cola Company, and PepsiCo. These companies often go into markets where the per capita consumption of their products is still relatively low. With economic expansion and the resulting improvement in personal incomes, these companies expect to experience substantial growth later on—though operations in the United States are showing little growth. A recent report showed Coca-Cola sold 189 12-ounce servings per person annually in the United States. Its international average was only 37 servings, although this varied between 215 in Iceland, 173 in Mexico, 111 in West Germany, 61 in the United Kingdom, 35 in Japan, and 26 in France. China trailed with 0.3 servings per capita. These figures are heavily influenced by the fact that in Europe soft drinks rank only number four for choice of drink, whereas in the United States soft drinks rank number one. With per capita consumption in Europe only 30 percent of the U.S. levels, Coca-Cola sees a considerable future in pushing more in Europe where colas have not yet reached maturity.[7]

Pursuing Potential Abroad

Despite its size as the world's largest economy, the United States market accounts usually for little more than one-half the business in many high technology product categories. For some of the more common product or industry categories such as food, the U.S. market represents a much smaller portion of the overall world market. As a result, many firms are attracted by the sheer size of the potential business abroad. For example, H. J. Heinz built a baby food factory in China because 16 million babies are born annually in China, compared to 3.5 million in the United

---

5. "A Strategic Guide to the Rim," *Fortune,* Special Issue: Asia in the 1990s, Fall 1989, pp. 72–84.

6. "Coke Gets Off its Can in Europe," *Fortune,* August 13, 1990, p. 69.

7. Ibid.

States.[8] With a population that is exceeding that in the United States, the European market, although fragmented into many countries, offers a market that is economically as large as the U.S. market. The Pacific Rim countries of Korea, Taiwan, Japan, and China have very large populations and are attracting many newcomers who want to go where they see new potential.

Internationalizing for Defensive Reasons

Sometimes companies are not interested in pursuing new growth or potential abroad but decide to enter international business for largely defensive reasons. When a domestic company sees its markets invaded by foreign firms, that company may react by entering the foreign competitor's home market in return. As a result, the company can learn valuable information about the competitor that will help in its operations at home. A company may want to slow down a competitor by denying it the cash flow from its profitable domestic operation which could otherwise be invested into expansion abroad. As a result, companies who had not needed to compete internationally find themselves suddenly forced to expand abroad.

Many U.S. companies opened operations in Japan because it allowed them to get closer to what was the most important competition for them. For example, major companies such as Xerox and IBM use their local subsidiaries in Japan to learn new ways to compete with the major Japanese firms in their field. Likewise, many European firms want to be represented in the U.S. market because they can learn about new opportunities more directly than if they waited in their home markets for U.S. firms to arrive with new products or technologies.

Leveraging Key Success Factors Abroad

Although many companies joining the ranks of internationally active firms still do so largely to search for new opportunities, there are also those companies that internationalize to achieve additional leverage for key resources or investments. Leveraging key success factors, or KSFs,[9] requires a firm to first become aware of the key functions it must concentrate on to beat both domestic and international competitors. Typically, to outdo competitors within these functions requires additional investment. Such investments can frequently be justified only if the market is large enough. Many times, a single domestic market cannot support the required outlays to stay competitive, forcing such firms to eye the international market from the very beginning.

In the pharmaceutical industry, the basic research and development of a new

8. Joseph O. Eastlack, Jr. and Roberta Lucker, "Is China Moving from Marx to Mastercard?" *The Journal of Consumer Marketing,* Summer 1986, pp. 9–10.
9. Kenichi Ohmae, *The Mind of the Strategist* (New York: McGraw-Hill, 1982), p. 42.

drug from inception to market launch may cost some $150 million. This cost will be incurred even if the drug is for only one market. Adding more markets to the product launch does not significantly increase the research costs. Since pharmaceutical companies can usually not afford to spend more than 15 percent of sales on research costs, the implication is that such a new drug must reach some $1 billion in sales over the product's lifetime, which tends to be seven to ten years before patents expire. Since few countries offer sales large enough for just one drug category, pharmaceutical companies are forced to look for many markets so that the development costs can be spread over a larger volume. Since these development expenditures are of a fixed nature, independent of eventual volume or number of markets covered, we have called them Critical Input Variables or CIVs. Such variables, which occur in many other industries as well, frequently are why companies pursue international or even global strategies in their quest to make such heavy fixed investment requirements more affordable.[10]

CIVs may not only be research and development. For a company that manufactures construction equipment, such as Caterpillar, an efficient dealer network with ample stocks of spare parts may be the key to success. In this case, the company will obtain more volume through its spare parts system by expanding internationally; and thus it can afford to maintain a more elaborate system than if it were based in only one market. In some product categories such as watches, luxury products, and many consumer electronics items with high brand recognition, companies may consider the cost of supporting a brand globally in advertising as a CIV. Consequently, companies need to become keenly aware of their relevant CIVs so that appropriate strategies can be devised that will make them more competitive both at home and abroad. How leveraging CIVs will influence strategic decisions will be discussed in greater detail later in this chapter.

DETERMINING GEOGRAPHIC CONCENTRATION

Once a company has made a commitment to extending its business internationally, management will soon be confronted with the task of setting some geographic or regional emphasis. A company may decide to emphasize developed nations, such as those of Europe and North America, or Japan. Alternatively, some companies may prefer to pursue primarily developing countries in Latin America, Africa, or Asia. Management must make a strategic decision to direct business development in such a way that the company's overall objectives are congruent with the particular geographic mix of its activities.

10. Jean-Pierre Jeannet, "Achieving Global Integration: Globalization versus Regionalization in Manufacturing and Marketing." Proceedings, Pharm Tech Conference 90, Aster Publishing, Eugene, Oregon, 1990, pp. 57–63.

Concentrating on Developed Countries

Developed countries account for a disproportionate share of world GNP (68 percent in 1984) and, thus, tend to attract many companies.[11] In particular, firms with technology-intensive products have concentrated their activities in the developed world. Although competition is usually more intensive in those markets, both from other international firms and local companies, doing business in developed countries is generally preferred over doing business in developing nations. This is primarily because the business environment is more predictable and the investment climate is more favorable. Kraft Inc., a large U.S. food company with business worldwide, has 95 percent of its international sales in countries considered economically advanced and politically of low risk. In the developing countries, the company prefers not to own any assets and utilize distribution or licensing agreements or work through joint ventures.[12]

Developed countries are located in North America (the United States and Canada), Western Europe, and Asia (Japan, Australia, New Zealand). Although some very large international firms such as IBM have operations in all of these countries, many others may be represented in only one or two areas. Very early in their development U.S. international companies established strong business bases in Europe and more recently in Japan. Japanese firms tend to start their overseas operations in the United States and Canada and then move into Europe.

The importance of developing a competitive position in the major developed markets was first articulated by Kenichi Ohmae. Referred to as the Triad, Ohmae maintained that for most industries it was important to compete effectively in the three parts of the triad, U.S.A., Europe, and Japan. Companies were said to need at least two areas where they were strong and a representation in the third. Real global competitors were advised to have strong positions in these areas. The three areas of the strategic triad account for about 80 percent of most industries, thus determining the outcome of the competitive battle.[13]

Three German companies made heavy investments into the U.S. market in the late 1980s which could be related to strengthening their position in the triad. Bertelsmann, a German publishing company, acquired the RCA record and music company and Doubleday, a publisher. Continental, the German tire producer, acquired General Tire in 1987. And finally, Hoechst, a large German chemical firm, acquired Celanese, a U.S. fibers and organic chemicals company. In all three cases, the acquisitions were aimed at strengthening the U.S. side of the business and eventually to use this as a way to expand into Japan and the Pacific Basin, the third and final part of the triad.[14]

11. *World Economic Survey 1986* (New York: United Nations, 1986), p. 16.

12. "Kraft: Its Global Strategy," *World Food & Drink Report,* October 29, 1987.

13. Ohmae, Kenichi, *Triad Power: The Coming Shape of Global Competition* (New York: Free Press, 1985).

14. "A Strategically Necessary Invasion," *Financial Times,* July 12, 1989, p. 11.

Emphasizing Developing Countries

Developing nations differ substantially from developed nations by geographic region and by the level of economic development. Markets in Latin America, Africa, the Middle East, and Asia are also characterized by a higher degree of risk than markets in the developed countries. Due to the less stable economic climates in those countries, a company's operation can be expected to be subject to greater uncertainty and fluctuation. Furthermore, the frequently changing political situations in developing countries often affect operating results negatively. As a result, some markets which may have experienced high growth for some years may suddenly experience drastic reductions in growth. Mexico and Brazil are good examples of countries that grew rapidly in the 1970s but whose economic expansion came to an abrupt halt with their sudden inability to service their extensive foreign debt. In many situations, the higher risks are compensated for by higher returns, largely because competition is often less intense in those markets. Consequently, companies need to balance the opportunity for future growth in the developing nations with the existence of higher risk.

One firm that considered itself overexposed to Third World countries was Nestlé. This Swiss-based multinational food company found itself with a substantial business volume in developing countries. To balance this risk, the company took specific steps to increase its business in North America, with special emphasis on the U.S. market. The company acquired several U.S. firms, including Stouffer Foods and Carnation and, thus, was able to achieve a more balanced distribution of its global sales as well as a corresponding decrease in its risk on investments in the Third World.

However, there are also industries that will certainly profit from a move to developing countries. The tobacco industry, for one, is moving heavily into developing countries because it sees more growth there than in the developed world of North America and Europe.[15] The cigarette consumption of Third World countries amounts to about one third of world consumption and is rapidly rising. Whereas cigarette consumption in Europe's largest markets has experienced a decline, it has grown substantially in Africa. Tobacco companies also meet less stringent laws in developing countries with respect to advertising regulations; thus many of the leading tobacco firms have emphasized their business development efforts in those regions.

Philips, the Dutch consumer electronics company, decided in 1985 to rapidly increase its investment in China. With investments totaling about $500 million, the company entered several ventures that are aimed at strengthening its position in this critical part of the world. These investments represent a long-term view on the part of Philips anticipating the future role China may play in the world economy.[16]

15. "Cigarette Companies Develop Third World as a Growth Market," *Wall Street Journal,* July 5, 1985, p. 1.
16. "Philips Sees Promise in China Affair," *Financial Times,* February 14, 1991, p. 20.

Expanding in Eastern Europe

The liberalization of the countries in Eastern Europe has opened a large new market for many international firms. Typically accounting for about 15 percent of a given worldwide demand in an industry, about two-thirds of that is accounted for by the Soviet Union. Although many companies consider this of a longer-term potential with little profit opportunity in the near term, many firms have moved to take advantage of operating in areas where they were prohibited from doing business.

One example is Otis, the large U.S.-based elevator company. Already represented in all major markets of the world, the company considered the Eastern European area of strategic importance signing a series of deals since 1989. In former East Germany, Otis acquired a local company and several service companies with a total of 2,000 employees. In Hungary, Otis entered a joint venture with a formerly state-owned elevator company which operates a factory and 500 employees. In the Soviet Union, Otis signed two joint ventures with two different elevator companies. In each venture, Otis will have 55 percent ownership and will produce and market elevators for the local market. Otis was not alone in its expansion strategy. Its principal rivals, Schindler of Switzerland and Kone of Finland, ranking number two and number three respectively worldwide, have both signed ventures in the same countries.[17]

Selecting Lead Markets

A lead market is a particular country where new developments show up first. A company aware of such trends can capitalize on its lead market presence by leveraging that experience to its other markets or countries. The United States tends to be the lead market for new electronic office equipment including computers. For many years, Olivetti, an Italian office equipment company, operated a subsidiary in the United States but never achieved much market success. However, the operation was justified by the company's management in Italy on the grounds that it allows the company to learn firsthand how to compete in the most advanced and sophisticated market of the world for the industry. By learning such lessons in the U.S. market, Olivetti was able to quickly apply them to Europe, its prime market. Consequently, the U.S. operation could be justified for the overall benefit of the company even if it did not become profitable. Companies are increasingly sensitive to lead markets and are taking actions to assure that they are adequately represented in such markets wherever they may be.[18]

The United States is no longer the only lead market in many key industries. When it comes to electronics or semiconductor manufacturing, Japan has captured the lead in a number of segments, as indicated in Figure 8.2. This loss of leadership

---

17. "Setting Sights on New Heights," *Financial Times,* March 1, 1991, p. 29.

18. Jean-Pierre Jeannet, "Lead Markets: A Concept for Designing Global Business Strategies." Working Paper, IMEDE, International Management Development Institute, Lausanne, Switzerland, May 1986.

FIGURE 8.2 ● Technology: The United States versus the World

Technology	Lagging	Holding its own	Leading
Biotech Create an array of new materials through biotech methods	■		
Gallium arsenide Develop semiconductor materials that increase chip performance	■		
High–power microwaves Apply this technology to weapons	■		
Integrated optics Use light instead of electric charges for chip memories and signal processing	■		
Machine intelligence and robotics Incorporate human "intelligence" and actions into mechanical devices	■		
Microchips Reduce size of high–speed computers and sensitive receivers	■		
Pulsed power Develop portable devices that fire pulses of laser microwave energy	■		
Superconductors Make substances with little or no electrical resistance at up to room temperature	■		
Advanced composites Create materials that will withstand high temperatures		■	
Air–breathing propulsion Make efficient, lightweight jet engines		■	
Fiber optics Produce highly efficient fibers for communications and navigation		■	
Hypervelocity projectiles Develop hardened, high–velocity missiles with increased penetrating power		■	
Automatic target recognition Create devices to detect, classify, and track targets			■
Computational fluid dynamics Simulate flow of fluids or gases by computer			■
Data fusion Process and present large amounts of raw computer data in usable form			■
Highly sensitive radars Detect Stealth–type targets			■
Parallel processing Run processors simultaneously for high–speed computing			■
Passive sensors Monitor surroundings without emitting signals			■
Phased arrays Develop advanced radar technology with no movement of antenna			■
Signature controls Limit the telltale signals that vehicles and weapons emit			■
Simulation and modelling Test concepts and designs without building replicas			■
Software development Create more affordable and reliable software			■

Source: "Getting High Tech Back on Track", *Fortune,* January 1, 1990, p. 76. From Department of Defense data, as reprinted in *Fortune,* January 1, 1990. Copyright © 1990 The Time Inc. Magazine Company. All rights reserved.

Gray = U.S. lagging in some important areas; Black = U.S. leading in most areas.

has become pronounced in a number of areas of the electronics industry. In those areas, the lead markets have shifted out of the United States into Japan. The worldwide share of U.S. semiconductor manufacturers has slipped to less than 40 percent in 1990.[19] This loss was primarily a function of less investment than Japanese firms, often caused by higher financing costs in the U.S. The lack of capital investment in the semiconductor industry has also caused difficulties to U.S. manufacturers of semiconductor testing equipment. In 1979, the top nine rankings were occupied by U.S. firms led by Fairchild, Perkin-Elmer, and Applied Materials. In 1988, the list was led by two Japanese firms, Nikon and TEL Electron, and the top U.S. firm had dropped to fourth place. When Japanese firms became the world leaders in semiconductors, their position was also exploited by Japanese test equipment manufacturers.[20]

Even in the computer industry, lead markets have started to change hands. While the United States still leads in the larger computers, Japanese firms have begun to compete effectively in the smaller generation machines. While IBM and Apple lead in PCs, it is Toshiba of Japan that is a leader in portable computers, with NEC, another Japanese company, another leading contender, behind Compaq and Zenith, both U.S. firms. The potential for still smaller computers is enormous and has shifted towards the Japanese. For laptops, notebook, or palm-size type computers, the market is just emerging and the experience of the Japanese firms with miniaturizing is a decided advantage.[21] Furthermore, a key component in all very small computers is a flat-panels display screen. The largest maker of these is Sharp of Japan, and no credible U.S. source exists. Even those pocket-sized computers made in the United States depend on these critical components and, thus, on Japanese suppliers. These developments have forced U.S. computer makers to link up with the Japanese in small models. Apple also is expected to eventually source its own lap-top from Sony.[22]

In recognition of the Japanese lead in many technology areas, IBM has begun to use the Japanese market as a testing ground worldwide for new technology. With sales of about $8.4 billion in 1989, IBM Japanese is already a major player in that market. However, the company first implemented a number of important policy changes in Japan only to apply them to other markets later on. This included a shift to the selling of solutions rather than hardware and the use of alliances to round out product lines. One of these alliances included working with Toshiba on flat-panel displays for use in the new lap-top computers. IBM had more than twenty-five such alliances in Japan alone. And when major competitors brought out note-book style

19. "U.S. Semiconductor Industry Slips Further in World Markets," *Financial Times,* February 22, 1991, p. 14.

20. "Pillar of Chip Industry Eroding," *New York Times,* March 3, 1989, p. D1.

21. "Japanese Portables Threaten American Lead in Computers," *New York Times,* November 24, 1990, p. 1.

22. "Made in the U.S.A., but by Sharp," *New York Times,* February 22, 1991, p. D1.

computers in 1989, IBM commissioned an independent company to produce one of its own.[23]

{ developing /developed. c.

△ COUNTRY SELECTION *{ countries*

At some point, the development of an international marketing strategy will come down to selecting individual countries where a company intends to compete. There are about 150 members at the United Nations, which is some indication as to how many different countries companies have to select from. Very few international firms end up competing in all of these markets. The decision on where to compete is referred to as the country selection decision and is one of the components of developing an international marketing strategy.

Why is country selection a strategic concern for international marketing management? Adding another country to a company's portfolio always requires some additional investment in management time and effort, and capital. Although the opportunities for additional profits are usually the driving force, each additional country also represents a new business risk. It takes time to build up business in a country where the firm has not previously been represented and profits may not show until much later on. Consequently, companies need to go through a careful analysis before they decide to move ahead.

△ Analyzing the Investment Climate

A complete understanding of the investment climate of a target country will help in making the country selection decision. The investment climate of a country is made up of its political situation, its legal structure, its foreign trade position, and its attitude towards foreign investment or the presence of foreign companies. In general, companies will try to avoid countries with uncertain political situations. The impact that political and legal forces can have on the operations of a foreign company abroad was described in detail in Chapter 4.

A country's foreign trade position can also determine the environment for foreign firms operating there. Countries with a strong balance of payments surplus or strong currencies that are fully convertible are favored as good places to invest. Countries with chronic balance of payments difficulties and those where there are great uncertainties about the transferability of funds are viewed as risky and as such are less favored by foreign investors. These aspects were described in greater detail in Chapter 2. Consequently, assessing a country's investment climate will require a thorough and skillful analysis. However, investment climate is not the only determinant for a country being selected for entry.

23. "Strategic Testing Ground for IBM," *Financial Times,* May 4, 1990, p. 23.

Determining Market Attractiveness

Before a country can be selected or targeted for addition to a firm's portfolio of countries, management needs to assess the overall attractiveness of that country with respect to the firm's products or services. Initially, this requires a clear indication of the country's market size. This may consist of analyzing existing patterns of demand. Also needed is some data on growth—both past and future—that will allow a firm to determine market size not only as it relates to the present situation but also with respect to the future potential of that country.

Analyzing demand patterns allows a company to plot where on the product life cycle a given product or service can be located. Also, a firm may want to analyze potential competitors in that country to achieve an understanding of how it can compete. Finally, companies entering a new country should get to know that market enough to be able to determine if their way of competing and marketing is allowed in that country. Some markets may be very attractive but if the firm's key strength cannot be employed success is questionable.

The analytic approach required for an in-depth analysis of a country's market attractiveness was covered in great detail in Chapters 5 and 7. Analyzing international markets and the company's prospective international buyers—the ability to perform marketing research and analysis on an international scale—is a prerequisite to sound country selection decisions.

MARKET ENTRY DECISIONS

Once a company has decided to select a certain group of countries for further market development, the company will then be confronted with market entry decisions. In this phase, a company will face a series of options as to how it wants to enter the selected country. The options range from a very low level of involvement and investment, such as various forms of exporting, to more involved and investment intensive forms of entry, such as a company owned sales subsidiary or even a manufacturing base.

Entry strategies are of strategic importance because most companies will not be able to shift quickly from one alternative to another following initial market feedback. Depending on the type of entry strategy selected, market success may differ substantially. Furthermore, some entry strategies require a substantial amount of initial investment and the results cannot be realized until much later. As a result, companies are very careful in finding the right amount of commitment combined with the expected results and the type of market they want to enter.

Given the importance of managing entry strategies for success in international marketing, Chapter 9 is entirely devoted to this topic. The chapter will concentrate on documenting the various analytic steps companies go through in making entry strategy decisions for their foreign ventures while describing influencing factors such as costs, investments, market potential, and sales volume.

GLOBAL MARKETING PROGRAMS

Although companies face a host of important decisions when developing marketing programs for international markets, the most important strategic decision they face relates to the amount of standardization versus differentiation aimed for in the various target markets. As we explained in considerable detail in our first chapter, companies face many barriers that prevent using or make it very difficult to offer standardized marketing programs. Standardization is not only to be understood in terms of product hardware but includes the "software" of marketing programs such as distribution, pricing, and promotion strategies.

It will not always be clear whether a marketing program needs to be tailored to each individual market. Although local conditions may signal on the surface that such an approach may be advantageous, other concerns need to be considered. Substantial changes in a company's marketing program naturally bring additional costs. Such cost increases may occur in the production of new or additional product models with corresponding research and engineering costs. Such incremental costs are not always justified by the incremental business volume expected. Consequently, in some cases a company may not be in a position to differentiate even though management believes the market will require it. Similar concerns apply for other marketing aspects such as advertising, distribution, or logistics.

Increasingly, companies need to consider the broader issues of globalization of their marketing programs, which will force such issues as globalized advertising, global products, or global pricing. These issues have become important as more and more international marketing decisions are made across many markets, or even worldwide, rather than the more traditional country-by-country decision making. Developing such global programs and understanding the implications will be the focus of Chapters 10 through 15, with particular emphasis on the various elements of the marketing mix.

MANAGING GLOBAL MARKETING

How a company manages, organizes, and controls its operations greatly influences the direction it takes. Executives, both domestically and abroad, tend to adapt to a company's organizational systems, which makes the choice of organizational system important. Although the impact of the organization's design or planning and control systems are less obvious to an outside observer, these factors are nevertheless considered of strategic importance because the effect is often realized only years after such systems have been put in place.

Of major concern to a company are the organizational structure to be selected for its international operations, the location of its decision-making authority with respect to international marketing, and the nature of its planning process as it impacts on international marketing. Chapters 16 and 17 are devoted entirely to these important concerns.

GENERIC INTERNATIONAL MARKETING STRATEGIES

Having explored some of the key strategic decisions faced by international marketing executives, our focus will now shift to the generic global and international marketing strategies companies can adopt. Generic strategies are general classifications used to organize a large number of possible individual strategies. This is done to highlight certain general principles—no company will neatly fall into any one of these categories. Instead, it is expected that most companies will fall somewhere in between categories, or they may use a combination of strategies from different categories. Furthermore, many companies actually pursue several types of strategies at once, varying them according to product line or business unit.

Generic international marketing strategies can be classified along two dimensions. The geographic dimension deals with the extent of international expansion, ranging from purely domestic, single country strategy to a global, multicountry strategy. Secondly, we can distinguish strategies by the extent of market/product lines offered. This can range from a narrow line, or niche strategy, all the way to a broad or multisegment line. For a graphical depiction of these dimensions, see Figure 8.3.

GEOGRAPHIC EXPANSION STRATEGIES

To succeed in international marketing competition, companies need to carefully look at their geographic expansion. To some extent, a firm makes a conscious decision about its extent of internationalization by choosing a posture that may range from entirely domestic without any international involvement to a global reach where the company devotes its entire marketing strategy to global competition. Each level of internationalization will profoundly change the way a company competes and will require different strategies with respect to marketing programs, planning, organization, and control of the international marketing effort.

Domestic Strategy

A company with a strictly domestic strategy has decided not to actively involve itself in any international marketing. To use our terminology from Chapter 1, such a firm will not develop globetrotting skills as no sales take place outside its domestic or home market. Clearly, such companies are not the main interest for our text but there are nevertheless situations in which a company should not or cannot become an active participant in international marketing.

When a company has a very limited product range that only appeals to its own local market, international marketing will not be advisable unless the company is prepared to expand its product line. In many service oriented businesses, customer relations are such that business is only done within a narrow or limited geographic trading range. To expand to new business centers other affiliates will have to be built,

FIGURE 8.3 ● Generic International Marketing Strategies

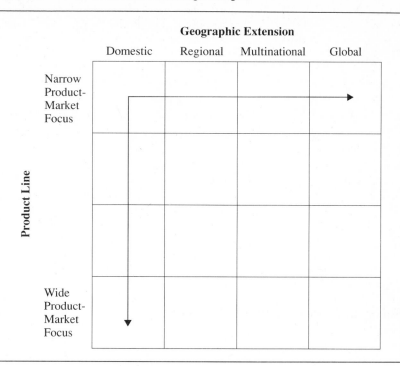

again requiring considerable capital assets. Also, some industries are substantially domestic, with individual companies not directly competing beyond their own local markets. And newly started companies may not be in a position to expand abroad before their domestic market is satisfied.

What has become evident is that, over the past two decades, an ever increasing number of domestic industries are becoming international. These developments may have been triggered by a foreign company arriving on the scene and changing the competitive situation. The U.S. major appliance industry serves as an excellent example of an industry that has turned from purely domestic to international in scope. Although only about 2 percent of all major appliances sold in the United States are imported, and exports account for about 6 percent, foreign competitors, such as Electrolux, control almost 20 percent of the U.S. market. That position was achieved through the acquisition of White Westinghouse and brands such as Frigidaire, Gibson, Kelvinator, and Tappan. With foreign competition invading its home territory, and with Europe growing faster than the North American market, the major U.S. players have become active internationally: GE, through a joint venture with British-owned GEC, Whirlpool, through a venture with Philips of the Netherlands, and Maytag, through the acquisition of Hoover, which gave it a strong position in the United Kingdom and some continental European markets. Occurring within weeks of each other, these actions show how quickly a purely domestic industry can turn into an international industry.[24] Consequently, today fewer and fewer industries can view themselves from a purely domestic point of view and more and more companies must move on to some level of internationalization.

Regional Expansion Strategies

Mapping out a regional strategy implies that a company will concentrate its resources and marketing efforts on one or possibly two of the world's regions. Emphasizing North America or Europe can be the result of a regional strategy. Other regions a company may want to concentrate on are Latin America, the Pacific Basin, or Asia. In such a situation, the company has expanded beyond a domestic environment but, as we will see later, has not yet reached a multinational or global state.

There are a number of reasons that make companies pursue a regional expansion strategy. Such firms are competing in the region that is part of their home market. Neighboring markets within the same region are invaded because of market or product similarity requiring few adaptations. Regional strategies are also encouraged when the customer requirements in one region are substantially different from others. Under those circumstances, different sets of competitors and market structures may exist, and industry participants may not invade each other's regions or market territories. When such a fragmentation exists, a firm can compete on the basis of knowing its own region best by being closer to its customers.

Examples for regional strategies can be found in a number of industries including the automobile, home appliance, and telecommunications industries. Among some of the leading automobile manufacturers, both Chrysler and Fiat can be classified as pursuing regional strategies. Chrysler withdrew from most overseas markets in the mid-1970s as a result of poor performance and a need to retrench to its major market, the United States. By the mid-1980s, Chrysler was competing largely in the United States, Canada, and Mexico. Another regional manufacturer in the automobile industry is Fiat of Italy. This company competes primarily in Europe with a few small operations in Latin America. Fiat does not play a major role in the North American markets or in Asia. Fiat has been very successful in leveraging its strong position in Italy into a sufficient volume to compete primarily in the small car segments in European countries. There are dangers in pursuing a regional strategy as Fiat has experienced. Many of its rivals, such as Ford or some Japanese firms, have a larger market to write off major car development expenditures. As a result, small regional rivals, just as domestic companies, find it increasingly difficult to compete against other firms with broader market coverage.[25]

Considerable attention has been given to companies pursuing integrated

24. "A Heartland Industry Takes on the World," *Fortune,* March 12, 1990, p. 110.
25. "The Turin Cloud," *Financial Times,* February 12, 1991, p. 21.

regional strategies in Europe. These integrated approaches, dubbed Euro or Pan-European strategies, have been triggered by the increasing European integration fostered by the Europe 1992 initiative. Among the U.S. firms switching to Pan-European strategies is Scott Paper. Until the mid-1980s, Scott pursued a country-by-country approach in Europe and developed important market positions in the major countries for disposable tissue paper. Many of these markets were developed with the help of local partners. These ventures had to be dissolved before the company could begin to integrate its operations across Europe. Because of the transportation costs involved, Scott still needs to produce close to major markets running several plants. However, a Pan-European approach is credited with a number of advantages. Scott established the Scottex brand across Europe and then leveraged its experience gained with product launches, positioning, and marketing from one country to another. In manufacturing, the company is building the same type of plant ordering identical machinery so that technical experience can be pooled.[26]

Companies may pursue one single regional strategy, such as to compete only in Europe or in the Asia Pacific region. Alternatively, companies may also decide to develop several regional strategies, even covering most of the world, on the basis that integration beyond a given region does not make much sense. Such a multiregional strategy is currently pursued by Sony, the Japanese consumer electronics firm. For Asia, Europe, and the United States, the company is building three largely self-sufficient industrial infrastructures that will be able to handle all products from development through production. Corporate functions currently handled in Japan will be decentralized to North America and Europe. Sony, with some two thirds of its sales outside Japan, is further along in this strategy of "global localization" than other Japanese firms.[27]

Multidomestic Strategies

Although we will present organization issues in more detail in Chapter 16, some general principles of how multidomestic firms are organized should be introduced at this point. To a large extent, international firms operating as multidomestic firms have organized their businesses around countries or geographic regions. While some key strategic decisions with respect to products and technology are made at the central or head office, the initiative of implementing marketing strategies is largely left to local country subsidiaries. As a result, profit and loss responsibility tends to focus on each individual country. At the extreme, this leads to an organization that runs many different businesses in a number of countries, therefore the term multidomestic. Each subsidiary represents a separate business that must be run profitably.

As we discussed in Chapter 1, multinational corporations tend to be represented in a large number of countries and the world's principal trading regions. The major-

---

26. "Crossing Frontiers with a Pan-European Plan," *Financial Times,* November 2, 1988, p. 27.
27. "The Emergence of a Global Company," *Financial Times,* October 2, 1989, p. 18.

ity of today's large internationally active firms may be classified as pursuing multidomestic strategies.

A large number of U.S. firms listed by *Fortune* magazine in its *Fortune* 500 list have traditionally operated multidomestically. This includes such well-known firms as General Motors, Ford, IBM, Gillette, General Electric, Kodak, as well as major service businesses including Citibank or Chase Manhattan, two of the largest U.S.-based financial services organizations. Common to most of these firms is their very large percentage of sales and profits generated from overseas business. For IBM and Gillette more than half of their volume is generated overseas.

Overseas firms such as Unilever, Royal Dutch-Shell, and Nestlé are foreign based firms with only a small portion of their sales coming from their domestic or home market. The ranks of international firms have also been joined by many Japanese firms, as well as firms from newly industrialized countries such as Korea, Taiwan, and some developing countries. Nestlé, the world's largest food company, though represented in most markets of the world, is a typical practitioner of the multidomestic strategy.[28] Nestlé, including its operating companies such as Carnation, Rowntree, or Buitoni, among others, has always practiced a decentralized approach to its management. Local operating managers thought to be much more in tune with local markets and, thus, are given the freedom to develop marketing strategies tailored to local needs. In the foods business where considerable differences exist between countries along cultures and consumer habits, the competitive environment, market structures, and practices, decentralization was judged by its management as imperative.[29]

GLOBAL STRATEGIES

To many readers the term *global strategy* probably suggests a company represented everywhere and pursuing more or less the same strategy. However, global strategies are not to be equated with global standardization, although this may be the case in some situations. A global strategy represents an application of a common set of strategic principles across most world markets. It may include, but not require, similarity in products or in marketing processes. When a company pursues a global strategy, it looks at the world market as a whole rather than at markets on a country-by-country basis, which is more typical for the multinational firm.

Standardization deals with the amount of similarity companies want to achieve across many markets with respect to their marketing strategies and marketing mix. Standardization may also apply to general business policies or the modes of opera-

28. "Nestlé Shows How to Gobble Markets," *Fortune,* January 16, 1989, p. 74.

29. Helmut Maucher, "Global Strategies of Nestle," *European Management Journal,* vol. 7, no. 1, March 1989, pp. 92–96.

tion a company may want to pursue. Globalization, on the other hand, deals with the integration of the many country strategies and the subordination of these country strategies to one global framework. As a result, it is conceivable that one company may have a globalized approach to its marketing strategy but leave the details for many parts of the marketing plan to local subsidiaries. Few companies will want to globalize all of their marketing operations. The difficulty then is to determine which marketing operations will gain from globalization. Such a modular approach to globalization is likely to yield greater returns than a total globalization of a company's marketing strategy.[30]

Reasons for Globalization

Several factors may drive companies toward the pursuit of a global marketing strategy. These factors range from a need to generate internal efficiencies, to take advantage of homogeneous markets, or to look for added synergies across a wide range of organizations. Wherever the causes may be, managers must understand or uncover if a "global logic" exists in their businesses, isolate that logic, and develop strategies accordingly.[31]

Globalizing for Internal Efficiency   What are the advantages to pursuing a global strategy? Internal efficiency is one advantage. By coordinating its operations for maximum efficiency, a company reduces costs and, thus, becomes more competitive.[32] Some companies may encounter new technological breakthroughs that represent substantial costs. These up-front research and development costs cannot be paid off by one or a few markets alone; consequently, companies become global out of a need to gain more volume. As we discussed earlier in this chapter, this need for more global volume triggered by the presence of critical input variables (CIVs) causes many firms to expand their global reach.

Globalizing to Compete in Homogeneous Markets   Another factor that encourages companies to pursue a global strategy is the homogenization of markets. In a much discussed article, Theodore Levitt encouraged companies to pursue globalization of products by looking at the similarities of their markets as opposed to differences. As a result, companies will gain economies of scale through cost reductions because the multitude of model variations may drive up costs and prevent internal efficiency from standardizing volume. Levitt also pointed out that lower prices,

30. John Quelch, "Customizing Global Marketing," *Harvard Business Review,* May-June 1986, pp. 59–68.

31. Robert B. Reich, "Who is Them?" *Harvard Business Review,* March-April 1991, pp. 77–88.

32. Thomas Hout, Michael E. Porter, and Eileen Rudden, "How Global Companies Win Out," *Harvard Business Review,* September-October 1982, pp. 98–108.

which can be offered as a result of standardization, will often overcome the resistance of customers against products with unique features tailored at individual markets.[33]

Originally considered one of the most important factors driving companies towards global marketing strategies, many firms incurred difficulties in their attempts at standardization. Today, most marketers are aware that few markets are similar, and significant differences remain. However, the other drivers, such as a need to pursue internal efficiency or leverage, are so important that companies have begun to adopt global marketing strategies in spite of marked differences. These partial global strategies allow for modularization and combine a portion of the strategy on a global basis with room for localization of products and marketing strategies.

Globalizing for Added Synergies While the international firm tends to see its investments in each market as separate and nonconnected, the global company aims at managing the interdependence between various foreign subsidiaries. This managing for interdependency tries to leverage strong positions in one market to help shore up weak positions in another. If one company showing a strong market in Japan brings about extra business in Europe, the global company will pursue such moves by looking at its total position in all markets rather than justify additional market share in Japan with incremental profits from Japan only.[34]

Leveraging strong positions to help weaker markets, also called *cross-subsidization,* is a move away from the traditional principle that each subsidiary should financially stand on its own. Cross-subsidizing foreign subsidiaries allows the global company to selectively slow a competitor's development in markets where it is most difficult for it to strike back. The global company will try to maximize its profits for the entire system of subsidiaries whereas the traditional MNC aims at maximizing profits for each subsidiary independently.[35]

Indicators for Globalization

Before a company will be able to decide on a particular global strategy, the evidence needs to be collected as to how far its environment has globalized. The extent of globalization can be measured at various levels. The company needs to look at its *customers* and have a clear view to what extent they have been subject to globalization. In addition, the company needs to have an idea on the nature of its *markets* which describes the particular way its customers purchase. Thirdly, a clear idea on the nature of its particular *industry* will tell a company whether it operates in a global

33. Theodore Levitt, "The Globalization of Markets," *Harvard Business Review,* May-June 1983, pp. 92–102.

34. Hout, Porter, and Rudden, "How Global Companies Win Out," *Harvard Business Review,* September-October 1982, pp. 98–108.

35. Gary Hamel and C. K. Prahalad, "Do You Really Have a Global Strategy?" *Harvard Business Review,* July-August 1985, pp. 139–148.

industry. And finally, the company will need to understand the nature of *competition* and the extent to which competition may have globalized. Understanding each of those four areas will result in a pattern that may help address the question if some form of global strategy may be appropriate for the company.

Globalization at the Customer Level   In its industry or segments, does the company actually meet a global customer? Global customers can be defined as group of customers with homogeneous needs, benefits sought, or product feature requirements across many markets or countries. The emphasis is on similarity because it is actually rare that a company meets identical customers across the world. The issue of customer globalization can be further analyzed on several levels. First, to the extent that the general need expressed by customers is similar across many countries, the company faces a *global need,* although product specifications may be different. A global need is an indication of a global product category. Companies facing global product categories realize that their products or services offered are present in most markets. In fact, there are few products that are so unique that they only exist in particular country segments. The majority of companies performing this analysis find that they actually are facing global product categories.

Beyond the general presence of a given product or service is the presence of *global customer segments.* Global segments are relatively homogeneous groups of customers with similar needs, interests, and preferences, present in many countries, although they may not be majority segments in many markets. Such global customer segments will exist only if there is the presence of a global product category. Analyzing global customer segments requires a company to go beyond country differences and to look for synergies and similarities across many national markets. The more specifically a global segment can be defined, the more likely that similarities within that segment outweigh differences present across countries.

Once the presence of the product or service across many markets has been ascertained, the company can look at the reasons for purchasing its products. The question shifts at this stage to the benefits sought by the customers. If a company markets a product that is purchased for similar reasons across the world, the company faces a *global benefit* which is going beyond the more general global product category. Global benefits deal with the communications and branding of a product and lead to different global marketing strategies. Globalization of benefits represents a more advanced form of globalization and, if present, directs companies to different strategies.

Finally, there is the question on whether a company can observe globalization of its products. This aspect centers on the product features, design, and functionality. True global products are more common in the industrial markets and less so in the consumer markets. A *global product* is described as consisting of largely the same features and functionality, although there can be differing degrees of globalization. Cars, definitely a global product category, are not truly global products because many countries have different requirements and regulations that do not allow car companies to produce complete standardized products worldwide. Instead, key components may be standardized, leading to global component strategies, while preserving the possibility for local customization or localization.

This discussion highlights one of the major developments in global marketing. The discussion has increasingly shifted from the absolute question of "Do we have global customers?" to the more differentiated question "At what level is the customer globalized?" The result of such an analysis is but one input into the understanding of how far globalization has progressed for a given industry.

Globalization at the Market Level   Analyzing globalization of markets, rather than customers, requires the company to get a clear understanding of the purchasing process. In particular, the interest now shifts towards the effort and range of the buying process. Global markets are characterized by customers who are both aware of and search out alternatives beyond their own country borders. In a globalized market, customers search the world for bargains or the best products and will buy from far away if a superior product is available. On the opposite side, local markets are characterized by customers who will only buy locally, do not go to great lengths to chase a bargain, and, therefore, ignore alternatives elsewhere. Companies can rely on many signals that will indicate whether they are facing a global market. The presence of parallel imports or gray markets, discussed in greater detail in Chapter 13, is a clear indicator that customers, by trying to take advantage of price differentials between markets or regions, are willing to purchase beyond borders. Furthermore, many firms are facing customers demanding to negotiate purchasing contracts for multiple countries or regions rather than buy on a country-by-country basis. Global markets are much more pronounced in standardized products or components and marketers of most commodities face them on a daily basis.

The presence of strongly globalized markets tends to force different global marketing strategies on companies. Coordinating pricing, logistics, sourcing strategies, and product launches are some of the strategies that will have to be adopted if a company faces global markets.

Globalization at the Industry Level   Strategists have learned to analyze industries and probe for the presence of Key Success Factors (KSFs) as we explained in earlier sections of this chapter. Globalization has occurred at the industry level if the key success factors, which are the basic competitive requirements a company must meet, are relatively similar across many countries. This will indicate that the experience in operating and competing in that industry is transferable. Rather than relearning how to penetrate a given industry when entering a new market, the company may be able to fall back on previous experience. Industries where such experience sharing is typical can be classified as having experienced globalization, although it is not a requirement that competitors already do so.

A second important development that is typical of globalized industries is the presence of CIVs (Critical Input Variables) as described earlier in this chapter. Their presence signals a strong benefit from globalization in a given industry. When CIVs are present, additional investment into opening new markets are relatively small and major benefits accrue to an integrative and global approach in that industry.

Globalization at the Competitor Level   Globalization at the competitor level is present when competitors can reach all major markets or when competitors are present in most markets. Here, globalization again may occur at several levels. First, the mere presence of the same competitor signals a different competitive environment than if a company faces a different set of competitors market after market. However, even if a company faces the same competitors, country after country, it may not yet mean that the competitors are actually competing with a coordinated strategy. True globalization at the competitors' level occurs when the company faces the same competitor and the same competitive strategy. Should only presence be the case, the competitive game may not be much different from facing different firms in each country. However, global presence in the first instance may signal eventual global competitive strategies in the future and this must be taken into consideration.

Under globalized competition, companies will need to review traditional assumptions on how to assign roles to subsidiaries in various markets. Issues of cross-subsidization for competitive leverage may apply now and measurement of market share in global terms may also become necessary if the company faces global competition. The difference of competitive strategies will be explained in more detail in the following section of this chapter.

Independence of Indicators of Globalization   As described in the previous sections, companies may gain valuable insights into the globalization process by examining their customers, their segments, their markets, their industry, and finally their competitors. Different levels of globalization may be observed in each area and it may not be necessary to have globalization emerge in equal patterns. Some companies may find that they are facing global competitors with coordinated strategies but their customers themselves may not qualify as global. Furthermore, it is conceivable that a company may come to the conclusion that globalization has progressed quite far in its markets, segments, and among its customers, but that competitors have yet to compete globally. As a result, different global marketing strategies may emerge as the global pattern differs for each company.

Global Marketing Strategies

In the early phases of development, global marketing strategies were assumed to be of one type only. Typically, these first types of global strategies were associated with offering the same marketing strategy across the globe. The debate had centered on whether a company could gain anything from this and what the preconditions for this type of strategy would be. As marketers gained more experience, many other types of global marketing strategies became apparent. Some of those were much less involved and exposed a smaller aspect of a marketing strategy to globalization. In this section, we will explore the various types of global marketing strategies and indicate the conditions under which they may best succeed.

Integrated Global Marketing Strategy When a company pursues an integrated global marketing strategy, all aspects of the marketing strategy have been globalized. Globalization includes not only the product, but also the communications strategy, pricing, and distribution, as well as such strategic elements as segmentation and positioning. Such a strategy may be advisable for companies who face completely globalized customers along the lines defined in the earlier section. It also assumes that the way a given industry works is highly similar, thus allowing a company to unfold its strategy along similar paths in each country.

Reality tells us today that those are rare situations, and complete integrated global marketing strategies will continue to be the exception. However, there are many other types of global marketing strategies; each of them may be tailored to specific industry and competitive circumstances.

Global Segment Strategies A company that decides to pursue the same segment in many countries is following a global segment strategy. The company may develop an understanding of its customer base and, thus, leverage that experience around the world. In both consumer and industrial industries significant knowledge is accumulated when a company gains in-depth understanding of a niche or segment. A pure global segment strategy will even allow for different products, brands, or advertising, although some standardization is expected. The choices may consist of competing always in the upper or middle segment of a given consumer market, or for a particular technical application in an industrial segment.

Global Product Category Possibly the least involved type of global marketing strategy is the pursuit of the global category. Leverage is gained from competing in the same category country after country and may come in the form of product technology or development costs. Selecting the form of global product category implies that the company, while staying within that category, will consider targeting different segments in each category, or varying the product, advertising, and branding according to local market requirements. Companies competing in the multidomestic way are frequently applying the global category strategy and leverage knowledge across markets without pursuing standardization. That strategy works best if there are significant differences across markets and when few segments are present in market after market.

Global Marketing Mix Element Strategies These strategies pursue globalization along individual marketing mix elements such as pricing, distribution, communications, or product. They are partially globalized strategies which allow a company to customize other aspects of its marketing strategy. Although various types of strategies may apply, the most important ones are global product strategies, global advertising strategies, and global branding strategies.

Global Product Strategy   Pursuing a global product strategy implies that a company has largely globalized its product offering. Although the product may not need to be completely standardized worldwide, key aspects or components may in fact be globalized. The company may elect to add a global product strategy if the product or services offered fit the description of global products discussed earlier. Global product strategies require that product use conditions, expected features, and required product functions be largely identical so that few variations or changes are needed. Examples of such strategies are Kodak and its films, many of the consumer electronics companies, and many computer firms offering largely identical products worldwide. Companies pursuing a global product strategy are interested in leveraging the fact that all investment for producing and developing a given product have already been made. Global strategies will yield more volume which will make the original investment easier to justify.

Global Branding Strategies   Global branding strategies consist of using the same brand name or logo worldwide. Companies want to leverage the creation of such brand names across many markets because the launching of new brands requires a considerable marketing investment. Global branding strategies tend to be advisable if the target customers travel across country borders and will be exposed to products elsewhere.

Global branding strategies also become important if target customers are exposed to advertising worldwide. This is often the case for industrial marketing customers who may read industry and trade journals from other countries. Increasingly, this has become important also for consumer products where cross-border advertising through international TV channels has become common. Even in some markets such as Eastern Europe, many consumers have become aware of brands offered in Western Europe before the liberalization of the economies in the early 1990s. Pursuing global branding allows a company to take advantage of such existing goodwill. Companies pursuing global branding strategies may include luxury product marketers who typically face a large fixed investment for the worldwide promotion of a product. In Chapter 15, we will look at the various alternatives to global branding in more detail.

Global Advertising Strategies   Globalizing advertising is generally associated with the use of the same brand name across the world. However, it is possible that a company may want to use different brand names, partly for historic purposes. Many global firms have made acquisitions in other countries resulting in a number of local brands. These local brands have their own distinguished market and a company may find it futile to change those names. Instead, the company may want to leverage a certain theme or advertising approach that may have been developed as a result of some global customer research. Global advertising themes are most likely advisable where a firm may market to customers with similar benefits sought across the world. Once the purchasing reason has been determined as similar, a common theme may be created to address it. The difficulties encountered with selecting common themes will be discussed at length in Chapter 15.

PRODUCT/MARKET STRATEGIES

As outlined earlier in this chapter, geographic extension is one of two key dimensions in the strategy of an international company. The other dimension is concerned with the range of a firm's product and service offerings. To what extent should a company become a supplier of a wide range of products aimed at several or many market segments? Should a company become the global specialist in a certain area by satisfying one or a small number of target segments, doing this in most major markets around the world?

Even some of the largest companies cannot pursue all available initiatives. Resources for most companies are limited, often requiring a tradeoff between product expansion and geographic expansion strategies. Resolving this question is necessary in order to achieve a concentration of resources and efforts in areas where they will bring the most return. We can distinguish between two models: on the one hand, we have the broad-based firm marketing a wide range of products to many different customer groups, both domestic and overseas. On the other hand we have the narrow based firm marketing a limited range of products to a homogeneous customer group around the world. Both types of companies can be successful in their respective markets.

Companies such as Procter & Gamble, Unilever, and Nestlé are all examples of consumer goods firms practicing a broad-based product strategy. In most markets, these firms offer many brands and product lines. Among industrial marketers, General Electric follows a similar strategy. Some of these firms, however, are broken down into a large number of strategic business units, or divisions with a limited product range aimed at a limited market segment, and within each business unit the chosen strategy may be much more focused.

Firms with a narrow product range include Hertz or Avis, the U.S. car rental companies, and Rolex, the Swiss watch manufacturing company. These firms have in common a narrow and clearly focused product line with the intent of dominating their chosen market segment across many countries. Many specialty equipment manufacturers in the fields of machine tools, electronic testing equipment, and other production process equipment tend to fit this pattern of niche or focus marketing.

Three concepts will help explain why some companies manage to achieve dominance of one small segment worldwide. As is the case with domestic business, to be successful the firm must combine a relevant competitive advantage, the mastery of key success factors (KSFs),[36] and the relationship between the target market and the

36. Ohmae, *The Mind of the Strategist* (New York: McGraw-Hill, 1982), p. 42.

firm's distinctive competence. To the extent that these three areas overlap and that the firm focuses them on its chosen target market, a much greater chance for success occurs (see Figure 8.4).

Competitive advantage includes the firm's relative advantage over other competitors. This may consist of an absolute advantage in technology or some other area, or a relative advantage where the firm is only relatively better. A competitive advantage may be based on marketing expertise, production technology, or better market contacts than competitors. The key success factors, KSFs, consist of those steps or business functions that a company must do well in to survive in a given industry. KSFs can consist of distribution, advertising, research, lower cost production, or other business steps. A company's distinctive competence consists of its acquired experience and usually covers a skill area where the firm has excelled over time. For one company that may be managing mass production; for another, it may consist of innovation in certain field or having served a certain customer group particularly well.

To stretch success geographically, companies must bring about an overlap of these three areas. Ideally, for any target segment the company brings together a competitive advantage, does well in the relevant key success factors, and has distinctive competence that is relevant for its market. As we extend this to other countries, firms that are active in markets where customer needs and market structures are relatively homogeneous can gain success with the same skill base and thus often find themselves dominating a certain segment worldwide. However, in markets where the KSF and the competitive advantage differ from country to country, it becomes much more difficult to leverage a company's experience base into other countries. This may either reduce the drawing range of the company to a limited number of markets or the company will have to acquire new skills to enter those more diverse markets. Such moves will increase risks because this adds greater uncertainty and requires more resources.

The trend today is for companies to expect their businesses to develop a worldwide position, and for some, such as GE, to become number one or two worldwide. This requires a business to develop its competitive position across all major markets, in particular across the major regions of North America, Asia/Pacific, and Europe. The preference is for businesses (or strategic business units in large corporations) to focus on a particular line or segment by extending that offering around the globe. This has also led companies to pursue global marketing strategies per business line rather than corporate wide. A company such as GE may pursue many different global marketing strategies, not just one. Each business is to develop its own, and there may well be different global marketing strategies for different businesses. In this sense, each business is given a global mandate which means that it is required to develop on a worldwide basis.[37]

37. "Jack Welch Reinvents General Electric—Again," *The Economist,* March 30, 1991, p. 59.

FIGURE 8.4 ● Focusing Key Skills for International Marketing Success

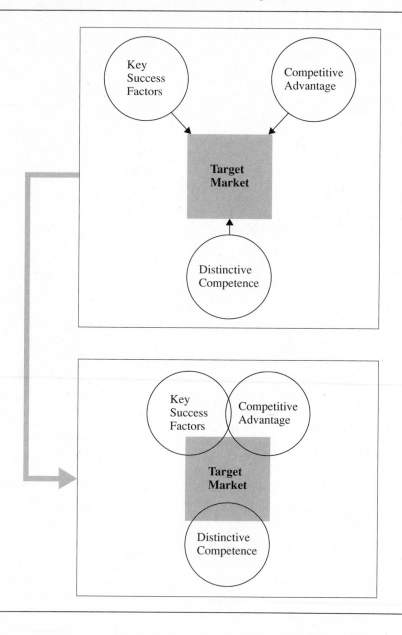

COMPETITIVE STRATEGIES FOR GLOBAL MARKETING

The focus of this section is on the various competitive strategies firms can adopt in the international field. The examples given will show the impact of various geographic and product/market structures on a firm's competitive position. For our purposes, we will define competitive strategy "as the way in which a firm can compete more effectively to strengthen its market position."[38] When firms compete in the international market, their competitive strategies are likely to depend on their relevant resources and the type of competition they are meeting. At the country level, companies are apt to meet a variety of different players, ranging from local firms to multinational companies and even global firms. As we outlined in detail in the previous section of this chapter, these types of firms operate differently. Consequently, a company will have to be able to adjust to any differences in competition on a country-by-country basis. Therefore the purpose of this section is to characterize some typical match-ups and to make it clear to the reader how competitive dynamics differ depending on the players involved.

We will look at competitive strategy by examining three prototype players: the local, the multidomestic, and the global firm. By describing some real competitive battles between such companies, we aim to distill some general concepts about which type of competitive strategy will work for each type of firm.

Local Company versus Global Firm

As we have learned, global firms are able to leverage their experience and market position in one market for the benefit of another. Consequently, the global firm is often a more potent competitor for a local company. The example of how Procter & Gamble dealt with two local competitors in the Swiss disposable diaper market will serve as an illustration of such a competitive dynamic.

In the mid-1970s, the Swiss market for baby diaper products consisted of cloth diapers, still the largest segment, and some disposable products such as inserts for traditional diapers.[39] Having observed the success of disposable diapers in the United States and in other larger markets, a Swiss company, Moltex, introduced its own version of the disposable diaper. Although a considerable habit change was needed, the company supported its product with little advertising and relied primarily on Switzerland's largest supermarket chain, Coop, for support. Moltex quickly gained a 35 percent market share.

When Procter & Gamble wanted to introduce its Pampers brand one year later, the large U.S. company found the channels blocked; Coop, its largest potential retail customer, was unwilling to stock another brand. Moltex had strengthened its hand

---

38. Michael E. Porter, *Competitive Strategy* (New York: The Free Press, 1980), p. x.

39. For more details, see Jean-Pierre Jeannet, *Competitive Marketing Strategies in a European Context.* IMEDE, International Management Development Institute, Lausanne, Switzerland, 1987.

with the trade by offering larger discounts and higher margins. In an effort to outflank the blocked channel, Pampers was introduced through drug stores, department stores, and in hospitals through heavy sampling. Once initial distribution was attained, Pampers brand was supported with considerable advertising aimed at the consumer. Despite its distribution handicap, Pampers became the brand leader.

When the large supermarket chain realized the profitability of the disposable diaper market, the chain introduced its own store brand. Moltex, up to that time the only brand carried by this chain, lost its most important distribution overnight. However, Procter & Gamble was able to continue to expand its market share and maintain dominance despite a substantial premium price because the company had continued to build its brand image with consumers by supporting it with advertising. In the end, the supermarket chain began to carry Pampers. Moltex, having lost distribution, was relegated to a minor brand.

Why was Procter & Gamble able to overcome substantial local competition despite a late entry into the Swiss market for disposable diapers? Moltex had learned from the considerable market potential in disposable diapers by observing market trends abroad. However, the company had adopted a marketing strategy that did not consider the marketing strength of its principal and most likely competitor, Procter & Gamble, though P&G was already on the Swiss market with other products and could be expected to follow suit soon. Local market connections to the retail trade were not sufficient to overcome the marketing expertise of a global firm.

Our second example should make clear to us that local firms can in fact compete effectively against much larger international companies if they compete wisely.

Ramlösa, the leading Swedish bottler of mineral water, is a local firm that was able to compete effectively against Perrier of France, probably the most successful marketer of mineral water worldwide. Ramlösa sold its mineral water primarily in Sweden with some minor export business to Norway and Finland, two neighboring countries. Ramlösa executives had watched Perrier invade market after market in Europe and finally dominate the premium segment for mineral water worldwide.[40]

In the early 1980s, when Perrier was repeating its attack on the premium segment of Denmark, Ramlösa executives realized that it would not be long before Perrier would invade their market also. In Sweden, Ramlösa enjoyed a market share of close to 100 percent, and it was feared an aggressive new entrant like Perrier might lower Ramlösa's share considerably. Having studied Perrier's strategy in other European markets, Ramlösa searched for a response and, in 1981, it finally decided to launch its own premium brand of mineral water. The company invested in expensive packaging and bottles, invested in advertising to obtain a premium image, and increased the price by almost 50 percent although the mineral water of the premium brand was identical to that sold under its regular label. The sales volume of the premium brand did end up decreasing the sales of the regular brand, but Ramlösa was not unhappy since the profitability of the premium brand per unit was substantially higher than its regular brand.

40. Ibid.

When Perrier finally entered the Swedish market in 1983, it followed its tried and proven strategy of aiming at the premium spot. However, with Ramlösa already owning the premium spot with its top brand, Perrier was forced to enter on a premium-premium strategy. This resulted in such a high price that Perrier gained very little market share over Ramlösa. By correctly spotting and predicting the Perrier strategy in advance, Ramlösa was able to design a response that prevented Perrier from unfolding the approach that had proven so successful elsewhere.

Although global firms have superior resources, they often become inflexible after several successful market entries and tend to stay with standard approaches when flexibility is called for. In general, the global firms strongest local competitors are those who watch global firms carefully and learn from their moves in other countries. With some global firms requiring several years before a product is introduced in all markets, local competitors in some markets can take advantage of such advance notice by building defenses or launching a preemptive attack on the same segment.

Multidomestic Corporation versus Multidomestic Corporation

When two multidomestic firms clash in a single market, the battles tend to be more expensive and more drawn out than when international firms compete against local competitors. This is largely so because international firms have sufficient resources to fight it out. Such clashes take place in many markets. However, when multinational firms compete in a certain market, there is normally no spillover into other markets since those firms view strategy mostly on a country-by-country basis.

How two multidomestic firms, the U.S.-based CPC International and the Swiss-based Nestlé, clashed in Denmark in the 1980s serves as a typical example of a head-on collision between two large international companies.[41] Both firms are large food companies operating subsidiaries in many countries. Aside from producing in Denmark for export, both companies operated two local marketing subsidiaries distributing a full line of products to the local retail trade. Nestlé marketed instant coffee, infant food products, and bouillons under its Maggi brand name. Maggi bouillons were Nestlé's most important product line in Denmark. Competing directly against Maggi was CPC's Knorr brand of dehydrated products, which included bouillons, but also soups and sauces. Nestlé controlled about 80 percent of the bouillon market compared to CPC's 20 percent. However, CPC's Knorr brand completely dominated the sauce and soup segments.

CPC's Knorr launched an attack in the bouillon segment by substantially underpricing Maggi. When Maggi realized that it suffered a disadvantage from a smaller shelf space area due to offering only one product in that category, it countered by introducing a new dehydrated line of mixes that were not sold by Knorr in Denmark.

41. See case series Nestlé Nordisk A/S (A) through (E), reprinted in Jean-Pierre Jeannet, *Competitive Marketing Strategies in a European Context.* IMEDE, International Management Development Institute, Lausanne, Switzerland, 1987.

This instantly gave Maggi more shelf space. Knorr followed suit, however. When Maggi realized that Knorr's funds for attacking in the bouillon segment came largely from its profitable sauce business, Maggi introduced a limited sauce line with low prices to reduce Knorr's cashflow. Although this paid for itself, Maggi was not able to have an impact on Knorr's profitability because the market grew due to higher competitive activity. In the end, Maggi also expanded into soups which enabled it to improve its position and to make up for lost profits in the bouillon segment, where price competition substantially lowered profit margins after several years.

Although both CPC International and Nestlé subsidiaries fought an intense marketing battle for several years, both subsidiaries relied largely on their own financial resources and had profit and loss responsibility on a local basis. Both multinationals made available to their subsidiaries the full product development resources of their international networks. The two companies offered full lines of dehydrated products in all major European markets including soups, sauces, mixes, and bouillons. As a result, the Danish subsidiaries could easily and quickly launch new products that were already marketed elsewhere. However, the two subsidiaries obviously had to bear all marketing costs on their own. At no time did this intensive battle spill over into other markets, nor was it a reflection of head-office strategy to expand certain product lines in Denmark.

Global Firm versus Global Firm

In some industries, developments have already reached a point where most key competitors have attained some level of globalization. In such situations, the type of competitive behavior has changed and global companies go beyond the leveraging of key developments or new product trends.

One of the longest running global competitive battles is the competition between the Coca-Cola Company and PepsiCo, both U.S.-based soft drink companies. Although the two companies are more evenly matched in the U.S. market, Coke's market share outside the United States amounts to 46 percent compared to Pepsi's 15 percent.[42] Differences abroad come from Coke's better market position in Europe and some Asian markets, whereas Pepsi has dominated some markets such as the Soviet Union. In one important market, India, Coke withdrew in the mid-1970s due to pressures to sell part of its local subsidiary. As a result, its rival Pepsi got a chance to enter and Coke has been trying to get back in.[43]

In its advertising, Coca-Cola is capitalizing on Coke's position as the world's most recognizable brand and product. The company spends some $240 million annually on advertising outside the U.S., most of it for its Coke brand. The company is using a pool of about nine commercials from which local country managers select

42. "Pepsi Keeps on Going After No. 1," *Fortune,* March 11, 1991, p. 62.

43. "The Real Thing: As a Global Marketer, Coke Excels by Being Tough and Consistent," *Wall Street Journal,* December 19, 1989, p. 1.

for their markets. By comparison, Pepsi spent $128 million outside the U.S., most of its on its snack food business.[44]

One of the biggest battle grounds for the two firms is Europe, and Germany in particular. Since the reunion, Germany's $1 billion soft drink market has become the center of attention. Coca-Cola had dominated West Germany with a 65 percent share of the cola market compared to Pepsi's 10 percent. In former East Germany, Pepsi had the lead with 30 percent of the cola market. Pepsi has increased its advertising expenditures from $7 million to $27 million in one year and is targeting a 20 percent cola share for the entire German market.[45] In the important French market, Coke has been outselling Pepsi by a ratio of almost 8 to 1. Coke's 80 percent market share is dominant partly because Coke entered first following U.S. soldiers after World War II and because France is one of the few countries in Europe where Coke owns its own bottling plants. This gives Coke greater control over its rival Pepsi, who is allied with Perrier in a joint venture.[46]

The battle for global dominance between Coke and Pepsi is not only fought in individual markets. It is fought at large sports events, such as the world cup for soccer. A company such as Coca-Cola who is dominant in some markets has the ability to cross-subsidize other markets where its competitive position is weaker.

Another major global battle is taking place between Eastman Kodak of the United States and Fuji Film of Japan. In the 1980s, Fuji attacked Kodak in its lucrative European and U.S. markets and forced the U.S. company into expensive price concessions. Eventually Kodak decided to strike back by attacking Fuji's own domestic market, Japan. Between 1984 and 1990, Kodak's presence in Japan grew from just 15 to 4,500 employees and sales grew from about $200 million to $1.3 billion over the same time period. The total investment amounted to some $500 million. Kodak judged this move important because it wanted to strike back at Fuji's domestic market where the Japanese firm enjoyed a market share of 70 percent in color film.[47]

Kodak's counterattack was combined with a number of changes in its Japanese marketing strategy. Kodak entered a joint venture with a chemical company to enhance its local distribution. It followed up with equity investment in Chinon, its local camera supplier, and its local photo finisher. Kodak began to place Japanese characters on its film products and opened a local research facility. In its promotions, Kodak became more aggressive with opening big neon signs in attractive locations and it eventually became the sponsor of the 1988 Olympics, in response to Fuji's official sponsorship of the 1984 Olympics in Los Angeles. Finally, Kodak invested $1 million in an airship with its colors and had it circling over Fuji's head office in

44. "Pepsi, Coke Focus on International Ad Efforts," *Advertising Age,* February 25, 1991, p. 32.
45. Ibid.
46. "C'est la Guerre for Coke and Pepsi," *Financial Times,* February 18, 1991, p. 15.
47. "The Revenge of Big Yellow," *The Economist,* November 10, 1990, p. 77.

Tokyo. This forced Fuji to bring back at great expense its own airship from a tour in Europe.

The results of this strategy, although costly, have yielded impressive market results. Kodak has increased its market share from 10 to 15 percent and may be passing Konica, Japan's number two, in a few years. The company has also become more aggressive in its professional segment in the United States where it is using its superior-size sales force to take business away from Fuji.[48] However, in the most important segment for color film used by amateur photographers, progress has been slow and Kodak's share is estimated to range around 10 percent. Observers believe that Kodak and Fuji each have about 10 percent of each other's home markets.[49] The basic strategy was to slow down Fuji's progress in the U.S. and Europe by hitting back at its domestic market where Fuji had been protected from substantial competition.

In some ways, global competition is like a global chess game with a few competitors blocking each other's moves in or around key markets. What a competitor may be doing in a given market becomes more important than what potential customers desire. However, to do well in this game requires that individual country aspirations and strategies become subordinated to the overall strategy directed from a central point.

CONCLUSIONS

Any company engaging in international and global marketing operations is faced with a number of very important strategic decisions. At the outset, a decision in principle needs to be made committing the company to some level of internationalization. Increasingly, firms will find that for competitive reasons international business must be pursued and that it is often not an optional strategy. Once committed, the company needs to decide where the international business should be pursued, both in terms of geographic regions and specific countries. A firm's entry decision into each market and the selection of the international marketing program are additional strategic decisions.

During this decade, a changing competitive environment has considerably affected these choices. In the past, companies have moved from largely domestic or regional firms to become global. As multidomestic companies, these firms competed in many local markets and attempted to meet the local market requirements as best they could. Although many firms still approach their international marketing effort this way, an increasing number of firms are taking a global view of their marketplace.

48. "Kodak Zooms in on Pro Photographers," *Wall Street Journal*, February 27, 1991, p. B1.
49. "Kodak Remains Out of Focus in Japan When it Comes to Key Color Film Market," *Wall Street Journal*, December 7, 1990, p. B1.

The global firm operates differently from the multidomestic or regional company. Pursuing a global strategy does not necessarily mean that the company is attempting to standardize all of its marketing programs on a global scale. Furthermore, a global strategy also does not imply that the company is represented in all markets of the world. Rather, global strategy is a new way of thinking about the business. Global companies are fully aware of their strengths across as many markets as possible. Consequently, the global company will build its strategy on the basis of its key skills and will enter markets where those skills are relevant.

A global company is also keenly aware of the value of global size and market share. As a result, a number of strategic decisions, such as which markets to enter, will become subject to the overall global strategy. Rather than making each market pay its way separately, a global firm may aim to break even in some markets if this will help its overall position by holding back a key competitor. As strategy begins to compare with that of a global chess game, companies will have to develop new skills and learn about new concepts to survive. Exploitation of the lead market principle and its understanding will become more important.

Globalization of many industries today is a fact. Some companies have no choice but to become globalized. Once key competitors in their industries are globalized, other firms must follow. This leads to a rethinking of the strategic choices and inevitably will lead to new priorities. Globalization is not simply a new term for something that has existed all along; it is a new competitive game requiring companies to adjust to and learn new ways of doing business. For many companies, survival depends on how well they learn this new game.

As we have seen in this chapter, globalization has become a multifaceted term requiring companies to carefully monitor their markets. Globalization may occur in several parts of a firm's business and require different responses whether it occurs at the customer level, or at the market, industry, or competitor level. As a result, now there are many types of global strategies a firm may choose from, moving the decision away from *whether* a global strategy toward *which* global strategy.

Questions for Discussion

1. Many companies have different reasons for internationalizing their operations. Contrast the reasons for a large firm, such as IBM, and a much smaller one, such as Apple or Compaq.

2. What reasons are there for small firms to pursue an international strategy? Should they do this at all?

3. Investigate the geographic portfolio of three large *Fortune* 500 companies. What differences do you see, and what do you think accounts for these differences?

4. Contrast global and other types of geographic expansion strategies. In particular, how does it differ from a multinational strategy?

5. Select three different industries you are interested in and compare them with regard to the factors for globalization. What implications are you making from your analysis?

6. How can a local company best compete against global firms?

For Further Reading

Alahutta, Matti. "Growth Strategies for High Technology Challengers." Acta Polytechnica Scandinavica, Electrical Engineering Series No. 66, Helsinki University of Technology, Helsinki, 1990.

Ayal, Igal, and Jehiel Zif. "Market Expansion Strategies in Multinational Marketing." *Journal of Marketing,* Spring 1979, pp. 84–94.

Bartlett, Christopher A. and Sumantra Ghoshal. *Managing Across Borders.* Boston: Harvard Business School Press, 1989.

Boddewyn, J. J. "Standardization in International Marketing: Is Ted Levitt in Fact Right?" *Business Horizons* (November-December, 1986).

Eckley, Robert S. "Caterpillar's Ordeal: Foreign Competition in Capital Goods." *Business Horizons,* March-April 1989, pp. 80–86.

Ghoshal, Sumantra. "Global Strategy: An Organizing Framework." *Strategic Management Journal,* vol. 8 (1987) p. 425–440.

Harrell, Gilbert D., and Richard O. Kiefer. "Multinational Strategic Market Portfolios." *MSU Business Topics* (Winter 1981), pp. 5–16.

Kaynak, Erdener, ed. *Global Perspectives in Marketing.* New York: Praeger Publishers, 1985.

Ohmae, Kenichi. *The Mind of a Strategist.* New York: McGraw-Hill, 1982.

Ohmae, Kenichi. *Triad Power: The Coming Shape of Global Competition.* New York: Free Press, 1985.

Porter, Michael. ed. *Competition in Global Industries.* Boston: Harvard Business School Press, 1986.

Reich, Robert B. "Who Is Them?" *Harvard Business Review,* March-April 1991, pp. 77–88.

Reich, Robert B. *The Work of Nations.* New York: Knopf, 1991.

Taylor, William. "The Logic of Global Business: An Interview with Percy Bernevik." *Harvard Business Review,* March-April 1991, pp. 91–105.

9

Global Market Entry Strategies

● **INTERNATIONAL COMPANIES MUST** *determine the type of presence they expect to maintain in every market where they compete. One major choice concerns the method of supplying the selected market. A company may want to export to the new market or it may prefer to produce locally. A second major choice involves the amount of direct ownership desired. Should the company strive for full ownership of its local operation or is a joint venture preferable? These initial decisions on market entry tend to be of medium- to long-term importance, leaving little room for change once a commitment has been made. Therefore, it is important to treat these decisions with the utmost care. Not only is the financial return to the company at stake, but the extent to which the company's marketing strategy can be employed in the new market also depends on these decisions.*

In this chapter, we concentrate on the major entry strategy alternatives by explaining each one in detail and citing relevant company experiences. We also treat the entry strategy from an integrative point of view and offer guidance as to how a specific strategy may be selected to suit a company's needs. For an overview of all chapter topics, see Figure 9.1.

FIGURE 9.1 ● Market Entry Strategies

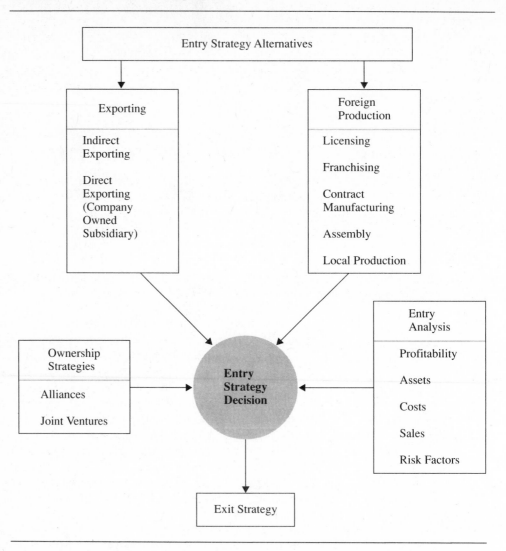

EXPORTING AS AN ENTRY STRATEGY

Exporting to a foreign market is a strategy many companies follow for at least some of their markets. Since many countries do not offer a large enough opportunity to justify local production, exporting allows a company to centrally manufacture its products for several markets and, therefore, obtain economies of scale. Furthermore, since exports represent incremental volume out of an existing production operation located elsewhere, the marginal profitability of such exports tends to be high. A firm has two basic options in carrying out its export operations. Markets can be contacted through a domestically located middleman (located in the exporter's country of operation)—an approach called *indirect exporting.* Alternatively, markets can be reached through a middleman located in the foreign market—an approach termed *direct exporting.* The use of various types of export middlemen is described in detail in Chapter 12.

Indirect Exporting

Several types of middlemen located in the domestic market are ready to assist a manufacturer in contacting foreign markets or buyers. The major advantage for using a domestic middleman lies in the middleman's knowledge of foreign market conditions. Particularly for companies with little or no experience in exporting, the use of a domestic middleman provides the exporter with readily available expertise. The most common types of middlemen are brokers, combination export managers, and manufacturers' export agents. Group selling activities can also help individual manufacturers in their export operations.

Direct Exporting

A company is engaged in direct exporting when it exports through intermediaries located in the foreign markets. Under direct exporting, an exporter must deal with a large number of foreign contacts, possibly one or more for each country the company plans to enter. While a direct exporting operation requires a larger degree of expertise, this method of market entry does provide the company with a greater degree of control over its distribution channels than will be the case under indirect exporting. The exporter may select from two major types of middlemen: agents or merchants. Also, the exporting company may establish its own sales subsidiary as an alternative to independent middlemen. Of the about 300,000 manufacturing companies in the United States, only about 10 percent are actively exporting. Almost 85 percent of the U.S. exports, however, is accounted for by the top 250 U.S. companies, which means that a substantial amount of exporting is performed by many small to medium-sized manufacturers. Most of these companies get started by using distributors overseas. But as Black Box Corp., a medium-sized company selling computer communications equipment, found out, most foreign distributors represented other competing brands as well. They frequently push whatever brand offers the best margin.[1]

1. "Made in the U.S.A.," *Business Week,* February 1988, p. 28–34.

The Company-Owned Sales Office (Foreign Sales Subsidiary)

Many companies export directly to their own sales subsidiaries abroad, sidestepping independent middlemen. The sales subsidiary assumes the role of the independent distributor by stocking manufacturers' products, selling to buyers, and assuming the credit risk. The sales subsidiary offers the manufacturer full control of selling operations in a foreign market. This may be important if the company's products require the use of special marketing skills, such as advertising or selling. The exporter finds it possible to transfer or export not only the product but also the entire marketing program that often makes the product a success.

The operation of a subsidiary adds a new dimension to a company's international marketing operation. It requires the commitment of capital in a foreign country, primarily for the financing of accounts receivables and inventory. Also, the operation of a sales subsidiary entails a number of general administrative expenses that are essentially fixed in nature. As a result, a commitment to a sales subsidiary should not be made without careful evaluation of all the costs involved.

Independent Distributor versus Sales Subsidiary

The independent distributor earns a margin on the selling price of the products. Although the independent distributor does not represent a direct cost to the exporter, the margin the distributor earns represents an opportunity that is lost to the exporter. By switching to a sales subsidiary, the exporter can earn the same margin by carrying out the distributor's tasks. For example, a manufacturer of electronic equipment exports products priced $7,500 each (at the factory in Boston). With air freight, tariffs, and taxes, the product's landed costs amount to $9,000 each. An independent distributor will have to price the products at $13,500 to earn a desired gross margin of 33⅓ percent. Instead, the exporter can set up a wholly-owned sales subsidiary, assumed in this case to consist of a manager, a sales manager, several sales agents, clerical staff, a warehousing operation, and the rental of both an office and a warehouse location. If the total estimated cost amounts to $450,000 annually, then the point at which the manufacturer can switch from an independent distributor to a company-owned sales subsidiary will be as follows:

$$\frac{\text{Operating costs subsidiary}}{\text{Distributor's gross profit per machine}} = \text{Unit breakeven volume}$$

$$\frac{\$450,000}{\$4,500} = 100 \text{ Pieces of equipment}$$

or

$$\frac{\text{Operating costs subsidiary}}{\text{Distributors' gross profit percentage}} = \text{Dollar sales breakeven volume}$$

$$\frac{\$450,000}{33\frac{1}{3}\%} = \$1,350,000 \text{ breakeven volume}$$

With increasing volume, the incentive to start a sales subsidiary grows. On the other hand, if the anticipated sales volume is small, the independent distributor will be more efficient since sales are channeled through a distributor who is maintaining the necessary staff for several product lines.

The lack of control frequently causes exporters to shift from an independent distributor to wholly-owned sales subsidiaries. Guinness, the British company that owns several well-known Scotch brands such as Johnnie Walker, had used independent distributors in Japan for many years. But after encountering substantial amounts of gray imports (unofficial imports by independent firms who took advantage of the official Japanese retail price and lower prices elsewhere in the world), the company bought out its two main distributors and regained control over its brands. Guinness employed about 500 people in its Japanese offices. This trend of selling through its own distributors was not limited to Japan alone, and Guinness estimated it was marketing 75 percent of its volume through such controlled distribution compared to less than 25 percent just a few years earlier.[2] Research has shown that firms marketing products that require the development of special skills or special working relationships tend to have their own sales subsidiaries.[3]

For years, Nissan, the Japanese car manufacturer, had used an independent importer for its business in the United Kingdom. This importer, named Nissan UK, was owned by a private individual, had achieved a volume of about 140,000 cars a year, and had exclusive rights to import and sell Nissan cars in the United Kingdom. However, a deep conflict erupted over the pricing of a new line of cars with the importer charging Nissan with overpricing for the U.K. market. Nissan used its right to terminate the exclusive dealership and as of the beginning of 1992 will open up its own subsidiary in the United Kingdom. It is the first time that a dealer cancellation has been implemented for such a large importer in the automobile industry.[4]

LICENSING AS AN ENTRY STRATEGY

Under licensing, a company assigns the right to a *patent* (which protects a product, technology, or process) or a *trademark* (which protects a product name) to another company for a fee or royalty. Using licensing as a method of market entry, a company can gain market presence without an equity investment. The foreign company,

2. "Guinness in Japan: A Combination of Luck with Some Judgment," *Financial Times,* July 13, 1989, p. 13.
3. Erin Anderson and Anne T. Coughlan, "International Market Entry and Expansion in Independent or Integrated Channels of Distribution," *Journal of Marketing,* January 1987, pp. 71–82.
4. "Nissan Gets Back in the Driving Seat," *Financial Times,* December 31, 1990, p. 10.

or licensee, gains the right to commercially exploit the patent or trademark either on an exclusive (the exclusive right to a certain geographic region) or unrestricted basis.[5]

Licenses are signed for a variety of time periods. Depending on the investment needed to enter the market, the foreign licensee may insist on a longer licensing period to pay off the initial investment. Typically, the licensee will make all necessary capital investments, such as in machinery, inventory, and so on, and market the products in the assigned sales territories, which may consist of one or several countries. Licensing agreements are subject to negotiation and tend to vary considerably from company to company and from industry to industry.

One company that is new to licensing is the largest brewer in the United States, Anheuser-Busch. As the first U.S. brewer to actively pursue foreign markets, Anheuser-Busch signed licensing agreements with several brewers in Canada, the United Kingdom, France, Germany, and Japan. The company's strategy is to enter a country through the leading brewer or beverage manufacturer rather than to export U.S. brewed beer. In Canada, the Anheuser-Busch brand Budweiser was licensed to Labatt Brewing Company and met with immediate success. In Japan, Budweiser is licensed to Suntory, the country's smallest brewer but a leader in the liquor business. Anheuser-Busch switched from exporting to licensing partly because it wanted to cut the retail price of its Budweiser brand in Japan in half. In Germany, the United Kingdom, and France, Budweiser is brewed by leading local brewing companies.[6]

Reasons for Licensing

Companies have used licensing for a number of reasons. For one, a company may not have the knowledge or the time to engage more actively in international marketing. The market potential of the target country may also be too small to support a manufacturing operation. A licensee has the advantage of adding the licensed product's volume to an ongoing operation, thereby reducing the need for a large amount of investment in new fixed assets. For a company with limited resources, it can be advantageous to have a foreign partner market its products by signing a licensing contract. Licensing not only saves capital since no additional investment is necessary, but it also allows scarce managerial resources to be concentrated on more lucrative markets. Also, some smaller companies with a product in high demand may not be able to satisfy demand unless licenses are granted to other companies with sufficient manufacturing capacity.[7]

5. For a thorough analysis of licensing among MNCs, see Piero Telesio, *Technology Licensing and Multinational Enterprises* (New York: Praeger Publishers, 1979).

6. "Anheuser Tries Light Beer Again," *Business Week,* June 29, 1981, p. 138; and "International Trend May Resume," *Financial Times,* April 7, 1984, p. 30.

7. "Licensing May Be the Quickest Route to Foreign Markets," *Wall Street Journal,* September 14, 1990, p. B2.

In some countries where the political or economic situation appears uncertain, a licensing agreement will avoid the potential risk associated with investments in fixed facilities. Both commercial and political risks are absorbed by the licensee.

In other countries, governments favor the granting of licenses to independent local manufacturers as a means of building up an independent local industry. In such cases, a foreign manufacturer may prefer to team up with a capable licensee despite a large market size because other forms of entry may not be possible. International paint firms, with operations in both Europe and North America, have had difficulties penetrating the Japanese market. As a result, many have signed licensing agreements with Japanese firms. PPG of the United States and Courtolds of the United Kingdom both licensed Nippon Paint for automotive and marine paints, respectively. DuPont has licensed Kansai, the other leading Japanese company, for its automotive paints. It is expected that these agreements, while not providing any penetration of the Japanese market, will keep the Japanese out of Western markets.[8] In other markets, however, PPG decided to stay away from licensing.[9]

The same applies for countries where trade restrictions prohibit the free import of products. A licensing agreement is ideal to overcome such barriers. Sulzer-Rueti, a Swiss-based company leading in the production of weaving machines, signed licensing agreements with companies in the Soviet Union, Iran, and Japan. The first two were countries that could not have been penetrated on an export basis because the hard currency necessary to purchase and import weaving machines would not have been available.

Competitive factors also influence the use of licensing. In industries with high visibility or national importance, local governments or buyers often prefer to purchase from local manufacturers. This may result in the formation of a "club" whereby foreign competitors find it difficult to gain any market share. In industries such as telecommunications, defense, or aerospace, where governments are the major buyers and often direct their purchases toward local firms, foreign competitors are forced to join such "clubs" via licensing to some of its members. Some companies use licensing as a means of preventing competitive technology from achieving market success, thereby assuring themselves of a larger market share. Sun Microsystems, the California-based manufacturer of computer workstations with sales of about $2 billion, licenses its technology to Toshiba of Japan, a major computer manufacturer with interests in the same market segment. Despite the obvious competitive threat for licensing technology to a potential competitor, Sun has customarily licensed its technology to companies around the world. But Sun expects to receive improvements via a feedback clause. Furthermore, the more computers are used with Sun's software and operating systems, the more independent software will be

8. "The Pace of Change Slows," *Financial Times,* World Paints and Coatings, Survey (Section III), March 27, 1991, p. 1.
9. Ibid.

written for them. This eventually results in an expanded market and the licensing revenue, an important profit contributor, helps to finance other important projects.[10]

Disadvantages of Licensing

A major disadvantage of licensing is the substantial dependence on the local licensee to produce revenues and, thus, royalties. Once a license is granted, royalties, usually paid as a percentage on sales volume only, will only be paid if the licensee is capable of performing an effective marketing job. Since the local companies' marketing skills may be less developed, revenues from licensing may suffer accordingly. Traditionally, Johnson & Johnson, the large U.S.-based health care company, had been licensing its newly discovered drugs in markets where it had little penetration. In 1985, the company licensed Hismanal, a nonsedating antihistamine, to Mochida, a Japanese pharmaceutical company. The drug, now selling in some 116 countries and the company's fastest growing drug, earns only thin royalties from the Japanese market. As a result, the company has moved into developing its own sales force in Japan by hiring about 300 sales representatives through its majority-owned affiliate. Several drugs are now in the process of being licensed and none are planned to be licensed to third companies.[11]

PepsiCo experienced the limitations of relying on a licensing partner in France. Pepsi was licensed through Perrier, the French mineral water company. However, the retail structure in France changed and supermarkets emerged as important channels. Other French brands, such as Badoit and Evian, did better in those channels. The resulting decline for Perrier also had a negative impact for Pepsi losing almost half of its market share.[12] This led to the breakup of the relationship and PepsiCo will in the future develop the French market on its own.

Another disadvantage is the resulting uncertainty of product quality. A foreign company's image may suffer if a local licensee markets a product of substandard quality. Insuring a uniform quality requires additional resources from the licensor that may reduce the profitability of the licensing activity.

To many companies, the possibility of nurturing a potential competitor is viewed as a disadvantage of licensing. With licenses usually limited to a specific time period, a company has to guard against the situation in which the local licensee will use the same technology independently after the license has expired and, therefore, turn into a competitor. Although there is a great variation according to industry, licensing fees in general are substantially lower than the profits that can be made by exporting or local manufacturing. Depending on the product, licensing fees may range anywhere between 1 percent and 20 percent of sales with 3 to 5 percent being more typical for industrial products.

10. "Computer Technology: Land of the Licensing Sun," *The Economist,* June 3, 1989, p. 80.
11. Global Push for Profit at Johnson," *New York Times,* September 3, 1990, p. B1.
12. "C'est la for Coke and Pepsi," *Financial Times,* February 18, 1991, p. 15.

Conceptually, licensing as an entry strategy should be pursued if the amount of the licensing fees exceeds the incremental revenues of any other entry strategy, such as exporting or local manufacturing. A thorough investigation of the market potential is required to estimate potential revenues from any one of the entry strategies under consideration. Unfortunately, research has shown that many licensing decisions are made without a complete comparison of the respective incremental profitabilities.[13]

Franchising

Franchising is a special form of licensing in which the franchisor makes a total marketing program available, including the brand name, logo, products, and method of operation. Usually, the franchise agreement is more compehensive than a regular licensing agreement inasmuch as the total operation of the franchisee is prescribed.

Numerous companies that have successfully exploited franchising as a distribution form in their home market are exploiting opportunities abroad through foreign entrepreneurs.[14] Among these companies are McDonald's, Kentucky Fried Chicken, Burger King, and other U.S. fast-food chains with operations in Latin America, Asia, and Europe. Service companies such as Holiday Inns, Hertz, and Manpower, Inc. (a temporary employment agency) have also successfully used franchising to enter foreign markets. Some of the most extensive franchising networks are those maintained by the two leading soft drink manufacturers, Coca-Cola Company and PepsiCo.[15]

In 1985, about 25,600 foreign outlets were maintained by U.S. franchise operators.[16] Some 37 percent of U.S. franchisers were operating abroad in 1985 and another 27 percent planned to expand abroad in the near future. Among those starting to expand in 1985 were Tandy Corporation with its Radio Shack stores.

LOCAL MANUFACTURING AS AN ENTRY STRATEGY

A common and widely practiced form of entry is the local production of a company's products. Many companies find it to their advantage to manufacture locally instead of supplying the particular market with products produced elsewhere. Numerous factors such as local costs, market size, tariffs, laws, and political considerations may

13. David B. Zenoff, "Licensing as a Means of Penetrating Foreign Markets," *Idea,* Summer 1970, p. 292.

14. Donald W. Hackett, "The International Expansion of U.S. Franchise Systems: Status and Strategies," *Journal of International Business Studies,* Spring 1976, pp. 65–76.

15. Bruce Walker and Michael J. Etzel, "The Internationalization of U.S. Franchise Systems: Progress and Procedures," *Journal of Marketing,* April 1973, pp. 38–46.

16. "Franchising: Big Businesses Go Worldwide," *Financial Times,* October 7, 1985, p. 27.

affect a choice to manufacture locally. The actual type of local production depends on the arrangements made; it may be contract manufacturing, assembly, or fully integrated production. Since local production represents a greater commitment to a market than other entry strategies, it deserves considerable attention before a final decision is made.

International firms with plants in Taiwan, Hong Kong, Singapore, and other foreign countries have little intention of penetrating these markets with the help of their new factories. Instead, they locate abroad to take advantage of favorable conditions that reduce manufacturing costs, and the products are slated for markets elsewhere. This cost savings strategy has been employed by many U.S. companies in the electronics industry and has more recently been adopted by Japanese and European firms as well. The motivation behind the location of plants in foreign countries may, therefore, at times be related to cost-cutting rather than to entering new markets. Such decisions are of a sourcing or production nature and are not necessarily tied to a company's international marketing entry strategy and are, therefore, not of concern to us here.

Contract Manufacturing

Under contract manufacturing, a company arranges to have its products manufactured by an independent local company on a contractual basis. The manufacturer's responsibility is restricted to production. Afterwards, products are turned over to the international company, which usually assumes the marketing responsibilities for sales, promotion, and distribution. In a way, the international company "rents" the production capacity of the local firm to avoid establishing its own plant or to circumvent barriers set up to prevent the import of its products. Contract manufacturing differs from licensing with respect to the legal relationship of the firms involved. The local producer manufactures based on orders from the international firm but the international firm gives virtually no commitment beyond the placement of orders.

Typically, contract manufacturing is chosen for countries with a low volume market potential combined with high tariff protection. In such situations, local production appears advantageous to avoid the high tariffs but the local market does not support the volume necessary to justify the building of a single plant. These conditions tend to exist in the smaller countries of Central America, Africa, and Asia. Of course, whether an international company avails itself of this method of entry also depends on its products. Usually, contract manufacturing is employed where the production technology involved is widely available and where the marketing effort is of crucial importance in the success of the product.

Assembly

By moving to an assembly operation, the international firm locates a portion of the manufacturing process in the foreign country. Typically, assembly consists only of the last stages of manufacturing and depends on the ready supply of components or manufactured parts to be shipped in from another country. Assembly usually involves heavy use of labor rather than extensive investment in capital outlays or equipment.

Motor vehicle manufacturers have made extensive use of assembly operations in numerous countries. General Motors has maintained major integrated production units only in the United States, Germany, the United Kingdom, Brazil, and Australia. In many other countries, disassembled vehicles arrive in assembly operations that produce the final product on the spot. This method of shipping cars as CKDs (completely knocked down) and assembling them in local markets is also used extensively by Ford Motor Company, American Motors' Jeep subsidiary, and most European and Japanese car manufacturers.

Often, the companies want to take advantage of lower wage costs by shifting the labor-intensive operation to the foreign market. This results in a lower final price of the products. In many cases, however, it is the local government that forces the setting-up of assembly operations by sometimes banning the import of fully assembled products or by charging excessive tariffs on imports. As a defensive move, foreign companies begin assembly operations to protect their markets. However, successful assembly operations require dependable access to imported parts. This is often not guaranteed, and in countries with chronic foreign exchange problems, supply interruptions can occur. In some countries, as is the case for the automobile industry in Brazil where some 70 percent of the parts are produced locally, car manufacturers must to engage in more than just assembly to produce their markets.[17]

Integrated Local Production Operations

To establish a fully integrated local production unit represents the greatest commitment a company can make for a foreign market. Since the building of a plant involves a substantial outlay in capital, companies only do so where demand appears assured. International companies may have any number of reasons for establishing factories in foreign countries. Often the primary reason is to take advantage of lower costs in a country, thus providing a better basis for competing with local firms or other foreign companies already present. Also, high transportation costs and tariffs may make imported goods uncompetitive.

Establishing Local Operations to Gain New Business   Some companies want to build a plant to gain new business and customers. Such an aggressive strategy is based on the fact that a local production commitment represents a strong commitment and is often the only way to convince clients to switch suppliers. This is of particular importance in industrial markets where service and reliability of supply are main factors determining product or supplier choice.

17. "Imports Take on Brazil's Car Makers," *Financial Times,* January 10, 1991, p. 6.

Guardian Industries, a U.S.-based flat glass manufacturer, was not able to enter Europe until it committed to a floating glass plant in Europe. Challenging the European giants, Saint-Gobain of France and Pilkington of the United Kingdom, the company began to make inroads by concentrating on a smaller market niche and by working with glass fabricators and distributors. Its European rivals had begun to integrate forward and were buying up independent distributors. Once an alternative source of supply was established, European distributors could be convinced to buy from Guardian. The U.S. firms eventually built two plants in Luxembourg, and was in the process of building others in Spain, France, and Hungary. Its European glass business had grown to about $300 million or 9 percent of the European market.[18] But without the up-front investment, the company would not have been able to make inroads in the market.

LEGO Company, the Danish-based toy company well known for its plastic construction toys, built a factory in Brazil in the mid-1980s to penetrate a market with 140 million people but little access to its toys. As the only foreign toy company in Brazil, LEGO was able to provide the local market with products that the country was prohibited from importing, or if allowed only at very high duty. Brazil, with almost half its population under the age of 25 years, represented a great opportunity for LEGO.

Establish Foreign Production to Defend Existing Business   Many times, companies establish production abroad not to enter new markets but to protect what they have already gained. Changing economic or political factors may make such a move necessary. The Japanese car manufacturers, who had been subject to an import limitation of assembled cars imported from Japan, began in the 1980s to build factories in the United States to protect their market share.

The first one to start U.S. production was Honda who had been selling cars in the United States since 1970 and had begun motorcycle production at Marysville, Ohio, in 1979. In 1982, Honda began to produce cars as well. This was followed by an engine plant in 1986 and the start of a second car assembly plant in 1988 with startup in 1989. By 1988, the company had built its 1 millionth car in the U.S. This strategy was not only intended to protect its 7.5 percent market share but to expand it to some 10 percent by the mid-1990s.[19] By 1990, Honda's Accord model had become the best-selling model in the United States.

Other Japanese companies followed suit. Nissan Motors began in Smyrna, Tennessee, in 1983. One year later Toyota teamed up with GM in Fremont, California, with its own plant to open in 1988 in Georgetown, Kentucky. Mazda, Mitsubishi, Subaru-Isuzu followed suit within a few years. By 1990, Japanese transplants, as

---

18. "U.S. Raging Bull Charges at European Glass Market," Financial Times, June 7, 1990, p. 17.

19. "Aggressive Expansion at Honda Is Straining Both Staff and Finances," *Wall Street Journal,* October 9, 1989, p. 1.

these factories are called, accounted for 22 percent of all the cars built in the United States and the market share of the Japanese firms combined climbed to 26 percent of U.S. sales.[20]

Moving with an Established Customer Moving with an established customer can also be a reason for setting up plants abroad. In many industries, important suppliers want to keep their relationship by establishing plants near customer locations; and when customers build new plants elsewhere, suppliers move too. The automobile industry, with its intricate networks of hundreds of component suppliers feeding into the assembly plants, is a good example of how companies follow customers. As Japanese car manufacturers build plants in the United States and in Canada, Japanese parts suppliers are becoming concerned that U.S. production will partially replace car shipments from Japan and that a reduction in parts volume will result. To counter this possibility, some 400 component plants have been built in the United States and in Canada.

However, about 40 percent of those operations established to supply Japanese transplant car assembly units are joint ventures with local companies.[21] Bridgestone Tire Co., Japan's largest tire manufacturer, decided to set up shop in Tennessee only after Japanese automobile firms began to move manufacturing into the United States.[22] In 1988, Bridgestone acquired Firestone of the United States to become one of the largest tire companies and to help it to serve the U.S. market better.[23]

In similar fashion, Detroit's major automotive parts and component suppliers, such as tire companies and battery manufacturers, long ago opened manufacturing facilities abroad to supply General Motors' and Ford's various foreign facilities.

Shifting Production Abroad to Save Costs The experience of Compaq Computer illustrates the complex decision-making process involved in deciding on a foreign manufacturing plant and its location. This U.S.-based manufacturer of small personal computers was founded in 1982 and experienced rapid growth. The company entered the European market in 1984 and began to look for a plant location in 1985. Compaq researched many European countries for possible locations and was courted by many countries that wanted the company to set up the plant in their localities. Eventually, Compaq decided to locate in Scotland in an area dubbed "Silicon Glen" for its likeness to the famous Silicon Valley in California. The company justified its plant location with the prediction that the U.K. market was likely to become Compaq's most important and fastest growing single market in Europe, so it would

---

20. "Auto Industry in U.S. Is Sliding Relentlessly into Japanese Hands," *Wall Street Journal,* February 16, 1990, p. 1.
21. "Successful Transplants," *Financial Times,* March 27, 1991, Automotive Components Survey, p. 2.
22. "A Different Kind of Tiremaker Rolls into Nashville," *Fortune,* March 22, 1982, p. 136.
23. "The World Tire Industry Survey," *Financial Times,* December 1988, Section III.

make sense to be close to that market.[24] In less than two years, Compaq doubled the size of its original factory as sales rose quickly in Europe.[25]

JOINT VENTURES

Companies entering foreign markets not only have to decide on the most suitable entry strategy, they also need to arrange ownership either as a wholly owned subsidiary or as a joint venture. Under a joint venture (JV) arrangement, the foreign company invites an outside partner to share stock ownership in the new unit. The particular participation of the partners may vary with some companies accepting either a minority or majority position. In most cases, international firms prefer wholly-owned subsidiaries for reasons of control. Once a joint venture partner secures part of the operation, the international firm can no longer function independently, which sometimes leads to inefficiencies and disputes over responsibility for the venture. If an international firm has strictly defined operating procedures such as for budgeting, planning, and marketing, it may become difficult to get the JV company to accept the same methods of operation. Problems may also arise when the JV partner wants to maximize dividend payout instead of reinvestment, or when the capital of the JV has to be increased and one side is unable to raise the required funds. Experience has shown that JVs can be successful if the partners share the same goals with one of them accepting primary responsibility for operations matters.

Reasons for Entering Into Joint Ventures

Despite the potential for problems, joint ventures are commonly used because they offer important advantages to the foreign firm. By bringing in a partner, the company can share the risk for a new venture. Furthermore, the JV partner may have important skills or contacts of value to the international firm. Sometimes, the partner may be an important customer who is willing to contract for a portion of the new unit's output in return for an equity participation. In other cases, the partner may represent important local business interests with excellent contacts to the government. A firm with advanced product technology may also gain market access through the JV route by teaming up with companies that are prepared to distribute its products.

Corning Glass Works, a U.S.-based company in a number of technology-intensive businesses, has used joint ventures extensively to open up markets otherwise not accessible to the firm. The company operates some twenty-three joint ventures, two-thirds of them with foreign firms, which together account for more than half of Corning's operating profits. Corning's optical fibers business has six joint ventures abroad. Many of its customers are local telephone companies who favor local suppliers. By

24. "A Tactical Victory for Silicon Glen," *Financial Times,* January 5, 1987, p. 8.
25. "Compaq Expands with Europe Strategy," *Herald Tribune,* July 11, 1989, p. 9.

joining with local partners, Corning gets access to markets and customers that would otherwise be closed to the company. In the TV glass business, Corning used joint ventures with Asahi Glass of Japan and Samsung of Korea to provide it with new technology. This became important as Corning's traditional U.S. customers gave up TV manufacturing and the industry became dominated by Japanese and Korean companies.[26]

Joint Ventures to Enter Government-Controlled Economies

Joint ventures are sometimes necessary to enter countries where the economy is largely under state control. In such countries, foreign investors are only allowed to take minority positions in conjunction with local firms. In the case of government-controlled economies, this often means a joint venture must be signed with a government-owned firm. Given the country's large economic potential, many foreign firms have been attracted to China. Within two years of the adoption of China's law on joint ventures in 1979, more than 400 joint venture contracts had been signed between Chinese and foreign firms. By 1991, some 10,000 joint ventures involving foreign investors had been formed in China. At least one hundred of them have been closed, not including a number of dormant ventures.[27]

Schindler, a Swiss-based firm and a leading elevator manufacturer, was the first foreign firm taking advantage of China's law on joint ventures in 1979.[28] The company took a 25 percent equity position with the goal of becoming both a major supplier of elevators in China and using the venture as a production base for its growing business in the Far East. Growth in output has averaged more than 20 percent during the first six years of operation. The venture has been profitable for Schindler. The company has been able to beat out Hitachi and Mitsubishi, its two leading Japanese competitors, as the leader of the Chinese market. The venture developed to the satisfaction of Schindler and led to a second venture in 1988. Between the two ventures, Schindler is operating three factories on a joint venture basis with an annual output of several thousand lifts and escalators.[29]

Computer companies, typically resisting joint ventures in other parts of the world, have begun to enter into ventures in China. The major motivating force was to please the Chinese government in the hope of gaining trade concessions for imports at a later time. Several companies, including IBM and Hewlett-Packard, opened manufacturing operations for hardware in China. Others, such as Digital, decided to pursue software development. China offered a cheap labor force in an industry that was plagued by a shortage in software engineers worldwide. Although using Chinese ventures as a subcontractor for less complex parts of software, these

26. "Your Rivals Can Be Your Allies," *Fortune,* March 27, 1989, p. 66.

27. "Foreigners Find China Ventures Difficult to Quit," *Wall Street Journal,* March 12, 1991, p. A15.

28. "Schindler Gives Chinese Business a Lift," *Financial Times,* August 29, 1986, p. 6.

29. "Swiss Lift Maker Expands in China," *Financial Times,* December 14, 1988, p. 6.

companies were actually developing software for overseas markets and not for local use.[30]

Joint Ventures in Eastern Europe   With the liberalization of industry and trade in Eastern Europe over the past few years, many international firms have pursued joint ventures in those countries. Originally, Western firms were not allowed to own any stock, capital, or real estate and joint ventures were, thus, the norm. Although the political and economic situations were still in flux, in many countries restrictions on foreign investments were lifted and foreign firms were allowed to start new companies with full ownership. Due to the difficulties of operating in unknown environments, many foreign firms, nevertheless, continue to prefer JVs with local partners.

In the Soviet Union, about 150 JV deals were signed in 1990. Of those, about two-thirds were entered into by European firms and about 20 percent were with U.S. companies.[31] Overall, there are about 2,800 registered JVs but only about 1,000 were estimated to be active.[32] Other sources estimate that the number of properly working JVs is less than 50.[33]

The difficulties running a JV are enormous since the Soviet Union does not yet have a market economy as we have come to know it in the West. Because of the often unreliable nature of supplies, lack of modern machinery or technological know-how, ventures that intend to exploit cheap Soviet labor or raw material often fail. Much greater chances for success have ventures that are largely aimed at satisfying domestic demand, with exports a secondary goal have much greater chances for success.[34]

The structure of the McDonald's venture in the Soviet Union is such a classic way of operating as an island within the country and as much as possible independent of local suppliers. With its partner, the City of Moscow, McDonald's built a $45 million processing plant to make its own beef patties, pasteurize its own milk, and bake its own buns. Raw materials for this plant, however, are obtained from Soviet sources and the company has a number of specialists working with suppliers on quality. Transportation is arranged with its own trucks. Pizza Hut, a unit of PepsiCo, opened its own venture with the City of Moscow in 1990. Its strategy is to source all of its supplies from local companies.[35]

One of the most recent ventures announced is between Gillette of the United States and a Soviet consumer products company. Gillette will build a $60 million plant and have a 65 percent stake in the operation. The goal is to produce shaving

---

30. "Computer Makers Go in Search of Chinese Goodwill," *Financial Times,* February 20, 1991, p. 6.

31. "Little Joy Flows from Soviet Joint Ventures," *Financial Times,* March 20, 1991, p. 3.

32. "Russian Roulette With Six Bullets," *The Economist,* January 12, 1991, p. 65.

33. "Teaming Up to Score from Perestroika," *Financial Times,* March 28, 1990, p. 12.

34. "Hertzfeld, Jeffrey M., "Joint Ventures: Saving the Soviets from Perestroika," *Harvard Business Review,* January-February 1991, pp. 80–91.

35. "Setting Up An Island in the Soviet Storm," *New York Times,* December 30, 1990, Section 3, p. 1.

equipment and blades for the domestic Soviet market. As one of the largest shaving markets in the world, the Soviet Union is estimated to have 100 million male shavers compared to 80 million in the United States. The JV will emphasize twin-blade razors but will not produce the Sensor, Gillette's latest product generation. Eventually employing some 600 people, the Soviet plant will rank among the top three production units for Gillette's worldwide oeprations.[36]

Joint venture activity has also been high in Eastern Europe. Hungary has attracted some of the most attention so far. Few foreign ventures have attracted as much interest as General Electric's deal with Tungsram, a long-established Hungarian maker of electric light bulbs. Ranking fifth among light bulb manufacturers worldwide, Tungsram had its own subsidiaries in the West and had traditionally been an active exporter. GE bought 51 percent ownership for $150 million.[37] The company has annual sales of some $300 million, 70 percent of this from exports in convertible currency. The venture with Tungsram had to be seen in global terms, however. GE, number two worldwide behind Philips in lighting, had only a 2 percent market share in Europe. Tungsram's 7 percent share of the Western European market will be an excellent base to improve GE's overall European position.[38] The expected investment of some $50 million over the next five years to bring Tungsram up to Western standards, plus the initial stake, compare well with the estimated price of $300 million for a new plant for GE in Europe, not even counting the start-up losses until volume had been reached to justify the investment.[39]

In Czechoslovakia, German-based Volkswagen beat out Renault of France for a 31 percent stake in Skoda, the major Czech car manufacturer. VW is expected to raise that stake to some 70 percent by 1995. As part of the deal, VW committed to invest some $6 billion into Skoda over the next ten years to bring it up to Western standards and to expand the company's car output from presently 180,000 cars annually to about 400,000 by 1997. VW intends to increase the product range of Skoda by adding Golf and Passat-type cars over time.[40] The Skoda brand name will be maintained, as well as Skoda's existing dealer network in Europe. Their major direction will be the growing Eastern European car market that is expected to grow from presently two million to three million units annually, including cars for the Soviet Union.[41]

JVs in Eastern European countries have been known to be slowed down for lack of critical resources. Red tape is still a major problem for companies operating in Eastern Europe. Access to hard currency is very limited, with special concerns for the Soviet Union. Negotiating business deals takes up much time and in some coun-

36. "Gillette Forms Soviet Link to Make Shavers," *Financial Times,* March 5, 1991, p. 26.
37. "Barometer for a Changing Climate," *Financial Times,* April 10, 1990, p. 29.
38. "GE Carves Out a Road East," *Business Week,* July 30, 1990, p. 32.
39. "GE in Hungary: Let There Be Light," *Fortune,* October 22, 1990, p. 137.
40. "VW and Skoda Unveil DM 9.5 Billion Strategy," *Financial Times,* December 11, 1990, p. 19.
41. "Western Car Groups Make Their Marque," *Financial Times,* April 2, 1991, p. 19.

tries, negotiations are hampered due to a lack of laws governing property rights. As many experts have predicted, investing in Eastern Europe will require patience and companies cannot expect immediate returns.

The Constant Danger of Joint Venture Divorce

Not all joint ventures are successful and fulfill their partners' expectations. One study found that between 1972 and 1976 some 90 major ventures failed in Japan alone. Many of these ventures involved large U.S.-based firms such as General Mills, TRW, and Avis. Another study showed that 30 percent of investigated joint ventures formed before 1967 between American companies and partners in other industrialized countries failed. In most cases, the ventures were either liquidated or taken over by one of the original partners.[42]

Borden Inc., a U.S.-based dairy company with worldwide sales of some $7 billion, was one of the more recent companies to experience difficulties with its JV in Japan. Originally entered into the early 1970s, Borden joined up with Meiji Milk Products of Japan to form several joint ventures. Meiji had produced Borden branded ice cream since 1971 and margarine since 1983. Borden cheese was made part of a different venture in 1972. By 1990, sales for the three product categories in Japan had reached $192 million. However, Borden felt that with the liberalization of the dairy business in Japan, a major expansion to some $400 million was possible.[43] A major disagreement was reported over the ice cream business, where the Lady Borden brand had slipped from its 60 percent of imported premium to about 50 percent. Major competitors were now Haagen-Dazs and Dreyer, both U.S. entries.[44] Faced with increasing competition but also more opportunities, Borden was said to have demanded a higher performance from Meiji as a precondition for extending its arrangements. Over the talks, the companies broke up. The three agreements expired in 1990 and Borden is in the process of securing alternative partnerships for sales and production.[45]

Not all joint ventures in Japan end up as failures. One of the most successful is the collaboration between Caterpillar of the United States and Mitsubishi Heavy Industries. For years, Caterpillar had a JV with Mitsubishi for the production of bulldozers and other heavy construction equipment. However, the market in Japan, where building operations must take place under very tight space situations, became increasingly attractive for excavators. These machines were never at the center for

42. J. Peter Killing, "How to Make a Global Joint Venture Work," *Harvard Business Review,* May-June 1982, p. 121.

43. "Borden and Meiji Part Ways, Face a Tough Road Ahead," *Tokyo Business Today,* December 1990, p. 40.

44. "Borden's Breakup with Meiji Milk Shows How a Japanese Partnership Can Curdle," *Wall Street Journal,* February 21, 1991, p. B1.

45. "Borden and Meiji Part Ways, Face a Tough Road Ahead," *Tokyo Business Today,* December 1990, p. 40.

Caterpillar, so that when the market took off in Japan, it decided to form a second JV, Shin Caterpillar-Mitsubishi. But the new JV was not only for Japan. It was also made responsible for hydraulic excavator design worldwide for both Caterpillar and Mistubishi, and included the Mitsubishi manufacturing in Japan. Outside Japan, Caterpillar was to remain independent for manufacturing and distribution, while all excavator products were to carry the name Caterpillar. Excavator sales of the combined company grew 75 percent to $2.7 billion worldwide in four years, and in Japan Mitsubishi recovered its declining market share.[46]

Corning executives, who have extensive joint venture experience as detailed earlier, have learned a number of lessons to make joint ventures successful. Because a partner is involved in all dealings, time must be taken to explain any unilateral decisions. Richard Delude, one of its senior executives, prepared the following items for a checklist for successful joint ventures:

1. Do not enter into JVs with partners that are initially overconcerned with control or how to split up if the venture should fail.

2. The venture must be able to get the resources to grow and should not be restricted technologically or geographically.

3. The venture must develop its own culture.

4. Venture managers need good access to top management at the parent companies.

5. Stay away from partners who are overly centralized and have no experience in sharing responsibility.[47]

Despite the difficulties involved with joint ventures, it is apparent that the future will bring many more of them. Successful international and global firms will have to develop the skills and experience to manage JVs successfully, often in different and difficult environmental circumstances. And in many markets, the only realistic access to be gained will be through JVs.

STRATEGIC ALLIANCES

A more recent phenomenon is the development of a range of strategic alliances. Alliances are different from traditional joint ventures in which two partners contribute a fixed amount of resources and the venture develops on its own. In an alliance, two entire firms pool their resources directly in a collaboration that goes beyond the limits of a joint venture. Although a new entity may be formed, it is not a requirement. Sometimes, the alliance is supported by some equity acquisition of one or both of the partners. In an alliance, partners bring a particular skill or resource, usually one

46. "Digging a Mutual Trench," *Financial Times,* March 11, 1991, p. 10.
47. "Hard Work on Joint Ventures," *Financial Times,* January 22, 1990, p. 30.

that is complementary, and by joining forces both are expected to profit from the other's experience. Typically, alliances involve either distribution access, technology transfers, or production technology, with each partner contributing a different element to the venture.

Technology-Based Alliances

Exchanging technology for market access was the basis of the AT&T alliance with Olivetti of Italy, entered into in 1984. AT&T needed to enter the European computer market to obtain economies of scale for its U.S. operations, but it did not have any marketing contacts of its own. On the other hand, Olivetti was eager to add larger computers to its existing line. As a result, Olivetti marketed AT&T computers through its extensive distribution system in Europe. In return, Olivetti became the key supplier to AT&T for personal computers and was able to use AT&T as its distribution arm in the U.S. market. Both companies were attempting to benefit from each other's market access and each other's production and technology resources.[48] However, after a quick start that involved mostly the sale of Olivetti-produced PCs through AT&T sales offices in the United States, the alliance lapsed when the cooperation became too one-sided. In 1989, AT&T was able to take a 20 percent stake in Italtel, the Italian state-owned telecommunications equipment company. With this alliance, AT&T hoped to gain better access to Italian telecommunications orders and elsewhere in Europe.[49]

A similar alliance was struck between AT&T and Philips of the Netherlands. AT&T, following its divestiture in the United States, was looking for a way to market its large public-exchange switching technology abroad where it had never been sold. Philips, who had excellent market contacts in a number of countries, was in need of a digital public-exchange system that followed earlier generations of mechanical switching systems. Philips, however, regularly reduced its stake and it became clear that the venture could not succeed in its original format. Philips sold out its stake in several steps, and AT&T eventually assumed 75 percent of the equity. AT&T was joined by two other European partners, Telefonica of Spain and Stet of Italy, who own the remainder of the venture.[50] By joining into an alliance and forming a joint venture, AT&T gained immediate market access in a number of countries, whereas Philips gained immediate access to digital technology and, thus, saved a considerable investment. Despite some difficulties at the start, AT&T has been able to grow its international business from just 8 percent in 1984 to 15 percent of corporate in 1990. Although this does include payments for long-distance traffic and equipment, the

48. George Taucher, "Building Alliances (A): The American Telephone and Telegraph Company, Case GM 351, and Building Alliances (B): Ing. C. Olivetti & Co. S.p.A., Case GM 352, IMEDE International Management Development Institute, Lausanne, Switzerland, 1986.

49. "US Giant Plugs Into Global Ambitions," *Financial Times,* August 30, 1989, p. 10.

50. "Philips Ends European Venture with ATT," *Financial Times,* September 21, 1990, p. 26.

equipment side of its business was helped by ventures in Spain and Korea. Similarly, employment abroad leaped from just 50 in 1983 to over 21,000 across some 40 countries by 1990.[51]

Production-Based Alliances

Particularly in the automobile industry, a large number of alliances have been formed over the past years. These alliances or linkages fall into two groups. First, there is the search for efficiency through component linkages which may include engines or other key components of a car. Second, companies have begun to share entire car models, either by producing jointly or by developing them together. In the United Kingdom, the British Rover Group and Honda of Japan produce some cars jointly.[52] Regional cooperation also exists between Volkswagen and Ford in Latin America.

The most far reaching alliance, however, was recently signed by Renault of France and Volvo of Sweden. The two companies agreed to a series of interlocking deals. Both will own 45 percent of each other's truck and bus divisions. Separately, Renault will buy 25 percent of Volvo's car operation and another 10 percent of Volvo Corporation. In return, Volvo will acquire 20 percent of Renault with an option for another 5 percent later on. This cooperation is expected to result in much greater synergy first in trucks and buses, where the combined Renault-Volvo Group will advance to the number one spot worldwide. In cars, the level of integration is planned to be less. However, in both situations, substantial savings are expected from global purchasing, development, design, and joint production of important components.[53] This complex alliance has passed all regulatory hurdles and is expected to be accepted by its shareholders.[54]

Distribution-Based Alliances

Alliances with a special emphasis on distribution are becoming increasingly common. General Mills, a U.S.-based company marketing breakfast cereals, had long been number two in the United States with some 27 percent market share compared to Kellogg's 40 to 45 percent share. With no effective position outside the United States, the company entered into a global alliance with Nestlé of Switzerland. Forming Cereal Partner Worldwide, owned equally by both companies, General Mills intends to use the local distribution and marketing skills of Nestlé in Europe, the Far East, and Latin America. In return, General Mills will provide technology and the

---

51. "ATT Slowly Gets Its Global Wires Uncrossed," *Business Week,* February 4, 1991, p. 30.

52. "Car Industry Joint-Ventures: Spot the Difference," *The Economist,* February 24, 1990, p. 92.

53. "Strained Alliances," *International Management,* May 1990, p. 28.

54. "Commission Approves Renault-Volvo Link-up," *Financial Times,* November 8, 1990, p. 3.

experience of how to compete against Kellogg's. The latter has some 40 percent of the worldwide breakfast cereals business. Initially, the new venture will use Nestlé plants in Europe and utilize Nestlé local distribution companies.[55] The partnership needs to match Kellogg's $200 million dollar advertising spending outside the United States as soon as possible, and none of them can do it alone.[56] The first introductions were scheduled for France, Spain, and Portugal with Golden Grahams and Honey Nut Cheerios.[57]

While Nestlé was getting access to a new product line, breakfast cereals, from General Mills by making its distribution network available, the company engaged in a different alliance with Coca-Cola. Forming Coca-Cola Nestlé Refreshments, the two partner companies intend to market Nestlé's new, ready-to-drink coffees and teas through the Coca-Cola distribution system worldwide.[58] Nestlé has developed new, ready-to-drink products and has already a leading position in instant coffee. But ready-to-drink products are sold mainly through vending machines. This latter distribution is well known to Coca-Cola who actually has in Georgia Brand, a canned coffee, its leading product in Japan. It was also in Japan that Nestlé became aware of the opportunity in ready-to-drink coffees and where the company had already signed a JV with Otsuka Pharmaceutical.[59]

In Japan, the ready-to-drink market has sales of $4.4 billion and is growing rapidly. This fact inspired both Nestlé and Coca-Cola to work together to bring these products to other markets. Both invested $100 million into the venture which excludes the Japanese market where both already have their own arrangements. Success elsewhere depends very much on the development and distribution of vending machines. In Japan there are some 5.4 million vending machines with some 2.2 million just for canned drinks. However, vending machines in Japan can be displayed in the streets with little fear of vandalism. Elsewhere in the world, such a strategy is not possible. This was believed to impact on the growth of such drinks outside Japan.[60]

The Future of Alliances

Although global alliances have not been around for a very long time, there are a few lasting alliances that have become models through their success. One of the most successful is the alliance between General Electric in the United States and Snecma of France in their aircraft engine business. The partners have collaborated since 1970 and have combined their forces in the development of a new class of passenger air-

55. "The Coming Battle of the Breakfast Table," *Financial Times,* December 21, 1989, p. 13.
56. "McCann Lands International Cereals," *Advertising Week,* July 30, 1990, p. 1.
57. "Euro Joint Venture Sets First Cereals," *Advertising Week,* November 19, 1990, p. 56.
58. "Coca-Cola Names Teasley as Chief of Joint Venture," *Wall Street Journal,* March 14, 1991, p. B6.
59. "Ware of the Sales Robots," *Forbes,* January 7, 1991, p. 294.
60. "Getting The Coffee Market in the Can," *Financial Times,* December 10, 1990, p. 17.

craft engines. Commercialization did not come until 1982 but the jointly developed jet engine has been a huge success. State-controlled Snecma needed a new jet engine to compete with Rolls Royce and Pratt & Whitney of the United States to offer options for the European built Airbus passenger jets. As a result, Snecma has renewed the collaboration with GE and signed on to participate again in the next generation of engines.[61]

Although many alliances have been forged in a large number of industries, the evidence is not yet in as to whether these alliances will actually become successful business ventures. The evidence suggests that alliances with two equal partners are more difficult to manage than those with a dominant partner. Furthermore, many observers question the value of entering alliances with technological competitors, such as between Western and Japanese firms. The challenge in making an alliance work lies in the creation of multiple layers of connections, or webs, that reach across the partner organizations. Eventually, this will result in the creation of new organizations out of the cooperating parts of the partners. In that sense, alliances may very well be just an intermediary step until a new company can be formed or until the dominant partner takes over.[62]

PREPARING AN ENTRY STRATEGY ANALYSIS

Of course assembling the correct data is the cornerstone of any entry strategy analysis. The necessary sales projections have to be supplemented with detailed cost data and financial need projections on assets. The data need to be assembled for all entry strategies under consideration (see Figure 9.2). The financial data are collected not only on the proposed venture but also on its anticipated impact on the existing operations of the international firm. The combination of the two sets of financial data results in incremental financial data incorporating the net overall benefit of the proposed move on the total company structure.

For best results, the analyst must take a long-term view of the situation. Asset requirements, costs, and sales have to be evaluated over the planning horizon of the proposed venture, typically three to five years for an average company. Furthermore, a thorough sensitivity analysis must be incorporated. This may consist of assuming several scenarios of international risk factors that may adversely affect the success of the proposed venture. For each scenario, the financial data can be adjusted to reflect the "new" set of circumstances. Possibly, one scenario may include a 20 percent devaluation in the host country combined with currency control and difficulty of receiving new supplies from foreign plants. Another situation may assume a change in political leadership less friendly to foreign investments. With the help of a sensi-

61. "A Lasting and Successful Alliance," *Financial Times,* January 8, 1991, p. 18.

62. Taucher, George, "Beyond Alliances," IMEDE Perspective for Managers, No. 1, 1988, IMEDE, Lausanne, Switzerland.

FIGURE 9.2 ● Considerations for Market Entry Decisions

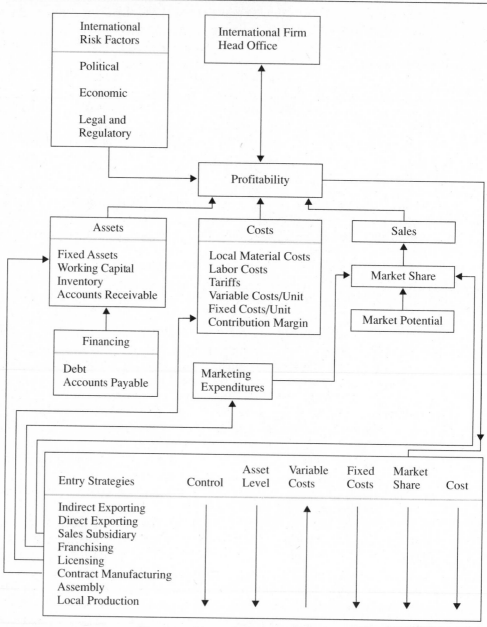

Direction of Arrow Indicates Increase in that Factor.

tivity analysis approach, a company can quickly spot the key variables in the environment that determine the outcome of the proposed market entry. The international company then has the opportunity to further add to its information on such key variables or at least closely monitor their development.

In the following section of this chapter we provide a general methodology for the analysis of entry decisions. It is assumed that any company approaching a new market is looking for profitability and growth. Consequently, the entry strategy must be subordinated to these goals. Each project has to be analyzed for the expected sales level, costs, and asset levels that will eventually determine profitability (see Table 9.1).

Sales

An accurate estimate of the market share or sales volume is crucial to the entry strategy decision. Sales results will largely depend on the company's market share and the total size or potential of the market. The market share to be gained primarily is competitively determined. The foreign company can influence the market share through a strong marketing mix which in turn is also dependent on the level of financial commitment for marketing expenditures. The various types of entry strategies also allow a foreign firm to unfold its marketing strategy to varying degrees. Typically, direct or indirect exporting results in a lower market share than local sales subsidiaries or local production due to the founder's weaker market presence. This weaker presence causes a loss of control over local middlemen. Also, to some extent, independent firms have to be depended on to carry out the company's marketing functions.

Of course market potential is not subject to the influence of the international firm seeking entry. The size of a local market combined with the expected market share often determines the outcome of an entry strategy analysis. Local assembly or production with correspondingly high levels of assets and fixed costs need large volumes to offset these costs, whereas exporting operations can usually be rendered profitable at much lower sales volumes than other entry strategies.

Particularly in markets with considerable growth potentials, it becomes essential to forecast sales over a longer period of time. A low expected volume right now may indicate little success for a new subsidiary, but data on expected volume later on may suggest a change in the future entry strategy. Since it is often impossible to shift quickly into another entry mode once a firm is established, special attention has to be focused on the need to ensure that the chosen entry strategy offers a long-term opportunity to maximize profits.

Costs

The international firm will have to determine the expected costs of its operation in a foreign country both with respect to manufacturing and general administrative costs. Unit variable costs may vary depending on local production, assembly, or

TABLE 9.1 ● Financial Analysis for Entry Strategy

Financial variables	Local values
Assets	
Cash	New amount of assets needed to
Accounts Receivable	sustain chosen entry strategy in
	local market
Inventory	
Equipment	
Buildings	
Land	
Liabilities	
Accounts Payable	New amount of liabilities
Debt	incurred due to entry strategy
Net Assets	

Costs	
Unit Variable Costs (VC)	Amount of VC in newly
	selected operations
Material costs	
Labor costs	
Purchases	
Fixed and Semifixed Costs	Local fixed costs due to selected
	entry mode
Supervision	
Marketing	
General Administrative	
Expenses	
Total Unit Costs	

Sales	Local sales of chosen entry
	mode
Total Sales	

exporting as the chosen strategy. To establish such costs, local material costs, local wage levels, and tariffs on imports will have to be taken into consideration. Again, unit variable costs should be expected to vary according to the entry strategy alternatives considered.

Necessary fixed costs represent another important element in the analysis. Administrative costs tend to be much smaller for a sales subsidiary compared to a

Decreases elsewhere (due to new operation)	*Incremental value*
Assets liquidated or no longer needed due to shift of operation	Net new assets required
Reduction or change in liabilities due to shift in operation	Net new liabilities incurred
	Net asset requirement
Diseconomies of scale due to volume loss by shifting production to new subsidiary	Net variable costs across all subsidiaries resulting from new entry mode
Lost contribution if production shifted elsewhere	Net fixed burden of new entry mode Incremental total costs
Lost sales in other units of the MNC subsidiary network	Net additional sales of entry strategy

local manufacturing unit. Through use of a contribution margin analysis, breakeven for several levels of entry strategies can be considered. Government regulations or laws may also affect local costs and substantially change costs over time.

Cost levels may differ substantially from country to country. Estimating and forecasting costs in the international environment requires a keen sense of awareness that environmental factors of a political, economic, or legal nature can render a careful analysis invalid. Consequently, such possibilities need to be considered from the outset.

Assets

The level of assets deployed greatly affects the profitability of any entry strategy. The assets may consist of any investments made in conjunction with the entrance (or exit, for that matter) into the new market. Such investments may comprise working capital in the form of cash, accounts receivable, or inventory, or it may include fixed assets such as land, buildings, machinery, and equipment. The amount of assets required depends to a great extent on the particular entry strategy chosen. Exporting or sales subsidiaries require an investment in working capital only with little additional funds for fixed facilities. Local assembly or production, however, demand substantial investments. Often it will be possible to use local financing to reduce the net investment amount of the international firm. For an adequate comparison of the various entry strategies, an asset budget should be established for each of the alternatives considered.

Profitability

Conceptually, a company should maximize the future stream of earnings discounted at its cost of capital. Other companies may prefer to concentrate on return on investment (ROI) as a more appropriate measurement of profitability. In either case, profitability is dependent on the level of assets, costs, or sales. Several exogenous international risk factors influence profitability and, therefore, must be included in the analysis. The outcome of such an analysis determines the selection of the entry strategy. In the following sections, each of these factors will be described and their possible impact on profitability will be indicated.

International Risk Factors

Aside from the normal business risk factors that every company also confronts in its home market, there are additional risks involved due to the existence of more than one single economy or country. Each country hosting a foreign subsidiary may take action of a political, economic, or regulatory nature that can completely obliterate any carefully drawn up business plan. As we discussed in Chapter 4, political turmoil in many parts of the world greatly affects business and investment conditions. Following the departure of the shah of Iran, the country's political stability deteriorated to such an extent that business could not be conducted as usual. Many foreign operations were taken over by the government or just ceased to exist. Similar effects could be witnessed on business in other countries, particularly Nicaragua (in 1979), and Turkey (1978 to 1980).

As we discussed in Chapter 2, different economic systems add to uncertainties and are reflected in currency changes or diverging economic trends. Manufacturing costs are particularly sensitive to various changes. Many times, a company has shifted production from one country to another on the basis of the latest cost data just to find out a few years later that costs have changed due to fluctuations of macroeconomic variables beyond company control. Local labor costs over the years have fluctuated considerably and are very sensitive to local inflation and foreign currency changes.

Labor cost data shows that the U.S. labor cost disadvantage increased from 1981 to 1983, when the U.S. dollar increased in value compared to other currencies. From 1985 to 1987, the U.S. dollar declined substantially compared to other leading currencies only to soar to new levels in 1991.

Since 1982, Caterpillar has increased its overseas production from 19 percent to 25 percent of total sales as a response to higher production costs in the United States. However, as the value of the U.S. dollar declined, so have Caterpillar's margins in its overseas units in the United Kingdom and France, whereas some of its U.S. competitors now have an advantage by producing in the United States. Caterpillar's largest competitor, Japan's Komatsu, however, had to absorb even larger cost increases in its Japanese production as a result of the rapidly rising yen.[63]

Maintaining Flexibility

The ability to switch from one mode of entry into another may be an important requirement of the initial arrangement. Data General of the United States was a company that was able to shift its entry strategy following the changes in the investment laws in Japan in 1978.[64] Data General had originally signed a licensing agreement with a consortium of seven Japanese companies in 1971 called Nippon Minicomputer. A few years later, Data General realized that most of its customers in Japan were other multinationals who wanted to make direct purchase agreements for buying Data General minicomputers with its head office in the United States. Since the company could not make a licensee obey such agreements, Data General negotiated first to buy a 50 percent stake in 1979 and finally up to 85 percent in 1982. The local organization was changed to Nippon Data General (NDG), but Japanese management was left in place. This stepwise approach to a integrated production and

63. "Weaker Dollar Isn't a Boon for Caterpillar," *Wall Street Journal,* February 20, 1987, p. 6.

64. "Data General Shows Friendly Takeovers Are Possible in Japan," *Business International,* August 6, 1982, p. 249.

sales organization was very successful for Data General and the company was able to obtain a leadership position in the Japanese market.

International Head Office

Once profitability on a local level has been established and the relevant international risk factors included, the proper analysis has to turn to the company as a whole. The expected profits of the new market entry have to be analyzed along with the overall impact on the total organization. Replacing imports with local production may cause a loss of sales or output at the existing facility, which may counterbalance the new profits gained from the plant opening. Consequently, such an impact may exist with respect to assets, costs, and sales depending on the entry strategy. As a result, the global firm aims at maximizing incremental profits achieved on incremental assets and sales. A promising opportunity abroad may suddenly appear less attractive when allowances are made for displacement in other parts of a global company.

Entry Strategy Configuration

This chapter has been dedicated to explaining the various entry strategy modes available to international and global firms. In reality, however, most entry strategies consist of a combination of different formats. We call the process of deciding on the best possible combination *entry strategy configuration.*

Although possible, most companies rarely employ one single entry mode per country. A company may open up a subsidiary that both produces some products locally and imports others to round out its product line. The same foreign subsidiary may even export to other foreign subsidiaries, combining exporting, importing, and local manufacturing into one unit. Furthermore, many international firms grant licenses to patents and trademarks to their foreign operations even when they are fully owned. This is done for additional protection or to make the transfer of profits easier. In many cases, companies have bundled such entry strategy forms into one single legal unit, *layering* in effect several entry strategy options on top of each other.

Bundling of entry strategies is the process of providing just one single legal unit in a given country or market. In other words, the foreign company sets up a single company in one country and uses that company as a legal umbrella for all its entry activities. However, such strategies have become less typical, particularly in larger markets where many firms have begun to unbundle its operations.

When a company *unbundles,* it essentially divides its operations in a country into different companies. The local manufacturing plant may be separately incorporated from the sales subsidiary. When this occurs, companies may select different ownership strategies, allowing for instance a JV in one operation while keeping full ownership in another part. Such unbundling becomes possible in the larger markets, such as the United States, Germany or Japan. It also allows the company to run several companies or product lines in parallel. ICI, the large U.K. chemicals company, operates several subsidiaries in the United States that report to different product line companies back in the United Kingdom and are independently operated. Global firms granting global mandates to their product divisions will find that each division will need to develop its own entry strategy for key markets.

EXIT STRATEGIES

Some circumstances may make companies want to leave a country or market. Other than the failure to achieve marketing objectives, there may be political, economic, or legal reasons for a company to want to dissolve or sell an operation. International companies have to be aware of the high costs attached to the liquidation of foreign operations; substantial amounts of severance pay may have to be paid to employees and any loss of credibility in other markets can hurt future prospects.

Exiting Markets for Consolidation Purposes

Sometimes an international firm may need to withdraw from a market because it has a need to consolidate its operations. This may mean a consolidation of factories from many to fewer such plants. Production consolidation, when not combined with an actual market withdrawal, is not really what we are concerned with here. Rather our concern is on *when* a company actually must abandon its plan to serve a certain market or country.

In the 1970s, several U.S.-based multinational firms had to retrench their international operations and shrink back onto a U.S. base. Chrysler sold its European operations in the United Kingdom and France to European car manufacturers, mostly Peugeot, and concentrated on the U.S. market. In Japan, Chrysler reduced its stake in Mitsubishi Motors and used the proceeds of about $600 million for operating purposes in the United States. Firestone, the U.S. tire company, consolidated its European operations and withdrew from many smaller markets.

More recently, Avon Products sold 60 percent of its successful Japanese company for some $400 million. This came after having offered 40 percent of its Japanese company to the public in 1987. The money was needed to reduce its debt in the United States.[65] Avon started its Japanese subsidiary twenty years ago and had sales of $285 million. This 4 percent market share was considered too small for a mature cosmetics market such as Japan and the company would have had to invest heavily into marketing in order to grow. Avon sold out to a Japanese mail order house and agreed to take a 5 percent royalty for the first eighteen months with a reduction to 3 percent thereafter.[66]

A company cannot always find a ready buyer for a firm. Several foreign companies found that closing ventures in China was rather difficult. One company, an

65. "Saying Sayonara Is Such Sweet Sorrow," *Business Week,* March 12, 1990, p. 52.
66. "Avon Agrees to Sell Rest of Japanese Unit," *New York Times,* February 22, 1991, p. D5.

Australian firm with a plant to build major appliances, found that its sales declined from 10,000 units a month to 1,000 units a month following the economic uncertainties in China in 1989. The company got the Chinese partner's consent to liquidate the venture, but progress slowed when the Chinese board chairman refused to make the public announcement that would have started the liquidation process. Another Australian firm with a pineapple venture, simply turned over its 50 percent holding to its partners.[67]

Exiting Markets for Political Reasons

Changing political situations have at times forced companies to leave markets. Procter & Gamble, the giant U.S.-based consumer goods manufacturer, sold its Cuban subsidiary in 1958, one year before Fidel Castro won the civil war. It also disposed of its Chilean subsidiary shortly before the election victory of Allende in Chile in 1970. Had the company insisted on staying in those markets, the subsidiaries would most likely have been expropriated.

Changing government regulations can at times pose problems prompting some companies to leave a country. India is a case in point. There, the government adopted its Exchange Regulation Act in 1973 to require most foreign companies to divest themselves of 60 percent of their subsidiaries by the end of 1977. Companies that manufactured substantially for export or whose operations comprised advanced technology were exempted. Since IBM's Indian operation did little exporting and sold mostly older computer models, the computer manufacturer was asked to sell 60 percent of its equity to Indian citizens.

The risks of leaving a market are demonstrated in the case of India where Coca-Cola decided to leave the market in 1977 rather than sell a controlling ownership to local investors. This gave its arch-rival, PepsiCo, a chance to negotiate its own deal with Indian partners and Pepsi went on sale for the first time in 1990 under the name of Lahar Pepsi. Although the law which caused Coca-Cola to leave in 1977 was eventually changed, the company was now trying for the third time to regain entry into that very fast growing market. When Coke left, soft drink sales were just 20 million cases compared to 110 million cases in 1990. However, the experience of PepsiCo indicates that gaining market share in India will not be easy as the local companies will defend market share vigorously.[68] The experience of Coca-Cola shows that leaving a market may give opportunities to rivals and when the market starts to take off, it will not be simply a matter of reentering at will.

The situation with South Africa shows that exit strategies can also be the result of negative reactions in a firm's home market. With the political situation in South Africa open to challenge on moral grounds, many multinational corporations have exited that country by abandoning or selling their local subsidiaries. In 1984, some

67. "Foreigners Find China Ventures Difficult to Quit," *Wall Street Journal,* March 12, 1991, p. A15.
68. "The Real Thing Returns to India," *Financial Times,* April 17, 1991, p. 18.

325 U.S. companies were maintaining operations in South Africa. Two years later, this number had decreased to 265. The total amount of U.S. direct foreign investment was estimated at U.S. $1.3 billion.[69] One of the U.S. firms leaving was Coca-Cola, the soft-drink bottler.[70] Other U.S. firms that have exited South Africa include General Motors, IBM, Motorola, and General Electric. Some European firms have withdrawn from that country also: Alfa-Romeo of Italy, Barclays Bank of the United Kingdom, and Renault of France among them.[71] Today, with the economic situation changing, some firms may reenter South Africa provided the international community withdraws the economic sanctions.

CONCLUSIONS

The world is comprised of more than 150 individual countries or markets. Thus, entry decisions are the strategy decisions international companies make most frequently. Since the type of entry strategy can be clearly related to later market success, these decisions need to be based on careful analysis. Companies often find that it is difficult to break out of initial arrangements, which is another reason why special attention must be given to this type of decision. In some of the more difficult markets, such as Japan, making the correct entry decision can become a key competitive advantage for a firm and it can unlock markets otherwise inaccessible to a foreign company.

To survive in the coming global battles for market dominance, companies have to become increasingly bolder and more creative in their entry strategy choices. Long gone are the days when entry was restricted to exporting, licensing, foreign manufacturing, and joint ventures. New concepts such as global alliances have become common, and international firms will have to include acquisitions, venture capital financing, and complex government partnerships as integral elements in entry strategy configurations. The myriad of new entry alternatives have raised the level of complexity in international marketing and will remain an important challenge for managers.

This added complexity will make detailed analysis of entry strategy alternatives and their comparisons more difficult. For adequate analysis, companies will have to take into consideration not only present cost structures but the ever changing economic and political environment. Rapidly changing foreign exchange rates have changed the cost of various entry alternatives and have forced companies to shift their approach. These economic changes are likely to remain and companies will be forced to reevaulate their entry strategy decisions on an ongoing basis. Entry strate-

69. "South Africa: Time to Stay—or Go?" *Fortune,* August 4, 1986, p. 45.
70. "If Coke Has Its Way, Blacks Will Soon Own 'The Real Things,'" *Business Week,* March 27, 1987, p. 56.
71. "High Risks and Low Returns," *Financial Times,* November 25, 1986, p. 10.

gies will rarely be made on a permanent basis but will have to be adapted to the most recent situation.

Although most companies have preferences as to which entry strategy they would pursue given no objections, increasingly firms will be adopting a flexible approach. Establishing a sales subsidiary may be the best alternative for entering some countries, whereas joint ventures may be necessary to enter other countries. Managers will be forced to learn to manage with a variety of entry strategies, and they will be less able to repeat the same entry patterns all over the world. A great amount of managerial flexibility will, thus, be required of international companies and their executives. We can also expect that the future will bring other types of entry strategies that will challenge international managers anew.

Questions for Discussion

1. Contrast the entry strategies practiced by Boeing and IBM. What differences do you find and what explains these differences?

2. Would entry strategies differ for companies considering Germany, Japan, or China? If so, in what way and for what reasons?

3. How will the entry strategy differ for a new start-up firm versus a mature multinational company?

4. What difficulties and special problems can be expected from a firm practicing only franchising as an entry strategy.

5. Perform a literature search on alliances and try to determine the reasons particular alliances were made.

6. It has been speculated that alliances between Japanese and Western firms work primarily to the benefit of Japanese companies. Comment.

7. Explain the concept of entry strategy configuration and the strategies of layering, bundling, or unbundling entry strategies.

For Further Reading

Alden, Vernon R. "Who Says You Can't Crack Japanese Markets?" *Harvard Business Review,* January-February 1987, p. 52.

Brasch, John J. "Using Export Specialists to Develop Overseas Sales." *Harvard Business Review,* May-June 1981, pp. 6–8.

Cavusgil, Tamer S., and John R. Nevin. "Internal Determinants of Export Marketing Behavior: An Empirical Investigation." *Journal of Marketing Research,* February 1981, pp. 114–119.

Harrigan, Kathryn R. *Strategies for Joint Ventures.* Boston: D.C. Heath, 1985.

Hertzfeld, Jeffrey M. "Joint Ventures: Saving the Soviets From Perestroika." *Harvard Business Review,* January-February 1991, p. 92–101.

Kanter, Rosabeth Moss. *When Giants Learn to Dance.* New York: Simon & Schuster, 1989.

Killing, J. Peter. "How to Make a Global Joint Venture Work." *Harvard Business Review,* May-June 1982, pp. 120–127.

Killing, J. Peter. *Strategies for Joint Venture Success.* New York: Praeger, 1983.

Kogut, Bruce, and Harbir Singh. "The Effect of National Culture of the Choice of Entry Mode." *Journal of International Business Studies,* Fall 1988, pp. 411–432.

Pekar, Peter Jr. "How Battle-Tested Managers Assess Strategic Alliances." *Planning Review,* July-August 1989, pp. 34–37.

Pekar, Peter Jr. *Making Strategic Alliances Work for Your Company.* A.T. Kearney, 1987.

Piercy, Nigel. "Export Strategy: Key Markets vs. Market Spreading." *Journal of International Marketing,* no. 1 (1981), pp. 56–67.

Reich, Robert B. and Eric D. Mankin. "Joint Ventures with Japan Are Giving Away Our Future." *Harvard Business Review,* March-April 1986.

Reid, Stan D. "The Decision-Maker and Export Entry and Expansion." *Journal of International Business Studies,* Fall 1981, pp. 101–112.

Root, Franklin R. *Entry Strategies for International Markets.* Lexington, Mass.: D.C. Heath, 1987.

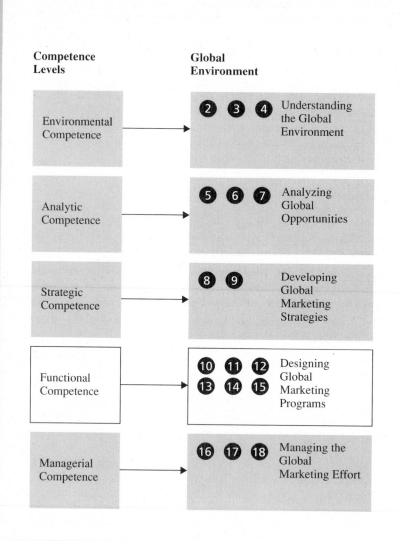

P A R T

F O U R

Designing Global Marketing Programs

ASSEMBLING AN INTERNATIONAL or global marketing program requires an analysis of how the international environment will affect the four major marketing mix elements: product, distribution, pricing, and communications. In Part 4, we focus on how companies adapt to different marketing environments by adjusting certain elements of their marketing programs to ensure market acceptance. In concentrating on these issues, our aim is to help you increase functional competence. Marketing managers must not only be knowledgeable about the international environment per se, they must also possess the solid, functional skills necessary to successfully compete in the international marketplace.

In Chapter 10 we concentrate on product strategy issues for international and global markets. In Chapter 11, we discuss how to manage the new product development process in an international environment. Important distribution and channel decisions are discussed in Chapter 12. Chapter 13 outlines the differences between domestic, international, and global pricing and how companies can deal with problems arising from different prices in different markets. In Chapter 14, we give an overview of communications strategies, sales force management, and promotional policies for international companies. The final chapter in this section, Chapter 15, looks at international and global advertising and the challenges faced by companies running different advertising programs simultaneously in many countries.

10

International and Global Product Strategies

● **THIS CHAPTER LOOKS** *at the strategies companies can pursue to adapt their products to international markets. Figure 10.1 highlights the elements involved in product strategy decisions. The chapter discussion first centers on the many possible environmental factors that tend to prevent the marketing of uniform and standardized products across a multitude of markets. Our attention then shifts to the various implications of selecting brand names for international markets. International firms are concerned not only with determining appropriate brand names but also with protecting those names against abuse and piracy. The following sections focus on packaging and managing product lines and support services. The chapter concludes with a section on the marketing of services on a global scale. We also highlight the enormous opportunities in the service industry and explain how various companies are pursuing such challenges.*

PRODUCT DESIGN IN AN INTERNATIONAL ENVIRONMENT

One of the principal questions in international marketing concerns the types of products that can be sold abroad. With respect to existing products, the international firm will want to know whether these products have to be adapted to certain international requirements or whether they can be shipped in their present form. For new products, the firm will have to select the particular features their products should incorporate and determine the desired function and performance of these features. The

FIGURE 10.1 ● International and Global Product Strategies

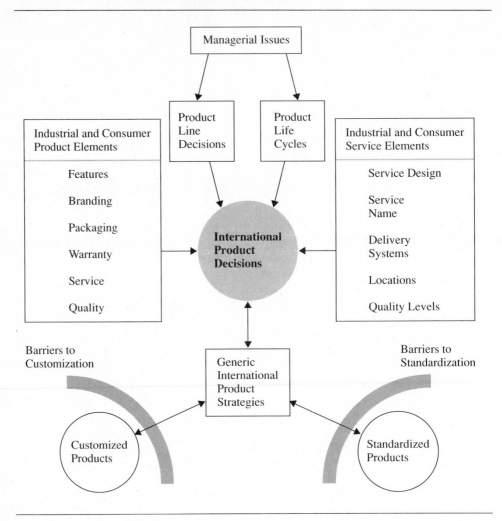

major elements of product design are explained in the following sections, with an emphasis on the effect of international complexities.

To select the most desirable product features is an involved decision for international marketers. The approach taken should include a thorough review of all the environmental factors that may affect product use (see Table 10.1). Furthermore, a thorough analysis should include the relative physical success factors developed in detail in Chapter 7. In all cases, however, a firm will have to picture its products in the targeted foreign market and ask the question: "How would our product be used

TABLE 10.1 ● Environmental Factors Requiring Product Design Changes

Environmental factors	*Design changes*
Level of technical skills	Product simplification
Level of labor costs	Automation or manualization of product
Level of literacy	Remaking and simplification of product
Level of income	Quality and price change
Level of interest rates	Quality and price change (investment in high quality may not be financially desirable)
Level of maintenance	Change in tolerances
Climatic differences	Product adaption
Isolation (heavy repair; difficult and expensive)	Product simplification and reliability improvement
Difference in standards	Recalibration of product and resizing
Availability of other products	Greater or lesser product integration
Availability of materials	Change in product structure and fuel
Power availability	Resizing of product
Special conditions	Product redesign or invention

Source: Richard D. Robinson, *International Business Management* (Hinsdale, Ill.: The Dryden Press, 1978), pp. 41–42. Reprinted by permission of the author.

in that country?" In some situations it may be necessary to send some units to the foreign market for testing purposes.

Product Dimensions for International and Global Use

Dimensions as expressed by size, capacity, or volume are subject to market and environmental influences that often require different approaches to any given market. One important factor, particularly for U.S. firms, is the selection of a metric versus a nonmetric scale. The firm must go beyond a single translation of nonmetric into metric sizes to help users or consumers understand the design of products. Simple translations do not lead to round standardized numbers, forcing companies actually to change the physical sizes of their products to conform to new standards. The U.S. market is the only remaining major nonmetric market, with Europe and Japan operating on the metric standard. Therefore, it is less of an issue for foreign firms than for U.S.-based companies that normally operate on a nonmetric basis at home.

The different physical characteristics of the consumers often influence product design. Swiss watch manufacturers have learned over the years to adapt their watch cases to different wrist sizes: the Japanese have smaller wrists than Americans, thus design changes are required that do not necessarily change the function or look of the watch. A leading Italian shoe manufacturer had a similar experience exporting shoes to the United States. Research revealed that feet were not the same in every country. Americans were found to have longer toes than Italians and smaller insteps.[1] Also, the company learned that Americans have thicker ankles and narrower, flatter feet. To produce a properly fitting shoe, the Italian company decided to make appropriate changes in its design to achieve the necessary comfort for American customers. Edmont, a division of Becton Dickinson, asked Japanese factory workers to test their new work gloves. They found that Japanese workers have smaller hands and shorter fingers than their counterparts in Europe and the United States.[2]

Size is often affected by the physical surroundings of product use or space. In some countries living space is limited, necessitating home appliances that are substantially smaller than those found in a country such as the United States where people live in relatively larger dwellings. Recently, U.S.-made major appliances have been imported into Japan by some discount chains. Although the volume is still small by international standards, some wealthier Japanese consumers favored these large appliances. Some of the customers had to return them after purchase, however, because they could not get the refrigerators through their own apartment doors.[3] Winnebago Industries, the U.S. maker of recreational vehicles, encountered difficulties selling its oversized vehicles in Japan through Mitsubishi Corporation, a larger international trading company. Narrow streets in Japan and a scarcity of campgrounds with camper hookups turned out to be major impediments to sales. This is similar to the experience of a U.S. furniture company, Richardson Brothers & Co. Its ornate oak dining room sets and 82-inch tall sideboards did not leave any room to put things on top because of low ceilings, and many did not even fit into existing apartments and houses.[4] In many countries, customers have come to expect certain products in certain sizes and, thus, international firms are forced to adapt to meet these expectations.

Matching Product Design Features with International and Global Markets

Invariably international firms find they must alter some components or parts of a product because of local circumstances. One worldwide manufacturer of industrial abrasives has had to adjust to different raw material supply situations by varying the raw material input according to country while maintaining abrasive performance

1. "Three Scientists Seek U.S. Data on Genetic Engineering," *New York Times,* March 8, 1978, p. A-19.
2. Robert Thomas, Vice President, Edmont Division of Becton Dickinson, in a discussion with authors on July 13, 1987.
3. "Japanese Eye the Western Kitchen," *Financial Times,* August 10, 1989, p. 18.
4. "Some Products Are a Tight Squeeze in Crowded Japan," *Wall Street Journal,* September 29, 1988, p. 26.

standards. Paint is another product that requires adaptation to climatic and surface circumstances. As a result, paint will differ from region to region even though the particular application may be identical.[5]

Procter & Gamble, the large U.S.-based consumer products company, found it had to adapt the formulation of its Cheer laundry detergent to fit the Japanese market requirements. Cheer, initially promoted as an all-temperature product, ran into trouble because many Japanese consumers washed their clothes in cold tap water or used leftover bath water. The Japanese also liked to add fabric softeners which tend to cut down on the suds produced by the detergent. P&G reformulated the product so that it works effectively in cold water with fabric softeners added and changed the positioning to superior cleaning in cold water. The brand is now one of P&G's best-selling products in Japan.[6]

Researchers have considered the U.S. customer to be particularly feature-conscious.[7] Consequently, features considered necessary in the United States may not be required abroad, although others may be in greater demand. Adding the desired features can strengthen a company's marketing effort and offset the added engineering and production costs. In some local markets customers may even expect a product to perform a function different from the one originally intended. One U.S. exporter of gardening tools found that its battery-operated trimmers were used by the Japanese as lawn mowers on their small lawns. As a result, the batteries and motors did not last as long as they would have under ordinary use. Because of the different function desired by Japanese customers, eventually a design change was required.

Adapting Products to Cultural Preferences   To the extent that fashion and tastes differ by country, companies often change their styling. Color, for example, should reflect the values of each country.[8] For Japan, red and white have happy associations, whereas black and white indicate mourning. Green is an unpopular color in Malaysia since it is associated with the jungle and illness. Green is also the national color of Egypt and therefore should not be used for packaging purposes there. Textile manufacturers in the United States who have started to expand their export businesses have consciously used color to suit local needs.[9] For example, the Lowenstein Corporation has successfully used brighter colors for fabrics exported to Africa.

5. "Paints & Coatings: The Battle for World Markets," *Financial Times,* March 10, 1989, Section III.

6. "After Early Stumbles, P&G Is Making Inroads Overseas," *Wall Street Journal,* February 6, 1989, p. B1.

7. Montrose Sommers and Jerome Kernan, "Why Products Flourish Here, Fizzle There," *Columbia Journal of World Business,* March-April 1967, pp. 89–97.

8. *International Marketing Management,* ed. Michael J. Thomas (Boston: Houghton Mifflin, 1969), p. 35.

9. Herbert E. Meyer, "How U.S. Textiles Got to Be Winners in the Export Game," *Fortune,* May 5, 1980, p. 260.

Scent is also subject to change from one country to another. S.C. Johnson & Son, a manufacturer of furniture polish products, encountered resistance to its Lemon Pledge furniture polish among older consumers in Japan. Careful market research revealed that the polish smelled similar to a latrine disinfectant used widely in Japan in the 1940s. Sales rose sharply after the scent was adjusted.[10]

Adapting Performance Standards   Manufacturers typically design products to meet domestic performance standards. As we have already seen, such standards do not always apply in other countries, and product changes are required in some circumstances. Products designed in highly developed countries often exceed the performance needed in developing Third World countries. These customers prefer products of greater simplicity, not only to save costs but to assure better service over a product lifetime. MNCs have been criticized for selling excess performance where simpler products will do. Stepping into this market gap are companies from some of the less developed countries whose present technology levels are more in line with those in the Third World.

The need for different product standards was behind a foreign acquisition by the Westinghouse Electric Corporation.[11] Standards for electrical equipment in the United States differed from those adopted by many foreign countries; relevant standards abroad were often set by the International Electrical Committee (IEC). Equipment based on IEC standards tended to be smaller and less costly than standard U.S. equipment. This led to a preference for IEC standard products among many developing countries. Rather than rebuilding the U.S.-made controls, Westinghouse decided to acquire a German firm specializing in IEC standard controls for use in its equipment.

Of course manufacturers from developing countries face the opposite challenge, requiring companies to increase the performance of their products to meet the standards of industrialized countries. In general, the necessity to increase performance tends to be more apparent as the need arises, whereas the opportunities for product simplification are frequently less obvious to the observer.

Sometimes manufacturers have to build design changes into products for overseas sales that are not apparent to the buyer. These internal design changes can increase product use or performance or adapt it to a new environment. As we have seen in the case of Westinghouse, different electrical standards require product adaptation. In color-television broadcasting, the prevalent U.S. system was not adapted worldwide. In Europe, countries installed either a French or a German designed system, each requiring specially equipped TV receivers. RCA offered only its standard models in Asia, disregarding the fact that both Singapore and Malaysia, two neighboring countries, had different broadcasting systems. With the RCA model the buyer

---

10. Vernon R. Alden, "Who Says You Can't Crack Japanese Markets?" *Harvard Business Review,* January-February 1987, pp. 52–56.

11. "Westinghouse's Gutsy Expansion Plans," *Business Week,* December 28, 1981, p. 61.

could receive only a picture but no sound. RCA distributors in Singapore had to wait several years for the company to make the necessary adaptations.[12]

Adjusting Quality to Global Requirements

The quality of a product reflects the intended function and the circumstances of product use. Consequently, as these circumstances change it is sometimes necessary to adjust quality accordingly. Products that receive less service or care in a given country have to be reengineered to live up to the added stress. At times, there may be an opportunity to lower product cost by reducing the built-in quality and, in turn, reducing price to the customary purchase levels of the local market. However, this may be dangerous if company reputation can suffer in the process. It may be preferable not to market a product at all.

Some companies go to great lengths to live up to different quality standards in foreign markets. The experience of BMW, the German automaker exporting to Japan serves as an excellent example of the extra efforts frequently involved. BMW found that its customers in Japan expected the very finest quality. Typically, cars shipped to Japan had to be completely repainted. Even very small mistakes were not tolerated by customers. When a service call was made, the car was picked up at the customer's home and returned when completed.

Adapting High Technology Products   Technology intensive and industrial products frequently find that standards for product performance differ from one country to the next. In telecommunications, the signaling standards used for U.S. public switching systems differ from those used in Europe. As a result, significant barriers exist when a company wants to become an exporter. In effect, the exporter often faces the decision to become a multi-standard firm. Designing and manufacturing such systems to several standards adds to the total cost and without minimum volume, a company may have to forego export opportunities if the adaptation costs outweigh the business opportunity. For their domestic clients Japanese manufacturers had long built machines similar to the standard U.S. machines offered by IBM, but they had their machines with special software packages.[13] These programs were geared to the often unique needs of Japanese clients and written in a mixture of Japanese and English. The programs were not subject to easy translation. To write entirely new software packages for export markets would have been not only expensive but also extremely difficult for Japanese programmers. Under those circumstances, Hitachi, after repeated requests from its U.S. sales partner, Intel, finally accepted the idea of producing computers that were plug-compatible with IBM machines and that could also run with IBM software packages. Neither Hitachi nor other leading Japanese

12. "RCA's New Vista: The Bottom Line," *Business Week,* July 4, 1977, p. 44.

13. Bro Uttal, "Exports Won't Come Easy for Japan's Computer Industry," *Fortune,* October 9, 1978, p. 138.

computer manufacturers sold machines domestically that were plug-compatible with IBM at that time. In this case the requirements of the export markets outweighed those of the domestic market.

Both Apple and IBM experienced the reverse in the Japanese market. Apple, first entering in 1979, made no significant changes in its product to meet local requirements. As a result, little software was written and the market share was always low. In 1988, however, Apple finally decided that it had to adapt and took the necessary steps to have local software houses write Japanese software. By aggressively pursuing Japanese software developers, more widely available Japanese software pushed up sales of its Macintosh line to about 50,000 units annually, double the amount of the year earlier.[14]

IBM, in response to the successful strategies of Japanese mainframe competitors Hitachi and Fujitsu, saw its market share in Japan plummet to under 30 percent compared to 70 percent in the rest of the world. IBM decided to offer an emulator that would let IBM mainframe machines run software originally written for Hitachi and Fujitsu machines. The required device, Prism, was offered for about $120,000. The strategy made IBM again a contender for companies that up to now had only used Japanese mainframes.[15]

Sometimes, different standards are mandated by governments leaving international marketers to scramble for compliance. Caterpillar manufactures backhoe-loaders type construction machinery for all of Europe in the United Kingdom. These machines are tractor types with a bucket up front and a digger at the back. Requirements for Germany are such that several special parts must be used. All tractors destined for Germany require a separate brake with an antidrive-through mechanism attached to the rear axle. The operating valve for the backhoe requires a special locking capability. The steering system needs to be equipped with specially positioned valves. The bucket must be equipped with a lock for traveling. The cost of these "extras" amounts to about 5 percent of total cost. In process is the establishment of European-wide standards for construction machinery. By avoiding such country-specific standards, the European Commission expects savings to industry and more competitiveness.[16]

Changing Proven Products to Meet Foreign Requirements   One of the most difficult decisions for international companies to make is whether or not to change a proven product that has sold well in the past. Sometimes, a company may be in a position to change a proven design to gain a competitive advantage because other more tradition-bound firms declined.

14. "Is It Finally Time for Apple to Blossom in Japan?", *Business Week,* May 28, 1990, p. 100.

15. "IBM Unit to Sell Device That Ties Mainframes to Hitachi's, Fujitsu's," *Wall Street Journal,* March 17, 1989, p. B3.

16. "A Bumpy Ride Over Europe's Traditions," *Financial Times,* October 31, 1988, p. 5.

Prior to 1974, French wines accounted for the largest volume of imported wines, with Italian suppliers a distant second. Since then, Italian vintners in the U.S. market have far surpassed their French competitors who concentrated on more expensive wines. In 1979, Italian vintners even outsold their French competitors in dollar volume. This remarkable upset of the world's most renowned wine producers was achieved by shrewd marketing and product adaptations that catered to the specific preferences of the American consumer. Whereas Italians preferred their Lambrusco wine dry, light, and fruity, the U.S. population, according to data supplied by the American importer, preferred a wine that was bubbly and slightly sweet, similar to popular drinks consumed with meals, such as soda. The Italians adjusted their fermentation process to produce such a wine significantly below the cost of French wines. This cost advantage was achieved with efficient bottling plants. Also, the Lambrusco wine was ready for consumption immediately upon fermentation, thus eliminating the customary two to four year aging process of more expensive wines. Lambrusco soon accounted for two-thirds of all Italian wines imported into the United States.[17]

INTERNATIONAL AND GLOBAL BRANDING DECISIONS

Selecting appropriate brand names on an international basis is substantially more complex than having to decide on a brand name for just one country. Typically a brand name is rooted in a given language and, if used elsewhere, may have either a different meaning or none at all. Ideally, marketers look for brand names that evoke similar emotions or associations around the world. By past learning experience, people around the world have come to expect the same thing from such brand names as Coca-Cola, IBM, Minolta, or Mercedes-Benz. However, it has become increasingly difficult for new entrants to become recognized unless the name has some meaning for the prospective customer. Language problems are particularly difficult to overcome. Colgate-Palmolive, the large U.S.-based toiletries manufacturer, purchased the leading toothpaste brand in Southeast Asia, "Darkie." With a minstrel in black face as its logo, the product had been marketed by a local company since 1920. After the acquisition in 1985, Colgate-Palmolive came under pressure from many groups in the U.S. to use a less offensive brand name. The company undertook a large amount of research to find both a brand name and logo that were racially inoffensive and yet close enough to be quickly recognized by consumers. The company eventually changed the name to "Darlie" after an exhaustive search.[18]

17. "Creating a Mass Market for Wine," *Business Week,* March 15, 1982, p. 108; and "The Toyota of the Wine Trade," *Fortune,* November 30, 1981, p. 155.
18. "Colgate Will Change Toothpaste's Name," *New York Times,* January 27, 1989, p. D1.

Brand Name Selection Procedures

Given almost unlimited possibilities for names and the restricted opportunities to find and register a desirable one, international companies spend considerable effort on the selection procedure. One well-known consulting company specializes in finding brand names with worldwide application. The company brings citizens of many countries together in Paris where, under the guidance of a specialist, they are asked to state names in their particular language that would combine well with the product to be named.[19] Speakers of other languages can immediately react if a name comes up that does not sound well in their language. After a few such sessions, the company may accumulate as many as 1,000 names that will later be reduced to 500 by a company linguist. The client company then is asked to select 50 to 100 names for further consideration. At this point, the names are subjected to a search procedure to determine which ones have not been registered in any of the countries under consideration. In the end only about ten names may survive this process, and from these the company will have to make the final selection. Although this process may be expensive, it is generally considered a small cost compared with the advertising expenditures invested in the brand name over many years.

When confronted with a search for a brand name with international applications, a company can use the following sources:

1. An arbitrary or invented word not to be found in any standard English (or other language) dictionary, such as Toyota's Lexus.

2. A recognizable English (or foreign language) word but one that is totally unrelated to the product in question, such as the detergent Cheer.

3. An English (or other language) word that merely suggests some characteristic or purpose of the product, such as Mr. Clean.

4. A word that is evidently descriptive of the product, although the word may have no meaning to persons unacquainted with English (or the other language), such as the diapers brand Pampers.

5. Within one or more of these categories, a geographical place or a common surname, such as Kentucky Fried Chicken.

6. A device, design, number, or some other element that is not a word or a combination of words, such as 3M Company.[20]

Selection of a brand name based on these six approaches is also closely related to another key issue in international branding: should the company use one brand name worldwide or should it use different names in different countries?

---

19. "Trademarks Are a Global Business These Days, But Finding Registrable Ones Is a Big Problem," *Wall Street Journal,* September 4, 1975, p. 28.

20. George W. Cooper, "On Your 'Mark,'" *Columbia Journal of World Business,* March-April 1970, pp. 67–76.

Single-Country versus Universal Brand Names

International marketers are constantly confronted with the decision of whether the brand name needs to be universal. Brands such as Coca-Cola or Kodak have universal use and lend themselves to an integrated international marketing strategy. With worldwide travel a common occurrence, many MNCs do not think they should accept a brand name unless it can be used universally. However, many product brands originated in a single market, typically the company's home market, and were given a brand name that reflected the home market's cultural background. Later extensions of such a brand name internationally can pose problems. When Bank Americard Inc. changed its logo and name to Visa in 1977, a primary consideration was bringing the card, which had been issued in over twenty countries with as many names, under the umbrella of a single, meaningful brand name.[21] The resulting name change, though expensive, nevertheless led to such strong growth that Visa surpassed Mastercard to become the most widely used card in the world. This was largely because the latter did not create such a unified worldwide image.

Of course it is not always possible to use the same name elsewhere, and a change in the home market may jeopardize the positive feelings for the original name gained after years of marketing efforts. In such instances different names have to be found. Procter & Gamble had successfully marketed its household cleaner, Mr. Clean, in the United States for some time. This name, however, had no meaning outside of countries using the English language. This prompted the company to arrive at several adaptations abroad, such as *Monsieur Propre* in France and *Meister Proper* in Germany. In all cases, however, the symbol of the genie with gleaming eyes was retained since it evoked responses abroad that were similar to those in the United States.

Private Branding Strategies

The practice of private branding or supplying products to a third party for sale under its brand name has become quite common in many domestic markets. Similar opportunities exist on an international scale and may be used to the manufacturer's advantage. Private branding offers particular advantages to a company with strong manufacturing skills but little access to foreign markets. Arranging for distribution of the firm's product through local distributors or companies with already existing distribution networks reduces the risk of failure and provides for rapid volume growth via instant market access. Some Japanese companies have used the private branding approach to gain market access in Europe and the United States. Ricoh serves as one of many examples.[22] Known as a manufacturer of cameras, Ricoh entered the market for small plain paper copiers (PPC) in the early 1970s. Supply contracts were signed with Savin for the U.S. market, with Nashua of New Hamp-

---

21. *Business Week,* July 14, 1980, p. 109.
22. "PPC Marketers Take Over American Distribution," *The Japan Economic Journal,* May 22, 1979, p. 7.

shire for Canada and Europe, and with Kalle of West Germany for Europe. With the help of these three firms, Ricoh gained 9 percent of the worldwide copier market within five years.[23]

These private branding arrangements are also called OEM contracts, short for original equipment manufacturer, in which the foreign manufacturer assumes the role of the OEM. As the market grows, they have become difficult to manage from the manufacturer's point of view. Nevertheless, these arrangements have opened markets more quickly and at much lower investment cost than would have been required for the Japanese firms to develop these markets on their own. Similar private branding or OEM strategies were pursued by Japanese manufacturers of video recorders (VCRs) in Europe, where Japanese companies were battling Philips of the Netherlands and Grundig of Germany for market dominance.[24] Japanese companies were supplying VCRs to European home electronic manufacturers with established distribution systems who did not want to invest research and funds to produce their own systems. Victor of Japan concluded long-term agreements with Saba, Nordmende, and Telefunken, all of West Germany, with Thorn Consumer Electronics of the United Kingdom, and with Thomson-Brandt of France. Matsushita Electric had similar arrangements with Blaupunkt Werke GmbH of West Germany, whereas Hitachi had an OEM arrangement with Granada TV Rental of the United Kingdom. The latest entrant, Toshiba, signed a long-term OEM contract with Rank Radio International of the United Kingdom. In all of these cases, the European companies placed their own labels on the VCRs imported from Japan.

Private branding or OEM contracts are not without drawbacks for the manufacturer. With control over marketing in the hands of the distributor, the manufacturer remains dependent and can only indirectly influence marketing. For long-term profitability, companies often find that they need to sell products under their own names, even where the OEM has achieved substantial marketing success. Such partnerships often end because of conflicting interests. The Japanese copier manufacturer Ricoh, which successfully used OEM arrangements to carve out a large market share in the United States for its plain copiers, reportedly paid Savin $14.5 million in compensatory royalties to obtain the right to sell copiers under its own name, Ricoh, as early as July 1981.[25]

Global Brands

Experts disagree on what makes a global brand. However, few brands are marketed in the same way, with the same strategy, and as identical products worldwide. Furthermore, many that are actually marketed as global brands with a largely identical strategy still have not yet received major recognition beyond their own home regions.

23. "Competition Heats Up in Copiers," *Business Week,* November 5, 1979, p. 115.
24. "Sony and Philips Seal Tie-up," *The Japan Economic Journal,* October 16, 1979, p. 8.
25. "PPC Marketers Take Over American Distribution," p. 7.

TABLE 10.2 ● Top Ten Brands by Region

Ranking	America	Japan	Europe
1	Coca-Cola	Takashimaya	Mercedes-Benz
2	Campbell's	Coca-Cola	Philips
3	Pepsi-Cola	National	Volkswagen
4	AT&T	Matsushita	Rolls-Royce
5	McDonald's	Sony	Porsche
6	American Express	Toyota	Coca-Cola
7	Kellogg's	NTT	Ferrari
8	IBM	Japan Air Lines	BMW
9	Levi's	All Nippon Airlines	Michelin
10	Sears	Seiko	Volvo

Source: The Economist. November 19, 1988, p. 80. © 1988 The Economist Newspaper Limited. Reprinted with permission.

Among the top twenty U.S. brands, all were of U.S. origin, and only a handful of the top twenty in Japan were foreign brands (see Table 10.2).[26]

Landor, an international consulting company, surveyed some 6,000 brands among 10,000 consumers to see how many brands are truly global in recognition and esteem. According to the results, only about twenty such brands have a major position in all three large markets of the United States, Japan, and Europe. The clear winner worldwide was Coca-Cola, finishing first in share of mind awareness and sixth in brand esteem. Other major global brands were Sony, Mercedes-Benz, Kodak, Disney, Nestlé, Toyota, McDonald's, IBM, and Pepsi-Cola. Other brands included in the global category were Rolls-Royce, Honda, Panasonic, Levi's, Kleenex, Ford, Volkswagen, Kellogg's, and Porsche. These brands all ranked among the top fifty in the three regions (see Table 10.3).[27]

That the status of a global brand can be made the expressed intent of a strategy is documented by Henkel, a large German company. It relaunched its Fa toiletries line consisting of shower and bath gel, deodorant, and soap, with a $41 million global campaign. The advertising was centralized in one agency with a target of fifty countries. In Japan, Henkel formed a joint venture with Lion, a leading toiletries company. Other new markets for entry are in Eastern Europe. The Fa line accounted for $177 million worldwide in 1988 and had been growing rapidly but had been selling only in a few European countries, the Middle East, Canada, and the United States.[28]

26. "Brands: It's The Real Thing," *The Economist,* November 19, 1988, p. 80.
27. "Coke's Kudos," *The Economist,* September 15, 1990, p. 120.
28. "Henkel Eyes Global Status for Fa Brand," *Advertising Age,* May 28, 1990, p. 46.

TABLE 10.3 ● Top Ten Global Brands

	"Share of mind"	*"Esteem"*
Coca-Cola	1	6
Sony	4	1
Mercedes-Benz	12	2
Kodak	5	9
Disney	8	5
Nestlé	7	14
Toyota	8	23
McDonald's	2	85
IBM	20	4
Pepsi-Cola	3	92

Source: The Economist. September 15, 1990, p. 120. © 1990 The Economist Newspaper Limited. Reprinted with permission.

Pan-Regional Brands

Brands actively marketed in a geographic region, such as Europe, are considered pan-regional, or as is the case in Europe, pan-European or Eurobrands for short. In the strictest sense, packaged goods that are marketed across Europe with the same formula, the same brand name, the same positioning strategy, package, and advertising are said to amount to less than 5 percent of total volume in Europe.[29] Examples of such products include P&G's Pampers and Head & Shoulders, Michelin tires, and Rolex watches. Experts expect their share of all brands to rise, however. Another group of products, marketed with semistandardized strategies but with changes in one or more of the marketing variables, are estimated to account for as much as 40 percent of the European consumer goods business. Consequently, purely national brands may decline in share from more than 50 percent today to about one third in the next decade.

In a survey of European consumers to determine leading brand names, about one-fifth of the leading fifty brands are of U.S. origin, with equal amounts from Germany and France. Mercedes-Benz was the winner, followed by Philips, Volkswagen, Rolls Royce and Coca-Cola.[30]

29. Beatson, Ronald, "The Americanization of Europe," *Advertising Age,* April 2, 1990, p. 16.

30. "Recognition and Respect—The Big Divide," *Financial Times,* November 17, 1988, p. 16.

In Japan, the leading non-Japanese brands were Coca-Cola, Nestlé, Porsche, Kentucky Fried Chicken, McDonald's, BMW, Gucci, Dunhill, Louis Vuitton, and other luxury brands. Nestlé was leading among the mass-marketed brands.[31]

Trademarks

Because brand names or trademarks are usually backed with substantial advertising funds, it makes sense to register such brands for the exclusive use of the sponsoring firm. However, registration abroad is often hampered by a number of factors.

Different interpretations exist in different countries and may affect filing. In some countries, registration authorities may object that the name lacks the inherent distinctiveness needed for registration or that the chosen word is too common to be essential to the promotion of the product, thus allowing other firms to continue to use the name in a descriptive manner. Other countries allow registration of trademarks and renewals for actual or intended use, thus increasing the possibility that some other firm may already have registered the name. In countries where the first applicant always obtains exclusive rights, companies risk the possibility of having their brand names pirated by outsiders who apply for a new name first. The foreign company is then forced to buy back its own trademark. When a country does not allow registrations until all objections are settled, registration may be postponed for years.

Trademark and Brand Protection

Violations of trademarks have been an ever-present problem in international marketing. Many companies have found themselves subject to violations by people who use either the protected name or a very similar one. Deliberate violations can usually be fought in court, though often at great expense. Violations of trademarks, or counterfeit products, are estimated to account for 3 percent of world trade, or some $60 billion in U.S. dollars, according to the International Chamber of Commerce. The Swiss watch industry estimated its own losses to $750 million per year. French perfume makers believe that they lose 10 percent of sales to fake products each year;[32] and the U.S. Department of Commerce estimates that some 750,000 U.S. jobs have been lost due to foreign forgeries of U.S. products.

Hennessey, the French cognac producer, became alarmed when sales in some Far Eastern markets dropped by as much as 30 percent. In those areas, businessmen brought friends and clients to bars and the choice of the cognac ordered signaled the status of both the host and guests. Cognac was ordered by the bottle making the brand very pronounced to all. Bar operators saved the empty bottles and later refilled them with cheap cognac. In some areas, empty Hennessey bottles brought $5 in the

31. Ibid.
32. "Stop, Thief," *International Management,* September 1990, p. 48.

black market. The company retaliated by placing a tamper-proof Polaroid label on each bottle and advertising this to the target market.[33]

In India, an entire cottage industry has developed making counterfeit Scotch whiskey. Legal imports into India are virtually nonexistent and restricted to a few 5-star hotels. In large cities such as Bombay or Delhi, diplomats and businesspeople sell their duty-free allocation of genuine Scotch through peddlers. The counterfeit industry, supplying identical labels, bottles, and packaging, sells its locally-made liquor through these very same channels. Because customers believe they are buying genuine bottles, they are paying about $25 a bottle.[34]

Counterfeiting has been injurious to both businesses and consumers alike. In some cases, trademark violations can result in the potential harm of the customer. Glaxo, the British pharmaceutical company, experienced counterfeiting of its best selling Zantac anti-ulcer drug. The counterfeit drug was produced in Greece where police helped with the seizure of several thousand packages. These packages were to be shipped to the United Kingdom and sold as regular drugs in the open market.[35]

A British manufacturer of surgical instruments found forged items appearing in several European and Third World markets originating in Pakistan. These miniature vascular clamps used to pinch arteries during heart surgery on children posed the risk of snapping during surgery.[36]

Abuses of trademarks and patents are particularly acute in these ten developing countries: Taiwan, South Korea, Thailand, Singapore, Malaysia, Indonesia, the Philippines, Mexico, Brazil, and India.[37] Although many industries have suffered from the effect of counterfeiters, expensive consumer goods, automobile parts, and pharmaceuticals have encountered particular problems.

International companies have been going on the offensive to defend themselves against counterfeiting. The United States passed the Trademark Counterfeiting Act of 1984 which makes counterfeiting punishable by fines of up to $250,000 and prison terms of up to five years.[38] The U.S. government has also put pressure on some foreign governments, particularly on Taiwan, to prosecute its own counterfeiters more aggressively.[39] International companies are increasingly focusing on methods to stop illegal counterfeiting. Many firms find that subcontractors, who know manufacturing processes, are becoming a problem. These companies may fulfill their regular contract to an international company while selling extra volume on the black market. To stop such practices, new marketing systems are developed to allow companies to monitor abuses and customers to spot counterfeit products. Polaproof by

33. Ibid., p. 49.

34. "Bell Toll for Indian 'Scotch' Makers," *Financial Times,* August 29, 1990, p. 5.

35. "Stop, Thief," *International Management,* September 1990, p. 48.

36. Ibid.

37. "Intellectual Property: Foreign Pirates Worry U.S. Firms," *Chemical & Engineering News,* September 1, 1986, p. 8.

38. "The Counterfeit Trade," *Business Week,* December 16, 1985, p. 64.

39. "Taiwan Curbs Its Counterfeiters," *New York Times,* March 30, 1986, p. 74.

Polaroid is one such tamper-proof label, holograms are another, and many invisible marketing devices or inks exist. However, given the difficulty of tracking counterfeiters and the obvious opportunities for making quick profits, counterfeiting is a problem that international companies will have to deal with for some time to come.

PACKAGING FOR GLOBAL MARKETS

Differences in the marketing environment may require special adaptation in product packaging. Changed climatic conditions often demand a change in the package to ensure sufficient protection or shelf life. The role a package assumes in promotion also depends on the market retailing structure. In countries with a substantial degree of self-service merchandising, a package with strong promotional appeal is desirable for consumer products. These requirements may be substantially scaled down in areas where over-the-counter service still dominates. In addition, distribution handling requirements are not identical the world over. In high-wage countries of the developed world, products tend to be packaged to reduce further handling by retailing employees. For consumer products, all mass merchandisers have to do is place products on shelves. In countries with lower wages and less developed retailing structures, individual orders may be filled from larger packaged units, entailing extra labor by the retailer.

R. J. Reynolds of Winston-Salem, North Carolina, exported cigarettes to 160 countries and territories.[40] The company observed more than 1,400 different product codes covering its various brands in all markets. For its leading brand, Winston, the company needed more than 250 different packages to satisfy different brand styles and foreign government requirements. The U.S. package design was used for fewer than six markets. Differences were due to various regulations on health warnings. In Australia the number of cigarettes contained in a package had to be printed on the package front. Some countries such as Canada require bilingual text. To avoid errors in the printing process when working with alphabets as diverse as Greek, Arabic, or Japanese, replicas of the original package were prepared in the foreign market and forwarded for production to the United States.

Specific decisions affected by packaging are size, shape, materials, color, and text.[41] Size may differ by custom, or by existing standards such as metric and non-metric requirements. Higher income countries tend to require larger unit sizes, since these populations shop less frequently and can afford to buy larger quantities each time. In countries with lower income levels, consumers buy smaller quantities, and more often. Gillette, the world's largest producer of razor blades, sells products in

---

40. "Tobacco Companies Face Special International Packaging Obstacles," *Marketing News,* February 4, 1984, p. 20.

41. Philip Kotler, *Marketing Management,* 5th ed. (Englewood Cliffs, N.J.: Prentice-Hall, 1984), pp. 490–492.

packages of five or ten in the United States and Europe, whereas singles are sold in some developing countries.

Packages can assume almost any shape largely depending on customs and traditions of each market. Materials used for packaging can also differ widely. Whereas Americans prefer to buy mayonnaise and mustard in glass containers, consumers in Germany and Switzerland buy these same products in tin tubes. Cans are the customary material to package beer in the United States, whereas most European countries still prefer glass bottles. The color and text of a package have to be integrated into a company's promotional strategy and, therefore, they may be subject to specific tailoring by country. The promotional effect is of great importance for consumer goods and has led some companies to attempt to standardize their packaging in color and layout. In areas such as Europe or Latin American where the consumers frequently travel to other countries, standarized colors help identify a product quickly. This strategy is naturally dependent on a set of colors or a layout with an appeal beyond one single culture or market. An example of a company pursuing a standardized package color is Procter & Gamble, the U.S. manufacturer of the leading detergent, Tide. The orange and white box familiar to millions of U.S. consumers can be found in many foreign markets, even though the package text may appear in the language or print of the given country.

MANAGING A PRODUCT LINE FOR GLOBAL MARKETS

In the early sections of this chapter, we covered decisions about individual products in detail. Most companies, however, manufacture or sell a multitude of products; some, such as General Electric, produce as many as 200,000 items. To facilitate marketing operations, companies group these items into product groups consisting of several product lines. Each product line is made up of several individual items of close similarity. A company with several product lines is faced with the decision to select those most appropriate for international marketing. As with each individual product or decision, the firm can either offer an identical line in its home market and abroad or, if circumstances demand, make appropriate changes.

In most cases, a firm would look at the individual items within a product line and assess marketability on a product-by-product basis. As a result, the product lines abroad are frequently characterized by a narrower width than those found in a company's domestic market. The circumstances for deletions from product lines vary, but some reasons dominate. Lack of sufficient market size is a frequently mentioned reason. Companies with their home base in large markets such as the United States, Japan, or Germany will find sufficient demand in their home markets for even the smallest market segments, justifying additional product variations and greater depth in their lines. Abroad, opportunities for such segmentation strategies may not exist because the individual segments may be too small to warrant commercial exploitation. Lack of market sophistication is another factor in product line variation. Aside from the top twenty developed markets, many markets are less sophisticated and their stage of development may not demand some of the most advanced items in a product line. And finally, new product introduction strategies can impact product lines abroad. For most companies, new products are first introduced in their home markets and introduced abroad only after the product has been successful at home. As a result, the lag in extending new products to foreign markets also contributes toward a product line configuration that differs from that of the firm's domestic market.

Firms confronted with deletions in their product lines sometimes add specialized offerings to fill the gap in the line, either by producing a more suitable product or by developing an entirely new product that may not have any application outside a specific market. Such a strategy can only be pursued by a firm with adequate research and development strength in its foreign subsidiaries.

Exploting Product Life Cycles in International and Global Marketing

The existence of product life cycles immediately opens opportunities to the international firm but, on the other hand, poses additional hurdles that may complicate product strategy. Experience has shown that products do not always occupy the same position on the product life-cycle curve in different countries.

New products receiving initial introduction in the world's developed markets tend to move into later life cycle stages before those in countries that receive the product at a later date. As shown in Figure 10.2, it is possible for a product to be in different stages of the product life cycle for different countries. Other countries follow, usually according to their own stage of economic development. Consequently, although a product may be offered and produced worldwide, it is common for a product to range over several stages in the product life cycle. The principal opportunity offered to the firm is the chance to extend product growth by expanding into new markets to compensate for declining growth rates in mature markets. A risk arises when a company enters new markets or countries too fast, before the local market is ready to absorb the new product. To avoid such pitfalls and to take advantage of long-term opportunities, international companies may follow several strategies.

During the introductory phase, a product may have to be debugged and refined. This job can best be handled in the originating market or in a country close to company research and development centers. Also, the marketing approach will have to be refined. At this stage, the market in even the more advanced countries is relatively small, and demand in countries with lower levels of economic development will hardly be commercially exploitable. Therefore, the introductory stage will be limited to the most advanced markets, often the company's home or domestic market.

Once the product has been fully developed and a larger group of buyers has become interested, volume will increase substantially. Domestic marketing policies foresee price decreases due to volume gains and to the entry of new competitors with an expansion of the entire market. It is at this stage that many firms start to investi-

FIGURE 10.2 ● Possible Product Life Cycle for a Product in Different Countries

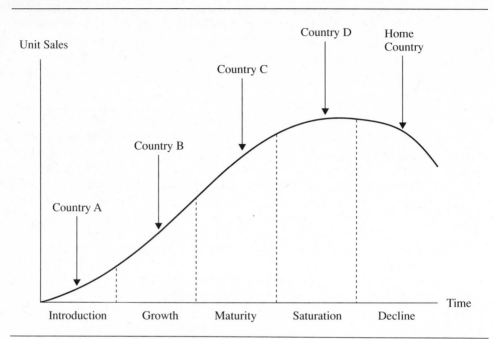

gate opportunities elsewhere by introducing the product in selective markets where it would be in the introductory phase. This requires some adaptation of communication strategy to parallel earlier efforts in the home market, as the approach designed for the second phase, the growth stage, cannot be used.

Bicycles are a product category that has remained in different stages of its life cycle in various countries. Of the world's 800 million bicycles, some 300 million are owned by the Chinese, up from 200 million only ten years ago. Another 45 million are owned by Indians. In China, a two-bicycle family may have as much status as a two-car family in wealthier Western nations. As a result, bicycles are considered to be still in the growth phase for China but hardly are in the same category in industrialized nations.[42]

A product facing life-cycle decline may be withdrawn in stages, similar to its introduction. The most advanced countries will see such a withdrawal earlier than some of the less developed markets. Volkswagen, the German auto maker, offers an example of how an old design may still sell in some countries while being long gone in others. Its famous Beetle car, originally introduced in the 1930s, has been with-

42. "Pedal Power," *The Economist,* January 20, 1990, p. 71.

drawn from production everywhere but Mexico. There, the Beetle remains the best selling car and helps make VW a leading car producer. The model has been adapted for modern environmental requirements but comes only in a simple version without any extras or options. The car is priced at $5,300 and the company has pledged to keep the price pegged to rises in the minimum wage. As a result, VW obtained some important tax relief.[43] Beetles still account for two thirds of the VW's Mexican output.[44]

Stahel & Koeng, a Swiss-based maker of weaving loom shuttles, is one of the few remaining companies still supplying wooden shuttles. Modern weaving machines all are shuttleless with annual production of some 50,000 machines compared to the 13,000 older types still produced. The company still produces some 100,000 shuttles, most of those exported to Third World countries. The old-style looms are only produced in Asia as production in industrialized countries has shifted to the newer looms. The company has been diversifying into other products to plan for what is expected to be a limited demand for another fifteen years.[45]

As we have seen, a product cannot automatically be assumed to reach the various stages in its life cycle simultaneously in all countries, thus flexibility in marketing strategy is required. To introduce a product abroad in stages represents a strategic decision in itself, as described later in this chapter. Though typical, the phased introduction to foreign markets may not always be in the best interest of the firm, as it may offer competitors a chance to expand locally.

INTERNATIONAL AND GLOBAL WARRANTY AND SERVICE POLICIES

Buyers around the world, like domestic consumers, expect more than just the physical benefits of a product. Clients purchase products with certain performance expectations and will consider company policies for backing promises. As a result, warranties and service policies have to be considered as an integral aspect of a company's international product strategy. Companies interested in doing business abroad frequently find themselves at a disadvantage with local competitors when competing on warranties and service. With the supplier's plant often thousands of miles away, foreign buyers sometimes want extra assurance that the supplier will back the prod-

43. "Miss the VW Bug? It Lives Beyond the Rio Grande," *New York Times,* October 20, 1990, p. 2.

44. "VW's Humble Hunch-back Makes a Comeback in Mexico," *The Financial Times,* October 23, 1990, p. 8.

45. "Hinwiler Webschuetzen mit grosser Tradition," *Neue Zuercher Zeitung,* August 15, 1990, p. 49.

uct. Thus, a comprehensive warranty and service policy can become a very important marketing tool for international companies.

Product Warranties

A company must address its warranty policy for international markets either by declaring its domestic warranty valid worldwide or by instituting a policy of tailoring warranties to specific countries or markets. Although it would be administratively simple to declare a worldwide warranty with uniform performance standards, local market conditions often dictate a differentiated approach. In the United States, most computer manufacturers sell their equipment with a 30- or 60-day warranty whereas 12 months is more typical in Europe or in Japan.

Aside from the two technical decisions as to what standards should be covered under a warranty and for how long, a company would be well advised to consider the type of actual product use. If buyers in a foreign market subject the product to more stress or abuse, some shortening of the warranty period may become necessary. A company may be able to change product design to allow for different standard performance requirements. In developing countries, where technical sophistication is below North American or European standards, maintenance may not be adequate, causing more frequent equipment breakdowns. Another important factor is local competition. Since an attractive warranty policy can be helpful in obtaining sales, a firm's warranty policy should be in line with that of other firms competing in the local market. But no warranty will be believable unless backed with an effective service organization, which is the subject of the following section.

Just how important international product warranty expectations have become is demonstrated by the experience of Perrier, the French bottled water company. In February 1990, the company had to withdraw its Perrier water from U.S. retail stores after the product was found to contain benzine above the legal limit. This U.S. test result triggered similar tests in other countries as health authorities elsewhere started to test. Soon, Perrier had to withdraw its products in other countries eventually resulting into a worldwide brand recall. This illustrates the interdependence of many products in today's open and accessible markets. Failure to maintain quality, service, or performance in one country can rapidly have a negative impact in other areas.[46]

Product Service

Although important to the consumer, service is even more crucial to the industrial buyer, since any breakdown of equipment or product is apt to cause substantial economic loss. This risk has led industrial buyers to be conservative in their choice of products, always carefully analyzing the supplier's ability to provide service in case of need.

46. "Brit Helps Perrier Move Beyond the Recall Crisis," *Advertising Age,* November 12, 1990, p. 54.

To provide the required level of service outside the company's home base poses special problems for international companies. The selection of an organization to perform the service is an important decision. Ideally, company personnel are preferable since they tend to be better trained. However, this can only be organized economically if the installed base of the market is large enough to justify such an investment. In cases where a company does not maintain its own sales subsidiary, it is generally more efficient to turn to an independent service company or to a local distributor. To have adequate services via independent distributors requires extra training for the service technician, usually at the manufacturer's expense. In any case, the selection of an appropriate service organization should be made so that fully trained service personnel are readily available within the customary time frame for the particular market.

Closely related to any satisfactory service policy is an adequate inventory for spare parts. Because service often means replacing some parts, the company must place sufficient inventory of spare parts within reach of its markets. Whether this inventory is maintained in regional warehouses or through sales susbidiaries and distributors depends on the volume and the required reaction time for service calls. Buyers will generally want to know how the manufacturer plans to organize service before making substantial commitments.

Firms that demonstrate serious interest in a market by committing to their own sales subsidiaries are often at an advantage over other firms using distributors. One German truck manufacturer that recently entered the U.S. market advertised the fact that "97 percent of all spare parts are kept in local inventory," thus assuring prospective buyers that they can get spares readily. In some instances, the difficulty with service outlets may even influence a company's market entry strategy. This was the case with Fujitsu, a Japanese manufacturer of electronic office equipment. By combining forces with TRW Inc., a U.S.-based company, Fujitsu was able to sell its office equipment in the U.S. market with the extensive service organization of TRW.

Since the guarantee of reliable and efficient service is such an important aspect of a firm's entire product strategy, at times investment in service centers must be made before any sales can take place. In this case, service costs must be viewed as an investment in future volume rather than as a recurring expense.

MARKETING SERVICES GLOBALLY

The international trade in services has increased to about $600 billion worldwide.[47] By far the United States is the world's leading service exporter with an annual volume of $56 billion for 1987.[48] This represents some 18 percent of total U.S. exports. With Japan alone, the U.S. trade in services (excluding investment income for financial

47. "GATT Brief: Center Stage for Services," *The Economist,* May 5, 1990, p. 88.
48. "US Takes the Flak for Failure," *Financial Times,* November 14, 1990, p. 16.

holdings) amount to a positive balance of $9 billion in 1989, up from $7.2 billion in 1988 and 5.3 billion in 1987.[49] International trade in services ranges from banking to insurance, credit cards, consulting, advertising agencies, accounting, law, shipping, and even entertainment services.

Decisions about marketing services are related to the structure of the service itself. A firm has to decide which services to sell or offer and how the service should be designed. Again the issue of standardization needs to be addressed, although there are fewer opportunities for economies of scale by standardizing services worldwide. A company needs to decide on the content of the service it wants to offer and the manner in which the service is performed or consumed. Business services tend to be more standardized, and more in demand worldwide, since the needs of companies are more uniform than those of individual consumers. To a much greater degree, personal services are subject to cultural and social influences and exhibit a greater need for tailoring to local circumstances.

Business Services

The services aimed at business buyers that are most likely to be exported are those that have already met with success. The experience of U.S.-based service companies can be used as an example. Some of the services most successfully marketed abroad include financial services. Commercial banks such as Citibank, Chase Manhattan, and Bank of America have built extensive branch networks around the world, to the extent that foreign deposits and profits make up nearly half of business volume. Advertising agencies have also expanded overseas either by building branch networks or by merging with local agencies.[50] Similar strategies were followed by accounting and management consulting firms. More recently, many U.S.-based marketing research firms have expanded into foreign countries.

Opportunities for New Service Firms

A great many opportunities exist for service companies abroad. Just as the U.S. economy is slowly moving to become a service economy, similar trends can be found in the economies of other developed countries in Western Europe and Japan.

Some examples demonstrate the many types of services that are in great demand abroad. The international courier service is an area where several companies are vying for global positions. The U.S.-based Federal Express built up its overseas business by buying Flying Tiger, the largest international cargo airline, and merging it with its international small documents and parcel service.[51] Federal Express had

49. "Service Exports: Better Than You Think," *Fortune,* June 4, 1990, p. 287.

50. Arnold K. Weinstein, "The International Expansion of U.S. Multinational Advertising Agencies," *MSU Business Topics,* Summer 1974, pp. 29–35.

51. "A Fragile Air Freight Strategy," *New York Times,* September 6, 1989, p. D1.

international revenue of $1 billion, or about 20 percent of the total. However, the building up of its courier service worldwide resulted in tremendous losses, estimated to have reached about $200 million since 1985 and, in 1991, are still running at about $100 million.[52] The company had experienced initial difficulties building a European hub in Frankfurt and ended up centering its European operations in Brussels.[53]

Another major company in the small parcels business with global ambitions is UPS (United Parcel Service). Although about two and a half times larger than its rival Federal Express, UPS is still smaller abroad operating in some 180 countries resulting in operating losses of about $200 million for a 15-month period ending June 1990.[54] It took UPS some twelve years to build its German operation to 6,000 employees. To help its overseas strategy, UPS has acquired several local courier companies in various countries, resulting in acquisitions costing almost $100 million.[55] However, UPS is using its considerable cash flow from U.S. operations to build its international network.

International accounting and consulting services is an area that has seen tremendous growth in the 1980s. Major firms started to think in global terms and to expand their operations into many markets. Among the leading accounting firms, international revenue typically was larger than domestic (or U.S.) revenue. Several firms merged so that the former "Big 8" are now down to six.[56] Ernst & Whinney wanted to merge with Arthur Young because of the latter firm's strong international network. Peat Marwick merged with KMG, a company that was traditionally strong in Europe. Overseas expansion is important to these U.S.-based firms since revenue is growing faster abroad and margins are also better for international business. Furthermore, many of the firm's accounting clients have recently gone through globalization themselves and demand different services. Finally, the impending liberalization of trade in Europe under the 1992 initiative has also boosted cross-national business and mergers.

Such international mergers also create their own challenges. KPMG Peat Marwick McLintock was formed in 1987 through a merger of Peat Marwick Mitchell and KMG Thompson McLintock. The KPMG initials stand for Klynveld Peat Marwick Goerdeler. The KPMG abbreviation was to become the firm's distinctive logo or brand name. This abbreviation typically appeared before the local name of the firm's local company, such as KPMG Geutsche Treuhand in Germany. The company has had difficulty in making the KPMG part a consistent brand to the financial community wherever the firm operated. International clients had a tendency to look

52. "Is Federal Express An Innocent Abroad," *Business Week,* April 2, 1990, p. 34.
53. "Mr. Smith Goes Global," *Business Week,* February 13, 1989, p. 72.
54. "Can UPS Deliver the Goods in a New World," *Business Week,* June 4, 1990, p. 80.
55. "Mr. Smith Goes Global," *Business Week,* April 2, 1990, p. 69.
56. "The Partners Revolt at Peat Marwick," *New York Times,* November 18, 1990, Section 3, p. 1.

upon the firm as KPMG, but local clients tended to associate more with the older local name of the various local operating firms, such as Treuhand in Germany.[57]

Selling Technology Overseas

Some companies have switched from selling products to selling technology. One company that has achieved considerable success in this area is Kawasaki Steel, one of the largest steel producers in Japan.[58] Faced with a stagnant market at home and with growing reluctance by foreign governments to increase Japanese steel imports, Kawasaki turned to its 800 scientists and engineers to produce better steel more efficiently. This effort led to substantial cost savings at Japanese plants while tempting foreign steel operators to purchase the technology. A specially organized division composed of engineering and marketing experts began exporting this know-how. The company had engineers who could engage in a one-shot technical consulting assignment or furnish an entire turnkey plant. Other engineers were available to help important steel users, such as builders of pipelines, off-shore platforms, and shipping berths around the world. Kawasaki was not concerned about exporting technology as long as its own engineers and scientists continued to develop the new techniques. Since it took years to bring a new steel mill on stream, its own scientists were expected to have advanced beyond currently installed technology. Similar opportunities were pursued by other Japanese steel manufacturers and by other companies all over the world.

United Breweries of Denmark, brewers of Carlsberg and Tuborg beer, started to exploit opportunities for selling brewing technology to those markets in which the company would have had great difficulty exporting beer.[59] The company formed Danbrew Consult Ltd. in 1970 to sell its brewing process know-how around the world. Even large U.S. breweries, such as Philip Morris's Miller brewery, have availed themselves of Danbrew services. The company believed that in some markets it could make more money selling services and technology than marketing beer.

Services for Consumers and Individual Households

Marketing services to consumers turns out to be more difficult than selling to industrial users. Since consumer purchasing and usage patterns between countries differ to a greater degree than industry usage patterns, many services have to be adapted to local conditions to make them successful. The U.S.-based fast-food chains were some of the first consumer service companies to pursue foreign opportunities.

57. "KPMG or Not To Be," *Financial Times,* November 8, 1990, p. 10.

58. "Kawasaki Steel: Using Technology as a Tool to Bolster Exports," *Business Week,* January 29, 1979, p. 119.

59. "Denmark's United Breweries Prospers by Selling Its Expertise as Well as Beer," *Wall Street Journal,* February 16, 1984, p. 40.

McDonald's, Kentucky Fried Chicken, Dairy Queen, and many others opened restaurants in Europe and Asia in large numbers.[60]

Though eventually successful, initial results were disappointing for McDonald's in Europe. The company had anticipated differences in taste by serving wine in France, beer in Munich and Stockholm, and tea in England, where the company also lowered the sugar content of its buns by 4 percent.[61] But McDonald's based its first store locations on U.S. criteria and moved into the suburbs and along highways. When volume did not develop according to expectations, McDonald's quickly moved into the inner cities. Once this initial problem had been overcome, McDonald's grew very quickly abroad. In 1985, international revenue accounted for 24 percent of revenue. Although some local food variations have been allowed, the company operated using the same standardized manual worldwide indoctrinating all of its franchise operations abroad with the same type of operating culture.[62]

The success of U.S.-based restaurant chains has encouraged foreign companies to venture abroad. Yoshinoya & Co., a Japanese restaurant chain, started its U.S. operations in 1973.[63] The company planned to set up some sixty beef-bowl shops around Los Angeles and another forty around San Francisco by 1981. Yoshinoya was originally motivated to move abroad because of Japanese restrictions on beef imports. The United States was selected because beef prices were lower than those in Japan, and beef was widely available. The food served in the United States is virtually the same in taste and menu. However, Yoshinoya did adjust the size of portions by serving between 30 to 50 percent more beef per bowl than was served in Japan, where beef was two to three times more expensive.[64] American consumers, unlike the Japanese, were found to be dissatisfied unless they were served food in quantity.

Even producers of films for American television have come to court foreign food buyers.[65] In 1970, exports of American-made television movies, serials, and full-length motion pictures shown on television amounted to $97 million. By 1980 sales had reached $365 million, an increase of more than 300 percent. Britain, Canada, Japan, Australia, and Brazil were believed to be the major customers. The only hurdle so far has been government quotas. In England, only 14 percent of daily air time can go to imports; and other countries enforce similar limitations. However, as governments abroad have begun to tolerate more competition, independently owned stations are being opened in many countries. This greatly increases the demand for imported programming. In Italy for instance, independent commercial television

60. Donald Hackett, "The International Expansion of the U.S. Franchise Systems: Status and Strategies," *Journal of International Business Studies,* Spring 1976, pp. 65–76.

61. *New York Times,* April 13, 1979.

62. "McWorld?" *Business Week,* December 13, 1986, p. 78.

63. "Yoshinoya Eyes Beef Bowl Chain Operation on U.S. West Coast," *Japan Economic Journal,* April 10, 1979, p. 14.

64. Ibid.

65. "American T.V. Abroad," *New York Times,* January 18, 1981, p. 18F.

was not allowed until recently. Suddenly fifty stations opened in Rome alone, all looking for attractive programming.

CONCLUSIONS

To be successful in foreign markets requires that companies be flexible in product and service offerings. Although a given product may have been very successful in a firm's home market, environmental differences can often force the company to make unexpected or costly changes. While a small group of products may be marketed worldwide without significant changes, most companies will find success abroad to be dependent on a willingness to adapt to local market requirements. Additional efforts are also frequently required in product support services to assure foreign clients that the company will stand behind its products. For those companies that successfully master the additional international difficulties while showing a commitment to foreign clients, success abroad can lead to increased profits and more secure market positions domestically.

Questions for Discussion

1. Generalize about the overall need for product adaptations for consumer products versus high technology industrial products. What differences exist? Why?

2. Which one of the factors in Table 10.1 would be of particular importance for a company such as GMC (trucks) as opposed to Atari (electronics)?

3. What are the major reasons for a company to have a worldwide brand name?

4. Under what circumstances would it be advisable to use different brand names in different countries?

5. Are there any differences between the international marketing of services versus the international marketing of products?

For Further Reading

Ayal, Igal, "International Product Life Cycle: A Reassessment and Product Implications." *Journal of Marketing* (Fall 1981), pp. 91–96.

Bartels, Robert. "Are Domestic and International Marketing Dissimilar?" *Journal of Marketing* (July 1968), pp. 56–61.

Britt, Stewart H. "Standardizing Marketing for the International Market." *Columbia Journal of World Business* (Winter 1974), pp. 39–45.

Buzzell, Robert D. "Can You Standardize Multinational Marketing?" *Harvard Business Review* (November-December 1968), pp. 1, 2, 113.

Davidson, William H., and Richard Harrigan. "Key Decisions in International Marketing:

Introducing New Products Abroad." *Columbia Journal of World Business* (Winter 1977), pp. 15–23.

Hill, John S., and Richard R. Still. "Adapting Products to LDC Tastes." *Harvard Business Review* (March-April 1984), pp. 92–101.

Keegan, Warren J. "Multinational Product Planning: Strategic Alternatives." *Journal of Marketing* (January 1969), pp. 58–62.

Levitt, Theodore. "Globalization of Markets." *Harvard Business Review* (May-June 1983), pp. 92–102.

Samli, A. Coskun, and Rustan Kosanko. "Support Service Is the Key for Technology Transfer to China." *Industrial Marketing Management* (April 1982), pp. 95–103.

Sorenson, Ralph Z. II. "U.S. Marketers Can Learn from European Innovators." *Harvard Business Review* (September-October 1972), pp. 89–99.

Sorenson, Ralph Z., and Ulrich E. Wiechmann. "How Multinationals View Marketing Standardization." *Harvard Business Review* (May-June 1975).

Ward, James J. *The European Approach to U.S. Markets: Product and Promotion Adaptation.* New York: Praeger, 1973. Chapter 4.

11

New Product Development Strategies

● **IN CHAPTER 10** *we focused on individual product decisions. In this chapter, we concentrate on the strategic issues of product design and development for international and global markets (see Figure 11.1). Following an in-depth analysis of the standardization versus adaptation issue, the first segment of this chapter covers a series of alternatives involving product extension, adaptation, and innovation strategies. This leads into a segment on global products which deals with the complexities of designing products for many markets simultaneously. This part of the chapter is devoted to a discussion of product development strategies for international companies. Emphasis is placed on organizational issues, sources, and approaches that will enhance a firm's ability to innovate in a changing marketplace. We conclude the chapter with a section on the process of new product introductions.*

INTERNATIONAL PRODUCT STRATEGIES[1]

The purpose of this section is to outline the basic product strategies a firm may select and to demonstrate their close relationship with a company's communication policy, particularly with respect to advertising. A company's decision to pursue a spe-

1. This section is based on Warren J. Keegan, "Multinational Product Planning: Strategic Alternatives," *Journal of Marketing,* January 1969, pp. 58–62.

FIGURE 11.1 ● International and Global Product Development Strategies

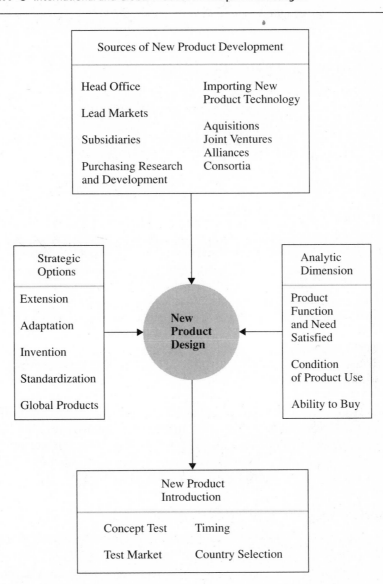

cific product strategy primarily depends on three factors: first, whether the product function or the need satisfied is the same or different in a new market; second, whether particular conditions surrounding product use can affect company strategy; and third, whether target market customers are financially able to buy the product. These three factors greatly influence the product strategy chosen. Before we turn to a company's strategic options, we first will examine the three elements in some detail.

Product Function or the Need Satisfied

The key to this factor is the role the product plays in a given market. Although certain types of products may be consumed by individuals in many countries, a company cannot automatically assume that the underlying motivation to purchase is identical. Take, for example, the difference between Americans and Russians with respect to purchasing and wearing T-shirts and blue jeans (which we discussed earlier in Chapter 3). In the United States, T-shirts and jeans convey an informal attitude toward clothing and a lack of interest in any status that clothing may convey. In fact, by dressing this way Americans give the appearance of wanting to be ordinary rather than stand out. In Russia the opposite is true. Because real blue jeans and T-shirts are in short supply, those who wear such clothing signal to society that they are aware of current fashions and are highly status conscious. In Russia, jeans and T-shirts clearly separate the individual from the rest of society. Thus the rationale for buying them is different in these two countries and appears quite contradictory.

On the other hand, products for industrial use, such as plant machinery, are purchased the world over for the same intention or reason. Therefore, very little difference in product function or satisfied need is expected. Also, many examples of consumer goods can be pointed to for which the need to be satisfied is identical. For one, the motivation behind the purchase of razor blades is homogeneous across countries and cultures.

Differences in product function or satisfied need, even when present, do not necessarily call for a change in product design or features. The primary focus here is on the buyer and the motivation that triggers a purchase. As a psychological concept, motivation requires a corresponding response. Therefore, dissimilar purchasing motives require unique communications responses, or a change in a firm's advertising, to relate the product to these different motives.

Conditions of Product Use

Physical environmental variables combine into a physical event that determines the salient factors surrounding a product's actual use. To the extent that these events are identical within any two countries, a product may be marketed without any changes or alterations. The conditions of product use reflect the actual use or consumption of a product regardless of the motivation that triggered its purchase. In seeking opportunities for product standardization, marketers must consider the physical events surrounding product use that substantially determine the viability of the strategy.

The Ability to Buy

Although purchasing power is generally not an issue in the developed countries of Europe, North America, and Asia, there are, nevertheless, hundreds of millions of potential customers in countries that simply do not have the economic resources found in more affluent countries. The motivation to purchase a product and actual use conditions may be identical to those in affluent societies, but the products used to satisfy these demands are beyond the price that buyers in developing countries can afford. Consequently, such situations may require an entirely different strategy. The product can be changed so that it can be made available at a substantially lower price. Thus, substantial differences in the nature of the economic event can have a significant influence on international product strategy. General Motors' attempt to market its Basic Transportation Vehicle (BTV) in developing countries serves as an excellent example. The BTV was designed at costs substantially below those of traditional cars by sacrificing comfort, style, and performance.[2]

Three Strategic Choices: Extension, Adaptation, Invention

A company can follow one of three basic strategies when moving into a foreign market. With respect to both its product and its communications policy, the firm can opt for an *extension* strategy, basically adopting the same approach as in its home market. The strategy of *adaptation* requires some changes to fit the new market requirements. When an entirely new approach is required, the company can adopt the strategy of *invention.* These three basic strategies can be further refined into the five strategies shown in Table 11.1. These five strategies are explained in the following sections.

Strategy One: Product Extension—Communications Extension This extension strategy calls for marketing a standardized product with the same communications strategy across the globe. Although this strategy has considerable attraction because of its cost effectiveness, it is rarely realizable for consumer products. The few exceptions include companies in the soft drink industry and some luxury goods firms. Industrial products, with a greater homogeneity of buyers internationally, offer a somewhat greater opportunity for this strategy, but again the extension strategy is far from the norm.

The cost effectiveness of this strategy should not be underestimated, however. Product adaptations entail additional research and development expenses and tool-

2. Harvard Business School, *"General Motors Malaysia Adm. Bhd.,"* HBS Case Services, Boston, Mass., 9-574-065, 1974/1981.

TABLE 11.1 ● International Product Strategies

Strategy	Product function or need satisfied	Conditions of product use	Ability to buy product	Recommended product strategy	Recommended communications strategy	Relative cost of adjustments	Product examples
1	Same	Same	Yes	Extension	Extension	1	Soft drinks
2	Different	Same	Yes	Extension	Adaptation	2	Bicycles, Motorscooters
3	Same	Different	Yes	Adaptation	Extension	3	Gasoline, Detergents
4	Different	Different	Yes	Adaptation	Adaptation	4	Clothing, Greeting cards
5	Same	—	No	Invention	Develop New Communications	5	Hand-powered washing machine

Source: From Warren J. Keegan: "Multinational Product Planning: Strategic Alternatives." Reprinted from *Journal of Marketing,* vol. 33, January 1969, pp. 58–62, published by the American Marketing Association.

ing costs, and they do not allow economies of scale to the extent possible under an extension strategy. Though less substantial, savings from the creation of only one communications strategy should also be considered. In any case, a decision should consider the anticipated impact on demand in the foreign market if the product is not fully suited to local tastes or preferences, as well as the potential savings. Past experience shows that rigidly enforcing a product and communication extension policy can lead to disaster and, therefore, should only be adopted if all requirements with respect to product function, need, use condition, and ability to buy are met.

Strategy Two: Product Extension—Communications Adaptations When the sociocultural event surrounding product consumption differs from country to country, but the use conditions as part of the physical event are identical, the same product can be marketed with a change in the communication strategy. Examples can be found among bicycle and motorcycle manufacturers. In the developing countries of Asia, Africa, and Latin America, a bicycle or motorcycle is primarily a means of transportation, whereas the same products are used in sports or for recreation purposes in the United States. This strategy is still quite cost effective, since communications adaptation represents a low-cost approach to tailoring a product to a local market.

Strategy Three: Product Adaptation—Communications Extension This strategy is appropriate when the physical event surrounding product use varies but the sociocultural event is the same as in the company's home market. Although changes in a product are substantially more costly than changes in the communications approach, a company will follow this course when the product may not sell otherwise in a foreign market. In some cases product formulations may be changed without the consumer knowing it, as with detergents and gasoline, so that the product can function under different environmental circumstances.

Strategy Four: Product Adaptation—Communications Adaptation   When both the physical and sociocultural events vary, a strategy of dual adaptation is generally favored. To make this strategy profitable, however, the foreign market or markets need to be of sufficient volume to justify the costs of dual adaptation. Nike, a leading U.S. manufacturer of running shoes, soon found that its continued growth in Europe could not be built on jogging shoes alone. In Europe jogging never developed to the extent it did in the United States. By far the largest sports-shoe category in Europe was soccer, prompting Nike to develop a shoe specifically designed for that market. To market the new product, Nike developed a unique promotional campaign that took into consideration the dominating positions of Adidas and Puma in the soccer shoe segment.[3]

Strategy Five: Product Invention   When the ability to purchase a product is generally missing, some companies have elected to invent an entirely new product, usually by redesigning the original product to a lower level of complexity. As a result, a substantially cheaper product leads to more purchases. An example was the strategy followed by Philips, the Dutch multinational corporation. In response to the desire of many developing countries to own their own television manufacturing plants, the Dutch company redesigned its equipment and tools to suit the volume requirements of some of the world's poorest countries. The molding machines used in its European plants to produce TV cabinets cost about $150,000, an amount justified by a factory output of about 100,000 units per year. But many African countries could only support plants with an average annual output of 3,000 to 5,000 sets. By borrowing from existing technology found in automobile dashboard manufacturing, Philips eventually invented a press that cost only $2,150.[4]

Advantages of Product Standardization

Complete standardization of product design results in a substantial saving of production and research and development costs and will allow a company to take full advantage of economies of scale. Often, several markets can be supplied from a regional or central manufacturing plant with efficient and long production runs. Aside from these obvious advantages, production sharing and simultaneously supplying markets from several plants are important factors that support standardized output. Managers in the U.S. subsidiary of Liebherr, a large German company producing construction machinery, decided to make some changes in the basic design of an excavator that was made to identical specifications elsewhere in Europe and

3. "Fitting the World in Sports Shoes," *Business Week,* January 25, 1982, p. 73.
4. *Wall Street Journal,* February 27, 1981.

Latin America. To make the excavator more acceptable to U.S. customers, the Virginia-based subsidiary enlarged the fuel tank and strengthened the undercarriage. When U.S. sales dropped in the recession of 1974–1975, the company accumulated a substantial inventory of excavators. However, it could not help its European plants, filled with back-orders, because of the difference in design. Obviously the advantages gained from adaptation have to be compared to the overall loss in manufacturing flexibility.[5]

Despite the advantages of economies of scale, there are few companies that can fully standardize their products for the many markets they serve. To bridge the gap between various local adaptations and the need to standardize some components, some international firms have moved to a new breed of products, the global product, which we will discuss in the following section.

GLOBAL PRODUCTS

In response to the pressure for cost reduction and considering the relatively few opportunities for producing completely standardized products, many firms have moved to the creation of a *global product.* The global product, based on the acknowledged fact that only a portion of the final design can be standardized, builds on flexibility to tailor the end product to the needs of individual markets. This represents a move to standardize as much as possible those areas involving common components or parts. This modularized approach has become of particular importance in the automobile industry, where both U.S. and European manufacturers are moving toward the creation of world components to combat growing Japanese competitiveness.

One of the first world cars was introduced by Ford during the 1981 model year. Ford's Escort model was simultaneously assembled in the United States, Great Britain, and Germany from parts produced in ten countries. The U.S.-assembled Escort contained parts made in Japan, Spain, Brazil, Britain, Italy, France, Mexico, Taiwan, and West Germany.[6] The European assembly plants in return bought automatic transmissions from a U.S. plant. Ford was estimated to have saved engineering and development costs amounting to hundreds of millions of dollars because the design standardized engines, transmissions, and ancillary systems for heating, air conditioning, wheels, and seats.[7] Still, the U.S. and European Escorts were two very different cars.

The second generation of global products was started in 1981, the year the first original Escort rolled off the line, to be ready for production in 1991. Created with a budget of some $2 billion, Ford designed its second generation Escort with Mazda,

5. "It's Tough Digging in the U.S.," *Fortune,* August 11, 1980, p. 146.
6. *New York Times,* November 9, 1980.
7. "Ford's Financial Hurdle," *Business Week,* February 2, 1981, p. 66.

the Japanese car manufacturer partly owned by Ford. The design was done by Ford engineers in the United States with the engineering and manufacturing planning performed by the Japanese engineers at Mazda. This new model was planned for assembly in twelve different locations where Ford will sell the car under its Escort name while Mazda will use its various brand names (the 323, Protege, or Familia). By pooling their development resources, Ford was estimated to have saved as much as $1 billion in development costs.[8]

Ford's strategy was driven by the fact that product development duplication was a very costly process amounting to billions of dollars per new model. Between North America and Europe, Ford produced seven different four-cylinder engines when two would suffice. Ford's long-term strategy was to shrink its models down to three basic global designs, a small, a medium, and a large type. They would be marketed in Europe, the United States, and Japan with the largest possible number of common components. As a result, the planned replacement for the Sierra line in Europe and the Tempo/Topaz line in the United States would be standardized down to a common platform. Because of the present differences between the two designs, Ford could not justify developing and manufacturing the three-door and five-door versions in the United States. It would have required new development costs. Using the European models was prevented by the differences in the basic versions. This process of globalization in the product design was made a challenge because Ford maintained full development staffs both in its European and North American car operations.[9]

As Ford was moving toward common designs for markets on three continents, some Japanese car companies were moving in the opposite direction. Honda has steadily added to its development and design function in North America. Its new Honda Accord station wagon introduced in 1990 was developed from the standard Accord power train in the United States and built only in its U.S. factory. The model will be exported to Japan and elsewhere.[10]

Toyota plans to launch a new version of its popular Camry in 1991. Making it three inches wider than its Japanese version, the new Toyota Camry will be better able to challenge the standard North American sedans of Ford and General Motors. Toyota is also developing a new large pick-up truck that will be unsuitable in Japan with its much narrower roads.[11]

The strategy pursued by the Japanese companies has been called a "tri-polar strategy" by a Nissan executive. This allows them to spread the expensive research and development costs across a worldwide production system. The regions can help each other when demand shifts or shortages occur. Furthermore, it allows the com-

8. "How Ford and Mazda Shared the Driver's Seat," *Business Week,* March 26, 1990, p. 94.

9. "Ford's Internal Battle to Supply a Global Common Market," *Financial Times,* May 22, 1989, p. 15.

10. "Honda's New Wagon: A U.S. Auto, Almost," *New York Times,* December 14, 1990, p. D1.

11. "Japan's New U.S. Car Strategy," *Fortune,* September 10, 1990, p. 65.

panies to put design teams closest to the markets, thus assuring maximum acceptance of the models.[12]

The challenge faced by Ford or other automobile manufacturers is similar to that faced by manufacturers and marketers of both industrial and consumer products all over the world. Cost pressures force them to standardize while market pressures require more customization. Conceptually these companies will gain from increasing the standardized components in their products while maintaining the ability to customize the product at the end for each market segment. International firms will have to respond by achieving economies of scale on the core of their products, or the key portion offered as a standard across all markets. This core will be built on a series of standardized components resulting in economies of scale. Different firms will have different levels of standardization, but they will rarely be able to standardize the product 100 percent. For one company, moving from a global core representing 15 percent of the total product to 20 percent of the total product may result in a considerable cost improvement, and this may be the maximum level of standardization desirable. For another firm, the core may have to represent some 80 percent of the total product to achieve the same effect. These levels will depend on the market characteristics faced by the company or industry. The limits to possible standardization were explained in the previous chapter.

NEW PRODUCT DEVELOPMENT FOR INTERNATIONAL AND GLOBAL MARKETS

To develop new products or services for international and global markets offers unique challenges to a firm. In contrast to the strictly domestic company, international firms must assign development responsibilities to any one of their often numerous international subsidiaries. Aside from the question of who should perform development work, there are organizational problems to be overcome that pertain to participation by experts in many subsidiaries. There is no doubt that the future success of international firms to a substantial degree will depend on how well firms marshal their resources on a global scale to develop new products for foreign markets.

The Organization of Head Office-Sponsored Research and Development

Most companies currently engaged in research and development on a global scale originally conducted their development efforts strictly in centralized facilities in the firm's domestic market. Even today, the largest portion of research and development monies spent by international firms is for efforts in domestically located facilities. As

12. Ibid.

a result, new product ideas are first developed in the context of the domestic market, with initial introduction at home, followed by a phase-in introduction to the company's foreign markets.

There are several reasons for this traditional approach to research and development. First, it must be integrated into a firm's overall marketing strategy. This requires frequent contacts and interfacing between research and development facilities and the company's main offices. Such contacts are maintained more easily with close proximity. The argument for a centralization of research and development is based on the concern that a duplication of efforts will result if this responsibility is spread over several subsidiaries. Centralized research and development is thought to maximize results from scarce research funds. A final important reason for centralization is the company's experience in its home or domestic market. Typically the domestic market is very important to the company and, in the case of international companies based in the United States, Germany, and Japan, it is often the largest market as well. As a result, new products are developed with special emphasis on the domestic market, and research and development facilities, therefore, should be close by.

Although there are many good reasons for centralizing product development at the company's head office, it will remain a challenge for the engineering and development staff of the firm to keep in mind all relevant product modifications before the design is frozen. Experience shows that later changes or modifications can be expensive. To keep a product acceptable in many or all relevant markets from the outset requires the product development staff to become globalized in the early creation. Only a globally-thinking product development staff will assure the global acceptability of a product by incorporating the maximum possible number of variations in the original product.

International Lead Markets and Research and Development[13]

Prior to 1960, new developments in industry, marketing, or management tended to emerge primarily in the United States. Such developments, once accepted in the United States, were apt to be adopted later in other countries. As a result, the U.S. market served as the lead market for much of the rest of the world. In general, a lead market is a market whose level of development exceeds that of the market in other countries worldwide and whose developments tend to set a pattern for other countries.

Lead markets are not restricted to technological developments as embodied in product hardware. The concept covers developments in design, production processes, patterns in consumer demand, or methods of marketing. Therefore, virtually every phase of a company's operation is subject to lead market influences, although those focusing on technological developments are of special importance.

13. This section is based on Jean-Pierre Jeannet, "Lead Markets: A Concept for Designing Global Business Strategies," working paper, IMEDE, 1986.

During the first half of the twentieth century, the United States achieved a position of virtual dominance as a lead market. Not only were U.S. products the most advanced with respect to features, function, and quality, but they also tended to be marketed to the most sophisticated and advanced consumers and industrial buyers. This U.S. advantage was partially based on superior production methods, with the pioneering of mass production in the form of the assembly line. The U.S. advantage extended to management methods in general, and particularly to access to new consumers. The rapid development of U.S.-based international firms was to a considerable degree based on the exploitation of these advantages in applying new U.S. developments abroad and in creating extensive networks of subsidiaries across a large number of countries.

But the U.S. lead over other countries did not last. Foreign competitors from Europe and Japan eroded the U.S. firms' advantages and, as a result, no single country or market now unilaterally dominates the world economy. Though the United States may have lost its lead in steel, television, radios, shoes, textiles, and automobiles, it still leads the world in electronics, the biosciences, computers, and aerospace. (See Figure 11.2.)

Although the general purpose computer industry is still dominated by mostly U.S. companies with the United States still serving as the lead market, there are many signs that this position may be challenged in the future. In 1983, U.S. companies had an 81 percent share of computer sales compared to 61 percent in 1989. Over the same period, the share of Japanese companies rose from 8 percent to 22 percent. Nowhere is this more visible than in the personal computer market. Here, U.S. companies dominate the PC segment with IBM and Apple in the lead. Epson was actually the first Japanese company with a unit volume of about one-fifth that of IBM. In the rapidly growing portable segment, including lap-top or pocket-size portable PCs, Japanese companies are in the lead (Toshiba, NEC). Japanese firms are able to leverage the Japanese skills of miniaturizing into the computer field and Japan is generally expected to become the lead market for such small PCs.[14]

The fragmentation of lead markets led to a proliferation of centers, substantially complicating the task of keeping abreast of the latest developments in market demands, products design, and production techniques. Even formerly developing countries, such as Korea, have reached lead market status in some categories. In some areas of chip development, Korea is now less than twelve months behind Japan and efforts are being made to close that gap.[15] However, to prosper in today's increasingly internationalized business climate, corporations must keep track of evolving lead markets as major sources for new product ideas. New product ideas can stem from influences in demand, processes of manufacture, and scientific discoveries; and no single country should expect to play a lead role in all facets of a firm's business. This means any corporate research and development effort must look for new devel-

14. "Japanese Portables Threaten American Lead in Computers," *New York Times,* November 24, 1990, p. 1.
15. "In Korea, All Circuits Are Go," *Business Week,* July 9, 1990, p. 69.

FIGURE 11.2 ● How the U.S. Stacks Up in a Dozen Emerging Technologies

	Compared to Japan			Compared to Europe		
	R & D	New Products		R & D	New Products	
Advanced Materials	↔ ↓	↓ ↓		↑ ↔	↔ ↔	
Advanced Semiconductor Devices	↔ ↔	↓ ↓		↑ ↔	↔ ↔	
Artificial Intelligence	↑ ↔	↑ ↔		↑ ↑	↑ ↔	
Biotechnology	↑ ↓	↑ ↓		↑ ↑	↑ ↔	
Digital Imaging Technology	↔ ↓	↓ ↓		↔ ↓	↓ ↓	
Flexible Computer-Integrated Manufacturing	↑ ↔	↔ ↔		↑ ↓	↓ ↓	
High–Density Data Storage	↔ ↔	↓ ↓		↑ ↔	↔ ↔	
High-Performance Computing	↑ ↔	↑ ↓		↑ ↑	↑ ↑	
Medical Devices and Diagnostics	↑ ↔	↑ ↓		↑ ↔	↑ ↓	
Optoelectronics	↔ ↔	↓ ↓		↔ ↔	↑ ↔	
Sensor Technology	↑ ↓	↔ ↔		↑ ↔	↔ ↔	
Superconductors	↔ ↓	↔ ↓		↔ ↔	↔ ↔	

U.S. Status   ↑ Ahead   ↔ Even   ↓ Behind

U.S. Trend   ↑ Gaining   ↔ Holding   ↓ Losing

Source: U.S. Commerce Dept. Reprinted from the June 15, 1990 issue of *Business Week* by special permission, copyright © 1990 by McGraw-Hill, Inc.

opments abroad rather than solely in the domestic market. Foreign-based firms adjusted long ago to this fact and organized research and development with the U.S. lead market role partially in mind. However, multinational corporations based in the United States conduct about 90 percent of research and development in their home market and, thus, run the risk of excluding themselves from important developments in foreign markets unless provisions are made.[16]

The rapid international expansion of U.S.-based firms depended to a large extent on their capacity to take advantage of lessons learned in the U.S. market. This strategy was characterized by centralized research and development functions and initial product introductions in the United States. Naturally, to a large degree, the success of this strategy depends on the inputs the central research and development staff derives from its own market environment. Should any part of a company's market become subject to foreign lead market influences, the organization of a firm's research and development function will have to be adjusted. Steel companies in the United States and manufacturers of automobiles, shoes, and textiles cannot disregard developments elsewhere in the world, since the lead market for these industries is no longer the United States. To expose itself to lead market developments, Kodak has invested $65 million in a research and development center in Japan, which employs a staff of about 200 people.[17] The company hired about one hundred professional researchers and directed the lab to concentrate on electronic imaging technology.[18] Other U.S. companies have built up their own R&D facilities in Japan, including Corning, Texas Instruments, IBM, Digital Equipment, Procter & Gamble, and several chemical and pharmaceutical companies such as Upjohn, Pfizer, Du Pont, and Monsanto. In 1990, U.S. companies spent $491 million to license technology from Japan compared to just $89 million eight years earlier. This speaks for the fact that Japan is increasingly becoming a lead market for many technology areas.[19]

The Role of Foreign Subsidiaries in Research and Development

Foreign subsidiaries of international firms rarely play an active role in research and development unless they have manufacturing responsibilities. Sales subsidiaries may provide feedback to the central organization on product adjustments or adaptation, but generally this participation does not go beyond the generation of ideas. Past research has shown that subsidiaries may assume some research and development

16. D. B. Creamer, *Overseas Research and Developments by U.S. Multinationals, 1966–1975* (New York: The Conference Board, 1975).

17. "Kodak Invades Japan to Fight Fuji—and Learn," *Providence Sunday Journal,* December 21, 1986, p. 71.

18. "When the Corporate Lab Goes to Japan," *New York Times,* April 28, 1991, Section 3, p. 1.

19. "Picking Japan's Research Brains," *Fortune,* March 25, 1991, p. 84.

functions if the products require some adaptation to the local market.[20] The ensuing research and development capability is often extended to other applications unique to the local market. In many instances, however, the new product may prove to have potential in other markets and, as a result, these developments get transferred to other subsidiaries and to the central research and development staff.

International subsidiaries assume special positions when lead markets change from one country to another. Countries that can assume lead market status tend to be among the most advanced industrial nations of North America, Europe, and Asia. Larger international firms quite often have subsidiaries in all these markets. A subsidiary located in a lead market is usually in a better position to observe developments and to accommodate to new demands. Consequently, international firms with subsidiaries in lead markets are in a unique position to turn such units into effective "listening posts."[21] For quite some time now, U.S.-based firms have profited from technological advances made by their European subsidiaries, leading to a reverse flow of technology.[22] Much of this flow however has occurred on an ad hoc basis without any attempts to exploit deliberately the capabilities of foreign subsidiaries in newly emerging lead markets.

In the future, international companies will have to make better use of the talents of local subsidiaries in the development of new products. Increasingly, the role of the subsidiary as a selling arm or production arm of the company will have to be abandoned and companies will have to find innovative ways to involve their foreign affiliates into the product development process. This involvement can be patterned around several role models.[23] The strategic leader role for developing a new range of products to be used by the entire company may be assigned to a highly competent subsidiary in a market of strategic importance. Another subsidiary with competence in a distinct area may be assigned the role of contributor by adapting some products in smaller but nevertheless important markets. Most subsidiaries, being of smaller size and located in less strategic markets, will be expected to implement the overall strategy and contribute less either technologically or strategically.

Purchasing Research and Development from Foreign Countries

Instead of developing new products through its own research and development personnel, a company may acquire such material or information from independent outside sources. These sources are usually located in foreign countries that have

20. Jean-Pierre Jeannet, *Transfer of Technology Within Multinational Corporations* (New York: Arno Press, 1980).

21. Raymond Vernon, "Gone Are the Cash Cows of Yesteryear," *Harvard Business Review,* November-December 1980, p. 150.

22. Jeannet, *Transfer of Technology Within Multinational Corporations* (New York: Arno Press, 1980).

23. Christopher A. Bartlett and Sumantra Ghoshal, "Tap Your Subsidiaries for Global Reach," *Harvard Business Review,* November-December 1986, p. 67.

acquired lead market status. Managers commonly read literature published by lead markets. Also, through regular visits to foreign countries and trade fairs, managers maintain close contact with their lead markets. Increasingly, however, these ad hoc measures are becoming insufficient for maintaining the necessary flow of information in rapidly changing markets.

For companies without immediate access to new technology embodied in new products, the licensing avenue has been the traditional approach to gain new developments from lead markets. United States technology has been tapped through many independent licensing arrangements. Japanese companies have made extensive use of the licensing alternative to acquire technologies developed in countries that were lead markets from Japan's point of view. In the early 1960s, several Japanese manufacturers of earth-moving equipment signed licensing agreements with the U.S. manufacturers to obtain expertise in hydraulic power shovels.[24] Though some Japanese companies attempted to develop a new product line from their own internal resources, it was Komatsu who, based on a licensing agreement with a U.S. company, achieved leadership in Japan. By 1989, Japanese companies manufacturing earth-moving equipment owned some twenty-one facilities abroad, some partly owned and others fully owned. Many firms that were originally licensers to those Japanese firms are no longer independent or have even become Japanese partners, joint ventures, or subsidiaries.[25] Though the advantage of licensing lies in its potential to teach new product technologies, there are typically some restrictions attached, such as limiting the sale of such products to specific geographic regions or countries.

A variation of the licensing agreement is the technology assistance contract with a foreign company, allowing a constant flow of information to the firm seeking assistance. Such agreements have been signed by several U.S. steel companies. Japanese steel makers have achieved world leadership. Consequently, steel companies all over the world, Americans among them, have tapped the former's knowledge and experience. Sumitomo Metal signed contracts with clients in nineteen countries, including U.S. Steel, for steel making, plate rolling, and pipe manufacturing. Other U.S. companies purchasing from Japanese companies included Armco, from Nippon Steel; Inland Steel, from Nippon Kokan; and Bethlehem Steel, from Kawasaki Steel.[26]

The Korean firm Lucky-Gold Star is an example of a company that aggressively buys technology abroad to assist in the development of its technologically advanced products. Over the years, the company has formed some twenty joint ventures and maintained technology cooperation agreements with more than fifty foreign firms. Lucky-Gold Star linked up with the U.S.-based AT&T to manufacture electronic telephone switching gear, fiber-optic cables, and semiconductors. Entering such

24. *Japan Economic Journal,* October 2, 1979 and August 5, 1980.
25. "Japan's Earth Movers Look Abroad," *Financial Times,* April 11, 1989, p. 25.
26. *New York Times,* October 28, 1980.

agreements offered the Korean firm quick access to modern technologies while allowing AT&T to build contacts within a new market.[27]

Importing as a Source of New Product Technology

Some corporations have decided to forego internally sponsored research and development, importing finished products directly from a foreign firm. Sometimes the importer assumes the role of an original equipment manufacturer (OEM) by marketing products under its own name. Some agreements made between Japanese suppliers and European and U.S. manufacturers serve to illustrate this strategy.

When IBM was looking for a small desk-top copier to fill a gap in its product line, the company turned to a Japanese supplier, Minolta Camera Co., Ltd., instead of developing its own machine.[28] IBM's product line included photocopying machines ranging from $6,000 to $40,000, after it dropped an older model that had sold for $4,000. But in 1980 the company opened its first retail outlets, which were targeted at small businesses. The need for a small desk-top model became apparent and had to be filled quickly. The Minolta-supplied model was sold as the IBM Model 102 and resembled the Model EP-310, which was marketed by Minolta in the United States through a network of independent dealers.

Though the importing method gives a firm quick access to new products without incurring any research and development expenditures, a company could become dependent and lose the capacity to innovate on its own in the future. As was the case with General Electric's color TV production, economic changes can lead to reversals later on. GE had stopped production of color TV sets in the United States in the mid-1970s and sourced all such products from Matsushita in Japan. When the value of the yen rose to record levels in 1986, GE switched back to U.S. sourcing. This move was made possible because the company had earlier acquired RCA which still operated a color TV plant in the United States.[29] Consequently, such a strategy of importing new products should be pursued with great care and possibly only in areas that do not represent the core of the firm's business and technology.

Acquisitions as a Route to New Products

To acquire a company for its new technology or products is a strategy many firms have followed in domestic markets. To make international acquisitions for the purpose of gaining a window on emerging technologies or products is developing into an acceptable strategy for many firms. Several European firms have acquired U.S.-

27. "Lucky-Gold Star: Using Joint Ventures to Sprint Ahead in the High-Tech Race," *Business Week,* July 9, 1984, p. 94.

28. *Wall Street Journal,* February 18, 1981; *New York Times,* February 18, 1981.

29. "GE Will Resume Some US Production of Color TVs Instead of Buying Abroad," *Wall Street Journal,* February 13, 1987, p. 6.

based electronics companies for that purpose. Siemens of West Germany bought into Advanced Micro Devices.[30] Robert Bosch, another German firm, acquired an interest in American Microsystems; and Philips of Holland purchased Signetics. In all these cases, the foreign firms had to pay substantial premiums over the market value of the stock as a price for access to new product development.

Japanese companies lend a good example of how the acquisition strategy can be used to get access to new products and technologies. Japanese firms are reported to have invested about $350 million in some sixty deals for a wide range of minority positions in U.S.-based high technology firms through either joint-ventures, licensing, or direct investments as minority shareholders. In 1989, Chugai Pharmaceutical acquired Gen-Probe of San Diego for $110 million to get access to the firm's products including test kits for the detection of cancer and viral infections. The same year, Fujisawa, another Japanese pharmaceutical company, acquired Lyphomed, an Illinois-based maker of generic drugs.[31]

At the same time, Apple was rumored to be negotiating with Sony of Japan to become its supplier for lap-top models. Japanese companies had begun to take the lead in the smallest computer models based on their skill of miniaturization and Apple's first line of lap-tops was both too heavy and too small. Sourcing from Sony would be cost efficient and would give Apple the needed "notebook" type computer model.[32]

The Joint Venture Route to New Product Development

Forming a joint venture with a technologically advanced foreign company can also lead to new product development, often at lower costs. In the 1960s and 1970s, it was largely Japanese companies that sought to attract foreign technology for the manufacture of advanced products in Japan. Many of these Japanese companies can be found in the front ranks of their industries today. Typically, these joint ventures were set up as separate entities, with their own manufacturing and marketing functions.

Other examples of this strategy can be found in France, where two French firms, Saint-Gobain-Pont-a-Mousson and Matra, entered into joint ventures with two American semiconductor manufacturers, National Semiconductor and Harris Corp., with the goal of manufacturing chips in France.[33] In a similar move, the French manufacturer of machine tools, Ernault-Somur, agreed to enter a joint venture with Toyoda Machine Works of Japan, a major machine tool supplier for Toyota.[34] The French company is a major supplier of machine tools to the French auto-

30. *Business Week,* October 17, 1977.
31. "A Shopping Spree in the U.S.," *Business Week,* June 15, 1990, p. 86.
32. "Sony, Apple Negotiating Laptop Deal," *New York Times,* October 1, 1990, p. D1.
33. "Europe's Wild Swing at the Silicon Giants," *Fortune,* July 28, 1980, p. 76.
34. *Japan Economic Journal,* September 2, 1980.

mobile industry and hopes to gain access to Toyoda's experience with industrial robots, an area where Japan has assumed the lead position.

United States car manufacturers have also acquired parts of Japanese and other Asian firms to participate in the development of new small cars. General Motors owns a significant investment in Isuzu Motors, Ford in Mazda, and Chrysler in Mitsubishi.[35]

General Motors also entered into joint ventures with Daewoo, a large Korean conglomerate, to build cars to GM's specifications. In the United States, GM jointly operated a plant with Toyota for the production of subcompact cars.[36]

More recently, joint ventures have taken the form of alliances in which entire companies pool their resources for competitive advantage. Although in the more traditional joint venture the cooperation restricted the legal entity of the venture, in an alliance the cooperation goes beyond a joint venture company. In some instances the agreement is made directly between two large firms without even forming a new legal entity. The strategic importance of alliances has already been discussed in Chapter 9. Our concern here is the ability to develop new products and how an alliance can help an international firm to accomplish this objective better, faster, and with less investment funds.

When Motorola of the United States and Toshiba of Japan decided to pool their resources by swapping technology and creating a joint venture in Japan, both firms had important strategic objectives in mind. Motorola was to get access to Toshiba's production technology for mass-produced memory chips with a chance to get back eventually into producing both one mega and four mega ram chips in large numbers—a production segment that Motorola had to abandon under intense price pressure from Japanese competitors. In return, Motorola was to give Toshiba access to its logic chips, particularly the large 32-bit microprocessors that are key components for the production of computers.[37]

Toshiba was no newcomer to such alliances. The Japanese company, which is a major force in electronics, concluded other deals with Olivetti of Italy (by buying into Olivetti's Japanese subsidiary), with AT&T of the United States, and with LSI Logic Corp. of the United States (to develop and sell specialized chips). Other development contracts were concluded with General Electric and Siemens of Germany. To strengthen its competitive position compared to other Japanese electronics firms, Toshiba needed access to the most advanced technology. By working with foreign partners the company expected to save both valuable time and development costs.[38]

Alliances can sometimes be formed by firms for some part of their business while they remain competitors in other segments. Olivetti of Italy and Canon of Japan decided to join forces for the development and marketing of office equipment

35. "Detroit's New Asian Strategy," *Fortune,* December 10, 1984, p. 172.

36. *Business Week,* July 16, 1984.

37. "Toshiba's Motorola Tie-Up Is Latest Bid to Bolster Its Semiconductors Business," *Wall Street Journal,* December 5, 1986, p. 35.

38. Ibid.

in Europe. The companies created a new joint company in Italy consisting of Olivetti production and research facilities for copiers and an infusion of capital and technology from Canon. With access to Canon's latest technology, particularly in the laser printing and electronic publishing area, Olivetti managers hoped that the new company would triple present volume—supplying both Olivetti and Canon distribution channels in Europe. Despite this cooperation, the two firms would remain competitors in the typewriter market.[39]

The Consortium Approach

To share the huge cost of developing new products, some companies have established or joined consortia to share in new product development. Under the consortium approach, member firms join in a working relationship without forming a new entity. On completion of the assigned task, member firms are free to seek other relationships with different firms. Consortia have been used for some time in marketing entire factories or plants, or in the banking industry, but they are a relatively new approach to new product research and development.

Since the development of new aircraft is a particularly cost-intensive business, the aircraft industry offers several examples of the consortium approach to product development. The high development costs require that large passenger aircraft must be built in series of 200 or 300 units just to break even. Under these circumstances, several companies form a consortium to share the risk. One of the first highly successful efforts was the European Airbus, developed and produced by French, British, and German manufacturers.

For its latest generation of long-range aircraft, the 777, Boeing was facing development and launch costs of some $4 billion. Such programs could not be justified unless several airlines, including foreign ones, could be involved from the outset with large commitments. To reduce the risk, Boeing asked three Japanese companies to take a 25 percent share in the project: Mitsubishi Heavy Industries, Fuji Heavy Industries, and Kawasaki Heavy Industries. These same Japanese companies had already been major suppliers of subassemblies for the 767 model range. It is believed that such Japanese participation was not only invited to share development costs but to help in the marketing of the planes. Japanese airlines are the largest buyers of long-range planes. The fact that All Nippon Airlines is the largest operator of Boeing 767 planes outside the United States was linked to the strong participation of Japanese firms in the production of the plane. Both Japan Airlines and All Nippon Airlines are among the key accounts sought for the launch of the Boeing 777 model range.[40] Japan Airlines is already the world's largest operator of Boeing 747s with a present fleet of sixty-seven airplanes and another sixty-four on order for the latest version,

39. "Olivetti and Canon Form Venture for Office Equipment Production," *Financial Times,* January 20, 1987, p. 1.

40. "How Boeing Does It," *Business Week,* July 9, 1990, p. 46.

thus underscoring the need to bring in Japanese partners in the early stages of any long-range passenger plane project.[41]

Responding to the same pressures as those faced by the airplane manufacturers, the major jet engine companies have also engaged in a number of consortiums. The U.S.-based General Electric has had a long-term agreement with Snecma of France. The French partner has taken a 20 percent interest in the new GE90 Model CF6 jet engine design which is projected to cost about $1.5 billion to develop.[42] Pratt & Whitney, the other leading U.S. firm, recently joined a partnership with MTU, a subsidiary of the German firm Daimler-Benz.[43] MTU had previously planned to become a partner with GE which prompted GE to look for Fiat as a new partner after the German firm decided to proceed with Pratt & Whitney.[44]

British Rolls Royce, the smallest of the major jet engine firms, made a series of collaborative ventures with different firms. Rolls Royce strategy has been to make project-specific ventures (see Figure 11.3). The most recent deal was made with BMW of Germany for the production of jet engines for the civil aviation market.[45]

The advantage of a consortium approach also lies in sales. The widespread participation of companies from the United States, Europe, and Japan gives partial reassurance for future sales, thus further reducing the risk to each participating company.

The consortium approach is becoming increasingly popular in several technology-intensive industries.[46] Companies in the automobile, computer, and biotechnology industries have formed cooperative agreements to share in the development and exploitation of technology. What is new to this trend is that sometime competitors will become partners, whereas previously no cooperation would have been possible.

The Internationalization of the Product Development Process

The previous sections dealt primarily with the sources of product development. To bring about a total integration of the product development process for a multinational enterprise often requires the adoption of new organizational forms and the restructuring of the development process as a whole. The challenge in multinational product development is finding a way to combine domestic and foreign expertise so that truly international or global products can result.

41. "JAL to Buy into Lockheed Jet Maintenance Offshoot," *Financial Times,* January 7, 1991, p. 12.

42. "Snecma to Take Share in New GE Engine," *Financial Times,* January 8, 1991, p. 18.

43. "Revving up for a Clash of Blades," *Financial Times,* September 6, 1990, p. 11.

44. "Fiat May Take 10% Stake in GE Jet Engine Development," *Financial Times,* July 4, 1990, p. 1.

45. "Modest Alliance Between Two Pioneers," *Financial Times,* May 4, 1990, p. 21.

46. Kenichi Ohmae, *Triad Power: The Coming Shape of Global Competition* (New York: The Free Press, 1985), pp. 125–148.

FIGURE 11.3 ● Rolls Royce's Main Relationships

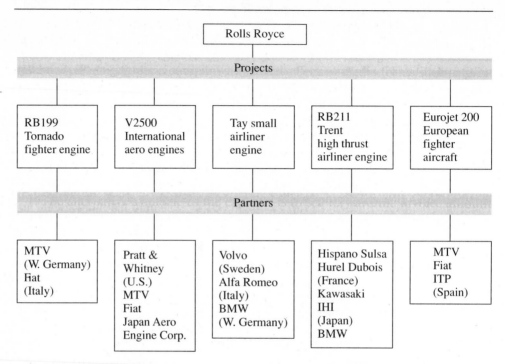

Source: Financial Times, May 4, 1990, p. 21. Reprinted by permission.

The international approach to new product development is best described by an executive of Fiat, the Italian car manufacturer. "Fifteen years ago we designed cars for the Italian market. Ten years ago we began designing 'European' cars. Now we develop them for the country with the biggest market—the United States—and scale them down for the others."[47] This shift from localized to worldwide development requires that the unique or special concerns for major markets be considered from the outset of the process, rather than attempting to make various adaptations on the initial model or prototype. This early introduction of global considerations not only ensures that the product will achieve wide acceptance, but also aims at maximizing the commonality of models to achieve economies in component manufacturing. A global product then is not identical in all countries. Instead, a world product is engineered from the outset with the goal of maximizing the percentage of identical components, design, or parts, to the point where local needs can be met with a minimum of additional costs in tooling, engineering, and development.

47. "To a Global Car," *Business Week,* November 20, 1978, p. 102.

To internationalize its own research, Japanese companies have begun to make heavy investments in U.S.-based research facilities. Hundreds of Japanese scientists already work side-by-side with Americans in research laboratories on exchange programs. This investment aims at getting access to U.S. scientific talent. One company, Kobe Steel, announced the opening of its research center near Stanford University and another, NEC, opened a laboratory for artificial intelligence in Princeton, NJ.[48]

To develop a global product also demands a different organizational setup. Changes instituted by General Motors are an indication of moves made by other international firms. With the advent of world cars, GM realized that the company needed closer coordination between its domestic units and its overseas subsidiaries. GM moved its overseas staff from New York to Detroit in 1978 in order to speed up communication between domestic and international staffs.[49] GM adopted the "project center" concept to manage its engineering effort. Each division or subsidiary involved in a new car design would lend engineers to a centrally organized project center, which would design, develop, and introduce the new model. Upon introduction of the model, the project center is disbanded. Of course, not every firm will find a project center approach feasible. Other alternatives include assigning primary responsibility to a subsiidiary with special capability in the new product field.

INTRODUCING NEW PRODUCTS TO THE MARKET

Once a product has been developed for commercial introduction, a number of complex decisions still need to be made. Aside from the question of whether to introduce the product abroad, the firm has to decide on a desirable test marketing procedure, select target countries for introduction, and decide on the timing or sequence of the introduction. With the large number of alternatives due to numerous possible markets, decisions surrounding new product introduction often attain strategic significance.

The determination of which product to introduce abroad of course depends on sales potential. Following a careful analysis, a list of target countries can be developed. A company then has to determine the next steps leading to actual introduction in the target countries.

Concept Tests

Once a prototype or sample product has been developed, a company may decide to subject its new creation to a series of tests to determine commercial feasibility. It is particularly important to subject a new product to actual use conditions. When the

48. "Japan: A Shopping Spree in the U.S.," *Business Week,* June 15, 1990, p. 87.
49. "GM Plans an Offensive for Growth Overseas," *Business Week,* March 27, 1978, p. 46.

development process takes place outside the country of actual use, a practical field test can be crucial. The test must include all necessary usage steps to provide complete information. When CPC International tested the U.S. market for dehydrated soups made by its newly acquired Knorr subsidiary, the company concentrated primarily on taste tests to assure that the final product suited U.S. consumers. Extensive testing led to soups different in formulation from those sold in Europe. CPC, however, had neglected to have consumers actually try out the product at home as part of their regular cooking activities. Such a test would have revealed consumers' discontent with the relatively long cooking time of up to 20 minutes, compared to 3 minutes for comparable canned soups. The company realized these difficulties only after a national introduction had been completed and sales results fell short of original expectations.

The concept testing stage would be incomplete if the products were only tested in the company's domestic market. A full test in several major markets is essential so that any shortcomings can be alleviated at an early stage before costly adaptations for individual countries are made. Such an approach is particularly important in cases where product development occurred on a multinational basis, with simultaneous inputs from several foreign subsidiaries. When Volkswagen tested its original Rabbit models, test vehicles were made available to all principal subsidiaries in order to ensure that each market's requirements were met by the otherwise standardized car.

There may be some differences between concept testing for consumer products and for industrial products. Industrial products tend to be used worldwide for the same purposes under very similar circumstances. Factories for textile machinery are relatively standardized across the world so that a test in one country may be quite adequate for most others. As a result, single country market testing may be more appropriate for industrial products.

Test Marketing

Just as there are good reasons to test market a product in a domestic market, an international test can give the firm valuable insights into potential future success. A key question is where should the test market be held? Companies in the United States have largely pioneered test marketing procedures because it has been possible to isolate a given market in terms of media and distribution. This may not always be possible in smaller countries, and even less so in countries where most of the media are national rather than local. If a test market were considered in a country with national TV only, and print media were substituted for TV for the purpose of the test, the test would not be a true replication of the actual full-scale introduction. As a result, the opportunities for small local test markets are substantially reduced outside the United States.

To overcome the shortage of test market possibilities, international firms often have substituted the experience in one country for a test market in another. Although test markets were typical for many U.S.-based firms before full-scale introduction in the U.S. market, subsidiaries tended to use these early U.S. results as a basis for analysis. Such a strategy requires that at least one subsidiary of an international firm have actual commercial experience with a product or any given aspect of the marketing strategy before introducing the product elsewhere.

Use of the U.S. market as a test market depends on the market situation and the degree to which results can be extrapolated to other countries. Since circumstances are rarely exactly the same, early U.S. results must be regarded with caution. Also, extrapolation may only be appropriate for other advanced countries in Europe and Asia. See also our explanation of the comparative-analytic approach in Chapter 7.

For firms with extensive foreign networks of subsidiaries, test markets can be used beyond the traditional mode. Another approach to test marketing is to use a foreign country as a first introduction and proving ground before other markets are entered. In Europe, smaller markets such as the Netherlands, Belgium, Austria, or Switzerland may be used to launch a new product. Because of their size, a test would include national introduction with results applicable in other countries. When Toyota started its European sales drive, Switzerland was used as a test, and the strategy developed by its independent Swiss distributor was later adopted elsewhere.

Special attention should be given to the lead market as a potential test market. Any new product that succeeds in its lead market can be judged to have good potential elsewhere as other markets mature. Philips, the Dutch electronics company, intends to use the United States market as its proving ground for consumer electronics products.[50] Though new products may be developed in the Netherlands, U.S. subsidiaries will market them first. Having to compete with major Japanese and U.S. manufacturers in the largest market for consumer electronics should provide input for European markets. European markets are believed to follow ultimately the consumption patterns set by U.S. consumers.

Timing of New Product Introductions

Very early in the introduction process a company will be faced with a decision to establish the timing and sequence of its introduction. Timing determines when a product should be introduced in a foreign market. Sequencing becomes an issue when a firm deals with several countries and must decide on a phased or simultaneous entry approach. Traditionally, firms have introduced new products first in their domestic markets to gain experience in production, marketing, and service. Foreign market introductions have been attempted only after a product has proven itself in the domestic market. Research has shown, however, that the time lag between domestic and initial foreign market introduction has substantially

---

50. "In Consumer Electronics The U.S. Is a Top Target," *Business Week,* March 30, 1981, pp. 97–100.

declined.[51] From 1945 to 1950, only 5.6 percent of investigated firms introduced new products abroad within one year. By 1975, the percentage had increased to 38.7 percent, and about two-thirds were introduced abroad within five years. This time lag reduction reflects the increased capability by U.S. firms to introduce products abroad rapidly. It also reflects the rapid economic development of many advanced countries, to the point where the United States no longer leads in a number of fields. It can be safely assumed that the average time lag will continue to decline.

Some companies are now in a position to introduce products simultaneously in several countries. When Apple revamped its product line in 1990, the launch of the Macintosh Classic line was communicated via television broadcasts to 121 countries and a total campaign costing $45 million worldwide. Previously, Apple introduced products in the United States first while announcing shipping dates weeks to several months later for its other markets. For its new line, most European countries were shipped localized versions of the original product the same week as the selling started in the United States. Japan and other Asian countries were expected to follow within just a few weeks with localized versions.[52] Simultaneous introduction depends on the company's foreign market development stage and the ability to satisfy demand. When the primary function of foreign subsidiaries is the sale of products shipped from one or a small number of central manufacturing centers, simultaneous introduction is possible, as long as marketing efforts can be coordinated. This structure is typical for electronics firms. Other companies produce in many markets; thus the manufacturing function would be strained if simultaneous introduction was attempted.

Increasingly, companies have to invest ever larger amounts for developing new technologies or products. As these investments rise, the time requirement to bring new generations of products on the market has increased, leaving less time for the commercialization of products until patent protections run out or until new competitors come out with similar products. As a result, companies have been forced to move into a rapid introduction of new products, so that we can now often talk of a global product roll-out. Global roll-out was practiced by Gillette with the introduction of its new Sensor razor with simultaneous introduction in both Europe and North America.

Country Selection

Although international firms have subsidiaries in numerous countries, initial product introductions have always been limited to the industrialized nations. William Davidson and Richard Harrigan documented that for the forty-four U.S.-based firms investigated, 83.5 percent of first introductions took place in developed countries for

51. William H. Davidson and Richard Harrigan, "Key Decisions in International Marketing: Introducing New Products Abroad," *Columbia Journal of World Business,* Winter 1977, p. 15.

52. "The Fruits of Flexibility," *Financial Times,* October 17, 1990, p. 17.

the 1945–1976 time period.[53] Leading target countries for the 1965–1975 period were the United Kingdom, Japan, Australia, France, and West Germany.[54]

Other research has shown that some companies use a two-step approach to new product introduction. At first, products are introduced in the most advanced markets, with developing countries following in a second stage.[55] Many U.S.-based international firms have used their European subsidiaries as stepping stones to Latin America or Eastern Europe. One electronics manufacturer transferred an innovation first to its Italian subsidiary; the Italian subsidiary then introduced it in Spain through another subsidiary there. The same company has also used its Dutch subsidiary to transfer innovations to Poland.

A firm's competitive situation abroad influences its country selection. Major subsidiaries tend to get new products first, and manufacturing subsidiaries are usually favored over sales subsidiaries. Also, each local market expects to face different competitors. This often means that the international firm first will choose a country where the firm is well entrenched over a market where competitive pressures make operating results less favorable.

CONCLUSIONS

When companies search for new markets for their products, they face the difficult choice of adapting their products to new environments. Such adaptations are frequently expensive when done after the fact. In the future, companies will increasingly consider international opportunities early in the development cycle of a new product. Incorporating international requirements early will allow new products to be immediately usable in many markets. Such a move toward internationalization of the product development cycle will result in the development of more world products. These products will be produced in modularized forms to include as many world components as possible, and they will incorporate a set of unique components to fit the product needs of individual markets. The challenge for international marketers is to find the best tradeoffs between the standardized world components of a product and the tailor-made components designed for specific markets.

Another major factor that is increasingly having an influence on new product development processes is speed. For competitive reasons, companies want to be among the first to enter with a new product or service because early entrants tend to obtain the biggest market share. To increase speed, companies work on collaborative

53. William H. Davidson and Richard Harrigan, "Key Decisions in International Marketing: Introducing New Products Abroad," *Columbia Journal of World Business,* Winter 1977, p. 15.

54. Ibid.

55. Jeannet, *Transfer of Technology Within Multinational Corporations* (New York: Arno Press, 1980).

development processes. Furthermore, they will shrink the time it will take from first, domestic introduction, until launched worldwide. In the end, many firms will launch multi-country launches or simultaneous global product roll-outs. The risk with such global launches will increase because less time is available to test the product, make sure it meets the market performance, and is sufficiently tailored to a given country.

Questions for Discussion

1. Analyze three different products (freezers, compact disks, and contact eye lenses) according to Table 11.1. What general marketing strategy recommendations do you arrive at?

2. What, in your opinion, is the future for global products?

3. How should international firms organize their new product development efforts today and in the future?

4. What is the impact of a loss of lead market position in several industries for U.S.-based corporations?

5. If you were to test market a new consumer product today for worldwide introduction, how would you select test countries for Europe, Asia, and Latin America?

For Further Reading

Afriyie, Koti. "International Technology Transfers." In *Cooperative Strategies in International Business,* ed. Farok Contractor and Peter Lorange. Lexington, Mass.: D.C. Heath 1987.

Behrman, J. N., and W. A. Fischer. "Transnational Corporation: Market Orientations and R&D Abroad." *Columbia Journal of World Business* (Fall 1980), pp. 55–60.

Crawford, Merle C. *New Products Management.* Homewood, Ill.: Irwin 1983.

Gerstenfeld, Arthur, and Lawrence H. Wortzel. "Strategies for Innovation in Developing Countries." *Sloan Management Review* (Fall 1977), pp. 57–68.

Hill, John S., and Richard R. Still. "Cultural Effects of Technology Transfer by Multinational Corporations in Lesser Developed Countries." *Columbia Journal of World Business* (Summer 1980), pp. 40–50.

Kaikati, Jack G. "Domestically Banned Products: For Export Only." *Journal of Public Policy and Marketing* 3 (1984), pp. 125–133.

Leroy, Georges. *Multinational Product Strategy.* New York: Praeger, 1976.

Ronstadt, Robert. "The Establishment and Evolution of R&D Abroad." *Journal of International Business Studies* (Spring-Summer 1978), pp. 7–24.

Terpstra, Vern. "International Product Policy: The Role of Foreign R&D." *Columbia Journal of World Business* (Winter 1977), pp. 24–32.

Wind, Yoram. "The Myth of Globalization." *The Journal of Marketing* (Spring 1986), pp. 23–26.

12

Managing International Channels

● **INTERNATIONAL MARKETING DISTRIBUTION** *decisions are similar to those in a domestic setting. What differs, of course, are the environmental influences that, in the end, may lead to substantially different policies and channel options. The international marketer needs to understand how environmental influences may affect these distribution policies and options. Using this knowledge, the international company must structure an efficient channel for products on a country by country basis.*

This chapter discusses the structure of international distribution systems; developing a distribution strategy; and selecting, locating, and managing channel members (see Figure 12.1). We also explain the issues of international logistics, gaining access to channels, and global trends in international distribution.

THE STRUCTURE OF INTERNATIONAL DISTRIBUTION SYSTEMS

The structure of the distribution systems available in a country is affected by the economic development of the country, the personal disposable income of consumers, and the quality of the infrastructure, as well as environmental factors such as the culture, the physical environment, and the legal/political system. Marketers who develop a distribution strategy must decide how to transport the goods from the manufacturing locations to the consumer. Although the distribution of goods can be

FIGURE 12.1 ● International Distribution

Players	Process
Home Market Channel Members	Developing an International Distribution Strategy
Export Management Company	Factors Affecting Selection of Channel Members
Export Agent	Locating and Selecting Channel Members
Direct Exporting	Managing the Distribution Channels
Foreign Market Channel Members	Gaining Access to the Distribution Channels
Import Middlemen	
Local Wholesalers	International Logistics
Retailers	Trends in Global Distribution

handled completely by the manufacturer, often the goods are moved through middlemen, such as agents, wholesalers, distributors, and retailers. An understanding of the structure of the available distribution systems is extremely important in the development of a strategy. The various channels available to a manufacturer are shown in Figure 12.2.

There are two major categories of channel members: (1) home country middlemen and (2) foreign middlemen. In the home country, a manufacturer can utilize the services of an export management company or an export agent, or it can export the products using company personnel. In Chapter 9, we discussed whether or not any of these channel members should be used. In this chapter, our focus is on how to locate, select, use, and manage channel members.

Home Market Channel Members

Within your home market there are a number of different types of channel members who can help with the export process. The most common types of export-related channel members in a home market are export management companies and export

FIGURE 12.2 ● International Marketing Channel Alternatives

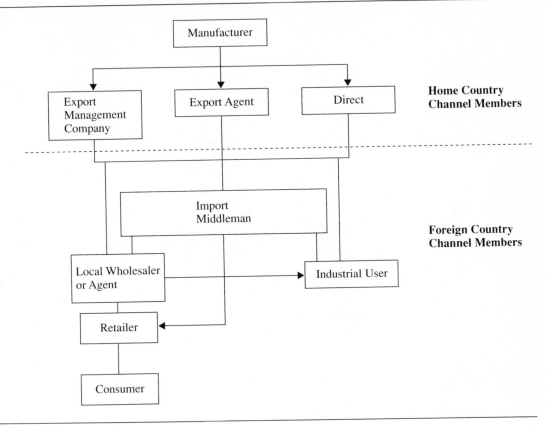

agents. Also, a firm can bypass the help of these specialists and use internal expertise to export.

Export Management Company   The Export Management Company (EMC) is a firm that handles all aspects of export operations under a contractual agreement.[1] The EMC will normally take responsibility for the promotion of goods, marketing research, credit, physical handling of the product, patents, and licensing. The population of EMCs is estimated to be 1,200 firms, representing some 10,000 manufacturers and accounting for 10 percent of U.S.-manufactured exports.[2] The arrange-

1. Bruce Seifert and John Ford, "Export Distribution Channels," *Columbia Journal of World Business,* Summer 1989, p. 22.
2. Franklin R. Root, *Entry Strategies for International Markets* (Lexington, Mass.: D.C. Heath, 1987), p. 78.

ment between an EMC and a manufacturer will vary, depending on the services offered and the volume expected. The advantages of an EMC are that (1) little or no investment is required to enter the international marketplace; (2) no company personnel are required; and (3) the EMC will have an established network of sales offices and international marketing and distribution knowledge. One disadvantage is that the manufacturer gives up direct control of the international sales and marketing effort. Also, if the product has a long purchase cycle and requires a large amount of market development and education, then the EMC may not devote the necessary effort to penetrate a new market.

Export Agents   Export agents are individuals or firms that assist manufacturers in exporting goods. Export agents are similar to EMCs, except that they tend to provide limited services and focus on one country or one part of the world. Export agents understand all the requirements for moving goods through the customs process. Export agents do not provide the marketing skills that an EMC provides; these agents focus more on the sale and handling of goods. The advantage of using an export agent is that the firm does not need to have an export manager to handle all the documentation and shipping tasks. One disadvantage is the export agent's limited market coverage, which requires the use of numerous export agents to cover different parts of the world.

Direct Exporting   Instead of using an EMC or export agent, a firm can export its goods directly, through in-house company personnel. Due to the complexity of trade regulations, customs documentation, insurance requirements, and worldwide transportation alternatives, people with special training and experience are necessary to handle these tasks. Also, the current or expected volume must be sufficient to support the in-house staff. As a company expands its international operations and sets up local production, the need for exporting will decrease.

Foreign Market Channel Members

As shown in Figure 12.2, once the goods have left the home market, there's a variety of channel alternatives in the international marketplace. These are import middlemen, local wholesalers or agents, and retailers.

Import Middlemen   Import middlemen identify needs in their local market and find products from the world market to satisfy these needs. The import middlemen will normally purchase goods in their own name and act independently of the manufacturers. As independent middlemen, these channel members will use their own marketing strategies and will keep in close contact with the markets they serve. A manufacturer desiring distribution in an independent middleman's market area should investigate this channel partner as one of the ways to get its product to wholesalers and retailers in that area.

TABLE 12.1 ● Wholesale Patterns in Selected Countries

	Number of wholesalers	*Retailers per wholesaler*
Belgium	60,589	2.2
Brazil	46,000	19.3
Chile	561	2.0
Domican Republic	589	19.0
El Salvador	396	3.6
Hungary	220	259.3
Kenya	2,277	1.8
Kuwait	2,819	4.9
Portugal	4,522	1.1
U.K.	108,392	2.1
U.S.	337,900	4.7
Singapore	20,103	.8
Yugoslavia	1,413	58.4

Source: Statistical Yearbook 1985/86, Table 138, pp. 656–679. Copyright, United Nations 1988. Reproduced by permission. Retailers per wholesaler was calculated by the author by dividing the number of retailers by the number of wholesalers for the same year by the author. The data is for the latest available year.

Local Wholesalers or Agents   In each country, there will be a series of possible channel members who move manufacturers' products to retailers, industrial firms, or in some cases other wholesalers. Local wholesalers will take title to the products, while local agents will not take title. Local wholesalers are also called distributors or dealers. In many cases the local wholesaler has exclusive distribution rights for a specific geographic area or country.

The structure of the wholesale distribution varies greatly from country to country, as shown in Table 12.1. The number of wholesalers and the number of retailers per wholesaler vary according to the distribution structure and wholesale pattern of the country. For example, although Kenya and Kuwait have approximately the same number of wholesalers, the Kenya wholesaler will indirectly serve 1.8 retailers whereas in Kuwait a wholesaler will serve 4.9 retailers. In state-controlled economies, the wholesalers serve a larger number of retailers, as shown by Hungary wholesalers who served 259 retailers.

The functions of wholesalers can vary by country. In some countries, wholesalers provide a warehouse function, taking orders from retailers and shipping them appropriate quantities. Wholesalers in Japan provide the basic wholesale functions

TABLE 12.2 ● Retail Patterns in Selected Countries

Country	Number of retailers	Population per retailer
Argentina	787,000	40
Ecuador	1,800	294
France	518,700	102
Hungary	63,700	157
Egypt	2,100	20,000
Iran	214,000	175
Indonesia	121,000	1210
Italy	849,600	64
Japan	1,628,600	68
Nigeria	22,200	4045
South Korea	673,600	63
Malaysia	96,000	142
Philippines	280,000	173
United Kingdom	345,500	162
United States	1,441,200	228
West Germany	382,300	160

Sources: Euromonitor International Marketing Data and Statistics,15th edition, 1991; European Marketing Data and Statistics, 26th edition, 1991. Reprinted by permission of Euromonitor Publications.

but also share risk with retailers by providing financing, product development, and even occasional managerial and marketing skills.[3]

Retailers   Retailers are the last members of the consumer distribution channel. Retailers purchase products for resale to consumers. The size and accessibility of retail channels varies greatly by country, as shown in Table 12.2. The population per retailer varies from a low of only 40 people per retailer in Argentina to 68 people in Japan, to 228 people in the United States, and to 20,000 people in Egypt. Although this data gives a general picture of the number of retailers and the population served per retailer, the data also varies by type of retailer. For example, a country may have an extremely large number of electronics retailers, but few bookstore retailers. Table 12.2 shows that there is a great diversity in retailer distribution systems from country

3. "Why Japanese Shoppers Are Lost in a Maze," *The Economist*, January 31, 1987, p. 62.

to country. Until recently, all retailing in China was through state-owned stores.[4] The number of retail outlets in China has grown from 1.4 million in 1980 to 8.8 million in 1987. The ratio of state owned to private or collective/owned stores has gone from 92/8 percent to 40/60 percent.[5] The international marketer must evaluate the available retailers in a country and develop a strategy around that structure.

DEVELOPING AN INTERNATIONAL DISTRIBUTION STRATEGY

The environmental variables of culture, physical environment, and the legal/political system combined with the unique structure of wholesale and retail distribution systems complicate the development of an international distribution strategy. A distribution strategy is one part of the marketing mix, and it needs to be consistent with other aspects of the marketing strategy. The distribution strategy must be consistent with product policies, pricing strategy, and communications strategy (see Figure 12.3).

Within the structure of the marketing mix, the international marketer makes the following distribution decisions:

1. *Distribution Density.* Density refers to the amount of exposure or coverage desired for a product, particularly the number of sales outlets required to provide for adequate coverage of the entire market.

2. *Channel Length.* The concept of channel length involves the number of intermediaries involved in bringing a given product to the market.

3. *Channel Alignment and Leadership.* The area of alignment deals with the structure of the chosen channel members to achieve a unified strategy.

4. *Distribution Logistics.* Logistics involves the physical flow of products as they move through the channel.

These four major decision areas cannot be approached independently. The decisions are interrelated, and they need to be consistent with other aspects of the marketing strategy. While it is important to evaluate the distribution strategy logically, often marketing managers are left with an international distribution structure from previous managers. While the present system may limit the flexibility of a company to change, there are often numerous opportunities around the current arrangement. For example, Nordica of Italy had been selling in Japan since 1960. In 1985, the company decided it needed to change its distribution system from its exclusive dis-

4. Heidi Vernon-Wortzel and Lawrence H. Wortzel, "The Emergence of Free Market Retailing in China," *California Management Review,* Spring 1987, pp. 59–76.
5. Guo Qiang and Phil Harris, "Retailing Reforms and Trends in China," *International Journal of Retail and Distribution Management,* vol. 18, no. 5, 1990, pp. 31–39.

FIGURE 12.3 ● Distribution Policies

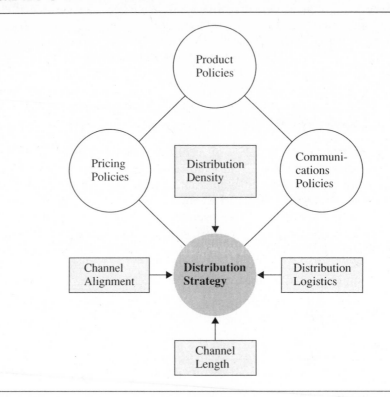

tributor Daiwa Sports. Nordica reached a financial agreement with Daiwa sports and hired the 85 employees who had been handling their line. These employees made up most of Nordica Japan, the company-owned sales organization in Japan which has been very successful.[6] The following sections deal primarily with a company's distribution policies, their dependency on distribution-specific variables, and their relationship to the other elements of the marketing strategy.

Distribution Density

The number of sales outlets or distribution points required for the efficient marketing of a firm's products is referred to as the density of distribution. The density is dependent on the shopping or buying habits of the average customer. An optimum distri-

6. Ian Rodger, "Nordica and Salomon Put The Boot In," *Financial Times,* August 30, 1990, p. 12.

bution network requires the marketer to examine how customers select dealers and retail outlets by segment.[7] For consumer goods, an extensive or wide distribution is required if the consumer is not likely to exert much shopping effort. Such products, also called convenience goods, are bought frequently in nearby outlets. Other products, such as appliances or clothing, are shopped for by visiting two or more stores; and these require a more limited or selective distribution, with fewer outlets per market area. For products that inspire consumer loyalty to specific brands, called specialty goods, a very limited or *exclusive* distribution is required. It is assumed that the customer will search for the product desired and is willing to stop at several places until the item is located.

The key to distribution density then is the consumer's shopping behavior, the expended effort to locate a desired item. This behavior, however, may vary substantially from country to country. In the United States, for example, where per capita income is high, consumers shop for many regular-use items in supermarkets and other widely accessible outlets, such as drugstores. In other countries, particularly for some with a much lower per capita income, the purchase of such items may be a less routine affair, causing consumers to exert more effort to locate such items. This would lead to a less extensive distribution of products. It is therefore necessary for the international marketer to assess the shopping behavior of various countries' consumers. Where consumers will buy certain goods vary a great deal from country to country. In Germany, contact lens solution is only found in stores that sell eye glasses, but in France it is also found in most drug stores. While magazines are sold in many grocery stores in the United States, in the United Kingdom they are sold almost exclusively through news agents. It is important to check where consumers buy certain types of products early in your distribution analysis.

In the industrial sector, differences in buyer behavior or the use of a particular product may require changes in distribution density. Since industrial products applications are more uniform around the world due to the similarity in application and use conditions, what constitutes capital equipment in one country typically is also classified as capital equipment in another nation. Differences may exist, however, among the decision makers. In the United States, for instance, radiology supply products are sold directly to hospitals and radiology departments though hospital supply distributors. However in France, patients must pick up radiology supplies by prescription from a pharmacy before visiting the radiology department at the hospital. In this latter case, radiology supplies have to be presold to physicians and stocked with pharmacies to be successful. This is the same strategy pursued by pharmaceutical firms. Of course, when selling to both physicians and pharmacies, the necessary distribution in France is much more extensive than it is in the United States where only hospitals need to be contacted.[8]

7. Allan J. Magrath and Kenneth G. Hardy, "How Much Distribution Coverage Is Enough?", *Business Horizons,* June 1989, p. 20.

8. Warren J. Keegan, *Multinational Marketing Management* (Englewood Cliffs, N.J.: Prentice-Hall, 1974), p. 175.

Channel Length

The number of intermediaries directly involved in the physical or ownership path of a product from the manufacturer to the customer is indicative of the channel length. Long channels have several intermediaries, whereas short or direct channels have few or no intermediaries. Channel length is usually influenced by three factors: (1) a product's distribution density, (2) the average order quantities, and (3) the availability of channel members. Products with extensive distribution, or large numbers of final sales points, tend to have longer channels of distribution. Similarly, as the average order quantity decreases, products move through longer channels to add to the distribution efficiency.

Since distribution density does affect channel length, it is clear that the same factors that influence distribution density influence channel length; namely, the shopping behaviors of customers. The average order quantity often depends on the purchasing power or income level of a given customer group. In countries with lower income levels, people often buy food on a daily basis at nearby small stores. This contrasts substantially with more affluent consumers who can afford to buy food or staples for one week, or even a month, and who don't mind traveling some distance to do this more infrequent type of shopping. In the first case, a longer channel is required, whereas a shorter channel is adequate in the latter case. The type of distributors available in a country affect the channel length. Also, the culture may demand a specific type of channel member.

Channel length does have important cost considerations. Salomon of France originally entered the Japanese ski equipment market with the giant Mitsui trading company. Mitsui insisted on taking delivery of goods through its Paris subsidiary, then transferring them to wholesalers, and then to retailers. This long channel resulted in Salomon bindings being very expensive in Japan. By the time all the intermediaries took their cut there was not much left for the manufacturer. As the company entered the ski boot business in 1980 they set up their own sales company which sold directly to a new breed of sport shops. In 1982, Mitsui did not renew the distribution contract on Salomon bindings.[9]

Channel Alignment

One of the most difficult tasks of marketing is to get various channel members to coordinate their actions so that a unified approach can be achieved. The longer the channel, the more difficult it becomes to maintain a coordinated and integrated approach. On an international level, the coordinating task is made all the more difficult since the company organizing the channel may be removed by large distances from the distribution system, with little influence over the local scene. In each country, the strongest channel member will be able to dictate policies to the other channel

9. Ian Rodger, "Nordica and Salomon Put The Boot In," *Financial Times,* August 30, 1990, p. 12.

members, though situations will vary by country. The international company will find it much easier to control the distribution channel if a local subsidiary with a strong sales force exists. In countries where the company has no local presence and depends on independent distributors, control is likely to slip to the independent distributor. This loss of control may be further aggravated if the international company's sales volume represents only a small fraction of the local distributor's business. Of course, the opposite will be true when a high percentage of the volume consists of the international corporation's products.

To achieve maximum efficiency in a channel of distribution, one participant emerges as the channel captain, or dominating member. Differences exist among countries as to who typically emerges as the dominating member. In the United States, for example, the originally strong wholesalers have become less influential, with manufacturers playing the dominant role in many channels. In Japan, on the other hand, wholesalers continue to dominate the channel structure. In many developing countries, independent distributors are very strong because they are the only authorized importers.

Different countries may require different channel strategies. Linear, a U.K. manufacturer of weather stripping for aluminum windows uses six different distribution methods to sell into 13 European countries. The size of the market, the distribution customers, and the way manufacturers buy dictated that different systems be used in different markets.[10] The international marketer will analyze each country with respect to the best operating mode, recognizing that it may be impossible to pursue the same strategy in all countries.

The international company used to its usual distribution arrangements in the domestic market often faces the problem of how to adapt the channel to foreign market situations. One U.S. company that abandoned its customary arrangement when entering Japan was the cosmetic firm Max Factor. Franchised corners were opened in large department stores or specialty shops with generous advertising and sales help from the company. The use of a multistage Japanese wholesale channel supported this strategy, which was patterned after the leading Japanese competitors Shiseido and Kanebo.[11] This strategy allowed Max Factor to far outdistance any foreign competitors in Japan.

A different approach was chosen by Caterpillar, the large U.S. manufacturer of earth-moving equipment, for its entry into Japan. At first, the company's joint venture partner, Mitsubishi, suggested marketing equipment through existing channels. (In Japan, the manufacturers sell through large trading houses who resell and provide financing to dealers. The dealers are relatively small and leave parts inventory and service to independent repair shops.) Caterpillar preferred to market its equipment through large independent dealers who not only sell but also service the equipment

10. Christopher Lorenz, "Where Variety is the Stuff of Success," *Financial Times,* October 26, 1988, p. 31.

11. "Shiseido Will Set Up French Cosmetics Venture," *Japan Economic Journal,* October 23, 1979, p. 12.

and maintain a sufficient parts inventory. Caterpillar recognized its distribution strategy is a critical global strength, which is difficult for competitors to match, so it has invested heavily in building and training its dealers.[12] Thus Caterpillar implemented its traditional strategy in Japan. It was successful and Caterpillar emerged as one of the leading earth-moving equipment manufacturers in Japan.

Distribution Logistics

Distribution logistics focuses on the physical movement of goods through the channels. An extremely important part of the distribution system, logistics will be discussed in detail later in the chapter.

FACTORS INFLUENCING THE SELECTION OF CHANNEL MEMBERS

After developing a distribution strategy, a marketer then needs to identify and select appropriate distribution partners who support the overall distribution strategy. This selection of distribution partners is an extremely important decision because often the partner will assume a portion or the entire marketing responsibility for a set of markets. The distribution decision is one of the most important elements of the entry strategy. A poor decision will often lead to lackluster performance. It is often expensive or sometimes impossible to change your distribution partner due to local laws. PepsiCo recently completed a year-long court battle to terminate their twenty-two year contract with Perrier to bottle and distribute Pepsi in France. PepsiCo contends that Perrier underperformed and let Pepsi-Cola's share decline.[13] Also, the distribution partner usually is involved in the physical movement (logistics) of products to the customers. Therefore, the success of a firm's international efforts depends on the partners it selects. A number of factors influence the selection of distribution partners. The factors that significantly affect selection are the following:

1. Cost
2. Capital requirement
3. Product and product line
4. Control
5. Coverage
6. Synergy

12. S. Tamer Cavusgil, "The Importance of Distributor Training at Caterpillar," *Industrial Marketing Management,* vol. 19, 1990, pp. 1–9.
13. William Dawkins, "PepsiCo Gets Go-Ahead to End Perrier Contract," *Financial Times,* November 28, 1990, p. 32.

Cost

Channel costs fall into three categories: initial costs, maintenance costs, and logistics costs. The initial costs include all the costs of locating and setting up the channel, such as executive time and travel to locate and select channel members, cost of negotiating an agreement with channel members, and the capital cost of setting up the channel. The capital cost is discussed separately in the next segment of this chapter. The maintenance cost of the channel includes the cost of the company's salespeople, sales managers, travel expenses, and the cost of auditing and controlling channel operations, local advertising expenses, and the profit margin of the middlemen. The logistical costs include the transportation cost, storage costs, the cost of breaking bulk shipments into smaller lot sizes, and the cost for customs paper work.

Although it is often difficult to predict all of these various costs when selecting different channel members, it is necessary to estimate the cost of various alternatives. High distribution costs usually result in higher prices at the consumer level, which may hamper entry into a new market. Companies often will establish direct channels, hoping to reduce distribution cost. Unfortunately, most of the functions of the channel cannot be eliminated, so these costs show up later. A study of five different international channels of distribution found that the least profitable is exporting directly to the retailers in the host country. The most profitable channel is selling to a distributor in a country that has its own marketing channels.[14]

Capital Requirement

The capital cost of different channel alternatives can be very high. The capital cost includes the cost for inventories, the cost of goods in transit, accounts receivable, and inventories on consignment. The capital cost is offset by the cash flow patterns from a channel alternative. For example, an import distributor will often pay for the goods when received, before they are sold to the retailer or industrial firm. On the other hand, an agent may not receive payment until the goods reach the industrial customer or retailer. This is also true of direct sales efforts. The establishment of a direct sales channel often requires the maximum investment, whereas use of distributors often reduces the investment required. The capital cost of various distribution channels affects the company's return on investment. In the early stages of the life cycle of organizations (see Chapter 16), companies often export through a distributor or agent, because they cannot afford the capital cost of setting up a direct sales effort.

Product and Product Line

The nature of a product can affect channel selection. If the product is perishable or has a short shelf life, then the manufacturer is forced to use shorter channels to get

---

14. Warren J. Bilkey, "Variables Associated with Export Profitability," presented at the 1980 Academy of International Business Conference, New Orleans, October 23, 1980.

the product to the consumer faster. A technical product often requires direct sales or highly technical channel partners. For example, Index Technology of Cambridge, Massachusetts sells a sophisticated software product to automate the development of software systems called computer aided systems engineering. The company entered the United Kingdom and Australia with a direct sales effort, but to avoid start-up costs it used distributors in France, Germany, Scandinavia. Insufficient revenues from distributors led the company to set up its own sales efforts in France and Germany, and purchase the distributor in Scandinavia. The highly sophisticated nature of the product required a direct sales effort. Nonperishable or generic, unsophisticated products that are available in many types of retail stores, such as batteries, may be distributed through a long channel that reaches many different types of retailers.

The size of the product line also affects selection of channel members. A broader product line is more desirable for channel members. A distributor or dealer is more likely to stock a broad product line than a single item. Limited product lines often must be sold through agents. If a manufacturer has a very broad, complete line, it is easier to justify the cost of a more direct channel. With more products to sell, it is easier to generate a high average order on each sales call. With a limited product line, an agent or distributor will group your product together with products from other companies to increase the average order size.

Control

Each type of channel arrangement offers a different level of control by the manufacturer. With a direct sales force a manufacturer can control price, promotion, the amount of effort, and the type of retail outlet used. If these are important, the increased level of control may offset the increased cost of a direct sales force. Longer channels, particularly with distributors who take title to goods, often result in little or no control. In many cases, a company may not know who is ultimately buying the product.

Limited control is not necessarily bad, however. If the volume of sales is adequate, the manufacturer may not necessarily care where the product is being used. Also, a manufacturer can increase its level of market knowledge, its influence on channel members, and its channel control by increasing its presence in the market. For example, the manager of international sales and marketing may be located in Europe and spend all of his or her time traveling with distributor salespeople.

Coverage

Coverage refers to the geographic coverage that a manufacturer desires. Though it is usually easy to get coverage in major metropolitan areas, it can be difficult to gain adequate coverage of smaller cities or sparsely populated areas. Selection of one channel member over another may be influenced by the respective market coverage. To determine an agent, broker, or distributor's coverage the following must be deter-

TABLE 12.3 ● Process of Establishing an International Distribution System

1. Develop distribution strategy.
2. Establish criteria for selecting distribution partners.
3. Locate potential distribution partners.
4. Solicit the interest of distributors.
5. Screen and select distribution partners.
6. Negotiate agreements.

mined: (1) location of sales offices, (2) salespersons' home base, and (3) last year's sales by geographic location. The location of sales offices indicates where efforts are focused. Salespeople generally have the best penetration near their homes. Past sales clearly indicate the channel member's success in each geographic area.

Synergy

The choice of channel members or partners can sometimes be influenced by complementary skills that can increase the total output of the distribution system. This normally occurs where the potential distributor partner has some skill or expertise that will allow quicker access to the market. For example, when Compaq entered the international personal computer market, it decided to sell only through a network of strong authorized dealers. While Compaq focused on developing market applications like sales force automation, computer aided design, and office productivity, it used the dealers to penetrate the market place. Compaq's international sales have grown from $20 million in 1984 to $1.33 billion in 1989 through the combination of marketing and technical expertise from Compaq and sales and implementation expertise from the authorized dealers.[15]

LOCATING AND SELECTING CHANNEL PARTNERS

The process of building an international distribution system normally takes one to three years. The process involves a series of steps which are shown in Table 12.3. The critical aspect of developing a successful system is locating and selecting channel partners.

The development of an international distribution strategy in terms of distribution density, channel length, channel alignment, and distribution logistics will establish a framework for the "ideal" distribution partners. The company's preference regarding key factors that influence selection of channel partners (cost, capital

15. Compaq—in the Spirit of Europe 1992," *The Economist,* May 5, 1990, pp. 32–33.

requirements, product, control, and coverage) will be used with the distribution strategy to establish criteria for the selection of partners. The strategy normally focuses the selection on one or two types of channel partners, for example, export manager's company and import distributors.

Selection criteria include geographic coverage, managerial ability, financial stability, annual volume, reputation, and so on. The following sources can be used to locate possible distribution partners:

1. *U.S. Department of Commerce.* The Agent Distributor service is a customized service of the Department of Commerce that locates distributors and agents interested in a certain product line. Also, the Department's Export Marketing Service can be used to locate distribution partners.

2. *Banks.* If the firm's bank has foreign branches, they may be happy to help locate distributors.

3. *Directories.* Country directories of distributors or specialized directories, such as those listing computer distributors, can be helpful.

4. *Trade Shows.* Exhibiting at an international trade show or just attending will expose managers to a large number of distributors and their salespeople.

5. *Competitor's Distribution Partners.* Sometimes a competitor's distributor may be interested in switching product lines.

6. *Consultants.* Some international marketing consultants specialize in locating distributors.

7. *Associations.* There are associations of international middlemen or country associations of middlemen. For example, Japan has numerous industry associations.

8. *Foreign Consulates.* Most countries have a commercial attaché at their embassies or a separate consulate, both of which are helpful in locating agents/distributors in their country.

After compiling a list of possible distribution partners, a letter may be sent to each with product literature and distribution requirements. The prospective distributors can be asked to respond if they have an interest in the firm's product line, with relevant information such as lines currently carried, annual volume, number of salespeople, geographic territory covered, credit and bank references, physical facilities, relationship with local government, and knowledge of English or other relevant languages. The firms that respond should be checked against the selection criteria. Before making a final decision, a manufacturer's representative should go to the country and talk to the industrial end-users or retailers to determine the best two or three distributors.[16] Also, while in the country, the manufacturer's representative should meet and evaluate the possible distribution partners before making a final decision.

16. G. Beeth, "Distributors—Finding and Keeping Good Ones," in *International Marketing Strategy,* ed. Hans Thorelli and Helmut Becker (New York: Pergamon Press, 1980), p. 261.

MANAGING THE DISTRIBUTION SYSTEM

Selecting the most suitable channel participants and gaining access to the market are extremely important steps in achieving an integrated and responsive distribution channel. However, without proper motivation and control over that channel, sales may remain unsatisfactory to the foreign marketer. The following sections discuss the steps that must be taken to ensure the flow of the firm's products through the channel by gaining the full cooperation of all channel members.

Motivating Channel Participants

Keeping channel participants motivated is an important aspect of international distribution policies. Financial incentives in the form of higher than average gross margins can be a very powerful inducement, particularly for the management of independent distributors, wholesalers, or retailers. The expected gross margins are influenced by the cultural history of that channel. For example, if a certain type of retailer usually gets a 50 percent margin and the firm offers 40 percent, the effort may be less than expected. Inviting channel members to annual conferences and introductions of new products is also effective. By extending help to the management of distributorships in areas such as inventory control, collections, advertising, and so on, goodwill can be gained that later will be of advantage to the international firm. Special programs may also be instituted to train or motivate the channel members' sales forces.

Programs to motivate foreign independent middlemen are likely to succeed if monetary incentives are considered along with efforts that help make the channel members more efficient and competitive. To have prosperous middlemen is, of course, in the interest of the international firm as well. These programs or policies are particularly important in the case of independent middlemen who distribute products on a nonexclusive basis. Often these middlemen are beleaguered by the principals of other products they carry; everyone is attempting to get the greatest possible attention from the distributor for their own purposes. Therefore the international firm must have policies that make sure the channel members devote sufficient effort to its products.

The motivation of channel partners and the amount of effort devoted to the firm's product line is enhanced by a continuous flow of two-way information between the manufacturer and distributor. The amount of effort an international firm needs to expend depends on the marketing strategy for that market. For example, if the firm is using extensive advertising to pull products through a channel, the middleman may be expected only to take orders and deliver the product with no real sales effort. If the marketing strategy is dependent on the channel member developing the market or pushing the product through the channel, then a significant sales effort will be required. As much as possible, the manufacturer should send letters, public relations releases, product news, and so on to encourage attention to its product line and reduce conflict. A study of manufacturer-distributor relationships found that more intense contact between the export manufacturer and the distributor resulted in better performance by the distributor.[17]

In addition to telephone and mail communication, periodic visits to distribution partners can have a positive effect on their motivation and control. Visits can provide other benefits as well. By visiting the distribution partner, any difficulties can be resolved. Also, sales volumes can be reviewed and emphasis placed on the most important products or types of customers. Often it is helpful to travel with a channel member salesperson to gain knowledge of the marketplace and to evaluate the skills of the salesperson. The most important benefit of a visit to the channel member is that it gives a clear message that the member's performance is important to the firm. Visits strengthen the personal relationship between the manufacturer and the channel member.

During these personal visits, the manufacturer can identify other ways to help and support the channel member. Strong advertising support either through national advertising or cooperative advertising can help strengthen the manufacturer's consumer franchise. Effective advertising makes it easier for the channel member to sell the manufacturer's products, which leads to increased sales and often more attention devoted to the product line.

Beware of strategies that cause conflict between manufacturers and channel members. The most common causes of channel conflict are (1) bypassing channels to sell directly to large customers, (2) oversaturating a market with too many dealers/distributors, (3) establishing too many levels in the distribution system; that is, requiring smaller distributors to buy from large ones, and (4) opening new discount channels that offer the same goods at lower prices.[18]

Recent research has shown that efforts by manufacturers to train and educate dealers in developing countries lead to increased revenue.[19] Caterpillar has faced the strong Japanese competitor, Komatsu, in the world earth-moving equipment market. Caterpillar found that dealer training could develop a strong competitive advantage difficult for Komatsu to copy. In fact, during the pilot of the dealer sales training program, participating dealers increased revenue by 102 percent.[20]

Controlling Channel Participants

Although motivated middlemen will expend the necessary effort on an international company's products, there is generally no assurance that these efforts will be chan-

17. Philip J. Rosson and I. David Ford, "Manufacturer-Overseas Distributor Relations and Export Performance," presented at the 1980 Academy of International Business Conference, New Orleans, October 1980, p. 10.

18. Allan J. Magrath and Kenneth G. Hardy, "Avoiding the Pitfalls in Managing Distribution Channels," *Business Horizons,* September-October 1987, p. 31.

19. Gary L. Frazier, James D. Gill and Sudhir H. Kale, "Dealer Dependence Levels and Reciprocal Actions in a Channel of Distribution in a Developing Country," *Journal of Marketing,* January 1989, pp. 50–69.

20. S. Tamer Cavusgil, "The Importance of Distributor Training at Caterpillar," *Industrial Marketing Management,* vol. 19, 1990, p. 5.

neled in the right direction. Therefore the company will want to exert enough control over its channel members to help guarantee that they interpret and execute the company's marketing strategies. The firm wants to be sure that the local middlemen price the products according to the company's policies. The same could be said for sales, advertising, or service policies. Since the company's reputation in a local market can be tarnished due to the ineffective handling of local distribution by independent middlemen, international companies closely monitor the performance of local channel members. After the takeover of United Distillers by Guinness, the company reorganized to become a worldwide marketer of high quality branded alcoholic drinks. In 1986, 75 percent of United Distillers volume was sold through 1,304 distributors. The company had very little control over the distribution. By 1990, the number of distributors was reduced to 470 and through acquisition or joint ventures, United Distillers has direct control over 80 percent of its distribution.[21]

One way to exert influence over the international channel members is to spell out the specific responsibilities of the middleman, including minimum annual sales, in the distribution agreement. Attainment of the sales goal can be required for renewal of the contract. Also, the awarding of exclusive distribution rights can be used to increase control over middlemen. Typically, the firm's business is channeled through one middleman in a given geographic area only, raising its importance to the middleman.

Frequently, such exclusive rights are coupled with a prohibition against carrying directly competing products. When the small British company, Filofax, entered the Japanese market in 1984, it decided to use Apex Inc. as its exclusive distributor. The exclusive distributorship gave Apex the incentive to push Filofax, and was successful in getting the product into 300 outlets, 60 in Tokyo, supported by heavy advertising showing Diane Keaton and Steven Spielberg using their Filofaxes. While there are thirty makers of imitation products, Filofax sells at a 50 percent price premium with high quality packaging and a leather binder. The relationship has been very profitable for both Filofax and Apex.[22] The exclusive distributors' leverage is their knowledge and expertise in the market. The leverage of manufacturer is the patent on the product, the brand name, and possible economies of scale. Of course, it is possible that the exclusive distributor can become too powerful and even evolve from a collaborator into a competitor. Many international companies limit the distribution rights to short time periods with periodic renewal. Caution is advised, however, since cancellation of distribution rights is frequently subject to local laws that do not allow a sudden termination.

Although termination of a distributor or agent for nonperformance is a relatively simple action in the United States, termination of international channel members can be very costly in many parts of the world. For example, in Honduras, the termination of an agent can cost up to five times the annual gross profits plus the value of the agent's investment, plus all kinds of additional payments. In Belgium,

21. Philip Rawstorne, "Re-shaping United Distillers," *Financial Times,* June 13, 1990, p. 12.
22. "Organized, But Not Personally," *The Economist,* November 12, 1988, pp. 82–83.

termination compensation for agents and distributors includes the value of any goodwill, plus expenses in developing the business, plus the amount of compensation claimed by discharged employees who worked on the product line. The minimum termination notice is three months.[23] As you can see, the termination of a channel member can be a costly, painful process, which in almost all cases is governed by local laws that tend to protect and compensate the channel member. Nissan, Japan's second largest car manufacturer is expected to enter a legal battle with its exclusive U.K. distributorship of twenty-one years. Nissan-U.K., owned by Mr. Botnar, a British entrepreneur, oversaw a network of 400 Nissan dealers who sold 138,000 cars in the U.K. in 1989. Nissan sent a fax to terminate the agreement at the end of 1990.[24]

GAINING ACCESS TO DISTRIBUTION CHANNELS

To actually gain access to distribution channels may well be the most formidable challenge in international marketing. Decisions on product designs, communications strategies, or pricing can be very complex and pose difficult choices, but once a company has made the choices, the implementation requires significant management expertise and resources. The distribution system is critical to implementing the marketing strategy.

The entry into a market can be accomplished through a variety of channel members described earlier in the chapter (see Figure 12.1). Often the most logical channel member already has a relationship with one of your competitiors, therefore limiting your access. This poses some special challenges to international marketers. Therefore this section is aimed at illustrating alternatives to companies that, while offering an excellent product or service, encounter difficulties in convincing channel members to carry their products.

The "Locked-up" Channel

A channel is considered locked up when a newcomer cannot easily convince any channel member to participate despite the fact that both market and economic reasons suggest otherwise. Channel members customarily decide on a case by case basis what products should be added or dropped from their line. Retailers typically select products that they expect to sell easily and in volume, and they can be expected to switch sources when better opportunities arise. Similarly, wholesalers and distributors compete for retail accounts or industrial users on economic terms. They can expect to entice a prospective client to switch by buying from a new source if they

23. "Guidelines for Terminating Agents and Distributors," *The Export Advisor,* November 1981.
24. John Griffiths, "Nissan to Split With U.K. Dealer After Row," *Financial Times,* December 28, 1990, p.1.

can offer a better deal. Likewise, manufacturers compete for wholesale accounts with the expectation that channel members can be convinced to purchase from any given manufacturer if the offer exceeds those made by competitors.

Often there are barriers that limit a wholesaler's flexibility to add or drop a particular line. The distributor may have an agreement not to sell competitive products. Or the distributor's business may include a significant volume from one manufacturer, so he or she does not want to risk upsetting the manufacturer. In Japan, relationships between manufacturers, wholesalers, and retailers are long-standing in nature and do not allow channel participants to change allegiance quickly to another source because of a superior product or price. Japanese channel members develop strong personal ties, and a sense of economic dependence develops. These close ties make it very difficult for any participant to break a long-standing relationship. In some cases, most existing wholesale or retail outlets may be committed in such a way that a newcomer to the market may not find qualified channel participants.

These cultural forces may not be the only influence in blocking a channel of distribution. Competitors, domestic or foreign, may try to obstruct the entry of a new company; or the members of a channel may not be willing to take any risks by pioneering unknown products. In all of these instances, the result is a locked-up channel that severely limits access to markets.

Manufacturers in the United States are not entirely new to the situation of the locked-up channel. Marketers of consumer goods developed the pull-type communication strategy to circumvent nonresponsive channel members by concentrating advertising directly on consumers. Manufacturers of industrial products usually can make use of independent manufacturers' representatives or agents to gain quick access to users. To use the same strategies abroad requires equally free access to communications channels in other countries. However, this access is restricted in some countries (see Chapter 15) due to government regulations that forbid TV or radio advertising or allow only limited availability of these media. In the case of industrial markets, the frequent entry of new entrepreneurs as independent agents is also considerably less prevalent. With fewer chances to outflank nonresponsive channels abroad, international marketers have developed new approaches to the difficult situation of gaining access to distribution channels.

Piggybacking

When a company does not find any channel partners with sufficient interest to pioneer new products, the practice of piggybacking may offer a way out of the situation. *Piggybacking* is an arrangement with another company that sells to the same customer segment to take on the new products as if it were the manufacturer. The products retain the name of the manufacturer and both partners normally sign a multi-year contract to provide for continuity. The new company is, in essence, "piggybacking" its products on the shoulders of the established company's sales force.

A Japanese manufacturer of soy sauce, Kikkoman, decided to piggyback on Del Monte's sales force for its entry into Mexico. The two companies had signed an earlier technical agreement allowing Kikkoman to sell Del Monte's tomato juice in Japan. Following Kikkoman's successful entry into the U.S. market, the company planned to enter several South American countries. The company also wanted to use Del Monte's existing strong retail sales network.[25] As a result of this move, Kikkoman was in a position to gain immediate distribution, a process that it would have taken years to develop on its own.

Under a piggyback arrangement, the manufacturer retains control over marketing strategy, particularly pricing, positioning, and advertising. The partner acts as a "rented" sales force only. Of course this is quite different from the private label strategy whereby the manufacturer supplies a marketer who places its own brand name on the product.

Joint Ventures

As we discussed in Chapter 9, when two companies agree jointly to form a new legal entity, it is called a joint venture. Such operations have been quite common in the area of joint production. Our interest here is restricted to joint ventures in which distribution is the primary objective. Normally, such companies are formed between a local firm with existing market access and a foreign firm that would like to market its products in a country where it has no existing market access. One of the best ways to enter the Japanese market is a joint venture with a Japanese partner that is in a similar but not competitive field.[26] Many such joint ventures have been signed between Japanese firms and foreign companies eager to enter the Japanese market. Through access to the distribution channel, the Japanese partner either acts as a sales agent or opens the doors for the joint venture's sales force.

Many such joint ventures expand into production, though the original intention on the part of the foreign partner clearly was to gain access to the distribution system. Kodak began selling in Japan in 1989, but found itself in a weak position in the mid-1980s with only fifteen people in its Tokyo office selling through four distributors. Kodak had 1 percent of the market, while Fuji had 70 percent and was attacking Kodak in the United States and Europe. Kodak formed a joint venture with Nagase Sangyo, an Osaka-based trading company specializing in chemicals, to attack Fuji in its home market. With heavy investment in plant, promotion and distribution, Kodak now has 4,500 employees in Japan and has 15 percent of the market.[27]

The largest Japanese computer company, Fujitsu Ltd., chose the joint venture route to expand its marketing operation in the United States. The company joined forces with TRW, which had the largest independent network of electronic equipment service personnel available in the United States. Using the joint venture tie,

25. "Kikkoman Is Due Actively to Sell Soy Sauce in Mexico in January," *Japan Economic Journal,* November 6, 1979, p. 14.

26. "Beating the System," *The Economist,* January 31, 1987, p. 63.

27. "The Revenge of Big Yellow," *The Economist,* November 10, 1990, p. 103.

Fujitsu got immediate access to a large service network.[28] As Komatsu, the Japanese earth moving equipment company, realized it could not overcome the strength of Caterpillar's dealer network in the U.S., it formed a joint venture with Dresser Industries to strengthen its distribution.[29]

Original Equipment Manufacturers (OEM)

In a situation in which the international manufacturer signs a supply agreement with a domestic or local firm to sell the international manufacturer's products but under the established brand name of the local firm, the arrangement is termed an OEM agreement or private labeling (for consumer products). The foreign company uses the already existing distribution network of the local company, whereas the local company gains a chance to broaden its product lines.

The French automobile manufacturer Renault signed an OEM agreement with the U.S. truck builder Mack. The agreement provided that medium-duty diesel trucks built by Renault would be sold under the Mack name through Mack's more than 300 dealers. Due to fuel prices, U.S. truck operators have shown a preference for the diesel trucks that always were very popular in Europe. Recognizing the opportunity, Renault signed the agreement and got immediate access to a well-entrenched distribution system. This was much easier than building one from scratch. Furthermore, selecting a well-known U.S. partner was viewed as less costly than joining a foreign company attempting to enter the same segment. The agreement was solidified by Renault's purchase of 20 percent of Mack's equity. Mack, of course, received an already proven line of medium-duty diesel trucks, thus saving the costs that it would have taken to develop its own line.[30]

Japanese companies have been particularly adept at using the OEM strategy to build whole alliances of captive markets. Matsushita, for example, marketed a substantial portion of its video tape recorders (VTRs) through OEM arrangements with RCA, Magnavox, Sylvania, Curtis Mathes, and General Electric—all U.S. companies. Likewise, another Japanese VTR-producer and joint venture company distributed its products in Europe through Thorn (UK), Thompson-Brandt (France), Saba, Normende, and Telefunken (Germany). All of these OEMs sold joint venture company products under their own brand names.[31]

In the computer field, Japanese companies have adopted strategies that differ from those customarily chosen by U.S. computer manufacturers. For example, Hitachi sold its mainframe computers which compete directly with IBM, through National Advanced Systems, the marketing arm of National Semiconductor in the United States. In Europe they sell through Comparex, a joint venture of BASF and

---

28. "TRW: Fujitsu's Key to the U.S.," *Business Week*, May 19, 1980, p. 118.

29. "For Caterpillar the Metamorphosis Isn't Over," *Business Week*, April 1987, p. 72.

30. "Signal Unit Plans to Sell Trucks of Renault Unit," *Wall Street Journal*, July 27, 1978, p. 7.

31. Ibid.

Siemens. In 1990, Hitachi formed a joint venture with Electronic Data Systems (part of General Motors) to buy National Advanced System, therefore switching from an OEM arrangement to a joint venture.[32]

Distributing in foreign markets under OEM agreements has its dangers as well. Since the local OEM will put its own label on the imported product, the international company does not get any access to local customers and, therefore, will find it difficult to achieve a strong identity in the market. This reliance on the local OEM can pose problems when the local company's performance declines. An excellent example is the situation faced by Mitsubishi International Corporation, a large Japanese automobile manufacturer that supplied Chrysler Corporation with small cars under an OEM agreement. With Chrysler's weak financial situation from 1983 to 1985, Mitsubishi would have preferred to sell its cars directly to the U.S. market under Mitsubishi's brand name. As long as the agreement was in effect, Mitsubishi was prohibited from doing that and its fortune in the U.S. market continued to depend on Chrysler's efforts. The OEM tie-up allows a company to reach a high volume more quickly by sacrificing independence and control over its own distribution system. Of course, a company selecting this route is partially motivated by the corresponding savings of expenses by not building its own distribution system.

Acquisitions

The acquisition of an existing company can give a foreign entrant immediate access to a distribution system. Although it requires a substantial amount of capital, operating results tend to be better than starting a new venture that often brings initial losses. It is often less important to find an acquisition candidate with a healthy financial outlook or top products than one with a good relationship to wholesale and retail outlets. A good example of the acquisition strategy to gain access to distribution channels was the purchase of 51 percent of Japan's Banyu pharmaceutical company by Merck. Sales and profits have more than doubled since the acquisition and Banyu is one of the fastest growing drug companies in Japan.[33]

The Japanese car market has been difficult to enter due to the stiff tax on big cars and limited distribution. The tax was dropped in April 1989 and Ford acquired a 35 percent stake in Autorama, a nationwide distributorship, to expand its sales. As a result, sales of Ford cars rose from 53,000 in 1988 to 75,000 in 1989.[34]

Starting New Ventures

To build one's own distribution system is not only costly but also requires patience and time. Aware of these risks, IVECO, a European truck manufacturer jointly

32. "Hitachi Acquires Route to U.S. Market With GM Link," *Financial Times,* February 28, 1989, p.1.

33. Carla Rapoport, "You Can Make Money in Japan," *Fortune,* February 12, 1990, p. 45.

34. Ibid., p. 46.

owned by Italy's Fiat and Germany's Klockner-Humboldt-Deutz, first attempted to enter the U.S. market with an arrangement with a U.S. truck manufacturer, but an agreement could not be reached because IVECO refused to have its vehicles sold under an OEM contract allowing the U.S. company to put its own name on the trucks. When it started out on its own, IVECO began to realize the difficulty ahead. Each individual dealer had to be separately recruited and sales had to be limited to the eastern and southern part of the United States. To overcome its low profile, IVECO budgeted $2 million for an advertising campaign. The company accepted the fact that break-even volume would be at least two years away with the actual outcome uncertain.[35] Though this strategy is higher in initial risk, it offers a company the chance to eventually control its own distribution system.

The Japanese retail market has been protected since 1973, when new stores over 500 square meters needed to get the permission of local store owners to open. Obviously, permission usually was denied! In mid-1990, the restriction was rescinded. Toys "R" Us plans to open its first store of 5,000 square meters in Niigata, a town of 500,000 people that already has sixty-three stores selling toys. Toys "R" Us plans to do $13.3 million in its first year, which is 80 times the average of the current toy stores and a 50 percent share of the Niigata market. It is too early to tell if Toys "R" Us will be successful, but it plans to open six stores in Japan by 1992.[36]

INTERNATIONAL LOGISTICS

The logistics system, also called physical distribution, involves planning, implementing, and controlling the physical flow of materials and final goods from points of origin to points of use to meet customer needs at a profit.[37] On an international scale, the task becomes more complex since so many external variables have an impact on that flow of materials or products. As geographical distances to foreign markets grow, competitive advantages are often derived from a more effective structuring of the logistics system, by either saving time, costs, or increasing a firm's reliability. The emergence of logistics as a means of competitive advantage is leading companies to focus increased attention on this vital area. Many manufacturers and retailers are restructuring their logistics efforts and divesting of their in-house distribution divisions in favor of outside logistics specialists.

A logistics system is expensive. It is a capital and labor-intensive function outside of the core business of most companies, that has become increasingly complex. For many concerns, it represents 16 to 35 percent of total revenues. Marks and Spen-

35. "A New Challenge in Trucks," *Business Week,* July 3, 1978, p. 88.

36. "Japanese Retailing—Uncorking the Bottleneck," *The Economist,* June 16, 1990, pp. 116–118.

37. Philip Kotler, *Marketing Management,* 5th ed. (Englewood Cliffs: N.J.: Prentice-Hall, 1984), p. 591.

cer, a U.K. retailer that operates in eight countries, has found it can increase the sales per square foot and eliminate the need for most stock rooms by increasing the frequency of delivery. To guarantee reliability the company used outside contractors.[38] The following sections describe the objectives of an international logistics system and the individual organizational operations that have to be managed into an efficient system.

Determining Service Levels

The principal objective of the logistics system is to provide the service of dependable and efficient movement of materials or products to the user. Since any combination of logistics arrangements involve expenditures, the firm is urged to first determine the level of service desired before any implementation is made. The determination of these service levels is marketing management's responsibility and requires attention in the following four areas:

1. *The maximization of the number of orders shipped compared to the number of orders received.* For most firms it is important to be able to ship products for orders received. It is generally accepted that a level of 100 percent is unrealistic since it requires the company to be prepared for all eventualities and most likely will result in high inventories. Marketing managers have to decide on an appropriate percentage given the existing competition, both here and abroad, and taking into consideration the delivery systems in the particular foreign market. Since it is not possible to fill all orders received, managers have to balance the costs of maintaining a sufficient inventory with the cost of lost business since clients may place orders elsewhere if delivery is not forthcoming immediately.

2. *The minimization of the time between order submission and actual order shipment.* Aside from having the products physically on hand, the firm must reduce its reaction or order-filling time; there should be speedy delivery to customers. Any reduction of this order processing time results in a reduction of the client's inventory needs and can, therefore, be turned into a competitive advantage. On an international level, it is unlikely that customers in all countries have the same expectation of this reaction time. Consequently, management has to pay special attention to local requirements or, where necessary, to ensure that orders submitted to one regional distribution center from different markets receive the necessary attention. It may not be feasible to have a unified or single policy for all markets.

3. *The minimization of the variance between promised delivery and actual delivery.* Once a customer has been promised delivery by a set date, the customer will draw down on inventory in anticipation of the new delivery.

---

38. "Distribution Services—The World's the Limit," *Financial Times,* November 6, 1990, Section III, p. 1.

Consequently, a delay can substantially affect the client's operation, maybe even cause a loss of orders. Minimizing the variance between promised and actual delivery does not always require the fastest mode of transportation. Reliability is the key. International logistics often involves various modes of transportation subject to unexpected occurrences that upset delivery schedules. The firm that manages to insulate its clients from such unexpected events can gain a substantial advantage over competitors.

4. *The minimization of damage in transit.* Any shipment that reaches its destination in damaged form represents an opportunity loss to the buyer who planned for the arrival of the product. Even if an insurance settlement replaces the actual value of products damaged, the loss of business due to the absence of additional inventory cannot be replaced. International shipments are often subject to numerous adverse physical stresses due to long transit times, changes in climate, or numerous handling at ports for trans-shipments. Adequate protective packaging is therefore required and may far exceed standards for domestic shipments.[39]

Logistics Decision Areas

The total task of logistics management consists of five separate, though interrelated, jobs. The areas include:

1. Traffic or transportation management

2. Inventory control

3. Order processing

4. Materials handling and warehousing

5. Fixed facilities location management

Each of these five jobs or decision areas offers unique challenges to the international marketer and is described below in more detail.

Traffic or Transportation Management Traffic management deals primarily with the mode of transportation. Principal choices are air, sea, rail, or truck, or some combination thereof. Since transportation costs contribute substantially to the costs of marketing products internationally, special attention has to be given to the selection of the transportation mode. Such choices are made by considering three principal factors: lead times, transit times, and costs. Companies operating with long lead times tend to use slower and therefore low-cost transportation modes such as sea or freight. For short lead-time situations, faster modes of transportation such as air or truck are used. Also important are transit times. Long transit times require higher

---

39. Adapted from John F. Magee, "The Logistics of Distribution." *Harvard Business Review,* July-August 1960, pp. 89–101.

financial costs since payments arrive later, and there are normally higher average inventories at either the point of origin or destination. Modes of transportation with long transit times are of course sea or rail, whereas air and truck transportation result in much shorter transit times. Costs are the third factor considered for the decision of a mode of transport. Typically, air and truck transportation are more expensive than either sea or rail for any given distance.

Overloaded ports or transportation facilities can be hazardous and costly. With coal again in great demand worldwide, U.S. coal exporters were restricted in their export shipments by bottlenecks in major ports.[40] With volumes of 90 million tons in 1980 and 110 million tons in 1985, U.S. coal exporters decided it was in their own best interest to expand port facilities. In one year alone, foreign customers paid about $1 million for waiting charges to foreign vessels waiting to load coal. At one point, 150 coal transport vessels waited at one Virginia port for an average delay of 60 to 70 days. If U.S. producers cannot guarantee speedy unloading, foreign customers may turn to other suppliers in Canada, South Africa, or Australia.

Rank Xerox found by centralizing inbound deliveries from fifteen different trucking companies to one, they reduced transport costs by 40 percent in its Holland plant. Through this and further moves to centralize logistics, they expect to save $200,000 a year. Rank Xerox expects to reduce transport cost, inventories, and warehouse costs while at the same time improving the management and control of the logistics system.[41]

Inventory Control The level of inventory on hand substantially affects the service level of a firm's logistics system. Due to the substantial costs of tied-up capital, inventory is reduced to the minimum level needed. In international operations, adequate inventories are needed as insurance against unexpected breakdowns in the logistics system. To reduce inventory levels a number of companies are adopting the Japanese system of just-in-time deliveries of parts and components. Also, companies are developing regional manufacturing strategies to minimize cost. For example, Rank Xerox produces its models for the entire world market (except the U.S. market) in four European plants. Prior to adopting a just-in-time system, they kept buffer stocks of 10 to 40 days and an inventory of finished goods of 90 days. Now there is no stock for just-in-time parts and components and an inventory of finished goods of only 15 days. The improvements are the result of a just-in-time strategy: a reduced number of suppliers, improved quality control, and a more efficient logistics system.[42]

40. "Inadequacy of U.S. Coal-Export Terminals Sparks Oil Money Push to Expand Capacity," *Wall Street Journal,* February 27, 1981, p. 25.
41. Michael Terry, "Logistics Firms Don New Clothes for 1992," *Financial Times,* November 6, 1990, Section III, p. 2.
42. Ibid.

Order Processing Since rapid processing of orders shortens the order cycle and allows for lower safety stocks on the part of the client, this area becomes a central concern for logistics management. The available communications technology greatly influences the time it takes to process an order. Managers cannot expect to find perfectly working mail, telephones, or telex systems everywhere. Aside from the United States, Europe, and Japan, the communications systems are inferior and tend to delay order processing. To offer an efficient order processing system worldwide represents a considerable challenge to any company today. However, doing this can be turned to a competitive advantage since customers reap added benefits from such a system.

Materials Handling and Warehousing Throughout the logistics cycle, materials and products will have to be stored and prepared for moving or transportation. How these products are stored or moved is the principal concern of materials handling management. For international shipments, the shipping technology or quantities may be different, causing firms to adjust domestic policies to the circumstances. Warehousing in foreign countries involves dealing with different climatic situations, and longer average storage periods may require changing warehousing practices. In general, international shipments often move through different transportation modes than domestic shipments. Substantial logistics costs can be saved if the firm adjusts shipping arrangements according to the prevalent handling procedures abroad.

Automated warehousing is a relatively new concept for the handling, storage, and shipping of goods. Warehouses are often adjacent to the factory and all goods are stored automatically in bins up to twelve stories high. The delivery and retrieval of all goods are controlled by a computer system. While automated warehouses require significant up-front capital and technology, they reduce warehousing costs significantly.

Fixed Facilities Location Management The crucial facilities to the logistics flow are, of course, production facilities and warehouses. To serve customers worldwide and to maximize the efficiency of the total logistics system, production facilities may have to be placed in several countries. In doing this, there is a tradeoff between economies of scale and savings in logistics costs.

At times, an advantage can be gained from shipping raw materials or semiprocessed products to a market for further processing and manufacture instead of supplying the finished product. These advantages arise from varying transportation costs for given freight modes or from different rates for each product category. Some companies compare the costs for several operational alternatives before making a final decision. The location of warehousing facilities greatly affects the company's ability to respond to orders once received or processed. A company with warehouses in every country where it does business would have a natural advantage in delivery, but such a system greatly increases the costs of warehousing and, most likely, the required level of inventory systemwide. Thus a balance is sought that still satisfies the customer's requirements on delivery and at the same time reduces overall logistics costs.

Managing the International Logistics System

The objectives of a firm's international logistics system are to meet the company's service levels at the lowest cost. Costs are understood as total costs covering all five decision areas. Consequently, a company has to combine cost information into one overall budget typically involving many departments from several countries. The key to effective management is coordination. A situation in which managers all try to reduce costs in their individual areas either will reduce the service levels provided or force other areas to make up for the initial reduction by possibly spending more than the original savings. Consequently, companies have to look carefully at opportunities to save in one area by comparing additional costs accruing in another. This process of comparison has caused some managers to refer to the logistics system as tradeoff management.

High quality logistics does pay off. With 50 percent of all customer complaints to manufacturers being the result of poor logistics, there are substantial rewards for good logistics that result in better service. Research by the Strategic Planning Institute reveals that companies with superior service receive 7 percent higher prices and grow 8 percent faster than low service companies. Also, on average they are twelve times more profitable.[43]

With markets becoming more scattered and dispersed over numerous countries, the opportunities for competitive advantages in international logistics grow. The firms that manage to combine the various logistics areas under the responsibility of one manager have a chance at achieving either substantial cost savings or an enhancement of their marketing position by increasing service levels at minimum costs.

GLOBAL TRENDS IN DISTRIBUTION SYSTEMS

Distribution systems throughout the world are continually changing due to economic and social change. As a manager develops a worldwide distribution strategy he or she must consider not only the current state of distribution but also the expected state of distribution systems in the future. Five major trends seem dominant throughout the world: (1) the growth of larger scale retailers, (2) an increased number of international retailers, (3) the growth of direct marketing, (4) the spread

43. Neil S. Novich, "Leading-Edge Distribution Strategies," *Journal of Business Strategy,* November/December 1990, p. 49.

of discounting, and (5) the increased role of information technology to support a distribution strategy.

Growth of Larger Scale Retailers

There is a trend toward fewer but larger-scale retailers. As countries become more economically developed, they seem to follow a pattern of fewer, larger stores. Three factors that contribute toward this trend are an increase in car ownership, an increase in the number of households with refrigerators and freezers, and an increase in the number of working wives. Although twenty years ago the European housewife may have shopped two or three times a day in local stores, the increase in transportation capacity, refrigerator capacity, cash flow, and the reduction of available shopping time have increased the practice of one-stop shopping in supermarkets. In 1987, 64 percent of households had one or more cars in the United Kingdom, making the large out-of-town store accessible. Tesco, one of the largest supermarket chains in the United Kingdom has shut down two-thirds of its small in-town stores (less than 10,000 square feet) in favor of large stores.[44] The reduction in the number of grocery stores per 1,000 people is shown in Table 12.4.

With the exception of Brazil and Japan, the number of grocery stores per person declined between 1970 and 1979. The increased size of retailers, along with the reduction of the number of small retailers, reduces the cost of distribution and increases the sophistication of retailers.

Retail concentration is increasing in most countries. Between 1980 and 1984, chains and cooperatives increased their total share of grocery trade from 75 percent to 81 percent in Britain, from 58 percent to 67 percent in West Germany, and from 44 percent to 60 percent in Holland. During the same period, the chains and cooperatives stayed at 69 percent in the United States and 43 percent in Japan.[45]

IKEA, the Scandinavian retailer, has been very successful in Europe and in the United States in luring customers into its 200,000 square foot stores. The company had eight-three stores in twenty countries at the end of 1989.[46] Once in the store, customers are given tape measures, catalogues, paper, and pencils. Child-care strollers are available as well as free diapers. Each store has a restaurant with Scandinavian delicacies such as smoked salmon and Swedish meatballs. Customers can also borrow roof racks to help bring furniture home. IKEA has created a fun shopping experience which encourages people to enjoy themselves and make purchases. The sales per square foot is three times higher than traditional furniture stores. IKEA's success has attracted the attention of Wal-Mart, Circuit City, and Stor (a U.S. retailer) who are all adopting some of IKEA's techniques.[47]

44. Suzanne Bidlake, "High Street Revival in Store," *Marketing,* October 26, 1989, p. 19.
45. "Retailing: Grocer Power," *The Economist,* January 10, 1987, p. 56.
46. John Thornhill, "Retailers Broaden Their Outlook," *Financial Times,* December 17, 1990, p. 3.
47. "Why Competitors Shop for Ideas at IKEA," *Business Week,* October 9, 1989, p. 88.

TABLE 12.4 ● Number of Grocery Stores per 1,000 Inhabitants in Different Countries

Country	1970	1979
Australia	1.2	.7
United States	1.1	.8
South Africa	1.3	1.0
Netherlands, The	1.3	1.0
Sweden	1.7	1.1
Canada	1.7	1.3
Great Britain	2.1	1.3
New Zealand	1.7	1.4
Switzerland	2.4	1.5
Germany, Federal Republic of	2.8	1.6
France	2.7	1.8
Austria	2.7	1.9
Brazil	1.9	2.0
Belgium	3.6	2.1
Japan	1.4	2.2
Ireland	5.9	2.6
Mexico	3.2	3.1
Spain	3.9	3.2
Portugal	5.7	4.5

Source: E. Dichtl and G. Finck, "Public Policy Towards Distribution in the Federal Republic of Germany," Institut für Marketing, Universität Mannheim, 1982, p. 6. Reprinted by permission.

International Retailers

There has been a growth in the number of international retailers. Most of these international retailers originate in advanced industrial countries and spread to the developed countries of the world. For example, Sears is now in Mexico, South America, Spain, and Japan; Walgreen's is in Mexico; and Tandy is in Belgium, the Netherlands, Germany, the United Kingdom, and France. The internationalization of retailing includes firms originating in the United States, Canada, France, Germany, and Japan. The internationalization of retailing was started by a number of large retailers in mature domestic markets that saw limited growth opportunities at home that matched the opportunities overseas. This is the principal reason for the trend toward international retailers. This has led Habitat, IKEA, McDonald's, Pizza Hut, Kentucky Fried Chicken, Carrefour, Marks and Spencer, Laura Ashley, and many others to see opportunities in Europe, the United States, and Japan. The path towards an international presence has been made greater by a number of facilitating factors like enhanced data communications, new forms of international financing, and lower barriers to entry. The Single European Market has also motivated retailers to expand overseas as they see a number of new international retailers entering their domestic markets.[48] This trend toward international retailers allows manufacturers to build relationships with retailers who are active in a number of markets.

European retailers have found that it is essential to establish a unique selling position. C&A, the privately owned Dutch chain of clothing stores; The Body Shop, the U.K. natural cosmetics group; Benetton, the Italian fashion chain; IKEA, the Swedish furniture store; and Aldi, the low-priced German food retailer are all successful international retailers that have developed a distinctive style. Each has a clearly defined trading format and product range which enables it to distinguish itself in every European market. Retailing formats can be translated into other countries as long as the message is clear enough in the first place.[49]

Direct Marketing

Selling directly to the consumer by telephone, mail, or door-to-door grew to a $150 billion industry in 1985, almost triple the $60 billion it made in 1975 in the United States. There is also a growth of direct marketing around the world. The complex multilayered Japanese distribution system has encouraged some foreign companies to skip the stores and go direct to consumers. The German publisher of Spiegel catalogues started selling dresses in 1986. Sharper Image and Sears have also marketed directly to Japanese consumers. High fees on bulk mailing and the difficulty of purchasing good lists have made direct marketing difficult in Japan. Shop America Ltd. has taken a new approach. They have combined forces with 7-Eleven—Japan, which has 4,000 stores and 4 million customers, to distribute catalogues and place orders. Executives of 7-Eleven expect sales to reach $70 million in the first twelve months as Shop America offers high quality brand names electronic goods at 30 to 50 percent less than retail store prices.[50]

Nonstore retailing in Japan is expected to grow from $10 billion in 1989 to $62 billion in 1998. This includes catalogue sales, door-to-door selling, and online shopping by videotex. The growth in direct marketing in Japan is supported by a number of demographic and technical factors. The dramatic increase in employed women from 50 percent in 1980 to 75 percent in 1987 has resulted in less available shopping

48. Alan D. Treadgold, "The Developing Internationalization of Retailing," *International Journal of Retail and Distribution Management,* vol. 18, no. 2, p. 5.

49. Thornhill, "Retailers Broaden Their Outlook." *Financial Times,* December 17, 1990, p. 3.

50. "Can This Catalogue Company Crack the Japanese Marketing Maze," *Business Week,* March 19, 1990, p. 60.

hours. Recent introduction of toll-free telephone, cable TV, videotex, and smart cards all make it easier to shop at home.[51]

Avon had an Asian sales force of 10,000 salespeople in 1981, selling more than $200 million in cosmetics directly to the consumer.[52] The increased affluence of consumers in developed countries, a reduction in the amount of time devoted to shopping, changing lifestyles, increased acceptance of credit cards, and improved postal and telephone services have all contributed to the growth in direct marketing.

Discounting

The growth of international brands having strong consumer support due to advertising has helped discounting become a major international force. Also, the elimination of required list prices has contributed to a growth in discounting. Innovative retailers have used price reductions with limited high volume assortments to develop successful discount stores. While the Japanese are known to pay among the highest prices in the world on the Ginza, Tokyo's premier shopping district, twelve miles away in Chiba you will find discount stores and giant hypermarkets with reasonable prices. Sales at discount stores in Japan are growing at twice the rate of ordinary department stores.[53]

Information Technology

The worldwide retail industry is moving fast toward the use of electronic checkouts that scan the bar codes on products speeding up the checkout, reducing errors, and eliminating the need to put a price label on each item. The electronic checkout also improves the stores' ability to keep track of inventory and purchase behavior. Mr. Ratner, head of the British jewelry chain which owns Ratners, Zales, H. Samuel, and Kay Jewelers, reports that twice a day each of 1,000 stores are polled and every item sold is replaced by 8:30 A.M. the following day. This computerized system gives the company a good appreciation of how fast items are selling so it can adjust its inventory. Lines are reviewed every three months and replaced if they are not moving fast enough.[54]

Computerized retail systems have led to better monitoring of consumer purchases, low inventory, quicker stock turns, better assessment of product profitability,

51. Nitin Sanghaui, "Non-Store Retailing in Japan," *International Journal of Retail and Distribution Management,* vol. 18, no. 1, 1990, p. 20.

52. "Business Briefs," *World Press Review,* February 1981, p. 55.

53. Carla Rapoport, "Ready, Set, Sell—Japan is Buying," *Fortune,* September 11, 1989, p. 159.

54. John Thornhill, "A Sense of Urgency Makes Good Business Says Ratner," *Financial Times,* November 6, 1990, Section III, p. VII.

and the possiblity of just-in-time retailing.[55] 7-Eleven—Japan coordinates sales through its 4,000 franchised convenience stores via a computerized point-of-sale network. The typical store has only 1,000 square meters of shelf space to sell 3,500 products. The network tracks sales of products by time of day and replenishes supplies automatically with three deliveries per day.[56] The 7-Eleven—Japan empire, which is owned by Ito-Yokado, the largest retail food group in Japan, has been so successful they recently took a majority stake in Southland, the Texas parent of 7-Eleven. Ito-Yokado hopes to use its advanced information technology techniques to revitalize 7-Eleven in the United States and the twenty other countries where stores are located.[57]

CONCLUSIONS

To be successful in the marketplace, a company needs market acceptance among buyers and market access via distribution channels. Companies entering foreign markets often do so without substantial acceptance initially. Consequently, the company must guarantee some degree of market access either through effective marketing programs or sheer financial strength. To achieve access the firm must select the most suitable members or actors of a channel, keeping in mind that substantial differences exist among countries both on the wholesale and retail levels. There are major differences in distribution country to country. Local habits and cultures, planning restrictions, and infrastructure can all affect your success in a new country. For example, Greece has idiosyncratic shopping hours, Germany does not allow stores over 10,000 square feet, and Italy has stringent planning restrictions. Any entrant to the Danish market needs to contend with the cooperative stores who account for 35 to 40 percent of the market.

It can also be a mistake to assume you know the market's needs, as Marks and Spencer found when they entered France. They thought the fashion conscious French shopper would want chic clothes. But, they wanted practical clothes from M&S, and went to fashion stores for their chic items.[58] Proper distribution policies have to allow for the local market's buying or shopping habits. A company should not expect to be able to use the same distribution density, channel alignment, or

55. Richard Ford, "Managing Retail Service Businesses for the 1990s: Marketing Aspects," *European Management Journal,* March 1990, p. 60.

56. "Networks' Net Profits," *The Economist,* Survey of Telecommunications, March 10, 1990, p. 30.

57. Robert Thomson, "Lesson in Store for 7-Eleven Chain," *Financial Times,* March 23, 1990, p. 37.

58. Thornhill, "Retailers Broaden Their Outlook." *Financial Times,* December 17, 1990, p.3.

channel length in all its markets. The logistics system must reflect both local market situations and additional difficulties due to longer distances. To actually find willing and suitable channel members may be extremely difficult; access may only be achieved by forging special alliances with present channel members or local companies with access to them. Once the distribution system has been designed, participants still have to be motivated and controlled to assure that the firm's marketing strategy is properly executed.

Questions for Discussion

1. Your firm is just beginning to export printing equipment. How would you assess the decision to use an export management company or an export agent versus direct exporting?

2. What are the key elements of a distribution strategy?

3. If you enter a new marketplace and decide to distribute the product directly to the consumer, what are the types of costs you will incur?

4. You have been assigned the task of selecting distributors to handle your firm's line of car batteries. What criteria will you use to select among the twenty possible distributors?

5. The performance of your agents and distributors in South America has been poor over the past three years. How will you improve the management of these agents and distributors?

6. What are the elements of an international logistics system, and how will they differ from a domestic logistics system?

7. Your firm has just entered the South Korean market for automobile parts. The major distributor is owned by a competitive manufacturer of automobile parts. What strategies can you use to gain access to this market?

8. Given the trends in distribution, what distribution strategies should a worldwide manufacturer of women's clothing consider?

For Further Reading

Bello, Daniel C., and Lee D. Dahringer. "The Influence of Country and Product on Retailer Practices." *International Marketing Review* (Summer 1985), pp. 45–52.

Bello, Daniel C., and Nicholas C. Williamson. "Contractural Arrangements and Marketing Practices in the Indirect Export Channel." *Journal of International Business Studies* (Summer 1985), pp. 65–82.

Brasch, John J. "Export Management Companies." *Journal of International Business Studies* (Spring-Summer 1978), pp. 59–72.

Czinkota, Michael R. "Distribution of Consumer Products in Japan." *International Marketing Review* (Autumn 1985), pp. 39–51.

Damon, Stewart W. "Establishing a Foreign Distributor and Agent Network," *Business America* (June 25, 1984), pp. 12-13.

Green, Robert T., and Arthur W. Allaway. "Identification of Export Opportunities: A Shift Share Approach." *Journal of Marketing* (Winter 1985), pp. 83–88.

Hall, R. Duane, and Ralph J. Gilbert. *Multinational Distribution: Channel, Tax and Legal Strategies.* New York: Praeger, 1985.

Kacker, Madhav P. *Transatlantic Trends in Retailing.* Westport, Conn.: Quorum Books, 1985.

Kaynak, Edener. "The Global Spread of Supermarkets: The Case of Turkey." In *Global Perspectives in Marketing.* Ed. Edener Kaynak. New York: Praeger, 1985.

Lowe, David. *The Transport and Distribution Managers Guide to 1992.* London: Kogan, Page, 1989.

Magrath, Allan J., and Kenneth G. Hardy. "Selecting Sales and Distribution Channels," *Industrial Marketing Management,* vol. 16 (1987), pp. 273–278.

McIntyre, David R. "Your Overseas Distributor Action Plan." *Journal of Marketing* (April 1977), pp. 88–90.

Perlmutter, Howard W., and David A. Heenan. "Cooperate to Compete Globally." *Harvard Business Review* (March-April 1986), pp. 136–152.

Rosson, Philip J., and I. David Ford. "Manufacturer-Overseas Distributor Relations and Export Performance." *Journal of International Business Studies* (Fall 1982), pp. 57–72.

Rosson, Philip J., and I. David Ford. "Stake, Conflict and Performance in Export Marketing Channels." *Journal of International Business Studies* (Fall 1982), pp. 57–72.

Shimaguchi, Mitysuaki, and Larry J. Rosenberg. "Demystifying Japanese Distribution." *Columbia Journal of World Business* (Spring 1979), pp. 32–41.

Stock, James R., and Douglas M. Lambert. "Physical Distribution Management in International Marketing." *International Marketing Review* (Autumn 1983), pp. 28–41.

13

Pricing for International and Global Markets

● **THIS CHAPTER PROVIDES** *an overview of the key factors that affect pricing policies in an international environment. We assume that you are already aware of the basic pricing decisions that companies must make in a single-country or domestic environment. In this chapter we concentrate exclusively on the unique aspects of international pricing. (See Figure 13.1 for a chapter overview.)*

The material is organized around four major issues. First we look at internal factors and company policies as they affect international pricing policies. Costs and how they affect price determination are major concerns. The second section is devoted to the market factors companies must consider in setting prices, such as competition and the income levels of various countries. The third segment focuses on the environmental variables, such as foreign exchange rates, inflation, and legal constraints, that are not controlled by individual firms but that play an important role in shaping pricing policies. The chapter ends with a section on the managerial pricing issues, such as transfer pricing—price arbitrage and countertrade—issues of great concern to companies active internationally. Also covered are the issues of financing and noncash pricing, two areas that have received increased attention from international firms.

FIGURE 13.1 ● International and Global Pricing Strategies

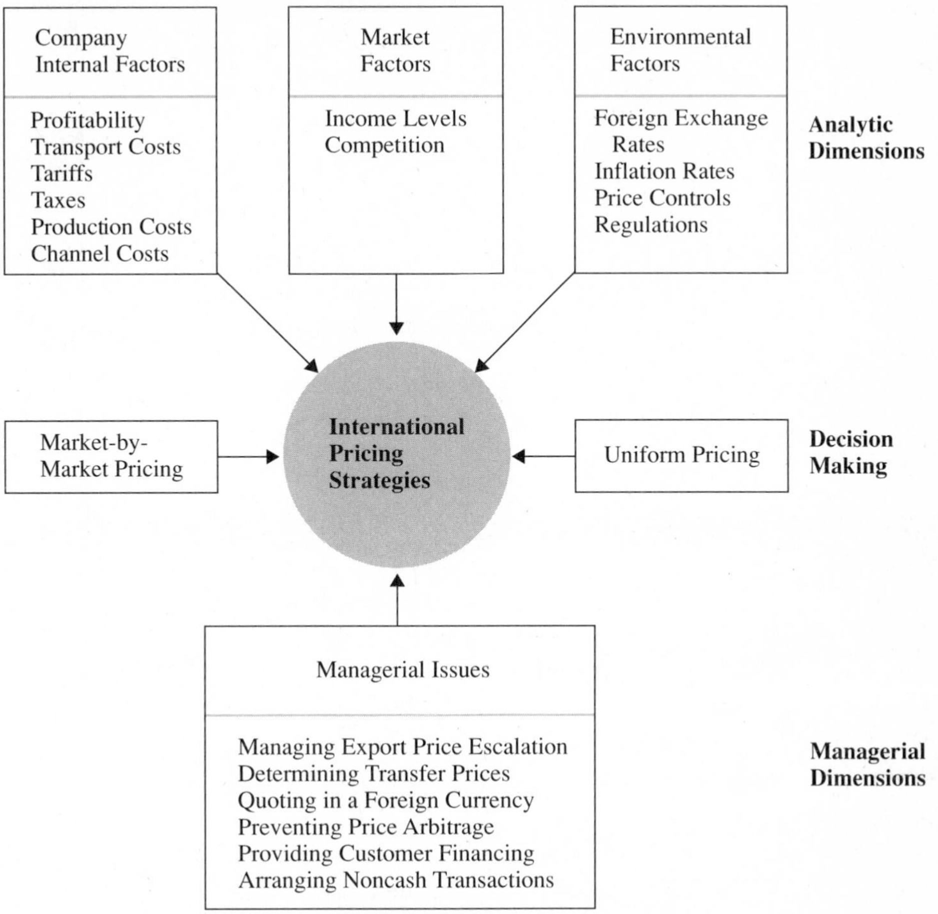

Company Internal Factors	Market Factors	Environmental Factors	
Profitability Transport Costs Tariffs Taxes Production Costs Channel Costs	Income Levels Competition	Foreign Exchange Rates Inflation Rates Price Controls Regulations	**Analytic Dimensions**

| Market-by-Market Pricing | → | **International Pricing Strategies** | ← | Uniform Pricing | **Decision Making** |

Managerial Issues	
Managing Export Price Escalation Determining Transfer Prices Quoting in a Foreign Currency Preventing Price Arbitrage Providing Customer Financing Arranging Noncash Transactions	**Managerial Dimensions**

COMPANY INTERNAL FACTORS

Most companies begin pricing deliberations based on their own internal cost structure. Therefore it makes sense to look first at internal cost before considering other issues. Included under internal factors are profits and the requirement for profits as they impact internal pricing procedures. Also of concern to us are international transfer costs, such as tariffs, transportation, insurance, taxes, and local channel costs.

Such costs frequently make exported products more expensive than domestic ones, and this fact must be taken into consideration if a company wants to compete

TABLE 13.1 ● Profit and Cost Calculation for Western Machine Tool, Inc.

Selling price (per unit)		$60,000
Direct manufacturing costs		
Labor	10,000	
Material	15,000	
Energy	1,000	$26,000
Indirect manufacturing costs		
Supervision	5,000	
Research and development contribution	3,000	
Factory overhead	5,000	$13,000
General administrative cost		
Sales and administrative overhead	10,000	
Marketing	5,000	$15,000
Full costs		54,000
Net profit before tax		6,000

effectively. However, such costs do not have to be taken as given. Companies can, through various actions, affect the level of these costs. It is the purpose of this section to point out the options available to companies in managing their international costs.

Profit and Cost Factors

The basis for any effective pricing policy is a clear understanding of the cost and profit variables involved. Experience shows that a clear definition of relevant costs or of profits is often difficult to achieve. On the other hand, the field of international marketing offers many examples of firms that have achieved substantial profits through flexible or nonconventional costing approaches. Therefore understanding the various cost elements can be considered a prerequisite for a successful international pricing strategy.

According to standard accounting practice, costs are divided into two categories: fixed costs and variable costs. Fixed costs do not vary over a given range of output, whereas variable costs change directly with output. The relationship of these variables is shown in Table 13.1 using a fictitious example, Western Machine Tool, Inc., a manufacturer of machine tools selling at $60,000 per unit in the U.S. market.

The total cost of a machine tool is $54,000. Sold at $60,000, the company will achieve a profit of $6,000 before taxes from the sale of each unit. However, if one

TABLE 13.2 ● Marginal Profit Calculation for Western Machine Tool, Inc.

Selling Price (per unit)			$60,000
Variable costs			
Direct manufacturing costs			
Labor	10,000		
Material	15,000		
Energy	1,000	$26,000	
General administrative costs			
Marketing	5,000	5,000	
Total variable costs			$31,000
Contribution margin (Selling price minus Variable costs)			$29,000

additional unit is sold (or not sold), the marginal impact not only amounts to an additional profit of $6,000 (or loss of the same amount), but the extra cost of an additional unit will be limited to its variable costs only, or $31,000, as shown in Table 13.2. For any additional unit sold, the marginal profit is $29,000, or the amount in excess of the variable costs. This amount may also be referred to as the contribution margin.

Another example is used to illustrate the relationships between variable costs, fixed costs, and contribution margin. Western Machine Tool has a chance to export a unit to a foreign country, but the maximum price the foreign buyer is willing to pay is $50,000. Machine Tool, using the full cost pricing method, argues that the company will incur a loss of $4,000 if the deal is accepted. However, since only $31,000 of additional variable cost will be incurred for a new machine because all fixed costs are incurred anyway and are covered by all prior units sold, the company can go ahead with the sale and claim a marginal profit of $19,000, using a contribution margin approach. In such a situation, a profitable sale may easily be turned down unless a company is fully informed about its cost composition.

Cost components are subject to change. By adding new output to a plant, such as new export volume, a company may achieve economies of scale that allow operation at lower costs, both domestically and abroad. Furthermore, as the experience curve indicates, companies with rapidly rising cumulative production may reap overall unit cost reductions at an increasing rate due to the higher output caused by exporting.[1]

1. For a detailed discussion of the experience curve concept, see Derek F. Abell and John S. Harmon, *Strategic Market Planning* (Englewood Cliffs, N.J.: Prentice-Hall, 1979), Chapter 3.

Transportation Costs

International marketing often requires the shipment of products over long distances. Since all modes of transportation including rail, truck, air, or ocean, depend on a considerable amount of energy, the total cost of transportation has become an issue of growing concern to international companies. High technology products are less sensitive to transportation costs than standardized consumer products or commodities. In the latter case, the seller with the lowest transportation costs often has the advantage.

For commodities, low transportation costs can decide who gets an order. For expensive products, such as computers or sophisticated electronic instruments, transportation costs usually represent only a small fraction of total costs and rarely influence pricing decisions. For products between the two extremes, companies can substantially affect unit transportation costs by selecting new transportation methods. The introduction of container ocean vessels has made large scale shipment of many products possible. Roll-on-roll-off ships (ro-ro carriers) have reduced ocean freight for cars and trucks to very low levels, making exporters more competitive vis-à-vis local manufacturers. The international firm must continuously search for new transportation technologies to reduce unit transportation costs and, thus, enhance competitiveness.

Tariffs

When products are transported across national borders, tariffs have to be paid unless a special arrangement exists between the countries involved. Tariffs are usually levied on the landed costs of a product, which includes shipping to the importing country. Tariffs are usually assessed as a percentage of the value.

Tariff costs can have a rippling effect and increase prices considerably for the end-user. Middlemen, whether they are sales subsidiaries or independent distributors, tend to include any tariff costs in their costs of goods sold and add any operating margin on this amount. As a result, the impact on the final end-user price can be substantial whenever tariff rates are high.

The intricacies of managing through duty and regulations are illustrated by Land Rover, the British producer of the Range Rover 4WD utility vehicle market in the United States since 1987. When the U.S. tariffs for trucks were increased from 2.5 percent to 25 percent to stem the imports, 4WD vehicles were classified as multipurpose vehicles subject to a higher tariff. But Land Rover complained that its $40,000 vehicle was classified as a truck and finally got by by pointing out that it has four doors, and not just two as the typical light truck. Thus the higher duty was avoided. In 1991, however, the United States began to charge a 10 percent surtax on luxury vehicles above $30,000, thus potentially affecting the sales of the Range Rover. The U.S. tax authorities classified four wheel drive vehicles as trucks and the Range Rover again avoided the tax. To assure compliance, however, the Range Rovers are shipped to the United States as cars to avoid the truck surcharge but has

TABLE 13.3 ● VAT Standard Rates

	0%	5	10	15	20	25
May 1990	· ·
Spain				●		
Luxembourg				●		
West Germany				●		
Britain				●		
Portugal				●		
Italy				●		
Greece				●		
France					●	
Belgium					●	
Holland					●	
Denmark					●	
Ireland					●	

Source: The Economist, May 12, 1990, © 1990 The Economist Newspaper Limited. Reprinted with permission.

increased the weight from 5,997 pounds to 6,019 pounds because the tax authorities, truck definition starts at vehicles of 6,000 pounds.[2]

Although tariffs have declined over recent years, they still influence pricing decisions in some countries. As we have seen in Chapter 9, to avoid paying high duties, companies have shipped components only and established local assembly operations because tariffs on components are frequently lower than on finished products. The automobile industry is a good example of how companies can reduce overall tariff costs by shifting the place of production, with the shipment of knocked-down cars to be assembled on the spot. Such a move may be called for when tariffs are especially high.

Taxes

Local taxes imposed on imported products also affect the land cost of the products. A variety of taxes may be imposed. One of the most common is the tax on value added (VAT) used by member countries of the European Community.

Each EC country sets its own value-added tax structure (see Table 13.3). However, common to all is a zero tax rate (or exemption) on exported goods. A company exporting from the Netherlands to Belgium does not have to pay any tax on the value added in the Netherlands. However, Belgian authorities do collect a tax on products shipped from the Netherlands at the Belgium rate. Merchandise shipped to any EC

2. "What's in a Name," *The Economist,* February 2, 1991, p. 60.

member country from a nonmember country, such as from the United States or Japan, is assessed the VAT rate on landed costs in addition to any customs duties that may apply to those products. Eventually the EC is planning to align VAT rates among the various countries and to have it paid in the country of consumption, thus eliminating the payment of VAT at each border. This plan is to take effect by 1996.[3]

Local Production Costs

Up to this point we have assumed that a company has only one producing location, from which it exports to all other markets. However, most international firms manufacture products in several countries. In such cases, operating costs for raw materials, wages, energy, or financing may differ widely from country to country, allowing a firm to ship from a particularly advantageous location to reduce prices or costs. Increasingly, companies produce in locations that give them advantages in freight, tariffs, or other transfer costs. Consequently, judicious management of sourcing points may reduce product costs and, thus, result in added pricing flexibility.

Channel Costs

Channel costs are a function of channel length, gross margin, and logistics. Many countries operate with longer distribution channels than the United States, causing higher total costs and end-user prices because of additional layers of middlemen. Also, gross margins at the retail level tend to be higher outside the United States. Since the logistics system in a large number of countries is also less developed than that in the United States, logistics costs are also higher on a per unit basis. All of these factors add additional costs to a product that is marketed internationally.

Campbell Soup Company, a U.S.-based firm, found that its retailers in the United Kingdom purchased soup in small quantities of twenty-four cans per case of assorted soups, requiring each can to be hand-packed for shipment. In the United States, the company sold one variety to retailers in cases of forty-eight cans per case which were purchased in large quantities. To handle small purchases in England, the company had to add an additional level of distribution and new facilities. As a result, distribution costs are 30 percent higher in England than they are in the United States.[4]

MARKET FACTORS AFFECTING PRICING

Companies cannot establish pricing policies in a vacuum. Although cost information is essential, prices also have to reflect the realities of the marketplace. The challenge

3. *The Economist,* May 12, 1990, p. 83.
4. Philip R. Cateora, *International Marketing,* 7th ed. (Homewood, Ill.: Irwin, 1990), p. 540.

of pricing for international markets is the large number of local economic situations to be considered. Two factors stand out and must be analyzed in greater detail: income levels and competition.

Income Levels

The income level of a country's population determines the amount and type of goods and services bought. When detailed income data is not available, incomes are expressed by Gross National Product (GNP) divided by the total population. This measure, *GNP per capita,* is a surrogate measure for personal income and is used to compare income levels among countries. To do so, all GNPs have to be converted to the same currency. If you look back at Table 5.7, you'll see that GNP per capita figures for key countries were expressed in U.S. dollars. Since the U.S. dollar has fluctuated substantially over the years, GNP per capita figures of countries such as Switzerland, Germany, and Japan have fluctuated correspondingly when translated into U.S. currency, placing these countries at times well ahead of the United States on a per capita income basis.

As a result of widely differing income and price levels, elasticity of demand for any given product can be expected to vary greatly. Countries with high income levels often display lower price elasticities for necessities such as food, shelter, or medical care. These lower elasticities in part reflect a lack of alternatives such as "doing it yourself," which forces buyers in these countries to purchase such goods even at higher prices. For example, in many countries with low income levels, a considerable part of the population has the additional alternatives of providing their own food or building their own shelters should they not have sufficient money to purchase products or services on a cash basis. Availability of such options increases price elasticity, as these consumers can more easily opt out of the cash economy than consumers in developed economies. International companies theoretically set product price by considering the price elasticity in each country. However, there are forces at work that do not always allow this practice because prices may vary widely across several countries. See Table 13.3 for different rates on value added taxes in Europe. The danger of disparate price levels is examined later in the pricing issues segment of this section.

Competition

The nature and size of competition can significantly affect price levels in any given market. A firm acting as the sole supplier of a product in a given market enjoys greater pricing flexibility. The opposite is true if that same company has to compete against several other local or international firms. Therefore the number and type of competitors greatly influence pricing strategy in any market.

Also important is the nature of the competition. Local competitors may have different cost structures from those of foreign companies, resulting in different prices. On the other hand, if all major competitors are international companies based in the

TABLE 13.4 ● Domestic Japanese Prices vs. Prices of Imported Products in Japan (in U.S. Dollars)

	Imported	*Japanese made*
20-inch color TV	$375	$617
Refrigerator	547	625
Play-only VCR	194	250
VCR	280	374
Radio/tape player	31	70
Portable compact disk player	154	232
Cordless phone	78	186
35mm camera	39	123
BMX bike	100	233
26-inch bike	155	389
Golfballs (one dozen)	23	35
Skateboard	20	38
Baseball mitt	20	51

Source: Wall Street Journal March 11, 1988, p. 1. Reprinted by permission of *The Wall Street Journal,* © 1988 Dow Jones & Company, Inc. All Rights Reserved Worldwide.

United States, cost similarities may equalize pricing policies. Market prices for the same product may vary from country to country, based on the competitive situation. Heinz, the U.S.-based food company and the world leader in ketchup with 50 percent world market share, began to expand on its 1 percent market share in Japan after a liberalization of the policy regarding some food imports. The company faced major price competition by the leading Japanese ketchup producer. However, Heinz decided not to follow suit but to keep prices at the higher level because it was believed to indicate quality and to protect its profitability.[5]

But foreign companies do not always have to be at a disadvantage when competing with local companies. In the wake of the substantial appreciation of the Japanese yen in the mid-to late 1980s, many importers found themselves in a situation where they could considerably underprice local Japanese firms. See Table 13.4 for a price comparison.[6]

5. "Ketchup War Will Be Fought to the Last Drop," *Financial Times,* February 21, 1990, p. 18.
6. "Japanese Learn Thrill of Bargain Shopping from Mentors Abroad," *Wall Street Journal,* March 11, 1988, p. 1.

TABLE 13.6 ● Currency Changes 1981/1982 to 1991

February 1	*Morgan** Guaranty Changes %*
Sterling	−18.3
U.S. Dollar	−18.7
Canadian Dollar	−0.5
Austrian Schilling	+12.5
Belgian Franc	−1.2
Danish Krone	+5.2
D-Mark	+26.4
Swiss Franc	+23.8
Dutch Guilder	+17.2
French Franc	−11.8
Lira	−19.1
Yen	+66.8

Morgan Guaranty changes: average 1980–1982 = 100.

**Rates are for Jan. 31, 1991.

Source: Financial Times, February 4, 1991, p. 31. Reprinted by permission.

differed from country to country. In some cases, inflation rates have risen to several hundred percent. When this happens, payment for products may be delayed for months, harming the economy because of the local currency's rapid loss of purchasing power. A company would have to use a LIFO (last-in-first-out) method of costing or, in the extreme, a FIFO (first-in-first-out) approach to protect itself from eroding purchasing power. A company can usually protect itself from rapid inflation if operating margins (gross margin, gross profit, net margin) remain constant combined with constant price adjustments, sometimes on a monthly basis.

International companies competing in Brazil have had to cope with inflation running at 850 percent in 1989. To cope with this, companies have had to develop sophisticated information systems in their prices, costs, and cash balances. Because money received from a customer in thirty days is substantially less than payments made today, companies have resorted to indexing of most contracts. Substantial discounts are granted for customers paying right away, and considerable penalties are levied on customers who fail to pay within agreed time periods.[9]

In countries with extremely high inflation, companies may price in a stable currency, such as the U.S. dollar, and translate prices into local currencies on a daily basis (see Table 13.6).

9. "Juggling With 850 Percent Inflation in Brazil," *Financial Times,* June 5, 1989, p. 18.

Price Controls

In many countries government and regulatory agencies influence the prices of products and services. Controls may be applied to an entire economy to combat inflation; or regulations may be applied only to specific industries, such as the Civil Aeronautics Board regulations for air fares in the United States (although they were phased out in the early 1980s). Cases in which price controls apply equally to all industries are often temporary or, as was the case in the United States, of a voluntary nature. In other cases, price increases might only be permitted when a real improvement in a product or its quality has taken place.

Other measures may be taken to prevent excessive pricing by individual companies. One such case involved Hoffmann-LaRoche & Co., A.G., a large producer of drugs and vitamins located in Switzerland. The company had a monopoly in tranquilizers known under the brand names Valium and Librium. As a result, in 1973 the British Monopolies Commission ordered the company to reduce prices by 35 to 40 percent. Similar action was brought against Hoffmann-LaRoche by the German cartel office and by the Danish and Dutch governments. After years of litigation, Hoffmann-LaRoche was forced to reduce prices, even though the reductions were smaller than originally demanded. Higher courts, however, later rolled back all price concessions in these countries after Hoffmann-LaRoche filed suit. The Hoffmann-LaRoche experience indicates that international firms cannot always make independent pricing decisions in each country.[10]

Even in the European Community, where many aspects of the countries' economies are coordinated, methods of controlling prices for drugs may vary considerably. In the United Kingdom, drug prices are established through the Pharmaceutical Price Regulation Scheme (PPRS). Though companies are allowed to set prices for individual drugs, the government limits their overall profitability. However, company profit targets are established through confidential negotiations and are set differently for each company. Furthermore, the British National Health Service recently introduced price limits for drugs that qualify for customer reimbursement. In Italy, a similar restrictive list is used combined with price controls and varying levels of reimbursements. France uses a method of strict price controls to contain overall health costs, and Germany also maintains a restrictive list for some drugs but otherwise lets the companies set their own prices. In the United States, by contrast, prices for some drugs are established through negotiations between the drug company, the federal government Medicare program, and several private insurance companies that reimburse their customers for drug costs. Otherwise, prices are set by the pharmaceutical companies, with most U.S. consumers paying out-of-pocket for their own drugs.[11]

In Japan, the system is different again. The Japanese government determines the prices for reimbursement of drugs made to physicians who in turn obtain the

10. "The EEC Cracks Down on Price Discrimination," *Business Week,* December 7, 1981.

11. "Schools Brief: A Regulatory Overdose," *The Economist,* October 18, 1986, p. 78.

drugs through wholesale channels of their own. Frequently, physicians end up obtaining a discount on list prices for drugs resulting in a reimbursement that is above the physicians' own cost and, thus, allowing them to make an extra profit. The Japanese government is combating this along with mandated reductions in the reimbursement price which amounted to 9.2 percent in 1989 alone. This reduction is forced back on the pharmaceutical companies who have to lower their own prices to keep the distribution channel at the same discount levels.[12]

As a result of widely differing pricing controls, wholesale pharmaceutical prices may vary by a factor of 3 among some European countries. In general, prices tend to be higher in countries with large pharmaceutical industries, such as Great Britain and West Germany, and lower in other countries, such as France or Italy. Due to the substantial price difference for some pharmaceuticals, some wholesalers of drugs have taken to the practice of buying some drugs in countries with low price levels and selling in countries with a higher level.[13]

Price controls are of special concern in countries with high inflation rates. To compensate for inflation, companies must raise prices periodically. In Brazil, the government publishes a consumer price index quarterly, and companies try to increase prices quarterly with the rate of inflation. With rates of inflation over 100 percent, pricing flexibility is of great importance. This flexibility can at times come under pressure as when in Brazil a newly elected government announced a temporary freeze on all prices and wages. With inflation running at 3 percent per day, such a loss of pricing flexibility can become a handicap even for the most astute companies.[14]

Regulatory Factors: Dumping Regulations

The practice of selling a product at a price below actual costs is referred to as *dumping*. Most governments have adopted regulations that prevent dumping because of potential injuries to domestic manufacturers. Antidumping actions are allowed under Article 6 of the GATT as long as two criteria are met: "sales at less than fair value" and "material injury" to a domestic industry.[15] The first criterion is usually interpreted as selling abroad at prices below those in the country of origin. However, the GATT rules adopted in 1968 prohibit assessment of retroactive punitive duties and require all procedures to be open. The United States differs from GATT in its dumping regulations, determining "fair market value" and "material injury" sequentially rather than simultaneously. Also, the U.S. government will assess any duty retroactively and has on numerous occasions acted to prevent antidumping practices from injuring domestic manufacturers.

12. "Long Term Benefits from Japan's Bitter Pill," *Financial Times,* June 15, 1990, p. 21.

13. "Schools Brief: A Regulatory Overdose," *The Economist,* October 18, 1986, p. 78.

14. "How Business Is Hog-Tied in Brazil," *Business Week,* May 14, 1990, p. 52.

15. Franklin R. Root, *International Trade and Investment,* 3rd ed. (Cincinnati: Southwestern, 1973), p. 296.

TABLE 13.7 ● Past Antidumping Actions of Governments

Reporting party	Reporting period	*Initiation* No. of countries involved	*Provisional measures* No. of countries involved	*Definitive duties* No. of countries involved	*Price undertaking* No. of countries involved	*Outstanding actions*
Australia	A	40	12	8	2	150
	B	20	10	5	1	49
Brazil	B	1	—	—	—	—
Canada	A	24	12	8	2	150
	B	20	20	18	5	159
EC	A	17	12	7	11	na
	B	30	10	4	5	na
Finland	A	5	3	—	3	na
	B	5	3	—	—	na
South Korea	A	1	—	—	2	na
	B	—	—	—	—	na
Mexico	C	2	12	2	—	na
New Zealand	C	4	1	1	—	na
Sweden	A	—	2	—	2	na
	B	—	—	—	—	na
US	A	41	55	38	2	151
	B	31	13	22	—	167

A: July 1 1986–30 June 1987

B: July 1 1987–30 June 1988

C: January 1 1988—June 30 1988

na = not available

Source: General Agreement on Tariffs and Trade (Geneva). *Financial Times,* January 30, 1990, p. 3. Reprinted by permission.

The U.S. government has taken antidumping actions on numerous occasions over the past decade. In one recent case, the U.S. government charged Asian sweater makers with dumping on a volume of $1.25 billion. In another case, dumping charges were leveled against ball-bearing imports on the basis of a suit filed by a U.S. producer.[16]

16. "When One Man's Dumping Is Another Man's Good Price," *Financial Times,* May 9, 1990, p. 10.

The United States is not alone in taking antidumping action. Numerous European governments have also initiated antidumping duties for steel and other low-priced imports. In one typical action, the European Commission found Japanese exporters of dot-matrix printers in violation of dumping regulations. Covering a volume of some $1.3 billion, fifteen Japanese firms will be charged up to 47 percent of excess duties on their products. According to EC rules, these dumping charges cannot be absorbed as extra costs by the manufacturer but must be passed on as price increases to the customers.[17] International marketers have to be aware of antidumping legislation that sets a floor under export prices, limiting pricing flexibility even in the event of overcapacity or industry slowdown. On the other hand, antidumping legislation can work to a company's advantage, protecting it from unfair competition (see Table 13.7).

MANAGERIAL ISSUES IN INTERNATIONAL & GLOBAL PRICING

Now that we have given you a general overview of the context of international pricing, we direct your attention toward managerial issues. These issues are recurring and require constant management attention as they are never really considered solved. The issues are export price escalation, transfer pricing, quoting in foreign currencies, and price arbitrage.

Determining Transfer Prices

A substantial amount of international business takes place between subsidiaries of the same company. In 1983, it was estimated that among the world's largest 800 multinational companies, accounting for about 90 percent of world trade, in-house trading between subsidiaries accounted for 34 percent of those companies' volume. In 1985, Digital Equipment Corporation alone had worldwide sales of $6.7 billion, of which intercompany transfers accounted for $2 billion. As a result, the cost to the importing or buying subsidiary depends on the negotiated transfer price agreed on by the two involved units of the international firm.[18]

How these prices are set continues to be a major issue for international companies and governments alike. Because negotiations on transfer prices do not represent arms-length negotiations between independent participants, the resulting prices frequently differ from free market prices.[19]

Companies may deviate from arms-length prices for two reasons. They may

---

17. "Printers Reflect Pattern of Trade Rows," *Financial Times,* December 20, 1988, p. 3.

18. "The World's In-House Traders," *The Economist,* March 1, 1986, p. 61.

19. For a thorough conceptual treatment, see Jeffrey S. Arpan, *International Intracorporate Pricing,* (New York: Praeger Publishing, 1972).

want to (1) maximize profits or (2) minimize risk and uncertainty.[20] To pursue a strategy of profit maximization, a company may lower transfer prices for products shipped from some subsidiaries while increasing prices for products shipped to others. The company will then try to accumulate profits in subsidiaries where it is advantageous and keep profits low in other subsidiaries.

Impact of Tax Structure on Transfer Pricing   Different tax, tariff, or subsidy structures by country frequently invite such practices. By accumulating more profits in a low-tax country, a company lowers its overall tax bill and, thus, increases profit. Likewise, tariff duties can be reduced by quoting low transfer prices to countries with high tariffs. In cases where countries use different exchange rates for the transfer of goods as opposed to the transfer of capital or profits, advantages can be gained by increasing transfer prices rather than transferring profits at less advantageous rates. The same is true for countries with restrictions on profit repatriation. Furthermore, a company may want to accumulate profits in a wholly owned subsidiary rather than in one that is minority owned; by using the transfer price mechanism, it can avoid sharing profits with local partners.

Companies may also use the transfer price mechanism to minimize risk or uncertainty by moving profits or assets out of a country with chronic balance-of-payment problems and frequent devaluations. Since regular profit remittances are strictly controlled in such countries, many firms see high transfer prices as the only way to repatriate funds and, thus, reduce the amount of assets at risk. The same practice may be employed if a company anticipates political or social disturbances or a direct threat to profits through government intervention.

In actual practice, companies choose a number of approaches to transfer pricing. Market-based prices are equal to those negotiated by independent companies or at arms length. Of thirty U.S.-based firms, 46 percent were reported to use market-based systems.[21] Another 35 percent used cost-based systems to determine the transfer price. Costs were based on a predetermined formula, which may include a standard markup for profits.

Internal Considerations for Transfer Pricing   Rigorous use of the transfer pricing mechanism to reduce a company's income taxes and duties and to maximize profits in strong currency areas can create difficulties for subsidiary managers whose profits are artificially reduced. In such cases, managers may be subject to motivational problems when the direct profit incentive is removed. Furthermore, company resource allocation may become inefficient since funds are appropriated to units whose profits are artificially increased; conversely, resources may be denied to subsidiaries whose

20. Sanjaya Lall, "Transfer-Pricing by Multinational Manufacturing Firms," *Oxford Bulletin of Economics and Statistics,* August 1973, pp. 173–175.

21. Scott S. Cowen, Lawrence C. Phillips, and Linda Stillabower, "Multinational Transfer Pricing," *Management Accounting,* January 1979, pp. 7–22.

income statement was subject to transfer price-induced reductions. It is generally agreed that a transfer price mechanism should not seriously impair either morale or resource allocations, since gains incurred through tax savings may easily be lost through other inefficiencies.

External Problems with Transfer Pricing   Governments do not look favorably on transfer pricing mechanisms aimed at reducing their tax revenues. United States government policy on transfer pricing is governed by tax law, particularly Section 482 of the United States Revenue Act of 1962.[22] The act is designed to provide an accurate allocation of costs, income, and capital among related enterprises to protect United States tax revenue. The U.S. Internal Revenue Service accepts the following transfer price methods:

> Market prices are generally preferred by the IRS, either based on a comparable uncontrolled price method or a resale price method. As far as cost-plus pricing is concerned, the IRS will accept cost-plus markup if market prices are not available, and economic circumstances warrant such use. Not acceptable, however, are actual cost methods. Other methods, such as negotiated prices, are acceptable as long as the transfer price is comparable to a price charged to an unrelated party.[23]

As a result of a perceived abuse of transfer pricing methods, the U.S. Internal Revenue Service undertook a major investigation of foreign subsidiaries operating in the United States. As a group, the more than 36,000 foreign-owned subsidiaries had a negative table income and, thus, paid no taxes in the mid-1980s. In particular, the IRS investigated pricing practices of foreign companies for excessively high transfer prices that tended to reduce the income produced by the foreign subsidiary in the United States. Underpayments were reported to amount to some $12 billion for the group of companies investigated. The IRS has the authority to recompute income and tax owed by using "fair" transfer prices and, thus, assess income taxes retroactively.[24]

Quoting in a Foreign Currency

For many international marketing transactions, it is not always feasible to quote in a company's domestic currency when selling or purchasing merchandise. Although the majority of U.S. exporters quote prices in dollars, there are situations in which

22. Cowen, Phillips, and Stillabower, "Multinational Transfer Pricing," *Management Accounting,* January 1979, p. 18; and Larry J. Merville and T. William Petty: "Transfer Pricing for the Multinational Firm," *The Accounting Review,* vol. 53, October 1978, pp. 935–951.

23. Cowen, Phillips, and Stillabower, "Multinational Transfer Pricing," *Management Accounting,* January 1979, p. 19.

24. "IRS Seeks to Determine if Foreign Firms Owe Billions in U.S. Taxes," *Wall Street Journal,* February 20, 1990, p. A6.

customers may prefer quotes in their own national currency. For most import trans-actions, sellers usually quote the currency of their own country. When two currencies are involved, there is the risk that a change in exchange rates may occur between the invoicing date and the settlement date for the transaction. This risk, the foreign exchange risk, is an inherent factor in international marketing and clearly separates domestic from international business. Astro-Med Inc., a small manufacturer of high quality printers based in Warwick, Rhode Island, experienced firsthand the reaction of a customer when the export price list was quoted in U.S. dollars. During the nego-tiations for a printer quoted at $200,000, its German customer balked at being pre-sented with a price list, sales manual, and brochures, all for the U.S. market.[25] Situ-ations occur in which an exporter is able to sign an order only if the buyer's currency is used. In such circumstances special techniques are available to protect the seller from the foreign exchange risk.

The tools used to cover a company's foreign exchange risk are either (a) hedging in the forward market or (b) covering through money markets. Foreign exchange futures or options are also available but still represent only a small fraction of total volume. These alternatives are given because of the nature of foreign exchange. As we discussed in Chapter 2, for most major currencies, international foreign exchange dealers located at major banks quote a spot price and a forward price. The *spot price* determines the number of dollars to be paid for a particular foreign currency if pur-chased or sold today. The *forward price* quotes the number of dollars to be paid for a foreign currency bought or sold 30, 90, or 180 days from today. The forward price, however, is not necessarily the market's speculation as to what the spot price will be in the future. Instead, the forward price reflects interest rate differentials between two currencies for maturities of 30, 90, or 180 days. Consequently there are no firm indi-cations as to what the spot price will be for any given currency in the future. For a review of foreign exchange markets, please see Chapter 2.

A company quoting in foreign currency for purchase or sale can simply leave settlement until the due date and pay whatever spot price prevails at the time. Such an uncovered position may be chosen when exchange rates are not expected to shift, or if any shift in the near future will result in a gain for the company. With exchange rates fluctuating widely on a daily basis, even among major trading nations such as the United States, Japan, Germany, and the United Kingdom, a company will expose itself to substantial foreign exchange risks. Since many international firms are in business to make a profit from the sale of goods rather than from speculation in the foreign exchange markets, management generally protect themselves from unex-pected fluctuations.

One such protection lies in the forward market. Instead of accepting whatever spot market rate exists on the settlement in 30 or 90 days, the corporation can opt to contract for future delivery of foreign currency at a firm price, regardless of the spot

25. "Learning the Language of EC Trade," *Providence Journal-Bulletin,* March 1, 1989, p. C1.

price actually paid at that time. This allows the seller to incorporate a firm exchange rate into the price determination. Of course, if a company wishes to predict the spot price in 90 days and is reasonably certain about the accuracy of its prediction, a choice may be made between the more advantageous of the two: the expected spot or the present forward rate. However, such predictions should only be made under the guidance of experts familiar with foreign exchange rates.

An alternative strategy, called *covering through the money market,* involves borrowing funds to be converted into the currency at risk for the time until settlement. In this case, a company owes and holds the same amount of foreign currency, resulting in a corresponding loss or gain when settling at the time of payment. As an example, an exporter holding accounts receivable in deutsch marks (DM), and unwilling to absorb the related currency risk until payment is received, may borrow deutsch marks for working capital purposes. When the customer pays in the foreign currency, the loan, also denominated in that same currency, is paid off. Any fluctuations will be cancelled, therefore resulting in neither loss nor gain.

How to Incorporate a Foreign Exchange Rate into a Selling Price Quote   To illustrate the incorporation of a foreign exchange rate into a price quote for export, let us assume the following: a U.S. company needs to determine a price quote for its plastic extrusion machinery sold to a Canadian customer. The customer requested billing in Canadian dollars. The exporter, with a list price of U.S. $12,000, does not want to absorb any exchange risk. The daily foreign exchange rates on February 7, 1991 are U.S. $.8624 spot price for one Canadian dollar, or $.8545 in the 90 days forward market.[26] The exporter can directly figure the Canadian dollar price by using the forward rate, resulting in an export price of $14,043.30 in Canadian currency. Upon shipping, the exporter would sell at $14,043.30 (in Canadian money) forward with 90 days delivery and, with the rate of $.8545 per Canadian dollar, receive U.S. $12,000. Consequently, wherever possible, quotes in foreign currencies should be made based on forward rates, with respective foreign currency amounts sold in the forward market.

Selection of a Hedging Procedure   To illustrate the selection of a hedging procedure, let us assume the following situation: A U.S. exporter of computer workstations sells two machines valued at $24,000 to a client in the United Kingdom. The client will pay in British pounds quoted at the current (spot) rate (February 7, 1991) of $1.9920, or £12,048.20. This amount will be paid in three months (90 days). As a result, the U.S. exporter will have to determine how to protect such an incoming amount against foreign exchange risk. Although uncertain about the outcome, the exporter's bank indicates that there is an equal chance for the British pound spot rate to remain at $1.9920 (Scenario A), to devalue to $1.8000 (Scenario B), or to appre-

---

26. "Foreign Exchange," *Wall Street Journal,* February 8, 1991, p. C10.

ciate to $2.1800 (Scenario C). As a result, the exporter has the option of selling the amount forward in the 90 days forward market, at $1.9597.

	A	B	C
Spot rate as of February 7, 1991	$1.9920	$1.9920	$1.9920
Spot rate as of May 7, 1991 (estimate)	$1.9920	$1.8000	$2.1800
U.S. dollar equivalent of £12,048.20 at spot rates on May 7, 1991	$24,000.00	$21,686.75	$26,265.10
Exchange gain (loss) with hedging	—0—	($2,313.25)	$2,465.10

The alternative available to the exporter is to sell forward the invoice amount of £12,048.20 at $1.9597 to obtain a sure $23,610.85, a loss of $389.15 on the transaction. In anticipation of a devaluation of the pound, such a hedging strategy would be advisable. Consequently the $389.15 represents a premium to ensure against any larger loss. However, a company would also forego any gain as indicated under Scenario C. Acceptance for hedging through the forward market depends on the expected spot rate at the time the foreign payment is due. Again, it should be kept in mind that the forward rate is not an estimate of the spot rate in the future.

Dealing with Parallel Imports or Gray Markets

One of the most perplexing problems international companies face is the phenomenon of different prices between countries. When such price differentials become large, individual buyers or independent entrepreneurs step in and buy products in low-price countries to re-export to high-price countries while profiting from the price differential. This arbitrage behavior creates what experts call the "gray market" or "parallel imports" because these imports take place outside of the regular trade channels controlled by distributors or company-owned sales subsidiaries. Such price differences can occur as a result of company price strategy, margin differences, or currency fluctuations.

Pricing differently for its domestic market and export markets, the U.K. car manufacturers created a price gap that caused an active parallel import market. During the late 1970s, prices for cars in the United Kingdom were increased in line with the relatively high inflation. However, the British were not in a position to pass on these increases in European export markets, thus resulting in very high car prices in the United Kingdom.[27] As shown in Table 13.8, U.K. car prices were considerably higher than those of the lowest country (Denmark) when adjusted for local taxes.[28]

27. "Car Prices: What Common Market?" *The Economist,* May 3, 1980, p. 75.
28. "European Car Prices: Single Market, Double Cross?" *The Economist,* January 13, 1990, p. 48.

TABLE 13.8 ● Average Pre-Tax Car Prices

	1987	1989
Denmark	100	100
Greece	n.a.	107
Belgium	121	123
Luxembourg	122	127
Holland	122	130
France	128	132
West Germany	128	137
Portugal	127	140
Ireland	130	145
Italy	129	148
Spain	142	149
Britain	144	161

Cheapest = 100

Source: The Economist, January 13, 1990, p. 48 © 1990 The Economist Newspaper Limited. Reprinted by permission.

In response to this difference, British buyers started to go to Belgium to purchase their cars. When British Leyland and other U.K. car manufacturers tried to contain the flow of parallel imports, or gray market cars, the British government stepped in to protect the private consumer.[29] As a result, car companies could not take direct measures against these practices other than by lowering prices in their domestic market or increasing prices abroad. Both the European Commission and the British government have continued to investigate price differences. The British government has pointed out that prices for cars in the United Kingdom remain some 30 percent higher than those in Belgium, a country with typically lower prices. European regulations permit British buyers to buy cars in Belgium and prohibit policies of car manufacturers aimed at stopping such practices.[30]

Fluctuating currency values can also create opportunities for parallel imports as we have observed earlier in this chapter. This can affect even U.S. companies, as experienced by Duracell, the U.S. battery producer.[31] This company maintained a manufacturing facility in Belgium as well as in the United States. When the dollar began to appreciate against European currencies, some U.S. retailers and wholesalers

29. "The Coming Car Price Crash," *The Economist,* December 12, 1981, p. 62.
30. "UK Car Pricing to be Investigated," *Financial Times,* May 10, 1990, p. 22.
31. "Duracell Attacks U.S. Gray Market," *Financial Times,* February 23, 1984, p. 6.

realized they could profit by importing Belgian-made batteries. Such purchases turned out to be at least 20 percent below those of Duracell's list price in the United States. Duracell saw its profitability threatened because it earned more on U.S.-produced batteries. Although the company tried to have this practice ruled illegal, in most countries parallel imports are not against the law.

For the United States alone, parallel or gray market volume was estimated to be $6 billion at retail level in 1984.[32] However, parallel imports are not restricted to consumer products. With the legal situation in the United States favoring the official importer or distributor, companies have used other methods in the United States. Vivitar began to code all of its products according to the intended market. The company notified its distributors that agreements would be terminated if parallel export products were traced to them. Other camera producers changed their names on products or did not extend warranty coverage to parallel exports.

International companies can deal with parallel or gray markets at two levels. Once such practices occur, a firm may use a number of strategies in a reactive way. This may range from confronting the culprit to price cutting, supply interference, emphasis of product limitations, all the way to acquisition of the diverter involved. A number of proactive strategies may be implemented to prevent the practice from occurring at all. A company may provide product differentiation solely to prevent gray markets from developing. Strategic pricing may be used to keep prices within limits. Cooperation may be achieved with dealers willing to cooperate. And finally, companies may use strict legal enforcement of contracts and even resort to lobbying governments with the aim of adding regulations that may prevent the practice.[33]

In some industries, independent businesses have sprung up to take advantage of such price differentials. These businesses, often referred to as diverters, work worldwide and are very quick to spot opportunities. A Belgian businessman acquired low-priced Colgate toothpaste in Brazil where it was made under license for local and regional markets. This Brazilian version was sold in the United Kingdom where it was marketed some 15 percent below regular retail prices. However, the Brazilian version was made with locally sourced chalk, a lower quality version than that used by Colgate elsewhere. Furthermore, the unexpected export volume created a local shortage in a country where imports were not allowed. The practice was eventually stopped as the diverter was found guilty of selling inferior merchandise by a British court.[34]

Product arbitrage will always occur when price differentials get too large and when transport costs are low in relation to product value. International companies will have to match price differentials more closely for standardized products in particular. Products that are highly differentiated from country to country are also less likely to become parallel traded.

32. "The Assault on the Right to Buy Cheap Imports," *Fortune,* January 7, 1985, p. 89.

33. S. Tamer Cavusgil and Ed Sikora, "How Multinationals Can Counter Gray Market Imports," *Columbia Journal of World Business,* Winter 1988, p. 75–85.

34. "Colgate Takes a Diverter to Task," *Financial Times,* April 14, 1989, p. 6.

Managing Export Price Escalation

The additional costs described earlier may raise the end-user price of an exported product substantially above its domestic price. This phenomenon, called export price escalation may force a company to adopt any one of two strategic patterns. First, a company may realize its price disadvantage and adjust the marketing mix to account for its "luxury" status. By adopting such a strategy, a company sacrifices volume to keep a high unit price. Alternatively, a company may grant a "discount" on the standard domestic price to bring the end-user price more in line with prices paid by domestic customers. Such discounts may be justified under marginal contribution pricing methods. Because of reduced marketing costs at the manufacturer's level, particularly when a foreign distributor is used, an export price equal to a domestic price is often not justified. Legal limits such as antidumping regulations prevent price reductions below a certain point. Customary margins, both wholesale and retail, may differ considerably among countries, with independent importers frequently requiring higher margins than domestic middlemen.

Global Pricing Strategies

As international companies deal with market and environmental factors, they face two major strategic pricing alternatives. Essentially, the choice is between the global, single-price strategy and the individualized country strategy.

To maximize a company's revenues it would appear to be logical to set prices on a market-by-market basis, looking in each market for the best combination of revenue versus volume yielding maximum profit. This strategy had been common for many firms in the early part of their international development. For many products, however, noticeable price differences between markets are taken advantage of by independent companies or channel members who see a profit from buying in lower-price markets and exporting products to high-price markets. For products that are relatively similar in many markets, and where transportation costs are not significant, substantial price differences will quickly result in the emergence of the gray market. As a result, fewer companies have the possibility of pricing on a market-by-market basis. As the markets become more transparent, the information flows more efficiently; and as products become more similar, the trend away from market-by-market pricing is likely to continue.

McDonald's, the leading U.S. fast food chain, has taken the route of pricing its products according to local market conditions. Its key product, the Big Mac, ranges in price from $1.10 (U.S.) in Hong Kong to $6.25 in the Soviet Union, with most countries in the range from $2 to $4.00.[35] (See Table 13.9 for more comparisons.) Certainly, McDonald's can maximize its pricing according to the competitive forces of each individual country without much fear of parallel imports.

For many consumer products, there are still substantial differences in the price

35. "The Hamburger Stand," *The Economist*, May 5, 1990, p. 128.

TABLE 13.9 ● International Prices of McDonald's Big Mac in Key Foreign Countries

Country	Price in local currency	Actual exchange rate April 30, 1990	Price at actual exchange rates in U.S. dollars	Purchasing power parity*	Percentage over (+) or under (−) valuation of the dollar
Australia	A$2.30	1.32	1.74	1.05	+20
Belgium	BFr 97	34.65	2.80	44.00	−21
Britain	£ 1.40	0.61	2.30	0.64	−5
Canada	C$2.19	1.16	1.89	1.00	+16
Denmark	DKr 25.50	6.39	4.00	11.00	−45
France	FFr 17.70	5.63	3.14	8.05	−30
Holland	FL 5.25	1.88	2.80	2.39	−21
Hongkong	HK$8.60	7.79	1.10	3.90	+100
Ireland	IR£ 1.30	0.63	2.06	0.59	+7
Italy	Lire 3900	1230	3.17	1773	−31
Japan	¥ 370	159	2.33	168	−5
Singapore	S$ 2.60	1.88	1.38	1.18	+50
S. Korea	Won 2100	707	2.97	955	−26
Soviet Union	Rouble 3.75	0.60	6.25	1.70	−65
Spain	Ptas 295	106	2.78	134	−21
Sweden	SKr 24	6.10	3.93	10.90	−44
United States	$ 2.20	—	2.20	—	—
W. Germany	DM 4.30	1.68	2.56	1.95	−14
Yugoslavia	Dinar 16	11.72	1.37	7.27	+61

*Received by dividing the local currency price of a Big Mac by its U.S. dollar price.
Source: The Economist, May 5, 1990, p. 128. © 1990 The Economist Newspaper Limited. Reprinted with permission.

across many countries. For a selective list of consumer products across major European cities, see Table 13.10. Differences in pretax retail prices tend to hide a number of inefficiencies in retail distribution systems, such as the preponderance of large-volume and low-price chains in the United Kingdom versus the dominance of small retail shops in Italy. Other factors are competitive, such that Heinz tends to price its products lower in countries where it is not leading, and Levi's jeans prices are high in Spain where they are viewed as fashion items rather than casual wear.[36]

Employing a uniform pricing strategy on a global scale requires that a company can determine its prices in local currency but, when translated into a base currency,

36. "Counting Costs of Dual Pricing in the Run-up to 1992," *The Financial Times,* July 9, 1990, p. 4.

TABLE 13.10 ● Price Comparisons of Consumer Products Across European Cities

	Lowest*		Highest*		Price coefficient**
Bosch 500-2 power drill	Brussels	70.94–56.75	Milan	99.34–83.48	1.47
Bosch 4542 washing machine	London	462.69–402.34	Milan	672.74–565.33	1.40
Braun Silencio hairdryer	London	18.44–16.03	Athens	50.60–43.62	2.72
Coca-Cola, 1.5l bottle	Amsterdam	.82–.69	Copenhagen	2.04–1.45	2.10
Colgate toothpaste, 100ml	Athens	1.33–1.15	Milan	1.88–1.72	1.50
EMI Compact disc: Tina Turner "Foreign Affair"	Athens	14.39–12.41	Madrid	21.72–19.39	1.36
EMI cassette of same	London	8.7–7.57	Copenhagen	21.84–17.9	2.36
Financial Times	London	.67–.67	Copenhagen	1.54–1.54	2.30
Gillette Contour razor blades, 5-pack	Athens	1.99–1.72	Copenhagen	3.53–2.76	1.60
Heinz ketchup, 570gm	London	.86–.86	Madrid	2.04–1.92	1.98
Hitachi 630 videorecorder	London	452.17–393.19	Athens	749.64–551.21	1.40
Hoover 3726 vacuum cleaner	Luxembourg	118.31–105.63	Amsterdam	260.31–219.67	2.08
IBM 30-021 personal computer, 20MB, color display	Athens	1629.21–1404.49	Copenhagen	4065.75–3332.58	2.37
Kelloggs cornflakes, 375gm	Amsterdam	1.26–1.06	Cologne	1.95–1.82	1.72
Kodak 35mm Gold 100 film	Cologne	3.4–2.98	Copenhagen	5.98–4.90	1.64
Levi's 501 jeans	London	50.01–43.49	Madrid	74.65–66.85	1.53
Mars Bar	London	.27–.27	Copenhagen	.67–.55	2.04
Nescafé, 200gm	Athens	3.67–3.16	Milan	7.78–7.14	2.26
Olivetti ET65 electronic typewriter	Brussels	331.37–278.48	Lisbon	638.37–545.62	1.96
Pampers, Midi 52, boy's	Dublin	10.47–8.51	Milan	11.70–10.73	1.26
Sony 2121 television	London	536.45–466.48	Copenhagen	1091.74–894.87	1.92
Timotel shampoo, 200ml	London	1.23–1.07	Amsterdam	2.09–1.76	1.64
Toblerone, 100gm	Amsterdam	.85–.72	Lisbon	1.49–1.38	1.92

*Prices in Ecu, converted at rate of April 27, 1990. The first set of figures in each column is the retail price, the second the price before tax. **Ratio of highest to lowest pre-tax prices.

Source: *Financial Times*, July 9, 1990, p. 4. Reprinted by permission.

will always charge the same price everywhere. In reality, this becomes very difficult to achieve whenever different taxes, trade margins, and customs duties are involved. As a result, there are likely to be price differences resulting from those factors not under control of the company. Keeping prices identical aside from those noncontrollable factors are a challenge. Firms may start out with identical prices in various countries but soon find that prices have to change to stay in line with often substantial currency fluctuations.

Although it is becoming increasingly clear for many companies that market-by-market pricing strategies will cause difficulties, many firms have experienced that moving to a uniform pricing policy is rather like pursuing a moving target. Even when a global pricing policy is adopted, a company must carefully monitor price levels in each country and avoid large gaps that can then cause problems when independent or gray market forces move in and take advantage of large price differentials.

FINANCING INTERNATIONAL MARKETING TRANSACTIONS

As many international marketers have observed, the ability to make financing available at a low cost can become the deciding factor that beats competitors. In the context of international marketing, financing should be understood in its broadest sense (see Figure 13.2). Not only does it consist of direct credits to the buyer, it also includes a range of activities that enable the customer to afford the purchase. In this section we examine financing provided by the selling company, as well as financing through the financial community and government-sponsored agencies.

Financing international marketing transactions involves a host of risks over and above those encountered by strictly domestic operations. International companies have to be aware of these risks and understand the methods available for reducing risk to an acceptable level. The four major risks include commercial risk, foreign currency risk, transfer risk, and political risk.

Commercial risk refers to buyer ability to pay for the products or services ordered. This risk is also typical for a domestic operation. As a result, companies are accustomed to checking the financial stability of their customers and may even have internally approved credit limits. Although checking credit references in a domestic environment poses no great difficulty, such information is not always readily available in many overseas markets. Companies can rely on their banks or on foreign credit reporting agencies where such organizations exist. Past experience with a commercial customer abroad may frequently be the only indicator of a firm's financial stability.

Foreign currency risk exists whenever a company bills in a currency other than its own.[37] For U.S. companies billing in Japanese yen, a currency risk exists because

37. Chuck C. Y. Kwok, "Hedging Foreign Exchange Exposures: Independent versus Integrative Approaches," *Journal of International Business Studies,* Summer 1987, p. 33.

FIGURE 13.2 ● Financing International Marketing Transactions

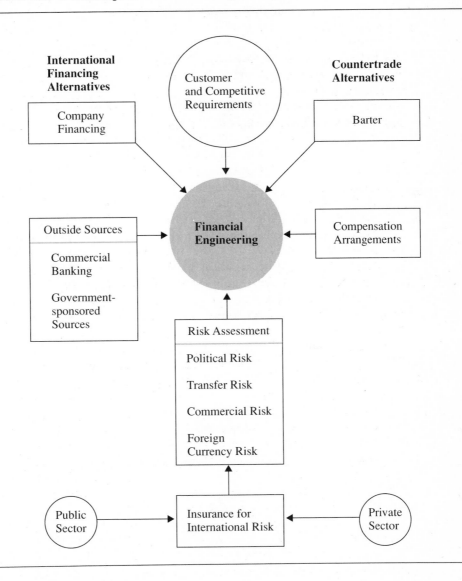

the value of the yen versus the dollar is subject to market fluctuations and, therefore, cannot be determined at the outset. Foreign currency risk grows with the length of credit terms and with the instability of a foreign currency. Suppliers can insure themselves against foreign currency fluctuations, as was described in more detail earlier in this chapter.

Invoicing in their own currency, suppliers shift the currency risk to the customer. The customer may not be in a position to cover that risk, as is the case in many countries with unsophisticated financial markets. In such a case, the exporting company frequently must choose between selling in a foreign currency or no deal at all.

Although the customer may be able to pay, payments often get delayed by bureaucracies, creating a *transfer risk.* Transfer delays prevail in countries where the foreign exchange market is controlled and where the customer has to apply for the purchase of foreign currency before payment takes place. Delays of up to 180 days beyond the credit terms agreed on are not unusual and add to the costs of exporter or supplier. In countries where a foreign exchange shortage prevents immediate payment of all foreign currency denominated debts, complex debt restructuring negotiations may take place, causing additional delays. Many countries have had to negotiate such extensions at one time or another, including Brazil, Mexico, Argentina, Turkey, Poland, and Zaire.

Financing for international marketing operations is also subject to *political risk,* which includes the occurrence of war, revolutions, insurgencies, or civil unrest, any of which may result in nonpayment of accounts receivable. In some instances, civil unrest may demand rescheduling of foreign trade debt, as was the case in Poland in the early 1980s. In other situations, political unrest may bring about a new government that cancels foreign debt, as was the case in Iran following the downfall of the shah.

The international marketer needs to understand the risks of providing financing to customers. In cases where the supplier shoulders all international risks, companies may want to build extra costs into their prices. Smaller price adjustments may be required when only a portion of the international credit risk is carried.

CUSTOMER VERSUS SUPPLIER-ARRANGED FINANCING

As discussed in this section, financing arranged by suppliers goes beyond the open account practices that will be described in Chapter 18. In this context, supplier financing is viewed as any term beyond the usual 30 to 90 days customary for open account shipment.

Because credit risks are higher for clients abroad, companies have a preference for shorter payment terms with foreign clients. However, many customers may not be able to purchase under shortened credit terms. Consequently, companies may charge an interest rate on the outstanding amount. When companies cannot get at least market interest rates, they may try to capture the additional cash through higher prices. However, most clients today are adept at comparing total costs to themselves, and opportunities for hiding interest cost behind higher list prices are limited.

Since most companies do not consider themselves to be in the business of financing their customers, they prefer to assist clients in finding suitable financing opportunities. One such exception is financing without recourse, a relatively new method for financing shipments abroad, which is explained below.

SOURCES OF FINANCING

Companies can choose from a wide selection of alternatives to finance international marketing transactions: traditional financing through commercial banks, government-sponsored loans, or countertrade. The international marketer is increasingly expected to be knowledgeable about complicated financial arrangements. As buyers compare acquisition costs, including any necessary financing, providing such financing becomes a matter for international marketing management to handle. The following sections are intended to offer you a general background on the most common financing alternatives practiced by many international companies today.

Financing Through Commercial Banks

Commercial banks, whether domestic or foreign, are usually willing to finance transactions only to first-rate credit risks. This fact makes financing unavailable to any but the largest companies. Furthermore, commercial banks avoid long-term financing and prefer short maturities. Commercial banks that have loaned heavily to developing countries have recently experienced difficulties with repayment and interest payments on outstanding loan portfolios. Therefore banks located in developed countries have hesitated to loan further to developing countries, forcing exporters to look elsewhere to finance their clients.

Clients outside the developed countries of Europe and Asia have also found local financing difficult. Especially for purchases in currencies other than their own, foreign buyers in developing countries are increasingly dependent on financing from abroad. For larger industrial projects, this is now almost the rule. With commercial banks only partially able to close the gap, both buyers and suppliers are availing themselves of other financing sources.

Forfaiting: Financing Without Recourse[38]

Forfaiting or financing without recourse means that the seller of merchandise can transfer a claim, resulting from a transaction in the form of a bill of exchange, to a

---

38. This section is based upon *Forfaiting,* Finanz A. G., Zurich, Switzerland, 1986, p. 6.

forfaiting house by including the term "without recourse" as part of the endorsement. The collection risk is thus transferred to the forfaiting house, and the seller receives on presentation of documents the full amount minus a discount for the entire credit period. The discount varies with the country risk and the currency chosen for financing. Typical maturities range from six months to several years.

Nonrecourse financing offers the advantage of selling products over medium terms at market rates. Such transactions are not possible through commercial banks. An exporter may obtain a firm quote on a given business deal ahead of time, allowing inclusion of the discount rate into the price calculation. This assures that the net payout meets normal profitability standards. For capital equipment exporting countries such as Germany and Switzerland, approximately 5 to 10 percent of exports are arranged through this financing technique. However, there are limitations to this financing method. For countries that are poor credit risks, forfait transactions are not possible.[39] Transaction size is usually under ten million dollars, although larger amounts may be financed through several institutions that together form an ad hoc consortium or syndicate.

Government-Sponsored Financing

With ability to assemble the best financing package often determining the sale of capital equipment or other large volume transactions, governments all over the world have realized that government-sponsored banks can foster exports and, therefore, employment. Government-subsidized financing now exceeds that which commercial banks and exporters formerly provided. For this purpose the United States created its Export-Import Bank (Exim for short) in 1934. Other countries, particularly members of the Organization for Economic Cooperation and Development (OECD), have established their own export banks also aimed at assisting their respective exporters with the financing of large transactions.

Japan committed $7.9 billion in 1987 to provide export insurance for developing countries and political risk insurance for Japanese companies investing overseas. The export insurance plan will cover up to 97.5 percent of the value for prepaid contracts.[40]

The Export-Import Bank[41]

The Export-Import Bank and its affiliated institutions, the Foreign Credit Insurance Association (FCIA) and the Private Export Funding Corporation (PEFCO), make a

39. Gino Giuliato, "Forfaitierung," Der Monat (Swiss Bank Corporation), March 1989, p. 24.

40. "Japan to Commit Almost $8 Billion to Trade Insurance," *Wall Street Journal,* March 31, 1987, p. 48.

41. This segment draws heavily from official publications of the Export-Import Bank of the United States, Washington, D. C., 1979.

number of services available to U.S. exporters. Exim has special services for short-term, medium-term, and long-term financing requirements. See Figure 13.3 for a depiction of the financing process.

Short-Term Financing Financing requirements of 180 days or less are considered short-term. For such commitments Eximbank does not make direct financing available. Instead, through the Foreign Credit Insurance Association (FCIA), Eximbank offers export credit insurance to the U.S. exporter. This insurance covers the exporter for commercial risk, such as nonpayment by the foreign buyer; political risk, such as war, revolution, insurrection, expropriation; and currency inconvertibility. The cost of such insurance averages less than half of 1 percent per $100 of gross invoice value. With such insurance in force, the exporter has the choice of carrying accounts receivable on the company records or refinancing with a commercial bank at domestic interest rates, provided the transaction is insured. In general, commercial risks are insured up to 90 percent of the invoiced value. Political risks are covered for up to 100 percent of the merchandise value, depending on the type of policy selected.

In 1983, about 7.5 billion dollars or 3.8 percent of U.S. exports were insured by FCIA.[42] Total premium costs were about 0.2 percent of the insured volume. In the same year, FCIA paid out $193 million to exporters or banks financing such trade. For the past few years, U.S. firms have enjoyed lower export insurance rates than those available in other countries. Companies in Sweden and Western Germany paid 3.4 and 2.3 percent respectively.

Medium-Term Financing Eximbank classifies terms ranging from 181 days to 5 years as medium-term. To serve exporters, four special programs exist: the medium-term export credit insurance (FCIA) programs, the U.S. Commercial Bank Guarantee program, the Discount Loan Program, and the Cooperative Financing Facility.

Several insurance alternatives are available through FCIA. Provided the foreign buyer makes a cash payment of 15 percent on or before delivery, and subject to a deductible of 10 percent, Eximbank will insure each specific transaction. Through the cooperation of nearly 300 U.S. commercial banks, Eximbank organized the U.S. Commercial Bank Guarantee Program. Under this program, Eximbank offers protection against commercial and political risks on debts acquired by U.S. banks from U.S. exporters. This coverage is now extended to more than 140 countries. Conditions for the guarantee program include a cash payment of 15 percent by the foreign buyer, a deductible of 10 percent, and passing credit checks imposed by Eximbank and the participating commercial bank. The interest rate is set by the commercial bank according to prevailing domestic market conditions.

42. *Der Monat,* publication of Swiss Bank Corporation, Basle, Switzerland, April 1985.

FIGURE 13.3 ● Export Import Bank Financing

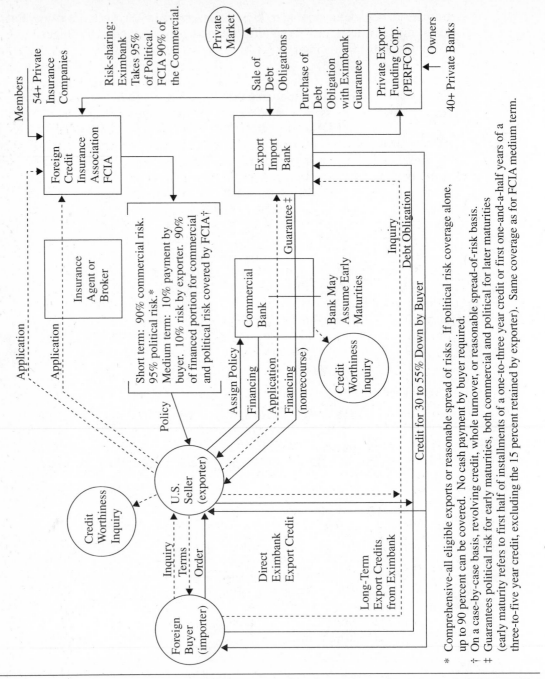

Source: Figure from *International Business Management,* Second Edition, by Richard D. Robinson, Copyright © 1978, by the Dryden Press, reprinted by permission of the publisher.

Long-Term Financing   Long-term financing by Eximbank extends from five to ten years. Under special circumstances, as in the case of conventional or nuclear power plants, financing may be arranged for longer periods. Financing may occur either by direct credit to the foreign buyer or by a guarantee assuring repayment of private financing arranged by the buyer. Eximbank requires a 15 percent downpayment by the foreign buyer and assurance that private financing is not possible on similar terms. In the past, foreign airlines and utilities have made frequent use of such facilities to finance purchases of aircraft and power-generating equipment.

In general, Eximbank programs do not extend direct financing to the U.S. exporter. Rather, the bank closes the gap between commercial bank financing and foreign buyer needs by guarantees or financing for the foreign buyer.

The Value of Eximbank Loans to U.S. Exporters   Although less than 10 percent of U.S. exports are financed through Eximbank, loans at lower than market rates are crucial to exporters of many products. In 1980, about $3 billion of Boeing Company's $5 billion in exports were financed by Eximbank.[43] In 1981, more than 2,600 firms used the services of Eximbank.[44] Researchers estimated that Eximbank operations in 1980 supported about 570,000 U.S. jobs.

Another U.S. company that has relied heavily on Eximbank financing is J. I. Case, one of the nation's leading farm equipment manufacturers. With foreign sales accounting for nearly half of company business, Eximbank credit helps it compete with European and Japanese manufacturers that can profit from low-cost government export financing. In 1980, a $10.4 million contract with the Dominican Republic was facilitated by an 8 percent loan for $3.5 million to the buyers. Also in 1980, a five-year loan at 7.75 percent helped clinch a deal with Israel.[45]

Eximbank support of U.S. exporters depends on funding from the U.S. government. United States exporters have in the past lobbied heavily to expand Eximbank funding, hoping to receive more loans at more favorable rates. However, many critics argue that Eximbank serves large firms that are already profitable. It is expected that the political debate surrounding Eximbank will continue and that its lending authority will vary as Congress appropriates differing fund levels from year to year.

For smaller companies, access to the full range of government-sponsored export financing is still difficult. Large commercial banks with the sophistication to help do not like to make small loans. On the other hand, the small local banks who handle the banking business for small companies do not have the resources and experience to assist in international export financing. As a result, several U.S. states, California among them, have set up their own state-sponsored export financing schemes for

43. "U.S. Firms Already Cut Back Work as Result of Ex-Im Bank Restraints," *Wall Street Journal,* March 31, 1981, p. 35.
44. "U.S. Companies and Unions Fight to Save Exim Bank from Budget Knife," *Business International,* May 14, 1982, p. 153.
45. "Banking on Ex-Im," *Time,* March 2, 1981, p. 28.

transactions of about $500,000 or less. California guarantees 85 percent repayment on loans used to finance working capital or accounts receivable tied to export orders. Illinois will even lend the bank of the small firm up to 90 percent of the funds needed to make export-related loans. More than ten U.S. states have started similar programs.[46]

COMPETING AGAINST EXPORT CREDIT BANKS OF FOREIGN NATIONS

Most developed nations of North America, Europe, and Asia maintain programs to finance exports from their own countries. To the extent that internal loan conditions differ from those offered by other countries, an exporter from a given country may have an advantage. United States Eximbank rates are usually higher than those offered by other export banks in other countries. To prevent an interest rate "war" from developing, leading industrial nations have agreed to minimum rates and loans for various groups of countries. Such agreements are renegotiated periodically, and the U.S. government has taken a lead in such negotiations.[47]

The Eximbank has an active intermediary program to loan money to banks at 150 basis points below OECO consensus rates for loans valued at less than one million dollars. These funds are designated to finance medium and small exporters for small transactions.[48]

FINANCIAL ENGINEERING: A NEW MARKETING TOOL

With financing costs becoming ever more important for capital goods, many companies have moved toward exploiting the best financial deal from bases around the world. A company with manufacturing bases in several countries may bid on a contract from several subsidiaries to let the client select the most advantageous package, or it may preselect the subsidiary that will bid based on available financing. Devising such financial packages is known as financial engineering. It is practiced by independent specialists located in leading financial centers and by international banks that have developed expertise in this field.

46. "States Launch Efforts to Make Small Firms Better Exporters," *Wall Street Journal,* February 2, 1987, p. 25.

47. "U.S. Overcomes EEC Resistance," *Financial Times,* July 5, 1982, p. 4.

48. Business International, "What's New at Eximbank and Why U.S. Exporters Should Take Another Look, *Weekly Report to Managers of Worldwide Operations,* March 30, 1987, pp. 98–99.

An example of financial engineering is offered by Massey-Ferguson, Ltd., a Canadian farm machinery manufacturer.[49] Massey-Ferguson had traditionally supplied tractors to Turkey from its U.K. plants. Turkey experienced balance of payments difficulty, and the company met problems obtaining credit for the country. Massey-Ferguson looked to its other manufacturing bases for new sources of financing. The best deal was offered by Brazil, a country eager to expand its exports. Brazilians helped convince the Turkish customer Mafer to buy Brazilian-made equipment in U.S. dollars.

Massey sold 7,200 tractors worth $53 million to a Brazilian agency which in turn sold to the Turkish buyer. Massey was to be paid cash and a Brazilian state agency guaranteed payment. Thus, Brazil was able to take business of about 20,000 tractors annually from the United Kingdom because it assumed all risk for Massey-Ferguson.

Other companies are now institutionalizing financial engineering in their global operations. Some maintain full-time specialists at their international divisions who are prepared to advise operating divisions on financial engineering opportunities in bidding. One division of a company with manufacturing operations in several countries frequently submits bids from several of its plants and lets the customer select the most desirable package. This strategy works best if products are highly standardized and quality differences between the various plants are minimal.

NONCASH PRICING: COUNTERTRADE

International marketers are likely to find many situations in which an interested customer will not be able to find any hard currency financing at all. In such circumstances, the customer might offer a product or commodity in return. The supplier must then turn the product offered into hard currency. Such transactions, known as countertrade, are estimated to have accounted for 8 to 10 percent of world trade or more than $200 billion in 1985. Other private sources have estimated countertrade as high as 30 percent of world trade and expect it to climb steadily in the future.[50]

The U.S. International Trade Commission surveyed 500 of the largest U.S. companies accounting for some 60 percent of U.S. exports on their use of countertrade. For 1984, the survey found that 5.6 percent of those firms' exports were covered by some part of a countertrade arrangement, totaling U.S. $7.1 billion. About 80 percent of this volume was accounted for by military equipment sales. Nonmilitary countertrade grew from $285 million in 1980 to $1.4 billion in 1984.[51]

49. "How Massey-Ferguson Uses Brazil for Export Financing," *Business Week,* March 17, 1978, p. 86.
50. "Beleaguered Third World Leads the Barter Boom," *Financial Times,* February 28, 1984, p. 6.
51. "Countertrade Comes Out of the Closet," *The Economist,* December 20, 1986, p. 89.

Forms of countertrade have always been popular between Comecon countries (U.S.S.R. and Eastern Europe) and Western countries. For that region, countertrade was estimated to represent about 15 percent of international trade, twice the average for the rest of the world.[52] A study by a private research firm reported that in the early 1970s some fifteen countries insisted on countertrade in some circumstances. By the end of the 1970s, this number had doubled, and by 1985 it had risen to more than fifty countries.[53] The recent changes in the political situation in the Comecon area have not eliminated the need for countertrade. The Eastern European countries, including the Soviet Union, remain plagued by a scarcity of foreign exchange. Instead of involving just government-sponsored foreign trade organizations, many more private or privatized companies are now looking to help themselves through such methods. Kotva, Czechoslovakia's leading department store, could not get access to sufficient Western goods even after the liberalization there in late 1989. The store traded Czech paper for Lego toys and Czech cheese for Italian vermouth.[54] To respond to this challenge, international marketers have developed several forms of countertrade (see Figure 13.4). The purpose of the following sections is to explain each one and then examine the problems associated with each.[55]

Barter

Barter, one of the most basic types of countertrade, consists of a direct exchange of goods between two parties. In most cases, these transactions take place between two or more nations (three in case of triangular barter). Barter involves no currency and is concluded without the help of intermediaries. Barter has become less common while other forms of countertrade have become more popular.[56]

One of the largest barter deals in recent years valued at about $3 billion was signed by PepsiCo and the Soviet Union. Since 1974, PepsiCo had engaged in business with the Soviet Union shipping soft-drink syrup, bottling it into Pepsi-Cola, and marketing it within the Soviet Union. By 1989, the business had reached some 40 million cases (each containing twenty-four 8-ounce bottles). Within the Soviet Union, PepsiCo was running some twenty-six bottling plants, all running at full capacity. The volume amounted to about $300 million for 1989. Since hard currency was not available for take out profits, PepsiCo had entered an agreement to export Stolichnaya vodka to the United States where it was sold through an inde-

---

52. David B. Yoffie, "Barter: Looking Beyond the Short-Term Payoffs and Long-Term Threat," *International Management,* August 1984, p. 36.

53. "Countertrade Comes Out of the Closet," *The Economist,* December 20, 1986 p. 89.

54. "Czech Retailer Leads in Effort for Western Goods," *New York Times,* November 26, 1990, p. D7.

55. The terminology used in this section is based on *Barter, Compensation and Cooperation,* Credit Suisse, Publication Vol. 47 IV, Zurich, Switzerland, 1978.

56. See Henry Ferguson, "Tomorrow's Global Manager Will Use Countertrade," *Corporate Barter and Countertrade,* July 1987.

FIGURE 13.4 ● Forms of Countertrade

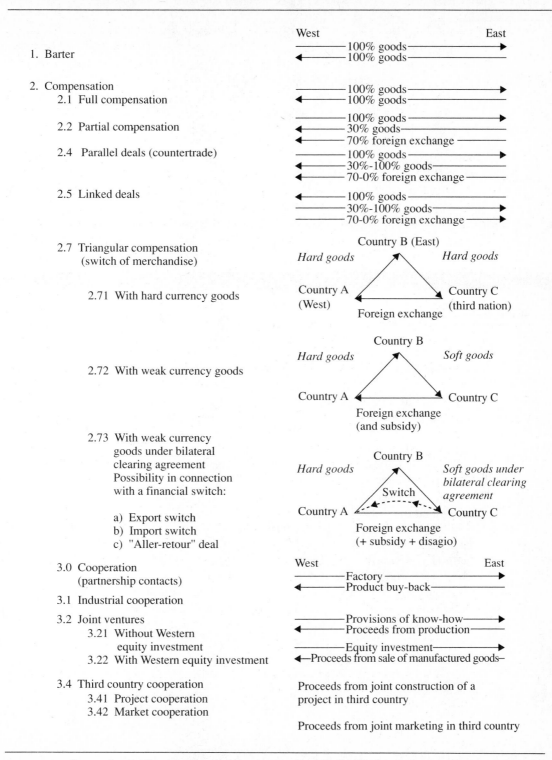

1. Barter

2. Compensation
    2.1 Full compensation

    2.2 Partial compensation

    2.4 Parallel deals (countertrade)

    2.5 Linked deals

    2.7 Triangular compensation
        (switch of merchandise)

        2.71 With hard currency goods

        2.72 With weak currency goods

        2.73 With weak currency
            goods under bilateral
            clearing agreement
            Possibility in connection
            with a financial switch:

            a) Export switch
            b) Import switch
            c) "Aller-retour" deal

    3.0 Cooperation
        (partnership contacts)

    3.1 Industrial cooperation

    3.2 Joint ventures
        3.21 Without Western
            equity investment
        3.22 With Western equity investment

    3.4 Third country cooperation
        3.41 Project cooperation
        3.42 Market cooperation

Source: Barter, Compensation and Cooperation, Credit Suisse, Zurich, Switzerland, Vol. 47, IV, 1978, pp. 8–9. Reprinted by permission.

pendent liquor company. That volume had reached some one million cases (each containing twelve 25-ounce bottles) or about $156 million in sales. In 1990, a new deal was signed that included the sale or the lease of at least ten Soviet tanker ships ranging from 28,000 to 65,000 tons. The proceeds of these transactions are to be used to expand the on-going PepsiCo business in the Soviet Union by expanding Pepsi-Cola into national distribution and to fund the expansion of the Pizza Hut restaurant chain.[57]

Compensation Arrangements

Compensation arrangements are transactions that include payment in merchandise or foreign exchange. Depending on the type of arrangement, the method or structure of the compensation transaction may change. One usually speaks of a compensation transaction when the value of an export delivery is offset by an import transaction or vice versa. Compensation transactions are typical for large governmental purchases, such as for defense, when a country wants to obtain some extra exports for the import of defense systems. Currently outstanding offset trade obligations were estimated at about $50 billion worldwide, a large amount of that incurred by U.S.-based aerospace and defense contractors.[58] Compensation transactions may be classified into several categories as described below.

Full Compensation versus Partial Compensation   Full compensation is similar to barter in that a 100 percent mutual transfer of goods takes place. However, deliveries are made and paid for separately. Upon signing the sales agreement, the exporter commits to purchase products or services at an amount equal to that specified in the export contract. An option exists to sell such a commitment to a third party who may take over the commitment from the exporter for a fee.

Under partial compensation, the exporter receives a portion of the purchase price in hard currency and the remainder in merchandise. The exporter will actually not be able to convert such merchandise into cash until a buyer can be found, and even then only at a discount.

A partial compensation transaction was concluded in 1981 by Honda, a Japanese car manufacturer, and the Algerian government to cover 15,000 passenger cars valued at $50 million. When Algeria could not pay in hard currency as a result of depressed crude oil volumes, Algeria offered to pay the entire value in oil. However, Algeria's official export price of $37.50 per barrel was above the valid spot price of $33. This would have resulted in a price discount of about 10 percent by Honda. The parties eventually agreed to compensate 40 percent of the contract value of Algeria's

57. "Pepsi Will Be Bartered For Ships and Vodka in Deal With Soviets," *New York Times,* April 9, 1990, p. 1.

58. "Excitement of Bartering is Fading Away," *Financial Times,* June 1, 1989, Section 3, p. 111.

official export price for crude oil with the rest paid in hard currency. This was the first such deal for Honda.[59]

Parallel Deals   In a parallel deal the exporter agrees to accept the merchandise equivalent of a given percentage of the export amount. Payment is received on delivery. This arrangement is intended to offset the outflow of wealth from the country when a very large purchase has been made. Within a given amount of time, the exporter searches for a specific amount of merchandise that can be bought from the country or the company that purchased the products originally. Eastern European countries often include a penalty fee in case the Western exporter defaults on the countertrade portion of the arrangement. Offset arrangements are a type of parallel deal gaining popularity today.

Linked Deals   Linked deals, sometimes called junctions, are a form of countertrade not frequently used. A Western importer finds a Western exporter willing to deliver merchandise to a country in Eastern Europe or the Third World. At the same time, the inporter is released from a counter-purchase agreement by paying a premium to the exporter, who in turn organizes the counter-purchase. This transaction requires agreement of the state-controlled trading nation.

Triangular Compensation   Triangular compensation arrangements, also called switch trades, involve three countries. The Western exporter delivers hard goods (saleable merchandise) to an importing country, typically in Eastern Europe. As payment, the importing country may transfer hard goods (easily saleable merchandise) or soft goods (heavily discounted merchandise) to a third country in the West or in Eastern Europe, which then reimburses the Western exporter for the goods received. Such negotiations may become complex and time consuming. Often the assistance of skilled traders, switch traders, is required to assure profitable participation by the Western exporter.

Offset Deals   One of the fastest growing types of countertrade is offset. In an offset transaction, the selling company guarantees to use some products or services from the buying country in the final product. These transactions are particularly common when large purchases from government-type agencies are involved, such as public utilities or defense-related equipment. To land the large order for its airborne early radar system (AWACS) from the United Kingdom, the Seattle-based Boeing company offered to offset the purchase by 130 percent. This would commit the Boeing company to spend 130 percent of the purchase value on U.K. products to offset the purchase, which was competed for by a British company as well. These types of transactions were first popularized by Canada and Belgium some twenty years ago and are now common for very large defense contracts in Western Europe, Australia, and

59. Ibid.

New Zealand. This technique is now also spreading to orders involving state railways or state airlines.[60]

Cooperation Agreements Cooperation agreements are special types of compensation deals extending over longer periods of time. They may be called product purchase transactions, buy-back deals, or pay-as-you-earn deals. Compensation usually refers to an exchange of unrelated merchandise, such as coal for machine tools. Cooperation usually involves related goods, such as payment for new textile machinery by the output produced by these machines.

Although sale of large equipment or of a whole factory can sometimes only be clinched by a cooperation agreement involving buy-back of plant output, long-term negative effects must be considered before any deal is concluded. In industries such as steel or chemicals, the effect of high volume buy-back arrangements between Western exporters of manufacturing technology and Eastern European importers has been devastating. Western countries, especially Europe, have been flooded with surplus products. Negotiations among European Community members are aimed at drafting a general policy on such arrangements to avoid further disruption of their domestic industries.

International Harvester is one U.S. company with experience in buy-back arrangements.[61] In 1973, the company sold the basic design and technology for a tractor crawler to Poland. At the same time, International Harvester agreed to buy back tractor components manufactured by the Polish plant. These components were shipped to a subassembly plant in the United Kingdom which served the European market. In 1976, the company sold Hungary the design for an axle. To offset this sale, the company agreed to purchase complete axles for highway trucks.

Dangers in Compensation Deals

The greatest danger in compensation arrangements stems from the difficulty of finding a buyer of the merchandise accepted as part of the transaction. Often such transactions are concluded with organizations of countries where industry is under government control. Since prices for goods in these countries are not determined by the supply and demand forces of a free market economy, merchandise transferred under compensation arrangements is often overvalued compared to open market products. In addition, such merchandise, obviously not saleable on its own, may be of low quality. As a result, the exporter may be able to sell the merchandise only at a discount. The size of these discounts may vary considerably, ranging from 10 percent to 33 percent of its value.[62] The astute exporter will raise the price of the export contract to cover such potential discounts on the compensating transaction.

60. "Countertrade Comes Out of the Closet," *The Economist,* December 20, 1986, p. 89.
61. "Countertrade," *Commerce America,* June 19, 1978, p. 1.
62. "Algeria: When Barter Is Battery," *The Economist,* October 3, 1981, p. 80.

FIGURE 13.5 ● Countertrade with International Chemical Company

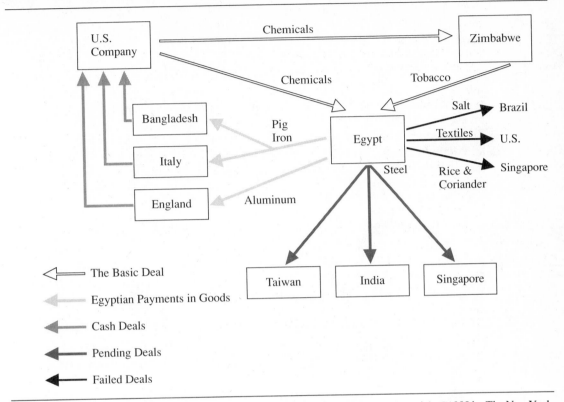

Source: New York Times, Special Business Supplement, September 25, 1988, p. 34. Copyright ©1988 by The New York Times Company. Reprinted by permission.

The experience of a multinational chemical company serves as a good example of the difficulties encountered in barter deals. The company had sold $8 million worth of chemicals to Zimbabwe and agreed to take payment in tobacco which was sold to Egypt, selling in the process another $12 million worth of chemicals to that country. To pay for this transaction, Egypt was offering a whole range of basic commodities and materials as payment in lieu of the $20 million cash price. A specialty company was engaged that selected appropriate products and found buyers elsewhere in the world, collecting the cash. All told, the $20 million deal with Egypt involved nine different countries and six different product categories (see Figure 13.5).[63]

63. "Barter is His Stock in Trade," *New York Times, Special Business Supplement,* September 25, 1988, p. 32–36.

Precautions for Countertrade

A study of fifty-seven British companies involved in countertrade reported that the most difficult problems with countertrade were that there was no in-house use for the goods offered and the negotiations were complex and time consuming.[64]

At the conclusion of the sales agreement, the exporter should obtain a clear notion of the merchandise offered for countertrade. The description, origin, quality, quantity, delivery schedules, price, and purchasing currency in local or hard currency should be determined. With a detailed description given to a specialized trader, an estimate on the applicable discount may be rendered. The sale price of merchandise offered may be structured to include the difference between purchase amount and actual cash value. It is paramount that the Western exporter not agree on any price before these other items are determined. Maintaining flexibility in negotiation requires skill and patience.

Organizing for Countertrade[65]

International companies are moving toward organizing countertrade for higher leverage. Many larger firms have established specialized units whose single purpose is to engage in countertrade. Many independent trading companies offer countertrading services. Recently, several large U.S. banks have formed their own countertrade units.

Daihatsu, a Japanese automobile manufacturer, offers a good example of how a willingness to engage in countertrade can lead to a competitive advantage. Although the company is the smallest Japanese automobile manufacturer, Daihatsu has managed to become the market leader for imported cars in Comecon countries such as Poland or Hungary. In Hungary, the company went as far as to schedule its parties for retiring Japanese workers through Hungary, allowing that country to earn additional foreign exchange, which resulted in the sale of another forty cars.[66]

CONCLUSIONS

Managing pricing policies for an international firm is an especially challenging task. The international marketer is confronted with a number of uncontrollable factors out of the economic, legal, and regulatory environment that all have an impact on how prices are established in various countries. Though these influences are usually

64. David Shipley and Bill Neale, "Industrial Barter and Countertrade," *Industrial Marketing Management,* February 1987, p. 6.

65. See also Christopher M. Korth, *International Countertrade* (Westport, Conn.: Quorum Books, 1987).

66. "Daihatsu Sets Sights on Europe," *Financial Times,* March 5, 1986, p. 4.

quite manageable in any given country, the difficulty for pricing across many markets arises from the price differentials that evolve out of environmental factors working in various combinations in different countries. Managing these price differentials and keeping them within some tolerable limits is a major task in international pricing.

One of the most critical values affecting price levels are foreign exchange rates. Today, managers find currencies moving both up or down, and the swings have assumed magnitudes that may substantially affect the competitiveness of a company. Understanding the factors that shape the directions of the foreign exchange market and mastering the technical tools that protect firms against large swings have become required skills for the international marketer. To the extent that a company can make itself less vulnerable from exchange rate movements compared to its competitors, may enable it to gain additional competitive advantage.

Because the relevant factors that affect price levels on an international scale are always fluctuating, the international pricing task is a never-ending process in which each day may bring new problems to be resolved. Whenever a company is slow to adapt or makes a wrong judgment, the market is very quick at adapting and at taking advantage of any weaknesses. As long as uncontrollable factors such as currency rates and inflation are subject to considerable fluctuations, the pricing strategies of international companies will have to remain under constant review. The ultimate goal is to minimize the gap between the price levels of various markets.

In this chapter we have also examined the rather technical aspects of trade financing and countertrade. Many executives have realized that they cannot leave these trade forms to the occasional specialist but must use them as a competitive weapon against aggressive competition. If knowledge of financial engineering and countertrade is to become a competitive advantage, marketing executives negotiating such transactions must master these techniques. International companies will be forced to expose and train their executives in these aspects of trade. We can expect an increasing world trade to be attached to one or the other of these techniques.

As competition in many industries increases, companies that have maintained a policy of "cash or no deal" often face a situation of "countertrade or no deal." Companies established in industrialized countries have seen that expansion into state-controlled economies or Third World countries and the hard-currency poor countries of Eastern Europe requires a willingness to engage in countertrade. Understanding countertrade has become a required background for an international marketing executive.

Questions for Discussion

1. Discuss the difficulty or desirability of having a standardized price for a company's products across all countries.

2. Why should a company not go ahead and price its products in each market according to local factors?

3. You are an exporter of industrial installations and have received an order for $100,000 from a Japanese customer. The job will take six months to complete and will be paid in full at that time. Now your Japanese customer has called you and also wants a price quote in yen. What will you quote him?

4. What strategies, other than through pricing, do companies have to combat parallel imports?

5. What should be the government's position on the issue of parallel imports? Should the government take any particular actions?

6. What is meant by the term *financial engineering?*

7. How should a firm approach the decision on whether or not its exports should be insured?

8. Explain the major forms of countertrade. Under what circumstances should a company enter into such transactions?

9. What are the major risks to a firm engaging in countertrade?

For Further Reading

Arpan, Jeffrey S. "International Intracorporate Pricing." *Journal of International Business Studies* (Spring 1972), pp. 1–18.

Baker, James C., and John K. Ryans, Jr. "International Pricing Policies of Industrial Product Manufacturers." *Journal of International Marketing,* 1, no. 3 (1982), pp 127–133.

Farley, John U., James M. Hulbert, and David Weinstein. "Price Setting and Volume Planning by Two European Industrial Companies: A Study and Comparison of Decision Processes." *Journal of Marketing,* 44, no. 1 (Winter 1980), pp. 46–54.

Burns, Jane O. "Transfer Pricing Decisions in U.S. Multinationals." *Journal of International Business Studies* (Fall 1980), pp. 21–39.

Cavusgil, S. Tamer, and Ed Sikora. "How Multinationals Can Counter Gray Market Imports." *Columbia Journal of World Business* (Winter 1988), pp. 75–85.

Dunhan, Dale F., and Mary Jane Sheffet. "Gray Markets and the Legal Status of Parallel Importation." *Journal of Marketing* 52 (July 1988), pp. 75–83.

Elderkin, Kenton W., and W. E. Norquist. *Creative Countertrade: A Guide to Doing Business Worldwide.* Cambridge, Mass.: Ballinger Publishing Company, 1987.

Ferguson, Henry. "Tomorrow's Global Manager Will Use Countertrade." *Corporate Barter and Countertrade,* 1, no. 6 (July 1987).

Frank, Victor H., Jr. "Living with Price Control Abroad." *Harvard Business Review* (March–April 1984), pp. 137–142.

Ghoshal, Animesh. "Flexible Exchange Rates and International Trade." *International Trade Journal,* 1, no. 1 (Fall 1986), pp. 27–66.

Gut, Rainer E. "Ten Principles of International Financing." In *The International Essays for Business Decision Makers.* vol. 5. Ed. Mark B. Winchester. The Center for International Business and Amacom, A Division of American Management Association, 1980, pp. 217–225.

Kim, Seung H., and Stephen W. Miller, "Constituents of the International Transfer Pricing Decision." *Columbia Journal of World Business* (Spring 1979), p. 71.

Korth, Christopher M. *International Countertrade.* Westport, Conn.: Quorum Books, 1987.

Lecraw, Donald J. "Pricing Strategies of Transnational Corporations." *Asia Pacific Journal of Management* (January 1984), pp. 112–119.

O'Burns, Jane. "Transfer Pricing Decisions in U.S. Multinational Corporations." *Journal of International Business Studies* (Fall 1980), pp. 23–39.

Weigand, Robert E. "International Trade Without Money." *Harvard Business Review* (November-December 1977), p. 28.

Yoffie, David B. "Barter: Looking Beyond the Short-Term Payoffs and Long-Term Threat." *International Management* (August 1984), p. 36.

14

International and Global Promotion Strategies

MANAGING THE COMMUNICATIONS *process for a single market is no easy task. However the task is even more difficult for international marketers who must communicate to prospective customers in many markets. In the process, they struggle with different cultures, habits, and languages.*

In this chapter, we describe the communications process when more than one country is involved and how a company structures its international promotion mix. Advertising, a key element of the promotional mix, will be covered in detail in our next chapter (Chapter 15). After a closer look at the differences between a single country versus a multicountry communications process, we will turn to the challenge of developing a personal selling effort on an international level. Various methods of sales promotion are analyzed, and special problems involving the selling of industrial goods are highlighted.

THE SINGLE COUNTRY PROMOTION PROCESS

Before we embark on a detailed discussion of the various tools available to firms in the international promotion area, we first need to discuss the international dimension of the communications process. From studying basic marketing, you should be familiar with the generalized single country communications process. Communications flow from a source, in this case the company, through several types of channels to the receiver, in this case the customer. Channels are the mass media, both print or electronic, and the company's sales force. Communications takes place when intended content is received as the perceived content by the receiver or customer. Through a feedback mechanism, the communications sender will be able to verify that the intended and perceived content were in fact identical.

This communications process is typically hindered by three potentially critical variables. A *source effect* exists when the receiver evaluates the received messages based on the status or image of the sender. Secondly, the level of noise caused by other messages being transmitted simultaneously tends to reduce the chances of effective communication. Finally, the messages have to pass through the receiver's, or target's, perceptional filter, which keeps out any messages that are not relevant to the receiver's experience. Consequently, effective communications require that the source, or sender, overcome the source effect, noise level, and perceptional filter. This is the communications process that most students of marketing are familiar with, involving a domestic, or single country, situation.

THE MULTICOUNTRY COMMUNICATIONS PROCESS

Research evidence and experience have demonstrated that the communications model adopted for the single country or domestic situation is applied to consumers in other countries as well. Consequently, the communications model covering international situations is the same as discussed above. What we do find, however, are some additional barriers to overcome: the cultural barrier, different source effects, and different noise levels. Figure 14.1 contains a multicountry communications model with the cultural barrier arising at different times or steps in the process.

What is meant by a cultural barrier? In any multicountry communications flow, the source and the receiver are often located in different countries and, thus, they have different cultural environments. The kind of influence culture can have on the marketing environment has already been discussed at length in Chapter 3. The difficulty of communicating across cultural barriers, however, lies in the danger of substituting, or falling back on, one's own self-reference criteria in situations in which no particular information exists. This danger is particularly acute for executives who are physically removed from the target country. By moving additional decision-making responsibility into the local market, the cultural barrier will have to be overcome at a point closer to the source.

Even in situations where a local subsidiary has substantial decision-making authority, there will be some input from a regional or corporate head office operation. For most firms, then, some effort of overcoming this cultural barrier will have to be made. This means that in virtually all cases some executives will be involved in bridging two cultures. The result of not successfully bridging this gap can be failure and substantial losses.

FIGURE 14.1 ● Barriers in the Multicountry Communications Process

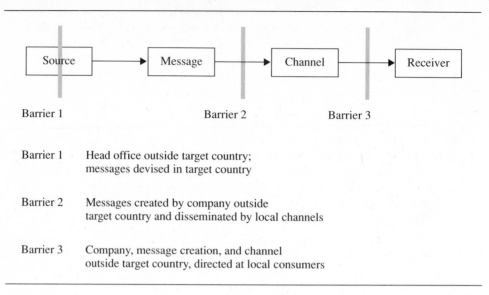

Barrier 1   Head office outside target country;
               messages devised in target country

Barrier 2   Messages created by company outside
               target country and disseminated by local channels

Barrier 3   Company, message creation, and channel
               outside target country, directed at local consumers

Multicountry communications may also have an impact on the source effect. A foreign company's communications may trigger different reactions than the communications of a local firm. In cases where a positive reference group effect exists, an international company may want to exploit the situation. Frequently, however, the reaction to international firms is negative, forcing companies to de-emphasize their foreign origins.

The noise level may differ due to different economic and competitive circumstances. In highly developed countries such as the United States, "noise" from competing companies for the attention of target customers is extremely high. In some developing countries, fewer companies may vie for the attention of prospective clients. With media availability differing widely from country to country, the nature of channels used to reach target customers tends to vary accordingly. And finally, the feedback mechanisms are subject to additional delays due to the distances involved.

Consequently, we can characterize the multicountry communications process as similar to the single country process, though subject to considerable additional difficulties that make this a highly challenging task. The purpose of this chapter is to develop strategies that international companies can employ to overcome these additional difficulties and barriers. Therefore, we will begin our analysis by concentrating first on the different elements of the communications mix.

FIGURE 14.2 ● International and Global Promotion Strategies

THE INTERNATIONAL PROMOTION MIX

How to manage the promotion mix internationally is a critical question for many companies. Most firms do business in a certain way and do not rethink their promotion mix regularly. However, international marketers cannot take the full availability of all promotion elements for granted. As a result, many companies find themselves in countries or situations that require an adjustment or a substantial change in their promotion mix. This section is devoted to understanding how different international environments affect promotion mix decisions (see Figure 14.2).

Elements of the Promotion Mix

In a domestic or single country environment, companies achieve a balance in their promotion mix on the basis of experience, costs, and effectiveness. For most companies, communications mix decisions require the selection of an appropriate balance between advertising and personal selling. This translates into a push versus pull strategy decision. How different is the company's approach to marketing its products internationally?

Push Oriented Strategy

In a domestic setting, push oriented marketing strategies emphasize personal selling rather than advertising in their promotion mix. Although very effective as a promotion tool, personal selling, which requires intensive use of a sales force, is relatively costly. Companies marketing industrial or other complex products to other firms or governmental agencies have relied on personal selling. Personal selling is usually more effective when a company is faced with a short channel. International marketers basically look at the personal selling requirements in the same way that marketers do in a domestic situation. However, some of the key inputs into the decision-making process need to be reviewed.

The complexity of a product usually influences how extensively personal selling is used. Although most companies market products of equal or less complexity abroad, the level of complexity has to be compared to the readiness level of the clients. Consequently, a U.S. company selling the same products abroad as those sold domestically may find that more personal selling may be necessary abroad because some foreign clients are less sophisticated than domestic clients. A U.S. company may use the same amount of personal selling in Europe as it does in the United States, but may need to put forth a greater personal selling effort in developing countries.

How a firm's products are purchased abroad can also lead to adjustments in the push policy. When a company markets industrial equipment, push policies usually are employed both at home and abroad. There are some product categories, however, for which buying may not be the same. What may be minor equipment or supplies purchased on a limited involvement basis in one country, such as the United States, may be considered major equipment for smaller firms abroad and, thus, require a more involved personal selling effort.

Though they may prefer personal selling as a promotion mix, many U.S. companies increasingly are using more advertising due to the high cost of maintaining a personal sales force. These costs, which are estimated to have passed $200 for a typical sales call, have motivated some companies to shift a part of the selling job to advertising. In foreign markets where salary levels may be lower than in the United States, companies may gain by making more use of personal selling.

Channel length can also be an important factor determining the amount of personal selling or push strategy to be used. To the extent that a company faces the same channel lengtn abroad as it does in the United States, no change is needed in the push strategy. However, when a company does face a longer channel because other intermediaries such as local distributors are added, the firm may be better off shifting to a pull campaign.

Pull Oriented Strategy

Pull strategy is characterized by a relatively greater dependence on advertising directed at the end-user for a product or service. Pull campaigns are typical for consumer goods firms that need to approach a large segment of the market. For such companies, the economies of using mass communications such as advertising have dictated a reliance on pulling the product through the distribution channel. Pull campaigns are usually advisable when the product is widely used by consumers, when the channel is long, when the product is not very complex, and when self-service is the predominant shopping behavior.

Increased or decreased reliance on pull campaigns for international marketers depends on a number of factors. Most important are access to advertising media, channel length, and the leverage the company has with the distribution channel.

Marketers accustomed to the large number of media available, such as in the U.S. market, will find that in overseas markets the choice may be substantially limited. For many products, pull campaigns work only if access to electronic media, particularly TV, is guaranteed. This is the case in Japan and in some developing countries where radio and TV stations tend to be commercially operated. However, in many European countries, advertising is restricted to print media only. In Scandinavia, no commercial television or radio stations were in existence in 1987.[1]

In many other countries, access to those media is restricted through a limit on time imposed by governments. Consequently, companies will find it difficult to duplicate their strategies when moving from a free environment such as the United States to the more restricted environment in Europe. Although in many countries a company may be able to shift advertising from one medium into another, it is nevertheless true that the unfolding of a full-blown push campaign as it is practiced in the United States is usually much more difficult if not impossible to do in other countries.

Channel length is a major determinant of the use of a pull campaign. Companies in markets such as the United States often face long channels in consumer goods and, thus, try to overcome channel inertia by directing their advertising directly to end-users. When a company markets overseas, it may face an even longer channel because local distribution arrangements are different. In the case of a country such as Japan, channels tend to be very long compared to those in the United States. As a result, a greater reliance on a pull strategy may be advisable or necessary in such countries.

Distribution leverage is also different for each company from market to market. Getting cooperation from local selling points, particularly in the retail sector, is often more difficult than it is in the domestic market. The fight for shelf space may be very intensive; shelf space in most markets is more limited than it is in the United States where it is customary to carry several competing brands of a product category. Under these more difficult situations, the reliance on a push campaign becomes more important. If consumers are demanding the company's product, retailers will make sure they carry it.

Push versus Pull Strategies

In selecting the best balance between advertising and personal selling for the push versus pull decision, companies have to analyze the markets to determine the need for these two major communications mix elements. However, as we have seen, the availability or access to any one of them may be limited. This is particularly the case for firms depending a great deal on pull policies. Many such companies find them-

1. "Media Fact Europe," *Focus,* January 1987, p. 21.

selves limited in the use of the most powerful communications tool. How shall a company adjust its communications policy under such circumstances?

When lack of access to advertising media makes the pull strategy less effective, a company may have to resort to more of a push strategy, making a greater use of personal selling. In some instances, this may already be the case when access to television advertising forces a company to use less effective media forms such as print advertising. In such circumstances, a company will be employing a larger sales force to compensate for the lesser efficiency of consumer directed promotions.

Limited ability to unfold a pull strategy from a company's home market has other effects on the company's marketing strategy. Limited advertising tends to slow the product adoption process in new markets, thus forcing the firm to accept slower growth. In markets crowded with existing competitors, newcomers will find it difficult to establish themselves when access to pull campaigns is limited.

Consequently, a company entering a new market may want to consider such situations for its planning and adjust expected results accordingly. A company accustomed to a given type of communications mix usually develops an expertise or a distinctive competence in that use. When suddenly faced with a situation in which that competence cannot be fully applied, the risk of failure or underachievement is increased. This can even affect entry strategies or the market selection process.

PERSONAL SELLING

Personal selling takes place whenever a customer is met in person by a representative of the marketing company. When doing business internationally, companies will have to meet customers from different countries. These customers may be accustomed to different business customs and may speak in a different language. That is why personal selling in an individual context is extremely complex and requires some very special skills on the part of the salesperson.

In this section, we differentiate between international selling and local selling. When a company's sales force travels across countries and meets directly with clients abroad, it is practicing international selling. This type of selling requires the special skill of being able to manage within several cultures. Much more often, however, companies engage in local selling; they organize and staff a local sales force made up of local nationals to do the selling in only one country. Managing and operating a local sales force involves different problems from those encountered by international salespersons.

International Selling (Multicountry Sales Force)

The job of the international salesperson seems glamorous. We imagine a professional who frequently travels abroad, visiting a large number of countries and meeting a large number of different businesspeople with various backgrounds. However, this type of work is quite demanding, and becoming a globetrotter (defined in Chapter 1) requires a special set of skills.

International salespersons are needed only when companies deal directly with their clients abroad. This is usually the case for industrial equipment or business services and rarely for consumer products or services. Consequently, for our purposes, international sales will be described in the context of industrial selling.

Purchasing Behavior   In industrial selling, one of the most important parts of the job consists of finding the right decision maker in the client company. The seller must locate the key decision makers who may hold different positions from company to company or from country to country.[2] In some countries, the purchasing manager may have different responsibilities or the engineers may play a greater role. The international salesperson must be able to deal effectively with buying units that differ by country.

A Japanese study investigated the purchasing process of a large corporation for packaging machinery.[3] The entire decision-making process took 121 days and involved twenty people from the purchasing company. In Japan, middle management is given considerable authority for purchasing. However, the staff departments responsible for the purchasing process involve all interested and affected departments in the decision-making process. In the case of the company purchasing packaging machinery, the process involved the production manager and the entire production department staff, the new product committee, the laboratory of the company, the marketing department, and the department for market development. For a detailed chart see Figure 14.3.

Buying Criteria   Aside from the different purchasing patterns found, the international salesperson may have to deal with different decision criteria or objectives on the part of the purchaser. Buyers or users of industrial products in different countries may expect to maximize different goals. However, it should be pointed out that for standardized uses for specific industries, relatively little difference between countries applies. Particularly for high technology products, such as production equipment for semiconductor components used in the electronics industry, the applications are virtually identical regardless of whether the factory is located in Korea or in the United States.

Language   Overcoming the language barrier is an especially difficult task for the international salesperson. The personal selling effort is substantially enhanced if the salesperson speaks the language of the customer. A summary of languages spoken in European countries is shown in Table 14.1

2. Thomas V. Bonoma, "Major Sales: Who Really Does the Buying?" *Harvard Business Review,* May-June 1982, p. 112.
3. "Japanese Firms Use Unique Buying Behavior," *Japan Economic Journal,* December 23, 1980, p. 29.

FIGURE 14.3 ● Organizational Buying Behavior in Japan: Packaging Machine Purchase Process

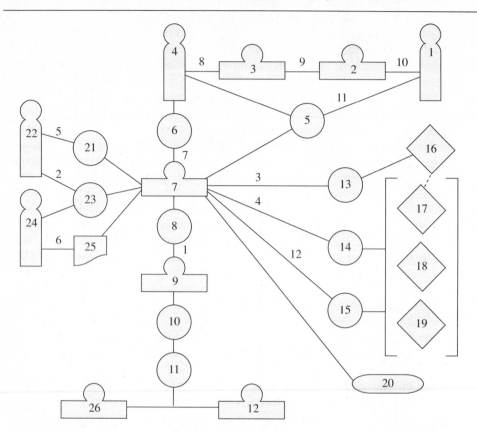

1 President	10 Request for Consultation	20 Overseas Machine
2 Financial Dept.	11 Production	Exhibitions
3 Sales Headquarters	of New Product	21 Request for Testing
4 Production Chief	Marketing Plan	of Prototype Machines
5 Decision	12 Product Development Dept.	22 Research Staff
6 Discussion	13 Discussion On Design	23 Production
of Production	of Prototype Machines	of Basic Design
and Sales Plans	14 Prototype Machine	24 Foreman
7 Production Dept.	15 Placement of Orders	25 Production
8 Production	16 Makers Design	of Draft Plans
of Packing	and Technical Staff	26 Marketing Dept.
Process Plan	17 Supplier A	
9 New Products	18 Supplier B	
Development Committee	19 Supplier C	

Source: "Japanese Firms Use Unique Buying Behavior," *The Japan Economic Journal,* December 23, 1980, p. 29. Reprinted by permission.

TABLE 14.1 ● Languages Spoken in European Households

	Belgium	Denmark	France	Germany	Ireland	Italy	Netherlds.	Norway	Spain	Switzld.	UK
Households (m)	3.6	2.1	20.3	25.3	0.85	18.5	5.3	1.55	10.3	2.5	21.03
Adults who speak:											
English (%)	26	51	26	30	99	13	50	80	n.a.	26	100
French (%)	71	5	100	12	12	27	16	10	n.a.	55	16
German (%)	22	48	11	100	2	6	61	20	n.a.	81	9
Italian (%)	4	1	8	2	1	100	2	4	n.a.	17	2
Spanish (%)	3	1	13	2	1	5	2	2	100	3	3
Flemish-Dutch (%)	68	1	1	3	—	—	100	—	—	—	1

Source: Data from a Gallup survey, as published in "European Satellite Battle Looms," *Financial Times*, September 16, 1985. Reprinted by permission.

For some of the products marketed by an international sales force today, two trends are evident. First, the dependency on the local language for many industries is not as strong today as it was just one or two decades ago. For many new and highly sophisticated products, such as in the electronics or aerospace industry, English is the language spoken by most customers. Consequently, with more and more executives speaking English in many countries, more firms have been in a position to actually market their products directly, without local intermediaries. English is widely spoken in Scandinavia and in Europe, just as it is the leading second language in Asia and Latin America. Consequently, we now see that the ability to speak a number of foreign languages is less of a necessity. However, the learning of a foreign language should be considered an excellent way to understand a foreign culture.

In industries where knowledge of the local language is important, companies tend to assign sales territories to salespersons on the basis of language skills. A European multinational manufacturer of textile equipment assigns countries to its salespersons according to the languages they speak. This is more important in the traditional industries such as textile manufacturing, where businesses are more local in orientation and where English is not spoken that well by management.

Even executives who speak fairly good English may not understand all the details of product descriptions or specifications. As a result, a company can make an excellent impression by having its sales brochures translated into some of the key languages. European companies routinely produce company publications in several languages. Such translations may not be needed for Scandinavia, but may go a long way in others parts of the world where the level of English language skills is not that high.

Business Etiquette   International marketers selling to overseas markets are likely to encounter a diverse set of business practices as they move from one country to another. Since interpersonal behavior is intensely culture bound, this part of the salesperson's job will vary by country. Many differences exist for how an appointment is made, how (and whether) an introduction is made, and how much lead time is needed for making appointments. The salesperson must also know whether or not gifts are expected or desired. When a salesperson is traveling to the same area repeatedly, familiarity with local customs can be expected. But for newcomers or experienced executives traveling to a new area, finding out the correct information is necessary.

For example, visiting businesspeople must attend long banquets when engaging in negotiations with the Chinese. These banquets may start in the late morning or early in the evening. Sitting mostly at a round table, the visitors will normally be seated next to the host who is expected to fill the visitor's plate at regular intervals. Foreigners are cautioned that frequent toasts are the norm and that many Chinese business hosts expect that the guest should become drunk; otherwise, the guest is believed not to have had a good time.[4] Also, business etiquette can change from one country to another. While it is acceptable for visitors to arrive late in China, India, or Indonesia, arriving late in Hong Kong is not acceptable. Lateness causes the visitor to "lose face," which is an extremely serious matter among Hong Kong businesspeople.[5]

Important information can be obtained from special sources, since no manager can be expected to know the business customs of every country. For one, the company's own foreign market representatives or sales subsidiary can provide important information or suggestions. Also, when such access is not available, governments tend to collect data on business practices through their commercial officers posted abroad. For example, the United States Department of Commerce (DOC) publishes a regular series entitled "Doing Business in. . ." which offers a wealth of helpful suggestions. Some business service companies, such as accounting firms or international banks, also provide customers with profiles of business practices in foreign countries.

Foreign businesspersons receiving visitors from the United States or any other foreign country rarely expect the foreign visitor to be familiar with all local customs. However, it is always appreciated when the visitor can indicate familiarity with the most common practices and some willingness to try to conform. Learning some foreign customs helps to generate goodwill towards the company and, therefore, can enhance the chance of doing business.

Negotiations Strategies   Negotiations in the international arena are complicated because the negotiating partners frequently come from different cultural backgrounds. As a result, misunderstandings or misjudgments can occur that will lead to failure. To maximize the outcome in the often difficult, long, and protracted negotiations, international sales personnel must be in tune with the cultural differences.

Although a myriad of negotiation strategies exist, concentrating on the mutual needs rather than the issues is a much practiced approach. In international marketing, the salesperson, or negotiator, must first determine the true objectives and needs of the other party. When negotiating within an unknown cultural setting, this is often a challenging task. However, careful assessment of the negotiating party's needs can enhance the chance for success.

For successful negotiation, understanding the *mindscape* of the counterpart can be very important.[6] Wenlee Ting, a noted anthropologist, defined mindscapes as "a structure of reasoning, cognition, perception, design, planning, and decision making that may vary from individual to individual and from culture to culture." Ting

4. "Chemicals in China: Capacity for Enjoyment," *Financial Times,* September 30, 1986, p. VI.

5. "Hong Kong: Executive Guide to the Territory," *Financial Times,* June 27, 1986, p. XV.

6. Alf H. Walle, "Conceptualizing Personal Selling for International Business: A Continuum of Exchange Perspective," *Journal of Personal Selling and Sales Management,* November 1986, pp. 9–17.

developed mindscape models based on the earlier work of another anthropologist, Maruyama. Building on Maruyama's work, Ting identified three common mindscapes for Hong Kong executives. Executives with an H-type mindscape tended to be interested in structured competition and the scientific organization of business. The tendency of executives with the I-type mindscape was to see separation of individual efforts as a key to higher efficiency. The G-type mindscape considered heterogeneity as a basis for mutually beneficial competition and tended to encourage differences among units. I-type mindscapes were said to be predominant among players in international finance or real estate; H-type mindscapes were predominant in family businesses; and G-type mindscapes were typical in international trading and business.[7]

The evidence further suggested that Hong Kong businesspersons negotiate well in Eastern and Western cultures. Skilled Hong Kong negotiators are able to engage in reasoning with Western counterparts while simultaneously employing other reasoning and negotiation techniques when dealing with local groups, family members, and other business associates.[8] This suggests that successful negotiation may depend on the foreign businessperson's ability to scout out the mindscape of his or her foreign counterpart. Careful preparation of the cultural norms prevalent in the foreign country is the starting point to successful negotiations and selling.

Timing is also an important aspect for negotiating abroad. In some countries, such as China, negotiations tend to take much more time than in the United States or some other Western countries. One European company that operated a joint venture in China observed that during one annual meeting, two weeks were spent in a discussion that elsewhere might have only taken a few hours. In this situation, however, much of the time was used for interdepartmental negotiations among various Chinese agencies rather than for face-to-face negotiations with the European company.

In another instance, a European firm negotiated with a Middle Eastern country over several months for the delivery of several hundred machines. When the company representatives went into that country for the final round of negotiations, they found that the competing firm had already been there several weeks before their arrival. The European firm's representatives decided to prepare themselves for long negotiations and refused to make concessions, figuring that the competitor had most likely been worn out in the prior weeks. As it turned out, that assessment was correct and the European company won the order by outstaying its competitor in a rather difficult negotiating environment. Obviously, unprepared sales executives may lose out to competitors if they do not understand the negotiation customs of a foreign country as they relate to the amount of time necessary to conclude a deal.

7. Wenlee Ting, *Business and Technological Dynamics in Newly Industrialized Asia* (Westport, CT: Greenwood, 1985); and Magorah Maruyama, "Mindscapes and Social Theories," *Current Anthropology,* 1980, pp. 589–608.

8. Walle, "Conceptualizing Personal Selling for International Business," *Journal of Personal Selling and Sales Management,* November 1986, pp. 9–17.

International Selling at Soudronic[9]   The sales function at Soudronic AG, a medium-sized manufacturer of welding equipment used primarily in the can-making industry, offers a good example of how an international sales force is organized and operated. Located in Switzerland, where all of its machines were produced, the company sold to can-makers in some eighty countries. The selling of these machines, which welded the bodies of metal cans at very high speeds, rested with a small sales force of seven sales managers. These managers reported to two regional sales managers, who in turn reported to the manager for sales and marketing. The entire world territory had been divided into seven parts in such a way that made travel schedules more efficient, that maximized the language competency of the sales force, and that balanced overall workloads.

Each sales manager was responsible for all client contact in his territory. In the assigned countries, the sales manager usually worked with local agents who indicated when a prospective client needed to be visited. The sales manager scheduled a visit on the next trip to that country and visited the client along with the local agent. The sales manager was technically trained to the extent that most questions could be answered on the spot. The sales manager also negotiated with the client for delivery and price terms within limits. Once a contract had been negotiated, the sales manager turned the client contact over to the service technician; although in many cases, the sales manager remained in contact with the client who preferred to deal primarily with one person.

Sales managers were expected to spend 50 percent of their time with clients either in the form of local contact, telephone contact, or correspondence. As a result, the Soudronic salespersons traveled a good percentage of the time. The availability of sales managers for such positions was limited. The company preferred to hire people who had a technical or engineering background together with several years of sales experience in the capital goods sector, not necessarily in the can-making industry. Prospective sales managers were also expected to have good firsthand knowledge of their assigned region, preferably through one or more years of work experience, and to have acquired the language locally. Compensation was partially on a commission and incentive basis.

Local Selling (Single Country Sales Force)

When a company is able to maintain a local sales force in the countries where it does business, many of the difficulties of bridging the cultural gap with its clients will be minimized. The local sales force can be expected to understand the local customs, and the international company typically gains additional acceptance in the market. This is primarily because local sales forces are usually staffed with local nationals. However, many challenges remain, and the management of a local sales force often

9. Jean-Pierre Jeannet, *Soudronic AG,* Case, IMEDE, International Management Development Institute, Lausanne, Switzerland, 1983.

requires different strategies from those used in running a sales force in the company's domestic market.

Role of Local Sales Force and Control   When a company has decided to build up a local sales force, the decision has already been made for forward integration in its distribution effort. As we learned in Chapter 9, establishing a sales force means that the company has moved to assume the full role of a local sales subsidiary, sidestepping the independent distributor. Depending on the distribution strategy adopted, the company may sell directly, as often is the case for many industrial products or business services, or indirectly through local wholesalers, as is the case for many consumer products and services. Although international companies will not make such a move unless present business volume justifies it, there are substantial benefits associated with having their own sales forces.

Control over a firm's sales activities is a frequently cited advantage for operating a company-owned local sales force. With its own sales force, the company can emphasize the products it wants to market at any time; and the company has better control over the way it is represented. In many cases, price negotiations, in the form of discounts or rebates, are handled uniformly rather than leaving these decisions to an independent distributor with different interests. Having a company sales force also ensures that the personnel is of the necessary level and qualification. Control over all of these parameters usually means higher sales compared to using a distributor sales force.

Also, the local sales force can represent an important bridge with the local business community. For industries where the buying process is local rather than international, the sales force speaks the language of the local customer, can be expected to understand the local business customs, and thus can bring the international firm closer to its end-users. In many instances, local customers, though not objecting to buying from a foreign firm, may prefer to deal with local representatives of that firm. As a result, the ability of the international company to make its case heard with prospective customers is substantially enhanced.

However, local sales forces are single country, or single culture, by nature. While they do speak the language of the local customers they often do not speak any other language. As many U.S. firms have experienced, the local sales force abroad may have a very limited understanding of English, and its understanding of the head-office language is, in general, not sufficient to conduct business in that language. Furthermore, a local sales force cannot be expected to speak the languages of neighboring countries sufficiently in order to deal directly with such customers. In Europe, where this problem is particularly acute, language competency usually precludes a German firm from sending its sales force into France, or a French firm from sending its sales force into Italy or Spain. In some countries, there are several different languages spoken and this tends to further reduce the mobility of a sales force.

Local Sales Job   The type and extent of local sales effort a company will need is dependent on its own distribution effort and the relationship to the other communications mix elements. For firms who still use distributor sales forces to a large extent, a missionary sales force with limited responsibilities may suffice. This missionary sales force would concentrate on visiting clients together with the local distributor's sales force. If the international company's sales force needs to do the entire job, a much larger sales force will be necessary. As for the international firm's domestic market, the size of the local sales force depends to a large extent on the number of clients and the desired frequency of visits. This frequency may differ from country to country, which means that the size of the sales force will differ from country to country.

The role of the local sales force needs to be coordinated with the promotion mix selected for each market. As many companies have learned, advertising or other forms of promotion can be used to make the role of the sales force more efficient. In many consumer goods industries, companies prefer a pull strategy concentrating their promotion budget on the final consumer. In such cases, the role of the sales force is restricted to gain distribution access. However, as we have mentioned previously, there are countries in which access to communications media is severely restricted. As a result, companies may place greater emphasis on the local sales force, which affects both role definition and size.

Foreign Sales Practices   Although sales forces are employed virtually everywhere, the nature of their interaction with the local customer is unique and may affect local sales operations. For most Westerners, Japanese practices seem substantially different. Here is an example reported by Masaaki Imai, President of Cambridge Corporation in Tokyo, a management consulting and recruiting firm.

When Bausch & Lomb Japan introduced its then new soft lens line into Japan, the company had targeted influential eye doctors in each sales territory for its introductory launch. The assumption was that once these leading practitioners signed up for the new product, marketing to the majority of eye doctors would be easier. One salesperson was quickly dismissed by a key customer. The doctor said that he thought very highly of Bausch & Lomb equipment but preferred regular lenses for his patients. The salesperson did not even have a chance to respond; but he decided, since it was his first visit to this clinic, to stay around for awhile. He talked to several assistants at the clinic and talked to the doctor's wife who was, as was typical for Japan, handling the administration of the practice.

The next morning, the salesman returned to the clinic and observed that the doctor was very busy. He talked again with the assistants and joined the doctor's wife when she was cooking and talked with her about food. When the couple's young son returned from kindergarten, the salesman played with him and even went out to buy him a toy. The wife was very pleased with the well-intentioned babysitter. She later explained to the salesman that her husband had very little time to listen to any sales presentations during the day, so she invited him to come to their home in the evening. The doctor, obviously primed by his wife, received the salesman very warmly and they enjoyed *sake* together. The doctor listened patiently to the sales presentation and responded that he did not want to use the soft lenses on his patients right away. However, he suggested that the salesman try them on his assistants the next day. So on the third day, the salesman returned to the clinic and fitted soft lenses on several of the clinic's assistants. The reaction was very favorable, and the doctor placed an order on the third day of his sales call.[10]

It is probably fair to say that salespersons in many countries would have taken the initial negative response as the final answer from the doctor and would have tried elsewhere for success. In Japan, however, the customer expects a different reaction from the salesperson. Japanese customers often judge from the frequency of the sales calls they receive whether the company really wants to do business. When the salesperson of one company makes more frequent calls to a potential customer than the competition, he or she may be regarded as more sincere.

This also means that companies doing business in Japan have to make frequent sales calls to their top customers often only for courtesy reasons. Customers get visited twice a year, usually in June and December, without necessarily discussing any business. Although this may occasionally be only a telephone call, the high frequency of visits significantly affects the staffing levels of the company-owned sales force.

Recruiting Many foreign companies have found recruiting sales professionals quite challenging in many overseas markets. Although the availability of qualified sales personnel is a problem even in such countries as the United States, the scarcity of skilled personnel is even more acute in developing countries. Multinational companies, accustomed to having salespersons with certain standard qualifications, may not find it easy to locate the necessary salespersons in a short period of time. One factor limiting their availability in many countries is the local economic situation. Depending on the economic cycle, the level of unemployment may be an excellent indicator as to the difficulty of finding prospects. This will limit the number of people a company can expect to hire away from existing firms unless a substantial increase over present compensation is offered.

More importantly, the image sales positions hold in a society may differ substantially. Typically, sales as an occupation or career has a relatively high image in the United States. This allows companies to recruit excellent talent, usually fresh from universities, for sales careers. These university recruits can usually consider sales as a career path toward middle-management positions. Such an image of selling is hardly found elsewhere in the world. In Europe, many companies continue to find it difficult to recruit university graduates into their sales forces, except in such highly technical fields as computers, where the recruits are typically engineers. When sales is a less desirable occupation, the quality of the sales force may suffer. If the company wants to insist on top quality, the time it will take to fill sales positions can be expected to increase dramatically.

---

10. "Salesmen Need to Make More Calls Than Competitors to Be Accepted," *Japan Economic Journal,* June 26, 1979, p. 30.

How then can a company approach its formation of a company-owned sales force in a local market? When the firm already operates a limited-function sales subsidiary with responsibility to deal with local distributors, existing local executives can be entrusted with the recruiting function. Where such a beachhead does not exist, the company may want to find an international sales executive presently active in one of its other markets who knows the situation and cultural context of the new market. That executive, sometimes called an *expatriate* because he or she is living outside of his or her own country, can be expected to build up the sales force step by step. Alternatively, executive recruiting firms have now sprung up in many countries, and these can be contacted to find the necessary personnel.

Compensation   In their home markets where they usually employ large sales forces, multinational companies become accustomed to handling and motivating their sales forces in a given way. In the United States, typical motivation programs include some form of commission or bonus for meeting volume or budget projections as well as vacation prizes for top performers. When an international company manages local sales forces in various countries, the company is challenged to determine the best way to motivate them. Not all cultures may respond the same way, and motivating practices may differ from country to country. For example, Fiat produces trucks in Yugoslavia under an agreement with Zavodi Crvena Zastava. At one of its training sessions, the idea of paying salespeople an incentive based on profit margins was met with laughter.[11]

One of the frequently discussed topics in motivating salespersons is the value of the commission or bonus structure. In particular, U.S. companies have tended to use some form of commission structure for their sales force. Although this may fluctuate from industry to industry, U.S. firms tend to use more of a flexible and volume dependent compensation structure than European firms. Japanese firms more often use a straight salary type of compensation. To motivate the sales force to achieve superior performance, the international company may be faced with using different compensation practices depending on the local customs.

Local Sales Force Examples

Managing a local sales force tends to be different according to the requirements of any given country. Local selling is one of the marketing elements that displays relatively great variety and is frequently adjusted for local customs even for companies where other marketing elements are standardized, such as advertising. The following sections are intended to give the reader some background on local sales force issues and practices.

11. "American Abroad: IVECO's Man in Yugoslavia," *Sales & Marketing Management,* June 1987, pp. 77.

Selling in Brazil[12]   Ericsson do Brasil was the Brazilian affiliate of L. M. Ericsson, a Swedish multinational firm with a strong position in the telecommunications industry. The company marketed both central switching equipment for telephone companies and private exchanges (PBXs) to individual firms. The sales force for the PBX business numbered about one hundred persons and was organized geographically.

In the southern sector of Brazil where industry was concentrated, the sales force was divided into specialists for either large PBXs, with up to two hundred external lines and several thousand internal lines, or for smaller systems called key systems, which could accommodate up to twenty-five incoming lines or up to fifty internal lines. In the northern, more rural part of Brazil, this specialization could not be achieved due to fewer accounts. As a result, the northern sales offices had sales representatives that sold both large and small systems.

Ericsson's sales force was compensated partially with a fixed salary and partially with commissions. Fixed monthly salaries amounted to about $400. A good salesperson could earn about $2,000 per month when the 4 percent sales commission was added to the base salary. Special government regulations required that each salesperson be assigned an exclusive territory. If a salesperson were reassigned, the company was then liable to maintain his or her income for another twelve months. As a result, changes in sales territory had to be considered carefully. When Ericsson do Brasil was faced with the introduction of a new paging system that was to be sold to corporate clients, most of whom also bought telephone equipment, the company found it difficult to assign territories to each of its present salespersons. If it wanted to reassign territories later on once it became clear who was good at selling paging systems over and above the telephone systems, the company would not be able to easily reassign territories without incurring compensation costs. In the end, Ericsson decided to assign the new paging system to its salespersons on a temporary basis only, thus preserving the chance to make other assignments later on without extra costs.

Wiltech India[13]   Selling in India is very different from selling in other countries. India, with the second largest population in the world, is an example of a typical developing country. Wiltech, a joint venture between the British company Wilkinson and a large Indian conglomerate, was founded to market razor blades in India based on Wilkinson technology. Founded in the early 1980s, the company needed to build up its sales force to compete against local competition. In India, there are more than 400,000 retailers or distributors of razor blades, and about 20 percent of them carry Wiltech blades.

The sales force of sixty persons primarily concentrates on urban markets. The sales representative working in a big metropolitan city directly handles one distrib-

12. Jean-Pierre Jeannet, *Ericsson Do Brasil: Ericall System,* Case, IMEDE, International Management Development Institute, Lausanne, Switzerland, M-296, 1983.

13. Jean-Pierre Jeannet, *Wiltech India,* Case, IMEDE, International Management Development Institute, Lausanne, Switzerland, M-336, 1988.

utor and about 600 to 700 retail outlets. He or she is expected to visit the distributor every day and to make another forty to sixty sales calls per day. The sales representative accomplishes this largely on foot because the sales outlets are relatively small and are clustered close to each other. The goal is to see important retailers at least twice per month and smaller retailers once a month. The sales representative working in smaller cities may cover about a dozen distributors and some 800 to 1,000 outlets. He or she sees distributors once or twice per month and sees from thirty-five to forty outlets per day. Travel is by railway or by bus, whichever is more convenient.

Wiltech sales representatives are paid a fixed salary of 800 rupees to 1,200 rupees per month (about U.S. $70 to $100). Sales representatives that achieve their quotas and productivity targets can earn another 400 to 500 rupees per month in a bonus. Expenses are paid on the basis of daily allowances for transportation, lunch, and hotel stays when necessary. For sales representatives selling from a fixed location, this daily allowance amounts to 30 rupees per day. When traveling away from home, the daily allowance amounts to 50 rupees plus the actual transportation costs for first-class train or bus fare. Although these costs appear very low compared to typical salaries and travel expenses paid in a developed country, they nevertheless represent a very good income in India where per capita GNP cost of living is very low by Western standards.

Alternatives to a Local Sales Force

Because the building up of a local sales force is both a costly and time-consuming task, come companies have looked for alternatives without necessarily falling back on independent distributors. When competitive pressures require a rapid access to a sales force, piggybacking has been practiced by some companies.

Recently, companies have entered into a wide variety of international distribution alliances. The sales alliance format differs from other ventures because the two firms who join forces do so as independent firms and not necessarily in the form of a limited joint venture. In an alliance, two companies may swap products, with one company carrying the other firm's products in one market and vice versa. Such swaps have been used extensively in the pharmaceutical industry. The short period of time left for marketing once the products have been approved and before the patents expire has called for a very rapid product roll-out in as many countries as possible.

INDUSTRIAL SELLING

Many of the promotion strategies discussed so far are geared toward the marketing of consumer goods and industrial goods. However, there are some specific promotion methods that are oriented largely toward the industrial market and that play an important role in the international marketing of such products. The use of international trade fairs, bidding procedures for international projects, and consortium selling all have to be understood if an investment or industrial products company wants to succeed in international markets.

International Trade Fairs

Participation in international trade fairs has become an important aspect for companies marketing industrial products abroad. Trade fairs are ideal for exposing new customers and potential distributors to a company's product range and have been used extensively both by newcomers and established firms. In the United States, industrial customers can be reached through a wide range of media, such as specialized magazines with a particular industry focus. In many overseas countries, the markets are too small to allow for the publication of such trade magazines in only one country. As a result, prospective customers usually attend these trade fairs on a regular basis. Trade fairs also offer companies a chance to meet with prospective customers in a less formalized atmosphere. For a company that is new to a certain market and does not yet have any established contacts, participation in a trade fair may be the only way to reach potential customers.

Companies have a large number of fairs to select from. International shows of general orientation include the Hanover Fair of West Germany, usually held in April each year. More than 500,000 visitors attend the fair coming from all industry sectors and representing many European countries. Many U.S. firms, both small and large, exhibit at the fair each year. More companies are represented through their European offices or distributors. The Hanover Fair is considered the largest industrial fair in the world.[14] Other large general fairs include the Canton Fair in China and the Milan Fair in Italy.

Specialized trade fairs concentrate on a certain segment of the industry or user group. Such fairs usually attract limited participation both in terms of exhibitors and visitors. Typically, they are more technical in nature. Some of the specialized trade fairs may not take place every year. One of the leading specialized fairs is the Achema for the chemical industry in Germany held every three years. Annual fairs having an international reputation include the air shows of Farnborough, England, or Paris, where aerospace products are displayed.

Participation in trade fairs can save both time and effort for a company that wants to break into a new market and does not yet have any contacts. For new product announcements or demonstrations, the trade fair offers an ideal forum for display. Trade fairs are also used by competitors to check on each other's most recent developments. They can give a newcomer an idea of the potential competition in

14. "World's Biggest Industrial Trade Fair Lures 500 U.S. Firms," *Industrial Marketing,* February 1981, p. 24.

some foreign markets before actual market entry. Consequently, trade fairs are both a means of selling products and of gathering important and useful market intelligence. Therefore marketers with international aspirations will do well to search out the relevant trade fairs that are directed at their industry or customer segment and to schedule regular attendance.

Selling Through a Bidding Process

The bidding process for industrial products tends to be more complicated, particularly when major industrial equipment is involved. For companies competing for such major projects, a number of stages have to be passed before negotiations for a specific purchase can ever take place. Typically, companies go through a search process for new projects, then move on to prequalify for the particular project before a formal project bid or tender is submitted. Each phase requires careful management and the appropriate allocation of resources.

During the search phase, companies want to make sure that they are informed of any project worth their interest that is related to their product lines. For particularly large projects that are government sponsored, full-page advertisements may appear in leading international newspapers. More likely, companies have to have a network of agents, contacts, or former customers who will inform them of any project being considered.

In the prequalifying phase, the purchaser will frequently ask for documentation from interested companies who would like to make a formal tender. At this phase, no formal bidding or tender documents are submitted. Instead, more general company background will be required that may describe other or similar projects the company has finished in the past. At this stage, the company will have to sell itself and its capabilities. A large number of companies can be expected to pursue prequalification.

In the next phase, the customer will select the companies to be invited to submit a formal bid. Usually, there will be only three to four companies. Formal bids consist of a proposal of how to solve the specific client problem at hand. For industrial equipment, this usually requires personal visits on location, special design of some components, and the preparation of full documentation including engineering drawings for the client. The costs can be substantial and can range from a few hundred thousand dollars to several million for some very large projects. The customer will select the winner from among those submitting formal proposals. Normally, it is not just the lowest bidder who will obtain the order. Technology, the type of solution proposed, and the financing arrangements all play a role.

Once an order is obtained, the supplying company may be expected to ensure its own performance. For that purpose, the company may be asked to post a performance bond which is a guarantee that the company would pay certain specified damages to the customer if the job was not completed within the pre-agreed specifications. Performance bonds are usually issued by banks on behalf of the supplier. The entire process, from finding out about a new prospect until the order is actually received in hand, may take from several months to several years depending on the project size or industry.

Consortium Selling

Because of the high stakes involved in marketing equipment or turnkey projects (a plant, system, or project in which the buyer acquires a complete solution so that the entire operation can commence at the turn of a key), companies have frequently banded together to form a consortium. A consortium is a group of firms that share in a certain contract or project on a pre-agreed basis but act almost like one company towards the customers. Joining together in a consortium can help share the risk in some very large projects. A consortium can enhance the competitiveness of the members by offering a turnkey solution to the customer.

Most consortiums are formed on an ad hoc basis. For the supply of a major steel mill, for example, companies supplying individual components may combine into a group and offer a single tender to the customer. The consortium members have agreed to share all marketing costs and can help each other with design and engineering questions. The customer gets a chance to deal with one supplier only, which substantially simplifies the process. Ad hoc consortiums can be found for some very large projects that require unique skills from their members. The consortium members frequently come from the same country and, thus, expect to have a greater chance to get the contract than if they operated on their own. In situations where the same set of skills or products are in frequent demand, companies may form a permanent consortium. Whenever a chance for a deal arises, the consortium members will immediately prepare to qualify for the bidding.

Companies that market equipment that represents only a small part of a much larger project may find the consortium approach helpful because marketing costs can be shared. Preparation of bid documents is expensive and a time-consuming process. Participating in a consortium may be the only chance for a company that is faced with a client demanding a turnkey project. The selection of appropriate partners is important in this context, and chances for overseas orders may be improved if the foreign firms participating in the consortium understand the foreign buying environment.

OTHER FORMS OF PROMOTION

So far, our discussion has been concentrated on personal selling as one key element of the communications mix. However, next to advertising, various forms of promotion play a key role in international marketing. Usually combined under the generic title of promotions, they may include such elements as in-store retail promotions or coupons. Many of these tools are consumer goods oriented and are used less often in industrial goods marketing. In this section, we will look at sales promotion activities, as well as sports promotions and sponsorships.

Sales Promotion

In many ways, the area of sales promotion has largely a local focus. Although some form of promotions, such as coupons, gifts, or various types of reduced-price labels, are in use in most countries, strict government regulations and different retailing practices tend to limit the options for international firms (as shown in Table 14.2).

In the United States, coupons are the leading form of sales promotion. Consumers bring product coupons to the retail store and obtain a reduced price for the product. Second in importance are refund offers. Consumers who send a proof of purchase to the manufacturer will receive a refund in the form of a check. Also used, but less frequently, are cents-off labels or factory-bonus packs, which induce customers to buy large quantities due to the price incentive. Marketers of consumer goods in the United States, who are the primary users of these types of sales promotion, find a full array of services available to run their promotions. Companies such as A. C. Nielsen Company specialize in managing coupon redemption centers centrally so that all handling of promotions can be turned over to an outside contractor.

In other countries, the primary sales promotion tools tend to be different. Coupons, the most frequently used tool in the United States, are frequently prohibited in such countries as Germany or Greece. Where they are being used, they tend to play a minor role, such as in Sweden or the United Kingdom. In most overseas markets, price reductions in the store are usually the most important promotional tool, followed by reductions to the trade, such as wholesalers and retailers. Also of importance in some countries are free goods, double-pack promotions, and in-store displays.

Most countries have restrictions on some forms of promotions. Frequently regulated are any games of chance, but games in which some type of skill is required are usually allowed. When reductions are made available, they often are not allowed to exceed a certain percentage of the product's purchase price. As a result, international firms will encounter a series of regulations and restrictions on promotions that differ among countries. Consequently, there is little opportunity to standardize sales promotion techniques across many markets. This has caused most companies to make sales promotions the responsibility of local management who are expected to understand the local customs and restrictions.

Sports Promotions and Sponsorships

With major sports events becoming increasingly covered by the mass media, television in particular, the commercial value of these events has increased tremendously over the last decade. Today, large sports events, such as the Olympics or world championships in other sports, can not exist in their present form without funding by

TABLE 14.2 ● Concise Guide to Sales Promotion

	Austria	Australia	Belgium	Brazil	Canada	Switzerland	Germany	Spain	Ireland	France
Top 3 sales promotion techniques	Reduced price in store	Reduced price in store	Reduced price in store	Gift Banded pack	Reduced price in store	Reduced price in store	Reduced price in store	Coupons	Reduced price in store	Reduced price in store
	Open competitions	Trade discounts	Trade discounts	Extra product free	Trade discounts	Trade discounts	Displays	Free goods	Trade discounts	Trade discounts
	Trade discounts	Promotional pack sizes with extra free product	Extra product free	Reduced price in store	Coupons	Merchandising contribution by manufacturers to trade	Trade discounts	Reduced price in store	Extra product free	Free samples
Restrictions on sales promotion techniques	No coupons, restrictions for on-pack deals	Individual state coupons restrictions. Promotions and trade support must be available for all stores. Lotteries and games of chance subject to government authorization. Some restrictions on proof of purchase.	No free draws. No sweepstakes.	Distribution of prizes via vouchers, contests, etc. is subject to government authorization. Ethical products, alcoholic beverages, cigarettes, cigars, not permitted any type of sales promotion.	Promotions must be offered to all stores. No promotions of pharmaceuticals except as samples to doctors. Competitions require skill testing questions.	Laws against unfair competition exist. No competitions. No free draws, sweepstakes, money-off vouchers, or money-off next purchase.	No coupons. Free goods restricted to value of about 0.10 DM. No in-pack premiums. No cross product offers. No free draws. No money-off vouchers.		Below cost selling. License required for competitions which must inspire a degree of skill.	Games of chance are usually forbidden. Premiums and gifts are limited to 5% of product value and no more than 1% off.

492

	Great Britain	Greece	Italy	Japan	Mexico	Netherlands	New Zealand	Portugal	Argentina	Sweden	United States	South Africa
Top 3 sales promotion techniques	Reduced price in store	Trade discounts	Reduced price in store	Reduced price in store	Reduced price in store	Trade discounts	Reduced price in store	Trade discounts	Reduced price in store	Co-op advertising and money-off	Coupons	Reduced price in store
	Trade discounts	Special offers	Banded packs	Trade discounts	Bonus packs	Reduced price in store	Banded packs	Reduced price in store	Trade discounts	Local activities	Refund offers	Trade discounts
	Coupons	Reduced price in store	Coupons	Premiums	On-pack premiums	Display promotions, premiums	Coupons	Competitions	In-store displays, promotions	Coupons	Cents-off label, factory packs, bonus packs	In-store coupons, promotions
Restrictions on sales promotion techniques	Legislation on bargain offers, lotteries, sweepstakes. Competitions must include a degree of skill. No price promotion on categories like pharmaceuticals.	No coupons. Gifts limited to 5% of product value.	No coupons on butter, oil, coffee. No self-liquidating offer or contest or gifts. Gifts limited to 8% of product value.	Some regulations regarding lotteries. Some regulations on excessive gifts or premiums.	Government authorization required. No promotions based on collecting a series of labels etc. No promotions of alcohol, tobacco products.	Legislation on gift schemes, pharmaceuticals, tobacco, games of chance.	No pyramid selling. No trading stamps. Coupons redeemable for cash only. Competitions require a degree of skill. Legislation on Christmas Club funds.	Some rules regarding lotteries and sweepstakes.	Rules regarding lotteries, special prizes. Products like pharmaceuticals cannot be promoted through prices.	No premium redemption plans. Competitions must include a degree of skill. Mixed offers are restricted. Cross-coupons "in-" or "on-pack" not allowed.	All promotion & trade support must be equally available to all retailers. Restrictions on frequency of use of "cents-off" and special packs. Numerous voluntary industry standards.	No lotteries or games of chance. Restrictions on coupons, especially no conditional purchase. No comparative advertising.

Source: From William J. Hawkes' Presentation to the International Marketing Workship AMA/MSI, March 1983, of A. C. Nielsen Company material. Reprinted by permission of A. C. Nielsen Company. Updated December 1990.

companies who do this either through advertising or through different types of sponsorships.

In the United States, companies have for some time purchased TV advertising space for such events as regularly broadcasted baseball, basketball, or football events. Gillette is one company that regularly uses sponsorship of the World Series to introduce new products. This is just another extension of the company's media strategy to air television and radio commercials at times when its prime target group can be found in large numbers watching TV or listening to the radio. More recently, companies have purchased similar time slots for the Olympics when they are broadcast in the United States.

In many foreign countries where commercial television advertising is restricted or not even allowed, companies do not have the opportunity to purchase air time. A U.S. firm that has invested heavily in U.S. television time for the Olympics will find itself unable to do the same in Germany, where TV advertising is shown only during some very limited time blocks during the day and not interspersed during sports shows. Therefore, companies that still want to expose their products to the large audience of these sports shows need to use different methods.

For the 1992 Winter Olympics in Albertville, France, the U.S. CBS TV-network paid $243 million and had already signed up about $100 million in advertising revenue by mid-1990. NBC had purchased the U.S. rights to the 1992 Summer Olympics to be held in Barcelona, Spain, for $401 million. By mid-1990 some $38 million of advertising had been sold. The majority of revenue is expected to come from pay-per-view package events.[15]

In order to circumvent restrictions on commercial television during sports programs, companies have purchased space for signs along the stadiums or the arenas where sports events take place. When the event is covered on television, the cameras will automatically take in the signs as part of the regular coverage. No mention of the company's product is made in any way either by the announcer or in the form of commercials.

It is the visual identification that the firms are looking for. In the case of the 1990 Football World Cup in Italy (referred to as soccer in the U.S.), the event extended over almost eight weeks and involved some twenty-four national teams. It was estimated that fifteen billion viewers watched either all the games or parts of them on television, which meant nine billion exposures for any company that had managed to obtain sign space along the playing field. Most of this was delivered in countries where from the very beginning it was difficult to get TV space and, thus, of great importance to the firm. Ten official sponsors for the entire series of fifty-two games played by the twenty-four teams obtained exclusive advertising rights in the stadiums and in official publications. Among the sponsors were Coca Cola, Mars, Gillette, Canon, JVC, Fuji Film, Philips, and Anheuser-Busch together with Carlsberg.[16]

15. "Grabbing the Rings: Marketers Tie in Early With Olympics," *Advertising Age,* August 6, 1990, p. 4.

16. "World Club Scores Big with Sponsors," *Advertising Age,* April 30, 1990, p. 42.

With the opening of the economies of Eastern Europe, sports event sponsoring is also used as a way to reach potential consumer markets. Promoters purchased the rights to the United Jersey Bank Classic and moved it to Leipzig, Germany, where several corporate sponsors paid almost $4 million to have the tennis tournament. The attraction for the sponsoring companies, which included Volkswagen, Kraft-General Foods, and American Airlines, was the TV coverage by German TV with some 30 million viewers. Also present were TV networks of several Eastern European countries.[17]

To take advantage of such global sports events, a company should have a logo or brand name that is worth exposing to a global audience. It is not surprising to find that the most common sponsors are companies producing consumer goods with a global appeal such as soft drink manufacturers, consumer electronics producers, or film companies. To purchase sign space a firm must take into consideration the popularity of certain sports. Few sports have global appeal. Soccer, which is the number one spectator sport in much of the world, still has little commercial value in the United States or in Canada. In contrast, baseball and American football have little appeal in Europe or parts of Asia and Africa. Many other sports also have only local or regional character, which requires a company to know its market and the interests of its target audience very well.

A Japanese financial services company, Orient Leasing, purchased one of Japan's twelve professional baseball teams, the Braves. As a result, the company was allowed to call them by the company's name and promptly changed its name to the shorter Orix. Within a short time, the national awareness of the company rose from 25 to 85 percent. The total cost of running the team was estimated at about $30 million. However, the company was reducing regular advertising due to the constant exposure of the Japanese public to Orix. This was assured not only through the name but also by placing the Orix name on the players' uniforms.[18]

Aside from sponsoring sporting events, companies have also moved more aggressively into sponsoring direct competitors or teams. Manufacturers of sports equipment have for some time concentrated on getting leading athletes to use their equipment. For sports that have achieved international or even global reach, such as tennis, skiing, or soccer, an endorsement of sports products by leading athletes can be a key to success. This is why manufacturers of sports equipment have always attempted to get their equipment used by world class athletes. In 1984, Puma sold only 15,000 tennis rackets a year. In 1985, following Boris Becker's first victory in Wimbledon and his endorsement of Puma rackets, sales jumped to 150,000 rackets.[19]

17. "Look Out Wimbledon, Here Comes Leipzig," *Business Week,* September 24, 1990, p. 54.

18. "Sponsorship in Japan: Benefits of Keeping an Eye on the Ball," *Financial Times,* May 25, 1989, p. 16.

19. "Puma Hopes Superstar Will Help End U.S. Slump, Narrow Gap with Adidas," *Wall Street Journal,* February 6, 1987, p. 24.

To exploit the media coverage of spectator sports, many nonsporting goods manufacturers have joined the sponsoring of specific athletes or teams. These are firms who intended to exploit the visual identification created by the media coverage. Many will remember the pictures of winning race car drivers with all the various corporation names or logos on their uniforms. Although these promotions once tended to be mostly related to sports products, now sponsors increasingly have no relationship to the sports. Sponsoring a team for competition in the sixteen Grand Prix races all over the world is estimated to cost about $45 to $60 million for one year. The main sponsor is expected to carry about half to two thirds of the cost and gets to paint the cars in its colors and have it carry its logo. The expenses are substantial because the winners do not get very high purses and yet leading race car drivers are reported to get salaries as high as $9 million for one year. In 1988, the races were broadcast in 81 countries over 100,000 minutes and attracted 3.3 billion viewers resulting in some 17 billion "viewings." Major sponsors were tobacco companies (Marlboro, Camel, John Player, Gitanes/Loto) and other consumer goods firms (Benetton).[20]

Companies have also become involved in bicycle racing. The U.S. convenience store chain, 7-Eleven, began to sponsor a team of U.S. professional riders during the 1986 Tour de France. Although the race took place in France, the company had intended to exploit its sponsorship in the U.S. through extensive coverage of the race in the U.S. news media.[21] Other companies who sponsored teams included Hitachi, Toshiba, and Panasonic, all of Japan. Other companies sponsored the official drink or the official computer for keeping the results. All of them were attracted by the 60 million viewers all across Europe who watched the daily reports on television.[22]

Through the intensive coverage of sports in the news media all over the world, many companies continue to use the sponsorship of sporting events as an important element in their international communications programs. Successful companies have to track both the interest of various countries in the many types of sports and exhibit both flexibility and ingenuity in the selection of available events or participants. In many parts of the world, sports sponsoring may continue to be the only available way to reach large numbers of prospective customers.

DIRECT MARKETING

Direct marketing includes a number of marketing approaches that involve direct access to the customer. Direct mail, door-to-door selling, and telemarketing are the primary direct marketing tools used in the United States. Some companies have been

20. "Motor Sport Industry," *Financial Times,* January 26, 1990, Section III, p. 1.
21. "Big Money Catches Up With the Tour de France," *Business Week,* July 28, 1986, p. 45.
22. Ibid.

able to achieve considerable success in their fields through aggressive direct marketing. Many of these firms realize that not all markets respond equally well to direct marketing. For the most part, the United States has the most developed direct marketing field.

Direct marketing, covering products purchased from an individual's home or office, covered some $70 billion in the United States in 1990. According to industry statistics, some 92 million Americans bought something from the home. Just as in the United States, direct marketing grew substantially in other countries. In the United Kingdom, the Benelux countries, France and Scandinavia, direct mail business doubled in the 1980s.[23] The market is also growing rapidly in Asia where it is well established in Hong Kong and Singapore. Prospects in Eastern Europe are not yet clear but experts expect it to grow there rapidly.

In Europe, despite the growth, direct marketing expenditures still only account for about one-third of all marketing expenditures compared to two-thirds in the United States. Total sales in the twelve EC member states is about one-third of the U.S. volume. Future growth appears to be largely dependent on expected regulation. In line with the EC 1992 initiative, new regulation for the direct marketing sector is under debate. Presently, direct marketing regulation is most restricted in Germany, where everything is forbidden unless specifically allowed. On the other hand, the United Kingdom or the Netherlands has more liberal regulations. As part of the EC 1992 regulations, a directive from the EC Commission is expected that will regulate the activity at the same level throughout Europe.[24]

Direct Mail

Direct mail, largely pioneered in the United States by catalogue houses such as Sears, Roebuck and Montgomery Ward, is being used extensively in other countries. Successful mail order sales require an efficient postal system and an effective collection system for the shipped products. In countries where these preconditions exist, direct mail is being used extensively by retail organizations and other service organizations such as *Reader's Digest* or credit card suppliers.

Austad, a leading U.S. catalog company marketing golf supplies, with sales of $60 million, achieved international sales of 20 percent in 1990. From a small start, international sales really took off when the company developed special catalogs for some key foreign markets. The company mailed some 140,000 catalogs to Japanese customers, some 60,000 to the United Kingdom, and another 40,000 to Sweden. The company customized its catalogs to the local requirements mailing local language catalogs to Japan, Sweden, and "English-English" to the United Kingdom. So

23. "International Direct Marketing: On the Brink of Maturity," *Financial Times,* April 18, 1990, p. 15.

24. "International Direct Marketing: Largely Uncharted Territory Ahead," *Financial Times,* April 18, 1990, p. 15.

far, all orders were shipped from the U.S. incurring considerable shipping expenses per order. In the future, Austad hopes to stock its products locally and, thus, cut expenses to its customers.[25]

Companies who may want to engage in direct mail will have to ensure that their mail pieces or catalogues are translated into the respective foreign language. Obtaining accurate mailing lists may also be difficult, although list brokers exist in many countries as they do in the United States. Direct mail offers an opportunity for companies that want to extend their business beyond a limited location and even into foreign countries. In general, however, mailing of packages abroad always involves the receiver country's customs system, which tends to delay parcels considerably.

Door-to-Door Sales

Companies such as Amway or Mary Kay Cosmetics have met with considerable success in the United States. These and other firms have grown entirely by the use of door-to-door selling techniques and by employing large numbers of part-time salespersons. Some firms employ women who sell through organized home "party" demonstrations or by contacting friends in their own neighborhoods or at work. Expansion of these and other companies into foreign markets has met with mixed success.

The concept of door-to-door selling is not equally accepted in all countries. Moreover, it also may not be equally accepted to make a profit from selling to a friend, colleague at work, or neighbors. The willingness to find suitable sales people on a part-time basis may also be limited because in some countries women or even students are not necessarily expected to work. One company that successfully transferred its direct door-to-door selling strategy from the United States to Japan is Amway. Within just eleven years, Amway sales reached $555 million in 1990 representing about one-fourth of total worldwide sales.[26] As a result, the Japanese operation has become Amway's largest foreign unit with some 700,000 distributor/salespeople. Many of its distributors are working full time and are paid on a commission-only basis as in the United States. Amway's strategy of selling directly to households is a big plus in a country where the regular distribution of goods is complicated and typically goes through many steps of wholesalers and retailers. As a result, Amway can circumvent the difficult Japanese distribution channel structure and is now one of the most profitable foreign companies operating in Japan.[27] Amway's success has also brought it attention from Japanese companies. Japanese firms marketing competing household products through regular channels are starting to bring new products to the market to slow Amway's expansion. Other companies, such as Sharp, a leading consumer electronics firm, have hired Amway to

25. "Translating a Technique into Overseas Success," *Advertising Age,* September 24, 1990, p. s-8.
26. *Wall Street Journal,* September 21, 1990, p. B1.
27. *Business Week,* September 4, 1989, p. 47.

Blake, David H., and Vita Toros. "The Global Image Makers." *Public Relations Journal* (June 1976), pp. 10–16.

Dunn, S. Watson. "Effect of National Identity on Multinational Promotional Strategy in Europe." *Journal of Marketing* (October 1976), pp. 50–57.

Ferguson, Henry. "International Exhibit Marketing: A Management Approach," *Dimensions* (1986).

Hoke, Peter. "Wunderman's View of Global Direct Marketing." *Direct Marketing* 48 (March 1986), pp. 76–88, 153.

Japan External Trade Organization. *Sales Promotion in the Japanese Market.* Tokyo: Jetro, 1980.

Still, Richard R. "Sales Management: Some Cross-Cultural Aspects." *Journal of Personal Selling and Sales Management* (Spring-Summer 1981), pp. 6–9.

Thomas, L. R. "Trade Fairs: Gateways to European Markets." *Business American* (April 20, 1981), pp. 7–10.

Tung, Rosalie L. "Selection and Training of Personnel for Overseas Assignments." *Columbia Journal of World Business* (Spring 1981), pp. 68–78.

Weser, Robert E. *The Marketer's Guide to Selling Products Abroad.* Westport, Conn.: Quorum Books, 1989.

15

Managing International and Global Advertising

● **AT THE BEGINNING** *of this book we defined international marketing as those marketing activities that applied simultaneously to more than one country. In the case of advertising, the volume of activity that is directed simultaneously toward targets in several countries is actually very small. The majority of advertising activity tends to be directed toward one country only. Despite the "local" nature of international advertising, it is important to recognize that the initial input, either in terms of the product idea or the basic communications strategy, largely originates in another country. Consequently, although there is a largely local aspect to most international advertising, there is also an international aspect to consider. Therefore, there are two important questions to be answered in international advertising: (1) how much of a local versus an international emphasis should there be and (2) what should be the nature and content of the advertising itself? The first part of the chapter is organized around the explanation of key external factors and their influence on international advertising. The second part of the chapter focuses on the major advertising decisions and helps to explain how external factors affect specific advertising areas. Special emphasis is given to advertising in Japan, where the advertising environment differs considerably from that in the United States or Europe. (For a chapter overview, see Figure 15.1.)*

FIGURE 15.1 ● International and Global Advertising

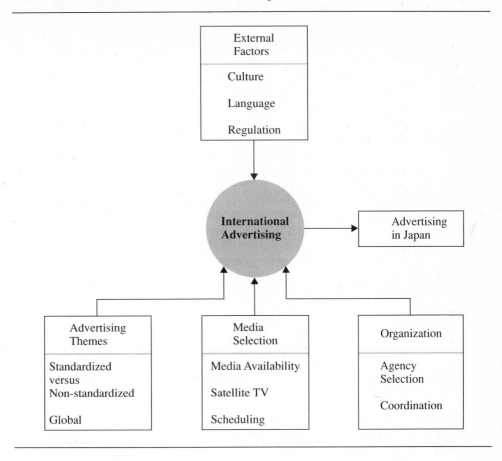

CHALLENGES IN INTERNATIONAL ADVERTISING

Probably no other aspect of international marketing has received as much attention as international advertising. Consider the following examples:

In Italy, "Schweppes Tonic Water" had to be reduced to "Schweppes Tonica" because "il water" turned out to be the idiom for a bathroom.

General Motors, translating its slogan "Body by Fisher" into Flemish for its Belgium campaign, found out belatedly that the meaning was the equivalent of "Corpse by Fisher."[1]

1. David A. Ricks, Jeffrey S. Arpan, and Marilyn Y. Fu, "Pitfalls in Advertising Overseas," *Journal of Advertising Research,* December 1974, p. 48.

These are only a few of the many examples of mistakes that were made in translating advertising copy from one language into another. Most of these mistakes, however, occurred in the 1960s when international advertising was in its infancy. Today, most companies and advertising agencies have reached a level of sophistication that has reduced the chance of translation error. This does not mean that language is not a factor to consider in today's international communications strategy. However, we have moved from a primary concern about translation to concerns about ways to be more efficient.

A second major cause of international advertising mistakes has traditionally been the neglect of cultural attitudes of consumers in foreign countries. Benetton, the Italian clothing manufacturer selling through stores all over the world, was one of the more recent examples of a company that ran into cultural problems with its advertising. The company launched a new campaign in the Fall of 1989 under the theme of "United Colors of Benetton" which had won awards in France. One of its ads featured a black woman breast feeding a white baby and another ad had a black and a white man locked together in handcuffs. The ads came under protest from U.S. civil rights groups and had to be withdrawn. Benetton also fired its advertising agency, Eldorado of France, the creator of the ads.[2]

These and the other examples we have cited point out that, even when the language or translation hurdle is correctly overcome, there still remains the need to consider the cultural and social background of the target market. Mistakes based on a misinterpretation of cultural habits are more difficult to avoid, though substantial progress has been made by international marketers to stay away from the most obvious violations. However, the avoidance of either translation or cultural errors will not be enough to produce an effective advertising campaign. Although we will initially concentrate on approaches to overcome such cultural difficulties, we will eventually emphasize critical issues around organizing campaigns internationally.

Overcoming the Language Barrier

Most of the translation blunders referred to in the previous section were due to literal translations performed outside of the target country. The translators, not always in contact with the culture of the target country, were unable to judge the actual meaning of the translated copy for the target audience. Furthermore, the faulty translation could not be checked by the executives involved since they too were from a different culture and did not possess any foreign language skills.

Given the opening of the economies in Eastern Europe to advertising, many companies had been looking for translators. Some had found out that those translators who had fled those countries many years ago wrote correct but outmoded copy.[3]

Today, the traps of faulty translations can be avoided through the involvement

2. International Advertising Supplement, *Financial Times,* December 7, 1989, p. 3.
3. "How to Advertise in Eastern Europe," *Financial Times,* October 31, 1989, p. 14.

of local nationals or language experts. Typically, international marketers have any translations checked by either a local advertising agency, its own local subsidiary, or an independent distributor located in the target country. Because international firms are active in a large number of countries and, thus, require the use of many languages, today's international marketers can find an organizational solution to the translation errors of the past. Many errors can still occur, however, if the foreign language copy is typeset incorrectly or by inexperienced typesetters. This is particularly true for non-Roman letters.[4]

In the European Community there are nine official languages. As a result, this puts a special emphasis on the ability to communicate visually rather than through the various languages. It is expected that graphics will be used more effectively in print media, too. Even the satellite TV service Sky Channel has discovered that not everyone in Europe speaks English and that, if given a chance, most people like to watch programs in their own language. Super Channel, the other satellite channel, moved to trilingual program service and rather than offer pan-European programs, the operators of satellite channels in Europe are moving into the direction of multiregional programming.[5]

Overcoming the Cultural Barrier

When international marketers fail due to misinterpretation of the local culture, they usually do so because they advocated an action that was inconsistent with the local culture or because the appeal chosen was inconsistent with the motivational pattern of the target culture. Advocating the purchase of a product whose use is inconsistent with the local culture will result in failure, even if the appeal chosen did not violate that culture per se. However, companies can also fail if only the appeal, or message employed, is inconsistent with the local culture, even if the action promoted is not. Consequently, a foreign company entering a new market has to be aware of both cultural aspects: the product's use and the message employed.

When Procter & Gamble, the U.S. consumer goods manufacturer, promoted its Camay soap in Japan in 1983 it ran into unexpected trouble. In the TV commercial, a Japanese woman was bathing when her husband walked into the bathroom. She began telling him about her new beauty soap but the husband, stroking her shoulder, hinted that suds were not on his mind. This very popular ad from Europe flopped because it was bad manners for a Japanese man to intrude on his wife.[6]

To ensure that a message is in line with the existing cultural beliefs of the target market, companies can use resources similar to those used to overcome the translation barriers. Local subsidiary personnel or local distributors can judge the cultural

4. "A Not-So-Funny Thing Happened on the Way to the Printer," *Business Marketing,* February 1987, p. 113.
5. "Reaching United Europe Won't be a Simple Task," *Advertising Age,* April 9, 1990, p. 31.
6. "After Early Stumbles, P&G Is Making Inroads Overseas," *Wall Street Journal,* February 6, 1989, p. B1.

content of the message. Also helpful are advertising agencies with local offices. The international marketer can not possibly know enough about all the cultures he or she will come into contact with. However, it is the responsibility of the international executive to make sure that knowledgeable local nationals have given enough input so that the mistake of using an inappropriate appeal with respect to the local culture will be avoided.

For successful advertising in Nigeria, Africa's largest and most populous nation, the standard advertising patterns used in other countries will not necessarily work.[7] Gulda beer ads showed a large, rough-hewn man in a blue-jean jacket based on the American movie character Shaft. The person is shown holding a mug, and the brown glass bottle of Gulda beer was on the table. The slogan "Gulda man, Gulda man, sure of his taste, proud to be different" was used. However, this ad did not appear to promote the brand. Research showed that Nigerian consumers of beer felt that good beer came only in green bottles. They noted that the person in the Gulda ad was always drinking alone. For many Nigerians, drinking beer was a social activity. The ad was finally changed. Gulda was presented in a green bottle, and the theme was changed to "Gulda makes you feel real fine," and the setting was changed to show elegant people drinking together. Sales volume increased dramatically.

Helene Curtis, a major company in the hair care market, tailored its advertising to suit the cultural differences of the various national markets while keeping intact the underlying theme of catering to the changing needs of the customer's hair. Hair care is different by national character and hair type also differs by region. Middle class women in Spain rarely wash their own hair whereas the opposite is true among British women. In Japan, Japanese women are fearful of overwashing their hair and losing its protective oils. As a result, the company needed to tailor its messages carefully to each national culture.[8]

The judgment on the appropriateness of a product or service for a culture is substantially more difficult than making a judgment only on the type of advertising to be employed. In Chapter 3 we discussed the nature of cultural and social forces, and in Chapter 7, we covered the evaluation of market potential for products. Therefore here we have restricted ourselves to a discussion of the advertising aspects of cultural analysis.

Selecting an Advertising Theme

For international marketers with products sold in many countries, the basic decision tends to center around the appropriate level of standardization for the advertising theme and its creative execution. As a result of early failures by inexperienced international companies in the early 1950s that employed a totally standardized approach, companies shifted to the other extreme by allowing each market to design

7. "Of Ads and Elders: Selling to Nigerians," *New York Times,* April 20, 1987, p. D10.
8. "Haircare Creates a Parting of the Ways," *Financial Times,* September 7, 1989, p. 12.

its own campaign. In the mid-1960s, European-based advertising executives started to discuss the possibility of greater standardization. Erik Elinder has been among the first to advocate the benefits of a more standardized approach.[9] Elinder argues that European consumers are increasingly "living under similar conditions although they read and speak different languages."[10]

Elinder has also pointed out that much of the European consumption has become international and that mass media coverage in several areas overlaps national boundaries. With people thinking and living more and more alike, why should advertising be different for each market?

Some of the barriers to standardized advertising are pointed out by Illmar Roostal, who indicated that many structural and organizational problems existed that could prevent companies from selecting a more standardized approach.[11] Among the factors preventing standardization are the absence of international advertising agencies with offices in many countries, the lack of interest among some companies to impose stricter controls over their local operations, the proliferation of languages, and the diversity of media characteristics by country.

What are the advantages of, or even the needs for, standardizing more of the firm's international advertising? First, there is the concern that *creative* talent is scarce and that one effort to develop a campaign will produce better results than forty or fifty efforts. This particularly applies to countries for which the marketing or advertising experience is limited. A second advantage centers around the economics of a global campaign. To create an individual campaign in many countries creates costs for photographs, layouts, and the production of television commercials. In a standardized approach, these production costs can be reduced and more funds can be spent on purchasing space in the media. One company, Levi Strauss, paid as much as $550,000 for one series of TV commercials. By reusing its commercials in many countries, the company saved in production costs. Furthermore, the company was able to spend more on the original version and, thus, produce a better advertisement.[12] A third reason for a standardized approach is found in global brand names. Many companies market products under a single brand name in several countries within the same region. With the substantial amount of international travel occurring today and the considerable overlap in media across national borders, companies are interested in creating a single image to avoid any confusion caused through local campaigns that may be in conflict with each other. L'Oreal, the French cosmetics

9. Erik Elinder, "How International Can Advertising Be?" *The International Advertiser,* December 1961, pp. 12–16; "How International Can European Advertising Be?" *Journal of Marketing,* April 1965, pp. 7–11.

10. "How International Can European Advertising Be?" *Journal of Marketing,* April 1965, p. 9.

11. Illmar Roostal, "Standardization of Advertising for Western Europe," *Journal of Marketing,* October 1963, pp. 15–20.

12. "Ads Astride the World," *Financial Times,* April 13, 1989, p. 16.

company, was one of the companies that aimed for a uniform identity for its international customer group.[13]

One of the best recent examples of a successful standardized campaign was Philip Morris' Marlboro campaign in Europe. Marlboro's success as a leading brand began in the 1950s when the brand was repositioned to assure smokers that the flavor would be unchanged by the effect of the filter. The theme *"Come to where the flavor is. Come to Marlboro country"* became an immediate success in the United States and abroad. The brand was the brand leader in West Germany with a 22 percent market share and was listed mostly among the top three brands in most European markets.[14] In all overseas markets, the advertising theme makes use of the same type of ad used in the United States. The cowboy has become a symbol of freedom and evokes the same feelings among Americans, Brazilians, or Germans. (This phenomenon was discussed earlier in Chapter 3 under the subject of reference groups.) Consequently, the cowboy is a relevant reference group for the German smoker, causing a positive identification. Marlboro's worldwide market share has shown an increase every year since 1965 and has reached sales of $9.4 billion in 1989. It was the world's most profitable consumer good surpassing even Coca-Cola.[15]

Levi Strauss, the world's largest clothing manufacturer, created a very successful advertising campaign for its European operations. Focusing on its traditional denim jeans, the "Launderette" commercial showed a young man walking into a 1950s launderette, stripping to his boxer shorts, and washing his Levi jeans to the sound of Marvin Gaye's soul music "I Heard it Through the Grapevine."[16] The commercial was later used in many international markets. Local rules, however, required a number of adaptations. Levi could not show the original commercial in the United States because another company held the copyright to the music. For Brazil and Australia, Levi had to re-shoot the commercials because local regulations required that commercials had to be made in those countries. In many Southeast Asian countries, local censors denied the company the right to run the commercial.

Levi Strauss's other successful commercial featuring denim jeans was the "Refrigerator" which features a young man driving his motorcycle up to a run-down hotel diner set in the Midwest, retrieving his 501-type Levi jeans from the refrigerator, putting the jeans on while a woman was looking on, and finally taking off with his Harley-Davidson.[17] To adjust to Australian requirements where women are important purchasers of jeans, the tone of the commercial was softened and the woman ended up roaring off on the motorcycle too.

13. "The Issue Globalists Don't Talk About," *International Management,* September 1987, p. 37.

14. "Cigarette Makers Now Look to Enhanced Big Grand Fire Power," *Financial Times,* April 26, 1990, p. 13.

15. "Defending the Rights of Marlboro Man," *The Economist,* April 21, 1990, p. 84.

16. "Ads Astride the World," *Financial Times,* April 13, 1989, p. 16.

17. Ibid.

As these examples show us, there are some specific factors that either allow or prevent some or parts of an advertising campaign to be standardized. The nature of these factors will be the topic of the following section.

Requirements for Standardized Campaigns

For a company to launch a worldwide standardized campaign, some requirements first have to be met. These requirements center around the name, packaging, awareness, competitive situation, and consumer or customer attitudes.

The need for a standardized brand name or trademark is viewed by many companies as a prerequisite to a standardized campaign. Not only should the name be written in identical format, but it should also be pronounced identically. The major product 7UP, which is sold in about 80 markets worldwide, is consistently pronounced in the English language in all countries.[18]

Trademarks or corporate logos can also help in achieving greater standardization of corporate campaigns. Such well known logos as Kodak's or General Electric's are used the world over.

Whirlpool, one of the world's largest manufacturers of domestic appliances, formed a joint venture in Europe with Philips in 1989. The two companies combined their European operations with Whirlpool as majority partner. As a result, Whirlpool became the world's largest appliance maker, overtaking Electrolux of Sweden. All appliances were to be marketed under Philips Whirlpool. The joint venture resulted in a market share of 12 percent in Europe compared to leader Electrolux of 22 percent. In the U.S. market, the positions were reversed with Whirlpool 30 percent and Electrolux with a 15 percent market share.[19]

Since Whirlpool was largely unknown to European consumers, the company undertook a Pan-European advertising campaign costing some $110 million over the next few years. The advertising was the result of some exhaustive testing of housewives in the United Kingdom, France, Spain, and Austria. The resulting two test campaigns were not universally accepted, forcing Whirlpool to develop a new campaign that was based on features that had tested positive in both test campaigns.[20] The introductory TV spot featured a woman and her son moving through an ultra-modern, computer-animated house from one electric appliance to another while a voice over described the economic and ecological advantages of using Philips Whirlpool and its reliability. However, some parts of the commercials had to be reshot to account for different washing machine configurations in Europe: the French and Finnish version show top-loading washers, the others feature front-loaders.[21]

18. Man in the Green Box Sells 7UP in World Markets," *Advertising Age,* May 19, 1975, p. 25.
19. "Whirlpool Striving to Clean Up Europe," *Advertising Age,* March 5, 1990, p. 30.
20. "Women of Europe Put Whirlpool in a Spin," *Financial Times,* March 1, 1990, p. 11a.
21. "Whirlpool Striving to Clean Up Europe," *Advertising Age,* March 5, 1990, p. 30.

The TV campaign will use the same ads in eleven countries. The strategy was to combine Philips' reputation for reliability with the U.S. firm's image of innovation and eventually create a Pan-European brand recognition that will completely phase out the Philips name by 1998. The phase-out is planned to take place country-by-country depending on how fast Whirlpool can establish its own identity.[22]

The Whirlpool entrance into Europe with a Pan-European campaign also prompted Electrolux to review its approach. The company had been using some twenty agencies for its thirty-six brands in Europe. For launching new brands and institutional advertising, more international advertising was planned.

To aid the prospective customer in identifying the advertised product with the actual one placed in retail stores, consumer products manufacturers in particular aim at packages that are of standardized appearance. Despite differences in sizes, these packages carry the same design in terms of color, layout, and name. Nonstandardized packages can not be featured in a standardized campaign, of course. Naturally, this concern is of much greater interest to consumer products companies since the package has to double both as a protective and a promotional device.

As products may be at different stages of their product life cycles in some countries, a need for different types of advertising may emerge due to the various levels of awareness customers have. Typically, a campaign during the earlier stages of the product life cycle concentrates on the product category since many prospective customers may not have heard about it. In later stages, with more intensive competition, the nature of the campaign tends to shift towards emphasizing the product's advantages over competitive products.

Consider the experience of Procter & Gamble when advertising first became available in former East Germany.[23] P&G developed a series of advertisements for TV that feature specific product information on a product's function rather than the typical ads situated in lifestyle situations aired for West German consumers. The company found that basic knowledge of consumer products such as fabric softeners, liquid detergents, and household cleaners were misused and the reusable containers intended to cut down on garbage were given to children as toys. The company expected that at some future time it would be able to air the same TV commercials throughout reunited Germany.

As companies enter new markets, they can expect to find different competitive situations that require an adjustment in the advertising campaign. Competing with a different group of companies and being placed in the position of an outsider often demands a change from the advertising policy used in the domestic market where these firms tend to have a strong position. The French company, Source Perrier, entered the U.S. market with its Perrier mineral water using a snob appeal. Emphasizing the product's noncaloric attributes, Perrier was positioned as an alternative to soft drinks or alcoholic beverages. With a premium price, Perrier was geared towards

22. "Whirlpool Seeks European Identity," *Financial Times,* January 13, 1990, p. 10.
23. "Lifestyle Ads Irk East Europeans," *Advertising Age,* October 8, 1990, p. 56.

the more affluent adults.[24] In European markets where Perrier was well entrenched and the drinking of mineral water accepted by a vast number of consumers, such an approach would not have yielded the same results.

Suntory, the leading Japanese whiskey distiller, dominates its domestic market with about a 60 percent market share. When entering the United States, however, the company also chose the snob appeal for people who looked for something special. Suntory's print advertising promoted its whiskey as "slightly east of Scotch." This campaign was specifically created for the U.S. market and differed substantially from Suntory's Japanese advertising which included a substantial amount of television commercials.[25]

A U.S. company that found itself in the role of an outsider in foreign markets was Anheuser-Busch. The largest U.S. beer brewer started to invade several foreign markets with tailor-made campaigns. In both Germany and France, the company promoted its beer as "The beer for the men of the West."[26] This campaign took into account the company's situation as a newcomer competing against highly reputed local brewers.

These three examples show companies with solid leadership positions at home entering foreign markets as outsiders. They were forced by this circumstance to develop advertising programs that were substantially different from those used in their home markets.

The Impact of Regulations on International Advertising

Although there are many situations where different customer needs require tailor-made advertising campaigns, in many instances it is the particular regulations of a country that prevent firms from using standardized approaches, even when they would appear desirable. When Coca-Cola internationally launched its theme, "Coke adds life," in the late 1970s, Scandinavian countries and Thailand refused the slogan because it was considered an overclaim. Eventually, the company was able to overturn the countries' prohibition after some considerable lobbying effort.[27] In countries such as Malaysia, regulations are a direct outgrowth of changing political circumstances. Following the growing influence of Moslem fundamentalists in many parts of the world, Malaysia, a country with a large Moslem population, outlawed ads showing women in sleeveless dresses and pictures showing underarms. These were

24. "Perrier: The Astonishing Success of an Appeal to Affluent Adults," *Business Week,* January 22, 1979, p. 64.

25. "The Liquor Industry's Aggressive New Ad Blitz," *Business Week,* March 20, 1978, p. 174.

26. "Anheuser Tries Light Beer Again," *Business Week,* June 29, 1981, p. 136.

27. "Curbs on Ads Increase Abroad as Nations Apply Standards of Fairness and Decency," *Wall Street Journal,* November 25, 1980, p. 56.

considered offensive by strict Moslem standards. Obviously, this caused considerable problems to marketers of deodorant products.[28]

Advertising for cigarettes and tobacco products are under strict regulations in many countries.[29] In France, R. J. Reynolds, the manufacturer of Camel cigarettes, was prohibited from showing humans smoking cigarettes. The company finally overcame the restrictions by showing a smiling camel smoking a Camel cigarette.[30] On the other hand, cigarette advertising is permitted in Greece, the only member of the Economic Community to do so. Although a ban exists on cigarette ads for television and radio, no limits exist for print advertising and posters.[31] On March 14, 1990, the European Parliament voted a complete ban of tobacco advertising throughout the European Community.[32] By the end of 1990, few of the largest fifty tobacco markets were expected to be without significant regulations on tobacco advertising, and in as many as twenty of them outright bans may be in effect.[33]

Advertising to children is also an area facing considerable regulation. General Mills, when marketing its Action Man soldiers in Germany, could not simply translate its copy into German. The company was forced to produce a very different television commercial by reducing the tone of the speaker's voice and the violence. Instead of showing the toy soldiers holding machine guns and driving tanks, they were shown unarmed and driving a jeep.[34] Kellogg could not use a commercial produced in the United Kingdom for its continental European business. The reference to Kellogg's cereals' iron and vitamin contents were not permissible in the Netherlands. The child wearing the Kellogg T-shirt in the original commercial had to be edited out for use in France, where children are forbidden to endorse a product. And the key line "Kellogg's makes their cornflakes the best they have ever been" would have been disallowed in Germany because of a prohibition against making competitive claims.[35]

As part of the Europe 1992 initiative, the European Community is debating a series of rulings that could have great impact on advertising in Europe. The discussions involve both efforts towards greater harmonization and the extent of regulation. Greater harmonization is generally viewed as desirable throughout Europe and potentially would result in equal regulations for advertising. This would greatly enhance the potential for Pan-European marketing campaigns and bring greater advertising efficiency. At issue is also the extent of regulation. Draft directives cov-

28. Ibid.

29. "Defending the Rights of Marlboro Man," *The Economist,* April 21, 1990, p. 84.

30. Ibid.

31. "Greece: No Limits on Ads for Cigarettes," *International Herald Tribune,* October 1, 1984, p. 15.

32. "Advertising: Single Marketing," *The Economist,* March 24, 1990, p. 64.

33. "Defending the Rights of Marlboro Man," *The Economist,* April 21, 1990, p. 84.

34. "Countries' Different Ad Rules Are Problem for Global Firms," *Wall Street Journal,* September 27, 1984, p. 33.

35. Ibid.

ering such areas as tobacco advertising, pharmaceuticals, or food claims tend to incorporate the most restrictive national regulations in many areas. Consequently, marketers are afraid that the end effect is "harmonizing the restrictions instead of harmonizing the freedoms."[36]

Other regulations companies may encounter cover the production of advertising material. Some countries require all advertising, particularly television and radio, to be produced locally. As a result, it has become a real challenge for international advertisers to find campaigns that can be used in as many countries as possible to save on the production costs. Such campaigns are, however, only possible if a company has sufficient input from the very beginning on the applicable legislation so this can be taken into account.

Advertising in the Japanese Market: The Land of the Soft Sell

Japan is the world's second largest advertising market with a total of $28 million (in 1988) growing at a faster rate than most other markets.[37] Advertising accounted for 1.2 percent of GNP in 1988, although still behind the 2.5 percent for the United States.[38] The dominating style of advertising in Japan was characterized by a subtle approach of "soft sell" compared to the "hard sell" typical in the United States or the "wit" prevalent in the United Kingdom.[39]

Given different cultural backgrounds, it is quite normal to expect differences in advertising appeals due to varying consumer attitudes. Japan offers us several examples that can be contrasted with experiences in the United States or Europe. In Japan, consumers tend to be moved more by emotion than by logic compared to North Americans or Europeans.[40] According to Gregory Clark, a European teaching at Sophia University in Tokyo, the Japanese are culturally oriented to consider the mood, style, and sincerity demonstrated by a deed more important than its content. Consequently, consumers are searching for ways to be emotionally convinced about a product. This leads to advertising that rarely mentions price, occasionally even omits the actual features or qualities of a product, and shies away from competitive advertising aimed at competing firms. This type of advertising is further supported by the Japanese language, which even has a verb *(kawasarern)* to describe the process of being convinced to buy a product contrary to one's own rational judgment.

Some differences are further elaborated by James Herendeen, an American executive working for one of the largest Japanese advertising agencies, Dai-Ichi

36. "Next Challenge: Re-regulation: 1992 Adding Up To Tough Ad Restrictions," *Advertising Age,* September 10, 1990, p. 57.

37. "Where Global Ambitions Come Unstuck," *Financial Times,* February 1, 1990, p. 9.

38. "Land of the Hardening Sell," *The Economist,* September 10, 1988, p. 89.

39. "In the Land of the Soft Sell," *Financial Times,* February 9, 1990, p. 20.

40. "Emotion, Not Logic, Sways the Japanese Consumer," *Japan Economic Journal,* April 22, 1980, p. 24.

Kikaku.[41] Japanese advertising has a strong nonverbal component, uses a contemporary Japanese language, frequently shows man-woman, mother-child, or even father-daughter relationships, demonstrates Japanese humor, and above all stresses long-term relationships. There is also some evidence of the individual's place in Japanese society in the use of evocative pictures or events to indicate individual values. With respect to the emotional tendency, Herendeen suggests the use of nonverbal communication or things that lead to inference rather than direct understanding. Also important is the product origin and the need to present the product as being right for the Japanese. This requires a strong corporate identity program to establish a firm's credibility in the Japanese market.

Research conducted for the Nikkei Advertising Research Institute in Japan on advertising expressions used in Japan, Korea, Taiwan, the United States, and France showed the high degree of nonverbal communication in Japan.[42] The study found that sentences of less than four phrases or words appeared in 50.1 percent of Japanese ads, 81.6 percent in Korea, 80.6 percent in Taiwan, but only 22.6 percent in the United States and 21.3 percent in France. The same study also compared the number of foreign words appearing in advertising headlines. Japan, with 39.2 percent, used the highest amount of foreign words, followed by Taiwan with 32.1 percent, by Korea with 15.7 percent, and by France with 9.1 percent. The United States used foreign words in only 1.8 percent of the headlines investigated. This underlines the strong Japanese interest in foreign countries and words, particularly those of the English language. A more recent study has confirmed the Japanese preference for less wordy advertising copy and a greater reliance on mood or symbolism.[43]

The need for a strong corporate image was emphasized in an annual survey of leading Japanese and foreign firms.[44] Table 15.1 contains the ratings for both domestic- and foreign-based food manufacturers active in the Japanese market. The Japanese firms with high ratings tended to be of long standing, technologically superior, diversified, and employing high quality personnel. Japanese consumers tended to buy these companies' products even if prices were high. The products were also used as gifts. The need for a strong corporate image also exists in the Japanese industrial goods market.

Although you may now conclude that American products do not sell in Japan, the reality shows that this is not necessarily so. Japanese television commercials are full of U.S. themes, use many U.S. stars or heroes, and are frequently using U.S. landscapes or backgrounds. By using U.S. stars in their commercials, Japanese companies give the impression that these products are very popular in the United States.

41. James Herendeen, "How to Japanize Your Creative," *International Advertiser,* September-October 1980, p. 22.

42. *Japan Economic Journal,* December 23, 1980, p. 33.

43. Jae W. Hong, Aydin Muderrisoglu, and George M. Zinkhan, "Cultural Differences and Advertising Expression: A Comparative Content Analysis of Japanese and U.S. Magazine Advertising," *Journal of Advertising,* 1987, vol. 16, no. 1, pp. 55–62.

44. *Japan Economic Journal,* December 23, 1980, pp. 33, 34.

TABLE 15.1 ● Ratings of Food Manufacturers in Japan (Percentage of Respondents Rating Companies as Excellent)

Foreign-affiliated companies			Japanese makers		
1	Coca-Cola (Japan)	66.4	1	Ajinomoto	83.7
2	Ajinomoto General Foods	56.7	2	Snow Brand Milk Products	83.5
3	Lipton Japan	46.5	3	Suntory	82.2
4	Twinings	45.0	4	Kirin Brewery	81.6
5	Nestlé Japan	43.9	5	Morinaga Milk Ind.	80.7
6	PepsiCo (Japan)	30.7	6	Kikkoman Shoyu	77.3
7	McDonald's	29.9	7	Taiyo Fishery	71.0
8	Brookbond	27.5	8	Nippon Suisan	68.2
9	Kirin-Seagram	20.8	9	Lotte	62.8
10	Yamazaki Nabisco	20.8	10	Calpis	61.3

Source: The Japan Economic Journal, December 23, 1980, p. 33. Reprinted by permission.

Given the Japanese interest and positive attitudes towards many American cultural themes, such strategies have worked out well for Japanese advertisers. This is why Nissan asked Paul Newman to drive its new car, Skyline, in its ads, and why John Travolta was asked to appear in an ad sipping a new semialcoholic fruit juice.[45] When Mitsubishi Electric paid rock-singer Madonna a reported $650,000 for the right to use fragments of a rock tour, the company's VCR sales doubled in three months while competitors experienced only a 15 percent increase.[46] Actress Faye Dunaway was paid some $900,000 by the Tokyo department store Parco for saying only, "This is an ad for Parco.[47]" In contrast to U.S. testimonials, however, Japanese advertisers tend to use foreign stars as actors using the product but not openly endorsing it.

A more recent development is the use of Japanese in an international setting. This leads to the use of Japanese models or business persons in foreign settings such as Matushita's ad depicting a jazz-loving employee visiting the United States where he is given a welcoming embrace by his friend who happens to be a black New Orleans saxophone player. Asahi, a successful Japanese brewery who launched the dry beer, used actual Japanese professionals working in the United States in a series of ads in Japan to show that "the brains created in Japan are becoming successful abroad."[48] It is part of a Japanese tendency to strive for product awareness only;

45. "U.S. Sets the Pace Despite Growing Pride in Things Japanese," *International Herald Tribune,* October 1, 1984, p. 12.
46. "Madonna in Japan," *Fortune,* September 15, 1986, p. 9.
47. Ibid.
48. "Tokyo TV Ads Portray Japanese as the Savvy International Type," *Wall Street Journal,* October 11, 1990, p. B6.

advertisements are devoid of any mention of the product itself. As a result, comparative advertising rarely exists in Japan; and before and after claims are also seldom used. According to some experts, Western advertising is designed to make the product look superior, whereas Japanese advertising is aimed at making it desirable.[49]

Advertising in Japan differed also from Western practice in its management and structure. In Japan, the conflict of interest rules did not apply and competing brands could be handled by the same agency. The market was dominated by Dentsu, by far Japan's largest agency and one of the world's largest advertising agencies. Dentsu is the Japanese media's largest single customer accounting for some 20 percent of all newspaper ads and about 15 percent of all TV advertising. As such, Dentsu usually commands the best price and the best space in the press.[50] None of the other major advertising markets in the world is dominated by a single local agency.

The Impact of Recent Changes in Eastern Europe on Advertising

With the political changes in Eastern Europe, advertising has suddenly become available to foreign companies and is developing as an acceptable economic activity. It has been hampered by the fact that commercial advertising as known in the open economies had been used largely for political purposes and to advertise excess goods. When the markets in Eastern Europe opened up, changes had to come both in the media policy of these countries and in the acceptability of advertising.

Residents of East Germany had been exposed to advertising through access to West German TV and some publications. However, because East German residents have had little exposure to some of these new consumer goods, the approach to advertising there is usually different than that for the same company in West Germany.[51] Ford purchased one-minute TV commercials in each of the forty-one soccer world championship games aired in East Germany. Its approach was less creative than that used for West Germany, described as a "down-to-earth good commercial." Many companies about to launch their products in East Germany had to postpone advertising efforts until distribution to local residents was assured.

In other Eastern European nations, advertising is likewise in the early phases of development. The present infrastructure is radically different from what international firms are used to. Few full-service advertising agencies exist. Many Western agencies are now developing local offices, some as joint ventures with local managers.

In Hungary, about 150 advertising agencies are said to exist. About 100 of those have been formed since the early 1980s. Total advertising spending is estimated at no more than $140 million (1990). Of the top ten agencies, four are government-owned, including the top 2. The other six have foreign partners, including some leading international agencies such as McCann-Erickson since 1988. Some of these joint ventures are expected to be turned into wholly-owned agencies in the near future.

---

49. "Advertising: Upping a Youthful Image," *Financial Times,* October 22, 1986, p. VI.
50. "In the Land of the Soft Sell," *Financial Times,* February 9, 1990, p. 20.
51. "E. Germany Gets New Ad Efforts," *Advertising Age,* July 2, 1990, p. 4.

These agencies attract both Hungarian and international companies.[52] The liberalization of the Hungarian economy has also brought new media. Aside from the opening of local print, *Business Week* and *Playboy* were two among many other international publications offering Hungarian language editions and accepting print advertising.[53]

Nowhere have the changes been more pronounced than in the Soviet Union. The Soviet government had decided only in February of 1988 that marketing would become a priority under perestroika.[54] Total advertising spending in the Soviet Union by foreign companies was estimated at only $10 million annually with most of it going towards trade fairs.[55] Outside posters and neon signs were among the first signs of advertising to appear with Samsung and Goldstar, both of South Korea, to be among the first firms to pay the $200,000 in annual fees for two spots in Moscow or Leningrad.[56]

Procter & Gamble was one of the first U.S. companies to pursue commercial TV advertising in the Soviet Union. The company sponsored the homecoming concert in Moscow of the famous Russian cellist, Mstislav Rostropovich, and was allowed to air a 12-minute commercial explaining its long company history and its various brands.[57] P&G is exporting several brands to the Soviet Union, among them Crest toothpaste and Camay soap. Colgate Palmolive, one of the world leaders in toothpaste, is importing Colgate toothpaste from an Indian company. Both companies can sell whatever they can ship.[58] Colgate had previously given away hundreds of thousands of toothpaste samples. When the company exhibited in a trade show in Moscow and gave away free samples, local residents stood in line for two hours. Many were reported to have returned to the end of the line for another sample. With strong interest among international firms to eventually be present in the large Soviet consumer market, several international advertising agencies have set up shop in Moscow, with Young and Rubicam and Ogilvy & Mather among them.

GLOBAL ADVERTISING

Global advertising has received a considerable amount of attention in the 1980s and can now be considered the most controversial topic in international advertising. The debate was triggered by Professor Theodore Levitt who argues in an article and in his

52. "Western Ad Agencies Push into Hungary," *Advertising Age,* June 11, 1990, p. 43.

53. "Playboy Shifts Image in Hungary," *Advertising Age,* August 6, 1990, p. 24 and "Business Week to Break Into Hungary," *Advertising Age,* March 12, 1990, p. 56.

54. "UK Helps to Make Advertising and Promotion a Priority of Perestroika," *Financial Times,* December 8, 1988, p. 12.

55. "Look But Don't Touch," *The Economist,* June 16, 1990, p. 118.

56. "UK Helps to Make Advertising and Promotion a Priority of Perestroika."

57. "Mad Ave. Takes the Perestroika Challenge," *Business Week,* March 5, 1990, p. 68.

58. "Colgate, P&G Pack for Road to Russia," *Advertising Age,* March 12, 1990, p. 56.

recent book, *The Marketing Imagination,* that markets are becoming increasingly alike worldwide and that the trend is toward a global approach to marketing.[59] Levitt's ideas were applied to the field of international advertising by Saatchi & Saatchi, a British advertising agency, who rose to prominence on the basis of its global campaigns.[60] Saatchi & Saatchi claimed that worldwide brands would soon become the norm and that such an advertising challenge could only be handled by worldwide agencies. One such advertising campaign for Procter & Gamble's Pampers has been used successfully throughout the world.

The proponents of global advertising cite several trends as indicators of what the future of international advertising will be.[61] Consumer tastes, needs, and purchasing patterns are said to be converging. This can be supported by the converging trends in demographics across many countries. At the forefront of these trends has been the decline of the nuclear family, both in the United States and in many countries around the globe. In most countries, more women are working. Similarly, divorce trends are increasingly pointing in the same direction in both the United States, Europe, and other developed countries. This has changed the role of women in society almost everywhere. Standards of living have risen in many countries and earlier differences among nations have been reduced. In addition to these demographic trends, common media such as films, television, and music are creating cultural convergence as well. These developments are said to reduce cultural barriers among countries; and these barriers are expected to be reduced even more through satellite television networks covering many countries with identical programs.

One of the stronger believers in global advertising, British Airways, broke new ground in its industry by airing the well-known "Manhattan" TV commercial in 1983. Designed by Saatchi & Saatchi, the spot showed the flight across the Atlantic and the landing on the island of Manhattan as an expression of British Airways flying as many passengers annually across the Atlantic as people lived in Manhattan. In 1989, the same advertising agency designed a new global campaign for British Airways featuring some 4,000 people greeting each other and interspersed with the creation of a smiling face when viewed from the air. The commercial was produced in the Midwest and directed by a well-known movie director. The company believes that the strong visual value allows it to use the production everywhere resulting in a global campaign production cost of about half the traditional cost of creating advertising for each market.[62]

For a global strategy to be successful, indications are that four requirements must be fulfilled. First, the product must be able to deliver the same benefit in each market. Second, the market or the product category development in each market

59. Theodore Levitt, "The Globalization of Markets," *Harvard Business Review,* May-June 1983, p. 92; *The Marketing Imagination* (New York: Free Press, 1983); and *International Herald Tribune,* October 1, 1984, p. 7 (interview with Theodore Levitt).

60. "Saatchi & Saatchi Will Keep Gobbling," *Fortune,* June 23, 1986, p. 36.

61. "Advertising by Saatchi & Saatchi Compton," *New York Times,* January 22, 1984, p. 87.

62. "BA's Warm Approach," *Financial Times,* December 28, 1989, p. 8.

must be at the same level in terms of product life cycle, penetration, and usage. Third, the competitive environment must be similar in each market. This refers to the type of competition and the nature of the competitive products encountered. And fourth, the heritage of the brand must not be restricted to particular countries and the brand history must be similar in the various markets.[63]

Many marketing professionals remain skeptical about the claims for global advertising.[64] Although many observers agree that for products aimed at the very affluent market in many countries, global marketing may be an advantage since these highly affluent and mobile consumers can be thought of as living in a global village.[65] Products included may range from diamonds to whiskey, to very expensive watches. Because of the many local differences that become evident in making up a global advertising campaign, many advertising agency executives remain dubious about the prospect for large-scale global advertising. Instead, indications are that more regionalized approaches, such as for Europe or for Asia, may be more appropriate at this time than going directly to a global approach.[66]

What may be more likely to happen is a modularized approach to international advertising. A company may select some features as standard for all its advertising while localizing some others. Pepsi Cola chose this approach in its 1986 international campaign. The company wanted to use modern music in connection with its products while still using some local identification. As a result, with the assistance of Ogilvy and Mather, its advertising agency, Pepsi Cola hired the U.S. singer, Tina Turner, who teamed up in a big concert setting with local rock stars from six countries singing and performing the Pepsi Cola theme song. In the commercials, the local rock stars are shown together with Tina Turner. Except for the footage of the local stars, all the commercials are identical. For other countries, local rock stars are spliced into the footage so that they also appear to be on stage with Tina Turner. By shooting the commercials all at once the company saved in production costs. The overall concept of the campaign can be extended to some thirty countries without forcing local subsidiaries or bottlers to come up with their own campaigns.[67]

MEDIA SELECTIONS

Across the world, the international marketer is faced with a variety of different media. Difficulties arise because not all media are available in all countries; or if they

63. M. Roland Jeannet, "Global Advertising," presentation made at 1988 Annual Conference of UK Advertising Agency Planners, London, 1988.

64. "Global Marketing Debated," *New York Times,* November 13, 1985, p. D21.

65. Rena Bartos, "And What About the Consumer Who Brushes His Teeth With Shampoo?" *International Herald Tribune,* October 1, 1984, p. 8.

66. "Prof. Real World's Lesson for Levitt," *Advertising Age,* January 6, 1986, p. 17.

67. "Advertising: Tina Turner Helping Pepsi's Global Effort," *New York Times,* March 10, 1986, p. D13.

are available, their technical quality or capability to deliver to the required audience may be limited. Therefore, aside from the considerations that concern domestic operations, international media decisions are influenced by the availability or accessibility of various media for advertisers and the media habits of the target country.

Media Availability

Advertisers in the United States have become accustomed to the availability of a full range of media for advertising purposes. Aside from the traditional print media consisting of newspapers and magazines, the U.S. advertiser has access to radio and television as well as billboards and cinemas. In addition, there is the availability of direct mail to any prospective client group.

Aside from the socialist and communist countries of the Eastern bloc, commercial radio is still not available in Norway, Denmark, Sweden, Finland, Switzerland, and Saudi Arabia. In Norway, Denmark, Sweden, and Saudi Arabia not even commercial television is available for advertisers.[68] Consequently, a company marketing its products in several countries may find itself unable to apply the same media mix in all markets. Even when some media are available, access may be partially restricted. The use of commercials interspersed throughout programs on radio or television is common in the United States, Japan, and Latin America among others, but less so in Europe. In Germany, advertisers have access to commercial television only during a few blocks of time, several minutes long at several time slots.[69] Because the commercials are not shown during frequent intervals as interruptions to TV programming, viewership of these preannounced commercial blocks tends to be very low. In addition, the time available for commercials is limited to forty minutes daily. For the most preferred block on German television, the evening program, less than half of the firms applying will ever be able to obtain media time. Therefore some firms have avoided television altogether because they were unable to obtain frequent showings, which are necessary for a successful campaign. Similar restrictions exist in several other European countries. Difficulties also exist for companies with existing television schedules. In some countries, the available time for commercials is allocated for various product groups, often regardless of the number of competitors or products on the market. For some competitive product categories, new products may only be launched by reallocating a company's television time among its existing products. This lack of flexibility inhibits new product introduction in some consumer product categories where television would be the most efficient advertising media.

Existing government regulations have also had a substantial impact on how much television advertising is used. In Europe, television time is freely available in

68. *Fifteenth Survey of Advertising Expenditures in 1983,* by International Advertising Research Associates (INRA), New York, 1985.
69. "Werbung: Bis Zum Spaten Abend," *Der Spiegel,* November 22, 1981, p. 81.

the United Kingdom, Greece, Ireland, Portugal, Spain, and Italy.[70] In Italy, the breakup of the state monopoly in 1976 resulted in the creation of several hundred commercial television stations alone.[71] In those countries, television advertising equals 30 to 50 percent of the print advertising volume. In European countries with restricted or limited access, television advertising amounts to about 5 to 20 percent of the total amount spent on print advertising. In Sweden, television advertising is not allowed and all advertising is in print (see Table 15.2).

The availability of media may also be limited by law. Most countries do not allow advertising for cigarettes or alcoholic beverages on television or radio, though they are usually permitted in print media. When the leading Japanese whiskey distiller Suntory entered the United States market, the company had to do without television, its preferred medium.[72] In Japan, Suntory was estimated to have spent about $50 million annually on television advertising because no restrictions existed with respect to alcoholic beverages there.

According to industry data, Europeans spend about .75 percent of GNP on advertising compared to 1 percent for Japan and 1.5 percent for the United States. In 1983, TV advertising amounted to $4.3 billion or only 20 percent of total European advertising expenditures. This compares to some $16.2 billion for the United States (32.5 percent of all advertising expenditures). If Europeans increased TV advertising to 1 percent of GNP and spent 30 percent of all advertising on TV, instead of only 20 percent, TV revenue could double and would require much more airtime to accommodate the new demand.[73]

These examples demonstrate that, on an international basis, companies have to remain flexible with respect to their media plans. A company cannot expect to be able to use its preferred media to the fullest extent everywhere. Consequently, international advertising campaigns will have to be designed with delivery over several media in mind.

Credibility of Advertising

Countries view the value of advertising in very different ways. In the United States, one study found that about two-thirds of the population felt abused by advertising.[74] In the United Kingdom, approval amounted to about 77 percent. In Germany, where television commercials are bunched up in a few blocks of about 10 minutes each, viewership is very low. Viewership rates have been steadily decreasing—

---

70. "European Ads' Potential 'Vast'," *Financial Times,* March 24, 1983, p. 10.

71. "U.S. Style TV Turns on Europe," *Fortune,* April 13, 1987, p. 95.

72. "The Liquor Industry's Aggressive New Ad Blitz," *Business Week,* March 20, 1978, p. 174.

73. "Pan-European Television: The Sky's Limit for Broadcasters," *The Economist,* February 8, 1986, p. 71.

74. "Are Ads Your Favorite Reading?" *The Economist,* September 5, 1981, p. 31.

TABLE 15.2 ● Concise Guide to Advertising in Twenty-Two Countries

	Austria	*Australia*	*Belgium*	*Brazil*
Total advertising expenditure 1979 Local Currency	7,900 Million A.S.	1,482 Million Dollars	9,500 Million Francs	50,700 Million Cruzeiros
Total expressed as a % of Gross National Product	0.88%	1.46%	0.3%	0.95%
Breakdown of Advertising Expenditure by principal media. %				
TV	16.5	30.3	12.8	42.0
National Press	⎫	10.6	31.0 ⎤	
Regional Press	25.3 ⎬	29.4 ⎫	10.8 ⎦	22.5
Magazines/Periodicals	⎭	7.6 ⎬	28.7 ⎤	9.5
Trade & Technical	In Other	2.6 ⎭	⎦	
Radio	6.5	8.8	1.2	16.0
Cinema	0.3	1.6	1.2	0.5
Outdoor	4.2	9.1	14.3	3.5
Other	47.2	NA	NA	6.0
Proportion of households with TV sets	91%	96%	93%	54%
Proportion of households with color TVs	44%	75%	50%	30%
Number of TV channels accepting advertising/ sponsorship	2	50	None but RTL Luxembourg is received	89
Advertising time in 24 hour period. Approximate minutes	20	154	62 (RTL)	360
Restrictions on TV advertising	No tobacco, hard liquor; regulated drugs and foods. Restrictions on children's advertising	No cigarettes	No tobacco, alcohol	No alcohol, cigarettes, cigars, until 9 PM
	+DM, −AC, PC	−DM, PC, PC	−DM, PC, +AC	+DM, AC, PC

Note: NA = not available. * = insignificant amount. O = medium not used. DM = direct mail. AC = agency commission. PC = production cost.

Source: From William J. Hawkes' presentation at the International Marketing Workshop AMA/MSI, March 1983, of A. C. Nielsen Company material. Reprinted by permission of A. C. Nielsen Company.

TABLE 15.2 ● Concise Guide to Advertising in Twenty-Two Countries (*cont.*)

Canada	*Switzerland*	*Germany*	*Spain*	*Ireland*	*France*
3.008 Million Dollars	981 Million Francs	10,786 Million D. Marks	64,800 Million Pesetas	45.1 Million Punts	17,400 Million Francs
1.16%	0.6%	0.8%	0.5%	0.6%	0.83%
16.6	12.1	9.6	33.0	32.1	9.5
*	55.9	48.1 ⎱	29.4	32.6 ⎱	
28.6 ⎱	NA ⎱	⎰		7.9 ⎰	17.5
17.9 ⎰	32.0 ⎰	18.4 ⎱	16.9	1.5 ⎱	
19.1	NA	* ⎰		* ⎰	21.1
11.4	0	3.3	12.3	9.9	6.5
O	NA	0.8	1.9	*	1.0
6.4	NA	3.6	6.5	6.0	9.3
*	NA	16.2	NA	*	35.2
97%	84%	85%	95%	85%	92%
81%	53%	62%	30%	32%	33%
95	3	2	2	2	2
216 Per Channel	60	40	85	85	48
No cigarettes, liquor. Regional restrictions on beer and children's advertising.	No alcohol, tobacco, drugs, politics, religion.	No cigarettes, religion, charities, narcotics, prescription drugs, children's advertising, cures.	No tobacco, hard drinks.	No tobacco, contraceptives, religion, politics.	Many categories are excluded: alcohol, margarine, slimming products, tobacco products, etc.
+DM, PC, −AC	−DM, AC, PC	+DM, −AC, PC	−DM, AC, PC	−DM, AC, PC	+DM, AC, −PC

TABLE 15.2 ● Concise Guide to Advertising in Twenty-Two Countries (*cont.*)

	Great Britain	Greece	Italy	Japan	Mexico
Total advertising expenditure 1979 Local Currency	2,219 Million Pounds	3735.6 Million Drachmas	1,186 Billion Liras	2,113 Billion Yen	9,660 Million Pesos
Total expressed as a % of Gross National Product	1.34%	0.32%	0.35%	0.95%	0.36%
Breakdown of Advertising Expenditure by principal media. %					
TV	22.1	46.4	19	⎰ 35.5	⎰ 65.0
National Press	⎱		⎰ 24	31.0	8.0
Regional Press	⎱ 48.0	27.8	⎱	⎱	⎱ NA
Magazines/Periodicals	⎰		⎰ 53	5.3	4.0
Trade & Technical	⎱ 22.3	20.0	⎱ NA	In "other"	1.0
Radio	2.4	4.6	4	5.0	15.0
Cinema	0.8	NA	NA	In "other"	4.0
Outdoor	4.4	1.1	NA	In "other"	2.5
Other	NA	NA	NA	23.1	0.5
Proportion of households with TV sets	94%	95%	96%	98%	43.8%
Proportion of households with color TVs	65%	5%	27%	96%	None
Number of TV channels accepting advertising/sponsorship	1	2	2+ Many private stations	93	15
Advertising time in 24 hour period. Approximate minutes	80	120	27 excluding private stations	230	12 Hour/station
Restrictions on TV advertising	No contraceptives, cigarettes, politics, gambling, religion or charities	No cigarettes, ethical drugs	No jewels, furs, newspapers, magazines, cigarettes, gambling, clinics & hospitals	No overstatement, comparison with competitors, sensual messages on commercial films	No liquor before 10 PM
	−DM, +AC, PC	−DM, PC, +AC	−DM, PC, +AC	+DM, AC, PC	−DM, PC, +AC

TABLE 15.2 ● Concise Guide to Advertising in Twenty-Two Countries (*cont.*)

Netherlands	New Zealand	Portugal	Argentina	Sweden	United States	South Africa
3,825 Million Florins	195.5 Million Dollars	1462.5 Million Escudos	1,028 Billion Pesos	2,004 Million Kronor	49,690 Million Dollars	290 Million Rands
1.29%	1.12%	0.2%	1.27%	0.46%	2.1%	1.8% (G.D.P.)
5.0	25.4	55	24.6	0	20.5	19.3
46.9	0			36	4.2	35.3
	48.1	29	42.3	41	25.1	4.1
8.7	6.6			16	5.9	16.3
3.6	NA		15.7		3.4	6.5
0.7	8.2	16	9.0	0	6.6	12.0
0.3	1.2	NA	1.4	1	0	2.1
6.1	0.3	NA	6.1	5	1.1	4.4
28.7	10.2	NA	0.9	NA	33.2	NA
97%	95%	NA	86%	93%	98%	26.5%
65%	70%	NA	18%	71%	83%	18.4%
2	2	2	38	None	728	1
30	260	30	10 Hour/channel	—	Voluntary code: hour/station	24
No tobacco, political, religion. Special legislation for pharmaceuticals, sweets, alcohol	No cigarettes, alcohol, feminine hygiene products, contraceptives, politics	No tobacco, gambling, liquor only after 9 P.M. Restrictions on medicines	No use of foreign words or slang. No attitudes against morals. No misuse of country symbols	—	No tobacco, contraceptives, fortune tellers	No Sunday advertising, no spirits, wine, beer, cigarettes after 9 PM except Saturday. No "sensitive" products
+DM, AC, −PC	+DM, AC, +PC	−DM, PC, +AC		−DM	+DM, AC, PC	−DM, AC, PC

observers believe that this low rate is a direct result of the German's critical opinion of advertising in general and the television medium specifically.

In Eastern Europe, where TV commercials had been used to sell products generally considered too shoddy to sell, consumers became skeptical of advertising in general. This skepticism was enhanced by the fact that the former communist regimes frequently used advertising for propaganda purposes, thus undermining its credibility.[75]

In other countries, particularly those of the developing world, advertising tends to be held in much higher regard. Advertised products have more prestige and those advertised on television are viewed by consumers as the most prestigious. Experts believe that the Japanese basically believe in the message of an advertisement, quite the opposite from U.S. consumers.

Differences in the credibility of advertising in general, and some media in particular, will have to be taken into consideration by the international firm. Companies may want to place a greater reliance on advertising in countries where its credibility is very high. In other countries, the use of alternative forms of communication may be stressed.

Media Habits

As the experienced media buyer for any domestic market knows, the media habits of the target market are major factors in deciding which media to use. The same applies on the international level. However, substantial differences in the media habits exist due to a number of factors that are of little importance to the domestic or single country operation. First of all, the penetration of various media differs substantially from one country to another. Secondly, we encounter radically different literacy rates in many parts of the world. And finally, we may find different cultural habits or traits that favor one media over another regardless of the penetration ratios or literacy rates.

Ownership or usage of television, radio, newspapers, or magazines varies substantially from one country to another. Whereas the developed industrial nations show high penetration ratios for all three major media carriers, other countries of the Third World have few radio and television receivers or low newspaper circulation (see Table 15.2). In general, the use or penetration of all of these media increases with the average income of a country. In most countries, the higher income classes avail themselves first of the electronic media and newspapers. International marketers have to be aware that some media, though generally accessible for the advertiser, may be only of limited use since they reach only a small part of the country's target population.

The literacy of a country's population is an important factor influencing media decisions. Though this is less of a concern for companies in the industrial products market, it is a crucial factor in consumer goods advertising. In countries where large

---

75. "Lifestyle Ads Irk East Europeans," *Advertising Age,* October 8, 1990, p. 56.

portions of the population are illiterate, the use of print media is of limited value. (Please see Table 3.2 for literacy rates of selected countries.) Both radio and television have been used by companies to circumvent the literacy problem. Other media that are occasionally used for this purpose are billboards or cinemas. The absence of a high level of literacy has forced consumer goods companies to translate their advertising campaigns into media and messages that communicate strictly by sound or demonstration. Television and radio have been used most successfully to overcome this problem, but they cannot be used in areas where the penetration of such receivers is limited. Frequently, this applies particularly to countries that have low electronic media penetration and low literacy rates.

In most developed countries, detailed statistics are available to advertisers documenting the time people spend in contact with any given medium. A survey conducted by the A. C. Nielsen Co. in 1980 determined that the average family in Tokyo, Japan used a television set for 8 hours and 12 minutes a day.[76] The corresponding figure for the United States amounted to 6 hours and 4 minutes. The difference between the U.S. and Japanese attitudes becomes even more apparent in a poll conducted in both countries.[77] People were asked which of the following items they would keep if they had to make do with all but one: television, newspapers, telephone, automobile, and refrigerator. The answers were as follows:

	United States	*Japan*
Television	3%	31%
Newspapers	6%	23%
Telephone	9%	16%
Automobile	39%	15%
Refrigerator	42%	13%

Consequently, 31 percent of the polled Japanese would rather give up all other four items to keep their television, whereas only 3 percent of the Americans felt that way.

In both the United States and Europe, viewership of television appears on the decline. This has caused some companies to make adjustments in the media mix for those areas. In other countries, particularly those of the Third World, media habits are rapidly shifting towards electronic media as ownership of radio and television receivers is becoming more common. For a more detailed summary of media habits in various countries, see Table 15.3.

Satellite Television

Satellite television channels, which are not subject to government regulations, have revolutionized television in many parts of the world. The impact of satellite television channels is nowhere felt more directly than in Europe.

76. *International Herald Tribune,* July 26, 1982.
77. Ibid.

TABLE 15.3 ● Advertising Expenditure Survey

1989 Total Advertising Expenditure Current Prices in Local Currency			Percentage Distribution of Measured Media				
			Print	TV	Radio	Cinema	Outdoor/ Transit
Austria	10,535	(m AS)	55.1	30.4	13.5	1.0	—
Belgium	47,095	(m BF)	57.3	28.8	0.9	1.8	11.1
Denmark	7,569	(m DKr)	87.9	8.1	1.4	0.7	1.8
Finland	5,136	(m FIM)	80.6	13.0	3.8	0.1	2.5
France	55,311	(m FF)	50.3	28.0	7.7	0.9	13.1
Germany	22,616	(m DM)	80.6	11.2	4.1	1.0	3.1
Greece	57,001	(m Dra)	45.1	40.8	7.3	—	6.8
Ireland	173	(m Punt)	52.6	29.9	10.4	—	7.2
Italy	6,276	(bn Lire)	42.8	51.5	1.6	—	4.1
Netherlands	7,932	(m FL)	83.8	11.6	2.2	0.3	2.1
Norway	4,745	(m NKr)	94.3	1.6	0.8	1.2	2.1
Portugal	45,044	(m Esc)	37.0	47.6	8.8	—	6.6
Spain	860,000	(m Ptas)	52.9	30.1	11.1	0.8	5.1
Sweden	12,907	(m SKr)	94.3	—	—	0.9	4.8
Switzerland	4,776	(m SF)	75.7	7.5	2.0	1.1	13.7
United Kingdom	8,313	(m £)	63.6	30.3	2.1	0.5	3.6
Japan	5,072	(bn Yen)	43.1	37.2	5.3	—	14.5
USA	123,930	(m $)	58.1	31.0	2.1	0.5	3.6

Source: From *World Advertising Expenditures 1989,* Twenty-Fourth Survey (Marmoroneck, NY: Stardon Inra Hooper, Inc.) 1989, pp. 10, 11, 42, 43.

The leader in this field of privately owned channels is Sky Channel owned by Rupert Murdoch, who also has substantial media interests in many countries. Sky Channel had reached 4.7 million homes in thirteen countries by the end of 1985, and it transmitted a maximum of 17 hours per day. Sky claimed that about 10 percent of all TV viewers served watched its channel. About one-third of all advertising revenue is generated from U.S. companies, another one-third from Japanese, and some 20 percent from continental Europe. Advertisers include such well-known companies as Canon, Digital, NEC, Kodak, Mattel, Nikon, Panasonic, Ford, Toyota, Xerox, Remington, Siemens, and Unilever.[78]

Originally only available as English speaking television, satellite channels are now available in several European languages such as German, French, or Swedish. Some 42.9 million viewers tuned into satellite TV in Europe in 1989.[79] This represents a 70 percent increase over 1988. The average weekly viewing almost doubled to 7 hours. One of the largest winners was CNN with an increase of almost 184 percent.

With the advent of local language satellite TV more attractive than the traditional national TV channels, many viewers left the English speaking channels of Sky and Super Channel.[80] Sky is still operating in the red after eight years. Furthermore, satellite TV has not attracted as much advertising expenditures as first anticipated with major advertisers only scheduling about 2 percent of their budgets on satellite TV.[81]

The presently existing satellite networks have not yet attracted a large number of advertisers. Companies still prefer an entire national audience, such as all of Germany, to a small segment throughout Western Europe. However, a recent deal arranged between Gillette and the Murdoch group of broadcasting channels may be an indication as to what companies may be able to do in the future. In October 1986, Gillette began to air through Sky Channel in Europe. The same advertisement had been carried earlier by Murdoch's Fox Broadcasting System in the United States and Network Ten, the group's Australian system. This arrangement allowed Gillette to show the same commercial in all three continents.[82]

Different firms are using satellite television for different purposes. Polaroid used it to advertise its sunglasses on Super Channel, an English language channel, to reach mostly younger people in the Netherlands. Polaroid found that the domestic Dutch TV channel reached an older audience, which was less appropriate for its products. On the other hand, Nissan used Super Channel to promote its corporate image in Europe. Nissan executives believed that the English language channel would get superior results for the unification of its image.[83]

For satellite-shown commercials to be effective, companies would have to be able to profit from a global brand name and a uniform logo. Also, language remains a problem, with English being the only language of the majority of satellite channels.

---

78. "Advertising Potential Elevated by Satellite," *Financial Times,* November 14, 1985, p. 12.

79. "Europe's Satellite TV Viewers Soar," *Advertising Age,* September 24, 1990, p. 39.

80. "Auf Wiedersehen, Roops," *The Economist,* September 17, 1988, p. 80.

81. "Satellite Broadcasting: Healthy Long-Term Outlook," *Financial Times,* March 14, 1989, p. V.

82. "Advertising: Global Network Beams Nearer," *Financial Times,* October 22, 1986, p. IV.

83. "Super Channel: A Test for the Global Concept," *Financial Times,* February 17, 1987, p. 11.

FIGURE 15.2 ● Commercial TV Advertising Time in European Countries in Minutes per Day

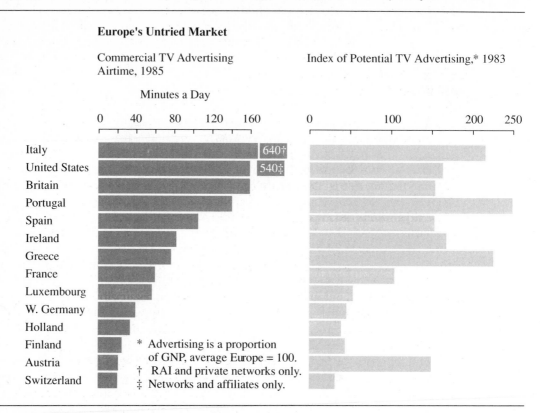

Source: "Pan-European Television: The Sky's the Limit for Broadcasters," *The Economist*, February 8, 1986, p. 71. © 1986 The Economist Newspaper Ltd. Used by permission.

But most observers admit that the availability of satellite commercial networks has already had an impact on the national regulatory boards of countries that have tended to restrict or limit commercial air time (see Figure 15.2). It is now expected that even in Scandinavia, commercial television will become the norm. In other parts of Europe, existing commercial television time is not expected to lose out to other channels. This may substantially enlarge the TV advertising market in Europe.

SCHEDULING INTERNATIONAL ADVERTISING

The general rule in scheduling advertising suggests that the company more or less duplicates the sales curve or seasonality of its product. Furthermore, depending on the complexity of the buying decision or the deliberation time, the media expenditures tend to peak before the actual sales peak. This practice, though somewhat generalized here, applies as well to foreign or international markets. Differences may exist, however, due to different sales peaks in the year, vacations, or religious holidays, and differences in the deliberation time with regard to purchases.

Sales peaks are influenced both by climatic seasons or by customs and traditions. Winter months in the United States or Europe are summer months in some countries of the southern hemisphere; namely Australia, New Zealand, South Africa, or Argentina. This substantially influences the purchase of many consumer goods such as clothing, vacation services, travel, and so on. Vacations are particularly important for some European countries. In Europe, summer school vacations tend to be shorter than in the United States, but employees are granted typically four to five weeks, which is more than those granted to the average employee in the United States. With vacations concentrated in a few weeks during the summer, this can have a substantial impact on the advertising scheduling. A company will not want to engage in a major media campaign when a substantial amount of the population is traveling away from home. In Sweden, many public places are closed in July; and Italy and France concentrate their holidays in August. In Germany, vacations are staggered by region over the period of July and August. There are also religious holidays that may affect the placement or timing of advertising. During the Islamic Ramadan, usually celebrated over a month during July, many Moslem countries do not allow the placement of any advertising.

For industrial products, the timing of advertising in support of sales efforts may be affected by the budgetary cycles prevailing in a given country. For countries with large state-controlled sectors, heavy emphasis needs to be placed on the period before a new national or sector plan is developed. Private sector companies tend to be more influenced by their own budgetary cycles usually coinciding with their fiscal years. In Japan, many companies begin their fiscal year in June rather than on January 1. To the extent that capital budgets are completed before the new fiscal year commences, products that require budgetary approval will need advertising support in advance of the budget completion.

The time needed to think about a purchase has been cited as a primary factor in deciding on the appropriate time by which the advertising peak is to precede the sales peak. In its domestic market, a company may have become accustomed to a given purchase deliberation time by its customers. Since the deliberation may be determined by income levels or other environmental factors, other markets may show different patterns. The purchase or replacement of a small electrical household appliance may be a routine decision for a U.S. household, and the purchase may occur whenever the need arises. In another country with lower income levels, such a purchase may be planned several weeks or even months ahead. Consequently, a company engaged in international advertising needs to carefully evaluate the underlying assumptions of its domestic advertising policies and not automatically assume that they apply elsewhere.

REACH VERSUS FREQUENCY

Invariably, an advertiser will be forced to make a tradeoff between the number of target customers to be reached and the number of messages placed through the media. This reach versus frequency tradeoff is created by advertising budget limitations which exist even in the largest organizations. Typically, consumer interest in the product is used as a guide to determine the frequency needed. This interest in any given product category may vary from country to country. Furthermore, in countries with otherwise extensive advertising, the existing "noise" may require a step-up in the frequency to ensure that the messages actually get through to the targets. Consequently, international advertisers should not assume that the reach versus frequency tradeoff will be the same in different countries.

ORGANIZING THE INTERNATIONAL ADVERTISING EFFORT

A major concern for international marketing executives centers around the organization of their company's international advertising effort. Key concerns are the role of centralization at the head office versus the roles subsidiaries and the advertising agency should play. Marketers are aware that a more harmonious approach to the international advertising effort may enhance both the quality and efficiency of the total effort. Thus, organizing the effort deserves as much time as individual advertising decisions about individual products or campaigns. Thus, in this section, we will look in greater detail at advertising agency selection and the managerial issues of running an international advertising effort in a multinational corporation.

Agency Selection

International companies face a number of options with respect to working with a given advertising agency. Many companies first develop an agency relationship domestically and have to decide at one point if they expect their domestic agency to handle their international advertising business as well. In some foreign markets, companies need to select foreign agencies to work with them—a decision that may be left to the local subsidiaries or may be made by the head office alone. Recently, some agencies have banded together to form international networks to attract more international business.

Working with Domestic Agencies When a company starts to grow internationally, it is not unusual for the domestic advertising agency to handle the international business as well. However, this is only possible when the domestic agency has international experience and international capability. Many smaller domestic agencies do not have international experience. Thus the companies are forced to make other arrangements. Frequently, the international company starts to appoint individual agencies in each of the various foreign markets where it is operating. This may be done with the help of the local subsidiaries or through the company's head office staff. Before long, the company will end up with a series of agency relationships that may make international or global coordination very difficult.

PPG Industries' Automotive Finishes Group had been using a domestic agency for ten years when the company was anticipating a substantial growth in its international business. PPG was looking to acquire several companies in Europe in addition to the two plants already in place. The company, therefore, switched all of its business from the domestic agency to Campbell-Ewald, which was organized as a network with many affiliates overseas.[84] To better coordinate its U.S. and international advertising campaigns, Goodyear requested that its domestic agency, J. Walter Thompson, closely work with its international agency, McCann-Erickson, on a global campaign even though the advertising would not be identical.[85] By having the two agencies work together, Goodyear was assured that the resulting campaign would be coordinated and that the company would speak with the same voice worldwide.

Working with Local Agencies   The local agency relationship offers some specific advantages. First of all, the local advertising agency is expected to fully understand the local environment and is in a position to create advertising targeted to the local market. However, many firms question the expertise and professionalism of local agencies, particularly in countries where advertising is not as developed as in the major markets of North America and Europe.

Jaguar has had some interesting experiences in penetrating the Saudi Arabian market.[86] Jaguar had its own advertising in the Middle East handled through a British agency. The Saudi audience reacted negatively to the Lebanese Arabic used in the copy. They also noticed that the visuals had been shot in the United Arab Emirates, because the drivers in the pictures were wearing black bands with long black strings at the back that weighted down the Arabian headdress. Though this type of headdress was typical for that part of the Arabian Gulf region it was not typical for Saudi Arabia. When the Jaguar importer in Saudi Arabia complained about the advertising, Jaguar looked for a local agency run by American and British expatriates. However, this attempt was also a failure and the account was finally shifted to a local agency run largely by Saudi managers. This agency heavily relied on high quality visuals from Jaguar in the United Kingdom but wrote all of its own copy.[87]

84. "PPG Finishes Switches Shops Citing New International Needs," *Industrial Marketing,* August 1981, p. 25.

85. "Goodyear Pulls Back From Print," *New York Times,* November 5, 1986, p. D19.

86. "The Sleek Cat Springs into the Saudi Market," *Financial Times,* November 2, 1985, p. 14.

87. Ibid.

Working with International Affiliates in Local Markets Increasingly, international companies have the option of working with local affiliates of large international agencies. Often these agencies were locally founded and at some time sold a minority stake to larger foreign agencies. More recently, international agencies have acquired majority stakes or started new branches from scratch. The capabilities of these agencies depend on the extent that they can be supported by the owner's network. However, this trend has brought new sophistication and expertise to countries where little existed.

Until recently, the advertising agency business in Korea was dominated by in-house agencies of large Korean companies controlling some 60 percent of billings. Smaller independent shops served the rest. With full-foreign ownership to be allowed as of 1991, many international agencies have decided to set up shop in Korea. International companies have been the major clients of these recently formed agencies.[88] Similar developments have been observed in the various Eastern European countries that are turning toward economic liberalization.

Working with International Advertising Networks Many companies with extensive international operations find it too difficult and cumbersome to deal simultaneously with a large number of agencies, both domestically and internationally. For that reason, multinational firms have tended to concentrate their accounts with some large advertising agencies that operate their own networks. Among the leaders are Saatchi & Saatchi, McCann-Erickson, Young & Rubicam, J. Walter Thompson, and Ogilvy & Mather.[89]

Kodak centralized all of its worldwide advertising in 1983 with just three international agencies which resulted in the replacement of fifty-three local agencies around the world.[90] Ford Motor Co. concentrated its advertising worldwide on three major agencies.[91] Gillette used to work with thirty agencies worldwide and reduced it to just two.

The first generation of international networks was created by U.S. based advertising agencies in the 1950s and 1960s. The major driving forces were their clients who encouraged their U.S. agencies to move into local markets where the advertising agencies were weak. Leaders in this process were J. Walter Thompson, Ogilvy and Mather, and Young & Rubicam. The second wave of international networks was dominated by British entrepreneurs, Saatchi & Saatchi and WPP, who assembled a series of international agency networks under one corporate name. Saatchi has two major international networks, Saatchi & Saatchi Advertising and BSB Worldwide.

88. "Agencies Vie for Slice of Korea," *Advertising Age,* September 10, 1990, p. 25.
89. "Advertising Age's Top 10 Agencies of 1969," *Advertising Age,* March 26, 1990, p. 5-1.
90. "Europe Sorts Out Alignments," *Financial Times,* October 13, 1983, p. VIII.
91. "Global Ad Buys in Ford's Future," *Advertising Age,* April 23, 1990, p. 4.

Other networks are being built by some of the French agencies, and the Japanese agencies are now also building their own networks through acquisition.[92]

International advertising networks are sought after because of their ability to quickly spread around the globe with one single campaign. Usually, only one set of advertisements will be made and then circulated among the local agencies. Working within the same agency guarantees consistency and a certain willingness to accept direction from a central location. If a company tries to coordinate a global effort alone without the help of an international network, the burden of coordination largely rests with the company itself. Not all firms are geared or equipped for such an effort. Therefore the international network is a convenience to multinational firms. The market share of multinational agencies had risen to 30 percent of world-wide billings in 1988. This trend toward international networks is continuing.[93] Table 15.4 provides a list of leading world advertising agencies.

Not all companies find a network a necessity. Some advertisers argue that a company may profit from a single strategy but that the execution of this strategy in the various markets should be left to local agencies that are willing to work in an ad hoc network geared only to the company's needs. Acorn, a British manufacturer of minicomputers, had its U.K. agency develop a campaign with independent agencies in Germany and in New York. Acorn had a clear strategy for attacking the educational segment in all markets. However, because of the differences in each market, the company did not opt for a standardized advertising campaign. In the United Kingdom, where the company faced a very high penetration of households with personal computers, Acorn capitalized on the fact that it was chosen by the BBC, the leading broadcasting network. Major targets were parents, but opinion leaders in schools were also addressed. In the United States, Acorn targeted mostly decision makers in schools and did not advertise to individual households. In Germany, the emphasis was more on creating a strong corporate identity. As a result, the company had three different campaigns, but all three of them aimed at the educational market segment that remained the cornerstone of Acorn's international marketing strategy.[94]

Coordinating International Advertising

The role the international marketing executive plays in a company's international advertising effort may differ from firm to firm and depend on several factors. Outside factors, such as the nature of the market or competition, and company internal factors, such as company culture or philosophy, may lead some firms to adopt a more

92. "Why the Colossal Cost Is Worth It," *Financial Times,* January 18, 1990, p. 13.

93. "The Tomato That Ate Chicago," survey on the advertising industry in *The Economist,* June 9, 1990, p. 8.

94. "A Dichotomy in Campaign Style," *Financial Times,* January 26, 1984, p. 12.

TABLE 15.4 ● World's Top Fifty Advertising Organizations in 1990

Rank	Advertising organization, headquarters	Worldwide gross income 1990	Worldwide capitalized billings 1990
1	*WPP Group*, London	$2,715.0	$18,095.0
2	*Saatchi & Saatchi Co.*, London	1,729.3	11,861.7
3	*Interpublic Group of Cos.*, New York	1,649.8	11,025.3
4	*Omnicom Group*, New York	1,335.5	9,699.6
5	*Dentsu, Inc.*, Tokyo	1,254.8	9,671.6
6	*Young & Rubicam*, New York	1,073.6	8,000.7
7	*Eurocom Group*, Paris	748.5	5,065.7
8	*Hakuhodo Inc.*, Tokyo	586.3	4,529.4
9	*Grey Advertising*, New York	583.3	3,910.4
10	*Foote, Cone & Belding Communications*, Chicago	536.2	3,554.8
11	*D'Arcy Masius Benton & Bowles*, New York	532.5	4,406.7
12	*Leo Burnett Co.*, Chicago	531.8	3,585.4
13	*Publicis-FCB Communications*, Paris	430.0	2,910.7
14	*Roux, Seguela Cayzac & Goudard*, Issy les Moulineaux, France	346.2	2,354.5
15	*BDDP Worldwide*, Boulogne, France	236.0	1,487.4
16	*Bozell, Jacobs, Kenyon & Echkhardt*, New York	214.0	1,570.0
17	*N W Ayer*, New York	185.9	1,469.2
18	*Tokyu Agency*, Tokyo	170.3	1,387.0
19	*Daiko Advertising*, Osaka, Japan	159.5	1,246.9
20	*Alliance International Advertising Group*, London	141.8	945.0
21	*TBWA Advertising*, New York	138.3	922.0
22	*Chiat/Day/Mojo*, Venice, Calif.	136.8	991.7
23	*Ketchum Communications*, Pittsburgh	134.2	1,030.4
24	*Dai-Ichi Kikaku Co.*, Tokyo	133.8	916.2
25	*Dentsu, Young & Rubicam Partnership*, New York/Tokyo	126.8	884.1
26	*Asatsu Inc.*, Tokyo	125.0	970.3
27	*Ross Roy Group*, Bloomfield Hills, Mich.	110.0	707.0
28	*Wells, Rich, Greene*, New York	105.0	845.0
29	*I&S Corp.*, Tokyo	104.2	833.2
30	*Yomiko Advertising*, Tokyo	102.9	795.6
31	*GGT PLC*, London	95.0	692.6
32	*Asahi Advertising*, Tokyo	88.9	522.7
33	*Man Nen Sha*, Osaka, Japan	87.0	566.0

TABLE 15.4 ● World's Top Fifty Advertising Organizations in 1990 (*cont.*)

Rank	Advertising organization, headquarters	Worldwide gross income 1990	Worldwide capitalized billings 1990
34	*FCAB*, Suresnes, France	83.1	600.7
35	*GGK International*, Zurich	79.3	556.7
36	*Cheil Communications*, Seoul	73.1	274.1
37	*MPM Propaganda*, Sao Paulo	65.2	189.5
38	*Armando Testa Group Worldwide*, Turin, Italy	63.3	481.8
39	*Nihon Keizaisha Advertising*, Tokyo	62.5	366.3
40	*Sogel Inc.*, Tokyo	57.8	364.6
41	*Orikomi Advertising*, Tokyo	57.5	440.0
42	*Telephone Marketing Programs*, New York	55.8	371.9
43	*W.B. Doner & Co.*, Southfield, Mich.	51.4	395.4
44	*Clemenger/BBDO*, Melbourne	50.7	317.0
45	*CDP Europe*, London	50.5	354.2
46	*Hill, Holliday, Connors, Cosmopulos*, Boston	50.1	333.9
47	*Admarketing Inc.*, Los Angeles	49.7	285.5
48	*Chuo Senko Advertising Co.*, Tokyo	49.1	356.4
49	*Earle Palmer Brown Cos.*, Bethesda, Md.	48.5	378.2
50	*Oricom Inc.*, Seoul	46.2	174.0

Note: Dollars are in millions.
Source: Reprinted with permission from *Advertising Age,* March 25, 1991, copyright Crain Communications, Inc. All rights reserved.

centralized approach in international advertising. Other firms, for different reasons, may prefer to delegate more authority to local subsidiaries and local agencies. The purpose of this final section is to review the key factors that may cause a firm to either centralize or decentralize decision making for international advertising.

External Factors Affecting Advertising Coordination   One of the most important factors influencing how companies allocate decision making for international advertising is market diversity. For products or services where customer needs and interests are homogeneous across many countries, greater opportunities for standardization exist. For companies with relatively standardized products, pressures also point in the direction of centralized decision making. Consequently, companies that face markets with very different customer needs or market systems and structures will work more towards decentralizing their international advertising decision making. Local knowledge would be more important to the success of these firms.

The nature of the competition can also impact on how an international firm plans for advertising decision making. Firms that essentially face local competition or different sets of competitors from country to country will find it more logical to delegate international advertising to local subsisidiaries. On the other hand, if a company is competing everywhere with a few sets of firms, which are essentially global firms using a similar type of advertising, the need to centralize will be apparent.

Internal Factors Affecting Advertising Coordination   A company's own internal structure and organization can also greatly influence its options of either centralizing or decentralizing international advertising decision making. The opportunities for centralizing are few when a company follows an approach of customizing advertising for each local market. However, when a company follows a standardized advertising format, a more centralized approach will be possible and probably even desirable.

Skill levels and efficiency concerns can also determine the level of centralization. Decentralization requires that the advertising skills of local subsidiaries and local agencies be sufficient to perform successfully. On the other hand, international advertising may not be centralized successfully in companies where the head office staff does not possess a good appreciation of the international dimension of the firm's business. Decentralization is often believed to result in inefficiencies or decreased quality because a firm's budget may be spread over too many individual agencies. Instead of having a large budget in one agency, the firm has created minibudgets that may not be sufficient to obtain the best creative talent to work on its products. Centralization will often give access to better talent, though knowledge of the local markets may be sacrificed.

The managerial style of the international company may affect the centralization decision in advertising as well. Some companies pride themselves on giving a considerable amount of freedom to local subsidiary managers. Under such circumstances, centralizing advertising decisions will only be counterproductive. It has been observed with many multinational firms that the general approach taken by the company's top management toward international markets relates closely to its desire to centralize or decentralize international advertising. However, since the company's internal and external factors are subject to change over time, it can be expected that the decision to centralize or decentralize will never be a permanent one.

This change in internal company policy is illustrated by Colgate-Palmolive, a firm with strong beliefs in global marketing strategies. The company had developed a strong central department with a director for worldwide advertising. This function was created several years ago following a long period of creating local advertising campaigns. Five years later, a new management reaffirmed its preference for locally created advertising and abolished the central control function.[95]

CONCLUSIONS

Few areas of international marketing are subject to hotter debate than international advertising. The complexity of dealing simultaneously with a large number of different customers in many countries, all speaking their own languages and subject to their own cultural heritage, offers a real challenge to the international marketer. International executives must find the common ground within these diverse influences so that coherent campaigns can still be possible.

The debate in the field has recently shifted from one of standardization versus customization to one of global versus nonglobal advertising. Proponents of global advertising point to the convergence of customer needs and the emergence of the "world consumer," a person who is becoming ever more homogenous whether he or she lives in Paris, London, New York, or Tokyo. However, many aspects of the advertising environment remain considerably diverse. Although English is rapidly becoming a global language, most messages still have to be translated into local languages. Regulations in many countries on the execution, content, and format of advertisements still make it very difficult to offer standardized solutions to advertising problems. Also, media availability to advertisers is substantially different in many parts of the world, so many companies still have to adapt their media mix to the local situation. Thus many executives believe that considerable local content is necessary. Therefore they will give the local country organizations substantial responsibility for input and decision making.

Most marketers realize that total customization is not desirable because it will require that each market create and implement its own advertising strategies. Top creative talent is scarce everywhere, and better creative solutions tend to be the costlier ones. As a result, companies appear to be moving towards modularization, in which some elements of the advertising message are common to all advertisements while other elements are tailored to local requirements. To make customization work, however, companies cannot simply design one set of advertisements and later expect to adapt the content. Successful modularization requires that companies, from the very outset, plan for such a process by including and considering the full range of possibilities and requirements to be satisfied. This offers a considerable challenge to international marketing executives and their advertising partners.

95. "Colgate Aftershock: Advertising Strategy Changes Looming," *Advertising Age,* September 24, 1990, p. 2.

Questions for Discussion

1. What are the major factors that affect the extension of an international advertising campaign into several countries?

2. How do you explain that some companies appear to be successful with very similar campaigns worldwide while others fail with the same strategy?

3. What advice will you give to a U.S. firm interested in advertising in Japan, and what will you suggest to a Japanese firm interested in advertising in the United States?

4. What future do you see for global advertising?

5. What will be the impact of increased commercial satellite television on international advertising, both in the United States and abroad?

6. How will the advertising industry need to react to the new trends in international marketing?

For Further Readings

"Advertising Regulations, Self-Regulations and Self-Discipline Around the World: Some Facts, Trends, and Observations." *Journal of International Marketing,* no. 1 (1981), pp. 46–55.

Aydin, Nizam, Vern Terpstra, and Attila Yaprak. "The American Challenge in International Advertising." *Journal of Advertising* 13, no. 4 (1984), pp. 49–57.

Boddewyn, J. J. "The Global Spread of Advertising Regulation." *MSU Business Topics* (Spring 1981), pp. 5–13.

Colvin, Michael, Roger Heeler, and Jim Thorpe. "Developing International Advertising Strategy." *Journal of Marketing* (Fall 1980), pp. 73–79.

Crunch, A. Graeme. "The Changing Faces of International Advertising." *The International Advertiser* 13, no. 2 (1972), pp. 4–6.

Donnelly, James H. Jr., and John K. Ryans, Jr. "Standardized Global Advertising, A Call As Yet Unanswered." *Journal of Marketing* (April 1969), pp. 57–60.

Dunn, S. Watson, and E. S. Lorimor. *International Advertising and Marketing.* Columbus, Ohio: Grid, 1979.

Harper, Malcolm. "Advertising in a Developing Economy: Opportunity and Responsibility." *European Journal of Marketing.* no. 3 (1975), pp. 215–223.

Killough, James. "Improved Payoffs from Transnational Advertising." *Harvard Business Review* (July-August 1978), pp. 102–110.

Neelankavil, J. P., and Albert B. Stridsberg. *Advertising Self-Regulation: A Global Perspective.* New York: Hastings House, 1980.

Peebles, Dean M., and John K. Ryans, Jr. "Advertising as a Positive Force." *Journal of Advertising* (Spring 1978), pp. 48–52.

Peebles, Dean M., John K. Ryans, Jr., and Ivan R. Vernon. "Coordinating International Advertising." *Journal of Marketing* (January 1978), pp. 28–34.

Ryans, John K., Jr. "Is It Too Soon to Put a Tiger in Every Tank? *Columbia Journal of World Business* (March 1969), pp. 69–75.

Stridsberg, Albert. "Can Advertising Benefit Developing Countries?" *Business and Society Review* (Autumn 1974), pp. 76–77.

"Colgate Aftershock: Advertising Strategy Changes Looming," *Advertising Age,* September 24, 1990, p. 2.

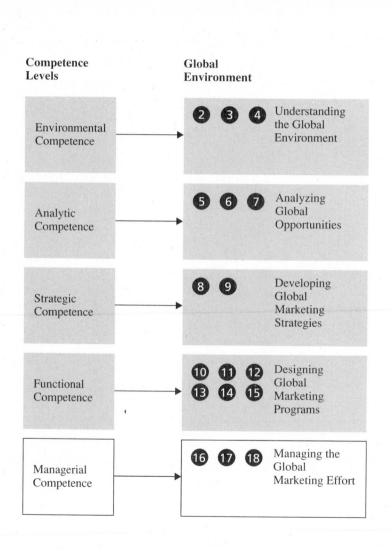

Competence Levels	Global Environment
Environmental Competence	**2** **3** **4** Understanding the Global Environment
Analytic Competence	**5** **6** **7** Analyzing Global Opportunities
Strategic Competence	**8** **9** Developing Global Marketing Strategies
Functional Competence	**10** **11** **12** **13** **14** **15** Designing Global Marketing Programs
Managerial Competence	**16** **17** **18** Managing the Global Marketing Effort

P A R T

F I V E

Managing the Global Marketing Effort

FOR A COMPANY to be successful at international marketing, it must do more than analyze markets and devise marketing programs. Increasingly, international companies are running complex organizations with operating units in many different countries. The managerial challenges of running such diverse organizations are substantial and require skills that are different from those required by single country organizations. This final part of our text is devoted to issues involving the managerial competence of international marketing managers. Our goal is to show how managers can guide their operations more effectively in this very competitive global marketplace.

In Chapter 16, we concentrate on organizational design issues for international firms and look at where the decision-making process should be concentrated. Chapter 17 focuses on how international firms should control their operations and marketing programs. The final chapter, Chapter 18, covers the various exporting and importing procedures faced by international marketing managers.

16

Organizing International and Global Marketing

● **AN IMPORTANT ASPECT** *of international marketing is the establishment of an appropriate organization. The organization must be able to formulate and implement strategies for each market. The objective of an international marketing organization is to develop a structure that will allow the firm to respond to distinct variations in each market while utilizing the company's appropriate experience from other markets and products. The key issue in establishing an international organization is deciding where to locate the international responsibility in the firm. The major dilemma facing international marketers involves the tradeoff between the need for an individual response to the local environment and the value of centralized knowledge and control. For companies to be successful, it is necessary to find a proper balance between these two extremes.*

There are a number of various organizational structures that are best suited for different internal and external environmental factors. No one structure is best. In this chapter, we will examine the elements that affect the international marketing organization, the alternative organizational structures, the common stages through which organizations evolve, the elements that affect the international marketing organization, the location of corporate global responsibility in an organization, and the recent trends in international organization design.

ORGANIZING: THE KEY TO STRATEGY IMPLEMENTATION

The global marketplace offers numerous opportunities for the astute marketer. To take advantage of these opportunities, the marketer will develop strategies to fit the needs of diverse markets while capitalizing on economies of scale in centralized operations, centralized control, and experience in other markets. These strategies will be adapted to the internal and external environment so that they will prevail over the competition.[1] The final success of the strategy will be influenced by the selection of an appropriate organization that successfully implements the strategy.

The structure of an international organization should be congruent with the tasks to be performed, the need for product knowledge, and the need for market knowledge. It is difficult to select an organizational structure that can effectively and efficiently implement a marketing strategy while responding to the diverse needs of customers and the corporate staff. Chapter 17, "Planning and Controlling International Marketing Operations," examines the simultaneous pressures for greater integration and greater diversity which also create a significant tension in the development and control of an ideal organizational structure.

ELEMENTS AFFECTING THE INTERNATIONAL MARKETING ORGANIZATION

The ideal structure of an organization should be a function of the products or services to be sold in the marketplace and the external and internal environments. Theoretically, the approach to developing such an organization is to analyze the specific tasks to be accomplished within an environment and subsequently design a structure that will complete these tasks most effectively. There are a number of other factors that complicate the selection of an appropriate organization. In most cases a company already has an existing organizational structure. As the internal and external environments change, companies will often change their organizational structure. It is important to understand the strengths and weaknesses of different organizational structures as well as the factors that encourage a change in the structure. The diagram shown in Figure 16.1 reflects the elements that affect organizational design. We will discuss each of these elements individually.

External Forces

The most important external factors are geographic distances, types of customers, and government regulations. In the international environment, each of the issues should be examined to determine their effect on the organization.

1. Alfred D. Chandler, *Strategy and Structure* (Cambridge, Mass.: The MIT Press, 1962).

FIGURE 16.1 ● Factors Affecting Organizational Design

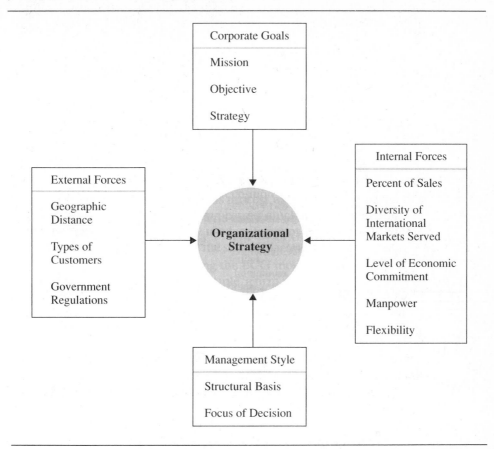

Geographic Distance   Technological innovations have somewhat eased the problem associated with physical distance. Companies, primarily in the United States and other developed countries, enjoy such conveniences as next-day mail, facsimile machines, teleconferencing, and rapid transportation. However, these benefits cannot be taken for granted. Distance becomes a distinct barrier when operations are established in less developed countries, where a simple phone call can take hours if not a few days to place. Even in developed countries, postal systems can be slow and telephone connections weak.

Geographic distance results in communication barriers, and one problem that even high technology cannot solve is the time differentials. Managers in New York who reach an agreement over lunch will have a hard time finalizing the deal with their headquarters in London until the following day, as most executives will be on their way home for the evening. The five hour difference results in lost communication time, which impedes rapid results in a divisional structure. Physical distance affects the relationship between a subsidiary and its headquarters, if regular face to face meetings are required. For example, Matsushita Electric, known for its Panasonic brand of consumer electronics, keeps tight control over its European management, requiring senior executives to fly 6,000 miles to the headquarters in Osaka as many as ten times per year.[2]

Types of Customers   A complete evaluation and understanding of the consumers within the marketplace enables companies to structure their organization appropriately. The more homogeneous the consumers with respect to the product or service, the easier it will be for a firm to consolidate its efforts. As the main purpose of most companies is to serve the needs of the consumer, "decisions about organizing should start with a profound understanding of consumers." Who are the consumers? Where are they geographically located? What drives their purchasing decisions? Are there groups of consumers with similar needs in different countries? And finally, how can we create an organizational structure to get to these consumers and evoke the desired response?[3]

For example, ICI, the U.K.-based chemical company, has reorganized its European operations from a set of product businesses that were marketed through national sales subsidiaries to a European organization. According to the company the reason for the change is to "meet the needs of our customers. The single European market will affect the way in which our customers organize their own businesses. They will be looking for fewer suppliers and a more integrated relationship with companies supplying them."[4] Yoshihisa Tabuchi, President and CEO of Nomura Securities, the largest financial institution in the world, says the company's strategy depends on its clients. "Some businesses are inherently domestic, so why try to make them global? Retail brokerage is a good example. The style and structure we use to sell securities in Japan can't work in America and we would be foolish to try."[5] Here again we see that the structure must fit the customers.

Government Regulations   How various countries attract or repel foreign operations affects the structure of the organization. Laws involving imports, exports, taxes, hiring, and so on differ from country to country. Local taxes, statutory holidays, and political risk can deter a company from establishing a subsidiary or management

2. "A Tortoise That Stays Within Its Shell," *Financial Times,* October 30, 1989, p. 13.

3. Sandra Vandermerwe, "Constructing Euro-Networks for Euro-Customers," paper presented to *The European League for Economic Cooperation Symposium on Social Europe,* May 1990 in Utrecht, Holland, p. 1.

4. Clive Cookson, "ICI Proffers More Corporate Clout to Its Customers," *Financial Times,* September 7, 1990, p. 12.

5. Michael Schrage, "A Japanese Giant Rethinks Globalization: An Interview with Yoshihisa Tabuchi," *Harvard Business Review,* July-August 1989, p. 71.

center in a country. Many developing countries require a firm that establishes plants on their territory to hire, train, and develop local employees and to share ownership with the government or local citizens. These requirements for local investment and ownership may require an organization with a local decision-making group.

Internal Forces

In addition to the external forces, there are often internal factors that will impact the international organization. The following section will examine these facts including the volume of international business, the diversity of the markets being served, the economic commitment to international business, the available manpower, and the flexibility within the company.

Percent of International Sales   The amount of international sales affects the type of organization. If only a small percentage of sales (1 percent to 10 percent) are international, a company will tend to have a simple organization with an export department. As the amount of international sales increases relative to total sales, a company is more likely to change from an export department to an international division to a worldwide organization.

Diversity of International Markets Served   The number and diversity of international markets served affects the choice of international organization. As the number and diversity of markets increase, the organization necessary to manage the marketing effort becomes more complex, and it requires a larger number of people to understand the markets and implement the strategies.

Level of Economic Commitment   A company unwilling or unable to allocate adequate financial resources to its international efforts will not be able to sustain a complex or costly international structure. The less expensive organizational approaches to international marketing usually result in less control by the company on the local level. It is extremely important to build an organization that will provide the flexibility and resources to achieve the corporation's long-term goals for international markets.

Manpower   Available and capable manpower is just as vital to a firm as financial resources. Some companies send top domestic executives to foreign operations and then find that they do not understand the nation's culture. According to statistics complied on U.S. corporations, 30 percent of the executives sent on overseas assignments have not worked out.[6] The hiring of local executives is also difficult because in many countries competition for such people is extremely intense. Panasonic U.K. recruits graduates from British universities to develop local talent. The graduate

6. Edwin R. Henry, "What Business Can Learn from Peace Corp's Selection and Training," *Personnel,* July-August 1965.

trainees are sent to Japan for one year to absorb Japanese culture and discipline. The program is extremely popular. With a long-term approach to developing local talent, Panasonic prefers "to grow their own" while arch-rival Sony uses headhunters extensively to recruit local managers.[7] Because people are such an important resource in international organizations, many companies structure their organizations based on the availability of internationally trained executive talent. Also, more companies are developing cross-cultural training programs to help prepare executives for new environments.[8]

Flexibility   Although a rigid structure enables a firm to gain more control over operations, it also restricts adaptability. When a company devises an organization structure, it must build in some flexibility, especially in the event of the need for future reorganization. A study of the implementation of a global strategy for seventeen products, found that organizational flexibility was one of the key success factors. The structure needs to be flexible enough to respond to the needs of the consumers.[9] Companies that establish a perfect design for the present find themselves in trouble later on if the firm grows or declines.

Management Style

The management style of a company can be described in terms of its structure and its decision making processes. These factors will influence the type of international organization the company will adopt.

Structural Basis   There are three basic options for the structure of an organization: functional, market-based, or matrix. These options provide the foundation on which to design an organization. Figure 16.2 depicts the options each company can take once it decides on the basic framework.

American Standard restructured its company from a geographic organization to a product-based organization. The purpose of the change was to encourage cross-fertilization of management skills and technology. Additionally, American Standard's corporate philosophy was to promote the best person. This policy meant that non-Americans not only ran most of the overseas divisions, but were moving into

7. "A Tortoise That Stays Within Its Shell," *Financial Times,* October 30, 1989, p. 13.

8. Mark Mendenhall and Gary Oddow, "Acculturation Profiles of Expatriate Managers: Implications for Cross-Cultural Training Programs," *Columbia Journal of World Business,* Winter 1986, p. 73.

9. Kamran Kashani, "Why Does Global Marketing Work—or Not Work?", *European Management Journal,* June 1990, p. 154.

FIGURE 16.2 ● Basis for Organizational Design

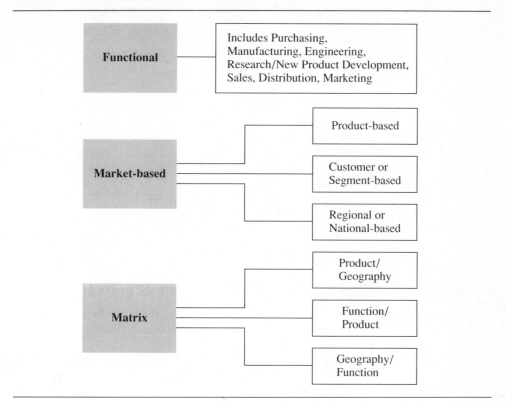

senior U.S. and global jobs. This philosophy enabled American Standard to shed its reputation as a U.S.-based company.[10]

The prospect of 1992 has given a number of firms the impetus to change their organizational structures. ICI, BP, Unilever, P&G, Electrolux, Philips, NCR, United Distillers, and many others have reorganized to improve their abilities to respond to the needs of the European markets. For example, in 1987, United Distillers was a loose federation of twelve brand-owning fiefdoms which included Johnnie Walker, Dewar, and Haig. Each had distilled its own whiskies and sold them around the world through third-party distribution. There was a great deal of interbrand competition and cannibalization. The company abolished the old product-based structure and introduced a simple regional structure that placed operational management

10. Hugh D. Menzies, "Happy Days at American Standard," *Fortune,* September 22, 1980, p. 136.

in market places—Europe, North America, Asia/Pacific, and International (South America, the Middle East, and Africa). A central strategic unit was established to research and produce individual brand marketing plans and portfolio strategies and to handle new product development in a liaison with regional managers. The new organization focuses on the needs of each market place, without cannibalizing its own brands.[11]

Focus of Decision   Who makes what decisions provides an orientation for the organizational design. If all decision-making responsibility is in the hands of headquarters, then the international operations should reflect this. There are many layers or types of decisions to be made from the purchasing of paper clips to the acquisition of a product line or a company. The focus of decision is very much a function of the CEO's management style. Texaco reorganized its structure to reflect the management style. August Long, the past CEO, made decisions on even minor expenditures and the company's success (or lack of success) reflected his authoritarian style. Subsequently, Texaco was restructured to provide more authority and responsibility to lower levels of management.[12]

Over a ten-year period, Electrolux has made over one hundred acquisitions to become one of the leading manufacturers of large appliances, vacuum cleaners, chain saws, and garden appliances. As the company has grown three-fold since 1981 there is pressure to develop a more formalized and centralized decision-making process. Sven Stork, one of the powerful product line managers, resists this trend. "Either Electrolux places trust in its product line manager or introduces a corporate control system like ITT's under Harold Geneen with 1,000 staff. That would be poison for this company, it wouldn't work; and so we'd have to sell two-thirds of our product lines."[13]

Corporate Goals

Every company needs a mission. The mission is a framework for the business, the values that drive the company and the belief the company has for itself. The mission is the glue that holds the company together. It answers these questions: (1) Why do we exist? (2) Where are we going? (3) What do we believe in? (4) What is our distinctive competence?[14]

After reviewing the mission, no company should begin establishing an international organization until it has reviewed and established its strategies and objectives. If the company anticipates future growth in international markets, then it must

11. Philip Rawstorne, "Re-shaping United Distillers," *Financial Times,* June 13, 1990, p. 12.

12. "Texaco Restoring Luster to the Star," *Business Week,* December 22, 1980, pp. 54–61.

13. Christopher Lorenz, "A Struggle Against Creeping Formality," *Financial Times,* June 26, 1989, p. 12.

14. Andrew Campbell, Marion Devine, and David Young, *A Sense of Mission* (London: The Economist Books, 1990), pp. 19–41.

establish a structure that can evolve into a larger operation effectively and efficiently. Too often, shortsighted executives establish international operations that do not enable the managers to grow with the company when markets begin to expand. These managers are not equipped to take on any added responsibility. Additionally, headquarters fail to communicate short-term goals, long-range objectives, and sometimes even the total mission of the company. Inadequate communications result in an ambiguous corporate image and the inability to facilitate coordination of all marketing elements.

Recent authors go beyond the need for goals and objectives and argue for "strategic intent." They argue that some of the companies that have risen to global leadership did so with a ten to twenty year quest for winning. Their leaders developed a strategic intent with slogans such as "Encircle Caterpillar" for Komatsu, and "Beat Xerox" for Canon. If the head of a company can develop this sense of winning throughout the company, it will stretch the organization to excel and achieve far greater goals.[15]

TYPES OF INTERNATIONAL ORGANIZATIONS

The international marketplace offers many opportunities. To take advantage of these opportunities, a company must evaluate the options, develop a strategy, and establish an organization to implement the strategy. The organization should take into account all the factors affecting organizational design shown in Figure 16.1. In the following segment of the chapter, we review the various types of international organizational structure.

Companies Without International Specialists

Many companies first begin selling products to foreign markets without a separate international organization or an international specialist. A domestically oriented company may begin to receive inquiries from foreign buyers who saw an advertisement in a trade magazine or attended a domestic trade show. The domestic staff will respond to the inquiry in the same fashion as it does other inquiries. Product brochures will be sent to the potential buyer for review. If sufficient interest exists on the part of both the buyer and seller, then more communication (telex, air mail, faxes, telephone, personal visits) may transpire. With no specific individual designated to handle international business, it may be directed to a sales manager, an inside salesperson, a product manager, or an outside salesperson.

Companies without an international organization will obviously have limited costs. Of course with no one responsible for international business, there will

15. Gary Hamel and C. K. Prahalad, "Strategic Intent," *Harvard Business Review,* May-June 1989, pp. 63–68.

FIGURE 16.3 ● Organization with an International Specialist

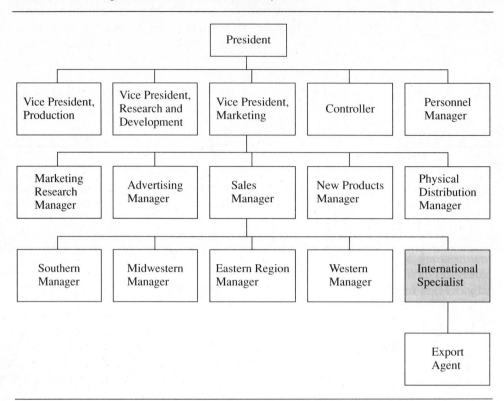

probably be little or no sales and profit from it. Also, when the firm attempts to respond to the occasional inquiry, no one will understand the difficulties of translation into another language, the particular needs of the customer, the transfer of funds, fluctuating exchange rates, shipping, legal liabilities, or many of the other differences between domestic and international business. As the number of international inquiries grows or management recognizes the potential in international markets, international specialists will be added to the domestic organization.

International Specialists/Export Department

The complexities of selling a product to a variety of different countries encourages most domestically oriented firms to establish an international expertise. This can vary from having a part-time international specialist to a full staff of specialists organized into an export department or international department. Figure 16.3 illustrates an organization with an international specialist.

The international specialist/export department is primarily a sales function. They will respond to inquiries, exhibit at international trade shows, handle export documentation, shipping, insurance, and financial matters. Also, the international specialist(s) will maintain contact with embassies, export financing agencies, and the Department of Commerce. All of these groups regularly publish requests for bid quotations from other countries. The international specialist or export department may use the services of an export agent, an export management company, or import intermediaries to assist in the process (see Chapter 12).

The advantage of hiring international specialists is that it gives firms the ability to respond, bid for, and process foreign business. The size of this type of organization will be directly related to the amount of international business that is handled. The costs should be minor when compared to the potential.

The international specialist/export department is often reactive, rather than proactive, in nature. Specialists do not usually evaluate the worldwide demand for a product or service, identify pockets of opportunities, develop a strategy to infiltrate these opportunities, or reap the rewards; they usually respond to inquiries. Also, the international specialist may have little opportunity to modify the current products or services to meet international market needs because the international sales are so small. In most cases the products are sold as is, with no modification.

International Division

As the sales to foreign markets become more important to the company and the complexity of coordinating the directing of the international effort extends beyond a specialist or a single department, a company may establish an international division. The international division normally will report to the president, thus having an equal status with other functions such as marketing, finance, and production. Figure 16.4 illustrates the organizational design of a firm using an international division.

The international division will be directly involved in the development and implementation of an international strategy. The head of the international division will have marketing, sales, and possibly production managers reporting to him or her. These individuals will focus their entire efforts on the international markets. It has been suggested that the international division is the best organizational alternative when international business represents 10 percent to 15 percent of the total business.[16]

The advantage of an international division is that it focuses on the international market at a high enough level in the organization to directly influence strategy. Also the international division will begin to actively seek out market opportunities in foreign companies. The sales and marketing efforts in each country will be supported through a regional or local office. This office will be able to understand the local environment, including legal requirements, customer needs, competition, and so on.

16. "Leaving the Rules for Global Selling," *Business Abroad,* November 1969, pp. 43–44.

FIGURE 16.4 ● Organization with an International Division

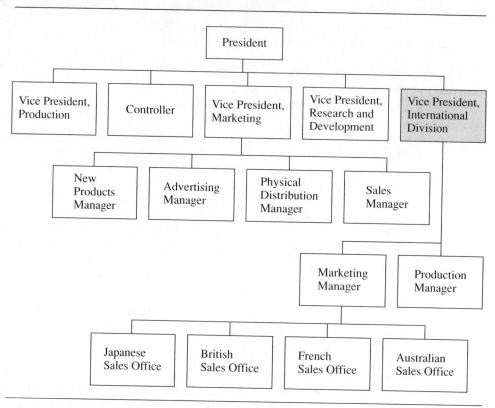

This close contact with the marketplace improves the organization's ability to perform successfully. Having an international division is obviously more expensive than having either no international focus or a specialist. However, the increased cost will be offset by increased sales. An international division can be the transition stage between a domestically oriented and a globally oriented company. As a company begins to adopt a worldwide focus, the international organization will evolve into a broader entity.

Worldwide Organizations

As a firm recognizes the potential size of the global market, it begins to change from a domestic company doing some business overseas to a worldwide company doing business in a number of countries. A worldwide focus will normally result in a worldwide organizational design. There are four dimensions around which a company can choose to organize: (1) geography, (2) function, (3) product, and (4) business unit.

We will discuss and illustrate each organizational alternative. The matrix organization, another type of worldwide organization, which combines two or more of the four dimensions, will also be discussed.

Geographic Organizational Structures

Geographic organizational designs focus on the need for an intimate knowledge of the company's customers and their environment. A geographic organization will allow a company the opportunity to understand local culture, economy, politics, law, and the competitive situation. There are two general types of geographic organizations, a regional management center and a country-based organization. In many cases, the regional management center and country-based organizations are combined.

Regional Management Centers   Regional management centers form a worldwide organization that focuses on a particular region of the world, such as Europe, the Middle East, Latin America, North America, the Caribbean, or the Far East. Figure 16.5 illustrates the regional management structure of a worldwide geographic organization.

The reason for a regional geographic approach to organizational design is twofold. First, there is the pressure of size. Once a market reaches a certain size, the firm must have a staff focused on that region to maximize revenues from that area of the world and to protect the firm's assets. The second reason for a regional focus is the regional nature of markets. A group of countries located close together, having similar social and cultural histories, climates, resources, and often languages, will have many similar needs for products. In many cases, these regional country groups have unified themselves for political and economic reasons; for example, the European Community is a regional group.

The regional approach to a worldwide organization has a number of benefits. It allows a company to locate marketing and manufacturing efforts to take advantage of regional agreements such as the EC or EFTA. Also, the regional approach puts the company in close contact with the distributors, customers, and subsidiaries. The regional management will be able to respond to local conditions and react faster than a totally centralized organization, in which all decisions are made at the headquarters.

One of the disadvantages of a regional management center is the cost. In general, the cost of overseas offices are expensive due to the following: international moving costs are high; executives living abroad usually receive additional compensation; and manpower, office space, communication, and travel expenses all result in increased costs. The increased costs of a regional office must be offset by increased organizational effectiveness, such as generating sales and controlling costs.

Prior to the euphoria regarding 1992, many large international companies were organized on a national basis. The national organizations, including those of France, Germany, Italy, and the United Kingdom, often were coordinated through a

FIGURE 16.5 ● Regional Management Centers

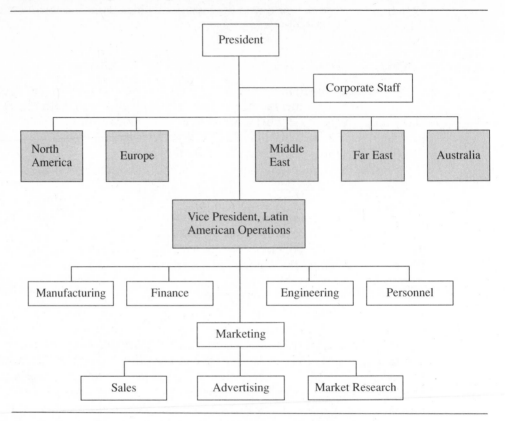

regional management center, the European headquarters. The prospect of a single European market has caused companies to rethink their European organization, often reducing the role of the national organization in favor of a stronger Eurocentric management. The year 1992 will bring the free flow of goods, people, and capital among the members of the European Community. Mergers and acquisitions have increased in Europe as large U.S., Japanese, and European firms acquire national companies.

Restructuring of manufacturing and logistics in Europe will proceed at a rapid pace as companies centralize production to lower costs and increase flexibility.[17] For example, Anglo Dutch Unilever, the world's second largest manufacturer of consumer products (after Procter & Gamble) set up a new organization in 1990 called

17. George Taucher, "1992: The End to European National Organizations," *International Business Communications* vol. 2, no. 3, 1990, pp. 4–7.

FIGURE 16.6 ● Country-Based Geographic Organization

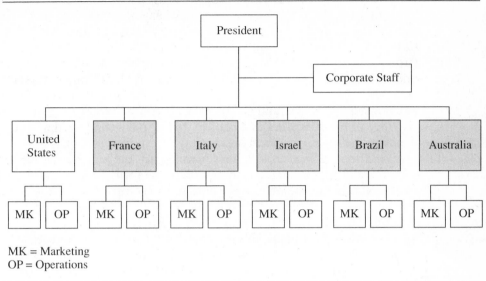

MK = Marketing
OP = Operations

Lever Europe. This was a surprise move for Unilever which has always been very decentralized with each national organization having full autonomy to modify and market products as dictated by local conditions. Of course, the decentralization led to a hodgepodge of brands, resulting in the same liquid abrasive cleaner being called Cif, Jif, Vif, or Viss depending on the country. Unilever will be centralizing both marketing and manufacturing and reducing the autonomy and power of the country managers.[18]

Country-Based Organizations   The second type of geographic organization is the country-based organization. This type of organization utilizes a separate organizational unit for each country. Figure 16.6 illustrates a simple country-based geographic organization.

A country-based organization is very similar to a regional management center, except that the focus is on a single country rather than a group of countries. For example, instead of having a regional management center in Brussels overseeing all European sales and operations, there is an organizational unit in each country. The country-based organization can be extremely sensitive to local customs, laws, and needs, which may be different even though the countries participate in a regional organization like the EC. With 1992 comes the acceptance of product standards from

18. Ian Fraser, "Now Only the Name's Not the Same," *Eurobusiness,* April 1990, p. 22–25.

country to country, the elimination of border restriction, and the moves to financial unity. These have caused many companies to look at Europe as a single market.

Country organizations are being eliminated or reduced in structure as pan-European organizations emerge.[19] Reckitt and Colman, the U.K.-based manufacturer of toiletries and household goods such as Brasso, has reorganized its corporate structure in response to 1992. Manufacturing operations have been consolidated so one or two factories will be making products for all of Europe, rather than having factories in each country making most products. Product marketing has also been reorganized into Eurobrand groups rather than by country.[20]

One of the difficulties of a country-based organization is that its cost is higher, therefore the benefit of a local organization must offset its cost. The second difficulty involves the coordination with headquarters. If a company is involved in forty countries, it is difficult and cumbersome to have all forty country-based organizational units reporting to one or more people in the company's headquarters. The third problem of a country-based unit is that it may not take advantage of the regional groupings of countries discussed in Chapter 5. The regional trading agreements such as the EC make it valuable to coordinate activities in EC countries. Also, there are regional media that often cut across country boundaries, such as television and print media, and require coordination. To deal with the shortcomings of a country-based organization, many firms combine the concept of a regional management center and a country-based unit, as shown in Figure 16.7.

The combination of a regional and country approach minimizes many of the limitations of both designs, but it also adds an additional layer of management. Some executives think that the regional headquarters' additional layer reduces the country-level implementation of strategy rather than improves it. In order to receive benefits from a regional center, there must be a value in a regional strategy. Each company must reach its own decision regarding the organization design, its cost, and its benefits.

Worldwide Functional Organizations

A second way of organizing a worldwide organization is by function. In such an organization, the top executives in marketing, finance, production, accounting, and research and development all have worldwide responsibilities. For international companies, this type of organization is best for narrow or homogeneous product lines, with little variation between products or geographic markets. As shown in Figure 16.8, the functional organization is a simple structure. Each functional manager has worldwide responsibility for that function. Usually the manager has people responsible for the function in regions or countries around the world.

19. George Taucher, "1992: The End to European National Organizations?" *International Business Communications,* vol. 2, no. 3, 1990, pp. 4–7.

20. Christopher Parkes, "Reckitt to Cut About 500 Jobs Over Two Years," *Financial Times,* July 1, 1989, p. 22.

FIGURE 16.7 ● Organization Using Both Country-Based Units and Regional Management Centers

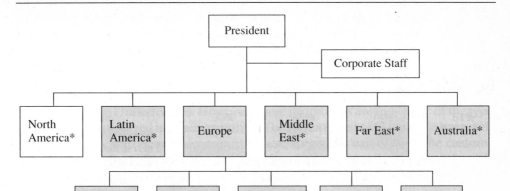

MK = Marketing
OP = Operations

*Under these regional offices would be country organizations similar to the European offices.

FIGURE 16.8 ● Functional Worldwide Organization

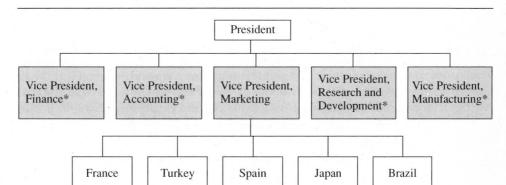

*Each functional vice president has managers of that function in the countries served reporting to him or her as illustrated with the Vice President, Marketing.

Though common in domestic companies, the functional organization is less common in international companies since few companies sell narrow homogeneous product lines with little region to region variations. The functional executives in American firms who do have international responsibilities usually work through a product or regional organization.

Worldwide Product Organizations

A third type of worldwide marketing organization is based on the product line rather than on the function or geographic area. The product group becomes responsible for the performance of the organizational unit, which incorporates marketing, sales, planning, and in some cases production. Other functions, such as legal, accounting, and finance, can be included in the product group or performed by the corporate staff.

Structuring by product line is common for companies with several unrelated product lines. The rationale for selecting a product versus a regional focus is that the differences between the marketing of the products is greater than the differences between the geographic markets. During the 1970s and 1980s many global companies used a dual structure referred to as a matrix of both geography and product, which is discussed later in the chapter. During the 1990s a number of companies such as Philips and ICI have switched away from their geographic and product matrix to strong product divisions.[21] Typically, the end-users for a product organization will vary by product line, so that there is no advantage to having the marketing for the different product lines done by the same group. The product is the focus of the organizational structure shown in Figure 16.9.

A product organization concentrates management on the product line, which is an advantage when the product line constantly changes due to technology. The product focus also gives the organization excellent flexibility. Within a product group the management can control the product life cycle, adding and deleting products with a marginal effect on overall operations. Also, the firm can add new product groups as they add new unrelated products through acquisition.

The product organization has its limitations.[22] Knowledge of specific areas may be limited, since each product group cannot afford a local organization. This lack of knowledge may cause the company to miss market opportunities. The managers of international product divisions can also be a problem. They can be ethnocentric and relatively disinterested or uneasy with the international side of the business. Another limitation of a product organization is the lack of coordination in international markets. If each product group goes its own way, the company's international develop-

21. Clive Cookson, "ICI Proffers More Corporate Clout To Its Customers," *Financial Times,* September 7, 1990, p. 12.

22. For a detailed discussion of a product organization, see William H. Davidson and Philippe Haspeslagh, "Shaping a Global Product Organization," *Harvard Business Review,* July-August 1982, pp. 125–132.

FIGURE 16.9 ● Worldwide Product Organizations

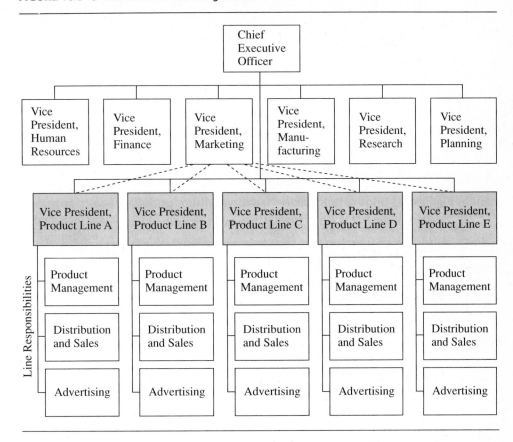

ment may result in inefficiencies. For example, two product divisions separately may be purchasing advertising space in the same magazine, which will be more expensive than if the purchases are combined. To offset the inefficiencies of a worldwide product organization, the organization must provide for global coordination of activities such as advertising, customer service, and government relations.

Matrix Organization

Companies have become frustrated with the limitations of the one-dimensional geographic, product, or functional organization structures. In response to the limitation of single dimension organizations, the matrix organization was developed. As shown in Figure 16.10, the matrix organization allows two dimensions of equal weight (here, geographic and product dimensions) in the organization structure and in

FIGURE 16.10 ● Matrix Organization

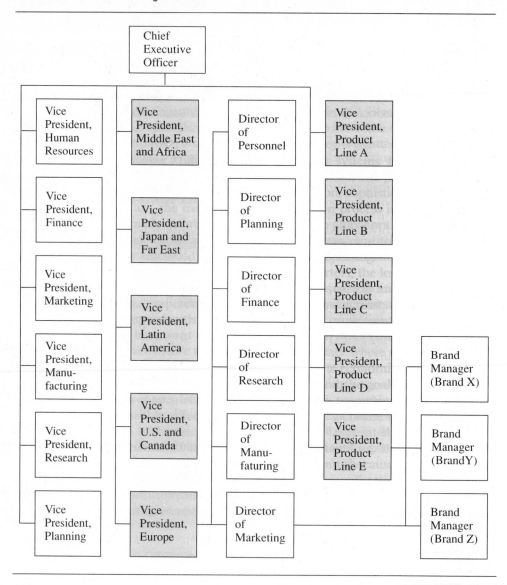

decision-making responsibility. A matrix organization structure has a dual, rather than a single chain of command, which means that many individuals will have two superiors. Firms tend to adopt matrix organizations when it is necessary to be highly responsive to two dimensions, such as product and geography; when there are stringent constraints on financial or human resources; and when uncertainties generate very high informational processing requirements.[23]

A matrix organization can include both the product and geographic management components. Product management has worldwide responsibility for a specific product line, while geographic management is responsible for all product lines in a specific geographic area. These management structures overlap at the national product/market level.

The combination of different organizational objectives and dual reporting relationships fosters conflict and complexity. Power struggles are a common problem when a matrix organization is first established. The power struggle is the result of the dual reporting relationship. The power limits of the two relationships are tested as each side attempts to identify its place in the organization.

Electrolux adopted a complex matrix organization that includes the following four dimensions:

Global Product Area Managers: Hot, Cold, Wet Appliances

Regional Marketing Coordinators: Europe, the United States, and the rest of the world

Country Level: Product Divisions

Country Level: Marketing/Sales Companies

The structure creates a number of tensions on the country, regional, and global level. Leif Johansson, product manager for white goods at Electrolux, says of the structure, "a quite impossible organization, but the only one that will work." Asked about eliminating or reducing the role of the country managers as done by ICI, Unilever, and others he said, "That would be wrong, because they're damned good at their jobs—which includes defending their national interests, dealing with large retail customers and trade unions, as well as overseeing national salary structures. There is too much of a tendency to try to solve organizational problems by designing a structure that quiets conflicts rather than bringing them to the surface."[24]

The key to successful matrix management is the degree to which managers in an organization can resolve conflict and achieve the successful implementation of plans and programs. The matrix organization requires a change in management behavior from traditional authority to an influence system based on technical competence, interpersonal sensitivity, and leadership.

23. Paul R. Lawrence, Harvey F. Kolodny, and Stanley M. David, "The Human Side of the Matrix," *Organization Dynamics,* Summer 1979, pp. 43–47.

24. Christopher Lorenz, "An Impossible Organization, But the Only One That Works," *Financial Times,* June 21, 1989, p. 14.

The advantages of a matrix or hybrid structure are that it

- Permits an organization to function better in an uncertain and changing environment
- Increases potential for control and coordination
- Gives more individuals the chance to develop from technical or functional specialists to generalists

There has been a shift away from the geographic/divisional matrix towards global divisions. These global divisions have responsibility for a set of products worldwide. The shift has been part of the multinationals' quest for simple structures, faster decision making, and greater global effectiveness.[25] Philips, Citibank, Ciba-Geigy, Texas Instruments, BP, and General Electric have all switched to worldwide product divisions away from matrix organizations. The main problem with matrix organizations is that it assumes that product and geographic consideration are evenly balanced; but in reality few large diversified companies have such a balance. A U.S.-based consumer goods firm with two major businesses, drugs and local brand candy bars, found that the matrix organization did not work for these two products. Therefore the company reorganized, putting its billion dollar ethical drug division on a worldwide basis with close ties to headquarters and retaining the matrix organization for the over-the-counter drugs and the candy divisions.[26]

The matrix organization requires a substantial investment in dual budgeting, accounting, transfer pricing, and personnel evaluation systems. The additional complexity and cost of a matrix organization should be offset by the benefit of the dual focus, increased flexibility and sales, and economies of scale.

Strategic Business Units with Global Responsibilities

One of the most recent forms of organizational design is the *strategic business unit* (SBU). The SBU is an organizational group of people supporting products and technologies that serve an identified market and compete with identified competitors. The SBU may either be a separate organizational design, similar to a product organization, or it can be an organizational unit that is used only for the purpose of developing a business strategy for many products in a geographic area.

The increased penetration of global competition has forced many firms to set up SBUs to address the global markets and assess competition in developing a global business strategy. For example, both Coors (beer) and Norton Company (grinding wheels) have set up separate business units to explore the markets for ceramic products based on new high performance ceramic technologies. These business units are

25. Christopher Lorenz, "Re-appraising the Power Base of Regional Barons," *Financial Times,* March 26, 1990, p. 12.
26. J. Quincy Hunsicker, "The Matrix in Retreat," *Financial Times,* October 25, 1982, p. 16.

particularly alert to the efforts of Japanese manufacturers such as Yokoyana, Suma-tomo, and many others who are engaged in ceramics research, as well as the Japanese Ministry of International Trade and Industry that sponsors long-term ceramics research and development.

LIFE CYCLE OF INTERNATIONAL ORGANIZATIONS

Companies evolve into different organizations over time. As their international involvement expands, the degree of organizational complexity increases and firms reorganize accordingly. When a firm moves from exporting a few goods to a world-wide organization, it finds that the company has gone through organizational changes with differing structures and focus. Organizations change to reflect the importance of different markets and the needs of the customer. As the amount of international business increases and the needs of the customers become more complex, the organization will change to reflect the market. The following diagram (Figure 16.11) depicts the typical progress of the international organizational life cycle. Because this is a dynamic and integrative process, most companies do not follow this life cycle exactly; but the framework does provide a method to evaluate the degree of focus and responsibility.

Export

When the domestic market becomes saturated or a need is identified in foreign markets, companies begin exporting their product or services. The export department is still a function of the company and normally reports and follows company procedures and strategies. Often, companies will first begin to receive inquiries from foreign companies about their products. Then, an export person or department is established to process and respond to the foreign inquiries.

Foreign Sales Office

If the demand for the product increases and there appears to be a need to establish an office either to ease administrative procedures or to investigate new markets or refine old markets, then a company will normally establish an office in a foreign country. Normally this office is under headquarters' control and acts according to home office directions.

Regional Market Center

Regional market centers act as filters between the headquarters and various country organizations. Regional market centers coordinate the marketing function of the

FIGURE 16.11 ● Life Cycle of International Organizations

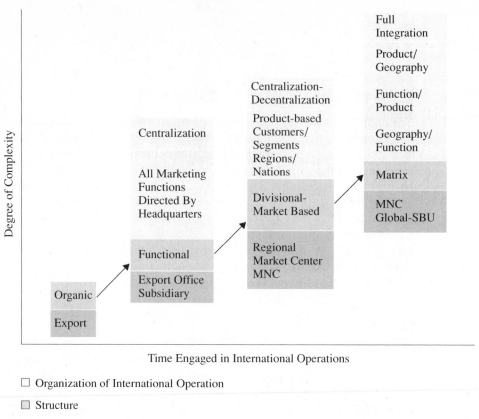

Time Engaged in International Operations

☐ Organization of International Operation

☐ Structure

▨ Focus

branches so that they remain in line with corporate objectives. Regional market centers are normally organized along geographic lines; however, these centers may be organized along product groups or similar target markets.

Matrix Organizations

The matrix organization is the most complex and sophisticated structure. It requires a firm to be fully competent in the following areas:

1. Geographic knowledge

2. Product knowledge

3. Functional aspects, such as finance, production, and marketing

4. Customer/Industry knowledge

Instead of choosing which one to adopt—a national organization or a product organization—the matrix incorporates both and each operates as a profit center. Matrix organizations allow low levels to have substantial authority; however, they require an open and flexible "corporate culture/orientation" for successful implementation.

Global Integration—Strategic Business Units

Fully advanced international companies with complete integration have begun to establish strategic business units. An SBU acts as a separate business and contains a group of products or technologies directed at a specific target market. SBUs are part of a formal structure but act primarily to determine strategies. As mentioned earlier in the chapter, a number of companies have moved from the geography/product division matrix to a global product division structure.

Trends in Global Organizations

Global companies are continually challenged by the need to adapt their organizations to the needs of the market place. The global company needs to respond to three major challenges:

The need for efficiency

The need for responsiveness

The need for learning[27]

As companies compete on a worldwide basis, they need to develop global economies of scale. Instead of supporting manufacturing plants in each major market, products or components are standardized. Electrolux, Black and Decker, Unilever, and many other firms have rationalized their manufacturing to yield economies of scale. While the washing machine or power tool may vary from country to country, the motors can be standardized and manufactured in large volumes to reduce costs. The organizational structure needs to encourage this trend toward efficiency, which is why as part of its complex matrix organization, Electrolux has Mr. Hot responsible for stoves and cookers, Mr. Cold for refrigerators and freezers, and Mr. Wet responsible for washers and dryers. These individuals coordinate the manufacturing and marketing of their product lines across all markets.[28]

While some products like soft drinks, watches, and perfume seem to be trending toward a single global brand, most markets vary by country. Even with the same

27. Christopher A. Bartlett and Sumantra Ghoshal, "Managing Across Borders," London: *Hutchinson Business Books,* 1989, pp. 3–17.

28. Christopher Lorenz, "An Impossible Organization But the Only One That Works," *Financial Times,* June 21, 1989, p. 14.

global product, market structure, competitors, regulations, and culture often will vary by country. Company organizations need to be able to balance their drive for global economies against the need to be responsive to local markets. Kao, the large Japanese detergent, soap, and personal care manufacturer, has developed technologically advanced factories with low costs. Unfortunately, Kao's attempts to enter America and Europe have stalled. Kao has failed because of its inability to understand the differences between markets and to adapt accordingly.[29] Failure to respond to local needs can undermine efforts towards global expansion.

The increased cost of R&D, shortened product life cycles, and consumer demand for the latest technology have increased the need for development and diffusion of worldwide learning. This learning is often related to R&D, but can also include marketing or manufacturing learning. ITT's strategy of individually developing its telecommunication switch technology for each country without gaining any global expertise is one of the factors leading to that company's decline. On the other hand, P&G's seven years of research to develop a heavy-duty, liquid laundry detergent in Europe was quickly and successfully transferred to the United States in the form of Liquid Tide.

Professors Bartlett and Ghoshal interviewed 236 managers in diverse groups of nine companies—P&G, Kao, Unilever, ITT, Ericsson, NEC, GE, Philips, and Matsushita. Based on their research, they suggest that the challenges of global efficiency, local responsiveness, and global learning have become so strong that the global organization must respond to all these challenges simultaneously.[30]

Kenichi Ohmae, argues against the trend toward global products. Being a global company begins with an attitude rather than a product. He suggests that the global company must position itself equidistant from the triad of major markets which are Japan, the United States, and Europe. While the tastes may vary, the broad movements among consumers are similar and offer opportunities. Ohmae believes the renaissance corporation should exploit whatever economies of scale, technology, or branding it has within the triad. In addition, the renaissance global corporation must be an "insider" in each of the triad markets. For example, Coke has 70 percent of the Japanese soft drink market. This is the result of heavy investment by the Coca-Cola Company in Japan to understand the market and build the functional specialties needed. That is, Coca-Cola became an insider in Japan.[31]

Much of this chapter has focused on the formal organizational structure. The formal structure establishes lines of authority and responsibility. In global organizations, the formal organization is important, but the formal organization is only one part of the organizational challenge. The interpersonal relationships, decision-making process, and individual behavior of managers must also be responsive to the

29. Bartlett and Ghoshal, "Managing Across Borders," London: *Hutchinson Business Books,* 1989, pp. 3–17.

30. Ibid., pp. 16–17.

31. Kenichi Ohmae, *The Borderless World* (London: Collins, 1990), pp. 26–30.

needs of the market place. Professors Bartlett and Ghoshal argue that *people* are the key to managing complex strategies and organizations.

The task of molding an organization to respond to the needs of a global market place involves building a shared vision and developing human resources. A clear vision of the purpose of the company that is shared by everyone gives meaning and direction to each manager. For example, NEC, the Japanese electronics company, has a vision of computers and communications. The vision is simple and can be easily communicated across borders. Every manager can see the direction and relate individual behavior to the goal of building systems where computers and communication are interlinked to solve business problems.

Managers are a company's scarcest resource. The process of recruiting, selecting, training, and managing the human resource must help build a common vision and values. Matsushita (Panasonic) gives new white collar workers six months of cultural and spiritual training. Philips has organization cohesion training and Unilever's new hires go through indoctrination. This initial training helps to build the vision and shared values. Managers also receive ongoing training. For example, Unilever brings 400 to 500 international managers from around the world to its international management training center. Unilever spends as much on training as it does on R&D, not only to upgrade skills, but also to indoctrinate managers into the Unilever club and help build personal relationships and informal contacts that are more powerful than the formal systems or structures.[32]

CONCLUSIONS

Organizing the marketing efforts of a company across a number of countries is a difficult process. As the scope of a company's international business changes, its organizational structure must be modified in accordance with the internal and external environments. As the number of countries a company is marketing in increases, as product lines expand, and objectives change, so will the organizations. In this chapter, we have reviewed the various organizations commonly used, showing the benefits of each. The dynamic nature of business requires a constant re-evaluation of organizational structure with necessary modifications to meet the objectives of the firm.

Questions for Discussion

1. What aspects of the external environment cause multicountry marketing organizations to be different from single country marketing organizations?

32. Christopher A. Bartlett and Sumantra Ghoshal, "Matrix Management: Not A Structure, a Frame of Mind," *Harvard Business Review,* July-August 1990, pp. 138–145.

2. What effect will the marketing strategy have on an international marketing organization? For example, if the key aspect of a computer manufacturer's strategy is to focus on three industries worldwide—banks, stockbrokers, and educational institutions—will the organization be different from that of another company that decides to focus on end-users who require mainframe computers?

3. How does a single country organization evolve into an international organization? What type of international organization is likely to develop first? Second? Why?

4. What actions will cause a company to develop an international marketing organization?

5. What are the pros and cons of a regional management center versus a product organization?

6. A country-based geographic structure responds well to the local culture and marketing. What will cause a company to switch from a country structure to a worldwide product organization?

7. Matrix organizations can be very costly and complex. What are the advantages of a matrix organization?

8. In addition to the formal organization structure, how does the global company assure it is responding to the market place and achieving efficiency, local responsiveness, and global learning?

For Further Reading

Bartlett, Christopher A. "MNCs: Get Off the Reorganization Merry-Go-Round." *Harvard Business Review* (March-April 1983), pp. 138–146.

Bartlett, Christopher A., and Sumantra Ghoshal. *Managing Across Borders:* The Transnational Solution. Boston: Harvard Business School Press, 1989.

Business International. *Designing the International Corporate Organization.* New York: Business International Corporation, 1976.

"Corporate Organization: Where in the World Is It Going?" *Business International* (August 15, 1980), pp. 257–258.

David, Stanley M., and Paul R. Lawrence. "Problems of Matrix Organization." *Harvard Business Review* (May-June 1978), pp. 134–136.

Davidson, William H., and Phillippe Haspeslagh. "Shaping a Global Product Organization." *Harvard Business Review* (July-August 1982), pp. 125–132.

Drake, Rodman, and Lee M. Caudill. "Management of the Large Multinational: Trends and Future Changes." *Business Horizons* (May-June 1981), pp. 88–90.

Handy, Charles. *Inside Organizations.* London: BBC Books, 1990.

Handy, Charles. *The Age of Unreason.* London: Hutchinson, 1989.

Holmen, Milton G. "Organizing and Staffing of Foreign Operations of Multinational Corporations." Paper presented at the Academy of International Business Meeting in New Orleans, October 25, 1980.

Hutchinson, J. "Evolving Organizational Forms." *Columbia Journal of World Business* (Summer 1976), pp. 49–50.

Ohmae, Kenichi. *The Borderless World.* London: Collins, 1990.

Parker, Herbert S. "Restructuring the Corporation." *Planning Review* (January-February 1987), pp. 46–48.

Picard, Jacques. "Determinants of Centralization of Marketing Decision Making in Multinational Corporations." In *Marketing in the 80's,* Proceedings of the Educators' Conference. Chicago: American Marketing Association, 1980, pp. 259–261.

Shetty, Y.K. "Managing the MNC: European and American Styles." *Management International Review,* no. 3 (1979), pp. 39–48.

17

Planning and Controlling International and Global Marketing

● **THE PROCESSES FOR** *planning and controlling are interrelated. Planning allows a company to understand the environment and develop a strategy. Controlling is the process of evaluating strategy implementation and managing the efforts of those people responsible for the strategy. The processes of planning and controlling are related to the specific organization (see Chapter 16), because the processes are completed within the organizational structure. As the environment changes and new strategies are developed, the organization may change, which may affect the planning and controlling processes. For example, if a company changes from a functional organization, with all marketing decisions made at the headquarters in New York, to a geographic organization, with regional management centers in Paris, Tokyo, New York, and Sao Paulo, the planning and controlling processes will change. Figure 17.1 shows how the planning and controlling processes relate to strategy implementation and to the organizational structure of the firm.*

THE INTERNATIONAL PLANNING PROCESS

Planning in the international environment is difficult because of the number of extraneous elements involved. Table 17.1 illustrates the differences between planning in a domestic setting and planning in an international one.

As shown in Table 17.1, there are numerous factors that increase the complexity

FIGURE 17.1 ● Planning and Controlling International Marketing

Planning Methods	Boston Consulting Group	General Electric/ McKinsey	Profit Impact of Marketing Strategy	Scenario Planning
Planning Process	Selecting Markets	Coordinating Planning Efforts	Decision Making	Standardized Versus Decentralized
Control Process	Standards	Measurements and Evaluations	Correcting Deviations	

of international planning, such as language, political differences, currency fluctuations, and a lack of market data. These differences increase the difficulty of developing and implementing international plans.

Strategic planning is a widely accepted practice of corporate business. The issue of globalization demands strategic research and thought in addressing increasingly complex and competitive world markets.[1] Often global strategic planning takes place at the highest levels of a company. It is common for relatively young, well-trained executives to provide the information and analysis for these high level discussions and decisions. It is important to understand the process that the board or executive committee takes to make a strategic decision, as you may be the marketing manager implementing that decision.

As businesses move into international markets, the decision makers are faced

---

1. See George Rabstejnek, "Let's Get Back to the Basics of Global Strategy," *Journal of Business Strategy,* September/October 1989, p. 34.

TABLE 17.1 ● Domestic versus International Planning

Domestic planning	*International planning*
1. Single language and nationality	1. Multilingual/multinational/ multicultural factors
2. Relatively homogeneous market	2. Fragmented and diverse markets
3. Data available, usually accurate and collection easy	3. Data collection a formidable task, requiring significantly higher budgets and personnel allocation
4. Political factors relatively unimportant	4. Political factors frequently vital
5. Relative freedom from government interference	5. Involvement in national economic plans; government influences business decisions
6. Individual corporation has little effect on environment	6. "Gravitational" distortion by large companies
7. Chauvinism helps	7. Chauvinism hinders
8. Relatively stable business environment	8. Multiple environments, many of which are highly unstable (but may be highly profitable)
9. Uniform financial climate	9. Variety of financial climates ranging from overconservative to wildly inflationary
10. Single currency	10. Currencies differing in stability and real value
11. Business "rules of the game" mature and understood	11. Rules diverse, changeable, and unclear
12. Management generally accustomed to sharing responsibilities and using financial controls	12. Management frequently autonomous and unfamiliar with budgets and controls

Source: William W. Cain, "International Planning: Mission Impossible?" *Columbia Journal of World Business,* July–August 1970, p. 58. Reprinted by permission.

with increasingly complex alternatives.[2] Should we license in Brazil, export to South Africa, establish a joint venture in Kuwait, or set up a wholly owned subsidiary in Hong Kong? Which project or combination of projects will meet our corporate objectives? The two dimensions that differentiate international from domestic strategic planning are the multiple countries that businesses market to and the modes of entry into those markets.

2. Noel Capon, Chris Christodoulou, John U. Farley, James Hulbert et al., "Comparison of Corporate Planning Practice in American and Australian Manufacturing Companies," *Journal of International Business Studies,* Fall 1984, pp. 41–54.

This chapter reviews the various types of planning processes being used, their application to the international market, and the advantages and disadvantages of each procedure when used with the international markets. The most widely used approaches to planning are the following:

Boston Consulting Group Approach (BCG)

General Electric/McKinsey Approach (GE)

Profit Impact of Market Strategy (PIMS)

Scenario Planning[3]

There are numerous articles and papers that review and compare the various planning models as they apply to domestic markets. Using these domestic systems as a base, each approach will be examined as it is used for international markets.

At any point in time, a firm really consists of a number of businesses, such as divisions, products, or brands. When these businesses were established, each of them was expected to grow. The firm would encourage growth by expanding research and development, advertising, and promotional budgets for all but the declining products. In recent years, the cost and availability of capital have caused corporations to be much more selective in the financing of their businesses. The tendency has been for a firm to look at its individual businesses and decide which ones to build, maintain, phase down, or close down. Therefore, the job of planning has become one of evaluating current businesses and searching out new opportunities so that the mixture of businesses within the firm will provide the necessary growth and cash flow for growth. For international markets, the breakdown of a firm's activities into the different businesses, usually referred to as strategic business units (SBUs), is normally done on a product-by-country basis. Once the firm is broken down into SBUs, planning must classify the firms based on expected future potential. While the concept of an SBU is widely accepted, it does have limitations. For example, in vertically integrated businesses it may not be easy to neatly sort out business units because they share facilities and their performances are interrelated.[4] One of the original classification schemes was developed by the Boston Consulting Group.

The Boston Consulting Group Approach[5]

The Boston Consulting Group (BCG) approach classifies all current strategic business units into a business portfolio matrix shown in Figure 17.2. This includes both current SBUs as well as potential or proposed opportunities. The proposed

3. Richard G. Hamermesh, "Making Planning Strategic," *Harvard Business Review,* July-August 1986, p. 115.

4. Rael T. Hussein, "A Critical Review of Strategic Planning Models," *The Quarterly Review of Marketing,* Spring/Summer, 1987, p. 17.

5. Bruce D. Henderson, "The Experience Curve Reviewed: IV. The Growth Share Matrix of the Product Portfolio," (Boston: The Boston Consulting Group, Inc., 1973), Perspectives No. 135.

FIGURE 17.2 ● Boston Consulting Group Matrix

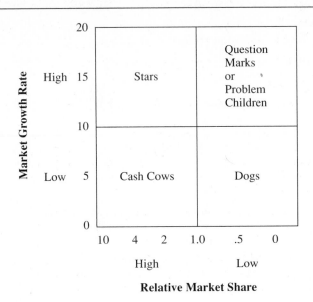

Source: Perspectives, No. 135, "The Experience Curve—Reviewed, IV. The Growth Share Matrix or The Product Portfolio." Adapted by permission from *The Boston Consulting Group,* Inc., 1973.

opportunities are normally an extension of the current business via expansion into a new country or new product. BCG's methodology classifies these businesses based on market growth rate and market share. The market growth rate is the expected total market demand growth on an annualized basis. The market share is the company's relative share compared to the largest competitor. For example, a rate of 1.0 means the SBU has the same share as the next competitor, a 0.5 means it has one-half the share of the next largest competitor, and a 3.0 means the SBU has a three times larger share than the next largest competitor.

A firm's SBUs are evaluated and classified based on this approach. Market growth rate relates to the stage of the product life cycle and relative market share is based on the concept of market dominance. According to their positioning, products are classified as follows:

Dogs: Low market share and low growth. Should break even. Not a source of cash.

Question Marks or Problem Children: Low market share and high market growth. These SBUs are cash users. Money must be spent to maintain market position. They could become either stars or dogs.

Stars: High growth and high share. May break even or use cash to support high growth rate. Eventually growth will slow down and they will become cash cows.

Cash Cows: High market share and low market growth. As expected, these SBUs throw off cash to support other SBUs.[6]

To survive in the long term, a firm needs the proper balance of business in each area. Over time, businesses will change their positions. Many SBUs start as problem children, then become stars, then cash cows, and finally dogs. The corporate planning function must work with the managers of each SBU to forecast the future mix of businesses in each area. Then, resources must be allocated based on this forecast as well as on the corporate objectives. Firms will use one of the following four strategies.

First, Build—invest for the future, forego short-term earning while improving market position.

Second, Hold—maintain the current position.

Third, Harvest—generate short-term cash flow regardless of the long-term effect.

Fourth, Divest—sell or liquidate.

The most difficult part of using the BCG method is determining which level or unit of analysis to examine. For example, a firm may only have 5 percent of the world industrial pipe market, but it has 35 percent of the world industrial pipe market over 15 inches in diameter and 58 percent of the Spanish industrial pipe market over 12 inches in diameter.

The method used most often when applying the BCG approach in international planning is to use one product compared by country, as shown in Figure 17.3.

The suggested procedure is to develop the market portfolio material for the firm's own products and for those of major competitors. Then, the analysis should be repeated in five years. This will assist management in deciding which countries to build, hold, harvest, or divest.

The major advantages of the BCG approach in international planning are the following:

- It requires a global view of the firm's business and its competition.
- The approach provides a framework for analysis and comparison of business.
- The procedure is a good basis for the formulation of marketing objectives for specific international markets.
- The methodology allows a convenient graphical form which is easily understood by executives.

Although the BCG approach has had wide acceptance, it has also received criticism. The main criticisms are oriented toward the oversimplification of the process.[7]

---

6. Bruce D. Henderson, *Henderson on Corporate Strategy* (Cambridge, Mass.: Abt Associates, 1979).

7. Peter W. Turnbull, "A Review of Portfolio Planning Models for Industrial Marketing and Purchasing Management," *European Journal of Marketing,* vol. 24, no. 3, 1990, p. 13.

FIGURE 17.3 ● Industrial Pipe—Market Portfolio

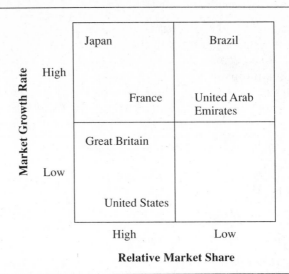

The BCG approach assumes that high market share and high growth rate will result in success. Research has raised some doubts about market growth and the market share. There are a number of low market share businesses with high profitability. Often problem children are the result of late entry to a market, which can change quickly with a leap frog strategy using new technology. If a cash cow is continually milked and not given sufficient attention, it can dry up. General Electric has been criticized for feeding off its cash cows too much and not investing enough to upgrade and protect its consumer products.[8] Obviously other internal and external factors also affect the success of a business. Even if you accept the basic premise of the BCG approach, there are still problems defining the product, defining the market, measuring market growth, and measuring market dominance. These limitations apply to both international and domestic applications.

When using the BCG method for international markets with one product compared in several countries, the following four problems arise. First, the elements chosen for analysis are the countries. This may be wrong. Instead of looking at the countries by country market growth and market share for hair shampoo, maybe we should be analyzing the world portfolio for hair shampoo, by product market. For example, the men's expensive shampoo market, children's shampoo market, young women's shampoo market, and so on. The original BCG model ignores the interdependence of international markets. While our Paris operation may be a dog, using

8. John O'Shaughnessy, *Competitive Marketing: A Strategic Approach,* London: Allen and Unwin, 1984, pp. 24–25.

Paris as a production point for Greece, Italy, Spain, Portugal, and France may result in a cash cow or star.

Second, the BCG approach assumes a firm has extended experience with a product. Therefore, a high market share and more production experience will result in decreased costs. This concept becomes very gray when we start to examine possible variations in input costs, such as capital, manpower, material, tariffs, inflation, exchange rates, and transportation for different countries.

Third, the BCG method assumes the motivations of international firms to be similar, that is, profits, return on investment, and so on. This is not always true. Different countries emphasize different things. For some it is full employment and a favorable balance of payments. Others may desire low inflation. A country's economic or social policies will affect the implementation of the BCG method.

Finally, the individual firm may have other objectives besides the generation of cash such as gaining technical information, preventing competition, or establishing good relations with a local government. For example, Philips, the Dutch electronics giant has argued that it must keep its semiconductor business which is a money-losing business. Philips executives maintain without proprietary access to semiconductor know-how, the company's ability to compete with the Japanese in consumer electronics will be fatally undermined.[9]

The General Electric/McKinsey Approach[10]

General Electric and McKinsey management consultants worked together to develop the GE business screen—a multifactor assessment based on an analysis of factors relating to profitability. The approach is an extension of the BCG approach.

The GE screen uses the following factors to evaluate SBUs:

Industry attractiveness	*Business strength*
● Market Size	● Relative Market Share
● Market Growth	● Price Competitiveness
● Market Diversity	● Size, Growth
● Profit Margins	● Product Quality
● Competitive Structure	● Profitability
● Technical Role	● Technological Position
● Cyclicality	● Strengths and Weaknesses
● Environment	● Knowledge of Customers/Market
● Legal, Human, Social	● Image, Pollution, People

9. Andrew Lorenz and Iain Jenkins, "The Powerhorse That Blew a Fuse," *The Sunday Times,* May 20, 1990, p. D9.

10. Information in this section is drawn from *Managing Strategies for the Future Through Current Crises* (Fairfield, Conn.: General Electric Company, 1975).

FIGURE 17.4 ● GE's Business Screen for Evaluating SBUs

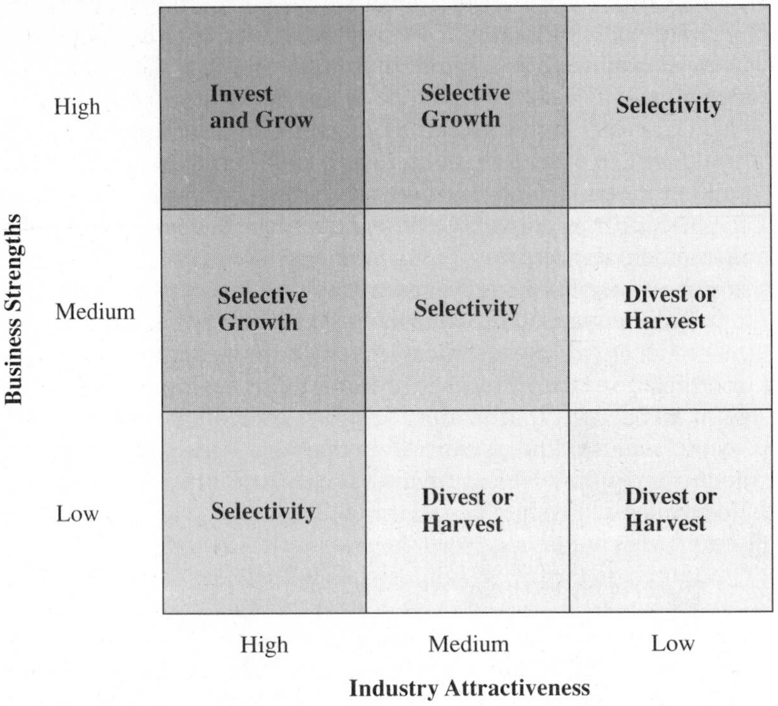

		High	Medium	Low
Business Strengths	High	Invest and Grow	Selective Growth	Selectivity
	Medium	Selective Growth	Selectivity	Divest or Harvest
	Low	Selectivity	Divest or Harvest	Divest or Harvest

Industry Attractiveness

The GE approach rates each SBU based on these factors for industry attractiveness and business strength.[11] Each of the factors is given a certain weight. A procedure of aggregating various executives' opinions on these weights results in a high, medium, or low attractiveness and business strength.[12] Each SBU is then located on GE's nine-cell business screen, shown in Figure 17.4.

As shown in the screen, the GE approach results in strategic decisions similar to those in the BCG approach. The three cells in the upper left show the SBUs in favorable industries with good business strengths. The firm should invest and grow with these cells. The three diagonal cells are in the middle. The firm needs to decide whether to maintain, improve, or harvest these SBUs. The three cells in the lower

11. Francis J. Aguilar and Richard Hamermesh, "General Electric: Strategic Position: 1981," Harvard Business School Case 9-381-174, p. 25.

12. Peter W. Turnbull, "A Review of Portfolio Planning Models for Industrial Marketing and Purchasing Management," *European Journal of Marketing,* vol. 24, no. 3, 1990, pp. 7–10.

right are those SBUs with an overall low attractiveness; this makes them candidates for harvesting or divesting.

The principles of the GE approach have been modified and used in the international environment. As we mentioned in Chapter 7, Ford Motor Company's Tractor Division has developed a strategic market portfolio evaluation system that focuses on country attractiveness and competitive strengths.[13]

The GE approach has the same limitations as the BCG method. However, the GE method is more adaptable to international markets. Each firm can determine which factors are important to its success in an international market and evaluate SBUs based on these factors. Unfortunately, little empirical work has been done on either approach in the international market. The GE approach is still two dimensional, using only the factors of country attractiveness and business strength. This ignores the form of entry. For example, the importance of political stability varies greatly depending on whether a firm is exporting or involved in direct foreign investment. In conclusion, the GE approach is useful for international companies. It provides more flexibility than the BCG approach, but its limitations should not be ignored.

Profit Impact of Marketing Strategy (PIMS)[14]

The PIMS project was started in 1960 at General Electric. Over the years the model was developed at the Harvard Business School, The Marketing Science Institute, and finally at The Strategic Planning Institute. The PIMS model data base includes the history and performance of over 450 companies and 3,000 businesses.[15] The model includes a computer-based regression model that utilizes the experience of the data base to determine what explains (or drives) profitability.

Each business is described in terms of thirty-seven factors such as growth rate, market share, product quality, investment intensity, and so on. The PIMS model uses multivariate regression equations to establish relationships between these different factors and two separate measures of performance, specifically, return on investment (ROI) and cash flow. PIMS research indicates that these performance measures are explained by general factors such as the following:

Market growth rate

Market share of business

Market share divided by share of three largest competitors

13. Gilbert D. Harrell and Richard O'Kiefer, "Multinational Strategic Market Portfolios," *MSU Business Topics,* Winter 1981, p. 12.

14. Information in this section is drawn from Sidney Schoeffler, Robert D. Buzzell, and Donald F. Henry, "Impact of Strategic Planning on Profit Performance," *Harvard Business Review,* March-April 1974, pp. 137–145.

15. Robert D. Buzzell and Bradley T. Gale, *The PIMS Principles: Linking Strategy to Performance* (New York: The Free Press, 1987).

Degree of vertical integration

Working capital requirements per dollars of sales

Plant and equipment requirements per dollars of sales

Relative product quality

The PIMS model uses many more variables than either the BCG or GE approach. Using the thirty-seven factors the model explains over 80 percent of the observed variation in profitability of the 3,000 businesses in the data base. Varta AG and Wiener-Verlag has $1 billion in sales through 20 profit centers in eight countries. Its business consists of paper manufacturing and printing. Through the BCG approach it found that most of its businesses were classified as cash cows, therefore they would be wise to take the cash and invest in high-growth businesses. Unfortunately, the group had very little surplus cash. So while the BCG technique was easy to apply and communicate, it gave little practical help. The company used the PIMS analysis to enhance its strategic planning. The twenty profit centers resulted in seventy SBUs, which were evaluated relative to the 3000 businesses in the database. The actual return on investment was calculated versus the return of companies with a comparable cost structure and competitive situation. The analysis showed a number of businesses that would achieve immediate profit improvement from operational changes such as reduced inventory. The analysis also showed which businesses were in a weak competitive position and the size of the investment needed to improve the business. The Varta AG and Wiener-Verlag group of companies found the PIMS far superior to the BCG model.[16]

There are three major criticisms of the PIMS model. First, since the model uses variables related to each other, multicollinearity results. Therefore, the impact of individual factors on performance cannot be clearly identified. Second, the PIMS results only include those companies still in the business. Maybe the higher profits are the result of taking higher risks, but that does not take into account other companies that tried and failed.[17] Third, the technical procedure for eliminating extreme values of data input tends to bias the results and improve the model's appearance. Although all these criticisms are valid, the methodology of the PIMS approach is one of the best approaches available to domestic planning.

The outlook for an international PIMS model is optimistic, with over 1,000 non-U.S. strategic business units. The PIMS model should analyze performance based on the traditional criteria as well as by mode of entry. The form that a multinational business takes has a significant impact on costs, profitability, risks, and so on. Also the PIMS model will probably be limited to product-by-country analysis. Although the data will be helpful, many products need to be analyzed on a product-

16. George Kellinghusen and Klaus Wubbenhorts, "Strategic Control for Improved Performance," *Long Range Planning,* vol. 23, no. 3, June 1990, pp. 30–40.

17. George S. Day, *Analysis for Strategic Market Decisions,* New York: West Publishing, 1986, p. 153.

by-market segment. Also, with the regional trade groups that have formed, such as ANCOM, ASEAN, EC, EFTA, and OPEC, many markets are becoming regionalized. This will also be an obstacle for the international PIMS model.

However, despite these limitations, the PIMS model may become one of the key international strategic planning models in the future. With the utilization of a multinational data base, the PIMS model will be able to assist planners in deciding how to allocate resources to meet corporate objectives.

Scenario Planning[18]

The three strategic planning models discussed so far are referred to as portfolio models. These models do not take into consideration the impact of various external factors such as economic growth, energy costs, inflation, East/West relations, war, and economic fluctuations.

Scenario planning is a unique approach to strategic planning. With scenario planning, the multinational's business is broken down into business/country segments. Then a central or most probable scenario is developed regarding significant external variables such as energy costs, world politics, inflation, and so on. Possible variants of this central scenario are also developed. Then, the business/country segments are evaluated based on the central scenario and the variant scenarios. Ideally, investment decisions can be made based on this analysis. A large U.K.-based oil company was using scenario planning in the early 1970s. The company had devised six possible scenarios, with a plan for each. When the Yom Kippur Arab-Israeli war took place in October 1973, followed by OPEC declaring an oil embargo, this company already had a plan which they implemented immediately to deal with limited supply and a slowdown in the worldwide demand for oil.[19]

The limitations of scenario planning are as follows. First, the development of a central scenario and variants will be difficult. There will be many inputs to this scenario with limited agreement. Second, analysis of the effect of each scenario will also be complex. For example, if a firm is selling pipe to the United Kingdom and the central scenario predicts oil prices will go up 10 percent per year, how will the firm evaluate the U.K. pipe market? Increased oil prices mean more tax revenues from North Sea oil, an increase in exports, a favorable impact on the balance of trade, the strengthening of the pound sterling, an increase in imports, and a decrease in the ability of the remaining U.K. industries to export.

Although the scenario planning or contingency planning are useful techniques, they should be used to augment the portfolio methods—BCG, GE, and PIMS.

18. Information in this section is drawn from Harold F. Klein and Robert E. Linneman, "The Use of Scenarios in Corporate Planning—Eight Case Histories," *Long Range Planning,* October 1981, pp. 69–77.
19. R. Jeffrey Ellis, *Managing Strategy in the Real World* (Lexington, Mass.; Lexington Books, 1988), pp. 107–119.

Global Business Planning—A Look to the Future

The models for business planning such as BCG, GE/McKinsey, and others when applied to international business have been criticized as being merely extensions of domestic models. The factors and criteria used in these approaches are too narrow and exclude factors that are international in nature. Researchers emphasize the need for adoption of a global portfolio perspective in order to determine the optional mix of countries, products, market segments, and modes of operation to achieve the desired long-term results.[20]

A global perspective on portfolio planning should allow a company to evaluate the extent of its involvement in international markets. Companies need to evaluate the opportunities for reallocating resources across countries, product line, and modes of operations. The benefits of participating in lead markets (see Chapter 11), understanding a major competitor's home market, and exploiting opportunities from specialized R&D talent must be assessed to identify the best allocation of resources to maximize the long-term profitabilty. When applying domestic approaches to the global environment, resources are often spread over wide geographic areas with little attention given to the interdependencies of management decisions. For an effective global portfolio strategy, there is the need for an integrated approach within the context of corporate objectives. Professors Wind and Douglas suggest that a global portfolio approach should

1. Be built on conceptually attractive dimensions of risks and returns as well as any idiosyncratic criteria considered to be important to the company.

2. Allow for differential weighting of the various dimensions.

3. Allow for sequential analysis to reduce the cost and complexity of data collection.

4. Integrate the available "hard" data with management's subjective judgments.

5. Allow for a flexible structure capable of dealing with any unit of analysis or portfolio components.

6. Be based on projected performance of the product/market/mode of entry and level and type of marketing activities under alternative scenarios.

7. Offer guidelines for resource allocation among the portfolio components.

8. Incorporate the scheduling of activities with the resource allocation procedure.

9. Allow for easily implementable sensitivity to assess the impact of changes in assumptions and judgments or to stimulate likely outcomes of competitive activities and other environmental forces.[21]

20. Peter W. Turnbull, "A Review of Portfolio Planning Models for Industrial Marketing and Purchasing Management," *European Journal of Marketing,* vol 23, no 3, 1990, pp. 14–15.

21. Yoram Wind and Susan Douglas, "International Portfolio Analysis and Strategy: The Challenges of the 80s," *Journal of International Business Studies,* Fall, 1981, p. 7. Reprinted by permission.

The International Marketing Planning Process

The complexity of international markets requires a structured approach to the planning process. Research into the practices of multinational companies have revealed a number of problems regarding the planning process. Among the problems identified were the following:

- Too much information of the wrong kind and a lack of useful information for planning.
- A neglect of strategic or long-term planning.
- Overemphasis on the plan as a control device instead of as a means to achieving the objectives.
- A belief that forecasting and budgeting were market planning.
- A separation of long-term and short-term plans which precluded operational management from considering more desirable alternatives.[22]

The heterogeneous nature of international markets and the difficulty of data collection require that the marketer take an organized approach to evaluating opportunities and preparing plans. Figure 17.5 illustrates an international marketing planning matrix.

The planning matrix is an organized approach to evaluating international opportunities. The matrix requires that the marketer evaluate the marketing planning variables at each level of decision making. The levels of decision making, which are located on the vertical axis, begin with the commitment decision. This first decision is whether or not to enter foreign markets; and this is based on the firm's objectives, its resources, and the opportunities available in international versus domestic markets. After making the commitment decision, a company will select the country it wishes to enter. The country decision is based on evaluation of the environment, the demand, the corporate resources, and the financial projections. The mode of entering the selected country will be based on the firm's commitment decision, the country selection, and the cost/benefit evaluation of different modes of entry.

As discussed in Chapter 9, the mode of entry will also be affected by a variety of other factors, such as risk assessment, laws of foreign ownership, and so on. The marketing strategy will flow logically from the firm's objective in a market, which will include the marketing mix required to differentiate products in that environment. The market organization decision is related to the objective and strategy for each market. The organization structure will determine which people will be where, how decisions will be made, what information and services will go back and forth between the organizational unit and headquarters, and the budgeting control process. A recent study of seventy-nine businesses from twenty countries found that all companies prepared some type of marketing plan. In fact, when given the following

22. Tom Griffin, "Marketing Planning: Observations on Current Practices and Recent Studies," *European Journal of Marketing,* vol. 24, no. 12, 1989, pp. 21–22.

FIGURE 17.5 ● International Marketing Planning Matrix

International Decisions	Marketing Planning Variables					
	Situation Analysis	Problems-Opportunity Analysis	Objectives	Marketing Program	Marketing Budgets	Sales Vol. Cost/Profit Estimate
A. Commitment Decision						
B. Country Selection						
C. Mode of Entry						
D. Marketing Strategy						
E. Marketing Organization						

Source: Reprinted with permission from Helmut Becker and Hans B. Thorelli: *International Marketing Strategy,* Copyright © 1980, Pergamon Press PLC.

standard model for a marketing plan 65 percent said their process was very similar and 28 percent said it was somewhat similar.[23]

Model Marketing Plan

Situational Analysis

　Environmental Trends

　Market Trends

　Strengths and Weaknesses versus Competition

Problems and Opportunities

　Based on Situational Analysis

23. Ibid.

Objectives of the Plan

Strategies to Achieve Objectives

   Product, Package, Price, Distribution, Advertising, Sales, Target Markets

Tactics to Implement the Strategies

   Sales Forecast

   Estimate of Income, Expense, Profit

   Method to Evaluate Overall Effectiveness of Plan

Selecting Markets

Only the largest international company with a product that appeals to all types of people in all environments can afford to be in all the countries of the world. Given the limited employee and financial resources of most companies, international activities must be limited to a selective set of countries. Given that most companies desire to be profitable in each market served, and that profitability will be determined by the level of resources required to meet the competitive demands of the marketplace, it is important to maintain a critical mass of marketing resources. These resources include the cost of modifying the product to be competitive, the distribution coverage, and the advertising and direct sales coverage required to be competitive. This set of marketing resources must reach a critical mass in order to be effective and profitable. Figure 17.6 shows a grid for evaluating new foreign markets. The horizontal axis measures the market attractiveness of each country and the vertical axis describes the company's position in each market with respect to the critical mass of marketing resources.

Using the grid for selecting new markets will help to focus a company's resources on the opportunities with the greatest profitability. It will also tend to concentrate market expansion in markets that are geographically close to current markets.

Coordinating the Planning Process[24]

Coordinating the strategic planning process between the product marketing functions and the country managers is a challenging process. There is a natural tendency to emphasize the product element that shortchanges the geographic element. To improve coordination of product management and country management while utilizing the expertise of each, General Electric has each *country* executive develop a comprehensive country opportunity plan that covers all products and strategies. The

24. The information in this section is drawn from "Many Subs in One Country? Getting More Coordination Without Stifling Initiative," *Business International,* January 15, 1982, pp. 17–19.

FIGURE 17.6 ● A Grid for Evaluating Foreign Markets

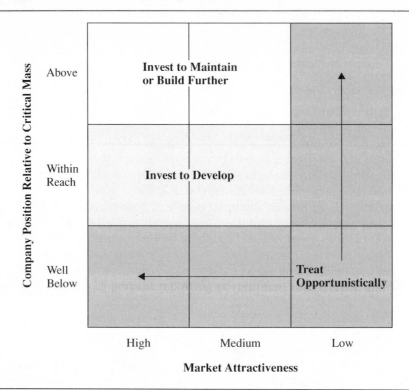

Source: Robert S. Attiyeh and David L. Wenner, "Critical Mass: Key to Export Profits," Reprinted from *Business Horizons,* December 1979. Copyright © 1979 by the Foundation for the School of Business at Indiana University. Used with permission.

country executive's plan is compared to the plans of G.E.'s individual strategic business units for that market. The combination of the two different organizations provides a rich pool of information on tactics and opportunities. The final plan will be an integration of the product and country point of view, with conflicts identified and solutions proposed.

Hoechst, one of the largest global chemical companies headquartered in Germany, uses a multilevel planning system to coordinate the different layers of management as well as to get the full benefit of its knowledge and coordinate strategy from different parts of the company. The Hoechst planning system is illustrated in Figure 17.7. The top layer is strategic planning covering a ten-year horizon for products and regions. For example, what is Hoechst planning over the next ten years for agricultural operations and pharmaceuticals? In addition, what are the plans for

FIGURE 17.7 ● Hoechst Planning System

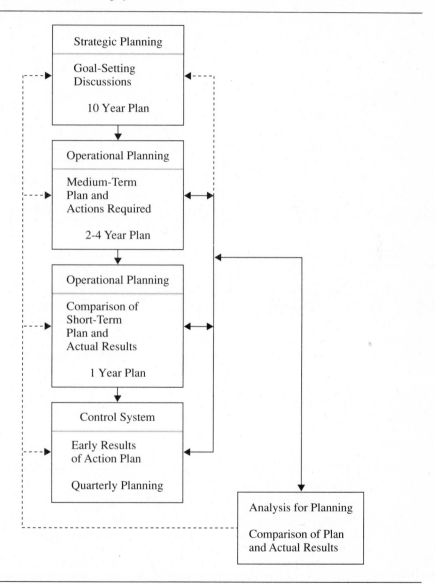

Source: Reprinted with permission from *Long Range Planning,* vol. 23, no. 3, Carol Kennedy, "Hoechst: Re-positioning for a Global Market." Copyright © 1990, Pergamon Press PLC.

Japan or France? Care is taken to ensure that the strategic goals match for products and regions. The strategic planning at Hoechst involves the following four steps:

1. Gathering internal data about markets, competitors, and capacities.
2. Gathering and analyzing external data on world economics, industry dynamics, market trends, and key success factors.
3. Development of strategic options and selection of a preferred solution.
4. Development of an implementation plan with milestones identified and target dates set.

The middle layer of Hoechst's system is operational planning. This process covers the next four years on a rolling forecast which is revised each year. The first year is in detail and the second to fourth years are in rougher outline. The bottom layer is a control system for following up and monitoring the progress of the operational plans on a quarterly basis. This allows deviations to be tracked and plans adjusted to deal with shocks, such as currency fluctuations. The planning system has proved successful with Hoechst achieving a 1988 profit of 2.0 billion Deutsche marks, the largest in its 125 year history.[25]

Siemens, the world's fifth-largest electrical and electronics equipment maker, has a formalized communication phase between the product groups and the geographic structures. During this formal communications phase of the planning process, the product and country management meet to establish an understanding of each other's position. Eaton Corporation, which is organized around a worldwide product structure, found it necessary to inform managers of methods to respond to common environmental issues such as political conditions, taxes, inflation, and joint ownership. To share information and experience, regional coordinating committees that meet monthly were set up in Latin America and Europe. Danish firms were found to be behind other Europeans in adopting formalized planning systems because they see planning as a matter of survival and prefer to minimize paper plans in favor of oral communication.[26]

Who Makes the Decisions?

Decision making responsibility is dependent on several internal and external factors. What decisions are made within each line of command differs from firm to firm.

Table 17.2 summarizes a study of eighty-six separate marketing programs in nine U.S.-based international companies that determined the degree of local man-

25. Carol Kennedy, "Hoechst: Re-positioning for a Global Market," *Long Range Planning,* vol. 23, no. 3, 1990, pp. 16–22.

26. Robert Ackersley and William C. Harris, "How Danish Companies Plan," *Long Range Plannng,* vol. 22, no. 6, December 1989, p. 115.

TABLE 17.2 ● Degree of Local Management Autonomy According to Type of Marketing Decision

	Local marketing decision			
Degree of local management autonomy	*PRODUCT DESIGN*	*ADVERTISING APPROACH*	*RETAIL PRICE*	*DISTRIBUTION OUTLETS/1000 POPULATION*
Primary authority rested with local management	30%	86%	74%	61%
Local management shared authority with other levels in organization	15%	8%	20%	38%
Decision primarily imposed upon local management	55%	6%	6%	1%
	100%	100%	100%	100%
N (Marketing programs observed)	N = 86	N = 84*	N = 84*	N = 86

*Classification information not available in two cases.

Source: R. J. Aylmer, "Who Makes Marketing Decisions in the Multinational Firm?" Reprinted from *Journal of Marketing,* October 1970, p. 26, published by the American Marketing Association.

agement autonomy with respect to various marketing decisions. Aylmer found that primary authority for the advertising, pricing, and distribution decisions were with local management. Only the product design decision was controlled primarily by headquarters and imposed on local management.

Standardized versus Decentralized Planning

When prospective markets can be grouped together as a result of homogeneous characteristics, then marketing decisions can often be standardized and applied to the markets. There are, however, certain marketing functions that cannot be completely standardized. A survey of one hundred senior executives in twenty-seven leading packaged-goods multinationals was conducted to determine the level of standardization for each of the elements in the marketing process. The results of this study are shown in Figure 17.8.

A recent study of seventeen attempts of standardization at American and European multinationals found that one-half of the attempts failed. The researcher recommends: (1) more uniform market research to determine the similarities and differences from country to country; (2) use of local initiative and decision making while implementing the strategy; (3) improved follow-up to identify and solve local

FIGURE 17.8 ● Standardization of Marketing Decisions Among European Subsidiaries of Selected Multinational Enterprises

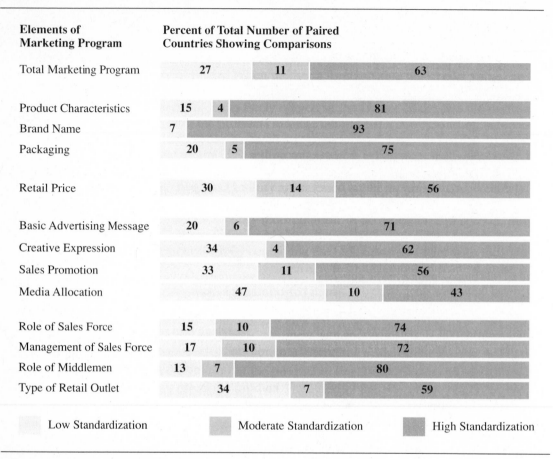

Elements of Marketing Program	Percent of Total Number of Paired Countries Showing Comparisons
Total Marketing Program	27 — 11 — 63
Product Characteristics	15 — 4 — 81
Brand Name	7 — 93
Packaging	20 — 5 — 75
Retail Price	30 — 14 — 56
Basic Advertising Message	20 — 6 — 71
Creative Expression	34 — 4 — 62
Sales Promotion	33 — 11 — 56
Media Allocation	47 — 10 — 43
Role of Sales Force	15 — 10 — 74
Management of Sales Force	17 — 10 — 72
Role of Middlemen	13 — 7 — 80
Type of Retail Outlet	34 — 7 — 59

Low Standardization   Moderate Standardization   High Standardization

Source: Reprinted by permission of the *Harvard Business Review.* "How Multinationals View Marketing Standardization" by Ralph Z. Sorenson and Ulrich E. Wiechmann (May/June 1975). Copyright © 1975 by the President and Fellows of Harvard College; all rights reserved.

implementation problems; (4) active participation from subsidiaries in the development of the strategy; (5) increased flexibility to allow global standards to be modified or developed when dictated by local conditions.[27]

The Single European Market offers a new opportunity for companies to standardize. A survey of forty companies inside the EC and forty companies outside the EC, from EFTA, North America, Australasia, and the Far East revealed their views

27. Kamran Kashani, "Beware the Pitfalls of Global Marketing," *Harvard Business Review,* September-October 1989, pp. 91–98.

about the opportunities that 1992 presented. Both insiders and outsiders reported that 1992 will encourage them to centralize strategic market decision making and advertising and promotion. Particularly the insiders think that marketing operations should be decentralized to get close to the customer and delivery quality by the account management staff.[28] Others have argued that the global product and centralized approach will only apply to cosmopolitan products like expensive watches and perfume so marketeers should continue to adapt products to meet local consumers' preferences.[29]

The annual operating plan is the most widely used process in most international firms.[30] Most firms combine their annual operating plan with a five-year plan. The planning process should be a major force for increasing the degree of integration and coordination between different entities of a global enterprise. According to James Hulbert and William Brandt, most of the problems with multinational planning lie with people, not with the planning systems.[31] According to John Lovering, Finance Director at Sears:

> Planning is very simple. It is deciding what to do, and making it happen. In my experience the second is much harder than the first. It is doomed to failure unless the necessary organizational steps are taken, and the use of strategic controls and reinforcing incentive and reward systems are central to this task. But as long as we remember that planning is a change agent, nothing more nothing less, we will not go far wrong. This means that the planning process must be consistent with the strategy and must help shape an appropriate culture and style. In these circumstances, the use of strategic planning processes can be genuinely helpful in ensuring a systematic approach to resource allocation and the maintenance of subsequent control."[32]

CONTROLLING INTERNATIONAL MARKETING OPERATIONS

Maintaining control of international operations is a growing concern in light of the increasing trend toward global companies. As a company becomes larger, it faces more critical decisions, and control over operations tends to dissipate. A company's planning process is usually based on a number of assumptions about country environments, competitors, pricing, government regulations, and so on. As a plan is

28. Sandra Vandermerwe, "Strategies for a Pan European Market," *Long Range Planning,* vol. 22, no. 3, June 1989, pp. 50–51.

29. Jurgen Reichel, "How Can Marketing Be Successfully Standardized for the European Market?", *European Journal of Marketing,* vol. 23, no. 7, 1989, pp. 60–67.

30. James M. Hulbert and William K. Brandt, *Managing the Multinational Subsidiary* (New York: Holt, Rinehart and Winston, 1980), pp. 35–64.

31. Ibid.

32. John Lovering, "Brief Case: Developing a Strategic Planning and Control Process," *Long Range Planning,* vol. 23, no. 2, April 1990, pp. 112–114.

implemented, the company must monitor its success as well as monitor the variables that were used to develop the plan. As the environment changes, so will the plan; therefore a critical part of planning is control. Establishment of a system to control marketing activities in numerous markets is not an easy job. But if companies expect to achieve the goals they have set, then a control system must be established to regulate the activities for achieving the desired goals.

Variables That Affect Control

There are several variables that affect the degree and effectiveness of a control system for international operations. A number of these are described in the following sections.

Communication Systems Effective communication systems facilitate control. Physical communication methods, such as the phone, mail, and personal visits, are greatly affected by both distance and location. The more sophisticated a country's telecommunications are, the easier the communication process is. Telecommunications technology greatly improved in the 1980s, with global optical fiber and satellite networks. Global voicemail, facsimile transmissions, and telephone communications have greatly enhanced communication and reporting.

Likewise, the closer the subdivision is to headquarters, the less chance there is to lose control. As physical distances separating headquarters and operating divisions increase, the time, expense, and potential for error increase. The physical distance also affects the speed with which changes can be implemented and problems can be detected.

Adequacy of Data The accuracy and lack of complete economic, industrial, and consumer data affect control. If the marketing plan and the goals for a particular country are based on inadequate data, then the ability to control and modify the marketing activities will be affected. For example, let's examine the goal of selling washing machines to Malaysia, maybe to achieve a 30 percent share of last year's market, which was estimated to be 100,000 units. Therefore, the goal would be 30,000 units. But if the actual sales were only 70,000 units because the government had exaggerated its report to indicate economic prosperity, then the goal of 30,000 units will be too high. It may also be difficult to get timely and accurate statistics, such as the level of inflation and disposable income, which will influence the marketing strategy.

Diversity of Environments Currency values, legal structures, political systems, advertising options, number and type of public holidays, and cultural factors all influence the task of developing and controlling a marketing program. Due to this diversity of the local environments there are continuous conflicts between the needs of the local situation and overall corporate goals. The issue of diversity must be reflected in the control system.

Management Philosophy   The management philosophy about whether the company should be centralized or decentralized will affect the development of a control system. A highly centralized management control system will require an effective communication system so that the headquarters staff has timely and accurate local input that may affect decision making. The communication system must also allow decisions to be made quickly and transmitted to the local management for quick implementation. A decentralized management control system may not require the same type of communication system for day-to-day decision making, but it will require a well-documented and communicated set of objectives for each autonomous unit. These objectives will help guide local decision making and control so that the corporate goals are achieved.

Size of International Operations   As the size of the international operation increases as a percentage of total sales, top management becomes more active in decision making. One author found that as the size of a local affiliate grew, the frequency of decisions imposed by headquarters declined and the frequency of decisions shared with headquarters increased.[33]

Elements of a Control Strategy

Control is the cornerstone of management. Control provides the means to direct, regulate, and manage business operations. The implementation of a marketing program requires a significant amount of interaction between the individual areas of marketing (product development, advertising, sales) as well as the other functional areas (production, research and development, finance). The control system is used to measure these business activities, competitive reaction, and market reaction. Deviations from the planned activities and results are analyzed and reported so that corrective action can be taken.

Many companies need to improve their control process. Without some type of control system, strategies that look good on paper never get implemented. Most strategies are long-term in nature and can often take a back seat to the short-term tactical decisions needed for quarterly results. One of the often overlooked strengths of Japanese companies is their ability to develop and implement long-term strategies.[34] Through interviews with over fifty companies regarding their control systems, Michael Goold assessed control systems on two dimensions—number of performance criteria and formality of the strategic control process. Figure 17.9 summarizes the control systems of eighteen multinational companies. The research on these companies found that strategic control systems add value through the following ways:

33. R. J. Aylmer, "Who Makes the Decisions in the Multinational Firm?" *Journal of Marketing,* October 1970, p. 26.
34. Warren J. Keegan, "Strategic Marketing Planning: Japanese," *International Marketing Review,* Autumn 1983.

FIGURE 17.9 ● Strategic Control Processes

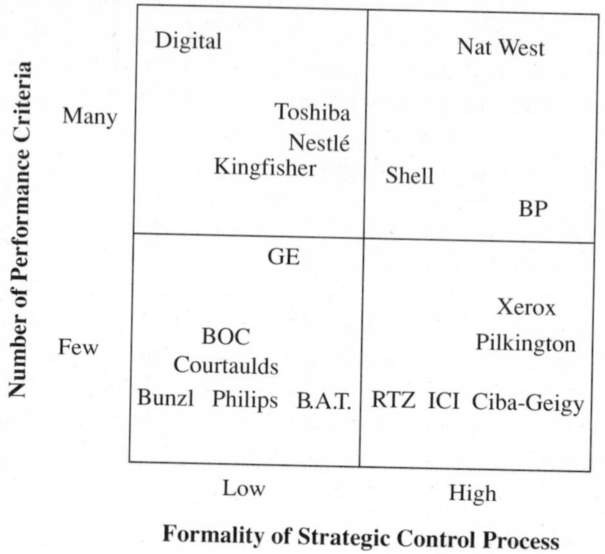

	Low	High
Many	Digital Toshiba Nestlé Kingfisher	Nat West Shell BP
Few	GE BOC Courtaulds Bunzl Philips B.A.T.	 Xerox Pilkington RTZ ICI Ciba-Geigy

Number of Performance Criteria

Formality of Strategic Control Process

Source: Michael Goold, *Strategic Control.* London: The Economist Books, 1990, p. 33. Reprinted by permission.

- Forcing greater clarity and realism in planning
- Encouraging higher standards of performance
- Providing more motivation for business managers
- Permitting timely intervention by corporate management
- Ensuring financial objectives do not overwhelm strategic objectives
- Defining responsibilities more clearly, making decentralization work better[35]

A control system has three basic elements: (1) the establishment of standards, (2) the measurement of performance against standards, and (3) the analysis and correction of any deviations from the standards. Although it seems that control is a conceptually simple aspect of the management process, there are a wide variety of problems that arise in international situations which result in inefficiencies and intracompany conflicts.

Developing Standards Setting standards is an extremely important part of the control process because standards will direct the efforts of individual managers. To effectively influence the behavior of the managers who direct the international mar-

---

35. Michael Goold, *Strategic Control* (London: Economist Books, 1990), p. 125.

keting programs, the standards must be clearly defined, accepted, and understood by these managers. Standard setting is driven by the corporate goals. The corporate goals are achieved through the effective and efficient implementation of a marketing strategy, on a local country level. The standards should be related to the sources of long term competitive advantage. In companies where the strategies are decentralized to a business, it is recommended that there only be four to six key objectives. Fewer objectives focus management's efforts without causing confusion about priorities.[36]

Control standards must be specifically tied to the strategy and based on the desired behavior of the local marketing people. The desired behavior should reflect the actions to be taken to implement the strategy as well as performance standards that indicate the success of the strategy, such as increased market share or sales. Examples of behavioral standards include the type and amount of advertising, the distribution coverage, market research to be performed, and expected price levels. Performance standards can include trial rates by customers or sales by product line.

The standards should be set through a joint process with corporate headquarters personnel and the local marketing organization. Normally the standard setting will be done annually, when the operational business plan is established.

Measuring and Evaluating Performance   After the standards are set, a process is required to monitor performance. In order to monitor performance against standards, management must be able to observe current performance. Observation in the international environment is often impersonal through mail, cable, or telex; but it also can be personal through telephone, travel, or meetings. Much of the numerical information will be reported through the accounting system, such as sales, expenses, and so on. Other items such as the implementation of an advertising program will be communicated through a report. The reporting system may be weekly, monthly, or quarterly.

Analyzing and Correcting Deviations from the Standards   The purpose of establishing standards and reporting performance is to assure achievement of the corporate goals. In order to achieve these goals, management must evaluate performance versus the standards and initiate actions where performance is below the standards set. The control process can be difficult in the international setting due to distance, communication, and cultural difference issues.

Control strategy can be related to the principle of the carrot and the stick, using both positive and negative incentives. On the positive side, outstanding performance may result in increased independence, more marketing dollars, and salary increases or bonuses for the managers. On the negative side, unsatisfactory performance can lead to the reduction of all the items associated with a satisfactory performance as well as the threat of firing the managers responsible. The key to correcting deviations is to get the managers to understand and agree with the standards, then give them

36. Ibid., p. 120.

TABLE 17.3 ● Making Formal Strategic Control Work

Issues	Recommendations
SELECTING THE RIGHT OBJECTIVES	Based on analysis of competitive advantage
	Few in number
	Milestones that measure short-term progress
	Leading indicators of future performance
	Projects or action programmes only if important for competitive advantage
SETTING SUITABLE TARGETS	Precise and objectively measurable, if possible
	Proposed by business managers, but stretched by the centre
	Competitively benchmarked
	Consistent with budget targets: trade-offs openly confronted and resolved
CREATING PRESSURE FOR STRATEGIC PERFORMANCE	Systematic progress monitoring and reviews
	Personal rewards indirectly tied to achievement of strategic targets
	Performance against strategic targets matters to top management and is the basis for corporate interventions
STRATEGIC PLANNING AND STRATEGIC CONTROL	High-quality strategic planning needed as basis for strategic controls
	Strategic planning process used to review strategic progress
FORMALITY WITHOUT BUREAUCRACY	Avoid large staff departments and lengthy reports
	Avoid specially gathered data
	Conduct reviews face-to-face
	Supplement formal reviews with informal contacts
	Be prepared to short-circuit formal process if necessary

Source: Michael Goold, *Strategic Control.* London: The Economist Books, 1990, p. 199. Reprinted by permission.

the ability to correct these deficiencies. This will often mean that the managers will be given some flexibility with resources. For example, if sales are down 10 percent, the ability to increase advertising or reduce prices may be necessary to offset the sales decline.

Making Strategic Control Work   Most companies do not have a formal strategic control system. Few companies define and monitor their strategic objectives as systematically as they monitor their budgets. While most managers can tell you within pennies how much the advertising expenditures are over or under the plan, few will be able to tell you the six milestones to implementing the 1993 strategy and the companies' progress on each. To establish and get full value from a formal strategic control system, Michael Goold has made a number of recommendations summarized in Table 17.3.

CONFLICT BETWEEN HEADQUARTERS AND SUBSIDIARIES

A universal problem facing international marketing executives is the internal conflict between headquarters and subsidiaries. A study of 109 large U.S. and European multinationals and their worldwide subsidiaries found that this conflict was a bigger problem than competition, political instability, or any of the other challenges of international marketing. Table 17.4 summarizes the results of the study.

Conflicts between two parts of a corporation are inevitable due to the natural differences in orientation and perception between the two groups. The subsidiary manager usually wants less control, more authority, and more local differentiation, whereas headquarters wants more detailed reporting and greater unification of geographically dispersed operations. This expected conflict is not bad. In fact, the conflict causes constant dialogue between different organizational levels during the

TABLE 17.4 ● Key Problems Identified by Large U.S. and European Multinationals

---

Key problems identified by headquarters executives
- Lack of qualified personnel
- Lack of strategic thinking and long-range planning at subsidiary level
- Lack of marketing expertise at the subsidiary level
- Too little relevant communication between headquarters and subsidiaries
- Insufficient utilization of multinational marketing experience
- Restricted headquarters control of the subsidiaries

Key problems identified by subsidiary executives
- Excessive headquarters control procedures
- Excessive financial and marketing constraints
- Insufficient participation of subsidiaries in product decisions
- Insensitivity of headquarters to local market differences
- Shortage of useful information from headquarters
- Lack of multinational orientation at headquarters

Source: Adapted and reprinted by permission of the *Harvard Business Review.* "Problems That Plague Multinational Marketers" by Ulrich E. Wiechmann and Lewis G. Pringle (July/August 1979). Copyright © 1979 by the President and Fellows of Harvard College; all rights reserved.

planning and implementation of strategies. This dialogue will result in a balance between headquarters versus subsidiary authority, global versus local perspective, and standardization versus differentiation of the international marketing mix.[37]

Some of the problems in planning and controlling international marketing operations can be reduced or eliminated. Common problems such as deficiencies in the communications process, overemphasis on short-term issues, and failure to take full advantage of an organization's international experience, require open discussions between headquarters and subsidiary executives.

Retaining Talented Global Managers

Many companies are shifting to a global marketing orientation. To successfully manage this shift to global marketing, companies must successfully utilize and integrate the talents of global managers. A recent survey of U.S. executives found that fewer than half of those sent abroad thought the posting helped their careers.[38] Companies that want to send good people overseas and keep them must change the status and handling of these posts. Five suggestions on how to motivate and retain talented global managers when making the shift to global marketing follow.

1. Encourage field managers to generate ideas and give them recognition for those ideas. R. J. Reynolds revitalized the Camel brand after a German subsidiary came up with a new positioning and copy strategy.

2. Include the country managers in the development of marketing strategies and programs. When Procter & Gamble introduced a sanitary napkin as a global product, local managers were encouraged to suggest changes in the global marketing program. Also, local managers were allowed to develop their own coupon and sales promotion programs.

3. Maintain a product portfolio of regional and global brands.

4. Allow country managers control of their marketing budgets, so they can respond to local consumer needs and competition.

5. Emphasize the general management responsibilities of country managers that extend beyond the marketing function. Country managers who have risen through the marketing function often do not spend enough time on local manufacturing, industrial relations, and government affairs. Global marketing can free them to focus on and develop their skills in these other areas.[39]

37. Ulrich E. Wiechmann and Lewis G. Pringle, "Problems That Plague Multinational Marketers," *Harvard Business Review,* vol. 57, July-August 1979, p. 124.

38. Thomas A. Stewart, "How to Manage in the New Era," *Fortune,* January 15, 1990, p. 32.

39. John A. Quelch and Edward J. Hoff, "Customizing Global Marketing," *Harvard Business Review,* vol. 64, May-June 1986, p. 68.

CONCLUSIONS

The processes of planning marketing programs and controlling their implementation are the first and last steps in international marketing. Marketers must first evaluate the global environment and select opportunities using one of the planning approaches. This process will lead to a strategy that is implemented by the organization. Sometimes the organization will be changed in order to effectively implement the strategy. Finally, a system must be put in place to evaluate the implementation and measure the progress toward the desired effect of the strategy.

The planning and controlling processes are critical parts of the marketing process that require communication and agreement from different parts of the organization. This is difficult. It is no surprise that the planning and controlling processes lead to conflict. However, it also promotes understanding the world market, developing effective strategies, and successfully implementing the strategies with excellent results.

Questions for Discussion

1. You have recently been transferred from a domestic marketing division to the international marketing staff. Part of your new job is to review the planning process of each geographic marketing group—Europe, Asia, and South America. What differences can you expect from domestic planning?

2. What are the advantages and disadvantages of the Boston Consulting Group planning method when applied to international markets?

3. What are the advantages and disadvantages of the PIMS model over other planning methods that can be used for international planning?

4. What types of marketing decisions are usually left up to the local management? Why?

5. What is the purpose of a control system? How do you differentiate a good control system from a poor one?

6. Recent feedback for sales, profit, and market share indicate that your subsidiary in Japan had not implemented the strategy that was developed. How will you influence the management to focus more effort on successful strategy implementation?

7. Recently you have lost four key international marketing people to other companies. You suspect that these losses indicate that the morale of your international executives is poor. What can be done to improve morale?

For Further Reading

Ansoff, H. Igor, and Edward J. McDonnell. *Implanting Strategic Management,* Second Edition. Englewood Cliffs: Prentice Hall, 1990.

Becker, Helmut, and Hans B. Thorelli. "Strategic Planning in International Marketing." In *International Marketing Strategy.* Eds. Hans Thorelli and Helmut Becker. New York: Pergamon Press, 1982, pp. 367–378.

Campbell, Andrew, Marion Devine, and David Young. *A Sense of Mission,* London: The Economist Books, 1990.

Chakravarthy, Balaji S., and Howard V. Perlmutter. "Strategic Planning for a Global Business." *Columbia Journal of World Business* (Summer 1985), pp. 3–10.

Day, George S. *Market Driven Strategy.* New York: The Free Press, 1990.

Dymsza, William A. "Global Strategic Planning," *Journal of International Business Studies,* Summer 1985, pp. 169–183.

Gale, Bradley T., and Ben Branch. "Allocating Capital More Effectively." *Sloan Management Review,* Fall 1987, p. 21.

Goold, Michael, and Andrew Campbell. *Strategies and Styles: The Role of the Centre in Managing Diversified Corporations.* Oxford: Basil Blackwell, 1987.

Hamel, Gary, and C. K. Prahalad. "Managing Strategic Responsibility in the MNC." *Strategic Management Journal* 4 (1983), pp. 341–351.

Hamel, Gary, and C. K. Prahalad. "Strategic Intent." *Harvard Business Review,* May-June 1989, pp. 63–76.

Hulbert, James M., William K. Brandt, and Raimer Richers. "Marketing Planning in the Multinational Subsidiary: Practices and Problems." *Journal of Marketing,* Summer 1980, pp. 7–15.

Nowakoski, Christopher A. "International Performance Measurement." *Columbia Journal of World Business* (Summer 1982), pp. 53–57.

Pink, Alan I. H. "Strategic Leadership Through Corporate Planning at ICI." *Long Range Planning* 21, no. 1 (1988), pp. 18–25.

Porter, Michael E., ed. *Competition in Global Industries.* Boston: Harvard Business School Press, 1986.

Wind, Yoram, and Susan Douglas. "International Portfolio Analysis and Strategy: The Challenge of the 80's." *Journal of International Business Studies* (Fall 1981), p. 7.

18

The Export and Import Trade Process

● **THROUGHOUT THE PREVIOUS** *chapters we have maintained that exporting and importing are subsets of international marketing. We have also indicated that international and global marketing may take place without any physical movement of products across country borders, thereby taking an even broader view of international marketing. However, most companies will, as part of their international marketing activities, engage in some form of exporting or importing. This can take place in the form of shipments from the headquarters location to a foreign market or through cross-shipments among various subsidiaries. Invariably, such export or import shipments cause specific problems that have not been discussed in the previous chapters and that can best be handled in the form of a specialized section such as this one.*

To deal with all the specific rules and regulations that can be found in today's complex international business environments is not possible or necessary for our purposes. In this chapter, we will view the export and import mechanics from the point of view of a U.S.-based firm. However, many aspects of the export section, such as those related to pricing, are of universal application and would be of interest to all readers. The structure and components of the chapter are depicted in Figure 18.1.

FIGURE 18.1 ● Export and Import Trading Process

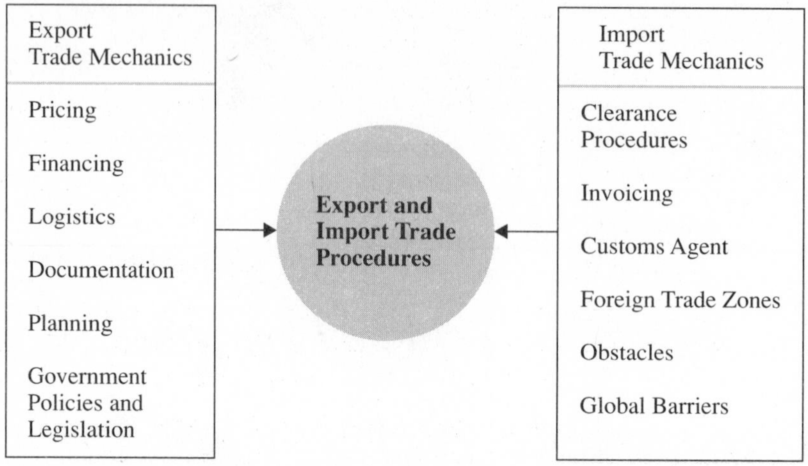

```
┌─────────────────────┐                    ┌─────────────────────┐
│ Export              │                    │ Import              │
│ Trade Mechanics     │                    │ Trade Mechanics     │
│                     │                    │                     │
│ Pricing             │      ╭───────╮     │ Clearance           │
│                     │      │       │     │ Procedures          │
│ Financing           │    ╱ │Export │ ╲   │                     │
│                     │   →  │and    │  ←  │ Invoicing           │
│ Logistics           │      │Import │     │                     │
│                     │      │Trade  │     │ Customs Agent       │
│ Documentation       │      │Proce- │     │                     │
│                     │      │dures  │     │ Foreign Trade Zones │
│ Planning            │      ╰───────╯     │                     │
│                     │                    │ Obstacles           │
│ Government          │                    │                     │
│ Policies and        │                    │ Global Barriers     │
│ Legislation         │                    │                     │
└─────────────────────┘                    └─────────────────────┘
```

EXPORT TRADE MECHANICS[1]

Any successful export activity of a firm should be based on a careful analysis of a company's export potential, as has been discussed in Chapter 9 on entry strategies. Potential techniques and approaches for such an analysis were covered in Chapters 7 and 8. Consequently, we start our discussion of export trade mechanics with the assumption that a potential market has been defined, measured, and located, and that the company has made the decision to exploit the opportunity through exporting. Our focus is on the execution of a firm's export operation, paying special attention to pricing, logistics, information, planning, and government policies that affect the individual firm.

Pricing for Export

In Chapter 13, we described in detail the process by which companies may determine prices for products to be shipped abroad. These methods of internal costing, profit analyses, and demand analyses can be applied to the export process. What is peculiar to exporting, however, is the method of quoting prices. Foreign buyers need to know precisely where they will take over responsibility for the product—or what shipping costs the exporter is willing to assume. In the United States, it is customary to ship

---

1. This section has been adapted and based on *A Basic Guide to Exporting,* U.S. Department of Commerce, International Trade Administration, 1991.

f.o.b. factory, freight collect, prepaid, charge, or C.O.D. However, in export marketing, different terms are used worldwide.

Figure 18.2 depicts commonly used export quotations for a hypothetical shipment by a Peoria, Illinois company to a client in Bogota, Colombia. The shipment is to go via truck to the railroad depot in Peoria and by rail to a New York pier. The products will then be shipped by sea to Barranquilla, Colombia. Following customs clearance, the shipment will go on by rail and truck to eventually reach the client's warehouse. In international trade, nearly twenty different alternatives exist to quote the price of the merchandise, all indicating different responsibilities for the U.S. company or its Colombian client.

The most common terms used in quoting prices in international trade are these:

c.i.f.: (Cost, insurance, freight) to a named port of import. Under this term, the seller quotes a price that includes the product, all transportation, and insurance to the point of unloading from the vessel or aircraft at the named destination.

c. & f.: (Cost and freight) is similar to c.i.f. except that insurance of the shipment is not included.

f.a.s.: (Free alongside) at a named port in the exporter's country. Under this term, the exporter quotes a price that includes the goods and any service and delivery charges to get the shipment alongside the vessel used for further transportation, but now at the buyer's expense.

f.o.b.: (Free on board) includes the price of placing the shipment onto a specified vessel or aircraft, but further transportation will be the buyer's responsibility.

Ex (named point of origin): Applies to a price for products at the point of origin and requires that the buyer assumes all transportation charges.

Incoterms is a booklet of terms and their definitions. These are the internationally agreed on terms used by international freight forwarders all over the world. The incorrect use of a delivery term can cause significant problems between the exporter and the buyer. (*Incoterms* can be obtained from the International Chamber of Commerce, 801 Second Avenue, Suite 1204, New York, New York 10017.)

When asked by a foreign buyer to quote a price, the exporter will have to quote a price that takes into consideration the methods of freight payment. In quoting a price, the company is advised to stipulate a price that easily allows the buyer to figure out total costs for the shipment. Usually, this means quoting a price c.i.f. foreign port. The foreign buyer can then estimate additional transportation charges for the final distance under known circumstances.

In the case of our example in Figure 18.2, the most meaningful quote for the Colombian buyer is c.i.f. Bogota. Quoting a price ex factory places the burden of estimating transportation entirely on the foreign buyer. But, as one may imagine, the estimation of costs can be quite difficult to do from abroad. However, an exporter can do a great service to the buyer by quoting prices that reflect the final destination charges based on information from freight forwarders with experience shipping to

FIGURE 18.2 ● Exporting Example

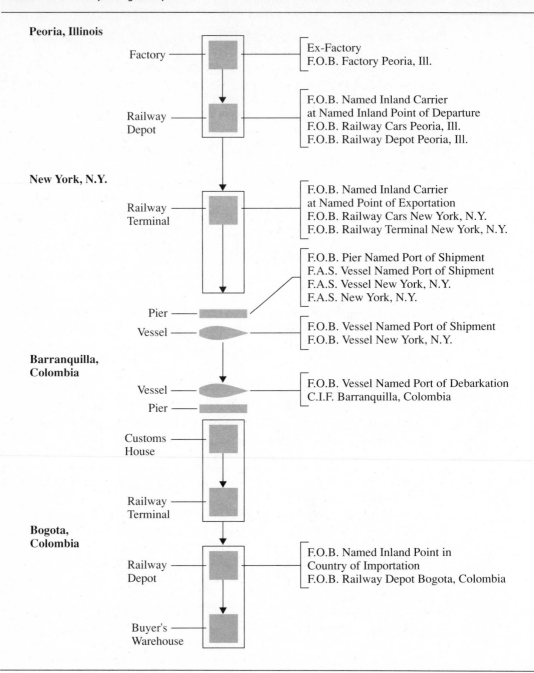

Source: Gerald R. Richter, "Basic Principles of Foreign Trade," in Leslie L. Lewis, ed., *International Trade Handbook* (Chicago: Dartnell Corporation, prepared in cooperation with The American Institute for Foreign Trade, 1965), p. 32.

the foreign country. It also makes it easier for the buyer to compare prices from different companies if they are all quoted to one point, such as Bogota. Sometimes the buyer will request a specific type of price. For example, if our Colombian buyer regularly imports from New York, he may request all prices be f.o.b. New York.

The computed freight, transportation, and insurance charges may also depend on the leverage the exporter or importer has with freight forwarders. To use the example shown in Figure 18.2 again, the U.S. exporter may only have this one shipment going to Bogota, Colombia. Therefore the shipping costs will be relatively high. Should the importer have several shipments that could be combined, average freight costs from New York to Colombia may be less. The exporter can facilitate the process by quoting several prices at various points along the shipment route and then leave the choice to the buyer who will select the best method.

Exporters should not underestimate the possibility of using the export pricing process as a selling tool, particularly when there are similar products available from other manufacturers. Also, there are obvious risks with different pricing strategies. For example, if you quote in a foreign currency rather than dollars, you assume the risk of exchange rate fluctuation. Even insurance costs can fluctuate. Insurance rates doubled for goods being shipped to the Gulf after Iraq's invasion of Kuwait on August 2, 1990.[2] Pricing for export involves many variables which require close examination. A miscalculation or misjudgment can often turn a profitable order to a losing order.

Financing Exports

Chapter 13 (Pricing) contained several sections on financing international marketing operations through, among others, export banks of various countries. Also discussed were noncash transactions such as barter and countertrade. These types of arrangements are not repeated in this chapter. This section focuses on the various arrangements exporters can make to ensure payment for their merchandise and credit methods that can be offered to foreign clients.

Although cash transactions can be desirable, payments in this form are rarely used. The shipment may be in transit for weeks or even months at a time, thus tying up the importer's capital. Also, the importer does not really know what was shipped until the products are in the importer's possession. Consequently, most forms of payment are designed to protect both parties. When an exporter knows the foreign clients and fully trusts their financial integrity, shipments on *open account* may be arranged. Usually, the terms are arranged such that the foreign client can wait to make payment until the goods have arrived at their final destination. However, in this case, the exporter will have risked capital in the transaction.

Consignment sales is the method whereby credit is extended by the exporter.

2. "Ship Insurance Rates Soar in Some Areas of Persian Gulf as Jan. 15 Deadline Nears," *Wall Street Journal,* January 10, 1991, p. A16.

The exporter is not compensated until the products are physically sold by the importer. The consignment goods are often held in free trade zones (discussed later in the chapter) or in a bonded warehouse until sold by an agent or needed by the buyer. With appropriate payment, the consigned goods will be released to the buyer. This approach increases the exporter's capital costs because no funds are received until the goods are collected by the buyer.

To control both ownership and payment terms for international shipments, traders have developed the *draft* or bill of exchange.[3] The draft is a formal order issued by the exporter to the importer specifying when the sum is to be paid to the third party, usually the exporter's bank. A triangular relationship is established with the issuer of the draft, or exporter, as drawer, the importer as drawee, and the payee as the recipient of the payment. Since the draft is a negotiable instrument, it can be sold, transferred, and discounted, and the exporter can use it to finance the shipment.

Exporters may use either a *sight draft* or a *time draft*. Sight drafts are used when the exporter desires to control the shipment beyond the point of original shipment, usually to assure payment. In practice, the exporter endorses the bill of lading (B/L) and adds a sight draft on the correspondent bank of the exporter's bank. Along with the bill of lading and sight draft, other documents will be provided such as the packing list, invoice, consular invoices, and certificate of insurance. Once the documents have arrived, a transfer by way of endorsement to the importer will be made on payment in full at that bank. Consequently, the importer cannot take possession of the goods until payment has been made (on sight of documents). Yet, the importer is assured that the goods have actually been shipped as indicated by the accompanying documents.

Alternatively, transactions can be made in time drafts. This method specifies the period in which the payment is to be made. The payment period beginning on receiving the documents may be 30, 60, 90 days, or longer. Drafts will not only allow the exporter to control the shipment until proper payment occurs, but they also allow further financing by having the properly signed draft discounted with a bank before the payment term agreed to expires. In such a case, the banking system assumes the role of the creditor, thus reducing the capital risks of the exporter.

Also used quite frequently is a financial instrument called a *letter of credit*. With a letter of credit the importer, or foreign buyer, finances the transaction, thus alleviating the credit burden on the exporter. With a letter of credit, the responsibility is in the hands of the importer. Once informed that the exporter will ship with a letter of credit (L/C), the importer will ask the bank to write an irrevocable L/C with a bank specified by the exporter on the latter's behalf. The importer will usually instruct the bank on the conditions of payment, typically against submission of all necessary documents including a bill of lading (B/L). When the exporter has placed the shipment on the appropriate vessel, the company will go to the bank and turn over all documents associated with the transaction. When satisfied, the exporter's bank will pay

3. Endel J. Kolde, *International Business Enterprise,* 2nd ed. (Englewood Cliffs, N.J.: Prentice-Hall, 1973), pp. 289–290.

out the funds and debit the importer's bank who will in turn debit the importing company.

Overall, the irrevocable L/C has distinct advantages for the exporter since it represents a firm order that, once issued by the bank, cannot be cancelled or revoked. For example, a firm that sells machinery that is built to order can use the irrevocable L/C to guarantee that payment will be made. Time limits are placed on the L/C that protect the importer against an open-ended transaction. Should the exporter fail to ship and submit documents before the expiration date, the L/C would expire without any further responsibility on the part of the importer to finance the transaction. Any bank charges associated with the transaction are usually paid by the buyer. Letters of credit are normally prepared at commercial banks by a staff of back office clerks. The paperwork required for each letter of credit, as well as the possibility of typing errors, can make the issuing of these instruments slow. Pressure from exports had focused many banks to automate this process with computer technology to speed up the process so payments could be processed quickly.[4]

Letters of credit are a widely used instrument that have developed into several specialized forms over and above the standard irrevocable L/C described above. The following additional forms exist:

Revolving or Periodic Letters of Credit allow for a repetition of the same transaction as soon as the previous amount has been paid by the bank that originated the L/C.

Cumulative Letters of Credit are opened to cover payments of partial shipments and/or the use of the unused portion of the L/C for another transaction between the same parties.

Red Clause Letters of Credit are used to permit partial cash payments to the beneficiary, or exporter, as an advance on the shipment without any documentation. Final payments are made only against full documentation, however.

Back-to-Back Letters of Credit are issued based on an earlier L/C. This may be done if an exporter, in whose favor an L/C was opened by a foreign client, will use the original L/C as a basis or security to issue a second L/C in favor of a supplier for materials connected with that particular transaction.

Circular Letters of Credit are issued without designating any particular bank. The exporter may send documents to the issuing bank or present them to any bank who will send them on for collection.

Performance Letters of Credit are used to guarantee the completion of a contract undertaken abroad. They can be drawn upon if the exporter fails to meet performance requirements and are therefore also known under the term *performance bonds.*[5]

---

4. Jon Marks, "Letters of Credit Are Beginning to Change, A Rich Link with the Past," *Financial Times,* June 1, 1989, Export Finance Section VII.

5. Ibid., p. 294.

When exporting to another country, such as a politically volatile area or with a new customer, guaranteeing payment of your invoices is always a concern. A letter of credit is a relatively safe instrument to guarantee payment. In some cases, letters of credit may not be acceptable to the buyer or they may not be practical. In the United States, exporters can turn to the Foreign Credit Insurance Association (FCIA) for assistance. The FCIA is an association of fifty marine and insurance casualty companies created in 1961 to insure U.S. exporters of goods and services against commercial and political risks. There are numerous risks with any foreign buyer. The firm can go out of business. The local government can change standards. Natural disasters like floods or earthquakes can eliminate the buyer's ability to pay. FCIA offers insurance to protect against a buyer's failure to pay. Most developed countries have some type of export insurance program similar to FCIA.

As we have seen, there are numerous options available to arrange for payment in export transactions. The exporting company can, of course, select the particular type of transaction, always keeping in mind the needs and requirements of the buyer who may, if offered better credit terms elsewhere, decide to place an order with a different company. The payment process is an important part of the transaction between the buyer and seller in an export situation; it can minimize the risks of exchange rate fluctuations and the process of dealing with a distant buyer or seller. Experienced exporters study government assistance and financing programs looking for creative ways to use these programs for the benefit of the buyer. For example, Biwater, a U.K. construction company, won a $550 million water supply contract in Malaysia through a combination of creative financing and support by the U.K. Aid and Trade Program.[6]

Export Logistics

The requirements of export logistics differ substantially from domestic operations requiring special care on the part of the exporting firm. Practices must ensure that the shipment arrives in the best possible condition and at the lowest possible cost.

To ensure that the products arrive in usable condition, export packages have to be prepared to avoid four typical problems: breakage, weight, moisture, and pilferage. Export shipments often are subject to additional handling procedures including the use of a sling for loading onto a vessel, nets to combine various items for loading, or conveyors, chutes, and other methods to put added stress and strain on the shipment and are frequently the cause of breakage. Once on board a vessel, the weight of other cargo placed on top of the shipment can also be hazardous. At the overseas destination, handling facilities are sometimes unsophisticated. Consequently, the cargo may be even dragged, pushed, or rolled during unloading, causing damage to the goods.

6. Peter Montagnon, "Export Credit: Unbundling—A Way Round Trade Barriers," *Financial Times,* November 7, 1990, p. 17.

While on a voyage, moisture is a constant problem due to condensation in the hold of a ship. This may even be so for vessels equipped with air conditioning and dehumidifiers. At the point of arrival, unloading may take place in the rain and many foreign ports do not have covered storage facilities. Furthermore, without adequate protection, theft or pilferage is common.

To avoid these problems, exporters are encouraged to add extra packaging to protect their cargo. However, overpacking should be avoided since both freight and customs are frequently assessed on the gross weight of the merchandise, resulting in unneeded charges for extra packaging. Air freight usually requires less packaging than ocean freight, and container shipments can be used to provide added protection for the goods. Exporters are encouraged to check with carriers or marine insurance companies for advice on proper packaging. For companies that are not equipped to do export packaging, professional companies exist that provide this service for a moderate fee.

Equally important is the proper marking of the shipment. Although the destination should be marked clearly and in large stenciled letters of black waterproof ink, experienced exporters advise that no additional facts be provided on the content of the packages to avoid pilferage or theft. Where necessary, special handling instructions should be added in the language of the port of destination.

Arrangements for the actual shipping of a company's products can be made through the services of an international freight forwarder. In general, a freight forwarder licensed by the Federal Maritime Administration should be used because these agents are familiar with foreign import regulations, methods of shipping, and the requirements of U.S. export documentation. Not only will freight forwarders advise on freight costs and other related fees, but they can also make recommendations on packaging. Since the cost for their services is a legitimate export cost, exporters can add such costs to their prices charged to foreign customers. Aside from advising exporters, forwarders also make the necessary arrangements to clear shipments through customs, arrange for the actual shipping, and check for the necessary documents as described in the section below.

Export Documentation

To facilitate the transfer of goods out of the United States and through a foreign country's procedures, a series of export documents have to be prepared. Exporters prepare such documents with care since frequently the export documents have been used as a basis for obtaining trade credit from banks or collection from the buyer.

One requirement is a detailed export packing list usually containing substantially more details about weight and volume than those used for domestic commerce. This packing list is used by shippers to reserve or book the necessary space on the vessel. Furthermore, port officials at the dock use this list to determine whether the correct cargo has been received. In addition, customs officials both in the United States and abroad use the packing list; and ultimately, the buyer will want to check the goods against the list to verify that the entire shipment was received. To satisfy all these users, the packing list must contain not only a detailed description of the products for each packaging unit but also weights, volume, and dimensions in both metric and nonmetric terms.

Most countries have specific requirements for the marking and labeling of imports. Failure to comply can result in severe penalties. For example, Peru requires that all imports are labeled with the brand name, country of origin, and an expiration date on the product. Custom officials will refuse clearance of any imports not complying with the regulations. The importer must ship the goods out of Peru within 60 days or they are seized and auctioned as abandoned goods. A basic guide for U.S. exporters published by the Department of Commerce will describe the required export documents and pertinent regulations for labeling, marking, and packing products for import. The pamphlet series entitled "Preparing Shipment to (Country)" helps avoid delays and penalties.[7]

The U.S. government requires that all export shipments be subject to a licensing procedure. Basically, there exist two types of export licenses. The *validated export license* must be secured for each individual order from the Office of Export Administration in Washington, D.C. Several types of products and commodities may fall into this category, such as chemicals, special types of plastic, advanced electronic and communications equipment, and scarce materials including petroleum. For defense products, licenses are issued by the Department of State. The requirement for a validated export license may apply for shipments of certain commodities to all countries or only to a limited number of countries. The entire mechanism was instituted to protect the United States' strategic position for reasons of foreign policy, national security, or to regulate supply for select scarce products. Regulations are also subject to frequent changes depending on the political or economic climate prevailing at the time of decision.

All other products are subject to several types of *general licenses.* These are published general authorizations, each with a specific license symbol that is dependent on product category. Exporters must inquire at the Department of Commerce to obtain the correct general license symbol. Exporters usually check with the Department of Commerce before an order is accepted to determine the type of license required. Obtaining export licenses from the government has often been a slow process that can cause delays for the exporter. To reduce the paperwork and speed up the process, the Department of Commerce has introduced two new systems. The Export License Application and Information Network (ELAIN) allows exporters to submit license applications electronically for all free world applications. When approved, the license is conveyed back to the exporter electronically. The System for Tracking Export License Applications (STELA) is a voice answering service that allows exporters to check the status of their license application. The new systems drastically cut processing time from an average of 46 days in 1984 to 14 days. For

---

7. "Tools of the Export Trade," *Business America,* October 28, 1988, pp. 2–5.

trusted trading nations, the processing time is often 5 days or less with the aid of the electronic systems.[8]

The exporter's *shipper's export declaration* has to be added to all shipments and requires a declaration of the products in terms of the U.S. Customs Service definitions and classifications. In this form, the exporter must note the applicable license for the shipment. A sample of the shipper's export declaration is shown in Figure 18.3.

Most exporters also submit a series of documents to their customers to facilitate additional financing or handling at the point of destination. These documents may vary by country, method of payment, mode of transportation, and even by customer. The following documents may be required:

Commercial Invoices. In addition to the customary content, the invoice should indicate the origin of the products and export marks. Also needed is an antidiversion clause, such as "United States law prohibits disposition of these commodities to North Korea, North and South Vietnam, Cambodia, or Cuba." When payment is against a letter of credit, the invoice should contain all necessary numbers and bank names. Some countries require even special certification, at times in the language of that country; and a few countries may need signed invoices with notarization. The Commerce Department keeps a current list of all requirements by country.

Consular Invoices. Some countries, particularly those of Latin America, require a special invoice in addition to the commercial invoice prepared in the language of the country and issued on official forms by the consulate. The forms are typically prepared by the forwarding agent.

Certificates of Origin. Some countries may require a specific and separate statement that is normally countersigned by a recognized Chamber of Commerce. Based on this statement, import duties are assessed; and if preferential rates are claimed, the inclusion of the certificate of origin is often necessary.

Inspection Certificate. A foreign buyer may request that the products be inspected, typically by an independent inspection firm, with respect to quality, quantity, and conformity of goods as stated in the order and invoice.

Bill of Lading. Bills of lading are issued in various forms depending on the mode of transportation. The exporter endorses the B/L in favor of either the buyer or the bank financing the transaction. The B/L identifies the owner of the shipment and is needed to claim the products at the point of destination. The bill of lading provides *three* functions: (1) receipt for goods; (2) content for shipment; and (3) title to the goods, if consigned "to the order of."

Dock Receipts or Warehouse Receipts. In cases in which the shipper or exporter is not responsible for moving the goods to the foreign destination but only to the U.S. port

8. "The Electronic Age of Export Licensing in ELAIN JOINS STELA To Cut Processing Time," *Business America,* February 29, 1988, pp. 7–11.

FIGURE 18.3 ● Shipper's Export Declaration

U.S. DEPARTMENT OF COMMERCE – BUREAU OF THE CENSUS · INTERNATIONAL TRADE ADMINISTRATION
FORM **7525-V** (1-1-88) **SHIPPER'S EXPORT DECLARATION** OMB No. 0607-0018

1a. EXPORTER *(Name and address including ZIP code)*				
	ZIP CODE	2. DATE OF EXPORTATION		3. BILL OF LADING/AIR WAYBILL NO.
b. EXPORTER'S EIN (IRS) NO.	c. PARTIES TO TRANSACTION ☐ Related ☐ Non-related			
4a. ULTIMATE CONSIGNEE				
b. INTERMEDIATE CONSIGNEE				
5. FORWARDING AGENT				
		6. POINT (STATE) OF ORIGIN OR FTZ NO.		7. COUNTRY OF ULTIMATE DESTINATION
8. LOADING PIER *(Vessel only)*	9. MODE OF TRANSPORT *(Specify)*			
10. EXPORTING CARRIER	11. PORT OF EXPORT			
12. PORT OF UNLOADING *(Vessel and air only)*	13. CONTAINERIZED *(Vessel only)* ☐ Yes ☐ No			

14. SCHEDULE B DESCRIPTION OF COMMODITIES,
15. MARKS, NOS., AND KINDS OF PACKAGES   *(Use columns 17–19)*

VALUE (U.S. dollars, omit cents)
(Selling price or cost if not sold)

D/F (16)	SCHEDULE B NUMBER (17)	CHECK DIGIT	QUANTITY – SCHEDULE B UNIT(S) (18)	SHIPPING WEIGHT *(Kilos)* (19)	(20)

21. VALIDATED LICENSE NO./GENERAL LICENSE SYMBOL   22. ECCN *(When required)*

23. Duly authorized officer or employee | The exporter authorizes the forwarder named above to act as forwarding agent for export control and customs purposes.

24. I certify that all statements made and all information contained herein are true and correct and that I have read and understand the instructions for preparation of this document, set forth in the **"Correct Way to Fill Out the Shipper's Export Declaration."** I understand that civil and criminal penalties, including forfeiture and sale, may be imposed for making false or fraudulent statements herein, failing to provide the requested information or for violation of U.S. laws on exportation (13 U.S.C. Sec. 305; 22 U.S.C. Sec. 401; 18 U.S.C. Sec. 1001; 50 U.S.C. App. 2410).

Signature   **Confidential** - For use solely for official purposes authorized by the Secretary of Commerce (13 U.S.C. 301 (g)).

Title   Export shipments are subject to inspection by U.S. Customs Service and/or Office of Export Enforcement.

Date   25. AUTHENTICATION *(When required)*

This form may be printed by private parties provided it conforms to the official form. For sale by the Superintendent of Documents, Government Printing Office, Washington, D.C. 20402, and local Customs District Directors. The **"Correct Way to Fill Out the Shipper's Export Declaration"** is available from the Bureau of the Census, Washington, D.C. 20233.

Source: U.S. Department of Commerce.

instead, a dock or warehouse receipt is usually required confirming that the shipment was actually received at the port for further shipment.

Certificate of Manufacture. Such a certificate may be issued for cases in which the buyer intends to pay for the order before shipment. The certificate may be presented, combined with a commercial invoice, to a bank appointed by the buyer for early payment. More typical is to pay only against a B/L indicating that the merchandise has actually been shipped.

Insurance Certificates. Particularly where the exporter is required to arrange for insurance, such certificates are usually necessary. They are negotiable instruments and must be endorsed accordingly.

Exporters pay careful attention to the specifications attached to letters of credit with respect to the required set of documents. The paying bank will only effect payment if all submitted documents fully conform to the specifications determined by the buyer. Mistakes can cause lengthy delays that can be costly to the exporter.

The Export Planning Process

The plan for a firm's export operations is central to any successful exporting effort. The planning activities are designed as a guideline for the future instead of depending on chance to pursue export business. The export plan ensures that all activities are directed towards the achievement of preformulated objectives that are selected to ensure the long-term profitability of the firm. Planning allows a firm to develop its export business on its own terms instead of having it be dictated by foreign clients' demands.

Several aspects are part of a successful export plan. Initially, the company will have to select an appropriate time horizon for its planning process. Root suggests that the planning horizon be chosen so that the firm will be forced to raise fundamental and basic questions about the future direction and extent of the firm's export business.[9] Secondly, planning horizons should be long enough to project the effects of the firm's decisions. The normal plan is three to five years, though for some it may be as short as one year or as long as ten years.

The planning unit will target specific countries for each product. The combination of the various country or product plans is the corporate export plan. However, the effort will almost always start at the country or product level. Viewing export planning as a process, one can identify the three major steps shown in Figure 18.4: identifying and measuring market opportunities, developing an export strategy, and implementing the strategy.

The process and analysis of identifying and measuring market opportunities has been described in detail in Chapter 7, International and Global Marketing Research.

9. Franklin R. Root, *Strategic Planning for Export Marketing* (Scranton, Penn.: International Textbook Company, 1966), pp. 4–7.

FIGURE 18.4 ● Export Planning Process

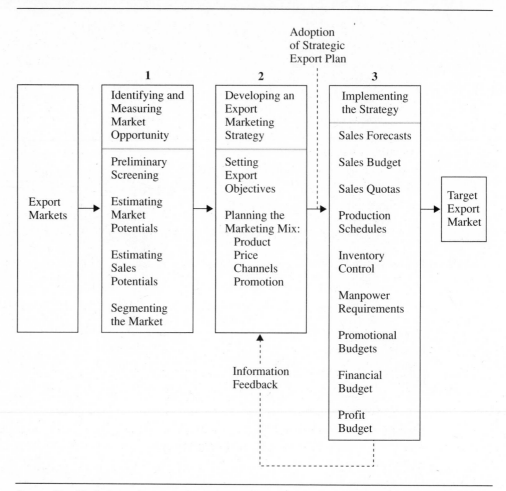

Source: Frankin R. Root, *Strategic Planning for Export Marketing* (Scranton, Penn.: International Textbook Company, 1966), p. 5.

Essentially, the plan has to start with a preliminary screening of the great many export markets that exist to identify those that may be pursued. The preliminary screening prevents any unnecessary effort spent on markets that do not warrant any resources at this time. For the targeted markets, the market potentials will be estimated always keeping in mind that the potential may be measured at various levels (see Figure 7.3). As a next step, an estimate of the firm's sales potential for each market will determine the best possible outcome given the firm's competitive position.

Where appropriate, market segments may be analyzed separately if the marketing strategy will require changes for each segment.

The development of the export strategy includes the setting of some objectives. Naturally, these objectives must be in line with the firm's capabilities and reflect the realities of the marketplace as derived from the analysis of the market opportunities. The specific objectives will differ by company. The objectives can include sales volume, market share, and profit expectations. The export plan should consider the potential market reaction to the firm's action and should recognize that competitors may adapt their marketing activities to planned changes.

Once export objectives have been clearly defined, the firm can go about planning the individual elements of the marketing mix. The product offering, including service, must be prepared, and allowances will have to be made for any adjustments if required. Prices will be predetermined based on both the internal price structure and the demand situation. The export plan will include a detailed promotional plan outlining all the steps to be undertaken to promote the product in the target market. Finally, the plans for the distribution strategy will have to be included as well, containing both entry and local distribution approaches. The key to a successful plan is the relationship between the objectives and the planned action. Management will have to ensure that the desired objectives can in fact be reached with the planned marketing mix.

Based on the detailed marketing mix plans, operational budgets are established. These budgets include:

1. Sales forecasts (in monetary and unit terms)
2. Sales budget (all planned sales-related expenditures)
3. Sales quotas (in monetary and unit terms)
4. Production schedules
5. Inventory control (including the requirements for inventories, both in domestic and foreign warehouse locations)
6. Employee requirements (the hiring of all necessary personnel to achieve the objectives set earlier)
7. Promotional budgets (with all expenses for advertising, exhibitions, and sales material)
8. Financial budget (for the capital requirements to carry out the planned effort)
9. Profit budget (as the final criterion and measuring device of the export operation)

Under ideal situations, operational budgets may be prepared for a number of alternative plans, with the final selection depending on the profitability of each of the scenarios. In a world where the present situation is constantly subject to new developments, a plan or the export effort over a period of three to five years may appear unnecessary or unwise. But even under rapidly changing situations, executives cannot avoid making some assumptions about the future. The export plan will bring discipline and cohesion to the process. Once the assumptions originally made have had to be changed, modifications in the plan may have to be as made as well. However, as with any planning process, the export plan forces the company to think about its future in an organized fashion.

GOVERNMENT EXPORT POLICIES AND LEGISLATION

There is no doubt that exports can greatly enhance the economy of any nation. The U.S. Congress found that exports were responsible for creating one out of every nine manufacturing jobs and generating $1 out of $7 of total U.S. goods produced.[10] Thus, governments frequently try to influence their country's export volume through legislation or direct government supports. To outline the export policies of all major countries is too difficult. Consequently, this section concentrates on the United States. Though the respective export policies of other countries may vary by specific objective or by approach, understanding the U.S. export policies will nevertheless give you some conceptual background for the understanding of the policies of all countries and an appreciation for the important role governments can play.

Organization of U.S. Export Policies

The execution of the U.S. government's export policies lies with the Department of Commerce, whereas negotiations and policy advisement to the president are the responsibilities of the Trade Representative, a cabinet position. Also part of the U.S. export policymaking is the Export-Import Bank, an independent agency whose activities were described in Chapter 13.

The U.S. Department of Commerce coordinates the activities of 162 commercial attaches in sixty-five countries.[11] Involved with U.S. embassies abroad, these attaches provide U.S. business with support at the local level. Also available are about 150 international trade specialists in thirty-two U.S. cities.[12] An important aspect of the Commerce Department's activities are trade promotion programs that include permanent overseas trade fairs and seminars on exporting for U.S. businesspersons in the United States. With a budget of several million dollars, the Department is now developing an Automated Information System that is expected to serve up to 50,000 subscribers in the United States.[13]

10. *Congressional Record,* vol. 128, no. 134, October 1, 1982.
11. "The New Export Policy Works Like the Old—Badly," *Business Week,* July 21, 1980, p. 89.
12. Ibid., p. 90.
13. Ibid., p. 89.

The office of the U.S. Trade Representative (USTR) has major responsibility for both multilateral and bilateral trade negotiations that of course include exports. Under the USTR falls the negotiation of the GATT agreements, any international commodity agreements, and many of the negotiations that take place within international organizations.[14] To provide for some coordination between the USTR office and the Department of Commerce leading government officials participate in the Trade Policy Committee. In 1987, thirty-six states maintained offices abroad and programs at home to encourage export trade, particularly with smaller companies.[15]

Most governments have some type of agency or program to support exporting initiatives. These programs are often targeted to the smaller company that does not have export experience. For example, Labelking, a small South London printer of adhesive labels for the food industry, relied on the advice of one of the thirty-one export development advisors hired and trained by the U.K. Department of Trade and Industry. The advisor helped Labelking assess the size of the European and U.S. market and enter the French and Iberian market.[16]

In addition to federal government programs, many states have established organizations and agencies to assist U.S. companies in their exporting efforts. For example, C. M. Magnetics, a three-year-old company in Santa Fe Springs, California, recently received a $2.7 million order from China. This order was the direct result of efforts by the state of California's World Trade Commission. "Without their help," company president J. Carlos Macrel said of the agency, "we probably wouldn't be in business today."[17]

Though the resources committed on behalf of U.S. exports may appear substantial, the $30.5 million spent on the export development program for fiscal 1981 is substantially less than the corresponding budget of the Japan External Trade Organization (JETRO). JETRO is endowed with a budget of $48 million and is able to maintain a staff of about 600 in Japan and another 650 persons overseas.[18] This discrepancy in budget is despite the fact that U.S. exports are almost twice the volume of Japan's exports. For many U.S. businesspeople, this difference in funding export programs is symbolic of a lack of interest on the part of many government officials and legislators who have accumulated a substantial amount of legislation that actually hinders U.S. exports. In the following section, we explore the various legislative and regulative disincentives that the United States and some other countries have accumulated.

14. "Service Exports Spell Relief FATT," *Business Marketing,* January 1987, p. 58.

15. "Big Plans for Small Business: Firm Try to Boost Exports," *Insight,* July 13, 1987, p. 40.

16. Charles Batchelor, "A Napoleonic Drive, With a French Partner into Iberia," *Financial Times,* September 5, 1989, p. 12.

17. "States Launch Efforts to Make Small Firms Better Exporters," *Wall Street Journal,* February 2, 1987, p. 25.

18. "The New Export Policy Works Like the Old—Badly," *Business Week,* July 21, 1980, p. 90.

Obstacles to U.S. Exports

The policies mentioned in this section are generally viewed as hindrances to commercial activity that ultimately affects domestic exports. Consequently, U.S. exports are below potential. These policies typically have been enacted by Congress to achieve other political goals such as environmental conservation.

The Foreign Corrupt Practices Act of 1977 was enacted as a result of published reports on corporate bribery of foreign nationals, initially triggered by the "United Brands Affair" in Honduras. The company reportedly paid funds to that country's president to get favorable tax treatment on banana exports. Subsequent investigations by the Securities and Exchange Commission (SEC) and the U.S. government found scores of other U.S. companies guilty of the same practices. The resulting "Act of 1977" places stringent restrictions on the type of payments that third party agents can receive. Consequently, some U.S. companies have the expense accounts of their foreign representatives certified by American consular officers. However, competitors from other major trading nations are not subject to such legislation, a fact that many U.S. businesspersons consider a disadvantage. A study of 207 U.S. exporters found that the most difficult aspect of international marketing in terms of ethical and moral problems is bribery. Thirty-four percent of the companies cited bribery as a problem followed by 15 percent reporting government interference and 7 percent citing customs clearance.[19]

Often to build a company's export business, the company will need to locate a staff of people in other countries. The cost of locating staff in other countries can be exorbitant. For example, a midlevel manager in the U.S. will earn $57,428 with salary and bonuses, while the same manager will be paid $103,550 in Switzerland, or $95,834 in Germany.[20] These comparisons do not include the additional costs of housing, moving, and air travel back to the States which most companies provide for overseas employees.

The policy instituted under the Carter Administration on nuclear power plant exports illustrates the effect of a political decision on foreign trade. The United States passed the Nuclear Non-Proliferation Act of 1978 requiring all governments that use enriched uranium from U.S. sources to obtain the U.S. government's permission in advance if the uranium is to be sent anywhere for reprocessing.[21] The retroactive law applied to most of the twenty-six loyal and trusted foreign customers who would face a cutoff in supplies if this new feature was not approved by them.

The U.S. Nuclear Non-Proliferation Act was enacted to enhance existing controls administered by the International Atomic Energy Agency (IAEA) based in Vienna, Austria. An international nonproliferation treaty had been in effect since 1970 and was signed by over one hundred governments, including those who had

19. Robert Armstrong, Bruce W. Stening, John K. Ryans, Larry Marks, and Michael Mayo. "International Marketing Ethics," *European Journal of Marketing,* vol. 24, no. 10, 1990, p. 10.

20. "Hay European Salary Comparisons," *Eurobusiness,* December 1990, p. 70.

21. "How Carter's Nuclear Policy Backfired Abroad," *Fortune,* October 23, 1978, p. 124.

purchased uranium under U.S. contracts. The act reflects the U.S. government's position that existing controls were not strict enough to prevent further proliferation of atomic weapons to nations that were on the verge of attaining such capabilities (Brazil, Argentina, Iran, Pakistan, and India among them).

Even before the enactment of the 1978 Act, U.S. export sales of nuclear reactors had been declining since 1974 due to a tremendous overbooking of orders.[22] In 1971, U.S. manufacturers supplied all eight foreign orders for nuclear reactors, but supplied only one of ten in 1976 and none of seven ordered in 1977. Foreign orders went to suppliers in Germany, France, and other countries that did not insist on rules such as those of the U.S. government. The loss of foreign orders for such nuclear reactors was further influenced by the U.S. government's decision to stop the development of the breeder reactor that allowed for reprocessing of spent uranium and would reduce the world's demand for raw uranium. However, other foreign governments, such as the French government, have continued to develop this new breeder technology and consequently are at an advantage over U.S. companies such as Westinghouse or General Electric who must compete with the older and simpler design. With each nuclear installation worth nearly one billion dollars, the effect on U.S. exports was substantial.

The U.S. government has also affected exports through politically motivated actions. Unilaterally, the United States has employed trade embargoes against Cuba, Vietnam, and the Soviet Union. Most of these actions were imposed by the U.S. government alone and were not followed by other nations, thus giving the clear advantage to foreign countries.

One of the most interesting examples of the effect of embargoes is seen in the trade relationship between the Soviet Union and the United States. Following the era of detente in the late 1960s and early 1970s, trade between the United States and the Soviet Union expanded considerably, as did trade between Europe and the Soviet Bloc and trade between the United States and the Soviet Union's allies, the Comecon countries. But the situation changed drastically with the Soviet invasion of Afghanistan in December 1979. The U.S. government quickly imposed an embargo that covered both grain shipments and strategic shipments. Besides the embargo of 17 million tons of grain, restrictions were placed on the export of high-technology items over and above those that always existed for military hardware.[23] Export licenses that had already been granted were suspended, which meant that U.S. companies could not ship products they had already contracted for. Some export license applications were denied, such as the one requested by Western Electric to supply $1 billion worth of telecommunications equipment and related technology to the Soviet Union.

The impact of the U.S. government's embargo on trade with the Soviet Union was severe.[24] United States agricultural exports declined from $2.9 billion in 1979 to

22. "Why the Nuclear Power Race Worries the U.S.," *Business Week,* August 23, 1976, pp. 68–69.

23. "What Trade Sanctions Will Cost," *Business Week,* January 28, 1980, p. 34.

24. "Russian Trade—Credit Where It Is Due," *The Economist,* June 6, 1981, p. 78.

$1.1 billion in 1980, and the total embargo was lifted in 1981. Nonagricultural exports suffered also. They declined from $750 million in 1979 to $360 million in 1980, depriving many U.S.-based companies of profitable business opportunities. Many opportunities denied to U.S. corporations are grabbed up by foreign-based companies whose governments may not enforce the same regulations or embargoes.

Sometimes, regulations that prevent exports are pushed by special interest groups. Exports of U.S. lumber in the form of logs were severely hurt by a rule that prohibited exports of logs cut on U.S. government land in raw form. Congress prevented such sales to satisfy U.S. sawmill owners and their workers who saw too many logs shipped to Japan where they were cut to Japanese specifications that differed from those used in the United States. Since the majority of U.S. logs are cut on government land, each year several hundred million dollars worth of export sales were lost. The Japanese simply bought logs elsewhere rather than buying cut timber in the United States.[25]

The limitations of exports can also be at an international level. The Coordinating Committee on Multi-lateral Exports Control (Cocom) was established in 1949 and includes fifteen nations—Belgium, Canada, Denmark, France, Germany, Greece, Italy, Japan, Luxembourg, The Netherlands, Norway, Portugal, Turkey, the United Kingdom and the United States. Cocom members agree on which products they will not sell to the Soviet Union and other Warsaw Pact countries such as Albania, North Korea, Vietnam, and China. Typical products include weapons, advanced computers, and atomic energy components. In 1985, Cocom limits cost U.S. industry $9.3 billion in lost sales according to a Natural Science Foundation report. With the opening up of Eastern Europe, Cocom is reducing its list of restricted products.[26]

Many business and political leaders have recognized the considerable negative effect of such rules for U.S. exports, and recent changes indicate a move towards fewer such restrictions. Occasionally, U.S. companies have diverted export orders to their foreign subsidiaries where such restrictions do not apply. In general, however, any company that depends on exports as a source of income is well-advised to carefully monitor government legislations and acts, both domestically and abroad, since the potential effect can be either to create new opportunities or to prevent the exploitation of existing ones.

IMPORT TRADE MECHANICS

In many ways, the importer is concerned with the same trade mechanics as the exporter. Communications with foreign suppliers can be difficult due to distances

25. Lee Smith, "The Neglected Promise of Our Forests," *Fortune,* November 5, 1979, p. 112.
26. "High-Tech Exports" Is the Dam Breaking?" *Business Week,* June 4, 1990, pp. 66–67.

involved, time changes, and cultural differences. Import trade makes use of the same price quoting vocabulary as exporting does, and the payment mechanism is the same with respect to the use of letters of credit or open accounts. Finally, the logistic concerns of the importer are identical to those of the exporter, so that many of the points covered in the earlier portion of this chapter need not be repeated.

A substantial amount of effort is expended by importers to bring products through local customs. Not surprisingly, import requirements vary by nation and are numerous. In this section, we concentrate solely on the major import procedures as they apply to the United States. However, these procedures are indicative of the type of procedures employed in other countries. The Department of Commerce has a staff of specialists to help companies export. These specialists can explain the customs clearance procedures for most countries. Also, freight forwarders are very knowledgeable about customers' requirements and will assist in preparing the necessary documents.

Importing into the United States[27]

On reaching the United States, the recipient, or consignee, of the shipment will have to file an entry for the products or goods with U.S. Customs. The importer has the choice of filing for consumption or filing for storage. Under the second alternative, imported products may be stored for some time before they are officially entered for consumption in the United States, or they may be re-exported.

Since the proper declaration of imported products requires some specific knowledge, many importers use the services of licensed customs brokers. A broker is empowered by the firm to act on its behalf at customs and file the necessary forms. To determine the customs status of a shipment, an examination is typically performed to check the following:

1. The value of the shipment to assess customs
2. The verification of required marking and labeling
3. Shipment of prohibited merchandise
4. Verification of invoicing and determination of either shortages or excess compared to the invoice

The importer will have to prepare all necessary forms to allow the U.S. Customs officials to make these determinations. Failure to meet these requirements may result in lengthy delays in clearing any shipment, unnecessary expenses on behalf of the importer, and higher fees charged by customs brokers.

27. The section on import trade mechanics was written based on a publication *Importing into the United States,* Department of the Treasury, United States Custom Service, January 1989. Since these regulations are subject to frequent revisions, the interested reader is advised to obtain the latest information directly from the Customs Service.

Valuation of Shipments   U.S. Customs officers are required by law to find the value of the imported merchandise. Basically, customs value is determined by selecting the higher of either foreign value nor export value. *Foreign value* is based on the prices at which the imported merchandise is freely placed for sale in the country of origin in the usual wholesale quantities. The *export value* is the price at which the merchandise is freely offered for sale as an export to the United States in the major markets of the country of origin. When neither a foreign value nor export value can be found, the merchandise may be entered at the corresponding U.S. value at which such or similar merchandise is freely offered in the United States less the necessary allowance for bringing the products into the country. If a corresponding U.S. value does not exist, valuation can be based on the cost of production. In a few cases, valuation can be based on the U.S. selling price, which is based on the typical price for the same product offered in the United States.

Products that are subject to duty are assessed either *ad valorem* (a percentage of the established value), with a *specific duty* (a specific amount per unit of measurement), or with a *compound duty* (combination of ad valorem and specific duty). Though the U.S. Customs Office publishes a list of the various duties by type of product, an importer can find out by contacting the U.S. Customs Office with the following information:

- Complete description of the imported item
- Method of manufacture
- Specifications and analyses
- Quantities and costs of component materials
- Commercial designation of the product in the United States and identification of the primary use of the product

Given sufficient material as described above, the U.S. Customs Service can provide importers with a binding assessment on import duties that make it possible to assess the entire landed cost for the importer for later use in pricing. No binding information is available via telephone or based on incomplete information.

Marking and Labeling   Unless otherwise stated, each product or article imported into the United States must be legibly marked in a conspicuous place with the name of the country of origin stated in English so that the U.S. purchaser can easily determine the country of origin. In some cases, markings may be made on the containers rather than the articles themselves. Importers are advised to obtain the particular regulations or exemptions from the U.S. Customs Service. In case of a lack of proper markings, the U.S. Customs Service can assess a special marking duty unless the imported products are marked under customs supervision. In either case, the lack or absence of the required markings can cause costly delays to the importer.

Prohibited or Restricted Merchandise   The importation of certain articles is either prohibited or restricted. It is impractical to list all the prohibited or restricted items.

TABLE 18.1 ● Classes of Products That Are Prohibited or Restricted for Import into the United States

---

- Alcoholic Beverages: Require a permit from Bureau of Alcohol, Tobacco and Firearms
- Arms, Ammunition, Explosives: Require a permit from Bureau of Alcohol, Tobacco and Firearms
- Automobiles: Must conform to Federal Motor Vehicle Safety Standards
- Coins, Currencies and Stamps: No replicas of U.S. or foreign items permitted
- Eggs and Egg Products: Subject to the Egg Products Inspection Act
- Animals and Plants: Subject to regulations of the Animal or Plant Health Inspection Service
- Electronic Products: Subject to the Radiation Control Act
- Food, Drugs, Devices, Cosmetics: Subject to the federal Food, Drug and Cosmetics Act
- Narcotic Drugs: Prohibited
- Nuclear Reactors and Radioactive Material: Subject to the U.S. Atomic Energy Commission
- Obscene, Immoral, Seditious Matter: Prohibited
- Pesticides: Subject to the federal Environment Control Act
- Wool, Fur, Textiles and Fabric Products: Subject to the Wool Products Labeling Act, the Textile Fiber Products Identification Act, the Flammable Fabrics Act, and the Fur Products Labeling Act

---

However, the major classes of items are shown in Table 18.1. Restricted items can be imported with proper clearance.

Import Invoicing Procedures For some special categories of merchandise, only a commercial invoice prepared in the same manner typical for commercial transactions is sufficient for U.S. Customs clearance. Quite frequently, either a special invoice or a commercial invoice is not available at the time of entry. In such instances, the importer can prepare a pro forma invoice by promising to deliver final invoices within six months of the date of entry. Also, a bond must usually be posted to cover the value of the estimated duties.

Inaccurate information can cause costly delays to both the importer and exporter. To provide for smooth clearance through customs the U.S. importer should assume the responsibility of properly informing the foreign supplier. The Journal of Commerce, a private company, has a service called PIERS, which is a data base of all imports and exports reported to the U.S. Customs in the forty-seven largest U.S. ports. The data is helpful for competitive and market research analysis.

Goods can be delayed at the port waiting for the necessary paperwork before being shipped. There is a trend toward the use of electronic transmission of customers' documentation. TRADANET is a global service that allows companies to send the commercial invoice and customs clearance document to the importer while the goods are in transit. With these documents, the importer can clear the goods through customs.[28]

The Role of the Customs Agent

Since the handling of shipments through customs requires specialized knowledge, most companies employ outside specialized firms that are registered with U.S. Customs. These agents will not only prepare the necessary invoices from information supplied by the importer, but they will also arrange for clearance through customs, inspection where necessary, payment of duties, and transport to the final destination. Frequently, such customs agents are also international freight forwarders, or freight forwarding firms with a specialized customs section. To allow the customs agent to act on behalf of the importer, a special power of attorney is granted that then identifies the customs agent as a legally empowered actor.

Free Trade Zones or Foreign Trade Zones[29]

Within the United States and elsewhere in the world, zones have been established where merchandise can be placed for unlimited time periods without the payment of duties. Duty will be assessed, however, as soon as the merchandise is transferred from the free trade zone.

Such zones offer many advantages to both exporters or importers. For one, duty payable can tie up a substantial amount of working capital. The use of a free trade zone allows a firm to keep an inventory close by without prepaying duty. In addition, many importers may later want to re-export products to other countries and would thus prefer to temporarily store the merchandise in a place where no duties have to be paid until the final destination is determined.

Free trade zones are also valuable as manufacturing sites. Any merchandise brought into such zones may be broken up, repackaged, assembled, sorted, graded, cleaned, or used in the manufacturing process with domestic material. The latter can be brought duty free into trade zones and reimported, again duty free, into the United States. Duty will only have to be paid on components or parts subject to duty, rather than on the entire value.

Free trade zones exist in most countries and are typically attached to ports or airports. In some countries with low labor costs, free trade zones were established to allow for the further processing of semimanufactured goods originating from devel-

28. Roy Price, "Towards Paperless Exporting," *Industrial Marketing Digest,* vol. 12, no. 3, 1987, pp. 63–66.

29. For a detailed discussion of the role of foreign trade zones in global marketing, see Patriya S. Tansuhaj and James W. Gentry, "Firm Differences in Perceptions of the Facilitating Role of Foreign Trade Zones in Global Marketing and Logistics," *Journal of International Business Studies,* Spring 1987, pp. 29–33.

oped countries.[30] These goods are later re-exported into the country of origin. Malaysia is one country that has allowed many foreign electronics companies to bring components for further assembly to Malaysian foreign trade zones. As a result, the foreign trade zones have ceased as a strictly distribution- or transportation-related phenomenon and are now incorporated by many international companies in their production or sourcing strategy.

Obstacles to Foreign Imports

Recently, there has been extensive political debate over protectionist measures for certain key U.S. industries. The trade law known as the "escape clause" authorizes the president to file a protecting grant for any industry that can prove that it is being hurt by imports.[31] The law dates back to the New Deal and President Franklin Roosevelt.

Nowhere have imports made a bigger impression than in the steel industry. In 1983, the United States imported roughly 20 percent of all our steel needs. United States companies claim that the steel is being "dumped" in our country at artificially low costs. Domestic companies blame foreign government subsidies for the low import cost. Hence, the steel workers and their companies are pushing government to protect U.S. markets against unreasonable foreign competition.

Yet, consumers are the main beneficiaries of these imports. They are able to purchase quality at low cost. In addition, there are countless numbers of jobs involved with trade firms in imports. A recent estimate states that 194,000 jobs are related to auto imports alone.[32] Quotas have been the recent political answer to the conflict. However, a 15 percent import quota on steel is estimated to have the effect of raising consumer prices over 20 percent.[33] The conflict boils down to lower prices versus jobs.

Global Import Barriers

Goods do not flow freely from country to country. There are a host of impediments to the smooth flow of trade such as import taxes, tariffs, quotas, and nontariff barriers which are discussed in Chapters 2 and 4. The importing country can take a number of actions to slow down, block, or make importing unprofitable. For example, South

30. "Export for the Future—Sameen (Kenya) Duty Free Industrial Park," *Eurobusiness,* December 1990/January 1991, Special Section-Kenya.

31. Clyde H. Farnsworth, "Industry's New Assault on Imports," *New York Times,* January 27, 1984, p. D1.

32. "Imports, Often Blamed for Killing U.S. Jobs, Create New Ones Too," *Wall Street Journal,* February 29, 1984, p. 1.

33. "Jobless Rate Off Despite Slowing of the Economy," *Wall Street Journal,* February 6, 1984, p. 5.

Korea's trade deficit quadrupled to $1.0 billion in 1990. In response, they have declared 94 percent of the U.S. exports to South Korea as luxury goods with tariffs and taxes. A large Westinghouse or Whirlpool refrigerator that sells for $1,700 in the U.S. costs $4,200 in Korea. If Korea does not relax some of these barriers, the United States may respond by slapping retaliatory duties on Korea's Hyundai cars and Lucky-Goldstar VCRs.[34] While the Office of the U.S. Trade Representative is working with Congress and the President to reduce export barriers, the single European Market of 1992 is producing new barriers. As the twelve countries of the European Community adopt over 280 directives to set business standards, U.S. businesses are finding many of the standards are in favor of European suppliers. For example, Hyster, the U.S. forklift truck manufacturer, found they needed to make twelve modifications to its forklift to comply with the new EC directive from Brussels.[35]

The manufacturers and farmers of the United States face a number of export barriers, which are being discussed through GATT negotiations, trade talks, and meetings of heads of state. The top ten barriers to trade are shown in Table 18.2.[36] Japan has received a great deal of pressure to open its markets.

The United States is a leader in the fight to ease barriers that prevent goods from entering Japan. Japan's trade surplus has averaged 30 billion dollars.[37] Many foreign countries insist that trade is a two-way street. Countries cannot expect to export unless they allow free and easy access to imports. Although the Japanese have been criticized for unfair trade practices, a recent survey indicated that 70 percent of Japanese consumers do not discriminate against imports.[38]

Japan has greatly simplified import procedures under a four-point plan.

1. Establishment or changes of specifications or standards with the aim of conforming to foreign standards.

2. The nature and aim of such establishment or changes will be made public in advance.

3. The views of those affected both at home and abroad will be sought. Efforts will be made to reflect these views in improving procedures as soon as possible.

4. Foreign inspection standards will be recognized as soon as possible and domestic inspection simplified.

34. "Seoul's Crackdown on Imports May be a Luxury It Can't Afford," *Business Week,* January 21, 1991, p. 46.

35. "AS EC Markets Unite, U.S. Exporters Face New Trade Barriers," *Wall Street Journal,* January 19, 1989, p. 1.

36. Rahul Jacob, "Export Barriers the U.S. Hates Most," *Fortune,* February 27, 1989, pp. 88–89.

37. "Japan—Headaches in the Labyrinth," *Financial Times,* September 19, 1983, Special Section—Japan, p. I.

38. "New Emphasis on Import Promotion," *Financial Times,* September 19, 1983, Special Section—Japan, p. VI.

TABLE 18.2 ● Export Barriers the U.S. Hates Most

Product	Countries	Barrier	Sales lost by U.S.*
Grain	European Community	Price supports, variable duties	$2.0 billion
Soybeans	European Community	Price supports	$1.4 billion
Rice	Japan	Ban	$300 million
Beef	European Community	Ban on growth hormones in livestock	$100 million
Commercial aircraft	Britain, France, Germany, Spain	Subsidies to Airbus Industrie	Over $850 million
Telecommunications equipment	European Community, S. Korea	Standards stacked against imports	No estimate
Telecommunications satellites	Japan	Ban on import by government agencies	No estimate
Pharmaceuticals	Argentina, Brazil	No patent protection	Over $110 million
Videocassettes, films	Brazil	Requirements to subsidize and market local films	Over $40 million
Computer software	Thailand	Poor patent protection	No estimate

*Annual, estimated

Source: Rahul Jacob, "Export Barriers the U.S. Hates Most." *Fortune,* February 27, 1989, p. 89. © 1989 The Time Inc. Magazine Company. All rights reserved.

It is hoped these four points will help to increase harmony among trading nations. However, if trade figures do not improve, one can predict more negotiations in the future.[39]

CONCLUSIONS

This chapter has explained some of the procedural aspects of international marketing. Thorough knowledge of these trade mechanics is often a prerequisite for international marketers. All too frequently, an international strategy fails because some of these mechanics have been neglected.

39. *Japanese Economic Journal,* June 26, 1979.

You should be aware, however, that this text cannot and does not specify all the regulations in force for any particular product category or country. We have provided a general background, listing the factors that may have to be investigated before a strategy can be implemented. The regulations described are also subject to change. Consequently, we suggest that close contact with specialists in this area be maintained so that executives responsible for international marketing activities can be kept abreast of new developments.

There is a trend around the world toward reducing barriers and opening markets. The rapid growth in global trade has made more countries interdependent. If Japan continues to protect its $6 billion rice market, the United States can limit the importation of Japanese cars. World leaders are working hard to open all markets, although it will take years to remove all the barriers. Close contact with your trade association will keep your firm up to date on the latest agreements between governments and the trade.

Questions for Discussion

1. Your company manufactures telephones at your plant in Scranton, Pennsylvania. South Korea wants a quote on 10,000 telephones. How should you quote so that it is convenient for the buyer?

2. Irrevocable letters of credit have become very popular. How do they protect the buyer and the seller?

3. When calculating the cost of a shipment of machinery for export, what additional costs will the exporter be faced with in addition to shipping and insurance?

4. Explain the possible uses of export documentation on a shipment of pipe from Los Angeles to Bolivia?

5. What are the critical elements of the export planning process? If you were asked to develop a plan for exporting gloves to South America, how would you do it?

6. What are the advantages and disadvantages of import limits in the United States? Use, for example, the import quotas on Japanese automobiles into the United States.

7. How can free trade zones be used by U.S. manufacturers?

For Further Reading

Attiyeh, Robert S., and David L. Wenner. "Critical Mass: Key to Exports." *Business Horizons* (December 1979), pp. 28–38.

Ayal, Igal. "Industry Export Performance: Assessment and Prediction." *Journal of Marketing* (Summer 1982), pp. 54–61.

Brasch, J. "Using Export Specialists to Develop Overseas Sales." *Harvard Business Review* (May-June 1981), pp. 6–8.

Carey, Ben. "Fine Tuning Harmonized System." *American Shipper* (September 1982), p. 100.

Dollar, David. "Import Quotas and the Product Cycle." *Quarterly Journal of Economics* (August 1987), pp. 615–632.

Filbert, William B. "The Licensing Process: Getting the Export License." *Export Today* (February 1984), pp. 60–63.

Fitzpatrick, Peter B., and Alan S. Zimmerman. *Essentials of Export Marketing.* New York: American Management Association, 1985.

"Export Activity in Developing Nations," *Journals of International Business Studies* (Spring-Summer 1978), pp. 95–102.

Hayes, John. "Who Sets the Standards?" *Forbes* (April 17, 1989), pp. 110–112.

McGuinness, Norman W., and Blair Little. "The Influence of Product Characteristics on the Export Performance of New Industrial Products." *Journal of Marketing,* (Spring 1981), pp. 110–122.

Rabino, Samuel. *Journal of Marketing,* "Tax Incentives to Export: Some Implications for Policy Makers." *Journal of International Business Studies* vol. 11, no. 1 (Spring-Summer 1980), pp. 74–85.

Root, Franklin R. *Entry Strategies for International Markets.* Lexington, Mass.: D. C. Heath, 1987.

Weiss, Kenneth D. *Building an Import-Export Business.* New York: John Wiley & Sons, 1987.

Yorio, V., *Adapting Products for Export.* New York: The Conference Board, 1983.

CASE 1

Gillette International's Trac II

In mid-1972, Gillette International's management was considering the introduction of its new shaving system, the TRAC II, in some of its foreign markets. The blade had been introduced only nine months earlier in the U.S. market with considerable success. However, existing blade production capacity was limited and the company could not serve all markets at the same time. Consequently, management was carefully evaluating which markets should get top priority for the TRAC II and how to combine this market selection process with an appropriate pricing strategy. In addition, the company was keenly aware of its main competitors, Schick of the United States and Wilkinson of the United Kingdom. The introduction of Gillette's newest product, the Platinum Plus, had been successful in most foreign markets, however a number of executives believed the Platinum Plus's performance was below potential and wanted to avoid some of these negative experiences with the TRAC II introduction.

●

The case was prepared by Robert Howard under the direction of Jean-Pierre Jeannet, Visiting Professor at IMEDE and Professor of Marketing and International Business at Babson College. This case was prepared for class discussion rather than to illustrate either effective or ineffective handling of an administrative situation. This case was based on earlier work by Robert Roland, M.B.A. candidate at Babson College. Copyright© 1988 by IMEDE, Lausanne, Switzerland. The International Institute for Management Development (IMD), resulting from the merger between IMEDE, Lausanne, and IMI, Geneva, acquires and retains all rights. Reproduced by permission.

COMPANY BACKGROUND

The Gillette Company was a Boston-based consumer goods manufacturer with annual sales in 1971 of $730 million. The company was best known for its shaving product line which was marketed worldwide and where Gillette continued to be the major company both in the United States and abroad.

The company's main operating units were Gillette North America, Gillette International, and other companies under the Diversified Companies group (see Exhibit 1). Gillette North America included four product divisions: Safety Razor, Paper Mate, Toiletries, and Personal Care.

The Safety Razor Division was responsible for the Gillette shaving business within the United States. The Toiletries Division marketed such products as deodorants, antiperspirants, shaving creams, and hair grooming products for both men and women, including the leading brands Right Guard and Foamy.

The Personal Care Division marketed women's toiletry products such as hair sprays, cream rinses, home permanents, and hair conditioners, as well as a line of portable hair dryers (Max, Super Max and Max Plus for Men). After only one year in national distribution, Gillette held second place in the competitive market for hand-held dryers.

Gillette's Paper Mate Division was responsible for marketing writing instruments in the United States and was the leader in porous point pens. The Paper Mate Division also sold ball point pens and refills, broadtip markers, glue, and had recently entered the lower price segment with a new line of ball point and porous point pens.

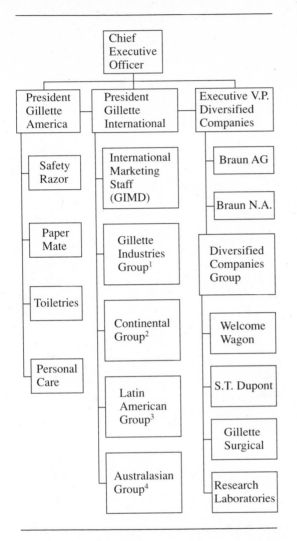

EXHIBIT 1 ● Gillette Organization Chart

1. United Kingdom, S. Africa and Export Depts to Ireland, Iceland, Greece, Eastern Europe, Near and Middle East, and African markets.
2. France, Germany, Italy, Spain and affiliated sales companies in Scandinavia, Benelux, Alpine, and Portugal.
3. Argentina, Brazil, Colombia, Mexico, Venezuela plus Latin American Sales Companies and Export to: Chile, Peru, Puerto Rico, Guatemala, Honduras, Costa Rica, Salvador, Nicaragua, Ecuador, Bolivia, Paraguay, Dominican Republic, Aruba, Curacao, Guyana, Surinam, Barbados, and the Bahamas.
4. Australia, New Zealand, Japan, Hong Kong, and Southeast Asia.

Source: Company records.

The Diversified Companies group included a range of recent acquisitions located both in the United States and abroad. Acquired in 1967, Braun AG of West Germany was a leading manufacturer of electric housewares. Its largest lines were electric razors, coffee makers, digital clocks, and some photographic products. In electric shavers, Braun was the market leader in Germany and its products were distributed in many European markets. Shavers were not sold in the United States due to a licensing agreement signed with an independent company in 1954 which was due to expire in 1975. Also part of this group was Welcome Wagon, a community service company acquired in 1971. Welcome Wagon was a service used by local businesses to acquaint new arrivals in the community with local companies and their services.

EXHIBIT 2 ● The Gillette Company
Development of Sales and Profits, 1967–1971 (In Millions of Dollars)

Year	*Total company*		*Blades and razors*		*Foreign operations*	
	SALES	*NET PROFITS*	*SALES*	*NET PROFITS*	*SALES*	*NET PROFITS*
1967	$428	$57	$193	$38	$167	$20
1968	553	62	238	40	221	23
1969	610	65	250	44	256	29
1970	673	66	262	46	289	33
1971	730	62	270	41	327	33

Safety Razor Division

The Safety Razor Division marketed Gillette's principal product line—shaving equipment and blades—in the U.S. market. Gillette was the world's leading blade manufacturer and the major factor in the U.S. market. The company marketed a full range of blades including double-edged stainless steel blades (Super Stainless Steel and Platinum Plus) as well as an older line of carbon steel blades (Super Blue, Blue, and Thin). Gillette sold its Techmatic Razor Blade and Lady Sure Touch on the band concept. In the United States, the Safety Razor Division also imported a line of disposable lighters under the name Cricket which was produced by Gillette's S.T. Dupont affiliate in France. Starting in the fall of 1971, the Division began marketing the TRAC II, Gillette's latest shaving product based on a twin-blade shaving system. 1971 had brought record sales and profits for the Division and the outlook for 1972 indicated another top performance.

International Division

Gillette International was responsible for marketing the majority of Gillette's products abroad. The company sold its products in more than 170 countries and territories with shaving products accounting for most of the volume. International sales had been steadily increasing as a percentage

of corporate sales and accounted for more than 40 percent of Gillette's volume. Because of the higher profitability of international operations, Gillette International accounted for half of the company's profits, as seen in Exhibit 2.

The president of Gillette International was also the executive vice president for international operations at corporate headquarters in Boston. The president was supported by a staff of international marketing experts located at Gillette's International Marketing Department (GIMD) in Boston. The staff was responsible for interacting with regional and country level managers on marketing, planning, and strategic issues and would set priorities for introduction when a supply of products was limited.

Reporting to Gillette International's president were four regional managers, each responsible for a group of markets. The Gillette Industries Group in London controlled Gillette operations in the United Kingdom and South Africa and export operations to Ireland, Iceland, Greece, Eastern Europe, the Middle East, and Africa. The group's only manufacturing facility was located in the United Kingdom.

Also located in London was the Continental Group with responsibility for subsidiaries in France, Germany, Spain, and Italy. The Continental Group also controlled the marketing operations of affiliated sales companies in Scandinavia, the Benelux countries, Portugal, Switzerland, and Austria. This group's plant facilities were located in Germany, France, and Spain.

Gillette International's other two regional operations were based in Boston. The Latin America Group headed subsidiary operations in Argentina, Brazil, Colombia, Mexico, and Venezuela and was responsible for export and sales in Chile, Peru, Puerto Rico, and all of the countries in Central America and the Caribbean area. The group's manufacturing plants were located in Brazil, Argentina, Colombia, and Mexico.

Gillette International's fourth regional group was the Australasian Group with responsibility for Australia, New Zealand, Japan, Hong Kong, and Southeast Asia. Its major plant facility was located in Australia.

THE DEVELOPMENT OF SHAVING TECHNOLOGY

Carbon Steel Blades

King C. Gillette, the company founder, introduced the first safety razor in 1895. The company was granted an exclusive patent in 1904 on an improved version of its blade which was followed by the development of the double-edged blade. In the 1930s, Gillette introduced carbon steel blades under the brand name Gillette Blue. These blades were thinner than earlier blades, had lacquer applied to the surface and offered an improvement in shaving comfort and blade life.

The introduction of the Super Blue blade in 1960 represented a quantum step in technology. The Super Blue came with a silicon coated treatment which was baked on to give it extra hardness. This new process significantly improved the quality of shaving, although the shave quality tended to decline more rapidly than with previous blades after reaching a certain point. The blade was priced at 6.9 cents per unit and quickly became the standard in the industry. Customers once accustomed to the more comfortable shave of the Super Blue found it very difficult to return to the older carbon blades. For about 18 months, Gillette was able to exploit this product advantage

before competitors could introduce similar products.

Stainless Steel Blades

In August 1961, another quantum leap in shaving technology occurred, when Wilkinson Sword, a U.K. company, introduced a Teflon coated stainless steel blade. The coating process was actually developed earlier by Gillette and Wilkinson paid a royalty to Gillette for its use. Stainless steel was much harder than carbon steel and could absorb the high temperature generated in the Teflon coating process. However, because of this hardness a stainless steel blade could not be sharpened as easily as a carbon blade. Stainless steel blades offered a high quality shave consistent over a relatively long time and were a considerable improvement for the user over carbon steel blades. Wilkinson introduced its new blade first in the United Kingdom and then launched it in the United States, but did not have sufficient supply to satisfy the entire U.S. market. In response, both Gillette and Schick, the principal U.S. competitors, countered with crash development programs before Wilkinson could become fully established in major markets.

In 1963, Gillette introduced a Teflon coated stainless steel blade under the brand name Stainless (Silver Gillette in Europe). The major hurdle to overcome was the manufacturing process as the new blades required specially designed equipment. The Stainless blades were improved by a factor of 2 to 3 in blade life over the carbon, double-edged blades. Gillette was able to maintain market leadership in the United States because Wilkinson moved too cautiously with its product roll-out and did not have a fully developed marketing function.

In 1965, Gillette introduced its first modern shaving system consisting of the Techmatic razor band technology. Rather than using single blades one after another, the Techmatic came equipped with a cartridge that contained a band of blades. The user would never have to touch a single blade, thus the Techmatic offered added convenience although blade quality was equal to the stainless steel blades. Techmatic's introduction was well-timed and had a lead of six months over all competitors, resulting in a 2 percent gain in market share. The Techmatic was Gillette's first entry into shaving systems other than the double-edged blade.

Platinum Treated Blades

In 1969, Gillette made another improvement in its blades by adding a platinum chromium alloy. This new blade, marketed in the United States under the brand name Platinum Plus, further increased blade life and shaving comfort, but was not considered a technological breakthrough. The blade was also introduced in European markets under various names which included the word "platinum."

In 1970 it was once more Wilkinson of the United Kingdom reaching the market with an innovation. Wilkinson launched its Wilkinson "Bonded" blade, consisting of a single blade enclosed in a plastic casing. The term "Bonded" meant that the blade remained permanently fixed in a cartridge. Although Gillette had been working on a twin blade cartridge, it was not ready for product launch at the time of the Wilkinson introduction. Fortunately for Gillette, Wilkinson did not have sufficient resources to make a major impact on the market.

In 1971, after combining Techmatic plastics knowledge with an innovative twin blade design, Gillette introduced the TRAC II. This was a major evolution from the single blade, double-edged razor and provided an entirely new concept in blade making. Although Wilkinson's "Bonded" razor gave the public its first experience with a cartridge product, the TRAC II represented the next step forward in cartridge design. Combined with Gillette's previous blade expertise, this shaving product was the most advanced in the industry in terms of quality and blade life (see Exhibit 3).

COMPETITION

Gillette Experience Prior to 1960

During the early development of the shaving industry, Gillette had almost no significant compe-

tition. The company got its first major break during World War I when U.S. soldiers were required to be clean shaven. By the end of the war, Gillette had sold some 3.5 million razors and about 52 million blades to the military forces giving Gillette a substantial advantage over other razor companies. Another big step occurred in 1939 when Gillette spent 50 percent of its entire advertising budget to sponsor the U.S. baseball World Series. By World War II, Gillette had the dominant share of the blade market. Market shares reached an all-time high in the early 1940s with 55–60 percent in the double-edged segment and about 40 percent of the entire market. The advent of television gave Gillette another boost.

Gillette did not face real double-edged blade competition in the United States or abroad until the early 1960s. Before that time, Wilkinson of the United Kingdom was not a major factor and Schick was only of minor concern in the United States. Gillette was much more concerned with electric razors, particularly abroad, where the pricing of electric shavers tended to be lower than in the United States. With a smaller price gap between electric and wet shaving and with many customers preferring electric over wet shaving, Gillette was gaining market share in a stagnant or even declining segment.

Recent Developments: The Platinum Plus Experience

Gillette International's latest worldwide product introduction was the launch of Platinum Plus blades in early 1970. The Platinum Plus represented a product improvement and had been well received in the United States in the fall of 1969. In 1970, a number of key foreign markets were offered access to the Platinum Plus technology. However, because production machinery was only available in limited volume, Gillette had to introduce the product selectively. By 1972, all markets had been introduced to the Platinum Plus blade albeit with varied success.

From the outset, Gillette International gave its local managers considerable freedom in selecting the positioning strategy for the new blade. As a result, different countries chose different strate-

EXHIBIT 3 ● Blade Quality vs. Blade Life

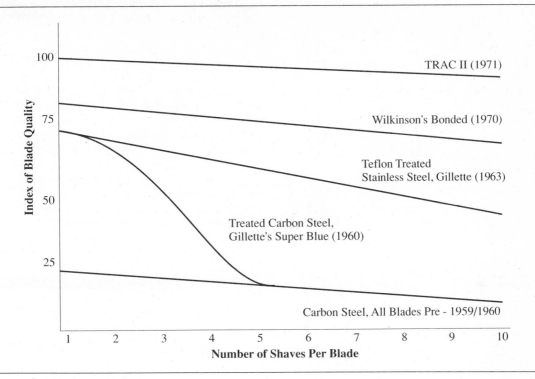

Source: Company records.

gies. Some market introductions were unsuccessful by Gillette standards, and the company wanted to learn from these mistakes before introducing the TRAC II.

After reviewing the introduction of Platinum Plus in Europe, management came to a consensus on what had gone wrong. To gain further insight on the European scene, management looked closely at the U.K., German, and Brazilian experiences.

The U.K. subsidiary, faced with intensive competition in the U.K. market and a scarcity of retail shelf space, had decided to introduce Platinum Plus as its new top-of-the-line blade in place of Super Silver. Super Silver and Wilkinson's top

blade had been similarly priced and selling at about the same volume. When Gillette withdrew Super Silver and introduced the higher priced Platinum Plus (with platinum coating), the company lost some of its share to Wilkinson because some users were unwilling to upgrade to the new product. As a result, Gillette lost overall market share and had not been able to regain it.

In Germany, the Gillette subsidiary also faced intensive competition from Wilkinson. With a surplus of blade products in the retail trade, the German subsidiary opted to provide an improved product by adding a platinum coating to its top-of-the-line brand Super Silver and introduce the new product as Super Silver Platine.

However, this variation brought only mixed success for Gillette.

By contrast, the Brazilian operations went ahead with the largely U.S. type strategy, by adding the new Platinum Plus to its existing product line which included the Super Silver. This strategy proved successful. As a result of the Platinum Plus experience, management at Gillette International felt that local management should not decide on the introductory program. Rather than local companies proposing their own strategies, Gillette International's management preferred to give the local subsidiaries detailed instructions. If the decision did not suit the local market, then local management could argue its case. At the start, however, there would be a more standardized marketing and positioning strategy largely based on the U.S. experience.

Schick in the US and Abroad

Schick, a fully-owned subsidiary of Warner Lambert, was Gillette's major competitor. Schick Safety Razor Co. manufactured injector and double-edged blades in the United States, Canada, Sweden, and the Netherlands as well as in Japan, where Schick was the dominant company in the wet shaving segment. Sales of Schick in 1972 were estimated at $47 million. In the United States and most other markets, Schick's market share was about one-third of Gillette's or less.

Schick's marketing strategy tended to emphasize print advertising or promotions such as free samples, in-store displays, or write-in offers. Schick was capable of introducing new blade types quickly and could be expected to react to Gillette within 12 to 18 months after a new product introduction. But, like Gillette, Schick was constrained by the scarcity of machinery needed to introduce new products. In January 1972, Schick had entered Schick Super II, a product similar to TRAC II, into the shaving system market on the West coast of the United States. By mid-1972, however, Schick Super II had still not reached full national distribution. Full-scale national television support had also not yet taken place. Most television ex-

posure in the U.S. market was through partial sponsorship of the 1972 summer Olympics which were going on at the time.

Wilkinson on All Continents

Wilkinson, a British company, was not a serious competitor to Gillette until it introduced a treated stainless steel blade in 1961. Wilkinson had been marketing an untreated stainless blade since the mid-1950s with little success. Total sales for 1971 amounted to about £24 million ($60 million) of which the shaving portion accounted for about £18 million ($40 million). Wilkinson had experienced growth rates of 20 percent in recent years and had approximately 75 percent of its sales overseas.

Wilkinson operated its main manufacturing facilities in the United Kingdom where it employed more than 1,300 people. The company's only other full manufacturing facility was in West Germany. Partial manufacturing and packaging were done in the United States, Australia, South Africa, and Spain.

When the treated, stainless steel blade was first introduced, Wilkinson did not have sufficient capacity to satisfy demand and the result was only a 20 percent erosion of Gillette's U.K. market share. After its introduction in the United Kingdom, Wilkinson moved into the West German market in 1962 and, on a limited basis, into the United States at the end of 1962. In addition to capacity constraints, Wilkinson did not have a fully developed marketing operation outside its key markets and, thus, could never capitalize on the Teflon coated stainless steel blade. The only exception was the U.K. market where Wilkinson's market share was larger than Gillette's.

Wilkinson's market share and market position differed considerably from market to market. As the major domestic producer, Wilkinson enjoyed a large share of the U.K. market. Its introduction of the "Bonded" razor ahead of Gillette had helped consolidate its market share further. It was estimated that Wilkinson's share was moving close to 50 percent for all blades sold in the United

Kingdom. In Germany, Wilkinson continued to defend its share of about 30 percent. The same local subsidiary was also responsible for selling in Austria and Switzerland, where the company's market share had been increasing.

In Italy, Wilkinson had been able to increase its market share to about 20 percent as a result of introducing the Wilkinson "Bonded" system. Although Wilkinson maintained its own subsidiary in Italy, sales and distribution were handled by Colgate-Palmolive. In France, distribution and marketing were in the hands of Reckitt & Colman. In Spain, the company had started construction of full-scale manufacturing facilities which were expected to come on stream in 1974.

In other European countries, Wilkinson also relied on the distribution arrangements with established consumer products companies. In Denmark, Norway, Sweden, and Holland, Wilkinson products were marketed by Colgate-Palmolive. Wilkinson blades were marketed in Greece by Unilever, one of the world's largest consumer products companies, and in Ireland by Beecham, a U.K.-based personal products company. Distribution was also handled by Reckitt & Colman in South Africa where Wilkinson's share had increased beyond 10 percent with the introduction of the "Bonded" blade. Wilkinson blades were also distributed in many Middle Eastern countries out of a Beirut office.

In Asia, Wilkinson blades were marketed in Japan, Australia, and New Zealand. The Australian market position improved considerably with the introduction of the "Bonded" blade. In Japan, Wilkinson was marketed through Lion, a major Japanese personal products company.

In the United States, where Wilkinson's share was about 10 percent, marketing had been handled exclusively since 1970 by Colgate-Palmolive, the large U.S.-based multinational consumer products company. In Canada, where Wilkinson had a market share of about 20 percent, its blades were distributed by John A. Houston Ltd. Throughout Latin America, Wilkinson used independent distributors to market in Brazil, Colombia, the Dominican Republic, Haiti, Paraguay, Uruguay, and Venezuela.

THE TRAC II OPPORTUNITY

Manufacturing Overview

The manufacturing process of the TRAC II system consisted of three distinct phases: the manufacturing of the blade, the manufacturing of cartridge parts, and the assembly of these blades and cartridge parts into the TRAC II system. Each one of these stages offered particular challenges to Gillette. The key problem, however, had turned from making the system work to adding sufficient capacity. Although it was difficult to forecast exactly how much blade capacity would be available for Gillette International, it was felt that each gain in annual volume of 150 million units would take 12 to 18 months.

Blade Manufacture

The blade manufacturing process alone consisted of six stages. In the first stage a continuous strip of soft steel, purchased in coils the width of one blade, was mounted on a wheel for perforation. Perforations in the steel served as guides for additional blade cartridge components and also enabled soap and water to pass through. Oil used in cutting these perforations was removed before the steel passed into a hardening furnace with three temperature zones. The hardening gave the blades an extended life of 11 to 14 shaves. After leaving the furnace, the steel was cooled in an annealing process before being rewound onto a wheel for sharpening.

In the sharpening process, the perforated and hardened steel strip was ground to remove rough steel from the blade's cutting edge, followed by rough sharpening and honing (refined sharpening process). Once the honing process had put a cutting edge on the blade, the steel strip was cut into individual blade lengths and the individual blades airblown onto blade holders. Blade holders transferred stacks of razor blades to blade magazines which passed through a washing cycle before vacuum phase sputtering.

The contents of each magazine were automatically unloaded onto a sputtering knife. Twelve sputtering knives were positioned around a sputtering post of chromium and platinum with the cutting edge of the razor blades facing the sputtering post. Using a technique known as ion deposition, chromium and platinum were transferred from the sputtering post to the blades' cutting edge.

In the final step, the blade edges were coated with Teflon and passed through a sintering furnace which baked the Teflon onto the blade and enhanced the bonding of chromium and platinum to the razor's cutting surface.

Cartridge Assembly

Each TRAC II cartridge contained two individual razor blades, as well as several plastic and metal parts. Cartridge assembly began with black plastic guard caps that were fed from a bowl of caps into a chute, with each cap positioned so that its plastic alignment studs were face up.

The first razor blade in the cartridge assembly was set on a guard cap with the plastic alignment studs passing through the blade perforations. A spacer was set on top of the first blade, followed by a second blade and, lastly, the top plastic guard cap. This was a very delicate operation since the relationship of the two blades to the cartridge was critical to providing shaving comfort. A slight pressure was applied to seal the assembled cartridge before it was moved to an automated inspection stage.

If the automated scanning device verified that all parts were included and properly aligned in the cartridge assembly, the cartridge was relayed to a dispenser tray. A plastic cartridge dispenser was positioned over the dispenser tray and five TRAC II cartridges pressed into place. Once assembled, these dispensers were transported to another area for final packaging. (For an overview of the manufacturing process, see Exhibit 4).

Equipment as Bottleneck

Manufacturing equipment for the production of razor blades had specific requirements and was not purchased on the open market. Instead, Gillette produced its own equipment in company-owned tool shops in Boston, the United Kingdom, and France. For TRAC II production, new equipment was needed for blade perforation, hardening, and sharpening. New equipment was also needed for the production of plastic elements such as guard caps and dispensers as well as for assembly and loading operations. The longest lead times (12 to 18 months) were for the procurement of sharpening equipment. For plastic parts production, molds had to be produced which also required high precision tools.

For years, Gillette tool shops had been operating at full capacity. In recent years, Gillette had suffered from undercapacity in production with output often a step or two behind actual demand for Gillette blades. As a result, Gillette's top management decided to add to existing capacity so that manufacturing capacity would always exceed demand by 10 percent. Consequently, just when the tool shops were busy providing this additional equipment, TRAC II increased the burden even more. It was estimated that Gillette was able to add about 150 million units of TRAC II (dispensers containing five cartridges) every 12 months, or about 12.5 million units per month. The Boston plant was using all its output to satisfy demand in the United States and the North American division wanted still more products out of the newly planned capacity expansion. Given the nature of tool production, there was no short-term solution for expanding total output beyond the rate of 12.5 million units per month.[1]

PRICING ISSUES

Pricing was a main consideration in the launch of TRAC II abroad. Gillette International viewed pricing as the key to increasing market share and to maintaining or improving margins in each market. Pricing was dependent on a number of factors, any one of which could be used as a basis for selecting a final price policy. These factors were: production costs, marketing costs, and competitor pricing.

1. The 150 million dispensers refer to annualized capacity increase, for example, after 12 months, the annualized output for the next 12 months would be increased by 150 million units (or 750 million blades).

EXHIBIT 4 ● Gillette TRAC II Manufacturing Overview

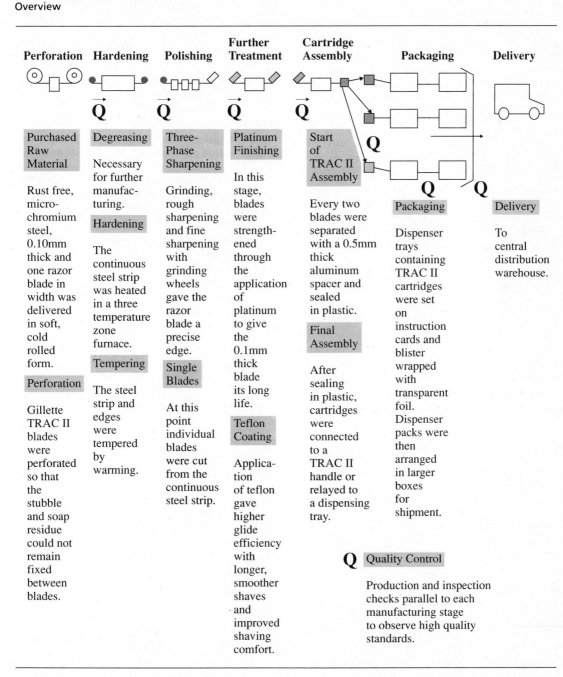

Perforation	Hardening	Polishing	Further Treatment	Cartridge Assembly	Packaging	Delivery

Purchased Raw Material

Rust free, micro-chromium steel, 0.10mm thick and one razor blade in width was delivered in soft, cold rolled form.

Perforation

Gillette TRAC II blades were perforated so that the stubble and soap residue could not remain fixed between blades.

Degreasing

Necessary for further manufacturing.

Hardening

The continuous steel strip was heated in a three temperature zone furnace.

Tempering

The steel strip and edges were tempered by warming.

Three-Phase Sharpening

Grinding, rough sharpening and fine sharpening with grinding wheels gave the razor blade a precise edge.

Single Blades

At this point individual blades were cut from the continuous steel strip.

Platinum Finishing

In this stage, blades were strengthened through the application of platinum to give the 0.1mm thick blade its long life.

Teflon Coating

Application of teflon gave higher glide efficiency with longer, smoother shaves and improved shaving comfort.

Start of TRAC II Assembly

Every two blades were separated with a 0.5mm thick aluminum spacer and sealed in plastic.

Final Assembly

After sealing in plastic, cartridges were connected to a TRAC II handle or relayed to a dispensing tray.

Packaging

Dispenser trays containing TRAC II cartridges were set on instruction cards and blister wrapped with transparent foil. Dispenser packs were then arranged in larger boxes for shipment.

Delivery

To central distribution warehouse.

Q **Quality Control**

Production and inspection checks parallel to each manufacturing stage to observe high quality standards.

Pricing Based on Production Costs

Production costs at Gillette were classified into two parts: manufacturing costs and initial investments costs. Manufacturing costs were defined as the sum of direct material, direct labor, and variable manufacturing overhead. The manufacturing costs of the new TRAC II were about twice the cost of the Platinum Plus blade which averaged $.03 per unit. Initial investment costs for new processes at Gillette were normally 20 percent higher than prior blade processes. Added capital investment for the TRAC II, however, was substantially higher than previous blade manufacturing processes because of the technology level and amounted to $10 million per 100 million units (dispensers at 5 blades each). As with the older line of blades, these investment costs would be reduced over time as volume increased and added equipment depreciated. A typical depreciation period was about six years. If the TRAC II were priced on the basis of total production costs, Gillette's typical ex-factory price for blades would give the company a gross margin of 70 percent. Out of this gross margin, the company would have to cover all direct marketing and general administrative expenses.

Pricing Based on Marketing Costs

Gillette's marketing costs tended to be higher for a new brand since the bulk of advertising expenditures would shift to the latest product. At the time of the TRAC II introduction, advertising expenditures for overseas markets were concentrated on Techmatic and Platinum Plus. If these expenditures were to be shifted to the TRAC II, management needed to decide on the changeover rate. Under ideal circumstances, these expenditures could be shifted at the same rate as customers upgraded brands. In the United States, the Marketing Research Group had charted trade-up patterns since 1960. When the Super Blue was introduced, it cannibalized Blue Blade sales, enabling Super Blue to achieve predominant market share after only 18 months. Similarly, when Platinum Plus was added to Gillette's product line, customers traded up from the stainless steel blade at roughly the same rate. This type of data was not

available for countries other than the United States, but management felt it could use these data as an estimate for trends in the European marketplace.

Initial interest in and purchase of the TRAC II was particularly dependent on two things. One was the newness of the product. Management in Boston felt that once the TRAC II was launched, there would be a certain period of vulnerability because of its level of sophistication. Whether trading up from a previous Gillette product or switching brands, a consumer would have to spend an initial $1.50 for a TRAC II handle to accommodate TRAC II cartridges. Secondly, therefore, the potential for cartridge sales was dependent on the number of TRAC II handles. The only experience Gillette had had with such a sophisticated trade-up was the Techmatic. Excluding the Techmatic, all of Gillette's other successor blades were compatible with the same razor handle. Hence, the level of advertising had to be sufficient to generate early sales of the sophisticated TRAC II while at the same time balance demand with a limited supply in each key market.

EXHIBIT 5 ● Size of Key Markets

Market	*Estimated blade sales (1972) (in millions of blades)*
United States	1772
United Kingdom	361
West Germany	296
France	429
Italy	266
Spain	160
Canada	170
Argentina	250
Brazil	500
Mexico	310
Sweden	35
Holland	50
Japan	1300

Source: Company records.

EXHIBIT 6 ● Key Market Shaving Data

	Male population in millions	Percentage of wet shavers	Share of market*			Manufacturing		
			G	S	W	G	S	W
U.S.A.	67.6	73	58	23	10	X	X	
U.K.	19.7	72	40	3	42	X		X
W. Germany	21.7	40	59	6	31	X		X
France	17.4	50	65	23	5	X		
Italy	17.2	74	65	3	19			
Spain	11.7	48	70	17	4	X		X
Canada	7.4	58	55	23	19	X	X	
Argentina	8.1	75	95	1	0	X		
Brazil	21.5	97	85	3	4	X		
Mexico	10.0	95	80	5	0	X		
Sweden	3.1	39	54	45	1		X	
Holland	4.6	32	60	30	3		X	
Japan	40.0 (approx.)	n.a.	14	64	n.a.			

Source: Company records.
*Share of Male Wet Shavers
n.a. = not available.

G = Gillette
S = Schick
W = Wilkinson

Pricing to Gain Market Share

The pricing policy chosen to cover production costs and advertising expenses would certainly influence market share. In the past, a new product would be priced at a certain premium over its predecessor. The size of this price premium would have varying effects on resulting market share. Given Gillette's pricing strategy with country by country differences, adding a 10–20 percent premium for a sophisticated new product such as TRAC II could result in success in some markets and low performance in others.

Past new product introductions served as an example. On average, Gillette's Super Blue sold at a 38 percent premium over Gillette's Blue. The first stainless steel blade, marketed as Super Silver in most European markets, was sold at about twice the retail price of the Super Blue.

The Gillette Techmatic was marketed at a substantial premium over the Platinum Plus. The amount of this price premium depended on the various competitive factors and differed from market to market. In 1971, the premium was about 50 percent over the Stainless Steel in both Germany and the United Kingdom. However, the price base was not identical and actual retail prices for the two markets differed.

Given the key market data in Exhibits 5 and 6, Gillette management was concerned with creating a pricing policy that would lead to intracompany trade up as well as intercompany brand switching.

Options for Gillette International

Having reviewed the manufacturing costs and anticipated demand patterns, Gillette management considered three pricing strategies: (1) in accordance with production cost differences; (2) at a constant premium over the now top Platinum Plus; or (3) at a uniform world price for all countries.

Pricing in relation to production costs would allow Gillette its existing margin structure and would take into consideration the new equipment investment. On the other hand, there were some markets where margins were lower than desired and a constant margin would not increase margins in these countries.

If management chose to price at a constant premium, there would be a real potential for price differences between markets. Such price differences between markets would not be easy to equilibrate once a product had been established at a certain price level. Furthermore, the differences could lead to product arbitrage (parallel imports).

The threat of parallel imports had always been a problem for Gillette and encouraged some managers to support the world pricing policy. Although this policy would alleviate parallel imports, it could put the TRAC II price out of reach in some markets which would affect market share. And, although this policy would reduce product arbitrage, a uniform price would open up doors to competitors with various lower cost products and with identical products priced at a lower level.

Whichever policy was chosen, Gillette's management constantly had to keep the competition in mind. Gillette had to continue and increase its TRAC II supply with one-third of all new output going to the U.S. market. The decision to go international had been made, but only the remaining two-thirds of new output could be spread among those key markets.

Gillette had to move rapidly to reach its overseas markets before Schick introduced its Super II and before Wilkinson had a replacement for its own "Bonded" blade. The importance of getting to a market first was reinforced by the Marketing Research Group's findings on timing and market share. That meant, all things being equal regarding pricing, quality of product, and distribution, that the market share potentials to the second, third, and fourth entrants would be no more than 30 percent, 18 percent, and 12 percent respectively, of the market leader.

Based on previous experience, the window of opportunity for the TRAC II would last 12 to 18 months. Given that this time lead represented the number of months Schick and Wilkinson needed to invest several million dollars to achieve production capability, management had to make its decisions soon. Furthermore, the precise combination of pricing policy and selected target markets had to match and preserve Gillette's image as world leader in the shaving industry.

CASE 2

Wiltech India Limited (A)

In August 1983, Malay Chadha and Suresh Metha,[1] General Manager and Marketing Manager of Wiltech shaving products, were reviewing the preceding year's sales. Wiltech had introduced a complete line of five products in July 1982 and had succeeded in associating the Wiltech name with the quality image and reputation of Wilkinson Sword. However, actual sales had been far below target figures and the low sales volume contrasted poorly to industry-wide sales of 1,850 million rupees vs Wiltech's 27 million rupees.[2] Therefore, Chadha and Metha had to consider what changes in Wiltech's marketing program could increase sales to the desired level. Such changes would require a complete review of Wiltech's pricing, advertising, and distribution strategies. Wiltech needed to improve the near-term situation, while also considering its long-term goal to become India's market leader in shaving products. In addition, an established multinational competitor was planning new plant construction.

Metha felt that prices could be maintained if Wiltech introduced one new blade and positioned its existing five brands more effectively. Chadha, on the other hand, believed that Wiltech had focused too much on India's wealthier segments and that prices should be adjusted. Chadha also saw that export opportunities existed and strongly favored trading with the Soviet Union. A detailed plan had to be ready in one week for presentation to the board. Despite this deadline, Chadha and Metha were unable after two days to agree on what Wiltech's problems were and how to correct them. High humidity and record temperatures did not help spirits as the two resumed their discussion.

1. Disguised names.
2. 10 rupees (Rs) = $1 in 1983.

WILTECH BACKGROUND

In 1979 Wilkinson Sword, the UK shaving systems company, entered into a licensing agreement to expand its international presence into India. Wiltech, for Wilkinson technology, was funded by Asian Cables Corporation Limited and the government-owned Karnataka State Industrial Investment Development Corporation. Equity participation was shared among Asian Cables (25 percent), the state government (26 percent), and the public (49 percent). The licensing agreement required Wilkinson to construct a manufacturing facility in Belagola, 100 miles from the central Wiltech office in Bangalore, Karnataka (see Exhibit 1). Wiltech's licensing terms included the following payments to Wilkinson:

This case was prepared by Robert Howard under the direction of Jean-Pierre Jeannet, Visiting Professor at IMEDE and Professor of Marketing and International Business at Babson College. This case was prepared for class discussion rather than to illustrate either effective or ineffective handling of an administrative situation. This case was based on earlier work by Sameer Kaji, M.B.A. candidate at Babson College. Copyright© 1988 by IMEDE, Lausanne, Switzerland. The International Institute for Management Development (IMD), resulting from the merger between IMEDE, Lausanne, and IMI, Geneva, acquires and retains all rights. Reproduced by permission.

EXHIBIT 1 ● The Indian Subcontinent

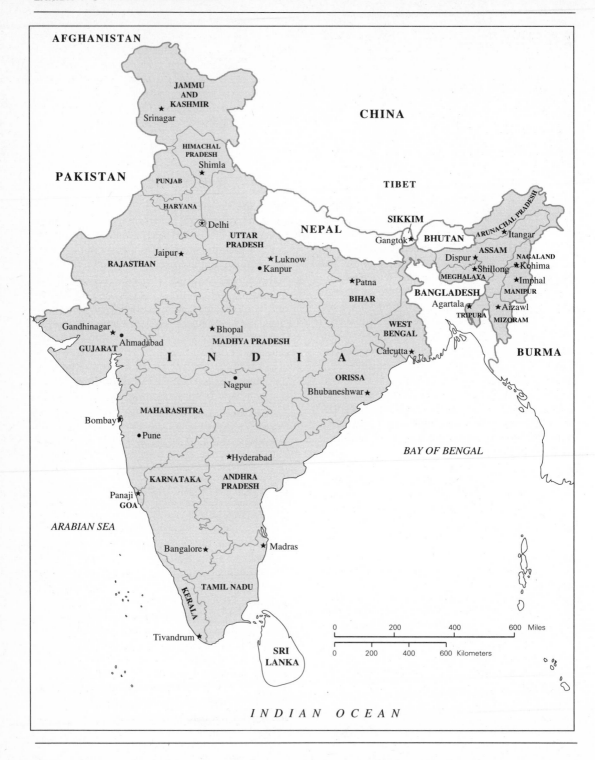

1. £130,000[3] for design, drawings, and documentation
2. £260,000 for plant installation and commissioning
3. From the start of commercial production, a 2 percent royalty on all products sold up to five years or £175,000 whichever came first

Wilkinson paid a tax of 20 percent to the Indian government on items 1 and 2 in three installments. A gratis time commitment of 7,840 man hours by Wilkinson engineers was also included in this payment plan. Moreover, to ensure continued interest in the project, Wilkinson's chief executive and technical director were appointed to Wiltech's board of directors.

Wilkinson's Role in Shaving History

Wilkinson Sword was founded by Henry Nock in 1772 to manufacture personal and military defense weapons. Nock and his partner, James Wilkinson, emphasized close tolerances, quality control, and innovation in the design of their products. This attention to detail led to being appointed gun and swordmakers for the British royalty—an honor which has continued to the present day. Henry Wilkinson, son of James, took full control of the business in 1825 and, in 1898, extended Wilkinson's image as a maker of quality steel cutting edges from swords to razor blades. Starting with the Pall Mall safety razor, Wilkinson maintained its position as a leader in shaving comfort and technology and pioneered several shaving breakthroughs.

One of Wilkinson's more recent innovations was the use of stainless steel. Double-edged carbon steel blades had been the industry norm until Wilkinson introduced its double-edged, stainless steel blades in 1956. Wilkinson developed their stainless steel blades further by coating them with Teflon and introduced these to the marketplace in 1961. A combination of product quality and a two-year lead time allowed Wilkinson to increase its UK market share from 7 percent to 45 percent with similar gains in other countries. In 1970 Wil-

3. £0.66 = $1.

kinson championed another first in shaving technology when it launched its bonded shaving system. The bonded shaving system, which contained a single blade permanently fixed inside a cartridge, was available throughout the world by the end of 1974. And, in 1976, Wilkinson introduced its adjustable twin blade cartridge system, similar to the Gillette TRAC II.

THE INDIAN MARKET

India in Transition

After gaining political independence from Great Britain in 1947, India attempted a series of centrally planned economic programs. From 1950 onward, however, the rate of economic expansion continued to remain only 1.5 percent ahead of the rate of population growth. Attempts to speed up India's growth rate began in the 1970s when forces emerged calling for reforms to move the country away from the planning process by freeing the private sector, reducing the dominance of the public sector and liberalizing import policy insofar as it restricted the importation of new technologies.

Indira Gandhi accelerated these efforts to attract foreign investment and raise the standard of living. Attempts to attract foreign business did not, however, include relaxing the laws on foreign ownership. India's leaders were concerned about foreign exchange shortages and, as a result, preferred to encourage the production of import substitutes and licensing arrangements with foreign firms. Although Wilkinson Sword was the first to negotiate such a licensing arrangement in the shaving industry, it was inevitable that other multinational competitors would soon follow.

Such firms were attracted to the Indian shaving market for a number of reasons, one of which was its potential size. In 1981, India's population was estimated at 685 million and was expected to reach 844 million by 1990 and 994 million by 2000. This population was slow at urbanization by Western standards and only 23 percent of the country resided in urban areas. Within this group of 156 million urban dwellers, 42 million (27 percent) lived in India's 12 metropolitan cities (see Exhibit 2). India's youth represented a dispropor-

EXHIBIT 2 ● Distribution and Growth of India's Population[1]

	1981	*1971*	*1961*	*1951*	*1901*
Number of Towns	3245	2636	2421	2890	1851
Urban Population (In Millions)	156.2	109.1	78.9	62.4	25.9
Urban as a Percentage of Total Population	23.3	19.9	18.0	17.3	10.8
Percentage of Towns					
Class I (Includes Metro. Cities[2])	6.7	5.6	4.3	2.6	1.4
Class II	8.3	6.9	5.4	3.3	2.3
Class III	22.8	22.1	19.0	11.6	7.4
Class IV	32.3	33.1	30.8	21.8	21.4
Class V	22.9	25.7	31.5	40.0	40.9
Class VI	7.1	6.5	9.1	20.6	26.7
Total	100.0	100.0	100.0	100.0	100.0
Percentage of Urban Population in					
Class I	60.4	55.8	50.2	43.4	25.8
Class II	11.7	11.3	11.1	10.4	10.8
Class III	14.4	16.3	17.5	16.0	16.0
Class IV	9.5	11.3	13.0	14.0	20.9
Class V	3.6	4.7	7.3	13.1	20.2
Class VI	0.5	0.5	0.9	3.2	6.3
Total	100.0	100.0	100.0	100.0	100.0

1. The definition of "urban" adopted in the 1981 census, as in the previous two censuses, was as follows
    (a) All statutory towns with a Municipal Corporation, Municipal Board, Cantonment Board or Notified Town Area, etc.
    (b) All other places with (i) a minimum population of 5,000, (ii) at least 75% of male working population engaged in non-agricultural and allied activity, and (iii) a density of population of at least 400 per square kilometer (1000 per sq. mile).
    An urban agglomeration is defined as one consisting of one or more towns including in some cases villages or parts of a village which can be considered as urbanized and contiguous to the town or towns concerned.
    Urban agglomeration has been treated as a single unit. Class I towns (called cities) are those with a population of 100,000 and above; Class II: 50,000 to 99,999;
    Class III: 20,000 to 49,999; Class IV: 10,000 to 19,999; Class V: 5,000 to 9,999 and Class VI: less than 5,000.
    All figures for 1981 except the All-India urban ratio (23.3%) exclude Assam and Jammu and Kashmir.
2. Metropolitan cities have populations of 1,000,000 or more and include: Calcutta, Bombay, Delhi, Madras, Bangalore, Hyderabad, Ahmadabad, Kanpur, Pune, Nagpur, Lucknow, and Jaipur.
Source: Statistical Outline of India 1986–1987. Tata Services Limited, Department of Economics and Statistics, Bombay House, Bombay, pp. 32, 46. Reprinted by permission.

EXHIBIT 3 ● Age Distribution of India's Population

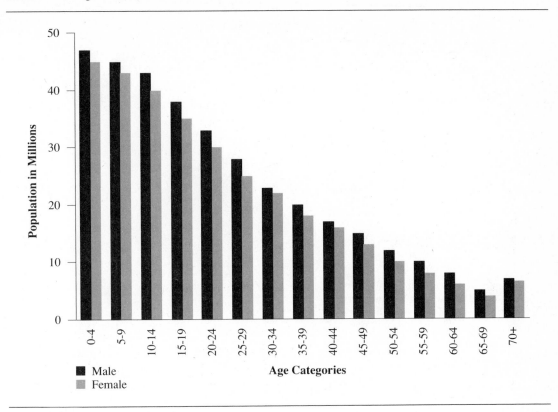

■ Male
■ Female

Age Categories

tionate amount of the total population with 40 percent of the country under the age of 15 and only 9 percent of the country 55 or older (see Exhibit 3).

Exacting descriptions of Indian society by income level were not available. Instead, the Center for Monitoring the Indian Economy classified Indian society into approximate income groups according to five member families (see Exhibit 4). Beyond an urban versus rural reference, information in Exhibit 4 did not indicate how India's consumer wealth was distributed countrywide. This data was available on a per capita income basis for each of India's states (see Exhibit 5).

In addition to a tremendous diversity in pop-

ulation and income distribution, there were 15 major languages, 1,650 dialects and several religions spread throughout India's 25 states and union territories. This diversity made it difficult to come up with any one best description of an "average" consumer in the shaving market. There was sufficient evidence, however, that indicated the majority of Indian males shaved each day and that it was considered a prerequisite prior to beginning the day's activities. Those who did not shave were considered unclean and unable to participate in religious practices or other daily activities. The research also revealed that consumers were dissatisfied with India's current shaving products yet were unaware of alternatives.

EXHIBIT 4 ● Structure of Indian Society

Position	Group	Annual income per five-member family	Education	Standard of living
Top 1%—ruling elites living in larger cities	(a) Big owners of all types of business and property (land, factories, trading, transport, contracting, and brokering) (b) Leaders of central, state, and local governments, cooperatives, and ruling parties; most members of central and state legislatures (c) Top leaders of large national or metropolitan trade unions	> Rs. 500,000	Varies	Opulent; conspicuous consumers
Next 4%—supporting power elite living in cities	(a) Medium owners of business and property, and very rich farmers (b) Second-rank political leaders of ruling parties and first-rank leaders of opposition parties (c) Top bureaucrats and technocrats at all levels of government (d) Top executives in large public- and private-sector business units (e) More affluent self-employed professionals (doctors, lawyers, etc.)	Rs. 100,000–500,000	Generally well-educated (tertiary level)	Fairly affluent; good housing, furnishings, cars, TVs, telephones, sound systems, other durables
Next 5%—relatively prosperous by Indian standards; living in urban areas	(a) Small property owners and rich farmers (b) Petty bureaucrats, junior and medium business executives, and other supervisory cadre (c) Workers and employees organized in unions (d) Second-rank leaders of large trade unions; (e) Less affluent self-employed (f) Others in "middle-class"	Rs. 15,000–100,000	Generally well-educated	Generally good housing, moderately furnished, some durables

EXHIBIT 4 ● Structure of Indian Society (*cont.*)

Position	Group	Annual income per five-member family	Education	Standard of living
Next 10%—above average by Indian standards; living in urban areas	(a) Upper-middle farmers (b) Owners of very small business and property (c) Supervisory and lower staff in unorganized business (d) Others regarded as lower middle class	Rs. 10,000–15,000	Poorly educated but literate	Barely tolerable housing and furnishing; some durables
Next 30%—barely above poverty line; living in towns and large villages	(a) Middle farmers (b) Lowest layers of employees in unorganized sector (c) Lowest layer of self-employed (d) Urban people in low-paid jobs	Rs. 6,000–10,000	Half literate, other half illiterate	Level of poverty visible to visitors
Last 50%—below poverty line; living in villages	(a) Poor farmers (b) Irregularly employed, underemployed, and unemployed (c)Tribals/scheduled castes (d) Landless agricultural laborers	< Rs. 6,000	Illiterate	Abject poverty, bare subsistence

Note: Indications and figures are approximate and indicate only broad magnitudes. Incomes include fringe benefits, open and hidden perquisites, and black-market income. Farmers generally live in villages, but some have been grouped with the urban population for simplification of presentation.
Source: India: Limited Avenues to an Unlimited Market, Business International, 1985, pp. 14–15. Reprinted by permission.

The government expansion of agricultural and social programs as well as the more liberal industrial policies created enthusiasm for investment as India entered the mid-1980s. Hence, with the indications that consumers were ready for alternative shaving products, Wiltech saw an excellent chance to secure a place in the Indian market.

The Indian Shaving Market

Worldwide, shaving markets were classified into wet and dry segments, the dry segment corresponded to electric and cordless razors, the wet segment to a variety of razors and blades. In India, the dry shaving market was insignificant and most males used wet shaving products. Razors and blades in India could be further classified by the type of steel used: carbon or stainless. Wiltech had two types of stainless steel products: (1) double-edged blades with a cutting edge on each side, and (2) twin blades where two blades were carefully positioned above each other in a cartridge. The term "shaving system" referred to blades packaged and purchased in conjunction with a razor.

EXHIBIT 5 ● 1983–1984 per Capita Income by State (In Rupees)

State	Per capita income
Andhra Pradesh	1,955
Assam	1,762
Bihar	1,174
Gujarat	2,795
Haryana	3,147
Himachal Pradesh	2,230
Jammu & Kashmir	1,820
Karnataka	1,957
Kerala	1,761
Madhya Pradesh	1,636
Maharashtra	3,032
Manipur	1,673
Orissa	1,339*
Punjab	3,691
Rajasthan	1,881
Tamil Nadu	1,827
Tripura	1,206**
Uttar Pradesh	1,567
West Bengal	2,231
Delhi	3,928
Goa, Daman & Diu	3,479
Pondicherry	3,693

Note: Owing to differences in source material used, the figures for different states are not strictly comparable.
*1982–1983.
**1980–1981.
Source: Statistical Outline of India 1986–1987. Tata Services Limited, Department of Economics and Statistics, Bombay House, Bombay, p. 22. Reprinted by permission.

Segmentation

In the shaving industry, market size, sales volume and market share were typically described in terms of blades sold. After 1961, stainless steel blades became the industry standard worldwide. In India however, the market transition from car-

bon steel to stainless steel did not begin until the mid-1970s and by 1983 was still not complete.

In 1983, the value of the entire Indian razor blade market was Rs. 439 million, three-quarters from stainless steel and the balance from carbon steel blades. Of a total 1,434 million blades sold, stainless steel blades accounted for 67 percent and carbon steel 33 percent. These two blade segments were also classified demographically, urban versus rural (see Exhibit 6), with urban consumers classified further according to town class (see Exhibit 7).

COMPETITION IN THE INDIAN RAZOR BLADE MARKET

Malhotra Group

The Harbanslal Malhotra Group of companies was formed in the late 1940s after India achieved its independence. In 1954 the government of India banned imports of several consumer goods to preserve scarce foreign exchange reserves. Razor blades were thus prohibited from legally entering the country, which gave the Malhotra Group a near monopoly. In the subsequent three decades, the Malhotra Group enjoyed substantial gains in market share and was virtually unchallenged until Wiltech entered the scene.

Malhotra's product lines consisted of four different double-edged blades and three shaving system products. Malhotra's biggest seller was the Topaz brand. Although the Topaz was made of local steel, it was Malhotra's popular blade. Aimed at users in cities and smaller towns, Topaz was priced at 45 paise[4] per blade and sold in packs of five. Malhotra also had slightly less expensive blades, each of which sold in packs of five. Their respective names and prices were Silver Prince at 35 paise, Ashok at 30 paise, and Panama at 30 paise. Malhotra had a near perfect monopoly with its three shaving systems—Ashok, Gallant, and SuperMax, all priced in the Rs. 7–12 category.

Malhotra's product line was able to meet the diverse needs of the entire Indian shaving market,

4. 1 rupee equals 100 paise

EXHIBIT 6 ● Urban vs. Rural Blade Consumption in India (In Millions of Blades)

| Area | Blade type | | |
	STAINLESS STEEL	CARBON STEEL	TOTAL
Urban	672.7	130.3	803
Rural	288.3	342.7	631
Total	961.0	473.0	1434

urban and rural as well as the carbon and stainless steel segments. This diverse market was reached by the Malhotra Group's 300 salesmen and 1,000 stockists (an inventory-carrying distributor). Malhotra maintained strong market awareness with a unique promotion strategy, sponsoring a variety of sporting events and musical concerts aimed at Indians in the 25–40 age group. The combination of a broad product line, an aggressive pricing policy, a promotion level three to four times that of Wiltech, and a long time presence in the Indian shaving market all contributed to Malhotra's 82 percent market share and its image as a leader in the Indian market.

Centron and Erasmic

Aside from Malhotra, the only other significant participants in India's razor market were Centron and Erasmic. Both firms made only blades and, hence, depended on Malhotra and black market shaving systems for the sale of their blades. Centron was a small manufacturer who concentrated sales in India's eastern region. Centron offered two blades in the 60–65 paise category: the Superswish and the Centwin, both in packs of five. In the 1970s, Centron was acquired by Brooke Bond, a large multinational which marketed tea all over the country. Although Centron's opera-

EXHIBIT 7 ● Urban Blade Consumption by Town Class Distribution (In Millions of Blades)

| Town class | Blade type | | |
	STAINLESS STEEL	CARBON STEEL	TOTAL
Metropolitan	193.3	23.4	216.7
Class I	229.8	35.2	265.0
Class II	90.2	16.9	107.1
Class III	82.3	24.8	107.1
Class IV	77.1	30.0	107.1
Total	672.7	130.3	803.0

Source: Company records.

tions concentrated on a limited region, Brooke Bond had an extensive, national distribution network which Wiltech management expected would be used countrywide to attack the razor market. Erasmic was another domestic manufacturer but marketed its blades primarily in Northern India. Erasmic's blades were priced at 45 paise and in packs of five.

Black Market Blades

Blades sold on the black market were either Wilkinson or Gillette and typically cost 70 paise to 1 rupee each. Gillette International marketed the majority of Gillette's products abroad and was Wilkinson's most serious competitor in the worldwide shaving market. Gillette knew that Indian consumers were willing to buy its shaving products on the black market and would, therefore, welcome an opportunity to enter the Indian marketplace legally. India's improved political and economic climate motivated Gillette management to establish a joint venture with Poddar of Calcutta. Gillette planned to manufacture its products by 1986 and, despite being a few years behind Wiltech, would use its full resources to secure a share of India's market.

Each of these competitors sought to differentiate itself from the others to protect the respective markets. One result of this differentiation was a wide range in razor blade prices. (The range of prices and product segments are summarized in a brand positioning chart in Exhibit 8.)

MARKETING PRACTICES IN INDIA

India's Distribution Channels

After leaving a factory, blades in India were shipped to and temporarily stored at company-owned depots. Depots were usually located in one or more states in such a way as to minimize interstate sales. Intrastate sales were preferred because of differing tax rates among India's states.

India's vast size affected physical distribution. Unlike North America or Europe, India did not have retail distribution chains organized at the national level; instead, outlets would receive merchandise from the nearest depot. As it was difficult to handle many towns from a single point, each town would have a stockist (distributor) to supply the town's retailers. Stockists, of which there were an estimated 25,000 in India, received their shipments from a nearby depot after conversing with a salesman. Stockists' stores typically averaged only 500 square feet, but they played an important role in the distribution process. These distributors served as wholesalers in India, granting credit and stocking the consumer products their retail customers requested.

Retail outlets also played a major role in India's distribution system. Large retail outlets (such as grocery stores, general stores, and pharmacists) averaged 175 square feet and sold items consumed on a daily basis. Each large retail outlet usually had two to three salesmen in addition to the owner.

Small retail outlets were so limited in space that they had virtually no shelf space for razor blade display, nor could they carry any inventory. Because of these space limitations a retailer never purchased case lots, only individual units usually less than 100 rupees in value. Small retail outlets were far more numerous than their larger competitors and could be found on almost every street corner even in residential areas. These small retail outlets also sold items consumed on a daily basis, but their limited space often required repeated same-day sales calls in areas with heavy sales, furthering the need for local stockists. Because of limited display space, the consumer could not usually see any blades and would simply ask for a package of blades, allowing the retailer to make the brand decision. To guarantee brand sales, it was customary in India to provide retailers with incentives such as cash or gifts (for example, imported Scotch) at festival times or as an end-of-year bonus. (For a distribution flowchart and 1983 data on blades sold through urban outlets, see Exhibits 9 and 10.)

Advertising in the Subcontinent

Media options for advertising in India consisted of television, radio, cinema, print and outdoor. Traditionally, television advertising had not been used as heavily as in the West. However, this practice began to change over the last decade as incom-

EXHIBIT 8 ● Pre Wiltech Brand Positioning of
Razor Blades in India

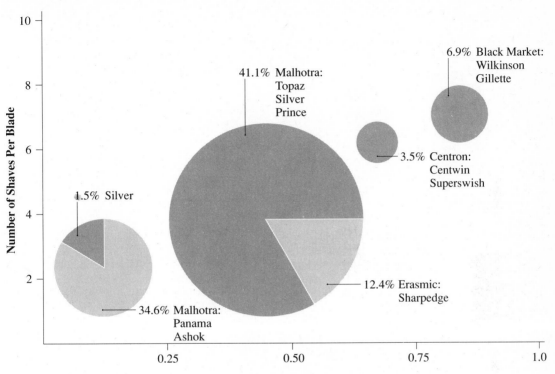

Price Per Blade in Rupees
With Market Share By Price Category and Blade Type

	Shaving Systems	Price in Rupees
▉ Stainless Steel		
▢ Carbon Steel		
Malhotra:	Ashok (Razor + 2 Twin Blades)	7.00
	Gallant (Razor + 2 Twin Blades)	12.00
	SuperMax (5 Twin Blades)	5.00

Source: Company records.

EXHIBIT 9 ● Flowchart of Wiltech Distribution
Channels

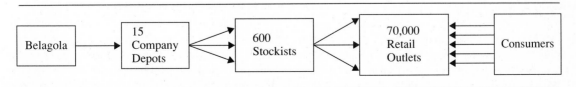

EXHIBIT 10 ● Volume of Razor Blades Sold Through Urban Outlets (In Millions of Blades)

| | Blade type | | |
Outlet	STAINLESS STEEL	CARBON STEEL	TOTAL
Groceries	262.4	58.8	321.2
General Stores	228.7	36.3	265.0
Other	174.9	33.9	208.8
Drug stores	6.7	1.3	8.0
Total	672.7	130.3	803.0

Source: Company records.

ing multinationals and other large companies responded to the rising number of television viewers. The advent of television advertising in India had, in fact, redefined the rules of consumer marketing. The success of products like Maggi, Vicco, Rasna, and Niki Tasha were attributed to television promotion. For most consumer products, television, cinema, and magazine advertising were preferred because they could project creative and colorful messages.

Statistics for television ownership were not available for smaller towns, but it was estimated that one television per 30 individuals was available in larger cities such as Bombay, Delhi, Calcutta, Bangalore, and Madras. Although the single, government-owned television channel would broadcast only in the late evening and at night, it reached 70 percent of India's population. Broadcasting began at 6:00 PM with the regional telecast via regional stations and was followed by a national broadcast from 8:00–11:00 PM, which usually included advertiser sponsored programs.

Advertising was only permitted before and after the news or program. Advertisements during the local broadcast were normally in the local language, while those aired on the national broadcast would be in Hindi or English. The Sunday feature film at 6:00 PM and televised sporting events were the most popular advertising spots. For satisfactory exposure, most firms purchased 30-second television spots at Rs. 7,000–10,000 which they would run for a three-month period.

Television advertisements could also be used in cinemas. Advertisements were aired before the film and during the ten-minute intermission. Cinema was India's most popular form of entertainment with approximately 11,000 theatres and an industry producing around 800 films a year. The cost of cinema advertising varied from town to town and within towns from locality to locality. Countrywide, costs could be as low as Rs. 25 per week or as high as Rs. 1,000 per week, with Rs. 300 per week considered average in urban markets. The shaving industry considered television and cinema to be the most effective media for advertising because the entire shaving process could be visualized with audio reinforcement of the message.

Unlike television, access to radio was more evenly dispersed throughout the country, reaching 87 percent of the population. In 1983, there was one radio for every eight individuals in India. The one national and several regional radio stations were all government owned. Advertisements from the national station were given in Hindi, the national language, whereas the local stations advertised in the local language. On average, radio spots lasted 30 seconds and cost Rs. 1,000–1,500 per slot, depending on the time of day. Although radio reached a larger population than television, it was not widely used by the shaving industry as it lacked a visual message.

Print media in India, various newspapers as well as twenty to twenty-five magazines, reached a total of 54 million people countrywide. These media were considered important in a campaign's introductory phase, but were not frequently continued, due to limited audio-visual capacity, after consumers had reached a certain level of awareness. A full-page advertisement in a daily with a circulation of 200,000 copies per day would cost between Rs. 10,000–15,000 per day. Magazines were read frequently and had a circulation of 20,000–100,000 copies per month. The cost of a single full-page advertisement would vary between Rs. 25,000–50,000 depending on the magazine and the advertisement's placement.

Outdoor advertising in India included billboards, posters at bus stops, outside buses, on overhead foot bridges, on the doors and sides of retail shops and on the external walls of buildings and compounds. Like newspapers, outdoor advertising tended to be used for special promotion campaigns or during the introductory phase of a new product. The cost of an average outdoor advertising campaign was Rs. 30,000 per month.

WILTECH'S COMPETITIVE POSITION

The Wiltech Product Line

All Wiltech blades had the traditional Wilkinson "Gothic Arch" shape, which enhanced blade strength and extended blade life by about 40 percent over normal blades. After the rough "gothic arch" production step, Wiltech blades were sharpened, smoothed and coated with Teflon. To ensure product continuity between the United Kingdom and India, Wiltech maintained strict quality control (QC) checks at each of its operations. Random samples from every lot were sent to Wilkinson in the United Kingdom for inspection. Each QC report through the middle of 1983 confirmed that Wiltech's products were meeting international standards. And, typical of many shaving products, Wiltech blades fit any brand of handle—both Indian and foreign.

Savage was Wiltech's premium blade with the same quality as imported Wilkinson blades due to a triple coating of chromium nitride, ceramic, and Teflon applied in the last stage of manufacturing. This coating gave each blade a 100 percent greater life than the regular Teflon-coated blades. Savage's packaging was also superior to Wiltech's other blades. Savage blades were wrapped in specially treated rustproof paper which had a dab of petroleum jelly on each corner to hold the blades firmly in place. Each pack contained five blades plus a top card that served both as a label and to give instructions on blade use. A purchase reminder card was placed between the fourth and fifth blades and each pack was wrapped in polystyrene and then cellophane before being shipped. A package of five Savage blades cost Rs. 4.90.

Wiltedge, with the same specifications as all Wilkinson blades, was marketed as Wiltech's most popular brand. Wiltedge had only Teflon coating and its packaging was less elaborate than Savage's. Wiltedge blades had both an inner wrapper and an outer wrapper and were packed in a cardboard tuck. A package of five Wiltedge blades cost Rs. 3.

Wilzor was India's only scientifically designed two piece razor and came with separable handle and shaving head. The shaving head contained double-edged blades adjusted to the optimum shaving angle. Alone, the Wilzor razor cost Rs. 13.10.

Wilman II represented Wilkinson's fixed twin blade shaving system. The Wilman was the only twin blade shaving product manufactured in India and had coatings of chromium, ceramic and Teflon. Designed with a lightweight, heat resistant holder, and two blades adjusted at a precise angle, the Wilman II was the newest shaving concept. Wilman II was offered as a system or a gift pack, both with two twin cartridges, and sold for 13.60 rupees and 28.40 rupees respectively. Wilman II refill packs of five twin blades were also available for Rs. 14.50.

Wiltessa was another first in the Indian shaving market, the only ladies' shaving system. The Wiltessa received the same process treatment as Wilman II and was specially designed for women's shaving needs. The Wiltessa was made of pink plastic and sold with two twin cartridges for Rs. 15.20.

Positioning the Wiltech Product Line

In 1982 Wiltech management felt that the superior quality of its products justified charging premium prices. As a result, Malay Chadha and Suresh Metha agreed to price Wiltech's line higher than the competition. Given India's market characteristics and the level of Wiltech's manufacturing technology, management decided to focus on stainless steel blades in the urban market. Within the urban market, management selected a target audience of males over 16 years old earning more than Rs. 1,000 per month. To win this audience, Chadha and Metha selected Savage and Wiltedge, the two brands felt to offer the greatest potential.

Savage was promoted as Wiltech's premium blade and aimed at those using black market blades and dissatisfied users of India's own premium blades. Wiltedge promotion was aimed at consumers of India's popular blades, offering higher satisfaction as well as a chance to upgrade to a higher quality product.

Wiltech's managers believed that a low awareness level of blade alternatives meant heavy promotion. Consequently, from May 1982 to March 1983, Wiltech spent Rs. 7,653,000 on advertising and promotion, scaling back in April 1983 when they felt initial brand awareness had been achieved. Press expenditures included six English magazines with nationwide coverage at a cost of Rs. 50,000 per magazine. Four regional magazines with local language were also used at a cost of Rs. 25,000 per magazine. The English magazines had a circulation of up to 100,000 versus the regional magazines with a circulation of about 60,000 each.

Advertising Expenditures (In Thousands of Rupees)

	May 1982–March 1983	*Proposed* *April 1983–March 1984*
Cinema Screening	773	1,546
TV Screening	238	987
Press	5,224	1,110
Others	416	285
Boarding	436	616
Film Production Costs	171	—
TV Production Costs	37	—
Radio Production Costs	—	155
POP Costs (leaflets, posters)	358	838
TOTAL	7,653	5,527

The Wiltech Distribution Network

To minimize the risk of product introduction, Wiltech test marketed its line with apparent success in Bangalore, Bombay, and New Delhi. As these cities were considered representative of countrywide market behavior, Wiltech felt encouraged and decided to pursue countrywide distribution. Wiltech's 15 depots throughout India housed stock on a transitory basis; the eight primary depots received stock directly from the plant, whereas the seven secondary depots received their stock from the nearest regional office or from a primary depot.

In addition to Wiltech's central office in Bangalore, the company had regional offices in New Delhi, Bombay, and Calcutta. Each office had a regional manager with 3 area sales managers, 6 sales supervisors, and 27 salesmen. Each Wiltech salesman was responsible for a particular territory and was paid a fixed salary of Rs. 800–1,200 per month. Additional incentives existed for meeting monthly target volume, market trends, competitive activities and stock availability. For successfully meeting targets, they received a Rs. 350 monthly bonus and for meeting quarterly targets, a bonus of Rs. 500.

Salesmen had to ensure that the orders of Wiltech's 600 stockists and all retailers were met, and that posters portraying the company's products were distributed to retail outlets. In metropolitan areas, a salesman handled one stockist and 600–700 retail outlets. Stockists were visited daily and retailers twice a month. Salesmen covering smaller towns handled an average of 10–12 stockists and 800–1,000 retail outlets. These stockists were visited once or twice a month. With stockists earning 7 percent and retailers 15 percent, Wiltech faithfully provided its distribution channels with standard operating margins. Classifying stockists and retailers as outlets, Wiltech's 81 salesmen reached 70,000 of India's 500,000 outlets by August 1983. Sales staff salaries, allowances and touring expenses accounted for 50–60 percent of Wiltech's marketing expenditures, excluding advertising and promotion.

OPTIONS FOR WILTECH INDIA

Price Reduction with New Advertising

Wiltech had anticipated a volume of 3 to 4 million blades per month for Savage and 4 to 5 million for Wiltedge, but actual sales were only one million and 700,000 blades per month respectively. Since each of Wiltech's brands were priced above the competition, Chadha felt that the pricing policy had caused the lower than expected sales volume.

He therefore proposed reducing prices along with a new communication policy.

If the Savage and Wiltedge, priced at Rs. 1 and 60 paise per blade respectively, were each lowered by 10 paise, they should be more competitive with black market blades at Rs. 0.7–1 and the 45 paise Topaz blade from Malhotra. Furthermore, if Wiltech did choose the price reduction strategy, Chadha felt that the company should reposition Wiltedge as a mass blade, which would require a new communication strategy. Having established Wiltech as a blade manufacturer of international standards, Chadha believed that a new advertising campaign should concentrate on product awareness rather than product quality.

Entry into the Rural Sector

Metha, on the other hand, felt that Wiltech needed more sales in India's rural sector, with consumers far from cities and modern telecommunications. Metha was aware that this segment, comprised primarily of farmers, provided half of India's market share and used mostly carbon steel blades in the 20–35 paise range. Unless Wiltech introduced a blade in the same price range, it could only sell brands priced about twice as high as rural customers were paying. To succeed with existing brands in this segment would require an educational campaign that demonstrated: (1) that stainless steel blades were more comfortable than carbon steel, and (2) Wiltech's blades, which were twice as expensive, could give at least twice as many shaves as Malhotra's Ashok, Panama, or Silver Prince blades.

India as an Export Base

In addition to taking corrective action for Wiltech's domestic strategy, Chadha wanted to review the advantages of using India as an export base to the U.S.S.R. and the Middle East. India's diplomatic relations with these countries had led to several successful commercial opportunities over the years; in 1981/1982 access to the Soviet market accounted for 19.3 percent of all Indian exports. Consumer goods were particularly important, as the U.S.S.R. purchased 83 percent of India's cosmetics and detergent exports and 45 percent of India's coffee exports. Their bilateral trade agreement provided India with Soviet crude oil and capital equipment. The biggest advantage was that neither had to pay with scarce hard currency; trade was conducted in Indian rupees, with rupee surpluses or deficits carried into the following year.

As an incentive to preserve scarce foreign exchange earnings, the Indian government granted tax breaks to firms committing production to exports. In 1982/1983, Wiltech's exports were only 2–3 percent of total sales but yielded a tax break of Rs. 47,000. The size of this tax break would be substantially larger if export volume were increased. Chadha did not foresee a problem in capacity utilization if domestic demand continued to be lower than originally expected.

Capacity Utilization

	Actual production (in millions of units)	Installed capacity (in millions of units)
Double-edged Blades	28.2	100.00
Shaving Systems and Twin Blade Units	5.4	20.00
Razor Handles	0.8	5.00
Two Piece Systems	0.2	0.25

Wiltech could continue to use the market channels originally developed by Asian Cables Corporation, which had provided its 2–3 percent export base. However, if Chadha decided to boost exports, he would have to increase contacts with Foreign Trade Organizations in the U.S.S.R. and attend exhibitions where contact with the right officials could be made. The Soviet reputation on negotiating was the only drawback to this option that Chadha could see. The Soviets could offer margins of 5–6 percent, but had been known to offer as little as 1–2 percent on certain products. On the other hand, Soviet central planners always placed bulk orders for an entire year. Success in the USSR and the Middle East would certainly be noted at Wilkinson headquarters in England. Market achievements in these regions would fit in with Wilkinson's worldwide perspective and could lead to a substantial career move for Chadha.

After two days, Chadha and Metha had little time left to work out Wiltech's strategy for fiscal 1984, but were still unable to identify the key issues and how they should be handled. They had to consider Gillette's anticipated 1986 market entry and how to respond if Malhotra used its standard tactic of flooding the marketplace with shaving products via product line expansion. Another concern was Centron's acquisition by Brooke Bond, a large multinational, clearly indicating that yet another international competitor with vast resources was targeting the Indian shaving market. All these factors reinforced the need for Wiltech to make the right moves and to do so in a timely manner. (Refer to Exhibit 11.)

EXHIBIT 11 ● Financial Data for Wiltech India 1982

Sales (In Rupees)	27,200,000
Variable Costs	21,729,000
Fixed Costs (depreciation, financing, staff salaries, and marketing costs)	8,856,000
	30,585,000
Operating Result	(3,385,000)

CASE 3

*Medical Equipment Company**

In 1981, Medical Equipment Company (MEC) faced a perplexing problem in its Latin American markets. Sales for its blood gas and electrolyte product lines in four countries typical of the Latin American market, Brazil, Argentina, Venezuela, and the Dominican Republic, were subject to substantial annual fluctuations. As an example, sales were increasing as much as 100 percent in one year in Argentina (1979–1980) while sales in Venezuela consistently moved in the opposite direction from the previous year's sales (see Exhibit 1). The marketing department was very concerned with these fluctuations and inconsistencies and sought to find reasons to explain the behavior of these markets. The regional management also wondered whether the markets were of sufficient interest, or whether they should be abandoned. What they could expect from these markets in the future was of particular interest to management.

COMPANY HISTORY

Medical Equipment, whose headquarters were located in the Greater Boston area, was a company

* Names and some facts are disguised.

●

This case was prepared by Visiting Professor Jean-Pierre Jeannet as a basis for class discussion rather than to illustrate either effective or ineffective handling of an administrative situation. Copyright© 1981 by IMEDE, Lausanne, Switzerland. The International Institute for Management Development (IMD), resulting from the merger between IMEDE, Lausanne, and IMI, Geneva, acquires and retains all rights. Reproduced by permission.

manufacturing sixty different instruments marketed through four different divisions. Each major product line was organized around a particular division, namely the Biomedical Division, the Analytical Instruments Division, the Micro Chemical Division, and the Sensorlab Division. The company's most recognized line was the blood gas line of the Biomedical Division.

The Biomedical Division included electrolyte, blood gas and chemistry analyzers for laboratory medicine, as well as parts, reagents and other expendables for these instruments. The electrolyte product line consisted of flame photometers which were among the most widely used instruments throughout clinical medicine. By measuring sodium and potassium, two elements vital to health, they provided valuable diagnostic information. Also measured were lithium levels which were important for the treatment of manic depressive patients (see Exhibit 2). The blood gas line included blood gas analyzers which measured blood parameters that were useful in critical care medicine and for the treatment of pulmonary diseases. MEC was one of the world's leading producers of blood gas analyzers, the company's first and original product line (see Exhibit 3).

The Micro Chemical Division manufactured a special instrument which was one of the most flexible chemistry analyzers on the market. It could be used in a hospital room or a doctor's office and could be operated by both paraprofessionals and highly skilled professionals. A cassette-programmable minicomputer made it possible to perform 120-350 tests per hour. Its disposable test motors and low reagents requirements helped hospitals combat rising costs.

EXHIBIT 1 ● Total MEC Exports of Electrolyte and Blood Gas Product Lines

	1980	*1979*	*1978*	*1977*	*1976*
Argentina	$ 208,833	$ 91,812	$ 16,530	$ 3,448	$ 6,861
Dom. Rep.	65,060	16,142	9,324	12,367	17,892
Brazil	255,099	131,400	175,527	297,657	205,213
Venezuela	98,478	243,367	197,628	473,293	137,254
Total*	$2,675,000	$2,280,000	$1,372,000		

*Export sales from the United States to unaffiliated customers.

EXHIBIT 2 ● Spectrophotometers

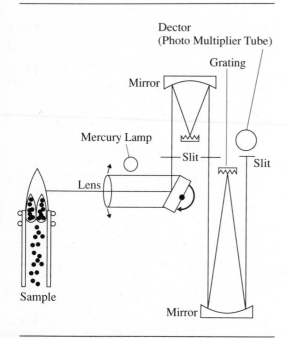

The optical system of this instrument had an innovative design which incorporated a double monochromator system to minimize errors due to stray light. Also included was an automatic wavelength-scanning system, internally calibrated mercury source, to ensure accurate wavelength selection.

The Analytical Instruments Division designed and manufactured atomic absorption spectrophotometers and inductively coupled plasma emission spectrophotometers. These instruments were used extensively to monitor the purity of water supplies. They were of great value to industries where parts-per-billion purity of materials, finished products and effluent were critical.

The Sensorlab Division technologies were also of great value to critical care medicine, as well as of use in food, beverage and drug processing industries. Among the instruments in this division, the MEC 501 System measured cardiac output and pulmonary artery pressure; the 200 CDE Monitor measured carbon dioxide; and the MEC 300 measured oxygen delivered during anesthesia. The industrial products group included, among others, instruments to monitor the beer brewing process or the fermentation process in cheese manufacturing.

INTERNATIONAL SALES

MEC's international sales accounted for some 40 percent of total 1980 sales of 99.1 million dollars, that is, 39.6 million dollars. This represented an increase of 2 percent over the 38 percent of total 1979 sales figures (see Exhibits 4 and 5 for financial data). Sales growth in Latin America and Mexico was attributed to products in the biomedical line, specifically blood gas analyzers and flame photometers. The two were considered to meet basic needs of health care facilities which were

EXHIBIT 3 ● Blood Gas Analyzer

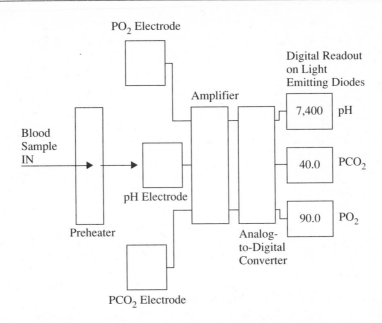

The blood gas analyzer heated blood samples up to body temperature. At this point an electrical charge built up and the electrodes were activated to measure the pH unit, carbon dioxide tension, and oxygen tension. This happened as blood gases transferred across the membrane.

being upgraded to include sophisticated diagnostic instrumentation where none had existed before. In Mexico the increase was significant for all

EXHIBIT 4 ● Price List

Model	Domestic retail	International retail*
Blood Gas 570	U.S.$ 9,900	10,395
Blood Gas 670	15,200	15,960
Electrolyte 290	6,700	7,035
390	4,900	5,145
590	9,500	9,975

*International prices were net 5% higher than domestic.

products, however, including those of the Analytical Instruments and Sensorlab Division.

MEC's international markets, besides Europe and Latin America, included Canada, Asia, Australia/New Zealand, the Middle East, Africa, and the People's Republic of China since 1980. MEC's International Division was comprised of two separate areas. Latin America, Asia Pacific and Canadian operations were managed through an area headquarters located in MEC's home office (see Exhibit 6 for an organization chart). MEC's international operations had just been reorganized toward the end of 1980. Its markets in Canada, Central and South America were now being served by an area division separate from the one in Europe. MEC expected continuing growth in the upcoming years although they realized that oil-importing countries had to restrict their purchases somewhat. Still, the fact that health care remained a

EXHIBIT 5 ● MEC Consolidated Statement of Income for the Years Ended March 31, 1980 and 1979
Medical Equipment Company and Subsidiaries

	1980	*1979*
NET SALES	$ 99,082,000	$ 87,866,000
COST AND EXPENSES:		
Cost of sales	50,311,000	45,112,000
Research and development	9,910,000	7,856,000
Marketing	21,305,000	16,718,000
General and Administrative	8,713,000	6,677,000
	90,239,000	76,363,000
INCOME FROM OPERATIONS	8,843,000	11,503,000
OTHER INCOME (EXPENSE):		
Interest	(2,450,000)	(1,501,000)
Foreign exchange adjustments	272,000	119,000
Other, net	(90,000)	(34,000)
	(2,268,000)	(1,416,000)
INCOME BEFORE PROVISION FOR INCOME TAXES	6,575,000	10,087,000
PROVISION FOR INCOME TAXES (note 2)	2,478,000	4,577,000
NET INCOME	4,097,000	5,510,000
EARNINGS PER SHARE	$ 1.39	$ 1.87

high priority for all of these countries was recognized by their political leaders.

DOMESTIC MARKETING POLICIES

In the U.S. market, MEC granted exclusive distribution rights to Scientific Products, a division of American Hospital Supply Corporation. MEC still had its own sales force organized geographically with specific salesmen reporting to their respective area managers, who in turn reported to the National Sales Manager. Also reporting to the Sales Managers were three Government/National Account Managers. The Area Technical Directors were included in another group which formed a part of the sales force.

The entire direct sales force consisted of sixty-five people and covered thirty sales territories. Besides the traditional duties attached to most sales positions, MEC's sales force was expected to coordinate dealer activities. Depending on the territory, each MEC representative worked with approximately 8–10 Scientific Product representatives. Their efficiency in communicating with their respective dealers helped them reach their individual sales quotas. The Area Technical Directors did not have direct sales responsibilities but provided customers with services through consulting about their problems and rendering technical assistance.

MEC's various divisions utilized "education" as a marketing tool. For its major customers the

EXHIBIT 5 ● MEC Consolidated Balance Sheet for March 31, 1980 and 1979
Medical Equipment Company and Subsidiaries (*cont.*)

Assets	*1980*	*1979*
CURRENT ASSETS:		
Cash, including time deposits of $350,000 in 1980	$ 2,059,000	$ 1,009,000
Accounts receivable, less allowances of $315,000 in 1980 and $189,000 in 1979	24,002,000	20,997,000
Inventories:		
Finished goods	8,499,000	8,425,000
Work-in-Process	4,854,000	5,003,000
Raw materials	9,389,000	7,595,000
	22,742,000	21,023,000
Prepaid expenses and other	1,395,000	1,004,000
Total current assets	50,198,000	44,033,000
PROPERTY, PLANT AND EQUIPMENT		
Land	1,780,000	758,000
Buildings and leasehold improvements	10,333,000	4,598,000
Laboratory and manufacturing equipment	11,640,000	9,902,000
Office and other equipment	2,082,000	1,856,000
	25,835,000	17,114,000
Less accumulated depreciation and amortization	8,880,000	7,123,000
	16,955,000	9,991,000
Construction in progress	2,152,000	2,102,000
Property under capital leases, less accumulated amortization	2,100,000	2,176,000
OTHER ASSETS	1,072,000	929,000
	$72,477,000	$59,231,000

Biomedical Division held three-day training seminars in applications, operations, routine maintenance and troubleshooting. In the past year about 600 laboratory professionals attended these seminars. Biomedical also provided Continu-ED audiovisual programs which were used to teach the theory and practice of clinical analysis in laboratories in the schools where technologists were being trained. The Analytical Instruments Division also held regular training sessions in its field laboratories. The division sponsored one-day seminars for chemists in major cities around the country. Over 5,000 current and potential users of spectrophotometers attended these seminars during the past year. Sensorlab conducted critical care symposia for respiratory therapists, anesthesiologists, cardio-pulmonary technicians and critical care nurses throughout the United States. These symposia included lectures and discussions on the theory and operation of the equipment as used to

EXHIBIT 5 ● MEC Consolidated Balance Sheet for March 31, 1980 and 1979
Medical Equipment Company and Subsidiaries (*cont.*)

Liabilities and stockholders' investment	*1980*	*1979*
CURRENT LIABILITIES:		
Notes payable to banks	$ 6,141,000	$ 8,085,000
Current maturities of long-term debt	523,000	487,000
Accounts payable	7,108,000	6,228,000
Accrued expenses	7,967,000	6,292,000
Accrued Federal and foreign income taxes	2,219,000	1,906,000
Total current liabilities	23,958,000	22,998,000
DEFERRED FEDERAL AND FOREIGN INCOME TAXES	2,239,000	1,654,000
LONG-TERM DEBT		
Notes payable to insurance companies	8,000,000	—
Bank term loan	7,000,000	7,000,000
Obligations under capital leases, less current maturities	2,112,000	2,208,000
Other	319,000	382,000
	17,431,000	9,590,000
COMMITMENTS AND CONTINGENCY		
STOCKHOLDERS' INVESTMENT		
Common Stock, $1 par value:		
Authorized 8,000,000 shares:		
Outstanding 2,926,888 shares in 1980 and 2,897,856 shares in 1979	2,927,000	2,898,000
Capital in excess of par value	6,230,000	6,030,000
Retained earnings	19,692,000	16,061,000
	28,849,000	24,989,000
	$72,477,000	$59,231,000

monitor the critically ill, plus hands-on demonstration of equipment.

LATIN AMERICAN OPERATIONS

In three of the four Latin American countries in question, that is, Argentina, Venezuela, and the Dominican Republic, MEC marketed its products through independent agents. Only in Brazil did MEC have its own sales force. The agents in the other three countries underwent the same educa-

tional process given in the seminars and symposia to domestic clients. The end users in these countries were therefore not given this information and instruction by MEC personnel but by the respective sales agents. (See Exhibits 7 to 17 for some background data on the Latin American market.)

The independent agents also carried the products of MEC's competitors, as MEC didn't have the same exclusive distribution system that they employed domestically. MEC, a leader in blood gas instruments, had the same competition

EXHIBIT 6 ● MEC International Division

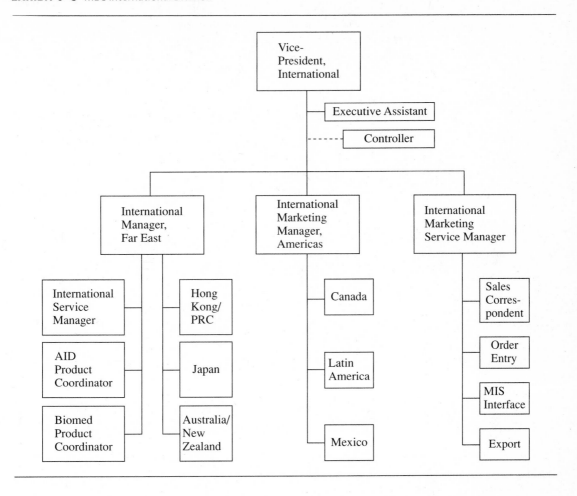

EXHIBIT 7 ● Population (in Millions)

	1975	*1976*	*1977*	*1978*	*1979*	*1980*
Argentina	25.38	25.72	26.06	26.39	26.73	27.1
Brazil	106.23	109.18	112.24	115.4	118.65	119.0
Dom. Rep.	4.7	4.84	4.98	5.12	5.28	5.3
Venezuela	11.99	12.36	12.74	12.98	13.12	13.52

EXHIBIT 8 ● Gross National Product (Billion US $) and GNP Per Capita (in US $)

	1975	1976	1977	1978
Argentina	44.257	42.972	44.788	42.939
(per capita)			(1,719)	(1,627)
Brazil	108.007	117.690	123.178	130.568
			(1,088)	(1,122)
Dom. Rep.	3.354	3.570	3.728	3.862
			(749)	(753)
Venezuela	22.826	24.603	26.277	27.985
			(2,063)	(2,127)

EXHIBIT 9 ● Growth Rates of GNP and GNP Per Capita

	1975	1976	1977	1978
Argentina	−1.3	−3.0	4.4	−4.1
(per capita)	(−2.6)	(−4.2)	(3.0)	(−5.3)
Brazil	5.7	9.2	4.7	5.9
	(2.7)	(6.1)	(1.8)	(3.1)
Dom. Rep.	5.0	5.9	3.3	3.6
	(1.6)	(2.4)	(− .1)	(.5)
Venezuela	5.2	7.4	8.1	6.5
	(1.7)	(3.9)	(4.6)	(3.1)

EXHIBIT 10 ● Exchange Rates (Local Currency per U.S. Dollar)

	1976	1977	1978	1979
Argentina				
(end of period	274.5	597.5	1,003.5	1,618.5
period average)	140	407.6	795.8	1,317.0
(pesos/$)				
Brazil	12.345	16.050	20.920	42.530
(cruz./$)	10.675	14.144	18.070	26.955
Dom. Rep.	1.0000	⟶		
(peso/$)				
Venezuela	4.2925	⟶		
(bolivars/$)	4.2899	4.2925	⟶	

EXHIBIT 11 ● Balance of Payments (in Million US $)

	1975	1976	1977
Argentina	−679	121	2,479
Brazil	−964	2,312	460
Dom. Rep.	28	−11	57
Venezuela	2,711	69	−79

EXHIBIT 12 ● Inhabitants Per Physician

Argentina	450 (1973)
Brazil	2,025 (1972)
Dom. Rep.	1,866 (1973)
Venezuela	921 (1976)

EXHIBIT 13 ● Average Number of Hospital Beds Per Thousand Inhabitants

Argentina	5.7 (1971)
Brazil	3.8 (1970)
Dom. Rep.	1.5 (1975)
Venezuela	2.9 (1976)

EXHIBIT 14 ● Hospitals Per Country

Argentina	2,864 (1971)
Brazil	4,067 (1971)
Dom. Rep.	306 (1972)
Venezuela	340 (1972)

EXHIBIT 15 ● Total Imports of Complete Electro-Medical Equipment (in US $)

	1980	1979	1978
Argentina	$2,287,000	$647,000	$462,000
Brazil	584,000	408,000	528,000
Dom. Rep.	N.A.	N.A.	73,443
Venezuela	462,000	646,000	819,000

EXHIBIT 16 ● Total Central Gov. Expenditure on Health*

	1972	1973	1974	1975	1976	1977
Argentina		.3%		.1%		.3%
Brazil	.2%			.8%		.23%
Dom. Rep.			1.7%	.9%		2.3%
Venezuela				2.7%		.9%

*Expressed as a percentage of Gross National Product.

EXHIBIT 17 ● Total U.S. Exports*

	1979	1978	1977	1976
Argentina	$4,159,113	$2,094,951	$ 888,218	$ 330,764
Brazil	7,058,969	7,079,688	2,554,142	1,468,369
Dom. Rep.	184,437	109,989	none reported	none reported
Venezuela	2,908,793	3,235,966	1,281,688	1,728,350

*Figures from U.S. Department of Commerce include only blood gases and electrolyte equipment, products which often took priority in developing countries.

internationally as domestically. This consisted of Beckman Instruments in California, Technicon Instruments of New York; Corning, Instrumentation Laboratories, Nova, Radiometer, and MCA, all located in the greater Boston area. While no data on market share was available, it was recognized that MEC was among the leaders in the blood gas analyzer line domestically and internationally. On an international level the extent of leadership might vary from country to country, however.

Although MEC could not identify who actually made the final decision in the purchasing process, it was believed to occur in a "ladder" type form. Initially, a group of laboratory managers would evaluate the product and then send their recommendations up to higher level management and eventually perhaps to a hospital administrator. How much influence any one group had, or who actually made the purchase decision, was unknown to MEC.

THE ARGENTINIAN MARKET

Argentina was a country with about 27 million people, growing at a rate of 2.9 percent. One third of the population lived in or around Buenos Aires, the nation's capital, and 72 percent lived in urban areas.

Argentina had been a republic since 1816. The Constitution of 1853, largely patterned after the U.S. model, remained in force for most of the time, though subject to alterations depending on the political situation. The country experienced its first military coup in 1930. A second coup by the military prepared the way for General Peron who assumed power in 1946. Assisted by his immensely popular wife, Evita, Peron formed a coalition of workers and the urban poor. He attempted to develop a modern welfare state and pursued extremely nationalistic policies. Overthrown in 1955, he went into exile in Spain but continued to play an important political role from abroad. In 1966, the military again overthrew the civilian administration and ruled for seven years. In 1973, Dr. Campora, a member of the Peronist party, won the elections, only to resign three months later to allow for another election won by General Peron as President and his second wife, Maria, as Vice-President (Evita Peron had died in 1952). When General Peron died in 1974 he was succeeded by Maria who could not control the increasing urban unrest and terrorism originally emanating from the Montenero guerilla group but later practiced by other political groups as well. In 1976, Maria Peron was overthrown by the armed forces under General Videla who was named President.

The Argentinian military continued to rule the country, and in October of 1980 General Viola was named successor to President Videla to assume power in spring of 1981. The military had made several important changes in the Constitution of 1853. Most power was centered in the hand of the Junta consisting of the leaders of the army, air force, and navy. It was this Junta that named the president, usually for three years, who must be a retired military officer. At the present time, a return to civilian rules was not planned.

The Argentinian economy was traditionally based upon agriculture with livestock and grains accounting for the majority of its output. In 1979, agriculture accounted for 12 percent of GNP and represented the largest export item.

At the time of Maria Peron's overthrow in 1976, the economic scene was rapidly deteriorating. Production was declining, inflation was accelerating rapidly, and Argentina was facing a moratorium on its foreign debt. Under the leadership of the Minister of the Economy, Martinez de Hoz, the government attempted to get to the root of these problems. In place of the Peronist populist programs designed to redistribute income and expand state activities, the government sought to establish more of a free market economy. The government emphasized an export-oriented growth strategy built around an improved agricultural sector. Major objectives were the reduction of the chronic fiscal deficit, rationalization of all public sector activities, monetary discipline, and the expansion of domestic and foreign private investment.

The peso was initially devalued in March of 1976 to 140 per one U.S. dollar, down from 109 previously, in an attempt to achieve these objectives. In May, further devaluations were announced. Now, exports could be financed with 65 percent of currency through the "official" market rate of 140 per U.S. dollar and 35 percent through the "free market" rate of 245–250 pesos per U.S. dollar. Free market pesos could be obtained outside the channels provided by the Central Bank of Argentina. A further devaluation occurred in July when 69 percent of exports could be financed in the "free market" and 31 percent in the "official" market. By November of 1976 the financing was set at 85 percent at the free rate and 15 percent official. Although GNP declined 3 percent in 1976, economic indicators at the end of the year were showing an upward trend. Despite the recession the government managed to keep unemployment at relatively low levels, but at the cost of keeping wages low. The government reduced its budget deficit from 12.8 percent of GNP in 1975 to 7.8 per-

cent in 1976. The Central Bank's reserves had increased by December of 1976 to 2.2 billion dollars, the highest level in Argentina's history. In 1976 Argentina's balance of trade showed a surplus of about $800 million. Inflation decelerated considerably in the second half of 1976 with an announced goal for 1977 to keep the rate of inflation below 100 percent.

By 1978, the rate of inflation was still at 170 percent, still not better than 1977's 160 percent rate. The budget deficit in 1978 could be financed for the first time without printing money, a common practice under earlier regimes.

In an effort to reduce inflation the government reduced some tariff barriers and thus hoped to cut the sizeable trade surpluses. Because authorities maintained a managed exchange rate, and determined in advance the dollar-peso exchange rate, the country suffered from an excess of dollars caused by the resulting surplus in the current account and government borrowing. Thus, the government decided to encourage imports in an effort to reduce the money supply. By early 1980 the Argentinian economic policy displayed strong liberal and classical tendencies. Price controls, interest rate ceilings, foreign exchange controls, credit controls, rent controls, state monopoly on exports, and import quotas had all been abolished. By now, real growth, fixed investments, and exports were rising at a healthy rate. Inflation was down to 45 percent from 900 percent just four years earlier. Whereas in earlier times the government had printed money to pay for its expenses, 80 percent of expenditures were now met by government revenues. Tax collections used to be a problem as people would delay payments in an attempt to pay in devalued pesos. By 1980, the peso's value was thought to be restored. The flight from real currency was no longer a necessity. Contrary to economic theories and the Phillips curve principle, unemployment had fallen together with the rate of inflation.

By the end of 1980 the liberal economic policies had come under fire. The number of bankruptcies of small businesses and the failure of the banks that had financed them had risen dramatically. Businessmen accused the government of setting the value of the peso at an artificially high level, making life easy for importers and causing great difficulties for domestic industries. In addition, considerable lines of short term subsidized credits to affected businesses were cut off by the government. In 1981, Martinez de Hoz admitted that his program had fallen short of expectations. Government expenses were viewed to be at the root of the problem as huge deficits still continued to exist. It was admitted that the exchange rate had been deliberately set to favor the importers.

With a new regime under General Viola to take power in March of 1981, a new economic team was appointed under the leadership of a new Minister of the Economy, Mr. Sigaut. It was believed that Mr. Sigaut would most likely take the "Japanese" approach which would include an all-out drive to promote exports, with subsidies, tariff barriers, and multi-tiered exchange rates likely to return. This would represent a return to the practices of the past. Many critics complained such a course should not be adopted, lest they end up in the economic nightmare they had experienced in the past.

THE BRAZILIAN MARKET

In terms of land area, Brazil was the fifth largest nation of the world and had an estimated population of about 118 million. There had been a growing trend towards urbanization with over 50 percent of the population currently living in urban areas.

Politically, the country had long been dominated by military leaders who last staged a coup in 1964 and had remained in power ever since. According to the present constitution, promulgated in 1967, Brazil was organized as a federal republic with broad powers granted to the federal government. At the national level, the constitution established a presidential system with three "independent and harmonious powers"—the executive, the legislative and the judicial. The president was elected for a six year term by an electoral college composed of members of the congress and representatives of state legislatures and municipalities.

Despite the superficial similarities between the governments of Brazil and the U.S., the Bra-

zilian president played a more prominent role in national affairs than did his U.S. counterpart. For example, the constitution gave the president the power to intervene in individual states and municipalities if he determined that conditions warranted such action. He could also issue decrees in matters concerning national security and public finance. In 1968, the president was given expanded powers, including the power to declare a state of siege for an unlimited time. He could also suspend the writ of habeas corpus in cases involving national security and was empowered to restrict traditional civil liberties. Furthermore, all actions carried out under this special authority were removed from judicial review. In April of 1979 these powers were exercised when then President Geisel closed the national congress and the country returned to a virtual dictatorship. This threatened the existence of civilian political participation in the government. This occurred because the opposition party in congress gained enough seats to block Geisel's control over the judicial system. Geisel had not anticipated that the "token" opposition would exercise their power in this manner. As a result, he took these actions to appease hard liners in the military who weren't keen about the recent liberalization policy.

General Baptista Figueiredo became President in 1979, winning in the electoral college by a vote of 355–266 over the opposition party candidate. Figueiredo had been hand picked to represent the ruling party of a group of military officers. He promised to continue the political opening process, allowing students the right to demonstrate and also granting their right to strike.

As a result of the military inspired revolution, the Brazilian government had focused on the following economic policy objectives: (1) maintenance of a high rate of growth, (2) control of inflation, and (3) gradual improvement of the welfare system. The years 1968–1973 were excellent ones for the Brazilian economy with the growth rate averaging 10 percent annually. In 1973, President Geisel announced a plan to equal the growth rates of these earlier years for the period 1975–1979. Investments in basic industries, sciences and technology, as well as economic infrastructure during the five-year plan were projected at about $100 billion. The priority industries in the plan included steel, fertilizer, non-metallic minerals, petrochemicals, paper and cellulose, pharmaceuticals, and all types of capital goods. A major reason why the economy was in need of adjustments stemmed from the pressure that the price of petroleum created on the balance of payments due to Brazil's position as a heavy oil importer. Underlining the nation's need to earn more foreign exchange, the government promoted a rapid growth of exports. Renewed efforts were made at strengthening domestic industries with special emphasis on import substitution, both as a means of conserving foreign exchange and as a step towards developing a modern industrial society.

Brazil's very recent international financial policy had also been aimed at its very large and increasing foreign debt. Brazil had been following a policy of frequently adjusting its exchange rates by small percentages to reconcile its own inflation rate with that of its major trading partners, which allowed it to maintain its international competitiveness.

Late in 1979, however, President Figueiredo saw the need for change as inflation rapidly approached 80 percent compared to the 1977 rate of 30 percent or the 1976 rate of 46 percent. Thus, he devalued the Cruzeiro 30 percent, departing from the system of mini-devaluations to prevent serious financial disruptions. He also weaned the private sector from over-generous subsidies and controls and ended export subsidies. Domestic concerns also lost import protection when the "law of similarity" was repealed which required that a domestically produced product be purchased over an imported one if the two products were similar. These actions, in essence, called for a gradual return to a free market economy.

Late 1980 saw another shift in emphasis as the Brazilian government tried to come to grips with 113 percent inflation and the deficit in its international payments account. The plan called for a more restrictive monetary policy with extremely heavy support for exports and priority treatment for agricultural developments. The goal was an inflation rate of 70 percent and to boost exports from 20 to 25 billion dollars. Domestic credit and the monetary base were supposed to increase by 50 percent in 1981.

Although Planning Minister Delfim had been criticized for abandoning the more classical economic approach in solving Brazil's problems, he viewed Brazil's case as unique because the young people in Brazil accounted for a very large percentage of its population. Substantial unemployment and underemployment existed in Brazil and trying to fight inflation and other problems with the classic tools of fiscal and monetary controls could provoke a recession, Delfim argued. This would be very detrimental to Brazil because of its low income levels and general impoverishment.

THE MARKET OF THE DOMINICAN REPUBLIC

The Dominican Republic was located on the eastern part of the island of Hispaniola which lay between Cuba and Puerto Rico. The western part of the island was occupied by the State of Haiti. About 70 percent of the country's population of 5.2 million lived in rural areas. The annual population growth rate was about 3 percent.

After a long period of control under General Trujillo, the country had entered a period of instability in the early 1960s followed by several terms of popularly elected governments. Under the constitution of 1966 the Dominican Republic was constituted as a representative democracy whose national powers were divided among the executive, legislative, and judicial branches of government. The president was directly elected for a four year term. In May of 1978, then President Balaguer was defeated in his try for a fourth consecutive term by Antonio Guzman of the Partido Revolucionario Dominicano (PRD). These elections were generally acknowledged to have been free and fair. Many parties, including the communist party, participated in an open and hard fought campaign. The inauguration of President Guzman was significant in that it represented the country's first peaceful transfer of power from one freely elected president to another in this century. President Guzman pledged that his administration would promote democratic institutionalization, economic development, and social justice, along with focusing public resources on the education, health, energy, and agricultural sectors of the Dominican economy.

The PRD participated for the first time in elections since 1966 and also gained a majority in the senate, but Balaguer's Partido Reformista retained control of the lower house. In 1980, the PRD claimed that President Guzman had deviated from party policies and disassociated itself from him.

In the early 1970s the Dominican Republic enjoyed one of the highest economic growth rates in Latin America. More recently the country had experienced an economic slowdown brought on by a fall in sugar prices and a rise in petroleum costs. Real GNP growth in 1977 was 3.3 percent, following increases of 2.9 percent in 1976, and 5 percent in 1975. Total real GNP for 1977 was 2.1 billion dollars, with real per capita income of $433.

Inflation, which had declined from a previous average of 14 percent to 7.8 percent in 1976, jumped to 16.4 percent in 1977. Its balance of payments rebounded from a $30 million deficit in 1976 to a $59.2 million surplus in 1977, thanks to increased coffee and cacao earnings and high capital inflows. Although the hurricanes Frederick and David devastated the country in 1979, the long term economic outlook was promising.

Agriculture continued to dominate foreign trade. In 1977, the Dominicans exported 1.4 million metric tons of sugar accounting for 32 percent of foreign exchange earnings. More than 80 percent of Dominican exports went to the U.S., and more than 50 percent of Dominican imports came from the U.S. The Dominican government was promoting foreign investment in industrial free-trade zones to foster employment. Free-trade zone firms were allowed to import and re-export goods duty-free, in addition to enjoying certain tax advantages such as tax holidays.

THE VENEZUELAN MARKET

Venezuela's population of about 14 million grew at an annual rate of 3 percent resulting in a dou-

bling of its entire population every 20 years. Venezuela's mostly oil based wealth was distributed very unevenly and a large segment of the population suffered from inadequate nutrition, housing, clothing, and education. These problems were aggravated by the rapidly growing population and an increasing number of illegal aliens, primarily from Colombia, who were attracted to Venezuela's booming labor market.

Though an independent state since 1830, Venezuela was governed primarily by dictators until 1958 when Romulo Betancourt became the country's first elected president to finish his term of office. In 1969, Caldera became the first Christian-democratic president, followed by Perez in 1974, who belonged to the opposition party, Accion Democratica. Since 1979, Herrera, again a Christian-democrat, had been president.

The present constitution guaranteed freedom of speech, religion, and assembly, and assigned substantial economic development responsibilities to the federal government. National elections were held every five years in which the president and members of congress, the state legislature, and the city councils were directly elected. The president could not be reelected until ten years after his most recent term. The executive, legislative, and judicial branches were separate. The president had extensive powers that included the power to appoint the council of ministers (the cabinet) and the state and territorial governors, by decree. The Democratic Republic Union (URD) and the Social-Christian Party (COPEI) were the two major parties in this democratic system although there were many smaller ones. The objectives of the Venezuelan government included the preservation and protection of free and democratic institutions and to maintain public order; promote, expand, and diversify agricultural and industrial production; to create new jobs, to carry out agrarian reforms, and to expand education, housing, public health, social welfare and community services. Venezuela's petroleum revenues provided excellent prospects for the country's continuing political, social, and economic development.

Venezuela's economy was totally dominated by its petroleum industry. Until 1970, the country was the world's third largest petroleum producer, and the leading exporter. Since 1971, the country had remained in fifth place with respect to production and third on exports. Petroleum had reached a peak of 3.7 million barrels a day in 1970 and averaged slightly over 2 million for the last 3 years. Petroleum accounted for 96 percent of Venezuela's export earnings in 1979. As a result of this over-dependency on oil, industrial diversification was a high government priority. Huge investments were made in agriculture, steel, and aluminum industries, and the latter had replaced iron ore as the second export earner.

Venezuela's historically positive balance of payments turned negative for the first time in 1977. The deficit had reached $5.7 billion in 1978 due to enormous public expenditures on ambitious development programs, and later fell to $228 million in 1978. Higher oil prices returned the balance of payments into surplus in 1979. When President Herrera assumed power in 1979, he pledged to place his emphasis on the development of agriculture and social services rather than on heavy industry as was done by his predecessor. The present 5-year plan aimed at economic expansion while placing renewed emphasis on social priorities. It anticipated an average annual growth rate of 6 percent, continued oil production at a level of 2.2 million barrels per day, and an annual increase of 15 percent in oil revenues.

MANAGEMENT APPRAISAL

As in most Latin American countries, MEC's management had identified three health care systems that existed in most countries. One system consisted of "social security" type hospitals catering to citizens who could not afford private hospitals, which represented the second system. A third system, also government funded, consisted of hospitals for military personnel and government employees. The two public systems and the private hospitals each contributed about equally to MEC sales. Among the public systems, the ones organized for military and government employees were always better funded than the social security hospitals.

MEC's management believed that politics and balance of payments played a major role in medical equipment sales. Also of importance was the country of education for medical doctors. And next to the official market always existed a parallel market of unauthorized imports representing about 15 percent of sales for each market. These sales were undocumented with products usually "smuggled" into the country.

MEC found independent agents of considerable importance in securing foreign currency under tight monetary situations. Particularly for private hospitals such agents had been able to occasionally arrange for creative financing to sell MEC instruments.

Over the past decade, only Mexico had shown a consistently increasing sales volume for MEC products. Though the Latin American market was considered to be growing overall, the considerable fluctuations were nevertheless cause for concern for MEC's regional management. A task force was formed that had collected the attached data. It was now up to the task force's members to form some conclusions on the reasons for this erratic sales pattern and to attempt to forecast future volume. Eventually, the task force would also have to make a recommendation to the company as to whether MEC should continue to serve these markets.

CASE 4

Nippon Vicks K.K.

In March of 1983, Masahiro Horita, product manager for Nippon Vicks' acne care business, was uncertain what to recommend to further grow the "Clearasil" business in Japan. "Clearasil" had been introduced nationally in 1979 and quickly reached a volume of 2.5 million packages. Nippon Vicks K.K. had been unable to expand volume beyond that point despite a general expansion of the market. Sales volume had recently dropped to a rate of 2 million packages per year. Horita felt under increasing pressure to remedy the situation, particularly given a period of intense competitive activity in early 1983.

During the last 12 months, Horita had held several discussions with head office executives on Clearasil strategy for Japan. He was expected to come up with a final proposal to be presented at the marketing strategy review meeting to be held at the end of this month. Despite extensive consultations, there still existed a substantial disagreement between Horita's views and those held by division head office personnel.

●

This case was prepared by Visiting Professor Jean-Pierre Jeannet, as a basis for class discussion rather than to illustrate either effective or ineffective handling of an administrative situation. Copyright © 1986 by IMEDE, Lausanne, Switzerland. The International Institute for Management Development (IMD), resulting from the merger between IMEDE, Lausanne, and IMI, Geneva, acquires and retains all rights. Reproduced by permission.

COMPANY BACKGROUND

Richardson-Vicks

Richardson-Vicks was a leading worldwide marketer of branded consumer products in the areas of health care, personal care, nutritional care, and home care. Corporate sales amounted to $1,115 million for the fiscal year ending June 30, 1982.

The Vicks name was recognized around the world for treatment of the common cold. In the United States, 25 percent of all consumer expenditures in this category went to purchase Vicks products. Abroad, Vicks cough drops were market leaders from Germany to Japan. VapoRub, originally introduced in 1906, was marketed in more than 100 countries. Cold care provided for the original base of Richardson-Vicks, and in 1983 the company continued to add new products to that segment. The company had recently moved to expand its non-cold health care products by adding an antacid, "Tempo," and acquiring "Percogesic" from DuPont's Endo Laboratories as an entry into the analgesic market.

Richardson-Vicks had been in the personal care business since 1958 and expanded this segment through product development and acquisitions. "Oil of Olay" was the leading adult skin care product in the world with sales of more than $150 million. The company marketed several teenage skin care products. Clearasil was the leading acne product in the United States, Germany, and Japan. Topex, another entry in the acne care category, was the leader in the benzoyl peroxide segment in many international markets. The company also sold several shampoo brands, toothpaste, and denture care products in many non-U.S. markets.

International Division

International operations accounted for slightly more than half of Richardson-Vicks' sales in 1982. With $303.8 million in sales for 1982, Vicks International Europe/Africa Division represented more than half of the company's foreign sales. Headquartered in Paris, the division's leading brands were Kukident denture care products, Vicks cough drops, Oil of Olay beauty fluid, and Clearasil acne care products.

The Vicks International Americas/Far East Division included Canada, Latin America, and the Far East. Sales for the Western Hemisphere (Americas) amounted to $136.9 million and other areas (mostly Far East) totalled $137.9 million. Headquartered in Westport, Connecticut, leading products of this division included "Choco Milk," a powdered chocolate nutritional supplement, Clearasil acne care products, Larin candy products, Oil of Olay beauty fluid, Colac laxative, Vicks cold products, and a line of insecticides.

Nippon Vicks K.K.

Nippon Vicks K.K. (NVKK) was a wholly owned subsidiary of Richardson-Vicks, Inc. The Japanese subsidiary was incorporated in 1964 and had experienced rapid growth. Sales grew from 1.8 billion yen in 1972/1973 to 11 billion yen in 1981/1982 and were expected to reach 13 billion yen in 1983/1984.[1] NVKK maintained its corporate offices in Osaka and operated a manufacturing plant near Nagoya, where about half of NVKK's staff was employed.

NVKK's leading product was "Colac," accounting for about one-half of the company's sales. "Colac" was the leading laxative in Japan with a market share of about 40 percent. Other products marketed were Vicks Cough Drops, Vicks VapoRub, and two infant care products, Milton and Milgard. With about 15 percent of NVKK's sales, Clearasil was an important con-

---

1. 250 yen = $1 U.S.; 1 billion yen = $4 million U.S.

tributor to the company's profitability. NVKK was one of the most successful foreign subsidiaries operating in Japan and its brands enjoyed a leadership position in their market segments. NVKK had been particularly successful in introducing consumer products in Japan for which domestic products did not exist.

THE U.S. MARKET FOR SKIN CARE PRODUCTS

When the Clearasil business was acquired by Richardson-Vicks in 1960, total value amounted to U.S. $2.3 million. By 1980, Clearasil sales represented about U.S. $30 million and consisted of Clearasil Regular Tinted Cream, Clearasil Soap, Clearasil Stick, Clearasil Vanishing Formula, Clearasil Medicated Cleanser, Clearasil Antibacterial Acne Lotion, and most recently New Super Strength Clearasil Creams and Clearasil Antibacterial Soap.

The target audience for acne care products were almost all teenagers. The most typical skin problems faced by this group were pimples, oily skin, and blackheads. It was estimated that about 20 percent of the target audience represented new users each year. Although this was a teenage product, mothers were believed to make the selection in six out of ten occasions for boys and three out of ten for girls.

About 50 percent of the target population used treatment products, up from 35 percent in 1975. Of the 50 million teenagers, only 25 million were users of treatment products, 10 percent had clear skin, and 40 percent represented potential new users. Clearasil was the market leader with Clearasil creams accounting for about 25 percent of dollar value and 30 percent of unit value.

The treatment market in the U.S. had undergone substantial changes in the 1970s. Prior to 1975, sulfur and resourcinol, used in Clearasil, were the only approved treatment agents for creams. In 1975, the Federal Drug Administration cleared benzoyl peroxide in strength of up to 10 percent. This provided an opportunity for a new brand, Oxy 5, and later Oxy 10 (indicating the percentage of benzoyl peroxide) marketed by Norcliff-Thayer, a unit of Revlon. Oxy began to erode

Clearasil's market share, a trend that was stopped only when Richardson-Vicks launched New Super Strength Clearasil Cream with 10 percent benzoyl peroxide in 1979. Clearasil's market share as a result rebounded and the brand continued to dominate the acne treatment segment.

In the U.S., Clearasil was heavily supported by advertising. Budgeted expenditures in 1980 accounted for about U.S. $5 million, or 25 percent of all advertising expenditures for the category. Richardson-Vicks employed a strategy in the U.S. that was closer to a two-way action benefit.

THE SKIN CARE MARKET IN JAPAN

In Japan skin care products were a part of the personal care industry. Since acne products were targeted for people in their teens and early twenties, the acne products were part of the young people's personal care segment. Two principal categories were offered: skin care, including facial and body care; and "other" cares, consisting of hair care, fragrances, etc. See Exhibit 1.

The youth skin care market included 21.6 million consumers between the ages of 12 and 24, both male and female. Some 77 percent, or 16.6 million young people, suffered some type of skin problems. About 51 percent or 11.0 million suffered from acne, or pimples. There was no difference between male or female populations when it came to acne suffering. See Exhibit 2.

About the remaining 47 percent, or about 5.2 million of acne sufferers, were characterized as treaters. A very small percentage of these would search out professional help. Treaters were described as acne sufferers using a specific acne product other than ordinary bar soap.

Some 53 percent of Japanese acne sufferers fell into the category of non-treaters. "Pimples are the symbol of youth" was a common saying in Japan according to Horita. "Japanese in general consider that the time will be coming for everyone to have pimples, and that they will disappear automatically. It was just a matter of time until they would disappear." Nontreaters used only ordinary bar soap to wash their face.

About 38 percent of treaters used "wash products" only, such as toiletry facial wash products, toiletry bar soaps, and cosmetic facial soaps. The wash-only group was 60 percent female. Wash products were marketed as preventatives.

About 44 percent of treaters used treatment products only. Of those, 70 percent were Clearasil users. Users of treatment products were about equally divided between male and female users.

The third and smallest group of treaters, 18 percent of all treaters, were simultaneous users of treatment products and wash products.

Products for Acne Treatment

"Before Clearasil's re-launch in 1978, there was no product on the market advertised exclusively for acne treatment. NVKK and Clearasil created this market," explained Horita.

Treatment products were classified either as drug or quasi-drug. The difference between the two categories depended on the product's ingredients and its registration with the Japanese Drug Administration. Clearasil was drug registered.[2]

Competitors in this category included a number of domestic and foreign brands including Upjohn Acne Lotion, Rexall Acne Lotion, Taisho Acneal Cream, Taisho Acneal Lotion. None of these products was actively supported by promotional campaigns and all were priced between 700 yen to 1200 yen per unit. Most of the manufacturers were pharmaceutical companies that tended to concentrate on ethical drugs that required promotion directed at the medical profession and distribution through drug store outlets.

The quasi-drug acne treatment products consisted of a number of products positioned largely for acne prevention. These products were licensed under a different procedure and were prevented by law to be positioned for treatment. Major competitors were Kanebo Asty, Shiseido Purit, Helene Curtis, Clear and Lovely, Noxema, and Acne Trio. These included some of the largest Japanese cosmetic companies. Prices for these products ranged from 500 to 1,500 yen.

There was a difference between the two product categories with respect to product claims and

---

2. The term *drug-registered* is identical with medicated product, and *quasi-drug* with nonmedicated, as used elsewhere in this case.

EXHIBIT 1 ● Japanese Skin Care Industry: Segmentation

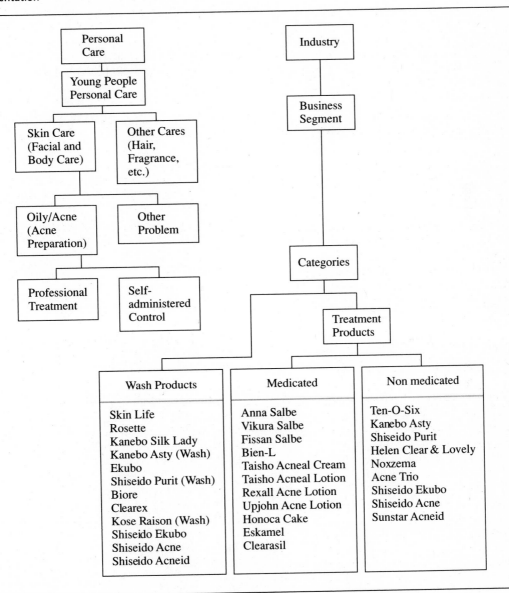

EXHIBIT 2 ● Japanese Skin Care Market: Young
People

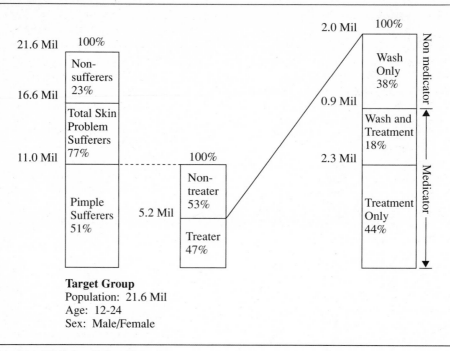

Target Group
Population: 21.6 Mil
Age: 12-24
Sex: Male/Female

Source: Post 24 A&U Tokyo (July, 1981).

distribution. Drug registered products could claim to treat and cure acne. Quasi-drug products at most could claim to prevent acne from occurring. If a company decided to license a product as a drug, that product's distribution was restricted to drug stores only. Quasi-drug products could be sold through a variety of outlets including drug stores, supermarkets, and department stores.

"Wash" Products

On a unit basis, "wash" products accounted for the largest share of the acne market in Japan. That share had been expanding and was estimated at more than 50 percent for the most recent two-

month Nielsen period. There were seven subcategories in this wash market. See Exhibit 3.

Major competitors included Gyunyu Sekken with its Skin Life soap priced at 150 yen for a 46 gram bar, and Kao Sekken Biore cleansing foam (300 yen for a 60 gram tube). Kao was Japan's leading soap and detergent company.

The wash category had consistently gained in market share compared to the drug and quasi-drug categories. However, the leading brands—Ekubo and Biore—had not been exclusively positioned as acne products. These three leading wash brands were supported by mass media and marketed for general skin care. It was in the "wash" products category that competitive activity was particularly strong. This category had witnessed several new product entries in the past two months. See Exhibit 4.

MARKET CHANNELS

All of NVKK's products fell into the proprietary drug category. Consequently, distribution was standardized for all products. About 2,000 companies competed in the proprietary trade but only about 175 employed 100 or more people. Proprietary drugs (OTC) accounted for 15 percent of all drug sales in Japan compared to ethical drugs with 85 percent.

NVKK used the same channels as its Japanese competitors. Sales were made from the factory to a group of primary wholesalers. Some of these in turn sold to a number of sub-wholesalers. The sub-wholesalers distributed NVKK's products through a large number of retail outlets which included general drugstores and various types of chain drugstores. Because NVKK products could only be sold through drugstores, the company did not maintain contacts with discount stores, department stores and convenience stores that did not have drug corners.

Wholesale Drug Distribution

NVKK used about 60 primary wholesalers which, together with their branches, maintained about 250 sales offices. Primary wholesalers were granted nonexclusive sales territories which resulted in at times very keen competition among various branch offices. "For this kind of trade, 60 primary wholesalers is probably a moderate figure," explained Nagata, NVKK's national sales manager. A large Japanese competitor would maintain up to 200 primary wholesalers. NVKK's top 5 primary wholesalers accounted for about 57 percent of NVKK's total sales volume, the next 5 for 14 percent, while the smallest 25 were responsible for only 8 percent of NVKK sales. See Exhibit 5.

The role of the primary wholesaler was to distribute the products both directly and through smaller sub-wholesalers. In the Japanese drug trade there existed about 2700 wholesalers of all types. Of those, about 500 carried ethical products only and 2200 carried both ethical and proprietary drugs or only the latter category. Among the top 100 wholesalers, 25 specialized in ethical products only. The rest carried both proprietary and ethical lines. Some of these also carried toiletry products. "Of the about 1000 wholesalers involved in proprietary drugs, we cover about 160," said Nagata, "and they maintain another 96 sales branches among themselves."

Of NVKK's primary wholesalers, only one concentrated in proprietary products accounting for 5 percent of NVKK's volume. Another eight primary wholesalers, accounting for 59 percent of sales, carried both proprietary and toiletry products. The remainder of its volume was accounted for by primary wholesalers carrying both drug categories.

Retail Drug Distribution

"NVKK has achieved virtually 100 percent penetration of the drug-related retail trade" declared Nagata. General drug stores were the most important retail segment, accounting for 70 percent of NVKK's volume. There were about 51,500 such stores in Japan. Most of these stores were small and had less than 6 employees. Two-thirds of all stores had only one or two employees. They accounted for 40 percent market share. In Japan, only 1 percent of all drugstores had more than 6 employees. These larger stores accounted for only 7 percent of the general drugstore sales volume.

The second most important group was the national and local chain drugstores. This category included about 2800 drugstores. They accounted for 20 percent of NVKK's volume. The local chains numbered about 1500 stores. Another 1300 outlets in this segment were accounted for by national chain stores, for example, Kokumin and Higuchi, or supermarkets with drug corners such as Daiei or Jusco. These chains maintained drug corners and employed a licensed pharmacist.

With about 300 outlets, local discount drugstores were small in numbers but accounted for 5 percent of NVKK's volume. These were individ-

EXHIBIT 3 ● Japanese Wash Market

Segment	Target	Benefits
Cosmetic cleansers (lotion, cream, gel)	Female adults Makeup users	Removes makeup and dirt thoroughly Refreshing Dirt free
Cosmetic facial soap (Honey cake, moon drops)	All females Normal/dry skin, primarily	After washing, leaves skin smooth and moist Less irritation
Toiletry bar soap by cosmetic company	Females	Keeps skin smooth and moist Refreshing
Toiletry facial wash (Biore, Silk Lady)	All females Normal/dry skin primarily	After washing, leaves skin smooth and moist Less irritation Good for preventing pimples (secondary) Good for delicate skin
Specialized facial soap	Females with delicate skin	Good for face washing for very delicate/sensitive skin
Medicated soap	Younger males/females	Sterilizes skin Good for preventing pimples Treatment for skin disease
Medicated soap for sterilization	Specifically for treating skin problem	Sterilizes skin

EXHIBIT 3 ● Japanese Wash Market (Continued)

Support	*Price/size/form*	*Distribution*	*Others*
Deep cleansing After feeling by product foam	Wide range of product forms	Cosmetic store	Use as part of daily make up routine
			Personal use only
			Double usage with facial soap
Ingredients (honey, lemon, etc.)	Transparent bar soap	Cosmetic store (Chain store)	Personal use
Appearance	Premium price		
Perfume	(1,000–1,500)		
Company image			
Product line by skin type	Medium price bar soap	All distribution channel	Personal–family
Special ingredient (MFP)	Mainly cream type	All distribution channel	Quasi drug
	Several sizes		Personal use– family use
Company image	Medium price 300–600		
No perfume	Premium price 1,000–2,000	Cosmetic/drug store (specialized)	Only for sensitive skin
No coloring			
No irritants			
Weak acidity same as skin			
Ingredients			
Antibacterial ingredients	Low–medium	Drugstore– Cosmetic	Specialized purpose only (pimple-allergy)
Drying effects			
Ingredients	Small size Medium–High	Drugstore only	

EXHIBIT 4 ● Competitive Actions

Acne Preparations
Trend of Consumer Sales (Units)

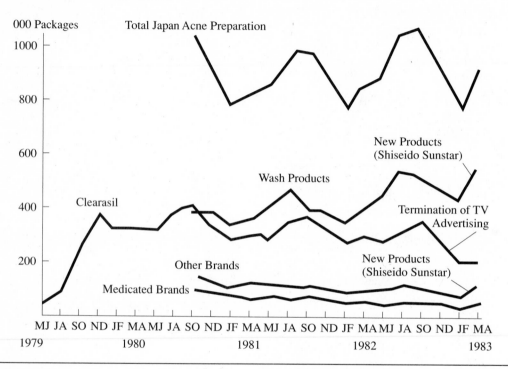

ually managed stores operated on a discount basis. The department store and convenience store segment included about 1500 outlets and accounted for only 3 percent of NVKK's volume. This last segment included 1000 drugstore corners in department stores and about 500 in convenience food stores. Most convenience food stores did not have drug sections.

In 1980, the typical drugstore's retail sales consisted of the following product categories:

Drugs	51%
Cosmetics	12%
Toiletries	9%
Medical supplies	9%
Other	19%

Drug sales were further subdivided into the following categories:

Nutritional and tonic drugs	30.8%
Psychotropic drugs (includes cold remedies and sleeping pills)	19.0%
Gastro-intestinal drugs	16.2%
External skin drugs	15.8%
Respiratory tract drugs	4.3%
Others	13.9%

NVKK's Sales Organization

NVKK's sales force consisted of 5 branch managers and 25 salesmen. They focused their activities on NVKK's primary wholesalers, the sub-

EXHIBIT 5 ● Distribution Channels

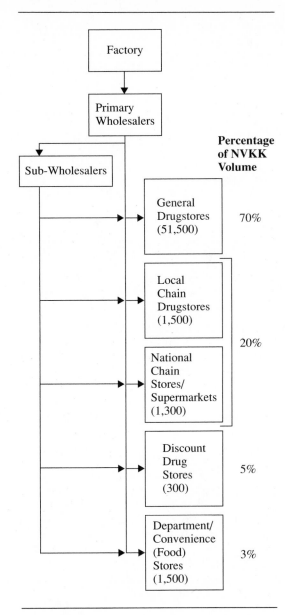

	Percentage of NVKK Volume
General Drugstores (51,500)	70%
Local Chain Drugstores (1,500) / National Chain Stores/ Supermarkets (1,300)	20%
Discount Drug Stores (300)	5%
Department/ Convenience (Food) Stores (1,500)	3%

wholesalers, and NVKK's largest 1500 retail customers. In urban areas, primary wholesalers were visited weekly, and twice per month in rural areas.

Both sub-wholesalers and top retailers were visited once per month.

NVKK's sales force was responsible for distributing all of the company's eight products in national distribution, as well as any test markets the company might run. For its size, NVKK maintained a small sales force. In accordance with NVKK's reliance on a pull strategy that included heavy use of consumer advertising, NVKK's sales force was primarily used to maintain good relationships with wholesalers and to solve minor problems. Almost all orders were telephoned to NVKK by its wholesalers. In contrast, NVKK's Japanese competitors in the drug market tended to follow more of a "push" campaign with a greater reliance on personal selling.

NVKK's price structure offered the average retailer a 30 percent gross margin. Sub-wholesalers bought at 64 percent of list, and the average primary wholesaler's purchase price was 60 percent of list. Although retailer margins for NVKK products were the same as for competitor products, NVKK wholesale margins were 3 to 4 percent below those of other major advertised brands. "NVKK follows much more of a pull strategy than other Japanese competitors in this field who tend to emphasize more of a push strategy," commented Nagata.

RECENT COMPETITIVE DEVELOPMENTS

Starting in February 1983, competition in the acne preparation market had been very active. This activity was largely concentrated on the quasi-drug and "wash" segments of the acne market. In February, Shiseido added "'Acne Wash Foam" as a line extension to its Ekubo "wash" product line. Also in February, Sunstar launched a set of "wash" products and a quasi-drug spot lotion under the brand name "Acneid." In March, Shiseido introduced a series of six wash products, including both wash and quasi-drug lotions, under the "Acne" brand name. That same month Kanebo added a drug registered acne cream "Mydate Acne Fresh" as an extension of its Mydate lotion and moisturizer wash products.

These new entries differed from existing cosmetic products insofar as they were exclusively positioned as acne products. Previously, products were either integrated into an existing line of cosmetics or represented a complete acne cosmetic line. These new wash products were registered as quasi-drug cosmetics with acne prevention as the key benefit. The new entries were distributed through a wide range of channels typical of cosmetic products.

The Ekubo line was produced and distributed by Shiseido, Japan's largest cosmetics company. The line included Ekubo Washing Foam, Milky Cream, Lemon Fresh, Milky Fresh, Milky Cream Soft, and Deodorant. The Ekubo Acne Foam came in two sizes of 20 grams and 80 grams, priced at 180 yen and 460 yen, respectively. The key benefit was "washing with it prevents acne." The line was supported by advertising in TV, magazines, outdoors, and informational leaflets and brochures.

Shiseido's later entry, Acne, was an entirely new line of six products consisting of:

Acne Soap	75 grams	600 yen
Acne Washing Foam	75 grams	1,000 yen (equals U.S. $4.00)
Acne Pack	75 grams	1,200 yen
Acne Lotion	75 grams	1,200 yen
Acne Skin Milk	75 grams	1,200 yen
Acne Spot Touch	10 ml	1,000 yen

These products appeared to be primarily targeted at consumers aged 15 to 17, both male and female, with the age group 18 to 24 as a secondary target. The introduction was supported with heavy TV, magazine, newspaper, and outdoor advertising.

Sunstar, Japan's leading marketer of toothpaste, introduced "Acneid," its first entry into the acne preparation market:

Acneid Washing Foam	60 grams	600 yen
Acneid Washing Foam S	60 grams	600 yen
Acneid Soap	60 grams	600 yen
Acneid Lotion	30 ml	700 yen

These products were fully supported with advertising in TV, magazine, outdoor, and point-of-purchase brochures.

Kanebo, Japan's second largest cosmetics company, introduced a medicated cream, Mydate Acne Fresh (30 grams at 600 yen) as a line extension for its Mydate series that included Clean Fresh cream, Milky Moist moisturizer, and Lotion Fresh.

CLEARASIL'S PERFORMANCE IN JAPAN

Skin toned Clearasil had been marketed without advertising support in Japan from mid 1961 until early 1974. It had reached a unit volume of only 44,500 units at a consumer price of 300 yen. It was taken off the market together with other small volume items in conjunction with a reorganization of NVKK's sales efforts.

Test Market Experience

NVKK decided to test market a reformulated version of Clearasil acne skin cream in 1978. The reformulated product was a "vanishing spot cream" that could be applied to acne on a person's face. Given its effective medicated ingredients, the product was designed to open the acne pimple head, drain the pimple without the need for squeezing, and finally to dry the acne pimples. The reformulated Clearasil was virtually identical to the product sold in the United States at that time. It did not contain benzoyl peroxide as it was not an approved ingredient in Japan. It was packaged in an 18 gram tube wrapped in a carton.

NVKK tested Clearasil in two test markets between July 1978 and June 1979. The two markets, Hiroshima and Shizuoka, represented about 4.5 percent of the total Japanese market and were supported with spot television advertising. Clearasil was priced at 700 yen per package at the consumer level and was distributed through drugstores only. Given Clearasil's registration as an OTC proprietary product, NVKK was restricted to the drugstore channel. "We choose to register Clearasil as a proprietary (OTC) drug product because we believe it was a marketing advantage," explained Horita.

The test market results were very encourag-

EXHIBIT 6 ● Clearasil Product Performance

		Sales units			*Value (000) yen*	
		Clearasil	*Clearasil share %*		*Clearasil*	*Clearsil share %*
1979	S/O	261,400	9.9		190,097	14.3
	N/D	373,380	11.0		271,092	17.0
1980	J/F	334,060	9.8		242,297	14.4
	M/A	314,280	10.9		228,591	15.0
	M/J	312,520	54.9		227,290	53.8
	J/A	385,340	45.3		298,146	45.9
	S/O	403,720	39.4		339,445	42.4
	N/D	325,870	36.2		227,498	40.6
1981	J/F	278,430	36.1		239,166	40.7
	M/A	295,680	36.1		251,942	39.9
	M/J	287,290	33.3		244,303	37.1
	J/A	358,610	36.2		306,242	41.1
	S/O	380,030	39.7		324,731	43.5
	N/D	320,350	37.0		273,877	41.9
1982	J/F	284,670	37.5		243,623	42.7
	M/A	305,290	36.0		260,285	40.2
	M/J	296,540	33.6		253,132	37.4
	J/A	333,300	31.8		283,883	35.8
	S/O	356,500	33.6		303,375	38.1
	N/D	300,210	32.2		252,702	36.7
1983	J/F	216,300	28.7		182,790	33.0
	M/A*	212,410	22.9		108,447	26.5

*Estimated by NVKK executives for period March/April 1983.

ing. Factory shipments amounted to about 122,000 packages over a twelve-month period. National roll-out was commenced in July 1979 and was completed by October. It was supported by TV advertisement exclusively and the consumer price was increased to 900 yen. Factory shipments for the first twelve months after national introduction amounted to 2,560,000 packages. The company had not expected to reach this sales level for at least another year. Factory ship-

ments remained at about the same level for the 1980/1981 fiscal year but began to decrease to 2,308,000 packages in 1981/1982 and 2,031,000 packages for the 1982/1983 fiscal year. For a detailed history of Clearasil's performance over the period 1979–1983, see Exhibit 6.

Throughout this time, NVKK supported Clearasil heavily with advertising. Advertising expenditures averaged about 70 percent of sales for the first three years after the national launch.

Dane Battiato, NVKK's marketing director, commented: "In our business it is typical to spend lots of money on advertising. When we first launch a new brand in a market, we are prepared to investment-spend beyond the normal level of advertising for a certain period. At Richardson-Vicks, we use a hurdle rate of 18 percent ROI for investment projects. With Clearasil, we can only reach normal product contribution if we cut marketing expenditures back to about 40 percent of the current level while holding sales."

Strategic Decisions on Clearasil

Horita believed NVKK management had reached a point where some critical decisions had to be made with respect to Clearasil's direction in Japan. "It bothers me that we cannot expand volume beyond the earlier reached levels of 2.5 million packages while the rest of the market is expanding rapidly."

In reviewing Clearasil's progress to date, management concluded that neither pricing nor product formulation were at the root of the problem. Horita pointed to indications that Clearasil's advertising was not communicating as well as it should. In order to restore Clearasil's volume growth, the advertising strategy might have to be changed.

Another opportunity for Clearasil was to expand into the "wash" segment by launching a Clearasil soap. This would give NVKK a chance to participate in the fastest growing acne preparation segment, the "wash" products, with the possibility of launching additional line extensions at a later time.

CLEARASIL ADVERTISING IN JAPAN

Clearasil's advertising was centered around the theme used worldwide by Richardson-Vicks. The key component was the documentation of Clearasil's three-way action:

1. Clearasil opens the acne/pimple head.
2. Clearasil drains the inside of the acne pimple without squeezing.
3. Clearasil dries the acne pimple.

From the outset, Clearasil was positioned as a unique and highly effective medicated cream with a special three-way action unsurpassed in its ability to clear up acne and thereby improve the appearance and social confidence of acne sufferers.

For the test market and the first year of national launch, NVKK used two TV commercials produced locally, both in a 30-second and 15-second version around two themes, "High School" and "Date." The same themes were used until mid-1980 when a revised version, "Adolescence," was introduced. Starting January 1981, a new commercial titled "Testimonial" was used in 30-second and 15-second versions to be followed a year later by still another new campaign titled "Disarming." See Exhibit 7.

The "High School" and "Date" Campaigns

The "High School" and "Date" versions of Clearasil were the initial commercials aired during both the test market period and during the first 12 months of national distribution. The campaign was designed to position Clearasil as *the* specific acne treatment product in a market where specific acne treatment products had never been actively marketed. See Exhibit 8.

The copy objectives were to make the point that Clearasil was specifically formulated to deal with acne, was a serious medicated product for treatment of acne, and would contribute to the improvement of the complexion of users. The advertising had to communicate Clearasil's three-way action and that it was suitable for all ages of the primary target audience, and to imply that it provided some form of social reward.

Change to the "Adolescence" Campaign

By the end of 1979, Horita concluded that the "High School" and "Date" campaigns worked well as introductory campaigns to build brand awareness. In fact, the campaigns had surpassed all NVKK objectives. However, Horita believed that the two commercials used did not wear very well over time. The commercials were too similar to each other because they both relied on the 3-way-action demonstration. Furthermore, low in-

EXHIBIT 7 ● Clearasil TV Campaign History

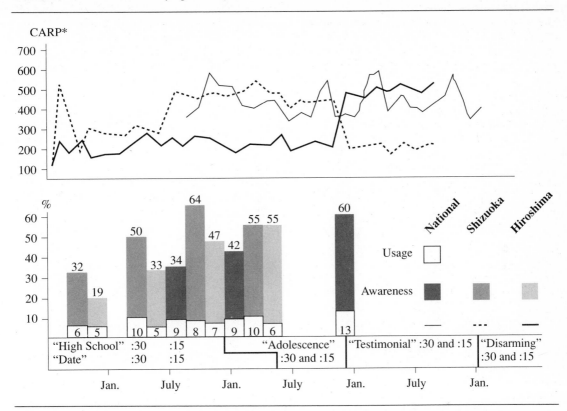

* CARP = *C*umulative *A*udience *R*ating *P*oint (People Rating) Shows Gross Coverage over the total people of each target area.

terest scores were indications of problems with the commercials.

Drawing on unused footage from the "High School" commercials, a new commercial entitled "Adolescence" was produced. There was, of course, little difference in copy compared to the earlier version. The major differences were new visuals on other aspects of school life. See Exhibit 9.

The "Testimonial" Campaign

Successive research indicated that the previous campaigns successfully communicated with and

generated trial among the sufferer/treater segment. The campaign failed to generate sufficient trial among the sufferer-nontreater segment because Clearasil was perceived as a very serious and specific product, possibly too medical, due to the overall serious tone of the commercials and the continuous use of the 3-way-action demonstration.

The "Testimonial" campaign was produced to increase trial among the nontreater segment which was identified as the key source for future volume growth for the brand. A documentary approach similar to Australian and Mexican testimonial commercials was used. These commer-

EXHIBIT 8 ● Story Board for "Date" Campaign, 1978/1979, June 14, 1978

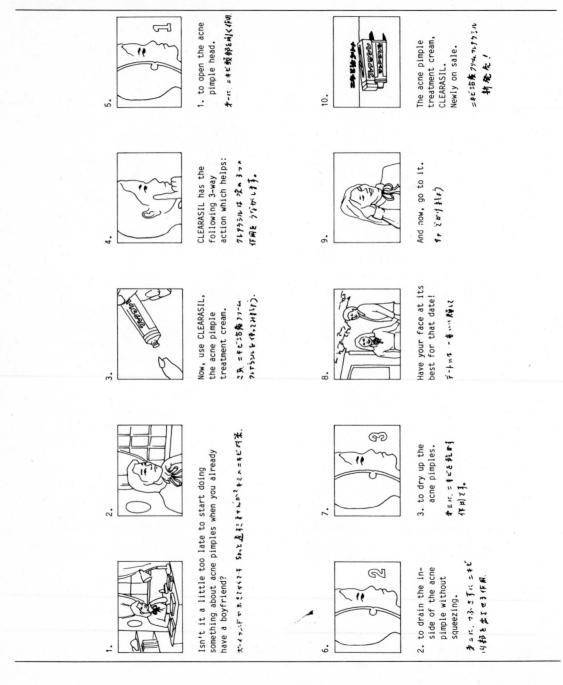

EXHIBIT 8 ● *(cont.)*

1.

When you're young, you have many small trials (and challenges). That's the essence of brimming youth . . . isn't it?

若さとは、様々な、いろいろ
悩みや 試みが あるから 若さです。

2.

You think about exams, sports,

試験とか スポーツも
上達 したい。

3.

girlfriends . . . acne pimples (are on your mind), too.

ガール フレンドゥに ニキビも。
ニキビも ぞう。

4.

Here is the acne pimple treatment cream, CLEARASIL.

さあ、ニキビ治療 クリーム
クレアラシルです。

5.

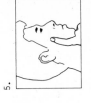

CLEARASIL has the following 3-way action which helps:

クレアラシルは、次の3つの
作用を うながします。

6.

1. to open the acne pimple head.

チーに、ニキビ 頭部を
開く作用。

7.

2. to drain the inside of the acne pimple without squeezing.

チニに、つぶさずに、ニキビ
内部を 出している作用。

8.

3. to dry up the acne pimple.

チニに、ニキビをかわかす
作用です。

9.

A bit of advice for your youth:

若さへ ひとつの
アドバイス

10.

The acne pimple treatment cream, CLEARASIL. Newly on sale.

ニキビ治療クリーム
クレアラシル
新発売

EXHIBIT 9 ● Story Board for "Adolescence"
Campaign, 1980, August 27, 1980

1.

When you're young,
you have many small
trials (and chal-
lenges). That's the
essence of brimming
youth . . . isn't it?

若さが輝やくには
いろんな消が
あるからこそですね

2.

You think about
your studies, your
future . . .

選択のこと。
将来のこと。

3.

girlfriends . . .

ガールフレンドのこと…

4.

and acne pimples
(are also on your
mind) . . .

そして、ニキビもそう。

5.

Here is the acne
pimple treatment
cream, CLEARASIL.

さあ ニキビ治療クリーム
クレアラシル です。

6.

CLEARASIL has the
following 3-way
action which helps:

クレアラシル・・らの次の
3つの作用を
うながします。

7.

1. to open the acne
pimple head.

第一に、ニキビ
頭部を開く作用。

8.

2. to drain the in-
side of the acne
pimple without
squeezing.

第二に、つぶさずに
ニキビの内部を
そうじ作用。

9.

3. to dry up the
acne pimple.

第三に、ニキビ
を乾かす作用
です。

10.

A bit of advise for
your youth.

若さに、ひとつの
アドバイス

11.

The acne pimple
treatment cream,
CLEARASIL.

ニキビ治療クリーム
クレアラシル

---

cials featured testimonial comments in quick cut sequences depicting teenagers who suffered from acne and who shared their various ideas on remedies and their advice with the television audience in a frank and natural way. The 3-way-action of earlier commercials was made slighly shorter and lighter in tone but NVKK retained the basic copy points and animation flow. NVKK added a new end benefit "clear and smooth" and dropped the reference to "acne treatment cream." Both a spring and summer version of the "Testimonial" campaign was produced. The media mix strategy remained unchanged. See Exhibit 10.

Testing of the "Testimonial" commercials against the earlier campaigns showed little improvement in interest, involvement and effectiveness. In those categories, the "Testimonial" cam-

paign was rated in the fourth, or lowest, quartile compared to average scores achieved by Japanese commercials.

The poor results of pre/post test among nontreaters despite high copy comprehension convinced NVKK executives that the "Testimonial" campaign could not live up to their expectations. An earlier study had shown that almost 70 percent of acne sufferers in the past year did not treat their acne other than washing with regular soap. It was increasingly clear that Clearasil could only grow as expected if an effective way to reach nontreaters could be found. Past campaigns were found amateurish (61%), dull (45%). A low interest test score of 480 was observed with a sharp drop during the explanation of the 3-way action. By comparison, for pharmaceutical products interest scores of 510

EXHIBIT 10 ● Story Board for "Testimonial"
Campaign

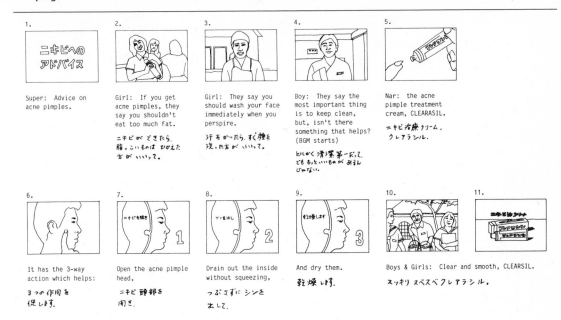

1.	2.	3.	4.	5.
Super: Advice on acne pimples.	Girl: If you get acne pimples, they say you shouldn't eat too much fat.	Girl: They say you should wash your face immediately when you perspire.	Boy: They say the most important thing is to keep clean, but, isn't there something that helps? (BGM starts)	Nar: the acne pimple treatment cream, CLEARASIL.

6.	7.	8.	9.	10. 11.
It has the 3-way action which helps:	Open the acne pimple head,	Drain out the inside without squeezing,	And dry them.	Boys & Girls: Clear and smooth, CLEARSIL.

to 520 were considered average; 550 or more was viewed as very good. Many commercials on the air scored in the 525 to 530 range. See Exhibit 11.

The Change to the "Disarming" Campaign

To more effectively communicate with nontreaters, a new "Disarming" commercial was produced. A new format for expressing the 3-way action was considered necessary. The previous approach created the impression that the product worked very quickly, that is, overnight, which was not the case. Furthermore, the 3-way action was perceived as having been worn out. However, the 3-way action was perceived to be the most impressive and important aspect of Clearasil. See Exhibit 12.

The new campaign also had to address the impression that Clearasil was for serious sufferers only and was not appropriate for light sufferers. The product was perceived as too strong for people with sensitive skin and was not "fashionable" because its image was inconsistent with that of a serious medicine. The previous execution of the "social reward" aspect was felt to be obvious, forced, and thus unpleasant to the viewer. While the concept of teenagers giving advice to other teenagers was acceptable, its execution was judged to be "preachy" in tone.

With respect to tone and image, the commercials were considered to be dark, gloomy, boring, repetitive, not lively, and lacking a modern contemporary "feeling." Contributing to this was the absence of music, the use of a male narrator, the execution of the 3-way action with its worn-out image and the fixed pattern of setting up the acne problem, on to 3-way action explanation, and then to end-benefit. Furthermore, some of the

EXHIBIT 11 ● Clearasil TV Commercials Test Ratings for "Testimonial" Campaign

	"High School"	"Date"	"Testimonial" Summer version	
			30 Sec	
	30 Sec score	30 Sec score	Score	Quartile
INTEREST				
Profile Curve Score	479	466	438	(4)
INVOLVEMENT				
Commercial Image Index	15%	12%	8%	(4)
COMMUNICATION				
A) Comprehension of Copy Point	48%	64%	42%	(2)
Comprehension of Sales Message	77	78	50	(1)
B) Recall of Brand Name	57	35	95	(1)
Recall of Copy Point	24	32	19	(2)
EFFECTIVENESS				
Pre/Post Score	+8%	+4%	+3%	(4)
			+5	(4)
Persuasion Score	37	30	25	(4)

characters in the commercials were not felt to be typical of contemporary teenagers.

A serious and direct approach to acne problems by highlighting disadvantages of acne sufferers was not responsive to nontreaters. Research showed that nontreaters were not seriously concerned about acne. "Do not worry about it" was the most often mentioned reason among nontreaters for not treating acne.

Dissatisfaction with Past Advertising Campaigns

During the first twelve months of the national campaign, Clearasil achieved an advertising intensity of about 14,700 GRP's in the two key regions of Japan, Kanto and Kansai, compared to a total of 18,888 GRP's and 19,947 GRP's respectively for all acne preparation products.[3] In March of 1980, Ekubo and Biore entered the market with budgets two to three times larger than Clearasil's for the March/June period of 1980. During the 1980/1981 period, Clearasil maintained its advertising at the same earlier level while Ekubo spent about 60% less and Biore maintained a level of

3. GRP = Gross Rating Point. GRP equals the sum of all airings of the program or spot announcement during a given time period. For example, a once-a-week program constantly recording a 15 percent rating (or 15 percent of TV homes covered) results in 60 GRP's for a 4-week period.

EXHIBIT 12 ● Story Board for "Disarming"
Campaign, Jan. 22, 1982

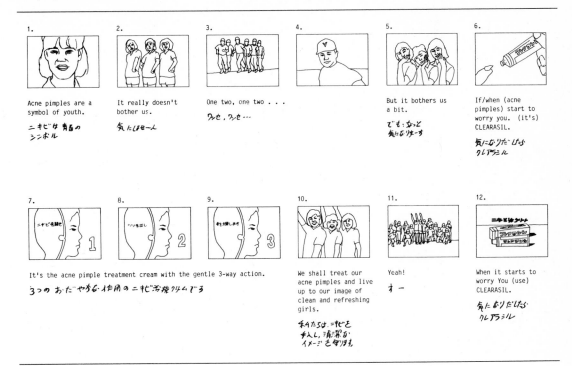

1. Acne pimples are a symbol of youth.
   ニキビな 青春の シンボル

2. It really doesn't bother us.
   気たにはせーん

3. One two, one two . . .
   フッセ, フッセ ---

4.

5. But it bothers us a bit.
   でも：ちょっと 気になります

6. If/when (acne pimples) start to worry you. (it's) CLEARASIL.
   気になりだしたら クレアラシル

7. 8. 9. It's the acne pimple treatment cream with the gentle 3-way action.
   3つの あたやかな 作用の ニキビ治療クリムである

10. We shall treat our acne pimples and live up to our image of clean and refreshing girls.
    私たちは ニキビ 手入し, 清潔な イメージを守ります

11. Yeah!
    オー

12. When it starts to worry You (use) CLEARASIL.
    気になりだしたら クレアラシル

sightly less than half of Clearasil's GRP's. During both years, Clearasil was the most advertised brand with a 45.9 percent share of GRP's. For more details, see Exhibit 13.

Horita, who had been off the brand from the end of 1979 due to an 18 months stay at the division's head office, became concerned about Clearasil's advertising in July of 1981. In his new position as creative development coordinator for all of NVKK's new products, he supervised some tests on Clearasil's advertising effectiveness on the "Adolescent" campaign. Interviewed teenagers connected the commercials with "dassai," a slang word used for a crumpled looking middle manager, somebody who was neither chic nor sophisticated. "In terms of U.S. equivalent, this comes close to the 'Columbo' role played by Peter Falk in the U.S. detective movie series," explained

Brian Taylor, one of the U.S. expatriate managers at NVKK. What Horita was concerned about was that the teenagers believed only a "dassai" could create such a commercial. Even worse was the connection between "dassai" and "kusai," the Japanese equivalent of "something disgusting."

Throughout this time period, NVKK had regularly measured consumer attitudes. Testing was done in the Tokyo area and in both of Clearasil's test markets. The results of the tests are shown in Exhibit 14.

"The data indicates a significant decrease in the satisfaction of Clearasil users," commented Mr. Horita, the brand manager. "At the same time, our brand awareness was ahead of objective. In our test markets, we expected a brand awareness of 50 to 60 percent after 12 months; instead, we achieved figures at 80 percent."

EXHIBIT 13 ● Acne Preparation Advertising Expenditures (in GRPs), 1979–1981

	Total	'79 July	Aug.	Sept.	Oct.	Nov.	Dec.	'80 Jan.	Feb.	Mar.	Apr.	May	June
Kanto													
Clearasil (7/79)	7,308	278	649	709	895	752	738	558	560	600	590	463	516
Ekubo (3/80)	4,847	—	—	—	—	—	—	—	—	1,805	1,185	1,271	588
Biore (3/80)	2,058	—	—	—	—	—	—	—	—	216	1,571	159	112
Skin Life	653	73	95	49	—	4	130	109	75	62	56	—	—
Noxzema	1,113	256	635	—	—	—	91	—	18	16	20	77	—
Asty	1,104	—	—	—	—	—	—	—	—	1,104	—	—	—
Clearex	60	—	—	—	—	—	—	—	—	—	—	—	60
Jelleje	—	—	—	—	—	—	—	—	—	—	—	—	—
Silk Lady	1,745	—	—	—	—	—	—	—	—	—	1,068	237	440
Total	18,888	607	1,379	758	895	756	959	667	653	3,801	4,490	2,207	1,716
Kansai													
Clearasil	7,447	262	682	671	848	626	626	611	474	574	941	560	572
Ekubo	4,741	—	—	—	—	—	—	—	—	1,605	1,195	1,354	587
Biore	2,164	—	—	—	—	—	—	—	—	68	1,781	183	129
Skin Life	612	59	97	28	—	7	132	110	54	68	57	—	—
Noxzema	973	181	601	—	—	—	67	—	18	15	23	68	—
Asty	1,072	—	—	—	—	—	—	—	—	1,072	—	—	—
Clearex	78	—	—	—	—	—	—	—	—	—	—	—	78
Jelleje	—	—	—	—	—	—	—	—	—	—	—	—	—
Silk Lady	2,860	—	—	—	—	—	—	—	—	—	1,819	526	515
Total	19,947	502	1,380	699	848	633	825	721	546	3,402	5,819	2,691	1,881

Source: MEH.

EXHIBIT 13 ● Acne Preparation Advertising Expenditures (in GRPs), 1979–1981 (Continued)

	Total	'80 July	Aug.	Sept.	Oct.	Nov.	Dec.	'81 Jan.	Feb.	Mar.	Apr.	May	June
Kanto													
Clearasil	7,089	513	812	456	468	442	812	848	509	625	569	478	557
Ekubo	4,197	1,574	916	443	255	284	212	105	80	93	80	94	61
Biore	3,138	674	170	83	208	614	109	260	46	71	558	165	180
Skin Life	736	35	15	27	16	7	100	166	95	137	116	22	—
Noxzema	1,865	121	260	212	156	170	128	3	—	125	126	415	149
Asty	—												
Clearex	79	79											
Acne Trio	515	—	—	—	—	—	—	—	—	—	—	—	515
Jelleje	—												
Silk Lady	1,445	—	—	—	—	—	—	—	—	—	922	523	—
Total	19,064 /	2,996	2,173	1,221	1,103	1,517	1,361	1,382	730	1,051	2,371	1,697	1,462
Kansai													
Clearasil	7,492	553	857	536	452	477	825	941	518	725	605	509	494
Ekubo	4,561	1,690	1,000	479	320	305	264	125	83	76	75	85	59
Biore	3,427	752	234	83	249	666	116	278	77	101	517	216	138
Skin Life	934	33	19	29	16	6	120	216	141	180	151	23	—
Noxzema	1,876	275	266	236	—	190	100	5	—	125	124	400	155
Asty	—												
Clearex	99	99											
Acne Trio	—												
Silk Lady	1,729	—	—	—	—	—	—	—	—	—	1,002	727	—
Total	20,118	3,402	2,376	1,363	1,037	1,644	1,425	1,565	819	1,207	2,474	1,960	846

Source: MEH.

EXHIBIT 14 ● Attribute Ratings on Clearasil (Among Clearasil Users)

Base	Tokyo			Shizuoka				Hiroshima			
	Post 6	*Post 12*	*Post 24*	*Post 6*	*Post 12*	*Post 18*	*Post 24*	*Post 6*	*Post 12*	*Post 18*	*Post 24**
	153 %	*75 %*	*85 %*	*142 %*	*155 %*	*150 %*	*98 %*	*111 %*	*148 %*	*155 %*	*115 %*
Leaves skin feeling clean	23	23	13	20	13	14	15	17	28	25	25
Leaves skin smooth	22	15	15	12	12	6	10	10	21	18	16
Not greasy	37	36	23	28	23	26	17	32	42	37	35
Does not irritate skin	34	33	20	19	19	20	21	24	37	29	38
Fast working	44	33	19	22	24	41	34	27	30	37	37
Dries up oily skin	37	29	22	25	21	47	28	26	34	37	38
Helps open pimples	35	35	23	22	20	34	33	20	28	31	46
Can use with assurance	NA	36	26	NA	NA	NA	23	NA	NA	NA	44
Disappears into skin	25	19	14	17	12	13	11	18	27	32	25
Helps prevent pimples	30	28	19	21	13	18	14	31	36	39	38
Improves appearance of facial skin	NA	15	14	NA	NA	NA	11	NA	NA	NA	21
Helps clear up pimples	47	36	23	24	21	35	28	32	37	41	45
Helps drain pimples	43	32	21	24	19	37	33	26	39	36	43
Is a medicine	NA	24	20	NA	NA	NA	15	NA	NA	NA	25
Is a product that suits me	NA	24	21	NA	NA	NA	18	NA	NA	NA	24
Is a contemporary product	NA	21	19	NA	NA	NA	10	NA	NA	NA	27
Is a cosmetic	NA	6	2	NA	NA	NA	4	NA	NA	NA	6

*Indicates 24 months after launch in that area.

EXHIBIT 15 ● Clearasil Consumer Off-Take, Spring 1983

	80/81	81/82	82/83	MAT	'83 J/F
Total Market	5,226	5,301	5,695	6,064	753
% Change Y/A		+1.4%	+7.4%	+6.5%	
Clearasil	1,973	1,943	1,642	1,660	216
% Change Y/A		+19.0%	−15.5%	+1.1%	
% Share	37.8%	36.7%	28.8%	27.4%	28.7%
Medicated Brands	354*	338	280	276	36
% Change Y/A		−4.5%	−17.2%	−1.4%	
% Share	6.8%	6.4%	4.9%	4.6%	4.9%
Other Brands	594*	567	661	702	84
% Change Y/A		−4.5%	+16.6%	+6.2%	
% Share	11.4%	10.7%	11.6%	11.6%	11.2%
Wash Products	1,831*	2,445	3,104	3,417	415
% Change Y/A		+33.5%	+27.0%	+10.1%	
% Share	35.0%	46.1%	54.5%	56.3%	55.2%

*These data '80 S/O–'81 M/J.
Units in thousands.

"Obviously, we are not getting our message across as effectively as we wanted. Our interest scores for both commercials were below average compared to the typical Japanese commercial. Where we did very well was in the comprehension of copy points, sales message, and copy point recall. However, despite the excellent comprehension scores, the Clearasil commercials scored low on pre-post effectiveness and persuasion." (See Exhibit 11.)

Withdrawal of Advertising Support in November 1982

In the fall of 1982, it became clear that Vicks' latest campaign, "Disarming," was no more successful than previous ones. Interest curves in theater testing dropped even more. "As it did not make sense to support Clearasil with a campaign that did not meet our communications objective, we decided to withdraw all advertising support in November 1982. For the last 5 months, we have not put any advertising expenditures behind Clearasil," explained Horita.

The impact of the advertising withdrawal was felt almost immediately in figures on consumer off-take collected regularly for NVKK. Market share for Clearasil dropped to a low of 23 percent as compared to more than one-third in earlier periods. The biggest winners were the wash products. The share of wash products reached 57 percent for the most recent period. See Exhibit 15.

Advertising in Japan

A specialist in Japanese advertising gave the following explanation: "When a Western businessman enters his hotel room in Japan and turns on the switch of his TV and watches the Japanese commercials, he invariably complains that they seem to be heavy on mood elements and often difficult to even understand what they were selling. On the other hand, Japanese businessmen complain on returning from the U.S. about the heavy verbiage in the U.S. commercials. How could the viewer, they would ask, stand being talked at so incessantly?"

When tested in Japan, U.S. and Japanese commercials ranked differently. Japanese commercials tended to score higher in "execution interest" whereas U.S. commercials scored higher on the "image index." The key difference was "copy recall" where Japanese commercials ranked overwhelmingly lower than U.S. commercials. There was little difference in brand recall, pre/post attitude shift, and product interest.

McCann-Erickson, NVKK's advertising agency in Japan, described the Japanese style of advertising as "understated" or "non-linear." There was a saying that in Japan "you don't go into somebody's living room without first taking your shoes off." Consequently, Japanese advertising showed more "respect" for the consumer by being less direct.

Japanese consumers perceived little difference in the quality or technical superiority of various products. Often they were not knowledgeable about product details such as ingredients in medicine. Because most products were in general believed to be equal, no comparative advertising was used in Japan. In the opinion of one of the executives, "you sell your product by becoming your consumer's friend."

For OTC products, word-of-mouth communications were very important and, together with store recommendations, outranked advertising as a source for product decisions. For both drug and cosmetics buyers, store recommendations are frequently solicited. Some 90 percent of buyers asked "always" or "sometimes" before purchasing.

THE OPPORTUNITY FOR LINE EXTENSION

As Horita was working on a solution for Clearasil's advertising problem he also investigated opportunities to participate in the rapidly growing wash segment. "With most of the competitive ac-

tivities right now taking place in the wash category, we should definitely consider entering with our own wash product," explained Horita. "Growth in the wash-only segment has outpaced growth in the treatment-only segment."

During the past few months, NVKK had a bar soap under test that could be marketed as Clearasil Soap. "We should see the Clearasil franchise as a business on its own with opportunities to expand into various categories, but all under the Clearasil franchise." The soap had been marketed by Richardson-Vicks in other countries under the Clearasil name and was thus available to NVKK. However, corporate policy did not allow a "prevents acne" claim which the Japanese government allowed as a claim for medicated soaps.

Product concept tests had already been carried out. Results indicated that a price of about yen 450 per package would be appropriate. The soap would be classified as a drug registered bar soap. Product usage tests indicated that treaters evaluated the product more positively than the general population. In general, test scores on Clearasil Soap were equal to or better than those for Clearasil Cream a few years ago. However, since NVKK had no prior experience with a drug-registered soap in Japan, there was no control group to compare its soap against.

Distribution Requirements for Entering Wash Category

Several options existed for NVKK's entry into the wash segment. Horita had to consider not only whether NVKK should enter this segment but also how this might be done. In addition, any initiative needed to be coordinated with actions for Clearasil cream.

"Entry into the wash product segment has some important consequences for distribution," commented Mr. Nagata, the sales manager. In Japan, bar soaps were sold primarily through supermarkets and department stores. Only cosmetic soaps were sold in important volumes through drug and cosmetic stores. Bar soap for bath use was a very popular gift item among Japanese with about 90 percent of the volume sold through department stores. Cosmetic soap was sold 75 percent through cosmetic stores or the cosmetic section in supermarkets, with drug stores accounting for 25 percent. "For us to be successful with a soap, we have to open more channels into the cosmetic stores, supermarkets, and department store segment. Right now, we don't have these channels."

"To appreciate the buying environment at the store level, you have to understand that soaps are treated as a toiletry product category. Although we may be selling to the same store, wholesaler and buyer choices are different from OTC products."

Japanese drugstores were notorious for their small size and crowded conditions. A typical drugstore was about 300 square feet in size. Arrangements included a U-shaped main counter and one or two middle aisles. Drug products, including Clearasil, were displayed behind the main counter and had to be specifically requested by the customer. Toiletries were typically displayed in one of the center aisles. In many instances, the wholesaler supplying toiletry products to a drugstore would differ from a wholesaler supplying drug products. In the case of chain drugstores, the buyer for toiletries was not identical to the buyer of drug products.

In cosmetic stores, a similar arrangement with a U-shaped main counter existed. Soaps would typically be displayed in one of the center aisles as a separate category with another aisle reserved for other toiletry products. Frequently, the supplying wholesalers for those categories were not identical, making it difficult, for example, for a drug wholesaler supplying a cosmetics store to add a product category that had traditionally been supplied by another wholesaler. Supermarkets and department stores typically bought from wholesalers that combined cosmetic and toiletry lines.

"Right now, only 5 of our primary wholesalers and 60 sub-wholesalers carry both proprietary drugs and toiletries" remarked Nagata, the sales manager. "To develop the same network in toiletries takes time. Ideally, we need other toiletry products and/or an entire new line to accomplish this. To give us adequate coverage in toiletries we need 60 to 70 primary and another 80 to 100 sub-wholesalers."

Competition in the Toiletry Sector

Japanese competitors in the toiletry segment employed various distribution and sales strategies. Sunstar, Japan's largest marketer of toothpaste, made non-exclusive use of primary wholesalers as did NVKK. Kao, the largest Japanese detergent and toiletry company, often referred to as the "Procter & Gamble of Japan," had its own sales company. This firm maintained numerous local joint-ventures with wholesalers. For Tokyo, the company operated under Tokyo Kao Sales Co. and was owned fifty percent by Kao. These joint-venture sales companies sold directly to retailers. Yet another approach was followed by Lion, a large toiletry company, whose major products were detergents, toiletry, and toothpaste. Lion also employed primary wholesalers but had its own sales groups inside each primary wholesaler that gave exclusive attention to its own products. Although Mr. Nagata was unsure, he believed that these sections were funded by Lion. Both Kanebo and Shiseido were classified as "affiliated chains." "Chain" products were marketed directly to retailers. The Kanebo "chain" included about 15,000 cosmetic stores. Kanebo's salesforce numbered 250 salesmen. The Shiseido "chain" consisted of 28,000 stores. Shiseido employed about 1,800 salesmen and about 10,000 demonstrators-merchandisers.

SEARCHING FOR A NEW ADVERTISING APPROACH

"Our original approach to advertising Clearasil in Japan has been to follow quite closely the approaches used around the world for this brand. The three-way action is the basic product support that has become the cornerstone to Clearasil advertising worldwide. It worked everywhere, and it certainly also worked in the early campaign in Japan," explained Horita. "Typical advertising in Japan is much more subtle than advertising used in the United States. There is clearly a soft-sell approach, and frequently the product is mentioned only briefly at the end."

Robert Whelan, the product manager for Vicks cough drops in Japan, explained Richardson-Vicks' advertising approach as follows: "In the United States, we believe that the advertising message should explain the benefit of a product, supply some rationale or reason for saying it, and offer some opportunity to distinguish the product from the competition with some credibility about the claimed advantages. To give up any of these elements would be a major change from past practices."

Harold Todd, President of NVKK, commented, "The Clearasil situation is very complex. Here we are with a commercial that scores very high on recall but low on interest. Horita would like to eliminate the three-way action part that has been the key to the product's success worldwide. Maybe it is true. But originally, we were successful with just that approach. Maybe we are simply telling the story the wrong way? There are pro's and con's on both sides. But certainly at this point I don't have enough confidence to simply take the 3-way action out."

NVKK's Advertising Approach for Other Products

With the exception of Colac, a laxative sold only in Japan, NVKK followed an advertising policy that was similar to the one used by other Richardson-Vicks subsidiaries. The TV commercials, while produced in Japan, followed the usual approach of product benefit and support claim. Virtually in all other product areas NVKK was the market leader by a wide margin.

Colac, the laxative, was different since it was only marketed in Japan. Accounting for almost half of NVKK's sales, Colac was a success story. Colac's advertising focused entirely on brand personality with no defined, rational exposition of support. Imagery and mood were used extensively in the earlier part of all Colac commercials to symbolize some of the key benefits promised. Later in

the commercials, what would appear to most observers to be just a conventional product introduction shot, is in fact the "clincher" in the eyes of the Japanese consumers.

Division Views

When the decision was made to relaunch Clearasil in Japan, the division argued strongly for the 3-way action approach which had proved successful in Brazil and Australia. Already at that time, Horita had felt uncomfortable with that approach. Although NVKK's top executives shared Horita's concern, they went along with the division's arguments of "why don't you try it." As a result, the Japanese campaign was built on the extensive documentation supplied by the division which included advertising strategy, logo, packaging, layouts, etc.

Following Horita's transfer to the divisional head office in Westport, Connecticut, NVKK followed the original strategy. Although Horita returned to Japan in mid-1981, he was not put back on Clearasil until spring of 1982. In the meantime, divisional management had changed and Horita, convinced that the existing policies would lead nowhere, tried again to get the division to accept a change. Two major meetings were held in Japan. "So far, the division has not accepted our point of view yet;" said Horita, "perhaps they felt that I did not listen to anyone and that I was stubborn. After all, other countries work with the 3-way action. Why should Japan be an exception?"

Horita's Views

Horita himself was uncertain as to what approach he should suggest. "We started out with a largely U.S. approach with emphasis on the three-way action argument. When our scores turned out low, we reduced the three-way action component by making it shorter or lighter, thus moving more into the direction of a Japanese approach. However, our scores got worse, not better. Now I am no longer convinced that moving to an even more typical Japanese style advertising would actually improve the situation. On the other hand, I have all along felt that the three-way action argument was kind of obvious to the Japanese consumer and it encouraged over-expectation of product performance. Its constant repetition just does not help."

For the upcoming meeting on Clearasil marketing strategy in Japan, Horita wanted to take an integrated approach to his business in Japan. "I don't see the Clearasil cream or the possibility of a Clearasil soap as two distinctly different issues. Instead, I would like to present an overall strategy for our Clearasil business in Japan and integrate both cream and soap under this umbrella."

CASE 5

Interactive Computer Systems, Corp.[1]

In September 1980, Peter Mark, Marketing Manager of Interactive Computer Systems Corporation, was faced with a perplexing conflict between his company's USA sales group and the European subsidiaries. The USA sales group had begun to sell a display controller which had been developed in Europe. The product had been selling in Europe for several years and sales were relatively strong. Now, however, several major European customers had begun to purchase the product through their USA offices and shipped it back to Europe. The Europeans were complaining that the U.S. pricing was undercutting theirs and that they were losing sales volume which was rightfully theirs. Both the U.S. and European groups claimed that their pricing practices followed corporate guidelines and met the profit objectives set for them.

INTERACTIVE COMPUTER SYSTEMS, CORP.

Interactive Computer Systems Corporation (ICS), headquartered in Stamford, Connecticut, was a

1. Names and data are disguised.

All prices and costs are stated in U.S. dollars.

●

This case was prepared by Visiting Professor Jean-Pierre Jeannet as a basis for class discussion rather than to illustrate either effective or ineffective handling of an administrative situation. Copyright © 1981 by IMEDE, Lausanne, Switzerland. The International Institute for Management Development (IMD), resulting from the merger between IMEDE, Lausanne, and IMI, Geneva, acquires and retains all rights. Reproduced by permission.

large multinational manufacturer of computer systems and equipment. The company made a range of computer systems and was best known for its small or "mini" computers. ICS was considered one of the industry leaders in that segment of the computer industry which included such companies as Data General, Digital Equipment, Prime Computer, Masscomp, and Hewlett-Packard.

The company was primarily a U.S. based corporation with the majority of its engineering and manufacturing facilities located in the eastern United States. In addition, ICS had manufacturing facilities in Canada, Singapore, West Germany, Brazil, and a joint venture in South Korea.

Sales were conducted throughout most of the non-Communist world by means of a number of sales subsidiaries with sales offices located in Canada, Mexico, Brazil, Argentina, Chile, Japan, Australia, and several European countries. Elsewhere, sales were conducted through a network of independent agents and distributors.

PRODUCT LINE

The ICS line of products was centered around a family of 16-bit mini computer systems. "Mini computer" was the popular term referring to small to medium sized computer systems which were used in a wide variety of applications including industrial control, telecommunications systems, laboratory applications, and small business systems. "16-bit" refers to the size of the computer "word" or unit of data. These systems were different from the large computer systems of IBM, Univac, and Honeywell which had word sizes of 32–36 bits.

In addition to the computer central processing units (CPU) and memory units, ICS produced a line of peripheral devices required for making complete computer systems. These included devices such as magnetic tape units, disk storage units, line printers, card readers, video and hard copy terminals, display units, and laboratory and industrial instrumentation interface units. These various peripherals were used as appropriate and combined with the final computer systems to meet the specific customer's requirements. ICS produced most of these products in-house but some, such as line printers and card readers, were purchased to ICS specifications from companies specializing in those products such as Data Products and Documentation.

ICS manufactured several central processing units (CPU) which were positioned in price and performance to form a product family. They all had similarity of design, accepted (executed) the same computer instructions, and ran on the same operating system (master control programs). The difference was in speed, complexity and cost. The purchaser was able to select the model which economically met the performance requirements of the intended application.

This family of CPU's, together with the wide range of available peripheral devices, formed a family of computer systems offering a considerable range of price and performance but with compatible characteristics and programming.

COMMUNICATIONS INTERFACES

A communications interface was a peripheral device used for transmitting data to or from the computer system. This could either be:

- A terminal on which a user could enter data, for example on a typewriter-like "keyboard," and have data displayed, typically on either a video screen, or "hard copy" on a typewriter-like printer.

- For other computers, either of the same type or from a different manufacturer.

MODEL 431 COMMUNICATIONS INTERFACE

The specific product in question was the model 431 communications interface, a 4 line programmable multiplexer.

The 431 consisted of one electronic circuit module which plugged into the I/O (input/output) "bus" of the computer (a bus was an electrical cable or wiring on which data signals flowed in some organized manner). It provided the interface for four separate communications lines which were connected by means of specially designed connectors on the module. Such multi-line interfaces were typically called multiplexers after the manner in which they worked internally. They offered the advantages of more efficient space utilization and lower per-line costs compared with the normal alternative of a separate single line interface per line. Depending on the computer vendor, multiplexers come in various sizes such as 2, 4, 6, 8, 16, 32, and 64 lines.

ICS already has 4, 8, and 16 line multiplexers in its line of high volume standard products. The specified advantage of the 431 was its programmable nature. It could be loaded with software to handle any of several different protocols directly in the interface using its own microprocessor on the module. It also performed error checking and moved data directly to or from the main computer memory. Since these functions had previously all been performed by a program running in the computer, the 431 relieved the computer of this load and freed it up to do other work. The result was a net improvement in system speed and power.

The model 431 was designed in 1977 at ICS's small European engineering facility assigned to its German subsidiary, Interactive Computers GmbH, in Frankfurt and was manufactured there for shipment world-wide to those ICS subsidiaries who were selling the 431. Sales had initially started in Europe and then spread to other areas. Sales volumes are given in Exhibit 1.

INTERSUBSIDIARY TRANSACTIONS

With the exception of the Korean joint venture, all of ICS's subsidiaries were wholly owned and

EXHIBIT 1 ● Model 431 Sales Volume (Units), Selected Countries

	1977	1978	1979	1980 (forecast)
Germany	30	100	110	100
UK	5	40	60	70
France	10	20	50	40
Canada	—	—	5	5
Switzerland	3	20	30	15
Australia	—	—	10	30
USA	—	2	80	200

EXHIBIT 2 ● Import Duties for Computer Equipment for Selected Countries[1]

USA	5.1%
Canada	8.8%
Japan	9.8%
Australia	2%
EEC[2]	None between EEC countries; 6.7% from outside EEC countries

1. These are typical amounts only. The topic of customs duties is quite complex. It varies with the type of goods, even within an industry (computer systems may be one rate while computer terminals may be another, higher rate and parts a third rate), and by country of origin.
2. European Economic Community (Common Market) consisting of the U.K., France, Germany, Italy, Belgium, Netherlands, Ireland, Denmark, and Luxemburg. *NOTE:* Duty calculated on a "C.I.F." basis—cost of the product plus insurance and freight.

products moved freely between them. ICS had set up its procedures and accounting systems in line with the fact that it was basically a U.S. based company manufacturing a uniform line of products for sales world-wide through various sales subsidiaries. For the major product lines, the only differences by countries were line voltages and some minor adaptations to comply with local government regulations.

Although the subsidiaries in the various countries were essentially sales subsidiaries functioning as sales offices to sell products in those countries, they were separately incorporated entities and wholly owned subsidiaries, operating under the laws of that particular country. Careful accounting of all transactions between the parent company and the subsidiaries had to be maintained for the purpose of import duties and local taxes.

When a customer ordered a computer system, the order was processed in the subsidiary and then transmitted back to the parent company (ICS) in the U.S. to have the system built. The order paperwork listed the specific hardware items (CPU, memory size, tape and disk units, etc.) wanted by the customer and each system was built specifically to order. The component pieces were built by ICS in volume to meet the requirements of these specific customer systems orders. Like most companies, ICS expended a great amount of

effort attempting to accurately forecast the mix of products it would need to meet customer orders.

When the customer's system, or any product, was shipped to the subsidiary, the subsidiary "bought" it from the parent at an intercompany discounted price or "transfer price" of list minus 20 percent. The level of subsidiary transfer price discount was established with two factors in mind:

● It was the primary mechanism by which Interactive repatriated profits to the U.S. parent corporation.

● The 20 percent subsidiary margin was designed to give the subsidiaries positive cash flow to meet their local expenses such as salaries, facilities, benefits, travel, supplies, etc.

Import duties were paid on the discounted (list minus 20 percent) transfer price value according to the customs regulations of the importing country. Some typical import duties for computer equipment are shown in Exhibit 2.

Most countries were quite strict on import/export and customs duties and required consistency in all transactions. Therefore, all shipments were made at the same discounted transfer price, including shipments among subsidiaries and shipments back to the United States.

PRICING

ICS set prices world-wide based on U.S. price lists which were referred to as "Master Price Lists" or MPLs. Prices in each country were based on the MPL plus an uplift factor to cover the increased cost of doing business in those countries. Some of these extra costs were:

- Freight and duty: in those countries where it was included in the price (in some countries duties were paid for separately by the customer).
- Extended warranty: in some countries, the customary warranty periods were longer than in the U.S., for example, one year versus 90 days.
- Cost of subsidiary operations and sales costs: to the extent that they exceed the normal selling costs in the U.S.
- Cost of currency hedging: in order to be able to publish a price list in local currency, ICS bought U.S. dollars in the money futures market.

Uplift factors were periodically reviewed and adjusted if needed to reflect changes in the relative cost of doing business in each country. Typical uplift factors for some selected countries are shown in Exhibit 3.

Each subsidiary published its own price list in local currency. The list was generated quarterly by use of a computer program which took a tape of all the MPL entries and applied the uplift and a fixed currency exchange rate which had been set for the fiscal year. This price list was used by all salespeople in the subsidiary as the official listing of products offered and their prices.

SPECIAL PRODUCTS

In addition to its standard line of products which were sold world-wide in volume, ICS had a num-

EXHIBIT 3 ● Typical Country Uplift Factors: Local Price = Master Price List + Uplift %

UK	8%
Germany	15%
France	12%
Switzerland	17%
Sweden	15%
Australia	12%
Brazil	20%
Canada	5%

ber of lower volume or specialized products. The model 431 communications interface was considered one of these. Specialized products were typically not on the MPL and prices were set locally by each subsidiary wherever they were sold. They were either quoted especially on request for quote basis or added to a special price list supplement produced by each country. This was a common procedure in the computer industry. IBM, for example, had several products "available on an RPQ basis" (Request Product Quotation) only.

To support the sales of the specialized products, ICS had a separate team of specialists with one or more specialists in each subsidiary. They were responsible for the pricing of their products and had a high degree of independence in setting prices in each subsidiary. The specialist or team in each subsidiary was responsible for all aspects of the sales of their assigned products and essentially ran a business within a business.

For the purposes of internal reporting to management, the specialists were measured on achieving a profit before tax, or PBT, of 15 percent which was the ICS goal. The results were shown on a set of internal reports which were separate from the legal books of the subsidiary. The purpose of the internal reports was to give ICS management more information on the profitability of its various product lines. These reports took the form of a series of profit and loss statements of operation by line of product with overhead and indirect costs allocated on a percentage of revenue basis. For these internal P&L reports, the cost of goods was the actual cost of manufacture (internal cost) plus related direct costs instead of the discounted price paid by subsidiaries and shown on their official statements of operation.

"431" SALES IN EUROPE

The model 431 communications interface was designed in 1977 by the European engineering group in Frankfurt as a followup to some special engineering contracts for European customers. It was introduced in the European market in 1978 where it had grown in popularity.

The 431 was produced in Frankfurt only on a low volume production line. The manufacturing and other direct costs amounted to U.S. $1500 per unit. Because there were no tariffs within the EEC and shipping costs were covered by allocated fixed costs, there were no other direct costs. The allocated fixed costs in Europe were running at 47 percent of revenue. Thus, a contribution margin of 62 percent was required to achieve a 15 percent PBT. Based on these costs, a list price of U.S. $3,900 had been set within the EEC. The resulting P&L is shown in Exhibit 4.

Because of the popularity of this product, it had been listed on the special products price list in most European countries. Within the EEC, the price had been set at the same level with any variation only due to local currency conversions. In

EXHIBIT 4 ● Model 431 European Profit Analysis (in U.S. dollars)

European List Price	US $3,900
Manufacturing and Other Direct Costs	1,500
Contribution Margin	2,400
	62%
Allocated Fixed Costs (47%)	1,833
PBT	US $ 567
	14.5%

European countries outside the EEC, the price was increased to cover import duties.

At the above price, the 431 had gained market acceptance and had grown in popularity, especially in Germany, the U.K., and France. Its customers included several large European based multinational companies who were of major importance to ICS in Europe. These customers designed specific system configurations and added programming to perform specified applications and shipped the systems to other countries, either to their own subsidiaries for internal use (for example, a factory) or to customers abroad.

"431" SALES IN USA

The 431 was brought to the attention of the U.S. sales group in two different ways. In sales contacts with U.S. operations of some European customers, ICS was told of the "431" and asked to submit price and availability schedules for local purchase in the USA. U.S. customers expressed irritation at being told that the model was not available in the U.S.

Secondly, the U.S. sales force also heard of the "431" from their European counterparts at sales meetings where the Europeans explained how the "431" had been important in gaining large accounts.

As a result of this pressure from customers and the sales force, the U.S. special products specialists obtained several units for evaluation and in 1979 made the "431" available for sale in the U.S.

Originally, the U.S. specialists set the price equal to the European price of $3,900. However, it became obvious that the market in the U.S. was more advanced and more competitive with customers expecting more performance at that price. As a result the price had to be reexamined.

The "431" was obtained from Frankfurt at the internal cost of $1,500. Transportation costs were estimated at $200. In the USA accounting system, import duties and transportation are not charged directly and were absorbed by general overhead. This came about because ICS was primarily an exporter from the U.S. with very little importing taking place. Consequently, it was felt

EXHIBIT 5 ● Model 431 USA Profit Analysis

USA List Price	$3,000
Manufacturing Cost	$1,500
Contribution Margin	$1,500
	50%
Allocated Fixed Costs (35%)	$1,050
PBT	$ 450
	15%

that import costs were negligible. Thus, the only direct costs was the $1,500 internal cost. Overhead and allocated fixed expenses in the U.S. averaged 35 percent.

The result was, as shown in Exhibit 5, a revised price of $3,000 with a contribution margin of 50 percent and a PBT of 15 percent—the ICS goal. Following this analysis, the U.S. price was reduced to $3,000. The "431" was not listed on the main USA price list but was quoted only on an RPQ basis. Subsequently, this price had also been listed on special products price list supplements which were prepared by the U.S. product specialists and handed out to the sales force in each district.

CURRENT SITUATION

The repricing of the "431" to $3,000 was instrumental in boosting U.S. sales. The sales volume continued to grow and some large customers were captured. These customers included existing ICS customers who previously used other, lower performance, communications interfaces, or had bought somewhat equivalent devices from other companies who made "plug compatible" products for use with ICS computers. Also, a good volume of sales was being obtained from the U.S. operations of European multinationals who were already familiar with the product. ICS's U.S. group, who had first viewed the European designed product with suspicion, was now more confident about it.

But the Europeans were not entirely happy with the situation. Recently, they started complaining to ICS management that the U.S. pricing of the "431" was undercutting the European price. This was causing pressure on the European subsidiaries to reduce their price for the "431" below the $3,900 they needed to meet their profitability goals. Pressure was coming from customers who knew the U.S. price and from European sales people who, as a result of travel to the U.S. or discussions with U.S. colleagues knew the U.S. price and what the uplifted European price "was supposed to be."

The price difference had also been noticed by several of ICS's larger European multinational customers. They started buying the "431" through their U.S. offices and reexported it, both back to Europe and to other countries.

So far, three customers had done this, two German firms and one French customer. Several additional customers were showing definite signs of "shopping around."

This loss of customers to the U.S. was particularly painful to the Europeans. They had invested considerable amounts of effort into cultivating these customers.

In addition, the customers still expected to receive technical and pre-sales support from their local ICS office (that is, European) as well as warranty and service support, regardless of where they placed the purchase order. Attempts to discuss this with the customers or persuade them to purchase in Europe had not been successful. Typical reactions had been "that's ICS's problem" (U.K. customer) and "but are you not one company?" (German customer).

In brief, the ICS European subsidiaries were complaining that they were "being denied the profitable results of their own work" by the unfair pricing practices of the U.S. parent company.

In the eyes of the U.S. team, however, they were pricing in accordance with corporate guidelines to achieve a 15 percent PBT. They also maintained that the market did not allow them to price the "431" any higher. Furthermore, they felt that they were simply exercising their right to set their own country prices to maximize profits within their specific country market.

The U.S. group was so pleased with the market acceptance of the "431" in the U.S. that they wanted to begin an aggressive promotion. As an important part of this, they were now planning to add the "431" on the official ICS U.S. price list. This was viewed as a key to higher sales since, especially in the U.S., products tended to be sold from the regular price list and the sales force tended to lose or ignore special price list supplements.

At this point, both the European and U.S. specialists were upset with each other. Both sides maintained that they were following the rules but that the actions of "the other side" were harming their success and profitability.

It had been a long day and it was time to go home. As he turned his car out into the traffic on High Ridge Road, Mark was still feeling confused about the issues and wondering what should be done.

P.T. Food Specialties—Indonesia (FSI)

On Tuesday morning, January 21, 1981, Ian Souter, Marketing Manager of FSI, was congratulating himself on having gotten an early start, as the Jakarta traffic seemed even worse than normal. He had allowed himself some extra time in order to prepare the agenda for a ten o'clock meeting with his staff. On the way to the office he asked the driver to turn on the radio in order to catch the beginning of the English language news. One block from the office he was reeling with shock as he learned that the Indonesian government was banning all TV advertising as of April 1, 1981. As the car pulled into his parking space it occurred to him that his entire organization, his marketing strategies and campaigns, and his own job structure had become obsolete in one single day.

P.T. FOOD SPECIALTIES (FSI)

FSI was owned jointly by Nestlé S.A., a large multinational food products company, and a group of Indonesian investors. Nestlé S.A. had been founded in Vevey, Switzerland in 1867 by Henri Nestlé as a small producer of milk products. In

This case was prepared by Barbara Priovolos under the supervision of Visiting Professor Jean-Pierre Jeannet as a basis for class discussion rather than to illustrate either effective or ineffective handling of an administrative situation. Copyright © 1982 by IMEDE, Lausanne, Switzerland. The International Institute for Management Development (IMD), resulting from the merger between IMEDE, Lausanne, and IMI, Geneva, acquires and retains all rights. Reproduced by permission.

1905, it merged with the Anglo-Swiss Condensed Milk Co. Between 1905 and 1980 this merged unit expanded rapidly, becoming Switzerland's largest multinational company and the largest company in the food industry in the world. In 1905, Nestlé already had 80 factories, 300 sales offices and 12 subsidiaries worldwide. By 1980, the Nestlé group produced revenues of almost SFr 24.5 billion through its sales offices and factories in more than 100 countries worldwide. Prior to 1972, Nestlé operated under the name Indonepro Distributors Inc. as the importer and distributor of Nestlé's products to Indonesia. In 1972, it began operating as a manufacturer and marketer of food products. It had discontinued its distribution operations after the introduction of an Indonesian law that restricted distribution activities to companies that were wholly owned by Indonesians. Since 1972, FSI had lost the right to sell its products directly to retailers or consumers.[1]

In 1981, FSI produced and marketed six products in Indonesia. The most important of these was MILKMAID SWEETENED CONDENSED MILK. Introduced in 1972 after a long history of importation. MILKMAID accounted for roughly 40 percent of FSI's annual turnover. It was perhaps the least profitable of its six products. The Indonesian sweetened condensed milk market was both very large and competitive. It was dominated by three large organizations, Frisian Flag (with 50 percent of the market), Indo Milk, in conjunction with the Australian Dairy Board, (with 34 percent of the market) and FSI (with 15 percent of the market). A 14 oz can of MILK-

1. In 1981, $1 = SFr 2.

MAID had a selling price of approximately 400 Rupiah in 1981.[2]

DANCOW powdered milk had also been introduced in 1972. It was sold in two forms, regular and instant. In 1981 DANCOW accounted for approximately 30 percent of FSI's total revenue. It was also one of FSI's most profitable products. The Indonesian powdered milk market was dominated by two large organizations. FSI had a 45 percent market share, and Frisian Flag had a 52 percent market share. The balance of the market was held by several imported brands. A 454 gram package (about one pound) of DANCOW regular carried a suggested retail price of 1,200 Rupiah in 1981.

In 1978, FSI had introduced two infant cereals into Indonesia. Neither of these products were to be used as breast milk substitutes. CERELAC contained powdered milk, whereas NESTUM did not. These had become two of FSI's most profitable products and accounted for approximately 10 percent of FSI's annual revenue. The infant cereal market was fairly small, but FSI controlled almost 63 percent of it. The balance of the branded cereals were supplied largely by one local producer P.T. Sari Husada, whose brand SNM had a 31 percent share of the market. All other brands, most of them imported, shared the remaining 6 percent of the market. Homemade cereals were very popular, and although little firm data was available on the subject, FSI executives believed that the vast majority of the children's cereal consumed in Indonesia was homemade. A 400 gram box of CERELAC and a 250 gram box of NESTUM had 1981 retail prices of 1000 Rupiah and 750 Rupiah, respectively.

MILO, a chocolate-malted powder that was mixed with milk to produce a high energy drink, accounted for eight percent of FSI's revenue. It was a moderately profitable product that had been introduced in 1974. The market for MILO was thought to be fairly small. It consisted primarily of children who used MILO as a "growing up" high nutrition drink and sports conscious adults who

used it as a high energy drink. FSI had approximately 45 percent of this market segment. It shared the market with the Ovaltine brand which had a 47 percent market share and the Malcoa brand which had an eight percent market share. In 1981, the retail price for MILO was 100 Rupiah for a 350 gram box.

PRODUCT DISTRIBUTION

Products found their way from the factory to the consumer's cupboard through a rather intricate series of distributors and wholesalers. SFI itself had only two customers. It sold all of its output to one of two main distributors, a Chinese-Indonesian company, and a Pribumi, or native Indonesian, company. These two main distributors sold FSI's products to subdistributors, or to agents for subdistributors. The approximately 45 subdistributors then sold the products to wholesalers or directly to small shops. As a result FSI's products changed hands a minimum of four times, and often as many as six times on their way from the factory to the consumer. See Exhibit 1 for a diagram of this distribution network.

FSI suggested price levels for both the retail and the wholesale outlets and paid for, although did not arrange, product transportation from the factory to the retailer. It also employed marketing personnel who served as advisors to the subdistributors and the retailers. Twenty area supervisors advised the subdistributors with regard to stock hygiene, merchandising and promotional activities. They also trained subdistributor sales personnel to set up in-store displays, point-of-sale selling materials and on-the-shelf product arrangement for maximum consumer impact. This type of support was considered by FSI executives as crucial. Many Indonesian retailers saw little difference between having a product in the store and making a product available to, or even attractive to, the customer. Many retailers ordered products that were left in cartons behind desks, in storage rooms, or in similar areas well out of reach of the consumer. This marketing support was also consistent with the marketing advice of businessmen based in In-

---

2. In 1981, 300 Rupiah = SFr 1; 625 Rupiah = $1.

EXHIBIT 1 ● Product Distribution

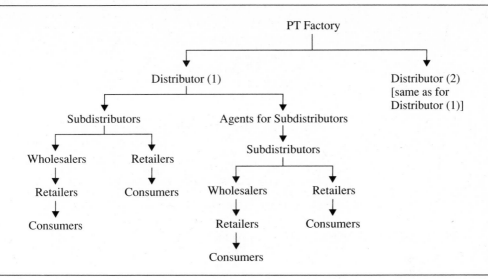

donesia who believed that personalized attention was an effective marketing tool in Indonesia.

In most cases, the subdistributors were grateful for the help provided by the area supervisors. Some conflicts of interest did occasionally occur. The subdistributors had a short-term view of business. They were generally most interested in products that were currently selling in large volumes. The area supervisor was interested in marketing every product and in building the market for new products, thus ensuring that the FSI brand was associated with goodwill and confidence in the mind of the extremely brand loyal Indonesian consumer. See Exhibit 2 for retail distribution data for FSI's products and its competitors' products.

The FSI marketing office also included one national sales coordinator to whom all of the area supervisors reported, and one product executive for each FSI product group. The product executives were responsible for developing and implementing supplemental promotional activities for their products, both trade oriented and consumer oriented, and for monitoring their products in the

Indonesian market. See Exhibit 3 for the FSI Marketing Department organization chart.

THE INDONESIAN BUSINESS CLIMATE

In 1981 Indonesia was the fifth largest country in the world in terms of population, behind China, India, the USSR and the USA. Its 150 million people lived on approximately 6,000 of the roughly 13,000 islands that, straddling 5000 km (3000 miles) of Equator, made up Indonesia. It was a country of uncharted jungles and densely populated cities. Twenty percent of all Indonesians were city dwellers and two thirds of them lived on the islands of Java, Madura and Bali. These islands contained only 7 percent of Indonesia's land mass and were among the most densely populated areas on earth. Indonesia's capital city of Jakarta was home to seven million people. See Exhibit 4 for a map of Indonesia.

The Indonesian people were of more than 300 different ethnic groups, most of them of Malaysian origin. More than 90 percent of the popu-

EXHIBIT 2 ● Retail Distribution—P.T.

MILKMAID	
	● Distribution largely urban
	● 80% Supermarkets, 16% Independent Shops, 20% Bazaar Shops stock[1] product
	● Sweetened condensed milk as a product category sells[2]

0.5% volume through Supermarkets
30% volume through Independent Shops
70.5% volume through Bazaar Shops

DANCOW

● Distribution largely urban

	Standard	Instant	
● Supermarkets	97%	90%	} stock
Independent Shops	15%	10%	} product
Bazaar Shops	30%	20%	}

● Full cream powdered milk as a product category sells
2% volume through Supermarkets
35% volume through Independent Shops
63% volume through Bazaar Shops

CERELAC/NESTUM

● Exclusively urban distribution

	CERELAC	NESTUM	
● Supermarkets	95%	94%	} stock
Independent Shops	10%	10%	} product
Bazaar Shops	20%	27%	}

MILO

● Exclusively urban distribution with concentration in 5 or 6 main Towns

● 98% of Supermarkets, 12% of Independent Shops, 37% of Bazaar Shops stock product

● Tonic food beverages sell
5% volume through Supermarkets
32% volume through Independent Shops
64% volume through Bazaar Shops

1. Percentage of retail shops who sell that particular Nestlé brand.
2. Percentage of total volume of that product category industrywide selling through specific retail trade category.

lation were followers of Islam giving Indonesia the world's largest Moslem population. Although more than 300 languages and dialects were in regional use, the national language of Bahasa Indonesia was believed to be understood by all but the most remote village dwellers.

Indonesia had been under Dutch colonial rule for almost 300 years prior to its occupation by the Japanese between 1942 and 1945. In 1945, two days after the surrender of the Japanese, Indonesia made a unilateral declaration of independence. In 1949, the Netherlands unconditionally recognized the Sovereignty of Indonesia. The po-

litical climate of Indonesia was stable. Its President, Suharto, had been in power since 1965. Although he was considered by many to be slow in initiating reforms that would stimulate economic growth, his leadership had been credited with reducing inflation from over 200 percent in the mid-1960's to under 10 percent in 1981, opening up Indonesia to some private and foreign investment, reducing the rate of its population growth and bringing the country to the brink of self sufficiency in rice production, after having been the world's largest rice importer for many years. Indonesia was a country very rich in natural resources, but

EXHIBIT 2 ● Retail Distribution—Competitors (Continued)

Competition to MILKMAID

Frisian Flag

91% of supermarkets
60% of independent shops } stock product
60% of bazaar shops

Indomilk

91% of supermarkets
31% of independent shops } stock product
39% of bazaar shops

Respective market shares

Frisian Flag   50%
Indomilk   34%
MILKMAID   16%

Competition to DANCOW

Frisian Flag Standard

97% of all supermarkets
27% of independent shops } stock product
46% of bazaar shops

Frisian Flag Instant

98% of all supermarkets
14% of independent shops } stock products
22% of bazaar shops

Respective market shares

DANCOW Std.   27%
DANCOW Inst.   18.3%
Frisian Flag Std.   43.2%
Frisian Flag Inst.   8.6%

Competition to NESTUM/CERELAC

SNM

84% of all supermarkets
11% of independent shops } stock product
22% of bazaar shops

Nutricia

91% of all supermarkets
3.5% of independent shops } stock product
4.3% of bazaar shops

Respective market shares

NESTUM   22%
CERELAC   41%
SNM   31%
All Others   6%

Competition to MILO

Ovaltine

98% of all supermarkets
10.7% of independent shops } stock product
24.7% of bazaar shops

Malcoa

91% of all supermarkets
4% of independent shops } stock product
10% of bazaar shops

Respective market shares

MILO   45.0%
Ovaltine   47.0%
Malcoa   8.0%

EXHIBIT 3 ● P.T. Food Specialities Marketing Department

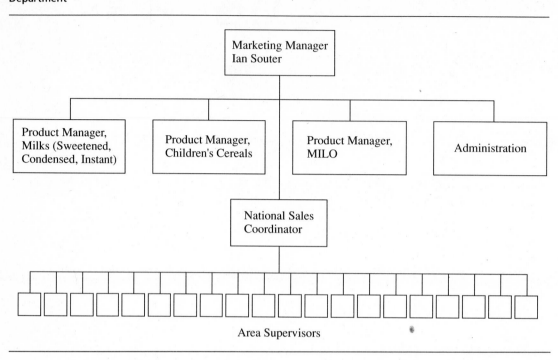

with a very poor population. It was a country that was deeply preindustrial, but one with a pocket of high technology industries.

Indonesia was a member of OPEC and the largest oil producer in South-East Asia. It had proven reserves of 14 billion barrels, and an estimated 50 billion barrels of reserves yet to be officially confirmed. Oil export earnings accounted for 75 percent of its foreign income in 1981. Oil was not the only important natural resource in Indonesia. Indonesia was the world's second largest producer of liquified natural gas and largest producer of tin. It also produced significant quantities of bauxite, nickel, coal, iron, manganese, gold, silver, copper, phosphates and sulphur. Nevertheless, the Indonesian economy was primarily agricultural. Agriculture, forestry and fishing employed two thirds of the Indonesian labor force

and accounted for almost one third of GNP. Small farms produced food for domestic consumption as well as natural rubber, coffee, pepper and tobacco for export. Large plantations, holdovers from its colonial days, produced Indonesia's most important agricultural exports: timber, rubber, coffee, tea, palm oil and sugar.

The Indonesian manufacturing sector was very small, accounting for less than 5 percent of exports and only 7 percent of GNP. The trading sector of the economy, wholesale and retail, accounted for approximately 16 percent of the GNP and was dominated by Indonesia's Chinese minority. Until 1965, Indonesia's five million Chinese had had a virtual monopoly of business and manufacturing activities within the country, and their influence in 1981 was still considerable.

In 1981, Indonesia had at least $10 billion in

EXHIBIT 4 ● Map of Indonesia

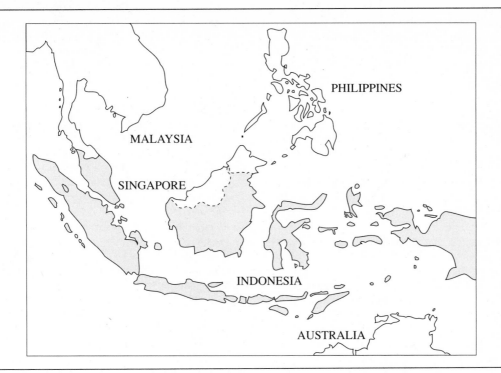

hard currency reserves that did not benefit the economy due to an underdeveloped banking and financial services sector. Poverty was acute in Indonesia, and many of its income statistics were misleading. Although the per capita income was about $370 per year, the concentration of wealth was such that certain economists estimated that 40 percent of the population existed on less than $90 per year.

The Indonesian population could be classified into five separate economic classes in terms of disposable household income.[3]

3. Each household contained approximately seven people. This classification was based on the best estimates of foreign businessmen operating in Indonesia during 1981.

Economic segment	Percentage of population	Monthly disposable income (in Rupiahs)
A	3%–5%	100,000
B	13%–18%	75,000–100,000
C	25%–30%	50,000–75,000
D	29%–30%	30,000–50,000
E	34%	30,000

FSI'S MARKETING MIX

As Marketing Manager, Ian Souter had generally emphasized developing customized campaigns for each of FSI's six products. The campaign budgets were divided between "above the line" mass media activities and "below the line" consumer promotion and trade promotion activities. In line with Nestlé and FSI company policy, which called for mass media promotion in order to build long term brand loyalty and confidence in their products, 60 percent to 90 percent of a campaign's budget was spent on mass media advertising. FSI executives felt that price promotions produced customers who only used the product while it was selling for the reduced price. These customers were likely to change brands again as soon as other manufacturers lowered their own prices. See Exhibit 5 for media spend data. Exhibit 6 for media cost data and Exhibit 7 for some magazine advertisement samples.

Souter felt that the 1980 MILKMAID campaign had been especially important. Souter had, in an effort to increase market share, attempted to reposition MILKMAID from a "growing up" children's drink to an "energy" drink for all ages. In 1980 FSI had for the first time created its own TV campaign for MILKMAID rather than adopting a campaign that had been developed by the Nestlé subsidiaries in Malaysia or the Philippines. This change in direction was seen by Souter as very important. Developing his own campaign had been both a lengthy and at times frustrating process. However it had given him the ability to adapt his campaign to the Indonesian market by using Indonesian actors, actresses and locations.

All of FSI's advertisements required approval by the Nestlé home office staff in Switzerland. In addition, working with the relatively inexperienced Indonesian film and creative personnel was frustrating even at the best of times. Thus the process of creating an Indonesian campaign required almost six months versus the two to three months that were required when already approved Malaysian or Philippine ads were adapted for use in Indonesia.

DANCOW powdered milk was promoted in two versions. The instant version received 90 percent of the promotional funds. DANCOW instant, or "the 4 second milk" had been the first locally produced instant milk in Indonesia. It had been a huge success. The instant form had, since its introduction, been advertised on TV and in women's magazines. Because the brand name was the same for both the instant and standard varieties it was believed that the standard form also benefitted from the advertisements for the instant form. The ad budget for the standard form was used for newspaper and cinema slide advertisements.

FSI's two infant cereals were both mass marketed and promoted to the medical profession with the help of samples and literature. CERELAC, the milk based cereal, had been introduced using TV ads that had been developed in Malaysia. This reliance on Malaysian TV advertisements had continued, as had the product's success in the market place. NESTUM, a non-milk cereal, had been introduced with magazine advertisements and had experienced very moderate initial sales. In mid-1979, a TV campaign for NESTUM was introduced, and sales increased dramatically. The TV campaign and the impressive sales results had both continued throughout 1980.

MILO was advertised primarily on television with some back up advertisements in women's magazines and children's comic books. It was also the only FSI product advertised in outdoor media. At selected sports events MILO had been advertised using A-boards (wooden signs placed back to back to form an A shape) around the entrance area to the event. Occasionally, these A-boards had also been used along parade routes.

TELEVISION ADVERTISING IN INDONESIA

Souter believed that:

> There is no substitute for television. Without television my job, the job of marketing these products, would be nearly impossible, and the job of introducing a new product would be entirely impossible. There is no other marketing tool in Indonesia that can ever come close to reaching exactly my market with exactly my message, the message that FSI products are consistently high quality products, products that one ought to use.

There were approximately two million television sets in Indonesia in 1981. They could tune

EXHIBIT 5 ● Media Spending—Per Product 1979 to 1981 (Planned)

1979, In Millions of Rupiah

Media product	T.V.	Radio	Newspaper	Magazine	Cinema	Outdoor (FORM & AMOUNT)	Trade promotion (FORM & AMOUNT)	Consumer promotion (FORM & AMOUNT)	Total
Sweetened Condensed Milk (MILKMAID)	40.55	7.73	—	7.66	0.01	—	0.60	—	56.55
DANCOW Instant	37.43	—	0.83	17.04	—	—	0.85	—	56.15
DANCOW Standard	22.46	—	8.69	—	11.90	—	0.52	—	43.57
NESTUM	29.82	—	—	—	—	—	—	3.87	33.69
CERELAC	42.97	—	—	—	—	—	—	3.59	46.56
MILO	33.07	—	—	—	—	2.00	0.07	0.45	35.59
TOTAL	206.30	7.73	9.52	24.70	11.91	2.00	2.04	7.91	272.11

EXHIBIT 5 ● Media Spending—Per Product 1979 to 1981 (Planned) (Continued)

1980, In Millions of Rupiah

Media product	T.V.	Radio	Newspaper	Magazine	Cinema	Outdoor (FORM & AMOUNT)	Trade promotion (FORM & AMOUNT)	Consumer promotion (FORM & AMOUNT)	Total
Sweetened Condensed Milk (MILKMAID)	65.14	12.91	—	12.23	0.03	—	0.50	0.07	90.88
DANCOW Instant	65.71	—	—	26.82	—	—	0.77	—	93.30
DANCOW Standard	36.97	—	13.19	—	11.40	—	0.65	—	62.21
NESTUM	72.90	—	—	—	—	—	0.11	2.40	75.41
CERELAC	51.73	—	—	—	—	—	0.11	2.24	54.08
MILO	90.82	—	6.29	21.21	—	0.24	2.79	2.04	123.39
TOTAL	383.27	12.91	19.48	60.26	11.43	0.24	4.93	6.75	499.27

EXHIBIT 5 ● Media Spending—Per Product 1979 to 1981 (Planned) (Continued)

1981, (Planned as of January 20, 1981), in Millions of Rupiah

Media product	T.V.	Radio	Newspaper	Magazine	Cinema	Outdoor (FORM & AMOUNT)	Trade promotion (FORM & AMOUNT)	Consumer promotion (FORM & AMOUNT)	Total
Sweetened Condensed Milk (MILKMAID)	120.0	20.1	—	17.6	2.3	—	18.0	3.0	181.0
DANCOW Instant	124.0	—	—	66.0	—	—	13.0	30.0	233.0
DANCOW Standard	50.0	—	—	38.8	11.2	—	18.0	4.0	122.0
NESTUM	91.0	—	—	29.0	—	—	5.5	5.5	131.0
CERELAC	90.0	—	—	—	—	—	5.5	6.0	101.5
MILO	120.0	—	—	30.0	—	—	20.0	28.0	198.0
TOTAL	595.0	20.1	—	184.4	13.5	—	80.0	76.5	966.5

EXHIBIT 6 ● January 20, 1981 Media Costs—
Development and Production

In Thousands of Rupiah

Media	Cost to Develop One Spot	Cost to Broadcast One Spot	
		Prime Time or Urban	Not Prime Time or Regional
TV		476.7	75.7
Radio	287.0	2.0	0.05
Newspaper	102.0	217.3	52.1
Magazine	2,300.0	1,358.9	

Outdoor Media	Fixed Investment /Unit*
A-Boards: Inside Stadium Outside Stadium	20,000 15,000
Billboards: Strategic Location Ordinary Location	25,000 15,000
Footbridges	140,000

* All Quotes Include Taxes and Annual Maintenance

A-Boards: In Stadium/Outside
Bill Board: Strategic Location/Ordinary
*All Quotes Include Taxes and Annual Maintenance

EXHIBIT 7 ● Ad Sample for MILKMAID

into one government owned network, Televisi Republik, Indonesia (TVRI). Television advertisements were carried during two "blocks" per day, as well as before, during and at the end of programs or sports events that the advertiser itself had sponsored. The early evening advertising block, from 17:30 to 18:00, was for regionally based commercials. The late evening block, from 21:00 to 21:30, was immediately before the late evening news break and carried national advertisements.

Some Western businessmen operating in Indonesia believed that television advertising in Indonesia, thanks to a happy and rare coincidence of business need and cultural forces working together, pleased just about everyone. Indonesia's television audience seemed to eagerly await the televised signals that one of the twice daily commercial breaks was about to begin. Cartoon type drawings of consumer product packages bearing generic names such as coffee, soap or milk lined

EXHIBIT 7 (Continued) ● Ad Sample for CERELAC

As a mother you want your baby to have nutritious food. CERELAC already contains milk, 11 vitamins and minerals necessary for good health. Your baby will love CERELAC with its biscuit base. CERELAC can be given to babies 4 months old and older, or according to the advice of your doctor.

EXHIBIT 7 (Continued)   ● Ad Sample for NESTUM

NESTUM—rice cereal which is ideal for your baby. If milk is no longer enough for your baby, give NESTUM rice cereal as a first solid food. NESTUM rice cereal contains many of the vitamins and minerals necessary for the health of your baby. NESTUM is for babies 4 months old and older or according to the advice of your doctor.

EXHIBIT 7 (Continued) ● Ad Sample for
DANCOW

The best milk for growth. Every child wants to grow healthy and
strong. DANCOW Instant is the best milk for growth. DANCOW
Instant is enriched with vitamins, is easy to prepare and is delicious.

EXHIBIT 7 (Continued) ● Ad Sample for MILO

MILO is full of nutrition and rich in energy because it is full of nutrients like malt, sugar, milk, the main vitamins and the main minerals. Your family needs MILO energy. Everyone uses energy every day, especially healthy, active children. This energy needs to be replaced. Chocolate flavored MILO gives this energy every day—at school, at home, and while exercising—to help one grow healthy and strong.

up on the screen and a butterfly flew into view to alight briefly on several packages, as if to select them for its own use. Many marketing executives felt that the television appearance of a commercial product was as appealing to the Indonesian consumer as those packages were to that butterfly. To the Indonesian consumer it was the sign that the product was of high quality, dependable, "real" and deserving of their confidence and trust.

Although firm statistics on television viewership did not exist, FSI executives believed that Indonesia's two million television sets were located almost entirely in urban areas. Beginning in the late 1970s, the Indonesian government supported a program to put a television set in every village for educational purposes. The number of sets involved in this program was never made clear. FSI executives also estimated that 11 percent of the televisions were in use during the early evening advertising break and that 24 percent were in use during the late evening advertising break. They were not sure who was watching. They felt that during the early break it was primarily children and domestic household help. Souter continued:

> I can control television advertising. I know, roughly, who sees it, and when they see it, I know what they see and I can judge how they interpret it because the visuals are so powerful. I can produce a TV campaign 1000 times more efficiently than any other mass media campaign. Or, for that matter, any other marketing or promotion effort whatsoever. That is not to say that producing a TV campaign is easy. It's not! But other campaigns are much more difficult to create—and much, much, much more difficult to implement.

When a television campaign was employed for a FSI product it was used to create the themes that were repeated and reflected by advertisements in other media. Souter believed that every product's ad campaign needed to be cohesive and self-reinforcing. To ensure this, he always developed TV campaigns first, and then designed the radio, magazine, cinema, outdoor and point of sale advertisements to reinforce and support the initially designed television message.

Not only FSI, but all its competitors as well, felt that television advertising was the most important factor in a product's marketing success. Competition for the 40 to 60 second advertising "spots" was breathtaking. Advertising spots were distributed by the government bureaucracy specifically charged with this mission. Simply filing a request for a spot entailed making one's way around an obstacle course of problems that governmental bureaucrats throughout the world seemed so skilled in designing. At this point, simple arithmetic brought the real scope of this situation into focus. FSI's experience, which they believed to be similar to that of most other advertisers as well, was that roughly one in every ten requests was granted. On average, FSI was granted three national and five regional spots per month. In order to increase their television presence, FSI sponsored each year eight to ten nationally televised series, 12 to 15 nationally televised sports events, and several regionally televised programs.

Television campaigns were also costly. One hundred million Rupiahs per year per product was required for an effective television campaign. Each regional spot cost about 300,000 Rupiahs to broadcast and each national spot cost about 750,000 Rupiahs to broadcast. In addition, the production costs for one spot, in both a 60 second and a 40 second version, were about ten million Rupiahs.

Two phrases highlighted both the advantages television advertising provided for a marketing manager operating in Indonesia in 1981 and the relative disadvantages of other media forms and promotional efforts: "ability to control" and "not labor intensive."

The production and broadcast of a television ad required the management and cooperation of a small team of professionals. Production required more people than might have been required in a country with a more experienced television establishment. However, one could identify fairly easily who was needed and what they needed to do. Similarly, to broadcast an advertisement was not a difficult task. Once permission had been granted, the result was available for all to see and to monitor. In addition to the ability to self-monitor a TV campaign, both TVRI and the advertising agencies provided certificates of broadcast for each broadcasted spot.

INDONESIA'S OTHER MASS MEDIA

Radio networks, in contrast with television, were operated only regionally. There was one government owned station that serviced major cities and many private stations that served both cities and rural areas. The radio networks were characterized by their variety in format, location and language. A radio campaign with national coverage cost 40 to 50 million Rupiahs and required the participation of 70 to 80 different radio stations. Local radio spots were arranged through local advertising agents. Neither the station nor the agents provided certificates to confirm that the ad had actually been broadcast. It was extremely difficult for FSI head office personnel to insure or confirm that the radio ads that they had paid for had been aired.

Obtaining the translations for the regional stations posed another problem when using radio advertisements. According to Souter "no two Indonesians will ever agree on an exact translation." The translation of only three advertisements into three dialects had recently required "months and months" to complete. The Indonesian radio "population" was believed to be many times that of its TV population, so that, theoretically at least, radio could have had as much, if not more, penetration value as TV.

Radio advertising could be booked throughout the day. The times most in demand, though, were early morning (workdays began around 7:00) and early evening before the TV was tuned in. During the Moslem fasting month in June or July advertisements for food and drink could be carried only after sunset.

Advertising in cinemas was fairly common in Indonesia. Most cinema advertising was in the form of slides that were shown before the start of the film. FSI had advertised MILKMAID in cinemas in smaller towns, but had not been very satisfied with the effectiveness of this media. Indonesian cinemas were of two classes. Class A cinemas were in major cities and were very expensive to attend, especially when good or well-known films were being shown. Class B cinemas were in smaller towns. They were less expensive to attend and were often rather shabby in appearance. Operational problems plagued both classes of cinema. In FSI's experience the slides, when they were shown at all, were often presented out of sequence or upside down.

FSI used some of Indonesia's magazines having national circulations for full page color advertisements that reflected their television advertisements. In magazine advertising their strategy was to cluster together several ads in several magazines in order to create an impact. They would then use these advertisements in cycles. For two months the clustered ads would appear in several different magazines and then, for one month, no magazine advertisements would be employed. When magazine advertising was the only mass medium used for a product as had been initially the case for NESTUM, a yearly ad budget of 56 million Rupiahs was required to obtain what they felt was an effective penetration.

High caliber magazines were costly to the consumer. They had newsstand prices of between 800 and 1000 Rupiahs per issue and were generally issued bimonthly. This high cost led to very high readership figures per issue. Advertising agency personnel multiplied circulation estimates by eight to compute actual readership. For its market, FSI executives felt that a multiple of five was more realistic. It was, however, very difficult, if not impossible, to estimate readership at all due to the very poor circulation figures that were available. Audited circulation figures were virtually unavailable and some FSI executives believed that the only way to really know who read which magazines was to survey the market by themselves.

Indonesia had six general interest magazines. Three of these were women's magazines which reported on fashion, decorating and cooking. These had very impressive European formats. "Femina" and "Kartini" were aimed at the upper class housewife and "Gadis" was designed for younger women. Research figures seemed to indicate that readership duplication was approximately 60 percent within this category. "Intisari," a Readers Digest style monthly, "Tempo," a Time style magazine, and "Executif," for high level business executives had not been used often by FSI. However these magazines were very popular among Indonesia's elite.

FSI used newspaper advertising primarily for special promotions and as a signal to the trade that FSI was very interested in supporting a given product. Souter felt that newspaper advertising was of strategic importance in dealing with the trade. Newspaper market penetration seemed to be fairly low. It was also a medium that was more effective in reaching a male audience than a female audience. Agency figures indicated that total readership was five times circulation figures. Although again circulation figures were considered to be very unreliable, FSI executives accepted a multiple of three in terms of their own market. New ads needed to be created for all newspaper campaigns because magazine artwork did not reproduce effectively in black and white. Souter estimated that 40 million Rupiahs were required, over a three month period, for an effective newspaper campaign.

The range of newspapers was very wide. Probably the most important ones were the two Jakarta based nationals "Kompas" and "Sinar Harapan." Their primary circulation was in Jakarta. In other important regional markets they were very often second in circulation after the local newspaper. There were two rather low circulation English language newspapers, the "Observer" and the "Indonesian Times"; these were not cited by FSI. In addition, a Chinese newspaper with a small but very influential readership was available. The advertising rates for the national and Chinese newspapers were much higher than those of the other newspapers.

Outdoor advertising was very popular in Indonesia, although FSI had rarely employed it. Billboards in shimmering or plain versions, footbridges, bus stop shelters and A-boards were all used for advertising purposes. Souter believed that few of the outdoor advertising opportunities were appropriate for FSI because of the nature of their products. Outdoor locations soon became dirty, especially those in crowded cities. He did not feel that a dirty environment was appropriate for food products. Nevertheless, many of FSI's competitors did make use of outdoor advertisements. A second problem with outdoor advertisements was the negotiations involved in arranging them. Various "fees" and taxes were often imposed on the advertisers for which no receipt was ever given.

Outdoor advertisements were not inexpensive and each form had its own particular drawbacks. Billboards needed to be leased for three to five years at a time, payable in advance. Bus stop shelters advertising different brands of the same products tended to line up one after the other. A similar problem arose with A-boards. These were often used temporarily at the entrance to sports events or along parade routes. They would often be massed so close together that the impact of each board was substantially reduced.

Pedestrian footbridges were an expensive, but popular, advertising medium. A company could build, for approximately 15 million Rupiahs, a pedestrian footbridge over a crowded street. The company would become liable for all maintenance charges and the ever popular annually negotiated tax. In return, advertisements could be painted on the bridge for five years. At one time FSI executives had considered building such a bridge but had decided against it on the basis of cost and their reluctance to negotiate the "taxes."

TRADE BASED PROMOTION

Indonesia's wholesalers and retailers always welcomed trade based promotions that involved distributing premiums such as drinking glasses, which were a particular favorite, or product samples. These were promotions that they could easily participate in. To them, the immediate nature of the reward was a tremendous allure. They disliked coupon type promotions that required them to give up something first by accepting less money for a product or accepting only a coupon for a product in anticipation of later reimbursement by the company sponsoring the promotion. The concept of a monetary society was new to some retailers, who were far more comfortable being barter traders.

TUESDAY AFTERNOON

It was late in the afternoon of Tuesday, January 21, 1981 and Ian Souter had spent the day reviewing the marketing campaigns for each of the six products FSI manufactured and marketed in Indonesia. He now had less than ten weeks to redesign and implement a "non-TV" campaign for each of those products. The campaigns needed to be finalized by mid-March for their April introductions. He needed to meet those deadlines despite the delays and interruptions that he had come to expect during his three years in Indonesia. He felt that his list of campaign and promotion ideas would serve as the basis of a very intensive review meeting the next day with the staff of the Fortune Advertising Agency, who had served FSI for twenty-two years, and his own superiors.

CASE 7

American Hospital Supply—Japan Corporation

In the spring of 1975, executives of AHS-Japan, under the direction of F. Nakamoto, the company president, met to discuss the possible method of entering the Japanese dental equipment market. The company was a subsidiary of American Hospital Supply, Inc., and had introduced two of its parent company's product lines very successfully during the last five years. It was now up to the executive team to select a strategy and to submit the proposal to its parent company for endorsement. The selection process was made particularly difficult by the nature of the distribution system and the strength of AHS-Japan's potential competitors.

AHS-JAPAN CORPORATION

AHS-Japan Corporation was originally established in 1968 as a branch of the American Hospital Supply Corporation. Just recently, its status had been changed to a subsidiary following the liberalization of the Japanese investment regulations that earlier had not allowed a foreign company to own the majority of the share capital of a subsidiary in Japan. The original mission of the branches

●

This case was prepared by Jean-Pierre Jeannet, Professor of Marketing and International Business at Babson College, while teaching as Visiting Lecturer at Keio University Graduate School of Business in Tokyo. This case was prepared for the sole purpose of class discussion rather than to illustrate either effective or ineffective handling of an administrative situation. Copyright © 1980, J. P. Jeannet.

was to sell a product line similar to the parent company's with a possibility for local production later on. At the outset, the company carried only medical equipment, such as surgical equipment for operating rooms, intensive-care or critical-care units. In 1971, diagnostic reagents were introduced as the second major product line. The planned introduction of dental equipment would represent the third major product line for AHS-Japan with further additions planned every one to two years. The company had been successful practically from its inception growing from originally three employees in 1968 to about fifty at the present time. Sales had shown a growth pattern of 50 percent compounded annually.

AMERICAN HOSPITAL SUPPLY CORPORATION BACKGROUND

American Hospital Supply was formed in 1922 as the first distributor specializing solely on products for hospitals. The company had concentrated on this segment for many years before introducing other product lines such as dental equipment and materials or scientific instruments. Today, the original hospital supply business accounted for about 50 percent of total sales of U.S. $1,002 million in 1974. The other major segments were science (32 percent of sales), medical and dental specialties (11 percent), and pharmaceuticals (7 percent). (See Exhibit 1.) The company had integrated backwards over the years producing approximately 45 percent of its sales through its own manufacturing subsidiaries. The approximately 24,100 employees serviced more than 140 countries through about 50 production centers and 120 sales or distribution centers. The product line comprised about 100,000 items.

AHS INTERNATIONAL OPERATIONS

AHS organized its international operations as a separate corporate group directed by a president. For 1974, net sales amounted to $104.2 million of which $33 million represented exports by U.S. subsidiaries to AHS companies and clients outside the U.S. and Canada. Net earnings amounted to $2.4 million on international group companies and another $6.1 million on the export transactions. The International Group had the responsibility for coordination of all domestic export shipments as well as direct responsibility for foreign-based operations. It has always been the strategy of AHS to concentrate on major markets with a sufficiently high level of health care to justify local operations. As a result, the group operated its 23 operations concentrated on just 14 markets.

PRODUCT LINES IN JAPAN

AHS-Japan's first product introduction consisted of a portion of the parent company's medical equipment line. Due to the competitive nature of the Japanese market, special emphasis was put on sophisticated products, particularly those with a focus on cardiac disease applications. As a result, the product line consisted of heart valves, pacers, bypass or intra-aortic balloon pumps, and surgical instruments for open heart surgery.

As a newcomer to the market, the company found the distribution problem particularly vexing. The market for medical instruments consisted of hospitals and clinical laboratories and some general practitioners. The larger hospitals and clinics sought their equipment directly from domestic manufacturers, importing companies, or foreign affiliated subsidiaries in Japan. All three of the above sources for medical equipment, however, also sold through a group of 27 specialized wholesalers who partially sold directly to smaller hospitals and clinics or resold to about 150 regional dealers. As it turned out, the 27 specialized primary wholesalers had strong ties to already established importers or domestic manufacturers

and were therefore not willing to adopt a product line that was competing with one of their established suppliers. Furthermore, AHS-Japan's cardiac equipment was of the highest sophistication that required the sales force to be fully trained in and knowledgeable about heart surgery, something that trade salesmen of both primary and regional wholesalers could not be expected to be. This situation led to AHS-Japan's decision to sell directly to end-users (see Exhibit 2).

Following the introductory period, AHS-Japan continued to monitor the activities of medical equipment wholesalers in Japan. The company discovered that operating margins were relatively low with net earnings averaging about 1 percent compared to 5.5 percent for AHS-US or 5 to 10 percent for typical U.S. dealers. While gross margins tended to be similar to those of the United States, Japanese intermediaries engaged in many additional activities and services of value to both suppliers and customers that were normally not performed by a wholesaler in the United States. Besides shipping goods to the customers, wholesalers gave general service, maintained excellent customer relations before and after the sale, collected valuable market information, sold repeat orders, and collected funds from their customers. Despite their gross margins,[1] these service functions tended to reduce the net profit margin below a level typical for the United States. AHS-Japan also noted that wholesalers in Japan were able to carry out all of these functions at a lesser cost than a U.S. subsidiary due to their lower wages.

As a result, AHS-Japan decided later to include wholesalers in its distribution effort for medical equipment. The resulting savings in manpower, particularly since salesmen did not have to make monthly collection calls, added to AHS-Japan's sales productivity. Today, close to 80 per-

---

1. Gross margins for medical products varied substantially and depended on individual products. Items with low unit value and a large volume in repeat orders might carry margins of as low as 15 percent. For equipment that required sophisticated service, long lead times, and relatively high unit value, the gross margins might be as high as 30 percent.

EXHIBIT 1 ● Group Net Sales and Net Earnings

NET SALES (IN MILLIONS OF DOLLARS)

	1975		1974		1973		1972		1971	
Hospital	$ 323.2	29%	$268.7	27%	$213.7	26%	$181.7	26%	$168.7	28%
Science Specialties	355.9	31	312.6	32	300.2	36	242.9	35	197.7	33
Medical Specialties	72.4	6	67.5	7	52.7	6	44.1	6	39.1	6
Pharmaceutical	91.1	8	74.8	8	62.0	7	54.9	8	51.0	9
Capital Goods	60.0	5	55.9	6	49.4	6	43.8	6	42.4	7
Dental	46.9	4	41.7	4	34.3	4	30.9	4	25.2	4
Dietary	43.8	4	39.6	4	30.0	4	24.0	4	21.2	4
Services	92.1	8	79.3	8	57.9	7	46.0	7	34.9	6
International	81.8	7	71.2	7	53.7	6	38.1	6	28.4	5
Unallocated eliminations and adjustments	(23.8)	(2)	(25.4)	(3)	(16.5)	(2)	(12.7)	(2)	(12.4)	(2)
	$1143.4	100%	$985.9	100%	$837.4	100%	$693.7	100%	$596.2	100%
Total international sales	$ 202.9	18%	$168.8	17%	$125.2	15%	$ 97.4	14%	$ 81.0	14%

NET EARNINGS (IN MILLIONS OF DOLLARS)

	$	%	$	%	$	%	$	%	$	%
Hospital	$ 19.3	35%	$ 13.7	29%	$ 10.0	25%	$ 7.5	21%	$ 6.1	21%
Science Specialties	16.5	30	14.6	31	13.6	33	12.3	34	10.7	35
Medical Specialties	6.8	12	5.9	13	3.7	9	3.4	10	2.6	8
Pharmaceutical	6.3	12	5.0	11	4.9	12	5.1	14	5.4	18
Capital Goods	3.0	6	2.3	5	2.2	5	2.0	6	2.1	7
Dental	2.4	4	2.6	6	1.8	4	1.5	4	0.4	1
Dietary	2.3	4	1.5	3	0.8	2	0.5	1	0.1	—
Services	1.8	3	3.0	6	1.6	4	0.9	3	0.6	2
International	.2	—	2.4	5	3.1	8	1.9	5	2.3	8
Unallocated interest, eliminations and adjustments	(3.4)	(6)	(4.4)	(9)	(0.7)	(2)	0.6	2	(0.1)	—
	$ 55.2	100%	$ 46.6	100%	$ 41.0	100%	$ 35.7	100%	$ 30.2	100%
Total international earnings	$ 10.5	19%	$ 10.9	23%	$ 7.9	19%	$ 4.9	14%	$ 3.2	10%

Sales and earnings for each market group include their respective export and Canadian operations. Appropriate eliminations have been made to reflect group results on a consolidated basis. Normal income tax provisions, less tax incentives and adjustments, are reflected within reported group earnings.

The International Group has responsibility for coordination of all domestic export shipments as well as direct responsibility for foreign-based operations. Total international net sales and net earnings shown as separate amounts include Canadian operations and United States exports, royalties from foreign sources, income from foreign investments, and foreign exchange gains and losses in addition to the International Group foreign-based operations.

Unallocated eliminations and adjustments reflect transactions between groups as well as corporate interest income and expense and other miscellaneous adjustments. Such unallocated interest expense after taxes amounted to $3.2 million in 1975 and $3.6 million in 1974. Other corporate office expenses have been allocated to group operations on the basis of sales and number of employees in each group.

EXHIBIT 2 ● Distribution Channels for Medical
Equipment and Devices

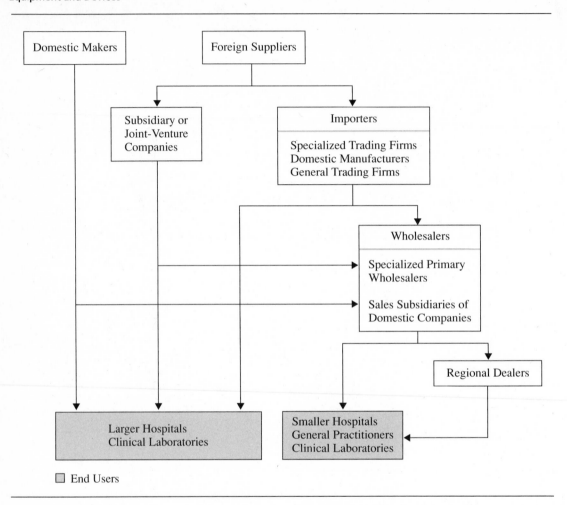

☐ End Users

cent of its sales were transacted through wholesalers or distributors. But the company believed these wholesalers to remain weak in promotion and technical after sales service. Consequently, these two aspects continued to be supplied by AHS-Japan. As a result, AHS-Japan has been very successful competing with medical equipment in Japan.

Following the successful introduction of medical equipment, American Hospital Supply

Corporation (AHSC) introduced clinical and diagnostic reagents. This product of the pharmaceutical industry was sold to the same targets as the medical equipment: hospitals, clinics, and general practitioners. Domestic producers only shipped about 30 percent of reagents directly, mostly to large hospitals or clinics; 70 percent was sold to 188 specialized primary wholesalers who partially sold directly to hospitals or supplied small regional wholesalers. These latter ones were not re-

EXHIBIT 3 ● Distribution Channels for Clinical
Diagnostic Reagents

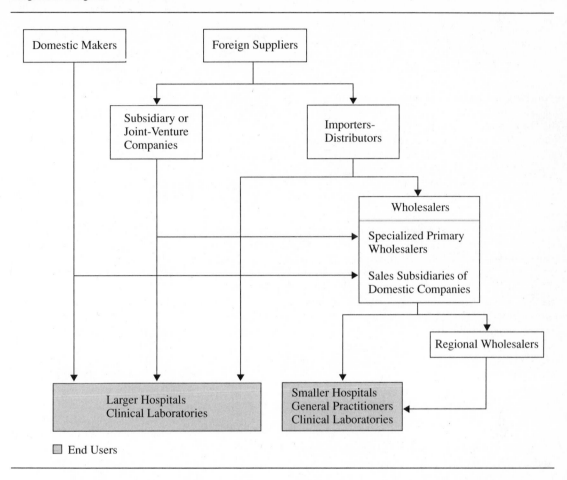

□ End Users

ally necessary except that local governments preferred to deal with regional wholesalers. Foreign
competitors could either sell through independent
importers or distributors or could form a joint
venture company in partnership with a Japanese
company. Since clinical reagents had to be kept
under refrigeration with special equipment,
AHSC had to find a way to obtain cooperation of
some of these primary wholesalers who supplied
the largest market segment. Since it was very dif-

ficult to obtain their cooperation as a newcomer,
AHS-Japan decided on a production joint-venture with Green Cross Co., a highly respected drug
manufacturer who also marketed whole blood. International Reagents Corporation, the JV manufacturing company, was then able to distribute its
reagents through 50 of the primary wholesalers
with the help of Green Cross Co. (See Exhibit 3 for
marketing channels.) Again, the product introduction was successful.

OPPORTUNITIES IN THE DENTAL EQUIPMENT MARKET

The market for dental equipment and materials in Japan was one of the largest in the world. There were approximately 40,000 dentists in Japan, and about 2,000 entered the field each year. They spent approximately $500 million in 1975 for both equipment and materials. Materials included all items that were actually used up or consumed by the dentist in his practice, or about $300 million annually. This amount was very high because it included precious metals, particularly gold, which accounted for 60 percent of the total used for fillings or tooth repair. Dental equipment, consisting of items such as chairs, lighting, handpieces, drills, etc., amounted to about $200 million annually. It was this latter segment of the market that was of prime interest to AHS-Japan Corporation. Japan's 40,000 practicing dentists were trained in the country's 27 dental colleges. Their income was relatively secure, because Japan's National Health Insurance Plan limited the amounts to be charged for a typical service. As a result, Japanese dentists had a tendency to see many more patients than their colleagues in Western countries—often 40 to 50 per day. Since the equipment of a dental practice represented a very large outlay, Japanese dentists turned to the equipment manufacturers for help to finance their initial costs.

The market for dental equipment was essentially dominated by three firms: Yoshida, Morita, and Osada. Together they accounted for 80 percent of the market. Yoshida, with a market share of 30 percent, was selling equipment manufactured by itself. Morita, also with a market share of 30 percent, had a licensing arrangement with Ritter, a major dental company in the United States. In contrast to the United States where a dentist might combine equipment from several manufacturers into a total package, the Japanese dentist only chose one manufacturer who then provided the total service. To attract dental college graduates, the leading companies even assisted in the planning, locating, and renting suitable buildings for dental practices and, in addition, provided the loans directly to the dentists to purchase or finance the practice. In the United States, the dentist typically received loans from a bank on his own without involving the dental equipment manufacturer. Of course, the Japanese system provided for a very strong tie between the dentists and the major manufacturers. To assist in the servicing of their equipment, each manufacturer provided expert repair service through an extensive servicing network. It was believed that the "new" market to dental college graduates represented about 60 percent of the equipment market.

The remainder of the market consisted of replacement sales to established dentists, or expansion of dental practices. This included most of the 40,000 practicing dentists. This segment of the market was dominated by 20 large wholesalers with strong contacts to the many retailers, or dealers, who were in almost daily contact with their dentists to supply them not only with replacement equipment but primarily with dental materials. The leading equipment manufacturers also used these intermediaries to sell in the replacement market.

Sharing the same distribution channel were the manufacturers of dental materials. This $300 million market consisted of 60 percent of precious metals, primarily gold and silver. The market had been growing at a rate of 10 to 15 percent. The market for materials in Japan was dominated by a few large firms, with the top three alone accounting for 70 percent of the market. G.C. Dental Industries was the leader with 28 percent, followed by Sankin with 22 percent and Shofu with 20 percent of the market. These manufacturers made extensive use of the 800 to 900 large and small retailers by selling to them either directly or through primary wholesalers (see Exhibit 4 for more details).

Sales to dentists took place almost on a daily basis. A retailer carrying one of the leading lines typically called the dentist in the morning and asked for the needs of the day. Orders were then accepted and shipped almost immediately. Contrary to equipment purchases, dentists sought materials from a number of manufacturers "cherry picking" each line for its best products.

EXHIBIT 4 ● Distribution Channels for Dental
Industry

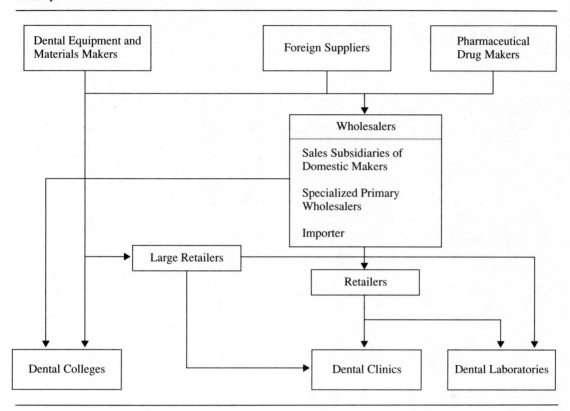

AHS-JAPAN'S LINE OF DENTAL EQUIPMENT

It was planned to introduce primarily handpieces, or "drills," and dental untis (see Exhibits 5 and 6) made by American Hospital Supplies' Midwest Subsidiary.[2] The handpieces and dental units were generally regarded as the best in the industry, both in the United States and in Japan. While more expensive than competitive products by about 25 percent, they offered considerable benefits com-

2. Midwest did not produce any other dental equipment such as chairs, lamps, etc.

pared to other handpieces. Drill speeds were as high as 450,000 R.P.M., though some local competitors' products achieved even higher speeds. The speed could be gradually adjusted from zero to top speed with a foot pedal, whereas local competitors had no adjustable speed or foot pedal. And finally, AHS units were generally considered to be superior to competitors in styling.

Japanese dentists were considering accuracy, quality, and high speed as the primary criteria in selecting handpieces. In general, American equipment was highly regarded among Japanese dentists, many of whom knew Midwest equipment from their trips to conferences in the United States

EXHIBIT 5 ● Midwest Handpieces

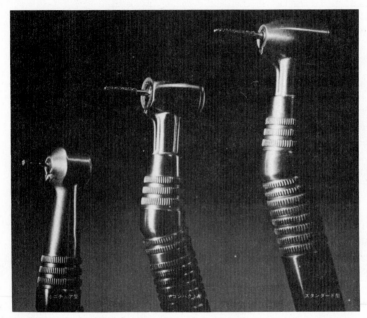

《エアータービン コントラアングル》
クワイエットエアー
スタンダード型
コンパクト型
ミニチュア型

回転ブレが無く、長寿命
磨耗の少ない特殊ボールベアリングと独特のメタルチャックシステムの採用により、バーのセンターリングは抜群。回転ブレが無いだけでなく、耐久性も連続回転試験で延べ800時間と、他社製品の2倍以上です。

強力で安定したトルク特性
高効率タービンと独自の軸受機構により、低速回転や加圧操作中においても安定した強いトルクを発揮します。

冷却効果の大きいスプレー
ヘッド先端のノズルからは冷却水が霧状になって噴出。形成歯牙を直接、効果的に冷やします。

ミッドウェスト社独自の4ホール方式
コントラ内には4本の（ドライブエアー用、エキゾーストエアー用、チップエアー用、水用）が独立して組込まれていますので――

①水 ②ドライブエアー ③エキゾーストエアー ④チップエアー

and Europe. In fact, some of them had purchased Midwest handpieces abroad or wrote directly to the factory in the United States. In the past, Midwest had filled these orders despite the absence of a servicing network to assist the dentists.

The dental units were to sell at about yen 4.5 million[3] compared to simpler ones available for as little as 2.5 million. Due to the expensive nature of AHS-Japan's equipment, the company considered the top 5 to 10 percent of practicing dentists as its main target market. Such a dentist typically had been in business for several years and achieved a relatively high income. When replacing equipment, he was more interested in status and willing to pay a premium price for what was considered the "Cadillac" of the industry. Of course, the products had to be adjusted to the Japanese environment. Because Japanese dentists were smaller than their American colleagues, they preferred somewhat smaller chairs and lighter handpieces. Also, electricity in Japan was not everywhere the same: the Western part used 60 cycles and Eastern part 50 cycles. Some adjustment to the dental units was required, since in rural areas Japanese dentists worked on the traditional

3. 250 yen = $1 U.S.

EXHIBIT 5 ● Midwest Handpieces (Continued)

《エアータービン ハンドピース》
ツルートルクショーティ I型 II型

低速使用時にも充分なトルク
エアータービンの高速回転を強力なトルクに変える画期的な
伝達装置。これが粘り強く安定した低速回転を実現しました。

優れた耐久性
回転部分の軸受けには特殊ボールベアリングを使用。長時間
にわたる苛酷な使用に耐えます。またエアーを動力源としますから電気的トラブルなどに悩まされることなく、ほとんど故障知らずです。

振動のないスムーズな回転
ボールベアリングの使用に加えて、ミッドウェスト社独自のメタルチャック方式の採用がバーの回転ブレを皆無にしました。ドリオット型のアタッチメント装置の場合もシッカリと安定します。

コントラ型の専用アタッチメントも用意
強力なトルクをそのままコントラアングルとしても使用できる専用アタッチメントを用意しました。特にバランスを重視。交換操作はワンタッチです。

回転速度が自由にコントロールできる
ミッドウェストアメリカン社のユニットと組合せればこの回転数をフットペダルで自由にコントロール。どの回転領域でも有効な力を発揮します。

チップエアー、スプレーが使用可能
必要に応じてスプレーホースを取付けることにより、チップエアー及びスプレーが使えます。

● I型
変速リングを切換えることにより、低速(200〜6,000rpm)から高速(6,000〜25,000rpm)まで自由に回転スピードをコントロールできます。

● II型
200〜6,000rpmの低速領域で高性能を発揮。回転スピードのコントロールは自在です。

■専用アタッチメント（別売）

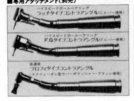

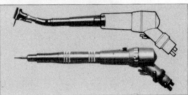

---

tatami (straw) mats and it was not possible to screw the equipment to the floor as was the case in urban areas or in the United States.

To facilitate such local adjustments, AHS-Japan planned to import the equipment initially from Midwest, and later to move into local assembly with local production as the ultimate goal. However, such adjustments to both dental units and equipment for an otherwise standardized product line would only be possible if AHS-Japan could guarantee sufficient sales volume to make the changes profitable.

SELECTION OF DISTRIBUTION CHANNEL

There were four basic options for AHS-Japan's entry into the dental equipment field. The company could (a) go directly to dentists with its own distribution set-up, or (b) AHS-Japan could use existing wholesalers and retailers to go to the market. The next two alternatives involved (c) some form of cooperation with one of the leading dental equipment manufacturers or (d) align themselves with a leading dental material supply manufacturer.

AHS-Japan had set several objectives for the introduction. The company wanted to become an important factor in the market with a goal of a 10 percent market share for handpieces and 5 percent for dental units. Also, it was important to portray reliability and, if some form of arrangement were to be negotiated, it would have to be with a first-class company. And, finally, AHS-Japan wanted to open up channels for additional dental product

EXHIBIT 6 ● Midwest Dental Unit

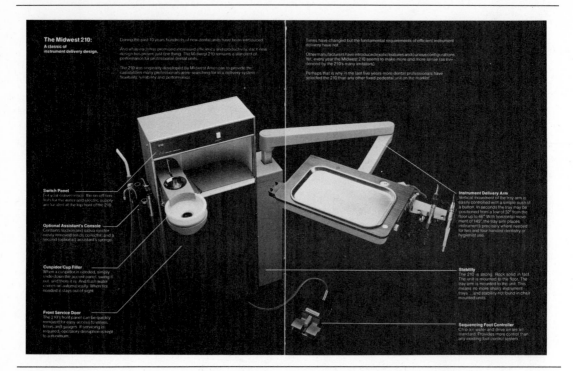

210 Dental Unit

Basic Unit (Right or Left Handed versions)	610090	Three Handpiece AUTOMATIC Activation and Syringe
		Two Handpiece AUTOMATIC Activation and Syringe
		Two Handpiece MANUAL Activation and Syringe
Basic Unit Includes:		Midwest Tri-Clear® Syringe and Hose

Counter Balanced Tray Arm with:
    a. Height adjustment button
    b. Spray control knob
    c. Water for handpiece cooling
    d. Stainless steel tray
    e. Warm water for 3-way Tri-Clear Syringe
    f. Air pressure gauge

Concealed Cuspidor with Automatic Flush and Gravity Drain

Concealed Cup Filler

Master Electric Switch

Flat Working Top

Variable Speed Foot Controller with Chip Air

Light Adapter Opening and Bracket
(Light Post Must Be Obtained from Light Manufacturer)

EXHIBIT 6 ● Midwest Dental Unit (Continued)

Duplex Electrical Outlet in Unit Base

Air Line Filter with Automatic Moisture Drain

Fused Electrical Service

Counter Balanced Accent Panel

Hydrocolloid and Drain Connection with Flow Adjustment

Dual Water Filtration System

Straight Handpiece Tubing with Midwest or Borden Back End

210 Dental Unit Accessories

Evacuation System	611467	Fittings for Central Suction Hi Volume Evacuation. Includes Solids Collector with Remote Switch for Central Pump and Saliva Ejector
	611472	Self-Contained Air Venturi Hi Volume Evacuation System with Fittings
Burner	303795	Bunsen Burner with Fittings
Syringe	611476	Tri-Clear® Syringe with Fittings (Auxiliary Syringe on Assistant's Console and Custom Installations)
Hoses	611328	Coiled Midwest 4-Hole Tubing (When Purchased with Unit) Also Available with Borden 2 and 3 hole Tubing.
	611329	Coiled Syringe Hose (When Purchased with Unit)
	731074	Fiber Optic Hose Installed 5′ Straight Hose with 10′ Fiber Optic Bundle
	731075	Coiled Fiber Optic Hose Installed
Oraluminator	731076	Oraluminator III Light Source with Remote Control Unit. Mounting Holes Predrilled in 210 Side Panel and Tray Bottom
HVE Hose	611481	Second HVE Hose (Central Vacuum only)
Syringe	280022	Tri-Clear® Syringe
Installation Kit	610117	Kit for Field Installation of Assistant's Tri-Clear Syringe on 210 Unit. (Does Not Include Syringe)
Tray Arm Lock	611494	U.S. Navy Tray Arm Locking Mechanism

introductions at a later time, both in the equipment and the materials segments of the market.

ALTERNATIVE A: GOING DIRECT

This would require AHS-J to sell directly to dentists, either to new graduates of dental colleges or established dentists, by use of a specially trained sales force. At this time, AHS-J did not have sufficient manpower to handle such a task, but additional personnel with sufficient qualifications could be hired and trained. AHS-J would also have to provide an extensive service network that could back up its selling effort. This was the option chosen for introduction of its medical equipment line.

ALTERNATIVE B: USING EXISTING INTERMEDIARIES

AHS-J had the option of selling to its targets through the 29 primary wholesalers and 800 to

900 large and small retailers. Essentially, this was the channel used by the leading manufacturers for the replacement portion of their business. It would be necessary to gain the cooperation of a number of the primary wholesalers, so that, in combination with their respective retail accounts, satisfactory coverage of the market could be established.

Using these intermediaries, however, would entail for AHS-J to assist in the sales task by training the distributor sales personnel. Technical service, however, would have to be provided by AHS-J, since wholesalers and retailers were historically weak in that area. To some extent, this was the alternative selected for the medical equipment line, following its successful initial introduction.

ALTERNATIVE C: COOPERATION WITH A DENTAL EQUIPMENT MANUFACTURER

The Japanese equipment manufacturers, which were now selling their own handpieces and dental units, were believed to be interested in using AHS-J's line as a new, top-of-the-line addition for dentists who were willing to pay for the added performance of Midwest equipment. Management believed that any one of the three leading manufacturers would be interested in carrying the line. Service could of course be handled by the Japanese manufacturer. However, management expected that whichever would be chosen as a distributor would require an exclusive arrangement for the Japanese market.

ALTERNATIVE D: COOPERATION WITH A DENTAL MATERIALS MANUFACTURER

Over the past few years, manufacturers of dental materials had made attempts to invade the equipment market with their own products. Management therefore believed that any of the leading three materials manufacturers would be willing to carry the Midwest line as its entry into the dental equipment market. Sales would take place primarily through wholesalers and retailers which was the customary channel for the material segment of the dental market. Service would have to

be provided in conjunction with AHS-J, since that was an important factor in the market.

THE REALITIES OF THE JAPANESE DISTRIBUTION SYSTEM

The choice of any of these basic alternatives greatly depended on AHS-J's objectives for its dental line in the Japanese market and on the "realities" of the Japanese distribution system, both in general and with respect to dental equipment and material.

One of the overriding factors in any Japanese distribution or business arrangement was the nature of the personal contact with one's business partners. In general, the Japanese did not like to conduct business with strangers, be that an unknown company or an unknown salesman. This often required that a businessman who wanted to see a particular person had to have an appropriate introduction. At best, this would be a good personal friend of the person to be visited, maybe even someone the latter was beholden to. Also, the higher the status of the person making an introduction, the better for later business. When no one could be found to give an introduction, sometimes a bank could serve as a reference. In any case, it was extremely difficult to see someone without an introduction, particularly when both the company and the person were unknown.

Another reality of business relationships was the loyalty displayed to existing contacts or associates. This was particularly strong in the channel structure. Over the years, manufacturers had become very close to their distributors and wholesalers, making it difficult for some to enact policies that would harm the other. Manufacturers would, whenever possible, tie wholesalers to their operations by granting liberal trade credit. Wholesalers in turn would do likewise with "their" retailers. As a result, a retailer would often be hesitant to carry a new, or even competitive, product from another wholesaler for fear of alienating his established supplier, and hence endanger his source of financing. Such ties also existed between retailers and customers. In the extreme, a market could at times be virtually "locked up" through existing relationships making it extremely difficult for a newcomer to enter.

With respect to trends in the dental market, one important factor was the attempt by both the equipment manufacturers and material producers to invade each other's territory. Both groups maintained strong controls with "their" loyal group of wholesalers and retailers, ensuring the "Big Three" of each group coverage of the entire Japanese market.

It was these general factors, combined with AHS-J's intermediate and long-term objectives, that the company's management had to consider. Whatever the company decided, it would also have to gain the support of its parent organization.

CASE 8

Biral International (A)

In the fall of 1979, the executive committee of Bieri Pumpenbau AG Biral International, located in Muensignen near Berne, Switzerland, met to discuss the implications of entering into a cooperation agreement with a Hungarian manufacturer to produce Bieri pumps. The committee had to decide if the company should pursue this opportunity along the lines negotiated by Vacano, the coordinator for sales to the COMECON area.[1] Negotiations had stretched over the better part of the last two years and had reached a critical point. A final decision on the part of Bieri's executive committee was required before the formal blessing of Hungary's Ministry of Foreign Trade could be obtained.

COMPANY HISTORY

The company was formed in 1919 by Bieri to produce a number of different pumps. In later years,

___

1. COMECON is an abbreviation for "Council of Mutual Economic Assistance" comprising the Soviet Union, East Germany, Poland, Hungary, Rumania, Bulgaria, Czechoslovakia, Cuba, North Korea, and a few associated members in Asia and Africa.

●

This case was prepared by Visiting Professor Jean-Pierre Jeannet as a basis for class discussion rather than to illustrate either effective or ineffective handling of an administrative situation. Copyright © 1985 by IMEDE, Lausanne, Switzerland. The International Institute for Management Development (IMD), resulting from the merger between IMEDE, Lausanne, and IMI, Geneva, acquires and retains all rights. Reproduced by permission.

the founder's two sons, Franz and Werner Bieri, took over management of the company. Under their direction, the company's manufacturing facilities were expanded in 1953 and 1961, and an entirely new factory was opened in 1971. The company's sales had reached a record of about 52 million francs by 1978, not including sales of the principal supplier of many of Bieri's electrical motors whose equity was partially owned by the principals of Bieri. In total, the company employed about 400 persons and, since 1978, had been under the direction of the third generation, Ueli and Peter Bieri, the two sons of Franz Bieri, and Hansrudolf, the son of Werner Bieri.

Bieri had been affected negatively during the recessionary period of 1974–1976 when residential construction, a major user of Bieri's products, went into a sharp decline in Switzerland. This happened at a time when the value of the Swiss franc moved up sharply against other currencies increasing the price of Bieri products in its major export markets while these countries also went through a recessionary period. Net profits (computed after funding of various reserves and depreciation) significantly dropped in 1975 but they had since recovered. For 1979, Bieri expected its profits to reach levels of the early 1970s. (See Exhibit 1 for sales and profit history.) The name Biral International had just been added to the company name. Originally, the Biral brand name applied only to a portion of the company's product line but now described all of Bieri's products.

PRODUCT LINES

Bieri had four major product lines: circulating pumps, general pumps, swimming pool pumps

EXHIBIT 1 ● Biral's Sales and Profit History

Year	Sales (SFr)	Profit (SFr)	Profit margin
1970	37,647,500	NA	NA
1971	42,165,200	191,600	0.4%
1972	49,284,000	82,140	0.1
1973	51,225,242	164,280	0.3
1974	51,474,400	10,952	0.2
1975	44,508,928	(39,701)	(0.08)
1976	53,527,900	(12,514)	(0.02)
1977	50,195,754	31,007	0.06
1978	51,917,486	100,518	0.19

and filters, and control systems. Circulating pumps accounted for 54.8 percent of 1978 sales. These pumps, traditionally marketed under the brand name Biral, were sold both in Switzerland, where Bieri was the undisputed market leader, and in other countries of Western Europe. Negotiations with the Hungarian cooperation partner covered exclusively circulating pumps, but the other product lines had also to be taken into consideration as additional orders could be expected if the agreement went into effect.

The second major product line, general pumps, or APB for "Allgemeiner Pumpenbau," accounted for 33.3 percent of sales. Included were pumps for water supply systems, irrigation systems, and wastewater pumps. These products were produced according to specifications submitted by the client. Sales were strongest in Switzerland with exports accounting for only about 10 percent of the output.

Bieri had two additional product lines of lesser importance. The swimming pool pumps, or SBF, accounted for 10.4 percent of 1978 sales. More than 90 percent of these sales were to customers in Switzerland. Control systems, Bieri's smallest product line, represented an extension of the company's efforts in the area of general pump construction. Control systems were suited for controlling large pump systems and had been manu-

factured in-house for several years. This capacity and knowledge was then also made available to other companies for different control applications. But volume never exceeded 1.5 percent of sales and amounted to only 0.3 percent in 1978.

BIRAL CIRCULATING PUMPS

Bieri company had for many years dominated the market in Switzerland with its circulating pumps. The pumps were used to circulate the water of heating systems in both commercial and residential buildings. Biral pumps, while more expensive than competitive products, were considered of the highest quality requiring minimal service. Also, their unique construction with the separating shell ensured that the pumps were effectively protected from penetrating water which could cause short circuits (see Exhibit 2). While the separating shell was, by itself, an easily understood concept, competitors had been unable to produce such a part for their own use. Bieri had developed a special 400-ton press to mass produce these separating shells with high precision.

Other advantages of Biral pumps were their highly efficient electric motors which ran with a minimum of noise and required lower electricity. The electric motors were produced by RCB Elektro-Apparate AG, a small company about 50 miles from the Bieri plant. Bieri was RCB's largest customer and owned the majority of RCB's share capital. Final assembly of Biral pumps took place at Bieri's plant in Muensingen. In 1979, Bieri expected to produce 200,000 to 250,000 units.

The separating shell technology was the property of RCB. Bieri had the shells produced by an outside contractor who used RCB's technology on an exclusive basis. All other parts were sourced by Bieri from independent contractors. At Bieri's plant in Muensingen, the circulating pumps were simply assembled from these purchased parts. Depending on product mix, output could be expanded by 100 to 200 percent on the part of Bieri without any substantial investments.

THE MARKETS FOR BIERI PUMPS

Circulating pumps were primarily sold in Europe under the Biral brand name. Forty-seven percent

EXHIBIT 2 ● Biral Circulating Pump (Cross Section)

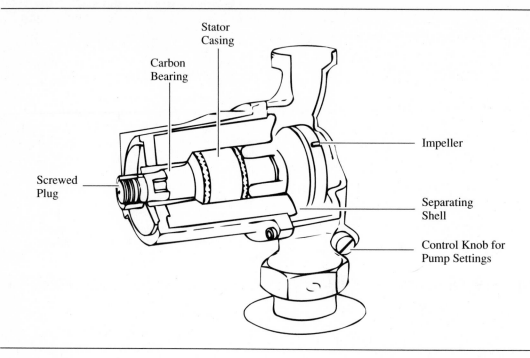

of the pumps were sold on the Swiss market, with the remainder exported to a few European countries with strong sales' networks such as Austria, Belgium, Germany, France, U.K., Italy, and the Netherlands (see Exhibit 3, 4, and 5). These Biral pumps were primarily used for heating systems, but could also be installed in connection with climate control systems and hot water supply systems. The pumps were generally bought by plumbing contractors who installed a heating system in a house. The pumps, valued at an average of between SFr 50 to SFr 1400, represented only a small portion of the approximately SFr 10,000 to SFr 20,000 for a complete system.[2] However, the pumps represented a crucial part since the proper circulation of the heated water throughout the pipe system of a building had a major influence on

2. In 1979 1 SFr (Swiss Franc) equalled U.S. $.60.

the efficiency of the heating plant. Plumbing contractors were particularly interested in trouble-free pumps that required little servicing. Should the pump fail, it was usually the plumber who was asked to service it.

Bieri offered Biral pumps in a large variety of sizes. Depending on the height of a building and the amount of water to be circulated, the plumber could determine exactly what pump was most appropriate. The correct selection was important since the right pump could run on lower rpms, resulting in lower energy costs and lower noise levels. Since circulating pumps had to run continuously during heating periods, energy consumption and noise level were important considerations for building owners.

Biral pumps were marketed directly by Bieri only to a few selected plumbing contractors in the canton of Berne, the particular area of Switzerland

EXHIBIT 3 ● Total Sales 1978 (in SFr)

Country	Circulating pumps	General pumps 'APB'	Swimming pool 'SBF'	Controls	Total
Switzerland	13,463,780	15,620,291	5,214,850	545,294	34,844,215
Algeria	—	42,475	7,803	—	50,278
Australia	56,681	—	—	—	56,681
Austria	2,650,860	5,742	38,295	236,522	2,931,419
Belgium	609,094	457	—	—	609,551
Denmark	5,282	11,187	—	—	16,469
W. Germany	3,623,573	167,315	5,899	9,108	3,805,895
France	1,121,639	3,313	—	—	1,124,952
Gt. Britain	1,627,906	63,747	11,579	—	1,703,232
Iraq	—	855,696	64,340	—	920,036
Ireland	—	79,261	—	—	79,261
Italy	2,813,158	2,097	30,527	—	2,845,782
Morocco	—	3,793	—	—	3,793
Netherlands	2,436,754	57,076	—	—	2,493,830
Norway	14,404	45,118	—	—	59,522
Poland	6,448	—	—	—	6,448
Singapore	—	1,512	—	—	1,512
So. Africa	—	13,936	—	—	13,936
Sw. Africa	22,794	—	—	—	22,794
USSR	—	20,890	—	—	20,890
Hungary	—	306,990	—	—	306,990
Total	28,452,373	17,300,896	5,373,293	790,924	51,917,486
As a Percentage of Sales	54.8%	33.3%	10.3%	1.5%	100.0%
Total Export	14,988,593	1,680,605	158,443	245,630	17,073,271
As a Percentage of Exports	87.8%	9.8%	.9%	1.4%	100.0%

where the company was located, and to manufacturers of heating furnaces (OEMs). In the rest of Switzerland, as well as in France, Italy, U.K., Netherlands, Austria and Belgium, Bieri had an exclusive sales agreement with Hoval. Hoval was a well-known manufacturer of furnaces with a technological advantage. Since furnaces were sold to plumbing and heating contractors, Hoval was in an excellent position to carry the Biral pumps as an addition to its own product line. Hoval had its own sales force in Switzerland, and operated sales subsidiaries in various European countries. Bieri, however, had an individual sales agreement with each Hoval subsidiary. This very close rela-

EXHIBIT 4 ● 1978 Sales Distribution by Product Line (in SFr)

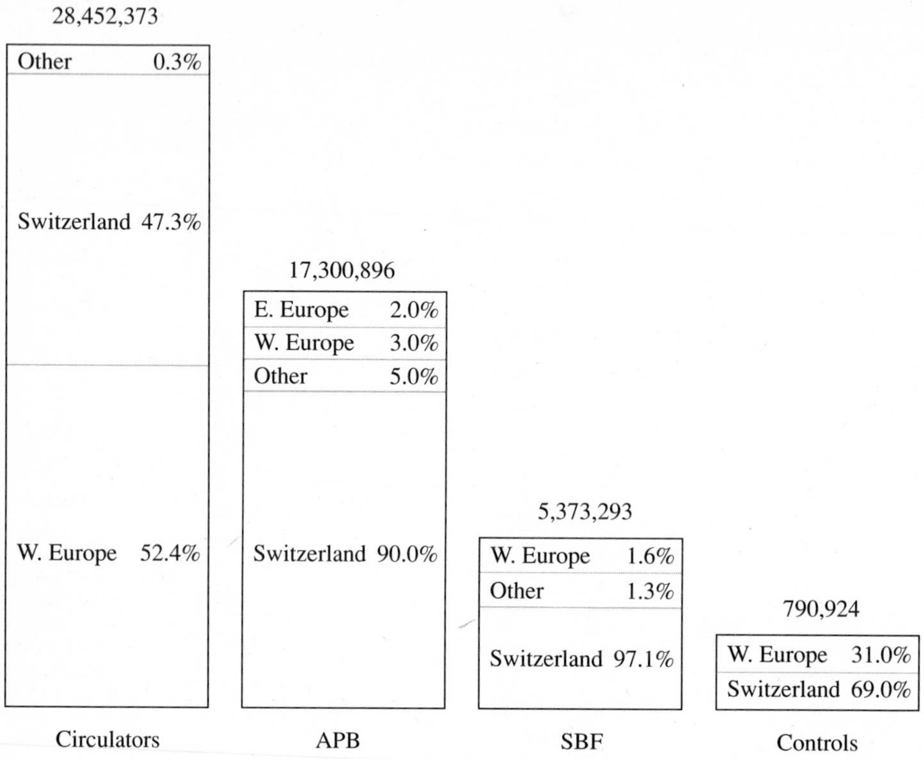

28,452,373

Other	0.3%

Switzerland	47.3%

17,300,896

E. Europe	2.0%
W. Europe	3.0%
Other	5.0%

W. Europe	52.4%

Switzerland	90.0%

5,373,293

W. Europe	1.6%
Other	1.3%

Switzerland	97.1%

790,924

W. Europe	31.0%
Switzerland	69.0%

| Circulators | APB | SBF | Controls |

tionship was further enhanced through a small stock ownership of Hoval in both Bieri and the producer of the pumps' electrical motors, RCB Elektro-Apparate AG. Hoval was also represented on the boards of both of these companies. Hoval's management has made it clear that it considered the Hungarian proposal to be Bieri's decision.

MARKET FORCES IN THE CIRCULATING PUMP MARKET

Sales of Biral pumps depended largely on building activity and Bieri's competitive advantage. Each new house or building in Bieri's market area required a heating system, and this usually meant an oil- or gas-heated furnace with hot water pumped throughout the house. Any such installation required a circulating pump. Electric heat, more popular in the United States, was not widely accepted, and in Switzerland a permit issued by the electric company was required to install it. Since electric generating capacity was barely sufficient to cover present demand, few such permits were granted. In other European countries, the situation was not much different from that in Switzerland.

The competitive situation, however, was quite dynamic and subject to rapid changes. Over the past eight years, currencies had fluctuated widely in the world markets. The free float of the

EXHIBIT 5 ● 1978 Sales Distribution by Region (in SFr)

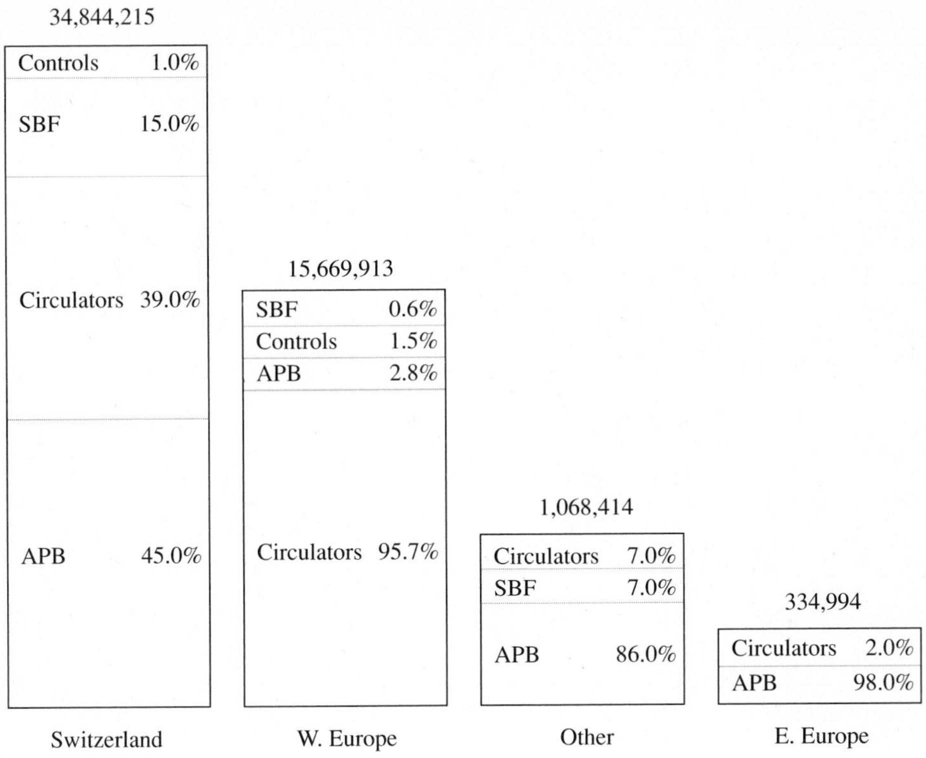

34,844,215

Controls	1.0%
SBF	15.0%
Circulators	39.0%
APB	45.0%

Switzerland

15,669,913

SBF	0.6%
Controls	1.5%
APB	2.8%
Circulators	95.7%

W. Europe

1,068,414

Circulators	7.0%
SBF	7.0%
APB	86.0%

Other

334,994

| Circulators | 2.0% |
| APB | 98.0% |

E. Europe

Swiss franc had resulted in a marked appreciation against other European currencies. Against the Italian lira, the French franc, and the British pound, the Swiss franc had more than doubled in value. While this was partially offset in these countries by inflation rates of 5 to 10 percent above the Swiss rate, Swiss production costs had increased relative to competitors located in those countries. Against the DM and the Dutch guilder, the Swiss franc appreciated about 25 percent, but these two latter countries had experienced an inflation rate similar to that of Switzerland. These currency changes left Bieri's prices 20 to 40 percent above those of its competitors. This had a particularly strong effect on Bieri's export markets where the company did not profit from the same strong brand loyalty that it enjoyed in Switzerland.

While Bieri had no significant competition in the circulating pump market in Switzerland, there were several European companies with substantially larger output and well entrenched positions in specific countries. The largest one, Grundfos, a Danish company, had operations in all major European countries and a total volume of more than 2.5 million circulating pumps annually. Grundfos was able to sell its pumps at prices of 20 to 30 percent below Bieri's due to its very large output. Next to Grundfos, there were three other major producers—Wilo in Germany, Euramo in France, and Myson in the U.K. These manufacturers had an annual output of about twice Bieri's volume and maintained strong positions in their home markets with only spotty coverage of the rest of Europe.

In its latest move, Grundfos started sales operations in Switzerland in 1978. This represented a major competitive threat to Bieri since Switzerland was its major market absorbing almost half of its Biral output at prices substantially above prevailing levels in other European markets. Grundfos pumps were not produced in Switzerland, resulting in greater price flexibility for the Danish company. Bieri believed that the Swiss plumbing and heating contractors were unlikely to buy an inferior product even at a very low price. This forced Grundfos to price higher than in other European markets, but still substantially below Bieri's prices. With Biral's reputation for quality and longevity, Bieri executives believed that the threat emanating from Grundfos was real but not critical.

From a long-term point of view, it was of importance to Bieri to increase its own annual output to obtain economies of scale and, as a result, to lower its unit costs. Combined with the already existing technological advantage, the company could look forward to a promising future.

BACKGROUND TO THE HUNGARIAN COOPERATION PROPOSAL

For several years, Bieri had employed a Marketing Manager for the Comecon Area, a position occupied by Vacano. He had made numerous trips to Eastern Europe to contact the various buying organizations. While each country in Eastern Europe had a somewhat different set-up, all had from 4 to 25 foreign trade organizations which bought and/or sold merchandise, as ordered by their "clients," all state-run manufacturing or trading companies. Typically, these foreign trade organizations would compete against each other for the same clients or business in their country. During the first phase of Bieri's marketing offensive in Eastern Europe, it was Vacano's task to make con-

tact with these organizations. Sales were never quite large, but had been steadily increasing as shown below:

Sales of Bieri Products to Comecon Countries

Year	Volume (SFr)	% BIRAL	% APB
1976	225,923	—	—
1977	145,272	8	92
1978	334,173	2	98
1979 (estimate)	520,220	—	—

General pumps (APB) accounted for the bulk of the business. Sales also tended to be concentrated by countries. In 1976 all sales were to Hungary, and Czechoslovakia accounted for 91 percent of 1977 sales. Hungary again absorbed 92 percent of sales to Eastern Europe in 1978. Bieri's had grown at about 50 percent per year despite strong competition from other European pump manufacturers. Direct annual marketing costs were relatively low averaging 40,000 francs and consisted mostly of trips by Bieri executives to the area and participation in trade shows.

Early in 1977, Bieri was approached by a Hungarian foreign trade corporation, Magyarexport (MAGEX) to open negotiations for a cooperative agreement with one of MAGEX's clients, Villamos.[3] The interest centered from the very beginning around Biral circulating pumps. Biral pumps were to be produced in cooperation with Villamos but payment for manufacturing know-how and licensing fees was, in part, to be made with output from the plant, either in the form of finished pumps or parts. Most Eastern European countries, and Hungary was no exception, were in need of western products and technology but they were usually unable to pay in convertible currency. To alleviate the problem, these countries

---

3. All Hungarian names are disguised.

imported technologies and preferred to pay primarily in merchandise.

Bieri's management quickly realized that such a cooperation agreement could offer an attractive way of entering the Hungarian or Comecon market provided the conditions were favorable. Vacano was authorized to commence negotiations, and, by 1979, he had gone through 8 revisions of the original proposal.

Villamos, the manufacturing enterprise, had no experience in the producing pumps. It was a relatively small company operating about 15 workshops. In 1979, a new factory was built allowing the company to centralize its operation just outside Budapest, Hungary's capital. The company's operations included an aluminum foundry and manufacturing of garden furniture and camping equipment. The negotiations were carried out by MAGEX on behalf of Villamos.

An abridged form of the latest version of the proposal is shown in the Appendix. The contract could be summarized as follows:

Cooperation Agreement:
Bieri was to deliver to MAGEX-Villamos the documentation and know-how to produce a specified number of Biral pumps. Included were all rights to the patents including those related to the electric motors with an additional responsibility of Bieri to provide 45 man-days of training at Bieri and a further possible 30 man-days at the Hungarian plant. Villamos was obligated to produce a minimum of 30,000 pumps over the 5 years the contract was to be in force plus pay an additional royalty fee of 3 percent for every pump produced. The fee could be paid in hard currency or parts shipment.

MAGEX and/or Villamos were prepared to buy pumps and parts from Bieri over the life of the contract and had a contractual obligation to give Bieri preference on such purchases. In return, Bieri would be obligated to buy back an equivalent value from the Hungarian companies. This obligation would remain in effect until termination of the contract. All money transfers were to take place in hard currency

and values would be calculated according to Bieri's price list.

PRELIMINARY EVALUATION OF THE AGREEMENT

For Bieri's executive committee's final evaluation, Vacano estimated that the direct costs arising from the agreement, such as training, would amount to about SFr 50,000. While it was difficult to estimate the size of the market for circulator pumps in Hungary, Vacano believed that 20,000 pumps annually was a "good figure." Sales of other pumps to Hungary had been very slow this year despite the fact that Bieri had submitted quotes for several installations totaling more than 1 million francs. Just this April, Bieri submitted a bid for a large project but all the orders went to the traditional suppliers. Sales so far had amounted to less than SFr 20,000 for 1979.

Negotiations had stretched over 2 years and were now at a point where he felt that Bieri could not obtain better terms. If Bieri would not go ahead with the contract, Villamos was certain to enter into an agreement with another European manufacturer, possibly even Grundfos.

As far as Vacano could determine, COMECON countries had for some time bought limited amounts of circulating pumps from Western sources. The major producer of circulating pumps was Czechoslovakia, but in amounts insufficient to satisfy domestic or COMECON demand. Once Villamos was in a situation to sell circulators, it would have to market its pumps through Szerelvenyertekesito, a Hungarian trading company that alone had the right to market such pumps in Hungary. With respect to those pumps covered in the corporation agreement, no competition existed in Hungary for those pumps covered in the corporation agreement. Once production started such pumps could be obtained only through Villamos. For larger circulating pumps, Hungarian foreign trade companies would continue to buy from western firms, including competitors of Bieri.

Under the proposed agreement Bieri would first supply the parts for the production of the

EXHIBIT 6 ● Prices and Delivery Conditions for Biral Pump Parts

		Pump types		
Number	Part	NRB 12 S-1 V	NRB 13 S-2 V	NRB 15 S V
	Completely assembled	SFr. 57.65	SFr. 76.75	SFr. 161.70
	Motor (complete)	41.09	58.17	132.47
1	Separating Shell (unfinished)	4.20	6.50	15.40
12, 13	Carbon bearing	1.81	3.50	3.50
15	Tolerance ring	.42	.50	.67
19/20	Impeller	1.22	1.91	8.14
8	Packing between pump motor	.32	.50	.92
23	Pump casing	7.08	8.47	10.66
7	Screw	.11	.11	.11
27	Control knob for pump settings	.38	.38	.49
26, 28, 31, 36, 53	O-Ring	.15	.15	.15
	Screwed Plug	.09	.17	.36
35	Name Plate	.32	.49	.78
56	Label	.03	.03	.03
	Connecting parts	2.63	2.63	3.81

All prices are valid for deliveries up to December 12, 1980 and do not include packaging or freight. Packaging and freight will be billed separately after each shipment. These conditions are subject to the agreement as covered in Article 12.

pumps. Within two years, it was planned to reduce these supplies to zero. The pumps covered by the contract ranged in price from SFr 57.65 to SFr 161.70 ex factory Muensingen. Contribution margin (covering variable costs of purchases, direct labor, but excluding factory overhead, depreciation, marketing, sales, and servicing costs) was approximately 50 percent. Consequently, the sales volume of the 30,000 pumps amounted to about SFr 3 million based on going Bieri ex factory-prices. For a detailed price list, see Exhibit 6.

THE HUNGARIAN BUSINESS CLIMATE

Ever since the end of World War II, Hungary had been under the influence of the Soviet Union. A member of COMECON, Hungary had a state-operated industry similar to those in other communist countries in Eastern Europe. The present political leadership, installed after the 1956 revolution, had over the years liberalized much of the economic activities. With a per capita income of approximately $2,500, Hungarians enjoyed a standard of living that surpassed those of other COMECON members except East Germany. The country's population amounted to about 11 million. Exports had reached a level of about 8 billion dollars but were still exceeded by imports amounting to $10 billion.

The negative balance of trade prompted the Hungarian government to take corrective action in 1972. Hungary became the second COM-

ECON government after Rumania to allow for joint ventures with western companies. However, due to restrictions and what western businessmen considered still unclear practices, only three ventures were formed. Since 1974, the Swedish firm Volvo produced a 4-wheel drive vehicle with the Csepel Company in Budapest that sold abroad through the Volvo organization.

Siemens of Germany established the second venture and, since 1975, Corning Medical of the United States produced medical equipment jointly with the Hungarian firm Radelhis. More activity could be found among strict licensing agreements. It was estimated that over the past few years alone, the Hungarian machinery industry had concluded more than 300 licensing agreements with Western firms. Moreover, Hungary had taken the leadership among COMECON countries for cooperation agreements. So far, it was estimated that Hungarian enterprises had concluded more than 500 such agreements.

Over the past few years, Switzerland had been an important trading partner for Hungary. Among the countries outside the COMECON area, Switzerland was Hungary's fourth important trading partner. Switzerland exported goods worth SFr 268 million to Hungary in 1976, up from only SFr 157 million in 1973. Imports from Hungary grew from SFr 155 million to SFr 170 million over the same time period. During the past few years, Swiss companies had signed many licensing agreements and cooperation arrangements. At the beginning of 1977, a total of 55 cooperation and 10 licensing agreements were in effect, and, by April 1978, it was reported that another 52 cooperation agreements were being negotiated. These agreements, however, still represented only 1.4 percent of Swiss-Hungarian trade compared to 5.3 percent for German-Hungarian trade and 7.5 percent for Swedish-Hungarian trade. The majority of these agreements were signed by machinery and chemical companies. Among others, there existed an agreement by Hermes Company to have its typewriters produced in Hungary; Sibir for the production of refrigerators; and Brown Boveri & Cie for the construction of steam turbines. Despite several attempts on the part of Vacano, Bieri had not been able to learn details of the experiences of these Swiss companies' operations in Hungary.

CONCLUSION

The latest version of the agreement had been made available to members of the executive committee. It was Vacano's strong belief that he had negotiated the best possible contract, particularly when considering the improvements over earlier versions. Should Bieri accept this agreement, it was then up to the Hungarian partners to have it ratified by the Hungarian Ministry of Foreign Trade. Only then would it become available for signature. It was now up to Bieri's management to decide if they wanted to proceed.

APPENDIX I
Licensing Agreement (Abridged)

Article I: Introduction

Bieri Pumpenbau AG, located in Muensingen, Switzerland, to be named "BIERI," and MAGEX Hungarian Export Commercial Enterprise, to be called "MAGEX," located in Budapest, Hungary, conclude a cooperation agreement for the manufacture, use and sale of BIRAL[1] circulating pumps and decide to engage in technical and commercial relations as follows:

- MAGEX will acquire from BIERI the know-how for the manufacture, use and sale of BIRAL circulating pumps type RB12S, RF12S, RB155, and RF15S. This know-how will be turned over to Villamos in Budapest, a Hungarian manufacturing company, and includes the know-how for the electric motors.

- BIERI is prepared to deliver to MAGEX the technical documentation and manufacturing know-how for the above pumps including the use of all relative industrial patents and rights. The only

1. The Biral brand name was not part of this agreement.

exception are rights related to the separating shell.

- Within the scope of this agreement, MAGEX is interested in obtaining a yet to be determined amount of components from BIERI.

- BIERI is prepared to accept from MAGEX a like amount of finished pumps, subassemblies, or individual parts manufactured by MAGEX in Hungary based upon the technical documentation of BIERI and provided they meet BIERI's requirements for quality, price, and delivery terms.

Article II: Purpose of Contract

It is the purpose of the cooperation between the partners of this contract to enable MAGEX to manufacture in Hungary the circulating pumps with the same characteristics and the same parameters of performance as those manufactured by BIERI in Switzerland and to sell these pumps in Hungary and some other countries specified later on.

Article III: Object of Contract

BIERI grants MAGEX the following rights:

- the right to manufacture in Hungary the circulating pumps BIRAL RB/RF 12 S/15S including all replacement parts and the electric motor with the exception of the separating shell that is not part of this agreement.

- the right to all new changes and developments with respect to the pumps under consideration for the duration of this cooperation agreement.

- the right to all industrial protective rights (patents, trademarks, etc.) granted to BIERI in relation to the pumps covered by this agreement.

- the right to sell these circulating pumps in all countries according to special stipulations set forth below.

Article IV: Sales and Export Rights

BIERI grants herewith MAGEX the unlimited non-exclusive right to offer and to sell the pumps in Hungary as well as the following countries:

To sell without any restrictions:

COMECON Territory: USSR, Poland, East Germany, Czechoslovakia, Hungary, Rumania, Bulgaria, Cuba

People's Republic of China, Yemen, Korea, Khmer Republic (Cambodia), as well as Laos and Burma

To sell upon consultation with BIERI and after determination of the relative range of export prices in the following countries in the world:

Afghanistan	Libya
Albania	Malaysia
Angola	Malta
Bangladesh	Morocco
Ceylon	Nepal
Egypt	Pakistan
Finland	Philippines
Greece	Portugal
Iceland	Sweden
India	Tunisia
Indonesia	Turkey
Iraq	Yugoslavia

plus in all states of Central and South America as well as in the remaining countries of the world, with the exception of those listed below where MAGEX has the right to export the subject matter upon consultation and solely through the existing sales organization of BIERI to the following countries:

Algeria	Netherlands
Australia	Norway
Belgium	Saudi Arabia
Canada	Singapore
Denmark	South Africa
Emirates of Persian Gulf	Spain
France	Syria
Great Britain	Thailand
Kuwait	USA
Luxemburg	West Germany

Pumps installed as a part of a turnkey plant may be exported by MAGEX without any restrictions. In the future, BIERI is prepared to enter an agreement about territorial expansion under consideration of the interest of the parties to this contract.

The contract parties will vote upon prices and conditions on the export markets at their regular biannual meetings.

As long as the contract is in force, Villamos may place a label on each pump indicating "Produced under license of Bieri Pump BIRAL International."

Article V: Technical Data

BIERI will turn over to MAGEX the entire technical documentation on the subject matter within 3 months of the signing of the contract. The total documentation passes into the possession of MAGEX which may dispose of it at liberty but with the restrictions of Article IX.

Article VI: Technical Assistance

BIERI will render technical assistance to MAGEX with respect to manufacturing the subject matter. BIERI will specifically instruct specialists of MAGEX at its manufacturing plant in Switzerland for the maximum of 45 man-days. The group of specialists is never to exceed 3 men and will have sufficient knowledge of the German language. BIERI will make one of its own specialists available to MAGEX at its Hungarian plant for a period not exceeding 30 man-days. The entire costs of traveling, lodging, and board for both the Hungarian and Swiss specialists will be paid for by MAGEX. BIERI will pay the Hungarian specialists a daily flat fee, according to Hungarian norms in effect at that time.

For any man-hours requested by MAGEX in excess of those specified, BIERI will supply the necessary personnel at the typical rates in force in Switzerland for the level of specialists made available. The partners agree to form a group of experts which is to meet twice annually, once in Hungary and once in Switzerland, to treat technical and commercial questions. The group should not exceed 3 experts on either side.

Article VII: Delivery of Components and Finished Products

MAGEX obligates itself to purchase during the course of the contract and, according to its requirements, pumps, subassemblies, or separate parts on the subject matter entirely from BIERI should MAGEX not be in a position to manufacture the subject matter itself. BIERI, in return, will undertake deliveries of entire pumps or parts and subassemblies, in order to assure the sufficient supply of MAGEX with the subject matter of this contract.

Article VIII: Guarantees

Provided that suitable manufacturing shops and equipment for the manufacturing of the subject matter of the contract are existing, and provided that all instructions, statements, and directions contained in the technical documents are strictly adhered to, BIERI guarantees that MAGEX will be in a position to produce the subject matter of the contract in the identical quality and with the same performance parameters as produced by BIERI.

In the case of difficulties, BIERI will indicate suitable measures to be taken by MAGEX to produce as indicated above.

Article IX: Secrecy

MAGEX obligates itself to treat the manufacturing know-how confidentially during the duration of the contract and for an additional period of 10 years after its expiration. Exempt from this are the manufacturing company in Hungary and Hungarian export trade enterprises with respect to information normally delivered to clients for quotations or orders. MAGEX will assure that the manufacturing company complies with the same rules of confidentiality.

Article XI: Licensing Fee

As compensation, MAGEX will pay BIERI 3% of the sales price for the pumps and parts manufactured in Hungary. MAGEX obligates itself to produce a minimum of 30,000 pumps within the 5 years of the contract. The basis for computing the licensing fee is the effective transfer price for fully assembled pumps as per Exhibit 5.

BIERI is prepared to purchase from MAGEX, up to the expiration of the contract, pump parts in compensation of the licensing fee at repurchase prices equal to 30 percent below list prices as per Exhibit 5.

In case MAGEX will produce less than the guaranteed minimum quantity, MAGEX will pay the 3% fee on the deficient quantity in Swiss Francs. The first payments will be made at the end of the second year of the contract, and then annually at the end of each calendar year until the contract expires.

Article XII: Compensation

BIERI is prepared to accept from MAGEX for the duration of the contract pump parts at the same value as MAGEX bought from BIERI, provided that MAGEX can actually effect delivery. The purchases by BIERI and the sales by MAGEX should be equalized annually as much as possible. Again, MAGEX will purchase parts at the full transfer price as per Exhibit 5 whereas BIERI would repurchase parts at 30 percent below these list prices.

To cover any goods delivered by BIERI, MAGEX will have opened irrevocable letters of credit through a large Swiss bank with payments due upon presentation of shipping documents. To guarantee its purchases, BIERI will establish a bank guarantee for 10% of the minimum sales agreed upon. MAGEX may cash the guaranteed amount should BIERI not make any purchases from MAGEX.

Article XIII: Priority as a Supplier

MAGEX will invite BIERI to tender offers when importing other pumps which are also contained in the manufacturing program of BIERI. MAGEX will exert its entire influence to insure that these pumps be bought from BIERI, provided that BIERI's quotes are competitive with regard to quality, price, and delivery terms. However, these transactions are on a cash basis and are not included in this cooperation agreement.

Article XIV: Higher Power (Acts of God)

The contract allows for cancellation given certain acts of God beyond the control of the partners. Any final dissolution, however, is subject to the court of arbitration.

Article XV: Court of Arbitration

Any disputes that cannot be settled by the parties is to be brought before the court of arbitration in Munich, West Germany. Each party nominates one member to the 3-person court, with the two selected members agreeing on a third person who is a citizen of Germany. In case an agreement on that 3rd person cannot be reached within 30 days, the chairman of the International Chamber of Commerce in Paris will be asked to nominate the 3rd member. The arbitrators decide by majority vote and their decision is final. The contractual relationship of this agreement is subject to the law of the Federal Republic of Germany. The court of arbitration decides on its own procedures.

Article XVI: Duration of Contract

This contract will be in force for 5 years. It will be prolonged automatically for one year at a time, provided that neither party gives notice by registered letter within six months prior to expiration of the contract.

After expiration of the contract, MAGEX will be authorized to continue to manufacture, use, and sell the products in Hungary according to Article II. However, Villamos is not allowed to use any labels on its exported pumps that may infer any relationship with BIERI.

Article XVII: Servicing

MAGEX assumes the entire servicing duties of customers and obligations of attendance as well as the entire servicing of replacement parts during the course of the contract, for pumps sold by itself. If MAGEX so desires, BIERI is prepared to offer suggestions and proposals free of charge for creation of a suitable service organization.

CASE 9

The World Paint Industry

In 1988, world paint sales were 12 billion liters, worth $30 billion at suppliers' prices. The paint market was evenly divided between decorative and industrial coatings (see Exhibit 1). Decorative included the cans of paint or stain purchased at local hardware stores. These products were almost a commodity, produced in high volume and marketed intensively. Industrial coatings, on the other hand, included paint for cars, ships, planes, boats, white goods, cans, and thousands of other applications. Of importance in this market were the paint's properties, that is, protecting from corrosion, abrasion resistance, and ability to withstand high temperature or wet weather.

In 1988, there were about 10,000 producers worldwide. A combination of takeovers, increasingly high technology, rising raw material costs, price wars and tighter environmental controls were taking their toll, however. The market share of the 10 largest producers rose from 20 percent in 1980 to 30 percent in 1987. Some industry observers predicted that the share of the top 10 producers would rise to 50 percent by 1995. A new hierarchy within the top 10 was emerging as only

●

This case was prepared by Arthur Gehring, Research Assistant, under the direction of Professor Jean-Pierre Jeannet, Professor of Marketing and International Business at Babson College, and Adjunct Professor at IMD. Both publicly available material and industry sources were used. Copyright © 1990 by IMEDE, Lausanne, Switzerland. The International Institute for Management Development (IMD), resulting from the merger between IMEDE, Lausanne, and IMI, Geneva, acquires and retains all rights. Reproduced by permission.

four were true global players: ICI, PPG, BASF, and International Paint-Courtaulds, and only the top three were well balanced in terms of geography and market sectors served. Others were primarily regional players (see Exhibit 2).

The paint industry was part of the much larger chemical industry (1988 sales of $1,500 billion). The world's top five chemical companies, BASF, Bayer and Hoechst (all of West Germany), ICI, (the United Kingdom), and Du Pont (the United States) were important players in paints and coatings, or participated indirectly as suppliers of raw materials. Chemical companies, which could make a huge variety of synthetic materials from a small number of basic substances, were in a good position to supply raw materials for the paint industry.

EXTERNAL FACTORS

Economic Pressures

The world paint industry was facing the twin pressures of over capacity and rising costs, particularly in raw materials, technical service needed to support high technology industrial coatings, and from increasingly tight antipollution laws.

Some observers suspected that the large paint manufacturers were prepared to live with tight margins, knowing this would speed the rationalization of the industry. Smaller members would be forced to sell if they occupied a desirable niche, or close down if they did not. Many smaller companies had long recognized that survival depended on successful international niche marketing of specialty industrial coatings. One alternative for

EXHIBIT 1 ● World Paints by Market Sector in 1988

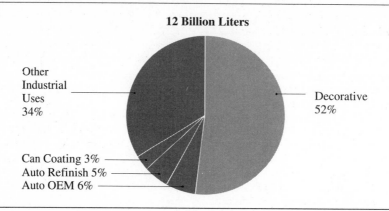

12 Billion Liters

Other Industrial Uses 34%

Decorative 52%

Can Coating 3%
Auto Refinish 5%
Auto OEM 6%

these companies was to start clubbing together, possibly through joint purchasing of raw materials, to have more bargaining clout with suppliers and then use the experience to try to increase co-operation further.

Environmental Factors

Standards of health, safety, and environmental protection were already getting tougher in antici-

EXHIBIT 2 ● World League Table

Approximate volume (in millions of liters)

1	ICI	U.K.	780
2	PPG	U.S.	460
	BASF	W. Germany	460
4	Sherwin-Wms.	U.S.	360
5	Akzo	Netherlands	350
6	Nippon	Japan	257
7	International	U.K.	235
8	Kansai	Japan	231
9	Du Pont	U.S.	228
10	Valspar	U.S.	200

pation of Pan European harmonization in 1992. Some seventy-two statutory instruments, codes and safety regulations had been published by various branches of governments in the past six months, fifteen times as many as in any previous six-month period. The Germans and French were imposing their standards on the rest of Europe. Environmental pressures affected what went into paints, how they were made, how effluents were disposed, and the application methods used by customers. New developments included using water rather than organic solvents, which reduced the emission of organic solvents into the atmosphere. Industrial coatings, which added more value and conferred marketable properties on the surfaces they covered, were more complicated and came under constant and closer scrutiny. Moreover, the pressure was not just from regulators, for the green issue was now being exploited in consumer marketing. This favored big paint makers with deep financial resources. With paint prices depressed, margins under pressure, and industrial customers trying to trim costs further, some medium-sized and smaller paint makers were beginning to get worried, especially with the continuing pressure of raw materials prices. Non-working capital had to be found for factory improvements, extra research, and compulsory testing to win approvals. As soon as everyone still surviving had met the eventual new standards, the goalposts would be moved to advance them further, shaking out even more companies. In the United Kingdom, "green" capital expenditures had risen to about 10 percent of total capital investments or about 0.7 percent of industry sales. It was estimated that the two largest German paint makers, Hoescht and BASF, were spending 1.4 percent and 1.2 percent of sales, respectively, on environmental investments due to the very stringent requirements in Germany.

PAINT MANUFACTURING

Paint was a mixture of several chemical products: solvents, resins, pigments, and additives. These chemical ingredients were typically purchased in bulk, then mixed, packaged by the paint manufacturer and distributed to the many customer segments.

Raw Materials

The cost of raw materials ranged between 30–55 percent of ex. factory costs depending on application. Resins, accounting for about 40 percent of raw material costs, were the binding component that resulted in the thick film, or smooth surface, once the paint had dried. It was resins that gave paint its required durability and other functional properties. Pigments were the elements that gave color to paint. White pigment, a powder largely made of titanium dioxide, gave white its opacity and was widely available. Pigments for other colors were fine chemicals. Overall, pigments accounted for 35–40 percent of raw material costs.

Solvents, accounting for some 10 percent of raw materials, were commodity chemicals in liquid form. Solvents allowed paint to assume a liquid form before application and evaporated during the drying process. Common solvents were a major environmental hazard contributing, among other things, to the destruction of the world's ozone layer. As a result, chemical solvents were being more frequently substituted by water. However, the use of water to dissolve paint required different resin formulations, which in turn only came through intensive research efforts. Additives, accounting for about 15 percent of raw material costs, included a wide range of items such as metals, catalysts, lead, chrome, many of which affected the drying process of paint.

The Decision to Make or Buy Raw Materials

Paint manufacturers showed various degrees of integration. Typically, paint companies that were not part of large chemical firms showed less integration. Many small paint firms essentially bought all raw materials in the open market, often from the same chemical firms that also operated paint companies.

Solvents, widely available in the open market, were of no strategic value. The situation for additives was similar, as several hundred suppliers created an open market. At times, the availability of certain additives might be constrained, but for most items, several suppliers existed.

In pigments, titanium dioxide was available from several suppliers, such as DuPont, SCM, Finn Titan, Dioxide (ICI), and Ishihara. Prices had been rising over time due to higher raw material prices. Although both DuPont and ICI had in-house or related suppliers, they also sold on the open market. Color pigments were supplied by specialist open market (or merchant) suppliers, including Ciba-Geigy, Hoechst, ICI, and Bayer. The pigment operations at Hoechst and ICI were separate from the paints businesses and supplied a limited range of pigments to all paint makers. Paint makers typically purchased their pigment from a range of suppliers.

Resins were available from merchant suppliers, captive sources, and a mixture of both. Major merchant suppliers were Rohm & Haas (number one worldwide), Union Carbide, Dow Chemicals, and Ciba-Geigy. Among the paint companies, ICI had both in-house capability and operated a merchant house (ICI Resins) independently. In the decorative paint and latex segment, a large number of suppliers existed. In general, paint makers purchased standard resins in the open market while trying to develop some proprietary resins for specialty applications.

The Paint Manufacturing Process

Typically, purchased resins and solvents were supplied by tanker truck and placed into large storage tanks at the plant. The liquids were metered into preliminary mixers and dispersed in a mixing process. Packaging was the final stage and was an important step. Finished paint took up a considerable amount of storage space as did the containers (labeled, pre-labeled, etc.).

Larger paint companies used dedicated lines for large volume paints, such as white, to avoid the time-consuming cleaning operation required when changing color. Low volume paints were produced in batch mode on different lines. Major manufacturing issues were the appropriate scale of plants, the required range of products, and the range of packaging sizes. Some companies switched to separating low from high volume plants because of the different manufacturing philosophies.

Paint Technology and Research

Most paint manufacturers concentrated their research efforts on resin technology. The properties of coatings could only be affected through improvements in resin technology. Over time, several generations of resins had been developed. The older types were solvent borne, whereas the later types were either water or powder borne, and had the advantage of reduced emissions. Understanding resin technology was thus considered a necessary core competence for paint makers. The formulation of new resins might result in a technological, and thus competitive, advantage. Although most paint manufacturers worked on some resin developments, standard resins were sourced from merchant suppliers.

Paint development could take place in two forms. Traditionally, paint companies concentrated on the recombination of existing building blocks, or resins, into new formulations. Increasingly, resources were shifted into creating new building blocks, or new resins. While the development of a new variation from existing ingredients might take 2 to 3 man/months, the development of a new resin would require 25 to 30 man/years, if successful.

Only those paint manufacturers that were part of major chemical firms engaged in serious resin development work. The others relied on merchant suppliers. Rohm & Haas was believed to have some 300 to 500 scientists working on resin development. But resin suppliers were often removed from paint applications and were thus interested in collaborating with their customers on research projects. Research at major chemical firms was carried out either centrally (Hoechst, Du Pont), or in smaller dedicated groups that were part of the paint organizations (BASF, ICI). Major paint companies were spending about 4 to 5 percent of sales on R&D with a trend towards higher levels.

Paint Industry Economics

Paint economics differed considerably by application segment. Raw material costs tended to average 30 to 55 percent of ex. factory price. Direct labor conversion costs averaged 5 to 10 percent. Indirect manufacturing costs, which included depreciation for equipment, averaged 15 percent. Distribution, transportation, and logistics accounted for about 5 percent. R&D was as much as 7 percent. Marketing and selling ranged from 5 to 15 percent, overhead about 10 percent, and pre-tax profit 7 to 15 percent of sales. Successful paint companies experienced an asset turnover of 2.5 to 3.0. Assets tended to be equally split between fixed and working capital. With a 10% return on sales, a company could thus achieve a return on net assets (RONA) of 25 to 30 percent (see Exhibit 3).

MARKET SEGMENTS

Although paint was sold for a large number of industrial and decorative uses, some major segments stood out due to their importance. Decorative, which included paints for professional and Do-It-Yourself (DIY) purposes, was the largest single segment. Industrial paints could be further subdivided into automotive OEM (original equip-

EXHIBIT 3 ● Paint Manufacturing Cost Structure

	Raw material	Direct labor conversion	Indirect manufacturing plus depreciation	R&D & technical service	Logistics & transport	Marketing & selling	Overhead	PBT	Av. ex. factory price/liter
Decorative Paint	40%	5%	15%	3%	5%	15%	10%	7%	$2.25
Can Coating	50%	7%	15%	7%	—	5%	9%	7%	$2.00
Refinish	30%	7%	12%	7%	5%	7%	6%	15%	$5.00
Automotive OEM	50%	5%	15%	7%	—	5%	8%	10%	$2.75
Powder	60%	5%	10%	7%	—	5%	6%	7%	$3.50

EXHIBIT 4 ● Major World Decorative/
Architectural Competitors by Region

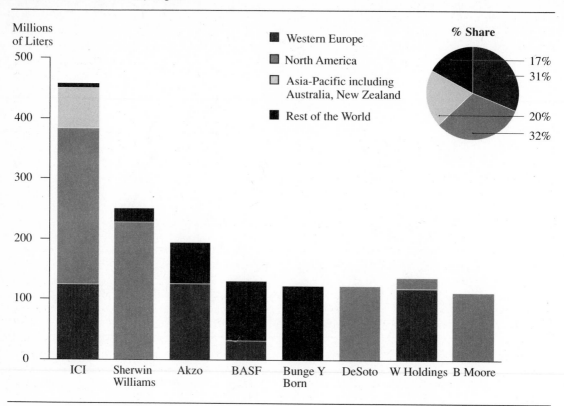

ment manufacturers), automotive refinishes, marine, can coatings, and powder. Each segment had its own particular customer group and usually required its own technology and application base.

Decorative Paints

Accounting for 52 percent of the 1988 value, about 6.25 billion liters, decorative paint was a major request in most geographic regions. North America accounted for 32 percent, Western Europe 31 percent, Asia-Pacific 20 percent, and the rest of the world 17 percent. Major competitors were, in order of importance, ICI (U.K.), Sherwin-

Williams (U.S.), Akzo (Netherlands), and BASF (W. Germany). (See Exhibit 4.)

Decorative paint had two major segments. The trade segment included sales to professional painters doing both redecoration and new housing, as well as to large professional painting firms. The second segment consisted of individual DIY users, who bought paint through retail stores. This segment had increased its share and now had slightly over half the decorative market.

From the position of a lowly commodity, domestic paint was increasingly being considered as a household fashion accessory, adding more value as this concept developed. Women were gaining influence in the selection process, because of retailers' efforts to make DIY shopping a pleasurable leisure activity. Most manufacturers had attempted to segment the market by offering special purpose products, such as anti-condensation paint, for specific tasks. Promotion, novel packaging, and segmentation were expected to remain important.

Retail Trade Developments

For paint manufacturers competing in the decorative segment, sales to retailers and DIY customers accounted for about half the volume. The other half was accounted for by the trade, or professional market. Professional painters were further subdivided into restoration (that is, mostly indoors), new housing contractors, and commercial contractors. Sales to this segment could be either through small independent stores or branches of manufacturers.

The developments in the retail/DIY segment were significantly changing the retailing process. This fact was most evident in advanced Anglo-Saxon countries such as the United Kingdom, the United States, and Australia, as well as to a lesser degree in such countries as France and Germany, but were considerably less pronounced in countries like Italy and Spain.

Traditionally, paint had been sold in small paint shops or hardware stores. In the late 1960s and early 1970s, specialist store chains like High Street (U.K.) and Sherwin-Williams (U.S.) replaced most of the small shops. In the 1970s and early 1980s, variety department stores and supermarkets took the lead (Woolworth, Sears, JC Penney, and Montgomery Ward in the United States, Tesco in the United Kingdom). Sears, partly through private branding, reached as much as 30 percent U.S. market share at its peak.

In the mid-1970s, large DIY super stores, or sheds, became dominant. In the U.S., stores like Home Depot were typical. In the U.K., Texas and B&Q were two leading examples. In the U.S., Sears saw its market share cut in half to 15 percent as a result of this development. The industry was already bracing itself for the next wave which

some experts speculated might lead back to specialty paint stores with enhanced service compared to the simple barn-type DIY stores.

The U.K. decorative market exhibited the trends that were typical of most major decorative markets. The market for household paint, like that for beans, soap, and fish fingers, had become retail led and susceptible to all the pressures which afflicted grocery producers. Price competition had intensified and margins had tightened as major retailers with vast bulk buying orders had demanded ever more advantageous terms. In the U.K., retailers' own label products had cut through the ranks of established brands, growing 150 percent since 1981 to claim almost 40 percent of the market. As in the supermarket trade, the policy of most companies dictated that only leading brands would be stocked.

Persistent promotion had helped ICI's Dulux brand retain its position as the leading paint in the United Kingdom, with a steady 33 percent share of the market. This market was undergoing a retailing revolution similar to the one which had transformed the grocery trade. The main difference was that while the supermarket's rise to preeminence in food and packaged goods took thirty years, the storming of the Do-It-Yourself trade by the superstore brigade happened in only ten years. The number of DIY specialist stores had shrunk from about 20,000 in 1979 to some 11,000 in 1988. The large DIY chains, led by B&Q, Texas, and Pay Less, accounted for 65 percent of all sector sales. Advertising expenditures for paint by DIY stores far outweighed paint makers' expenditures. The DIY stores had become brands in their own right.

Throughout this retailing cycle, the marketing task of the paint manufacturer changed at each turn. In the first cycle, independent distributors and wholesalers gave way to manufacturer-owned stores and outlets. When the chains took over, increased buying power led to bargaining over shelf space. The supermarket or departmentalized variety stores brought private labels. And finally, the super stores narrowed the brand choice by typically carrying just one advertised brand and their own private label. The reduced number of brands

EXHIBIT 5 ● Major World Auto OEM Competitors
by Region

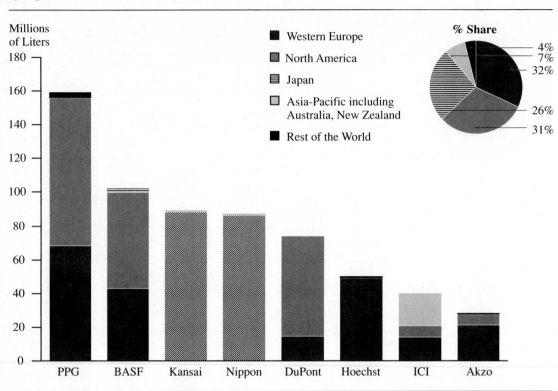

Millions of Liters

Legend:
- Western Europe
- North America
- Japan
- Asia-Pacific including Australia, New Zealand
- Rest of the World

% Share: 4%, 7%, 32%, 26%, 31%

Companies (x-axis): PPG, BASF, Kansai, Nippon, DuPont, Hoechst, ICI, Akzo

carried led to the disappearance of many retail paint suppliers and brands.

Automotive OEM

The automotive paint segment consisted of paint sales made to automobile manufacturers for use in their assembly plants. Worldwide, this segment represented six percent of the paint market. Major markets were North America (31 percent), Western Europe (32 percent), and Japan (26 percent). Leading competitors were, in order of importance, PPG, BASF, Kansai, Nippon, Du Pont, Hoechst, and ICI (see Exhibit 5).

In 1988, the paint sales to car manufacturers amounted to about 720 million liters, averaging $2.80/liter in price or $2.0 billion total. Only PPG with 19 percent share and BASF with 18 percent share were true world players. PPG's great strength was its 45 percent share of the U.S. home market. Kansai was Nissan's paint maker in Japan. In Europe, the race was on to be third in 1992, when the car industry would narrow down its suppliers on U.S. lines. In the running were Herberts, Akzo and an ICI/DuPont joint venture.

The customer base, mainly globally operating companies, was technologically very demanding. The technical service requirements of customers required paint suppliers to station technical service personnel permanently on location. As a result, the automotive companies preferred suppliers located at their doorsteps. This led to scattering factories close to assembly plants. In the United States, major paint companies would typically have several plants. The trend had moved away from multiple sourcing, which had kept local players alive, towards single sourcing and worldwide deals. Typically, a customer maintained a major supplier each for top coats and base coats, with a second supplier for smaller volume applications "to keep the big ones honest."

The trend was to build an applied research center close to manufacturers. Austin O'Malley, head of PPG/Europe, said, "Ownership of the automotive industry has gone global. Supplies and suppliers must go global, too. We are going for global sales to key customers. Naturally, we are concentrating very hard on the customer. We supply material with high value added to help motor manufacturers cope with their cost and production problems." The trend had already been established on a continental scale in the U.S., with only three main suppliers: PPG, BASF, and DuPont. The arrival of the single European market in 1992 was expected to have a similar effect.

There was a technological dimension to this market. Electrolytic application techniques ensured an even spread of the first coat. This had an important influence on appearance and protection after other coats had been applied. Several paint makers developed this technology. Both PPG and Hoechst licensed their technology to others. Hoechst linked to DuPont which linked to Kansai. PPG linked to Nippon which linked to International Paint. PPG developed a method that produced more stable and rust resistant coating. In 1988, 83 percent of the electrolytic tanks in the world used this technology, either supplied or licensed.

Although particular paint applications such as color, etc., were developed for each customer, a substantial part of the basic research had worldwide applications. Technical spin-offs were also possible for other paint segments such as for the refinishing sector (with modifications in formulations due to the different paint application meth-

ods), and for industrial components in areas such as the domestic appliance industry. This was one reason why many players stayed in this segment despite low profitability or losses.

PPG had formed a worldwide team for each major manufacturer, so that the same people serviced the same customer wherever a car plant was located. PPG was also selling a complete paint shop staffed with PPG employees. An exemplary relationship was in Korea, where General Motors and Daiwoo chose PPG. The specifications for the plant's coating system was designed by Opel in West Germany; pre-treatment chemicals came from the U.S., the sealant from Spain, the electrocoat and top coats from France.

Some experts believed the way to get ahead in this business was to develop new products that would leapfrog over competitors, such as water-based paints which would not emit the organic solvents contributing to acid rain. There was considerable cross-licensing occurring in this market.

Automotive Vehicle Refinishing

The refinish segment included paints and coatings for repairing automobiles. This segment accounted for 5 percent of world sales, had the highest price per liter ($5.00) and was considered the most profitable paint segment. North America accounted for 36 percent of the world market, followed by Western Europe (30 percent), and Asia-Pacific/Japan (25 percent) (See Exhibit 6).

Only ten paint manufacturers competed significantly in the refinishing sector. Among those, only Sherwin-Williams of the United States and Rock of Japan did not also compete in the automotive OEM market. No new competitor had entered since the 1950s. The world leader was BASF, due to its recent acquisition of Inmont in the United States. BASF led with 17 percent of the world market, followed by DuPont, ICI, and PPG.

Although the volume of paint sold in this market was smaller than the OEM segment, it was a larger segment by value due to its far higher sales price: 480 million liters at an average price of $5.00, making the total market worth $2.4 billion.

Customers were largely small paint shops

EXHIBIT 6 ● Major World Refinish Competitors by Region

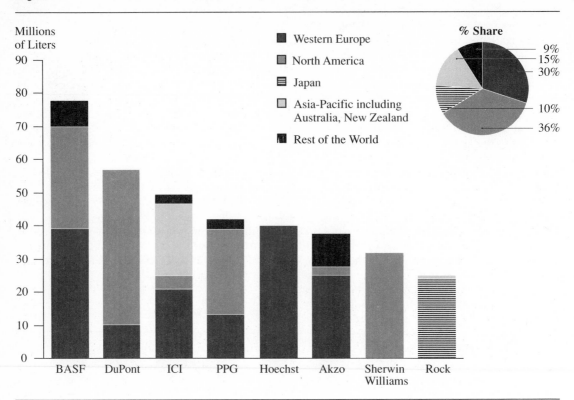

Millions of Liters

Legend:
- ■ Western Europe
- ■ North America
- ▤ Japan
- ☐ Asia-Pacific including Australia, New Zealand
- ▦ Rest of the World

% Share
- 9%
- 15%
- 30%
- 10%
- 36%

who needed quick and frequent deliveries, typically on a daily basis. Paint manufacturers supplied their customers with mixing schemes through local distributors who would combine the basic colors and shades with solvents to obtain the correct color match. There were some 10,000 different shades and some 60 different colors to select from.

To compete in this business, a company had to have access to the color and paint shops of the car manufacturers to obtain the needed information. Automobile manufacturers wanted to make sure that their customers could get their cars repaired wherever they marketed. As an example, a company like Toyota was interested in worldwide coverage. Refinish paint manufacturers profited if they could have access to all car manufacturers wherever they were located, so that they could supply the widest possible color range in any geographic market.

Marine Paints

This $800 million market was dominated by a handful of companies. International Paint had 30 percent of the market. Other important manufacturers were: Chugoku, and Nippon Oil and Fats of Japan, Hemel of Denmark, Jotun of Norway, and Sigma Coatings from Belgium. These six companies accounted for 85 percent of the paint applied to the world's ships. The fortunes of this market followed those of the shipping industry. Outlook

EXHIBIT 7 ● Major World Can Coatings
Competitors by Region

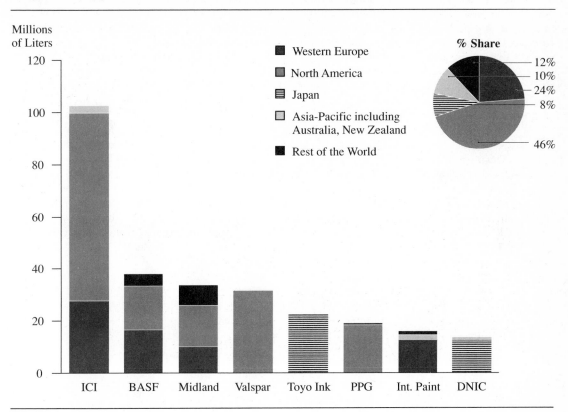

for the 1990s looked bright as the aging fleet of merchant vessels would be replaced.

Typically, a ship had at least five outside layers of paint. On top of the primer were two coats of corrosive paint, then two coats of anti-fouling paint below the waterline. Anti-foulings released a biocide to prevent barnacles, seaweed and other marine organisms from growing on the hull. A common ingredient of anti-foulings, TBT, was under attack by environmentalists. New tin-free alternatives were being developed, but were not as effective. A new "self-polishing" anti-fouling released by International Paint had saved the shipping industry $200 million a year in fuel costs. Other important segments of the marine paint in-

dustry were coatings for cargo tanks and offshore oil rigs. Tank coatings had to resist a wide range of liquid chemicals. The deck areas of a rig had to survive exposure to seawater, rain, sun, and spillage of oils and chemicals.

Can Coatings

The can coating segment, with worldwide sales of $1.2 million, accounted for only 3 percent of the world paint market. Some 46 percent of the market was in North America, followed by Western Europe (24 percent), and Asia-Pacific (18 percent). Major competitors were ICI, BASF, Midland, and Valspar (see Exhibit 7).

The coatings were applied inside the tin and aluminum cans used as food or beverage containers, to make them corrosion resistant. This thin layer on the inside of every can was crucial for a successful canning operation. Consequently, this segment of the paint industry was viewed as a high technology application. Customers were concentrated, with major use in the hands of four groups and their licensees: Continental Can, Pechiney-Triangle (included former American and National Can), Carnaud-Metal Box, and Crown Cork and Seal. These can manufacturers operated canning lines all over the world, and they expected the suppliers to follow them everywhere with a consistent product, insuring the same taste for globally marketed products such as Coca-Cola.

Coating products had to be developed for each application, as they depended on the particular food or beverage as well as on the type of metal or aluminum container used. Customers were increasingly seeking ways to simplify and tended to look for a narrower technology range. In this business, it was important to be able to make the development effort go around. A new product for sardines might be developed in Portugal, but might have applications for Norwegian packers as well. Success depended on avoiding duplication of effort in applications development. Although coatings were usually not identical, a considerable part of the concept development could be used again for other customers with the same applications.

Powder Paints

Powder coatings were a precisely formulated mixture of pigment and resin which were sprayed, using electrostatic spray guns. The sprayed item, a metal object, was then heated for some 10 minutes to cure the surface. Coatings had been developed for heat resistance or chemical resistance. The major benefits for users were the reduced emissions such as solvents used with wet paints and the reduced need for waste disposal. Major user groups were the automotive component suppliers, the metal furniture industry, and domestic appliance manufacturers. Powder paint could conceivably substitute up to 50 percent of paint being applied to metal. In Europe, where the product was pioneered, the substitution already amounted to about 20 percent, compared to about 10 percent in the United States, an amount that was, however, growing rapidly.

The market for powder coatings was growing between 10 percent and 20 percent per year. This had attracted hot competition, resulting in low margins, which were squeezing many medium-sized and smaller companies. International Paint was fighting with Ferro (U.S.) for the world's number one position. DSM (Netherlands) had a dominant position in Europe (see Exhibit 8).

Potential new markets included: car engine blocks, baskets inside automatic washing machines, and the steel reinforcement bars used in concrete. Finally, powder paint was a potential weapon against colored plastics, a big threat to paint makers. There was talk of a powder which could be cured without heat, so that it could be used with cheap plastic that had no inherent aesthetic properties. Most manufacturers were also experimenting with high gloss finishes that could eventually be used for car body work.

GEOGRAPHIC MARKETS

The markets of North America (32 percent) and Western Europe (30 percent) dominated the world market. The remainder was accounted for by Latin America, Africa and the Middle East combined (14.5 percent), Japan (13 percent), Southeast Asia (9 percent), and Australasia (1.5 percent) (See Exhibit 9.)

Western Europe

The Western European market was dominated by the major economies of West Germany, the United Kingdom, France, and Italy. All major segments were represented in Western Europe, with decorative, automotive OEM, and the refinish portions of the market reflecting their relative importance worldwide. Europe was somewhat ahead of the other regions in powder paints, but can coatings volume was below the representative size of its market, primarily due to the domination of the U.S. market in this area. (Throughout this

EXHIBIT 8 ● Major World Powder Competitors by Region

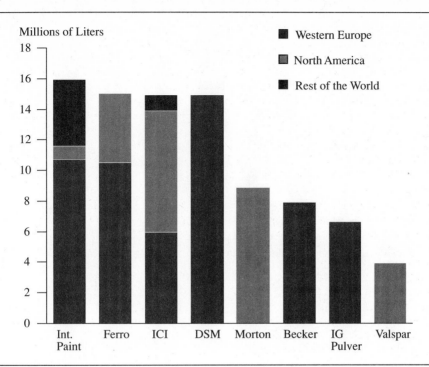

Millions of Liters

Legend:
- Western Europe
- North America
- Rest of the World

Categories: Int. Paint, Ferro, ICI, DSM, Morton, Becker, IG Pulver, Valspar

---

analysis, the paint markets of Eastern Europe have been excluded. Representing the equivalent of about 1.5 percent of world paint volume, or 1.8 billion liters, this market was not yet open to international competitors.)

North America

The North American market, consisting of the United States and Canada, was the largest paint market in the world, with 32 percent of world paint volume in liters. In the decorative and the automotive OEM segments, the United States accounted for its respective share. Both in refinish, and particularly in can coatings, the North American share was relatively higher than the region's share in the entire paint market.

Japan

Although the Japanese market accounted for only 13 percent of world paint sales, it accounted for 26 percent of world automotive OEM. As a result, two Japanese companies were among the world's top ten producers. Decorative paint was not a key market. Traditional domestic architecture, with its paper partitions, meant that millions of square feet of walls were not decorated. More modern buildings were being constructed, but decorative still only accounted for 22 percent of the market. The market's strength came from its industrial base.

Japan's paint industry mirrored the Japanese economy. A large home market was a mixed blessing as it provided little experience in operating

EXHIBIT 9 ● World Paint Markets by Region

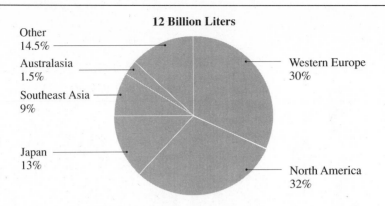

Southeast Asia includes China, Southeast Asia, Indian Sub-Continent.
Other-Rest of World includes Latin America, Africa, Middle East.
Excludes U.S.S.R. and Eastern Europe at 15% of world total.

outside Japan. The only Japanese paint exported was that already on Japanese goods. Paint production had virtually stopped growing in recent years with the worldwide reaction to trade imbalances with Japan (see Exhibit 10). Many companies were setting up factories abroad. The former was costly and risky, as the race to buy the most promising targets had been won by European and U.S. paint companies. It seemed likely that cross-licensing of technology would be the most frequently chosen course.

Nippon, the largest paint company in Japan, was also very active in the rest of Asia. Shinto and Nippon Oil & Fats had licenses for ICI's Queens awards winner, Aquabase, the waterborne car paint. "NOF and Shinto are like ICI's children. We have good cooperation with Shinto to develop this product," said Mr. Teruji Ogawa, Chairman of NOF. Nippon and Kansai were the market leaders in the car factories. Kansai had wanted ICI's technology but ICI was too "slow moving", so Kansai developed its own alternative by making use of its relationship with DuPont.

Part of the strength of the Japanese economy was the sheer bulk of intra-trading that took place within six major informal corporate groups. The presidents of the twenty-nine companies of the Mitsubishi group met once a month. These social gatherings were reinforced by more formal links, such as capital relationships between companies, interlocking directorships, and cross holdings of stock.

Kansai belonged to the Sanwa Group, along with Daihatsu Motor. Dai Nippon Toryo belonged to the Mitsubishi Group, Shinto to the Sumitomo Group and NOF to the Fuyo or Fuji Group, along with Nissan. There was no motor manufacturer in the Sumitomo Group, but there was no paint maker in the Mitsui Group, in which Toyota Motor had observer status. Shinto had filled the gap with Toyota. Meanwhile, BASF had developed a close relationship with Dai Nippon Toryo, which was inevitably close to Mitsubishi Motors. By going with NOF and Shinto, ICI had an insider's introduction to both Nissan and Toyota, the two Japanese car manufacturers building

EXHIBIT 10 ● Japanese Paint Production

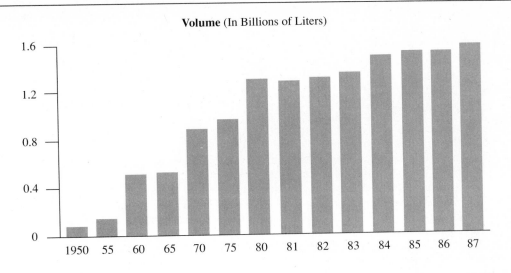

Volume (In Billions of Liters)

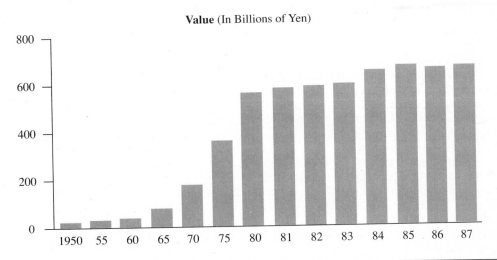

Value (In Billions of Yen)

the most factories abroad. Even in the United States, where Nissan's relationship was with DuPont, there should have been an inside track, since DuPont and ICI had a joint venture on car paints in Europe. Nippon Paint, which did not belong to any corporate group, was pursuing a strategy of keeping its cross-licensing agreements simple. Nippon had relationships with International Paint and PPG.

The relationships were becoming increasingly confusing: Kansai had a long-standing relationship with both ICI and Hoechst. As a result of their alliance, NOF and Shinto would be attacking Kansai's market share using ICI technology. Kansai's defense would be through its relationship with DuPont, ICI's partner in Europe. European and U.S. paint makers did not have these problems; they were used to legal watertight agreements about specific technology in specific geographic markets.

Southeast Asia

The battle for the Far East markets was heating up. The prizes were potentially vast; in terms of population the markets compared to Europe. There was continuous, fast economic growth. In developing countries, growth and affluence led to more people painting their homes, and to growth in industrial markets as cars and consumer goods were manufactured locally.

Few foreign paint companies were operating seriously in Southeast Asia, as paint markets were just starting to develop. In 1987, the economy of Singapore grew by 10 percent, Malaysia by 7 percent, Thailand by 8 percent, the Philippines by 6 percent, and Indonesia by 4 percent. Among the international paint companies, ICI had built factories in Thailand, Malaysia, Singapore, and Indonesia. International Paint had set up in Singapore, where there was a growing market for their marine paints, in Malaysia, where it had targeted the canning industry as a principal customer, and in Bangkok. Nippon Paint was the only other producer approaching the region with the same levels of investment. Early entry into foreign markets was part of its corporate strategy. They had had to follow their customers abroad. The low labor costs of Southeast Asia had encouraged two strategies: first, to develop there ahead of others and second, to develop low-cost products by making them locally.

Lim Say Chong, Managing Director of ICI Paints in the region explained, "Don't judge us by European perceptions of risk taking and ways of doing business. Our competition is basically Japanese. They are prepared to make little profit and live with low prices for a long time. They gain in total market share, building up a strong position to give them leverage among distributors and sales outlets, and then start fighting you with better,

higher priced products. We have to make profits acceptable to the city of London year after year. They take a twenty-five-year view of their business. If we stick to the European way, they will walk all over us in the end."

Four-fifths of Malaysia's market was decorative, of which there were three major segments. The quality end comprised about 15 percent, the middle 52 percent of the volume, and the cheap market accounted for a third of sales. Lim of ICI stated, "Simple emulsion costs U.S. $1.50 per liter. The Japanese sell it at U.S. $.60 per liter." Nippon quickly established share, then started to bring some better-quality paints onto the market. "When the Japanese got into the mid-tier of the market from the bottom tier, we decided to give them some trouble," Lim said. In the early 1980s, ICI moved into the mid-tier from the quality end of the market with a lower priced brand. The effect was to put a lid on Nippon's march upmarket. In 1988, ICI's share was 27 percent versus Nippon's 24 percent. Berger Malaysia, and Seasons, two local brands, each had 10 percent.

A rush of investment was expected during the next two years. Foreign companies could set up joint ventures in the region with Asian countries taking a 5 percent stake and the company keeping a 60 percent stake as long as the deals were concluded by 1991. Only the makers of industrial paints already there were likely to be able to benefit by supplying coatings for goods made in the new factories, an advantage for ICI, International Paint, and Nippon. "Japanese paint makers will make deals in industrial products because they know now that we will fight and cause them a lot of trouble if they try to come in directly," Lim said.

Australia

Although the Australian market was small, it was a microcosm of things to come. Trends showed up quickly because of the small population. The first two-piece cans outside the United States appeared here. In 1988, there were 116 paint companies in Australia, but the top three controlled 80 percent of the market. Australia showed the effect of monopoly, and duopoly, on prices and choice more rapidly than anywhere else, so the world was watching.

ICI was spending (Australian) $5 million[1] on Dulux, its decorative brand, equalling the total spent by the entire industry in the past. Taubmans Industries, owned primarily by International Paint, was responding by spending (A) $6 million. ICI planned to spend A$100 million during the next five years to upgrade seven factories. ICI had planned to buy Berger's Australian operations with its two major brands, Berger and British, and then sell one to Taubmans, but Taubmans backed out. As a result, ICI was stuck with too many brands. Although ICI's Dulux had 40 percent market share compared to Taubmans' 22 percent, having so many brands was resulting in cannibalization. This gave an advantage to specialist paint shops, which liked receiving three brands from one company. However, big retailers were concerned, as they had limited space and wanted competition amongst suppliers. ICI Australia had stayed in heavy duty protective coatings, while ICI Paints had long since abandoned the sector as a core business. The reason for this decision was that Taubmans led this segment, thanks to International Paint, and while Dulux stayed, Taubmans had to keep its prices low. When things settled down, no one expected ICI's Dulux to be anything other than the market leader. It was too far in the lead and too well managed to fall far, if at all, no matter what Taubmans planned to do.

MAJOR PAINT MANUFACTURERS

By 1988, the ten largest paint companies in the world accounted for almost one-third of the world paint volume. Most of these players had grown by acquisition (see Exhibit 11). In the process, the ranking by volume was considerably changed. PPG (United States) had lost the number one position to ICI (United Kingdom). Hoescht (Germany) and Dupont (United States) dropped out of the top league, while Inmont and Glidden (both United States) were acquired. Newcomers were

1. U.S. $1.00 = A $0.80.

Nippon and Kansai (both Japan), and Valspar and DeSoto (both United States). (see Exhibit 12.) The leading paint companies tended to be concentrated differently by paint sector (see Exhibit 13) and by geographic concentration (see Exhibit 14).

International Paint-Courtaulds

International Paint-Courtaulds' worldwide sales were 235 million liters a year. The company was pre-eminent in marine and protective coatings. International Paint's (IP) share of profits from the yacht and marine sectors had dropped from 60–80 percent in 1980 to 30 percent, despite having 40 percent of the world market. Its profit contribution from Europe was reduced to 35–40 percent from 60 percent in 1980. Currently, 30–35 percent came from North America, with the rest coming from all over the globe. IP had been aggressively expanding its powder business internationally through acquisitions, despite not being profitable until 1986. Recent acquisitions included: Germany (1980); France and Brazil (mid 1980s); Korea, the United States, and Australia (late 1980s); and Spain and Italy (late 1980s). Far East locations included: Singapore, Hong Kong, Malaysia, Taiwan, and Thailand. IP led the Australian market in oil and can coatings.

The powder segment was growing significantly for IP due to its industrial marketing skill and global presence in marine coatings. Pragnell of International Paint explained, "Transfer of marketing technology, standards, and operations from marine to powder has been crucial. Powder is a technology, not a business." IP was expanding Porter Paints, the U.S. decorative manufacturing and marketing company bought for $140 million in 1987. IP was emphasizing technology, marketing and computerized systems. Shipowners could arrange to have exact quantities of paint delivered at a wide range of ports. IP was determined to defeat ICI in a race to dominate waterborne coating for steel cans.

Sherwin-Williams

The company celebrated its 122nd year of business in 1988 with an increased operating profit of

EXHIBIT 11 ● Restructuring the World Paint Industry

Company	Acquisition	Year	Sector
Akzo	Wyandotte (U.S.)	1983	Motors
(Netherlands)	Levis (Belgium)	1984	Decorative/motors/industrial
	Bostik (U.S.)	1984	Aircraft
	Blundell-Permoglaze (U.K.)	1985	Decorative
	Sandtex (U.K.)	1986	Decorative
	Procolor (Spain)	1986	Decorative/industrial
	Brink Molyn (Netherlands)	1986	Decorative
	Ypiranga (Brazil)	1987	Decorative/industrial
BASF	Valentine (U.K.)	1984	Vehicle refinishing
(West Germany)	Inmont (U.S.)	1985	Motors/refinishing/can coatings
	Mobil Coatings (Netherlands)	1985	Cans coatings
	Lusol (Argentina)	1988	Motors/industrial
DuPont	Ford Motor Paints (U.S.)	1986	Motors
(United States)	SFDUCO (France) - part	1988	Motors
	IDFAC (joint venture with ICI)	1988	Motors
Hoechst	Renault Paint (France)	1986	Motors
(West Germany)	Ault & Wiborg (U.K.)—part	1986	Motors/refinishing/industrial
	Divested-part W. Germany	1984	Decorative
	Berger (U.K.)	1987	Decorative
ICI	Holdens (U.K.)	1982	Can Coatings
(United Kingdom)	Valentine (France)	1984	Decorative/refinishing
	Ault & Wiborg (U.K.) - part	1985	Can coatings
	HGW Paints (Ireland)	1985	Decorative/refinishing/industrial
	Knopp (W. Germany)	1988	Powder coatings
	Glidden (U.S.)	1986	Decorative/can coatings/powder
	Bonaval (W. Germany)	1986	Refinishing
	Attiva (Italy)	1988	Can coatings
	DuPont (Spain)	1988	Powder
	Berger (Australasia)	1988	Decorative/industrial
	IDAC (joint venture with DuPont)	1988	Motors
International	Silap (France)	1982	Powder
Courtaulds	Litoverti (Brazil)	1982	Can coatings
(United Kingdom)	Oxyplast (Australia)	1985	Powder
	Porter Paint (U.S.)	1987	Decorative/yacht
	Extensor (Sweden)	1987	Marine
	La Minerva (Italy)	1988	Powder

EXHIBIT 11 ● Restructuring the World Paint Industry (Continued)

Company	Acquisition	Year	Sector
	Suministros (Spain)	1988	Powder
	Epiglass (New Zealand)	1988	Yacht (marine)
PPG	Cipisa (Spain)	1982	Motors
(United States)	IVI (Italy)	1984	Motors/refinishing/industrial
	Wulfing (W. Germany)	1984	Motors
	International (U.K.) - part	1985	Motors

EXHIBIT 12 ● Major World Paint Competitors by
Sales Volume (In Millions of Liters)

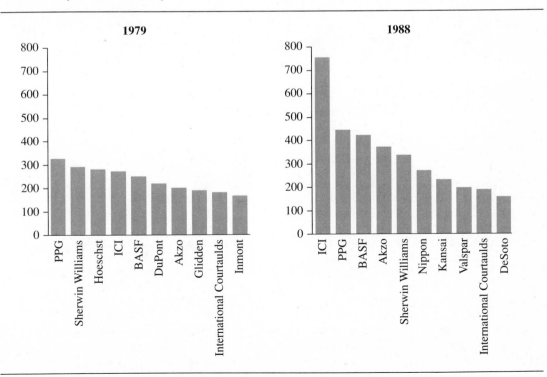

EXHIBIT 13 ● Major World Paint Competitors by
Market Sector

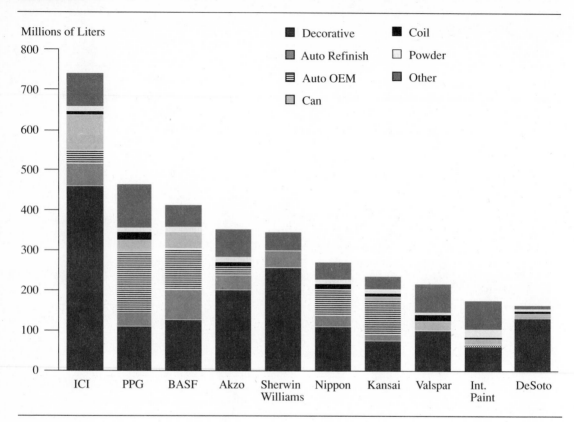

7.7 percent of sales, to $101 million. Net sales increased by 8.3 percent to reach $1,950 million. Sherwin-Williams had 2,000 company-operated paint and wall covering stores across the United States, which accounted for an 8 percent sales increase over the past year and were the backbone of the company's Paint Stores segment. The segment's overall operating profit dropped slightly during the year, however, due to provisions established in the fourth quarter for the closing of certain unprofitable stores, as well as to reduced margins caused by the required increase in reserves resulting from the escalating costs of products sold. Sherwin-Williams

planned increasing its prices in 1989 to improve operating margins.

In addition to the main Sherwin-Williams brand paint and coatings, the company produced and marketed the brands Dutch Boy, Martin-Semour, and Kem-Tone. Sherwin Williams also produced private label brands for sales through independent dealers, mass merchandisers and home improvement centers, as well as special purpose coatings for the automotive refinish market, industrial maintenance, and traffic paint.

Sherwin-Williams International Group was divided into four sectors: Canada, Mexico, the West Indies, and Brazil. The company operated

EXHIBIT 14 ● Major World Paint Competitors by
Region

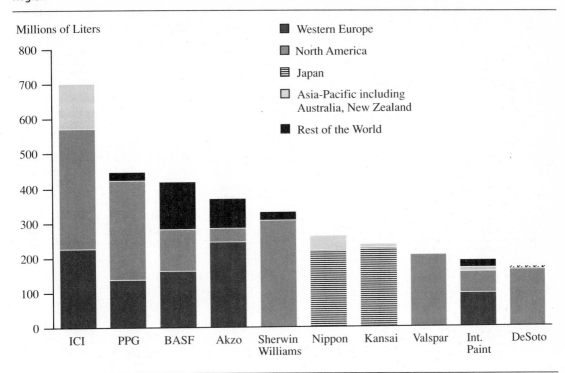

seventy-eight of its own stores in Mexico and had
forty-two stores throughout Jamaica, Trinidad,
Puerto Rico, and Panama. Licensing rights had
been extended to twenty-five other countries
around the world for production and distribution
of decorative coatings, industrial and automotive
paint finishes, and a variety of home decorative
products. The group's primary markets included
dealers, contractors, automotive body shops,
commercial and industrial maintenance accounts, original equipment manufacturers, and
Do-It-Yourself customers.

BASF

With corporate sales of $24.4 billion (1988),
BASF was the world's largest chemicals company.

The company jumped from fifth place ranking in
paints to sharing second with PPG by acquiring
Inmont, the U.S. paint and inks giant, for $1 bil-
lion in 1985, beating out ICI and Akzo. BASF
then had to cope with a different corporate culture, the more North American "can do, profits
now" style of management demanded by shareholders wanting ever-better yearly results. Like
many German companies, BASF's backers were
institutional, they took a longer view of the marketplace and did not burden management with
the need to show continuous short-term progress.
"Cross-fertilization of research findings has been
very beneficial," said Geoffrey Watson of BASF.
It had a joint venture with Tanabe in Japan and
was close to Dainippon Toryo, which was in the
same corporate group as Mitsubishi Motors.

BASF set the pace in minimizing the environmental impact which was driven by ever-tighter West German regulations. BASF achieved this goal with a massive capital spending program. Having spent DM 200 million[2] already, it had committed DM 1 billion by 1993. Dr. Jürgen Kammer, Chairman, explained, "In West Germany, we have the highest standards already. What today is a burden, tomorrow will be an advantage." Because of the sophisticated chemistry involved, such things could not be learned overnight or bought. BASF's profile in the industry had been strong on reliable products, high technology and quality, but less noted for its marketing skills. This area tended to be weak in many German paint companies.

BASF had already spent DM 200 million over four years on its Munster factory, the largest concentration of paint making facilities in the world, occupying nearly 100 acres and employing more than 2,800 people. This plant included a new, flexible manufacturing system for paint making, a batch process which had previously defied such advances. BASF's engineers realized that the bottleneck was in the blenders where all the ingredients were mixed. Conventionally, they either had to be cleaned out before the next batch was mixed, or use a less efficient system whereby a strict progression from lighter to darker colors had to be followed. BASF's revolutionary solution had been to install moveable blenders which could be slotted into line as required. The answer was to convey the several ton blenders around on hovercraft and hoists. Labor savings had been considerable. The principles were being copied in a new factory in Spain and would be introduced whenever new plants were built on existing sites.

Hoechst

With total sales of $23.4 billion, Hoechst ranked second among all chemical companies. The group's paint sales were DM 443 million. Herberts, its English subsidiary and major paint unit,

claimed 36 percent of the West German vehicle refinish market, 23 percent in Western Europe, and 7 percent in the world. It regarded nineteen countries in Western Europe as its home market and sold in twenty-four other countries worldwide.

In 1987 Hoechst decided to leave the decorative segment due to its unenviable third place position in many markets, as well as escalating promotional costs. The company's decorative arm, Berger, was sold to International Courtaulds of the United Kingdom and merged with another newly-acquired company, Crown Paints. Hoechst concentrated on both automotive segments—OEM, where it had leading technology, and refinishing. Hoechst was looking toward North American and Japanese markets for expansion. However, other paint makers had been much quicker to realize that globally-based customers wanted globally spread suppliers. Herberts' problem outside Europe was similar to that of leading Japanese paint makers outside Japan; nearly all its major competitors had arrived first, limiting slow starters to their home markets.

ICI

In 1988, ICI had total sales of $20.8 billion and ranked as the world's fourth largest chemicals company. ICI's paint sector was viewed as a laggard within its own group while being an outstanding performer in the industry. Sales were up £70 million[3] to £1.36 billion; profits rose to £98 million, reaching an ROS of 7.19 percent. Although twice the level of Japan's paint makers and 50 percent better than BASF, it was poor compared to ICI's pharmaceutical business of 26 percent, and 12.6 percent for the entire company. The weakness of ICI's paint sector was compounded by having to satisfy the shareholders year after year.

ICI's marketing of decorative paint was acknowledged as the best in the world. It excelled in highly specialized paints for repairing car bodies

---

2. U.S. $1.00 = DM 1.75.

3. U.S. $1.00 = £0.70.

and dominated the can coating sector. The goal for the European joint venture with DuPont was to have 20 percent of the Western European market in vehicle refinishing by the early 1990s. ICI manufactured in twenty-nine countries and sold in fifty.

ICI had been investing up to 5 percent of sales in R&D and £525 million for capital projects during the last three years. The ICI dilemma appeared to have crystallized into making more of its present strengths and being committed to its customers worldwide so as to build up long-term loyalty. Herman Scopes, Principal Executive Officer of ICI, stated, "We have got to stop being a paint manufacturer and become a service organization that has paint manufacturing as part of its operations."

ICI's corporate goals were: (1) to consolidate after the 1986 acquisition of Glidden, (2) to focus growth, and (3) to improve quality so as to achieve better margins and service despite rising costs and static prices. These goals would be pursued utilizing its global spread and balance, very large financial resources, good technological and commercial base, and a general management which competitors acknowledged as being good as well as having clear strategies. There were problems. Surveys showed that the staff was disquieted about big company bureaucracy, inadequate internal communications, a lack of recognition of people's contributions, and internal rather than customer orientation. Only a large minority of customers rated ICI better than the competition. The bulk opted for the "much the same" category, while a small minority declared ICI worse. These results had sprouted 400 voluntary "customer focus" groups. Benefits so far had been a flow of good ideas, better commitment to the customer at all levels, pinpointing the things that irritate customers, better teamwork, and the identification of training needs.

PPG Industries

With corporate sales of $5.7 billion (1989), PPG had traditionally been the world's largest paint company until ICI acquired Glidden Paints in the United States. Aside from its paints business, PPG was the world's third largest producer of float glass and the second largest producer of fiberglass. PPG was a major global supplier of automotive original equipment glass. PPG also operated a chemical division selling a range of products to several user industries.

PPG's paint and resins sales of $2.07 billion (1989) resulted in operating earnings of $287 million. PPG was the world's leading supplier of automotive and industrial finishes, and a major supplier of trade paint (decorative) and stains. In automotive (OEM), PPG offered a wider range of services and products compared to competitors, ranging from finishes to metal pretreatments, electrodeposition prime coats, top coats, sealants, and adhesives. PPG was able to expand its OEM business in North America by supplying "transplants" of Japanese car manufacturers, and through acquisitions of paint suppliers in Europe. Major R&D work had been undertaken to make top coats chip resistant, including the development of a top coat from powder paint. PPG gained from specific development centers in Flint, Michigan, and Cordstonn, Ohio, as well as a new corporate automotive technology center near Detroit, Michigan, housing fiber, glass, and coatings specialists to serve automotive clients' needs.

Automotive refinishes continued to be a high profit growth segment for PPG. The company maintained a 17,000 color library. The market grew due to longer manufacturer's warranties which enticed customers to hang on to their cars longer. In Europe, PPG consolidated its marketing under the PPG brand name, as it had done previously in the U.S. In 1969, PPG acquired a major Swedish supplier. The European refinish segment was managed out of the U.K. with other technical color teams in France. National refinish marketing managers were maintained in all major European markets. In industrial coatings, PPG continued to build on its electrodeposition technology by expanding into the appliance sector in Europe and into container coatings.

The decorative segment, where PPG competed with its Pittsburg Paint products in the United States, acquisitions of Olympic (leading stains in the United States), and Lucite, strengthened its channel position into home centers and mass merchandisers. Due to its size and volume stability, PPG considered the decorative sector important. PPG particularly emphasized its finishes for building claddings. Applied to pretreated metal, then oven-cured, PPG's Duranar coatings protected more area of architectural metal worldwide than any other formulations.

Akzo

Akzo was Holland's largest chemical company with sales (1989) of D. fl. 18.7 billion,[4] operating income of D. fl. 1.39 billion and net income of 954 million guilders. Originally strong in fibers, the fibers and polymer group accounted for 29 percent of sales. Other sectors were chemical products (35 percent), coatings (22 percent), and health care and miscellaneous (22 percent). Akzo ranked 12th among the world's largest chemicals companies.

Akzo's coating division achieved sales of 3,659 million guilders (1989), up from 2,794 guilders in 1988. Operating value for 1989 was 281 million guilders, or 7.7 percent. The coating division reported an operating income of 18.7 percent of average invested capital based on a net sales/average capital ratio of 2.44. Of the total sales increase of 31 percent, 19 percent were due to acquisitions, 3 percent to higher value, and 6 percent to price increases.

In the decorative sector, which included decorative, Do-It-Yourself, and architectural paints, Akzo introduced its color consultancy system with the installation of computers for color research in the Netherlands and Germany. In car refinishes, Akzo made progress everywhere, particularly in the U.S. Akzo was working on an integrated system for the color mixing process, calculations, and management, and was introducing this system in its trading courses in Car Refinishing Information Centers around the world. A

4. U.S. $1.00 = D. fl. 2.00.

new plant in Pontiac, Michigan, came on stream in 1989.

In industrial coatings, volume was up and margins were slightly down. The automotive OEM sector yielded "inadequate" returns in 1989. For some of its major customers, Akzo operated on-line and offered water-based finishes, particularly primers. Of increasing importance were coatings for plastics. Akzo also competed in coatings for aircraft. A major development in 1989 was Akzo's acquisition of Reliance Universal (U.S.). This company was a major producer of industrial coatings for wood, metal, plastics, metal packaging, paper, and coil coatings. Reliance was integrated with Akzo's other operations in the United States.

To enhance its operations, Akzo had started to consolidate manufacturing in fewer plants. The company was streamlining its product range, which had grown as a result of various acquisitions. Akzo had major operations in Europe (The Netherlands, Germany, Belgium, Austria, Denmark, Spain, the United Kingdom, Greece), in North America (the United States, Canada), Latin America (Brazil, Mexico, and Argentina), and Asia (Indonesia, Malaysia, and Thailand).

Nippon Paints

With a total volume of 257 million liters, Japan's largest paint company, Nippon Paint, had 1989 sales of about U.S. $1 billion. Operating profit was about $40 million, net profit $25 million. This was the highest net profit earned during the last ten years. Synthetic resin paints represented 80 percent of its volume. Thinners, lacquers, and other chemicals represented the rest (resin printing plate materials).

Nippon Paint was the leader in Japan in electrodeposition paint, and number two in metal surface treatment. Paint for automobiles was about 40 percent of sales, while strong developments in paint for exteriors and industrial machinery were taking place. Nippon's R&D expenditures amounted to $41 million. Total employment stood at 2,700. The company had plans to expand its European operations based in Germany.

Kansai Paint

As Japan's second largest paint company, with a volume of 230 million liters worth $1 billion, Kansai Paint's operating profits amounted to $45 million, with a net profit of $28 million. Some 81 percent of sales were in synthetic resin paints. The rest was accounted for by lacquers, thinners, oil paints, and other chemicals. About 40 percent of sales were in the automobile industry. Also represented were paints for construction, building materials, and other metals. The company had recently built a new technology center and was spending $26 million on research.

CASE 10

Alfa-Laval Filters Product Center

In December 1980, Rune Glimenius, General Manager of the product center for Alfa-Laval filters, and David Webster, Marketing Manager, were reviewing marketing options. All year they had collected information on the world market for ultrafiltration. Management intention was to secure a worldwide lead position in this market which was growing at 20 percent annually. Glimenius and Webster were uncertain which of many possible applications to select for emphasis. Other pending decisions were which countries to target and what channels to use. The new product center had to be organized either by product, by geographic area, or by application. Glimenius struggled to resolve these issues before detailing a plan for group management.

COMPANY BACKGROUND

Alfa-Laval, a diversified manufacturer of industrial equipment with applications in many fields, was a leading Swedish multinational with annual sales of 6.5 billion Swedish Krona (SEK).*

*1 SEK = U.S. $0.25 = SFr 0.40.

●

This case was prepared by Visiting Professor Jean-Pierre Jeannet as a basis for class discussion rather than to illustrate either effective or ineffective handling of an administrative situation. Copyright © 1983 by IMEDE, Lausanne, Switzerland. The International Institute for Management Development (IMD), resulting from the merger between IMEDE, Lausanne, and IMI, Geneva, acquires and retains all rights. Reproduced by permission.

Founded under the name AB Separator in 1878 by Gustav de Laval and Oscar Lamm, it produced the first continuously operating cream separator, invented by de Laval and used to separate cream from milk. Alfa-Laval became one of the first multinational companies when it established a subsidiary in the United States in 1883 and constructed a plant in Poughkeepsie, N.Y., in 1892. It formed sales subsidiaries in several European countries at about the same time. Although all foreign subsidiaries had operated under the name Alfa-Laval, the parent company in Sweden did not adopt that same name until 1963. In 1980 Alfa-Laval employed 18,000 persons in 140 countries. Alfa-Laval included 140 companies, subsidiaries, or units with forty factories located in thirty-five countries. Sales were worldwide with 15 percent in Sweden, 55 percent elsewhere in Europe, 15 percent in North and South America, and the remainder spread throughout Asia and Africa (Exhibit 1).

PRODUCT LINES

Product lines had evolved from the cream separator to include separators for oil and water purification, for yeast, and for many other applications. Alfa-Laval was the lead company worldwide for centrifugal separators. In the 1920s Alfa-Laval had added milking machines to its product line. With growing popularity of automated milking machines in the 1950s, this product gained importance and Alfa-Laval became a household word among farmers worldwide. Alfa-Laval was also a leading manufacturer of heat exchangers and separation equipment. Company technical expertise included separation and thermal technology, liquid handling, and continuous processes with plants for both separation and thermal technology. Alfa-Laval had in-depth knowledge of milking, milk refrigeration, feeding, and all activities centered around cattle farming and barns.

ALFA-LAVAL WORLDWIDE ORGANIZATION

Alfa-Laval was structured to meet the needs of a multi-application product line with worldwide manufacturing and sales. Corporate staff was located in Tumba near Stockholm. Three business groups and the marketing companies were located in over 140 countries.

Eight executives directed the corporate staff group, in turn supported by 20 departments. The three business groups, a unit called "Regional Management," and the larger composite marketing companies all reported to the executive group. Regional Management was a central unit recently formed to coordinate marketing activities in controlled-economy and developing countries. Composite marketing companies were sales companies marketing both agricultural and industrial equipment. They were relatively large units assigned to report directly to certain members of the executive group (Exhibit 2).

Alfa-Laval had segmented into three units, each with its own business group. The Agri unit had three product divisions: milk production, barn equipment, and farm supplies. Milk production manufactured milking and feeding equipment. Barn equipment manufactured equipment to cool milk, milking parlours, and equipment for manure handling. Farm supplies produced accessories, other equipment, and spare parts. Agri had two sales divisions. The farm supplies unit delivered entire projects such as the SAADCO project in Saudi Arabia, a farming and dairy complex to house 10,000 milk cows and 15,000 young stock. The export unit handled sales to state-controlled economies and to countries where Agri was represented only by agents. Ten local marketing subsidiaries selling Agri products exclusively reported to the export unit. Exports conducted its own re-

search worldwide, employed 5000 people, and accounted for one third of sales.

Eight independent companies produced specialized products unrelated to the three main units. These eight contributed 20 percent of sales. Based in Nordic countries, these eight produced electric steam boilers, marine refrigeration plants, heat pumps, products for animal feeding and fish breeding, rotary machines, and heat exchangers.

ALFA-LAVAL INDUSTRIAL GROUP

The industrial group with nearly half of worldwide sales volume was Alfa-Laval's largest. Each of its four product divisions had worldwide responsibilities. The separation engineering division manufactured centrifugal separators, decanter centrifuges, and filters. The thermal engineering division made plate heat exchangers. The flow equipment division produced pumps, control valves, and fittings. The automation division made electronic products.

The industrial group also had three application divisions responsible for sales of the four product divisions in certain target markets worldwide. The marine and power engineering division marketed equipment for ships and for the power industry: separators, heat exchangers, and freshwater distillers. The dairy and food engineering division sold process equipment to dairies and food processing plants. The food technology division marketed components, equipment, and complete installations for fish processing, starch production and vegetable oil processing. Also in the industrial group were fourteen sales companies which specialized exclusively in product lines for their countries or areas. The newly formed filters product center was part of the separation engineering division of the industrial products group. The separation engineering division had three product centers: high speed separators, decanters, and filters.

Alfa-Laval had a complex international structure. Product groups had worldwide responsibility for manufacturing and sales. In countries where marketing companies existed, customer contacts were limited to the marketing company for that geographic area. Marketing was the responsibility of the applications divisions except

EXHIBIT 1 ● Activities in Summary*

	1980	1979	1978	1977	1976	1975	1974	1973	1972
Net sales by business group									
Agri-group	1 922	1 805	1 530	1 329	1 127	1 023	960	842	652
Industrial group	3 135	2 562	2 443	1 899	1 795	1 701	1 506	1 091	881
Other companies	1 445	1 119	1 013	980	834	817	708	521	372
Income Data									
Net sales	6 502	5 486	4 986	4 208	3 756	3 541	3 174	2 454	1 905
Income after net financial items	477	391	321	305	303	264	249	207	122
As percentage of net sales	7.3	7.1	6.4	7.3	8.0	7.5	7.8	8.4	6.4
Adjusted income per share	22.9	18.8	15.4	14.7	14.6	14.1	13.4	11.1	6.5
Income before taxes	297	275	212	172	153	139	124	154	107
Provision for taxes	102	108	114	90	89	77	68	78	52
Balance Sheet Data									
Liquid assets	1 056	1 138	1 278	1 228	935	572	334	358	314
Inventories	2 313	2 023	1 790	1 656	1 486	1 295	1 108	850	685
Other current assets	1 833	1 754	1 677	1 309	1 139	1 131	1 048	853	786
Long-term assets	1 485	1 350	1 175	996	855	564	456	395	351
Current liabilities	2 754	2 666	2 587	2 230	1 678	1 440	1 200	971	769
Long-term liabilities	1 010	978	954	821	694	645	515	390	356
Untaxed reserves	1 464	1 282	1 151	1 034	910	544	431	325	271
Equity capital	1 459	1 339	1 228	1 104	1 133	933	800	770	740
Total assets	6 687	6 265	5 920	5 189	4 415	3 562	2 946	2 456	2 136

Number of employees									
Sweden	7 363	7 081	6 875	6 895	6 781	6 739	6 464	6 152	5 202
Outside Sweden	10 711	10 815	10 888	10 890	11 039	11 269	11 258	10 157	9 635
Profitability									
Return:									
On average operating capital before taxes	14.0	12.3	11.4	12.2	13.3	15.1	16.4	14.8	9.9
On equity capital after taxes	11.4	10.3	9.4	9.5	10.2	11.9	12.8	11.5	7.1
Ratios									
Current assets to current liabilities	1.9	1.8	1.8	1.9	2.1	2.1	2.1	2.1	2.3
Solidity ratio	32.8	31.6	30.5	31.2	36.0	33.8	34.5	38.0	41.0
Interest coverage	4.3	4.3	4.3	4.4	4.7	4.2	4.8	5.5	4.9
Other data									
Dividend									
As percent of earnings	26.3	25.5	31.2	27.3	27.4	25.2	21.3	25.6	43.6
SEK per share	6.0	4.8	4.8	4.0	4.0	3.6	2.9	2.9	2.9
Capital stock, December 31	521	417	417	417	417	333	267	267	213
Share price, December 31 (SEK)	137	98	115	118	122	106	79	79	71
Price/earnings ratio, per share	6	5	7	8	8	8	6	7	11

*As originally stated except for 1976, which is restated in accordance with accounting principles adopted in 1977. (Amounts in MSEK)

EXHIBIT 2 ● Worldwide Organization

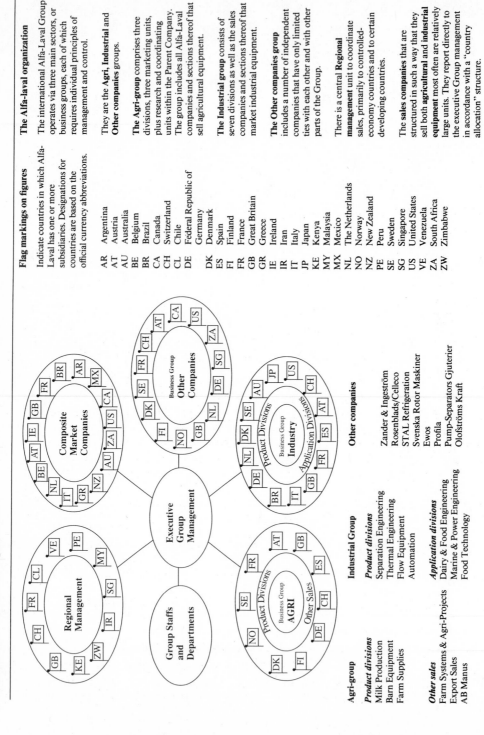

The Alfa-laval organization

The international Alfa-Laval Group operates via three main sectors, or business groups, each of which requires individual principles of management and control.

They are the **Agri, Industrial** and **Other companies** groups.

The Agri-group comprises three divisions, three marketing units, plus research and coordinating units within the Parent Company. The group includes all Alfa-Laval companies and sections thereof that sell agricultural equipment.

The Industrial group consists of seven divisions as well as the sales companies and sections thereof that market industrial equipment.

The Other companies group includes a number of independent companies that have only limited ties with each other and with other parts of the Group.

There is a central **Regional management** unit to coordinate sales, primarily to controlled-economy countries and to certain developing countries.

The **sales companies** that are structured in such a way that they sell both **agricultural and industrial equipment** most often are relatively large units. They report directly to the executive Group management in accordance with a "country allocation" structure.

The Executive Group Management—the management for the Alfa-Laval Group—consists of eight people with some twenty Group staffs and departments at their disposal.

Flag markings on figures

Indicate countries in which Alfa-Laval has one or more subsidiaries. Designations for countries are based on the official currency abbreviations.

AR Argentina
AT Austria
AU Australia
BE Belgium
BR Brazil
CA Canada
CH Switzerland
CL Chile
DE Federal Republic of Germany
DK Denmark
ES Spain
FI Finland
FR France
GB Great Britain
GR Greece
IE Ireland
IR Iran
IT Italy
JP Japan
KE Kenya
MY Malaysia
MX Mexico
NL The Netherlands
NO Norway
NZ New Zealand
PE Peru
SE Sweden
SG Singapore
US United States
VE Venezuela
ZA South Africa
ZW Zimbabwe

Agri-group

Product divisions
Milk Production
Barn Equipment
Farm Supplies

Other sales
Farm Systems & Agri-Projects
Export Sales
AB Manus

Industrial Group

Product divisions
Separation Engineering
Thermal Engineering
Flow Equipment
Automation

Application divisions
Dairy & Food Engineering
Marine & Power Engineering
Food Technology

Other companies
Zander & Ingeström
Rosenblads/Celleco
STAL Refrigeration
Svenska Rotor Maskiner
Ewos
Profila
Pump-Separators Gjuterier
Olofströms Kraft

where local marketing companies existed. Transfer prices were set so that product divisions would show balanced results. Consequently, profits were usually realized in applications divisions or in marketing companies. Alfa-Laval was a federation of companies. This loose federation had been enhanced during both world wars when communications with the parent company were extremely difficult. As a result, unit independence was an important characteristic of Alfa Laval.

THE FILTERS PRODUCT CENTER

Before 1978, filter activities had been spread throughout the industrial group. The new product center was formed to concentrate filter activities into one unit. A broad product line had formerly concentrated around filter centrifuges, a low technology item sold to another company. Management decided to eliminate half the product line by selling, licensing, and discontinuing operations. Traditionally Alfa-Laval had emphasized high margin products within a limited product range. Product line reorganization allowed the filters center to benefit from global operations with high market shares in some applications. The company enjoyed an excellent reputation and was known for its service. To foster a high technology image, the center emphasized new filtration methods. High speed separators, the major product of the separation division, had existed for 100 years. Alfa-Laval held a strong market share in high speed separation. With the total world market growing slowly, and with new competitors entering the market, this segment was viewed as mature and saturated. Alfa-Laval had long regarded high speed separators as subject to considerable substitution risk from new technologies and processes. The filters product center was intended to gain a strong position in new technology as a hedge against obsolescence of traditional lines.

SEPARATION TECHNOLOGY

Separation was any process whereby particles were separated from a liquid. Different separation methods were employed depending on particle size. The following techniques were used at each level:

Particle Size

Particle size (in microns)

	100	Conventional filters
	10	High speed separators
Bacteria	1	Microfiltration
Microemulsions	0.1	Ultrafiltration (UF)
Macromolecules	0.01	
Sugar	0.001	Reverse Osmosis (RO)
Salts		

Conventional filters were used for solid/liquid filtration and high speed separators for liquid/liquid and liquid/solid. Other methods employed membrane technology. For microfiltration, ultrafiltration, and reverse osmosis, pressure was combined with cross-flow. Ultrafiltration and reverse osmosis depended on the availability of efficient membranes, which lasted for about 10 years. Industrial processes fell within one category, and no substitution occurred among filtration technologies.

Alfa-Laval separation had concentrated on high speed separators for a wide range of applications. Industry increasingly demanded new processes for separation of ever smaller particles. Of five technologies for separation, ultrafiltration was the most recently developed. The new product center was therefore directed to concentrate on membrane technology and ultrafiltration.

ULTRAFILTRATION TECHNOLOGY

Ultrafiltration (UF) was a pressure-driven membrane process to separate and fractionate components of liquids. Separation was performed by a porous membrane allowing water and other low molecular substances to pass. Larger molecules, micro-emulsion droplets, and suspended solids were held back. Ultrafiltration could selectively concentrate solutes, particles, colloids, and emulsions. Separation problems previously requiring expensive and complicated methods could now be solved using ultrafiltration, at low pressure and without heat or chemical additives. Process and waste liquids could be treated at a fraction of the cost of traditional evaporation.

Alfa-Laval membranes were hollow fibers of slightly over 1 mm inner diameter. Inside each fiber was a thin skin with small pores uniform in size. The inner skin was surrounded by a highly permeable sponge-like support structure, thicker and with larger open pores. The process liquid was pumped into one end of the fiber. Smaller molecules such as water and salts were forced radially outward through the membrane skin and support structure and discharged as ultrafiltrate or "permeate." Pore size was chosen so that molecules with different weights and micro-emulsions could not follow the same path through the fiber. Some molecules thus continued with the flow inside the fiber. This crossflow prevented build-up of the material retained inside the fiber. Without the crossflow, the flow rate of the ultrafiltrate would be reduced. This method allowed high flow rate even under low pressure (Exhibit 3).

The frame of reference used to measure ultrafiltration ability was the capacity of the membrane to retain a given macromolecule of known molecular weight. A "cut-off" was the molecular weight of the test macromolecule used because molecular shape and other factors could affect membrane performance.

The concept of ultrafiltration had existed for some time. Alfa-Laval had sold its first installations in 1973/1974 to pharmaceutical companies processing human albumin. The new company strategy called for marketing ultrafiltration equipment outside a laboratory environment, targeting companies already using expensive methods of filtration. Technology had to be re-engineered to fit industrial processes and capacity requirements.

THE ALFA-LAVAL UF SYSTEM

The Alfa-Laval ultrafiltration system was modular in design. All system elements were included, and it was adaptable to individual client needs. Hollow fiber cartridges were available with different characteristics depending on the applications desired. To accommodate either batch or continuous-flow operations, the system could be equipped with a batch tank or a feed inlet. All systems were equipped with feed pump, circulation pump, strainer, ultrafilter cartridges, and a collector for the permeate and the end concentrate (Exhibit 4). Permeate from cartridges was collected in a common outlet manifold and continuously discharged.

Alfa-Laval's system had several important characteristics. Permanent parts such as piping, pumps, strainers, valves, fittings, and control panels, were manufactured by Alfa-Laval, simplifying service and spare-part requirements. Cartridges had to be cleaned at regular intervals, but the optimum operating period between cleanings varied according to application. Circulating a detergent solution usually sufficed. Alfa-Laval offered a back-flush system using a hollow fiber cartridge. This process prevented membrane fouling and concentration polarization. Hollow fiber cartridges required lower material consumption and lower plant pressure. The technology permitted a short residence time for treated fluids and gave higher product yields. Romicon, a subsidiary of the U.S.-based chemical company Rohm & Haas, manufactured the cartridge from durable polymers. After several years of experience in this field, Alfa-Laval enjoyed in-house expertise and knowledge of all UF and RO applications.

Alfa-Laval offered four plant configurations. The UFP I was designed as a pilot plant with only one membrane cartridge, at SEK 60,000. The UFS 4 was designed for batch processing with four membranes, SEK 100,000. Two larger configurations, the UFS 14 with 14 membranes and the UFS 30 with 30 membranes, cost SEK 150–200,000 and SEK 200–300,000 respectively. Any of these single units could be combined into a "cascade" of units to achieve higher purification,

EXHIBIT 3 ● Membrane Technology

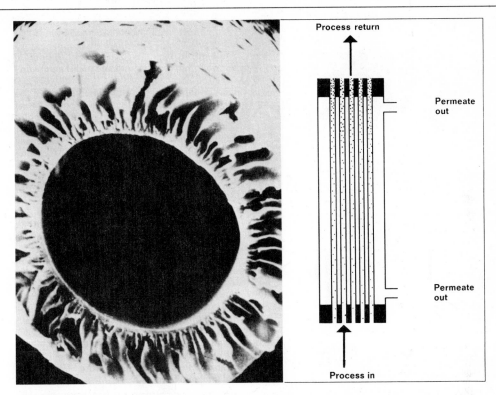

The Hollow Fiber consists of a thin inner skin surrounded by a porous "sponge-like" outer support. The inner skin is the separating membrane surface. The pore size in this skin determines the size of molecules which can pass through the membrane. Larger molecules are retained on the inside of the fiber.

A large number of Hollow Fibers is imbedded on both ends in epoxy resin. The cartridge shell and adapters are made of inert clear polysulfone.

Shipping data

	Long type cartridges	Short type cartridges
Height	180 mm	180 mm
Length	1 170 mm	710 mm
Width	205 mm	205 mm
Weight	4.6 kg	2.5 kg

EXHIBIT 4 ● The Ultrafiltration Process

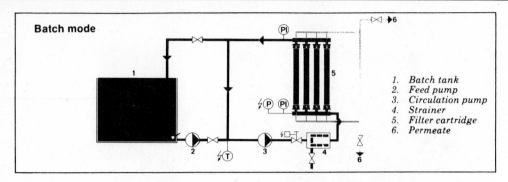

Batch mode

1. Batch tank
2. Feed pump
3. Circulation pump
4. Strainer
5. Filter cartridge
6. Permeate

The plant can be designed for batch or continuous operation in relation to concentrate production. In the batch mode the process liquid is recirculated through the cartridges until the desired level of concentration is achieved in the batch tank.

In continuous operation process liquid is continuously fed into the circulation loop. The concentrated liquid is constantly discharged. As in the batch mode, permeate production is continuous during the process.

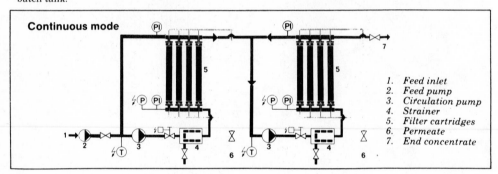

Continuous mode

1. Feed inlet
2. Feed pump
3. Circulation pump
4. Strainer
5. Filter cartridges
6. Permeate
7. End concentrate

or as parallel units to obtain more capacity (Exhibit 5).

THE WORLD MARKET FOR ULTRAFILTRATION

When the filters product center was formed, Alfa-Laval had estimated the 1980 market for ultrafiltration, microfiltration, and original equipment as follows:

Dairy	SEK 55 million
Electrophoretic paint	55
Oil/water	30
Pharmaceutical & biotechnology	20
Process water	15
Others	15
Total	190 million (at customer prices)

Given the 20 percent annual growth rate, the total market was expected to grow as follows:

EXHIBIT 5 ● Membrane Separator Ultrafiltration
Unit, UFS-14

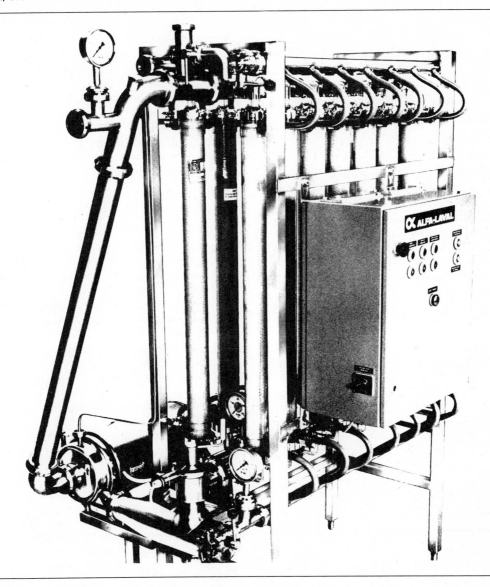

1980	SEK 190 million
1981	225
1982	270
1983	325
1984	390
1985	470
1986	560

Potential applications existed in pulp and paper production, foods, chemicals, sewage treatment, and farming.

DAIRY APPLICATIONS

The dairy industry offered opportunities to use ultrafiltration for two purposes: concentration of whey to recover protein, and preconcentration of milk for subsequent production of dairy products. Market size in 1980 for these applications was estimated at SEK 55 million.

Whey, a by-product of cheese, had high protein content. Protein recovery using traditional filtration methods was difficult, and therefore whey had been generally discharged as waste. UF preconcentration of milk offered applications for cheese making. Ymer in Denmark was a very popular fermented milk product similar to sour milk and high in protein. Ymer producers converted to UF for a top-grade product with yields 18 percent above those from standard methods. UF could achieve similiar results for cheeses such as Camembert, cream cheese, ricotta, and feta. Although the final product had different composition and structure, consumers could discern no difference in taste.

Alfa-Laval executives believed UF provided substantial advantages: higher yield, increased nutritional value, simpler product composition, reduced space requirements, capability to produce sweet permeate, and ease of continuing processing.

Two customer groups used UF in the dairy industry: newly built cheese operations and dairies adding a UF system to an already existing plant. Installation at an existing plant required changes often discouraging to the customer. Newly built plants offered greater promise. Addition of UF whey processing to existing or new cheese plants was much easier.

Buying habits differed by size of cheese producers. Small dairies were likely to buy new equipment for prestige purposes and could easily be talked into buying. Large dominant producers such as Sweden's two coops showed little interest in new technology or new products. Multinationals such as part of Kraft in the U.S. purchased according to engineering specifications.

Cheeses most likely to benefit from UF were produced in small plants, particularly common in France. Fewer than 50 cheese plants were built annually worldwide, and the trend was to larger, more centralized operations.

ELECTROPHORETIC PAINT PROCESSES

Electrophoretic processes, a market of SEK 55 million, deposited paint by electrolysis. A painted part had to be rinsed to give it an acceptable finish. Using water to rinse created waste that could not be re-used. A UF recycling loop could rinse and recover the paint, allowing the customer to use more expensive paint because of reduced losses.

Fifty percent of all users in this segment, automobile manufacturers maintained extensive paint operations. Automobile manufacturers hesitated to install UF without approval of their paint suppliers and manufacturers. Installation of a UF system could be viewed as an equipment change invalidating a paint supplier's guarantee. Dürr, one of the largest paint suppliers, had integrated UF systems made by Abcor, a U.S. company, into its paint systems. If automobile manufacturers specified UF equipment when ordering a new paint line, UF might account for 5 to 10 percent of the cost of an entire paint unit.

Non-automotive users composed the other half of the paint segment. Producers of consumer durable goods and furniture parts were more likely to adopt UF if contacted directly. Alfa-Laval's UF system offered reduced investment need, operating costs, down-time, and maintenance costs.

Approximately 100 paint systems of varying

sizes were installed annually. Car manufacturers especially in the U.S. could be persuaded to install UF systems on the basis of cost savings. Manufacturers would often adopt UF systems when switching from older anionic paint to newer catiodic paint.

Glimenius considered this segment the most price sensitive. Having a similar company already using a UF system in the same country was an important reassurance for the prospective customer.

THE OIL/WATER SEGMENT

UF could be used to treat oil waste or to recover oils from soluble oil waste produced by mechanical engineering. Wherever cutting or lubrication fluids were needed, companies faced a disposal problem. Users could either contract for the collection of effluent and return usable oil for a fee, or install their own treatment systems. Some types of oil/water emulsions used for cooling and lubrication in metal and mechanical industries could not be split with a high speed separator unless chemical splitting agents were added and the emulsion heated. Such separation was often used before UF to remove "tramp" oil that had contaminated the emulsion and was present in unemulsified form. Tramp oil could adversely affect UF performance but could be removed by paper band filters or a simple settling tank.

The advantage of UF was its ability to concentrate oil into less than one tenth of the original volume. For example, if 100 liters of water with 3 percent oil content were subjected to UF, the 3 liters of oil could be concentrated into 5 liters of emulsion, returning 95 liters of water in pure form. The concentrated oil emulsion could be reused. UF functioned mechanically and required no chemical substances which were often a greater environmental hazard than the effluent.

Oil-water applications were evenly split between factory and commercial contractors. Purchase of a UF system depended on cost comparison between in-house treatment and outside collector services. In Sweden 20 to 25 plants could justify an in-house UF system, and in France, 50 to 100. Commercial collectors needed efficiency and flexibility for a variety of effluents and sold extracted material for additional income.

Commercial collectors and their organizational structures varied from country to country. In Sweden there was one government-owned collector agency. In the U.K. there were two or three large collectors and 10 of medium size. In Germany a fully developed system existed. In some countries waste could be dumped in old mines leaving little demand for UF. However, worldwide attitudes were quickly changing with regard to waste treatment.

THE PHARMACEUTICAL AND BIOCHEMICAL SEGMENT

The pharmaceutical industry held potential for UF in the areas of enzyme processing, human blood, antibiotics, process water, and biochemistry. Most enzyme processing companies already had or were considering UF. Ten companies with worldwide operations produced 80 percent of total enzyme output. Enzymes were used for bulk chemicals, detergent additives, and in the U.S., corn syrup. The industry leader by volume was Novo of Denmark, followed by Gist Brocard in Holland, and Miles Laboratories and Pfizer in the U.S. UF's advantage was that it reduced the need for purification and spray drying because the process concentrated and purified simultaneously.

UF advantages in human blood processing were less marked than in enzyme processing. UF lowered salt and ethanol concentration in albumin and other products during a complicated fractioning process. Major customers were blood collection centers, depending on size and volume. Germany, France, and the U.K. had three or four blood centers with enough volume to consider UF plants. U.K. centers got blood for free and were less interested in economics.

UF could also be used to produce animal blood albumin and blood plasma for processing into concentrated or dried products. UF was an alternative to concentration by evaporation or a pre-treatment before drying. UF offered lower operating costs and improved quality. It also minimized the time that plasma or albumin were kept at temperatures capable of supporting bacterial growth. Whereas many industrial products did not have a high enough market value to justify a UF process, pharmaceutical products were of sufficient value to make UF attractive.

Many companies used UF to process antibiotics. A major advantage of UF was the simultaneous removal of undesirable low-molecular compounds and salts during concentration. The cost of one more step in producing a high-value antibiotic was minimal. Since national drug control agencies licensed the composition and application of a drug and also its production process, introducing UF into an existing plant required reapproval by the local drug administration agency. UF increased yield and resulted in higher return, necessitating custom designed systems and engineering advice. Margins were highest where development work was done concurrent with new process introduction. Potential customers were 50 well-known pharmaceutical manufacturers with a few hundred installations worldwide. Decision makers were difficult to find.

UF was also suited for the production of high quality water, used to remove microorganisms, bacteria, toxins, and pyrogens from water for final washing and rinsing of pharmaceutical product containers. Such processed water was required by both antibiotics manufacturers and "pill makers," which bought raw materials from pharmaceutical companies and packaged them into pills. Several thousand such companies existed worldwide. Similar potential applications existed for cosmetics manufacturers.

Biochemistry offered opportunities for UF applications in downstream processing, an area currently in development. Biotech companies existed in the U.S., Japan, and Europe. An unknown company could become a leader tomorrow.

SMALLER SEGMENTS

The process water segment with volume estimated at SEK 15 million was the smallest application segment. Two sub-segments were the electronics industry, needing high resistivity 18 Mega Ohm water to rinse electronic components or chips, and the water treatment industry.

A limited number of large plants could be equipped for a specific application, such as indigo recovery or vinegar processing. UF sales depended on knowledge of the existence of these unique opportunities, which were difficult to identify.

POTENTIAL UF APPLICATIONS

Alfa-Laval executives had identified four areas where UF was not currently used but might have a bright future. The pulp and paper industry had five projects expected to be built over the next five years in the U.S., Canada, and Scandinavia.

In the food industry, starch, vinegar or fish production, and waste recovery were possible applications. In the fruit juice industry, UF could be used for juice clarification and recovery of citrus oil. UF also had applications for production of wine, beer, and soft drinks.

Individual dairy farms could become buyers of UF systems to separate, concentrate, or filter milk. Although farm-based UF plants were not economical for fewer than 100 cows, France, New Zealand, the U.S., and Canada offered excellent potential. The great distances between farm and dairy in these countries made attractive the potential to reduce the number of times products had to be transported. Sewage treatment was believed to have the largest number of potential UF users.

COMPETITION

Ten competitors including Alfa-Laval marketed UF systems, three from the U.S., four from Europe, and two from Japan. All 10 competed worldwide, but only two or three competed directly in any given country.

Abcor, located in Wilmington, Massachusetts, was the largest U.S. competitor. Abcor was owned by Koch Industries, a diversified company, and employed 200 persons. Abcor dominated the segment for electro-coat industrial applications and had a tie-in with Dürr of Germany, the leading supplier of large paint systems to the car industry. Oil-water applications were another Abcor strength, with 60 percent of sales in replacement membranes. Abcor was market leader in the U.S. and also sold systems in Europe, Australia, and Comecon countries. Except for the U.K., where Abcor sold through a subsidiary, the company relied on agents or distributors. Abcor appointed several agents in one country, each specializing in a different application. Alfa-Laval management considered Abcor its most aggressive price competitor.

Another U.S. competitor, and a unit of the chemical company Rohm & Haas, Romicon had 60 employees and specialized in supplying membranes. It also competed for entire UF systems. Outside the U.S. Romicon was active in Japan and Europe, using distributors for local contacts and a small subsidiary in Holland to coordinate European business. A specialist in the production of hollow fibre cartridges, Romicon supplied cartridges for Alfa-Laval UF systems and for other UF systems on an OEM basis.

Millipore was the third U.S. firm, a leading supplier of filtration equipment for food and beverage manufacturers and laboratories. Millipore was very profitable and had considerable financial resources. UF was small compared to its total operations. The company was strong in laboratory size UF equipment but weak in industrial scale systems. Millipore had concentrated on UF applications in the pharmaceutical and beverage industries and in potable water, marketing worldwide through its own subsidiaries.

The Danish Sugar Company (DDS) was the largest European competitor. With ample financial resources, this company sought new growth opportunities. There was only low growth potential in sugar refining. DDS marketed UF equipment through two subsidiaries, Pasilac and Niro Atomisor. Similar to Alfa-Laval, Pasilac had concentrated on buying components, on contracting, and on turnkey plants. It was one of Alfa-Laval's principal competitors for plate heat exchangers. DDS employed 150 people in its membrane business and concentrated in hygienics, food and dairy, and pharmaceuticals. DDS was not in paint or water-oil applications. Strong in Europe, it also competed in the U.S., Japan, and Australia, selling through subsidiaries and agents.

Paterson Candy International, PCI, was the second largest European competitor. PCI employed 1200 persons, of which 70 were in separation technology. PCI concentrated on nondesalination applications and was the world leader in reverse osmosis. Only 15 persons worked in UF membranes. The company competed in the dairy and food industries for reverse osmosis but had not concentrated on any given UF application. PCI sold UF in Europe through sales subsidiaries or agents.

Two other European firms were both French. Rhone-Poulenc, a very large multinational chemical company, had no other filtration activity. Twenty people composed its membrane unit. In France the company was strong in dairy applications because of the French cheese industry. Rhone-Poulenc sales outside France were relatively small. The company had an agreement with Eisenmann of Germany, a paint specialist and major competitor of Dürr. The other French company, SFEC, was state-owned and associated with the French Atomic Energy Commission. SFEC had acquired UF technology from Union Carbide, a U.S. chemical company. Its new UF unit was still small and as yet had no commercial opportunities.

Activities of the two Japanese companies marketing UF systems remained unknown to Alfa-Laval executives. Both Nitto and Toray concentrated in Japan and were believed to be in the system-perfecting stage.

ACCEPTANCE OF UF BY REGION

Various parts of the world showed different levels of acceptance for UF. The U.S., Australia, New Zealand, and parts of Europe showed high acceptance. High acceptance occurred in the U.K., France, Germany, and Italy. Scandinavian countries showed average acceptance. Spain had low acceptance. Knowledge and use of UF was low in Latin America and Africa, with the exception of

South Africa. Glimenius knew too little about Japan to assess penetration.

The U.S. and Canada had one half of world UF capacity. Europe had 35 percent, Japan 10 percent, and Australia and New Zealand combined, 5 percent. Installed capacity in Europe had not been broken down by country. Current sales were believed to approximate the distribution of installed capacity, with Europe holding a somewhat higher share due to faster growth in this region.

Glimenius was concerned about selection of a geographic area for future concentration. He preferred proximity to his unit, expecting a need for close contacts until his product center gained sufficient experience.

SELLING THROUGH ALFA-LAVAL SUBSIDIARIES

Utilizing Alfa-Laval subsidiaries was a major question for Glimenius and Webster. Each subsidiary was an independent marketing company responsible for all sales within its country. Product divisions marketed through the marketing companies. Although Glimenius was not forced to utilize the marketing companies, he did not know where else to turn. He knew the flow equipment division used non-Alfa-Laval channels to market valves and fittings. If he chose to utilize the marketing companies, he had to recognize their strengths and weaknesses.

The marketing companies had varying structures, depending on applications. Divisions corresponded to the industrial groups used by Alfa-Laval in Sweden. Each division had product departments. The regional organization included the salesforce. The number and size of divisions and departments depended on sales volume. Regional agents were sometimes used instead of company salesmen.

Department financial results were the performance measure. Training new people showed no short-term results. It was likely that one or two specialists would be selected to be trained in UF while keeping other responsibilities. Engineers were excited about the prospects in UF, as were executives at the division level in various marketing companies.

The regional salesforce was familiar with only one type of product. UF was not among them because of its recent introduction. The salesforce did not quote prices but handed specifications to the product department which concluded deals. The salesforce consisted of technical people recruited and trained as salesmen. Despite their title as area sales engineers, there was a natural product specialization. Training for a new UF line would take time and reduce sales in other applications. An obstacle to UF was the need to train both the salesforce and the service division for selling and servicing UF equipment.

MARKETING COMPANY STRUCTURES

In the United Kingdom, the marketing company had six divisions: separation and thermal, food and dairy, marine and power, farming, contracting, and service. The service division was responsible for all after-sales service. The separation and thermal division consisted of two departments: separation and thermal. The separation department employed twelve engineers, each specializing by product line. There was no UF specialist in the department. Regional sales were the responsibility of six sales engineers. Four specialized in separation machines and two sold the entire division product range. In France, the salesforce specialized by division and operated out of the head office in Paris.

The German company resembled the U.K. company. The separation department employed 12 specialists by application. Regional sales offices were located in 10 cities. The salesforce was organized by types of customers or industries and reported to a separate division head for field sales. A salesman's strength was his knowledge of individual customers and his personal contacts. A salesman could not know more than one or two product lines in depth and therefore required support from the head office in Hamburg, which if necessary could contact the respective product center in Sweden.

German high speed separator salesmen had

good contacts with the dairy industry and also for applications such as chemicals and oil/water where high speed separators were easiest to sell. Separator salesmen did not visit paint application customers, although thermal heat exchanger salesmen did. No contacts existed in process water applications. The high speed separation division had lost control of pharmaceutical and biochemical applications. The German salesforce exerted strong influence which might conflict with corporate planning.

The U.S. salesforce operated from regional offices. Salesmen of all divisions were combined into one regional center while remaining under division control. The separation division salesforce specialized by customer type. High salesforce turnover was a problem. Selling separation equipment was more an art than a science. Experience was essential, and it took three or four years to learn. With greater job mobility in the U.S. than elsewhere, the salesforce was constantly changing. Consequently, most salesmen did not even have knowledge of all Alfa-Laval older separation products.

The special unit selling Alfa-Laval products to government trading countries was a staff group paid by the corporate units. With no P&L responsibility, this unit had good connections in COMECON countries and operated an office in Moscow. There was a possibility of using this government trading unit as a means for geographical concentration. It would take time to show results. No short-term arrangements were possible through this channel.

ORGANIZATIONAL ISSUES FOR THE FILTERS PRODUCT CENTER

When the filters product center was formed as S-5 in the separation division, it included four other product ranges. Three of these, sieve band presses, foam scrubbers, and rotoshears, were dropped. Rotary vacuum filters was targeted for harvesting. Only UF was selected for further investment. The product center had no manufacturing facilities and sourced all components from Sweden or from outside vendors when necessary.

The filters product center had a small administrative unit, an R+D unit, a marketing department, and an engineering department. Marketing under David Webster included one assistant and one secretary. Glimenius had to decide whether to organize the marketing department by application or by geographical area. The engineering department could be organized by function, such as service, design, purchasing, and procurement, or by application, by geographic area, or by product line. There were three engineers and a department head. Growth was expected.

In marketing Glimenius had been limited by availability of qualified personnel with sufficient background. Two different postures were possible for the marketing department. It could assist the marketing companies in quoting for UF plants and projects, or it could employ its own sales engineers who would contact prospective clients. A new salesman would require 3 months to start finding customers and another 9 months to generate orders. For UF lines, negotiation time was 3 to 6 months, with delivery and invoicing 6 months later. Volume for a good sales engineer would be SEK 3 million, possibly only after one or two years.

FINANCIAL CONSIDERATIONS

Glimenius had full profit and loss responsibility for his product center. Costs averaged SEK 300,000 per person, including fringe expenditures. The company charged 18 percent on capital. SEK 200,000 in capital were required for every one million in sales. Average A/R turnover of 45 days was standard for Alfa-Laval marketing companies, which earned 25 percent margins on prices. Product center gross margin was one third.* Glimenius could ask for a supplemental budget, but he would have to demonstrate need.

DEVELOPMENT OF A BUSINESS PLAN

Glimenius knew that Alfa-Laval would look at the long-term perspective. The option was for rapid

*Estimates by case writer.

EXHIBIT 6 ● Ultrafiltration—Alfa-Laval Dairy Applications (To Date)

Customer	Type of application		Product	Commissioning
Denmark				
CM, Århus	UFS-14	35m²	Skimmilk	1977
Dan-Maelk, Århus (includes the CM, Århus, installation)	3 × UFS-14	105 m²	Skimmilk	1978
Esbjerg	UFS-14	35m²	Skimmilk	1978
Fynsk Malek, Odense	UFS-14	35m²	Skimmilk	1978
Randers	UFS-14	35m²	Skimmilk	1978
Plumrose A/S Alka-Assens	UFS-4	10m²	Skimmilk	1978
Jaegersborg	UFS-4	10m²	Skimmilk	1978
Snejbjerg	UFS-14	35m²	Skimmilk	1979
Horsens	UFS-6	15m²	Skimmilk	1979
Hilleröd Research Dairy	3 × UFS-4	25m²	Milk, Whey	1979
*	3 × UFS-4	25m²	Cheese	1981
France				
Laiterie	UFS-14	12 × 35m²	Lactic Acid	1976–80
Mont St. Michel			Casein Whey	(Expansion from 3 × 35m²)
Montfaucon	UFS-10	53m²	Whole milk	
	UFS-20		Camembert	
*	3 × UFS-30	281 m²	Feta	1981
Switzerland				
Nestlé	UFS-4	10m²		1978
Germany				
	UFS-14	35m²	Acid Whey	1980

*Confidential.

EXHIBIT 7 ● Alfa-Laval Ultrafiltration Plants for Soluble Oil Wastes

Customer	Year commissioned	Address	Type of plant	Membrane surface m²	Pretreatment	Application	Average plant capacity l/h
BELGIUM							
Fabrique National		Herstal	UFO-4	7.5	Separator WSB 104B-74	Washing liquid	
Fabrique National		Herstal	UFO-4	7.4	Separator WSB 104B-74	Washing liquid	
Fabrique National	1976–1978	Hauts-Sarts	UFO-4	7.5	Separator WSB 104B-74	Emulsions	
Fabrique National		Harze	UFO-4	10	Separator WSB 104B-74	Washing liquid	450
FRANCE							
Citroën		Various factories	Pilot unit UFO-1	2.5	MAB 103	Test on various fluids	—
Le Compresseur Frigorifique	1977–79	Montluel	UFO-4	7.5	Settling tank	Emulsions Wash water	120 180
Recyclage Industrial Chimique (RIC)		Beynes	UFO-12	30.0	Separator FUVPX 207	Emulsions Wash water	800 1 500
Poly Oil Chemie		Bassens	UFS-14/8	20.0	Separator FUVPX 207	Mixture of emulsions and wash water	950
Glanzer-Spicer	1980	Le Mans	UFS-14/8	20.0	Separator WSPX 204	Emulsions Wash water	500 900
Gaz de France	1980	St Clair Sur Epte	UFS-4/5	12.5	—	Oily water from air compressor	400
UNITED KINGDOM							
Lanstar	1980	Manchester	UFS-14N	35	Separator WSPX 213	Emulsions	1 000

EXHIBIT 8 ● Alfa-Laval Ultrafiltration Plants for Pharmaceutical and Biochemical Applications

Customer	Country	Application	Membrane surface (m^2)	Start-up year
Merck, Sharp & Dohme	France	Vaccine manufacturing	25	1979
*	Scandinavia	*	40	1980
*	Scandinavia	*	40	1981
*	Denmark	Enzyme processing	10	1981
*	U.K.	Pilot	.3	1981
*	Asia	Enzyme processing	10	1981

*Denotes confidential.

growth in volume or smaller growth with emphasis on profits. The company expected him to raise UF market share from less than 5 percent to one third of the worldwide market while earning at least the company average of 7 percent return on sales. Organizational issues had to be resolved for the product center. (For a listing of existing Alfa-Laval U.S. installations, see Exhibits 6–8.)

Given the present competitive and market situation. Glimenius had to chart a strategy for presentation to management. He knew that such a presentation would entail both general strategy and financial forecasts. He wondered which industry applications he should emphasize. Looking at the structure of Alfa-Laval marketing companies, he was unsure how to market the UF product line and which geographic areas to select for concentration.

CASE 11

General Concepts

During Spring of 1977, William P. Edwards, Director of Corporate Marketing Communications of General Concepts, was conducting a review of his company's approach to international advertising. During the last four years, the European subsidiaries had become more independent in their approach to advertising causing General Concepts to present a sometimes different image to its worldwide clientele. It was up to Edwards to choose from several possible alternatives a workable structure for General Concepts' international advertising keeping in mind General Concepts' corporate goals and the realities of the marketplace.

COMPANY HISTORY

General Concepts was incorporated in 1966 as a manufacturer of small and medium sized general purpose digital computers. The company grew very quickly from sales of 2 million dollars in 1969 to sales of over 180 million dollars for fiscal year 1976 (see Exhibits 1 and 2 for financial summaries). At the same time, the company expanded its product line to include peripheral computer equipment, software and software services, and maintenance and training services for its clients.

●

This case was prepared by John Bleh, Research Assistant, under the direction of Jean-Pierre Jeannet, Professor of Marketing and International Business at Babson College, as a basis for class discussion rather than to illustrate either effective or ineffective handling of an administrative situation. All names and confidential data were disguised. Copyright © 1987 by Jean-Pierre Jeannet.

Traditionally, the electronic data processing industry had been characterized by a rapid technological process and price reductions. Some of the company's competitors, such as Digital Equipment Corporation, were long established companies, with substantially greater resources than General Concepts. There were, however, also a number of competitors smaller than General Concepts. Since small and medium scale general purpose digital computers were usually sold outright rather than leased, manufacturers were attracted by the relative ease of entry into this market segment compared to large computers where leasing terms required substantial financial resources on the part of the seller. Despite this tough competitive climate, and without benefit of exact industry statistics, General Concepts' management felt the company was one of the major manufacturers of small and medium scale general purpose digital computers for industrial and scientific applications. By the end of fiscal year 1976, a total of 33,900 units had been shipped to customers, compared with 3150 units just four years ago.

PRODUCT LINES

The company's product line consists of three basic segments: central processors, software, and peripheral equipment.

Central processors were marketed under the trademarks of *Orion, MicroOrion,* and *Satellite.* From a design point of view, all *Orion* line computers used the same central processor and peripheral equipment, although performance and price of each model was different. All *Orion* computers were 16-bit binary computers using medium and large-scale integration, with four accumulators,

EXHIBIT 1 ● Financial Summary (In Thousands of Dollars)

	1976	1975	1974	1973	1972	1971	1970	1969
Expenditures for property, plant, and equipment	15,277	7,344	6,458	6,674	3,897	770	456	102
Current assets	137,523	102,865	61,137	41,227	30,232	23,020	5,225	854
Current liabilities	50,337	25,721	26,595	14,152	7,600	2,677	1,175	523
Working capital	87,186	77,144	34,542	27,075	22,632	20,343	4,050	331
Stockholders' equity	114,787	92,224	48,809	37,245	27,080	21,446	4,377	429
Per share data: Outstanding shares (000)	9,839	8,787	8,386	8,421	7,980	6,976	5,946	4,841
Net income	$2.11	1.53	1.21	.81	.49	.22	.11	(.06)
Return on average assets	14.4%	13.6%	16.0%	15.4%				
Return on average equity	20.1%	19.1%	23.5%	20.8%				
Cumulative computers shipped	33,900	25,500	19,300	11,000	4,170	1,710	690	110
Employees at year end	6,190	3,610	3,650	1,910	840	480	240	90

Fiscal Year Ended (In Thousands of Dollars)

	1977 (estimate)	1976	1975	1974	1973	1972	1971	1970	1969
Net Sales	250,000	180,000	119,611	92,952	59,558	30,324	15,341	7,035	2,000
Costs and Expenses		141,104	94,659	73,910	47,491				
Income from Operations		37,649	24,952	19,042	12,067	3,897	1,561	433	(300)
Other Income, principally interest		2,832	1,368	889	1,145			200	32
Interest Expense		(406)	(365)	(437)	(141)				
Income before Income Taxes		40,075	25,955	19,494	13,071				
Provisions for Income Taxes		19,295	12,479	9,368	6,220				
Net Income		22,780	13,476	10,126	6,851	3,897	1,561	633	(268)

EXHIBIT 2 ● Consolidated Balance Sheet

	September 25, 1976
ASSETS	
Current assets:	
Cash	$ 597,000
Short-term investments, at cost and accrued interest which approximates market	35,716,000
Accounts receivable, less allowance for doubtful accounts of $2,500,000 in 1977 and $2,200,000 in 1976	46,853,000
Inventories	54,009,000
Prepaid expenses	348,000
Total current assets	137,523,000
Property, plant and equipment, at cost	39,676,000
Less accumulated depreciation	12,075,000
Total property, plant and equipment, net	27,601,000
	$165,124,000
LIABILITIES AND STOCKHOLDERS' EQUITY	
Current liabilities:	
Notes payable, including accrued interest	$ 5,466,000
Accounts payable	19,576,000
Accrued payroll and commissions	2,685,000
Federal, state and foreign income taxes	15,665,000
Deferred income taxes	4,515,000
Other accrued expenses	2,430,000
Total current liabilities	50,337,000
Stockholders' equity:	
Common stock, $.01 par value:	
Authorized—20,000,000 shares	
Issued—	
9,574,000 shares at September 24, 1977	
9,474,000 shares at September 25, 1976	95,000
Capital in excess of par value	58,245,000
Retained earnings	56,488,000
	114,828,000
Less: Treasury stock at cost (48,000 shares)	1,000
Note receivable from sale of stock	40,000
Deferred compensation	—
Total stockholders' equity	114,787,000
	$165,124,000

EXHIBIT 3 ● Chart of Computer Families

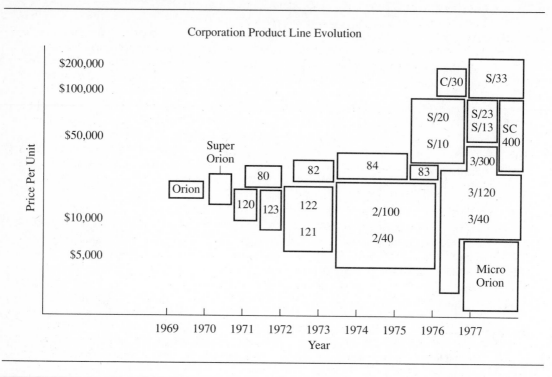

Corporation Product Line Evolution

two of which could be used as index registers. Parts, service, and additional equipment for old and new models were continuously kept available. *Orion* computers were mostly sold to Original Equipment Manufacturers (OEMs) to be added to machines or systems for controlling discrete assembly line operations, monitoring continuous production processes, testing, production planning, inventory management, and environmental surveillance. Furthermore, *Orion* computers had been successfully employed in scientific and engineering problem solving, medical and scientific laboratory analysis, and education. Orion models were marketed under model number Orion 120/121/122, Orion 80/82, Orion 84, ORION 2, ORION 83, ORION 3/300 and SC/400 (see Exhibit 3).

As a more powerful extension of the Orion models, the *SATELLITE* line was developed in 1975. The three models S/10, S/20, and C/30 were aimed at large and complex applications in both general scientific and business operations. For this latter segment, the C/30 was equipped with a commercial instruction set, Report Generating Program, and a data file management system. Within the first 12 months of introduction, over 1000 SATELLITE systems had been installed at an average value of about $60,000 per system.

The *MicroORION,* introduced in 1976, was a family of microprocessors, but also available as a fully equipped computer with software and peripheral equipment.

General Concepts also marketed a number of peripheral equipment to satisfy the needs of clients who preferred to purchase systems as complete packages. Produced and sold were teletypewriters, paper tape readers and punches, cathode ray tube terminals, magnetic disc memories, magnetic tape equipment, line printers, plotters, card readers, communications controllers, multiplexors, and analog-to-digital as well as digital-to-analog converters.

In conjunction with its central processors, General Concepts developed and offered an extensive list of *software products* to be used with its ORION, SATELLITE, and microORION lines. Such software systems could be sought on a prepared basis, or if contracted by the customer, developed to fit special needs.

Not yet on sale, but planned for introduction within the next few months, was a new family of small business computers, the SC/400 family. The product family was designed for business information processing for small to medium sized companies with sales ranging from $500,000 to $20 million. Also, the SC/400 computers could be used by departments or regional offices at large corporations as part of a distributed processing network. Operated on a transaction-by-transaction basis rather than batch process, and with as many as 9 stations operating simultaneously and independently, the system offered advantages not presently available in other small business systems. The SC/400 family, made up of three models, was priced from $30,000 to $90,000 per system.

SALES AND DISTRIBUTION

While manufacturers of large computer systems, such as IBM, sold their products directly to end users, small computers were generally sold through intermediaries. General Concepts was typical of such small computer manufacturers selling about 30 percent of its products directly to end users and 70 percent through 4 major types of intermediaries: Original Equipment Manufacturers (OEMs), systems integrators, industrial distributors, and retail stores or dealers (see Exhibit 4).

Direct sales were made by more than 420 sales engineers and 220 systems engineers operating from various sales offices in the United States and abroad. With the increase in direct sales activities, General Concepts developed a more specialized sales force such as for micro products, technical systems, or commercial systems. In some cases, sales representatives were targeted at special industry segments such as medicine, banking, or government.

OEMs had long been the most important segment for small computer manufacturers. These companies combined computer hardware (central processors, terminals, storage equipment, etc.) with other equipment to produce products such as electronic cash registers, body scanning equipment, microfiche developers, or numerically controlled machine tools to be sold under the OEMs' own name. The small computer was actually "buried" inside the OEMs' product. In many instances, the end user of the product was not aware of the supplier of the computer portion contained in the end product.

Systems Integrators (SIs) and Small Business Systems Suppliers formed the fastest growing segment in the distribution of small computers. Unlike OEMs, SIs bought their computers already assembled into a system from a single computer vendor, such as General Concepts. SIs added value to the product they resold in the form of application software designed to do a specific job: inventory control, order entry, accounting, etc. Many SIs were originally service bureaus that had accepted data processing work for clients who had insufficient in-house information processing capacity or capabilities. Some SIs also offered installation assistance, diagnostic help, and field maintenance. Since the demand for application software and support had exceeded the capabilities of both the traditional and minicomputer vendors, this segment could be expected to continue its rapid development and growth.

Industrial Distributors were an important distribution channel for all those computer products sold in large numbers approaching the sale of a commodity. Microprocessors (also called computer on a chip) or operator terminals were bought by users on that basis as components for their own products. The strength of the industrial distributor was to offer an immediate local supply of the components to the OEMs.

Retail distributors formed the latest distribution segment. The "computer store" displayed small computer systems or microprocessors of several manufacturers for purchase by individu-

EXHIBIT 4 ● Channels of Distribution

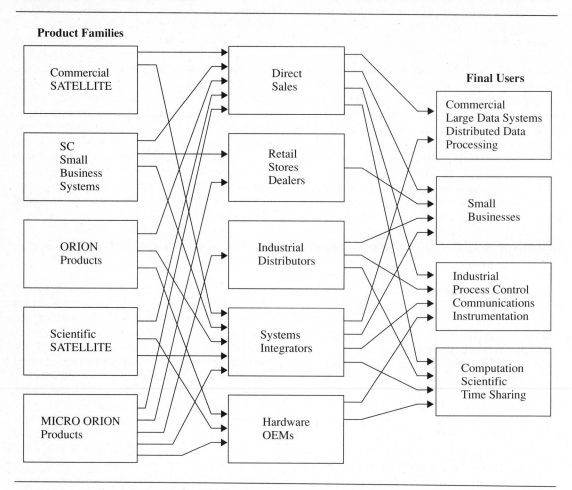

As can be seen in the graph above, while sale of computers directly to users by General Concepts has increased substantially the systems integrators, distributors, and retail channels have become increasingly important. Many of the product and service departments described in this section should stimulate this rapid growth further in the year ahead.

als. Originally frequented by hobbyists, computer stores increasingly served small businesses by assisting them in selecting computers on the basis of ease-of-use, pricing, and overall capability.

Service and maintenance of General Concepts' products was supported by about 800 field engineers, both to fulfill product warranty service and to service installed machines on a service contract basis.

GC'S ADVERTISING STRATEGY

GC's communication strategy was dominated by the existence of three primary customer groups:

OEMs, Systems Houses, and Direct End-Users. GC's advertising was primarily directed at this latter group, the clients that bought GC equipment directly from the manufacturer and, to a smaller degree, from Systems Houses. These customers again could be divided into two main user groups: clients for business data service processing and clients who used GC products primarily for science, industrial computing, and process control of manufacturing operations. GC had to communicate its products' features to these prospective clients.

GC believed that there was a difference in target group for computers for business use vs. scientific or manufacturing control use. The main target group for computers with application for business data processing were corporate managers, particularly presidents, VP of finance, and chief operating officers, in addition to data processing executives. The important aspect was to justify a choice of acquiring little known GC computers instead of machines manufactured by larger main frame companies such as IBM, Honeywell, etc. GC's strategy was to reduce the risk as perceived by company executives for such a decision by using a message that was essentially non-technical. This approach was selected since non-technical executives, or generalists, had to make a technical, or data processing, decision with little knowledge of the hardware aspects of the computers to be chosen.

GC therefore occupied the position of a newcomer or outsider in the market for small computers. To compete against its better known competitors such as Digital Equipment Company or Hewlett-Packard, GC selected a communications strategy that depicted the company as unique, often bizarre, a company with a chip on its shoulder, using advertising copy that paid little attention to plain facts. Recognizing that technical or line managers paid greater attention to the products themselves whereas corporate officers were primarily risk averse, GC often chose testimonials of successful applications of its computers as a basis for its message development.

With respect to the scientific and industrial applications, corporate managers were involved to a lesser extent. Technical managers such as manufacturing managers, research directors, se-

nior systems engineers, and scientists had a somewhat greater influence on the selection process. These technical managers were more likely to select a piece of equipment on its technical merit alone. As a result, technical or product oriented copy played a somewhat larger role for this market segment than for business data processing applications.

GC advertising in the United States was almost exclusively in print. Due to the fact that corporate management was the primary audience, about 75 percent of the advertising expenditures was concentrated on the *Wall Street Journal* and *Business Week*. Additional space was bought in other leading executive magazines such as *Forbes, Dun's,* and *Fortune.*

GENERAL CONCEPTS' INTERNATIONAL OPERATIONS

From its early existence, General Concepts had been selling abroad. Total international sales as a percent of total corporate sales grew from 23 percent in 1971 to 41 percent in 1976. This rapid growth brought about the formation of many subsidiaries, particularly in Europe, and the establishment of production units in South Korea and Hong Kong. General Concepts' international sales developed as follows for 1971–1977.

	Sales in dollars	Percentage of consolidated sales
1971	$ 3.4M	23%
1972	7.8	26
1973	17.2	29
1974	25.1	27
1975	42.8	39
1976	72.3	41
1977 (est.)	80.0	—

General Concepts had 17 wholly owned foreign sales subsidiaries and two production subsidiaries. Aside from European sales subsidiaries, General Concepts maintained subsidiaries in Canada, Australia, New Zealand, Brazil, Venezuela, and Israel. Japan was served through a licensing agreement with Nippon Computer Corp. since 1971. Whenever new products were introduced, they were made available to all the sales subsidiaries simultaneously, both in the U.S. and abroad.

GENERAL CONCEPTS EUROPEAN OPERATIONS

General Concepts maintained 11 wholly owned sales subsidiaries in each of the following countries.

	Year Formed
United Kingdom	1971
Germany	1971
Spain	1971
France	1972
Netherlands	1972
Austria	1972
Italy	1973
Sweden	1974
Switzerland	1974
Denmark	1975
Belgium	1975

European sales had shown the same rapid development as sales in the domestic market or other international sales, quickly growing from about 1 million dollars or 7% of corporate sales in 1971 to about 50 million dollars or about 30 percent of corporate sales in 1976. In general, European area sales represented 70 percent of General Concepts' international sales. The bulk of these European sales was accounted for by the subsidiaries in the U.K., Germany, and Spain, in that order of importance.

As a result of General Concepts' rapid growth in Europe, several changes in its operational set-up had to be made. The most important move came in 1972 when General Concepts consolidated under the direction of Jack Bailey, since succeeded by Steve Blair, all its European subsidiaries into General Concepts Europe, Inc., with operations headquartered in Paris. Blair, Vice-President Europe for General Concepts, controlled the European subsidiaries through four area managers, each of whom had three to four subsidiaries assigned. A specialized group of staff personnel was maintained at the office of General Concepts Europe in Paris. (See Exhibit 5.)

The managers of the local subsidiaries maintained a considerable degree of autonomy over their operations inasmuch as each subsidiary was a separate profit center. In line with their P&L responsibility, subsidiary managers decided which products to carry in their product line, and how to budget for their marketing expenditures, including advertising.

INTERNATIONAL ADVERTISING AT GENERAL CONCEPTS THROUGH 1976

In its early stages of market development, all advertising for Europe was done in the United States by Henderson, Sloan, Williams, Inc., New York, one of the leading advertising agencies in the United States. Henderson also made all media purchases in New York. With the formation of General Concepts Europe in 1972, the newly appointed Vice President Europe had a communications manager reporting to himself, located in Paris. This communications manager also worked on PR assignments. Essentially, all creative work, however, was done by Henderson and then sent to Europe. No clearcut advertising policy existed, and Europe's largest subsidiary, General Concepts Limited in the United Kingdom, had about 10 advertisements produced locally by a small technically oriented advertising agency.

In 1973, Edwards was hired as Director, Corporate Communications. During his first trip to Paris that same year, Edwards hired Alain Ray to fill the recently vacated position of communications manager. Ray had come to General Con-

EXHIBIT 5 ● Organization Chart

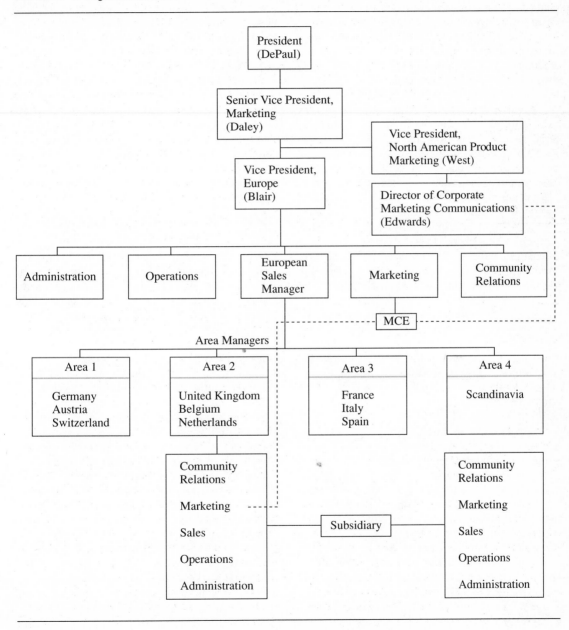

cepts from Hewlett-Packard's European head-quarters in Geneva, Switzerland.

While in Paris, Edwards made a number of changes in the reporting structure as well. He decided to centralize all advertising for Europe under Ray. Each major subsidiary hired its own marketing communications expert, called MCE, responsible to Ray in Paris who in turn reported directly to Edwards in General Concepts' headquarters in Connecticut.

Creative work continued to be done by Henderson in New York for the U.S. market. This material was sent to Ray in Paris, who, together with his MCEs for the various countries, made suggestions as to how the advertising could be adapted to each individual market. All space purchased for print media continued to be handled in New York by Henderson, Sloan, Williams.

In 1973, Henderson introduced an independent agency "network" to better control the series of changes made in the various countries' advertising. These agencies, selected by Henderson in Germany, Spain, and the United Kingdom, allowed the adaptations to be made with the same degree of continuity or oneness throughout all markets but with changes for each local market as needed. This additional measure of decentralization was felt necessary to allow local changes while continuing to project the same image in all European countries. So by 1974, Ray had about 7 MCEs reporting to himself, but continued to report to Edwards.

In 1975, two important events substantially affected General Concepts' approach to international advertising. First, Edwards left the company (to return about two years later to assume the same position). In the same year still, Henderson, Sloan, Williams, General Concepts' advertising agency for several years, was fired and the account was assigned to Nazzaro Associates, Inc., in Los Angeles, with E. Richard Steele as Account Executive. Since Nazzaro was not asked initially to handle European advertising, Ray at General Concepts Europe assumed greater control continuing to work with each local agency. Local subsidiaries were allowed to appoint and/or continue with their own local advertising agencies to either

adapt U.S. creative work from Nazzaro's or to create their own material. Only after the creation of the advertising did it have to be submitted to Ray in Paris. As a result, General Concepts' advertising began to assume a different look in each country with Nazzaro in Los Angeles essentially used for General Concepts' North American business only. By 1976, General Concepts Europe had, in the eyes of the U.S. parent company, become sufficiently mature to handle its advertising more independently. As a result, Ray reported now directly to the new V.P. in Europe, Larry J. Bailey. Any adaptations made in Europe were only checked by William P. Edwards who had returned to General Concepts in 1977, with the title of Corporate Director of Marketing Communications.

PROBLEMS WITH GENERAL CONCEPTS' EUROPEAN ADVERTISING

Ever since its entry into the European market General Concepts had to face situations that at times differed significantly from its U.S. environment. General Concepts' approach of being unique, at times even bizarre, led to the creation of advertisements that in the eyes of General Concepts' European subsidiaries were ill suited for their markets and could not be adapted.

General Concepts had experienced three basic difficulties with the extension of all its ads to Europe. First, General Concepts in the United States used minority groups in its advertisements. European subsidiaries were opposed to using such pictures with minority members on the grounds that Europeans could not identify with black computer specialists since many companies had no blacks in such positions. Secondly, the direct naming of a competitor, a practice often used by General Concepts, was only accepted in the United Kingdom and against the law in most other countries. For all other European subsidiaries a different message had to be created. And finally the sweepstake campaigns so successful in the United States were outlawed in many European countries, Germany among them, and were eventually only instituted in the United Kingdom and Sweden.

The difficulty of General Concepts' advertising situation was best expressed by three very successful U.S. ads that all were either substantially changed or not run at all in Europe. General Concept used one ad with "Hillbillies" capitalizing on the wide knowledge and positive general attitude towards such persons in the United States. However, when General Concepts tried to run the same ad in Europe its subsidiaries objected since such "Hillbillies" did not exist as a separate identifiable group in Europe nor was there an appropriate concept to express it therefore completely losing the desirable message of the ad.

A similar reaction was found towards General Concepts' "Redneck" ad depicting General Concepts' computers as breaking the speed barrier without paying the price. Hence identification with the "Redneck" sheriff as a folk hero. But this image did not exist in Europe, and the ad would have lost its punch line. Furthermore, the Italian subsidiary objected since in Italy nobody wearing a uniform, either police, military or otherwise, could be depicted in advertising. And one ad, showing a picture of a man hanging by his thumbs to visualize the result of "One test of a computer company is the kind of support you get after the sale," was rejected by General Concepts' German subsidiary since the meaning of the ad conveyed a sense of terrorism in Germany. Another successful U.S. ad with the slogan "With some computer companies you can end up paying for more company than computer," showed a steak with a lot of fat indicating the overhead associated with General Concepts' bigger competitors. However, when translating the message for German customers, the meaning communicated by the picture turned out to be just the opposite one, since the steak with fat had a positive connotation to Germans. And finally, General Concepts had some problems with the ad "When your business expands and your computer can't, where does that leave you?" combined with the picture of a single hand holding a bag. In the United Kingdom, the same meaning was expressed by the phrase "don't get left holding the baby" while in France the expression centered around "being in a basket of crabs."

In general, General Concepts' creative philosophy did not always translate very well since the U.S. idiom both in terms of copy and visual could not be extended abroad. These problems were most extreme with Germany, somewhat less with Italy and France, while both Scandinavia and particularly the United Kingdom offered greater opportunities for General Concepts' U.S. approach.

An additional problem was created by General Concepts' U.S. advertising emphasizing products only and therefore not developing any company image ads as requested by its subsidiaries. Since in many European countries General Concepts was not very well known, some subsidiaries, notably the Italian unit, were authorized to create special advertisements to improve their markets' awareness of General Concepts, as a small computer manufacturer. In 1976, Nazzaro had recommended that each area develop testimonial ads for its area. That program was ongoing and apparently successful.

ALTERNATIVES TO GENERAL CONCEPTS' APPROACH TO ADVERTISING IN EUROPE

Upon his return to General Concepts, Edwards and Nazzaro felt that General Concepts' advertising in Europe had to be revised to follow general corporate philosophy and present a uniform image to all customers, both domestic and foreign. Over the last two years, General Concepts' advertising in the various European countries had become fragmented and did not offer the uniform image it once had.

General Concepts aimed at presenting a unified look to all its customers all over the world, and this goal was presently not achieved in Europe. This desire for a unified look had already resulted in a corporate identity program to cover the corporate mark, stationery, business cards, printed sales promotion material, personal identifications, product identification, and signage. The program was put forward in a manual with a cover letter written by DePaul, General Concepts' President (see Exhibit 6). The program did not pertain to the company's worldwide advertising effort. Furthermore, Edwards felt he lacked leverage with

EXHIBIT 6 ●

A CORPORATE IDENTITY PROGRAM
FOR GENERAL CONCEPTS CORPORATION

General Concepts is one of the world's fastest growing organizations, in one of the fastest growing industries.

As we continue to expand worldwide, it is essential that the company maintain a clear and consistent visual identity with customers, employees, and other important audiences.

The enclosed is an interim guideline that covers the major aspects of General Concepts' corporate identity program.

The elements of the program reflect the "face" of the company—progressive, experimental, innovative, fast moving.

Through these elements, we hope to create a thread of graphic continuity woven into our worldwide corporate identity program in all areas whether it be brochure, sending a bill, plus all of the numerous other ways you influence and communicate with our public.

I urge everyone to use this manual as the standard for corporate identity.

Robert DePaul
President

Ray reporting to Blair to exercise any kind of control or influence over Europe's advertising. While the mechanics of the advertising side were well taken care of, General Concepts Europe depended largely on these small local agencies for creative input as well as for marketing expertise.

In Edwards' view, leverage, mechanics, creative input, and marketing expertise combined with people relationships among different ad agencies and subsidiaries substantially affected productivity and advertising quality. Since the subsidiaries had selected their own agencies, people relationships were likely to be good. However, Edwards believed that without additional control he could not significantly influence the European subsidiaries' advertising approach. In his words, "control does not necessarily mean direct control. It means a method to project a better understand-

ing of what General Concepts wants in all of its communication endeavors."

As he approached the decision, Edwards believed he had four basic alternatives to improve General Concepts' present set-up in Europe: (a) assign authority to Nazzaro Associates for both domestic and European advertising; (b) have General Concepts create a "network" of European different advertising agencies selected by Edwards for better control and assigned to each subsidiary; (c) keep present European agencies but coordinate their efforts through General Concepts in Southern California; and finally (d) assign the creative strategy and execution of the international advertising program to a large New York agency with its own network of international affiliates in place.

At about the same time as Edwards was reviewing his alternatives in Europe, Nazzaro Associates also became dissatisfied with General Concepts' setup and proposed its own solution to the problem. Nazzaro wanted the responsibility to create advertising for General Concepts' domestic and international business which meant that it was Nazzaro who supplied the creative work for all General Concepts ads. However, Nazzaro did not have any foreign affiliates to carry out this proposal on its own. To compensate for this lack of foreign contacts, Steele proposed that Nazzaro affiliate with Ed Hopkins Europe, a large and well known international advertising agency headquartered in New York, who would supply the foreign expertise to Nazzaro. Ed Hopkins had its European headquarters in Paris and subsidiaries in European countries where General Concepts' own subsidiaries were located. Under Steele's plan, Nazzaro would supply drafts of all creative work to Ed Hopkins in Paris. Ed Hopkins' people would review the potential need for changes by contacting their own locally affiliated agencies who would discuss each proposed advertisement with General Concepts' local MCEs. The reviewed proposals would then be returned to Nazzaro with any changes indicated. Proposed concept changes would also be added. The final result would be advertising concepts and copy that could be adopted by all subsidiaries with only local translation done under the supervision of the local Ed Hopkins affiliate. Advertising media space would be purchased by Ed Hopkins Europe under coordination with local subsidiaries.

Of course, as an alternative General Concepts could create its own network of affiliated advertising agencies. Such a network would be coordinated through General Concepts Europe in Paris. General Concepts would select in each country an appropriate agency who would be assigned to work with its local subsidiary. Nazzaro creative work would be circulated to each advertising agency who would discuss the proposal with its assigned General Concepts subsidiary and review the creative necessary changes. These comments would be sent to John Clarke, (who reported to Ray) at General Concepts Europe who in turn would confer with Richard Steele at Nazzaro. Ed-

wards believed it would not be easy to select good agencies in each country. At the present time, he had no particular agencies in mind. Besides, Nazzaro had worked with the present network and found it wholly lacking. In production requirements alone (film screens for publication, etc.) the problems were monumental when you added the language barrier and the constant need to convert to metric measures.

A third alternative for Edwards was to work with those agencies already selected by each subsidiary but to attempt to control their creative output. He felt that if each agency were required to execute its creative work locally under the guidance of General Concepts' general advertising directives, and if each agency were required to submit all creative to General Concepts Southern California office for approval, some measure of common approach to General Concepts' image in Europe could be achieved. In fact, it would be up to Edwards and his office to coordinate Nazzaro creative strategy with the proposals from Europe to provide for the common image desired by General Concepts.

A fourth alternative available to Edwards was the selection of a large New York based advertising agency with good connections in Europe through either affiliates or subsidiaries. This agency would be given authority to execute General Concepts' advertising strategy outside the U.S. based upon Nazzaro's initial creative proposals. This move meant to revert to the pre-1974/75 policy. While no serious discussions had taken place, Edwards thought that Marsteller might be a possibility to take charge under this alternative.

POTENTIAL REACTION BY AFFECTED PARTIES

In Edwards' view, all four alternative proposals reflected a considerable improvement over status quo. The adaptation of any of the alternatives would present General Concepts with additional leverage over the execution of its advertising in Europe, improve the creative input, and add some additional marketing expertise for the subsidiaries. While all four alternatives increased General

Concepts' control over its European advertising, the four proposals of course did so to varying degrees, with Nazzaro's alternative or the big New York agency approach to be favored over the other alternatives.

An important consideration was also the views and possible reaction among General Concepts' European subsidiaries. Edwards knew that personal chemistry played a very important role in advertising and that the imposition of any agency selection in General Concepts' local subsidiaries might create tensions along that way. If the four proposals were presented to the subsidiaries for a free vote, he was convinced that the subsidiaries would prefer to continue to work with their own agencies over any other choice.

Edwards knew it was up to him to determine the direction of General Concepts' advertising approach in Europe. With present European measured media expenditures for 1977 at $500,000 and European budget expenditures for the next fiscal year of about $700,000, he was determined to reach a decision that could be acceptable to most parties concerned.

CASE 12

Puritan-Bennett Corporation Boston Division

As he stepped into the elevator at the Skyline Hotel in London, John Sweeney, Vice President and General Manager of the Boston Division of Puritan-Bennett Corporation, reflected on his problems and frustrations with the British market. He had been with Ray Oglethorpe, Vice President for Sales and Marketing, and Bob Taylor, Vice President for International Operations, since early morning. It was a typical day for London in late November of 1983. They had been trying to determine the best distribution for Puritan-Bennett medical products in Europe for next year. John Sweeney suspected that some parent company current channels did not meet Division needs.

Earlier that day they had met with Adamson and Carr Ltd., Puritan-Bennett's British distributor, to discuss plans and forecasts for Division and corporate product lines. The three vice presidents had then reviewed the situation in the United Kingdom and the rest of Europe.

PURITAN-BENNETT CORPORATION

Puritan-Bennett Corporation was founded in 1913 as the Puritan Company, a welding supply

●

This case was prepared by Susan Nye under the direction of Visiting Professor Jean-Pierre Jeannet as a basis for class discussion rather than to illustrate either effective or ineffective handling of an administrative situation. Copyright © 1984 by IMEDE Lausanne, Switzerland. The International Institute for Management Development (IMD), resulting from the merger between IMEDE, Lausanne, and IMI, Geneva, acquires and retains all rights. Reproduced by permission.

manufacturer and distributor. The company emphasized the manufacture and supply of medical gas and equipment. It had pioneered development of oxygen as a medicinal agent. The company manufactured and sold three product lines: medical, aviation, and industrial, with medical products accounting for the largest percentage of sales (Exhibit 1).

In 1956, acquisition of the Bennett Company accelerated corporate growth in the United States and abroad. The company, now known as Puritan-Bennett, had sales offices worldwide for medical, aviation, and industrial product lines. Expansion continued in the late 1970's and early 1980's through acquisition and research and development. In 1978 the medical line was extended by purchase of the Foregger Company, a manufacturer of operating room equipment. The Boston Division was acquired in 1981 (Exhibit 2).

DEVELOPMENT OF THE BOSTON DIVISION

In 1978, John Sweeney acquired the assets of a bankrupt company and started LSE Corporation. The firm initially employed a total of four people, including Sweeney. LSE had a small manufacturing facility. Included in the purchase was a line of screening spirometers in process of development. The company specialized in developing and selling a full line of spirometers, used in doctors' offices and industrial clinics as screening devices to diagnose lung dysfunction (Exhibit 3). Until this time most spirometry had been done in hospitals. While the test took only a few minutes of a patient's time, evaluation of test results was time-consuming (about 30 minutes) and cumbersome.

EXHIBIT 1 ● Five-Year Financial Summary, Corporate and Subsidiaries

(All dollar amounts in thousands, except common share data and number of employees)	1983	1982	1981	1980	1979
Operating Results					
Net Sales					
Bennett Division	$ 48,525	$ 47,505	$ 53,382	$ 47,464	40,817
Puritan Division	37,944	35,859	33,889	29,431	26,903
Boston Division	5,614	5,208	1,282	—	—
Total Medical	92,083	88,572	88,553	76,895	67,720
Aviation Division	12,772	14,161	18,437	17,863	14,764
Industrial Division	4,890	4,424	5,562	5,361	5,262
Total Net Sales	109,745	107,157	112,552	100,119	87,746
Gross Profit	45,551	40,757	47,748	38,910	34,289
Percent of Sales	41.5%	38.0%	42.4%	38.9%	39.1%
Marketing, Research & Administrative Expense	41,348	40,877	37,401	30,517	26,425
Operating Profit (Loss)	4,203	(120)	10,347	8,393	7,864
Other Income (Expense)	(407)	(6,551)	540	20	(81)
Income (Loss) Before Income Taxes	3,796	(6,671)	10,887	8,413	7,783
Percent of Sales	3.4%	—	9.7%	8.4%	8.9%
Provision for (Benefit from) Income Taxes	1,220	(4,412)	4,335	3,628	3,118
Effective Tax Rate	32.1%	66.1%	39.8%	43.1%	40.1%
Net Income (Loss)	2,576	(2,259)	6,552	4,785	4,665
Percent of Sales	2.3%	—	5.8%	4.8%	5.3%
Financial Data					
Net Working Capital	$ 39,126	$ 36,037	$ 39,079	$ 37,789	$ 34,761
Current Radio	2.5	3.3	3.9	4.6	4.3
Long-Term Debt	9,131	6,089	7,599	7,327	8,813
Debt/Equity Ratio	13.0%	9.4%	10.9%	11.5%	14.3%
Stockholders' Equity	60,922	58,622	61,932	56,464	52,805
Return on Average Stockholders' Equity	4.3%	—	11.1%	8.8%	9.1%
Common Share Data					
Earnings (Loss)	$ .87	$ (.78)	$ 2.27	$1.66	$ 1.62
Dividends Declared	.40	.40	.40	.40	.40
Net Book Value	20.62	20.28	21.45	19.62	18.37
Average Number of Shares Outstanding	2,947,652	2,889,444	2,883,588	2,876,471	2,873,084
Other Data					
Depreciation and Amortization	$ 4,677	$ 4,865	$ 4,672	$ 4,197	$ 4,305
Capital Expenditures	7,287	6,415	7,057	3,933	4,851
Plant and Equipment, Net	30,710	27,996	28,666	26,682	27,087
Total Assets	99,894	83,204	86,241	77,015	74,479
Number of Employees	1,893	1,869	2,080	1,978	1,837

EXHIBIT 2 ● Corporate Organization Chart

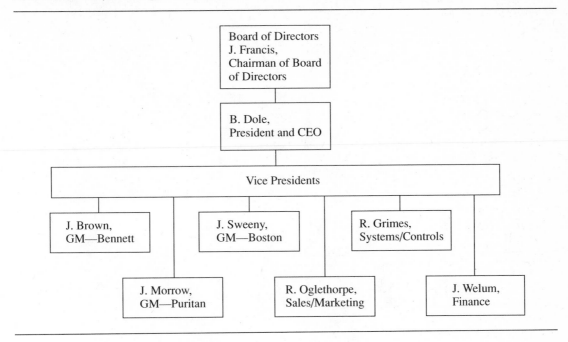

When a physician suspected a patient might be suffering from COPD (Chronic Obstructive Pulmonary Disease), he or she would recommend the patient be tested at a hospital.

A pioneer in the field, LSE offered within three years a broad range of microprocessing spirometers which allowed a doctor or nurse to evaluate test results in only five minutes. Improvements in technology led to a competitive price. In 1979 the top-of-the-line spirometer sold for $7,000 in the United States, and in 1981 for $4,500. John Sweeney's small company had grown to $3 million in sales and to an approximate 30 percent market share in the United States.

Puritan-Bennett acquired LSE Corporation in 1981 as part of an expansion program to increase the number of product lines and to upgrade the level of its microprocessing technology. An innovator in microprocessing spirometers, LSE met the parent company's need. Shortly after the merger, the re-named Boston Division joined another Puritan-Bennett acquisition, a firm manufacturing noninvasive blood pressure monitors. Noninvasive blood pressure monitors measured blood pressure during surgery, during stress testing, and for chronically or critically ill patients (Exhibit 4). The newly organized Boston Division developed, coordinated, and manufactured spirometers and monitoring devices. Sales and responsibilities were divided between the Division, which sold to individual physicians, and the company, which sold to hospitals and clinics. The Boston Division manufactured all spirometers in-house. Some monitoring devices were assembled from a combination of in-house product parts and purchased components. Others were imported through an arrangement with a Finnish company.

The Boston Division had recently moved to a larger manufacturing and sales facility in Wilmington, Massachusetts. The Division employed seventy people to manufacture and sell spirome-

EXHIBIT 3 ● PS600 Spirometer

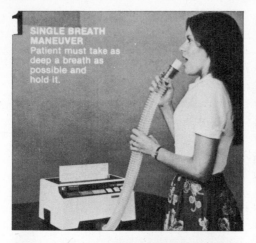

1 SINGLE BREATH MANEUVER
Patient must take as deep a breath as possible and hold it.

2 Place mouthpiece inside mouth with teeth on **outside** of barrel and seal lips tight...

3 Exhale the air as **forcefully** as possible from the beginning and keep exhaling until all the air is emptied out...

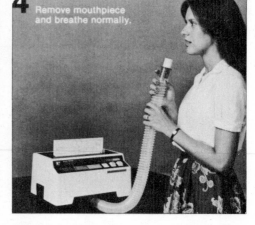

4 Remove mouthpiece and breathe normally.

MVV MANEUVER (Page 21 in Manual)

CAUTION: The MVV (Maximum Breathing Capacity) is a breathing stress test and should not be performed on patients with heart problems unless supervised by a physician.

1. Subject should take a deep breath before placing mouthpiece inside mouth with teeth on outside of barrel and lips sealed tight.

2. Instruct the subject to then breathe out and in as **rapidly** and **deeply** as possible.

3. Encourage the subject to continue to breathe in and out for a minimum of 10-12 seconds before telling them to stop.

FEF$_{25-75}$

This is the Forced Expiratory Flow during the middle 50% of the FVC curve.**

FEF$_{200-1200}$

This is the Forced Expiratory Flow between 0.2 liters and 1.2 liters.**

**If desired, this parameter may be calculated using the technique described on page 19 of the VS400 Operating Manual.*

 PURITAN-BENNETT CORPORATION

PURITAN-BENNETT CORPORATION OF MASSACHUSETTS
BOSTON DIVISION
265 BALLARDVALE STREET, WILMINGTON, MA 01887
(617) 657-8650 (800) 225-5344 TELEX 94-9467

EXHIBIT 4 ● D4000 Noninvasive Blood Pressure
Monitor

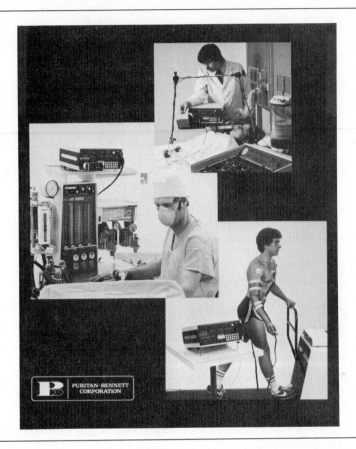

ters and other Division products. Three engineers researched and developed innovative pulmonary diagnostic and monitoring products.

The Boston Division was most closely aligned with the Bennett Division, one of several Puritan-Bennett units. The Bennett Division sold life supporting medical equipment, primarily ventilators, to hospitals. Ventilators assumed respiratory function, either short term for patients under anesthesia in the recovery room or in intensive care, or long term for terminally ill patients.

The Bennett Division had succeeded with its newest product, the 7200 Microprocesser Venti-lator, which had sold well in the United States since introduction in 1983. Benefits of the new product included increased breathing ease for the patient, better operator control over ventilatory parameters, and lower operating costs. Products were competitively priced in the United States at $10,000 to $12,000 (Exhibit 5).

BACKGROUND ON SPIROMETRY

Spirometers were used to measure lung capacity and to diagnose lung dysfunctions. Lung dysfunctions could be categorized as restrictive, reducing

EXHIBIT 5 ● 7200 Microprocessor Ventilator

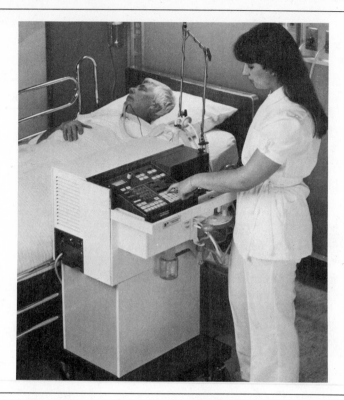

volume (vital lung capacity), or obstructive, reducing flow through the airways, or a combination of both.

Spirometers were used in early diagnosis of chronic obstructive pulmonary disease (COPD), the sixth leading cause of death in the United States in 1980. Grouped under COPD were bronchitis, asthma, and emphysema. Leading causes of COPD were smoking, air pollution, occupational pollution, infection, heredity, aging, and allergies.

As depicted in Exhibit 6, air initially enters the body through the nose and mouth, then passes through the pharynx, larynx, trachea, bronchi, and bronchioles. At the chest cavity the trachea branches into two bronchi. Each bronchus subdivides forming tiny tubes called bronchioles which open into small air sacks called alveoli. The alveoli

form clusters around the bronchioles and unite into lobes. Each alveolus contains a mesh-like network of capillaries, or tiny blood cells. The lungs carry oxygen to the body by the air passage to the thin walls of the alveoli. Blood then absorbs the oxygen. The average office worker inhales 400 cubic feet of air each day, and the body absorbs an average of 20 cubic feet of oxygen.

Spirometer manufacturers had benefited in 1979 when U.S. health officials mandated spirometry for certain high risk groups. High risk groups included textile industry employees exposed to cotton dust, miners susceptible to black lung, and asbestos industry employees. A voluntary medical group had determined standards for spirometry, and government regulations later incorporated these standards. Some spirometer manufacturers

EXHIBIT 6 ● The Respiratory System

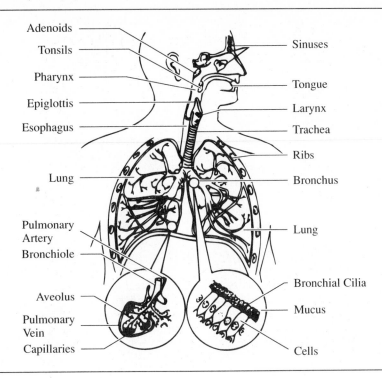

Adenoids

Tonsils

Pharynx

Epiglottis

Esophagus

Lung

Pulmonary
Artery

Bronchiole

Aveolus

Pulmonary
Vein

Capillaries

Sinuses

Tongue

Larynx

Trachea

Ribs

Bronchus

Lung

Bronchial Cilia

Mucus

Cells

---

were temporarily forced out of the market when their products failed to meet the new standards.

BOSTON DIVISION SPIROMETRY PRODUCT LINE

Puritan-Bennett spirometers analyzed volume displacement and rate of airflow. The VS400 and the PS600 measured the volume of air inspired and expired and calculated flow. The DS705 and the ES800 measured the flow of air expired and calculated volume based on expiration speed and time (Exhibit 7). To perform the test a patient inhaled deeply and exhaled forcefully into a tube connected to the spirometer. The test was repeated three times.

The VS400 and PS600 produced tracings of individual single breaths and maximum volun-

tary ventilation (MVV). While the VS400 still required hand calculations of pulmonary function parameters, the more advanced PS600 included a microprocessor to compute test results automatically. This innovation was considered key to the Division's continued growth. The Boston Divi-

EXHIBIT 7 ● Spirometers

sion was also working on an Apple software package allowing a physician to automate storage and retrieval of patient records on an Apple personal computer.

MONITORING PRODUCT LINE

Puritan-Bennett's Boston Division also manufactured monitors. Noninvasive blood pressure monitors were the only line of monitors produced in-house. Other monitors were imported from Europe for sale throughout the Western Hemisphere.

Blood pressure monitors measured the pressure blood exerted on arteries throughout the body. Blood pressure level depended on the rate of heart contraction, the amount of blood in the circulatory system, and the elasticity of arteries. Blood pressure was continuously monitored during surgery. Patients with chronic diseases and those convalescing from acute diseases also required monitoring. Serious illness and surgery could alter blood pressure and thus needed to be controlled. A regular part of health checks, blood pressure screenings were particularly important for older people because blood pressure may rise with age.

Blood pressure was measured by pumping air into a bag or cuff fastened around the arm. Inflation continued until blood flow stopped. This measure, called systolic pressure, represented blood pressure when the heart contracted. Pressure when the heart relaxed between beats was called diastolic pressure.

The Puritan-Bennett D4000 and D4001 monitors could be used anywhere in a hospital and provided automatic inflation and deflation. The devices employed a patented infrasonde technique to monitor blood pressure continuously. Digital display of the blood pressure reading facilitated use by physicians or nurses. The product was designed for continuous monitoring rather than one-time screening.

THE U.S. MARKET FOR SPIROMETERS

The Boston Division, particularly strong in the U.S., enjoyed a 25 percent market share. Spirometer sales had reached $4 million in 1983 and were expected to account for 50 percent of Boston Division sales in 1984. There were 467,000 practicing physicians in the U.S. Spirometers were used in doctors' offices, hospitals, and clinics. Boston Division strength lay in the doctors' office segment which included more than 100,000 physicians. The U.S. medical profession had begun to emphasize preventive health care, and John Sweeney believed that approximately 38 percent of practicing physicians could benefit from owning a spirometer. He estimated that only 30 percent of respiratory specialists or general practitioners currently employed spirometers in office. Spirometers were Puritan-Bennett's only medical product marketed to physicians' offices.

Physicians used spirometers primarily as a screening device. Lung screening was common in a variety of medical situations in the U.S. Hospital admissions, pre-operative checks, and annual checkups for senior citizens and smokers required lung screening as a part of regular test procedure. Many industries such as asbestos and mining regularly screened employees for lung dysfunction due to inhalation of dust or chemicals.

Most U.S. hospitals maintained respiratory therapy departments and pulmonary laboratories. Respiratory therapy departments treated lung problems early and monitored changes in patient progress during therapy. The spirometer was used for a five minute simple screening test of patients undergoing therapy before and after medication. The pulmonary laboratory evaluated chronically ill patients. Large pulmonary laboratory equipment cost from $50,000 to $75,000. Tests using such equipment were more extensive than those using spirometers and took longer to perform. The spirometer quickly screened large numbers of people, while the pulmonary laboratory equipment was used to evaluate treatment of patients identified as already having a lung dysfunction.

PURITAN-BENNETT CORPORATE MARKETING EFFORT IN THE U.S.

Puritan-Bennett employed 55 salespersons to sell medical products to all operating divisions of a hospital. This salesforce accounted for approximately $80 million in sales in 1983. Until 1983

Puritan-Bennett had sold through distributors in the U.S. market, with a trained salesforce giving missionary support for all product lines. In early 1983 Puritan-Bennett began to sell equipment directly to hospitals. The decision to develop a direct salesforce was based on two criteria. First, many distributors were not expanding sales volume according to company expectations. Second, the company expansion program was creating conflict. As Puritan-Bennett added new products to its line, it found that some dealers already carried similar competitive products. Furthermore, Puritan-Bennett's new technology for its 7200 microprocessing ventilator required extensive training for a highly technical sale. As the company continued to expand, these problems were expected to continue. Puritan-Bennett also used the cost savings on distribution margins to lower its prices. Selling costs now averaged 20 percent of sales.

BOSTON DIVISION U.S. MARKETING EFFORTS

Three segments composed Division spirometry sales: hospitals accounting for 20 percent of total volume, industry with 20 percent, and physicians with 60 percent. Hospital sales were made by Puritan-Bennett's corporate salesforce. The Boston Division had sole responsibility for marketing spirometers to private physicians and industrial users through 100 dealers. Most Division volume came from the top 40 percent of these dealers. Dealers ranged from highly specialized ones to others carrying a broad line of medical equipment, accessories, and disposables. The best distributors were specialized either by area of medical expertise, such as cardiac or respiratory, or by end-user, such as hospitals or physicians' offices. Dealers were supported by a ten person missionary salesforce reporting to the Division office in Wilmington, MA. Three area managers representing East, Central, and West regions reported to sales manager Bob Glinski. The missionary salesforce was divided among the three regions. Bob Conley, one of the original employees at LSE, acted as marketing manager. Sales were strong in regions of the U.S. where environmental or industrial influences created respiratory problems.

John Sweeney liked the combination of dealers and support sales staff and felt they had been key to Division success in the United States, particularly in the physician segment.

The physician's office spirometry market was still developing. The selling approach was less technical but required that the salesperson be able to stimulate primary demand by identifying potential users and key customers and by offering creative financial plans. Key customers were doctors or researchers who, through speeches and/or publications, were influential within their professions.

Monitor equipment sales were expected to grow to 50 percent of Division sales. Noninvasive blood pressure monitors were to account for one third of this volume. Noninvasive blood pressure monitors represented a rapidly growing market and required a highly technical sale. Unlike spirometers, monitors did not represent a new concept in medicine, but successful selling required a thorough technical understanding of the product. These products were sold directly to hospital users. John Sweeney estimated market share worldwide at 5 percent.

The United States represented about 50 percent of the world market for spirometers. Major industrial nations composed the remaining 50 percent. Sweeney estimated the spirometry market in Europe at $2.5 million, including hospital sales, which accounted for 80 percent of the spirometry market abroad.

Puritan-Bennett and the Boston Division sold medical products through dealers at 25 percent off list price. Division gross margin was 55 percent, with selling costs averaging 20 percent of sales.

BOSTON DIVISION INTERNATIONAL MARKETING EFFORT

John Sweeney believed that to survive in today's medical equipment industry a company must have an international sales base. The bankrupt company Sweeney acquired in 1978 had sold nearly $1 million in spirometers in Europe in 1977. Reorganization of that company into LSE Corporation had left ill feelings with its German distributor, prompting Sweeney to seek a new distribution network. In 1979 he visited trade shows and signed on new distributors.

In spite of John Sweeney's efforts, initial attempts at European sales for LSE were not successful. Sweeney feared the small size of his organization was a major drawback in dealing with European distributors. LSE merged with Puritan-Bennett in 1981, partially in the hope that as part of a larger company the new division would gain greater leverage with distributors. Continual spirometer improvements had been made, and Sweeney was convinced that spirometers would sell in the European market if distributors paid more attention to his products. Special sourcing was required, however, to overcome limitations caused by the relative strength of the U.S. dollar versus other currencies.

Marketing spirometers in Europe required changing electrical wires and switches and programming for "normal" reference values by country. These changes had already been made for the United Kingdom, and the Division was working on changes for other countries as well.

Whereas in Europe pulmonary laboratories existed for treatment of chronically ill patients, there were no respiratory therapy departments. Furthermore, little screening occurred for hospital admission and preparation for operations. Screening in physician offices was developing at a slower rate than in the United States. John Sweeney believed this market had potential. Rising cost of hospital care worldwide evoked interest in products for use in doctor's office or at home. European and Japanese participants at conventions of the American Lung Association, as well as other pulmonary specialists, voiced growing interest in nonhospital screening and treatment techniques.

PURITAN-BENNETT INTERNATIONAL SALES ORGANIZATION

Following the merger, the Boston Division depended upon Puritan-Bennett's international sales division for overseas sales.

The International Division channeled all sales through independent distributors. International sales reached $20 million in 1983. The vice president of international sales, Bob Taylor, was based at the head office in Kansas City. International operations were divided into three geographical areas. Les Fuller was area manager for Europe and the Middle East. The other divisions were Latin America, smallest of the three in terms of sales, and the Far East, largest in sales but employing fewer people than the European division.

There were three European area sales representatives. One representative based in Germany covered German speaking countries, including Germany, Austria, and Switzerland, as well as Eastern Europe. Another representative based in France covered France, Italy, Belgium, and Spain. A third representative in the United Kingdom covered the United Kingdom and Scandinavia. A fourth representative responded for the Middle East.

Puritan-Bennett had entered Europe before 1970 on an export basis. In the mid-1970s, the company had expanded its international commitment by forming a service organization in England. Puritan-Bennett's International Division had sold only ventilators, marketing directly to hospitals. Hospital doctors and nurses were the key decision makers in the purchase decision.

Puritan-Bennett U.K. Limited was the company's only wholly owned sales and distribution subsidiary. Based in Chichester, England, it imported and sold medical equipment to European distributors and performed technical service for distributors. Contact with end users was restricted to key customers or new product introductions. The U.K. Operation employed ten people.

In Europe, Puritan-Bennett's larger distributors carried a full line of medical equipment and supplies. Smaller distributors concentrated on a specific medical expertise. It was very difficult to find distributors which fit the entire product line but were not already carrying a competitor's product.

Spirometers were sold to Puritan-Bennett U.K. Ltd. at 25 percent off U.S. list price. Duty and freight added 11 percent to landed costs. Puritan-Bennett U.K. Ltd. used a markup of 20 percent. Average transportation costs of 10 percent within the European marketplace were paid by the final distributor. The local distributor expected a 50 percent markup on landed costs.

Stiff price competition threatened any U.S. company operating in Europe. The strong U.S. dollar, as well as transportation and tariff costs, made price competition difficult. Puritan-Bennett relied on technical superiority of its products. Continued strength of the U.S. dollar intensified the price differential between U.S. and European or Japanese products.

EXPERIENCE IN THE U.K.

Puritan-Bennett's U.K. distributor for 10 years, Adamson and Carr was owned by a larger firm which manufactured cardiac care equipment. Adamson and Carr distributed products not only for its parent company but also for other medical equipment manufacturers. Following their visit earlier this day, Sweeney, Taylor, and Oglethorpe worried about low 1984 forecasts for ventilators, projected by A&C at five to eight units. When pressured, A&C revised to 10 to 20 units, still far below the estimate of 50 to 100 units predicted for Germany by Puritan-Bennett's German distributor. John Sweeney believed that sales in the United Kingdom should be similar to those in Germany. Touring the A&C plant, Sweeney noticed what appeared to be inventory build-up of A&C parent company products. Parent company cardiac care equipment had an average price of $3,000 to $12,000.

With A&C, Puritan-Bennett benefited from an installed sales base. Sales management, sales training, order processing, accounting, and inventory management adequately met the needs of both Puritan-Bennett and A&C's parent.

The distributor employed twelve salespeople who had established key contacts at hospitals with recovery rooms (RR), intensive care units (ICU), and critical care units (CCU), all important in marketing A&C cardiac care line. These contacts provided access to anesthesiology departments which were major users of monitoring and support equipment.

A&C had recently sold few noninvasive blood pressure monitors or spirometers and hesi-tated to expand that part of its product line. Prior to this time, A&C had carried Vitalograph spirometers. Vitalograph, a major European competitor of Puritan-Bennett, had now decided to sell direct in the United Kingdom.

Under socialized medicine the government provided almost all health care. This meant that most testing and screening, including spirometry, was done in hospitals.

Previously the International Division had enjoyed good sales results with Bennett ventilators in the United Kingdom. Price increases and greater sophistication lowered late generation sales. The International Division had experienced similar distribution problems in other European countries. Ventilators sold well in the Middle East, Japan, and Germany. Sales in Spain were building, and sales in Italy held promise.

EXPERIENCE IN GERMANY

Strong ventilator sales in Germany had reached $3 million, 10 percent of U.S. sales. Puritan-Bennett Corporation used Carl A. Hoyer GmbH as its independent distributor. The International Division had enjoyed a good relationship with Hoyer for many years. Hoyer specialized in ventilation and respiratory products. Hoyer distributed for several companies, and Puritan-Bennett ventilator sales represented 50 percent of volume. Hoyer had a strong technical orientation and employed ten salespersons for Germany and Switzerland.

Hoyer was a good source of new product information for Puritan-Bennett. Because of their technical orientation, Hoyer salespeople helped Puritan-Bennett define new needs in the medical equipment market and identified new products in development by Puritan-Bennett competitors. Hoyer desired to expand its product line but only within the hospital segment. Already Hoyer carried a competitor's noninvasive blood pressure equipment. Germany had a large industrial base, making spirometry viable. Spirometry and blood pressure monitoring were both reimbursable through public and private health insurance programs.

The Puritan-Bennett U.K. subsidiary supported Hoyer activities. As in other European countries, this support included active missionary sales work. Puritan-Bennett participated in medical conventions, sponsored direct mailings, sought and referred dealer leads from other regions, and supported medical research using papers mentioning Puritan-Bennett products. Almost all missionary efforts in Europe centered on ventilators.

EXPERIENCE IN JAPAN

Amco Japan Ltd. was Puritan-Bennett's Japanese distributor. Amco Japan distributed throughout Japan, emphasizing high tech medical equipment. The medical equipment industry consisted of two segments: instruments and accessories or added features, and disposables. Disposables were those products which were consumed or would wear out and had to be thrown away. They included patient circuits, tubes, and mouthpieces. Amco Japan had emphasized technical equipment sales, featuring disposables and accessories as incremental business.

The Japanese distributor had no manufacturing facility. Amco Japan had begun with kidney dialysis equipment and broadened its product line to high tech medical equipment as the industry matured. Amco was second only to Hoyer in international sales volume for Puritan-Bennett. Twelve to fifteen salespeople, organized by specialty in terms of product function, called almost exclusively on hospitals. Amco Japan carried products from several different companies and desired to maintain a broad product line.

Most other Japanese distributors were large firms with internal specialization, either by end user or by area of medical specialty, such as respiratory or cardiac care.

Amco Japan was Boston Division's largest distributor of noninvasive blood pressure monitors. Introducing the Boston Division spirometer, Amco would face strong domestic competition. Heavy industry and heavy smoking habits created a viable market for spirometry, a reimbursable medical expense.

Bream headed sales for the Far East. The International Division maintained two offices to serve the Far East, one in Hong Kong and one on the U.S. West Coast. Puritan-Bennett had no representative based in Japan. Amco provided warehouses.

COMPETITION FOR VENTILATORS, SPIROMETERS, AND MONITORS

Puritan-Bennett was one of three leading competitors in the worldwide ventilation market. The others were Siemens and Bourns. Based in Germany, Siemens sold direct throughout Europe and the U.S. Bourns Ltd., a British company, sold its Bear ventilator direct in the U.S. and the U.K. Bourns was less active on the continent than Puritan-Bennett or Siemens.

Siemens ventilators had microprocessors and cost $15,000. The Bourns Bear 20 ventilator at $10,000 had no microprocessor.

Noninvasive blood pressure monitoring was rapidly expanding and attracting new entrants. First in the market with its Dinamap monitor, Critikon became world leader and marketed direct in the U.S. and Europe, selling elsewhere via distributor. John Sweeney counted eight international competitors selling noninvasive blood pressure monitors. Most used a mix of direct sales and distributors. Many, like Datascope, were between one and two years old, rapidly gaining sales volume.

Competition in spirometry existed in countries where industry, pollution, and smoking prevailed and where government or private medical insurance reimbursed spirometry.

Puritan-Bennett dominated U.S. office spirometry with 30 percent market share but held only a negligible share of the non-U.S. market. Tariffs and duties impeded manufacturers in this price competitive market. These extra costs resulted in end user prices sometimes 50 percent above prices of European manufactured spirometers.

Vitalograph, Ltd., a British company and Puritan-Bennett's largest competitor, dominated the European spirometer market. Vitalograph sold direct in the United Kingdom but used distributors throughout the rest of Europe.

Before technological developments by LSE and later by the Boston Division, Vitalograph had sold the most widely used spirometer in the U.S. Vitalograph European prices ranged from $1,150 for the basic model to $5,000 for the top-of-the-line model. Vitalograph offered no spirometer with microprocessing but had designed personal computer software to sell with the spirometer. A physician or nurse would connect the volume mechanism with a computer.

Puritan-Bennett's International Division and Vitalograph shared many European distributors, notably in Italy, Austria, and the Netherlands. Vitalograph was not represented in Japan, and its U.S. market share had declined. Vitalograph did all manufacturing in the United Kingdom. Its sales volume equalled that of the Boston Division.

Litton Industries operated two subsidiaries, Hellig A.G. in Germany and Mijnhardt A.G. in the Netherlands. Both produced spirometers under the name Vicatest. Vicatest, a small part of this very large company, was fighting to gain a stronger position in the spirometry market. Vicatest sold direct in the Netherlands and Germany but used distributors throughout the rest of Europe. Vicatest had entered neither Japanese nor U.S. markets. The product line included Vicatest 3 with microprocessing. Vicatest priced items 33-35 percent below those of the Boston Division.

The Chest Co., a Japanese firm new to the European market, sold spirometers priced below Puritan-Bennett by 50 percent in Europe and 25 percent in the United States.

The Warren E. Collins Company of Braintree, Massachusetts, sold in both the U.S. and Europe but had not substantially dented the spirometry market in Europe. Jones Medical Instrument Company competed primarily in the United States but had begun to compete overseas. Other U.S. companies attempted to enter the international market as industrialized countries increased concern for preventive health care. A U.S. National Health Institute study showed strong correlation between lung capacity and heart disease. Early detection of reduced lung capacity might decrease patient risk if followed by early treatment or behavior change.

Spirometer manufacturers faced a new group of competitors. With technological breakthroughs leading to cost and time savings, manufacturers of large pulmonary laboratory systems showed interest in the screening market. System manufacturers included Warren E. Collins and the Gould Company in the United States and Jaeger A.G. in Germany.

CORPORATE STRATEGY

The late 1970s and early 1980s marked significant change for Puritan-Bennett. Through acquisitions and intensified R&D activities, the company adopted a more innovative position in the marketplace, incorporating electronics and microprocessing into its products. Puritan-Bennett also broadened its product line. This dual positioning strategy of broad and innovative product lines increasingly mandated international rather than domestic focus.

In the past decade European and Japanese competitors had entered the U.S. market. Entry into foreign markets would allow Puritan-Bennett to know foreign competitors before they entered the U.S. John Sweeney felt that presence in a foreign market could buy time for an American firm. By competing well on foreign soil, Puritan-Bennett could instill reluctance by European or Japanese firms to enter the United States.

International presence supported the company desire to maintain a leading edge in technology. "This allows us a window on technology," said John Sweeney. "U.S. doctors do not have all the answers. We need worldwide contacts with doctors and researchers." An example of new techniques developed outside the United States, high frequency ventilation was most widely used in Germany, and therefore the German market provided the best place for feedback.

Different regulatory environments confirmed the importance of an international base. The U.S. Federal Drug Administration (FDA) could inhibit rapid introduction of new technologies. If Puritan-Bennett introduced a product in its foreign markets first, it would begin earlier pay-back of the initial investment. Puritan-Bennett discovered that despite approvals required, the process was fast in the United Kingdom and in Germany. In

France, the process known as "homolugation" was cumbersome and difficult. The "Koseisho" procedure in Japan was well defined and predictable within a clear time frame.

With greater emphasis on innovation, Puritan-Bennett rapidly increased its R&D investment. Seeking a larger sales base would allow the company to spread initial investment cost over larger unit sales. This was true for all medical products, both hospital and physician office segments.

U.S. firms were at a cost disadvantage in many international markets because of labor, tariffs, transportation, and the strong U.S. dollar. Product quality and differentiation were therefore essential for success in Europe or Japan.

INTERNATIONAL PARTNERSHIP WITH A FINNISH FIRM

In 1981 Puritan-Bennett entered a partnership with the Datex Division of Instrumentarium, a Finnish company manufacturing hospital monitoring products. Instrumentarium had sought U.S. market entry as a first step to expansion throughout the western Hemisphere.

The initial agreement focused on one product, a carbon dioxide monitor that measured carbon dioxide [CO_2] level of patients in surgery or patients under ventilation in respiratory therapy. The monitor measured carbon dioxide levels breath to breath, providing continuous feedback on the oxygen-carbon dioxide exchange.

Because John Sweeney's division marketed all monitoring products, he was asked to oversee the partnership. Monitors were produced in Finland and sold by Puritan-Bennett in the U.S. through its distribution network. In 1983 when Puritan-Bennett began direct sales to hospitals, Finnish products were handled by the Kansas City based corporate sales group. The Boston Division continued to coordinate all activities with the Finnish company.

Since conclusion of the original agreement, the two companies had broadened their cooperation, expanding the produce line to include an anesthesia brain monitor. This equipment monitored the brain waves of a patient under anesthesia and functioned with other Puritan-Bennett products. The two companies were in negotiation to add monitoring devices to both Instrumentarium and Puritan-Bennett product lines. Further agreement gave Puritan-Bennett responsibility for the entire Western Hemisphere by adding sales to Canada and Latin America.

Puritan-Bennett and Instrumentarium had entered joint product development projects. Instrumentarium was to develop specific products to fit the Puritan-Bennett line, either by complementing it or working in conjunction with an existing Puritan-Bennett product.

Elsewhere Instrumentarium sold monitors through dealers. In Germany and Switzerland it had used Carl A. Hoyer G.m.b.H. The Finnish company used a different dealer in the U.K. and enjoyed strong sales there.

Both Puritan-Bennett and Instrumentarium were pleased with the relationship to date. They considered the possibility of a marketing joint-venture in one or two key markets. The joint-venture could market both the current line and any new products. Both companies felt that a joint-venture could maximize their effectiveness. They were still in the early stages of target identification.

ALTERNATIVE DISTRIBUTION CHANNELS

As Taylor, Sweeney, and Oglethorpe reviewed distribution channels at their meeting in the Skyline lobby, they recognized several viable alternatives. Considering the United Kingdom as an example, they knew they could keep their current distributor, seek a new distributor, or use a direct salesforce.

All three gentlemen agreed that ventilator sales projected by Grant at A&C were unacceptably low. The new generation 7200 model had sold well in the U.S. Previous experience with A&C had been satisfactory, and Puritan-Bennett did not want to create tensions in its European distribution chain by dropping an established distributor after an extended relationship.

Puritan-Bennett could seek a new distributor. Bob Taylor was concerned about the time it would take to establish and to train a new distributor. He believed it might require two or three years to reach adequate volume.

A direct salesforce was also possible. Puritan-Bennett currently sold $500,000 in disposables for ventilators already installed in the United Kingdom. Bob Taylor considered this to be "captive" business regardless of any change in channels. Disposables revenue would adequately cover the cost of adding salespeople to Puritan-Bennett U.K. Ltd. John Sweeney estimated that the cost of maintaining a sales force approached $70,000 per salesman.

CONCLUSION

Growing product lines and innovations were important for the three vice presidents to consider when examining distribution channels. Training a new distributor and subsequent high volume could take two or three years, particularly for ventilators because this equipment required a highly technical approach. Medical equipment sales demanded commitment from a sales organization, and finding a strong distributor could be difficult. A direct salesforce guaranteed early commitment but might not have immediate access to necessary channels. Hard feelings by distributors already providing good volume and service should not be risked.

John Sweeney considered how his division's products could and should fit with Bennett Division ventilators. One reason LSE had joined Puritan-Bennett was to improve international distribution by better access to European distributors. Another consideration was future broadening of Boston Division product line. Expansion was expected to continue in all medical product lines. Sweeney wanted to determine which channels could best accommodate expansion.

CASE 13

The SWATCH Project

"This watch is the product which will reintroduce Switzerland to the low and middle price market. It is the first step of our campaign to regain dominance of the world watch industry," said Dr. Ernst Thomke, President of ETA SA, a subsidiary of Asuag and Switzerland's largest watch company. Ernst Thomke had made this confident declaration about SWATCH to Franz Sprecher, Project Marketing Consultant, in late spring 1981. Sprecher had accepted a consulting assignment to help ETA launch the watch, which was, at that time, still in the handmade prototype phase and as yet unnamed. This new watch would come in a variety of colored plastic cases and bracelets with an analog face. ETA had designed an entire production process exclusively for SWATCH. This new process was completely automated and built the quartz movement directly into the watch case. Sprecher's key concern was how to determine a viable proposal for moving this remarkable new product from the factory in Grenchen, Switzerland into the hands of consumers all over the world.

●

This case was prepared by Susan.W. Nye and Barbara Priovolos under the direction of Visiting Professor Jean-Pierre Jeannet as a basis for class discussion rather than to illustrate either effective or ineffective handling of an administrative situation.
Copyright © 1985 by IMEDE, Lausanne, Switzerland. The International Institute for Management Development (IMD), resulting from the merger between IMEDE, Lausanne, and IMI, Geneva, acquires and retains all rights. Reproduced by permission.

COMPANY BACKGROUND: ETA, EBAUCHES AND ASUAG

SWATCH was only one brand within a large consortium of holding companies and manufacturing units controlled by Allgemeine Schweizer Uhrenindustrie (Asuag, or General Company of Swiss Watchmaking). SWATCH was to be produced by ETA, a movement manufacturer, which was part of Ebauches SA, the subsidiary company overseeing watch movement production within the Asuag organization.

Asuag was founded in 1931 when the Swiss government orchestrated the consolidation of a wide variety of small watchmakers. The major purpose of this consolidation was to begin rationalization of a highly fragmented, but vital, industry suffering the effects of one world war and a global depression. By 1981 Asuag had become the largest Swiss producer of watches and watch components. Asuag was the third largest watchmaker in the world behind two Japanese firms, Seiko and Citizen. Asuag had a total of 14,499 employees, 83 percent of whom worked within Switzerland. Asuag accounted for about one third of all Swiss watch exports, which were estimated at SFr 3.1 billion in 1980.* Major activities were movement manufacture and watch assembly. Bracelets, cases, dials and crystals were sourced from independent suppliers.

Ebauches SA, a wholly owned subsidiary of Asuag, controlled the various movement manufacturers. The Swiss government played an important role in encouraging and funding Ebauches' formation in 1932. An "Ebauche" was

*U.S. $1 = SFr 2.00 or SFr 1 = U.S. $0.50

the base upon which the movement was built and Ebauches companies produced almost all of the movements used in watches produced by Asuag group companies. Sixty-five percent of Ebauches production was used by Asuag group companies, and the rest was sold to other Swiss watch manufacturers. Ebauches SA recorded sales of SFr 675.0 million in 1980, a 3.1 percent increase over the previous year. Ebauches companies employed a total of 6,860 people, 90 percent of them in Switzerland.

ETA SA, the manufacturer of SWATCH, produced a full range of watch movements and was known as the creator of the ultra-thin movements used in expensive watches. The quality of ETA movements was so renowned that some watches were marked with "ETA Swiss Quartz" as well as the name brand. ETA movements were distributed on a virtual quota basis to a select group of watch manufacturers. The demand for its movements had always equalled or exceeded its production capacity. In 1980 ETA employed over 2000 people and produced more than 14 million watch movements for revenues of approximately SFr 362 million and profits of about SFr 20 million.

Dr. Ernst Thomke had joined ETA as president in 1978. Early in his career, he had worked as an apprentice in production at ETA. He left the watch industry to pursue university degrees in chemistry and cancer research earning both a Ph.D. and a medical degree. He then moved on to a career in research at British-owned Beecham Pharmaceutical. Thomke did not stay in the lab for long. He moved into the marketing department where he boosted Beecham sales with ski trips and concerts for physicians and their families. His unorthodox selling techniques led to skyrocketing sales. He looked for a new challenge when faced with a transfer to another country. His colleagues at Asuag and throughout the watch industry described Thomke as a tough negotiator and as iron willed. After joining ETA he agreed to provide advertising and support allowances to movement customers. However, these agreements stated that ETA only provided aid if it had a role in product planning and strategy formulation.

THE GLOBAL WATCH INDUSTRY

To understand the global watch industry three key variables were considered: watch technology, watch price and the watch's country of origin.

Watch Movement Technology

Watch design underwent a revolutionary change in the early 1970s when traditional mechanical movement technology was replaced with electronics. A mechanical watch's energy source came from a tightened mainspring which was wound by the user. As the spring unwound it drove a series of gears to which the watch hands were attached, the hands moved around the analog (or numerical) face of the watch to indicate the time. Highly skilled workers were required to produce and assemble the movements in accurate mechanical watches and the Swiss were world renowned in this area.

The first electronic watch was built by a Swiss engineer, Max Hetzel, in 1954, but it was U.S. and Japanese companies that first commercialized electronic technology. Bulova, a U.S. company, was the first to bring an electronic watch to market in the early 1960s, based upon tuning-fork technology. A vibrating tuning-fork stimulated the gears movements and moved the hands on a traditional analog face. At the end of the decade, quartz crystal technology began to appear in the market place. An electric current was passed through a quartz crystal to stimulate high frequency vibration. This oscillation could be converted to precise time increments with a step motor. Quartz technology was used to drive the hands on traditional analog watches and led to an innovation: digital displays. Digital watches had no moving parts and the conventional face and hands were replaced with digital readouts. Electronic watches revolutionized the industry because for the first time consumers could purchase an inexpensive watch with accuracy within one second per day or less.

Ebauches owned companies had been involved in electronic watch technology since its pioneering stages. In 1962, Ebauches was among a number of Swiss component manufacturers and watch assembly firms which established the "Centre Electronique Horlogère" (CEH). The center's immediate goal had been to develop a movement which could compete with Bulova's tuning-fork movement. CEH was never able to successfully produce a tuning-fork movement which did not violate Bulova's patents. In 1968 Ebauches entered into a licensing agreement with Bulova to manufacture and sell watches using Bulova's tuning-fork technology. In 1969 CEH introduced its first quartz crystal models and Ebauches subsequently took over manufacture and marketing for the new movement, introducing its first quartz line in 1972.

Ebauches also worked with the U.S. electronic firm, Texas Instruments, and FASEC[1] in the early 1970s to pursue integrated circuit and display technology. By 1973 Ebauches was producing movements or watches for three generations of electronic technology: tuning-fork, quartz analog and digital. Ebauches did not stay in the assembled watch market for long, and returned to its first mission of producing and supplying watch movements to Asuag companies. Between 1974 and 1980 the Swiss watch industry as a whole spent SFr 1 billion towards investment in new technology and Asuag accounted for half the expenditure. Ebauches Electronique on Lake Neuchâtel was a major use of investment funds and was created to produce electronic components.

Price

Price was the traditional means of segmenting the watch market into three categories. "AA" and "A" watches were sold at prices above SFr 1200 and accounted for 42 percent of the total value of watches sold and 2 percent of total volume. "B" watches priced at SFr 120-1200 made up 25 percent of the market in value and 12 percent in units. "C" watches were priced under SFr 120 and accounted for 33 percent of the market in value and 86 percent of total units.

---

1. FASEC was a laboratory for joint research in semiconductors, integrated circuits and lasers. It was formed in 1966 by the Swiss Watch Federation (FHS), Brown Boveri, Landis & Gyr and Philips of the Netherlands.

PLAYERS IN THE GLOBAL WATCH INDUSTRY

Japan, Hong Kong and Switzerland, together accounted for almost 75 percent of total world watch production. In 1980 watch producers worldwide were faced with inventory buildups at factory warehouses and retail stores. A worldwide recession had slowed demand for watches and overproduction compounded the problem. 1980 projections were not being met, and factory-based price cutting, particularly by large producers, was becoming common as a substitute for production cuts.

The Swiss Watch Industry

The Swiss watchmakers' position was viewed by many industry observers as being more precarious than others. Since 1970, when the Swiss accounted for 80 percent, their share of the world watch market in units had declined to 25 percent of the world's watch exports. The Swiss ranked third in unit production but remained first in the value of watches sold. Twenty-five percent of all Swiss watch factories were permanently shut down during the 1970s and 30,000 workers lost their jobs.

Despite extensive factory and company shutdowns within the Swiss industry, in 1981 the Swiss still owned the rights to 10,000 registered brand names, although less than 3,000 were actively marketed. Most Swiss watches were priced in the mid- to expensive price ranges, above SFr 100 ex-factory and SFr 400 retail. In 1981, industry analysts were congratulating the Swiss for their adherence to the upper price segments, as the low-price segments were beginning to turn weak. Industry observers noted that the Swiss seemed to be emerging from a decade of uncertainty and confusion and were focusing on higher quality segments of the watch market. Swiss component manufacturers had been supplying their inexpensive components to Far East assemblers and it was felt that this practice would continue.

Swiss watch manufacturers generally fell into one of three categories. First, there were the well established, privately owned companies which produced expensive, handmade watches. These firms included Rolex, Patek-Philippe, Vacheron Constantin, Audemars-Piguet and Piaget. For the most part, these firms were in good health financially. Stressing high quality as the key selling point, these manufacturers maintained tight control through vertical integration of the entire production and marketing processes from movement and component production through assembly and out into the market. The recession had cost them some customers, but these had been replaced by new Middle Eastern clients.

Second, there were a number of relatively small privately owned companies that concentrated on watch components—bracelets, crystals, faces, hands or movements. This group included an ETA competitor Ronda SA. The financial health of these companies was mixed.

The third sector of the industry were the largest participants, Asuag and Société Suisse pour l'Industrie Horlogère (SSIH). SSIH was an organization similar to, but smaller than Asuag, producing 10 percent of all Swiss watch and movements output. Its most famous brand, Omega, had for years been synonymous with high quality. Omega had recently run into trouble and had been surpassed by the Asuag brand Rado as Switzerland's best selling watch. In June 1981, SSIH announced a loss of SFr 142 million for the fiscal year ending March 31, 1981. This loss gave SSIH a negative net worth of SFr 27.4 million. A consortium of Swiss banks and the Zurich trading group Siber Hegner & Co., AG were brought together to save the company.

In the late 1970s Asuag and SSIH began working in a cooperative effort to cut costs through the use of common components. However, this effort did not affect individual brand identities or brand names. Industry analysts did not rule out the eventual possibility of a full merger. Asuag was noted for its strength in production and quality, but was reported to have a weakness in the marketing function. SSIH was noted for strong marketing skills, but had recently been faced with a slippage in product quality. It was believed that both companies would stand to gain from closer ties in research and production.

The watch industry played a significant role in Switzerland's economy. The banks and the government took a serious interest in its operations and the performance of individual companies. Between 1934 and 1971 the Swiss government made it illegal to open, enlarge, transform or transfer any watch manufacturing plant without government permission. This action was justified as a defensive move to combat potential unemployment due to foreign competition. It was also illegal to export watch components and watch making technology without a government issued permit. The government essentially froze the industry by dictating both prices and the supplier-manufacturer relationship. These constraints were gradually removed, beginning in 1971, and by 1981 were no longer in effect.

The Japanese Watch Industry

Japan was the world's second largest watch producer in 1980 with approximately 67.5 million pieces, up from 12.2 million pieces in 1970. The growth of the watch industry in Japan was attributed to the Japanese watchmakers' ability to commercialize the electronic watch. K. Hattori, which marketed the Seiko, Alba and Pulsar brands, was Japan's largest watchmaker, and responsible for approximately 42 million units. Selling under three different brand names allowed Hattori to compete across a broad price range. Seiko watches fell into the "B" category. Alba and Pulsar competed in the "C" range.

Casio entered the watch market in 1975 selling low cost digital watches. Philip Thwaites, the U.K. marketing manager, described Casio as follows: "Casio's strategy is simple, we aim to win market share by cutting prices to the bone." Casio's product line was exclusively digital. The company was noted for adding "gadgetry" to its watches, such as timers, stop watches and calculators. In Casio's view the watch was no longer just a time piece but a "wrist instrument."

In contrast to Switzerland, Japan's "big 3" watch producers: the Hattori group, Casio and Citizen, had a combined product line of fewer than 12 brands. All three firms were fully integrated: producing movements, most components, assembling and distributing worldwide through wholly owned distribution subsidiaries. These watchmakers made extensive use of automated equipment and assembly line production techniques.

The Watch Industry in Hong Kong

Hong Kong manufacturers had only entered the market in 1976 but by 1980 unit output had reached 126 million units. Ten major producers accounted for an estimated 70 percent of total volume. Watch design costs were minimized by copying Swiss and Japanese products. As many as 800 "loft workshops" were in operation in the late 1970s. These facilities could be started at low cost and ran with minimum overheads. The expanded capacity led to the rapid fall of Hong Kong watch prices: prices of simple watches in the SFr 15-20 range in 1978 and dropped to SFr 10 the next year with margins of less than SFr 1. Hong Kong watches were sold under private label in minimum lot sizes of 1000–2000 units with average ex-factory costs of SFr 20 for mechanical watches and SFr 50 for quartz analog and SFr 10 for electronic digitals. Most watchmaking activity in Hong Kong was concentrated on assembly. The colony had become Switzerland's client for watch components and movements. Swiss movement exports to Hong Kong had grown from 13.3 million pieces in 1977 to 38.5 million pieces in 1980.

THE "POPULARIUS" PROJECT

The SWATCH project began under the code name "Popularius." Thomke's goal had been to discover what the market wanted and then to supply it. He told his engineers that he wanted a plastic, analog watch that could be produced at less than SFr 10 and sold ex-factory at SFr 15. He also wanted to use the technology which ETA had developed for its high priced, ultrathin "Delirium" movements to enter the low priced watch segment. Thomke was convinced that ETA's long term viability and profitability depended on increasing the company's volume and integrating

downstream into fully assembled watch production and marketing. Thomke had seen the demand for ETA movements dwindle when exports of finished Swiss watches declined from 48 million pieces in 1970 to 28.5 million in 1980. The mass market "C" watch all but disappeared from Swiss production and was replaced by inexpensive Japanese and Hong Kong models. The Swiss manufacturers pushed their products up-market and sales value of exports moved from SFr 2,383.7 million in 1970 to SFr 3,106.7 million in 1980.

With electronic technology, movements were no longer a major cost factor in the end price of a watch. The average price of an ETA movement was SFr 18 and applied whether the watch sold ex-factory at SFr 80 or SFr 500. Thomke wanted to increase ETA volume output and knew that Asuag transfer pricing policies made this difficult. Asuag was a loose consortium of companies, each operating as an independent profit center. Transfer pricing reflected this fact. At each point of production and sales: movements, components, assembly and through the distribution channels, a profit was taken by the individual unit. Thomke believed that this system weakened the Swiss brands' competitive position for the volume business which his movement business needed to be profitable. Thomke believed that if he wanted to introduce a successful new product, he would need to sell it to one percent of the world's population, which amounted to about ten percent of the "C" market segment. He knew that the Japanese companies were fully integrated and that the Hong Kong assemblers, which already operated with low overheads, were moving increasingly towards full integration.

Thomke knew he could turn over the "Popularius" project to another Asuag unit, but he did not have a great deal of confidence in the production and marketing capabilities of Asuag branded watch assemblers. ETA was the only company within the Asuag group which had extensive experience in automated manufacturing. If the "Popularius" was to succeed as the latest entry in the low price market, it would have to be produced in an automated environment. Furthermore, Thomke had watched many of the finished watch companies steadily lose market share to Japanese and Hong Kong competitors over the last decade and he had little confidence in their marketing capabilities. ETA currently sold sixty-five percent of its output to Asuag companies and Thomke wanted to reduce this dependence. He planned to use the "Popularius" as ETA's own entry into the finished watch market(Exhibit 1).

ETA engineers and technicians, responding to Thomke's specifications, developed the "Popularius." To meet the low unit ex-factory price was no small accomplishment. A cost analysis at that time showed that the required components without assembly would have cost SFr 20. Quartz technology provided accuracy within one second per day, and the watch was waterproof, shock resistant, and powered by a readily available and inexpensive 3 year battery. The watch weighed 20 grams and was 8mm thick with an analog face. The face and strap were made of durable mat finished plastic and the strap was attached with a special hinge that was flush with the face. It was considered stylish and attractive. Further aesthetic enhancements could be made with the careful selection of color and face design. Ultrasonic welding produced a finished product which would not be reopened after it left the assembly line. In the event of failure, designers believed that the watch was essentially unrepairable and would be replaced rather than repaired. Batteries were replaceable by the owner and inserted in the back of the watch (Exhibit 2).

The product line was, at that time, limited to one size, a large "man's" watch, which could be produced in a number of solid colors with several designs or patterns on the face. Although a twenty-five percent smaller version for women and children was being considered, no definite introduction plans had as yet been developed. Management believed that the young were a potentially strong secondary market for the new product. A number of ideas were in development for "novelty" watches with special functions, a button watch and special colors and motifs. A day/date calendar with a quick reset feature was available. The production system was designed for strict quality control conditions to produce highly reliable watches. The movement was designed with a theoretical life of thirty years and "Popularius" would be sold with a one year guarantee.

Manufacturing Systems for "Popularius"

The ability to produce and sell a watch with the "Popularius" features, for a low price, was largely dependent upon unique production technology developed at ETA. ETA's product development staff was respected throughout the watch industry for its technical abilities in mass production. Its production technology was considered by industry observers to be equal to that of the best Japanese companies. In the early stages of electronic movement production, even with high priced luxury movements, automated assembly was not only possible but a practical means of production. The production equipment planned for "Popularius" was entirely Swiss made, and would in its final form consist of a fully automated production line that consumed raw materials at one end and delivered complete watches at the other.

ETA technology built the movement right into the base of the watch and required only 51 parts versus the 90 to 150 parts found in most electronic and mechanical watches. ETA had already used this technology to create the "Delirium," the world's thinnest movement measuring .98 mm at its thickest point. These movements were used in high precision, luxury watches measuring 2.4mm at their thickest point and selling at retail SFr 40,000.

The "Popularius" production process and the equipment that made the technology possible were protected by seven patents. The ETA technical staff felt that it would be impossible for a competitor to duplicate "Popularius," especially at low ex-factory price, because the watch was closely linked to its unique production process. ETA engineers had already invested nearly two years on this project, including the efforts of 200 employees and more than SFr 10 million in research and development funds.

Production was still limited to hand production of prototype watches and watches for test marketing purposes. ETA expected the line to

EXHIBIT 1 ● Comparison of Ebauches SA Sales to World Market

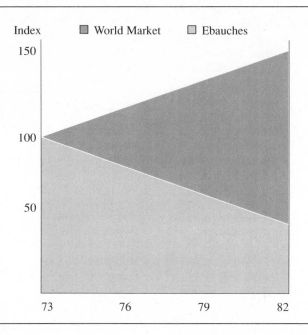

have semi- but not full automation with forecasted production levels of 600,000 men's watches and 150,000 smaller versions for women or children in the first year. Fully automated lines which would produce 2 million units per year were targeted for the second year. Production goals of 3 million units had been set for the third year. Production quotas for later years had not yet been finalized. Management expressed the desire to reach production and sales levels of 5 million units after 3 years.

Initially it was expected that full unit cost could go as high as SFr 16. As volume increased the per unit cost would drop and the full unit cost was expected to be less than SFr 10 at production levels of 5 million watches per annum. The project was not considered technically feasible at annual production levels below 5 million, and higher volume was expected to drive the unit price just below SFr 7. Asuag pricing and costing policy suggested that individual projects should reach con-

tribution margins of 60 percent for marketing, sales and administrative expenses, fixed costs and profits. Each size model would require a separate production line. Within each line economic order runs were 10,000 units for each color and 2,000 units for each face style. Maximum annual production per line was 2 million units and the initial cost of installing a line was SFr 5 million including engineering costs of SFr 2 million. Additional assembly lines could be installed at an estimated cost of SFr 3 million. Production costs included depreciation of this equipment over four years. The equipment occupied space which was already available and no additional real estate investments were expected.

ETA had applied for special financing packages with local authorities. No response had as yet been received. However, obtaining the necessary financing was not viewed as a problem.

Initial plans suggested a marketing budget of SFr 5 per unit. The brand was expected to break

EXHIBIT 2 ● Photograph of the Product

SWATCH.
THE REVOLUTIONARY NEW TECHNOLOGY.

swatch⊞

SWATCH. THE NEW WAVE IN SWISS WATCHES.

even in the third year and begin earning profits for ETA in the fourth year. Per unit marketing costs were expected to decline as volume increased. Decisions as to how the budgeted marketing funds would be distributed had not been finalized. It was expected that they would be divided between ETA and its distributors, but on what basis and how the "campaigns" would be coordinated could not be decided until distribution agreements had been finalized. Thomke was a firm believer in joint ventures and wanted to develop 50/50 relationships with distributors.

Still to be decided were questions of packaging, advertising, production line composition and distribution. Packaging alternatives centered around who should do it. ETA needed to decide if the product would leave the factory prepackaged and ready to hang or display, or shipped in bulk and packaged by the distributor or retailer or even

sold "as is." Advertising budgets and campaigns had not been finalized. The size of the budgets and the question of whether or not advertising costs would be shared between ETA and the distributors were still open. The advertising agencies had not yet been chosen and no media decisions had been finalized.

DISTRIBUTING "POPULARIUS"

Sprecher felt that distribution was the most important and problematic of the issues still outstanding. Discussions at ETA on developing an introduction strategy were confined to five industrial markets. Although, it was not as yet definitive, the emerging consensus seemed to be that distribution would begin in Switzerland, the United States, the United Kingdom, France and West Germany. Distribution in Japan, other industrialized countries and certain developing countries was also being discussed for a later date.

Market and Country Selection

A major motivation in choosing the target entry markets would be the probability of gaining high volume sales and meeting Thomke's goal of selling a watch to 1 percent of the world population. The U.S. would be an important market for "Popularius" success. It was the world's single largest watch market and success with a product in the United States often signaled global success. Thomke planned to keep the watch priced below $30 in the United States. Germany, and the United Kingdom were significantly large in terms of population, but could be difficult markets to enter because they were known to be particularly price sensitive. Germany was also noted as being particularly slow in accepting new innovations in consumer goods. Switzerland was chosen because it was the home market. ETA management assumed that their next move would be into Canada and the rest of Europe. If ETA decided to enter Japan and the LCDs, management would have some special considerations. Japan would be a particularly difficult market to crack because almost all "B" and "C" class watches sold in Japan were produced domestically. Furthermore,

EXHIBIT 3 ● Projected Marketing Costs and Profits
for SWATCH

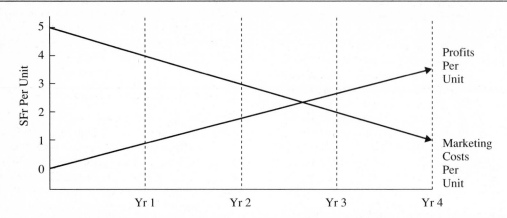

Per Unit:
Full Cost to Produce = SFr 10 (with Long Range Target of Less than SFr 7
                                     Including Depreciation for Production Machinery)
Ex- Factory Price = SFr 15
Contribution Margin for Marketing Costs and Profit = SFr 5

Sprecher had heard that Seiko was considering plans for introducing a new quartz analog watch which would be priced under SFr 50. The LCDs of Africa and Latin America provided ETA with opportunities for volume sales. Sprecher expected that consumers in these markets would use price as the only criteria for choosing a watch. Selling the "Popularius" to LCDs would put ETA in competition with the Hong Kong producers' inexpensive digital watches.

Selecting Distributing Organizations

Within each market there was a range of distribution alternatives. But a fundamental need was a central marketing, sales and distribution unit within ETA with sole responsibility for "Popularius." However, at that time, there was no marketing or sales department within the ETA organization. ETA's products, watch movements, had always been distributed to a select and consistent

group of users. Distribution at ETA had essentially been a question of arranging "best way" shipping, letters of credit and insurance. The annual costs of establishing a central marketing division within ETA was estimated at SFr 1–1.5 million. This figure would cover management and administrative salaries for a marketing manager, regional managers, product managers, service, sales planning and advertising and promotion planning. Sprecher believed that eight to ten people would be required for adequate staffing of the department. Furthermore, he estimated that wholly owned subsidiaries in any of the major target markets could be staffed and run at a similar cost.

Contracting individual, independent marketing organizations in each country and then coordinating the marketing, sales and distribution from the Grenchen office would, Sprecher believed, allow ETA to retain a much greater degree of control over the product. He felt that this type of organization would allow ETA to enter the market slowly and to learn about it gradually without having to relinquish control.

Following Thomke's suggestion, throughout the summer of 1981 Sprecher took a number of trips to the U.S. to determine possible solutions to this and other marketing problems. Sprecher's agenda included visits to a number of distributors, advertising agencies and retail stores. Sprecher completed his investigation with visits to some of the multinational advertising agencies' Zurich offices. Sprecher made his rounds with a maquette which he described as an "ugly, little black strap." The "Popularius" prototype still had a number of bugs to iron out and Sprecher could only make promises of the variety of colors and patterns which were planned.

The U.S. would be essential to "Popularius" success because it was the world's largest watch market. Thomke and Sprecher also believed that the U.S. market would be more open to this new idea and felt they would gain the best advice from U.S. distributors and advertising agencies (Exhibit 4).

Retailer and Wholesaler Reactions

Sprecher began his first U.S. trip with a visit to Zales Corporation. The Zales organization included both a large jewelry and watch wholesale business and a chain of jewelry stores. Sprecher met with a high level marketing manager who responded positively to the product, but said that Zales could not seriously consider it at this early

EXHIBIT 4A ● Retail Watch Purchases in the U.S. (Summary of Market Research)

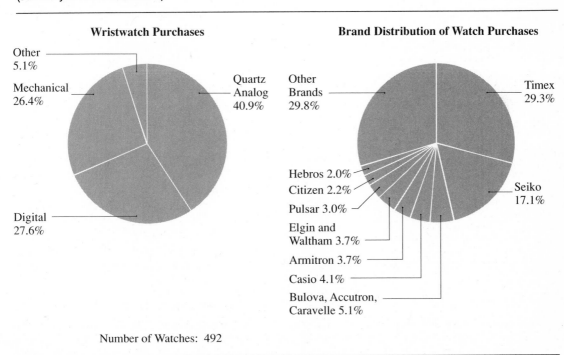

Wristwatch Purchases

Other 5.1%
Mechanical 26.4%
Quartz Analog 40.9%
Digital 27.6%

Brand Distribution of Watch Purchases

Other Brands 29.8%
Timex 29.3%
Hebros 2.0%
Citizen 2.2%
Pulsar 3.0%
Elgin and Waltham 3.7%
Armitron 3.7%
Casio 4.1%
Bulova, Accutron, Caravelle 5.1%
Seiko 17.1%

Number of Watches: 492

EXHIBIT 4B ● Watch Purchases by Retail Price (Sample size = 465)

	% Quartz analog	% Digital	% Mechanical
(Number of watches)	(200)	(135)	(130)
Price categories			
$1,000 or more	.5	.7	1.5
$300 to $999	4.0	.7	1.5
$100 to $299	38.0	8.9	14.6
$50 to $99	33.5	31.9	35.4
$30 to $49	24.0	57.8	47.0

Note: 46.6 percent of all watches are purchased on sale or discount.

stage. He invited Sprecher to return when the project was further along. Zales management did advise Sprecher that if ETA decided to go ahead with the project and start production and sales, then "do it right." Doing it "right" meant heavy spending on advertising, point-of-purchase displays, merchandising and aggressive pricing.

Sprecher also paid a visit to Gluck and Company. Gluck was a jewelry, watch and accessory wholesaler operating in the low price end of the market. An aggressive trader, Gluck operated mainly on price and much of its business involved single lots or short term arrangements to catalogue and discount houses. Gluck executives told Sprecher that they did not believe in advertising, but relied on low prices to push goods through the distribution chain and into the hands of the customer. If Gluck agreed to take on "Popularius" it

EXHIBIT 4C ● Retail Watch Purchases in the U.S.(Watch Purchases by Outlet Type. Sample Size = 485.)

	% Watches (all)	% Analog quartz	% Digital
(Number of items)	(485)	(198)	(134)
Jewelry Store	27.6	34.3	12.0
Department Store	26.2	26.3	27.6
Discount Store	16.7	14.7	23.1
Catalog Showroom	10.3	14.7	10.4
Mail Order	5.4		11.2
Wholesaler	2.1		1.5
Drug Store	5.1		6.0
Flea Market	0.4		
Other Outlets	6.2		7.5

EXHIBIT 4D ● Distribution of Watch and Jewelry Purchase Prices by Age of Purchaser

	18–24 yrs.	*25–34 yrs.*	*35–54 yrs.*	*55 and over*
(Number of customers)	(150)	(419)	(821)	(431)
$25 to $49	39.4%	39.6%	35.7%	32.3%
$50 to $99				
$100 to $299	20.7%	24.8%	25.3%	28.5%
$300 to $999	27.3%	25.3%	26.7%	27.6%
$1,000 or more	11.3%	8.8%	9.0%	10.4%

would have to be sold with a retail price of under SFr 40. Sprecher attempted to discuss the possibility of a long term relationship between ETA and Gluck, but the wholesaler did not appear particularly interested.

Sprecher's reception at Bulova's New York offices was very different from Gluck. Andrew Tisch's, president of the company, first reaction was that the "Popularius" should be packaged as a fashion watch. Tisch had had substantial experience in consumer goods marketing and believed that "Popularius" should be heavily advertised and promoted, suggesting a budget of SFr 20 million. He was sufficiently impressed with the project, and voiced some interest in establishing a separate company with ETA to market the watch.

Considering OEM Arrangements

Sprecher was concerned that he might be taking a "hit-or-miss" approach to his investigation and decided to pay a visit to Arthur Young and Company. Arthur Young was among the largest accounting firms in the world, one of the "Big Eight," and was noted for its industry analysis and consulting. Sprecher visited Arthur Young to see if their consultants might have some suggestions on potential partners for ETA. The accounting firm put together a proposal on how to attack the problem of finding a distribution partner. Sprecher was well aware that his investigation was still incomplete, and he returned to Switzerland

with the Arthur Young proposal to work out a new agenda of visits.

Included in the Arthur Young proposal was the possibility of turning all marketing responsibilities of "Popularius" over to an independent company. Sprecher investigated this possibility and entered into negotiations with two well-known multinational consumer good companies: Timex and Duracell. Both of these companies had their own extensive and established distribution channels. ETA executives believed that an agreement with either of these two firms might provide "Popularius" with a virtual guarantee of high volume sales due to the extensive and intensive marketing resources at both.

The Duracell Proposal

Duracell produced and distributed high quality batteries worldwide and was interested in becoming the exclusive distributor of "Popularius." Contact was initiated with the U.S. battery company's general manager in Zurich and followed up with a visit at Duracell's U.S. headquarters. The company had a distribution system in place which covered the entire globe. Duracell batteries were sold through drug stores, supermarkets and hardware stores. Duracell made batteries for watches as well and therefore had some contacts in the retail watch trade. The company employed an experienced and well trained sales force and had a wealth of marketing knowledge. Duracell had unused distribution capacity and its management was looking for extensions to the product line and felt that an electronic watch could be complementary to and a logical extension of Duracell batteries.

Sprecher felt that an agreement with Duracell could be interesting but was concerned that ETA was being relegated to the role of product supplier with little or no impact on marketing decisions. Duracell wanted to establish itself in an original equipment manufacture relationship with ETA. Duracell would buy the watch from ETA and then control the product's marketing strategy. ETA would be supplying the product, the product's name and some marketing funds, but would be left out of most mass marketing decisions. Furthermore, while Duracell continued to express interest, they were proceeding at what ETA executives considered to be a snail's pace. In late summer, Duracell management informed ETA that they were continuing their evaluation of "Popularius" as a product and that their investigation of its potential market was still incomplete.

The Timex Organization

Timex was known for producing durable, inexpensive watches. The U.S.-based company had become famous in the late 1950's and 1960's for circumventing traditional watch outlets, jewelry stores and distributing through mass outlets such as drug, department and hardware stores and even cigar stands. At its peak, Timex had sold watches through an estimated 2.5 million retail outlets. In 1982 Timex had an estimated 100,000 to 150,000 worldwide. Timex and ETA were considering the possibility of ETA production of a limited range of watches under the Timex name. The Timex "Popularius" would be produced in black with a different, but ETA approved, design. The hinge which attached the plastic strap to the watch case would be different and "Swiss Made" would not be stamped on the face. Timex was willing to guarantee a minimum annual order of 600,000 units, at SFr 10 ex-factory price.

Sprecher knew that ETA executives considered private label production as a viable option which could be implemented in either the intro-

ductory phase of distribution or later when the brand was well established. However, they felt that the Timex arrangement had some drawbacks. First, they perceived the Timex organization as somewhat stodgy and bureaucratic and ETA executives were unsure as to how close a working relationship they could establish with Timex management. Second, Timex seemed to want "Popularius" for "nothing." Sprecher did not think that they could keep "Popularius" to a SFr 50 retail price and gain a profit in the Timex agreement. Sprecher considered the Timex distribution system very costly. Sprecher estimated that Timex watches were distributed with a retail price of 4 to 4.5 times the ex-factory watch price. ETA wanted to maintain a 3 to 3.5 ex-factory ratio. Sprecher believed that the Timex system was costly because it used a direct sales force as well as two middlemen (distributor and broker) to get watches into the retail store. Finally, ETA management was also concerned with Timex's most recent performance. The company had been steadily losing market share.

Positioning Options

Towards the end of his second trip to the States, Sprecher hit upon the "perfect" name for the new product—SWATCH. He had arranged to spend two weeks with the advertising agency Lintas SSC&B to work on developing a possible product and advertising strategy. This arrangement initiated a quasi-partnership between the two firms; Lintas invested its time and talent in the "Popularius" project and would receive payment later if they were to get the advertising account.

Lintas had been influenced by their work with another client, Monet, a producer of costume jewelry. Monet supported its products with heavy point of sale promotion activities. Lintas believed that this kind of promotion would be beneficial to "Popularius."

Lintas saw a number of positioning options for the "Popularius," a (new) Swiss watch, a second watch, an activity watch, a fashion watch or a combination of images. The agency had suggested approaching the "Popularius" positioning with a combination of a fashion and sports image while emphasizing the watch's Swiss origin. The copy staff was excited about stressing the Swiss watch concept and the contraction S'watches was repeated throughout their notes. Sprecher looked at the abbreviation and was struck by the idea of taking it one step further to SWATCH and the "Popularius" finally had a name.

Considering Direct Mail

Back in Switzerland, Sprecher continued interviewing advertising agencies. He visited the Zurich office of McCann-Erickson, a large multinational advertising agency to discuss advertising strategy and to look into the mail order market. McCann-Erickson made an investigation of the mail order market for the SWATCH in West Germany. The purpose of this study was to demonstrate what a mail-order approach might accomplish for SWATCH.

McCann-Erickson's proposal suggested using mail order as an initial entry strategy for SWATCH. This arrangement would later be expanded into a mail-order business through specialized companies with a full range of watches and jewelry. Target group would be young men and women between 20 and 29 years as well as people who "stay young." The target group would be motivated and interested in fashion, pop culture, and modern style.

To achieve sufficient penetration of the target market which the agency estimated at 12.5 million, advertising support of about SFr 1 million would have to be spent. Orders were estimated anywhere from 50,000 units to 190,000. This estimate included volume of 4,500 to 18,000 for a test market with total advertising costs of about SFr 150,000. The effort would be organized in two waves, one in spring and a second in the fall.

Additional costs to be considered were mailing a SFr 2.50 per unit as well as an unknown amount for coupon handling. Furthermore, experience indicated that about 10 percent of all orders would not be paid.

Considering an Exclusive Distributorship

Zales had suggested that Sprecher contact Ben Hammond, a former Seiko distributor for the

southwestern region of the U.S. Sprecher was unable to make this contact, but Thomke followed up on this lead on a separate visit to the U.S. in late summer. Ben Hammond, president of Bhamco, was interested in the exclusive distribution rights for North America for SWATCH and a second Asuag brand, Certina. Bhamco was a gem stone firm and Hammond had been in the jewelry and watch business in the southwest for several years. Up until the recent past he had been the southwest distributor for Seiko. Hammond reported that he and Seiko had had a falling out when the Japanese manufacturer opened a parallel distribution system, selling its watches through new distributors to mass merchandise and discounters in direct competition to its traditional outlets and "exclusive" distributors. He proposed to start a new company, Swiss Watch Distribution Center (SWDC) and wanted an agreement for three years. Hammond was very enthusiastic about the SWATCH and told Thomke that he could "sell it by the ton." Hammond projected first year sales of 500,000 units growing to 1.2 million and 1.8–2 million in years two and three and then leveling off at 2.5 million.

Hammond felt that the watch should be positioned as a fashion item and sold through jewelry and fine department stores. He believed that a heavy advertising and point of sale budget would be important to gaining large volume sales and felt that a SFr 5 per watch was a reasonable figure. Furthermore, after his experience at Seiko, he promised a careful monitoring of consumer take-off and a close relationship with retail buyers to avoid discounting and to give service support. Based in Texas, Hammond had substantial financial backing from a group of wealthy investors. He planned to begin initial efforts in the southwest and then promised to spread rapidly to all major U.S. cities and Canada.

Next Week's Meeting

Thomke had just returned from the United States and briefed Sprecher on his meeting with Ben Hammond. Thomke was anxious to get moving on the project and planned to make a proposal to Pierre Renggli, the president of Asuag in mid-September, less than three weeks away. At the end of the briefing they had scheduled a strategy planning session for the next week. Sprecher now had less than one week to evaluate his information and to prepare his proposals for Thomke in preparation for their final presentation to Renggli. Sprecher knew that Thomke expected to receive approval for ETA production and marketing of SWATCH at that presentation. Sprecher knew that his proposals to Thomke needed to be operationally feasible, and with target launch date of 1 January 1982, available implementation time was short. Sprecher knew that they could pursue negotiations with some of the companies which he had visited or "go it alone" with a direct sales force. Sprecher needed to balance the economic restraints which required minimum annual sales volume of 5 million with Thomke's desire to keep strategic control of the product within ETA. Sprecher needed to consider ETA's lack of marketing experience and what that would mean in the international marketplace.

CASE 14

Tissot: Competing in the Global Watch Industry

One sunny afternoon in May 1985 Dr. Ernst Thomke drove his Porsche through the Jura mountains; he was on his way to Bienne for a Tissot strategy session. After more than a decade of declining sales, layoffs and factory closings the popular business press was proclaiming the return of the Swiss watch industry. Much of the credit for the resurrection had been given to Thomke, president of Ebauches SA, one of the SMH companies, and initiator of a new low priced Swiss fashion watch: the SWATCH. Thomke believed that the predictions of a revived Swiss watch industry were premature. He had accepted the considerable task of giving the Asuag brands, and particularly Tissot, a hard look to formulate new strategies to bring the Asuag group profitably in the second half of the 1980s and beyond. Specifically, his goal was to increase SMH total volume from 7 million to 50 million units. As his Porsche sped through the countryside he considered the past and future trends for the global watch industry and he asked himself. "How can Tissot grow and profit?"

In 1985, the future trends for the global watch industry were anything but clear. Over the past fifteen years, the industry had experienced radical changes. Innovation in products, production and marketing were all key factors in the volatility which marked a period of rapid entry (often followed by rapid exit) of new competitors and the departure of some established producers.

In 1970 the global watch industry was dominated by Swiss watch manufacturers. By 1975 the competitive field had expanded and key players came from Switzerland, Japan, and the United States. By the early 1980s the U.S. had all but disappeared as a contender and Hong Kong was the world's largest exporter in units in the industry with 326.4 million watches and movements in 1984. Japan ranked second in number and value of units produced. Between 1970 and 1984, the Swiss dropped to third place in unit volume as their assembled watch exports dwindled from 48 million to 17 million pieces. However, Switzerland continued to rank first in value of watch exports, SFr 3.4 billion in 1984 (see Exhibit 1).

THE WATCH INDUSTRY IN SWITZERLAND

The Swiss watch industry was concentrated in the Jura along the western border of Switzerland. The Swiss had conquered the world market with mechanical watches and had developed a reputation for fine craftsmanship, elegance and style. Swiss companies produced 80 percent of the watches selling for SFr 1,200 or more and virtually all top priced watches. A large portion of these watches were still mechanical.

Until the early 1970s, Swiss watchmaking was intensely specialized and fragmented, with a rigid structure which had remained unchanged for centuries. Major changes began in the 1970s with

This case was prepared by Susan W. Nye under the supervision of Visiting Professor Jean-Pierre Jeannet as a basis for class discussion rather than to illustrate either effective or ineffective handling of an administrative situation. Copyright © 1985 by IMEDE, Lausanne, Switzerland. The International Institute for Management Development (IMD), resulting from the merger between IMEDE, Lausanne, and IMI, Geneva, acquires and retains all rights. Reproduced by permission.

849

EXHIBIT 1A ● Total Production of Watches and Watch Movements Worldwide 1960–1984 (In Millions of Pieces)[1]

1960	1970	1975	1980	1982	1983	1984
98.0	174.0	220.0	300.0	330.0	370.0	n.a.

[1]Without other timepieces as penwatches, and so on.
Source: Swiss Watch Federation. Used by permission.

EXHIBIT 1B ● Watch Production by Country 1960–1983 (Percentage of Worldwide Unit Production)

	1960	1970	1975	1980	1982	1983
Switzerland	43.0%	42.0%	32.0%	18.4%	10.8%	9.3%
Japan	7.2	13.7	14.0	22.5	24.7	26.1
Hong Kong	—	—	—	18.5	30.0	35.0
USA	9.7	11.5	12.5	4.0	—	—
E. Ger.	20.5	14.5	16.7	15.7	14.8	13.2
France	5.6	6.3	7.6	3.3	2.9	2.2
W. Ger.	8.0	4.7	4.3	2.2	1.2	1.1

Source: Swiss Watch Federation. Used by permission.

EXHIBIT 1C ● Watch Exports—Watches and Movements 1960–1984 (In Millions of Frs)

	1960	1970	1975	1980	1982	1984
Switz.*	1159.2	2383.7	2764.3	3106.7	3091.9	3397.3
Japan	16.4	399.3	835.1	1911.1	1908.5	2876.2
Hong Kong	—	63.1	246.1	1855.6	1779.0	2091.2
France	26.2	78.1	209.3	265.0	218.3	233.7
Germany	83.6	129.6	140.2	171.7	175.4	231.4

*Including nonassembled movements.
Source: Swiss Watch Federation. Used by permission.

EXHIBIT 1D ● Watch Exports—Watches and Movements 1960–1984 (In Millions of Pieces)

	1960	1970	1975	1980	1982	1984
Switz.*	42.6	73.4	71.2	51.0	45.7	46.9
Japan	0.1	11.4	17.1	48.3	63.6	94.7
Hong Kong	—	5.7	16.1	126.1	213.7	326.4
France	1.3	4.4	9.5	9.8	8.4	6.2
Germany	3.8	4.1	9.5	4.5	4.7	5.5

*Including nonassembled movements.
Source: Swiss Watch Federation. Used by permission.

EXHIBIT 1E ● Exports As a Percentage of Total Pieces Produced 1960–1984

	1960	1970	1975	1980	1982	1984
Switz. (E)	97%	97 %	97%	97%	97%	97%
Japan	2	48	57	72	80	n.a.
Hong Kong	—	100	100	100	100	100
France	24	40	57	*	*	*
Germany	48	50	*	*	*	*

(E) = Estimation.
n.a. = not available.
*Not available; because of reexports, exports are larger than production.
Source: Swiss Watch Federation. Used by permission.

EXHIBIT 1F ● Assembled Watches As a Percentage of Watches and Movements Exported (value)

	1960	1970	1975	1980	1982	1984
Switz.	81.3%	86.1%	87.9%	85.9%	91.5%	92.9%
Japan	51.6	83.6	92.1	90.6	87.6	85.0
Hong Kong	97.1	100.0	96.6	95.4	96.9	96.7
France	87.7	93.8	93.8	88.7	91.5	94.4
Germany	91.1	88.7	90.6	89.0	92.0	94.8

Source: Swiss Watch Federation. Used by permission.

EXHIBIT 1G ● Assembled Watches As a Percentage of Watches and
Movements Exported (pieces)

	1960	1970	1975	1980	1982	1984
Switz.	73.7%	73.6%	71.7%	55.9%	59.3%	55.2%
Japan	29.0	64.8	78.1	75.5	67.5	60.6
Hong Kong	98.2	100.0	98.1	94.4	95.6	92.1
France	n.a.	89.5	90.4	81.6	79.0	94.4
Germany	89.3	88.9	85.5	69.0	74.4	72.6

n.a. = not available.

Source: Swiss Watch Federation. Used by permission.

several mergers involving sizeable firms and important initiatives in both horizontal and vertical integration.

The Swiss watch industry was essentially a group of industries. Traditionally, the Swiss had operated on a two tier system: component manufacturing and assembly. In 1934 the Swiss government had instituted laws that made it illegal to open, enlarge, transfer or transform any watchmaking facilities without government permission. Exports of components and movements were also illegal without permission, as was the export of watchmaking machinery. These regulations were instituted to protect the Swiss watch industry against foreign competition. The government began de-regulating the industry in 1971 and in 1985 these laws were no longer in effect.

Swiss watch firms generally fell into one of three categories. First, there had been a large number of "one-man-and-a-boy" and other small enterprises which produced components, movements or put purchased parts into cases. These firms marketed on the basis of long-established personal contacts. Included in this category were the piece work assemblers. A significant portion of inexpensive mechanical watches were assembled by Jura farmers during the winter as in-home piece work. Second were the well-established, privately owned watchmakers which produced expensive, handmade watches. And finally, there

was the Asuag-SSIH organization which was a group of companies representing approximately 35 percent of total Swiss exports of watches and movements.

Watches and movements declined from 11.9 percent to 7.2 percent of total Swiss exports from 1970 to 1980. At the start of the 1970s there were 1,618 watchmaking firms in the industry; this figure had fallen to 634 by 1984. Between 1970 and 1984 the full-time labor force producing watches shrank from 89,500 to 31,000. Layoffs due to the shrinking demand for mechanical watches were exacerbated by automation, rationalization and concentration initiated throughout the Swiss watch industry.

SMH

Corporate Background

In an effort to resuscitate the industry, a consortium of seven Swiss banks orchestrated a merger between SSIH and Asuag in 1982. They provided the merger with a capital and cash infusion totaling more than SFr 700 million. In return the bank gained 97 percent ownership of the combine and planned to sell shares to the public when it returned to profitability, estimated at five to ten years. Turn around began in 1984 with sales totaling SFr 1,582.4 million and after tax profits of

SFr 26.5 million. In February 1985, it was announced that control would be returned to private investors.

Asuag, short for Allgemeine Schweizer Uhrenindustrie, had been the largest producer of watches and watch components in Switzerland, accounting for about one-third of total Swiss watch exports and 25 percent of production in Switzerland. Asuag had been founded in 1931 when the Swiss government orchestrated the consolidation of a wide variety of small watchmakers to strengthen the industry during the worldwide depression.

Movements were produced by the twelve subsidiaries of Ebauches SA, including ETA. ETA was the largest Swiss movement manufacturer. ETA produced a full range of movements, but was best known as a producer of high quality, expensive ultra-thin watch movements used for luxury watches. Ebauches companies sold 65 percent of their production volume to the Asuag-SSIH brands. Ebauches' sales had dropped from 51.1 million to 32.1 million pieces between 1973 and 1984. During this period the world market for movements had grown from 215 million to 350 million units. Ebauches world market share dropped from 23.8 to 9.2 percent.

Asuag's brands of finished watches included: Longines, Eterna, Certina, and Rado. Rado was the largest selling mid priced Swiss watch with annual sales of about 1 million units. Fifty-five percent of Asuag's production was in finished watches. Asuag began losing money in 1977, reporting an accumulated net loss of SFr 129 million in 1982.

Société Suisse de l'Industrie Horlogère (SSIH) had been the second largest watch company in Switzerland, responsible for 10 percent of total output. SSIH was made up of a diverse group of companies producing watches and movements in all price categories. SSIH group companies included Omega, Tissot and Economic Time.

SSIH had encountered severe financial problems in the late 1970s. In 1977 the Zurich-based trading group Siber Hegner & Co. AG, a major international distributor of Swiss watches, including Omega and Tissot provided SSIH with a capital infusion of SFr 32.5 million. A rescue plan was devised which de-emphasized the lower price end of the market. Siber Hegner management concentrated on electronic quartz models which sold at prices above SFr 235. Tissot watch prices were pushed upwards and Tissot models were sold in the SFr 235 to 1500 range. Omega watches were priced above SFr 600 at retail. Companies producing at the low price end of the market were sold off and inexpensive watch production was reduced from 69.2 to 19.7 percent of total. At the same time, the product mix was shifted and electronic watches increased from 8.9 percent of total in 1976 to 47.9 percent of total sales in 1980. Siber Hegner provided a cash infusion for research and development and a worldwide advertising campaign. Acquisitions and joint ventures were arranged to improve integration, although management, production, marketing and sales remained decentralized.

Initially, turn-around was successful with profits in 1979 allowing for the first dividend payment since 1974. Profitability was short lived and in June 1981, SSIH announced a loss of SFr 142 million for the year ending March 31, 1981, giving the company a net loss of SFr 27.4 million. A consortium of Swiss banks in an effort to bail out the company provided cash and credit valued at almost SFr 230 million in return for 96.5 percent equity in the recapitalized company.

Tissot SA

Thomke described Tissot, and most Asuag-SSIH watches, as a "branded commodity." The individual companies produced their products under recognized brand names, but Thomke felt that the watches had been poorly developed in terms of brand image and personality. Thomke believed the weak image had led to the decline in Tissot sales (Exhibit 2). His goal was to create a workable brand strategy and identity for Tissot. In May 1985, Thomke believed that Tissot had gained the reputation of an "inexpensive" Omega.

The company produced about 400,000 watches in 1984, for watch sales of SFr 42 million. The average retail price for a Tissot watch was

EXHIBIT 2 ● Tissot World Sales 1981–1984

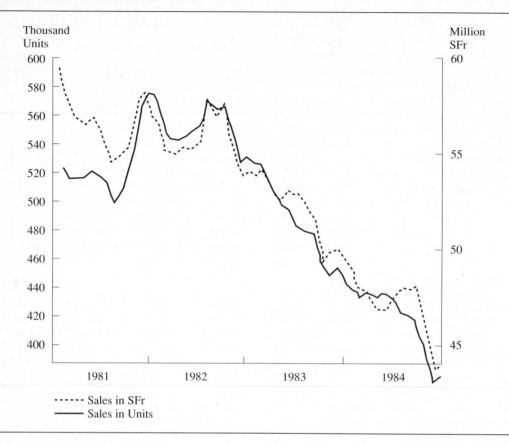

about SFr 375. Strongest sales volume was from watches in the SFr 300–700 range. Retail prices ranged from SFr 75 to 800 for stainless steel and gold plated watches. A second smaller line of gold watches sold for between SFr 1000 and 5000. Tissot watches were sold in Europe: Switzerland, West Germany, Italy, Scandinavia and the U.K. Tissot was also sold in Brazil, South Africa, Hong Kong, Singapore and Japan. Tissot had been withdrawn from the U.S. market in the 1970s but Thomke wanted to re-introduce it to the U.S. as soon as possible.

Tissot production was limited to assembly.

Employment at the factory had declined from a high of 1200 to 200. All components and movements were purchased from Asuag-SSIH or independent companies. At the start of 1985 Tissot workers were assembling a product line of some 300 styles, each produced in a woman's and man's model and in a number of different metals and combinations. Thomke had already assigned ten engineers at Tissot to review the product line and production process.

Tissot shared Omega's distribution at both the wholesale and retail level. Almost all Omega wholesalers were independent distributors. A total of 12,000 retail stores, mostly jewelry stores and a few "high class" department stores carried Tissot watches. The majority of its watch sales came from the top 3,000 stores. Ex-factory prices ranged from SFr 60 to 2,000. Both wholesalers and retailers provided advertising and promotion support, but all promotion activities had to be initiated by Tissot.

Thomke was aware that if he wanted to build up a strong image for Tissot, he would have to increase his marketing and promotion expenditure. Asuag-SSIH set targets for marketing and profit margins (MPM) for each brand. Thomke felt that a 50 percent margin would give a brand adequate funds for marketing and profit. Only his latest product, SWATCH, came close to that figure, followed by Rado with almost 30 percent. A target MPM* of 15 percent had been set for Tissot for 1984, but Thomke had learned that the actual margin had been closer to 10 percent.

Thomke believed that the MPM had been squeezed by wholesalers because of the slow turnover for Tissot watches. Wholesalers demanded a margin of 28 to 45 percent for Tissot watches. Explaining the situation, Thomke said, "Tissot has never recovered the sales and market share it lost to Seiko and Citizen in the 1970s. Sales to retailers have slowed considerably and consumer demand is down. To encourage wholesalers to keep Tissot in inventory, the company granted more liberal wholesaler margins, at the expense of marketing funds and profits."

Thomke felt that it was still possible to build up the brand and re-establish a strong wholesale network. However, he realized that this was an expensive proposition. He was prepared to invest 18 to 20 percent of sales in promotion, but to have any effect he needed a promotion budget of SFr 12 million for Europe alone. Thomke estimated that the company could spend SFr 6–8 million in Germany, Tissot's largest market in 1985. This figure would be divided with one half targeted for media advertising and the rest for point-of-sale promotion. If handled correctly, promotion activities

would give Tissot the strong image which Thomke felt was essential to successful watch sales.

WATCHMAKING TECHNOLOGY

Designing a Watch Collection

Watches covered a broad spectrum in terms of style and price, ranging from sport watches for informal or daytime wear, to luxury dress watches which were pieces of jewelry. It could take three years to bring a watch from the drawing board to the market. A watch collection was made up of as many as thirty to forty lines. Each line had up to 1000 models. A watch line was differentiated by case shape, design and the movement. The differences between models were cosmetic variations in color and types of materials or due to slight variations in technology, such as day/date calendars or self-winding mechanisms.

Watch cases were made in precious metals, standard steel, brass and plastic. The cases of many expensive luxury watches were decorated with semi-precious and precious stones, such as lapis lazuli, diamonds and sapphires. Watch cases were made in two or three pieces. Two pieces, the back and front, were standard and held the watch together. For better watches a separate rim held the crystal in place. The rim provided designers with more flexibility when developing new models and gave the watches a finer finish.

Watch crystals were pieces of thin glass or plastic which protected the hands and dial and came in three types. The most expensive were plastic, followed by mineral glass and sapphire glass. Sapphire glass was very hard and could not be scratched or chipped.

Straps or bracelets held the watch on the wrist and came in a variety of materials. Straps came in leather, plastic and cloth ribbons. Bracelets were made from precious metals, standard steel, brass and plastic. Precious and semi-precious stones were often set into the bracelets of luxury watches. Up until the 1970s most watches were sold with leather straps. In the past 15 years fashion had changed and most watches were purchased with bracelets.

*MPM = Marketing and Profit Margin.

Timekeeping Technology

Every watch was composed of four basic elements: a time base, a source of energy, a transmission and a display. The movement was the watch's time base. Movements came in two major categories: mechanical and electronic. Mechanical movements were driven by the release of energy from an unwinding spring. Electronic watches ran on an electric battery. Energy was transmitted through a series of gears, a motor or integrated circuits to the hands of analog watches. These hands moved around the dial to display time. Integrated circuits were used to transmit time to digital watches, and time was displayed numerically in a frame on the watch case.

Mechanical Watch Movements

The movement was a complex set of 100 or more tiny parts. While all mechanical watch movements operated on the same principle, there was a great deal of variety in watch quality. Friction and wear had to be minimized to insure long term accuracy of the tiny moving parts. To minimize friction, jewels were placed at all the movement's critical pivot and contact points. Fifteen was the standard number of jewels but high-quality movements might contain as many as thirty. Contrary to popular belief, adding more jewels did not necessarily indicate increased quality, or cost to production. These internal jewels were synthetic and relatively inexpensive. It was the overall care and craftsmanship that went into the watches that created the expense and not the jewels themselves.

The precision and accuracy found in high quality jewel-lever watches required micromechanical engineering expertise. A variety of modifications could be made to a spring-powered watch which added to the complexity of the interior design but not the basic mechanism. Refinements, such as improved accuracy, miniaturization, water resistance and self-wind technology, rather than radical new developments had occurred. Calendars and chronographs, as well as watches with start/stop mechanisms were also possible.

Pin-lever watches, also called "Roskopfs" after their inventor, had metal pins instead of jew-

EXHIBIT 3 ● Wristwatch Purchases in the U.S.

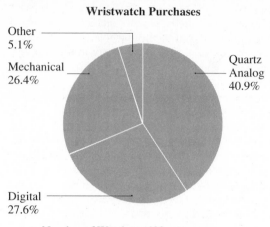

Wristwatch Purchases

Other 5.1%
Mechanical 26.4%
Quartz Analog 40.9%
Digital 27.6%

Number of Watches: 492
(Total Number of Surveyed Buyers: 492)

Source: National Jewelers/HTI.
Consumer Survey 1983.

els on the escapement mechanism gear teeth. Roskopf's original goal in inventing this watch had been to make the movement so simple that watches could be made affordable to everyone (Exhibit 3).

Electronic Movements

A Swiss engineer, Max Hetzel, invented the first electronic watch in 1954. This development was largely possible due to advances in miniature batteries and electric motors during World War II. Initially, electronics did not represent a big departure from mechanical technology, nor offer substantially better accuracy. While the energy source was replaced with electronics, the transmission and regulating components remained unchanged.

The tuning-fork watch, developed in the 1960s, represented a significant change to the traditional principles of determining time. A small battery in the watch sent an electric current to the tuning-fork and stimulated it to vibrate at 360 cycles per second. The vibrations were transmitted to a set of gears which drove the hands on the watch face. Tuning-fork watches if properly adjusted were accurate to within one minute per month.

The quartz crystal watch began appearing in the marketplace at the end of the 1960s. An electric current was passed through a quartz crystal to stimulate high frequency vibration which could be converted into precise time increments. Microcircuitry subdivided the crystal's frequency into an electric pulse which drove the watch. The pulse operated a tiny electric stepping motor or was transmitted through conductors and integrated circuits to drive the gears and watch hands.

In 1972, digital watches appeared for the first time. These watches had no moving parts and the conventional face and hands were replaced with digital readouts. Early digital watches used light emitting diodes (LED) to show the time. With this technology, users pressed a button for time display. LED watches required a great deal of power and batteries lasted no longer than one year. Liquid crystal diodes (LCD) came on the market in 1972; these watches displayed the time continually. These watches were considerably more conservative in energy usage, and batteries lasted from 3–5 years or longer.

Early electronic watches were not fully water and shock proofed and the batteries often malfunctioned in hot, humid climates. However, within a short period of time, technological advances led to electronic watches which were water proof to depths of 30 meters, shock proofed and able to withstand tropical climates.

Designing electronic watches for women had initially created problems, as well as opportunities. To create models which fit a woman's smaller wrist required considerable miniaturization of the movement and battery. Creating smaller movements led to increased design flexibility. Improvements in miniaturization and advancement in large-scale integrated circuits (LSI) and battery technology allowed manufacturers to add special functions without excessive bulk. Watches began to take on the appearance of multifunction instruments. Runners, skin divers, sailors, and other sports enthusiasts bought watches which would provide them with waterproofing and sophisti-

cated chronograph functions. Travelers were afforded the opportunity to buy watches with multi-time zone functions and alarms. Watches were also available with calculators and radios, and progress was being made toward a television watch (Exhibit 3).

Producing Watches

Movements, hands, cases and bracelets were assembled to produce a complete watch. Mechanical watch quality was dependent on the care taken in assembly as well as the quality of the individual components. High quality mechanical movements were made by hand and a combination of semi- and highly skilled craftsmen was needed. Mechanical watch assembly was done in batches. Highly skilled workers were essential at the final stages of production, for finishing and adjusting to produce high quality, finely finished, accurate movements and watches.

While the term *pin-lever* refers specifically to the replacement of jewels with metal pins, roskopfs were made from lower quality grade materials. Labor requirements for roskopfs were reduced with semi- or unskilled labor working in batch production.

Electronic movements for analog watches combined micro-mechanical and electronic engineering. The electronic regulating mechanism simplified the production process which could be run in an automated setting with semi-skilled labor. Movements for digital watches were radically different from analog watches. These watches had no moving parts and time was programmed onto a silicon chip. Unskilled labor could be used to assemble digital watches which were assembled in batches and on automated assembly lines.

Both mechanical and electronic watch reliability was tied to the number of inspections the manufacturer made. For mid-priced and expensive watches 100 percent inspection occurred at several points during the process. Tests were made for water- and shock-proofing as well as accuracy.

Costs of production were a function of a company's degree of integration and automation, material costs and the local wage rates. Material costs were based on the quality of the watch produced. With roskopf watches labor constituted a significant portion of variable costs, but as the watches moved up-market the materials, fine stainless steel, sapphire crystals and eventually precious metals and decorative jewels played the major role in the watch's ex-factory price. Watchmakers could improve their variable costs by assembling

at volumes above 10,000 pieces. Assemblers producing 100,000–500,000 units per year could benefit from component supplier discounts which were as high as 20–25 percent. Beyond this point, cost improvements could only be realized with new production processes, automation and robotics. Wages for the Swiss watch industry averaged SFr 12 per hour. Most Swiss watchmakers sought

EXHIBIT 4A ● Breakdown of Production Costs

For a Swiss watch with an ex-factory price of SFr 390 variable cost breakdown was estimated as follows:

case	70
bracelet	90
dial	50
crystal	18
movement	18 (50 for mechanical)
hands	5
Total materials costs	251
Assembly and quality control	25
Margin	114
Ex-factory	390
Wholesalers' margin	260
Retailers' margin	650
Consumer price	1300

For Japanese watchmakers producing a watch with ex-factory of SFr 250 breakdown of costs and margins as follows:

Total variable costs	150
Margin	100
Ex-factory	250
Wholesalers' margin	60–90
Retailers' margin	310–340
Consumer price	630–700

For Hong Kong makers producing a watch with ex-factory cost of SFr 80 break-down of variable costs were as follows:

case and dial	15
bracelet	15
crystal	15
movement	18
hands	2
Total materials costs	65
Assembly and quality control	6
Manufacturer's margin 10%	8
Ex-factory	80
Wholesalers' margin	30
Retailers' margin	55–110
Consumer price	165–220

Source: Asuag-SSIH and interviews with industry experts.

EXHIBIT 4B ● Breakdown of Costs and Margins for
Traditional "B" Watches (By Country of Origin)

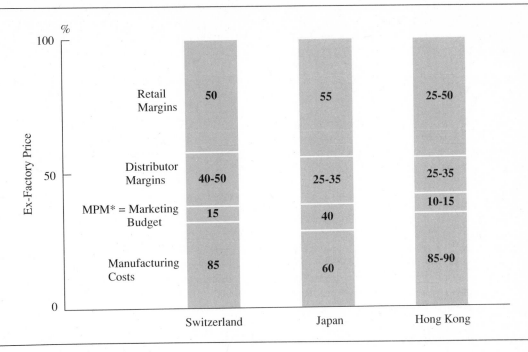

*Manufacturing and Profit Margins

a 30 percent gross margin. In Japan average
hourly wages for factory workers were SFr 7.20.
Japanese producers had an average gross margin
of 40 percent. In Hong Kong manufacturers kept
their ex-factory prices low with inexpensive, but
highly productive piece-work labor, averaging
under SFr 10 per day, fewer inspections and
cheaper materials. Gross margins of approximately 10–15 percent were typical for Hong Kong
manufacturers (Exhibit 4).

SEGMENTING THE GLOBAL WATCH INDUSTRY

Price Segments

Price has been a traditional means of segmenting
the watch market into three categories. The first
group were low price, "C," watches and included

all watches sold at retail for under SFr 120. Roskopf watches and inexpensive digitals competed
in this market. These watches accounted for 33
percent of total value of global watch sales and 86
percent of unit volume. The mid-price or "B"
watches ranged from SFr 120–700 at retail. This
sector represented 25 percent of sales in Swiss
francs and 12 percent of total units for 1984. Electronic watches dominated both the "C" and the
"B" price segments.

The third category were the top priced
watches. The retail price of "A" watches ranged
from SFr 700–5,000. Manufacturers of luxury
watches "AA" class, sold to a small exclusive
group willing to pay several thousand Swiss francs
for a special custom design jeweled watch. Precious stones and/or metal used in the watch face
and bracelet accounted for the major portion of
the "A" and "AA" watch prices. This was partic-

EXHIBIT 5 ● Watch Purchases in the U.S. at Retail Prices

No. of items	% Watches (490)*	% Quartz analog (200)	% Digital (135)	% Mechanical (130)
$1,000 or more	.8	.5	.7	1.5
$300 to $999	2.4	4.0	.7	1.5
$100 to $299	23.5	38.0	8.9	14.6
$50 to $99	33.5	33.5	31.9	35.4
$25 to $49	39.8	24.0	57.8	47.0

*Total 490 responses for consumer survey.

Source: National Jeweler/HTI.
Consumer Survey 1983.

ularly true for electronic watches where movements averaged SFr 18. About 27 percent of the value of total watches and 2 percent of pieces sold worldwide were from the "A" tier. "AA" watches accounted for 16 percent of global watch sales in Swiss francs, but less than .5 percent of total units. Mechanical watches still dominated the high priced segments (Exhibit 5).

Evaluating timekeeping technology was difficult for consumers. When shopping for watches, consumers chose a particular price level and expected a certain level of technical proficiency, style, and intangibles such as prestige. Quartz technology had changed the price/accuracy ratio. Before the electronic watch, accuracy was bought with expensive, finely engineered jewel-lever watches. With the introduction of electronics, watches with accuracy of plus or minus 15 seconds per month could be purchased for as little as $9.95.

Geographic Segments

Technologies and price have had an impact on the world markets for watches. Historically, the U.S. has been the major importer of finished watches. The U.S. was often the launching ground for new products and success in this market indicated strong possibility of global success. The strong dollar and improving U.S. economy in 1984–1985 had had a positive impact on the sales and profits of Swiss and Japanese watch companies. Europe and Japan were also strong markets for watches in all price categories. However, throughout the 1960s and 1970s, new opportunities for watch sales opened up in the oil producing countries in the Middle East and in less developed countries (LDC).

In the 1960s watch producers began to move into the LDC with inexpensive roskopf watches. This market was taken over by inexpensive digitals in the early 1970s. However, the initial success of the cheap digital in this market was short-lived and consumers returned to mechanical watches. The miniature batteries in the quartz watch were very expensive in these regions, sometimes more than the original cost of the watch. By 1984, this problem had been solved and inexpensive electric watches again dominated the LDC market.

A new opportunity for watch manufacturers developed in industrialized countries with young children providing a new and growing market for inexpensive watches. Until the 1960s most children received their first watch in their mid- to late teens, often as a gift. Roskopf watches opened up the market to children in the 7 to 10 year range. A significant portion of these purchases were novelty watches, with cartoon and storybook characters which were sold as gifts for young children.

The market for expensive watches moved to

the Middle East in the early 1970s. The rest of the world was caught in a recession, largely due to escalating oil and gas prices, and demand for high price luxury items fell off. Buyers in the oil producing countries had both the money and the interest to purchase luxury goods. The Swiss were particularly adept at meeting the changing fashions and tastes of this new luxury segment and provided expensive, luxury watches with lapis-lazuli, coral, diamonds and turquoise (Exhibit 6).

TRENDS IN WATCHES DISTRIBUTION

Wholesale Distributors

Watch distributors played an essential role in linking the manufacturer to the retailer. Distributors generally sold one or perhaps two non-competing brands. Wholesalers expected exclusive distribution rights for the brand for a given region. Distributors maintained a sales force to sell to and service retailers. They purchased watches outright and maintained a local inventory.

Manufacturers expected their distributors to participate in promotion activities. Distributors attended trade fairs and contributed to advertising, mailing expenses and point-of-purchase display materials.

The distributor was responsible to find and oversee adequate watch repair services. Watch repair was a key issue for watches in the "B," "A" and "AA" categories. This service need had led to a close working relationship between the producer, distributor and retailer. The distributor found and licensed watch repair services and jewelers with watch repair capabilities. For especially difficult repairs the distributor helped arrange for work to be sent back to the factory. With inexpensive, "throw-a-way" watches repairs were less critical or non-existent. Importers of "C" level watches had greater freedom in channel selection. Mass merchandisers, drug stores and even supermarkets were used to distribute watches to end users. Some of these watches were sold with a guarantee, and rather than repair, a replacement was offered.

EXHIBIT 6A ● Major Importers of Swiss Watches and Movements (In Millions of Pieces)

	1960	1970	1975	1980	1982	1984
Hong Kong	1.9	10.0	11.3	12.5	4.1	4.9
United States	12.4	19.2	12.0	5.9	3.6	4.6
Germany	1.3	2,9	5.0	4.9	3.6	4.0
Italy	1.2	2.6	2.6	2.5	2.3	3.0
France	0.2	0.7	0.8	1.6	1.9	2.2
Japan	0.2	1.0	1.6	0.7	0.7	2.0
United Kingdom	1.7	6.1	6.3	3.2	1.9	1.9
Saudi Arabia	0.2	3.4	1.1	1.0	1.2	0.9
Arab Emirates			1.4	1.9	1.3	0.8
Spain	0.8	2.5	1.9	1.3	1.1	0.8
Total 10 largest markets	19.9	48.4	44.0	35.5	21.7	25.1
Total worldwide	41.0	71.4	65.8	51.0	31.3	32.2

Source: Swiss Watch Federation. Used by permission.

EXHIBIT 6B ● Major Importers of Swiss Watches and Movements (In Millions of Swiss Francs)

	1960	1970	1975	1980	1982	1984
United States	250.6	482.2	348.6	379.7	407.8	598.7
Hong Kong	76.6	242.6	257.6	401.6	344.1	351.5
Italy	70.1	153.9	194.0	256.4	287.7	300.3
Germany	48.2	135.3	195.6	241.7	212.4	246.6
Saudi Arabia*	12.2	92.0	84.0	201.9	271.9	233.1
France	10.6	38.6	75.6	123.3	152.0	169.8
Japan	14.1	88.0	172.5	109.0	120.3	167.1
Singapore	38.3	45.1	58.3	79.7	106.2	150.3
United Kingdom	43.1	131.3	176.6	125.3	127.2	139.9
Arab Emirates*	—	—	59.4	71.7	94.9	82.1
Total 10 largest markets	563.8	1,409.0	1,622.2	1,990.3	2,124.5	2,439.4
Total worldwide	1,146.3	2,362.2	2,720.3	2,917.5	3,011.0	3,298.8

*Saudi Arabia with Arab Emirates in 1960 and 1970.

Source: Swiss Watch Federation. Used by permission.

EXHIBIT 6C ● Major Importers of Japanese Watches and Movements (In Millions of Pieces)

	1980	1982	1983
Hong Kong		14.2	23.0	28.3
United States	7.5	10.3	11.8	
Germany		3.4	2.7	3.1
Italy		0.8	0.8	1.1
France		1.1	1.9	2.6
Canada		0.8	0.7	1.0
United Kingdom	1.1	1.7	2.2	
Saudi Arabia	2.1	2.8	3.9	
Arab Emirates	0.6	1.3	1.4	
Spain		0.5	2.0	2.1
Total 10 largest markets		32.1	47.2	57.5
Total worldwide		48.3	63.6	76.0

Source: Swiss Watch Federation. Used by permission.

EXHIBIT 6D ● Major Importers of Japanese Watches and Movements (In Millions of Swiss Francs)

	1980	1982	1983
United States	316.9	372.9	403.4	
Hong Kong		383.7	471.0	580.8
Italy		40.9	33.3	47.6
Germany		142.4	94.4	88.0
Saudi Arabia	107.3	94.8	158.3	
France		72.0	73.0	95.5
Canada		44.6	39.6	51.1
Singapore		18.3	29.9	23.0
United Kingdom	54.3	56.0	56.7	
Arab Emirates	24.5	42.4	58.9	
Total 10 largest markets		1205.0	1306.4	1563.2
Total worldwide		1918.5	1925.4	2224.7

Source: Swiss Watch Federation. Used by permission.

EXHIBIT 6E ● Major Importers of Watches and Movements from Hong Kong (In Millions of Pieces)

	1980	1982	1983
Canada	2.9	8.6	10.2
United States	32.6	81.7	119.2
Germany	11.5	15.6	20.5
Italy	4.6	5.2	8.0
France	6.6	4.8	4.2
Japan	5.9	8.2	12.4
United Kingdom	9.7	10.4	12.6
Saudi Arabia	2.4	6.4	7.1
Arab Emirates	1.4	3.9	6.2
Spain	4.2	9.5	14.8
Total 10 largest markets	81.8	154.3	215.2
Total worldwide	126.1	213.7	284.1

Source: Swiss Watch Federation. Used by permission.

EXHIBIT 6F ● Major Importers of Watches and Movements from Hong Kong (In Millions of Swiss Francs)

	1980	1982	1984
United States	469.4	591.3	671.7
Canada	56.7	63.3	57.8
Italy	62.7	34.9	40.8
Germany	194.9	129.4	145.9
Saudi Arabia	58.9	102.3	100.5
France	88.5	34.2	22.8
Japan	69.5	65.1	84.7
Singapore	43.8	46.8	34.2
United Kingdom	139.0	82.6	76.3
Arab Emirates	25.7	59.6	57.0
Total 10 largest markets	1209.0	1209.4	1291.5
Total worldwide	1859.7	1779.6	1915.3

Source: Swiss Watch Federation. Used by permission.

Most watch manufactueres had agreements with independent distributors. The Japanese and some of the private Swiss firms operated wholly or partially owned marketing and sales subsidiaries in their foreign markets. Twenty-five to 35 percent was the standard markup granted wholesalers and importers of Japanese and Hong Kongese watches. This figure increased to 40 percent or more for importers of most Swiss watches.

Retailers

A wide variety of retailers sold watches to the end user, including jewelry and department stores, mass merchandisers and mail order catalogues.

An estimated 40 percent of worldwide watch sales came from jewelry stores. Watch manufacturers benefitted from the jeweler's selling expertise and personal interaction with consumers. Watches sold in exclusive jewelry and department stores benefitted from the store's deluxe or fashion image. Fine gold, mechanical watches were a nat-ural extension of the jeweler's product line and most were capable of minor watch repairs and cleaning. When electronics were initially introduced, some jewelry stores resisted the new technology. Electronics were not within the jeweler's extensive training. Within a short period of time, however, customer demand and refinements to the technology moved quartz watches into jewelry stores worldwide.

Jewelry stores had been the traditional outlet for watch sales until the mid-1950s. The rapid growth in roskopf and later in inexpensive digital watch sales was accompanied by channel diversification and watches moved into new outlets: drug stores, department stores and supermarkets. Retail watch sales in the U.S. had been influenced by channel diversification and in 1983 less than 30 percent of watches sold in the U.S. were purchased in jewelry stores (Exhibit 7).

Stock turn for a "B", "A" or "AA" watch

EXHIBIT 7A ● Watch Purchases by Outlet Type in the United States

Number of items	% Analog	% Digital	% Watches (485)
Jewelry store	34.3	12.0	27.6
Department store	26.3	27.6	26.2
Discount store	14.7	23.1	16.7
Catalog showroom	14.7	10.4	10.3
Mail order	14.7	11.2	5.4
Wholesaler	2.5	1.5	3.1
Drug store	2.0	6.0	5.1
Flea market*			2.4
Other outlets	3.0	7.5	6.2

*Flea markets accounted for less than 1% of all categories

EXHIBIT 7B ● Cost of Purchases in Main Outlets

Number of items	$1000+ (40)	$300–999 (173)	$100–299 (485)	$50–99 (466)	$25–49 (657)
Jewelry Store	70.0%	69.4%	49.1%	34.6%	27.2%
Department Store		6.9	16.7	22.5	27.9
Discount Store	2.5	1.7	5.8	9.7	10.5
Catalog Showroom	5.0	5.2	8.9	9.4	7.3
Other Outlets	22.5	16.8	19.5	23.8	27.1

could be as low as two times per year at retail and phasing out older models and cleaning out the pipeline could take 2 to 3 years. "C" watches generally moved more quickly, with 4 to 6 stock turns per year.

Jewelry stores and department stores were accustomed to a 50–55 percent markup. Mass merchandisers' margins varied and went as low as 25 percent.

COMPETITORS IN THE GLOBAL WATCH INDUSTRY

Timex

Timex, a U.S. company, began selling inexpensive, mechanical watches in the late 1950s. Most Timex watches fell into the "C" range, with prices ranging from under SFr 15 to just over SFr 250.

EXHIBIT 7C ● Brand Distribution of Watch
Purchases in the United States

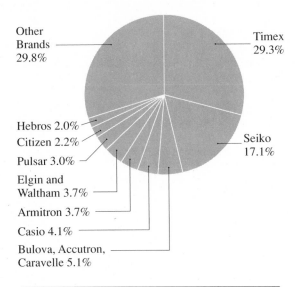

Brand Distribution of Watch Purchases

Other
Brands
29.8%

Timex
29.3%

Hebros 2.0%

Citizen 2.2%

Pulsar 3.0%

Seiko
17.1%

Elgin and
Waltham 3.7%

Armitron 3.7%

Casio 4.1%

Bulova, Accutron,
Caravelle 5.1%

Source: National Jeweler/HTI.
Consumer Survey 1983.

The company developed into a manufacturer of mass-produced, hard alloy pin-lever watches. Manufacturing was mechanized, simplified and standardized. When the company's pricing plan called for a 30 percent markup at the retail level, jewelry stores refused to carry the watches. Timex moved into mass outlets such as drug, department and hardware stores, and even cigar stands. The number of outlets for Timex watches in 1985 was estimated between 100,000 and 150,000. This figure was down from a high of 2.5 million in the 1960s. By the late 1960s, 50 percent of all watches sold in the U.S. were Timex. In 1985 Timex had capacity to produce 15 million watches.

Timex had an advertising budget of approximately SFr 20 million, most of which was spent on television sports events. Timex produced a large number of styles, but did not promote any single model or style. The company was known for its "takes a licking and keeps on ticking" slogan, promoting Timex durability.

Timex began limited production of digital watches in 1972. By the mid-1970s the company was feeling pressure from new entrants from Japan and the U.S. Sales support for mechanical watches was withdrawn and Timex attempted to increase its digital capacity and to gain electronics capabilities rapidly. As a mechanical watch manufacturer Timex had been fully integrated, but used outside sources for electronic components. The company's initial entries to the digital market were poorly received and sales declined to SFr 1 billion in 1979. During the 1970s the company faced significant losses which amounted to SFr 260 million by the end of 1982. These losses were expected to escalate.

In the 1980s, Timex moved into consumer electronics, computers, home health care products and refocused its watch business to try to halt its profit slide and plant closings. In 1981 Timex invested in a British home-computer company founded by inventor Clive Sinclair. The computer had little capacity but had the lowest price on the market. In 1982, fierce price competition in the home-computer market squeezed margins and the price was cut in half to approximately SFr 100. The company also lost sales to competitors such as Commodore which offered more power for about SFr 180. Timex management viewed the watch industry as splitting into two parts: jewelry and wrist instruments. Timex reported that its development plans would emphasize the wrist-instrument business with multi-function watches.

Texas Instruments, Inc.

In 1975 a number of U.S. electronics companies entered the industry with digital watches and circuits for electronic movements. Finding themselves with excess capacity an estimated 100 chip producers entered the watch market. Most started as suppliers of movements and components and integrated forward into production and assembly of complete watches. In the early days of digital watch sales, demand far outstripped capacity. In spite of this fact, the electronics companies continually pushed price down in a market share war which eventually destroyed this attempted entry into the watch business.

Texas Instruments (TI) was the largest of the semi-conductor and computer companies to enter the watch industry. Its consumer electronics division began in the early 1970s with handheld calculators. The company then broadened this line with watches, home computers and educational products.

Watch manufacturing at TI began in 1976, when its first LED, plastic-cased watch with a SFr 40 price tag was introduced. One month later the price was cut in half. TI developed a digital watch that could be made from TI built parts on automated equipment. Prices were set to undercut the mechanical watch competition with a goal to gain a large piece of both the U.S. and global market. Prices were set to reflect budgeted, future volumes.

While TI had surprised the competition with reduced prices, it was caught off-guard with advances in digital display readouts. To provide a full line of products the company imported 7 out of 13 of its basic lines from Hong Kong, including its multifunction watches. The corporation reported SFr 6.4 billion in sales in 1979, SFr 800 million of which came from consumer goods. The division showed a pre-tax profit of SFr 4 million down from pre-tax $28 million in 1978. Profits continued to slide and TI moved out of the watch industry in 1982.

Casio Computer Company

In 1974 Casio, a Japanese computer company entered the market and claimed 12 percent share of all Japanese watches sold within five years. Casio watches were sold in the "C" price range. Casio manufactured its watches in highly automated factories. Its product line was limited to digital watches, many of them multi-functional with stop watches, timers and calculators. Casio management has been quoted as saying: "People should own at least 3 watches." In 1985 Casio was selling an estimated 30 million watches per year. The Casio name was clearly linked worldwide with multifunction watches.

Casio's first entry into the digital market was priced at SFr 180 and initial sales were weak. As the company's watch prices began to fall, sales doubled annually from 1974-1980.

Casio was among the first electronic watch producers to determine that the electronic watch's greatest appeal was technical rather than aesthetic. The company urged its department and mass merchandise store retailers to display its watches in the camera, calculator or stereo department, rather than the jewelry department. Casio management felt that sales personnel at these counters understood electronic equipment better than jewelry salespeople and could therefore answer customer questions.

The Hong Kong Watchmakers

Hong Kong entered the watch market in a major way in 1976, specializing in inexpensive electronic and mechanical watches. Hong Kong watch manufacturers did not sell under their own company or brand name. Private label watches were produced and sold in minimum lots of 1000-2000 pieces per model.

Ten major producers accounted for an estimated 70 percent of total volume, but as many as 800 "loft workshops" were also operating. These production facilities could be started at low cost and run with minimum overheads. Hong Kong was the world's largest watch exporter, and was responsible for 326.4 million units in 1984; total value was SFr 2,091.2 million. Most watch production in Hong Kong was limited to assembly. Inexpensive components and movements were purchased in large lot sizes. Hong Kong manufacturers kept their design costs minimal or non-existent by producing copies and near-copies of watches displayed at trade fairs and in jewelry stores. Average ex-factory prices were SFr 25 for a mechanical, SFr 60 for quartz analog and SFr 12 for electronic digitals. Hong Kong watch prices began to fall rapidly in the late 1970s. Simple watches selling for SFr 18-20 in 1978 dropped to SFr 12 in one year and margins shrunk to less than SFr 1.

Counterfeiting was a fairly common practice among small Hong Kong manufacturers. A counterfeit copied the original watch design and was marked with the brand name. This practice was generally avoided by the large producers who beginning in the early 1980s were seeking entry into the international watch establishment. Counterfeiting was a significant problem faced by European and Japanese producers. Unlike technological innovations, it was very difficult to establish patents or copyrights on designs. Firms could begin to protect their brand name by establishing a company or joint-venture within Hong Kong.

SWATCH Watch SA

SWATCH was a plastic, quartz analog watch. SWATCH was sold at SFr 15 ex-factory and SFr 50 at retail in Switzerland. Prices outside of Switzerland were slightly higher and the top price was $30 in the United States. The product was available in 12 styles, which changed twice per year, in a woman's and a man's model.

SWATCH WATCH was an Asuag-SSIH company under the direction of Ernst Thomke. It was founded in 1985 when it was split off from its original producer ETA. SWATCH WATCH remained within the Ebauches group of Asuag-SSIH. Within two years of its introduction in 1982, the brand had hit sales of 3.5 million units. Sales for 1985 were expected to reach 7.5 million units. In 1985 SWATCH management was concerned that the company's already constrained capacity could become an increasingly significant problem over the next few years. The product was produced on a fully automated and robotized assembly line and the hands were the only component purchased from an outside source. The company had enjoyed rapid decline in production costs per watch. Thomke had met and surpassed his original target production cost of SFr 10 per watch.

From introduction it had been positioned for active people, a sport or fashion accessory and not as a time piece. The watch sold in jewelry and department stores. The company had spent heavily on promotion and advertising, budgeting approximately SFr 5 per watch for marketing expense and profits.

SWATCH invested SFr 20 million in marketing efforts and was expected to spend SFr 30 million in 1985. SWATCH was sold in 19 industrial countries and approximately 50 percent of all SWATCHes were sold in the U.S. In the majority of markets independent distributors were employed. However, SWATCH WATCH USA was a wholly owned subsidiary which controlled distribution in the United States. SWATCH WATCH USA played a significant role in the creation of marketing strategy and planning for the watch.

Seiko

Seiko, part of the K. Hattori Company, began marketing an electronic, quartz watch in 1969 and emerged as the market volume leader in the global watch industry within ten years. In 1984 the company reported annual sales of SFr 3.8 billion for watches and clocks. Seiko brand watches fell within the "B" category. But the company competed in the "C" segment watches with the Alba and Larus labels; high "C" or low "B" segment with the Pulsar label and "A" segment with the Jean Lassale brand. In 1984 the company sold 55 million watches, 22 million under the Seiko brand.

Seiko had been using assembly line production since the mid-1950s. Following the example of the Detroit automobile factories, its engineers designed assembly lines and unskilled laborers were employed in most production. The firm was fully integrated: manufacturing key components, jewels and even watchmaking machinery. Seiko was among the first to initiate large scale production and sales of electronic watches.

Seiko had been protected from foreign competitors in its domestic market. Only expensive watches, about 5 percent of total units and 20 percent of total value of Japanese purchases, were imported. Almost all of the low- to mid-price watches purchased in Japan were produced by Seiko or one of its two domestic competitors, Citizen and Casio. Japanese companies produced some low priced movements for Hong Kong manufacturers. However, movements for "B" watch production were not exported to Hong Kong.

Seiko used the U.S. as a market for initial entry, where they gained a reputation which they then sold worldwide. The company offered fewer than 400 quartz and mechanical models in the U.S., but over 2,300 worldwide. These models included analog, digital and multifunctions watches. Plans called for an expansion of the number of styles sold in the U.S. and a broadening of the price range at the upper and lower ends of the market.

Seiko owned sales subsidiaries in all of its major markets. Seiko watches were sold in jewelry and department stores. It had also established service centers in all of its major markets. This service allowed the customer to bring or mail a repair problem directly to the company by-passing the jeweler. Seiko spent as much as SFr 80-100 million annually in worldwide advertising, mostly television, to sell its quartz watches. Seiko had created a strong brand image based on its quartz technology and accuracy.

While Seiko was a formidable competitor for the Swiss watch industry, Japanese consumers were a major market for Swiss luxury watches. Throughout the 1970s and 1980s Swiss luxury watches were considered a status symbol in Japan. In 1981 Seiko moved into the luxury market, at home and abroad, when it purchased a small Swiss watch producer Jean Lassale. The company's plan was to combine Swiss design and elegance with Japanese engineering and technical skill in electronics.

By 1970 both Seiko and its Japanese competitor Citizen had diversified into new businesses with internal development, mergers and acquisitions. Included in the expanded product line were: consumer electronic products such as computers, software, calculators, high-speed printers, miniature industrial robots, office equipment and machine tools and even fashion department stores.

As Seiko faced the 1990s, these product lines were expected to become an increasingly important part of the company's total sales and profits. In 1970 clocks and watches represented 99 percent of Seiko sales; but by 1983 that share had dropped to 40 percent. Top executives at Seiko expected this figure to continue to decline to 30 percent by 1990.

Longines SA

Longines was well-known internationally but losing money when it was acquired by Asuag in 1974. Longines was developed into the group's premiere, or top-priced, brand and began contributing to profits in 1976.

After joining ASUAG, Longines' prices began to climb, as the company edged its way into the high-priced "A" watch segment. The first Swiss manufacturer to produce electronic watches in 1969, Longines' product mix was 50 percent electronic. In 1985 average ex-factory price for Longines watches was SFr 450 to 500.

Longines produced at levels of about 500,000 watches per year. Investments were made in more efficient machines to reduce dependence on skilled labor and the number of different types of movements and other precision parts was cut back. Longines continued to make about 30 lines, each with many variations.

Longines put all of its promotion money behind its leader model, the "Conquest." Management felt that the top priced "Conquest" best represented the overall style of the collection. "The Longines Style" campaign was supported with an advertising and promotion budget of 10 percent of total sales and this sum was matched by Longines agents. Advertisements were placed in international and local media.

In 1984 Longines introduced a new watch line, the Conquest VHP. VHP stood for "very high precision" and the watch promised accuracy within 1 second per month. The gun metal-colored titanium and gold watch contained two quartz crystals. The first was the timekeeper and the second compensated for vibrations and effects of the weather. The watch sold for SFr 1,650 at retail and initial response from the marketplace was very positive. Advertising for the new line stressed the watch's Swiss origin with the heading "Swiss Achievement."

Rolex

Rolex, with its prestigious "Oyster" line was perhaps the best known of the Swiss luxury watch manufacturers. Rolex was a private company, owned by a foundation. The company was responsible for about 5.5 percent of Switzerland's watch exports by volume, with estimated annual export of 400,000 units, valued at SFr 700-800 million. Rolex did not disclose its domestic sales.

Ninety percent of all Rolex watches were produced with mechanical movements housed in gold or platinum cases. The "Oyster" line was described as a premium sports watch. Retail "Oyster" watch prices ranged from SFr 800 for stainless steel watches to SFr 14,000 for solid gold watches. Production was semi-automated and Geneva housewives made up a large part of the semi-skilled labor. Skilled workers were required for hand-assembly in the final stages of production. The company always allowed production to lag slightly behind demand.

Throughout the turbulent 1970s, the company had stayed consistently with the luxury sport watch market. Rolex limited advertising to the higher-priced "Oyster" line. Rolex also had a second line: "Cellini," of high priced luxury dress watches. The company resisted entry into the electronic age; only 10 percent of the Rolex line was electronic. There was some speculation that in the next 3 to 5 years quartz watches would rise to 30 percent of total output. In 1983, quartz production was limited to watches under the Tudor brand, at the low end of Rolex's market and were priced below SFr 1200. The Tudor watches were not advertised and did not bear the Rolex name. In 1985, Rolex catalogue included 3 "Oyster-quartz" models.

Rolex employed wholly owned, marketing subsidiaries in 19 countries. The Geneva headquarters worked through the subsidiaries to license jewelers to sell and service its watches. The subsidiaries provided sales and service support to local retailers and watch repairers. Maintaining adequate service coverage was important in an era of throw-away watches. For example, the New York subsidiary licensed 70 watch repairers to service Rolex watches. Distribution to retail outlets was based on a quota system. Subsidiaries were also used to maintain tight control over retail prices; Rolex did not permit any discounting. Promotion and advertising expenditures were estimated at 10 percent of sales. This expenditure was matched by the wholesalers and retailers.

Piaget SA

Piaget SA was founded by George Piaget in 1874, and in 1985 was still a family business directed by the founder's grandsons and great-grandsons. The company's workshops produced approximately 15,000 handmade watches each year at prices ranging from SFr 4,000 to 400,000. The company carried a large collection of luxury watches for both men and women, producing approximately 1200 models.

Only gold and/or platinum were used to encase the watch movements, and many of the watches were decorated with precious stones. Both mechanical and quartz models were included in the Piaget's collection. Piaget was the only producer of luxury dress watches which was fully integrated. The company produced the world's thinnest mechanical watches: 1.2mm for a hand wind model, and 2mm for an automatic. Historically, the Piaget line was limited to dress watches, but the company entered the sports watch market in 1980.

Worldwide, Piaget watches were carried by 400 retailers. They tended to be the most prestigious stores in their areas and were located to be accessible to potential luxury watch buyers. Whenever possible, the watchmaker preferred retailers to carry only Piaget in their luxury dress watch line. Annual advertising expenditure for Piaget was estimated at SFr 3 million, excluding the U.S. About 55 percent of this expense was paid for by Piaget, and the rest was contribution from distributors and retailers.

Other Swiss manufacturers producing luxury dress watches included: Audemars-Piguet, Patek-Philippe and Vacheron & Constantin. All three were smaller than Piaget, producing less than 15,000 watches per year and followed similar strategies.

Ebel

Ebel was founded in 1911 by Eugene Blum. The company described its transition in the 1970s as a renaissance.

In 1974 the third generation of Blums, Pierre-Alain, took over the company. When Pierre-Alain Blum became president Ebel's 50 employees were making private label watches. With new management, Ebel began to take a closer look at the customers of its chief client Cartier. Within a short period of time, Ebel began branded watch production and employment grew to 500 people. 1984 sales were estimated between SFr 150 and 170 million.

The company's growth came about with the development of a unique one piece watch case and bracelet construction which became the base for the Ebel collection. Ebel's goal was to design and maintain a "classic," timeless collection and the company did not plan to make major annual changes to its line. Ebel watches sold at retail SFr 1,000 to 15,000. The company had five models and realized 90 percent of its sales from the top three. The company's goal was to create a strong brand image. Using its leader model, Ebel promoted its watch lines with the slogan "architects of time."

Ebel moved into electronic movements in 1978. With that change in technology the company enjoyed a boost in sales. In 1985 Ebel was assembling 300,000 units per year. The company maintained tight control over its suppliers. Ebel had production and development contracts with its movement suppliers and partial ownership of its case and bracelet manufacturer. The company still assembled private label watches for Cartier. In 1975 sales to Cartier had represented 90 percent of sales, 10 years later these sales represented less than 50 percent of total. It was estimated that Cartier sales provided about 25 percent of Ebel's profits in 1984.

Blum maintained close personal contact with

the end customer with frequent visits to jewelry stores. His goal was to keep a close eye on stock levels at jewelry stores and avoid a build up of stocks in the distribution channels. He also wanted to insure that the jewelry store's image was in line with the Ebel image.

In addition to its "architects of time" media advertising, Ebel also used sports sponsorship as a means of building an image with the public. Ebel became one of the first watch companies to actively use sporting events for its watches' promotion. Ebel sponsorships included a soccer team in Geneva and tennis and golf matches.

In the 1980s Ebel was broadening its business activities. It expanded its product line by becoming the distributor for Schaeffer pens. Ebel also entered the clothing business with the American firm, Fenn, Wright and Manson. They opened a boutique in Geneva and others were in the planning stages. Finally, Ebel was the agent for Olivetti computers for the French speaking part of Switzerland. The distribution company employed 12 people including programmers.

Recent Entrants in the Watch Industry

A new group of "outsiders" and "newcomers" has entered the global watch industry. Many of these companies (or current ownership) have been operating for ten years or less. With few exceptions, these "watchmakers" subcontracted all production and assembly, mostly in Switzerland. The watches were then positioned in the market as high fashion pieces.

Included in this group were Raymond Weil, founded in 1976. Within ten years the company had reached annual sales levels of approximately 300,000 quartz watches, at prices ranging from SFr 500 to 1700. All work was subcontracted to companies and individual component manufacturers and assemblers in the Jura region of Switzerland. The company employed 15 people for design, marketing and sales and administration. One-third of all wholesale activities were captively held.

Weil's success in the watch industry was attributed to the company's sense of style and fashion. A new collection was introduced each year with six woman's and six man's watches. Weil was constantly responding to changes in consumer tastes and the latest trend. His 1985 spring collection was named for a hit movie, Amadeus, a biography of the life of Mozart. Raymond Weil had a limited budget for its advertising and promotion expenditures, relying on a few well-placed messages and style to sell its products.

Cartier watches were classic in design and limited to 15 different models. Cartier subcontracted its watches from Ebel. The Cartier watch lines did include models which sold for as much as SFr 100,000. Most Cartier watches sold at prices ranging from SFr 1,200-25,000. Most Cartier watches were quartz. Selling at a level of 450,000 units per year, the watch was an addition to the company's collection of accessories and jewelry. The watches were sold through the company's specialized retail stores and independent boutiques, jewelry and fashionable department stores all over the world. Watch advertising and promotion expenses were minimized because the company's name was well recognized in the market place and the watch fell under the umbrella of the company's other accessories.

Gucci watches were sold by an independent entrepreneur who licensed the Gucci name. These "A" watches were sold at Gucci shops and by independent jewelers and high fashion department stores and boutiques. Annual volumes for Gucci watches were estimated at 400,000 units. The company did not advertise heavily and relied on the Gucci name for prestigious name brand identity.

SUMMARY

Thomke knew that there were a number of options open to him to bring Tissot from its current status of a "branded commodity." He estimated that relaunch in Europe would be a minimum of SFr 12 million. Costs for reintroducing Tissot to the U.S. would be even greater. To afford these marketing expenses, Tissot marketing and profit margins would have to improve and sales volumes would have to grow. Thomke knew he could shift prices and was considering pushing Tissot prices downward to the bottom of the "B" group. A downward price shift would require a considerable increase in volume if the Tissot brand was to be profitable. The producer's margin decreased as watches moved down market to the "B" and "C" segments. Thomke knew that producers of expensive watches which had a strong positive image with consumers could command high ex-factory prices. This provided the luxury watch firms with considerable margins for marketing expenditures and profit.

Thomke believed that to operate profitably a watch had to capture at least 10 percent of its market segment. He wanted to produce a workable brand strategy which would allow Tissot to gain at least 10 percent of its segment. Thomke had several key factors to consider. The fast paced technological changes of the 1970s had slowed and the traditional watch buying market was maturing. However, he saw that nontraditional approaches in the industry had allowed new entrants such as Raymond Weil and SWATCH to successfully gain footholds and profits in the global watch industry.

CASE 15

ICI Paints (Abridged)

"We at ICI Paints aspire to the number one position globally in the paint business. Our goal is to make ICI Paints the first choice among paint suppliers to whom a customer anywhere in the world would turn if he were seeking a long-term supply relationship," said Herman Scopes, PEO of ICI Paints. "Now, we are already the world's leader if measured in market share, sales volume, or liters of paint produced. However, we have not yet been able to translate this position into superior financial performance. To get there, we will have to become much better at learning from each other and at transferring best practice from one operation to another."

INDUSTRY PROFILE

The world paint market was estimated at some £ 20 billion[1] at ex. factory level and some 12 billion liters. Growth was expected to average 2 to 3 percent through the next decade.

1. In 1988, £1.00 = $1.50

●

This case was prepared by Jean-Pierre Jeannet, Professor of Marketing and International Business at Babson College, and Adjunct Professor at IMD, as a basis for class discussion rather than to illustrate either effective or ineffective handling of a business situation.
Copyright © 1990 by IMEDE, Lausanne, Switzerland. The International Institute for Management Development (IMD), resulting from the merger between IMEDE, Lausanne, and IMI, Geneva, acquires and retains all rights. Reproduced by permission.

North America accounted for 31 percent of the market by volume, followed by Europe (29 percent), Japan (13 percent), Asia-Pacific (11 percent), and the rest of the world (16 percent). In the more mature paint markets of North America and Europe, annual growth was expected to be below GNP growth whereas in the newly industrializing countries growth was expected to be in line with GNP growth. Long term, the three principal paint user areas of Europe, North America, and Asia-Pacific were expected to become of equal size and account for 75 percent of the world market (see Exhibit 1).

Major application segments included decorative uses (52 percent), industrial uses (37 percent), coatings for cans (3 percent), automotive OEM (6 percent), car repair/refinishing (5 percent). See Exhibit 2.

There were approximately 10,000 paint manufacturers worldwide. Leading paint companies, aside from ICI, PPG, and BASF, were Sherwin-Williams (the United States), Akzo (Netherlands), Nippon (Japan), International-Courtaulds (the United Kingdom), Kansai (Japan), DuPont (the United States), and Valspar (the United States). The top ten companies shared 30 percent of the world paint market in 1988. That share was expected to increase over the next decade.

COMPANY PROFILE

ICI Paints was the world's largest paint manufacturer with a sales volume of £1.5 billion, or 8 percent of the world market, and an annual output of 800 million liters, or 7 percent of world volume. The company operated some sixty four manufac-

EXHIBIT 1 ● World Paint Industry Profile by Region

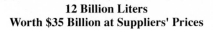

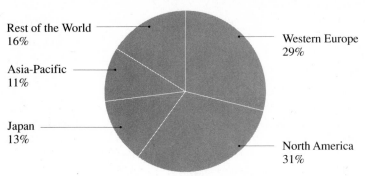

12 Billion Liters
Worth $35 Billion at Suppliers' Prices

Rest of the World 16%

Western Europe 29%

Asia-Pacific 11%

Japan 13%

North America 31%

turing plants in twenty nine countries. Licensees operated in another fourteen countries (see Exhibit 3). ICI was about 70 percent larger than its next biggest competitor, PPG Industries.

ICI Paints was part of the Consumer and Specialty Products sector of ICI. The division accounted for about 12 percent of total ICI turnover and 7 percent of its operating profit. Sales in 1988 (excluding sales by related companies) had reached £1.363 billion with a trading profit of £98 million resulting in a return of 7.2 percent of sales. ICI Paints' profitability was on a par with BASF, its leading European competitor, and about twice that of its Japanese competitors. ICI Paints had

EXHIBIT 2 ● World Paint Volume by Market Segment

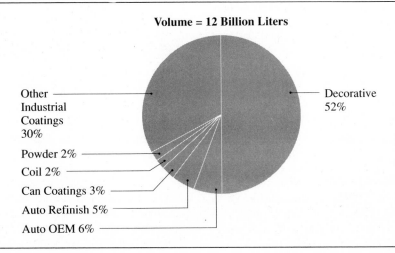

Volume = 12 Billion Liters

Other Industrial Coatings 30%

Decorative 52%

Powder 2%

Coil 2%

Can Coatings 3%

Auto Refinish 5%

Auto OEM 6%

EXHIBIT 3 ● ICI Paints Territorial Spread

ICI Paints manufacturing companies

Australia	Malaysia	Taiwan
Canada	Mexico	Thailand
Ireland	New Zealand	United Kingdom
Fiji	Pakistan	Uruguay
France	Papua New Guinea	United States
India	Singapore	West Germany
Italy	Spain	
Madagascar	Sri Lanka	

ICI Minority holdings

Botswana	Indonesia	South Africa
Malawi	Nigeria	Zimbabwe

Companies manufacturing under licence

Colombia	Korea	Turkey
Cyprus	Portugal	Venezuela
Japan	Saudi Arabia	Yemen
Jordan	Sudan	
Kenya	Trinidad	

---

been a consistent performer in an industry that had been characterized by considerable restructuring (see Exhibit 4).

ICI's market position varied considerably by market segment. The company was the world leader in the decorative and can coatings areas, a major player in automotive refinishes, one of the smaller automotive OEM players, and it also held positions in powder, coil coatings, and other industrial coatings. ICI was absent from the marine paints sector (see Exhibit 5).

Decorative Paint Segment

About 57 percent of ICI Paints' business was accounted for by the decorative segment which included paints and coatings used for the protection and decoration of industrial, commercial, and residential buildings. ICI was the world's largest producer of decorative paints, both for professional and do-it-yourself (DIY) users. The company marketed its Dulux brands in the United King-

dom, Australia, New Zealand and a few other Asian markets, the Valentine brand in France, Ducolux in Germany, and Glidden Spred in the United States which was acquired as part of the acquisition of Glidden in 1986. Glidden was the inventor of waterborne latex paints for popular emulsions. Although operating under different brands, ICI was the leader in most of these markets, particularly in the premium end of the market.

Most decorative paint was used where produced with little cross-shipping due to its low value. ICI tended to meet different local players country by country. The wholesaling structure and retailing industry as well as the role of the DIY market varied considerably from one country to another. Furthermore, there was little economy of scale effect in this business. Some 500 paint companies competed in this segment in Italy alone. Paint formulations used also had to be adjusted to local use conditions such as prevailing surfaces, building materials, and climate.

EXHIBIT 4 ● ICI Paints Financial Performance 1985-1989

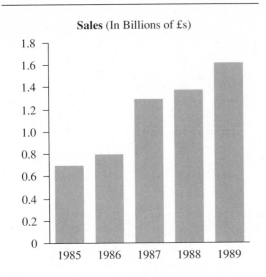

Sales (In Billions of £s)

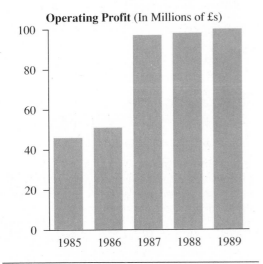

Operating Profit (In Millions of £s)

Despite these local differences, some commonalities existed. "Attitudes to what consumers want are far more common than different," commented John Thompson, ICI Paints Planning Manager. "We have done market research in Turkey, Italy, and Columbus, Ohio, and the same overall pattern emerges: the woman in a household determines when a surface is to be painted and she determines the color. The husband selects the brand, usually on the basis of price and technique, although women are increasingly also making this decision. In terms of paint application, it is about evenly split between husbands and wives."

Can Coating Segment

Although the can coating segment with worldwide sales of £800 million accounted for only 3 percent of the world paint market, it accounted for 11 percent of ICI business, or £165 million, representing about 28 percent market share and giving it world leadership. Some 46 percent of the market was in North America, followed by Europe (24 percent) and Asia-Pacific (22 percent). Major competitors were BASF, Midland, and Valspar.

The coatings were used on the inside of tin or aluminum cans for food or beverage containers, making them corrosion resistant. This thin layer on the inside of every can was a crucial part for a successful canning operation. Consequently, this part of the paint industry was viewed as a high technology application.

Customers were concentrated with major use in the hands of four groups and their licensees: Continental Can, Pechiney-Triangle (included former American and National Can), Carnaud-Metal Box, and Crown Cork and Seal. These can manufacturers operated canning lines all over the world, and they expected the suppliers to follow them everywhere with a consistent product insuring same tastes for globally marketed products such as Coca-Cola.

Coating products had to be developed for each application and depended on the particular food or beverage as well as on the type of metal or aluminum container used. Customers were increasingly looking for simplifications and tended to look for a narrower technology range.

In this business, it was important to be able to make the development effort go around. A new product for sardines might be developed in Portugal but might have applications for Norwegian packers as well. Success depended on avoiding du-

EXHIBIT 5 ● ICI Volume by Market Segment

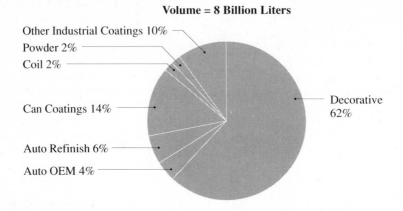

Volume = 8 Billion Liters

Other Industrial Coatings 10%
Powder 2%
Coil 2%

Can Coatings 14%

Auto Refinish 6%

Auto OEM 4%

Decorative
62%

plication of effort in applications development. Although coatings were usually not identical, a considerable part of the concept development could be widely applicable to other customers with the same applications.

ICI had acquired some eleven coatings companies over the years including Holden (Birmingham) with operations in Europe, Marsden (the United Kingdom), Wiederhold (Germany), Attivilac (Italy), and Glidden (the United States). In Europe, ICI had strong operations in Rouen, France, where its Holden operation was located near the Carnaud company. The French operation had thus always been strong in food applications. Glidden, on the other hand, enjoyed an 80 percent market share in the US for beverage cans.

ICI had targeted the can coating segment for major growth and planned to increase its market share to 40 percent of the world market, up from 28 percent currently. A new production facility was planned for Taiwan. As part of this expansion strategy, the company combined all of its various can coatings businesses under the same leadership in a single packaging group. Prior to that change, can coatings had been part of the larger group for general industry coatings.

Major changes were also contemplated for

development. Work was conducted to transfer Glidden's aluminum can coatings technology to steel and tin plate. Also under review was a decision whether or not to site a new development center in Singapore or Malaysia to service the growing Asia-Pacific markets. Other research initiatives were considered on basic background chemistry and how to develop this for the canning industry.

Automotive OEM Paint Segment

The automotive paint segment consisted of paint sales made to automobile manufacturers for use in their assembly plants. Worldwide, this segment represented 5 percent of the paint market. Major markets were North America (31 percent), Europe (32 percent), and Japan (26 percent). Leading competitors were PPG, BASF, Kansai, Nippon, DuPont, Hoechst, and ICI, in order of importance.

ICI's market share was about 6 percent worldwide, ranking it number 7 out of 8 international players. Most of its sales were in Europe, followed by the Asia-Pacific area (exclusive of Japan) and North America, with major local markets in Malaysia, Australia and Canada. ICI was considered technically good but commercially weak in this segment. The company was a leader in the initial development of electrolytic paint and in the development of waterbased top coat paints (Aquabase) for automotive users. The latest product was first introduced by GM in Canada and was now being introduced by Volvo in Sweden. Other European manufacturers were testing it, and ICI had granted a license to a Japanese company.

"This is an incestuous industry," remarked John Thompson, ICI Paints' Planning Manager. The customer base was largely globally operating companies and technologically very demanding. The technical service requirements of customers required paint suppliers to station technical service personnel permanently on location. As a result, the automotive companies preferred suppliers located at their doorsteps. This led to scattering factories close to assembly plants. In the United States, major paint companies would typically have several plants. Trends were away from multiple sourcing, which had kept local players alive, towards single sourcing and worldwide deals. Typically, a customer maintained a major supplier each for top coats and base coats with a second supplier for smaller volume applications "to keep the big ones honest."

This segment was technically very demanding. PPG had reached segment leadership by developing electrolytic techniques key for the important base coating of car bodies. The initial development was actually made by ICI but it was PPG which had made a commercial success out of the invention. At that time, PPG occasionally achieved single-source status through the installation of "hole-in-the-wall" plants where the company was producing adjacent to the paint shops of the assembly plant.

Although the particular paint applications such as color, etc., were developed for each customer, a substantial part of the basic research had worldwide applications. Technical spin-offs were also possible for other paint segments such as the refinish sector (with modifications in formulations due to the different paint application methods) and for industrial components in areas such as the domestic appliance industry. This was one

of the reasons why many players stayed in this segment despite low profitability or losses.

ICI had a very narrow geographic base in this segment and currently lacked platforms for major expansion. As a result, ICI engaged in a joint venture with DuPont called IDAC on a 50:50 basis to supply the Western European automotive market. DuPont had most of its automotive paint business in the U.S. and was therefore relatively weak in Europe. DuPont's area of strength was in the top coat business, with GM and Ford as major customers in the U.S. The IDAC goal was to reach a 20 percent market share in Europe during the early 1990s.

Automotive Refinish Paint Segment

The refinish segment included paints and coatings for repairing automobiles. The segment accounted for 4 percent of world sales and had the highest price per liter (£3.34). It was considered the most profitable paint segment. North America accounted for 36 percent of the world market, followed by Europe (30 percent), and Asia-Pacific (25 percent).

Only 10 paint manufacturers competed significantly in the refinish sector. Among those, only Sherwin-Williams of the United States and Rock of Japan did not also compete in the automotive OEM market. No new competitor had entered since the 1950s.

The world leader was BASF as a result of its recent acquisition of Inmont in the United States, followed by DuPont and ICI. ICI was the largest refinish supplier outside the United States. Its Autocolor brand led in the United Kingdom and was well known in Europe. In France, the company was the leader with its Valentine brand. ICI had a color inventory of some 30,000 formulae to match the stock colors of virtually all vehicle manufacturers. ICI's matching capability was developed in the UK market where a wide variety of car models were on the road following the decline of the local UK car industry.

Customers were largely small paint shops who needed quick and frequent deliveries, typically on a daily basis. Paint manufacturers supplied their customers with mixing schemes through local distributors who would combine the basic colors and shades with solvents to obtain the correct color match. There were some 10,000 different shades and some 60 different colors to select from. For ICI, this resulted in some 30,000 different formulae, partly as a result of different application techniques for the same shades and colors. A recent trend was in the direction of color mixing at the end-user location using color systems supplied by the paint manufacturer. Recently, ICI had placed a computerized management system at the disposal of its customers.

To compete in this business, a company had to have access to the color and paint shops of the car manufacturers to obtain the needed information. Automobile manufacturers wanted to make sure that their customers could get their car repaired wherever they were marketed. As an example, a company like Toyota was interested in worldwide coverage. Refinish paint manufacturers profited if they could have access to all car manufacturers, wherever they were located, so that they could supply the widest possible color range in any geographic market.

Powder Paint Segment

Powder paints was the fastest growing segment and represented an alternative technology for traditional wet paint rather than a particular application segment. Growing 10 to 20 percent annually, the segment had attracted many large companies as well as smaller suppliers. Leaders were International-Courtaulds (the United Kingdom), Ferro (the United States), ICI, and DSM (Netherlands).

Powder coatings were a precisely formulated mixture of pigment and resin which were sprayed using electrostatic spray guns. The sprayed item, a metal object, was then heated for about 10 minutes to cure the surface. Coatings had been developed for heat resistance or chemical resistance. The major benefits for users were the reduced emissions such as solvents used with wet paints and the reduced need for waste disposal. Major user groups were the automotive component suppliers, the metal furniture industry, and domestic appliance manufacturers. Powder paint could conceivably substitute up to 50 percent of the paint being applied to metal. In Europe, where the product was pioneered, the substitution already amounted to about 20 percent, compared to about 10 percent in the U.S., an amount that was, however, growing rapidly.

While the technology itself had become basic, there was room to develop many applications. ICI had selected some specific applications for further development, such as domestic appliances and architectural components. ICI had concluded a joint venture with Nippon Oil & Fats of Japan in Malaysia. About half of ICI's powder volume was in the U.S., about 40 percent in Europe, and the rest spread over many countries. In the United States, ICI was tied for first place with Morton, but was only sixth in Europe.

General Industrial Paint Segment

Some £250 million of ICI Paints' business was part of the general industrial paint category, which included general industrial liquid paints, wood finishes, adhesives, ink, and others. Two-thirds of this segment was allied in some way to its four core business areas, such as adhesives in the U.S. or metal can printing. Another part consisted of stand-alone businesses, not necessarily connected to core sectors, such as inks for screen printing in Germany. In these segments, ICI did not compete consistently throughout the world and had only selected local pockets of excellence.

STRATEGY

ICI Paints aimed at world leadership and profitable growth. The company intended to concentrate on its key paint businesses on a global basis and wanted to exploit particular regional opportunities in the EC and Asia-Pacific regions. ICI believed that a commitment to R&D and innovation was an essential part of industry leadership.

Organizationally, ICI aspired to become a marketing driven organization that was quality and customer focused, health and safety conscious, and environmentally responsible.

Organization

ICI management believed it was essential to have a global organization and management structure which would be both global and territory centered, support R&D centers of excellence in certain locations, and would maximize resources and synergy between businesses, operations, and locations.

ICI Paints was organized both along geographic and business lines (see Exhibit 6). Reporting to the PEO were three regional heads (Chief Executives) for Europe, North America, and Asia-Pacific. Each Chief Executive had P&L responsibility for the entire paint business in his area. The North American Chief Executive was also the head of Glidden, ICI Paints' major operating unit.

Reporting to each Chief Executive were several managers with country or territorial responsibility, called TGMs (Territorial General Managers) and BAGMs (short for Business Area Managers) for the four core sectors: decorative, can, automotive refinish and OEM, and powder. In some situations, BAGMs were identical with TGMs. In general, P&L results were a joint responsibility of BAGMs and TGMs.

At the territory or country level, BAGMs existed for the core business areas to the extent that each country had business in each of the four core sectors. Each territory also had other paint businesses. The percentage of sales in the latter category varied across territories, with higher percentages reported for some developing markets in Asia and lower percentages in the developed markets of Europe and North America.

Decision Making

Major decisions were always discussed and decided by the International Business Team (IBT) chaired by Herman Scopes, its PEO. Eight executives were members of the IBT, including the PEO and the three Chief Executives. The ICI Paints Group was led by Herman Scopes as its PEO and the seven members of the International Business Team (IBT). Part of the IBT were the three Chief Executives for North America, Europe, and Asia/Pacific/Australia regions, as well as four other executives with either functional or segment responsibility (see Exhibit 7). The IBT met six to eight times per year at various locations.

Executives were nominated to the IBT because of their ability to contribute broadly to the development of the ICI Paints Group rather than their specialties or specific skills. Once part of the IBT, members were assigned "portfolios" based on their own talents and experience, occasionally resulting in changes when the personnel constellation changed in the IBT.

An important aspect of the way ICI Paints operated was its use of International Leaders (ILs). IL positions existed for each of its four core business areas (decorative, can coatings, automotive, and powder) as well as for five functional areas: finance, information technology, operations, R&D, and management development. The ILs for three of these five areas were members of the IBT.

The ILs of the core sectors had the roles of facilitators or coordinators. These international leaders did not have P&L responsibility. However, they were responsible for the development of global strategies for each of their assigned core sectors. Powder was coordinated out of the U.S., decorative out of Europe (by the Chief Executive Europe), and automotive and can coatings from Europe (head of that sector for Europe).

Strategies were developed at the business level by the international leaders and their teams, and were then proposed to the International Business Team.

COORDINATING CORE BUSINESS SEGMENTS

The strategy making and coordination process differed considerably across the four core business areas.

The *decorative world strategy* consisted of three major elements. First, ICI Paints was to pursue quality leadership in all markets where the company was competing. It was understood that this meant setting the pace in the sector and pursuing a premium price. Second, there was to be a drive towards running a world brand, Dulux, the only world consumer paint brand in existence. This goal included having a consistent role for Dulux as the aspirational brand in all ICI decora-

EXHIBIT 6 ● Organization Chart

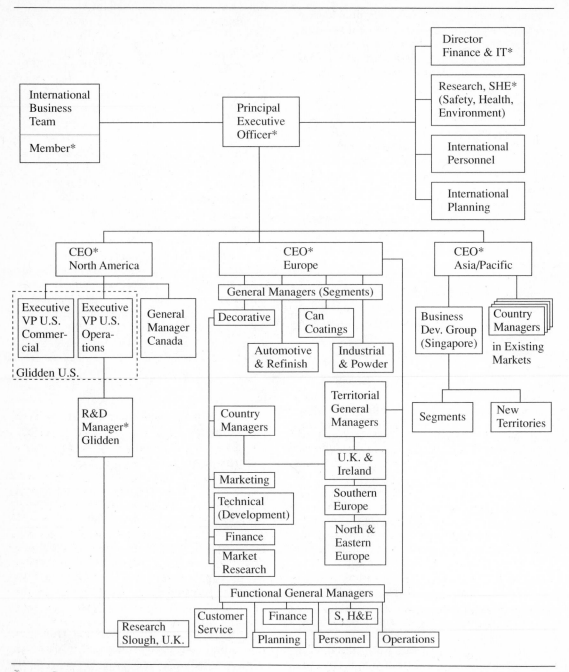

Source: Company records.

*International Business Team Member

EXHIBIT 7 ● Members of the International Business Team (IBT)

Herman Scopes	PEO ICI Paints
John Dumble	Chief Executive North America, President Glidden
Doug Curlewis	Chief Executive Europe International Leader Decorative Paint
Richard Stillwell	Chief Executive Asia-Pacific/Australia
John Danzeisen	Finance Director International Leader Powder International Leader Finance Function International Leader IT Function
Alex Ramig	International Leader R&D
Brian Letchford	International Leader Automotive Refinish and OEM (designated International Leader Can)
Quintin Knight	International Leader Can Coatings (retiring in March 1990)

Other International Leaders not part of the IBT:

June Thomason	Operations Manager, Glidden International Leader Operations
Ian Cope	International Leader Management Development

tive paint markets. Third, ICI was to use the fact that it was the largest paint producer worldwide and should thus be able to maximize its resources in key functional areas.

Coordination was hampered by the fact that local operating companies considered their competitive situations to be unique. Glidden in the United States did not compete in the premium sector at all and its market share was only about 10 percent, compared to 40 percent in the United Kingdom, or the three brand product line in Australia. To launch Dulux as a premium brand in the United States would entail a marketing investment of about $50 million over 4 to 5 years with a seven-year payback period for a required 5 percent market share. Glidden executives were not convinced that this strategy would be successful in the United States.

Due to the differences encountered, the IL for the sector had pursued a "consultative mode," meeting about twice annually with the key executives from the various operating companies. In addition, the IL had frequent individual meetings with operating executives and territorial managers.

In the *automotive sector,* the IL positions for the OEM and refinish segments were combined. For refinishes, where ICI had major positions in Europe and Australia only, the strategy was fairly heavily led from the center. Involved were key managers from Europe and Australia with others "mostly along for the ride." A major point of discussion was ICI's future strategy in the U.S. where it had no position at that time. Glidden executives were very interested in entering the refinish sector. However, a "greenfield approach" (that is, starting up with no previous capability) was considered difficult and, as yet, no ready candidates for acquisition existed.

In the automotive OEM segment, the IL role consisted largely of outside contacts with DuPont, ICI's partner for Europe, and frequent negotiations with Japanese companies on technology transfers that might result in obtaining business for ICI from Japanese transplant operations in Canada, Australia, Southeast Asia, India, and Pakistan, all countries where ICI was active in the OEM business.

Coordination in the *can coatings sector* was very close and involved a formal business area review team under the leadership of the IL for can coatings. The team consisted of the key players worldwide in ICI Paints, who met several times each year. A major challenge here was to devise a strategy in view of the increased concentration among customers. Despite ICI's leading market position, the company could not dictate prices. The resulting squeeze on margins had reduced profitability, and a new strategy would have to be devised to lead the company out of this "commodity hole".

For the *general industrial paint sector,* no IL had been appointed. These businesses were led in various ways. Businesses that were closely affiliated with one of the four core areas were attached to the IL teams of those areas. Others were left under the direction of the territorial management. Some businesses not directly tied to the paint business were kept as long as they were meeting required profitability targets.

Coordinating at the Functional Level

The ILs for the five key functions undertook their roles in different ways. For all functional ILs, however, the objectives were similar. ICI wanted to transfer skills, experience, and best practice around its group operating companies. It also wished to accelerate the innovation process (as distinctly different from the invention process). And finally, the desire, as elsewhere in the business, was to simplify and focus on operational aspects, not just "spin wheels."

For the finance area, this largely involved the

enforcement of corporate guidelines and practice around the Paint Group. For information technology (IT), the mission was still vague. One of the jobs was to encourage and promote the use of IT where appropriate, often convincing Chief Executives to make the necessary investments. The coordinating activities had led to a policy of using DEC equipment for technical applications, and IBM for commercial and operational tasks.

In operations, efforts were undertaken to spread efficient production procedures across the group. Here, ICI relied on Glidden's skill as a low-cost producer.

In the R&D area, there had been a long-held conviction that technology was driven by the automotive and industrial market, such as coil coatings. ICI Paints was now moving the emphasis of its R&D brainpower to new fields such as decorative, can coatings, and powders, which was beginning to yield exciting results.

Coordinating the various functions was a challenging task since many of its operating companies had different corporate origins, were acquired from various sources, and represented different nationalities and cultures.

Current Organizational Issues for ICI Paints Worldwide

Over the past years, ICI's organization had undergone considerable changes. Aside from its territorial focus, it introduced the idea of ILs for segments and functions. However, the company encountered a major obstacle in the fact that much of its production assets were shared. It was believed that some fifty of its sixty-four plants were common sites for a number of paint products and segments. This meant that the business segments were largely responsible for business volume, but the BAGMs did not have full asset responsibility. At this time, not more than 75 percent of the company assets could be clearly attributed to individual business lines.

Aside from the organization issues and the challenges faced by each of the four core sectors, ICI Paints needed to leverage the benefit of its being the largest global player into a superior financial performance.

Name and Company Index

Subject Index